AF663554

THREE MOUNTAINS AND SEVEN RIVERS

PROF. MUSASHI TACHIKAWA

Three Mountains and Seven Rivers

Prof. Musashi Tachikawa's Felicitation Volume

Edited by

Shoun Hino
Toshihiro Wada

MOTILAL BANARSIDASS PUBLISHERS
PRIVATE LIMITED • DELHI

First Indian Edition: Delhi, 2004

ISBN: 81-208-2468-7

MOTILAL BANARSIDASS
41 U.A. Bungalow Road, Jawahar Nagar, Delhi 110 007
8 Mahalaxmi Chamber, 22 Bhulabhai Desai Road, Mumbai 400 026
120 Royapettah High Road, Mylapore, Chennai 600 004
236, 9th Main III Block, Jayanagar, Bangalore 560 011
Sanas Plaza, 1302 Baji Rao Road, Pune 411 002
8 Camac Street, Kolkata 700 017
Ashok Rajpath, Patna 800 004
Chowk, Varanasi 221 001

Printed in India
BY JAINENDRA PRAKASH JAIN AT SHRI JAINENDRA PRESS, A-45 NARAINA, PHASE-I, NEW DELHI 110 028 AND PUBLISHED BY NARENDRA PRAKASH JAIN FOR MOTILAL BANARSIDASS PUBLISHERS PRIVATE LIMITED, BUNGALOW ROAD, DELHI 110 007

Preface

We planned this volume in Autumn 2000 to felicitate the sixtieth birthday of Prof. Dr. Musashi Tachikawa. Unfortunately it took more time to publish than we expected, but we hope that the volume will be a fitting felicitation of his sixtieth birthday.

Prof. Tachikawa was born in Nagoya in 1942. As a student at Tokai High School in Nagoya, he was much influenced by Rev. Reiho Hayashi and felt a keen interest in Buddhist philosophy. In 1960 he entered Nagoya University, and in 1964 the Graduate School of Letters of the same university. During his studies at Nagoya University. Prof. Tachikawa learned Buddhist philosophy from Prof. Yoshihumi Ueda, and Sanskrit philology from Prof. Hidenori Kitagawa. During the period 1965 to 1967 he studied Tibetan Buddhism under Rev. bSod nams rgya mtsho and Rev. mKhas btsun bzang po at The Oriental Library in Tokyo. From 1967 to 1970 he studied at Harvard University under the guidance of Prof. Daniel H.H. Ingalls, and was awarded a Ph.D. degree in 1975: His Ph.D. dissertation, *The Structure of the World in Udayana's Realism,* was published in the Netherlands (and now being reprinted at Motilal Banarsidass). This book presents a translation and analysis of Udayana's *Lakṣaṇāvalī* and *Kiraṇāvalī* and gives us not only a view of Vaiśeṣika philosophy but also a sketch of Indian philosophy. Prof. Tachikawa's research at Harvard University seems to have provoked him to use working concepts such as Indian realism and nominalism in analyzing Indian classical texts. In 1970 he took up a post at Nagoya University, where in 1976 Prof. Yūsho Miyasaka arrived at his post. Prof. Tachikawa took the opportunity to carry out research on Buddhist tantrism with him. In 1985 Prof. Tachikawa was awarded a Doctor of Letters by Nagoya

University, and in 1994 this dissertation was published: *Chūron no Shisō (The Thought of the Madhyamakakārikā)*. This book too provides us a new viewpoint in analyzing Sanskrit texts involving contradictory statements, such as those of Nāgārjuna and the *Prajñāpāramitāsūtras*. In 1991 he left Nagoya University for the National Museum of Ethnology in Osaka, and now he is striving to synthesize his research on wide areas.

Prof. Tachikawa's study comprises five different fields of Indology. These are, in chronological order, Nāgārjuna's Madhyamaka Philosophy, Indian realism, Buddhist tantrism and Hindu tantrism, and Buddhist Theology. The study of Buddhist tantrism and Hindu tantrism covers both iconography and rituals. At first glance their mutual relationship is not clear, but Prof. Tachikawa's methodology makes us understand just how deeply related they are. His study is deeply rooted in philology, involving Sanskrit and Tibetan original texts, and is characterized by making use of comparative philosophical working concepts such as Indian realism and Indian nominalism, the sacred and the profane. He has used these concepts since his early days while studying the first four fields, and established their place in Indological and Buddhist studies in Japan.

To apply what he calls working concepts to one of four fields is not so surprising. In fact Indian realism and Indian nominalism were used in the study of Indian realism. Furthermore the sacred and the profane were used in the study of Buddhist or Hindu tantrism. He did not use them as an introduction to an article or a book, but rather he presented a whole picture of the entire study by means of working concepts. Thereby readers understand where individual topics are located in the whole picture of his study. This methodology appears easy to employ, but in fact requires both deep knowledge of the subject matter and insight into the holistic idea about how to grasp Indian thought. Prof. Tachikawa is a rare scholar having thus achieved this deep knowledge and insight into such a complex field of study.

His study is characterized by his use of multiple (not single) working concepts in all of the fields. Taking the study of Madhyamaka Philosophy for instance, he presented a logical interpretation of Nāgārjuna's contradictory passages by using the sacred and the profane and at the same time made a clear-cut distinction between other Buddhist thoughts and Hindu philosophical systems by using Indian realism and Indian nominalism. In such a methodology, there is room for some criticism, for we do not have the relevant Sanskrit words which can be applied to working concepts. Furthermore, some object to the use of working concepts. But we should understand that his study is based on his attitude of grasping an individual object of study with a bird's eye view. This is useful in Indian thought and religion and can be related to the study of other philosophical systems and religions in the world as well.

His fifth field of study, viz. Buddhist Theology or Buddhology, is in the same line as his four other fields of study. This develops his fundamental matter of concern, that is, what Buddhism can do for us humans presently. He creatively speculates and discusses how Buddha, Buddhists and this World of Buddhists are related to one another and how they should be related. In this fifth field he is not content with finding out something practical and useful among the philosophical viewpoints of the Buddhism of the past, but is also developing his Movement of Thought toward constructing a positive and new Buddhist system. Currently Prof. Tachikawa is pursuing his studies and we scholars do not know what the final outcome will be. We can only speculate.

To commemorate Prof. Tachikawa's sixtieth birthday, scholars from various fields have shared and contributed their articles. We feel proud of this volume which celebrates Prof. Tachikawa's academic contributions, and we cordially wish him continued academic success and good health.

January
2004

S. Hino
T. Wada

Contents

Section IV
ICONOGRAPHY

Section V
JAINISM

Section VI
LOGIC

SECTION VII
POETICS

SECTION VIII
VEDIC THEMES

SECTION IX
SOCIAL PRACTICES

SECTION X
TIBETAN THEMES

SECTION XI
VEDĀNTA AND MĪMĀṂSĀ

Section XII
SĀṂKHYA AND YOGA

Section XIII
TANTRISM

Contributors

(1) Major, (2) Position, (3) Department/Division/Faculty/School, (4) Institute/University, (5) Institute/University Address

AKIMOTO, MASARU [*Mahāyāna* Buddhism] Professor, Faculty for the Study of Contemporary Society, Kyoto Women's University, 35 Kitahiyoshi-cho, Imakumano, Higashiyama-ku, Kyoto 605-8501, Japan

ASANO, GENSEI [Yoga and Jainism] Professor, Dept. of Buddhist Culture, Doho University, 7-1 Inabaji-cho, Nakamura-ku, Nagoya, 453-8540, Japan

BAHULKAR, SHRIKANT [Vedic and Tibetan Studies] Professor and Head, B.L. Centre of Sanskrit and Asian Studies, Tilak Maharashtra Vidyapeeth, Pune 411037, India

BRONKHORST, JOHANNES [Indian Linguistics, Philosophy, and Religion] Professor, Section de Langues et Civilisations Orientales, Faculté des Lettres, Université de Lausanne, B. F.S.H. 2, 1015 Lausanne, Switzerland

CÜPPERS, CHRISTOPH [Tibetan Studies] Director, Lumbini International Research Institute, P.O. Box 39, Bhairahawa, Dist. Rupandehi, Nepal

DEEG, MAX [Sanskrit Etymology and Buddhist Culture in China] Professor, Section Religious Studies, Faculty of Protestant Theology, University of Vienna, Rooseveltplatz 10, 1090 Wien, Austria

DEEGALLE, MAHINDA [Theravāda Buddhism] Senior Lecturer, Study of Religions, School of Historical and Cultural Studies, Bath Spa University College, Newton Park, Bath BA2 9BN, U.K.

DEODHAR, LALITA [Vedānta and Kashmir Śaivism] Assistant Editor, Sanskrit Dictionary Project, Deccan College, Pune 411006, India

DOUGLAS, WILL [Newar Buddhism] Visiting Lecturer at Tribhuvan University; Fellow, Wolfson College, OX2 6UD, U.K.

EHRHARD, FRANZ-KARL [Tibetan Studies] Professor of Tibetan and Buddhist Studies, Dept. of Asian Studies, University of Munich, Geschwister-Scholl-Platz 1, 80539 Munich, Germany

EINOO, SHINGO [Vedic and Hindu Ritual] Professor, Institute of Oriental Culture, The University of Tokyo, 7-3-1 Hongo, Bunkyo-ku, Tokyo 113-0033, Japan

ENDO, KO [Yoga] Professor, Dept. of Comparative Cultures, Aichi Bunkyo University, Nenjozaka 5969-3, Okusa, Komaki 485-8565, Japan

FRANCO, ELI [Indian Philosophy] Research Fellow, Institute for the Cultural and Intellectual History of Asia, Austrian Academy of Sciences, Vienna, Austria

GRANOFF, PHYLLIS [Vedānta and Jainism] Professor, Dept. of Religious Studies, McMaster University, Hamilton, Ontario, L8S 4K1 Canada

HATTORI, MARI [Alaṅkāra] Visiting Lecturer, Japanese Red Cross Aichi Junior College, 3-35 Michishita-cho, Nakamura-ku, Nagoya 453-0046, Japan

HIKITA, HIROMICHI [Hindu Tantrism and Early Buddhism] Professor, Dept. of Buddhist and Religious Studies, Faculty of Letters, Aichi Gakuin University, 12 Araike, Iwasaki-cho, Nisshin 470-0195, Japan

HINO, SHOUN [Vedānta and Hinduism] Professor, Gifu Pharmaceutical University, 5-6-1, Mitahora-higashi, Gifu 502-8585, Japan

HIRANO, KATSUNORI [Vaiśeṣika] Research Fellow, COE Office Graduate School of Letters Nagoya University, Nagoya International Center Bldg., 47-1, Nagono 1-chome, Nakamura-ku, Nagoya 450-0001, Japan

HIROTA, DENNIS [Japanese Buddhism] Professor, Dept. of Asian Studies, Chikushi Jogakuen University, 2-12-1 Ishizaka, Dazaifu 818-0192, Japan

HOSODA, NORIAKI [Upaniṣad and Early Buddhism] Associate Professor, Graduate School of Letters, Hokkaido University, Kita 10, Nishi 7, Kita-ku, Sapporo 060-0810, Japan

ISHIGURO, ATSUSHI [History of Indian Art] Professor, Dept. of Japanese Culture, Faculty of Letters, Aichi Gakuin University, 12 Araike, Iwasaki-cho, Nisshin 470-0195, Japan

ISHITOBI, MICHIKO [Indian Logic] Komazawa School of Nursing and Welfare, Iwanizawa, Japan

IWATA, TAKASHI [Buddhist Logic] Professor, Dept. of Asian Philosophy, Faculty of Letters, Waseda University, 1-24-1 Toyama, Shinjuku-ku, Tokyo 162-8644, Japan

JACKSON, DAVID P. [Tibetan Studies] Professor and Head, Dept. of Indian and Tibetan Studies, Asia and Africa Institute, Hamburg University, Neue Rabenstrasse 3, 20354 Hamburg, Germany

JHA, V.N. [Nyāya, Vaiśeṣika, Mīmāṃsā, Vyākaraṇa, Sanskrit Literature, Linguistics and Vedic Studies] Director, Centre of Advanced Study in Sanskrit, University of Pune, Pune 411007, India

KIMURA, BUNKI [Vedānta and Contemporary Buddhism] Associate Professor, Junior College Division, Aichi Gakuin University, 1-100 Kusumoto-cho, Chikusa-ku, Nagoya 464-0037, Japan

KOLHATKAR, MADHAVI [Brāhmaṇa] Assistant Editor, Sanskrit Dictionary Project, Deccan College, Pune 411006, India

KUDO, NORIYUKI [Vyākaraṇa and Buddhist Sanskrit Philology] Lecturer, The International Research Institute for Advanced Buddhology, Soka University, 1-236 Tangi, Hachioji, Tokyo 192-8577, Japan

MINOWA, KENRYO [Japanese Buddhism] Associate Professor, Dept. of Japanese Culture, Faculty of Letters, Aichi Gakuin University, 12 Araike, Iwasaki-cho, Nisshin 470-0195, Japan

MIYAJI, AKIRA [Art History of India and Central Asia] Professor, Dept. of Aesthetics and Art History, Graduate School of Letters, Nagoya University, Furo-cho, Chikusa-ku, Nagoya 464-8601, Japan

MIYAMOTO, KEIICHI [Vaiśeṣika and Buddhism] Professor, Department of Philosophy, Kokugakuin University, Higashi, Shibuya-ku, Tokyo 150-8440, Japan

MOCHIZUKI, KAIE [Madhyamaka] Associate Professor, Faculty of Buddhism, Minobusan University, 3567 Minobu, Minobu-cho, Yamanashi Prefecture 409-2597, Japan

MORI, MASAHIDE [Ritual and Iconography of Tantric Buddhism] Associate Professor, Faculty of Letters, Kanazawa University, Kakuma-machi, Kanazawa 920-1192, Japan

MOTEGI, SHUJUN [Sāṃkhya and Epic] Professor, Faculty of Education, Shinshu University, 6 Nishinagano, Nagano, 380-0871, Japan

MURAKAMI, SHINKAN [Vaiśeṣika, Sāṃkhya, Vedānta, and Buddhism] Professor Emeritus, Dept. of Indology and History of Indian Buddhism, Graduate School of Arts and Letters, Tohoku University, Kawauchi, Aoba-ku, Sendai 980-8576, Japan

NOZAWA, MASANOBU [Vaiśeṣika] Professor, Division of Liberal Arts, Numazu College of Technology, 3600 Ooka, Numazu 410-8501, Japan

ONODA, SHUNZO [Tibetan Studies] Professor, School of Literature, Bukkyo University, 96 Kitahananobo-cho, Murasakino, Kita-ku, Kyoto 603-8301

PAUL, GREGOR [Comparative Study of Logic] apl. Professor, Dept. of Philosophy, Karlsruhe University, Kollegium am Schloss, Bau II, 76128 Karlsruhe, Germany

SAKUMA, RURIKO [Buddhist Tantrism and Iconography] Research Fellow, The Eastern Institute, Inc, 2-17-2 Sotokanda, Chiyoda-ku, Tokyo 101-0021, Japan

SAKURAI, MUNENOBU [Buddhist Tantrism] Associate Professor, Dept. of Indology and History of Indian Buddhism, Graduate School of Arts and Letters, Tohoku University, Kawauchi, Aoba-ku, Sendai 980-8576, Japan

SHIMA, IWAO [Vedānta and Medieval Hinduism] Professor, Faculty of Letters, Kanazawa University, Kakuma-machi, Kanazawa 920-1192, Japan

STAAL, FRITS [Linguistics, Indian Logic and Vedic Ritual] Professor Emeritus, Dept. of Philosophy and of South Asian Studies, University of California at Berkeley, California 94720, USA

TANAKA, KIMIAKI [Esoteric Buddhism and Buddhist Iconography] Research Fellow, The Eastern Institute, Inc, 2-17-2 Sotokanda, Chiyoda-ku, Tokyo 101-0021, Japan

TANAKA, MASAKAZU [Social Anthropology of South India] Associate Professor, Institute for Research in Humanities, Kyoto University, Ushinomiya-cho, Yoshida, Sakyo-ku, Kyoto 606-8501, Japan

TANI, TADASHI [Buddhist Logic] Professor, Dept. of Humanities, Kochi National College of Technology, 200-1 Monobe, Nankoku-shi 783-8508, Japan

TANIGUCHI, FUJIO [Indian and Tibetan Buddhism] Associate Professor, Faculty of Literature, Nagoya Women's University, 1302 Takamiya-cho, Tenpaku-ku, Nagoya 468-8507, Japan

THITE, GANESH [Veda] Professor and Head, Department of Sanskrit and Prakrit Languages, University of Pune, Pune 411 007

TILLEMANS, TOM [Buddhist Logic, Mādhyamika and Tibetan Buddhism] Professor, Section de Langues et Civilizations Orientales, Faculté des Lettres, Université de Lausanne, B. F.S.H. 2, 1015 Lausanne, Switzerland

UNEBE, TOSHIYA [Vyākaraṇa and Buddhism] Associate Professor, Dept. of Indian Studies, Graduate School of Letters, Nagoya University, Furo-cho, Chikusa-ku, Nagoya 464-8601, Japan

WADA, TOSHIHIRO [Nyāya and Vaiśeṣika] Professor, Dept. of Indian Studies, Graduate School of Letters, Nagoya University, Furo-cho, Chikusa-ku, Nagoya 464- 8601, Japan

YAMAGUCHI, SHINOBU [Buddhist Tantrism] Associate Professor, Dept. of Asian Studies, Chukyo Women's University, 55 Nadakayama, Yokone-cho, Obu-shi 474-0011, Japan

YOKOTA, JOHN SHUNJI [Philosophy of Religion and Inter-Religious Studies] Professor, Faculty for the Study of Contemporary Society, Kyoto Women's University, 35 Kitahiyoshi-cho, Imakumano, Higashiyama-ku, Kyoto 605-8501, Japan

YORITOMI, MOTOHIRO [Buddhist Tantrism and Iconography] Professor and President, Shuchiin University, 70 Nishijyouke, Mukaijima, Fushimi-ku, Kyoto 612-8156, Japan

YOSHIMIZU, CHIZUKO [Indo-Tibetan Buddhist Epistemology and Madhyamaka] Lecturer, Institute of Modern Languages and Cultures, Tsukuba University, Tennodai 1-1-1, Tsukuba, 305-8571, Japan

YOSHIMIZU, KIYOTAKA [Mīmāṃsā] Associate Professor, Graduate School of Letters, Hokkaido University, Kita 10, Nishi 7, Kita-ku, Sapporo 060-0810, Japan

YOTSUYA, KODO [Tibetan Buddhism] Associate Professor, Faculty of Buddhism, Komazawa University, 1-23-1 Komazawa, Setagaya-ku, Tokyo 154-8525, Japan

I

ANCIENT GEOGRAPHY

CHAPTER 1

Three Mountains and Seven Rivers

FRITS STAAL

1. *A Geographical Mirror*

There are many links between Buddhism and the Vedas. One is the god Indra, others may be found in the Upaniṣads. The features of kinship between the two traditions on which I shall focus in this essay lie on the roads, routes and treks of Central Asia. For it is an undeniable fact of geography that the movements of speakers of early Indo-Aryan, the language of the Vedas, which came from Central to South Asia, and those of Buddhism in the opposite direction mirror each other to some extent. I stumbled upon this topic in earlier papers,[1] first in the course of a discussion of Lake Manasarovar and Mount Kailāsa, both located in western Tibet, less than a hundred miles north of the Himalayan Range. Known to Buddhism but not yet to the Veda,[2] the geographical constellation there is extraordinary. Mount Kailāsa is the source, or close to the source of four great rivers that flow in the four cardinal directions, either around the extremities of the Himalayas or cutting through them before reaching their final destination. The first two reach the Arabian Sea, the third and fourth flow into the Bay of Bengal: (1) The Indus, the longest, flows north towards Gilgit before it makes a dramatic turn to the south and reaches the Punjab; (2) The

Sutlej flows west, close to the steep northern flanks of the Himalayas, then turns south to cut through them and also reach the Punjab; (3) The Karnali goes south through Nepal before it ultimately flows into the Ganges; and (4) the Tsangpo or Brahmaputra, almost as long as the Indus, goes east and traverses central Tibet before turning south and entering the Bay of Bengal together with the Ganges. See the accompanying map.

More recently, in search of the best Soma,[3] I examined a well-known dialogue in Vedic ritual. The chief priest asks the Soma merchant: "Is it from Mount Mūjavat?" and the merchant replies: "It is from Mount Mūjavat". Mūjavat is the name of the mountain from which, according to *Ṛgveda* 10.34.1 and other early sources, the best Soma came. We do not know its location but a recent etymology of the name suggests an answer. The common *-vat* possessive suggests the meanings "having *mūja-*" or "inhabited by the Mūja tribe." The element *mūj(a)* is not Indo-European and Michael Witzel considered several possible etymologies in 1980.[4] More recently, Witzel[5] has suggested that it may be related to the element *muz* of Muztagh Ata, (Uighur) "Father of Muz Mountain(s)", a giant mountain towering over a mountain complex on the border of Tajikistan and Xinjiang, close to the source of the Oxus and Yarkand-Tarim rivers—also on our map. My 2001a article[6] concludes that the Soma ritual depicts the movements of Indo-Aryan speakers from the areas or drainage basins of Oxus and Tarim toward Indus and Ganges and represents the Indo-Aryan or Vedic contribution to Indian civilization.

Witzel's suggestion is purely linguistic but in geographical terms it raises questions, not because Muztagh Ata is far to the north (where Indo-Aryan came from), but to the east. Speakers of Indo-Iranian came from south of the Ural mountains.[7] At some time they split into Iranian and Indo-Aryan (and a third smaller branch to which I shall briefly return). Around the beginning of the second millennium BCE, speakers of these languages trekked further south, east of the Caspian Sea, and reached the Oxus somewhere west of modern Samarkand, formerly Marakanda, capital of Sogdiana where, according to Arrianus, Alexander of Macedon suffered his first defeat in 329 BCE.[8] Why *west* of Samarkand? Because to its *east* there are mountain ranges, leading up to the Pamirs, a desolate highland where the extremities of the Tien Shan, Kun Lun, Hindukush, Karakoram and Himalayan

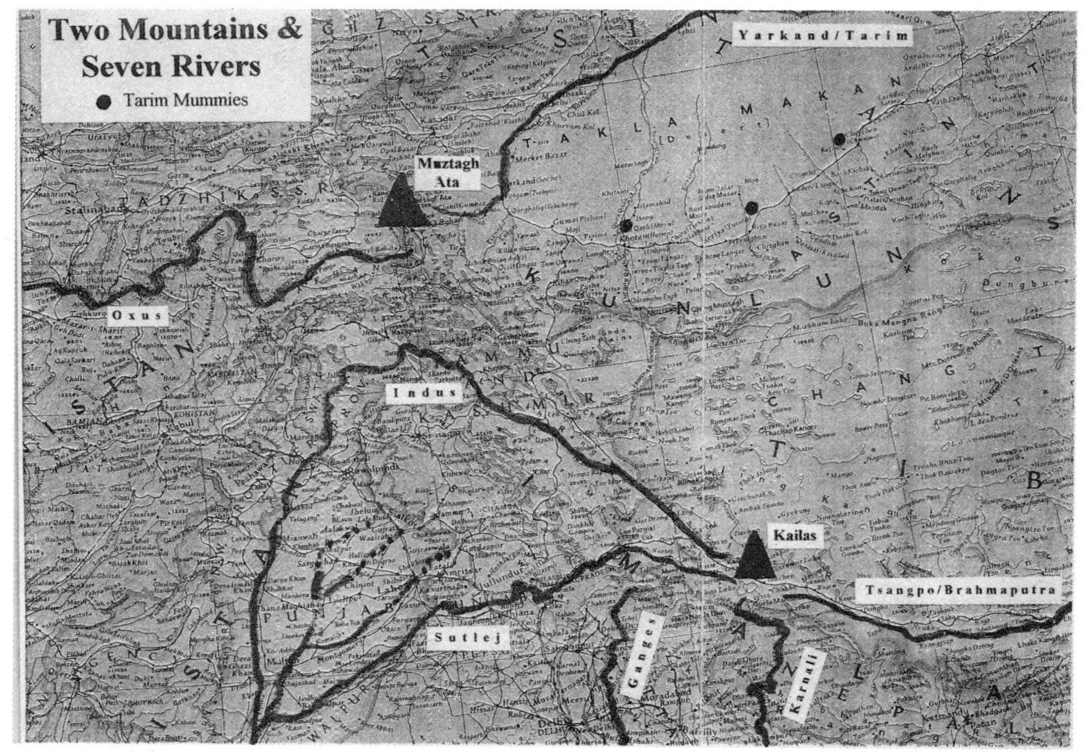
Two Mountains &
Seven Rivers
● Tarim Mummies
Yarkand/Tarim
Muztagh Ata
Oxus
Indus
Sutlej
Ganges
Karnali
Kailas
Tsangpo/Brahmaputra

ranges meet. It seems unlikely that Indo-Iranian speakers would have wandered that far east, cut through the mountains all the way to their eastern flanks and met with Muztagh Ata. What, then, happens to Witzel's suggestion? I shall argue that it depends on the relation between Indo-Iranian and Tocharian, the easternmost Indo-European language, attested late, in Buddhist manuscripts from the end of the first millennium CE. It is a topic on which opinions diverge widely.

The accompanying map "Two Mountains and Seven Rivers"[9] raises two questions that are more easily answered: (1) Why does its caption mention *seven* rivers when the two mountains are connected with only *six*? and (2) Why does it mention *two* mountains when the title of the present essay and volume mention *three?*

The *Ṛgveda* mentions more than thirty-five rivers.[10] The answer to (1) is that the map includes the Ganges because it is not only the most renowned river of post-Vedic India, but also often described as flowing from Kailāsa although it originates in fact from south of the watershed of the Himalayan range.[11] The answer to (2) lies in the fact that, in India as elsewhere, some mountains are more real than others. High mountains are by their very nature inaccessible and it is not surprising that there is in their realm much category confusion between mythical and real. Mount Meru, centre of the universe, is mythical and has no place on a geographical map.[12] Muztagh Ata and Kailāsa and their rivers, by contrast, occur not only on modern maps but Buddhist sources refer or allude to them. Unlike the more mythical Indian epics and Purāṇas, these sources provide us with concrete information which I summarize here from Staal 1988 and 1990.[13]

Pali sources depict lake Anavatapta as surrounded by five mountains of which *Kelāsa* is one. Four channels flow from the lake and turn into four, then five rivers: Ganges, Yamuna and three smaller streams in northern India and Nepal. This knowledge is primarily based on travellers' knowledge for Anavatapta must be one of the two lakes immediately to the south of Kailāsa: Manasarovar or Rākṣasa Tāla. But early Buddhists did not regard Kelāsa as centre of the world.[14] That idea is "Hindu" (i.e., Indian) and refers to Kailāsa as well as Meru. Later Buddhist sources, originating in north-west India and often preserved in Chinese, provide a standardized picture: Sītā (= Tarim) flows north, Oxus west, Indus south and Ganges east. In actual fact, only the Indus originates from the Kailāsa region; the source of the Ganges lies elsewhere as we have just seen; Oxus and Sītā are much further north. None of the standard quadruplet originates from the Mānasarovar or Rākṣasa Tāla. It is the Sutlej that originates from the latter. Together with the Indus and three others, it makes up the five (*pañj*) streams (*āb*) of the Punjab.

The standard mythology is a mixture of facts and confusion. Muztagh Ata and Kailāsa are identified with each other though they are at least 600 miles from each other "as the crow flies" (i.e., in a straight line[15]). For human travellers, the distance is very much greater because one has to go part of the way on foot in this most mountainous region of the planet.

The entire construction enables us to extrapolate from Buddhism back to the Vedas and, vice-versa, extrapolate forward from the Vedas to Buddhism. The two movements have remained unconnected on account of the narrow perspectives of not only some followers of these "religions" (if that is what they are[16]) and the general public, but also of those scholars or scientists who adhere with almost equally religious zeal to labels, putting up barriers between Hindus and Buddhists, Indologists, Buddhologists, Central Asianists and Sinologists, religious scholars, philologists and linguists, anthropologists and historians. We gain insight by deconstructing such labels and replace them by people, ideas, rites and goods that have been continuously on the move in both directions.

Deconstruction in this area comes about by paying attention to features not of cultural theory but of geography. Mountains hardly change, at least from a human perspective (contrast the geological perspective of *note* 11). Rivers do to some extent. They change their course in more or less flat areas like the Tarim basin or the Punjab.[17] They hardly change in mountainous areas because of the unchanging nature of mountains. These facts imply that the movements of peoples through the Himalayas, Hindukush, Karakorams and Pamirs, often along or close to river valleys and gorges, has also changed little during recent millennia.

Steep gorges like those of the upper Indus as it traverses the western extremities of the Himalayas before it is forced to deflect its course by the Karakorams, may be crossed by bridges made from twisted twigs or ropes and later constructed with iron chains. In the fifth century BCE, the Sanskrit grammarian Pāṇini refers to *bhastrā* which also occurs in late Vedic and may already have denoted a boat made of inflated skins as it later does. Buddhist and epic *piṭaka,* similarly, may already have referred to a coracle made of wickerwork covered with watertight materials. Both are described and illustrated by Agrawala[18] but this must be used with caution because it tacitly includes later data.[19] Yet, early use of such vessels on the upper Indus is not excluded wherever river banks are flat. It may be difficult even at lower altitudes when water levels change rapidly as they do at Pāṇini's birthplace Śalātura near modern Attock, where the Kabul river joins the Indus at the point where it enters the Punjab plains.[20]

I referred to a myth that resulted from confusion but confusion is not confined to mythology and not all myths are triggered thus. Mountain perspectives are almost always confusing. Some 20 miles north of Muztagh Ata itself there is another mountain, Kungur or *Gongge'er Shan,* from which it was distinguished only in 1885. It is now, at 25,325 feet, the highest mountain of China. It may be seen from the direction of Kashgar from where it obscures Muztagh Ata which at 24,757 feet, is immediately behind it. That is was not recognized as the higher mountain is explained by the fact that it is merely the highest crest of an extended ridge. According to Curzon's still useful and readable monograph *The Pamirs and the Source of the Oxus,*[21] Muztagh Ata "is a far finer mountain, since it is conical and comparatively isolated." Perhaps its shape helps to explain its confusion with Kailāsa which is also perfectly shaped.[22]

The ranges of the Hindukush, Karakorams and Pamirs between Indus, Oxus and Tarim are confusing also on most modern maps which typically follow political frontiers and therefore have to be put together like a jigsaw puzzle. The ancients had no maps but even Aurel Stein, when crossing the Taghdumbash Pamir, thought that he had come close to the point "where the drainage areas of the three great river systems of the Indus, the Oxus and the Tarim meet, the representatives as it were of the still greater ethnic areas of India, Iran and Turkestan".[23] As we have seen, the Indus has nothing to do with it. Post-Vedic India lost all knowledge of the Pamir watershed and Muztagh Ata. Even Mount Kailāsa is known in Indian civilization almost entirely in mythical form.[24]

Mountain mythology may be triggered by facts. Reinhold Gruenendahl's 1993 studies two *Mahābhārata* episodes on Gandhamādana, a mountain south of Kailāsa. It is closely connected with the Manasarovara lake and *rākṣasas* and *yakṣas* who are followers and protectors of Kubera.[25] According to the epic, Gandhamādana is to the north of the Himalayas: the Pāṇḍavas reach the Himavat range *traveling in the northern direction* after which sage Lomaśa declares "Gandhamādana is our next goal".[26] The epic distinguishes Gandhamādana from three other mountains: Kailāsa, Meru and Mainaka.[27] Its chief characteristic is inaccessibility (*Unzugänglichkeit*). Yet, Gandhamādana and Kailāsa are also confounded. Following N. Nand and K. Kumar,[28] Gruenendahl concludes that Garhwal was the original region of Kailāsa.[29] According to him, the "transfer" to Mount Kailāsa in western Tibet is of later date and due to the "close connection" (*enge Verbindung*) between Kailāsa and Gaṅgā. However, not only was Kelāsa known to Buddhist travellers but that connection does not exist since the Ganges originates south of the Himalayan range, on the other side of the mountains from the perspective of Kailāsa as we have seen.

The map of Garhwal which Gruenendahl attaches to his study does not show the Manasarovara lake itself but its furthest point to the north-east is the Mana Pass from where one descends to Tsaparang and from there, following the Sutlej, to the two lakes at the feet of the Kailāsa and Gandhamādana mountains. Mana Pass (pictured on our accompanying map immediately to the north of Kamet, another Himalayan giant) may be reached from the south by following the Alaknanda stream beyond Badrinath and Mana where Vyāsa, composer of the *Mahābhārata,* is said to have lived in a cave.[30] It is a long distance to the Kailāsa region and Gruenendahl quotes with approval as "subtle"[31] the observation of cartographers Harley and Woodward[32] that that distance is greater than the entire breadth of Garhwal as shown on the map. And yet, all these authorities miss the point. Crossing Himalayan passes at 18,000 feet or more is much harder than trekking a long distance through the Tibetan plateau into which one descends *after* crossing the passes. That does not only explain India's China War, to which we return, but is illustrated again and again by Indian travellers at much earlier dates. Gandamādana is probably the same as what became later known as the Gurla Mandhata mountain.[33] At 25,355 ft, much higher than Kailāsa, it is the first mountain massif that travellers from the south meet on their way to Kailāsa—just as Lomaśa declared in the *Mahābhārata*.

In his recent book on the *Mahābhārata* epic, Alf Hiltebeitel pays direct attention to the question whether myths carry their own kind of truth. He shows that the great epic clearly distinguishes three mountains: Kailāsa, associated with Śiva and inhabited by *siddhas*; Himavat, the Himalayan silver-white range, equally earthly but in some respects related to the third, mythical Mount Meru, golden and yellow centre of the world. It is difficult to depict their relationships in more precise geographical terms and Hiltebeitel concludes that these mountains are "out of this world".[34]

I would not even think of suggesting that Hiltebeitel might be wrong. His book is the product of many years of informed reflection. And yet there may be exceptions where the epic provides reliable, even interesting information about the geography of our world. One seems to occur at the end of his book where Hiltebeitel discusses the epical topos of "The other side of the mountain".[35] Śuka, son of Vyāsa, departs from Kailāsa, "a real single mountain", in the direction of earthly Himavat and unearthly Meru. Then, "fully breaking through to the other side", he reaches the Ganges. Hiltebeitel invokes Chinese parallels that may be palatable to those indologists who are "allergic to importing French thought into the interpretation of a classical Sanskrit text." But even in this mythical context, a geographical interpretation will not have failed to occur to my readers. For we have seen that travelling from Kailāsa in the southern direction, one has to "break through to the other side of the Himalayas" before one can get to the Ganges. It is tempting to believe that Vyāsa was familiar with the geological explanation of note 11.

2. *BMAC and the Tarim Mummies*

Numerous historical events illustrate the fact that mountains and rivers in mountainous areas have not changed their positions or courses during recent millennia. One is the sixties' war between India and China, another that of President Bush in Afghanistan which continues at the time of writing. Speaking of real world features, I taught a seminar at Berkeley in the fall of 2001, meeting every Tuesday. We started with a discussion of the itineraries of speakers of Indo-Aryan into South Asia and concentrated on the geography of Afghanistan where part of the older *Ṛgveda* was composed. As it happens, our third meeting was on September 11. Soon thereafter, U.S. military intelligence began to explore the geography of Afghanistan, a subject with which my students were already familiar. When Bush looked for bases in Pakistan, all predicted that he would be looking next at the former Soviet Republics north of the Afghan border. When it became known that the Taliban began to escape into Baluchistan, we knew already why because near Quetta, just below the Bolan Pass, Pirak had been an outpost of the BMAC or "Bactrian-Margianian Archaeological Complex"—topics we had explored because they yield early archaeological evidence for the shapes and configurations of bricks in Vedic altars. When combined with the evidence for "Western Aryan", they explain the connectedness between Greek and Vedic geometry.[36]

It has long been known that the "Mitanni Aryan" or "Western Aryan" of modern Syria and northern Irak, attested on clay tablets dated to the fourteenth century BCE, exhibits forms of early, Vedic and slightly pre-Vedic, Indo-Aryan.[37] Why did Indo-Aryan split into two groups, the smaller that went west to become "Mitanni Aryan" before disappearing and the larger group that went east and settled in South Asia? It has been widely assumed that this split may be due to the fact that Indo-Aryan speakers went south first and were followed by a massive intrusion of Iranian which acted as a wedge, forcing them out of the way, the majority across the Khyber and Bolan passes into the Indus Valley. That speakers of Indo-Aryan formed the vanguard of the Indo-Iranian movement is strongly supported by the carefully argued and formulated etymological reconstructions of Lubotsky.[38] These reconstructions also support the idea held earlier by Hiebert, Parpola, Witzel and others, that speakers of Indo-Iranian incorporated loanwords from the Central Asian towns of the BMAC, but Lubotsky is more specific: he shows how some of these words were first accepted by the Indo-Aryans before they were passed on to the Iranians.

After the decline of the Indus Valley Civilization (about 1900 BCE), the BMAC flourished for a few centuries on both sides of the Oxus. It spread to the south and served as a link between the Indus Valley and ancient Mesopotamia. The BMAC settlements were fortified: brick walls with towers surrounding a variety of structures, fire temples and altars, living quarters and working spaces for artisans including smiths and jewellers. Witzel's recent survey[39] has drawn attention to several unsolved problems. The vocabulary of the Veda contains words of BMAC and other Central Asian provenance, including animal names and terms associated with agriculture and brick-built settlements.[40] Similarly, archaeological BMAC influence has been found all over the Iranian plateau to its south.[41] And yet, these same areas have not been directly affected by the steppe influences to its north "as the older model of a massive Indo-Iranian or Indo-Aryan immigration would require".[42] Apparently, what happened instead is that small bands of people, speaking closely related languages, gradually trickled across the mountains.

We have seen that the movements of speakers of Indo-Aryan and Buddhist monks across the Oxus mirror each other. The Tarim-Yarkand basin of Xinjiang also played an important role in the expansion of Buddhism, so isn't it likely that it played a similar role in the movement of Indo-Aryan or Indo-Iranian? That could be predicted on logical grounds but there is also recent empirical evidence that supports it.

The Tarim-Yarkand Basin has recently drawn media attention because of the discovery of numerous so-called "mummies", really desiccated corpses, with tattooed skins and clothes surviving in excellent condition. These mummies do not look like the Egyptian paradigm, "wizened and eviscerated pharaohs wrapped in yards of dusty gauze".[43] Because of the extraordinary dryness, the facts that the tombs were well aerated and the dead probably died in midsummer so that the corpses quickly lost fluids and dried,[44] they are so well preserved that they seem to be merely asleep. They are often accompanied by small bags containing Ephedra. The earliest of these discoveries date from approximately 2000 BCE and the latest from the second or third century

CE. They started earlier and lasted longer than the BMAC, but all the early finds coincide in time with the movements of Indo-Iranian speakers.

The newsworthy feature of these corpses is that their physical appearance suggests and DNA analysis demonstrates that they belong to people who have been called by various terms: European, Europoid, Caucasian or Caucasoid. Corpses found after the third century CE are increasingly Mongoloid and Chinese. It has been widely assumed that the language spoken by these mummies before they were mummies was Indo-European.[45] If that is so, their language must have been an early form of Tocharian—the easternmost member of the Indo-European language family—or Indo-Iranian.

The evidence for Tocharian is Buddhist and of much later date: end of the first millennium CE,[46] but it was spoken in the same Tarim Basin of Xinjiang. That recent form of Tocharian, the only one that is known, has links with Chinese and Altaic[47] but is chiefly and more basically connected with western Indo-European.[48]

The origin of Tocharian remains controversial. Pulleyblank argued on linguistic grounds, in various contexts between 1966 and 1983,[49] that Tocharian must have been spoken in the Tarim basin at a much earlier period, perhaps as early as 2000 BCE. Some such view, going back another one or two millennia, has been adopted, partly on archaeological grounds, by Mallory and Carpelan & Parpola 2001.[50] It has also been assumed, on analogy with the Iranian "wedge", that Indo-Iranian itself acted as a wedge and separated Tocharian from the Indo-European languages to its west.

According to others, Tocharian arrived in Central Asia later than Indo-Iranian. Adams[51] argued that the Tocharians entered the Tarim Basin from the north but borrowed irrigation and its vocabulary from eastern Iranians who had entered or were entering from the south-west. The question we raised before (page 4) remains: why would speakers of Indo-Iranian, having reached the Oxus, trek east through the mountains? There is no solid evidence for Indo-Iranian, let alone Iranian, existing that far east during the early periods.

Leaving aside Tocharian uncertainties, what are solid facts

regarding the Tarim mummies and the Indo-Iranian languages? As for the first, mummies have been found along the northern and southern branches of the Silk Road both. In the north, they are mostly concentrated near Lop Nor, far to the east and close to China proper, just off the right border of our map. Along the southern branch, a series of finds leads close to the source of the Yarkand-Tarim river, the Muztagh Ata ridge. The three most important of these discoveries are represented on our map by black dots. The westernmost of these is immediately to the north of Khotan.[52]

As for the second, Indo-Iranian is the language or group of dialects spoken by those who wandered in the southern direction east of the Caspian Sea. What may be concluded from that? The first point is that there would have been no reason for these wanderers after they had reached the area of Samarkand, to change course, turn east and enter the mountains. If any eastward move took place, it would have been easier and, therefore, more likely, at a much earlier period. Starting, for example, from the Sintashta-Arkaim culture,[53] some speakers of Indo-Iranian could easily have continued in a south-eastern direction through the extensive steppe and forested regions of what is now Kazakhistan, pass through the "Dzungarian Gates" and enter the Tarim Basin from the north. Those speakers, before they became mummies, are likely to have spoken what became an "eastern" form of Indo-Iranian. The western and eastern groups would soon be separated from each other by the Tien Shan, the Pamirs and other mountain ranges.

Could the movements of these two branches constitute the cause for the unexplained split of Indo-Iranian into Iranian and Indo-Aryan? If that were so, the Tarim mummies, being the eastern group, are likely to have spoken (an early form of) Indo-Aryan. After establishing themselves in the basin, they would have reached Khotan, from where the westernmost finds of Tarim mummies come, and the Muztagh Ata range still further to its west. I conclude that it likely that it is these Indo-Aryans who discovered the Soma and became the vanguard of the Indo-Iranian movement. It follows that Witzel's etymology is vindicated by speakers of Indo-Aryan who moved not from west to east, but from east to west, passing through the Wakhan corridor and entering what is now Afghanistan where they composed part of the *Ṛgveda*.

There is a third branch of Indo-Iranian along with Iranian and Indo-Aryan: the presently small group of Kafiri or Nuristani languages. Perhaps the Tarim mummies spoke some of its early forms. Why do none of the contributors to the 1998 volumes edited by Victor Mair[54] mention Indo-Aryan or Kafiri as possible languages of the mummies? Why do all assume that their language must have been (early forms of) Tocharian or Iranian: Douglas Q. Adams (already in 1995), John Colarusso, Jeannine Davis-Kimball, J.P. Mallory, Asko Parpola, Colin Renfrew and Mair himself? Are not Indo-Aryan, and even Kafiri, at least equally likely candidates? Is not Indo-Aryan a more likely candidate than Iranian since all Iranian languages that spread to the east belong to the first millennium CE? And isn't it telling that the ancient Iranians, who had many *haoma* substitutes, probably did not know the original Soma[55]?

It may take some time before we have answers to these questions. There are also others for Tarim Indo-Aryans could have taken other routes to South Asia. What we can do is answer the question, how people at different periods of history moved from the Tarim Basin to the Indus valley—the topic of our third and final section.

3. *From Tarim to Indus*

The many possible routes may be roughly subdivided into three groups: the easiest "western" (A) the "middle" (B) and the "eastern" (C).[56]

(A) Speakers of Indo-Iranian trekked south and crossed the Oxus west of Samarkand. Some Chinese Buddhist pilgrims support that traditional picture by following part of the same route. Xuan zang (Hsüen-Tsang), regarding Samarkand as a veritable paradise, went there first before he turned south, crossed the Oxus at Termez and reached Bamiyan. Like the early speakers of Indo-Aryan, he then turned east again and reached the Indus valley via the Khyber Pass. His probable route, long but relatively easy is depicted by Foucher.[57]

We have seen that the Tarim mummies, before they were mummies, may have followed a similar route. They would have reached the Taghdumbash Pamir, located at the eastern extremity of the Wakhan corridor, where Sir Aurel Stein got confused.[58] It is true that it is "a wide, grey desolate valley. . . with a bitter wind blowing over the grass night and day".[59] All the same, that corridor has always been a link between east and west because the watershed there is very much lower than the axial range of the Hindukush to the south of it—an important geographical and geopolitical fact emphasized by Curzon.[60]

(B) Swat with its numerous Buddhist remnants may be reached from the south-west via the Swat river or more directly from the north where the terrain is much more difficult.[61] The entire "central area" between the Oxus and Indus rivers and the Hindukush and Karakoram mountain ranges has long been known for the extreme hardships it imposes upon travellers. Klimburg[62] refers to Chinese sources describing "ravines and canyons which enclose unfordable streams", "hanging passages", paths of about one foot wide where travellers "walk step-by-step clasping each other"[63] and mentions modern comments on bridges made of twisted twigs: "very unpleasant to cross in a high wind".[64]

Many such descriptions have been corroborated in more precise geographical terms by a series of recent discoveries on the upper Indus. The opportunity was opened by the construction of the Karakoram Highway between Pakistan and China. First discovered by A.H. Dani and Karl Jettmar, these sites are now being made available through the magnificent series *Materialien zur Archäologie der Nordgebiete Pakistans*. The second of four volumes that have been published so far is especially relevant to our present context. Edited by Gérard Fussman and Ditte König,[65] it deals with Shatial, a "station of rock carvings and inscriptions" (*Felsbildstation*) not far east of Swat. Oskar von Hinüber, Karl Jettmar, Nicholas Simms-Williams and others have contributed to their translation or analysis. Their dates fall within the period 350-650 CE. There is no unanimity about their significance. Why did people come together in this remote place on the upper Indus and constructed a bridge from iron chains?

Shatial might have been a caravanserai, an exchange market or a religious centre (not exclusively Buddhist since there are numerous theriomorphic forms and phallic representations). The number of Sogdian inscriptions, 565, is larger than in any other known upper Indus site. Many are graffiti in which a person states his name and adds some information, e.g. "I arrived here yesterday. . .". The writing exhibits a style that has been found in Dunhuang in Kansu, close to the eastern border of Xinjiang.[66] The majority of names suggest that these Sogdian speakers came from families that originated in the neighbourhood of Samarkand, but there is one exception that clearly refers to western Xinjiang because it states: "I (so-and-so, son of so-and-so) have come here on the tenth and have invoked the spirit of this holy place Kart (= Shatial?) to enable me to get speedily to Kharvandan and be happily reunited with my brother".[67] Kharvandan has been identified by Yutaka Yoshida[68] with modern Tash Qurghan at the foot of Muztagh Ata, visible on our map at the right bottom angle of the large triangle that indicates that mountain.

Why did so many Sogdians come to Shatial? According to Karl Jettmar, Sogdian merchants may have had a monolopy on trade with people coming from the south who are responsible for more than 400 Brahmi inscriptions (similarly numerous in other upper Indus sites). The Sogdians, in other words, came to Shatial from the north to exchange goods.

In our present context, the inscription that refers to Tash Qurghan is relevant because it suggests that a millennium or so earlier, Indo-Aryan speaking mummies, before they were mummies, may also have trekked south through the difficult "central" area. They could have used bridges made of twisted twigs or some of the simpler types of boat mentioned in Pāṇini, Late Vedic or the epic.

(C) The "eastern" routes start from Khotan and all are very difficult but the second I shall mention becomes easier afterwards. It is worthy of note that south of Khotan there is another Muztagh mountain. Not as high as its "father" (*ata*), it stands north-east of the Soda Plains of Aksai Chin to which we shall return.

(C1) Any trek from Khotan in the south-western direction has to cross one of the high passes of the Karakoram Range. The most dangerous is the Muztagh Pass which, at 19,030 feet, cuts through the heart of the Karakorams, next to K2. Following a tributary of the Yarkand river, the ascent is not bad but the descent on the other side almost impossible. The first and only people known to have done it are Sir Francis Younghusband

and his small party of Baltis and Ladakhis.[69] That was in 1887 and due to a misunderstanding that arose on the spot. Younghusband wrote afterwards in a letter how his guide Wall started hewing steps across the ice slope which led to the precipe: "I freely confess that I myself could never have attempted the descent and that I—an Englishman—was afraid to go first." Sven Hedin called the descent of the Muztagh "the most difficult and dangerous achievement in these mountains so far."

(C2) Another trail from Khotan goes via the Karakoram Pass, formidable at 18,290 feet. Skirting the southern extremities of the Karakoram range, it reaches the Indus in the valley of Ladakh. Those who perservere in the southern direction are in for a pleasant surprise: the valley of the upper Indus in western Tibet—a wide tract of land at an altitude of about 12,000 feet which does not change much between Ladakh and Mount Kailāsa. Some Chinese Buddhist pilgrims (perhaps also Vedic Indians[70]) followed the latter part of this route. They were in the same position as China in the 1950's when it sought access for large trucks and equipment into Tibet.

The causes and outcome of the India-China war are largely dictated by the enduring facts of geography. It is difficult to enter Tibet from the east because the rivers there—the upper stretches of the Yangtze, Mekong, Salween and other rivers of east and south-east Asia—run north-south through steep gorges that can easily be controlled by Tibetans. Reliable access from China is through Xinjiang and then following the route I just outlined. China, therefore, may lose Buddhist Tibet if and when it loses Muslim Xinjiang.

In the middle fifties, India and China were friendly neighbors, not contemplating military expeditions through each other's territory. India had inherited British-Indian boundaries that were chiefly based on British fear or paranoia about Russia.[71] Since the Karakoram Pass had been accepted as a boundary by British and Chinese in the late nineteenth century, Chinese troops did not cross it. East of the Karakoram Pass the situation was less clear and China built a road through the Soda plains of Aksai Chin, as legitimate or illegitimate a part of China on Chinese maps as it was of India on Indian, that is, old British maps. Bordering on the Karakorams at over 18,000 feet, Aksai Chin is a barren wasteland, difficult of access from any side. But the Chinese road was targeted to reach the wide tract of land that is the Indus valley in Western Tibet and runs in the south-eastern direction up to the region of Kailāsa as I just described it.

Whether Tarim mummies travelled south along this trek is left for Chinese archaeologists to discover. Giuseppe Tucci pointed out that archaeology in Tibet, until the time of his writing, had been confined to objects found by chance because the Tibetans did not like digging in their country. "When I sought to explore a cave at Luk in Western Tibet I was obliged to abandon the excavation, the hostility of the village people being all too evident." Tucci adds that Chinese archaeologists are now free to "carry out excavations of any kind".[72]

Having reached the Kailāsa region along the difficult eastern route, Indo-Aryan speakers from the Tarim basin could have continued to South Asia by following the Sutlej river downstream via Tabo, or crossing the Lipu Lekh Pass at the point where modern Tibet, Nepal and India meet. In so doing, they would have followed what became later a Buddhist trek or the route that Hindu pilgrims from India continue to take to the present day.

Conclusions

From a human perspective, mountains and rivers that flow through mountainous areas are enduring features of geography. This applies to the routes of speakers of Indo-Aryan, Buddhist pilgrims and later warriors or travellers through the Hindukush, Pamirs, Karakorams and Himalayas. Barring better boots, tents, concentrated foods and a few other amenities, modern travellers in these areas are in the same position as their ancient precursors.

A particular conclusion that may be drawn from these general considerations is that many ancient inhabitants of the Tarim Basin may not have spoken Iranian or Tocharian, as has been widely assumed, but an early form of Kafiri or Indo-Aryan. On their way to Afghanistan via the Wakhan corridor and perhaps the BMAC, they must have discarded their little bags with Ephedra and discovered the real Soma, all the while composing hymns. The *Ṛgveda* carries no explicit memories of Oxus or Tarim, but if the best Soma came from Mūjavat, Muztagh Ata or the Pamirs, that would be a clear recollection of its Central Asian past.

My conclusions are tentative for crossing the boundaries between civilizations and academic specializations is by its very nature risky. But fear of failure has never led to scientific progress.

I am grateful to participate in the Felicitation Volume in honour of my esteemed colleague and old friend Professor Musashi Tachikawa who has made valuable contributions to several disciplines. My essay has been inspired by this display of Buddhist *abhayam* which is also Vedic (*Ṛgveda* 10.152.2 = *Atharvaveda* 1.21.1). My contribution has been prompted further by the generous gift, many decades ago, of his only copy of the 1982 edition of

and his help in obtaining a magnificent photo of a world map from Horyu-ji with Meru/Kailāsa and the four rivers at its center.

NOTES

1. Frits Staal, 1986, with photographs by Adelaide de Menil, "In the Realm of the Buddha", *Natural History* 95, 34-45. 2531 (Thai Buddhist era) = 1988 CE, "Where was Lake Anodat?" in *Journal of the Faculty Arts* of *the Chulalongkorn University* 129-37. 1990, "The Lake of the Yakṣa Chief", in Tadeusz Skorupski (ed.), *Indo-Tibetan Studies, Papers in honour and appreciation of Professor David L. Snellgrove's contribution to Indo-Tibetan Studies* Tring, U.K.: The Institute of Buddhist Studies, 275-91. 2001a, "How a Psychoactive Substance becomes a Ritual: The Case of Soma", *Social Research. An International quarterly of the Social Sciences* 68, 745-78.—The present essay uses diacritics sparingly and only in textual or linguistic contexts.
2. Unless *Ṛgveda* 2.15.6. which declares that Indra after drinking Soma: "made the Indus through his power flow in the northern direction", refers to the only region where the Indus flows in that direction, viz., north of Kailāsa. I argued in Staal, 2001a (see *note* 1): 290-91 that the Vedic Indians would have discovered it if and when they went upstream to the source of their most important river. Michael Witzel (personal communication) considers it more likely that that reversal of direction is due to the river being dammed as the result of an earthquake.
3. Staal, 200la (see *note* 1).
4. Michael Witzel, 1980, "Early Eastern Iran and the Atharvaveda", *Persica* 9, 86-128: 104-5: *notes* 16-17.

5. Michael Witzel, 1999a, "Aryan and non-Aryan Names in Vedic India. Data for the linguistic situation, c.1900-500 B.C.", in Bronkhorst, Johannes and Madhav M. Deshpande (eds.), *Aryan and Non-Aryan in South Asia. Evidence, Interpretation and Ideology,* Cambridge Mass.: Harvard University, 337-404: 345, 363; (2000), "The Home of the Aryans", in Hintze, A. & E. Tichy (eds.), *Anusantatyai. Festschrift für Johanna Narten zum 70. Geburtstag* Münchener Studien zur Sprachwissenschaft, Beihefte NF 19. Dettelbach: J.H. Roell, 283-338: 295 *note* 23.
6. See *note* 1.
7. Witzel 2000 (see *note* 5): 283-86; James P. Mallory and Victor H. Mair. 2000, *The Tarim Mummies. Ancient China and the Mysteries of the Earliest Peoples from the West,* London: Thames & Hudson, 119; Christian Carpellan and Asko Parpola, 2001, "Emergence, Contacts and Dispersal of Proto-Indo-European, Proto-Uralic and Proto-Aryan in Archaeological Perspective" in Archaeological Perspective" in: Christian Carpellan, Asko Parpola and Petteri Koskikallio (eds.), 2001, *Early Contacts between Uralic and Indo-European: Linguistic and Archaeological Considerations,* Helsinki: Suomalais-Ugrilainen Seura, 55-150: 93-96. Cf. Victor H. Mair, 1998; "Die *Sprachamöbe.* An Archeolinguistic Parable," in Victor H. Mair (ed.), 1998, *The Bronze Age and Early Iron Age Peoples of Eastern Central Asia,* Washington: Institute for the Study of Man, and Philadelphia: The University of Pennsylvania Museum Publications, Vols. I-II: II: 852-53.
8. Gerhard Wirth and Oskar von Hinüber (eds.), (1985), *Arrian, Der Alexanderzug/Indische Geschichte,* Berlin: Akademie-Verlag, Vols. I-II: I: 290ff.
9. Adapted from a 1952 map of the *National Geographic Society.*
10. Witzel 1999a (see *note* 5): 368-76, with discussion of earlier studies.
11. Most of the rivers of northern India originate in the Himalayas, but some of the largest have their sources not in the Himalayas but further to the north. The reason is that these rivers are older than the mountains. Before the Himalayas existed, they flowed southward from present-day Central Asia and the Tibetan plateau into the Tethys Sea. During the Tertiary age, the chunk of land that was to become India drifted across that sea and collided with the Asian plateau, pushing up the Himalayas. The rivers now had to go around the mountains or cut through them. South of the new Himalayas, new rivers originated and flew in the southern direction (e.g., the Ganges).
12. Although it has been related to Tirich Mir, the highest mountain of the eastern Hindukush: Witzel 2000 (see *note* 5): 313, *note* 90.
13. See *note* 1.
14. Explanation in Staal 1990: 287 (see *note* 1).
15. In mountainous areas there are no straight lines. Moreover, it would be more appropriate to substitute for English "crow", the Himalayan *haṃsa* or "goose"; or the Bearded Vulture (*Gyps himalayensis*), perhaps the original *śyena* (Frits Staal in collaboration with C.V. Somayajipad and M. Itti Ravi Nambudiri, 1983, *AGNI. The Vedic Ritual of the Fire Altar,* Berkeley: Asian Humanities Press, Vols. I-II, 1983; Indian edition, 2001:. Delhi: Motilal Banarsidass, I: 89-90) which soars at 16,000 feet across the mountains (Arnold Heim and August Gansser, 1939, *The Throne of the Gods. An Account of the First Swiss Expedition to the Himalayas,* New York: The Macmillan: Plates 101 and 192).

16. Staal. 1982, "The Himalayas and the Fall of Religion", in Deborah E. Klimburg-Salter (ed.), *The Silk Route and the Diamond Path. Esoteric Buddhist Art on the Trans-Himalayan Trade Routes,* UCLA Art Council, Los Angeles, 1982, 38-50. 1985, "Substitutions de paradigmes et religions d'Asie", *Cahiers d'extrême Asie* 1, 21-57; 1989, 1993, *Rules without Meaning: Ritual, Mantras and the Human Sciences,* New York etc.: Peter Lang; Indian edition, 1996, Delhi: Motilal Banarsidass: Chapter 28.
17. See e.g., Michael Witzel, 1989, "Tracing the Vedic Dialects", in Colette Caillat (ed.), *Dialectes dans les littératures indo-aryennes,* Paris: Institut de Civilisation Indienne, 97-265: 116.
18. V.S. Agarwala, 1953, *India as known to Pāṇini. A Study of the cultural material in the Aṣṭādhyāyī,* Lucknow, University of Lucknow: 156-57.
19. Michael Witzel, 1999a (see *note* 5): 359 *note* 99.
20. The British bridge of 1885 "was difficult to construct owing to the rapidity of the current. ... It is 100 ft. high above low water" because "the river has been known to rise 90 ft. in flood": Murray's *Handbook of India, Pakistan, Burma and Ceylon,* 1959 (18th edition), London: John Murray: 505.
21. George N. Curzon. 1896, *The Pamirs and the Source of the Oxus,* London: The Royal Geographical Society, 51.
22. Curzon (see *note* 21) also describes (*pages* 49-50) two lakes in the Pamirs as "two sheets of water united by a narrowish strait in the centre" and continues with a description that perfectly fits the two lakes Mānasarovar and Rakshas Tal south of Mount Kailāsa. That resemblance may have been noted by early travellers and contributed to the confusions between the two mountains.
23. M. Aurel Stein, 1975 [1907], *Ancient Khotan. Detailed Report of Archaeological Explorations in Chinese Turkestan Carried Out and Described under the Orders of H.M. Indian Government,* New York: Hacker Art Books, New York: 22.
24. Of course, there are Indians who have been there and Hindu pilgrims continue to go. One of the best books on the Kailāsa region, published with a foreword by Jawaharlal Nehru was written by Swami Pranavananda. F.R.G.S. (*Fellow of the Royal Geographical Society*): 1949, *Kailāsa-Mānasarovar,* Calcutta: S.P. League, Ltd.
25. Cf. Staal 1990 (see *note* 1).
26. *Mahābhārata* 3:142 in Reinhold Gruenendahl. 1993, "Zu den beiden Gandhamādana-Episoden des Āraṇyakaparvan", *Studien zur Indologie und Iranistik* 18, 103-38:104.
27. Gruenendahl (see *note* 26): 117.
28. Nitya Nand and Kamlesh Kumar, 1989, *The Holy Himalaya. A Geographical Interpretation of Garhwal,* Delhi: Daya Publishing House.
29. Gruenendahl (see *note* 26): 136.
30. Gruenendahl (see *note* 26): 130, *note* 85.
31. Gruenendahl (see *note* 26): *note* 101 "*feinsinnig*".
32. J.L. Harley and D. Woodward (eds), 1992, *The History of Cartography,* Vol. 2, 1: *Cartography in the traditional Islamic and South Asian Societies,* Chicago and London: The University of Chicago Press, 439.
33. Staal 1990 (see *note* 1): 282-85.
34. Alf Hiltebeitel, 2001, *Rethinking the Mahābhārata. A Reader's Guide to the Education of the Dharma King,* Chicago and London: The University of Chicago Press: 305.

35. Hiltebeitel 2001 (see *note* 34): 312 ff.
36. Staal, 1999, "Greek and Vedic Geometry", *Journal of Indian Philosophy* 27, 105-27. 2001b, "Squares and Oblongs in the Veda", *Journal of Indian Philosophy* 29, 257-73. 2001c, "There is no Proof But...: Addendum to EJVS 7-3 on Vedic Geometry and the History of Science", *Electronic Journal of Vedic Studies (EJVS)* 7/5.
37. See, e.g., Paul Thieme, 1960, "The 'Aryan' gods of the Mitanni treatises", *Journal of the American Oriental Society* 80, 301-17; T. Burrow, 1973, "The Proto-Indoaryans", *Journal of the Royal Asiatic Society,* 123-40.
38. Alexander Lubotsky, 2001, "The Indo-Aryan Substratum" in Carpellan *et al.* (see *note* 7), 301-17.
39. Witzel 2000 (see *note* 5): 287-91.
40. Michael Witzel, 1999a (see *note* 5); 1999b, "Substrate Languages in Old Indo-Aryan (Rigvedic, Middle and Late Vedic)", *Electronic Journal of Vedic Studies (EJVS)* 5/1: Section 5; Alexander Lubotsky, 2001 (see *note* 38).
41. See the map in Fredrik T. Hiebert, 1998, "Central Asians on the Iranian Plateau: A Model for Indo-Iranian Expansionism", in Mair (see *note* 7), Vol. I, 148-61: 152, Fig. 2.
42. Witzel 2000 (see *note* 5): 290.
43. Mallory and Mair, 2000 (see *note* 7): 8.
44. Dexiu He, 1998, "A Brief Report on the Mummies from the Zaghunluq Site in Charchan County" in Mair (see *note* 7), Vol. I, 169-74: 174; contrast Wang Binhua in Mallory and Mair 2000 (see *note* 7): 178-79.
45. Victor H. Mair, 1998, "Priorities", in Mair 1998 (see *note* 7), Vol. I, 4-41; I: 16; Sinor in Mair 1998 II: 741, etc.
46. See above, page 5.
47. Georges-Jean Pinault, 1998, "Tocharian Languages and Pre-Buddhist Culture", in Mair (see *note* 7), Vol. I, 358-71; Alexander Lubotsky, 1998, "Tocharian Loan Words in Old Chinese: Chariots, Chariot Gear, and Town Building", in Mair Vol. I, 379-90.
48. e.g., Eric P. Hamp, 1998, "Whose were the Tocharians?" in Mair (see *note* 7), Vol. I, 307-46.
49. Pulleyblank, E. G. (1983), "The Chinese and their Neighbours in Prehistoric and Early Historic Times", in D.N. Keightley (ed.), *The Origins of Chinese Civilization,* Berkeley: University of California Press, 411-66.
50. James P. Mallory, 1989, *In Search of the Indo-Europeans: Language, Archaeology and Myth,* London: Thames and Hudson, endorsed by Werner Winter, 1998, "Lexical Archaisms in the Tocharian Languages", in Mail (see *note* 7), Vol. I, 347-57, and Carpelan & Parpola 2001 (see *note* 7).
51. Douglas Q. Adams, 1998, "On the History and Significance of Some Tocharian B Agricultural Terms" in Mair (see 7), Vol. I, 372-78.
52. The distinction between the northern and southern discoveries reflects the distinction between so-called 'Proto-European' and 'Indo-Afghan' or 'East Mediterranean' populations: Victor H. Mair, 1995, "Prehistoric Caucasoid Corpses of the Tarim Basin, "*Journal* of *Indo-European Studies,* 23: 281-308:190, Adams 1998 (see *note* 7).
53. Witzel 2000 (see *note* 7): 283-85; Carpelan & Parpola 2001 (see *note* 7): 95-96, 131-32, 131-38.
54. See *note* 7.
55. Staal 2001a (see *note* 1): 763-69 discussing David Stophlet Flattery and

Martin Schwartz, 1989, *Haoma and Harmaline: The Botanical Identity of the Indo-Iranian Sacred Hallucinogen "Soma" and Its Legacy in Religion, Language and Middle Eastern Folklore,* Berkeley: University of California Press.

56. For a further discussion of "B", see Maximilian Klimburg, 1982, "The Setting: The Western Trans-Himalayan Crossroads", in Deborah E. Klimburg-Salter (ed.), *The Silk Route and the Diamond Path. Esoteric Buddhist Art on the Trans-Himalayan Trade Route,* Los Angeles: UCLA Art Council, 24-37. Klimburg refers to "B" as "western" adopting a Himalayan perspective.
57. A. Foucher, 1947, *La vieille Route de l'Inde de Bactres a Taxila,* Paris: Les Editions d'Art et d'Histoire, Vols. I-II: II: 233.
58. Above, pages 8.
59. Patrick French, 1995, *Younghusband. The Last Great Imperial Adventurer,* London: Flamingo, 77.
60. *The Pamirs and the Source of the Oxus* (see *note* 21): 40.
61. Contrast the opening chapters with, e.g., chapters XIII and following in Sir Aurel Stein (1972) [1929] *On Alexander's Track to the Indus. Personal Native of Explorations on the North-West Frontier of India carried out under the orders of H.M Indian Government,* New York: Benjamin Blom, Inc.
62. Klimburg, 1982 (see *note* 56): 33 ff.
63. Following Luciano Petech, 1950, *Northern India according to the Shui-ching-chu,* Roma: ISMEO: 16.
64. After John Biddulph, 1880, *Tribes of the Hindukush,* Calcutta. Reprint Graz 1971: 2.
65. Gérard Fussman and Ditte König, 1997, *Die Felsbildstation Shatial,* Mainz: Philipp von Zabern. Cf. the review by Richard Salomon, 2001, *Journal of the American Oriental Society* 121: 663-64.
66. There are a few Chinese inscriptions. Some contain what may be the names of persons, others may be imitations and none can be dated: Thomas O. Hollmann in Fussman (see *note* 65): 61. Most of them occur on a large boulder which also carries a figure that Jettmar regards as Chinese (Wei) in style. Chinese inscriptions have been found elsewhere, e.g. Hunza (Fussman: 73, *note* 1). The Chinese occupied Gilgit later.
67. Fussman 1997 (see *note* 65): 207-8.
68. Yutaka Yoshida, 1991, "Sogdian Miscellany III", in Ronald E. Emmerick and Dieter Weber (eds.), *Corolla Iranica.* Papers in Honour of Prof. Dr. David Neil MacKenzie, Frankfurt – New: Peter *Lang,* 237-44: 237-38 referred to by Sims-Williams in Fussman 1997 (see *note* 65).
69. French 1994 (see *note* 59), Chapter 4.
70. See note 2.
71. In 1889, Lord Lansdowne wrote (Neville Maxwell 1972, *India's China War,* New York: Anchor Books: 16): "The country between the Karakoram and Kuen Lun ranges is, I understand, of no value, very inaccessible and not likely to be coveted by Russia. We might, I should think, encourage the Chinese to take it, if they showed any inclination to do so. This would be better than leaving a no-man's-land between our frontier and that of China. Moreover, the stronger we can make China at this point, and the more we can induce her to hold her own over the whole Kashgar-Yarkand region, the more useful will she be to us as an obstacle to Russian advance along this line."
72. Giuseppe Tucci, 1973, *The Ancient Civilization of Transhimalaya,* Geneva: Nagel Publishers, 33.

II
BUDDHISM

Chapter 2

Early Buddhism

JOHANNES BRONKHORST

This is the text of a lecture delivered at a small conference organised by Professor Richard Gombrich at the University of Oxford in April 2001. The aim of this conference was to bring a number of speakers together who occupy themselves with the theme of early Buddhism. They were invited to present their different approaches and results. The present paper primarily presents the approach and findings of my "Die Buddhistische Lehre" (Bronkhorst, 2000),[1] but does so in the light of a comparison with some of the views of Dr. Sue Hamilton[2] and Professor Richard Gombrich in particular.

Sue Hamilton, on p. 59 of her book *Early Buddhism: A new approach,* makes the following important observation: "...it is highly likely that records preserved orally from the beginning, in an environment in which communities were both dispersed and lacked anything like a kind of formal communication system, of a teaching that was novel, radical, and difficult to grasp, should include anomalies, variations, slightly distorted repetitions, and any number of oddities of various sorts. It would, I think, be surprising if they did not." I fully agree, and even a superficial aquaintance with the Pali canon supports Hamilton's observation, I think. I agree with Sue Hamilton as far as the nature of our material is concerned, but I disagree with her proposal as to how to deal with it. She continues namely with the words: "I think one should discount as unimportant the bulk of these", and it is clear from the context that it is the bulk of "anomalies, variations, slightly distorted repetitions, and any number of oddities of various sorts" that according to Hamilton have to be discounted as unimportant. This method, if it is one, opens the way to what Hamilton calls a "common-sensical approach to the material" (p. 4), one in which we allow our common sense to decide what early Buddhism is all about, and discard everything else. The history of Buddhist studies is strewn with the results of the common senses of various scholars, few of which have convinced other specialists. What is needed, I submit, is not one more subjective choice of preferred passages, but a serious attempt to make sense of all, or as many as possible, of them, including the "anomalies, variations, slightly distorted repetitions, and any number of oddities of various sorts". Far from discounting anomalies, I would think, it is important to try to explain them. This is a daunting task, and I am far from claiming to have accomplished it. However, by systematically studying at least some important anomalies, I do think that a better understanding can be reached of the doctrinal developments that have taken place during the decades, perhaps centuries, in which the Sūtra Piṭaka reached its more or less final form(s).

There is an obvious way to account for a number of the anomalies we find in the early Buddhist texts by considering a factor which, as Richard Gombrich points out,[3] is easily forgotten. Gombrich describes it as follows : "Often the Buddha's preaching was successful in making converts. By the same token converts came from a variety of backgrounds. At that time Buddhism had only rudimentary institutions, no schools and probably rather haphazard socialisation of converts. So many members of the Saṅgha must have gone on using some of their former terms and concepts. . . ." I find this description very plausible. Gombrich then however continues : "and the Buddha may well have gone on meeting them half way when he talked to them". Here we have to be careful, I think. It is true that there are passages in the early canon where the Buddha is presented as "accept[ing] as the starting-point of his own position the desirability of the act or condition prized by his opponent",[4] but these should not be confused with others where the positions of opponents are presented, not as the starting-point for a debate or a sermon, but as the Buddha's own. In these cases the Buddha presumably has not gone on meeting his opponents *half* way, but *all the way,* so much so that we might have to assume that the Buddha had actually been converted to those other positions. Unless, of course, we drop the idea that such passages correctly represent the position of the Buddha. The presence of such passages can then still be accounted for by remembering that "[s]o many members of the Saṅgha must have gone on using some of their former terms and concepts", but without the added supposition that they reliably express the Buddha's words. Since Professor Gombrich himself[5] believes that certain *suttas* postdate the Buddha's death, this would seem to me an elegant and plausible solution to some of the more problematic anomalies in the Sūtra Piṭaka that should also be acceptable to him.

What were the "former terms and concepts" of many new members of the Saṅgha? What do we know about the other religions that existed at the time of the Buddha? The religious movement that is perhaps most often mentioned as such in the canonical texts is Jainism. Mahāvīra was a contemporary of the Buddha, and many encounters of the Buddha with followers of the former are recounted. Mahāvīra, like the Buddha, was a wandering ascetic, both were called *Śramaṇa,* both preached practical ways to escape from the results of one's deeds, so there are plenty of reasons to assume that many early converts came from the kind of background to which Jainism belonged. Professor Gombrich agrees with this, but believes that there are practical problems. With regard to the Jainas he says:[6] "these allusions to opponents' arguments could well be distorted". He supports this with the following arguments:[7] "The Jain texts that have come down to us were probably first written down in the fifth century A.D.; some of the material is certainly very much older, but scientific study of the voluminous and very difficult Jain texts is in its infancy. However, what we do have is enough to show that some (not all) of the teaching ascribed by the Buddhist texts to Mahāvīra . . . is quite unlike what Jain tradition holds him to have taught." Perhaps under the influence of these remarks, Dr. Hamilton does not so much as mention the Jainas in her recent book, not even in the chapter on "The Indian context".[8]

And yet the situation is by far not so bleak as suggested by Gombrich. Whatever doctrinal developments Jainism has undergone during the centuries preceding the final constitution of its canon—to the research of which I have tried to contribute in a few articles[9]—, a number of essential positions of the earliest Jaina texts are confirmed by the Buddhist canon. Consider the following: Chapter 29 verse 37 of the Jaina *Uttarajjhayaṇa* states: "By being without activity the soul does not bind new karma and destroys the karma that was bound before." The *Cūladukkhakkhandha Sutta* of the *Majjhima Nikāya* (PTS edition vol. I, p. 93, 1.2-10) ascribes exactly the same point of view to the Jainas, in the following words: "As a result of the annihilation of former actions by asceticism, and of the non-performing of new actions, there is no further effect in the future; as a result of no further effect in the future there is destruction of actions; as a result of the destruction of actions there is destruction of suffering; as a result of the destruction of suffering there is destruction of sensation; as a result of the destruction of sensation all suffering will be exhausted." It hardly matters how exactly the Jainas of that early period conceived of the nature of *karma.* Both passages teach us that the Jaina ascetics of that time aimed at destroying the results of their deeds, and that the method they considered appropriate was total abstention from all activity. Other passages, from both the Buddhist and Jaina canon, confirm this.

It is equally clear from both canons that the Buddhists disagreed with the Jainas, both where the nature of the problem and that of its solution was concerned. One again I cite two passages, one from the Buddhist canon, the other one from the Jaina canon. In the *Devadaha Sutta* of the *Majjhima Nikāya* (PTS edition vol. II, p. 222) the Buddha is recorded to have said: "If the pleasure and pain that beings feel are caused by what was done in the past, then the Nigaṇṭhas (i.e., the Jainas) surely must have done bad deeds in the past, since they now feel such painful, racking, piercing feelings." An early Jaina text—the *Sūyagaḍa* (*Sūtrakṛtāṅga*) 2.6.26-28, as presented by Bollée[10]—pays back in kind by pointing out that a Buddhist who grills a child and eats it, but without knowing that he does so, is supposedly free of guilt, whereas that same Buddhist is guilty if he eats a gourd while thinking it is a baby. The passage reads, in Bollée's translation:[11] "If someone puts a ball of oilcake on a spit and roasts it with the idea: this is a man, or a gourd, thinking it to be a baby, he becomes for us soiled/soils himself for us with killing a living being. On the other hand, however, if a non-Āryan puts a man on a spit and roasts him, taking him for an oil-cake, or does the same to a child he thinks is a gourd, in our opinion he is not soiled with killing a living being. If (*ca*) someone puts a man or a child on a spit and roasts it on a fire taking it for a lump of oil-cake, it would be fit for Buddhists to end their vow of fasting with." From these and other passages it becomes clear that the Jainas had a different vision of karmic retribution from the Buddhists: unlike the Buddhists, the Jainas believed that one's actual deeds are what counts first of all; the Buddhists, on the other hand, attributed more, perhaps exclusive, significance to the motivation of the deeds, primarily desire, sometimes, especially later, it seems, intention. (There seems to be only one passage in the Sutta Piṭaka with identifies *kamma* with *cetanā* "intention", *Aṅguttara Nikāya* III.415; this one passage is often cited to justify far-reaching conclusions about the nature of early Buddhism. I would, for example, be very hesitant to conclude from this one passage that the Buddhists, or the Buddha himself, ethicised the world. In a recent article I have been able to show that the *Sūyagaḍa* has undergone the influence of Sarvāstivāda Abhidharma, and cannot therefore be as old as most of the Buddhist Sūtras.)[12]

This simple observation raised some fundamental questions. Jaina asceticism, with its emphasis on immobilisation, makes a lot of sense against the background of their view of karmic retribution. It made no sense at all from the point of view of those who believed that desire is the root cause of rebirth. The Buddhist method therefore *had* to be different: not suppression of deeds (whether physical or mental), but destruction of the roots of desire was required. The Buddhist path had to be psychological in some way, and that is what is was. But obviously the fit between the complex psychological method and the Buddhist, view of karmic retribution was not as crisply clear as that between the problem and its solution in the case of the Jainas. Moreover, there are reasons to think that the Jaina interpretation of the nature of karmic retribution was far more widespread at that time than the Buddhist one, which would seem to have been some kind of innovation.

This fundamental opposition between the Jaina and Buddhist methods to reach liberation, combined with the fact that many newly converted members of the Saṅgha must have gone on using some of their former terms and concepts, are able to explain a number of the more radical anomalies in the Buddhist texts. I have pointed out a number of them in several publications, and Professor Gombrich has added some. He draws attention,[13] for example, to the Padhāna Sutta of the Sutta Nipāta, where the Buddha is depicted as defeating Māra, death, by dint of mortifying the flesh. Gombrich comments:[14] "I see it as part—the losing side—of a debate among Buddhists, which may at the same time (we cannot tell) have been a debate with non-Buddhists." Elsewhere in the same book he says:[15] "another reason I posit for discrepancies is that monks were arguing about these topics and that the texts sometimes preserve more than one side of an argument." It is however not at all obvious that there was such a debate among Buddhists, nor that either side lost the debate. Jaina-like practices are found at numerous places in the canon, and still appear to have inspired Buddhists long after the closure of the canon (whatever that may precisely mean). But whether or not there was such a debate, it seems that almost everyone, including Professor Gombrich, but perhaps excluding Dr. Hamilton, agrees that there are very serious anomalies in the canon which cry out for an explanation. Among these explanations the ideological influence from the side of non-Buddhist ascetic movements appears to be an obvious candidate.

How can the identification of these alternative practices help us in establishing what the Buddha taught? Very simply by showing us that these alternative practices cannot have been part of it. That is to say, we have to search the method of the Buddha in the textual passages that do not present practices that had found their way into the canon under Jaina or related influence.

I now turn to another source of "former terms and concepts" of new members of the Saṅgha. I have already pointed out that certain scholars, among them Sue Hamilton, do not pay much attention to the influence early Jainism or related ideologies may have had on Buddhism. They usually concentrate on Vedic religion, especially on the form it takes in the early Upaniṣads.[16] Some scholars have drawn attention to parallels in the Buddhist canon to passages in the early Upaniṣads. The presence of such parallels is in itself perhaps not very surprising, for at least some of the Brahmins converted to Buddhism are likely to have known one or more Upaniṣads. I am less inclined to believe that the Buddha himself knew these Upaniṣads. The Buddha was, after all, not a Brahmin, and it is unlikely that he had learnt any Vedic texts by heart. Moreover, the doctrinal points which we associate with the Upaniṣads are attributed to outsiders by the Upaniṣads themselves. There are plenty of reasons to think that the doctrine of rebirth and liberation as we find them in the early Upaniṣads is a borrowing from elsewhere. Don't forget that the most orthodox of Vedic Brahmins, the Mīmāṃsakas, went on ignoring rebirth and liberation for another thousand years after the early Upaniṣads. This was not therefore a development of Vedic religion, but an intrusion in some Vedic texts of views and beliefs that were apparently popular outside the Vedic fold.

The importance of insight in the new doctrines of the Upaniṣads is well-known, and there is reason to think that insight was already important among those from whom the Upaniṣads borrowed these ideas. The reason why exactly insight was so important seems less well-known. Yet little reflection is required to see that exactly the same reason which induced Jaina and other ascetics to aspire for total motionlessness induced others to think that insight into the true nature of the self can secure the same result, viz., liberation. For the self in those movements, whatever other characteristics it may possess, is by its nature inactive. The notion of an inactive self pervades much of Indian religious and philosophical literature; other characteristics—such as being identical with Brahma, being conscious, being blissful, etc.—accompany this notion in some and don't do so in other of its manifestations.

Buddhism could not, it appears, resist for long the pull of an insight that would, all by itself, liberate the person who has it. Several scholars, among them Richard Gombrich,[17] have drawn attention to the inconsistencies in the canon in this respect. Gombrich goes further and claims "that Enlightenment without meditation was probably never envisaged by the Buddha or in the earliest texts",[18] and further that the change in soteriology involving the idea of an insight that by itself would bring about liberation did not take place until at least 65 years after the death of the Buddha.[19]

However that may be, the belief that insight into the true nature of the self was a, or rather the, method to attain liberation was current among certain contemporaries of the Buddha, and this is noticeable in the Buddhist texts. The repeated assertion that the *skandhas* are not the self, for example, is most easily explained as a rejection of the very notion that knowledge of the self—i.e., of the true self, which does not act—has a role to play in attaining liberation. Ironically, the knowledge of the fact that the *skandhas* are not the self is itself sometimes presented as a liberating insight, e.g. in the case of the first five converts to Buddhism. It is easy to see that this new insight structurally amounts to exactly the same as the insight into the true nature of the self: In both cases I am not identical with, or to be identified with, anything in me that acts. Since I have nothing to do with those acts, the results of those acts will not accrue to me.

By being aware of the alternative methods and ideologies that were around at the time of the Buddha and in the years following his death, it is possible to identify an important number of positions presented in the Buddhist canon as due either to influence from those alternative methods or due to resistance against them. All these positions and passages tell us little or nothing about the new message which the Buddha wanted to convey.

What, then, is my understanding of early Buddhism? My answer is likely to disappoint you. I have distilled no complex theory from the texts, nor do I have a new approach. I have rather tried to let the texts answer the questions suggested by those texts themselves. The texts considered are not, of course, the ones that betray outside influence. But once one removes those, much of what remains is rather straightforward. There are, to be sure, numerous passages—many of those in the *Saṃyutta Nikāya*—whose primary objective appears to be classificatory, and which may for this reason have to be understood as early manifestations of the classificatory tendency that characterises the development towards Abhidharma, which was soon to take over altogether. These passages, too, are not likely to provide us with straightforward information about early Buddhism. But beside these passages, there are many others that present us with a problem and with the solution to that problem. The main teachings of the Buddha as I have presented them in "Die buddhistische Lehre" can be resumed as follows.

Numerous passages repeat that the Buddha preached a method to put an end to suffering and to rebirth. Many of these passages, most of them well-known, emphasise that this aim is completely central to the Buddha's message, and that nothing else has any importance.[20] I insist, as ever, on an interpretation of the texts which is as direct as possible. I feel deeply sceptical, for example, with regard to those who at the end of many words come to the conclusion that a straightforward term like *duḥkha/dukkha* does not mean "painful" or "suffering" but "experience", as does Sue Hamilton.

Which is the method that puts an end to suffering and rebirth? A long passage that occurs numerous times in the *Majjhima* and *Dīgha Nikāyas,* and even a few times in the *Aṅguttara Nikāya,*[21] describes it in much detail. I assume that you all know it. Since however scholars go on searching the Buddha's method elsewhere, often ignoring this passage, I will read it out to you in the slightly modified English translation of Bhikkhu Ñāṇamoli and Bhikkhu Bodhi:[22]

> [H]ere a Tathāgata appears in the world, accomplished, fully enlightened, perfect in true knowledge and conduct, sublime, knower of worlds, incomparable leader of persons to be tamed, teacher of gods and humans, enlightened, blessed. He declares this world with its gods, its Māras, and its Brahmās, this generation with its recluses and brahmins, its princes and its people, which he has himself realised with direct knowledge. He teaches the Dhamma good in the beginning, good in the middle, and good in the end, with the right meaning and phrasing, and he reveals a holy life that is utterly perfect and pure.
>
> A householder or householder's son or one born in some other clan hears that Dhamma. On hearing the Dhamma he acquires faith in the Tathāgata. Possessing that faith, he con-

siders thus: 'Household life is crowded and dusty; life gone forth is wide open. It is not easy, while living in a home, to lead the holy life utterly perfect and pure as a polished shell. Suppose I shave off my hair and beard, put on the yellow robe, and go forth from the home life into homelessness.' On a later occasion, abandoning a small or a large fortune, abandoning a small or a large circle of relatives, he shaves off his hair and beard, puts on the yellow robe, and goes forth from the home life into homelessness.

Having thus gone forth and possessing the *bhikkhu*'s training and way of life, abandoning the killing of living beings, he abstains from killing living beings; with rod and weapon laid aside, gentle and kindly, he abides compassionate to all living beings. Abandoning the taking of what is not given, he abstains from taking what is not given; taking only what is given, expecting only what is given, by not stealing he abides in purity. Abandoning in celibacy, he observes celibacy, living apart, abstaining from the vulgar practice of sexual intercourse.

Abandoning false speech, he abstains from false speech; he speaks truth, adheres to truth, is trustworthy and reliable, one who is no deceiver of the world. Abandoning malicious speech, he abstains from malicious speech; he does not repeat elsewhere what he has heard here in order to divide [those people] from those, nor does he repeat to these people what he has heard elsewhere in order to divide [these people] from those; thus he is one who reunites those who are divided, a promoter of friendships, who enjoys concord, rejoices in concord, delights in concord, a speaker of words that promote concord. Abandoning harsh speech, he abstains from harsh speech; he speaks such words as are gentle, pleasing to the ear, and loveable, as go to the heart, are courteous, desired by many and agreeable to many. Abandoning gossip, he abstains from gossip; he speaks at the right time, speaks what is fact, speak on what is good, speaks on the Dhamma and the Discipline; at the right time he speaks such words as are worth recording, reasonable, moderate, and beneficial.

He becomes content with robes to protect his body and with alms-food to maintain his stomach, and wherever he goes, he sets out taking only these with him. Just as a bird, wherever it goes, flies with its wings as its only burden, so too the *bhikkhu* becomes content with robes to protect his body and with alms-food to maintain his stomach, and wherever he goes, he sets out taking only these with him. Possessing this aggregate of noble virtue, he experiences within himself a bliss that is blameless.

On seeing a form with the eye, he does not grasp at its signs and features. Since, if he left the eye faculty unguarded, evil unwholesome states of covetousness and grief might invade him, he practises the way of its restraint, he guards the eye faculty, he undertakes the restraint of the eye faculty. On hearing a sound with the ear. . . . On smelling an odour with the nose. . . . On tasting a flavour with the tongue. . . . On touching a tangible with the body. . . . On cognizing a mental property with the mind, he does not grasp at its signs and features. Since, if he left the mind faculty unguarded, evil unwholesome states of covetousness and grief might invade him, he practises the way of its restraint, he guards the mind faculty, he undertakes the restraint of the mind faculty. Possessing this noble restraint of the faculties, he experiences within himself a bliss that is unsullied.

He becomes one who acts in full awareness when going forward and returning; who acts in full awareness when looking ahead and looking away; who acts in full awareness when flexing and extending his limbs; who acts in full awareness when wearing his robes and carrying his outer robe and bowl; who acts in full awareness when eating, drinking, consuming food, and tasing; who acts in full awareness when defecating and urinating; who acts in full awareness when walking, standing, sitting, falling asleep, waking up, talking, and keeping silent.

Possessing this aggregate of noble virtue, and this noble restraint of the faculties, and possessing this noble mindfulness and full awareness, he resorts to a secluded resting place: the forest, the root of a tree, a mountain, a ravine, a hillside cave, a charnel ground, a jungle thicket, an open space, a heap of straw.

On returning from his alms-round, after his meal he sits

down, folding his legs crosswise, setting his body erect, and establishing mindfulness before him. Abandoning covetousness for the world, he abides with a mind free from covetousness; he purifies his mind from covetousness. Abandoning ill-will and hatred, he abides with a mind free from ill-will, compassionate for the welfare of all living beings; he purifies his mind from ill-will and hatred. Abandoning sloth and torpor, he abides free from sloth and torpor, percipient of light, mindful and fully aware; he purifies his mind from sloth and torpor. Abandoning restlessness and remorse, he abides unagitated with a mind inwardly peaceful; he purifies his mind from restlessness and remorse. Abandoning doubt, he abides having gone beyond doubt, unperplexed about wholesome states; he purifies his mind from doubt.

Having thus abandoned these five hindrances, imperfections of the mind that weaken wisdom, quite secluded from sensual pleasures, secluded from unwholesome states, he enters upon and abides in the first *jhāna,* which is accompanied by applied and sustained thought, with rapture and pleasure born of seclusion. . . .

Again, with the stilling of applied and sustained thought, a *bhikkhu* enters upon and abides in the second *jhāna,* which has self-confidence and singleness of mind without applied and sustained thought, with rapture and pleasure born of concentration. . . .

Again, with the fading away as well of rapture, a bhikkhu abides in equanimity, and mindful and fully aware, still feeling pleasure with the body, he enters upon and abides in the third *jhāna,* on account of which the noble ones announce: 'He has a pleasant abiding who has equanimity and is mindful.' . . .

Again, with the abandoning of pleasure and pain, and with the previous disappearance of joy and grief, a *bhikkhu* enters upon and abides in the fourth *jhāna,* which has neither-pain-nor-pleasure and purity of mindfulness due to equanimity. . . .

When his concentrated mind is thus purified, bright, unblemished, rid of imperfection, malleable, wieldy, steady, and attained to imperturbability, he directs it to knowledge of the destruction of the taints. He understands as it actually

> is: 'This is suffering'; . . . 'This is the origin of suffering'; . . . 'This is the cessation of suffering'; . . . 'This is the way leading to the cessation of suffering'; . . . 'These are the taints'; . . . 'This is the origin of the taints'; . . . 'This is the cessation of the taints'; . . . 'This is the way leading to the cessation of the taints'.
>
> When he knows and sees thus, his mind is liberated from the taint of sensual desire, from the taint of being, and from the taint of ignorance. When it is liberated there comes the knowledge: 'I am liberated'. He understands: 'Birth is destroyed, the holy life has been lived, what had to be done has been done, so that I will not return here.'

I would like to conclude this presentation with some reflections about method. There are many issues that could and perhaps should be addressed here, such as the claim (*my claim*) that in the search for early Buddhism the texts should be taken seriously, and to the extent possible literally. Instead I propose to draw a lesson from the great detective Sherlock Holmes. An inspection of many of the cases that he has been able to bring to a successful end shows that Mr. Holmes, in order to solve a crime, never hesitates to connect a number of at first sight unconnected facts. Most of his readers no doubt agree that this is the best method, probably the only possible method, to reach a solution to the problems Holmes has to deal with. Those readers themselves, as well as Holmes' companion Dr. Watson, normally start from the assumption that those unconnected facts are just that, viz., unconnected facts, and all marvel at Holmes' capacity to connect them up into a vision that leads to the solution of the crime. Not so Professor Gombrich,[23] who points out that only in the case of a physical phenomenon, such as a chemical reaction, do we try to find a unique set of conditions which triggers it. Social phenomena, and this includes no doubt also the crimes that Sherlock Holmes has solved, are supposedly not like that. When trying to solve crimes—that at least is what I conclude from Professor Gombrich's remark—we should leave unconnected facts unconnected. And indeed, it is not completely impossible (even if at times highly improbable) that each of the facts that draw the attention of Sherlock Holmes is really due to totally independent causes, or to chance as we might call it.

In this debate I sympathise with Sherlock Holmes and his method. I do think that a number of at first sight unconnected facts, if they allow of a common explanation, can be taken as supporting evidence for that explanation, also in the realm of human affairs. I am convinced that there are, or should be, important points of similarity between philologists and detectives, and I am inclined to follow Holmes in his observation to the extent that "[t]he more *outré* and grotesque an incident is the more carefully it deserves to be examined, and the very point which appears to complicate a case is, when duly considered and scientifically handled, the one which is most likely to elucidate it".[24] In my research on early Buddhism I have collected a number of at first sight irregular passages in the Buddhist canon, and proposed a theory that makes sense of these in the light of other information about the period concerned. This theory concerns the presence of a shared ideology in a number of religious movements contemporary with early Buddhism, an ideology which subsequently infiltrated Buddhism in various ways. You are free to disagree with me, but in that case the number of options open to you is rather limited. You may present a better theory than mine: I am not aware of anyone having done so. You also have the possibility to maintain that human events cannot be dealt with in this manner, that each irregular passage in the canon may have to be explained in its own special manner; if this is what you think, I can only advise you to read once again the adventures of Sherlock Holmes and ask yourself whether you really believe what you say. Or finally, you may proclaim that there are no irregularities to be explained; in that case I can only advise you to read the Buddhist canon once again, with your eyes wide open this time.

NOTES

1. Johannes Bronkhorst, "Die buddhistische Lehre," in Heinz Bechert *et al., Der Buddhismus I. Der indische Buddhismus und seine Verzweigungen,* W. Kohlhammer, Stuttgart (Die Religionen der Menschheit, vol. 24, 1), 2000, pp. 23-212.
2. Sue Hamilton, *Early Buddhism: A new approach. The I of the beholder,* Curzon Press, Richmond, Surrey, 2000.
3. Richard F. Gombrich, *How Buddhism Began. The conditioned genesis of the early teachings,* Athlone, London & Atlantic Highlands, N.J., 1996, p. 19.

4. T.W. Rhys Davids, *Dialogues of the Buddha,* translated from the Pali, Part I, 1899, reprint 1977, Pali Text Society, London and Routledge & Kegan Paul, Henley & Boston, p. 206; cited Gombrich, *How Buddhism Began,* p.17.
5. Gombrich, *How Buddhism Began,* pp. 20, 76, 96f.
6. Gombrich, *How Buddhism Began,* p. 13.
7. Gombrich, *How Buddhism Began,* pp. 13-14.
8. Neglecting Jainism when discussing the background of early Buddhism seems to have become a British tradition. In a recently published book (Paul Williams with Anthony Tribe, *Buddhist Thought. A complete introduction to the Indian tradition,* Routledge, London and New York, pp. 6-21) Paul Williams dedicates some 15 pages to "The Brahmanical doctrinal background", and none at all to Jainism.
9. Johannes Bronkhorst, "Remarks on the history of Jaina meditation," in Rudy Smet and Kenji Watanabe (eds.), *Jain Studies in Honour of Jozef Deleu,* Hon-no-Tomosha, Tokyo, 1993, pp. 151-162; "Abhidharma and Jainism," *Abhidharma and Indian Thought. Essays in honor of Professor Doctor Junsho Kato on his sixtieth birthday,* Shuju-sha, Tokyo, 2000, pp. 598-581 ([13]-[30]).
10. W.B. Bollée, "Adda or the oldest extant dispute between Jains and heretics (Sūyagaḍa 2, 6), Part two," *Journal of Indian Philosophy* 27(5), 1999, 411-37.
11. Bollée, "Adda or the oldest extant dispute between Jains and heretics (Suyagaḍa 2, 6), Part two," pp. 411-13.
12. Bronkhorst, "Abhidharma and Jainism".
13. Gombrich, *How Buddhism Began,* pp. 77f.
14. Gombrich, *How Buddhism Began,* p. 78.
15. Gombrich, *How Buddhism Began,* p. 97.
16. The relatively high number of Brahmins converted according to the ancient texts should remind us of the fact, pointed out most recently by Ian Mabbett, "The early Buddhist saṃgha in its social context," *Nagoya Studies in Indian Culture and Buddhism* (*Saṃbhāṣā*) 21, 2001, pp. 101-129, esp. p. 108, that "the references to conversions of brahmans and ascetics must be seen for what they are—a concern by later redactors to demonstrate to a critical audience that their master had been successful in impressing his superiority upon those classes which were the most dangerous potential opponents of his teaching". Mabbett then continues: "It is clear enough that the stories told in the suttas play fast and loose with a stock of floating anecdotes which are pressed into service for didactic purposes, and the line between fact and fiction is impossible to draw. Gombrich has pointed out the way in which a single brahman may appear in the canon in a number of different episodes which contradict each other." The reference is to Richard Gombrich, "Three souls, one or none: the vagaries of a Pāli pericope," *Journal of the Pāli Text Society* 11, 1987, pp. 73-78.
17. Gombrich, *How Buddhism Began,* chapter IV.
18. Gombrich, *How Buddhism Began,* p. 131.
19. Gombrich, *How Buddhism Began,* p. 132.
20. This characterisation of the central aim of early Buddhism is not controversial. Cp. Richard Gombrich, *Theravāda Buddhism: A social history from ancient*

Benares to modern Colombo, Routledge and Kegan Paul, London, 1988, p. 24 (cited in Paul Williams with Anthony Tribe, *Buddhist Thought. A complete introduction to the Indian tradition,* pp. 3-4): "[Buddhists] conceive salvation—or liberation, to use a more Indian term—as the total eradication of greed, hatred and delusion. To attain it is open to any human being, and is ultimately the only thing worth attaining, for it is the only happiness which is not transient. A person who has attained it will live on so long as his body keeps going, but thereafter not be reborn. Thus he will never have to suffer or die again. For Buddhists, religion is what is relevant to this quest for salvation, and nothing else."

21. L. Schmithausen, "On some aspects of descriptions or theories of liberating 'insight' and 'enlightenment' in early Buddhism," Klaus Bruhn and Albrecht Wezler (eds.), *Studien zum Jainismus und Buddhismus. Gedenkschrift für Ludwig Alsdorf,* Franz Steiner, Wiesbaden (Alt- und Neu-Indische Studien, 23), 1981, pp. 199-250, esp. p. 204 n. 15 gives references, and points out that this passage does not apparently occur in the *Saṃyutta Nikāya.*
22. *The Middle Length Discourses of the Buddha: A new translation of the Majjhima Nikāya,* original translation by Bhikkhu Ñāṇamoli, translation, edited and revised by Bhikkhu Bodhi, Wisdom Publications, Boston, 1995, pp. 272ff. This translates Majjhima Nikāya I 179ff.
23. Gombrich, *How Buddhism Began,* p. 19, n. 19.
24. Sir Arthur Conan Doyle, *The Hound of the Baskervilles,* twenty-sixth impression, John Murray, London, 1992, p. 231.

CHAPTER 3

Theravāda Pre-understandings in Understanding Mahāyāna

MAHINDA DEEGALLE

Most Pāli chroniclers began recording the history of Theravāda and Mahāyāna in Sri Lanka with a presumption that Mahāyāna was a doctrine deviated from the original teachings of the Buddha. This pre-understanding has colored the historical discourse and religious representation of Mahayana Buddhist movement in Sri Lanka. Because of this, the analysis of the prejudices and misunderstandings of Mahāyāna embedded in the traditional literary sources of the Sri Lankan Buddhist tradition is important. With a close examination of the fourteenth century *Nikāyasaṅgraha* of Jayabāhu Devarakkhita Dhammakitti Thera, this paper outlines the biases and misunderstandings that crept in comprehending Mahāyāna doctrines and practices.[1]

The Nikāyasaṅgraha and Sri Lankan Mahāyāna

Among Sri Lankan chronicles, the *Nikāyasaṅgraha*[2] stands as the most detailed Sinhala or Pāli literary account on the origin and development of Sri Lankan Mahāyāna Buddhism. Compared to other Pāli and Sinhala texts, the *Nikāyasaṅgraha* is a rather small work. The first printed edition (1890) of the *Nikāyasaṅgraha* included only 32 pages.[3] While the Hugh Nevill collection at

The British Library has three palm-leaf manuscripts[4] consisted of double-sided 22-27 palm-leaves, the Library of the Colombo Museum also possesses three palm-leaf manuscripts.[5] The author of the *Nikāyasaṅgraha,* Jayabāhu Devarakkhita Dhammakitti Thera[6] held an ecclesiastical position as the *saṅgharāja* (Chief of the Monastic Community). He composed a prominent Sinhala prose text, a *baṇapota* (preaching manual) entitled the *Saddharmālaṅkāraya* (The Ornament of the Good Doctrine, *c.* 1398-1410).

Living in the fourteenth century, on the basis of Pāli chronicles, oral accounts, traditions of Buddhist elders and contemporary events,[7] Dhammakitti Thera aimed at recording the history of Buddhism in Sri Lanka and India beginning with the arrival of King Vijaya in Sri Lanka to the reign of King Parākramabāhu V (1344-1359). While covering the same ground as did the previous Pāli chronicles, in his writing this author refers and directs the reader to the two previous Pāli chronicles—the *Mahāvaṃsa.*[8] and the *Cūlavaṃsa*—for more details on the issues that he recorded. In combination with the Pāli chronicles, this Sinhala work remains as a historical work valuable for the history of Buddhism in Sri Lanka. It covered areas of history that was not covered by previous works and included information on the history of *nikāya* (monastic fraternity) in Sri Lanka and documented the much valuable teacher lineage (P. *ācariya paramparā*) that emerged in Sri Lanka for active Buddhist scholarship. One of its important contributions is that it maintains that the Dhammaruci groups of monks at the Abhayagiri Vihāra in Anurādhapura were a branch of the Vajjiputtaka monks in India. It further records that the pupil of Dhammaruci of the Palārāma in India introduced it to Sri Lanka.

It is not explicit in the *Nikāyasaṅgraha* that its author's aim was writing the history of Mahāyāna in Sri Lanka. His purpose was not even recording the main facts of history. Rather his aim was narrating the way the early Buddhist *saṅgha* in India and subsequently in Sri Lanka became divided on religious grounds and the way the Theravāda monks of Mahāvihāra succeeded in establishing their point of view over and above the divisive forces within the Buddhist *saṅgha.* In other words, as he claimed his aim was writing 'a narrative that goes in accordance with *dhamma*' (*dharmānugata kathā prabandhayak*).[9] Because of this interest in monastic divisions in the history of Buddhism and true teachings of the Buddha, he wrote about divisive groups within the *saṅgha.* His interest on the development of Theravāda *saṅgha* in Sri Lanka, however, predominated his narrative. In his narration, he dwelled on the evils that fell on the Theravāda monastic establishment and attempted to portray its success in overcoming the negative challenges that it encountered in Sri Lanka. As a by-product of this effort,. in his treatment of the history of Buddhism, one can detect some information on the Mahāyāna movement in Sri Lanka and his attitude to its development within the history of Buddhism. Originally, though he wanted to cover only until the reign of Bhuvanekabāhu V (15th year, 1390 or 1375), he extended his account further covering until the reign of Vīrabāhu II (1408-1411).

As a historical document, the *Nikāyasaṅgraha's* weakness is that at times its author could not distinguish Mahāyāna schools from non-Mahāyāna schools. As I will demonstrate below, he had attributed ideas, thoughts and practices to non-Mahāyāna schools as if they belonged to Mahāyāna. Another important point that one should bear in mind is that within the *Nikāyasaṅgraha* itself the author has never used the term '*Mahāyāna*' but instead used different terms such as *vaitulyavāda* connoting the sense of Mahāyāna. Its critical statements about non-Mahāyāna schools resulted from its commitment to the elaboration of 'true *dharma*' and its interest in preserving the teachings of the Buddha (*buddhabhāṣita*). Because of this, without hesitation, it treated anyone, any thought or any movement that deviated from its own conception of *dharma* as heretical and subjected them to severe criticism.

The weaknesses of the *Nikāyasaṅgraha*'s account have been continuous building blocks for accurate understanding of Mahāyāna as a historical movement in Sri Lanka. The *Nikāyasaṅgraha*'s accounts have undermined the importance and contribution of Mahāyāna Bodhisattva cult to the development of Sinhala Buddhist practices in Sri Lanka. The *Nikāyasaṅgraha*'s bias is clearly visible in its technical terms. The religious terminology that the *Nikāyasaṅgraha* utilized to define, describe and represent Mahāyāna religious movement to a late medieval Sinhala Buddhist audience reflects its bias. Some of the terms that it used to describe non-Theravāda movements are *mithyādharma* (false teaching), *saddharmapratirūpa*[10] (counterfeit teaching), and *bhikku pratirūpaka tīrthaka*[11] (fake clerical non-believer).

For an adequate understanding of the textual representations of Mahāyāna in the *Nikāyasaṅgraha*, it is important to locate the *Nikāyasaṅgraha* in its socio-religious and historical contexts in the late medieval Sri Lanka. Unlike other Sri Lankan chronicles on the history of Buddhism, the *Nikāyasaṅgraha* was written rather late even after the unification of the divided *saṅgha* of the Mahāvihāra, Abhayagiriya and Jetavana Vihāra by Parākramabāhu I (1153-1186). When this Sri Lankan religious context is compared to that of India, it appears that the religious conditions of Buddhism in India was at a stage of gloom. Due to aggressive Hindu assimilations and the attacks of militant Islam, Indian Buddhism, the fountainhead of Mahāyāna and Tantra, disappeared completely from the Indian soil at the end of the twelfth century, two centuries before the compilation of the *Nikāyasaṅgraha*. In Sri Lanka, while Theravāda of the Mahāvihāra was active and flourished moving from the ancient capital Anurādhapura (*c.* 300 B.C.E–1000 C.E) to Polonnaruva (993-1235), Dambadeṇiya, Yāpahuva and Kurunegala (1232-1341) and finally to Gampola (1341-1411) where Dhammakitti Thera composed the *Nikāyasaṅgraha*, the fate of the Abhayagiri Vihāra was unfortunate that its power got gradually weakened to an unprecedented degree ultimately leading to a complete neglect of its buildings and monastic practices. While the legacy of the Abhayagiri Vihāra gradually disappeared from the historical memory of Sinhala Buddhists resulting complete neglect of its buildings until the pioneering work of J.G. Smither (1884), the Mahāvihāra began to flourish once it moved to Polonnaruva by spreading its power within Sri Lanka and in Southeast Asian Theravāda Buddhist countries. Within the late medieval Sri Lanka, the gradual growth of the inward 'local consciousness' gave birth to the regeneration of 'vernacular Buddhism'[12] centered around a vast corpus of vernacular Sinhala literature including Buddhaputra Thera's *Pūjāvaliya* (1266 C.E.); the *Nikāyasaṅgraha* emerged to record the disputed history of Buddhism in Sri Lanka among the Theravāda, Mahāyāna and Tantric Buddhist schools.

Previous scholarship has taken the *Nikāyasaṅgraha* as an important document recording the ecclesiastical history of Buddhism in Sri Lanka and Mahāyāna Buddhist movement. In writing

"Mahāyānism in Ceylon" (1928), Senarat Paranavitana cited the *Nikāyasaṅgraha* seven times.[13] Malalasekera praised the *Nikāyasaṅgraha* as "an authentic record" on Buddhist 'schisms' and in particular, information that it gives about the thirteenth and fourteenth centuries.[14] In *Mahāyāna Monuments in Ceylon* (1967), Nandasena Mudiyanse mentioned this text twelve times.[15] In "Mahāyāna Literature in Sri Lanka: The early Phase" (1977), Heinz Bechert referred to the Nikāya Saṅgraha three times and in "Buddhist Sanskrit Literature in Sri Lanka" (1982) four times.[16] Though it remains as a later work in the history of Sri Lanka, it has attracted many scholars because it gives clear and detailed accounts of Mahāyāna and other ecclesiastical affairs.

The Nine Episodes

As previous scholarship has identified,[17] the *Nikāyasaṅgraha* includes nine episodes dating to nine periods of Sri Lankan kings which have some relationship with Mahāyāna and Tantric Buddhist movements in Sri Lanka. As mentioned below these nine episodes cover the period from the third through twelfth centuries in which Mahāyāna was an active Buddhist movement in Sri Lanka as supported by archaeological evidence. The nine episodes of the history of Mahāyāna in Sri Lanka as narrated by the *Nikāyasaṅgraha* are the following:

(i) The reign of King Vohārikatissa (*c.* 209-231)[18] marked the suppression of the *vaitulyavāda*, the burning of religious books, and the punishment of Buddhist monks who took the *vaitulyavāda.* This is the first occasion that Sri Lankan chronicles mention the influence of non-Theravāda schools on Sri Lankan Buddhist affairs. While the *Dīpavaṃsa* identified the 'false doctrine' as the *vitaṇḍavāda* (sophism, false doctrine),[19] the *Mahāvaṃsa* and the *Nikāyasaṅgraha* identified it as the *vetulyavāda* or *vaitulyavāda.*[20] The *Dīpavaṃsa* and the *Mahāvaṃsa* maintain that through the assistance of minister Kapila, King Vohārikatissa suppressed the *vetulya* doctrine and subdued the heretical monks (P. *pāpaniggaha*). The *Nikāyasaṅgraha* mentions explicitly that the Abhayagiri monks of the Dharmaruci sect adopted the *vaitulya piṭaka* which was composed at the time of Dharmāśoka by "certain infidel Brahmans called Vaitulyas" who wore monk's robes for destroying the religion of the Buddha. When they preached it as the words of the Buddha, the monks of the Theriyanikāya rejected the *vaitulya* doctrines after comparing with authentic texts. After hearing this news, King Vohārikatissa collected the *vaitulya* books; after inquiring from minister Kapila, he burnt them and disgraced the 'sinful priests'.

(ii) In the reign of King Goṭhābhaya (*c.* 249-262),[21] the *vaitulyavāda* was reintroduced and Goṭhābhaya purged it by branding the bodies of 60 monks of Abhayagiri Vihāra who took *vaitulyavāda* and banishing them to Kāvira. Then Ussiliyātissa Thera left the Dharmarucinikāya and resided in Dakkhinagirivihāra. The monk Sāgala who lived there established the Sāgalanikāya.

(iii) The reign of King Mahāsena (*c.* 274-301)[22] was a turning point in the disputes among the monks of Theravāda and Mahāyāna. Persuaded by Saṅghamitta, a pupil of the banished sixty monks, King Mahāsena with the help of minister Soṇa destroyed the Mahāvihāra and persecuted Theravāda monks. The *Nikāyasaṅgraha* records that the number of destroyed monasteries were "about 364 colleges and great temples, including Lovāmahāpāya". After destroying the monastic premises, they ploughed their lands and planted *undu.* Though the *Mahāvaṃsa* mentions this persecution of Mahāvihāra, the *Dīpavaṃsa* is silent about it. The monks of Mahāvihāra vacated the Mahāvihāra for nine years and took residence in remote Malaya and Rōhana regions (*Mahāvaṃsa,* ch. 37:1-50). The *Nikāyasaṅgraha* adds that before leaving Anurādhapura, the monks of Mahāvihāra gathered at Lovāmahāpāya and declared that even if their lives are in danger they would reject the *vaitulyavāda.*[23] It also adds that the monks who deserted the capital belonged not only to the Mahāvihāra but also to the temples in the vicinity such as Mirisaveṭi Vihāra and Segiri Vihāra. The *Nikāyasaṅgraha* states that the Dhammaruci monks of the Abhayagiri Vihāra occupied the Segiriya. The *Mahāvaṃsa* records that King Mahāsena brought the great stone images to Abhayagiri Vihāra and constructed new buildings there. Furthermore, within the Mahāvihāra boundary, King Mahāsena constructed the Jetavaṇa Vihāra for the elder Tissa who resided at the Dakkhiṇārāma. However, an accusation against elder Tissa resulted his expulsion from the Buddhist order. Though the *Mahāvaṃsa* does not mention the name of the chief minister who judged the accusation against elder Tissa, the *Nikāyasaṅgraha* gives his name as Dharmika. The *Nikāyasaṅgraha* adds a narrative of a novice of Situlpavu Vihāra who possessed supernatural powers and saved the lives of some monks of Mahāvihāra by assuming the form of a *rākṣasa* who held an iron club raised in his hand and thereby dispersing the monks of the Jetavana Vihāra (Denānaka) in various directions. According to the *Mahāvaṃsa*, the king had removed the boundary stones from the Mahāvihāra *sīmā*. When the minister Meghavaṇṇābhaya rebelled, the king changed his attitudes towards Mahāvihāra and began restoring some Buddhist sites. The daughter of a scribe, the favourite wife of the king, assassinated both and it. The adds that she burnt *vaitulya* books. The Jetavanārāma Sinhala slab-inscription[24] mentions religious policy of King Mahāsena and also records the term *vaitulyavāda*.

(iv) For the *Nīlapaṭadarśana* that appeared during the reign of King Kumāra Dhātusena (*c.* 508-516),[25] please see the relevant section below.

(v) Both the *Cūlavaṃsa* and the *Nikāyasaṅgraha* record the incidents related to Mahāyāna during the reign of King Silākāla Ambasāmaṇera (*c.* 518-531).[26] This is the first occasion that Sri Lankan records mention *dharmadhātu*. According to the *Cūlavaṃsa*, in the twelfth year of King Silākāla Ambasāmaṇera's reign, a Sri Lankan merchant, whose name the *Nikāyasaṅgraha* gives as Pūrṇa, went to Kāsipura (Varanasi) and brought back a *dharmadhātu*, which the *Nikāyasaṅgraha* defines as "a book containing the Vaitulya doctrines." The *Cūlavaṃsa* states that the king was unable to distinguish the true doctrine from the false and "as a moth flying to a lamp" he took it "for gold," placed it in a house near the royal palace, took it to Jetavana Vihāra each year and arranged an annual festival for its honor. These statements with regard to the existence of *dharmadhātu* in Sri Lanka have been a subject of previous scholarly inquiry. As early as 1928, Paranavitana suggested that it was a Mahāyāna text, quite possibly, the *Saddharmapuṇḍarīka Sūtra*.[27] Mudiyanse (1967:82-3) believed that it was an object of much honour—a Mahāyāna text or an object of worship such as an image of either Vajrasattva or Vairocana. Though Bechert (1977:364-5) does not identify it by name, he also maintains that it was a Mahāyāna work of Indian origin written in Sanskrit.

(vi) The reign of King Aggabodhi I (*c.* 571-604),[28] is important since a debate has occurred in which the Indian monk Jotipāla[29] defeated the adherents of *vaitulya* school in Sri Lanka. According to the *Cūlavaṃsa*, an *ādipāda* (crown prince) called

Dāṭhāpabhuti; being ashamed of the defeat at the debate, though he raised his hand to strike Jotipāla, it was not successful since at that moment an ulcer appeared in the hand of Jotipāla. Being pleased with this incident, the King assigned a dwelling place for Jotipāla in that *Vihāra.*

(vii) In terms of the history of Mahāyāna and Tantric Buddhism in Sri Lanka, the reign of King Sena I (833-853)[30] marks two historical events: the arrival of a specialist of the Vajraparvatanikāya[31] and the introduction of the Ratnakūṭa collection.[32] Though *Cūlavaṃsa* devotes 87 verses to describe the activities in the reign of King Sena I, as a historical source, it fails to mention any of these two events related to the Mahāyāna movement in Sri Lanka. In this area, the *Nikāyasaṅgraha* remains the sole literary authority. According to the *Nikāyasaṅgraha,* during the reign of Sena I (Matvala Sen), an ascetic of Vajraparvatanikāya wearing monk's robes arrived from India (Dambadiva) and lived in Vīraṅkura. By giving 15 *kalandas* of gold, he bribed the royal cook Girivase Sen asking him to praise his virtues to the king. Since the king was not a man of learning, hearing the praises "as the grasshopper leaps into the fire" he went to the ascetic. Being impressed with his secret discourse called 'confidential teaching', he accepted the false *vājiriya* doctrines by abandoning the true doctrines such as the *Ratanasutta.*[33] According to the *Nikāyasaṅgraha,* because the king embraced the false doctrines he had to flee the city to Polonnaruva by giving it up to the Tamils. In this time, the *Ratnakūṭa* teachings were also introduced to Sri Lanka.[34]

Epigraphic and sculptural evidence supports the historical existence of Tantric Buddhism in Sri Lanka. The first arrival of Tantric Buddhism in Sri Lanka dates to the late Anurādhapura period (750-850). A bronze statue of Vajrapāṇi had been discovered near Ratkaravva Purāṇavihāra in Kurūṇegala District in 1988.[35] Another Vajrapāṇi image is carved on a rock at Buduruvagala with the images of Avalokiteśvara and Tārā. A passage from the Iñdikaṭusäya copper plaques (in Sanskrit) has been identified as a section of the *Kāśyapa-parivarta.*[36] Paranavitana dated these plaques to eighth or ninth century. It is not certain, however, whether the Iñdikaṭusäya copper plaques directly derived from the *Ratnakūṭa-Sūtra* mentioned in the *Nikāyasaṅgraha.*

(viii) In recording the events related to the Mahāyāna movement during the reign of King Sena II (853-887),[37] the *Nikāyasaṅgraha* differs from the *Cūlavaṃsa*. While the *Cūlavaṃsa* makes no reference to the penetration of Mahāyāna into Sri Lanka, the *Nikāyasaṅgraha* mentions that King Sena II activated the religious observances of the three *Nikāyas* and made them conform to the rules of the Buddhist teachings. Though the *Cūlavaṃsa* (ch. 51:49-50) states that the king set up guards at the coast to protect the country from enemies (*arīnaṃ duppadhaṃsiyaṃ*), even citing the *Cūlavaṃsa* inaccurately, the *Nikāyasaṅgraha* (p. 18) interprets the verse differently; it interprets king's placement of guards as a measure to prevent the 'false doctrines' and 'false priests' entering Sri Lanka. It further maintains that the ignorant and the foolish continued to practice the 'doctrines of *vājiriya*' since such doctrines continued to remain in Sri Lanka 'clandestinely' as a 'secret cult' since the time of Sena I. In this case, it is extremely difficult to judge which of these two historical chronicles record accurate information. Here, while it is acknowledged that the *Nikāyasaṅgraha* deliberately alternated some parts of the *Cūlavaṃsa* verse by replacing 'enemies' with 'false doctrines,' it cannot be maintained that the *Nikāyasaṅgraha* is factually wrong by recording the existence of the 'doctrines of *vājiriya*' since the *Cūlavaṃsa* itself has taken an orthodox position in not recording the anti-Mahāvihāra and anti Theravāda events within its treatment of historical events related to Buddhist schools in Sri Lanka.

(ix) The reign of King Parākramabāhu I (1153-1186)[38] is important because his reforms unified the divided *saṅgha*. The *Cūlavaṃsa* (ch. 78:1-27) narrates that King Parākramabāhu I purified the Mahāvihāra first and then unified it with the Abhayagiri and Jetavana fraternities. It describes the Abhayagiri monks as a group formed at the time of Vaṭṭagāmaṇī Abhaya (c. 89-77 BCE) and the Jetavana as formed at the time of Mahāsena (c. 274-301 CE) who accepted the *vetulla piṭaka*. However, it makes no direct reference to Mahāyāna as an independent movement. The *Nikāyasaṅgraha's* account (pp. 20-22) of the period is identical with that of the *Cūlavaṃsa*. However, the *Nikāyasaṅgraha* mentions (p. 22) the Vaitulya as a independent group separated from the Dhammaruci (Abhayagiri) and Sāgalika (Jetavana) when it refers to the monks of the three fraternities.

While these episodes often have similar or slightly changed

parallel accounts in previous Pāli chronicles, the episode of 'philosophy of the blue robe' that I discuss in detail below has no parallel account in other Sinhala or Pāli sources except in the later Sinhala text, the *Saddharmaratnākaraya* (The Mine Jewels of the Good Doctrine, *c.* 1417)[39] which was written by his pupil Dhammadinnācārya Vimalakīrti Thera.

The Philosophy of the Blue Robe (*Nīlapaṭadarśana*): *A Misrepresentation*

As an example of the *Nikāyasaṅgraha*'s misrepresentations of Buddhist religious movements, here let us discuss its account of the "philosophy of the blue robe". Fortunately, the *Nikāyasaṅgraha* quotes two verses[40] from an alleged *Nīlapaṭadarśana* text[41] which is lost for modern scholarship. As recorded by the *Nikāyasaṅgraha,* if such texts had been preserved until modern period our role of interpreting Mahāyāna movement in Sri Lanka becomes a much easier work. Since we are not in possession of the *Nīlapaṭadarśana* text today and are left with scant quotations our work becomes difficult. As can be seen below, the two *gāthās* preserved in the *Nikāyasaṅgraha* provides at least some information about this non-Theravāda movement.

> *veśyāratnaṃ surāratnaṃ ratnāṃ devo manobhavaṃ*[42]
> *etadratnatrayaṃ vande hyanyatkācamaṇitrayaṃ*[43]
>
> (I worship the three jewels—prostitute, liquor and love. Except these, other three jewels are mere glasses.)[44]
>
> *na kiṃ pibasi durmedha! narakaṃ gantumicchasi*
> *lavaṇodakasaṃyuktāssurāssvargepidurlabhāṃ*
>
> (Fool, why do not you drink! Do you wish to go to hell? Liquor mixed with salt is scarce even in heaven.)[45]

Quantitatively, though this quotation of two verses by the late medieval Sri Lankan Buddhist author is rather small to analyze an influential religious trend in ancient India, they nevertheless contain some non-traditional ideas. These two verses can be utilized in understanding Theravāda attitudes and perspectives toward radical religious views and practices that were against the accepted norms of the Theravāda tradition.

The importance of this quotation lies in its presentation of a radical view of the three jewels. Its *new* notion of three jewels included (a) the involvement in prostitution, (b) the consumption of liquor and (c) having a sexual life rich with love.[46] When seen from the Theravāda perspective, these *alternative* three jewels are quite radical and go against the accepted notion of three jewels (Buddha, *Dhamma,* and *Saṅgha*) in the Buddhist traditions. Because of this radical spirit, the *Nikāyasaṅgraha's* account of the *nīlapaṭadarśana* requires serious scholarly attention.

To explain the origin of the *nīlapaṭadarśana,* the *Nikāyasaṅgraha* inserted a narrative. When Kumāra Dhātusena (*c.* 508-516) ruled Sri Lanka,[47] his Indian contemporary was Śrī Harṣa[48] who ruled Southern Madhurā.[49] At that time, an 'impious' Sammitiya monk,[50] wearing a blue robe, visited a harlot at night; after spending the night there, he returned *vihāra* at daybreak. According to the *Nikāyasaṅgraha,* when his pupils questioned him whether his blue robes were appropriate for Buddhist monks, he praised their appropriateness. From then on, his devoted followers also began wearing blue robes rejecting the traditional saffron robes of the Buddhist monk. To that radical monk, the *Nikāyasaṅgraha,* attributes the authorship of the alleged *Nīlapaṭadarśana* text.[51] This Indian teacher of the 'philosophy of blue[52] robe' outlined the *nīlapaṭadarśana* despising the traditional three jewels as mere crystal stones and replacing them with (a) prostitutes, (b) liquor and (c) love. These two verses not only suggest a religious opinion contrary to Theravāda precept and practice, by replacing the traditional notion of the three jewels, they also challenge the entire soteriological system of Theravāda.

Among the Sri Lankan historical chronicles, the *Nikāyasaṅgraha* stands out as the only text which gives the origin and history of the *nīlapaṭadarśana.*[53] Though the Pāli chronicle *Cūlavaṃsa* (ch. 41:1-3) records the reign of Kumāradāsa (c. 508-516), it does not mention this incident related to the *nīlapaṭadarśana.* In recording this event, the *Nikāyasaṅgraha* relies on different sources, perhaps, oral, which other chroniclers did not use in recording the history of Buddhism in Sri Lanka. Its use of alternative sources may have resulted in inserting a narrative which was not available to other traditional historians. Another important point that one should bear in mind is that the *Nikāyasaṅgraha* does not record this event of the *nīlapaṭadarśana* in chronological order in the proper place; it has inserted this narrative of an early period after the discussion of a later king Sena II (853-887).

In examining 'the philosophy of the blue robe,' there is another point that one should keep in mind. In his work, the author of the *Nikāyasaṅgraha* wanted to discuss the influence of Mahāyāna movements which caused divisions within the early Buddhist *saṅgha.* With that goal of refuting Mahāyāna as a deviated thought, this Sinhala author included episodes related to Mahāyāna. However, his selection of episodes became defective since he was not well aware of the historical conditions related to Indian Mahāyāna. He seems to have selected episodes on the basis of mere assumptions and pre-understandings. This becomes clear when one reflects on the episode related to Sammitiya monk and the *nīlapaṭadarśana.* Though it appears that the author of the *Nikāyasaṅgraha* treated the Sammitiyanikāya as belonging to Mahāyāna, the research on the subject suggests that the Sammitiyanikāya was not a Mahāyāna school but a Hīnayāna fraternity. The Sammitiyanikāya was not even of Mahāsaṅghika lineage; it belonged to Vātsīputrīya lineage of Sthaviravāda. On the whole, there is a little that makes the monks of the Sammitiyanikāya differ from the monks of Theravāda. Because of inaccurate knowledge and prejudice, this Sinhala author has muddled the problem related to Mahāyāna existence in Sri Lanka. He has picked up a wrong episode to describe the negative aspects of wrongly perceived Indian and Sri Lankan Mahāyāna.

This *Nikāyasaṅgraha* account has some implications on established Buddhist practices. Let us take them one by one. First, let us take the issue of monastic robe—the attempt to replace saffron robes with blue robes. This replacement of the traditional saffron robes has some symbolical importance. As a radical religious movement, the *nīlapaṭadarśana* prescribed 'blue' as the color of monastic robe[54] by substituting the traditional custom of wearing saffron robes.

Theravāda traditions assign a supreme importance to the monastic robe. For Theravāda, the monastic robe symbolically represents true priesthood. Saffron robe was one of the four requisites recommended by the Buddha for his renounced followers. As a religious dress, it symbolizes two aspects—asceticism and purity. Taking a religious vow to wear only a robe made of rags taken from the heap of dust became a prominent ascetic (P. *dhutaṅga*) practice within Theravāda monasticism.[55]

In Sinhala Buddhism, the saffron robe has become a powerful symbol of purity. As a visual expression, it demonstrates one's commitment to the Buddhist path. It is a symbolic representation of one's connection to the Buddha through *civaraparamparā* (robe lineage). The *pabbajjā* (ordination) is both an act of receiving robes and committing oneself to observe the precepts. While precepts train one to be morally righteous, the robe that one wears symbolizes one's commitments. Both at the time of *pabbajjā* and *upasampadā* (higher ordination) the symbolic transition from the worldly life to the world of spirituality is symbolized through the removal of lay clothes to the monastic robes. Even after many years of training as a novice, one has to remove one's robes and wear a lay dress of white before receiving *upasampadā*. This rite of passage signify the importance of robe. While the typical color of Theravāda monastic robe remains saffron (though some wear the robes in yellow, brown or red), Theravāda monastics are not supposed to wear white or black robes and not definitely blue.

The *Nikāyasaṅgraha* attributes the act of wearing blue robes to Sammitiya monks. To determine the accuracy of this account which narrates the origin of blue monastic robe with specific reference to Sammitiya monks, non-Sri Lankan Buddhist scriptures can be utilized. Two scriptures in the Chinese Buddhist canon which deal with the subject of Hīnayāna *vinaya* discuss the color of the monastic robe. During the Later Han dynasty (25-220 C.E.), between the year 148 and 170 C.E., An-sei-kou of Parthia translated into Chinese the *Dai-biku-sanzen-igi* (*Taishō*, no. 1470).[56] Perhaps, it belongs to the Mahāsāṅgikas. During the Eastern Chin dynasty (317-420 C.E.), an unknown author has translated the *Sharihotsū-mon-kyō* (*Taishō*, no. 1465)[57] whose monastic affiliation is a mystery. These two scriptures contain identical passages (Taishō, vol. 24, pp. 925c-926a and 900c) and explain the distinctive features of the five *nikāyas* and the color of their monastic robe. From the former scripture, it is possible to know that even before the early second century C.E., the Hīnayāna monks chose robes of various colors. While Sarvāstivāda selected dark red, Dharmaguptaka, Mahīśāsaka and Mahāsāṅghika chose black, blue and yellow respectively. The robe of the Kāsyapīya monks was a mixture of yellow, pink and red. The only difference between these two Chinese accounts is that the latter scripture interchanges the color of the monastic robe of the monks of Sarvāstivāda and Dharmaguptaka. However, the important point is that both accounts agree that the monks of the Mahīśāsaka wore blue robes. If one relies on these two Chinese accounts, then it is clear that by the time of the second century C.E. some monastics belonging to different *nikāyas* had started wearing robes of various colors. This color differentiation of monastic robe may have originated due to practical needs of distinguishing monks of various *nikāyas*. When these two Chinese accounts are taken into consideration, the *Nikāyasaṅgraha's* attribution of 'blue' as the color of Sammitiya monks' robe becomes a problematic issue. Thus, on the basis of these two non-Sri Lankan sources, it can be concluded that it is not Sammitiya monks but rather the monks of the Mahīśāsakanikāya wore 'blue' colored robes.

The recommendation of a sexual life rich with love and of the use of prostitutes in gratifying one's sexual desires in the above two verses is quite striking. Suggesting that those two aspects are two alternative jewels is a further astonishment. This innovative suggestion pauses serious challenges to established Buddhist institutions. Celibacy has been a cornerstone of early Buddhist monastic practitioners. The celibate life of the Buddhist monastic was called *brahmacariya.* In addition, in the third precept of the five precepts which were meant for lay Buddhists, Buddhists are advised to lead a relatively controlled sensual life. In particular, the misconduct in sensual pleasure was called, '*kāmesu micchācārā.*' In this context, the recommendation to involve in prostitution is a radical change and a challenge for the established Buddhist practice.

The presentation of the use of liquor as one of the three jewels pushes Buddhist teachings into a radical context. The precept of refraining from taking alcoholic beverages is the fifth of the five precepts of the lay Buddhist. Both monastics and lay people abstain from taking alcoholic beverages. Here, the recommendation to take liquor contradicts the accepted practice.

On the whole, this movement has challenged the established Buddhist practices by encouraging to involve in prostitution by rejecting *brahmacariya,* accepting sensual pleasures with women, and advising to take alcoholic beverages. These recommendations challenge both the monastics and lay people to revise their precepts. It is also worth noting the two historical incidents that occurred in India (Śrī Harṣa) and Sri Lanka (Kumāradāsa). While the former suppressed the 'philosophy of blue robe,' the latter promoted it.

Concluding Thoughts

This paper began by mentioning the pre-understandings that the *Nikāyasaṅgraha* included in its representation of Mahāyāna movement in Sri Lanka. With one example taken from its description of the "philosophy of the blue robe," I have demonstrated that this fifteenth century Sinhala author did not possess an accurate understanding of Buddhist movements in India. In particular, his attribution of the blue robe to Sammitiya monks seems to be inaccurate when Chinese descriptions are taken into consideration which maintain that Mahīśāsaka monks wore the blue robes. Though some descriptions in the *Nikāyasaṅgraha* are inaccurate perhaps because of its pre-understandings, some details that it gives about the presence of non-Theravāda Buddhist movements in the late medieval Sri Lanka and the historical details of his contemporary period bear some historical and religious value for the inquisitive scholar.

NOTES

1. An early version of this paper was presented at the XIIth Conference of The International Association of Buddhist Studies, University of Lausanne, Lausanne, Switzerland, August 23-28, 1999.
2. The Sinhala title *Nikāyasaṅgraha* ('The Compendium of the Buddhist Monastic Community') is made up two Sinhala words *nikaya* ('group,' 'collection,' 'fraction') and *saṅgraha* (P. *saṅgaha,* 'compendium'). In Sri Lanka, the community of Buddhist monastics got divided into *nikā* and *gaṇa.* This text was also known by another name as *śāsanāvatāra* ('The Descent of the Buddhist Monastic Establishment').
3. In 1890, N. Don M. De Zilva Wickremasinghe edited the first printed edition (*Nikāya Saṅgahawa, or śāsanāwatāraya: A History of Buddhism in India and Ceylon* by Dewarakkhita Dharmakīrti Mahāthera who lived in the reign of Bhuwanekabāhu V (1378-97 C.E.), ed. N. Don M. de Zilva Wickremasinghe with an appendix by Weḷiwitiye Dhammaratana Sāmi, An Ācārya of the Vidyōdaya Piriwena (H.C. Cottle, Acting Government Printer, Colombo, Ceylon, 1890). This first printed edition (1890) included an introductory portion (i-viii), the main text (1-32) and an appendix (33-48). The 1907 edition (*Nikāya-saṅgraha or Śāsanāwatāraya: A History*

of Buddhism in India and Ceylon by Dewarakkhita Dharmakīrti Saṅgharāja, H.C. Cottle, Government Printer, Colombo, Ceylon, 1907) contained 28 pages of printed text. This edition had been used for making an English translation in 1908. The English translation Devarakkhita Jayabāhu Dharmakīrti Thera, *The Nikāya Saṅgrahawa: Being a History of Buddhism in India and Ceylon,* trans. C.M. Fernando and ed. Mudaliyar W.F. Gunawardhana (H.C. Cottle, Government Printer, Colombo, 1908) runs only 31 pages. It includes a valuable introduction (v-xix) and an essay entitled "Analytical Survey" (xxi-xxxvi) written by Mudaliyar W.F. Gunawardhana. While the 1924 edition of the Sinhala text has 28 pages, the 1935 edition contains 30 pages plus an extensive glossary (31-60) with an appendix (61-65).

4. The manuscript Or. 6606(10) dating to the early 19th century contains 22 leaves (ka-khū) written on both sides. While Or. 6606(11) dating to the late 18th century contains 27 leaves (ka-khḷ), Or. 6606(48) dating to the late 18th or early 19th century is an excellent copy with 24 leaves (ka-khṝ) (K.D. Somadasa, *Catalogue of the Hugh Nevill Collection of Sinhalese Manuscripts in the British Library* (The British Library and The Pali Text Society, London, 1990), vol. 4, pp. 32-34, 88-89).
5. W.A. de. Silva, *Catalogue of Palm Leaf Manuscripts in the Library of the Colombo Museum* (Ceylon Government Press, Colombo, 1938), vol. 1, p. 294.
6. Dēvarakkhita Jayabāhu Dharmakīrti *alias* Dvitīya Dharmakīrti (Dharmakīrti II) was a pupil of Dharmakīrti I who founded Saddhammatilaka Vihāra, Gaḍalādeṇiya. While the Nikāyasaṅgraha was his first work (p. 28), he also wrote *Bālāvatāra, Gaḍalādeṇi Sannaya* and the Sinhala prose work the *Saddharmālankāraya.* His pupil, Dhammadinnācārya Vimalakīrti Thera (Dharmakīrti III), wrote the *Saddharmaratnākaraya.*
7. Note that except the two Pāli chronicles, the *Mahāvaṃsa* and the *Cūlavaṃsa* he does not cite by name any other source that he used for writing the history of Buddhism in Sri Lanka.
8. The *Nikāyasaṅgraha* refers to the *Mahāvaṃsa* on three places (pp. 13, 15 and 16) and to the *Cūlavaṃsa* on two occasions (pp. 17 and 18). However, it does not make any reference to the oldest Pāli chronicle, the *Dīpavaṃsa.*
9. Unless indicated otherwise, all foreign language terms and phrases within parenthesis are from Sinhala language.
10. Devarakkhita Jayabāhu Dharmakīrti Thera, *Nikāyasaṅgahaya,* ed. Kumāraṇatunga (Vidyāsāgara Yantrālaya, Colombo, 1924), p. 16.
11. Devarakkhita Jayabāhu Dharmakīrti Thera, *Nikāyasaṅgraha,* 1924, p. 15. One commentary defines '*tīrthaka*' as 'a group of Hindu priests' (Devarakkhita Jayabāhu Dharmakīrti Thera, *Nikāya Saṅgrahaya hevat Śāsanāvatāraya,* ed. A.S. Perera (R.E. Perera, Kadavata, 1935), p. 4.
12. For 'vernacular' forms of Buddhism and the growth of 'local consciousness' within medieval Sri Lanka, see Mahinda Deegalle, "Vernacular Buddhism: Neglected Sources in the Study of Sri Lankan Theravāda," *Journal of the Japanese Association for South Asian Studies* 9 (1997), pp. 69-101 and "*Noviyat Hudījana:* Local Consciousness within Disappearing Cosmopolitan Buddhism," in G.D. Ratnapala et al. (ed.) *Sambhāṣā: Vidyōdaya 125 Vana*

Śāstrīya Samaru Saṅgrahaya (Pirivena Education Branch, Ministry of Education and Higher Education, Battaramulla, 1999), vol. 10, pp. 483-503.

13. S. Paranavitana, "Mahāyānism in Ceylon," *Ceylon Journal of Science* 1928, (2), pp. 38 (3 times), 39, 40, 68, 69.
14. "It gives much valuable information about schisms in the Buddhist church, and is an authentic record, specially of events which took place in the thirteenth and fourteenth centuries, where the *Mahāvaṃsa* accounts are often unreliable and seem to want supplementation," G.P. Malalasekera, *The Pāli Literature of Ceylon* (Royal Asiatic Society, London, 1928), p. 243; C.E. Godakumbura *Sinhalese Literature,* (Colombo Apothecaries' Co., 1955) also has cited this work several times: 7, 49, 61, 82, 92, 94, 96, 109, 120ff, 127, 129.
15. Nandasena Mudiyanse, *Mahāyāna Monuments in Ceylon* (M.D. Gunasena, Colombo, 1967), pp. 2, 6, 7, 8, 9, 10, 16, 18, 26, 81, 83, 115.
16. Heinz Bechert, "Mahāyāna Literature in Sri Lanka: The Early Phase," in L. Lancaster and L.O. Gómez (eds.), *Prajñāpāramitā and Related Systems: Studies in Honor of Edward Conze* (University of California, Berkeley, 1977), pp. 361, 364, 365; Heinz Bechert, "On the Identification of Buddhist Schools in Early Sri Lanka," in G.D. Sontheimer and P.K. Aithal (eds.), *Indology and Law: Studies in Honour of Professor J. Duncan M. Derrett* (Universität Heidelberg, Wiesbaden, 1982), pp. 10, 11, 13, 15.
17. For example, see Mudiyanse's work (1967) for clear divisions of these episodes according to the reign of Sri Lankan kings.
18. *Mahāvaṃsa,* ch. 36, vv. 39-41; *Nikāyasaṅgraha,* pp. 12-13
19. *Vitaṇḍavāda* literally means 'sophism' or 'sham doctrine'. The term *vitaṇḍavādin* is also found in the *aṭṭhakathā* literature. The content of *vitaṇḍavāda* and the views of the *vitaṇḍavādin* as represented in the *aṭṭhakathā* literature is highly varied and complex. It is extremely difficult to believe that *vitaṇḍavāda* belonged to a particular school. It could have been a general name used by Sri Lankan authors of the Mahāvihāra to identify views and doctrines that they viewed as to be sophistic or false. Because of innovative nature in doctrine and belief, Theravādins might have regarded Mahāyāna views as *Vitaṇḍavāda.* It becomes the earliest name that Theravādins gave to Sri Lankan Mahāyanists.
20. The *Vaitulyavāda* is the name given at the second stage. *Vi+tulya* ('*not* the same as oneself,' 'diverse,' 'heretics'). This term appears only once in the *Kathāvatthū-aṭṭhakathā* (N.A. Jayawickrama, (ed.), 1979), p. 168. In using the term *vaitulyavāda,* the *Nikāyasaṅgraha* follows the *Mahāvaṃsa.* In comparison with the two Pāli chronicles (*Dīpavaṃsa,* ch. 22:43-45; *Mahāvaṃsa,* ch. 36:39-41), the *Nikāyasaṅgraha* description of the *vaitulyavāda* is more detailed by adding the names such as "the priests of Abhayagiri of the Dharmaruci sect," "the Vaitulyan Piṭaka, which certain infidel Brahmans called Vaitulyas," and "Dharmāśoka Mahārāja." The attitudes of the *Nikāyasaṅgraha* is negative as can be seen in the following quotation: "the priests of Abhayagiri of the Dharmaruci sect adopted the Vaitulyan Piṭaka, which certain infidel Brahmans called Vaitulyas, who had assumed the garb of monks for the purpose of destroying the religion" (p. 12-13).
21. *Mahāvaṃsa,* ch. 36, vv. 110-112; *Nikāyasaṅgraha,* pp. 13-14.

22. *Dīpavaṃsa,* ch. 22, vv. 66-75; *Mahāvaṃsa,* ch. 37, vv. 1-50; *Nikāyasaṅgraha,* pp. 14-16.
23. *Nikāyasaṅgraha,* p. 14.
24. Mudiyanse, *Mahāyāna Monuments in Ceylon,* pp. 80-81.
25. *Nikāyasaṅgraha,* pp. 18-19.
26. *Cūlavaṃsa,* ch. 41, vv. 37-40; *Nikāyasaṅgraha,* pp. 16-17.
27. Paranavitana, "Mahāyānism in Ceylon," pp. 45-6; H.C. Ray et al. (ed.), *University of Ceylon, History of Ceylon* (Colombo: Ceylon University Press Board, 1959), vol. 1, Part 2, pp. 380-81.
28. *Cūlavaṃsa,* ch. 42, vv. 35-38; *Nikāyasaṅgraha,* p. 17.
29. *Nikāyasaṅgraha* clarifies his identity as a person from Dambadiva (P. Jambudīpa=India).
30. *Nikāyasaṅgraha,* p. 18.
31. In the history of Indian Buddhism, a school named Vajraparvatanikāya is not found. It is quite possible that this reference refers to the Vajrayāna or a Tantric school.
32. Its full Sanskrit title is *Mahāratnakūṭa-Sūtra.* This voluminous collection preserved in Chinese (49 "assemblies" and 120 fascicles, Taishō No. 310, vol. 11, pp. 1-685) and Tibetan is consisted of many independent *Sūtras.* In 713, Bodhiruci brought the Chinese version to its final form. The Tibetan version (Dkon-brtsegs I: Tibetan Tripiṭaka, Peking Edition, No. 760, vols. 22-24) is based on the Chinese collection. The original core text composed in India was initially was called the *Kāśyapa-paripṛcchā* which corresponds to the 43rd assembly of the Chinese version. This original text now is called the *Kāśyapa-parivarta.* The *Mahāratnakūṭa-Sūtra* belongs to the Mahāyāna scriptures of the second period composed after Nāgārjuna (c. 150-250). It includes the *Mahāprajñāpāramitā-Sūtra, Buddhāvataṃsaka-nāma-Mahāvaipulyā Sūtra, Mahāsaṃnipāta Sūtra, and Mahāparinirvāṇa-Sūtra.* See Akira Hirakawa, *A History of Indian Buddhism* (*Tokyo:* Shunjūsha, 1979), vol. 2, pp. 64-66; J. Takasaki, "Dai hoshaku kyō (Mahāratnakūṭa-sūtra)," in *Shin butten kaisetsu jiten* (*Tokyo:* Shunjūsha, 1961), pp. 93-94.
33. *Cūlavaṃsa* 51:79 records that King Sena II wrote down the *Ratana Sutta* (*Suttanipāta,* pp. 39-42) on gold plates and performed a great festival for its honor (*Mahāpūjā*).
34. *Nikāyasaṅgraha,* p. 18.
35. Ulrich yon Schroeder, *Buddhist Sculptures of Sri Lanka* (Hong Kong: Visual Dharma Publications, 1990), pp. 222, 258, 292-93.
36. Mudiyanse, *Mahāyāna Monuments in Ceylon,* pp. 90-92; Bechert, "Mahāyāna Literature in Sri Lanka: The Early Phase," p. 365.
37. *Nikāyasaṅgraha,* p. 18.
38. *Cūlavaṃsa,* ch. 71-79, 1,612 verses; *Nikāyasaṅgraha,* p. 22.
39. One considerably large section of the *Nikāyasaṅgraha* (1924, pp. 7-26) is similar to a section in the *Saddharmaratnākaraya* (ed. Kulupaluvāve Devānanda Thera, Colombo: Ratnākara, 1955), pp. 300-21. In this portion, there are only minor changes in wording. However, the last portion of the *Nikāyasaṅgraha* (pp. 23-26) characteristically differs from the *Saddharmaratnākara's* account (pp. 316-21). This overlap is perhaps due to the teacher-pupil relationship.

40. Verses 10 and 11 in the *Nikāyasaṅgraha* (1924, p. 17; 1935, p. 18; 1908, p. 19).
41. The Reiyūkai ('Society of Companions of the Spirits'), a modern Japanese new religion based on the *Lotus Sūtra*, founded in 1924 by Kakutaro Kubo and Kimi Kotani, the mother institution out of which Sōka Gakkai (f. 1930, 'Value Creation Society') and Risshō Kōseikai (f. 1938, 'Society for Establishing Righteousness and Personal Perfection through Fellowship') were born, has a prayer book with excerpts from the *Lotus Sūtra* entitled '*aoi kyōkan*' (The Blue Book). I am not sure how and why the Reiyūkai coined such a name for their prayer book which is used in communal gatherings of members held on the ninth and eighteenth day of each month. It is also important to note the existence of Buddhist scriptures often written on blue or black paper in Japan. The ninth century manuscript of the *Bonmōkyō* (Sūtra of Brahma's Net) in the Hōryuji Treasures at Tokyo National Museum is written on dark blue paper using gold ink (*Umarekawatta Hōryūji Hōmotsukan: Contemporary Vision, Ancient Art. The New Gallery of Hōryūji Treasures*, Tokyo National Museum, 1999, p. 236). I wonder whether this practice is limited only to the *Lotus Sūtra*. The Japanese term for 'blue' is *aoi*; this term, sometimes, means 'green,' though the term '*midori*' exists for the color green. Note also the existence of Blue Annals in Tibet and The Blue Cliff Records in China and Japan.
42. The Sanskrit term *manobhāva* means the 'god of love', 'Anañga' (Vāliviṭiyū Sorata Thera; *Śri Sumaṅgala Śabdakōṣaya*, Abhaya Prakāśakayō, Mt. Lavinia, 1970), p. 697.
43. The equivalents of the Sanskrit term *kāca* in Sinhala are *kadāva* (W. James Fernando, The *Sanskrit and Sinhalese Dictionary*, W. James Fernando, Panadura, 1922, p. 53), *kadāmäṭi* (Vāliviṭiyē Sorata Thera, *Śri Sumaṅgala Śabdakośaya*, p. 255), *kācakaya* (Carter (1924):163), *kadāmiṇi* (Sorata, p. 210), and *kadāpahaṇa* (Sorata, p. 226, M.D. Ratnasuriya and P.B.F. Wijeratne, *The Shorter Sinhalese-English Dictionary*, The University of Ceylon Press Board, Colombo, 1949, p. 377), with the meaning of 'glass,' or 'crystal.'
44. *Nikāyasaṅgraha* 1908, p. 19; 1924, p. 17.
45. Though both the *Nikāyasaṅgraha* (1924), pp. 16-17 and *Saddharmaratnākaraya* (1955), pp. 310-11 give the account of the *nīlapaṭadarśana*, the *Saddharmaratnākaraya's* account does not include these two verses of the *nīlapaṭadarśana* text.
46. Moraṭuwe Sāsanaratana Thera (*Lakdiva Mahāyāna Adahas*, M.D. Gunasena, Colombo, 1962, p. 59) is in the opinion that the *nīlapaṭadarśana* was quite probably a group of esoteric (*gupta*) teachings that spread during the age of Tantricism. As an example of esoteric teachings found in Theravāda scriptures, he cites the *Dhammapada* v. 294:
Mātaraṃ pitaraṃ hantvā (Having killed mother and father)
rājāno dveca ca khattiye (and two warrior kings)
Raṭṭhaṃ sānuvaraṃ hantvā (having killed a country with its retinue)
anīgho yāti brāhmaṇo (the ungrieving goes the Brāhmaṇa)
Furthermore, the *Devadūta Sūtra* is also believed to be a scripture produced by Sammitīya monks.
47. Kumāradāsa is famous as the Sri Lankan poet who composed the Sanskrit epic (*Mahākāvya*) *Jānakīharaṇa* (C.E. Godakumbura, *Sinhalese Literature*,

p. 4; Puñci Baṇḍāra Sannasgala, *Siṃhala Sāhitya Vaṃśaya*, p. 38). Kālidāsa, the author of *Meghadūta*, was his Indian contemporary Sanskrit poet. For a long time, only the Sinhala *sanne* (paraphrase commentary) of this epic–*Jānakīharaṇasannaya*–with *padārthakathana* (explanation of words and meaning) produced in the Polonnaruva period circulated in Sri Lanka. In about 1600, Rājasundara translated 15 chapters of it into Sanskrit. However, recently, a complete copy of the *Jānakīharaṇa* has been discovered in Malabar. Indian scholars accept that Kumāradāsa composed the *Jānakīharaṇa* when he was living in India (K.A. Nilakanthasastri, *A History of South India*, Oxford University Press, 1955, p. 331). See also Devahuti's *Harsha: A Political Study* (Oxford University Press, 1999).

48. According to the *Nikāyasaṅgraha*, King Śrī Harśa gathered the blue-robed priests with their sacred texts to a house and made a fire-offering of the house with them inside and their texts. This seems to be an act of persecution that they faced in India.

49. While the *Nikāyasaṅgraha* (p. 16) mentions the king of Southern Madhurā as Śrī Harśa, the *Saddharmaratnākaraya* mentions the king Bhoja who lived in Śrī Harśa of Dambadiva (p. 310); however, this reference to Bhoja is problematic. King Bhoja, the son of Sindhurāja (1018-1060) lived much later (K.A. Nilakantha Sastri, *History of India*, Part I: Ancient India (S. Viswanathan, Madras, 1950, pp. 203-204). However, on p. 311, the author mentions as "Śrī Harśa devayō." While there are differences in the very rendering of this particular account, it seems that the author of the *Saddharmaratnākara* is following the *Nikāyasaṅgraha* or any another source which gave the same account. According to Indian accounts, the king of Kanauj and Thaneswar was Harśavardhana (r. 606-47). Chronologically, he lived in few years later than Kumāradāsa. King Harśavardhana belonged to the Pushyabhuti dynasty. The Chinese pilgrim Hsüen-tsang mentions Harśa's acts of charity and warfare in his T'ang Hsi Yü Chi (Devahuti (1999): 3-11; Samuel Beal, (trans.), *Buddhist Records of the Western World*. 2 vols., London: 1884). In 643 C.E., Hsüen-tsang attended Harśa's sixth great act of distributing treasures and has left an account of it (Sachchidananda Bhattacharya, *A Dictionary of Indian History*, Calcutta: University of Calcutta, 1967, pp. 409-410). He ruled his vast empire having Kanauj as his capital and assumed the title of "mahārājādhirāja" (Surjit Mansingh, *Historical Dictionary of India*, Asian Historical Dictionaries, No. 20, Lanham, MD: The Scarecrow Press, 1996, p. 169). He also had diplomatic relations with the Chinese Emperor T'ai Tsung. He was eclectic in his approach to religion; he was devoted to Śiva and the Sun; in his latter part of life, he devoted himself to Mahāyāna Buddhism. As a Sanskrit poet, he composed 3 texts: (i) *Nāgānanda*, (ii) *Ratnāvali* and (iii) *Priyadarśikā*. He was also a patron of several internationally refuted scholars (a) Bāṇabhaṭṭa, the author of the *Kādambarī* and *Harśacarita* (620 C.E.), (b) Mayūra, the lyric poet (Vallabhadeva, *Subhāśitāvalī*, eds. P. Peterson and Durgaprasada, Bombay, 1886, pp. 28-29), (c) Hsüen-tsang (Yuan Chwang or Xuan Zang 600-64 C.E.) who arrived in India in 635 C.E. and remained there until 643 C.E. and returned to China in 645 C.E. D. Devahuti, *Harsha: A Political Study* (Delhi: Oxford University Press, 1999).

50. Both the *Nikāyasaṅgraha* and the *Saddharmaratnākara* agree that the monk belonged to Sammitīya Nikāya. A teacher named Sammata established Sammitīya Nikāya (Rockhill, *The Life of Buddha,* p. 184). It was also known as Ḥvantika, Kuru Kullaka (E.J. Thomas, *The History of Buddhist Thought,* p. 290). It spread widely during the fifth and sixth centuries and was the prominent school during the reign of Harśavardhana (Sāsanaratana Thera, *Lakdiva Mahāyāna Adahas,* p. 57). The seventh century Chinese traveller I-ching who visited Shih-li-cha-tō-lo (Śrīkṣetra, or Prome) records the presence of Theravāda (Ḥryasthaviras), Ḥryamahāsāṃghika, Ḥryamūlasarvāstivāda, and Ḥryasammatīya schools there (Donald K. Swearer, "Buddhism in Southeast Asia," in Joseph M. Kitagawa and Mark D. Cummings (eds.), *Buddhism in Asian History,* Macmillan Publishing Company, New York, 1989, p. 109). The Sammatīya was also known as Vātsīputrīya or Vajjiputtaka, came from Avanti (p. 109). Inscriptions record their presence in Sārnāth during the fourth century and in Mathurā during the fifth century. The early seventh-century ruler Harśavardhana is thought to have supported the Sammitīyas in the early part of his reign.
51. While the *Nikāyasaṅgraha* mentions that the monk composed a text (*nam vū grantharacanāvak,* p. 16) entitled *nīlapaṭadarśana,* the *Saddharmaratnākara* mentions that he composed a number of texts (*nam vū grantha sankhyāvak,* p. 311) bearing that name.
52. As a color, blue is related to several aspects of religious life. Nīlāmbara Vajrapāṇi refers to a statue of Bodhisattva Vajrapāṇi found in Tibet (*Sinhala Śabdakośaya,* 1986, Vol. 13, p. 6395). Nīlatārā is another name for Mahāyāna Buddhist goddess Tārā (p. 6391). Nīlagrīvayā (blue-necked) refers to Maheśvara (p. 6390). Nīlakasiṇa, is one of the ten *kasiṇas* belonging to the forty *kammaṭṭhāna* (p. 6389) and refers to the state of mental absorption (*samāpatti*) which one attains by meditating on *nīlakasiṇa* (p. 6389). Nīlakaṇṭhayantra protects one from diseases caused by planetary influences (p. 6389). Nīlaviṣṇu maṅgalyaya is performed in the low country of Sri Lanka to prevent planetary influences of Planet Śani (p. 6394). Nīlakūṭa rākṣasabaliya is a form of Bali (p. 6389). It cannot be ignored that the Buddha's one of the two prominent disciples Sāriputta is often sculptured in color blue and also the statues of Viṣṇu.
53. Mudiyanse (1967, p. 9) interprets *nīlapaṭa* as 'dark coloured robes'. He also suggests the possibility that they "practised extreme forms of Tantrism." Furthermore, it has already been suggested that *nil-sādana* was a name for Tantric practices (Charles Eliot, *Hinduism and Buddhism,* Arnold, London, 1957, vol. 3, p. 40).
54. In Sinhala *nīlapaṭa* means 'blue robe' (*Sinhala Śabdakośaya,* Vol. 13, 1986, p. 6391). In defining both *nīlapaṭa* and *nīlapaṭadarśana,* the Sinhala Dictionary accepts the *Nikāyasaṅgraha's* definitions and maintains that *nīlapaṭadarśana* was an 'ancient Indian philosophy' (*purāṇa bhāratīya darśanayak,* p. 6391). As a technical term, it identified the scripture that proposed the *nīlapaṭadarśana* philosophy and the Sammitīya monks who wore the blue robes. It also introduced two related terms *nīlapaṭadhara* and *nīlapaṭācāryaka.*
55. For a broad view on the importance of ascetic practices such as *dhutaṅga* in Asian Buddhist monastic traditions, see Mahinda Deegalle, "Asceticism:

Buddhist Perspectives," and "Marathon Monks," in William Johnston (ed.) *Encyclopedia of Monasticism* (Fitzroy Dearborn Publishers, Chicago, 2000), pp. 89-92, 891-22, and "Austerity as a Virtue: Spiritual Practices in Japanese and South Asian Buddhist Traditions," in W.D. Lakshman (ed.), *The Distant Neighbours: Fifty Years of Japan-Sri Lanka Relations* (Colombo: Faculty of Graduate Studies, University of Colombo, 2003), pp. 164-190.

56. For translation, see Mochizuki, vol. 4: 3372b-3373a; Bussho, vol. 4: 440b-441a.
57. See Mochizuki, vol. 3: 2194bc; Bussho, vol. 4: 375b-376a.

CHAPTER 4

Bodhisattvas and True Words (*satya*): A Note on the Origin of Mahāyāna Buddhism

KEIICHI MIYAMOTO

1. *True Words Create the World*

A notion that words have souls has been maintained since ancient times in Japan. It is even now recognized in the fact that we Japanese believe in the effect of ominous words. For example, if I might utter words such as 'to drop', 'to slip' and so on in front of a student preparing for an entrance examination, I should be blamed by others for having uttered ominous words. This is because words such as 'to drop' and so on are believed in Japan to have a power to bring out a situation that the student fails the examination. Namely words such as 'to drop' and so on are believed to have a power to create the world which contains a situation that the student fails the examination. In this way we Japanese have a sense a little that words create the world. But to our astonishment Indian people have had it very strongly since ancient times to today.

In the Aryan religion Vedic words are called '*brahman*'. The term '*brahman*' is one which is derived from the verbal root '*bṛh*' the original sense of which is 'to expand' and, therefore, means 'what expands' or 'what has a power of expanding'. That is to say, Vedic words as '*brahman*' are believed to expand and create the world which exactly corresponds to the words. Such words are called 'true' (*satya*) also.

The original sense of the term '*satya*' is 'what has a power to create things which correspond to it'. Though the term '*satya*' is sometimes associated with the term '*kāma*' (for example, '*satyakāma*' [one whose wishes always come true]), it is generally associated with terms such as '*vacana*' and so on, namely with terms which mean 'word'. In *the Story of the King Nala* (*Nalopākhyāna*) *Damayantī* moved gods by her own *satya* (the fact that she had never told a lie). *Satya* is conceived to accomplish anything.

2. *Satya, Śīla and Vrata*

The *Mahābhārata* 12.124.60 is a very interesting verse. It is as follows:

> "Law, what is true, good deed, power and I (happiness) are always based on precept. There is no doubt about it."

Here are enumerated powers or those which have powers. They are as follows:

law (*dharma*)	(what has) a power to maintain the order of the world,
what is true (*satya*)	(what has) a power to accomplish things corresponding to it,
good deed (*vṛtta*)	(what has) a power to invite a good life in the future,
power (*bala*)	power, and
happiness (*śrī*)	(what has) a power to make people happy.

That is to say, the verse tells that we need precept (*śīla*) or good mental attitude in order to make these items established. For example, to hold a good mental attitude on *satya* means not to betray words of a promise or of a vow which one ever presented and to make such a way of thinking complete and unshakable. Therefore, *satya* does not merely rank with law and so on, but is that which associates law and so on with a good mental attitude. Namely, *satya* and a good mental attitude compose one set.

One of the most important conditions required to Buddhists is to keep five precepts (*pañca-śīla*). They are as follows:

a precept not to hurt creatures,

a precept not to steal,

a precept not to commit adultery,

a precept not to tell a lie, and

a percept not to drink wine.

Among these a precept not to tell a lie is a moral wide-spread in India and is generally described in Sanskrit as *satya-vacana.*

There is a term 'a body of precept', which is likely a term made by Chinese Buddhists. According to them it is produced by keeping a precept by all means and is a power to stop evil and to promote good. Now it is clear that it is nothing but a power of *satya* in the Indian context. A precept not to hurt creatures means not to betray words of a vow not to hurt creatures. Therefore it is *satya* that penetrates all of the precepts.

But, as Buddhist *śīla* is a good mental attitude or a good character acquired by it, all of the precepts ought not to be performed perfectly. That is to say, according to Buddhism *satya,* which penetrates all of the precepts, is not necessarily perfect.

Therefore, for example, if a precept not to hurt creatures should be performed perfectly, monks should be prohibited to eat meats. But traditional Buddhists assert that they are permitted to eat meats when the meats concerned are recognized as pure by three ways. Besides Ambapālī became a believer in Gotama Buddha and taught by him kindly although she, a high-grade prostitute, can by no means perform a precept not to commit adultery.

On the other hand Jainism demands five vows (*pañca-vrata*) which resemble Buddhist five precepts. They are as follows:

a vow not to hurt creatures,

a vow not to steal,

a vow not to commit adultery,

a vow not to tell a lie, and

a vow not to possess (surplus) property.

Jainists, monks or seculars, are required to perform them perfectly. For, if a vow is not performed perfectly and does not come true (*satya*), it does not come to have any power. That is to say, a vow is believed to be completely of no use unless it comes true. Thus Jainists are much more traditional than Buddhists as to Indian old belief that *satya* has a power to accomplish wishes.

Brahmanas, who were deprived of their rich patrons by new comer religions such as Buddhism and Jainism, received former Indian habitants whom they had regarded as barbarians as legal members of Brahmanical society in order to get the necessary cost of living. As a result there arose a new religion named Hinduism that integrated Brahmanism and many religious elements of former habitants.

Brahmanas pursued the highest pureness as a new reason for the right that they continue to stand on the top of the society. So they abolished traditional rituals that require sacrifice of creatures and adopted worshipping reception (*pūjā*) as a new central ritual. Besides they rapidly turned into rigid vegetarians and quite impudently declared that only they had kept a perfect discipline not to hurt creatures.

Now brahmanas, when they come to be required to adopt a discipline not to hurt creatures and so on, selected Jainistic *vrata,* not Buddhistic *śīla.* This is because it is *vrata* come true (*satya*) that agrees with a Vedic belief in verbal power. In this way a notion that *vrata* come true should be highly esteemed got to dominate Hinduism.

Mahāyāna Buddhism was strongly influenced by the thought of relief by the absolute in Hinduism. Besides it adopted a notion of *vrata* come true from Hinduism and set it in the core of the idea which is the basis of bodhisattvas' austerities, namely a flag mark of Mahāyāna Buddhism. As this point has never been noticed by scholars, we shall clarify what it is.

3. *Pāramitā*

In the stream from the movement of glorification of Buddha to that of Mahāyāna Buddhism a concept of bodhisattva as an ideal ascetic came to be amplified.

Needless to say, a person named bodhisattva indicated originally only Gotama Buddha before enlightened. Then it came to be said that he could get enlightened (Buddha) only because he had kept various austerities with all his efforts in innumerable past lives. To keep austerities with all one's efforts by all means is nothing but *pāramitā*. The term '*pāramitā*' is interpreted as accomplishment or as reach to the other shore. I am not certain that such interpretations are right or not. But I am sure that from a functional point of view it is nothing but to keep austerities with all one's efforts by all means.

It is clear that *pāramitā*, to keep austerities with all one's efforts by all means, is based directly on *vrata*. The main point of the *Jātaka* is that Gotama Buddha accomplished a big wish to attain enlightenment by force of *satya* which is nothing but *pāramitā* or *vrata* kept with all his efforts by all means. This point is very important.

That is to say, a bodhisattva or an ideal ascetic is not required to master a system for ascetics named three kinds of discipline (*śikṣā-traya=śīla-samādhi-prajñā*) in order to across to the other shore, but to appeal to a power of true words or *satya*. The establishment of a new concept of bodhisattvas destroyed a traditional concept of discipline.

In Mahāyāna Buddhism all of the ascetics who devote themselves to *pāramitā* came to be called bodhisattvas. Here was completed a Mahāyānistic concept of discipline that bodhisattvas attain both enlightenment and a power to relieve all of the people.

There are enumerated six kinds or ten kinds of *pāramitā*. But, because Mahāyāna Buddhism as a popular religion aims at an easy way, it avoided difficult kinds of *pāramitā* and finally came to recommend wisdom (*prajñā*) *pāramitā*. Here came to be established a big stream which produced an amount of canons named *Prajñāpāramitā-sūtra*.

Hereby we can interpret correctly the latter part of the *Prajñāpāramitā-hṛdaya-sūtra* which is as follows:

> "Therefore it should be understood that *prajñāpāramitā* is a great true word (*mantra*), a great magical true word, a supreme true word, an unparalleled true word, what removes all of the pains and *satya* (what accomplishes all of the

wishes) because it does not betray us." (*tasmāj jñatavyaṃ prajñā-pāramitā mahāmantro mahāvidyā-mantro 'nuttara-mantro' samasama-mantraḥ sarva-duḥkha-praśamanaḥ satyam amithyatvāt.*)

The term '*mantra*' originally means a Vedic word, namely *brahman*.

This part advocates that to keep wisdom with all one's efforts by all means has a power to accomplish all of the big wishes. We should notice that it also advocates that to keep wisdom with all one's efforts by all means is nothing but *satya*. The essence of this canon is that, because to keep wisdom with all one's efforts by all means is a vow (*vrata*) come true (*satya*), it brings an unparalleled right enlightenment (*anuttra-samyak-sambodhi*) as well as a power to relieve all of the people by removing all of the pains. The conclusion is that *pāramitā* is a direct motive power that enables both self-interest (enlightenment) and interest for others (relief of all of the people). This is the key-concept of the *Prajñāpāramitā-hṛdaya-sūtra*.

4. *Praṇidhāna*

It is not only *pāramitā* that bodhisattvas should perform. What was invented as another discipline of bodhisattvas which depends on words of vow more deeply than *pāramitā* is aspiration-vow (*praṇidhāna* or *praṇidhi*). Though the term '*praṇidhāna*' is quite Buddhistic, its meaning overlaps that of the more general term '*vrata*', namely vow.

The most famous aspiration-vow is that of Dharmākara who became Amitābha Buddha. He thought out forty-eight articles of aspiration-vow in order to build Sukhāvatī, a sort of paradise, equipped with the most gorgeous ornaments after he contemplated for five kalpas. He kept them with all his efforts by all means and made them true (*satya*). He did not perform austerities named three kinds of discipline (*śikṣā-traya*). Only by force of *satya* he became Buddha, built *Sukhāvatī* equipped with the most gorgeous ornaments and attained a big power that relieve all of the people.

A Japanese Buddhist sect, Jodo-shinshu, uses terms such as 'a power of aspiration-vow' and so on. It is clear that such a power is nothing but a power of *satya* in the Indian context.

5. *Conclusion*

An old belief of Indian people that true words (*satya*) have a power to accomplish all of the wishes was inherited by Mahāyāna Buddhism through the medium of Hinduism and became a key-concept of austerities of bodhisattvas. Bodhisattvas should neglect the three kinds of discipline developed by Gotama Buddha and keep their vows with all their efforts by all means in order to make them true.

Mahāyāna Buddhism classified ascetics into three kinds, namely śrāvakas, pratyeka-buddhas and bodhisattvas, and declared that the former two are Hīnayāna Buddhists. That is to say, while the former two appeal to the three kinds of discipline in order to across to the other shore, bodhisattvas appeal to true words in order to across to the other shore and to let all of the people to do so.

By the way, bodhisattvas are given two alternative courses, namely *pāramitā* course and *praṇidhāna* course.

The representative bodhisattva who selected the former course is Avalokiteśvara. According to the *Prajñāpāramitā-hṛdaya-sūtra* he performed the easiest *pāramitā*, namely wisdom (*prajñā*) *pāramitā* with a result that he attained a magnificent power to relieve all of the people. Famous bodhisattvas who selected the latter course are Dharmākara, Kṣitigarbha and so on.

Thus we can conclude that Mahāyāna Buddhism was established under the strong influence of Hinduism.

CHAPTER 5

Remarks on the Orthography of the Kāśyapaparivarta Manuscripts:* 'Visarga-daṇḍa' in Verses

NORIYUKI KUDO

Introduction

The double dot is an orthographic sign that has long presented difficulties in the editing of Sanskrit texts. Though usually a visarga, this sign is occasionally employed as a punctuation mark as well, a fact noted already in the late nineteenth century by Georg Bühler in his *Indische Palaeographie.* Bühler, citing inscriptions and other materials, remarked as follows on this usage of the double dot as punctuation: "Ein doppelter Längsstrich, oft gekrümmt, erscheint vom 1.-8. Jahrh. p. Chr. als Vertreter des doppelten Verticalstrichs, und in den Kuṣana-Inschriften, sowie auch später, mitunter ein Doppelpunct."[1] He also noted that the double dot is ". . . in allen diesen und andern Fällen fälschlich als Visarga gelesen."[2]

Take its physical appearance and role into consideration, the double dot used as punctuation mark might be called a "visarga-daṇḍa" or a "double dot daṇḍa." The present study is an examination of this mark as found in the Sanskrit manuscripts of the

Kāśyapaparivarta[3] (= hereinafter *KP*), in which the double dot appears with at least three other types of punctuation marks. Owing to space limitations, the present article considers only the verse sections of the *KP*.

Four Sanskrit manuscripts of the *KP* have been identified: SI P/2[4] and SI P/85A[5] in the Petrovsky Collection; fragments in the Hoernle and the Mannerheim Collections;[6] and a fragment in the Turfan Collection.[7] Since all of the manuscripts were originally obtained from Central Asia,[8] philological study of them is necessarily limited to the peculiarities of the language(s) used in that area. Various linguistic features of the *KP* have been discussed already by Seishi Karashima,[9] the present paper focuses on the orthography in the above-mentioned *KP* manuscripts, especially the puzzling double dot punctuation mark. The text used for this article was the new version published by M. I. Vorobyova-Desyatovskaya, mentioned in note 3, above.

1. *Punctuation Marks Appearing in* **KP** *Manuscripts*

Friedrich Weller, who produced an annotated German translation of the *KP* on the basis of an extensive study of the Tibetan, Chinese, and Mongolian versions of the text, took notice of the "double dot daṇḍa," which had been mistakenly transcribed as *-ḥ* in the romanized text published by Staël-Holstein (see note 3, above). Weller suggested that it be read as a punctuation mark, in contrast to the position taken by V.S. Vorobyov-Desyatovsky, who transliterated the SI P/85A manuscript.

> "Ich bin mir dessen nicht sicher, ob V.-D. [= Vorobyov-Desyatovsky, noted by N.K.] zu Recht meint, ein solcher falscher Visarga sei dem Umstande zuzuschreiben, daβ danach ein Daṇḍa ausgefallen sei, Anm. 7, Ende. Ich halte es für möglich, daβ es sich um gar keinen Visarga handelt, jedenfalls von Haus aus, sondern eben um ein Interpunktionszeichen. In der Guptaschrift sind Visarga und Interpunktionszeichen (Daṇḍa) kaum voneininander zu unterscheiden. Vielleicht trifft dies auch für manche seltsame Formen zu, die in Baron v. Staël-Holsteins Textausgabe auf *-ḥ* ausgehen. Mir scheint sich die Frage eher so zu stellen, ob solche falsche Visarga nicht eher darauf hindeuten, daβ ein Zeichen miβdeutet wurde."[10]

As Weller states, it was the similarity of the double dot and the visarga ("similarity" is in fact too weak a word—there is absolutely no difference between the two signs' physical or graphic appearance) that caused Staël-Holstein to transcribe the former as a visarga. It is the purpose of the present paper to examine the signs once again and to clarify their functions, now that we have clear facsimiles of the *KP*.

Among the four extant manuscripts of the *KP*, only SI P/2 in the Petrovsky Collection has a verse portion. The punctuation marks used in the SI P/2 manuscript, in both the prose and the verse portions, can be classified into at least four types[11]:

(1) A double vertical stroke, with the strokes slanting upwards toward the left. This sign occurs at the ends of prose sections and verse sections (primarily after the verse-number). It appears a total of 180 times in SI P/2.

(2) A double vertical, bent stroke. This appears only five times, and is used in the same way as (1), above.

(3) A single dot located on the top line of an *akṣara.* This functions as a full stop or a comma, sometimes co-appearing with the mark described in (1), above. It appears 733 times.

(4) Two dots arranged vertically—that is, the mark this article is concerned with. This is the most ambiguous of the four marks—as noted by Bühler, it functions as both a daṇḍa or a visarga, and it is difficult in many cases to determine which function it is serving. We can tentatively evaluate its function as (i) visarga, (ii) daṇḍa, (iii) visarga-cum-daṇḍa and (iv) neither visarga nor daṇḍa, i.e., a superfluous mark.

SI P/2 manuscript and the other three manuscripts are all Central Asian works, and are thus written in some variety of Gupta Brāhmī script.[12] The "visarga-daṇḍa" or "double dot daṇḍa" is not, however, exclusive to the orthography of Central Asian manuscripts. It is widely seen in manuscripts from the Indian subcontinent and the surrounding area, and comments can be found regarding the occurrence of this type of punctuation in a number of the critical editions of the Buddhist Sanskrit literature. Therefore, before beginning our investigation of punctuation patterns in the *KP*, it would be useful to make a brief survey of others groups of MSS.

2. *The "Visarga-daṇḍa" in other Buddhist Sanskrit Manuscripts*

2.1 *Central Asian Manuscripts*

A.F. Rudolf Hoernle, in describing certain fragments of the *Saddharmapuṇḍarīkasūtra,*[13] noted several punctuation marks and gave the following descriptions: "The full stop is generally indicated by a dot placed on the line"; "we find the double dot, which occurs also in inscriptions and in the Bower MS"; "it is followed by a double vertical stroke, which appears also alone to mark the end of a sentence"; and, "the two vertical strokes are joined at their lower ends by a slanting line,"[14] It is obvious that his manuscript has exactly the same punctuation marks as those identified by us; his descriptions correspond, respectively, to our (3), (4), (2) and (1).

Louis de La Vallée Poussin, who published certain of the Sanskrit manuscripts in the Stein Collection, introduced a special symbol in his transliteration to denote the "visarga-daṇḍa": "Ce sigle représente, d'aoilleurs sans exactitude, les trais qui figurent le visarga, mais font aussi office de ponctuation, concurremment avec le point allongé en virgule (•)."[15]

Dieter Schlingloff gives a detailed analysis of visarga apparently used as punctuation marks.[16] He enumerates a number of instances in which a visarga, preceded by either '-*a*' vowel or non-'*a*' vowels, remains unchanged even before the vowel or voiced/voiceless consonant; that is to say, in which a visarga (by which the original final '-*s*' is replaced) is kept as it is, as if it were in the absolute final position:

> "Im ersten Falle ist das Trennungszeichen ein einfacher Punkt, wie er sich häufig am Satzende findet, im zweiten ein Doppelpunkt, also das Zeichen für den Visarga. Die häufige Verwechselung beider Zeichen in unserem Text weist darauf hin, daβ der Visarga von den Schreibern weitgehend als ein reines Wort- oder Satztrennzeichen aufgefaβt wurde. In dieser Verwendung findet sich auch in anderen ostturkistanischen Sanskrittexten statt eines besonderen Satzzeichens oft der Visarga, unter Nichtbeachtung der Sandhiregeln, am Ende eines Satzes, Halbverses oder sonstigen Sinnabschnittes. Eine auffallende Besonderheit unseres Textes

ist, daβ der Visarga in dieser Funktion in das Innere des Satzgerfüges gedrungen ist; die Wörter stehen also, mit Visarga (oder einfachem Punkt) im Auslaut, ohne Beachtung der Sandhiregeln, nebeneinander."[17]

This "double dot daṇḍa" is recognized even in the ancient manuscript of the *Udānavarga* found in Subhaši, which contains several script types (namely, Schrifttypus I : Kuṣāṇa—Brāhmī a~d and Schrifttypus II: Gupta group A, e-g).[18] Hideaki Nakatani, in deciphering this manuscript, uses the sign ";" (semi-colon) to indicate the "double dot daṇḍa."[19] There is a total of 24 examples, including ambiguous cases.

2.2. *Gilgit Manuscripts*

The same types of punctuation are also see in the Gilgit manuscripts. Adelheid Mette, in editing the *Devatāsūtra* and the *Alpadevatāsūtra* on the basis of the Gilgit manuscripts, comments, "Texte der fehlende Visarga ergänzt werden darf. Visarga am Ende von Strophen und Halbstrophen könnte in den meisten Fällen als Pausenzeichen im Sinne des Daṇḍa zu werten sein."[20]

Haiyan Hu-von Hinüber classifies seven fold signs used at the end of the sentence in her edition of the *Poṣadhavastu* of the *Mūlasarvāstivādavinaya* based on the Gilgit manuscript.[21] In her division, visarga is regarded as one of the punctuation marks as well as others such as double dot and single dot, etc.[22] We can see instances of {*ḥ*} which appear mainly at the end of a sentence in her text but they seem to be a punctuation mark followed by straight daṇḍa.

Christoph Cüppers' edition of the ninth chapter of the *Samādhirājasūtra,* based on twelve manuscripts from Nepal and one Gilgit manuscript, also makes brief mention of the "visarga-daṇḍa." The Gilgit manuscript utilized by Cüppers (abbreviated as C there) has a number of instances where the double dot functions as a punctuation mark at the end of pādas; the same double dot sign also appears in his Nepalese MSS, at the end of pādas followed by a straight vertical daṇḍa.[23] He illustrates this using boldface, such as **-ḥ**. It should be noted, however, that in reviewing Cüppers' text from the perspective of punctuation it is possible to find more instances than he took into consideration.

2.3. *Nepalese Manuscripts*

As with the other Buddhist Sanskrit manuscripts, the Nepalese manuscripts too show this kind of punctuation, as noted by Cüppers in his edition of the *Samādhirājasūtra.* John Brough also makes mention of it in his review of Franklin Edgerton's *Buddhist Hybrid Sanskrit Dictionary and Grammar:*

> "The two dots, as used for the visarga, are frequently employed in Newari manuscripts simply as a mark of punctuation, and this usage has occasionally found its way into Sanskrit manuscripts also. A distinction is sometimes made by writing the visarga as two small circles, or in the shape of a figure 8; but a confusion is possible, and editors should be on their guard."[24]

As an example of this "confusion" he cited a word-form (*ārabhyaḥ*, used for the absolutive of *ārabhya*) found in the Cambridge manuscript of the *Pāpaparimocana.* Brough comments that, if we accept Edgerton's principle in editing a Buddhist Sanskrit text,[25] "we should then doubtless explain it as a hyper-Sanskritism."[26] However, Brough continues, "I have little doubt that it arose simply from an earlier manuscript which used the two dots with the force of a comma."[27]

Nevertheless, it should be pointed out with regard to Brough's comments that, in view of the wide occurrence of the "visarga-daṇḍa" in other groups of Buddhist Sanskrit manuscripts, the double dot sign can no longer be characterized merely as something that is "frequently employed in Newari manuscripts simply as a mark of punctuation, and this usage has occasionally found its way into Sanskrit manuscripts also."

3. *"Double dot daṇḍa" in the Verse Portion of the KP*

In Vorobyova-Desyatovskaya's new romanized text of the *KP*, all examples of the "visarga-daṇḍa" are found at the end of pādas, with only two exceptions. The question is: When a noun or adjective ending in *-ḥ* appears in this position, should it be read as part of the case ending, or as a genuine punctuation mark? There may, in other words, be some room for reinterpreting the reading of the *KP.*

In the following description, I have adopted the term

"strophe" to indicate a single verse of the *triṣṭubh/jagatī* type, consisting of four pādas. Thus, 1 strophe = 4 [a~d] pādas.[28] When appropriate the strophe-number in the manuscript is given according to the section number, so that "2nd, § 1" would signify the second strophe in the first section (it must be born in mind, however, that since this system is based on the section division, in cases where the verse lines straddle several sections the numbers do not correspond with those in the manuscript). In case where the strophe in given is a last one, it is referred to as "**/last in § X"; when a section has only one strophe, its number is not given in my list. Readings of the *KP* are from Vorobyova-Desyatovskaya's text, and follow the convention adopted there, except for the use of different printing styles to indicate the restored *akṣaras.*[29]

3.1 *Punctuation Types* (*1*)~(*3*).

Punctuation type (1) (see section 1, above) appears, as a rule, at the end of the last strophe in each section. There are only three exceptions: in § 65 this type of daṇḍa appears at the end of first strophe[30]; in § 107 it appears at the end of the first strophe, followed by four other strophes; in § 126 it appears at the end of fifth strophe, followed by another strophe.

Punctuation type (2) is seen twice in the verse portion: at the end of the last strophe in § 1 (a restored occurrence), and at the end of the last strophe in § 128.

Punctuation type (3), a single dot, appears 139 times, always at the end of pāda: 'a' pāda: 3 times; 'b' pāda: 85 times[31]; 'c' pāda: 0 times; 'd' pāda: 51 times.

3.2 *Punctuation Type* (*4*): *double dot daṇḍa or visarga-daṇḍa*

There is a total of 72 examples of this type in the entire *KP*: 55 in the prose portion and 17 in the verse portion. We have two instances where the "double dot daṇḍa" appears in the middle of 'a' pāda. Let us examine all of these examples.

> Ex. 1: 'b' pāda of last strophe in § 2. [J.- Tr.]
> 3v.2-3 na vākpa + + +[32] taparo ca bhauti **:**

Unknown to Staël-Holstein; Vorobyov-Desyatovsky transliterates this pāda as "*na vākṣa. . . taparo bhoti*"[33]; Weller gives no comment on this form. Since the word *bhauti* itself is a hypersanskritized form [<*bhoti* < *bhavati* (3rd sg. form of /bhū)],[34] the double dot is apparently a puncuation mark.

Ex. 2: 'd' pāda of last strophe in § 2. [J.-Tr.]

3v.3 prajñām anāpnoti jinapraśastā :

Vorobyov-Desyatovsky transliterates this as *jinapraśastāḥ*; Weller reads it as a daṇḍa (p. 63, fn. 3-1; see above quotation in § 1). Acc. sg. form of *-śāstar* stem, adjective to *prajñām*: "He will obtain the wisdom eulogized by the Victorious one"; cf. *BHSG* § 13.10.

Ex. 3: 'd' pāda of 2nd strophe in § 3. [Tr.-J.]

4r.5 [m]ohen(t)i [c]it[t]aṃ va[r]ab(u)d(dh)abodhaye :

Staël-Holstein: *vara buddhabodhayeḥ*; Weller: *varabuddhabodhayeḥ* (p. 64, fn. 22).

Dative singular of *i*-stem: "their minds seeking for the buddhahood are confounded".

Ex. 4: 'd' pāda of last strophe in § 4. [Tr.- J.]

5v.2 cittaṃ na bodhāya kadāci muhyati : 3 ¶

Staël-Holstein: *muhayatiḥ*, resulting in a quite ambiguos word. This word is simply a verbal form of 3rd sg., cf. Karashima, "Some features," p.44, fn. 3: "... would be never embarrassed"; also cf. in prose: *na cāntar*[*ā*] (*mu*)*hyati* ...(4v.3).

Ex. 5: 'd' pāda of 2nd strophe in § 8. [J.- Tr.]

9r.1-2 karmasvako nānuśayaṃ vahaṃto : 2

Staël-Holstein reads: *vahaṃtoḥ*; Weller did not give any comment.

Nom. sg. masc. of *nt*-stem (present p. of √vahat), cf. BHSG §18.6: "[The bodhisattva,] thinking that it is a result of my action, has never a grudge [against others]"; cf. in prose: (*nā*)*śayaṃ vahati* (8v.2-3).

Ex. 6: 'd' pāda of 2nd strophe in § II. [Tr.-Tr.]

11r.5 <pā>paṃ ca dharman parivarjayeta :

Staël-Holstein reads: *parivarjayetaḥ;* Weller no comment.

Opt. 3rd sg. of √*pari-vṛj*-: "... [and he] should avoid [those who indulge] in bad teaching."

Ex. 7: 'd' pāda of 2nd strophe in § 14. [Tr.- Tr.]
13v.1-2 saṃbuddha[m](ā)rgasy(') upastaṃbhanāya :

Staël-Holstein reads: *ā̃upastaṃbhānayaḥ;* Weller no comment.
Dat. sg. neuter of *a*-stem: "[The Buddhas are a friend of those who are born from the Sugata(s),] being as an incitement to the way of the enlightened people"; cf. in prose: *sarvabuddha-dharmo[p] (astaṃ) bhāya saṃvartate* (13r.3-4).

Ex. 8: 'b' pāda of 2nd strophe in § 26. [Tr.- Tr.]
19v.3 dṛḍhāśayākṛtrimaprematāyā :

Staël-Holstein reads: *prematayāḥ;* Weller no comment.
Gen. sg. fem. of *ā*-stem, cf. *BHSG* § 9.49: ". . . having a firm intention, undissembled kindness. . ." In this strophe, a-c pāda ends in *-tāyā,* which seems to rhyme; cf. in prose: *(d)[ṛ]ḍhādhtyāśayatayā akṛtritimaprematayā* (18r.4-5).

Ex. 9: 'b' pāda of 3rd strophe in § 27. [Tr.- Tr.]
20r.3-4 upāyato saṃgṛhītā ca prajña :

Staël-Holstein reads: *prajñaḥ;* Weller no comment.
Nom. sg. fem. of *ā*-stem: ". . . [having] a wisdom followed by the means. . ."; ct. in prose: *upāyasa[ṃ]gṛhītā prajñā* (19r.1).

Ex. 10: 'c' pāda of a strophe in § 34. [Tr.-J.]
23 r.1 em eva śuddhāśaya bodhisatvo :

Staël-Holstein reads: *bodhisatvoḥ* but gives a note as "[sic.]"; Weller no comment.

Nom. sg. masc. of *a*-stem: "Thus, indeed, a bodhisattva of pure will. . .", cf. in prose: *āśayaśuddho bodhisatvah* . . . (22v.5).

Ex. 11: 'd' pāda of 2nd/last strophe in § 81. [Tr.-Tr.]
41 v. 3 jinātmajo vuccati śuddhasatvo : 3 ||

Staël-Holstein reads: *śuddhasatvoḥ;* Weller no comment.
Nom. sg. masc. of *a*-stem: "[a bodhisattva] is called 'a son of Victorious One,' 'a person of purity.'"

Ex. 12: 'c' pāda of 6th/last strophe in § 107. [Tr.- Tr.]
5 6v.1 evaṃvidhaḥ śīlavratoppapanno :

Staël-Holstein reads: *śīlavratopapannoḥ;* Weller no comment.

Nom. sg. masc. of *a*-stem: "In this way, one who is linked with *śīla* and *vrata*. . ."

Ex. 13: 'd' pāda of 1st strophe in § 114. [J.- Tr.]
58v.3-4 tau bodhisatvena vivarjaniyo : ¶

Staël-Holstein reads: *vivarjanīyoḥ;* Weller no comment.

Nom. du. masc. of *a*-stem *vivarjanīyo* (< -*au*), cf. Karashima, "Some features," § 9.5, p. 50: "It is said by the Victorious One that those two are impure; therefore those two should be avoided by a bodhisattva." Cf. This pāda is equal to 'd' pāda of 1st strophe in § 111 (57v.4-5) and 'd' pāda of 1st strophe in § 113 (58r.5-v.1).

Ex. 14: 'd' pāda of 3rd strophe in § 126. [Tr.-Tr.]
63r.5-v.1 ācāraguptiḥ kuhako dvitīyo : 3

Staël-Holstein reads: *dvitīyoḥ;* Weller no comment.

Nom. sg. masc. of *a*-stem: "this is a second group [of *śrāmaṇa*] who is keeping a good conduct but is hypocritical."

Ex. 15: 'd' pāda of 2nd strophe in § 136. [Tr.-J.]
68r.5-v.1 (sa) śī(lavā)n kāśyapa buddhaśāsane :

Staël-Holstein reads: *buddhaśāsaneḥ;* Weller: no comment.

Inst. pl. neuter of *a*-stem, cf. Karashima, "Some features," § 9.16, pp. 52-3 and fn. 49: "O, Kāśyapa, one who remains moral according to the Buddha's teachings is, . . ." Cf. This pāda is equal to 'd' pāda, 3rd and 5th strophe in § 136 (68v.2, 4: . . .buddhaśāsane. 3, 5).

Ex. 16: 'a' pāda of 4th strophe in § 136. [J.-J.]
68v.2-3 na lokalipto na ca lokaniśrito :

Staël-Holstein reads: *lokaniśritoḥ* Weller no comment.

Nom. sg. masc. of *a*-stem: "He is not defiled by this world, not reliant on the world,. . ."

Ex. 17: 'a' pāda of 3rd strophe in § 137. [J.-J.]
69r.2 na śīlaparamo na samādhita{ṃ}nmayo :

Staël-Holstein reads: *samādhitaṃnmayoḥ*; Weller reads as Staël-Holstein (144, fn. 10).

Nom. sg. masc. of *a*-stem: "He is not a person who believes the

Moral as supreme nor a person who is absorbed in samādhi,. . ."[35]

In the following two examples, the double dot sign should be deleted.

Ex.-odd 1: in 'd' pāda of 3rd/last strophe in § 3 [Tr. -Tr.]
4v.1 [v](a)rāgr(a)b(o)dh(iṃ) spṛś(a)t(i){ḥ} pr(a)ś[ā](s)[t](āṃ)

Both Staël-Holstein and Weller left this word as it is.[36]

Ex.-odd 2: in 'd' pāda of 1st strophe in § 107. [Tr.- Tr.]
56r.1 ādīnavān n(i)ḥsaraṇ[e]{ḥ} k(i)m eṣā

Staël-Holstein reads: *niḥsaraṇeḥkam*; Weller proposed to read: *kim* for *kam; niḥsaraṇaṃ* for *niḥsaraṇeḥ* (p. 126, fn. 4). A scribal error for *niḥsaraṇaṃ* (nom. sg. neuter), see Karashima, "Some features," p. 53, fn. 56: "What escape is there from this danger?"

3.3 *Patterns of Type (4)*

As noted above (3.2), the following pattern is seen with the double dot or visarga-daṇḍa signs that occur at the end of pāda:

'a' pāda: 2 cases; 'b' pāda: 3 cases[37]; 'c' pāda: 2 cases; 'd' pāda: 10 cases.

The above examples may be categorized into several patterns according to the relation to its preceding word-end:

(1) After the last word of 'a' pāda that takes a phonological permutation.

-aḥ > *-o* (nom. sg. masc.) – Examples 10, 11, 12, 14, 16, 17 (*BHSG* § 8.18);
-ntaḥ > *-nto* = ex. 5(*BHSG* § 18.6).

This morphology is found at the end of other pādas as well, sometimes followed by a single daṇḍa and sometimes followed by no mark. Let us see the instances where the ending *-aḥ* > *-o* • (ignore the difference of the stems!) occurs:

'a' pāda (1 case): *prasthito* • (10v.2, 2nd, § 10)
'b' pāda (7 cases): *sakto* • (14r.3, 2nd/last, § 15); *nirvikāro* • (21v.l, 2nd/last, § 29); *āśayato* • (22v.l, § 32); *asaṃtrasaṃto* • (23v.3, § 36); *bhramaṃto* • (41v.2, 2nd/last, § 81);

lakṣaṇapuṇyasatvo • (42v.5, 1st, § 83); *tanmayo* • (69r.1, 2nd, § 137).

'c' pāda (none):

'd' pāda (4 cases): *bodhisatvo* •(11r.4, 1st, § 11); *prasannacitto* •(11v.5, 1st, § 12); *bodhisatvo* • (23v.3, § 36); *vukto* • (63r.3, 1st, § 126)

In contrast to the "double dot daṇḍa", which appears at the end of 'd' pāda (i.e., at the end of strophe), the single dot daṇḍa is generally used at the end of 'b' pāda.

We have a dozen instances where this morphology appears without any mark.

- *aḥ* > *-o* [38]:

'a' pāda 24 cases; 'b' pāda 17 cases; 'c' pāda 26 cases; 'd' pāda 7 cases.

(2) After the nominal declension or verbal conjugation ending in a sound that is allowed to stand in final position.

Examples 2, 3, 7, 9, 13(*-au* > *-o*), 15 (nominal); 1,4,6 (verbal).

In cases of other pāda-ends, number of instances are as follows:

> nominal word ['a' pāda 56 cases; 'c' pāda 50]; verbal form ['a' pāda 19; 'c' pāda 20]; indeclinable ['a' pāda 11; 'c' pāda 10]. As to 'b' and 'd' pādas, see § 4 in this paper.

The above analysis deals with material in published sources, and thus, though meaningful in that it constitutes a reexamination of the earlier readings of Staël-Holstein, Weller, and Vorobyova-Desyatovsky, it concerns only those cases where we ourselves have already determined if a double dot sign signifies a visarga or a daṇḍa, and thus breaks little new ground. Let us therefore see whether there are any other instances where a double dot represents a punctuation mark rather than a visarga, or where it combines the functions of a punctuation mark and a visarga, and whether any discernible pattern exists in these usages. I will examine places that are not transcribed as double dot, and places where pauses would indicate the need for a daṇḍa, but where single dot occurs.

4. *Classification of the Signs Appearing at the End of the Pādas*

As mentioned above, in most cases it is at the end of 'b' or 'd' pādas that punctuation marks are found. At the end of 'a' pādas there are only 3 cases of punctuation marks, all of them single dot; the 'c' pādas have no punctuation. Therefore, in the following discussion only the 'b' and 'd' pādas are considered. Signs that can be regarded as representing pauses in the pāda are virāmas, numerals, and daṇḍas (vertical, single dot and double dot). In the manuscript there are many places in which pauses in the verse are not marked by daṇḍas, so I have taken into account the word-form occurring at the location of the pause.

In the analysis below, punctuation marks and understandable symbols are categorized from those locations closest to the words at the pāda-ends. That is, single or double dots that appear after the word with a virāma are all considered part of the virāma category, and are therein classified and assorted. In those places where it was felt necessary the words at the pāda-end are given. Also categorized are the endings of the words immediately preceding single dot. The word "sandhi" indicates cases where, according to Sanskrit sandhi rules, sandhi modifications are considered to have occurred despite the fact that a pause exists (especially in cases where the modification involves ending with a visarga; e.g., *-aḥ* > *-o*; *āḥ* > *-ā* [cf. § 3.3 above]; "nominal" indicates nominal declension (except the words ending in *-ḥ*); "verb" indicates conjugation (in words with personal endings); "ind." signifies examples ending in indeclinable words.

At the end of 'a' pāda (150):

A-1. virama = 2 cases.

56r.3, [illegible]th, § 107; 58v.3, § 114.

A-2. single dot = 3 cases.

pratiṣṭho • (10v.2, 2nd, § 10); *bhoti* • (26v.4, § 46); *āśrita* • (56r.2, 3rd, § 107).

A-3. double dot = 2 cases. [see above examples 16 and 17].

A-4. no mark (a large number of instances. Not enumerated here).

At the end of 'b' pāda (151):

B-1. virāma only = 24 cvases.

2r.5, 2nd, § [illegible]; 2v.2, 3rd/last, § 1; 6r.4, 2nd, § 5; 6r.5, 3rd/

last, § 5; 7v.l, 4th/last, § 6; 8r.2, 2nd/last, § 7; 8v.5, 1st, § 8; 9v.5, 3rd/last, § 9; 10v.3, 3rd/last, § 10; 15v.3, 1st, § 18; 17r.4, 5th/last, § 20; 21v.4, 1st, § 30; 23r.4, § 35; 25r.1, § 40; 26r.3, § 44; 37v.5, 1st, § 71; 40r.1, last, § 77 [incomplete]; 42r.2, 1st, § 82; 43v.5, § 85; 45v.3, § 90; 56r.5, 5th, § 107; 56v.1, 6th/last, § 107; 64v.3, § 128; 65r.2, 2nd/last, § 129.

B-2. single dot only = 85 cases:

sandhi 7 (14r.3, 2nd/last, § 15 [*sakto* •]; 21v.l, 2nd/last, § 29 [*nirvikāro* •]; 22v.l, § 32 [*āśayato* •]; 23v.3, § 36 [*asamtrasaṃto* •]; 41v.2, 2nd/last, § 81 [*bhramaṃto* •]; 42v.5, 1st, § 83 [°*puṇyasatvo* •]; 69r.1, 2nd, § 137 [*tanmayo* •]);

nominal 45[39] (4r.5, 2nd, § 3; 5r.4, 1st, § 4; 7r.3, 1st, § 6; 7r.4, 2nd, § 6; 9r.1, 2nd, § 8; 9v.3, 1st, § 9; 11r.4, 1st, § 11; 9v.4, 2nd, § 9; 11v.5, 1st, § 12; 12v.3, 2nd, § 13; 13r.5, 1st, § 14; 13v.2, 3rd/last, § 14; 14v.4, 2nd/last, § 16; 15r.3, 1st, § 17; 15r.4, 2nd/last, § 17; 15v.4, 2nd/last, § 18; 16r.4, 1st, § 19 16v.l, 2nd/last, § 19; 17r.l, 2nd, § 20; 19v.5, 3rd/last, § 26; 20r.5, 4th, § 27; 20v.1, 5th/last, § 27; 20v.5, 3rd/last, § 28; 21r.5, 1st, § 29; 24r.1, § 37; 24v.2, § 39; 25r.4, § 41; 25v.2, § 42; 40r.3, § 78; 40v.l, § 79; 41v.l, 1st, § 81; 43r.1, 2nd/last, § 83; 44v.4, 1st, § 87; 46r.2, 1st, § 91; 56r.l, 2nd, § 107; 57v.4, § 111; 58r.5, § 113; 59v.4, § 118; 63r.5, 3rd, § 126; 63v.4, 6th/last, § 126; 65r.1, 1st, § 129; 65v.1, § 130; 65v.3, § 131; 69r.2, 3rd, § 137; 69r.5, 5th/last, § 137);

verb 26[40] (2r.4, 1st, § 1; 3r.5, 1st, § 2; 4r.3, 1st, § 3; 4v[illegible], 3rd/last, § 3; 8r.l, 1st, § 7; 11r.5, 2nd, § 11; 12r.l, 2nd/last, § 12; 12v.l, 1st, § 13; 12v.4, 3rd/last, § 13; 17r.2, 3rd, § 20; 17r.3, 4th, § 20; 20v.4, 2nd, § 28; 23r.1, § 34; 25v.5, § 43; 27v.4, § 49; 40v.5, 1st, § 80; 44v.5, 2nd/last, § 87; 45r.3, § 88; 46v.2, § 92; 57r.l, § 108; 57r.3, § 109; 57v.l, § 110; 58v.3, § 114; 63v.1, 4th, § 126; 64r.3, § 127; 69r.3, 4th, § 137)

ind. 7 (3v.1, 2nd, § 2; 7r.5, 3rd, § 6; 14v.3, 1st, § 16; 22r.3, § 31; 24r.4, § 38; 33v.5, 2nd, § 65; 46r.3, 2nd/last, § 91).

B-3. double dot = 3 cases (For a detail, see above examples 1, 8, 9):

3v.2-3, last, § 2; 19v.3, 2nd, § 26; 20r.3-4, 3rd, § 27.

B-4. numeral = one (doubtful) case:

+ + *to* 2 (6r.3, 1st, § 5).

B-5. unknown = 4 cases:

5r.5, 2nd, § 4; 20r.1, 1st, § 27; 20v.2, 1st, § 28 [restored]; 66r.3, § 132.

B-6. no mark = 34 cases:

samādapeti (5v.2, 3rd/last, § 4); *yu[k]to* (9r.2, 3rd/last, § 8); *pratipattisusthitaḥ* (10v.1, 1st, § 10); *śīlasaṃvṛtaḥ* (10v.2, 2nd, § 10); *bodhisatvaḥ* (11v.1, 3rd/last, § 11); *vuktāḥ* (13v.1, 2nd, § 14); *arthikaḥ* (14r.2, 1st, § 15); *ni(rāmi)ṣeṇa* (16v.4-5, 1st, § 20); *adhimucyamānāḥ* (19v.3, 1st, § 26); *bhavaṃgatiṣu* (20r.3, 2nd, § 27); *vivar[dh]a[m]ā[n]aḥ* (21v.5, 2nd/last, § 30); *sapta* (26v.1, 1st, § 45); *bhoti* (26v.5, § 46); *sthitānā* (27r.3, § 47); *kkriyayāsamarthaṃ* (27v.1, § 48); *rogavinigrahāya* (33v.4, 1st, § 65); *putrāḥ* (41r.1, 2nd/last, § 80); *bodhisatvaḥ* (42r.3, 2nd/last, § 82); *lakṣaṇacitritāṅgaṃ*(44r.3, 1st, § 86); *jinarājaputraṃ* (44r.4, 2nd/last, § 86); *kṣiptaṃ* (55v.5, 1st, § 107); *vihanyamānā* (56r.2, 3rd, § 107); *mūḍhāḥ* (56r.3, 2nd, § 107); *ādaiḥ* [< *āryaiḥ*] (58r.2, § 112); *sevanā* (59v.1, § 117); *lubdho* (63r.3, 1st, § 126); *kuhanādisevī* (63r.4, 2nd, § 126); *ca* (63v.3, 5th, § 126); *niśrayaḥ* (68r.4, 1st, § 136); *niraṃgaṇaḥ* (68r.5, 2nd, § 136); *sarvabhavopapattibhiḥ* (68v.1, 3rd, § 136); (*aki*) *ñcanaḥ* (68v.2-3, 4th, § 136); *saktaḥ* (68v.4, 5th/last, § 136); *sudāntacittaḥ* (68v.5, 1st, § 137).

Among these, there are 17 cases in which the visarga sign is nothing but a "visarga-cum-daṇḍa," and 4 cases wherein the anusvāra is nothing but a "anusvāra-punctuation".[41]

At the end of 'c' pāda [omitted].

At the end of 'd' pāda (150).

D-1. virāma [in combination with ¶ / numeral/both/single dot] total: 28 cases:

D-1.1 virāma only = 10 cases:

2r.5, 1st, § 1; 6r.3, 1st, § 5; 9r.1, 1st, § 8; 9v.3, 1st, § 9; 15r.4, 1st, § 17; 15v.4, 1st, § 18; 21v.5, 1st, § 30; 44v.4, 1st, § 87; 65v.1, § 130; 69r.3, 3rd, § 137.

D-1.2. with ī or // = 9 cases:

2v.2, 3rd/last, § 1; 22v.2, § 32; 25r.4, § 41; 26v.5, § 46; 27r.4, § 47; 43v.5, § 85; 44r.5, 2nd/last, § 86; 44v.5, 2nd/last, § 87; 57v.2, 1st, § 110.

D-l.3 with numeral = 3 cases:

12v.3: 2nd, § 13; 20v.l, 4th, § 27; 20v.2, 5th, § 27.

D-l.4 With numeral followed by ¶ = 5 cases:

10r.1, 3rd/last, § 9; 15r.5, 2nd/last, § 17; 21v.l, 2nd/last, § 29; 22r.l, 2nd/last, § 30; 42r.3, 2nd/last, § 82.

D-l.5 with single dot = one case:

16v.5, 1st, § 20.

D-2 single dot [in combination with ¶ / numeral/both] total: 51 cases:

D-2.1 single dot only = 17 cases:

sandhi 4 (11r.4, 1st, § 11 [*bodhisatvo*; 11v.5, 1st, § 12 [*prasannacitto* •]; 63r.3, 1st, § 126 [*vukto* •]);

nominal 18 (2v.l, 2nd, § 1; 10v.l, 1st, § 10; 13v.l, 1st, § 14; 14v.4, 1st, § 16; 19v.3, 1st, § 26; 21r.5, 1st, § 29; 41v.2, 1st, § 81; 42v.5, 1st, § 83);

verb 14 (4r.4, 1st, § 3; 5r.5, 1st, § 4; 6r.4, 2nd, § 5; 12v.2, 1st, § 13; 41r.l, 1st, § 80).

ind. (65r.2, 1st, § 129).

D-2.2 with ¶ = 19 cases:

sandhi 1 (23v.3, 1st, § 36 [*bodhisatvo* • ¶]);

nominal 11 (16v.5, 1st, § 20; 22r.4, 1st, § 31; 24v.3, § 39; 27v.1, § 48; 27v.5, § 49; 33v.5, 1st, § 65; 37r.1, last, § 69; 40r.1, last, § 77; 40v.1, § 79; 55v.5, 1st, § 107; 59v.2, § 117);

verb 5 (23r.1,§ 34; 23r.5, § 35; 24r.2, § 37; 24r.4, § 38; 57r.1, 1st, § 108);

ind. 2 (45r.4, § 88; 65v.4, § 131).

D-2.3 with numeral = 7 cases:

case ending 4 (56r.4, 4th, § 107; 63v.2,4th, § 126; 68v.2, 3rd, § 136; 68v.4, 5th/last, § 136);

verb 3 (9v.4, 2nd, § 9; 69r.1, 1st, § 137; 69r.4, 4th, § 137).

D-2.4 with numeral followed by ¶ = 8 cases:

nominal 6 (12v.5, 3rd/last, § 13; 13v.3, 3rd/last, § 14; 17r.5, 5th/last, § 20; 56v.1, 6th/last, § 107; 63v.3, 5th, § 126; 69r.5, 5th/last, § 137);

verb 1 (12r.2, 2nd/last, § 12);

ind. 1 (46v.3, § 92).

D-3. numeral [in combination with ¶] total: 27 cases:

D-3.1 numeral only = 17 cases:

5v.1, 2nd, § 4; 7r.5, 2nd, § 6 [°*māṇo*]; 7v.1, 3rd, § 6; 10v.3, 2nd, § 10; 17r.4, 4th, § 20; 19v.5, 2nd, § 26; 20r.1, 3rd/last, § 26; 20r.2, 1st, § 27; 20r.3, 2nd, § 27; 20r.5, 3rd, § 27; 20v.3, 1st, § 28 [*anyāḥ*]; 20v.4, 2nd, § 28; 56r.3, 3rd, § 107; 56r.5, 5th, § 107 [*suratah*]; 63r.5, 2nd, § 126 [*parivarjayaṃto*]; 68v.3, 4th, § 136 [°*sīlaḥ*]; 69r.2, 2nd, § 137.

D-3.2 with ¶ = 10 cases:

8r.3, 2nd/last, § 7 [*bodhisatvaḥ* 12 ¶]; 9r.3, 3rd/last, § 8 [*niṣevitavyaḥ* 13 ¶]; 10v.4, 3rd/last, § 10 [*putrāḥ* 3 ¶]; 11v.1-2, 3rd/last, § 11 [*dharmapaṇḍitaḥ* 3 ¶]; 14r.4, 2nd/last, § 15 [°*varjanīyā* 2 ¶]; 14v.5, 2nd/last, § 16 [*ca* 2 ¶]; 15v.5, 2nd/last, § 18, [*vināyakā* 2 ¶]; 16v.1, 2nd/last, § 19 [*proktā* 2 ¶]; 20v.5, 3rd/last, § 28 [*proktā* 11 ¶]; 63v.4, 6th/last, § 126 [*nivṛtaḥ* 6 ¶].

D-4. double dot [in combination with ¶ / numeral/ both] total: 10 cases:

D-4.1 double dot only [examples 2, 3, 6, 7, 15] = 5 cases:

3v.3, 3rd/last, § 2; 4r.5, 2nd, § 3; 11r.5, 2nd, § 11; 13v.1-2, 2nd, § 14; 68r.5-v.1, 2nd, § 136.

D-4.2 with ¶ [ex. 13] = one case:

58v.3-4, § 114.

D-4.3 with numeral [ex. 5, 14] = 2 cases:

9r.1-2, 2nd, § 8; 63r.5-v.1, 3rd, § 126.

D-4.4 with numeral followed by ¶ [ex. 4, 11] = 2 cases:

5v.2, 3rd/last, § 4; 41v.3, 2nd/last, § 81.

D-5. double daṇḍa (¶) = 20 cases:

This daṇḍa appears at the last strophe of the section.

6r.5, § 5 [restored]; 7v.2, § 6; 25r.1, § 40; 25v.2, § 42; 25v.5, § 43; 26r.3, § 44; 70r.4, § 78; 41r.2, § 80; 42v.4, § 83; 45v.3, § 90; 46r.4, § 91; 57r.4, § 109; 57v.5, § 111; 58r.3, § 112; 58v.1, § 113; 59v.5, § 118; 64r.4, § 127; 64v.3, § 128[12]; 65r.3, § 129; 66r.4, § 132.

D-6. unknown = 6 cases:

4v.l, 3rd/last, § 3 [restored]; 7r.3, 1st, § 6 [unrestored]; 8r.l, 1st, § 7 [unrestored]; 16r.5, 1st, § 19 [restored]; 17r.2, 3rd,

§ 20 [unrestored but most probably a daṇḍa or numeral 3]; 68r.4, 1st, § 136 [restored].

D-7. no mark = 8 cases:

.y. taḥ (3v.1, 1st, § 2); *sthitaḥ* (3v.2, 2nd, § 2); *(cā)rthikaḥ* (14r.2-3, 1st, § 15); *sevitavyāḥ* (17r.4, 2nd, § 20); *samarthāḥ* (42r.2, 1st, § 82); *paurāḥ* (44r.4, 1st, § 86); *jātiḥ* (46r.2, 1st, § 91); *eṣā* (56r.2, 2nd, § 107).

Only eight pādas do not have any punctuation mark; however, our observation leads us to conclude that the scribe might have used visarga to denote a pause on purpose. In the last case, "visarga-cum-daṇḍa" is not used but the form *eṣā* might be "a corruption of *eṣāṃ*."[43] If so, we have here an instance of "anusvāra-punctuation" but anusvāra is mistakenly lost.

5. *Summary*

On the basis of the above data, we can more accurately assess the endings of 'b' and 'd' pādas. With 'd' pādas –that is, the last pādas of strophes –it is only in exceptional cases that the ending occurs with no mark. Since, in these exceptional cases, the pāda's final word almost always closes with a *-ḥ* (visarga), we may conclude that this visarga functions as a visarga-cum-daṇḍa; from the perspective of the morphology of Middle Indic or Buddhist (Hybrid) Sanskrit, this sign might be transliterated as **:**, rather than as *ḥ*.

The sign most frequently seen at the end of 'b' pādas is a single dot, in contrast to 'd' pādas, where double dot daṇḍas and numerals are most often found. In cases where no mark exists the double dot sign is regarded as a visarga-cum-daṇḍa. In cases where the last word does not end in *-ḥ* and there is no mark to represent the end of the pāda, a sort of Middle Indic morphology *-aḥ* > *-o* tends to occur.[44] In other words, although these cases are orthographically inconsistent in that the pāda-end is not marked by a daṇḍa, the scribe might have intended to denote the pāda-end by means of some symbol such as a single/double dot or a special word-form.

In conclusion, I would like to reiterate that there are cases where the double dot sign in the manuscript should or might be read as a visarga-cum-daṇḍa although in the new romanized text they are transliterated as *-ḥ*.

'a' pāda-end:

khedaḥ (20r.1, 1st, § 27); *°nirvṛtaḥ* (42r.3, 2nd/last, § 82); *prabhāsvaraḥ* (73v.4-5, § 85); *samādhiḥ* (63v.1, 4th, § 126); *upetaḥ* (65r.2, 2nd/last, § 129); *asaktamānasaḥ* (68v.5, 1st, § 137); *śuddhaḥ* (69r.4, 5th/last, § 137).

'b' pāda-end:

pratipattisusthitaḥ (10v.1, 1st, § 10); *śīlasaṃvṛtaḥ* (10v.2, 2nd, § 10); *bodhisatvaḥ* (11v.1, 3rd/last, § 11); *vuktāḥ* (13v.1, 2nd, § 14); *arthikaḥ* (14r.2, 1st, § 15); *adhimucyamānāḥ* (19v.3, 1st, § 26); *vivar*[*dh*]*a*[*m*]*ā*[*n*]*aḥ* (21v.5, 2nd/last, § 30); *putrāḥ* (41r.1, 2nd/last, § 80); *bodhisatvaḥ* (42r.3, 2nd/last, § 82); *mūḍhaḥ* (56r.3, 2nd, § 107); *ādaiḥ* (< *āryaiḥ*) (58r.2, § 112); *niśrayaḥ* (68r.4, 1st, § 136); *niraṃgaṇaḥ* (68r.5, 2nd, § 136); *sarvabhavopapattibhiḥ* (68v.1, 3rd, § 136); (*aki*) *ñcanaḥ* (68v.3, 4th, § 136); *saktaḥ* (68v.4, 5th/last, § 136); *sudāntacittaḥ* (68v.5, 1st, § 137).

'c' pāda-end:

paṇḍitāḥ (3v.3, 3rd/last, § 2); *pratirūpakoktāḥ* (14r.3, 2nd/last, § 15); *codanīyaḥ* (20r.2, 1st, § 27); *pratiṣṭh<it>aḥ* (25r.4, §41); *bhikṣoḥ* (65v.4, 1st, § 131); *vipramuk*(*t*)*aḥ* (68v.1, 2nd, § 136); *pratiṣṭhitaḥ* (68v.2, 3rd, § 136); *anāsravaḥ* (68v.4, 5th/last, § 136).

'd' pāda-end:

.y. taḥ (3v.1, 1st, § 2); *sthitaḥ* (3v.2, 2nd, § 2); *bodhisatvaḥ* 2 ¶ (8r.3, 2nd/last, § 7); *niṣevitavyāḥ* 3 ¶ (9r.3, 3rd/last, § 8); *putrāḥ* 3 ¶ (10v.4, 3rd/last, § 10); *dharmapaṇḍitaḥ* 3 ¶ (11v.1-2, 3rd/last, § 11); (*cā*)*rthikaḥ* (14r.2-3, 1st, § 15); *sevitavyāḥ* (17r.4, 2nd, § 20); *anyāḥ* 9 (20v.3, 1st, § 28); *bodhisatvaḥ* ¶ (26r.3, § 44); *buddhaputrāḥ* ¶ (41r.2, 2nd/last, § 80); *samarthāḥ* (42r.2, 1st, § 82); *putrāḥ* (44r.4, 1st, § 86); *śrrāvakaḥ* ¶ (45v.3, § 90); *jātiḥ* (46r.2, 1st, § 91); *sūrataḥ* 5 (56r.5, 5th, § 107); *nirvṛtaḥ* 6 ¶ (63v.4, 6th/last, § 126); *ucyamānaḥ* ¶ (64r.4, § 127); *śrrutābhiyogaḥ* ¶ (65r.3, 2nd/last, § 129); *viśuddhaśīlaḥ* 4 (68v.3, 4th, § 136).

NOTES

The author wishes to thank to Dr. M. I. Vorobyova-Desyatovskaya of St.-Petersburg, who provided him with the opportunity to read photocopies of *Kāśyapaparivarta* manuscript SI P/2, and who offered much valuable advice during her stay at the International Research Institute for Advanced Buddhology, Soka University, Japan. He also thanks his colleagues, Seishi Karashima and Stefano Zacchetti, who worked patiently with the author on the present manuscript, on several occasions until late into the night. His thanks go also to Mr. Thomas Kirchner who took great trouble in checking the unidiomatic English of the author. Needless to say, the author bears sole responsibility for any errors or misunderstandings presented here.

1. Bühler, *Indische Palaeographie: von circa 350 a.Chr. -circa 1300 p. Chr*, Strassburg: K. J. Trübner (Grundriss der Indo-arischen Philologie und Altertumskunde Bd. 1 Heft 11), 1896, § 36 C.5, p. 84.
2. Ibid., p. 87, note 30.
3. The Sanskrit text of the *KP* was first published by Baron A. von Staël-Holstein, under the title *The Kāśyapaparivarta—A Mahāyānasūtra of the Ratnakūṭa Class in the Original Sanskrit, in Tibetan and in Chinese*, Shanghai, 1926. Recently, M.I. Vorobyova-Desyatovskaya, in collaboration with Seishi Karashima and Noriyuki Kudo, published a new transliteration and the facsimiles of all the manuscripts except the Mannerheim fragment. Her work is entitled *The Kāśyapaparivarta: Romanized Text and Facsimiles* (Bibliotheca Philologica et Philosophica Buddhica V; Tokyo: the International Research Institute for Advanced Buddhology at Soka University, 2002).
4. This manuscript, except folio No.3, was used by Staël-Holstein in his editio princeps of the *KP*.
5. This single-folio manuscript was identified and published by V.S. Vorobyov-Desyatovsky in 1965 ("Vnov' naidennye listy rukopisei Kāshyapaparivarty", *Rocznik Orientalistyczny* 21, 1957, pp.491-500).
6. The two fragments in the Hoernle Collection were identified and published by Hōryū Kuno, with facsimiles ("Saiiki shutsudo bukkyō bonpon to sono seiten shiron-jo no chii [jō]. Daihōshakkyō to Zōagonkyō no genten 1. Uten shutsudo Daihōshakkyō bonpon to sono kachi", *Bukkyō kenkyū* [*Buddhist Studies*] 2/3,1938, pp. 71-110). The fragment in the Mannerheim Collection was transliterated by Julio Nathanael Reuter, without facsimile ("Some Buddhist Fragments from Chinese Turkestan in Sanskrit and 'Khotanese'," *Aikakauskirja* [*Journal de la Société Finno-Ougrienne*] 30:37, Helsinki 1913-18, pp. 1-37, 9 plates [Repr. with some minor changes in: C. G. *Mannerheim, Across Asia from West to East in 1906-1908*, vol. 2, Helsinki 1940, pp. 1-35]). Later J. W. de Jong found that all three fragments belong to one and the same folio and presented a reconstructed text ("Sanskrit fragments of the Kāśyapaparivarta," *Beiträge zur Indienforschung*, Berlin, 1977, pp. 247-55).
7. First transliterated in *Sanskrithandschriften aus den Turfanfunden*, (Verzeichnis der orientalischen Handschriften in Deutschland, Band X), Teil I, Ernst Waldschmidt (ed.), 1965, p. 165 (Tafel 36 [recto]), and later identified by Dieter Schlingloff in *Sanskrithandschriften aus den Turfanfunden*, (Verzeichnis der orientalischen Handschriften in Deutschland, Band

X), Teil 4, Lore Sander and Ernst Waldschmidt (eds.), Wiesbaden: Franz Steiner, 1980, p. 280.

8. Some fragmentary copper plates with *KP* engravings have been found in Sri Lanka: see S. Paranavitana, "Iṅdikaṭusāya Copper Plaques," *Epigraphica Zeylanica* III, 1928, pp. 199-212; do., "A Note on the Iṅdikaṭusāya Copper Plaques," *EZ* IV, 1939, pp. 238-42. Since the text retrieved from those plates is very fractional, I take no notice of it here.
9. See Seishi Karashima, "Some features of the language of the *Kāśyapaparivarta*," in: *Annual Report of The International Research Institute for Advanced Buddhology at Soka University for the Academic Year 2001*, vol. 5, 2002, pp. 43-66.
10. Weller, *Zum Kāśyapaparivarta* Heft 2: Verdeutschung des Sanskrit-Tibetischen Textes, Berlin (*Abhandlungen der Sächsischen Akademie der Wissenschaften zu Leipzig*, Philologisch-Historische Klasse 57-3), 1965, p. 63, En. 3. Weller's comments were based on the passages given in the present article as examples 1 and 2. These passages are found in folio No.3.
11. For the physical appearance of the marks, see Vorobyova-Desyatovskaya, *The Kāśyapaparivarta*, Conventions, p. xv.
12. For details on the scripts of the mauscript and fragments of the *KP*, see Vorobyova-Desyatovskaya, *The Kāśyapaparivarta*, Introduction. The punctuation marks found in the other *KP* MSS are as follows: SI P/85A and the two fragments in the Hoernle Collection contain (1), (3), and (4), while the Turfan fragment has (3) and (4) (although the facsimile of Mannerheim fragment has yet to be published, since it belongs to same folio as the two Hoernle fragments it must have the same punctuation).
13. Hoernle Nos. 142 and 148, written in "the Upright Gupta script of the calligraphic type" (Hoernle, *Manuscript Remains of Buddhist Literature Found in Eastern Turkestan*, Oxford, 1916, pp. 142-43).
14. Hoernle, op. cit.
15. La Vallée Poussin, "Documents sanscrits de la seconde collection M A Stein," *Journal of the Royal Asiatic Society* 1911, pp. 759-77, esp. p. 764, fn. 1.
16. Schlingloff, *Ein buddhistisches Yogalehrbuch*, Textband, Berlin: Akademie Verlag, 1964, (Sanskrittexte aus den Turfanfunden VII), esp. pp. 17-19. Quoted from p.17.
17. Schlingloff, op. cit., p. 17.
18. According to Nakatani, this manuscript might have been written between the last half of the third and the beginning of the fourth centuries *C.E.* (*Subasi shahon no kenkyū* [**A Study on the Udānavarga of Subhaši*], Kyoto: Jinbunshoin, 1988, §§10-19, pp. 10-20). As to the facsimiles of the Subhaṣi manuscript, see Nakatani, *Udānavarga de Subhaši. Edition critique du manuscrit sur bois rovenant de Subhaši*, Bibliothèque Nationale de Paris, Fonds Pelliot. Tome I: Texte et Facsimilés. Collège de France, Institut de Civilisation Indienne, Paris, 1987.
19. Nakatani, *Subasi shahon no kenkyū*, §23 b, pp. 25-26.
20. See Mette, "Zwei kleine Fragmente aus Gilgit," *Studien zur Indologie und Iranistik Heft* 7, 1981, pp. 133-51, esp. p. 141 [cf. also Mette, *Die Gilgitfragmente des Kāraṇḍavyūha*, Swisttal-Odendorf: Indica et Tibetica Verlag (Indica et Tibetica 29), 1997, p. 11]. Hisashi Matsumura later revised the same two texts, devoting particular attention to the punctuation marks, see

Matsumura, "Devatāsūtra to Alpadevatāsūtra," ["*The Devatāsūtra and Alpadevatāsūtra*"] *Indogaku Bukkyōgaku Kenkyū* [*Journal of Indian and Buddhist Studies*] 30-2, 1982, pp. 988-82 (54)-(60). And he says that "when a punctuation mark is not found inspite that it is expected (e.g. at the end of sentence or half-verse), it is because in most cases the sentence or half-verse ending in visarga or a consonant with virāma" (p. 987 tr. by N.K.). In his other article, he points out that "Two dots (:) denote, in some cases, visarga, but in other cases a punctuation mark; sometimes it is very difficult to judge what the two dots denote. In many cases the visarga itself, and virāma too, take a role of a period or a comma at the same time" (Matsumura, "On sūtra of the Ekottarikāgama on Triśaraṇagama and Pañcaśīla," *Archiv orientální* 57/4, 1989, pp. 359-71, esp. p. 368). In editing of the *Kaṭhinavastu* of the *Mūlasarvāstivāda Vinaya,* he also makes mention of "visarga-daṇḍa" in separate column (Matsumura, "The *Kaṭhinavastu* from the Vinayavastu of the Mūlasarvāstivādins," *Sanskrit-Texte aus dem buddhistischen Kanon: Neuentdeckungen und Neueditionen III,* Göttingen: Vandenhoeck & Ruprecht, 1996 (Sanskrit-Wörterbuch der buddhistischen Texte aus den Turfan-Funden Beiheft 6), pp.145-239, esp. p. 182).

21. Haiyan Hu-von Hiniiber, *Das Poṣadhavastu: Vorschriften für die buddhistische Beichtfeier im Vinaya der Mūlasarvastivādins,* (Studien Zur Indologie und Iranistik Monographie 13), Reinbek: Dr. Inge Wezler Verlag für Orientalistische Fachpublikationen, 1994.
22. Ibid., pp. 44-45, 11.6; p.46, 11.8 (3) <d>; p. 122, VI.5.2.(b) <4>; p. 125, VI.5.3. As for the symbols used in her transliteration in order to make a distinction between several puncutation marks, see the table in p. 44 and p. 127.
23. See Cüppers, *The IXth Chapter of the Samādhirājasūtra: A Text-critical Contribution to the Study of Mahāyāna Sūtras,* Stuttgart: Franz Steiner Verlag (Alt- und Neu-Indische Studien 41), 1990, esp. p. xx.
24. Brough, "The language of the Buddhist Sanskrit texts," *Bulletin of the School of Oriental and African Studies* 16, 1954, pp. 351-75, esp. p. 361.
25. Brough cites Edgerton's principle as stated in the *BHS Reader* (Brough, op. cit. p. 353). Edgerton says: "Any non-Sanskritic form presented in the mss. must, in general, be regarded as closer to the original form of the text than a 'correct' Sanskrit variant" (*Buddhist Hybrid Sanskrit Reader,* 1953, New Haven, Preface, p. vi).
26. Brough, "The language of the Buddhist Sanskrit texts," p. 361.
27. Brough, op. cit.
28. In the text of the *KP,* there are two metrical types, *triṣṭubh* (Tr., eleven syllables)/ *jagatī* (J., twelve syllables) type and *śloka.* The extant Sanskrit text contains 601 pādas of the former type (including three incomplete pādas) and 4 verses of the latter.
29. Regarding metrical problems, I shall confine myself to pointing out those closely related to the reading of the text. Other issues, such as influences from Middle Indic, metri causa, two shorts for one long, ligatures that do not make position, and so on, will be treated on another occasion.
30. Although we cannot know how many verses exist because the following three folios (Nos. 34-36) are missing, there must be some more strophe(s)

after this; according to the Tibetan and Chinese translations, this section might have two strophes. It means mat two-third of 'c' pāda and 'd' pāda are presumably lost.

31. In addition, two appear at the end of the 'b' pāda of a śloka.
32. These three sylables should be ⏕ – or – ⏕.
33. In his note on the word *bhoti*, he explained only its phonetic change: *bhavati* > *bh-o-ti*, see Vorobyov-Desyatovsky, "Vnov' naidennye," p. 495, n. 22.
34. Cf. Karashima, "Some features," p. 48, § 5.3.
35. Cf. Karashima, "Some features," p. 45, § 2.2.
36. This is a superfluous type of "double dot" sign but sometimes in this text *pr-* does not make position, resulting in a preceding syllable remaining short. If this is the case here, the sign becomes necessary to read a preceding syllable as long, although this explanation is too complicated. In the *KP*, ligatures that do not make position are as follows: *kṣ-*, *pr-*, *jñ-*, *str*, *śr*(*r*)-, *kr-*, *-vr-*. However, this tendency is not consistent.
37. There is only one instance where the numeral 2 occurs at the end of a 'b' pāda: + + *to* 2 (6r.3, 1st, § 5). This sole instance may be seen as a case in which the numeral 2—which makes no sense in this position—is simply a transcribal error for a double dot punctuation mark, because the two signs are quite similar, although its preceding word remains unrestored.
38. Besides, we have instances that *-ḥ* changed in *-s*/*-ś* permutating with the initial consonant of the 'd' pāda: *bodhisattvas tatrā*° (26v.1, § 45); *dharmāś caturau* (2v.2, 3rd/last, § 1).
39. In addition, at the end of 'b' pāda of *śloka* (59r.1, 1st, § 115).
40. In addition, at the end of 'b' pāda of *śloka* (59r.3, 1st, § 116).
41. As for the "anusvāra-punctuation," see Schlingloff, *Ein buddhistisches Yogalehrbuch*, pp. 19-20.
42. This double vertical daṇḍa is type *(2).
43. See Karashima, "Some features," p. 57, § 16.10, and fn. 97.
44. See *BHSG* §§ 8.17, 8.78, 18.6.

CHAPTER 6

Mārgajñatā in the *Abhisamayālaṅkāra*[1]

FUJIO TANIGUCHI

The *Abhisamayālaṅkāra* is a synopsis of the *Prajñāpāramitāsūtra* written from the standpoint that the sūtra shows a practical path to Emancipation.[2] Mārgajñatā is one of three types of omniscience mentioned in the text. In this short paper the auther will study how we should look at mārgajñatā in its proper practical perspective.

Mārgajñatā is originally one of three types of omniscience described in the *Twenty-five Thousand Stanza Prajñāpāramitāsūtra.* The *Abhisamayālaṅkāra* follows the sūtra and incorporates the three types of omniscience into its unique system of practice. It is the system of eight abhisamaya (realizations). The text distributes the eight abhisamaya into three categories.[3]

Three objects (viṣaya):

1. sarvākārajñatā (the omniscience in regard of all the aspects),
2. mārgajñatā (the omniscience in regard of the practical paths), and
3. sarvajñatā (the omniscience in regard of all the things).

Four applications (prayoga):

4. sarvākārābhisaṃbodha (the intuition of all the aspects),
5. mūrdhābhisamaya (the realization at its summit),
6. anupūrvābhisamaya (the gradual realization), and
7. ekakṣaṇābhisaṃbodha (the momentary intuition).

Fruit (phala):

8. dharmakāya (the truth body).

Haribhadra, a leading commentator on this text, explains the relationship among the first four abhisamaya as follows:

1. (The chapter of) Sarvākārajnatā will be indicated first because it will be a statement of the fruit so that a bodhisattva wishing for buddhahood could recognize all the aspects such as determination (cittotpāda).[4]
2. Mārgajñatā will be indicated because no one will be able to understand sarvākārajñatā without recognition of mārgajñatā.[5]
3. Sarvajñatā will be indicated because no one will be able to recognize the practical paths properly without recognition of all the things.[6]
4. In order to control the three types of omniscience one who has recognized them must meditate repeatedly on the three types of omniscience again through summarizing the knowledge of all the aspects, practical paths and things. Therefore sarvākārābhisaṃbodha will be indicated.[7]

According to this explanation of Haribhadra, a bodhisattva must recognize the first three abhisamaya, which are sarvākārajñatā, mārgajñatā and sarvajñatā, before he begins his practice along the system of the *Abhisamayālaṅkāra.* On the other hand, these three are defined as the wisdom of three types of sages respectively; sarvākārajñatā is the wisdom of buddhas, mārgajñatā is that of bodhisattvas, and sarvajñatā of both śrāvakas and pratyekabuddhas.[8] Therefore the first three chapters of this text ought to explain these three types of omniscience because their titles are named after them. Judging from the topics discussed in these chapters of the text, however, their subjects don't seem to be the wisdom of the three types of sages.

Mārgajñatā

The *Abhisamayālaṅkāra* defines mārgajñatā as the wisdom of bodhisattvas, and the text gives the title "Mārgajñatā" to its second chapter. Therefore the subject of the second chapter should be the wisdom of bodhisattvas. And it declares itself as a treatise showing a practical path to sarvākārajñatā, that is a process of attaining buddhas' wisdom. The first seven chapters among eight mainly illustrate the course for buddhahood and the last one alone describes buddhahood itself, dharmakāya. Then the seven chapters ought to show us bodhisattvas' practice. Judging from that interpretation and the definition of mārgajñatā we could regard this text as a work explaining mārgajñatā chiefly, because bodhisattvas' practice ought to be the scope or function of mārgajñatā. The structure of our object, however, denies that mārgajñatā is the chief subject of the *Abhisamayālaṅkāra.*

We will look first at the topics of the chapter II titled "Mārgajñatā."

1. The basis of mārgajñatā (v. 1)
2. The path of śrāvakas (v. 2)
2a. The aids to penetration of śrāvakas (vv. 3-5)
3. The path of pratyekabuddhas (vv. 6-8)
3a. The aids to penetration of pratyekabuddhas (vv. 9-10)
4. The path of vision (of bodhisattvas) (vv. 11-16)
5. The merits of the path of meditation (of bodhisattvas) (v.17)
6-11. The path of meditation (of bodhisattvas) (vv. 18-31)

Chapter II ought to explain the paths of śrāvakas, pratyekabuddhas, and bodhisattvas, for its subject is mārgajñatā or the omniscience in regard of the practical paths. Each practical course of these sages comprises five paths. They start at saṃbhāramārga and end up with niṣṭhāmārga according to Yogācāra School terminology. But the *Abhisamayālaṅkāra* mentions only darśanamārga (the path of vision) and bhāvanāmārga (path of meditation). It never uses such terminologies as saṃbhāramārga (the path of accumulation) and prayogamārga (the preparatory path), which are the first two stages of five. Its author prefers mokṣabhāgīya (the aids to emancipation) and nirvedhabhāgīya (the aids to penetration) to saṃbhāramārga and prayogamārga instead. And nirvedhabhāgīya of bodhisattvas is not explained in this second chapter. Some might conclude that this text does not regard these lower levels of practice as paths. But it is not true.

As for the paths of śrāvakas and pratyekabuddhas, Chapter II refers to nirvedhabhāgīya of the sages, which is a preliminary stage to their paths. And nirvedhabhāgīya of bodhisattvas is mentioned in the first, fourth, and fifth chapters.[9] In addition, mokṣabhāgīya of bodhisattvas, which is a lower level than nirvedhabhāgīya, is explained in the fourth chapter.[10] So it is clear that the *Abhisamayālaṅkāra* regards the two lower levels as parts of bodhisattvas' practice, even if they are not named "mārga". Chapter II treats only bhāvanāmārga and darśanamārga as bodhisattvas' paths. Though mārgajñatā (the omniscience in regard of the practical paths) is defined as the wisdom of bodhisattvas, it is not of all bodhisattvas but of those who have arrived at the level of Ārya or a Saint.

Sarvākārajñatā and Sarvajñatā

The *Abhisamayālaṅkāra* discriminates between sarvākārajñatā (the omniscience in regard of all the aspects) and sarvajñatā (the omniscience in regard of all the things) clearly. It mentions the wisdom of buddhas by the former, and the wisdom of both śrāvakas and pratyekabuddhas by the latter. In addition to that usage, sarvajñatā has another wide sense. It refers to the three types of omniscience in general. Tibetan translators put this same word into two terminologies. The wisdom of both śrāvakas and pratyekabuddhas is translated in a grammartically ordinary form, that is "thams cad shes pa nyid," while the three types of omniscience is given an equivalent in a respective form, "thams cad mkhyen pa nyid," because it includes the wisdom of buddhas.

On one hand, Chapter II titled "Mārgajñatā" describes the wisdom of bodhisattvas anyhow. On the other hand, judging from the topics dealt there, the first and the third chapters titled "Sarvākārajñatā" and "Sarvajñatā" respectively do not explain the wisdom of buddhas and that of both śrāvakas and pratyekabuddhas directly.

We will verify the topics of Chapter I titled "Sarvākārajñatā" then.

1. The determination (cittotpāda v. 18-20)
2. Instructions (avavāda vv. 21-24)
3. The four aids to penetration (nirvedhabhaṅga vv. 25-36)
4. The lineages (gotra vv. 37-39)
5. The objectives (ālambana vv. 40-41)
6. The goal (uddeśa v. 42)
7. The performances in armor (saṃnāha-pratipatti v. 43)
8. The performances of procession (prasthāna-pratipatti vv. 44-45)
9. The performances of equipment (saṃbhāra-pratipatti vv. 46-71)
10. The performances of departure (niryāṇa-pratipatti vv. 72-73)

The subject of this chapter ought to be sarvākārajñatā defined as object (viṣaya) of training according to the last verse of the *Abhisamayālaṅkāra.* But these ten topics are mainly connected with bodhisattvas rather than buddhas. So we could conclude that the first chapter does not describe the wisdom of buddhas directly, but the essential conditions for attaining sarvākārajñatā. On the other hand Haribhadra explains in his commentary that sarvākārajñatā is the object which a beginner bodhisattva should recognize before he begins his training.[11] In that context Chapter I ought to give a beginner a rough sketch of sarvākārajñatā, but it does not illustrate the object itself but just shows some accessories to it.

Now let us check the topics of Chapter III.

1/2 Not staying in cyclic existence nor staying in quietude (v. 1)

3/4 Far from prajñāpāramitā because of not being means, close to it because of being means (v. 2)

5. The discordant factors (v. 3)
6. Their antidotes (vv. 4-7)
7. Trainings (vv. 8-10ab)
8. The sameness of the trainings (v. 10cd)
9. The path of vision (vv. 11-15)

Among these nine topics 1 & 2 describe the standpoint of Mahāyāna. Topics 3 & 4 make a pair; the former explains for the standpoint of śrāvakas and the latter that of bodhisattvas. Similarly topics 5 & 6 make a pair; topic 5 shows Hīnayāna and topic 6 Mahāyāna. The trainings and the path of vision which are mentioned in the topics 7-9 do not belong to śrāvakas but to bodhisattvas. Haribhadra adds in his commentaries on them that implicitly these topics 7-9 refer to those of śrāvakas[12]. And in his Smaller Commentary he says at the end of the last topic of the third chapter as follows:

> A bodhisattva should recognize the path of śrāvakas in the course of sarvajñatā, but should not realize it. Therefore the path of meditation (belonging to śrāvakas) is not described here[13].

This comment indicates that the third chapter titled "Sarvajñatā" does not mention the wisdom of śrāvakas chiefly. Sarvajñatā is explained within the limits that a bodhisattva should recognize the wisdom of śrāvakas in his mahāyānistic practice. And he should recognize it in comparison with the wisdom of bodhisattvas. And the wisdom of śrāvakas mentioned here belongs to those who have not arrived at the level of arhat yet. This is more clear when we find the fact that the term "mārgajñatā" is used in parallel with the word "sarvajñatā" in the *Abhisamayālaṅkāra.*

We find seven cases of the word "mārgajñatā" and nine "sarvajñatā".

mārgajñatā: maṅgala, I.3, 9, II.2, 11, 16, IV.19
sarvajñatā: maṅgala, I.3, 11, III.7, 11, 15, IV.(1), 17, (V.33).

Among these nine cases of "sarvajñatā", IV.1 and V.33 do not indicate only the wisdom of śrāvakas but all three types of omniscience. So we have only to hold an inquiry into the other seven cases. The three types of omniscience is referred to in such cases as mangala, 1.3, 1.9 & 11, and IV.17 & 19, and "mārgajñatā" and the "sarvajñatā" are parallel there. Moreover "mārgajñatā" in the cases of Chapter II are parallel to "sarvajñatā" in the cases of Chapter III even though the topics of the two chapters are not parallel themselves.

The subject of II.11 is that the path of vision in the course of mārgajñatā consists of the sixteen *kṣaṇas* of *kṣānti* and *jñāna*, and II.16 is a part of verses explaining the sixteen *kṣaṇas*. The subject of III.11 is also that the path of vision in the course of the sarvajñatā consists of the sixteen *kṣaṇas* of *kṣānti* and *jñāna*, and III.15 is a part of verses explaining the sixteen *kṣaṇas*. The path of vision mentioned in Chapter III belongs to bodhisattvas. It means that the path of vision of the third chapter is equivalent to that of the second chapter.

Now let us examine II.2 and III.7, which are not inquired yet.

> This path of śrāvakas in the course of mārgajñatā should be recognized through non-apprehension of [sixteen] aspects of the Four Noble Truths. (II.2)
>
> No contact with signs, no rise of knowledges about either things or expressions. Those are the [sixteen] aspects of sarvajñatā. (III.7)

According to II.2, bodhisattvas should recognize as their objects of practice the sixteen aspects of the four noble truths belonging to the path of śrāvakas. They should do so by the way of non-apprehension. Here non-apprehension is a way of recognition of the objects; and the objects, the sixteen aspects, are the ways recognizing their objects, the four noble truths. So bodhisattvas have the same object of practice as śrāvakas do, but they recognize them in a different way. According to III.7, the standpoint of śrāvakas is a factor that bodhisattvas should negate after learning it. And their Mahāyānistic practice works as antidote for it.

The two verses, II.2 & III.7, make it clear that bodhisattvas should not accept the standpoint of śrāvakas even when they learn it, and that they study it in order to negate it.

Conclusion

The *Abhisamayālaṅkāra* presents a system of practice on which a practitioner trains himself after recognizing the three types of omniscience as his object of training. But the way of explanation of each three is different in this text. Sarvākārajñatā is explained indirectly just by presenting the essential conditions for attaining it. Mārgajñatā is illustrated directly by what a practitioner comprehends through mārgajñatā. Sarvajñatā is explained indirectly by comparison, showing how the wisdom of bodhisattvas is superior to that of śrāvakas.

It is difficult for a beginner practitioner to understand concretely and directly what and how sarvākārajñatā is even though it ought to be his ultimate goal. He must get satisfied at first to recognize its essential conditions so that he could vaguely know the direction to follow. A beginner practitioner who is still an ordinary person (pṛthagjana) need reach the state of ārya bodhisattva before attaining buddhahood. To become ārya he must recognize the paths of śrāvakas and pratyekabuddhas. On his way to buddhahood there is a possibility that he might take a means for an end. It means that he might fall into hīnayānistic path. In order to avoid the risk a novice bodhisattva must always keep in mind how the wisdom of śrāvakas and pratyekabuddhas are inferior to that of Ārya bodhisattvas.

Mārgajñatā in the *Abhisamayālaṅkāra* does not cover all the stages of bodhisattvas' wisdom. It is limited to the stages of the path of vision and meditation. The whole practical system of the *Abhisamayālaṅkāra* is the path to sarvākārajñatā, and this wisdom of buddhas is the ultimate goal of a practitioner of Mahāyāna. So the path to sarvākārajñatā means a whole system of Mahāyāna itself, while mārgajñatā consists of only two among five Mahāyānistic stages. Someone might not think mārgajñatā so important in the practical system of the *Abhisamayālaṅkāra*. But once a practitioner must recognize and then negate sarvajñatā, Hīnayānistic wisdom, before he attains buddhahood. If he denies sarvajñatā with any concept, "mārgajñatā" is a more effective idea than "sarvākārajñatā". That is because mārgajñatā is not an end of mahāyānistic practice but just a way to its ultimate goal, and because sarvajñatā is not necessarily an end of Hīnayānistic practice either.

Through the concept "mārgajñatā" one could claim superiority of mahāyāna and accept sarvajñatā without rejecting it completely. In that sense "mārgajñatā" is an important idea in the practical system of the *Abhisamayālaṅkāra*.

ABBREVIATIONS

AA: *Abhisamayālaṅkāra*

AAA: *Abhisamayālaṅkārālokā Prajñāpāramitā-vyākhyā,* (ed. by U. Wogihara), Sankibo Buddhist Book Store, 1973 (1932).

AAS: *Abhisamayālaṅkāra-kārikā-śāstra-vivṛti,* (ed. by H. Amano), Heirakuji-shoten, 2000.

(Associate Professor, Nagoya Women's University)

NOTES

1. This present paper is an English translation of my Japanese paper titled *Genkan-shogon-ron ni okeru Dochi (Journal of Indian and Buddhist Studies,* Vol. 50, No. 1, December, 2001, pp. 129-35).
2. *sarvākārajñatā-mārgaḥ śāsinā yo 'ra deśitaḥ/* I.1ab (*AAA* p.5 1.2)
3. *viṣayas tritayo hetuḥ prayogaś catur-ātmakaḥ/*
 dharmakāyaḥ phalaṃ karmety anyas tredhārtha-saṃgrahaḥ// (*AAA* p.992 ll.15-16)
4. *buddhatvārthino bodhisattvasya cittotpādādi-sarvākāra-parijñānāyādau phala-nirdeśena sarvākārajñatā kathitā/* (*AAA* p. 16 ll.1-2)
5. *sarvākārajñatādhigamo na vinā mārgajñatā-parijñāneneti mārgajñatāṃ vaktum āha/* (*AAA* p. 129 ll.11-12)
6. *sarva-vastu-parijñānaṃ vinā na mārgajñatā-parijñanaṃ samyag iti sarvajñatāṃ vaktuṃ.../* (*AAA* p. 413 ll.13-14)
7. *parijñāta-tri-sarvajñatā-vaśitvārthaṃ punaḥ sarvākāra-mārga-vastu-jñāna-saṃgraheṇa tri-sarvajātāṃ bhāvayatīti sarvākārābhisambodho vaktavyaḥ/* (*AAA* p.445 ll.11-12)
8. *sambhārāś ca sa-niryāṇāḥ sarvākārajñatā muneḥ//* I.6cd (*AAA* p. 17 l.11)
 vijñānāṃ bodhisattvānām iti mārgajñatoditā// I.9cd (*AAA* p. 18 l.11)
 dṛṅ-mārgaḥ śrāvakādīinām iti sarvajñateṣyate// I.11cd (*AAA* p.18 1.28)
9. *AA* I.vv.25-36; IV.vv.35-37, 40-45; V.vv.1-4.
10. *AA* IV.vv.32-34.
11. *AAA* p. 16 ll.1-2.
12. *sarvajñatādhikārād vyatireka-nirdeśena* (*AAS* p. 48 1.9); *arthād yathokta-viparyayeṇa śrāvakādīnām* (*AAS* p. 51 1.18); *etad-viparyayeṇa śrāvakādīnāṁ...* (*AAS* p. 53 l.11) etc.
13. *sarvajñatāyāṃ śrāvaka-mārgo bodhisatvena parijñeyo na sākṣāt-karttavya iti bhāvanā-mārgo na nirdiṣṭaḥ/* (*AAS* p. 53 ll.12-13).

CHAPTER 7

Buddhist Definition of Existence: *Kāritra* to *Arthakriyā*

MASARU AKIMOTO

1. *Introduction*

In the Buddhist tradition of epistemology and logic, it is Dharmakīrti who defined a real entity by means of the word "*arthakriyā*" or "*arthakriyāśakti*" [1] (the ability or power to cause effects). It refers to the intrinsic quality of any real entity which exists as a momentary (*kṣaṇika*) and particular existent (*svalakṣaṇa*) and is distinguished from both similars and dissimilars. Whatever has this quality really exists. This definition of existence is found in *Pramāṇavārttika* as follows:

Only existents which have the ability to cause their own effects are real entities.[2]

Where does this concept of the ability to cause effects come from? I think Dharmakīrti's definition resulted from the historical development of certain doctrinal disputes. In earlier Abhidharma texts there were various arguments about the relations between existence and time. In due course, they were well summarized by Vasubandhu (*c.* 400-480) who is regarded as having moved from the Hīnayāna position to the Mahāyāna position. We can see that, in a sense, some epochal developments in Buddhist ontological theories began from him. So we will use the *Abhidharmakośabhāṣya* of Vasubandhu as the starting point of this paper and survey certain aspects of these historical developments extending as far as "*arthakriyā*".

In the 5th chapter (Anuśaya-nirdeśaḥ) of *Abhidharmakośabhāṣya*, the Sarvāstivādin theory that all the dharmas really exist during the three periods is presented. This argument continues to develop in later texts and commentaries, and is thought to come to an end only in the *Tattvasaṃgraha* of Śāntarakṣita (*c.* 725-778) and *Tattvasaṃgrahapañjikā* of Kamalaśīla (*c.* 740-795). The argument begins with the following question: if the dharmas really exist during the three time periods, then "what determines whether they are past or present or future?" The Sarvāstivādin's answer is that present dharmas are differentiated from past or future one by means of their activity' (*kāritra*). I think this argument eventually led to the later, more rigid definition of existence.

2. *Traditional definitions of "kāritra" in the Sarvāstivāda and Vasubandhu's critique of them*

The Sarvāstivādins declare that the constituents of phenomenal existence (*dharma*) exist as real entities in all the three times: past, present, and future. Each constituent, which continues to have its own intrinsic quality (*svalakṣaṇa*) in each of the three times, is determined to be a present dharma according to the nature of its 'activity' (*kāritra*): A constituent is a future dharma when it is not yet in activity; it is a present dharma when it is currently in activity; and it is a past dharma when its activity has ceased. What, then, is its 'activity'?

Vasubandhu (*ca.* 400-480) presents the following argument for this in the *Abhidharmakośabhāṣya*:

> You (Sarvāstivādins) should answer the question why a dharma is called past or future, even though a past or future one exists as a real entity [just like a present one]. [The Sarvāstivādin's answer:] We said that the three time periods [of a dharma] was I determined by its activity (*kāritra*). [The opponents ask:] If so, in what activity is a present eye [engaged in] which is unable to see anything [because of the darkness and so on] (*tatsabhāga*)? [The Sarvāstivādin's an-

> swer:] They are [in the activity of] grasping and giving their effects (*phaladānapratigrahaṇa*). [The opponents say:] Then the error will occur that a past dharma is [also] in activity [i.e. present], or is half in activity [i.e. half present]. In this way, a confusion of the distinguishing characteristics of the three time periods will occur.[3]

Here, Vasubandhu summarizes the arguments developed in the *abhidharma* tradition, and narrows down the term 'activity' to two meanings. One is, in the example of the eye (as a dharma), the activity of seeing; the other is [the activity of] grasping and giving its own effect. But, he argues, neither of the two is able to determine a dharma as present. The former is unable because when it is in the darkness a present eye is not in the activity of seeing and so on; and the latter is unable because the activity of giving its effects (*phaladāna*) does not always take place in the present time. Now, grasping its effects (*phalapratigrahaṇa*) is a function whereby a dharma holds on to an effect which will come about at a time later than the present, and this function is considered to always be present. But the function of giving effects (*phaladāna*) is the ability to produce its effect in the present period alone, and this function, according to the Sarvāstivādin system, is sometimes present and sometimes past. Therefore, Vasubandhu argues, [the activity of] grasping and giving effects cannot define a dharma as present.

These arguments were already found in the *Vibhāṣā*, the fundamental text of the Sarvāstivādins. There it was argued that even an eye which is not in the activity of seeing is considered to be present because it is in the activity of grasping its own effect, of which it is itself the cause (*sabhāgahetu*). This is a response to the objection that an eye in the darkness and so on is not present because it is not presently in the activity of seeing. Here it is argued that an eye which is not in the activity of seeing, but only of grasping its own effect, which is the function of causing its own effect, does exist at the present and thus that the function determines that the eye is present.[4] But in the *Vibhāṣā* various kinds of activities are explained and grasping one's own effect alone is not always sufficient to determine a dharma as present. This is why, I think, Vasubandhu suggests that the Sarvāstivādins should declare that grasping its own effects is, in and of itself, sufficient 'activity' to determine a dharma as present. The response to this suggestion was given by Saṃghabhadra (*ca.* 430-490), one of the Sarvāstivādin thinkers.

3. *The Traditional "phalapratigrahaṇa" and Saṃghabhadra's "phalākṣepaśakti"*

We can say Saṃghabhadra was the first person who asserted, from the Sarvāstivādin position, that a dharma is determined to be present in every case on the sole basis of grasping its own effect (*phalapratigrahaṇa*), which will be produced by its cause.[5] Saṃghabhadra used the word "*phalākṣepaśakti*" (the power to project or 'draw' effects) instead of "*phalapratigrahaṇa*". I think it was in order to further clarify the meaning of 'activity' (*kāritra*) that its definition was restricted in this way. It is important that he used the term "power" (*śakti*), because it would be easy to extend this to the power to cause effects (*arthakriyā* or *arthakriyāśakti*), which was the definition of a real entity in later periods.

For his part, Saṃghabhadra defines *kāritra* and so on in *Nyāyānusāriṇī* as follows:

> Each dharma generally has two kinds of functions. One is its activity (*kāritra*), the other is its power or ability (*śakti* or *vyāpāra*). The power or ability to draw an effect is called activity. The term "activity," however, does not refer to all [kinds of] abilities, for there are some abilities that are different from activity.
>
> For example, the eye's ability to see some color and shape is interrupted by darkness, but its activity is not so. Namely, an eye cannot see any color and shape in the darkness because the ability to see is interrupted by some obstacle, e.g. the darkness etc.; but the ability to draw its own effect cannot be interrupted by it. Therefore, its activity always exists at the present because the eye can draw its effect even in the darkness.
>
> It is by its activity that a dharma is determined as present. The activity of each dharma, even when it ceases, does not become "invariable" (*asaṃskṛta*). And a dharma's ability to produce its effect (e.g. *phaladāna*, etc.) is not called activity, but merely ability. [This is] because the activity of drawing

> effects exists only in the present; "invariable" [dharmas, however,] cannot draw their own effects; and only the activity of drawing [their own] effects is called activity.
>
> Accordingly, Vasubandhu's view in his work that [the term] 'activity' includes some other abilities like giving effects, etc. indicates that he is ignorant of the established theories of Abhidharma. And although a past dharma can give some effect, we do not say it has activity. Therefore no confusion can exist in our definition of time.[6]

As Saṃghabhadra clearly explains, dharmas have various functions. Activity is one of them, but it is distinguished from other abilities. Activity is, in his view, the power or ability to draw effects. It is what is called 'grasping effects' in his tradition. For example, an eye has the ability to grasp its own effect, which will exist at the very next moment. This ability is its 'activity', which Saṃghabhadra calls the power to draw its own effects. For example, the eye which has no ability to see, but only the power to draw its own effect, surely exists in the present time. Therefore its activity is always the criteria by which a dharma is determined as present or not. This is the Saṃghabhadra's view.

4. *Saṃghabhadra's "phalākṣepaśakti" to Dharmakīrti's "arthakriyā"*

Saṃghabhadra declared that it is the power (*śakti*) of drawing effects that differentiates present dharmas from past and future ones. At the same time he still declared, from the Sarvāstivādin position, that each dharma continued to have its own quality during the three time periods.

Śāntarakṣita criticizes the Sarvāstivādin position in the 21st chapter, named Traikālyaparīkṣā (Study of Three Time Periods), in his *Tattvasaṃgraha*. The person whose positions are criticized is clearly Saṃghabhadra, since, in verse 1809, we find phrase, "*kāritrākhyā phalākṣepaśaktir*", which he discusses; and in *Tattvasaṃgrahapañjikā*, Kamalaśīla's commentary on this text, Saṃghabhadra and his positions are cited by name. He had already been criticized before Śāntarakṣita (*c.* eigth cent.), by Sthiramati (*c.* sixth cent.) who lived even before Dharmakīrti (*c.* seventh cent.), but we will not refer here to the arguments in Sthiramati's work, *Tattvārtha*; a commentary on the *Abhidharmakośabhāṣya.*

In the first eight verses of this section of the *Tattvasaṃgraha*, 1785-1792, Śāntarakṣita introduces the traditional Sarvāstivādin position according to *Abhidharmakośabhāṣya*, and in the next fifty-two verses, 1793-1844, criticizes their assertions concering activity (*kāritra*). The chapter then ends in verse 1855. The critique of the concept of activity is thus the main theme of this chapter. This is probably because he considered the arguments concerning activity to be the most important part of the discussion of the existence of dharmas during the three times.

The critique begins with the question—is its activity different from a dharma or the same as it?—and discusses difficulties in both cases. Eventually he concludes that it is impossible to escape the contradiction between a dharma and its activity, which according to the Sarvāstivādins are the same,[7] because a dharma really exists in the past, present and future, while its activity only exists in the present. In verse 1801 of *Tattvasaṃgraha*, the Sarvāstivādin theory is ironically denied as follows:

> Activity does not always exist, but every dharma always [exists]. And the activity is said to be the same as a dharma. It is clearly divine work.[8]

The arguments about activity begin in detail from verse 1803 on. In them Śāntarakṣita connects Saṃghabhadra's concept of *phalākṣepaśakti* (the power to draw effects) with Dharmakīrti's concept of *arthakriyāśakti*[9] (the power to cause effects). In verse 1809, Śāntarakṣita says that the power to draw effects, as defined by Saṃghabhadra, is in fact the intrinsic nature of a real entity:

> The power to draw effects, called activity (*kāritra*), is not any object of words (i.e. it is not conceptual). Because the power is just [the intrinsic quality of] a real thing (*vastu*)[10]. How could such [a power] be a [mere] semblance (*prajñaptisat*)?

Saṃghabhadra had said that the activity which determines a dharma as present is the power to draw its own effect. Now Śāntarakṣita says in the above verse that the power Saṃghabhadra refers to is neither conceptual, as an object of words, nor a mere semblance, but rather is just the intrinsic nature of a real entity itself. Kamalaśīla explains this in his commentary as follows,

> Therefore, we can say, the determination of the [present] time period by the criteria of the [power to draw effects, as defined by Saṃghabhadra,] has been admitted as true [by Śāntarakṣita].[11]

So I think that Śāntarakṣita's declaration amounts to nothing more than equating the power to draw effects, as defined by Saṃghabhadra, with the power to cause effects, as defined by Dharmakīrti—because Dharmakīrti defined a real entity as that which has the ability or power to cause effects. Śāntarakṣita does not explicitly state that the power to draw effects is the same as the ability to cause effects, but he surely identifies the one with the other.

By the way, Saṃghabhadra, from the Sarvāstivādin position, insists on the reality of all the dharmas during the three times. This also refers to the reality of dharmas which do not have the power to draw effects, i.e. the reality of past or future dharmas. And it is this power alone that differentiates present dharmas from past or future ones. But Śāntarakṣita, from the Sautrāntika position, denies the reality of dharmas during the three times and admits only the reality of present dharmas. So he declares that only entities that have this power really exist, and that past or future dharmas are not real entities because they do not have this ability to cause effects. He states this in verse 1820 of his work:

> Only things which have the ability to cause effects are real entities. They do not exist during the past or future times. No effect could be caused by such [an incapable thing].[12]

And then in verses 1834 and 1835 he states that things that have the ability to cause effects exist during the present time, and so are real entities, and that when they are not present they do not have that ability, and so are not real entities:

> Do past or future entities have the ability to cause effects or not? If they have the ability, it necessarily follows that they are present entities, just like any other [present entity, so admitting of no argument]. (1834) If they are not present, it necessarily follows that the past or future entities lack any such ability, just like red lotuses in the sky. (1835)

As we have seen above, according to Śāntarakṣita, the power to draw effects (*phalākṣepaśakti*), the criteria by which Saṃghabhadra defined the activity (*kāritra*) of dharmas, is the intrinsic quality of any real entity, and this was eventually equated with the power to cause effects (*arthakriyāśakti*), the criteria by which Dharmakīrti defined a real entity. And if it is this power that determinates entities as present, then only the entities with this power are real because only the entities in the present time are real. This is thought to be Śāntarakṣita's position.

5. *Conclusion*

The Sarvāstivādins insisted on a unique ontology in which each of the dharmas exists during the three time periods with its own intrinsic nature, and on the basis of this theory they tried to explain the cardinal Buddhist doctrines of "causality" (*pratītyasamutpāda*), "selflessness" (*nairātmya*) and so on. Nāgārjuna (*c.* second-third cent.), founder of the Mādhyamikas, explained "causality" by his theory of "emptiness" (*śūnyatā*), i.e. that everything lacks its own nature—which of course denies the Sarvāstivādin position.

The Sautrāntikas and the Yogācāras, however, responded to this Sarvāstivādin assertion in a different manner than the Mādhyamikas, for Vasubandhu took up the subject in his work from the Sautrāntika perspective. There he focused on the question of how a dharma was determined as present when it continued to hold its intrinsic nature during the future, present and past times. According to the Sarvāstivādins, the criteria by which a thing is determined as present is its activity (*kāritra*), but Vasubandhu argued that the definition of activity was so ambiguous that it could not always determine a thing as present. And eventually, I think, he suggested that the determinitive activity was nothing but the function of grasping effects (*phalapratigrahaṇa*), which is only one of a variety of activities.

Accepting this suggestion, Saṃghabhadra asserted it as a Sarvāstivādin theory, but he used the expression "the power to draw an effect" (*phalākṣepaśakti*) to clarify the meaning of the word *kāritra* much more precisely than before. That is to say, he asserted that *kāritra* means only the power to draw effects, and that present dharmas always have this power even if they lack any other ability. This assertion was provoked by Vasubandhu, but at the same time also protected the Sarvāstivādin position from the critiques of other schools. Moreover, I think, by using the word "śakti" (power or ability) Saṃghabhadra suggested a new and important criteria for defining what a real entity must be.

The power to draw effects is at the core of the Sarvāstivādin system, but I think its influence extended as far as Dharmakīrti's concept of the ability or power to cause effects (*arthakriyā* or *arthakriyāśakti*). This is thought to be the achievement of Saṃghabhadra.

The Sarvāstivādins insist on the reality of all the dharmas during the future, present and past. They claim that a present dharma has the power to draw its own effect which is said to neither the same as nor different from itself. The Sautrāntikas hold that the reality of an entity is defined by the power to draw effects, that is, the ability to cause effects. This ability alone is evidence of its reality. So only present entities are real according to them. Although both sides kept disputing the moot point about whether only dharmas in the present or in all three times were real, both of them seemed to agree on the point that only present dharmas have the ability to cause their own effects. We see that it is Śāntarakṣita who combined both of these concepts, but the concept of *arthakriyā* or *arthakriyāśakti* could be seen as already arising from the progression of concepts between Vasubandhu, Saṃghabhadra, Sthiramati and so on. We shall be pleased if we have clarified these points in this paper.

NOTE

1. Shōryu Katsura, "Dharmakīrti's Theory of Causality," *Journal of the Nanto Society for Buddhist Studies* 50, Todaiji Temple, Nara, pp. 96-114.
2. *Pramāṇavārttika* (in *The Pramāṇavārttikam of Dharmakīrti*, ed. by R. Gnoli, Instituto Italiano per il Medio ed Estremo Oriente, Rome, 1960), I, k.166ab: *sa pāramārthiko bhāvo ya evārthakriyākṣamaḥ.*
3. *Abhidharmakośabhāṣya* in *Abhidharmakośabhāṣya of Vasubandhu* ed. by P. Pradhan, K.P. Jayaswal Research Institute, Patna, 1967), p. 297, ll.13-17.
4. *Vibhāṣā* (in Taisho-Daizo-Kyo 27) p. 393c.
5. cf. Takumi Fukuda, "The Saṅghabhadra's Theory of *dharmas* existing in the Three Times as explained in *Nyāyānusārin*", *Buddhist Seminar* 48, Otani University, Kyoto, 1988, pp. 48-68. Norisato Aohara, "*Kāritra and Śakti* according to Saṅghabhadra," *The Studies in Buddhism*, 42, Ryūkoku University, Kyoto, 1986, pp. 21-42.

6. *Nyāyānusāriṇī* (in Taisho-Daizo-Kyo 29) p. 631 c5-17. These passages are cited in *Tattvārthā* (in Peking Edition), 273b8-274a4, by Sthiramati, and cited in brief in *Tattvasaṃgrahapañjikā* (in *Tattvasaṃgraha of Ācārya Śāntarakṣita with the commentary 'Pañjikā' of Śrī Kamalaśīla* ed. by S.D. Shastri, Bauddha Bharati, Varanasi, 1968), p .617, 19-23. Cf. Masaru Akimoto, "*Abhidharmakośabhāṣya* Commentary by Sthiramati—On the reality of the past, present and future (1)—," *Bulletin of the International Cultural Research Institute of Chikushi Jogakuen College* 4, p. 54.
7. *Abhidharmakośabhāṣya*, p. 298, 4-10.
8. Almost the same as the verse found in *Abhidharmakośa*, p. 298, 21-22.
9. The word "*arthakriyāśakti*" is found in *Tattvasaṃgraha*, k.1837, etc.
10. *Tattvasaṃgrahapañjikā* p. 622, 17-18: *yā ca phalākṣepaśaktiḥ sā nānyā vastusvalakṣaṇāt, kiṃ tarhi, tad eva.*
11. *Tattvasaṃgrahapañjikā* p. 622, 20-21: *tataś ca tadvaśād adhvavyavasthānaṃ tāttvikam eveṣṭam bhavatīti bhāvaḥ.*
12. *Tattvasaṃgraha*, k.1820, p. 624: *sa eva bhāviko bhāvo ya evārthakriyākṣamaḥ, sa ca nāsti tayor yo 'sti na tasmāt kāryasaṃbhavaḥ.* This verse parallels one of Dharmakīrti's *Pramāṇavārttika*, I, k.166: *sa pāramārthiko bhāvo ya evārthakriyākṣamaḥ, nānveti yo 'nveti na tasmāt kāryasaṃbhavaḥ.* The former denies the reality of past or future; the latter denies the reality of the principle (*pradhāna*) that the Sāṃkhya school insists on. Dharmakīrti's verse is as follows: "Only the thing which has the ability to cause effects is quite a real entity. It doesn't continue to exist. By a continuing thing [like *pradhāna*] no effect could be produced."

CHAPTER 8

Defining and Redefining *Svalakṣaṇa:* Dharmakīrti's Concept and its Tibetan Modification

CHIZUKO YOSHIMIZU

Recent contributions to the Tibetan development of Buddhist philosophical systems have attracted considerable attention, not only because of their significant results but also because of their methodological consciousness that any intellectual tradition must be examined in light of its historical and cultural circumstances. Continuity and discontinuity of thought as well as the characteristics of Tibetan interpretations first become clear through a thorough investigation of both Indian and Tibetan traditions, and yet the significance of individual thought is finally to be considered in its contemporary context. In this respect, the latest studies of the Tibetan development of Dharmakīrti's (7c.) epistemology were most successful in indicating the consistency and inconsistency of Tibetan interpretations with Dharmakīrti's original ideas.[1] Special attention has been paid to the originality of dGe lugs pa thinkers. They indeed made several theoretical modifications to, reinterpretations and reevaluations of Indian original thought, especially with regard to logicoepistemological issues in both major fields of Buddhist philosophy, viz., the Madhyamaka system and that of Dharmakīrti.[2] In order to gain a clear picture of the dGe lugs pa position on these Buddhist philosophical systems, we have attempted to reveal what might actually underlie their problematic commitments to traditional teachings, i.e., to reveal its historical background, probable textual sources, possible misinterpretations and wrong transmissions of text, as well as particular aims and motivations they may have had in mind.

The present paper too is an attempt to clarify the way dGe lugs pa scholars redefined the concept *svalakṣaṇa* (*rang mtshan*) and to specify the reasons for this redefinition on the basis of the writings by the three main figures from the earlier period of the school, i.e., Tsong kha pa Blo bzang grags pa (1357-1419), rGyal tshab Dar ma rin chen (1364-1432) and mKhas grub dGe legs dpal bzang po (1385-1438).[3] I also wish to consider the question of how Dharmakīrti and these Tibetan thinkers understood the meaning of the individuality and reality of existents under the concept of *svalakṣaṇa*, since defining *svalakṣaṇa* is none other than defining what an individual and real entity is. Through the following discussion, one will see that both Dharmakīrti and the dGe lugs pa thinkers define *svalakṣaṇa* not in isolation from, but in complete accordance with, their respective considerations of relating philosophical issues. As for the dGe lugs pa, however, it can be said that they aimed to comprehend such fundamental concepts as *svalakṣaṇa* from a wider perspective, namely they tried to formulate a version of individuality and reality which holds true not only for the Sautrāntika tradition of Dharmakīrti but for Buddhist philosophical systems in general, including Madhyamaka. I would like to focus on this point in the last part of the paper.

1. *Dharmakīrti on svalakṣaṇa*

Little needs to be said about the considerable significance of the term *svalakṣaṇa* which literally means 'own characteristic', and comes down to term for 'particular' or 'individual'. *Svalakṣaṇa* is characterized by Dignāga (6c.) as the object of direct perception (*pratyakṣa*), i.e., the object of a cognition which is free of conceptual construction (*kalpanāpoḍha*).[4] Dharmakīrti added to this epistemological notion a clear ontological ground by identifying it with that which has causal efficacy (*arthakriyāsāmarthya, arthakriyāśakti. don byed nus pa*), that is, an ability to produce an effect. He explicitly defines this alone (*eva*) as ultimately existent (*paramārthasat*) or as a real entity (*vastu*), in contrast to the 'universal' or 'common characteristic' (*sāmānya* or *sāmānyalakṣaṇa*). The latter, in contrast to *svalakṣaṇa*, refers to the object of conception or of words that lacks causal efficacy and hence is considered to be merely conventional and unreal.[5] We may be able to give the broad outlines of the development of the idea from Dignāga to Dharmakīrti, or from the epistemological to the ontological characterization of *svalakṣaṇa*, as follows: The fact that a thing is actually perceived by someone, sometime and somewhere indicates that this thing exists at that moment at that place, unless this perception is proven to be false by someone else. Since this thing causes a direct perception of its own image, it is admitted to be causally efficacious. Furthermore, this thing must be allowed to be real, for unreal things such as a horn of a rabbit or an abstract concept like 'eternity' cannot cause any direct perception. In other words, the arising of a direct perception should properly presuppose the presence of something real as its object. Hence the object of direct perception proves to be existent in reality. In this way, a *svalakṣaṇa* to be cognized by a direct perception can be identified as a real entity.

The term *svalakṣaṇa*, as opposed to *sāmānyalakṣaṇa* or common characteristic, entails from the beginning that the phenomenon is individual, unique and distinct. Dignāga's description of *svalakṣaṇa* as the object of direct perception may well reflect the idea that *svalakṣaṇa* is a substantially individual thing, since it is the function of perception to make substantial distinctions among its objects. To this extent, one could also say that *svalakṣaṇa* is a spatiotemporally individual and unique occurrence, which necessarily occupies a certain location in space and time, in contrast to a merely imagined object. The more strict spatiotemporal qualification of *svalakṣaṇa* can be derived from Dharmakīrti's definition of a real existent as having causal efficacy, if this qualification is linked to the theory of momentariness (*kṣaṇikatva*), viz., that whatever is existent in reality is exclusively momentary.[6] It is theoretically consistent to interpret *svalakṣaṇa* as a unique and single phenomenon that occurs and disappears every single moment, since *svalakṣaṇa* is a real existent to be defined as that which has causal efficacy, although such a momentary thing is far beyond the range of perceptual object.

Besides *svalakṣaṇa* being distinguished the one from the other in virtue of their distinct substances, we can also understand from the literal sense of the word that *svalakṣaṇas* are *known* to be unique because of their characteristics (*lakṣaṇa*). Although it is beyond the function of perception to specify the features of an entity as, for instance, being a pot, being gold, being round, and so on, these kinds of unique features of one *svalakṣaṇa* can be perceived through its image as a whole and help to differentiate this *svalakṣaṇa* from other *svalakṣaṇas*. Theoretically speaking, such a distinction of *svalakṣaṇa* by its nature too is grounded in its causal efficacy, because, according to Dharmakīrti, the difference of nature consists in the difference of causal efficacy[7] in the following manner: a *svalakṣaṇa* is known as individual and unique by its essential nature (*svabhāva*), since the essential nature of a real entity is determined by a particular ability of its cause to produce this entity, and this entity in turn arises being endowed with a particular ability that is its essential nature.[8] Thus considered, it may be proper to say that Dharmakīrti's identification of *svalakṣaṇa* as that which has causal efficacy provides a clear theoretical ground for both the reality and the individuality of the entity that is defined by Dignāga as the object of direct perception.

2. *The dGe lugs pa on rang mtshan*

The dGe lugs pa thinkers formulated the definition of *rang mtshan* according to their own interpretation of individuals and real entities. Let us look at the following definition, which mKhas grub proposes for *rang mtshan*, still claiming it to reflect a Sautrāntika position:

> "In their own system [of the Sautrāntika], the definition of *rang mtshan* is the thing (*dngos po*) which consists (*gnas*), not being conceptually imposed, but from its own side [i.e., intrinsically], in its essential nature (*rang bzhin*) uncommon [with other things]."[9]

Neither the object of perception nor causal efficacy is mentioned here as the definiens or the defining characteristic. Nor is it possible to interpret the phrase 'consisting in its essential nature' as implying 'consisting in its own causal efficacy' and the phrase 'not being conceptually imposed' as implying 'being directly perceived', once one takes account of the views peculiar to the dGe lugs pa with regard to *rang mtshan* and *spyi.*

One should first recall the dGe lugs pa position that *rang mtshan* is identical with a real existent which has causal efficacy (*don byed nus pa*), but not only *rang mtshan* is counted as real, nor is it determined for the object of direct perception alone, for they maintain that there exist real universals (*sāmānya, spyi*),[10] and that a *rang mtshan* appears in a conceptual cognition. Even it is not contradictory that one and the same thing is *rang mtshan* as well as universal (*spyi*) in its different aspects. They are not opposing notions but are relative. A pot, for instance, is a particular (*rang mtshan*) in relation to its property of being impermanent (*anitya, mi rtag pa*), but at the same time it is a universal as well in relation to its individuations, since the property of being a pot is common to all kinds of pots such as golden pots, silver pots, copper pots, and the like.[11] Under this condition, the dichotomy between *rang mtshan* and *spyi* according to whether it is real or unreal, or whether it is cognized by direct perception or conceptual cognition is on no account conducive to clarifying the dGe lugs pa idea of individuality and reality.

Nor can causal efficacy define the reality of *rang mtshan.* Although the dGe lugs pas accept the concepts 'that which has causal efficacy', 'that which is ultimately existent' and '*rang mtshan*' as synonyms in accordance with the statement of *Pramāṇavārttika* III 3, they explicitly note that neither causal efficacy nor *rang mtshan* is taught by Dharmakīrti as a definiens or a defining characteristic of ultimate reality, but just as an instance of those which are to be defined as such (*mtshan gzhi*).[12] That is to say, whatever is 'that which has causal efficacy' or '*rang mtshan*' is a real entity, but it is not just this alone that is ultimately real, since there are universals that exist in reality. Yet the dGe lugs pas maintain that the individuality of *rang mtshan* in the sense of 'consisting in its essential nature' is grounded in reality, as suggested in the aforecited mKhas grub's definition of *rang mtshan*, for the notion of 'not being conceptually imposed but from its own side' is adopted as the defining characteristic of ultimate reality (*don dam bden pa, parmārthasatya*) by Tsong kha pa:

> "The definition of ultimate reality is that which is not merely conceptually imposed (*rtog pas btags pa*), but established from the side of the object itself (*yul rang gi ngos nas*)."[13]

A *rang mtshan* is a real existent insofar as it meets this condition. In the same way, the *rang mtshan* is established as an individual insofar as it is intrinsically abiding in its essential nature. The essential nature is, however, not necessarily confined to causal efficacy, since mKhas grub propounds the aforecited definition of *rang mtshan,* after having denied causal efficacy together with the spaciotemporal uniqueness as being the defining characteristics of *rang mtshan,* by saying:

> "Such definitions of *rang mtshan* on which others insist as that which exists, without sharing (*ma 'dres par*) place, time and essential nature (*yul dus rang bzhin*) [with other things] and that which is causally efficacious are unacceptable."[14]

Neither substantial individuality nor causal efficacy is the definiens of *rang mtshan* either.[15] The uncommonness of essential nature is rejected here just because, in my conjecture, it lacks the qualification of being intrinsic (i.e., *rang ngos nas mthun mong ma yin pa'i rang bzhin du gnas pa*) in contrast to mKhas grub's own definition, for, as will be discussed below, the non-intrinsic or conventional uncommonness of essential nature is also accepted by those who refuse the real existence of *rang mtshan.* Accordingly, for the dGe lugs pas, *rang mtshan* is an entity that is individual and unique in reality solely because of the intrinsic abiding in its essential nature.

What then is the essential nature that determines a thing as an individual or *rang mtshan?* Let us consider this question with the example of 'golden pot' (*gser bum*), which the dGe lugs pas use for *rang mtshan* when explaining the theory that a *rang mtshan* appears to a conceptual cognition.[16] Since we have closely analyzed this problematic presentation in our previous studies,[17] I would just like to reconsider what it means to say that 'golden pot' is an example of *rang mtshan.*

First, one should note that such an example of *svalakṣaṇa* would not be acceptable to Dharmakīrti. Even not appealing to the theory of momentariness, the word 'golden pot' (*gser bum*) cannot directly refer to any substantially individual entity, which is the object of direct perception, but according to the *apoha* theory it solely refers to the universal. For the dGe lugs pa thinkers, however, 'golden pot' is an example of a particular (*rang mtshan*), and 'pot' is a universal (*spyi*). In Tibetan, this example is always simply given as '*gser bum*', i.e., 'golden pot', which is not accompanied by a demonstrative pronoun, nor by an indefinite article, nor by a suffix designating the plural. That is, neither 'this or that golden pot' (*gser bum di/ de*), nor 'some golden pot' (*gser bum zhig*), nor 'golden pots' (*gser bum rnams/ dag*) is specifically intended. Since the Tibetan language has no definite articles and only rarely use the indefinite *zhig*, the expression '*gser bum*' signifies either a golden pot or the golden pot in the sense of a generic singular (viz., *a* golden pot or the golden pot in general), which is to be cognized as such by its properties of being a pot and being gold. These properties are, on one hand, essential characteristics of a golden pot, whereby a golden pot is distinguished from other things such as silver pots, copper pots, glasses, tables, and so on. On the other hand, they are also common properties to all golden pots, viz., 18-carat golden pots, gold-plated golden pots, small golden pots, big golden pots, and so on. That is to say, any individuation or differentiation among individual golden pots is not, and cannot be, indicated by the expression '*gser bum*'. The fact that this example is nevertheless repeatedly applied to *rang mtshan* means that it completely meets the conditions of *rang mtshan* for the dGe lugs pa. That is to say, a golden pot consists in the essential nature of being a pot and being gold from its own side independent of any conceptual construction. To sum up, the essential nature in perspective of the dGe lugs pa does not actually differ from common properties, which are identical with real universals to be signified by generic concepts.

Despite the fact that their understanding of *rang mtshan* obviously deviates from that of Dharmakīrti, the dGe lugs pa scholars seem to have formulated such an idea of essential nature on the basis of Dharmakīrti's own words in *Pramāṇavārttika* I 40. It is even not far from the truth to speculate that mKhas grub's definition cited previously is a modification of *Pramāṇavārttika* I 40. Let us compare them with each other:

> *Pramāṇavārttika* I 40) "Since all things (*sarvabhāva*) by nature consist in their respective essential nature (*svabhāva*), they are distinguished from their homogeneous and heterogeneous [things]."[18]
>
> (mKhas grub's definition) "The definition of *rang mtshan* is the thing (*dngos po*) which consists (*gnas*), not being conceptually imposed, but from its own side [i.e., intrinsically], in its essential nature (*rang bzhin*) uncommon [with other things]."

The similarity in expression is evident. Taking the subject of *Pramāṇavārttika* I 40, 'all things' (*sarvabhāva*), to be identical with *svalakṣaṇas* in the sense of real existents,[19] the dGe lugs pa interpreters understand this verse to be intended to teach the mode of existence of real entities (*dngos po'i gnas lugs*).[20] In this regard, it seems reasonable to assume that they took this verse to describe the essential characteristic of *svalakṣaṇa* and adapted it to their own definition of *rang mtshan.* To conclude this section, I would like to propose the following tentative illustration of *Pramāṇavārttika* I 40 with the example of 'golden pot' in accordance with the dGe lugs pa interpretation: "The *svalakṣaṇa* such as a golden pot consists in its essential nature of being a pot, being gold, being impermanent, and so on. Therefore it is different from such homogeneous things as a silver pot as well as from such heterogeneous things as a table, space, etc."[21] So would the verse be elucidated by the dGe lugs pas.

3. *Reasons for redefining svalakṣaṇa*

From the theoretical point of view, the dGe lugs pa interpretation of *svalakṣaṇa* apparently goes beyond the range of sound interpretation. It is not exaggerated to regard it as a systematic revision of the Sautrāntika doctrine. This revision is, however, certainly an outcome of various external and internal factors. Such a realistic position as the dGe lugs pa thinkers have is actually considered to have originated with some Indian scholars and have been carried over by Tibetan gSang phu tradition.[22] The lack of semantic interest may also be described as a general-tendency of this Tibetan scholastic tradition. Of course one should also clarify, in addition to this historical background, the theoretical grounds for the dGe lugs pas' redefinition of *svalakṣaṇa*. We will devote the last section of the present paper to this inquiry.

mKhas grub explains the reason for his rejection of causal efficacy as a defining characteristic of real entity as follows:

> "The dBu ma thal 'gyur ba (i.e., the Prāsaṅgika-Mādhyamika) maintains that *rang mtshan* is the main [subject] to be negated (*dgag bya*) through the logical reason (*rtags*) to investigate the ultimate [reality]. Accordingly, he maintains that the ultimate reality consists in the negation of that very concept (*don ldog*) of *rang mtshan* asserted by substantialists (*dngos smra ba*). Hence, whatever is asserted by the substantialists as the very concept of *rang mtshan* is [none other than] that which the dBu ma thal 'gyur ba asserts to be unestablished as a [real] basis (*gzhi ma grub*) even according to verbal conventions (*tha snyad du yang*), for such [things] as that which [exists] not sharing (*ma 'dres pa*) place, time and essential nature [with other things], and that which is causally efficacious are, on the contrary, accepted by the dBu ma thal 'gyur ba too [according to verbal conventions]. Therefore, these [things] are the instances of that which is to be defined [as *rang mtshan*] (*mtshan gzhi*) but are not the definiens of *rang mtshan* here in the case (*skabs 'dir*) [in which the Sautrāntika tenet is treated]."[23]

Insofar as *rang mtshan* is a real entity, the 'concept of *rang mtshan*' or the defining characteristic thereof must, on one hand, correspond to the condition of real existent, the establishment of which the Prāsaṅgika-Mādhyamika refutes even conventionally. In other words, the concept of *rang mtshan* is, for the dGe lugs pas, from the beginning determined as the object of refutation (*dgag bya*) from the Madhyamaka point of view, since the core of the Madhyamaka ontology consists in negating such a substantial or real existent. On the other hand, the 'concept of *rang mtshan*' or the defining characteristic thereof may not correspond to that which the Prāsaṅgika-Mādhyamika accepts on the conventional level, for, supposing that such a thing be the defining characteristic of *rang mtshan*, it would follow that the *rang mtshan* itself must be conventionally accepted by the Mādhyamika too, which, however, contradicts his position in which the real existence of *rang mtshan* is not acknowledged, neither ultimately nor conventionally. Moreover, it is also an important thesis for the dGe lugs pas that, in the Prāsaṅgika-Madhyamaka system, all causal relations as well as causal efficacy are conventionally established. Hence the dGe lugs pas exclude causal efficacy from the defining characteristics of *rang mtshan* and ultimate reality.[24]

In relation to these Madhyamaka positions, the dGe lugs pas evaluate the ontplogical views of other schools, viz., Sarvāstivāda, Sautrāntika and Yogācāra, as being substantialist, for the reason that the latter assert such substantial or real entities as being *vastu* (*dngos po*) or *svalakṣaṇa* (*rang mtshan*), because they are 'not merely conceptually imposed but established from the side of the objects themselves' (*rtog pas btags pa tsam ma yin par yul rang gi ngos nas grub pa*).[25] In this manner, in order not only to include universals in the domain of real existents, but also to hold the consistency with the Madhyamaka ontology, the dGe lugs pas redefine even the most important concept of Dharmakīrti's tradition.

What the dGe lugs pa scholars thereby finally aimed at is, in my opinion, a systematization of the Buddhist philosophical teachings of the four main traditions, i.e., the Sarvāstivāda, Sautrāntika, Yogācāra, and Madhyamaka. For the dGe lugs pas, the question of what is a real entity or what is the reality should be answered not within the narrow scope of one tradition, but in a range of knowledge that extends over the entire historical development of Buddhist philosophy. In other words, the dGe lugs pas intended to connect the different systems, which had developed separately in different periods in India, by reinterpreting them systematically from one common perspective. What they actually did, however, is to reevaluate the teachings of other schools in light of the Prāsaṅgika-Madhyamaka of Candrakīrti (7c.), which they estimated as the highest among Buddhist philosophical systems.

This kind of attempt to systematize various philosophical thoughts in light of the Prāsaṅgika-Madhyamaka doctrine, indeed, can be seen in several discussions in the dGe lugs pa exegeses.[26] In its historical aspect, it is to be considered as a result of the fact that Candrakīrti's system had won a certain popularity among Tibetan Buddhists by the period of Tsong kha pa. At the same time, however, this attempt in turn resulted in accelerating the reevaluation of Buddhist philosophical traditions in the eyes of Tibetan thinkers. Firmly bound to tradition, but also creative, Tibetans intensively engaged themselves in the development of Buddhist philosophy. It is a remarkable phenomenon in Tibetan intellectual history that they rediscovered and reinterpreted many Buddhist philosophical concepts. Redefining *svalakṣaṇa* is one of Tibetan challenges to the traditional system of Indian Buddhist philosophy. In this regard, it remains a fascinating task for us to discover and analyze their philosophical commitments and their underlying motives. In this fashion, we can better establish the significance of the Tibetan developments in the history of the transmission of Buddhist thought.

NOTES

1. Cf. e.g., Georges Dreyfus, "Universals in Indo-Tibetan Buddhism," in Sh. Ihara and Z. Yamaguchi (eds.), *Tibetan Studies, Proceedings of the 5th Seminar of the International Association for Tibetan Studies, Narita* 1989, Naritasan Shinshoji, 1992, vol. 1, pp. 29-46; Id. (ed. in collaboration with Sh. Onoda), *A Recent Rediscovery: Rgyal tshab's Rigs gter rnam bshad, a Facsimile Reproduction of Rare Blockprint Edition*, Kyoto, 1994; Id., *Recognizing Reality, Dharmakīrti's Philosophy and its Tibetan Interpretations*, Albany, 1997; Tom Tillemans, "On the So-called Difficult Point of the Apoha Theory," *Asiatische Studien/ Études Asiatiques* 49-4, 1995, pp.853-889; Chizuko Yoshimizu, "Tsoṅ kha pa on *don byed nus pa*" in E. Steinkellner et al. (eds.), *Tibetan Studies, Proceedings of the 7th International Seminar of the International Association or Tibetan Studies Graz 1995*, Wien, 1997, Vol.2, pp. 1103-1120; Id., "Gelukuha ni yoru Kyōryōbu Gakusetsu Rikai (1) Nitaisetsu" (The dGe lugs pas' Interpretation of the Sautrāntika System (1): The Theory of the Two Kinds of Reality), *Journal of Naritasan Institute for Buddhist Studies* 21, 1998, pp. 51-76; Id., "Pramāṇavārttika I 40 no kaishaku ni tsuite" (On the Interpretation of *Pramāṇavārttika* I 40), *IBK* 47-2, 1999, pp. (97)-(101); Id., "*Dṛśya* and *vikalpya* or *snang ba* and *btags pa* Associated in a Conceptual Cognition," in Sh. Katsura (ed.), *Proceedings of the 3rd International Dharmakīrti Conference. Hiroshima 1997*, Wien, 1999, pp. 459-474; and Id., "Geluku-ha ni yoru Kyōryōbu gakusetsu rikai (2) Fuhen jitsuzai ron" (The dGe lugs pas' Interpretation of the Sautrāntika

System (2) The Theory of Real Universals), *Bukkyō bunka kenkyū ronsyū* (*Studies of Buddhist Culture*) 4, 2000, pp. 3-32.

2. As for the dGe lugs pa interpretation of Candrakīrti's negative position on the logical method to investigate reality, cf. e.g., Shirō Matsumoto, "Tsong kha pa no jiritsu ronshō hihan" (bTsong kha pa's Criticism of the Independent Argument), in Z. Yamaguchi (ed.), *Chibetto no bukkyō to shakai* (*Buddhism and Society in Tibet*), Tokyo, 1986, pp.475-508; David Seyfort Ruegg, *Three Studies in the History of Indian and Tibetan Madhyamaka Philosophy*, Part 1, Wien, 2000; Kōdō Yotsuya, *The Critique of Svatantra Reasoning by Candrakīrti and Tsong-kha-pa*, Stuttgart, 1999; Chizuko Yoshimizu, *Die Erkenntnislehre des Prāsaṅgika-Madhyamaka nach dem Tshig gsal stoṅ thun gyi tshad ma'i rnam bśad des 'Jam dbyaṅs bźad pa'i rdo rje*, Wien, 1996; and Id., "Tsong kha pa's Reevaluation of Candrakīrti's Criticism of Autonomous Inference," in G. Dreyfus and S. McClintock (eds.), *The Svatāntrika-Prāsaṅgika Distinction, What Difference does a Difference Make?* Wisdom Publication 2002, pp. 257-288.
3. This paper was presented at the University of Lausanne on the 26th of March, 2002, and originally written on the basis of my previous two Japanese articles, i.e., "Gelukuha ni yoru Kyōryōbu Gakusetsu Rikai (1)" and "(2)" as well as a German paper, "Das Individuelle und das Wirkliche bei den dGe lugs pa: Grundbegriffe buddhistischer Philosophie in tibetischer Modifizierung", read at the University of Munich on the 22nd of November 2001. For this revised version, I would like to thank Prof. Tom Tillemans for his valuable suggestions regarding both contents and English expressions.
4. *Pramāṇasamuccayavṛtti* ad *Pramāṇasamuccaya* I 2 (Masaaki Hattori, *Dignāga, On Perception.* Cambridge, 1986, p.79 n.1.14): *na hi svasāmānyalakṣaṇābhyām anyat prameyam asti. svalakṣaṇaviṣayaṃ hi pratyakṣaṃ sāmānyalakṣaṇaviṣayam anumānam iti pratipādayiṣyāmaḥ; Pramāṇasamuccaya* I 3c (Hattori, op.cit., p.82 n.1.25): *pratyakṣaṃ kalpanāpoḍham.*
5. *Pramāṇavārttika* I 166abc and its *Svavṛtti* (in *The Pramāṇavārttikam of Dharmakīrti, the First Chapter with the Autocommentary, Text and Critical Notes* ed. by R. Gnoli, Rome 1960): *sa pāramārthiko bhāvo ya evārthakriyākṣamaḥ. idam eva hi vastvavastuyor lakṣaṇaṃ yad arthakriyāyogyatā 'yogyatā ca.*; *Pramāṇavārttika* III 3 (in "Pramāṇavārttika-kārikā, Sanskrit and Tibetan," ed. by Yūsho Miyasaka, *Acta Indologica* 2, pp.1-206): *arthakriyāsamarthaṃ yat tad atra paramārthasat / anyat saṃvṛtisat proktaṃ te svasāmānyalakṣaṇe //*
6. Cf. e.g. *Pramāṇavārttika* I 269ab: *sattāmātrānubandhitvān nāśasyānityatā dhvaneḥ; Hetubindu* (in *Dharmakīrtis Hetubinduḥ, Teil I: Tibetischer Text und rekonstruierter Sanskrit-Text* ed. by E. Steinkellner, Wien 1967) 4*, 6f.: *yat sat tat kṣaṇikam eva, akṣaṇikatve 'rthakriyāvirodhāt tatlakṣaṇam*

vastutvaṃ hīyate. Regarding the theoretical link between impermanence and real existence in the proofs of momentariness, cf. e.g. E. Steinkellner, "Die Entwicklung des Kṣaṇikatvānumāna bei Dharmakīrti", *WZKSO* 12/13 (1968-69), 1968, pp. 361-377; Chizuko Yoshimizu, "The Development of *sattvānumāna* from the Refutation of a Permanent Existent in the Sautrāntika Tradition", *WZKS* 43, 1999, pp.231-354; and Id., "Kōjō na mono wa naze munōryoku ka—Setsunametu ronshō no riron teki haikei (Why is a Permanent Thing Inefficacious?—The Theoretical Background of *kṣaṇikatvānumāna*)", *IBK* 48-1, 1999, pp. (196)-(200).

7. One may take *Pramāṇavārttika* I 40 (cited in n.18 below) to state the uniqueness of *svalakṣaṇa* in this sense, as the dGe lugs pas do, if one supposes that the subject of this verse (*sarvabhāva*) refers solely to *svalakṣaṇa.*
8. Cf. E. Steinkellner, "Wirklichkeit und Begriff bei Dharmakīrti," *WZKS* 15, 1971, pp.179-211, p.183f., 188f. and Yoshimizu, "Kōjō na mono wa naze munōryoku ka", p. (197)f.
9. *Yid kyi mun sel* (in mKhas grub rje's *gSung 'bum Tha,* lHa sa Zhol version) 2lb2f. (tr. Dreyfus, *Recognizing Reality,* p.117): *rang lugs la / rang mtshan gyi mtshan nyid rtog pas btags pa min par rang ngos nas thun mong ma yin pa'i rang bzhin du gnas pa'i dngos po'o //* A similar description occurs in rGyal tshab's *Thar lam gsal byed* (in rGyal tshab rje's *gSung 'bum, Cha,* lHa sa Zhol version) 45b3f. with regard to the subject (i.e., *sarvabhāva*) of *Pramāṇavārttika* I 40 (see n.18 below), where rGyal tshab identifies as *rang mtshan* as 'the thing which consists, not being conceptually imposed but from its own side, in its essential nature uncommon [with other things]' (*rtog pas btags pa tsam min par rang bzhin gyis gzhan dang ma 'dres par rang gi ngo bo la gnas pa,* cf. Yoshimizu, "Geluku-ha ni yoru Kyōryōbu gakusetsu rikai (2), p. 23).
10. The dGe lugs pas differentiate *spyi* (*sāmānya*) from *spyi mtshan* (*sāmānyalakṣaṇa*). The latter signifies solely unreal, unconditioned and imagined object like space (*nam mkha', ākāśa*). Cf. Tillemans, op.cit., p.865f., Dreyfus, *Recognizing Reality,* p.181, and Yoshimizu, "Tsoṅ kha pa on *don byed nus pa*", p. 1114 n. 39.
11. As for the relation between *rang mtshan* and *spyi* for the dGe lugs pas, cf. e.g. *Yid kyi mun sel* 33a4 (tr. Dreyfus, *Recognizing Reality,* p.181 and Yoshimizu, "Geluku-ha ni yoru Kyōryōbu gakusetsu rikai (2), p.15 n.19): *rang mtshan yin kyang rang gi gsal ba la rjes su 'gro byed pa'i spyi yin par mi 'gal zhing/* Cf. also Dreyfus, *Recognizing Reality,* p.173ff. and note 16 below.
12. Regarding the synonyms of *rang mtshan,* see the explanations by dGe lugs pas cited in Yoshimizu "Gelukuha ni yoru Kyōryōbu Gakusetsu Rikai (1)", pp.58 and 63 n.9. As for their commitments to *Pramāṇavārttika*

III 3, see *Thar lam gsal byed* 210b6f., *mNgon sum le'u ṭik* (in *The Collected Works of Tsong kha pa* 22 of bKra shis lhun po version ed. by Ngawang Gelek Demo, New Delhi 1978) 17a5f., *Yid kyi mun sel* 44b 1 ff. (cited and translated in Yoshimizu, op.cit, p.65 n.14). Concerning the problematic Tibetan translation of *arthakriyāsamartham* in *Pramāṇavārttika* III 3 as *don dam don byed nus pa* and its interpretations, cf. e.g. *mNgon sum le'u ṭik* 166b1-4, *Thar lam gsal byed* 211a3ff. and the references cited in Yoshimizu, op.cit, p.61 n.8. rGyal tshab states the opinion in his *Thar lam gsal byed* 211a3ff. (cited and translated in Yoshimizu op.cit, p.62) that the qualification of 'being ultimate' is made to causal efficacy in *Pramāṇavārttika* III 3 in order to eliminate the 'false' conception that the causal efficacy is solely conventionally (*kun rdzob tsam du*) accepted. This 'false' conception most likely belongs to the Mādhyamikas, as will be discussed later. In this regard, it is interesting to remark that Se ra Chos kyi rgyal mtshan propounds the definition of ultimate reality as that which ultimately has causal efficacy (*don dam par don byed nus pa'i chos*) in his *Grub mtha'* (in *Textbooks of Se ra Monastery* ed. by Tshulkhrim Kelsang & Shunzo Onoda, *Biblia Tibetica series*, Kyoto 1985) 4b3 (cited in Yoshimizu, op.cit., p.64 n.11).

13. *Tshad ma'i brjed byang* (in *The Collected Works of Tsong kha pa* 22 of bKra shis lhun po version ed. by Ngawang Gelek Demo, New Delhi 1978) 34a1f.: *don dam bden pa'i mtshan nyid rtog pas btags pa tsam ma yin par yul rang gi ngos nas grub pa /* Cf. also *mNgon sum le'u ṭik* 17a6f.: *don dam bden pa'i mtshan nyid rtog pas btags pa la ma ltos par rang gi ngos bos dpyad bzod du grub pa /* Parallel definitions by other dGe lugs pas are cited in Yoshimizu, op.cit., pp.53 and 64 n.11. The dGe lugs pas presumably define the two kinds of reality on the basis of Dharmakīrti's own words in *Pramāṇavārttika* I 68-91, especially 68-70, as I have previously discussed in Yoshimizu, op.cit., pp.52-57 and *"Dṛśya* and *vikalpya"*, p.460 n.5.

14. *Yid kyi mun sel* 21a5f.: *gzhan dag yul dus rang bzhin ma 'dres par gnas pa dang / don byed nus pa sogs rang mtshan gyi mtshan nyid du 'dod pa mi 'thad do//* One should note the fact that the similar definitions of rang mtshan appear in the *sDe bdun 'jug sgo Yid kyi mun sel* (in *The Collected Works of Tsong kha pa* 27 of bKra shis lhun po version ed. by Ngawang Geleg De mo, New Delhi 1977) 3b6, which is a glossary of terms, concepts and their definitions ascribed to Tsong kha pa, but probably descended from Phya pa's tradition of gSang phu monastery. Yet it seems more plausible to assume that mKhas grub denies the traditionally acknowledged definitions, which Tsong kha pa and he himself have learned from their teachers, rather than to jump to the conclusion that mKhas grub thereby rejects Tsong kha pa's view, because, as will be seen below, mKhas grub

gives his own definition with a clear consciousness of the theoretical consistency with Tsong kha pa's fundamental ontology as well as his understanding of causal efficacy. Thus considered, the fact that the old type of definition of *rang mtshan* is found in the *sDe bdun 'jug sgo* might support the originality of mKhas grub's definition, as I have suggested in Yoshimizu, "Geluku-ha ni yoru Kyōryōbu gakusetsu rikai (2)", p.24f.

15. The substantial distinction according to place and time mentioned here by mKhas grub is, however, on no account concerned with momentary existents, since he himself describes the difference of place and time as a rough incompatibility of location such as east and west and morning and afternoon. See *Yid kyi mun sel* 33a1ff.: *snga dro'i ka ba phyi dro med pa dus ma 'dres pa'i don yin gyi / . . . shar la reg pa'i rdzas des nub la ma reg pa lta bu / yul ma 'dres pa'i don yin gyi / . . . khra bo la yod pa'i rang bzhin de ser skya la med pa sogs / rang bzhin ma 'dres pa'i don yin gyi /* Cf. also a parallel explanation in rGyal tshab's *Thar lam gsal byed* 451a-4 and the discussion in Dreyfus, *Recognizing Reality*, p.117ff. Moreover, it must be noted that the momentariness itself is differently understood by the dGe lugs pas as having a certain duration. Cf. e.g. *Yid kyi mun sel* 34a2, 34b5ff. (cited in Tillemans, 17 op.cit, p.884, Yoshimizu, op.cit., p.17 n.23) and the discussion in Dreyfus, op.cit., pp.109-114.
16. This explanation occurs for the first time in *Tshad ma'i brjed byang* 19a3f.: *rtog pa la yul ji ltar snang zhing 'jug pa'i tshul ni / gser bum bum par 'dzin pa'i rtog pa la gser bum yang bum par snang zhing rang gi dngos kyi gzung bya de'ang bum par snang la snang ba'i ngo na de gnyis gcig tu 'dres nas snang zhing snang ngor so sor dbyer med pas snang btags gcig tu bsres pa zhes bya ste snang ba rang mtshan dang btags pa sgra don no //* Cf. also *Yid kyi mun sel* 35a3ff., lCang skya's *Grub mtha'* (in *mDo sde pa* Chapter of Peking version, *Buddhist Philosophical Systems* ed. by Lokesh Chandra, *Śata-Piṭaka-Series* 233, New Delhi 1977) 74blff., and *Thar lam gsal byed* 59b5-60a3. This passage indeed has raised discussions among scholars because of its remarkable assertion that a *rang mtshan* appears to a conceptual cognition. For the details, see the references cited below in n.17.
17. As for the close analysis of this passage, cf. Tillemans, op.cit., p.866, Dreyfus, *Recognizing Reality*, p.323, Yoshimizu, "*Dṛśya* and *vikalpya*," p.466 and "Geluku-ha ni yoru Kyōryōbu gakusetsu rikai (2)", p.11f.
18. *Pramāṇavārttika* I 40: *sarve bhāvāḥ svabhāvena svasvabhāvavyavasthiteḥ/ svabhāvaparabhāvābhyāṃ yasmād vyāvṛttibhāginaḥ//*
19. See *Yid kyi mun sel* 41b6f and *Thar lam gsal byed* 45b3f. (cited in Yoshimizu, op.cit., p.22f.). It is Śaṅkaranandana who interpreted 'all things' to refer to both individuals and universals (*Pramāṇavārttika* D152b6). However, this does not necessarily suggest that

Śaṅkaranandana asserts the existence of real universals, for, to my knowledge, he expresses nowhere such a realistic view. He includes universals into 'all things' presumably in a hypothetical sense in accordance with Dharmakīrti's postulation '*sati vā*' in *Pramāṇavārttikasvavṛtti* 25, 12. For this issue, cf. Yoshimizu, "Pramāṇavārttika I 40 no kaishaku ni tsuite", p.(101) n.10 and "*Dṛśya* and *vikalpya*", p. 463 n.19.

20. See e.g., *Tharl lam gsal byed* 46b1. *Pramāṇavārttika* I 40 introduces together with 41abc (*tasmād yato yato 'rthānāṃ vyāvṛttis tannibandhanāḥ/ jātibhedāḥ prakalpyante*) the idea that such concepts of properties as 'being impermanent' (*anityatva*) and 'being produced' (*kṛtakatva*) are formulated on the basis of the essential nature (*svabhāva*) of things, although the real existence of universals, which are identical with or different from particulars, is unacceptable. Dharmakīrti is thereby demonstrating that an inference based on the essential property as a logical reason (*svabhāvahetu*) is valid for establishing the reality of entities such as their being impermanent. In fact, he opens with this verse the long discussion of the *apoha* theory. rGyal tshab, however, interprets this *apoha* section of *Pramāṇavārttika* I as contributing to the establishment of the two kinds of reality (see Yoshimizu, op.cit., pp. 460-463, 470 Appendix 2). As regards *Pramāṇavārttika* I 40 in commentarial tradition, cf. also Dreyfus, *Recognizing Reality*, p.118, Yoshimizu, "Pramāṇavārttika I 40 no kaishaku ni tsuite" and "*Dṛśya* and *vikalpya,*" p. 463 n. 19. For the dGe lugs pas, the question of how one can establish reality by means of inferences, if the meaning of words is mere elimination of others (*anyāpoha*), overlaps with the question of how the Mādhyamika can prove the non-substantiality and emptiness by means of empty words (cf. Yoshimizu, op.cit., p. 462 and "Geluku-ha ni yoru Kyōryōbu gakusetsu rikai (2), p. 28).

21. It is interesting to note that both rGyal tshab and mKhas grub offer a similar elucidation in their respective commentaries on *Pramāṇavārttika* I 40, as I have pointed out in Yoshimizu, "Pramāṇavārttika I 40 no kaishaku ni tsuite", p.(101) n.10 and "Geluku-ha ni yoru Kyōryōbu gakusetsu rikai (2)", p. 22f.

22. Cf. Dreyfus, *Recognizing Reality*, pp.193-200 and the references cited in Yoshimizu, "*Dṛśya* and *vikalpya*," p. 459 n.1.

23. *Yid kyi mun sel* 21a6-21b2 (cited and translated in Yoshimizu, "Geluku-ha ni yoru Kyōryōbu gakusetsu rikai (2)," p. 19): *dbu ma thal 'gyur ba / rang mtshan don dam dpyod pa'i rtags kyi dgag bya'i gtso bor 'dod pas / dngos smra ba 'dod pa'i rang mtshan gyi don ldog de bkag pa don dam bden par 'dod pa yin la / de'i phyir dngos smra bas rang mtshan gyi don ldog tu gang 'dod pa de / dbu ma thal 'gyur ba tha snyad du yang gzhi ma grub par 'dod pa yin la / yul dus rang bzhin ma 'dres pa dang*

don byed nus pa sogs dbu ma thal 'gyur ba yang khas len pa'i phyir ro// des na de dag skabs 'dir rang mtshan gyi mtshan gzhi yin gyi mtshan nyid min no //

24. Cf. the discussions and textual sources cited in Yoshimizu, "On *raṅ gi mtshan nyid kyis grub pa* III," *Journal of Naritasan Institute for Buddhist Studies* 16, 1993,pp.129, 132f and ibid., 17, 1994, p. 327, n.67.
25. This kind of real entity can be properly identified with 'that which is intrinsically established' (*rang gi mtshan nyid kyis grub pa*) in opposition to the unreal, mere conceptual existent (*btags yod*) or that which is postulated by names and signs (*ming dang brdas rnam par gzhag pa*). The expressions '*rang gi ngos nas grub pa*' and '*rang gi ngo bos grub pa*', which they use in their definitions of *rang mtshan* and ultimate reality, are no doubt synonyms of the former, i.e., '*rang gi mtshan nyid kyis grub pa*'. Also the expression '*rtog pas btags pa*' means the same as the '*btags yod*'. Cf. Helmut Tauscher, *Die Lehre von den zwei Wirklichkeiten in Tsoṅ kha pas Madhyamaka-Werken*, Wien, 1995, p.124 n.262 and Yoshimizu, "Tsong kha pa's Reevaluation," Appendix.
26. Cf. e.g., the synthesis of the Madhyamaka ontological doctrine of non-substantiality and the logicoepistemological system of Dharmakīrti's tradition by dGe lugs pa scholars, which is the object of studies such as Yoshimizu, *Die Erkenntnislehre des Prāsaṅgika-Madhyamaka* and Seyfort Ruegg, *Three Studies in the History of Indian and Tibetan Madhyamaka Philosophy.*

CHAPTER 9

The "Grammarian's Objection" in Sthiramati's *Triṃśikābhāṣya* and Bhartṛhari's Argument on the Secondary Application of Words

TOSHIYA UNEBE

1. More than sixty years ago, Jōshō Nozawa pointed out that the "Grammarian's objection" with reference to the concept of "*upacāra*" is recorded in Sthiramati's commentary (*bhāṣya*) on the first verse of the *Triṃśikā* of Vasubandhu.[1] Although he explicitly notified that an examination of grammatical literature was a desideratum, a comprehensive study of the objection in the context of Sanskrit grammatical tradition still needs to be done. With regard to the objection, a rather general reference to Bhartṛhari's *Vākyapadīya* II by Noritoshi Aramaki[2] is the only relevant one that I have seen so far. Although Jan E.M. Houben's study on the concept of *upacāra* as presented in the *Vākyapadīya* III.3 in comparison with that of the Vijñānavādins is valuable, his focus is not on the objection itself.[3]

Over these sixty years, many studies on the *Triṃśikā* and the

Vākyapadīya including the above mentioned ones have been published. My attempt in this paper is only to show that the connection between the objection recorded in the Sthiramati's commentary and the grammatical literature, especially, Bhartṛhari's *Vākyapadīya.* Using these earlier studies, we shall discuss it further in detail.

Musashi Tachikawa, to whom this volume is respectfully offered, is also one of these scholars who have clarified the meaning of "*upacāra*" in the first verse of the *Triṃśikā.* In one of his serial studies on this verse,[4] he collected more than ten translations of the verse, to which he submitted to a critical reviews. In section 6 of his paper, he reviewed the translation by Thomas E. Wood and said that his has an advantage over others in that his interpretation of the seventh case (locative) found in "*vijñānapariṇāme*" in the *pāda* c is not forced and, is indeed, natural. The text and Wood's translation of the verse is as follows:

> *ātmadharmopacāro hi vividho yaḥ pravartate/*
> *vijñānapariṇāme 'sau pariṇāmaḥ sa ca tridhā// Triṃśikā* 1[5]
>
> The usages of the terms "*ātman*" and "*dharma*" are manifold, but both terms just refer to the transformations of consciousness (*vijñāna-pariṇāma*). That transformation is three-fold.[6]

Tachikawa shows that we can interpret the seventh case found in "*vijñāna-pariṇāme*" as per Wood's translation, namely, in the sense of "to refer to," because when it is used with "*vṛt*" it means "to refer to." Although it remains to be discussed whether many other scholars' interpretations and Chinese/Japanese traditional interpretations as well justify Tachikawa's conclusion or not, I also would like to interpret this verse as Wood does for the present, for, in grammatical and lexical statements, the seventh case commonly means "in the sense of" or "referring to;" besides, "*pravartate*" means "to occur". We may take the following example from Bhartṛhari's *Mahābhāṣyadīpikā:*

> *kaścit śabdas tadbhāvāpādanena vādhyāropeṇa vā pravartate/ yathā vāhīke gośabdo rajjudravye ca sarpaśabdaḥ//*[7]
>
> Some word occurs through acquisition of the state of [other] thing or through superimposition. For example, the word "*go*" ("ox") [occurs] in the sense of a man from *Vāhīka*

> country (*vāhīke*), and "*sarpa*" ("snake") [occurs] referring to a rope-form object.[8]

Thus, "a word A is used referring to B (a referent)," or "A is applied to B" can be expressed as "A occurs (*pravartate*) in the domain of (i.e. literal meaning of the seventh case) B."[9]

Sthiramati's commentary does not reject this interpretation. According to him, the verse (*pāda* abc) means that various verbal expressions such as "*ātman*" or "*jīva*" for human beings and "*dharma*" or "*āyatana*" for other constituents of this world are used among people (*loka*) as well as in the scientific system (*śāstra*), but they just refer to the transformations of consciousness (*vijñāna-pariṇāma*) in reality and, therefore, they are mere secondary applications (*upacāra*).[10]

Here "*upacāra*" indicates an expression which does not refer to its referent directly. For the Vijñānavādins, all verbal expressions refer to the transformations of consciousness, although it looks as if they refer to their own referents.

Sthiramati, commenting on "*upacāra*" introduces some other's objection which claims that "*ātman*" and "*dharma*" cannot be *upacāra* if their referents, *ātman* and *dharma* do not exist. According to a subcommentator Vinītadeva, the upholder of this objection is, the Grammarian (*vaiyākaraṇa/brda sprod pa pa*).[11]

The essential point of the objection found in the Sthiramati's lengthy reference to it is as follows:

> *asaty ātmani mukhye dharmeṣu copacāro na yujyate/ upacāro hi triṣu* [*satsu*] *bhavati nānyatamābhāve mukhyapadārthe tatsadṛśe anyasmin viṣaye tayoś ca sādṛśye/*[12]
>
> Unless *ātman* as the primary [referent of its corresponding expression "*ātman*"] and *dharmas* [as the primary referents of their corresponding expressions "*dharmas*"] exist, their secondary application (*upacāra*) is illogical. Because *upacāra* can occur when three exist; if even the one [of the three], namely, primary referent of words, similar but another thing, or similarity between the two does not exist, [*upacāra*] does not occur.

As is explicitly stated above, the opponent insists that *upacāra*, a secondary application or transferring usage of words, is possible only when 1. the primary referent, 2. another thing resembling the primary one to which the word is actually applied, and 3. similarity (*sādṛśya*), or common property (*sādhāraṇa dharma*) between the two exist. According to the example referred by Sthiramati, a common expression (simile) "the boy is fire (*agnir mānavakaḥ*)," which means that "the boy looks red like a fire" or "the boy is sharp/resplendent/eye-catching/choleric like a fire" needs 1. fire as the primary referent of the word "fire," 2. a boy figuratively referred by the "fire," and similarity, or common property, that is, red color (*kapilatva*) or sharpness (*tīkṣṇatva*) of the fire and the boy.[13]

The Vijñānavādins insist that "*ātman* is nothing but the *vijñāna-pariṇāma*," which means that "the *vijñāna-pariṇāma* looks like *ātman*"; "*dharmas* are nothing but the *vijñāna-pariṇāma*," which means that "the *vijñāna-pariṇāma* looks like *dharmas*" because the expressions "*ātman*" and "*dharma*" are *upacāra*. If they are *upacāra*, there must exist 1. the primary referents (*ātman* and *dharma*), 2. another thing resembling, or looking like the primary one (*vijñāna-pariṇāma*) and 3. their similarity, as in the case of the simile above. But since the Vijñānavādins do not admit the existence of *ātman* and *dharma* as the primary referents, the expressions "*ātman*" and "*dharma*" as the secondary application (*upacāra*) are inevitably impossible for them. Thus the opponent considers.[14]

The counter-argument by Sthiramati is, in short, that even in the case of the common expression "the boy is fire", the similarity between the boy and the fire does not exist, and also, the fire primarily referred to by the word "fire" does not exist, because only *vijñāna-pariṇāma* exists in reality. Thus, there should be no problem in the Vijñānavādins' statement. To explain this counterargument in detail is far beyond the scope of this paper. I confine myself to examining how far the above-mentioned "Grammarian's objection" is related to the Grammarians' idea found in their existing treatises.

2. The example of *upacāra* referred by Sthiramati, "the boy is fire (*angir mānavakaḥ*)," is found in the *Mahābhāṣya* of the eminent grammarian Patañjali along with another expression "the man from *Vāhīka* country is an ox (*gaur vāhīkaḥ*)," which means that "the man from *Vāhīka* country is dull like an ox. He mentions them as examples of *guṇa-vacana* (secondary expres-

sions) to explain *Pāṇinisūtra* P 8.1.12 (*prakāre guṇavacanasya*).[15] To explain, "*go* (ox)" in the *gaur vāhīkaḥ* is *guṇa-vacana*, because it expresses an attribute (*guṇa*), dullness of the *Vāhīka* despite that the word "*go*" usually expresses the *jāti* (generic property) of oxen, and therefore this is secondary (*guṇa/gauṇa*). Patañjali, however, does not tell us much about these phrases themselves, for his purpose is only to give some examples for understanding the sūtra.[16]

The same examples are used in Bhartṛhari's works. The one in the *Mahābhāṣyadīpikā* which we have seen above, is also one of his remarks on the phrase "*gaur vāhīkaḥ*". A direct reference to those two examples is found in a section of the *Vṛtti* on the *Vākyapadīya* II,[17] where Bhartṛhari explains the primary (*mukhya*) and secondary (*gauṇa*) meaning of words.[18] Although he does not use the term "*upacāra*" to refer to the secondary usage of words in that section, Aramaki has suggested that Bhartṛhari's argument there has some relation to the above mentioned objection found in Sthiramati's *Triṃśikābhāṣya*, as noted above. One of the relevant verses in Bhartṛhari's lengthy argument, as given in the Puṇyarāja's commentary, is as follows:

sādṛśyam idānīṃ nimittatvenāha/
jātiśabdo 'ntareṇāpi jātiṃ yatra prayujyate/
saṃbandhisadṛśād dharmāt taṃ gauṇam apare viduḥ// VP 2.273
gośabdo gotvajātiṃ vināpi svavyaktigataguṇasādṛśyād vāhīke prayujayata iti sādṛśyaṃ gauṇamukhyabhāve nimittam//[19]

Now, some explain similarity as the ground [for explaining how a secondary meaning comes into existence]:

> Others consider: when a word expressing a generic property (*jātiśabda*) is applied to something even without the generic property (*jāti*) through a related similarity, the something is the secondary [meaning of the word].

The word "ox" ("*go*") [expressing the generic property of the oxen (*gotva*)] is applied to a *Vāhīka* even without the generic property of the oxen (*gotva*) through an attribute (*guṇa*), that is, the similarity which exists in its own particular. Thus, the similarity is the ground for being related as the primary (*mukhya*) and secondary (*gauṇa*).

As explained concretely in the Puṇyarāja's *Ṭīkā*, the example, "the man from *Vāhīka* country is an ox (*gaur vāhīkaḥ*)" is based on the similarity or common property (dullness and so on) of an ox and a *Vāhīka.* As a consequence, we can see that the example consists of three factors: the generic property of the oxen (*gotva*) which is originally expressed by the word "ox" ("*go*"), a *Vāhīka* to which the word is applied, and the similarity between the two.

The object of this section of the *Vākyapadīya* is to explain various criteria for distinguishing the primary and secondary meaning/application of words, and therefore, Bhartṛhari (or the upholder of the opinion above, called "others") does not intend to criticize the Vijñānavādins or other schools. In fact, this is just one of the various views about the ground for secondary meaning. But we may consider that this opinion is shared with that of the opponent recorded in the Sthiramati's *Triṃśikābhāṣya,* as both consider the three factors with reference to a secondary application of words: the word "ox" is applied to a *Vāhīka* through the similarity, or common property (e.g. dullness) of ox and *Vāhīka;* and the word "fire" is applied to a boy through their common red color or sharpness.

Such arguments regarding the secondary application of words are also discussed in many treatises of various schools.[20] The most detailed arguments on the secondary application of words are found in the scientific tradition of treatises dealing with the poetics of ornate poetry (*alaṅkāraśāstra*). Among them, one of the most eminent *alaṅkārikas,* Ānandavardhana classifies the secondary usage (*guṇa-vṛtti*) of words into *upacāra* (metaphorical one) and *lakṣaṇā* (relational one).[21] He refers to the phrase "the boy is fire (*agnir mānavakaḥ*)" as one of the examples of *upacāra* and says that it is based on a property belonging to the expressed object and on a suggested meaning e.g. the sharpness of the fire (and the sharpness of the boy).[22] The concept of *upacāra* defined by some *alaṅkārikas* roughly corresponds to that which is explained by Sthiramati. In contrast, Bhartṛhari does not use the term *upacāra* in this context, as stated above, although an idea close to it is found in his *Vākyapadīya.* According to Kunjunni Raja, the classification of secondary usage into two categories (one based on similarity and the other based on relations other than similarity) can go back to Kumārila, although he also does not use the term *upacāra.*[23]

3. In the same section of *Vākyapadīya* II, Bhartṛhari introduces various views on the phrase "*gaur vāhīkaḥ*" and examines them in detail. Although Bhartṛhari himself does not refers to them with the term *upacāra*, according to the commentator Puṇyarāja, three kinds of *upacāras* are presented in a sub-section (VP 2.250-256) under it. It is worth examining them following Puṇyarāja's classification.

yathā sāsnādimān piṇḍo gośabdenābhidhīyate/
tathā sa eva gośabdo vāhīke 'pi vyavasthitaḥ//
sarvaśaktes tu tasyaiva śabdasyānekadharmaṇaḥ/
prasiddhibhedād gauṇatvaṃ mukhyatvaṃ copavarṇyate// VP2.252-3
gotvānuṣaṅgo vāhīke nimittāt kaiścid iṣyate/
arthamātraṃ viparyastaṃ śabdaḥ svārthe vyavasthitaḥ// VP 2.255
tathā svarūpaṃ śabdānāṃ sarvārtheṣv anuṣajyate/
arthamātraṃ viparyastaṃ svarūpe tu śrutiḥ sthitā// VP 2.256[24]

1. *Secondary application of word (śabda-upacāra)*: Just as a mass endowed with a dewlap and so on is denoted by the word "ox" ("*go*"), it is in the same manner, that very word "ox" is established in [the sense of] a man from *Vāhīka* country (*vāhīka*).

But, depending on the difference of acceptations (*prasiddhi*), primary and secondary [usage] of the word which possesses many properties, or power to denote its all meanings, is talked about.

2. *Secondary application of outer referent* (*bāhyārtha-upacāra*): Some consider that because of a certain ground (*nimitta*) [e.g. dullness (*jāḍya*) in this case], the generic property of the oxen (*gotva*) adheres to the man from *Vāhīka* country (*vāhīka*). The actual referent itself is presented differently [i.e. not as an ox but a *Vāhīka*], [but] the word is established in its own referent (oxness).

3. *Secondary application of own form* (*svarūpa-upacāra*): And also, [some consider that] the own form of a word is adhered to its all referents. The actual referent itself is presented differently [i.e. not as its form but an ox or a *Vāhīka*], [but] the word is stationed in its own form (*svarūpa*).

All these three views hold the idea called *ekaśabdadarśana*, that is, one and the same word (*ekaśabda*) can denote many objects.[25]

The first view considers that the one and the same word "ox" is applied to both an ox and a man from *Vāhīka* country, but, since there is the difference in acceptation (*prasiddhibheda*), that is, the word "ox" for the latter is less known, it becomes secondary. Thus, the application of the word "ox" to a *Vāhīka* is called a secondary application of the word (*śabda-upacāra*).[26] This view, however, may be incompatible with the Grammarians' presupposition, the eternity of the relation between a word and its referent,[27] for the word now denotes one and now another in this view. This might be a reason why the following two other alternatives are called for.

In the second view, the idea which we have seen in the previous section is explained in a slight different way. According to this view,[28] there are three factors in the phrase: the generic property of the oxen (*gotva*) which is originally expressed by the word "ox," a *Vāhīka* to which the word is applied, and a common property, e.g. dullness (*jāḍya*) of the two. On the basis of the common property, the original referent (*gotva*) is superimposed on the *Vāhīka*. Thus, this is called a secondary application of outer referent (*bāhyārtha-upacāra*). On this view, the word "*go*" refers to *gotva* whether the word denotes an ox or a *Vāhīka*. And in this case, the eternity of the relation between a word and its referent is maintained.

The standpoint of the third view is totally different from the second. According to the view, the form of a word (*svarūpa*), namely, a particular pattern of phonemes, is invariably the primary referent of the word. It is superimposed on the object, which it denotes, and therefore this view is called a secondary application of own form (*svarūpa-upacāra*).[29] Since the word "*go*" primarily refers to its own form (it will be /gauḥ/ or some other form alike in its actual utterances), whether the word denotes an ox, a *Vāhīka*, or others, the eternity of the relation is maintained in this position also. We should note that this view does not see any difference between ox and *Vāhīka* as referents of the word "*go*". Only the form of a word is its primary referent and all meanings are secondarily denoted on the basis of the superimposition of the form. The proposition that the primary referent of the word is its own form (*svarūpa*) may look peculiar, but this has been traditionally accepted by the Grammarians, for grammar operates on forms, not meanings (certainly not on referents) as prescribed in *Pāṇinisūtra* 1.1.68, *svaṃ rūpaṃ śabdasyāśabdasṃjñā.*[30] Bhartṛhari repeatedly explains this standpoint of the Grammarians in his *Vākyapadīya.* We may say that in this context Bhartṛhari admits the third view as the conclusion from his standpoint as a Pāṇinian grammarian, although he does not thoroughly reject other views.

4. Sthiramati seems to know the third view of the Grammarians. In fact, his following statement in the last part of his counterargument seems to provide an argument against this very view:

> *evaṃ yāvac chabde saṃbandhābhāvāj jñānābhidhānābhāva evaṃ cābhidhānābhidheyābhāvān naiva mukhyaḥ padārtho 'sti/ api ca sarva evāyaṃ gauṇa eva na mukhyo 'sti/*[31]
>
> In the same way, since there is no relation to a word, any knowledge and expression [of the word] cannot exist first of all. And in the same way, because expression and expressed do not exist, there is no primary referent (*padārtha*). And also, everything here is secondary, not primary.

According to Vinītadeva, the first part of this passage is to refute an opponent who asserts that a word (as a particular pattern of phonemes, namely, a form of word) is the primary referent because both the knowledge and expression are primarily applied to it.[32] This opponent's idea corresponds well to the third view introduced by Bhartṛhari. As quoted above, Sthiramati rejects this saying that there is no relation to a word. Vinītadeva explains the reason for Sthiramati's rejection as follows:

> *sgra la yang de gnyis mngon sum du 'jug pa med pa nyid de / 'di ltar sgra'i rang gi ngo bo dang brjod pa ni 'brel ba med de / sgrai'i rang gi ngo bo dang brjod pa tha dad pa med pa'i phyir ro/ tha dad pa ni 'brel pa'i gnas yin na ni/ tha dad pa med pas de ji ltar rung bar 'gyur /*[33]
>
> Both [the knowledge and expression] cannot be applied directly to a word also. In this case, there is no relation between the own form (*rang gi ngo bo/svarūpa*) of the word (*sgra/śabda*) and expression (*brjod/abhidhāna*), because there is no difference between the own form of the word and expression. If the difference is the basis for the relation

('*brel pa/saṃbandha*),[34] how would it (the relation of them) be possible because there is no difference?

Here, Vinītadeva clarifies the "relation (*saṃbandha*)" in the Sthiramati's commentary as that of an expression (*brjod/abhidhāna*) to its own form (*rang gi ngo bo/svarūpa*). Thus, we may say that Sthiramati refers to the opponent who exactly has the corresponding ideas to Bhartṛhari's.

In spite of Sthiramati's refutation above, however, we can find some sort of affinity between the ideas of Sthiramati and Bhartṛhari. Sthiramati argues against the view correspond to the second view of the Grammarians at full length, but against that to the third view, which is probably most important to Bhartṛhari himself, he gave only the short remark quoted above. As we have seen above, this view holds that there is no difference between an ox and a *Vāhīka* as secondary referents of the word "*go*" since the primary referent of the word is nothing more than its form. And the Vijñānavādins may approve of this idea in the point that the referents of the word "*go*" such as an ox and *Vāhīka* are all secondary, since they admit *vijñāna* only.

Sthiramati attacks the opponent saying that "everything here will be secondary, not primary". This must be crucial criticism to the holders of the idea that *upacāra* invariably needs three factors: the primary referent of a word, a secondary referent to which the word is applied, and relation between the two. But, since every referent of our usual linguistic activity is secondary according to the third view introduced by Bhartṛhari also, Sthiramati's conclusion might not be crucial for him.

5. Most of Sthiramati's argument is, in fact, aimed at rejecting the view of those who explicitly distinguish the primary referent of a word (an ox for "ox", fire for "fire") from the secondary one (a *Vāhīka* for "ox", a boy for "fire"). Although this kind of view does not seem to be the final standpoint of Bhartṛhari, he, from this point of view, discusses the secondary usage of words in detail in his *Vākyapadīya*.

This discussion on the secondary usage of words is probably more related to the view of Sthiramati's opponent. As a matter of fact, the relevant section of the *Vākyapadīya* has already been examined by Hajime Nakamura as an objection of Bhartṛhari to the Vijñānavādins.[35] As Nakamura has shown, Bhartṛhari, using the examples frequently used by the Vijñānavādins such as a mirage looking like water, a rope looking like a snake, and a fire-wheel looking like a real wheel, asserts that we can distinguish between the primary and the secondary usage of words on the basis of the distinction between true and false cognition.

Here Bhartṛhari argues against those who hold that the distinction between the primary and secondary usage of words is subjectively established by us. According to this view, even if a speaker uses the word "water" for a mirage by mistake, the word is primarily used in this case because the speaker intends to speak about water; even though his word "water" is referring to the mirage in reality, this is not a secondary usage of the word.[36]

In reply, Bhartṛhari illustrates that the distinction of the primary and secondary usage of words is related to the distinction of the true and false cognition or expression. We can experience the difference between water and a mirage or a snake and a rope, even though we may mistake one for another under a certain condition. Thus we can say that the word "water" for real water is primary; the same word for a mirage is secondary. In this case, the distinction between the two is not subjective but clearly objective, because it is based on the distinction of outer objects.[37]

Bhartṛhari's opponent here is not the Vijñānavādins because the opponents' claim that even the word "water" for a mirage can be primary is totally opposite of that of the Vijñānavādins, since, as we have seen, every expression must be secondary for them. But the idea that even the word wrongly used by mistake is subjectively (believed to be) primary may be admitted by the Vijñānavādins also with regard to the worldly level of our linguistic activity.

Bhartṛhari's argument above—a word referring to its real object is primary and a word referring to the unreal or untrue object is secondary—is, in a sense, very stale and commonplace. In fact, he himself says that this view is actually based on the common sense of people (*loka*) as the conclusion of his argument on this topic:

deśakālendriyagatair bhedair yad dṛśyate 'nyathā/
yathā prasiddhir lokasya tathā tad avasīyate// VP 2.296

yac copaghātajaṃ jñānaṃ yac ca jñānam alaukikam/
na tābhyāṃ vyavahāro 'sti śabdā lokanibandhanāḥ// VP 2.297[38]

[Even] that which is seen the other way round due to differences of place, time, and sense-organs, can be ascertained as is accepted by people in this world.

Our linguistic activity is not from the knowledge based on defected sense-organs and the knowledge of the unworldly level. The ground of words is people in this world.

Our linguistic activity is not based on a mistake that happened during twilight, the seeing of two moons caused by an eye disease, or the supernatural knowledge of *yogins.* The words which we daily use are based on generally accepted ideas (*prasiddhi*) of people in this world. The task of the Grammarians is, in the first place, to examine these ordinary words used in our daily life. Thus, this view based on the point of view of our daily life in this world (*loka*), is also important to the grammarian, Bhartṛhari. We should, however, notice that Bhartṛhari also develops his argument from the point of view of the science of grammar (*vyākaraṇaśāstra*), as we have seen in the previous sections.[39]

6. In conclusion, let us summarize our discussion briefly. As we have examined, the close ideas to the "Grammarian's objection" presented in Sthiramati's *Triṃśikābhāṣya* are recorded in Bhartṛhari's *Vākyapadīya.* But it is doubtful that he intends to make an objection to the Vijñānavādins *per se,* as he seems to introduce just various views with reference to the secondary application or secondary meanings of words. Among the various views taken up by Bhartṛhari, the one particular to him is that a word primarily refers only to its form (*svarūpa*), a particular pattern of phonemes; whatever else the word may refer to is secondary. In spite of Sthiramati's rejection of this view, we can see some kind of affinity between Bhartṛhari and the Vijñānavādins on this point, since it is the Vijñānavādins who assert that whatever a word may refer to is secondary.

NOTES

* I would like to express my sincere gratitude to Professor Leonard van der Kuijp at Harvard University, Professor Ashok Aklujkar at the University of British Columbia and Professor Parimal Patil at Harvard University for

their invaluable comments, suggestions and corrections. I also would like to acknowledge the financial support from Japan Society for the Promotion of Science (Research Fellowship for Young Scientists and Grant-in-Aid for Scientific Research) which made my research at the Harvard University possible. Thanks are also due to the Harvard University itself, where, through the courtesy of Professor van der Kuijp and under the auspices of the Department of Sanskrit and Indian Studies, I could enjoy ten months of productive research as an Associate in 2002-2003.

1. Jōshō Nozawa, "Ujishōron ni okeru Kesetsu to Yuishikiron ni okeru Kesetsu ni tsuite (*Upacāra* in the *Svabhāvavāda* and *Vijñānavāda*)," *Shūkyō Kenkyū* 2(4), 1940, pp. 345-51 [In Japanese].
2. Noritoshi Aramaki, "Yuishikisanjūron (A Japanese Translation of the *Triṃśikābhāṣya*)," in *Seshinronshū* (*Works of Vasubandhu*), Chūōkōronsha, Tokyo, 1976, p. 369: note (7).
3. Jan E.M. Houben, *The Saṃbandha-Samuddeśa* (*Chapter on Relation*) *and Bhartṛhari's Philosophy of Language*, Egbert Forsten, Groningen, 1995, pp. 258-259.
4. Musashi Tachikawa, "Yuishikisanjūju ni okeru Kesetsu to Shiki ni tsuite (1)" (*Upacāra* and *Vijñāna* in the *Triṃśikā*, part 1), in *Indian Thoughts and Buddhist Culture, Essays in Honour of Professor Junkichi Imanishi on His Sixtieth Birthday*, Shunjūsha, Tokyo, 1996, pp. 345-56 [In Japanese].
5. *Triṃśikā* (in *Vijñaptimātratāsiddhi, deux traités de Vasubandhu Viṃśatikā* (*la Vingtaine*) *accompagnée d'une explication en prose et Triṃśikā* (*la Trentaine*) *avec le commentaire de Sthiramati* par Sylvain Lévi, 1re partie – texte, Librairie Ancienne Honoré Champion, Paris, 1925), p. 13.
6. Thomas E. Wood, *Mind Only*, University of Hawaii Press, Honolulu, 1991, p.49.
7. This example is reproduced from the following passage in the *Mahābhāṣyadīpikā of Bhartṛhari* (Fascicle IV: Āhnika I, ed. by Johannes Bronkhorst, Bhandarkar Oriental Research Institute, Poona, 1987), pp. 31-32.
   śabdo hi kaścit tulyarūpaḥ pravartamāno bhinnārtho bhinnanimittaḥ parasparam apekṣamāṇaḥ pravartate/ yathāśvaśabdaḥ subantas tiṅantaś ca/ kaścit tu nimittasya tulyatvāt pravartate/ yathā apśabdaḥ samudre bindau ca jātinimittaḥ/ kaścij jātibhede 'pi rūḍhiviṣayaḥ kriyā tulyeti pravartate/ yathā sarvaḥ aśnoter akṣaḥ padyateḥ pādaḥ mimīter māṣa iti/ tatra kriyāsāmānyāt siddham iti/ kaścit tadbhāvāpādanena vadhyaropeṇa vā yathā vāhīke gośabdo rajjudravye ca sarpaśabdaḥ/
   For translations of this passage, see Ibid., pp.95-96 and S.D. Joshi and J.A.F. Roodbergen, *Patañjali's Vyākaraṇa-Mahābhāṣya, Paspaśāhnika*, Poona University, Poona, 1986, pp. 159-160.
8. For the word "*vāhīka*" (or "*bāhīka*"), see S. D. Joshi and J. A. F. Roodbergen, *Patañjali's Vyākaraṇa-Mahābhāṣya, Karmadhārayāhnika*, Poona University, Poona, 1971, p. 115: fn.409 in detail. We will take up the phrase "*gaur vāhīkaḥ*" later.
9. My interpretation is, thus, slightly different from the one Tachikawa presents, as I do not think the seventh case here is used in an idiomatic combination with the verb "*pravartate*," unlike the combination of the seventh case and "*vartate*." The seventh case means "in the sense of" by itself.

10. *ātmadharmopacāro hi vividho yaḥ pravartate/ lokaśāstrayor iti vākyaśeṣah/ vijñānapariṇāme asau/ ātmadharmopacāra iti saṃbadhyate/ ātmā dharmāś copacaryante ity ātmadharmopacāraḥ/ sa punar ātmavijñaptir dharmaprajñaptiś ca/ vividha ity anekaprakāraḥ/ ātmā jīvo jantur manujo māṇava ityevamādika ātmopacāraḥ, skandhā dhātava āyatanāni rūpaṃ vedanā saṃjñā saṃskārā vijñānam ityevamādiko dharmopacāraḥ/ ayaṃ dviprakāro 'py upācāro vijñānapariṇāma eva na mukhye ātmani dharmeṣu ceti kuta etat/ dharmāṇām ātmanaś ca vijñānapariṇāmād bahirabhāvāt/* (*Triṃśikābhāṣya* in *Vijñaptimātratāsiddhi*, pp.15-16).
11. Vinītadeva/Dul ba'i lha in his *Triṃśikāṭīkā/Sum cu pa'i 'grel bshad* introduces the objection with the following leading phrase:
'dir brda sprod pa pa la sogs pas phyir rgol ba ston te/
Here showing an objection from the Grammarian (*vaiyākaraṇa*) and so on... (*Triṃśikāṭīkā/Sum cu pa'i 'grel bshad* 9b5-6, the *Tibetan Tripiṭaka sDe-de edition* (D), Tohoku University Catalogue no. 4070 [no. 4075 in vol. 41 of the Taipei edition]). *Tibetan Tripiṭaka Peking edition* (P), no. 5571 in vol. 114, 11a6 reads "brda spros pa pa," which seems to be meaningless.
12. *Triṃśikābhāṣya*, p. 17. For better understanding, I supplied "*satsu*," which is missing in the published text, according to the reading of a manuscript (National Archives, Kathmandu, Nepal Ms. No. 5-136 vi, Bauddhadarśana 40ka) and its (older) transcripts. See manuscripts C 3b4, E 6.10 and F 4a4 published in *Three Works of Vasubandhu in Sanskrit Manuscript*, ed. by Katsumi Mimaki, Musashi Tachikawa and Akira Yuyama, the Centre for East Asian Cultural Studies, Tokyo, 1989.
13. *tad yathā mukhye agnau tatsadṛśe ca māṇavake tayoś ca sādhāraṇe dharme kapilatve tīkṣṇatve vā saty agnir māṇavaka ity upacāraḥ kriyate/* (*Triṃśikābhāṣya*, p.17).
14. This is based on Vinītadeva's explicit explanation:
gal te de ltar rnam par shes pa gyur pa la bdag dang chos nye bar 'dogs par byed na/ yang de'i tshe bdag dang chos rnams dngos su yod par 'gyur te/ gzhan du na ni nye bar 'dogs par mi 'gyur ro zhes phyogs snga ma'o// Triṃśikāṭīkā (D) s10a2-3; (P) 11b2-3).
15. *prakāre guṇavacanasya//8/1/12// guṇavacanasyeti kim artham/agnir māṇavakaḥ/ gaur vāhīkaḥ/* (*The Vyākaraṇa-mahābhāṣya of Patañjali*), vol. 3, ed. by Kashinatha V. Abhyankar, Bhandarkar Oriental Research institute, poona, 1972, p. 368). For the meaning of the sūtra, see Sumitra M. Katre, *Aṣṭādhyāyī of Pāṇini*, University of Texas Press, Austin, 1987, p. 972.
Sthiramati also gives a remark on the phrase "*gaur vāhīkaḥ*" as follows: *yac ca yatra nāsti tat tatropacaryate/ tad yathā bāhīke gauḥ/* (*Triṃśikābhāṣya* p.16)
Here he explains that in the case of the example of *upacāra*, "*gaur vāhīkaḥ*", the word "ox" is secondarily applied (*upacaryate*) to that which is not an ox, and, in the same way, "*ātman*" and so on are secondarily applied to that which are not *ātman* and so on.
16. Patañjali elsewhere classifies secondary application of words or transfer of meaning into four categories according to four grounds i.e. location (*tātsthya*), quality (*tāddharmya*), proximity (*tatsāmīpya*) and association (*tatsāhacarya*). For details, see K. Kunjunni Raja, *Indian Theories of Meaning,*

The Adyar Library and Research Centre, Madras 1963, pp.235-236.

17. *śabdāntarābhisambandhenāgnir māṇavako gaur vāhīka iti/ Vṛtti* on VP 2.251 (*Vākyapadīya of Bhartṛhari, Containing the Ṭīkā of Puṇyarāja and the Ancient Vṛtti, Kāṇḍa II*, ed. by K.A. Subramania Iyer, Motilal Banarsidass, Delhi, 1983, p.255). These are examples of words, of which meaning is determined by the relation to another word (*śabdāntarābhisambandhena*).
18. The section is as long as seventy-five verses (VP 2.250-324). His lengthy discussion is summarized in K.A. Subramania Iyer, "Bhartṛhari on the Primary & Secondary Meanings of Words," *Indian Linguistics* 29(1), 1968, pp. 97-112.
19. *Vākyapadīya, Kāṇḍa II*, p. 111.
20. See Kunjunni Raja, *Indian Theories of Meaning*, pp.231-73.
21. See, for example, Daniel H.H. Ingalls, Jeffrey Moussaieff Masson, and M.V. Patwardhan, *The Dhvanyāloka of Ānandavardhana with the Locana of Abhinavagupta*, Harvard University Press, Cambridge, 1990, p.562: §3.33h, where Ānandavardhana says "It is true that secondary usage (*guṇavṛtti*), whether metaphorical (*upacāra*) or relational (*lakṣaṇā*), is also based on both [word and meaning]." See also Ibid., p.48: note 2.
    It is interesting to note that the commentator Abhinavagupta says that "the presence of three factors forms the seed from which secondary usage (*upacāra*) arises. They are: the blocking of the primary meaning; a cause [e.g., proximity to or similarity to the primary object]; and a purpose [e.g., one's eagerness to express forcefully this proximity or similarity]." (Ibid., p.65): *mukhyasya cārthasya bhaṅgo bhaktir ity evaṃ mukhyārthabādhā, nimittaṃ, prayojanam iti trayasadbhāva upacārabījam ity uktaṃ bhavati/* (*The Dhvanyāloka of Ānandavardhanācārya with the Lochana & Bālapriyā Commentaries*, ed. by Pt. Pattābhirāma Śāstri, Chowkhambā Sanskrit Series Office, Benares, 1940), p.30.
22. *guṇavṛttis tu vācyadharmāśrayeṇaiva vyaṅgyamātrāśrayena cābhedopacārarūpā sambhavati, yathā—tīkṣṇatvād agnir māṇavakaḥ, āhlādakatvāc candra evāsyā mukham itādau/* (*the Dhvanyāloka*, ed. by Pt. Pattabhirāma Śāstri, p.433). Ingalls et al. (*the Dhvanyāloka*, p. 570: § 3.33j) translates: whereas secondary usage may come into being in the form of metaphorical identity resting on a property belonging to the expressed object and on a suggested meaning of any sort [not necessarily a beautiful meaning]. For example, [we call] the young brahmin a fire because of the sharpness [of fire]; we speak of a woman's face as a moon because of the delightfulness [of the moon].
23. *Indian Theories of Meaning*, p.240. According to it, Kumārila uses the terms *gauṇī vṛtti* and *lakṣaṇā* respectively.
24. *Vākyapadīya, Kāṇḍa II*, pp. 104-5, 255-6.
25. The opposite point of view, *anekaśabdadarśana* is explained in VP 2.257 onward. See Iyer, "Bhartṛhari on the Primary & Secondary Meanings of Words", p. 104.
26. *evaṃ śabdopacāraḥ prasiddhyaprasiddhinimittakaḥ pradarśitaḥ/ Ṭīkā* on the VP 2.255 (*Vākyapadīya, Kāṇḍa II*, p. 105).
27. This is one of the most important topics of the *Patañjali's Mahābhāṣya, Paspaśāhnika*. For details, see Joshi and Roodbergen, *Patañjali's Vyākaraṇa-Mahābhāṣya, Paspaśāhnika*, pp.85-116. See also Houben, *The Saṃbandha-Samuddeśa*, pp. 36-40,

28. The following explanation is based on Puṇyarāja's commentary: *arthaḥ śabdasya dvividhaḥ, svarūpaṃ bāhyaś ca/ tatra nimittāj jāḍyāder gotvaṃ vāhīke 'py anuṣajyate, śabdas tu gotvaṃ evābhidhatta iti bāhyārthopacāraḥ/* *Ṭīkā* on the VP 2.255 (*Vākyapadīya, Kāṇḍa II,* p. 105).
29. *atha svarūpopacāram āha...*, *Ṭīkā* on the VP 2.256 (*Vākyapadīya, Kāṇḍa II,* p. 105).
   As Houben (The *Saṃbandha-Samuddeśa,* p.258) remarks, the commentator on the *Vākyapadīya* III, Helārāja glosses *upacāra* as *adhyāropa* "superimposition." In the case of Puṇyarāja's usage too, *upacāra* can be translated as superimposition: superimposition of a word to other thing (*śabdopacāra*), superimposition of the outer referent to other thing (*bāhyārthopacāra*), and superimposition of its own form to other thing (*svarūpopacāra*). (We should note the possibility of Herārāja's authorship of the (original) *Ṭīkā* suggested by Ashok Aklujkar, "The Authorship of *Vākya-kāṇḍa-ṭīkā,*" *Charudeva Shastri Felicitation Volume,* Vol. I, Delhi, 1974, pp. 165-188.) Bhartṛhari himself uses the word "*svarūpa-adhyāropa*" with reference to the phrase "*gaur vāhīkaḥ*" in the *Vṛtti* on VP 1.67 (*Vākyapadīya of Bhartṛhari, Kāṇḍa I,* Deccan College, Poona, 1966, p. 126).
30. Katre (*Aṣṭādhyāyī of Pāṇini,* p.27) translates the sūtra as follows:
   An expression denotes itself (*svam rūpam*) unless it is the name of a linguistic technical term (*śabda-saṃjñā*).
   This sūtra provides that a grammatical operation is to be applied to the form of a word, not to the referent of the word. In grammatical treatises, thus, a word denotes its form. For example, the word "agni" in a grammatical rule denotes a particular pattern of phonemes,/a/,/g/,/n/, and/i/ but not fire. See Hideyo Ogawa, "Bhartṛhari on *A.* 1.1.68," *Journal of Indian Philosophy* 29, pp. 531-543, for a detailed study on Bhartṛhari's view on this rule.
31. *Triṃśikābhāṣya,* p.17.
32. *sgra la blo dang sgra gnyis mngon sum du 'jug ste/ de'i phyir sgra de nyid dngos su 'gyur ro/ snyam pa la/ de'i phyir de bzhin du sgra'i bar du zhes bya ba la sogs pa smras so//* (Triṃśikāṭīkā (D) 12b4; (P) 14b4-5),
33. Triṃśikāṭīkā (D) 12b5-6; (P) 14b5-6.
34. The basis of this statement is found in grammatical treatises. See Joshi and Roodbergen, *Patañjali's Vyākaraṇa-Mahābhāṣya, Paspaśāhnika,* p.159: fn 642. The use of the sixth (genitive) ending, which indicates relations such as owner-owned relation as provided by the *Pāṇinisūtra* 2.3.50, requires difference (*vyatireka*), or the presence of different items.
35. Hajime Nakamura, "Bhartṛhari and Buddhism," *Journal of the Ganganatha Jha Kendriya Sanskrit Vidyapeetha,* vol. 28, parts 1-2, 1972, pp.395-405.
36. *atyantaviparīto 'pi yathā yo 'rtho 'vadhāryate/*
   yathāsaṃpratyayaḥ śabdas tatra mukhyaḥ prayujyate// VP 2.285 (*Vākyapadīya, Kāṇḍa II,* p.264)
   See Nakamura, "Bhartṛhari and Buddhism," p.396 for a translation and discussion on this verse (Nakamura cites it as VP 2.287).
37. *yady api pratyayādhīnam arthatattvāvadhāraṇam/*
   na sarvaḥ pratyayas tasmin prasiddha iva jāyate//
   darśanaṃ salile tulyaṃ mṛgatṛṣṇādidarśanaiḥ/
   bhedāt tu sparśanādīnāṃ na jalaṃ mṛgatṛṣṇikā// VP 2.286-7 (*Vākyapadīya, Kāṇḍa II,* p.264)

See also Nakamura, "Bhartṛhari and Buddhism," pp. 397-8.
On the page 397 Nakamura cites following Bhartṛhari's remark on *upacāra: upacāro hi mukhyasya saṃbhavād avatiṣṭhate/* (VP 3.8.13ab)
He translated it as "Truly metaphorical expression is established because of the existence of the original meaning." Although Nakamura understands it as insisting an objection to the Vijñānavādins and it may appear so, the verse needs to be understood in the context of the cognition of action (*kriyā*).

38. *Vākyapadīya, Kāṇḍa II,* p.267.
39. This reminds us of Sthiramati supplying "*lokaśāstrayor*" to the *pāda* ab of the first verse of the *Triṃśikā* as cited in note 10.

CHAPTER 10

Bhagavat in Chinese Buddhist Translation: An Indirect Example in Oral *Nirvacana* in Buddhist Text Translations?

MAX DEEG

It is a well-known fact that the study of Buddhist texts is depending heavily on translations in non-Indic languages. The main corpus of this literature is preserved in Chinese and Tibetan translations, the first group representing the earliest versions of Buddhist texts in a non-Indic language, starting from the 2nd century A.D. One of the main tasks for the first translators in and into these languages was the creation of a terminological corpus.

For the research on Tibetan we possess with the bilingual dictionary *Mahāvyutpatti* relatively good evidence for Buddhist terminology at least for the official translations whereas the motive and procedure behind particular translations is not always clear.[1] The matter is, however, different for the texts preserved in the huge Chinese Buddhist corpus called *sanzang* 三藏, the Chinese *tripiṭaka*. In both cases the same *crux* is that in most cases we do not possess the Indian original—if there was one at all — but in case of the Chinese texts there is even the heavier problem that there are texts of which we do not even know the title from other sources like the Tibetan and that, on the other hand, there are not few Indian *sūtras* of which exist two or more Chinese translations made in different periods and sometimes heavily differing from each other.

The two main types of rendering Indian Buddhist terminology and names in the translations are: 1. transcriptions[2], trying to copy the sounds of the original by the phonetic inventory of the language into which the translation was made, and 2. translations in a narrow sense by analyzing the meaning of the original Indian word or name and rendering it by semantic units of the language of the translation (Chinese, Tibetan, etc.).

In the case of no. 2 it is clear that some semantic analytical work had to be done by the translator before he came up with a result, a translation. As successors of the great philologists of the 19th and 20th century we would like to expect the analysis to be made on the sound and strict foundation of philology, already developed in India close to the time of the life of the Buddha through grammarians such as Pāṇini and his followers Kātyāyana, Patañjali and others. Reality, however, is a bit different. The analysis underlying a lot of the translations of Buddhist terms and names does not at all follow the laws of word-formation of Sanskrit and other Indian languages, as developed by the grammarians (*vaiyākaraṇa*) but show features which the modern philologist would describe euphemistically as fanciful at least. This kind of critic, however, does totally miss the point. The analysis done by Indian (or foreign) *paṇḍita* did not necessarily follow the strict rules of the *vaiyākaraṇa*, who only taught regular word formation anyway, but were mostly done in the traditional patterns of semantic exegesis which we know as the *nirvacana* of the *nairukta*, the scholars of this very branch of brahmanic learning. It has already been stressed by others, that it was not only the brahmanic tradition which used this method of semantic analysis, but also the Buddhists[3] (one may add the Jains). We find *nirvacana* in terms of etiological stories in the commentary literature of the Pāli canon over and over again; this points out the existence of such an exegetical tradition in the 4th, 5th century A.D. And we have further good evidence of "classical"

Indian word analysis in the translations of the Buddhist canon into other Asian languages, into Tibetan and into Chinese.[4]

As there are no dictionaries for the Sino-Buddhist vocabulary found in these texts and established on a sound philological and critical basis these Chinese texts very often challenge the patience and the nerves of the scholars, finding no entry of some name or expression in the dictionaries or only insufficient explanations. A lot of Sino-Buddhist words are treated as mistranslations or misunderstandings of the original Indian term which is usually taken to be Sanskrit. I will try to show by one example that *nirvacana*–analysis can help to understand the translation process in quite a lot of cases as not being incorrect but settled on the sound basis of traditional Indian methods of dealing with word analysis. It seems that especially in Buddhist monasteries with its variety of local and canonical languages the tradition of *nirvacana* survived in a particularly consequent form which then was even more reinforced and productive when Buddhist monks had to translate Buddhist terminology and names into such totally different languages as Tibetan or Chinese.

I will subsequently deal with a puzzling word from the stratum of early Buddhist terminology in Chinese, the word *shizun*, usually rendered as the "*World-Honoured*", which is supposed to be the equivalent for Skt., *bhagavat*, the "*Blessed One*"[5].

Everybody who studies Buddhist texts in an Indian language stumbles over this word already in the stereotypical beginning of a *sūtra:* "*Such I have heard: once the Blessed One was dwelling at X...* ". In Sanskrit this is the formula: *evaṁ mayā śrutam: ekasmiṁ samaye bhagavān ... viharati ...*; in Pāli it is: *evaṁ me suttaṁ: ekaṁ samayaṁ bhagavā ... viharati. ...* In Chinese this formula was already formalized in an almost interlinear style as *rushi wo wen: yishi for zai ...* 如是我聞 一時佛在[6]..., which is almost the standard translation of the traditionally so-called *jiuyi* 舊譯 "old translations", from around 400 A.D.[7] and which only strikes the knowing reader by the translation of *bhagavat* through *fo* 佛.

It should be noticed, however, that there were some early syntactic variants of the formula which do not exactly correspond in terminology and syntax: *An Shigao*, from which the earliest translations into Chinese are preserved, has: *wen rushi:*

yishi fo zai ... 聞如是。一時佛在 ... Here we have first a difference in syntax: where the later standard formula follows exactly, like an interlinear gloss, the Sanskrit, the early translators seem to give a more intelligible and natural Chinese rendering for their time by omitting the subject (*wo* 我 : Skt. *mayā*) and putting the modifier to the normal place behind the predicate (*wen rushi* ... 聞如是 instead of rushi wo wen ... 如是我聞)[8].

As we have already noticed the most interesting difference to the Indian version of the initial formula of a *sūtra* already in the earliest translations attributed to *An Shigao,*[9] is that we find what we could take as an avoidance of a translation of the term *bhagavat:* the fixed terminology of the Indian *sūtras* calling the Buddha *bhagavat* in the formula is not translated by most of the early translators who always use *fo* 佛, Buddha, for *bhagavat.* For the Indian originals — as far as we can see from the text preserved of the *Hīnayāna* as well as of the *Mahāyāna*-tradition — there is no doubt that the formula contained only *bhagavat* and not *Buddha.*[10] One can only speculate why the first translators did not translate the text verbatim,[11] i.e., did not translate *bhagavat* but *buddha* / *fo* 佛 (or, of cause, used the transcription *pojiapo*), but did never use *shizun* in the formula, despite the fact that its use in the running text was totally normal. It is quite possible that the translator who was first responsible for this translation (and his successors) did not want to overload his translation with epitheta of the Buddha, especially in the introductory formula, which were not known to his readers or hearers, or that he was not sure if he had made the right translation.

Let us now have a closer look on the other earlier translators and the terminology used by them for the formula and for an original Indian *bhagavat. An Shigao,* besides his use of the already mentioned standard formula, *wen rushi: yishi fo zai* . . ., sometimes transcribes *bhagavat* : *pojiapo* 婆伽婆.[12]

If we proceed to early commentary literature (*śāstra*), e.g. the *Mahāprajñāpāramitāśāstra,* attributed to Nāgārjuna and translated into Chinese by Kumārajīva, the formula is discussed at length and it is again the transcription *bhagavat* / *pojiapo* 婆伽婆 [13] which is found in the explanation of the initial formula—not *buddha* / *fo* 佛 (but also not *shizun* 世尊, which I will discuss below)!

Despite the fact that it is not used in the initial formula of the Chinese *sūtra*-translations the standard translation word for *bhagavat* in Chinese is *shizun* 世尊,[14] which is normally rendered as "*the world-honoured one*". *Shizun,* however, is traditionally thought to be a literal translation of a Skt. *lokajyeṣṭha,* the "*Best, Highest of the World*". This seems to be bolstered by an entry in the Tibetan dictionary *Mahāvyutpatti* (Mv.) and its Chinese gloss which gives exactly *shizun* 世尊[15]. There are, nevertheless, some points which raise doubt about the correctness of this equation: 1. *lokajyeṣṭha* does by far not occur as often in Indian texts as *shizun* in the Chinese translations. 2. both Tibetan and Skt. do only correspond to the first part of Chinese *shizun* (*loka-*: '*jig-rten shi* 世)[16]—not to mention that 3. the Chinese entries in the Mv. cannot be taken into consideration to solve the problem because they are much younger than the original bilingual dictionary itself.[17]

Considering the fact that shizun belongs to the oldest layer of Chinese translation words occurring over and over in these texts one should reconsider its formation and the question of the underlying Indian term. To take up the question which comes up very often when dealing with early Sino-Buddhist terms: how and why could a translator render Skt. *bhagavat* by *shizun* 世尊, "*world-honoured*"?

For a traditional Indian specialist for etymology and semantics, a *nairukta,* it would be evident that the word *bhagavat* has to be split into two parts: *bhaga* and *vat.* What is a secondary suffix for the Old-Indian grammarian (*vaiyākaraṇa*) and for the modern linguist, *-vat,* could be interpreted as a verbal element in the tradition of the *nairukta.* And *-vat* is indeed taken as belonging to verbal roots, as can be seen by the etymologists of the word *bhagavat* (see above). As there is not root *-vat* the rendering of *-vat* as *-zun* 尊 has to have happened over a different form of the word. Now, as is well known to every Sanskritist, *bhagavat* is a noun with alternating stems. Its so-called strong stem is e.g. (with the ending acc.sing.) *bhagvant-*(*am*). But for an explanation deriving word-formative elements from verbs so preferred by the *nairuktas* there is still no root *-vant.*

The solution of the problem is, as has been shown for other

words by the few scholars working on the field of Sino-Buddhist terminology and its formation, that the underlying language of the translation *shizun* for *bhagavat* was not Skt. but a Middle-Indian dialect, most probably a North-Western vernacular similar to what has been called *Gāndhārī*.[18] In this language *-vant* can be *-vand*[19] and this seems to be the solution for the equation *-vat*: *zun* 尊 : the root *vand-* does indeed mean "*to greet, to venerate, to honor*".

The question why the strong stem should have been the form for the translator to analyse *-vat/ vant-* as belonging to *vand-* can be answered by the actual situation we meet in the Chinese texts. If the underlying Prākrit would still have made the distinction between nom.sing. and acc.sing. the following explanation would be appropriate: because the entering formula, as we have shown above, does not render the original nominative *bhagavā̃*, but very often starts using the translation word in the *sūtra* exactly from the moment when the Buddha is asked a question by someone (. . . *bhagavantam avocat*) it was exactly the strong stem on — *vant-* which was taken as a basis for the analysis for the Chinese translation word. If, however — and this would be the explanation facilior — the underlying language was really a Prakrit similar to *Gāndhārī* or the dialect of the *Niya*-documents from Central Asia (*Kroraiṁna/ Shanshan* 善鄯) which do no longer distinguish nom.sing. and acc.sing. the case is even simpler because in these cases the word would[20] have been shifted to the vocalic declension under preservation of the strong stem.[21]

But what about *bhaga-*, which as an appellative normally means "*good fortune, happiness, welfare, prosperity, majesty, etc.*"[22]? Or: how and why should *bhaga-* have been translated as *shi-* 世, "*world*"? The later Chinese lexicographers at least had no problems of identifying the first character and element in *shizun* with Skt. *loka*, "*world*".[23] But this is only a pseudo-solution for the problem: *shizun* is definitely translating *bhagavat* in the first period of translations and so the problem how *bhaga-* should have meant "*world*" is still there. Having a look at the traditional explanations of the word *bhagavat* it becomes clear very soon that the element *bhaga-* indeed caused the interpretators some semantic problems.

If my suggestion how *-vat* (**-vand*) could become translated as *zun* in Chinese is correct, the solution for the problematic first element of the word *shizun* should also be sought and found in the context of Prākrit rather than Sanskrit. (Early) Skt. and Pāli have — beside the regular *bhagavat* — another word, *bhavat,* which is thought to be a contracted form of the former[24]). Unfortunately this is not found in a Buddhist Prākrit such as *Gāndhāri* but one could suspect by the frequency in Pāli-texts that a corresponding form also existed in the language of the Northwest. A word *bhava* in the sense of "*what comes into existence, i.e. this world*", or *bhū*[25], in the sense of "*earth, world*", fits well to the Chinese rendering *shi* 世, "*world*". The underlying word which was the Indic model for *shizun* could have had a pronounciation such as **bha'avand-*[26] > **bhaya-vand-* > **bhava-vand*[27] / **bho-vand* which would have been a perfect starting point—interpreted as *bhava* or *bhū*[28] as proposed above – for the Chinese translation *shizun* 世尊, the "*one honoured by the world*".

But there is more: another translation for *bhagavat* in an older layer of Buddhist translation texts — *An Shigao,* however, never uses it — is *tianzun* 天尊, usually rendered as "*the heavenly honoured*". The word is usually considered to be a Buddhist loanword from Daoist vocabulary[29]. I have some doubts with this interpretation. First there is no clearly dated pre-Buddhist reference to the term found in Daoist scriptures[30], and then our analysis of *shizun* on the grounds of Indian word analysis shows in the last element of the word, *zun,* that it has actually a parallel structure like *shizun.* This should lead us to the conclusion that *tianzun* is not a Daoist word but a Buddhist translation term created on a partially identical basis as *shizun,* and that the Daoists have taken over the word into their vocabulary because of the element *tian,* "*heaven*", so important to them. As we have the same element *-zun* for Skt. *-vant* it seems clear that *tianzun,* too, was a Chinese translation word for *bhagavat* of a *Gāndhārī* word as shown above. So here we have an early alternative translation term for *bhagavat* in Chinese with an identical second element for *-vat* which seems to prove at least that the translators were quite convinced that their Chinese rendering *-zun* was a correct one. But again: what about *tian-*? The correlation *bhaga-*: *tian-* is finally easier to explain than *bhaga-* : *shi-*; *bhaga* was after all a word used for god(s)[31], like a synonym for *deva*, and words for "god" were rendered in Chinese as *tian* without the traditional monolithic Chinese connotation of the "*God Heaven*", but rather the polytheistic meaning of an Indian *deva*. An interpretation of the word *bhaga* as synonym for Skt. *deva* under the influence of Iranian-speaking language-environment[32] is easily understandable. So the rendering *tianzun* for *bhagavat* as "*honoured by the gods*"[33] made perfect sense. Moreover, it fitted to the Buddhist idea that the Buddha as a supreme being was even venerated by the gods such as Brahmā or Indra. As an even more respectful epithet on for the Buddha in terms of meaning — the *one honoured by the gods*" versus the "*one honoured by the world*" — *tianzun* was in a finally lost competition with *shizun* in works translated by one and the same early translator and in different translations of the same work by different translators. This can be shown by various examples,[34] also for the Lotussūtra where Dharmarakṣa's/Zhu Fahu's translation uses both *shizun* and *tianzun*, whereas in Kumārajīva's text we only find *shizun*.[35]

The example of the early Chinese translations of *shizun* (and *tianzun*) for *bhagavat* may — besides providing a fascinating example of the process of word-analysis underlying the Chinese translations of a certain Indian word — serve as a warning against discarding Buddhist Chinese terminology as too fanciful and obscure before having tried to penetrate to the mechanism of semantic-formal analysis underlying these renderings. By accomplishing such a task by carefully investigating text by text, word by word, we may be able to estimate early Chinese translations of Buddhist texts in a different way as is usually done today.

NOTES

1. In general, however, the Tibetan translations, though of later date, were accepted as more reliable than the Chinese: cp. Nils Simonsson, *Indo-Tibetische Studien. Die Methoden der tibetischen Übersetzer, untersucht im Hinblick auf die Bedeutung ihrer Übersetzungen für die Sanskritphilologie*, Uppsala 1957, 7: "*Die augenfällige Treue der Vorlage gegenüber, die gegen den Hintergrund der grosszügigen Selbständigkeit der chinesischen Übersetzungen besonders scharf hervortrat, führte zu einer hohen Einschätzung der tibetischen*

Übertragungen, die allerdings in einigen ihrer Äusserungen über das rechte Mass hinausging".

2. Strictly speaking one has to make a distinction between transliteration—e.g. the Tibetan way or representing letter by letter of the original Sanskrit in Tibetan script—and transcription as the method of rendering the original sounds by similar sounds and the corresponding graphems of the goal language as in the case of the Chinese Buddhist translations.
3. See, Eivind Kahrs, *Indian semantic analysis. The nirvacana* tradition, Cambridge 1998, 34f., who gives a thorough description of the *nirvacana* tradition and its Kāśmīrian Śaiva-offspring.
4. Also in the case of translation of Buddhist texts into Central-Asian languages such as Khotanese, Tocharian, Uighur, which vocabulary becomes not so evident under the aspect of word-formation there is a high possibility that words were translated on the basis of *nirvacana*-analysis like in Tibetan and in Chinese.
5. [The data used in this article were retrieved by means of the digital *Chinese Electronic Tripiṭaka Series,* CBETA-*Dianzi-fodian-xilie* 電子佛典系列, procured by the *Chinese Buddhist Electronic Text Association/ Zhonghua-dianzi-fodien-xiehui* 中華電子佛典協會 and verified in the printed edition of the *Taishō-canon* (T.)] Even the dictionaries of the *Tang*- period were still aware of that equation: Huilin's 慧琳 *Yiqie-jing-yinyi* 一切經音義, T.2128.313c.: 薄伽梵 古譯爲世尊世出世間咸尊重 ("*bhagavān: . . . in old translations this is called "world-honoured"* (*shizun*), (*because he*) *is venerated by all beyond the world and in the world.*"), and 479c: 婆伽婆。此云世尊。 ("*pojiapo* (*bhagavā*)*: this means "world- honoured"* (*shizun*)."); both passages are almost identically quoted in the continuation of Huilin's work, the *Xu-yiqie-jing-yinyi* 續一切經音義, compiled by Xilin 希麟 : T.2129.934c.23ff. and 954c.2f., 966a.18f., 971a.16ff., 973a.11ff.
6. Or: *zhu* 住.
7. The most famous translator from the beginning of this period is Kumārajīva; for examples of the formula see T.262, his famous translation of the *Saddharmapuṇḍarīka-sūtra*.
8. Erich Zürcher, "A New Look at the Earliest Chinese Buddhist Texts" in Koichi Shinohara, Gregory Schopen (ed.), *From Benares to Beijing. Essays on Buddhism and Chinese Religion in Honour of Prof. Jan Yün-Hua,* Oakville, New York, London 1991, 288, thinks that the change to the more recent formula was caused by metric reasons. In a later article, "Vernacular Elements in Early Buddhist Texts: An attempt to define the optimal source materials", *Sinō-Platonic Papers* 71 (March 1996), 1-31), however, Zürcher comes to an interpretation (p.2) close to the one presented in the present article. Zürcher stresses the importance of this initial formula for the relative dating of a translation (p.3) and gives a helpful list of pre-*Kumārajīva*-translations with the formula *wen rushi* as "*criterium for selection*".
9. I leave aside T. 784, the "*Sūtra in forty-two chapters*", *Sishier-zhang-jing* 四十二章經, ascribed to the legendary earliest translators in China,

Kāśyapa Mātaṅga / Zhe (Jiaye) moteng 铄迦葉摩騰 and *Zhu Falan* 竺法蘭 / *Dharmaratna* (?) by the Chinese tradition, in which *pojiapo* 婆伽婆, *shizun* 世尊 or *tianzun* 天尊 are not found, but only *fo* 佛.

10. It is especially in the period of the *Tang* that "innovative" translators like *Xuanzang* 玄奘 (re)start to render *bhagavat,* or even more correct: the Skt. nominative *bhagavān,* by means of a transcription—cp. T.124 *rushi wo wen: yishi bojiafan zai* . . . 如是我聞。一時薄伽梵在 ("*Thus I have heard: once the bhagavān dwelt* (*at*) . . .").
11. In some cases they even seem to have elided the *evaṁ mayā śrutam*-part of the formula and starting — right to the point, one could say — : *fo zai*. . . ("*The Buddha was* (*at*) . . ."), or *fo shuo* ("*The Buddha said:* . . ."). It is rather unlikely that there were Indian originals of *sūtras* which have now been lost but which would have represented that form of cliché.
12. *Pojiapo* 婆伽婆 is obviously based on the nom. sing. *bhagavā* of a Prākrit form (like Pāli), while in later transcriptions like *bojiafan* 薄伽梵 are based on the nom. sing. of the Skt. *bhagavān.* The word is found in the beginning formula in T.131, 140, 149, 684, 791, while in the other cases the formula has always *fo* 佛 or omits it and start with direct action of the Buddha such as *fo zai*... 佛在 ("*The Buddha stayed in*. . .") (T. 729), or *fo shuo* . . . 佛說 ("*The Buddha expounded:* . . ."). Interestingly enough *pojiapo* or *fo* are only found in the formula — as to have the text look authentical — while in the text of the *sūtra* it is always replaced by *shizun* in case of *pojiapo* and sometimes in case of *fo.*
13. T.1509.70b.14ff. translated into French by É. Lamotte, *La traité de la grande vertu de sagesse de Nāgārjuna* (*Mahāprajñāpāramitāśāstra*) *tôme I,* Louvain 1944, 115ff.
14. HŌBŌGIRIN, Fasc.1, Tokyo 1929, s.v. *Bagaba* 婆伽婆, 46, and s.v., *Buts* 佛 191a. and 192b. *Shizun* became the epitheton of the Buddha to a degree that it could be used for all kind of other "secondary" epitheta such as *sugata, tathāgata, jinendra, bhadanta, mahāmuni, śāstṛ,* etc.: see Hirakawa Akira, *Buddhist Chinese-Sanskrit Dictionary,* Tokyo 1997, 69a., which however do also not reflect any semantic rendering of an Indian word *bhagavat.* The meaning of *shizun* was not at all clear for Chinese learned Buddhists: the *Song*-dictionary *Fanyi-mingyi-ji* 翻譯名義集, "*Compilation of meanings of words translated*", compiled by *Purun* 普潤, gives *lokanātha/ lujianata* 路迦那他, "*saviour of the world*", as corresponding to *shizun* (edition Taibei 1979, 5a.16f.) without any semantic but rather associative explanation: *tianshang-renjian suo gongzun* . . . 天上人間所供尊 ("(*Because*) *he is the one venerated by the gods* (*or: up the in the heavens*) (*and*) *by mankind,* (*he is called world-honoured* (*shizun*).)"), and the same equation, *Lokanātha* : *shizun,* is stated in the *Fan-fanyu* 翻梵語, T.2130.981b.13. originally compiled by *Xinxing* 信行. Modern Chinese scholars closely follow these traditional interpretations: cp. Zhu Qingzhi, *Fodian yu zhonggu-hanyu-cihui-yanjiu*

("*Studies in Buddhist literature and Middle-Chinese vocabulary*"), Taibei 1992, 27 朱慶之, 佛典與中古漢語詞彙研究, 臺北.

15. Mv.13: *Loka-jyeṣṭhaḥ, 'jig-rten-gyi gtso-bo,* 世尊 (edition Sakaki).

16. On the other side the Mv. gives a somewhat artificial distribution when it has as entry no. 2: *bhagavān, bcom-ldan- 'das,* 出有壞, 薄伽梵 (*bao-jia-fan/ *bak-gia-buam*^{h} = *bhagavan*(*t*)), the Tibetan translation—as intransparent as it is: *bcom*(*-ba*) in the sense of "*conquered, subdued, killed*" (which shows that the underlying word was taken as a *bahuvrīhi*), does not at all correspond to any meaning of *bhaga-* (reflecting the "classical' interpretation which puts *bhaga* to √*bhañj-*, "to break") + *ldan*: (modifier) *-vat* + '*das* from '*da'-ba* , "*to pass away*", to √*vṛt-* as in *Buddhaghosa's* explanation in the *Visuddhimagga:* cp. Lamotte, *La traité . . .,* 117, note. 1. The Tibetan rendering seems to be no equivalent to Skt. *bhagavat*—showing that even at a relatively late time when the Tibetan terminology was set up the word *bhagavat* was still subject to interpretations and "fanciful" translations. The Tibetan commentaries on the Mvy. show these problems, too: see Ishikawa Mie (ed.), *A Critical Edition of the Sgra Sbyor Bam Po Gnyis is Pa, An Old and Basic Commentary on the Mahāvyutpatti,* Tokyo 1990, 6 (Studia Tibetica No.18, Materials for Tibetan-Mongolian Dictionaries, Vol.2, The Toyo Bunko), where the explanation of *bhagavat* does not really analyse the Sanskrit word in the line of the Tibetan *bcom-ldan-'das* but gives a sound "Indian" analysis into *-bhaga/bhagna* (*bhañj-*) : *bcom-*(*pa*) and *-vat* / nom. *-van* : *ldan,* going then over to a rather disparate explanation of *'das* without a real connection to the Indian equivalent *bhagavat;* it may be that the commentators did not any more understand the motivation behind *'das* which may have been a tautological rendering for the element *-vat* as belonging to *vṛt-* in the sense "*to go* (*beyond*)". The *lectiones variae* in the different editions seem to indicate that the explanation was far beyond being transparent to the Tibetan editors (see e.g. the *bhagnamara-/ bhganamara-/ bhaganama/ bhagnama-*). On the problem of the analysis of *bhagavat* in Tibetan cp. also Simonsson, *Indo-Tibetische Studie . . .,* 266ff., with the somehow docetic differentiation between a "wordly" *bhagavat,* translated as *leg-pa-daṅ-ldan-pa* ("*the one possessing bless*"), and a "transcendent" *bhagavat*-Buddha for which the element '*das* ("*passing, transcending*") is added to *bcom-ldan* (includes also a quotation from *Abhisamayālaṅkārāloka,* which refers to the "*method of the nairukta*", *nairukta-vidhānena*).

17. It is highly probable that the Chinese gloss was chosen on behalf of its first character *shi-*, correlating with *loka-*.

18. This idea that some of the older Chinese translations were based on a North-West Prakrit original was already brought into discussion by Brough, v. Hinüber, and others, but was fully demonstrated by Karashima Seishi, *The Textual Study of the Chinese Versions of the Saddharmapuṇḍarīkasūtra in the light of the Sanskrit and Tibentan Versions,* Tokyo 1 992 (Bibliotheca Indologica and Buddhologica 3) and other subsequent works. On "Gāndhārī"

(G.) as underlying language of Chinese translations see also: Daniel Boucher, "Gāndhārī and the Early Buddhist Translations Reconsidered: The Case of the *Saddharmapuṇḍarīkasūtra*", *Journal of the American Oriental Society* 118.4 (1998), 471-506.

19. It would have been written as *-vad(a)*: cp. J. Brough, *The Gāndhārī Dharmapada (Edited with an Introduction and Commentary)*, Oxford 1962, 98ff. It is interesting to note that in *Bhārhut* in connection with a pictural relief we find an inscription *ajātasata bhagavato vaṁdate* (see Schopen, Gregory, "Two Problems in the History of Indian Buddhism: The Layman Monk Distinction and the Doctrines of the Transference of Merit", in: StII 10 (1985), 9–47, reprinted in (and quoted after): Schopen, Gregory, *Bones, Stones, and Buddhist Monks. Collected Papers on the Archaeology, Epigraphy, and Texts of Monastic Buddhism in India,* Honolulu 1997, 23–55, p.45, note 14), indicating that at least on the level of stylistic repetitions a connection was made between *bhaga-vat* and *vand-*.

20. Unfortunately the word does neither occur in the *G.–Dharmapada* nor is it found in the *Niya*–documents but the *Kurram*-casket inscription has *bhagavada* (Brough, *The Gāndhārī Dharmapada* . . ., 86) and the *Bimaran* vase *bhagavada* (Brough, *The Gāndhāri Dharmapada* . . ., 95).

21. See Th. Burrow, *The Language of the Kharoṣṭhī Documents from Chinese Turkestan,* Cambridge 1937, 29 (e.g. the PN *Viryavaṁda:* Skt. *Vīryavat*).

22. Cp. the meanings in Monier Monier-Williams, *A Sanskrit-English Dictionary,* Oxford 1899 (Indian Reprint Delhi 1963ff., 743b. s.v. The Chinese glossary-dictionaries may still reflect this meaning; cp. for instance *Huilin*'s *Yiqie-jing-yinyj,* T.2128.313c.21f.: 薄伽梵。五印度梵語也大智度論云如來尊號無量名略而言之有其六種是總稱也義曰衆徳之美尊敬之極 ("*Bhagavān:* (*comes from the*) *Brahma-language* (*Sanskrit*) *of the five Indias; The Da-zhidu-lun* (*Mahāprajñāpāramitā-śāstra, see below*) *says: there are unnumerous honorific titles of the Tathāgata; shortly speaking there are six categories; bhagavān is the* (*most*) *comprehensive name; its meaning is:* (*possessing*) *the beauty of all virtues* (*and receiving*) *the utmost of veneration.*") and even clearer in the quoted passage (line 23) from a work called "Hymn of the Treatise of the Buddha-lands", *Fodi-lun-song* 佛地論頌 (T.1530?), where the all-comprising title (*zonghao* 總號) of *bhagavān* is said to mean what is called luck and reference (*mingcheng jixiang ji zungui* 名稱吉祥及尊貴).

23. From the Chinese dictionary entries of the *Tang*-period and the various contexts it becomes clear that the meaning of *shi* 世 was rather "*world*" (cp. *shijian* 世間, *shijie* 世界) in a topographical-cosmological sense than "*generation*" in a more temporal-periodical sense; see *Yiqie-jing-yinyi* 一切經音義, T.2128.431b.11: 世尊爲世所尊也 ("... *the world-honoured means the one honoured by the world* ...").

24. J. Wackemagel, A. Debrunner, *Altindische Grammatik. Band III: Nominalflexion—Zahlwort—Pronomen,* Göttingen 1975, 259, § 142.c).

25. The Prākrit-form would have been *bho-* (<*bhava*) , taken for *bhu*; the G.-mss. in the British Museum have *bhu* where Pāli has *bhavaṁ* as a vok. of the contracted form corresponding to Skt. *bhavant* (see Richard Salomon, *Ancient Buddhist Scrolls from Gandhāra. The British Library Kharoṣṭhī Fragments,* Seattle 1999, p.25): **bhū-vand* hypercorrectly restituted to *bhava-vand* for sake of translation?
26. In the *Niya*-dialect for instance, *g* is sometimes taken as *y* and this could have caused a misinterpretation **bhayavanda* to **bhayavanda* (for intervocalic *y* for *v* in names: *Budha-deyu* : Skt. *Buddhadeva,* see Burrow, op.cit., 4). Even more important for the argumentation here is the occurrence of the G.-form in the discovered *Kharoṣṭhī*-fragments in the British Library (Salomon, *Ancient Buddhist Scrolls,* . . . 25): *bhayavadu,* and for the hiatus the form *mriaṁ* for G. *mrigo* (Skt. *mṛga*) in the *uddāna* of the G.-Rhinoceros *sūtra*: Richard Salomon, *A Gāndhārī Version of the Rhinoceros Sūtra. British Library Kharoṣṭhī Fragment 5B,* Seattle, London 2000, 37, 82, 190.
27. This form could also have been occurred ad hoc by haplological process on the basis of (Skt.) *bhavant* (*bhava-vant*).
28. Reinterpreted through "hypercorrect" reconstitution or scribe convention of or for G.– *o-* representing—*u-*, for which see Richard Salomon, A *Gāndhārī Version. . .,* 79f.?
29. Both *Hanyu-dacidian* 2, 1439a. and *Morohashi* 5833.964 seem to presuppose this by first giving the Daoist and secondly the Buddhist meaning. There is, however, no earlier evidence of the Daoist use of the term than its earliest Buddhist occurrence (personal communication by Livia Kohn; see also Yamada Yoshiaki, "The Lingbao School" in Livia Kohn (ed.), *Daoism Handbook,* Leiden, Boston, Köln 2000 (HdO4.14) (Chapter Nine), 225 and passim).
30. E.g. in *Han*-texts in which we would expect it given the context: cp. Anna K. Seidel, *La divinisation de Lao Tseu dans le Taoisme des Han,* Paris 1992.
31. Originally meaning "*dispenser*" (√*bhaj-*, "*to divide, distribute*") — Monier-Williams: "*gracious lord, patron*"; *Petersburger Wörterbuch,* vol. V, 169: "*reicher oder gnädiger Herr, Schutzherr*" — and being used for the Vedic god *Bhága* but also as an epitheton for other gods.
32. Corresponding Iranian words with the clear semantic "*god*": Avestan *baga,* Young-Avestan, *baγa,* Sogdian *βγ-*, Middle-Persian *βγ,* Parthian *bg*. Manfred Mayrhofer, *Etymologisches Wörterbuch des Altindoarischen,* vol.2, Heidelberg 1992, 239f., s.v., *bhága.* See also the strong presence of the Iranian word *baga* for god in *Kuṣāna*–epigraphy and — coinage: on a coin *Bagobosdo* ("*the god Buddha*"), John M. Rosenfield, *The Dynastic Arts of the Kushans,* Delhi 1993, 77, or *bagopouro* ("*Son of God*" : Skt. *devaputra*), *bagoshao* ("*God King*" : Skt. *deva rājā*) for the rulers: op.cit., 202. It may be of some interest, that at the very contact point of the Indian "sphere" and the Central-Asian–"sphere" of the *Kuṣāna*-empire the (royal) name

of *Bhāgadatta/Bhagadatta* is found in the *Paṭola-Ṣāhi* inscription of Hatun: Gérard Fussman, "Chilas, Hatun et les bronzes bouddhiques du Cachemire" in Karl Jettmar, Ditte König, Martin Bemmann (ed.), *Antiquities of Northern Pakistan, Reports and Studies,* Vol. 2, Mainz 1993, 9f. and 16f.; this name may well have meant "*given by the gods*" like its Skt. parallel *Devadatta.*

33. The *locus classicus* in Buddhist commentary literature — on the early *Wuliangshou-jing* 無量壽經 *Sukhāvatīvyūha* (T.360), attributed to *Kang Sengkai* 康僧鎧 *Saṅghavarman* from the middle of the 3rd century, but being shifted to the first half of the 5th century by modern scholarship (see Kenneth K. Tanaka, *The Dawn of Chinese Pure Land Buddhist Doctrine — Ching-ying Hui-yüan's Commentary on the Visualization Sutra,* Albany 1990, 16; more hesitating: Luis O. Goméz, *The Land of Bliss. The Paradise of the Buddha, Sanskrit and Chinese Versions of the Sukhāvatīvyūha Sutras,* Honolulu, Kyoto 1996, 126), the *Wuliangshou-jing-yishu* 無量壽經義疏 (T.1745) by *Huiyuan* 慧遠 (pseud. *Jingying* 淨影) of the *Sui* dynasty—has exactly this interpretation: 天尊是沸異名。天有五種。如涅槃經。佛於五中上。故曰天尊 ("*Tianzun is a different name for the Buddha. There are five kinds of gods* (*deva*). *As the Parinirvāṇasūtra* (*says*)*: The Buddha is the highest among the gods; that is why* (*he*) *is called the* '*one honoured by the gods*'.") (quoted after Ōda, *Bukkyō-daijiten,* 1251c.).

34. The early occurrences are rare: first in *Tanguo* 曇果 / *Dharmaphala* (?) and *Kang Mengxiang's* 康孟詳 *Zhong-benqi-jing* 中本起經, T.196.149a.23, where the Buddha is addressed as *tianzun* (which the *Song-*, *Yuan-* and *Ming*-editions change into the synonym *shenzun* 神尊 [sic!]), while in other places of the same *sūtra* we still find *shizun* (49 times). This *sūtra* has also a very special beginning: *A'nan yue: wu xi cong fo wen rushi. Yishi fo zai* . . . 阿難曰。吾昔從佛聞如是。一時佛在 ("*Ānanda said: I have heard from the Buddha: Once the Buddha dwelt* (*at*) . . ."), which is also the beginning of *Faju*'s 法炬 *Luoyun-renru-jing* 羅云忍辱經, T.500. *Kang Sengkai's* 康僧鎧 *Wuliang-shou-jing* 無量壽經 (T.360, see note ??) has *tianzun* once (266c.5), but 20 times *shizun*; here also the initial formula of the *sūtra* is interesting in terms of the syntax: *wo wen rushi: yishi fo zai* . . . 我聞如是。一時佛在, putting the pronoun *wo* 我 in front of the older *wen rushi* . . . 聞如是 . . . .*Kang Senhui's* 康僧會 *Liudu-ji-jing* 六度集經 (T.152) has two occurrences of *tianzun,* but 18 times *shizun. Zhi Qian* 支謙, in his *Fanmo-yu-jing* 梵摩渝經 (T.76), has far the most *tianzun* in one *sūtra* (883c.17, 884c.5, 885a.25, 886a.6, 886a.10), but again has one *shizun* (886a.18); see also the same translator's *Bashi-jing* 八師經 (T.581), where only *tianzun* occurs 3 times (965a.8, 965a.9, 965a.14). In *Fali's* 法立 and *Faju*'s *Zhu-defu-tian-jing* 諸德福田經 (T.683) *tianzun* is used twice (777a.16 and 17) and in *Faju*'s *Youzhen-wang-jing* 優塡王經 (T.332) once (70c.21).

35. Cp. Karashima Seishi, *A Glossary of Dharmarakṣa's Translation of the Lotus Sūtra* 正法華經詞典, Tokyo 1998 (Bibliotheca Philologica et

Philosophica Buddhica I), 409, s.v. *shì zūn* : 445, s.v. *tiān zūn;* see also on Kumārajīva's translation Karashima Seishi, A *Glossary of Kumārajīva's Translation of the Lotus Sūtra,* 妙法蓮華經詞典 Tokyo 2001 (Bibliotheca Philologica et Philosophica Buddhica IV), 244, s.v. *shi zūn.*

CHAPTER 11

Engaging Religious Language in the Pure Land Path: Repositioning Shin Buddhist Tradition in the Field of Buddhist Studies

DENNIS HIROTA

> It is a matter of neither practice nor good acts, neither sudden attainment nor gradual attainment, neither meditative practice nor nonmeditative practice . . . neither daily life nor the moment of death. . . . It is simply *shinjin* (authentic entrusting that is the Buddha's mind), inconceivable, inexplicable, and ineffable. It is like the medicine that eradicates . . . the poisons of our wisdom and foolishness.
>
> —Shinran, *The True Teaching, Practice, and Realization*[1]

> [B]reak off your thinking that it may be a thinking of God; break off your dialectic, that it may be indeed dialectic; break off your knowledge of God, that it may be what, in fact, it is, the wholesome disturbance and interruption which God in Christ prepares.
>
> —Karl Barth, *Epistle to the Romans*[2]

One of the most persistent voices among Japanese scholars of Buddhist Studies calling for the development of Buddhist theological thought has been that of Prof. Musashi Tachikawa. He states, for example:

> In Buddhist studies today, philological and textual research has established its own attitude and methods. Sectarian study has also, based on philological methods, functioned as a distinct field. It is time that, in addition to these established fields, a scholarly perspective that might be described as Buddhist theology be created. It should not be simply the interpretation of particular scriptures and should not belong to the traditional sectarian study of any school. While standing upon the results of textual research, it should attempt the theoretical formulation of personal Buddhist practice.[3]

Among Tachikawa's methods toward this goal is the use of comparative study, bringing modern Western philosophical thought and Christian theology to bear on Buddhist teachings, with a particular interest in strains of Pure Land tradition.

In this article,[4] I will consider the specific contribution that might be made to the field of Buddhist Studies, and particularly toward the development of Buddhist theological thought as a crucial and integral aspect of the academic understanding of Buddhist tradition, through a consideration of the Japanese Shin Buddhist tradition (*Jōdo Shinshū*), a form of Pure Land Buddhist path established by the medieval thinker and religious leader Shinran (1173-1263). If the theological study of a religious tradition investigates the understanding of the self and the world of the practitioner actually engaged with the tradition in the present, a theological approach must begin with an understanding of the nature of the teachings themselves and of the character of a person's engagement with them. Although Shin has been among the traditions of Japanese Buddhism largely neglected in modern Buddhist studies in the West (and relegated to sectarian institutions in Japan), I believe it has a distinctive contribution to make to the fields of Buddhist studies and that this contribution might be illuminated through a radical revision of the comparative presuppositions that have been imposed on Shin from Western perspectives in the past.

To clarify the kind of contribution that might be made, however, we must begin by grasping the reasons for its marginalization in Western Buddhist studies.

There is little need to make the case that the Shin Buddhist tradition, one of the largest Buddhist movements in the world today with a continuous, well-documented history of nearly eight centuries, has indeed received disproportionately little attention in Western Buddhist studies. The disparity between the significant role Shin Buddhism has played in Japanese society and its relative neglect by Western scholars has frequently been remarked upon. Recently, Galen Amstutz has vigorously argued: "In spite of the major, perhaps even central, role played by Shin in early modern and modern Japanese history, Shin is practically unknown outside of Japan; even among academics it is widely misunderstood."[5] Amstutz has gone on to record the views of Shin, both interested and dismissive, of Christian missionaries and other early Western observers as well as of recent scholars.

In addition, there is widespread agreement among most commentators that the fundamental reason for this imbalance in modern Western Buddhist studies, even given the general marginalization of Japanese Buddhist traditions as a whole as being historically and doctrinally distant from 'original' Buddhism, lies in the close resemblance of certain fundamental symbols and concepts to those of Protestant Christianity. This resemblance has been commented on since the earliest contact with Europe in the sixteenth century. Among some Jesuits who journeyed to Japan, the source of Shin teachings appeared all too obvious—the same devil who had served as Luther's inspiration.[6] In later times, visitors who had a more positive view of Protestant tradition made a correspondingly more favorable appraisal of Shin, particularly its egalitarian religious ideals and rationalist social influence. In any case, the perceived resemblance to Protestant Christianity has led many Western Buddhist scholars, even those initially attracted to Japanese Zen, to assume that Shin represents a debased and simplified Buddhism for the masses. Jan van Bragt, a Catholic priest with long experience in Japan, characterizes the general attitude:

[T]he West is mainly interested in Buddhism as its antipode,

> partly in distrust of its own religious tradition. It is therefore most attracted to these forms of Buddhism wherein that antipodal character appears most clearly—Theravāda, Zen, Tibetan Buddhism. The Pure Land school, on the other hand, is perceived as very close to Christianity and far removed from the mainstream of Buddhism.[7]

I do not believe that the generally accepted "benign" explanation of neglect is wholly adequate—that Shin, with its rejection of monasticism, contemplative practices, superstitious beliefs, and even Shinto rites, and its lack of a colorful pantheon of Buddhas or an aggressive social program, simply fails to interest Western researchers motivated by personal attraction to Buddhism as an alternative, exotic, or activist religion.[8] Historically, I suspect it further stems from various oversimplifications arising not only from "orientalist" attitudes in the West, including the impulse Edward Said emphasizes to explain Orientals to themselves, even when employing the Orientals' own scholarship, but also the desire for Western recognition operative among Buddhists in Japan, on both personal and institutional levels, and an eagerness to utilize Western interest for internal prestige. Nevertheless, my chief concern here is the positive contribution the study of Shin might make to the field of Buddhist studies at present, or more precisely—since historical, political, and sociological study will undoubtedly eventually expand to cover Shin institutions more fully—the possibilities for expanding the parameters of Buddhist studies that might be opened up through confronting the presuppositions at work in the marginalizing patterns of thought about Shin.

The Western Bifurcation of Shin Buddhism

While van Bragt's general account of the interests of many Western Buddhist scholars may be accurate, I believe that further analysis of the dominant views of Shin may be useful, for even in a case like van Bragt's, awareness of the fundamental predisposition that has colored Western attitudes toward Pure Land Buddhist traditions does not keep him from adopting its basic assumptions in his own discussion. In brief, treatment of Shin Buddhism in the West has been based on resemblance with Protestant Christianity and has therefore been cast in an analytic mode of discussion framed by similarity and contrast. Moreover, this mode of discussion has not been simply comparative, but has imposed from the outset an understanding of Shin as internally divided, as though religious features wholly familiar to the West have been incongruously grafted onto alien roots.

In essence, in the standard discussions of Shin Buddhism, including that of van Bragt, the elements of Shin have been divided in two, or separated out into two conceptual bins. On the one hand, there are the religious attitudes and social manifestations that have close correspondences within Christian tradition (Karl Barth, in his pioneering discussion of Shin in *Church Dogmatics*, lists: "religion of grace", "Reformation doctrines of original sin, representative satisfaction, justification by faith alone, the gift of the Holy Ghost and thankfulness").[9] On the other, there are the elements that present instead teachings or symbols that appear distinct from any Christian counterpart (Barth states, "we miss any doctrine of the law and also of the holiness, or wrath of Amida. ... In the Jōdo religion it is not Amida or faith in him, but this human goal of desire [for nirvāṇa] which is the really controlling and determinative power"). These latter characteristics are generally understood to represent the attitudes of "mainstream Buddhism" or "general Mahāyāna." In short, Shin is grasped as a tradition whose evolution has dislodged it somehow from general Buddhist soil, making it comprehensible only by situating it somewhere between Christianity and more "mainstream" Buddhism.

As I have discussed elsewhere, I find the lists of Karl Barth insightful.[10] His view of Shin as resembling Protestant Christianity so closely as to require explanation (or perhaps more accurately: as to afford a convenient example of human religious imagination) is well-known, but his notation of differences is also illuminating. A more recent but rougher pronouncement of substantially the same paradigm may be found, for example, in James Dobbins, a scholar of Japanese Buddhism:

> [L]ay religiosity consists primarily of reverence for the Buddha. ... Shin Buddhism is none other than one specific form of this general lay Buddhist outlook. Its specific aspects are its Buddha, Amida; its path to enlightenment, via Pure Land; its sacred story of how Amida established that path; and its

> practices, the nembutsu and otherwise. But if Shin is demythologized—that is, if its specific aspects are stripped away—then the religious sensibilities and practices remaining are not significantly different from those found in lay Buddhism throughout Asia. They are faith-oriented and devotional. ... What is unique about Shin is not the beliefs and practices it propounds but its advocacy of the lay path over the clerical one.[11]

In other words, when one ceases to be distracted by the superficial Pure Land Buddhist trappings, Shin's thoroughly recognizable core is disclosed: a "lay religiosity" that is "devotional" and "faith-oriented". Shin's significance lies in its explicit development of this "lay religiosity", which stands opposed to clerical Buddhism even while it emerges out of Buddhist tradition.

Jan van Bragt also expounds this basic model of Shin as double in nature:

> The Buddhist Pure Land school contains within itself an unresolvable, living, and possibly creative, tension between its own particular religiosity and the mainstream of Buddhism. When going away too far from that mainstream, it is apt to fall into a kind of folk religion that is hardly recognizable as Buddhism. But on the other hand, when trying to stick too closely to the logic of that mainstream, it tends to lose its own originality and religious dynamism—as well as its inner affinity with Christianity.[12]

According to van Bragt, the "particular religiosity" or "religious dynamism" of Shin Buddhism lies in those elements that at once lend it an "inner affinity with Christianity" and bring it into tension with "the mainstream of Buddhism". There are different ways of handling this dichotomizing model, but the central question here is less the particular manner in which it is shaped than the effect of taking it as a starting point. This is because once the conceptual split is made, there seems to be little interest in the possibilities of reintegrating the divided elements and also little willingness to relinquish the fundamental coordinates of resemblance to Christianity and difference from "mainstream" Buddhism.

In the case of Barth, despite his perceptive account of the

differences between Shin and Protestant Christianity, the polemical theological use of Shin to locate and underwrite the final uniqueness of Christianity caused him to disregard the differences he notes and to focus solely on the similarities. In his view, the entire significance of Shin lies precisely in its similarities with Christianity—which only highlights its character as a merely human creation and thus a foil to what he sees as true religion.

Even in the field of modern religious studies, where no theological interest such as Barth's is expected to be at work, one finds the same impulse to disregard the differences and focus primarily on the similarities alone as defining and significant. Of course, the significance in this case differs from Barth's theological notion of rejecting "religion" as a merely human creation. It will more probably be something like the notion of "lay" Buddhism consisting "primarily of reverence for the Buddha" that grounds Dobbins' appraisal of Shin. For Dobbins, Shin—in its resemblance to Protestant Christianity—serves as an aperture through which Buddhist traditions "throughout Asia" may be seen to harbor a broad "lay" element.[13]

A more subtle application of this same model is found in the field of interreligious dialogue. While from a sociological perspective the assertion of Shin Buddhism as fundamentally rooted in Mahāyāna is deemed "elitist" or "modernist," here it tends to be labelled "reductionist." In an ingenious sleight of hand, it is argued that Western scholars need to uphold the basic character of Shin in the face of those Shin scholars who may resist the notion that their tradition is in essence similar to Christian religiosity, and who may stubbornly insist on continuities with Mahāyāna tradition. In this view, the original bifurcation of Shin is once again simply assumed, and once again the significance of Shin tradition is located in its likeness to Christianity. What is new is the justification of these moves by labeling resemblance to Christian religiosity "Shin specificity" and non-resemblance "mainstream Buddhism."[14] Thus, for Shin Buddhists to give weight instead to elements of their tradition dissimilar to Christianity—for example, the aspiration to realize *nirvāṇa* that Barth notes—amounts to an act of effacement of what is distinctively Shin. It has even been suggested that Mahāyāna thought stands in a relation to Shin religiosity analogous to the relationship of Greek philosophy and Christianity.[15] In this view, as with Barth and Dobbins, Shin would seem to have its center in a Christian-like religiosity, and to stand in distant and uncertain relation to Mahāyāna tradition.

We see, then, that in the bifurcating method of comprehending Shin developed in the West, no justification is regarded as necessary for the original division into Christian-like and non-Christian-like elements, which is merely presupposed. Rather, justification may be necessary for minimizing the distinctive elements and emphasizing the similarities, but it is easily found. For a theologian like Barth, the justification is clear enough: his overriding interest is to illuminate Reformed Christianity or true religion, not to clarify Shin. For the student of religious studies who takes a historical-sociopolitical approach, the justification will lie in an emphasis on overt behaviors that fall easily into Western categories rather than private professions such as desire for *nirvāṇa.* So strong is the insistence on partitioning Shin Buddhism according to Western categories that any resistance to such an understanding is regarded as inherently suspect, a matter of mere apologetics, or ironically, of the influence of Western modernist demythologization, or even—a charge brought by some proponents of "interreligious dialogue" in both the West and Japan—of religious exclusivism.

Toward a New Triangulation of Shin Buddhism

As we have seen, Shin has most often been dealt with in the West, whether by those who have tended to dismiss it or those who have considered themselves favorably disposed, by means of a kind of triangulation, fixing it in relation to, and at some point between, the more stable and integral coordinates of Protestant Christianity and general Mahāyāna Buddhism. This view of Shin against the backdrop of a contrast between Mahāyāna Buddhist thought and Protestant religiosity is not necessarily entirely without grounds. It turns on the apparent shift from emphasis, in "general Mahāyāna", on meditative practices and eradication of egocentric attachments in order to achieve Buddhahood to emphasis, in the Shin tradition, on a conception of "shinjin", or the entrusting of oneself to the wisdom-compassion of Amida Buddha.

This shift, however, has been perceived in the West as moving across an unbridgeable gap, thereby distancing Pure Land teachings in fundamental ways from Mahāyāna tradition and bringing it, despite its use of traditional Buddhist symbols and concepts, into broad alignment with forms of religiosity familiar to Protestant Christianity. The disjunction between meditation and shinjin has sometimes been grasped as corresponding to a basic difference between Mahāyāna thought and Christian religiosity, and Shin has therefore been seen as best understood as hybrid, standing doctrinally on an inadequately acknowledged leap. Underlying such views is not only the initial Western interest in meditative practice and monastic discipline, and the tendency to view Buddhist tradition as normatively an abstruse philosophic system and a metaphysics that provided alternatives to Western systems, but also the reaction against such views resulting in attempts to locate Japanese Buddhist traditions within social and historical categories.

The problem is not with the comparative method itself, which is perhaps both natural and inevitable, but with the notion that progressive refining of the comparison as it has been framed will unfailingly lead to deepened understanding of Shin tradition and its significance. Rather, I wonder if it is not time to rethink the elements of the triangulation and devise a new approach to understanding—an approach that enables contemporary access to the resources of thought and religious life within the tradition. This would be a new triangulation that brings the historical manifestations and traditional formulations of teaching and practice into interaction with contemporary perspectives—whether Western (including Christian) or Asian—seeking to create an exposition of Shin Buddhism that genuinely deepens our present understanding of the tradition. How might such an approach be developed? What would be its characteristics, and what would it illuminate?

In order to achieve a sharpened, more illuminating comprehension of the lived significance of the tradition now or at various points in the past, an approach is necessary that would, I believe, have two characteristics. First, it would grasp Shin Buddhist tradition at a point prior to bifurcation into Christian-like and non-Christian-like elements, and would not originate from division of Shin into two aspects and deliberation about which is properly the focus of research and which is to be disregarded. It is not enough, of course, simply to focus on the established formulations of the tradition itself, which have often been shaped by concern for self-definition within the diversity and flow of Buddhist history. Simply to digest and repeat the Shin Buddhist institution's present representation of its teaching or the doctrinal formulations developed in the scholastic tradition would not necessarily go beyond objectifying the tradition within the framework described above, viewing it as a static entity within particular historical contexts. Research of this kind has already been attempted as a species of fieldwork by Western scholars, who tend nevertheless to treat Shin doctrine within the standard constricted framework of bifurcation.

Thus, an effective approach for a unitive grasp of Shin would, secondly, bring the tradition into a dialogical framework. By this, I mean that one would probe the resources of the tradition for presenting an intelligible self-understanding by being sensitive to the demands of engagement inherent in the tradition, and further, by bringing to bear questions of the contemporary context and of the nature of religious engagement itself. Such an approach may have resonances with the conversational hermeneutic model that Gadamer sets forth in *Truth and Method* to describe the relationship of the individual with cultural tradition in a Western context. There are, however, significant reasons within Shin Buddhist tradition itself for adopting such an approach.

As we have seen, the common perception of Shin tends to locate it in a line of tension between poles of mainstream Mahāyāna Buddhism and Christian religiosity. This framework is often regarded as characterized by a polarity between "emptiness" as metaphysical view or meditative realization and faith as belief. The issue of engagement, however, can encompass both various forms of practice *and* conceptions of "faith," and thereby open up inquiry at a point prior to the distinction between them and thus prior to the objectification of Shin under existing Western categories. This is critical, because Shin is precisely that stream of Buddhist tradition that most radically brought into question the nature of genuine engagement, and sought through that questioning to discover a form of engagement both authentic and available to persons of all capacities and all modes and stations of life.

It is impossible here to discuss in detail the resources within the Shin tradition that provide for an approach that is at once non-bifurcating and illuminating without the imposition of the usual polarized framework. In publications elsewhere I have sought to take up some of the issues involved, including Shinran's view of human existence, of language, and of the processes of engagement.[16] Here, I will simply mention and illustrate briefly several characteristics of the tradition that might contribute to the formation of such an approach.

The Character of Engagement in the Shin Buddhist Path

There are three central characteristics of the Shin Buddhist path that have not been adequately recognized, even in Japan, but now should be explored in order to achieve today a more penetrating grasp of the tradition. The Shin Buddhist path should be recognized to be centrally pragmatic in orientation; inherently concerned with language, most notably as the hearing of the teaching and the verbal act of practice (*nembutsu*, saying the Name of Amida Buddha), but also in relation to the fundamental linguisticality of human existence; and dialogic in its dynamics and conceptual structures. When engagement with Shin in understood in these terms rather than in terms of Christian-like religiosity and non-Christian-like metaphysics, an approach to comprehension opens up that allows for interpretation of the texts, practices, and historical manifestations of the tradition with significance resonances with contemporary thought.

By *pragmatic*, I mean that although Shin is commonly viewed as a system of "faith," it is not a set of "truth-claims" or doctrinal propositions to be accepted as true descriptions of the cosmos in the ordinary sense. Rather, as Karl Barth notes, "it is not Amida or faith in him ... which is the really controlling and determinative power" in Shin tradition. It is often assumed that the relationship between practice and shinjin in Shinran's thought is one of mutual exclusion, parallel to the Protestant Christian dichotomy of works and faith, so that his radical development of the conception of shinjin results in a Buddhism with no place for practice. In fact, however, as seen in the title Shinran applied to his magnum opus, *The True Teaching, Practice, and Realization of the Pure Land Way* (*Ken jōdo shinjitsū kyō gyō shō monrui*), it is practice that holds the pivotal position in his thought.[17] It is not that *shinjin* or persons' entrusting of themselves to Amida's Vow is understood as itself a kind of, or replacement for, practice; rather, genuine practice (*nembutsu*) is enacted by persons who have attained (i.e., been given) the Buddha's mind as shinjin (actual hearing of the teaching). Although Shinran states that shinjin is the true cause of birth in the Pure Land and of attainment of Buddhahood, this shinjin is inseparable from practice (*nembutsu*, Name as concretizing the practice of Buddha), and as in other forms of Buddhism, practice is the foundation of the conception of the path. Rather than "faith" simply as belief or worship, then, it is the category of engagement with the path that provides the appropriate means for approaching Shin tradition and that allows for a vision of Shin within the context of Buddhist tradition. Moreover, it is the linguistic character of the Shin path (hearing the teaching and saying the *nembutsu*) that constitutes its accessibility to human beings regardless of capacity for conventional religious practice.

I will focus here on the third of the intertwined characteristics of engagement mentioned above, its dialogical character. By this I mean not only that practicers understand that, while within their own historical and cultural context, they must fully engage and be engaged by the tradition so that it becomes present to them, but further that the character of the engagement itself is understood to be inherently dynamic and transformative. I wish to explore this aspect of engagement—the dialogical character of its conceptual structures—in part to show how such an approach might be employed to avoid the imposition of the bifurcating framework described above, but also because the approach may offer hints regarding other areas of Buddhist studies, where presuppositions about Buddhist "philosophy" in the reading of texts or "lay religiosity" as a sociopolitical category may tend to dissolve issues of the path.

The Dialogical Structures of Path and Reality in Shin Buddhism

Here, I will take up briefly the two sides or stances involved in engagement—that of the practicer and that of Buddha or dharma (reality and the verbal disclosure of reality). By sketching the conceptual dynamic on each side as conceived and experienced by practicers in engagement, it will be possible to suggest how Shinran delineates the process of engagement and the transformed existence of the practicer. This will serve as a means for grasping the Shin path—including the shift in Buddhist tradition found at its roots from meditative practices and disciplines to conceptions of entrusting oneself to wisdom-compassion—without presupposing the patterns of bifurcation we have considered above. In this way, it will be possible to stake out appropriate groundwork for the comparison of the Shin path both with other Buddhist traditions and with Christian forms of religiosity.

When focus is placed on issues of engagement, dharma in its verbal manifestations is considered not as a system of abstract propositions or truth-claims to be intellectually comprehended or believed but as an articulation of reality realized through a person's engagement. Similarly, the practicers addressed or described in the teaching are not simply ordinary persons in the world, but those transformed through their engagement with dharma. Therefore, whichever side we begin with, we inevitably find it inseparable from the opposite side. If we follow Shinran's basic organizing principle of the Buddha's "giving" or transferring the virtues of wisdom-compassion to beings (*ekō*), and his statement that Amida engages beings and gives them all of the elements of the path—teaching, practice, shinjin, and realization—then it is natural to begin with the side of dharma.

Although this has gone unrecognized in the scholastic tradition, Shinran's thought uniquely emphasizes two overlapping but distinct conceptual frameworks by which Amida Buddha is conceived. One is the concept of two kinds of dharma-body—dharma-body as dharma-nature or formless reality and dharma-body as compassionate means (*hōben hosshin*, Amida Buddha). Here, Amida is understood as reality taking conceptual form in order to make itself known to ignorant beings. The second framework for understanding Amida is the concept of "fulfiled body" (*hōjin, sambhogakāya*) of Buddha in all its virtuous adornments, which is the manifestation of Buddhahood attained through the fulfilment of bodhisattva vows and aeons of practice. For Shinran, Amida as fulfilled Buddha-body is above all characterized by the unhindered light of wisdom that pervades all worlds and works to awaken all beings, for the Primal Vow that informs Amida's Buddhahood was precisely the vow to bring all beings to supreme enlightenment.

Perhaps the concept of the two dharma-bodies may be understood to present a vertical paradigm by which Amida Buddha is seen to emerge into history and human awareness as form from formless reality. Amida as fulfilled Buddha-body would then be seen as a horizontal paradigm following a line of time formed by the narrative of the former king Dharmākara taking vows, performing bodhisattva practices, and at length becoming Amida Buddha and establishing the Pure Land. These two paradigms are interlocking but stand together somewhat like an optical illusion that can be grasped in either way, but only singly, not simultaneously.

Amida is seen either as Buddha compassionately emerging from formless reality or as the culmination of aeons of practice to save all sentient beings. In fact, it is above all the entire causal *narrative* of Dharmākara-Amida that is the emergence of dharma-body as compassionate means, that is, of comprehensible *form.* At the same time, the narrative progresses from the aeons of practice performed by Dharmākara toward Amida's Buddhahood as the formless light of wisdom. That is, conversely, the narrative itself moves toward attainment of the formless.

On the side of the practicer, there is a similar interplay of conceptual structures. Here, it turns on two ways of conceiving reality and two consequent modes of engagement with it. Reality is conceived of as the Pure Land and as Amida Buddha. Engagement, then, is informed by aspiration for the Pure Land and entrusting of oneself to Amida Buddha. These are distinct modes of engagement, although here again this has gone unrecognized in the scholarly tradition. Elsewhere, I have applied the term "teleological" to the former and "interpersonal" to the latter to indicate the difference in orientation.[18] If the former is comprehended as incorporating a horizontal vector characterized by spatial distances and temporal progression, the latter may be thought to embody vertical vectors of immediate relationship between practicer and Buddha. Since Shinran declares both the Pure Land and Amida to be the light of wisdom, we see that these two ways of conceiving reality and two modes of engagement are interlocking. Nevertheless, as with the conceptual frameworks applied to the apprehension of Amida Buddha, there remains an irresoluble and dynamic interplay between them for the Shin practicer. Shinran's notions that practicers realize wisdom-compassion as shinjin while remaining foolish beings, or that they attain birth in the Pure Land in the present while remaining in this world, arise from this dynamic.

What is the significance of this dynamic interplay of conceptual structures that comes to light when it is asked how the teaching engages practicers, or how the engaged practicers understand themselves and the teaching? Here it is possible only to note that the two forms of conceptual interplay are of course not unrelated; rather, they are integrated in the purpose and functioning of the Pure Land path as Shinran understood it. This was to bring unenlightened beings, who cannot break through the structures of their own conceptuality, to an apprehension at once of the falsity of modes of thought and perception rooted in a delusionally reified self, and of reality that cannot be grasped by false conceptuality. In order to achieve this purpose, a kind of thinking is necessary that enables, through engagement with it, apprehension of inconceivable reality while remaining in the realm of human conception and linguisticality, or, in traditional Mahāyāna terms, apprehension of nonduality through dualistic structures of thought. This thinking is manifested in the dynamic interplay of conceptual structures briefly outlined above, which are set in motion by the engagement of the practicer. As Shinran states:

> Supreme Buddha is formless, and because of being formless is called *jinen* ("spontaneously bringing beings to become so"). Buddha, when appearing with form, is not called supreme nirvāṇa. In order to make it known that supreme Buddha is formless, the name Amida Buddha is expressly used. ... Amida Buddha fulfills the purpose of making us know the significance of *jinen.*[19]

With regard to our theme here, it may be noted that there has been an inclination not to recognize an approach to Shin through issues of engagement, which would grasp the tradition through its roots in Mahāyāna. This has been the case both in the West and also in the sectarian scholastics of the temple bureaucracy in Japan, where a well-defined orthodoxy has been a primary concern. Western scholars have focused not on the dynamic process of engagement, but on more congenial categories such as emptiness or co-dependent origination as metaphysical concepts or doctrinal truth-claims as objects of faith. Both such categories are inappropriate to the core of Shin. Rather, focus on engagement would allow not only for more precise understanding of Shin, but also for new and more pertinent comparison with Christian forms of religiosity, for example, by bringing into conversation Shinran's conception of shinjin and the rich theology of love in Christian tradition. It is the dynamics of love—a term largely absent from Shin Buddhist thought—as paradoxically both divine gift and human capacity that might better illuminate the transformed existence of the person of shinjin than faith.[20] Moreover, it is the highlighting of the category of engagement that may be Shin Buddhism's greatest contribution, as a long-enduring Buddhist tradition with a highly articulated doctrinal and commentarial heritage, to Buddhist studies as a field.

Traditional Buddhist institutions in Japan are increasingly becoming the objects of academic study, even as they appear to be suffering from loss of confidence due to a general malaise among local temples, the unresolved complicity of the temple institutions in outdated hierarchical and authoritarian social structures, and the growing indifference of their congregations to now meaningless ritual practices. There is no question that such historical and sociological study of Buddhist traditions is necessary. For example, Shin institutions in Japan comprise extensive infrastructures of hereditarily-owned temples together with entrenched bureaucratic administrative systems, but they have not yet been adequately studied, either in Japan or the West, from sociological perspectives. Nevertheless, one wonders whether it is possible for sociological, political, historical, and textual study to advance without the development of complementary approaches that treat issues of engagement and the self-understanding of engaged practicers such as those outlined above. Without such approaches, sociological or historical study will tend to fall back on Western categories of religious studies—on emptiness and co-dependent origination as metaphysics, on dharma as truth-claims believed in by laity, on the temple systems as bureaucratic fixture—and thus fail to evolve the conceptual tools needed to achieve a more nuanced and precise understanding of the human significance of Buddhist traditions.

NOTES

1. From "Chapter on Shinjin," Section 51, *The True Teaching, Practice, and Realization of the Pure Land Way*, in Dennis Hirota, *et al.*, *The Collected Works* of *Shinran*, Translated with Introductions, Glossaries, and Reading Aids, Jōdo Shinshū Hongwanji-ha, Kyoto, 1997, vol. 1, p. 107.
2. Karl Barth, *Epistle* to *the Romans*, trans. Edwyn C. Hoskyns, Oxford University Press, London, 1933, p. 426.
3. Musashi Tachikawa, "The World and Amida Buddha," in Dennis Hirota, ed., *Toward a Contemporary Understanding of Pure Land Buddhism: Creating a Shin Buddhist Theology in a Religiously Plural World*, State University of New York Press, Albany, 2000, pp. 223-24.
4. This article was originally presented at a symposium of the Buddhist Studies Forum, Harvard University, March 1999.
5. Galen Amstutz, *Interpreting Amida*, State University of New York Press, Albany, 1997, p. ix.
6. E.g., Allessandro Valignano. Quoted in Amstutz, *Interpreting Amida*, pp. 45-46.
7. Jan van Bragt, "Buddhism—Jōdo Shinshū—Christianity: Does Jōdo Shinshū Form a Bridge between Buddhism and Christianity?," *Japanese Religions* 18(1), January 1993, p. 47.
8. Amstutz argues that it is above all the consequential political aspects of Shin tradition that have made it difficult for Western researchers to grant recognition.
9. Karl Barth, *Church Dogmatics*, T. & T. Clark, Edinburgh, 1961, vol. 1, 2, p. 342.
10. I have discussed Barth's exposition in "Breaking the Darkness: Images of Reality in the Shin Buddhist Path," *Japanese Religions* 16(3), January 1991, pp. 17-45, and also in Hirota, ed., *Toward* a *Contemporary Understanding of Pure Land Buddhism*, pp. 34-38.
11. James C. Dobbins, *Jōdo Shinshū: Shin Buddhism in Medieval Japan*, Indiana University Press, Bloomington, 1989, p. 160.
12. Jan van Bragt, p. 56.
13. Dobbins, pp. 160-61.
14. This is the tack of van Bragt and, under his direction, it was followed by Hee-Sung Keel in *Understanding Shinran*, Asian Humanities Press, Fremont, 1995. For a review of Keel that points out his simple adoption of sectarian formulations of doctrine, see Gregory G. Gibbs, "*Understanding Shinran* and the Burden of Traditional Dogmatics," *Eastern Buddhist* 30(2), Autumn 1997, pp. 267-286.
15. By van Bragt, p. 58.
16. See especially my article "Shinran's View of language: A Buddhist Hermeneutics of Faith," *Eastern Buddhist* 36(1), Spring 1993, pp. 50-93 and 36(2), Autumn 1993, pp. 91-130. For an exposition of Shinran's path within the framework of general Mahāyāna thought, see Yoshifumi Ueda and Dennis Hirota, *Shinran: An Introduction to His Thought*, Hongwanji International Center, Kyoto, 1989. In Japanese, see my book, *Shinran: Shūkyō Gengo no Kakumeisha*, Hōzōkan, Kyoto, 1998.
17. For a complete English translation of all Shinran's doctrinal writings, see Hirota, *et al.*, *The Collected Works of Shinran*.

18. In Hirota, "Breaking the Darkness: Images of Reality in the Shin Buddhist Path." See note 10.
19. Hirota, *et al.*, *The Collected Works of Shinran*, vol. 1, p. 428.
20. I have discussed a Pure Land Buddhist view of love in *Wind in the Pines: Classic Writings of the Way of Tea as a Buddhist Path*, Asian Humanities Press, Fremont (CA), 1995.

CHAPTER 12

The Mode of Existence of Japanese Buddhism: From a View of the Ceremonial Services

KENRYO MINOWA

1. *Introduction*

The Buddhist denominations of modern time in Japan seem to be divided into three types, one is the traditional Buddhist denominations, the second was newly lay Buddhist denominations and the third was new-newly lay Buddhist ones[1]. In this small paper I will make a brief survey of the character of the traditional Buddhist denominations. They are deeply influenced by the Japanese Buddhist tradition, whose most typical characteristic seems to be the ceremonial services (*hō'e*).

From the Nara period, the Japanese Buddhist world had an intimate relationship with the Imperial court and it came to have a similar hierarchical system as the bureaucracy of the Imperial court. Of course, there were some priests who had no interest in this hierarchy, and they made groups in the later Heian period. However, their successors were also brought into the same hierarchy sooner or later.

I will try to make clear the features of the traditional Buddhist denominations from the point of view of the ceremonial services.

2: *Supervising Group* (*sōgō*) *and Ceremonial Services* (*hō'e*)

Ceremonial Services are one of the characteristics of the mode of existence of Japanese Buddhism. Buddhism was established as a religion for the human heart and mind, but in Japan, Buddhism has had since its introduction strong relation with the Imperial court and the state. The Imperial court established the system of *Sōgō* for the sake of controlling the Japanese Buddhist world.[2] *Sōgō* means the group of *Sōjyō, Sōzu* and *Risshi,* like Archbishop, bishop and sub-bishop. In order to be enthroned with the status of *Sōgō,* at first it was necessary only to exhibit sincerity as monk.[3] Later, however, in Heian Period (794-1192), it became necessary to have a lectureship of the several ceremonial services in Nara. After cloisterd government era (1086-1192), services in Kyoto were also added.

After the era of emperor Kanmu (who reigned from 781-806), this became the standard and this system was used to make a hierarchy of the Japanese monk's world, even though it gradually loosened his actual functions. In this way, the method of advancing the Buddhist studies through ceremonial services came about. Debate especially, which was posted in the ceremonial service, had an important role in the advancement of the Buddhist studies. Most monks, of course, who were limited *Gakuryo* monks, were eager to focus the learning. Actually they were said to study very hard.

On the other hand, in the late Heian and Kamakura periods, there appeared the secluded monks (*tonsesō*) who had a different perspective on the sincerity of the mind. They had no interest in getting a higher position in the monk's hierarchical world. They formed the denominations that lead formation of the modern Japanese Buddhist denominations like Zenshū, Jyōdoshū, risshū, and Nichirenshū, etc. However, the tendency to emphasize the ceremonial service penetrates into those denominations too, so in this sense, we can put the ceremonial services as one of the characteristic features of Japanese Buddhism.

3. *Ceremonial Services in the Ancient Japan*

Now let us examine the movement of Buddhism in ancient Japan particularly during the Asuka and Nara Period. When the Buddhism was introduced to Japan officially in AD 538 year, our ancestors accepted it as being the same as our traditional religion, Shinto,[4] which is the oldest ethnic religion in Japan. For example, the old traditional text *Nihonshoki* reported the first official transit of Buddhism to Japan: Buddhism was introduced as the best religion to realize one's wishes.[5] At that time, MONONOBE no Moriya, a representative of the MONONOBE clan, said that Japan was a country with plenty of original deities, *Yaoyorozu no kami,* and it was not necessary to worship foreign ones. On the other hand, SOGA no Umako, a representative of the SOGA clan, who was a descendant of people visiting Japan, insisted that we should accept Buddhism. It seemed that SOGA's opinion made a base to accept Buddhism in Japan.

During the Asuka period (late sixth century–early seventh century), Buddhism was accepted as the religion for the clan, especially of the noble family. Meanwhile, the Japanese Emperor also accepted it as his own religion. After his acceptance, the Buddhism came to hold a close relationship with the Imperial court or state. TAMURA Yenchō said that it was after Emperor Jyomei (who reigned form 629-641) that Buddhism had a close relationship with the state,[6] and we cannot consider Japanese Buddhism without regarding the relationship with the State, especially in ancient times.

At that time there were many ceremonial services for wishing merit-transferring for the dead by the Emperor.[7] The ceremonial services for wishing the peacefulness of the state, which were done by reciting the Chinese version of *Mahā-prajñāpāramitā-sūtra, Dai-han'nya-kyō* or other sūtra like the Chinese version of the Lotus sūtra, *Saddharmapuṇḍarīka-sūtra,* were also held frequently by the Emperor. At the same time the ceremonies of providing food were also held and this type of ceremony was called "*Saiye*". In this way the mode of holding the ceremonial services of reciting the sūtra and providing food appeared. It can be said that the mode of wishing for peacefulness of the state by holding the ceremonial services was established in the Asuka and Nara

Periods. We can regard this type of Buddhism as the Buddhism for guarding the state (*Gokoku-bukkyō*).

The first accomplishment of this mode was found in the policy of Emperor Shōmu (who reigned from 724-749). He made state-established provincial temples in every province, such as Kokubun-ji and Kikubun-ni-ji, whose official names were *Konkōmyō shiten'nō gokoku no tera* and *Hokke metsuzai no tera*. And the central Kokubun-ji was the Tōdai-ji in Nara province and the central Kokubun-ni-ji, Hokke-ji in the same province.

In January the ceremony for the purpose of guarding the state was held in the Shinto style from the 1st to 7th in a court, and from the 8th to 14th, in the Buddhist style. This ceremony was called *Kyūchū Misaiye* or *Goshichinichi no mishuhō*. Discourse was made on the Chinese version of *suvarṇaprabhā-sūtra* in this ceremonial service. Simultaneously, discourse was made on the same sūtra in each state-established provincial temple, Kokubun-ji and Kokubun-ni-ji. These were all for the sake of guarding the state.

The sūtras discoursed upon in these ceremonies were the *Lotus sūtra, Myō-ho-ren-ge-kyō,* the Chinese version of *Saddharmapuṇḍarīka-sūtra, Kon-kō-myō-kyō,* the Chinese version of the *Suvarṇaprabhā-sūtra* and *Nin'no-hannya-kyo.* These were called the "Three sūtras for guarding the state" in Japan.

The monks were supervised by the state and they were called state monks, or *kansō:* The state made a law called *Sōni-ryō* to supervise them. The first law that supervised the monks and nuns was found in the *Yōrō-ryō* that was promulgated in AD 718. The monks were governed from the point of becoming the novice, and the document for certifying novices was called *do'en-chō*. When he received the higher ordination, the document certifying his monkshood was issued and it was called *kai-chō*. We can know that the state governed the monks personally under the Japanese Statute.

After the Chinese monk, Ganjin (688-763), who was famous for transmitting the official higher ordination to Japan came to Japan, becoming a monk in Japan was strictly governed. The State made three platforms for the higher ordination in Japan, one was in Tōdai-ji in Nara Province, one was in Yakushi-ji in Simotsuke and another was in Kanze'on-ji in Tsukushi. Every new applicant wishing to become a monk had to receive a higher ordination at either platform. It means that every monk had to be registered twice, once when becoming a novice and then again when becoming a monk, by the state. Of course, there were several monks who had no relation with the state, but they were not in the mainstream of the monks world. For example, a famous monk, Gyōki (668-749), who was regarded as the representative of that type, was an exceptional example.

4. *The Situation of the Heian Period*

Emperor Kanmu (who reigned from 781-806) promoted this system in the early Heian period inheriting the mode of Nara Buddhism. Emperor Kanmu added the Tendai denomination as an authorized religious denomination in the 25th year of Enryaku (806) and he admitted two members into the number of persons to be ordained annually for the Tendai denomination. The persons to be ordained annually seemed to be executives among the Buddhist monks. In this way the system by which 12 persons would be selected from the five denominations, Kegon, Tendai, Ritsu, Sanron and Hossō was established in the early Heian period.[8] Emperor Kanmu recommended for the Buddhist monks to study Buddhism hard and he made it as a central course of the Buddhism. We can say that his policy made the course of Japanese Buddhism.[9]

There were several famous ceremonial services in the temples of Nara, which continued from the Nara period. Three of those were important for the Buddhist hierarchical system. These three were called "Nanto sanne", and this was composed of Kōfukuji *Yuima'e*, Kyūchū *Misai'e* and Yakushiji *Saishō'e*. Kofukuji was the main temple of Fujiwara family, who located in a centre of political power in Heian period. Yakushiji was a temple established by the Emperor family in later seventh century. Kyūchū *Misai'e* was a ceremony held from 8th to 14th in January in a court and it was an official ceremony literally.

The main purpose of these ceremonies was to discourse on the sūtra. The sūtra seemed to be read in a Chinese way or Japanese-Chinese way at the first and then explained by the lecturer. We imagine that there would have been some questions when the lecturer discoursed on the sūtra. We guess these questions came to have a function as a very important role in the ceremony. It is guessed that this developed into the debate, *"rongi"*.

The original meaning of *rongi* is to discuss meaning and it is mainly to discuss the dogmatic thesis of Buddhist studies. It is not certain when the *rongi* appeared in a ceremony, but we have a guess that its origin appeared in the late Nara or early Heian period because there were several arguments that were called *"jyōron"* in that period. *Jyōron,* arguments of the Buddhist studies, seem to have had a relationship with *rongi.* We have several documents such as *Shugo-kokkai-shō* written by Saichō (767-822) and *Daijyō-sanron-daigi-shō,* by Gen'ei (?-840), these are the textbooks which are concerned with *Jyōron.* We guess that these *jyōrons* became the foundation for *rongi.* The topic that was argued in *jyōron* was divided into small detail, and it is supposed that this detail became a topic of *rongi.*

The oldest ceremony in *Nanto sanne* was the Kofukuji *Yuima'e.* It was established by the Fujiwara clan in commemoration of FUJIWARA no Kamatari's (614-669) recovering from disease in the seventh century. The ceremony was held at the Kofukuji. The *Sanbō-e-kotoba* said Yakushiji *Saisho'e* was established in the 7th year of Tenchō and Kyūchū *misai'e,* in the 2nd year of Jingo-kei'un.[10] The lecturer who finished the lectureship of the Kofukuji *Yuima'e* was selected for the position of lecturer of the Kyūchū *Misai'e* and Yakushiji *Saishō'e* of the next year. The lecturers who finished these three lectures, *Nanto sanne* were called *"ikō"*. Therefore the word of *iko* means a person finishing the three lectures *of Nanto Sanne.* They were appointed as *risshi, sōzu,* and *sōjyō* in the order of becoming *iko.*

5. *The Movement of Middle and Later Heian Period*

Nanto Sanne held in Nara were monopolized by the monks who lived in Nara in the middle Heian period. To deal with this situation the similar ceremonial services were established in the northern capital city, Kyoto. These came to be called *"Hokkyō sanne"* later.

When we examine the text *Sanbō-e-kotoba,* written in the tenth century, we can enumerate the famous ceremonial services as follows: *Kyūchū-misai'e, Hiei-senpō. Shu-nigatsu'e, Sai'in-anan-keka,*

Yamashinadera-nehan'e, Yakushiji-saishō'e, Takao-Hokke'e, Hokkeji-kegon'e, Sakamoto-kangaku'e, Yakushiji-bantō'e, Hiei-shari'e and so on.[11]

Generally speaking, the contents of these ceremonial services were divided into three parts. The first part was *Ganmon,* which carried out the explanations of the meaning of the ceremony and praising the donor who made donations and offerings to the ceremony itself. The second was *Kyōshaku,* the interpretation of the sūtra, the third was *rongi,* discussions of Buddhist teachings, or debates.

The original form of the ceremonial service seemed to be composed of two parts, *Ganmon* and *Kyōshaku.* When it was a ceremony sticking to formalities, the lecturer and listener were selected by a certain procedure, "*Kushō*". *Kushō* means official selections by the noble of the state. The total members who could attend the ceremony were strictly limited. Of course an audience was allowed to be there, but they were usually noble people.

There seemed to be another type of ceremony, which had no limitation, so we imagine that almost all people could attend and listen, if they wanted. Therefore the lecture was also called the *Shōdō,* oratory, that contributed to the people's cultivation and enlightenment.[12]

After Chōken (1126-1203) appeared in the late Heian period, *Insei-ki,* or the cloistered government period, the word *Shōdō* seems to have become a popular word. He was a monk who was famously good at preaching orally and was living at Agu'i, where there was a city branch of the Hieizan Enryakuji temple in Kyoto. The meaning of the *Shōdō* was to cultivate people and to have people get enlightenment by the discourse.[13] The opportunity for it was indeed ceremonial services.

In addition three more official ceremonies were established in the period of the cloistered government, which was situated above the *Nanto-sanne* and *Hokkyō-sanne.* Those were called *Sankō,* composed of *Kyūchū-saishōkō; Sentō-saishōkō* and *Hosshōji-mihakō.* This Sankō was the most formal ceremony in that period.

In the *Eiga-monogatari,* which illustrated the glory of the Fujiwara family, especially that of FUJIWARA no Michinaga (966-1027), we can find the statement that the monks in those days thought it was honor to be invited to those ceremonies by the official selection.[14] From these documents, we can know the situation of the ceremonial services of that time. Buddhist monks centered upon the ceremonial services, especially official ceremonies that had a relationship with the state.

Naturally, there were also other types of monks who had no interest in official ceremonies and success within the priesthood. Those were sometimes monks who dwelt in the small temples in the mountainsides. Anyway it is true that, concerning to the Gakuryo monks of the four big temples like Tōdaiji, Kōfukuji, Enryakuji and Onjyōji, they were willing to conduct themselves in relationship with the ceremonial services and studied very hard. They were eager to occupy high position in the hierarchy of the Buddhist monks of the temple.

6. *Development of the Kamakura period*

In the period of the cloistered government, new type of monk appeared, who did not want to conduct themselves under the official ceremonies. They were called *tonsesō,* secluded monks. We can guess that their ancestor were the group who had no relationship with the state, for example, *Jikyōsha, Hijiri* and *Shōnin.* They were separate not only from secular world but also worldly part of the Buddhist priests. They were usually called *tonsesha.* Judging from the Buddhist narratives, when *tonsesha* appeared, they were living in the mountainsides, had a faith in the Amida Buddha and were very negative toward the secular world. However, at the end of the period of the cloistered government, those appeared among monks who were very positive toward both the Buddhist world and the secular world. Although they were called by the same word *tonsesha,* they worked very positively toward the Buddhist world. We can enumerate the monks of *risshū* in Nara and of Zenshū in Kyoto as typical examples of this.[15] One of the remarkable monks was Yōsai (1141-1215), who was regarded as a founder of the Rinzai denomination. He went abroad and brought back the Rinzai Yōki denomination to Japan, but he did not want to have an aggressive relationship with the state. He was also a secluded monk.

7. *Secluded Monk in Nara and other Regional Province*

In Nara city one new development was seen.[16] That was the

Ritsu denomination. Jyōkei (1155-1213), Kakujyō (1194-1253) and Eison (1201-1290) were famous for their movements. Jyokei was probably a monk who made the ground work for precepts restoration. Kakujyō was a monk who constructed a new theory for higher ordination, and Eison was a monk who made a large group of the Ritsu denomination basing a centre at Saidaiji. Although they studied very hard in Buddhist studies, they had no interest in the hierarchy of Buddhist world, like *risshi, sōzu* and *sōjyō.* It is certain that they also studied under the circumstances of ceremonial services, but they did not pay any attention to getting a position in the Buddhist world rather paid attention to the question what is the most important for Buddhist monk. They became secluded monks and worked hard for the welfare of people.

Now let us look at the example of Eison. He made a discourse not only in the ceremonial services for sūtra explanations but also in the ordination ceremonies. Viewing from the *Kanjin-gakushō-ki,* his autobiography, we can know that he discoursed at the opportunity to give the bodhisattva precepts, or higher ordinations. In the case of praying for rain too, he discoursed for the sake of the cultivation of the people. However the most popular opportunities for the cultivation of people were the *Kō,* that is the ceremony to give a discourse on the Buddhist texts. He used the text concerned about the bodhisattva precepts like *Bonmō-kyō, Bonmō-koshaku-ki* and *Gyōji-sho,* etc., mainly when it was the case for the people's cultivation and welfare.

We have an interesting source document that was written by the monk Kyo'e, named *Shi'en-shōnin-dojin-gyōhō-kekka-ki.* The record of the number of discourses on the Buddhism was listed here. It said as follows:

> The number of giving discourses; from the 5th of Feb. in Katei 3rd year to the 13th of July in Shō'ō 3rd year, within the 55 years, total was 10,721 days, among them, at this (Saidaiji) temple, 9,634 days. Total of giving discourses for the sake of people's welfare was 1,085 days, among them, 437 days for the sake of people interior and 648 days for the sake of people exterior.[17]

It is made clear that the opportunities for people to come into contact with Buddhism were ceremonial services, even though they were cases produced by secluded monks.

Next, let us examine the case of Nichiren (1222-1282). He was born in the Awa region in *Jyō'ō* 1st year. He studied at Seichoji in Awa in his youth, and then he went to Kamakura, later, after 20 years old, to Hieizan Enryakuji. He seemed to be a secluded monk, and we can rarely find the record that he attended the official ceremonial services. He used to give a discourse on Buddhism by letters and thoughtful papers. Of course, it is possible to imagine that he had several opportunities to give discourses on his Buddhism through ceremonies, even though they were few.

It is certified that when he was 32 years old, he gave a discourse on Buddhism at the *Seichōzan Dōzenbō* for a few people. However, he was not willing to become a lecturer of the official ceremonial services judging from the document of *Hōmon-mōsarubeki-samanokoto*. In this document he rebuked his disciple who was pleased at being selected as a lecturer of the official ceremony.[18] Viewing from this incident, he was negative toward taking chances of giving discourses at the official ceremonial services, but this made us notice that official ceremonies were still working with formality and authority. Anyway, he seemed to be against official ceremonies, but it is also true that he had many opportunities to give discourses on his Buddhism to his followers, like at meetings for the sūtra explanation. We have one example. That was at the small hut of *Matsubagayatsu* in the Izu region and he delivered the lecture of the lotus sūtra there.

At very least during the middle era of Japan, the secluded monks appeared and some of them became founders of several Buddhist denominations that continue into modern times. They also held ceremonial services as the opportunities to contact with the Buddhism for the commonality. Of course, some of them were not willing to hold ceremonial services, but they also came to perform ceremonial services as an opportunity for spreading Buddhism to the common people. It seems that the time was probably after the Edo-period.

8. *The Examples of the Kyōshaku, Sūtra Interpretation*

We have remarkable documents about the ceremonial services,

which were classified as *Kyōshaku*. This is the record of a discourse on Buddhist texts and we can get some information from it. It is known that the narrative, which we could find in the textbook of the Buddhist narrative, was really spoken in the discourse of ceremonial services. However, the documents of *Kyōshaku* were limited mainly to those of Agu'i, Tendai denomination, and it seemed that they were concerned with the noble people mainly. It is a pity that we do not have many documents of *Kyōshaku* that were delivered for the common people in the Kamakura period. As a consequence, it is difficult to make clear the real situation of the discourse for the common people.[19]

Finally, let us examined the records of the *Kyōshaku,* sūtra interpretation that was thought to belong to the Tendai denomination. Studies on sūtra interpretation were strenuously done by several scholars like ABE Yasuro, KOMINE Kazuaki, YAMAZAKI Makoto and OSHIMA Kaoru, etc. According to their results,[20] it seems that there remains mostly the materials concerning the Hokekyo discourses. Those materials are supposed to be the record of the ceremonies which the nobles had relations with as donor or listener. The *Kyōshaku* has two styles, one is volume commentary, which is supposed to be used at the Hokke-hakkō, etc., and the other is chapter commentary, which is supposed to be used at the Hokke sanjjukō. etc. In case of the Tendai denomination, the Chigi's commentary, Hokke-mongu, lead those interpretations. There are few materials that conveyed the actual contents of sūtra interpretation which was really done in the ceremonial service, however, most of them are the digests of the contents of the sūtra, which was lead by the Chigi's commentary. Let us consider one example. We have material in Ishiyama temple in Shiga, which seems to belong to Tendai's *Kyōshaku*. The content is divided into three parts. One is a summary, the second one is an interpretation of the title, and the third one is an interpretation penetrating into the sentences.[21] It is also stated that there was a difference among the texts which were referred to according to the denominations.

9. *Conclusion*

The ceremonial services are a characteristic feature of Japanese Buddhism and they are still alive. They are an indispensable element of Japanese Buddhism. Of course, there are many elements or factors in Japanese Buddhism, like funeral ceremonies, syncretism of Buddhism and Shintoism so and on. However, the ceremonial service is one of the most important elements. We can imagine that Chinese culture, which emphasizes the importance of rites influenced Japanese Buddhism. At very least, the opportunities for the common people to have contact with Buddhism are through the ceremonial services. It is applied to both the old type Buddhist denominations like *Hossō, Kegon, Tendai, Singon* and Kamakura New Buddhist denominations like *Nichiren, Ritsu, Zen* denominations. At ceremonial services like *Shōgatsu'e, Higan'e* and *Segaki'e,* people go to the temple and listen to the lecture of Buddhism from the monks. It can be said that the ceremonial service is indeed an indispensable characteristic of Japanese Buddhism and it originated from the style of Buddhism of the Nara and Heian periods.

NOTES

1. This classification is made in religious studies. They divide the Japanese religious groups into three types, traditional, newly and new-newly. I think this is applicable to the Buddhist denominations too. Newly lay Buddhist denominations are established after the late Edo and Meiji periods, for example, *Honmon-butsuryūshū* and *Reiyūkai,* etc., and new-newly lay Buddhist ones are established in the modern time like *Kōfuku no kagaku,* I use the words "new-newly lay Buddhist denomination" in the sense that this is the newest among the newly lay Buddhist denominations.
2. The incident in which a monk knocked down his grandfather with an ox became an impetus to establish the *sōgō* See the 32nd year of Suiko *of Nihon-shoki,* Nihon Koten Bungaku Taikei, Iwanamishoten.
3. See the 12th year of Tenmu of the *Nihon-shoki.*
4. *Shinto* means Japanese traditional religion, but this word is sometimes misunderstood as the special religion, *Kokka-shintō* of the before second World War. Therefore *Jingi-shinkō,* the faith for the Japanese traditional deities, is used in these days.
5. See August of the 13th year of Kinmei of the *Nihon-shoki.*
6. TAMURA Encho, *Asuka Bukkyoshi Kenkyu,* Haniwa shobo, Tokyo, 1969, pp. 5-53, SONE Masato, Nihon Bukkyō no Reimei, Edited by MORI Kimiyukī, *Nihon no Jidaishi 3, Wakoku Kara Nihon he,* Yoshikawa Kōbunkan, 2002, 162-197.
7. HORI Ichiro considered the ceremonies held in Ancient times in detail. HORI Ichiro, *Nihon Bukkyo Bunkashi,* Rinsen Shoten, Tokyo, 1970, pp. 223-270.
8. Dajyō-kanpu, Nenbun-dosha no koto, the 25th year of Enryaku. *Ruijyū-sandai-kaku,* Former part, Sinteizoho Kokushi Taikei, pp. 74-75.

9. The study of Buddhism was regarded as the way of guarding the state and this concept formulated a direction for Japanese Buddhism. UEJIMA Susumu, "State and Buddhism in the Early Medieval ages", *The Journal of Japanese History, NIHONSHI KENKYU,* No.403, Kyoto, 1996, pp. 31-64.
10. *Sanbo'e Chukosen,* Sin Nihon Koten Bungaku Taikei, vol. 31, pp. 141-142, 166-167.
11. *Sanbo'e Chukosen,* Sin Nihon Koten Bungaku Taikei, vol. 31, pp.132-134.
12. See OSUMI Kazuo, *Nihon no Chusei No.2, Shinjin no Sekai/ Tonsesha no Kokoro,* Chūōkōron shinsha, 2002, Tokyo.
13. *Genkō-shakusho,* Dainippon Bukkyo Zensho, No.101, pp. 488.
14. *Eiga Monogatari,* vol. 2, Shinpen Nihon Koten Bungaku Zenshu, Shogakkan, pp. 188-189.
15. MATSUO Kenji said all Kamakura New Buddhist groups belonged to secluded monks. MATSUO Kenji, *Shinpan Kamakura Sin Bukkyo no Kenkyu—Nyumon Girei to Sosi Shinwa—,* Yoshikawa kobunkan, 1998, Tokyo.
16. MINOWA Kenryo made a brief survey of the precept restoration. MINOWA Kenryo, *Chusei Shoki Nanto Kairitsu Fukko no Kenkyu,* Hozokan, 1999, Kyoto.
17. *Saidaiji-Eison-Denki-Shusei,* Hozokan, Kyoto, 1977, p. 214.
18. Edited by Nichiren kyōgaku kenkyūjyo, *Showa teinan, Nichiren Shōnin Ibun,* Minobusan Ku'onji, p. 444.
19. OSUMI Kazuo says that the *Shasekishū* is the direct record of the discourse, if it is true, this text will be a very important document for understanding the real situation of the relationship between the Buddhist monk and the common people. See OSUMI, *Nihon no Chūsei,* vol. 2, Yoshikawa kobunkan, 2002.
20. YAMAZAKI Makoto & KOMINE Kazuaki, Agui Shōdō Siryō Sanshū 5, *Kokubungaku kenkyū siryōkan bunken shiryōbu Chōsa kenkyū hokoku,* No.16, Tokyo, 1995. YAMAZAKI Makoto & ABE Yasuro, Agui Shōdō Siryō Sanshū 6, *Kokubungaku kenkyu siryokan bunken shiryobu Chosa kenkyu hokoku,* No.17, Tokyo, 1996.
21. It is not made clear from when this style became popular and from which this style came out although this style is supposed to be an orthodox style. OSHIMA Kaoru, Agui Choken no "Seppo"—Shoan 4nen Kyuchu Saishoko ni okeru Kansho wo megutte—*Bukkyo Bungaku,* No.24, 2000, pp. 27-38 and OSHIMA Kaoru, Kamonshu Kaidai, *Hokekyo Kochushakushu, Sinpukuji Zenpon Sokan,* No.2, Rinsen shoten, 2000, Kyoto, pp. 630-654.

III

MĀDHYAMIKA

CHAPTER 13

A Note on Nāgārjuna and the Naiyāyikas[1]

ELI FRANCO

The clarification and interpretation of Madhyamaka philosophy, especially that of Nāgārjuna, have been an ongoing concern of Professor Tachikawa throughout his career.[2] Therefore, I hope that it would not be out of place here to contribute a short note, in an attempt to elucidate one of the most discussed problems in the history of early Madhyamaka.

The relationship between Nāgārjuna and the Naiyāyikas, or more precisely, between the *Vigrahavyāvartanī*[3] and the *Nyāyasūtras*, has been discussed many times over the last century. This relation was first pointed out by H. Ui in 1924.[4] A few years later, in his pioneering translation of the *Nyāyasūtras*, Ruben has remarked that *Nyāyasūtras* 2.1.16-19 were written in response to Nāgārjuna's question: "If the knowledge of the objects of cognition depends on the means of cognition, by what are these means of cognition determined?"[5] Similarly, Tucci maintained that "[t]here is no doubt that in this case the compiler of this section of the NS. [i.e. the section on *pramāṇas*] meant to refute the attacks of Nāgārjuna as contained in his Vigrahavyāvartan and implicitly in the MMK."[6] Tucci then proceeded to claim that the two texts are "interdependent" by which he probably meant that Nāgārjuna seems to be familiar with certain *Nyāyasūtras* while other *Nyāyasūtras* are formulated against Nāgārjuna.[7]

In more recent times, Bronkhost has courageously (and improbably) claimed that "The *Nyāya Sūtra* existed before Nāgārjuna and was known to him... . The *Nyāya Sūtra* known to Nāgārjuna appears to have been identical with the one known to us, except for at least one portion which anyhow does not fit organically."[8] Bronkhorst's approach to the interpretation of the *sūtras* has outraged Claus Oetke to the point that he wrote a whole monograph in response to Bronkhorst's paper.[9] His monograph was then reviewed by Bronkhorst,[10] whose review in turn provoked a response by Oetke.[11]

My purpose here is not to review the extensive literature on the subject,[12] nor to analyse the arguments employed in favor of one position or the other. Rather, I would like to shed some new light on the subject by adducing evidence from additional material that has not been available so far, at least not widely available. While editing the so-called Spitzer Manuscript[13] I came across two relatively small fragments (63 and 474) that deal, I submit, with precisely the same subject-matter as that of *Nyāyasūtras* 2.1.16-19 and *Vigrahavyāvartanī* 30ff. The two fragments fit perfectly together and I joined them (digitally)[14] as follows:

63a+474a

1 ///(pra?)māṇānā(ṃ) yadā hi pratyakṣan na ta///

2 ///[t]. ḥ siddha iti pramāṃāny api svāt(ma?)///

3 ///ddhāsiddhaḥ [na] ca pradīpaḥ ...i///

63b+474b

1 ///(sthā)ṇur u[tā]ho puruṣa iti viśe(ṣa)///

2 ///[n]y api kuta ity anavasthā atha pram(āṇa?)///

3 ///(au)[pa]m[y]am aupam[y]ād aitihyam iti///

In spite of the fragmentary nature of the above text we can see on side b (which is certainly the recto) line 1, the end of the discussion on the topic of doubt, which was the immediately preceding topic in the manuscript; the stock example of doubt ("Is it a man or a trunk?") is clearly formulated. In line 2 the topic of *pramāṇa* is already discussed and we find the remnants of the well-known argument that if everything is established by *pramāṇas,* then how are the *pramāṇas* themselves being established? If they are established by other *pramāṇas,* an infinite regress *(anavasthā)* would result. In line 3 one can observe the alternative explanation, namely, that the *pramāṇas* establish each other, e.g., tradition is established by analogy, analogy (by inference, inference by perception and perception by tradition).[15] For these arguments the parallels in the *VV* (e.g., 32, 51[16]) are well-known. On side a, which I consider to be the verso, one can discern the opinion that the *pramāṇas* are capable of establishing themselves as well as their objects, just as a lamp is capable of illuminating itself as well as its object (i.e., one does not need an additional lamp to see a lamp). The argument too is well-known from *Vigrahavyāvartanī* 33, *NS* 2.1.19, etc.[17]

What can we conclude from the fact that a discussion similar to the one in *Nyāyasūtra* and the *Vigrahavyāvartanī* appears in the Spitzer Manuscript? Given that this manuscript belongs to the Kuṣāṇa period, i.e., that it is roughly contemporary with Nāgārjuna, the most important conclusion is, in my opinion, that a discussion concerning the vexing question of how the *pramāṇas* themselves can be established was not unique, probably not even exceptional, in Nāgārjuna's time. The work partially preserved in the Spitzer Manuscript was not written by an original philosopher; it was a compilation in which standard Abhidharma topics were discussed, and among these topics the issue of *pramāṇas* was discussed as well, also as a standard topic. Consequently, there is no reason to assume that the author of the *Nyāyasūtra* responds specifically to Nāgārjuna; he may have been responding to any number of texts, Buddhist or non-Buddhist, where similar arguments about the *pramāṇas* were raised. The same holds good for the assumption that Nāgārjuna knew the *Nyāyasūtra* because he speaks of the same four *pramāṇas* that are accepted in this text. In the second-third centuries there were certainly any number of texts, such as the one preserved in the Spitzer Manuscript,[18] where these same four *pramāṇas* were discussed. Thus, there is no way to determine that Nāgārjuna must have known the *Nyāyasūtra* text in some earlier form. There is a widely spread tendency in Indological studies to arrange all surving works linearly and assume that each posterior author must have known his anteriors. The above note attempts to demonstrate that this tendency may lead us astray.

NOTES

1. I would like to thank my wife Karin Preisendanz for reading this note and making very helpful remarks. The following abbreviations are use below:
   NS: W. Ruben, *Die Nyāyasūtra's*. Leipzig 1928.
   VV: Bhattacharya, K. (tr.), E.H. Johnston and A. Kunst (eds), *The Dialectical Method of Nāgārjuna. (Vigrahavyāvartanī)*. Delhi, 1978.
2. The publications of Professor Tachikawa on Madhyamaka are numerous and stretch over several decades; to mention but a few cf. "A Study of Buddhapalita's *Madhyamakavṛtti* (1)," The Journal of the Faculty of Letters, Nagoya University 63,1974, pp. 1-19; "A logical analysis of the *Mūlamadhyamakakārikā*," in M. Nagatomi *et al.* (eds) *Sanskrit and Indian studies: essays in honour of Daniel H.H. Ingalls*, Dordrecht, 1980, pp.159-181; "*Pratītyasamutpāda* in the Dedication of the *Mūlamadhyamakakārikā*," The Adyar Library Bulletin, Dr. K. Kunjunni Raja Felicitation Volume, Vols. 44-45, Madras 1980-81, pp. 639-653; "Two Kinds of Negations in the Mūlamadhyamakakārikā," *Proceedings of the Thirty-First International Congress of Human Sciences in Asia and North Africa*, Toho Gakkai, 1984; "The Logical Structure of the Tetralemma in the Mūlamadhyamakakārikā"

Studies on Indian Culture and Esoteric Buddhism, 1993 401-421. For his most recent publication on Madhyamaka, which conveniently assembles several essays previously available only in Japanese cf. *An Introduction to the Philosophy of Nāgārjuna,* Delhi, 1997.

3. Occasionally the *Vaidalyaprakaraṇa* is also drawn into the discussion, but the considerations and conclusions about the *Vigrahavyāvartanī* are *eo ipso* valid for the *Vaidalyaprakaraṇa* and therefore the latter need not be further considered here. Further, the attribution of this work to Nāgārjuna is doubtful; cf. O. Pind, "Why the Vaidalyaprakaraṇa Cannot Be an Authentic Work of Nāgārjuna," *Wiener Zeitschrift für die Kunde Südasiens* 45, 2001, pp. 149-172.
4. For this and further references to early Japanese and Western scholarship on the *Vigrahavyāvartanī* cf. H. Nakamura, *Indian Buddhism. A Survey with Bibliographical Notes,* repr. Delhi, 1987, pp. 238-239, n. 21.
5. Cf. W. Ruben, *Die Nyāyasūtra's.* p. 24: "Nāgārjuna (in Vigrahavyāvartinī (sic.), zit. Mādhy. vṛ. S. 59,4) fragt: 'Wenn das Wissen der Erkenntnisgegenstände von den Erkenntnismitteln abhängt, durch was werden dann diese Erkenntnismittel festgestellt?' dagegen richtet der so angegriffene Nyāya das vorliegende Kapitel."
6. Cf. G. Tucci, *Pre-Diṅnāga Buddhist Texts on Logic from Chinese Sources.* repr. Madras, 1981, p. xxvii.
7. In the notes to the *Vigrahavyāvartanī* (*ibid.* pp. 36-37) Tucci maintains that the *traikālyāsiddhi* (*NS* 2.1.8) is "clearly enunciated" in *VV* 20 and 70-71 and is implicated in *VV* 43, 45; the argument in *VV* 31-32 is refuted in *NS* 2.1.17, and that of *VV* 45 in *NS* 2.1.18, etc. However, it is not clear to me where, according to Tucci, Nāgārjuna responds to the *Nyāyasūtras;* Tucci points out that the opponent in *VV* 20 seems to make the same objection as in *NS* 2.1.12, but that does not prove that Nāgārjuna responds to this particular *sūtra,* and in fact Tucci does not say so. He also claims (p. 37) that Vātsyāyana's new interpretation of *NS* 2.1.19 may have been proposed to avoid criticism by Nāgārjuna, but this cannot imply that Tucci thought that Nāgārjuna knew this *sūtra* because he says earlier (p. 36) that this *sūtra* is a reply of the *NS* to an objection of Nāgārjuna
8. Cf J. Bronkhorst, 'Nāgārjuna and the Naiyāyikas', *Journal of Indian Philosophy* 1985, pp. 107-132, on p. 126. On top of that Bronkhorst suggests (*id.* p. 123) that "[i]t seems that the so-called 'Nyāya system of philosophy' arose because someone who adhered to the Vaiśeṣika philosophy wrote a handbook on rules of debate." Further he claims that this handbook "came to be mistaken" for the basic work on a separate system of philosophy. Why such a book came to be mistaken for the basic work (i.e. *sūtra*-work) for a separate system of philosophy, and how one would know that such a mistake has occurred, are questions that Bronkhorst does not address in his paper.
9. Cf. C. Oetke, *Zur Methode und Analyse philosophischer Sūtratexte. Die Pramāṇapassagen der Nyāyasūtren.* Reinbek 1991.
10. In *Asiatische Studien/ Études/ Asiatiques* 47/3 (1993), pp 501-510 (this is a review of two books, only pp. 506-510 deal with Oetke's book.).
11. Cf. C. Oetke, "Pragmatic Principles & Bronkhorst's Maxims of Interpretation," *Studien zur Indologie und Iranistik 21,* 1977, pp. 133-152.

12. For a recent publication which also summarizes previous scholarship on the subject cf. A. Meuthrath, *Die Nāgārjuna zugeschriebene Vigrahavyavartanī und die Nyāyasūtras. Eine Untersuchung des Verhältnisses beider Texte zueinander.* Reinbek 1999.
13. On the Spitzer Manuscript in general cf. D. Schlingloff, "Fragmente einer Palmblatthandschrift philosophischen Inhalts aus Ostturkistan (Ms. Spitzer)," *Wiener Zeitschrift für die Kunde Süd- und Südostasiens* 12/13, 1968/69 [Festschrift Frauwallner], pp. 323-328. "Franco, The "Spitzer Manuscript"—A Report on Work in Progress," in: *Abhidharma and Indian Thought: Essays in Honour of Professor Doctor Junsho Kato on His Sixtieth Birthday,* Tokyo 2000, pp. 562-544 ([49]-[67]), and Franco, "The Earliest Philosophical Manuscript in Sanskrit," forthcoming in *Journal of Indian Philosophy.*
On specific issues addressed in this manuscript cf. Schlingloff, "The oldest extant parvan-list of the Mahābhārata," *Journal of the American Oriental Society* 89, 1969, pp. 334-338. Y. Miyasaka, "Kyōryōbu no danpen" [Fragments of Sautrāntika], *Journal of Indian and Buddhist Studies* 10, 1962, pp. 673-679. Repr. in Miyasaka's collected papers *Indo Koten Ron (Bhāratīyasaṃskṛtagranthanirūpaṇam)* I. August 1983, pp. 151-161. Franco, "The Earliest Extant Vaiśeṣika Theory of *guṇas,*" *Wiener Zeitschrift für die Kunde Südasiens* 44, 2000, pp. 157-163. Franco, "Lost Fragments from the "Spitzer Manuscript," in *Harānandalaharī,* [Festschrift Minoru Hara] ed. R. Tsuchida and A. Wezler, Reinbek 2000: 77-110 . Franco, "Fragments of a Buddhist *Pramāṇa* Theory from the Kuṣāṇa Period," *Bukkyō Dendō Kyōkai Fellowship Newsletter* 4. Tokyo 2001, pp. 2-12. Franco, "Towards a reconstruction of the Spitzer Manuscript –The dialectical portion," *Wiener Zeitschrift für die Kunde Südasiens* 2002, pp. 171-224.
My edition of the entire manuscript is forthcoming in Alt- un Neuindische Studien.
14. Slides of the fragments were kindly provided by the State Library, Berlin.
15. The words in brackets are my conjecture.
16. For further references cf Bronkhorst's review [n. 9 above], p. 507.
17. However, the parallels do not present completely identical argumentations; in the Spitzer Manuscript each *pramāṇa* seems to be established by a single other *pramāṇa,* whereas in *VV* 51 each *pramāṇa* is established by the three others.
18. Note, however, that in the Spitzer Manuscript the terminology differs slightly because the author uses *aupamya* instead of *upamāna,* just as is the case in the *Carakasaṃhitā.,* ed. G. Pandeya, 2nd ed. Varanasi 1983, *Vimāna* 8.33 nr. 4; cf. also *Vimāna* 8.27 nr. 21.

Chapter 14

Are the Mādhyamikas Śūnyatāvādins?

KAIE MOCHIZUKI

I. *Introduction*

If we have this question, how should we answer? As for Nāgārjuna, we must answer "yes", because he called himself Śūnyatāvādin in his *Vigrahavyāvartanī*[1] and *Vaidalyaprakaraṇa*[2]. But we must acknowledge that the Śūnyatāvādin are not only the Mādhyamikas, but also Yogācārin or Vijñaptimātravādins, who are the opposition to them. We can see easily the concept of emptiness also in their texts. I am going to reconsider the idea of emptiness in the Mādhyamika tradition in this small paper.

Based on the question of whether "marked with emptiness" is an orthodox theory of Buddhist philosophy, I will criticize the thought that the emptiness[3] is the central philosophy of the Mādhyamika school or Buddhism. I believed formerly that the idea of emptiness was the central idea of Buddhism and I did not doubt that the teachers of the Mādhyamika school were asserters of emptiness (*śūnyatāvādin*). As the title of this paper is ended with an interrogation mark, my standpoint to this question is a negative one. Because Shiro Matsumoto indicated this already[4], this is not a new viewpoint. I am going to state my personal interpretation of emptiness in this paper.

When I read the commentary to the *Prajñāpāramitāhṛdayasūtra* by Dīpaṃkaraśrījñāna[5], I saw the next passage in the Sanskrit text of this sūtra:

> *sarva-dharmāḥ śūnyatālakṣaṇā anutpannā aniruddhā amalāvimalā nonā paripūrṇaḥ.*[6]

In most of the translation of this text, from old Chinese to modern languages, people have read the compound, *"sarva-dharmāḥ śūnyatālakaṣaṇa"*, as "all things are marked with emptiness". This reading is not wrong in Sanskrit grammar and is supplemented with the idea that the main theme of the *Prajñāpāramitāsūtra* is emptiness. But I knew another reading of this compound which can be seen in commentaries by later Indian teachers, namely Kamalaśīla, Dīpaṃkaraśrījñana, and so on.

Comparing the Tibetan translations of the *Prajñāpāramitāhṛdayasūtra* with its Chinese translations, the latter read this compound as "marked with emptiness". We can judge that this reading was popular in Chinese tradition. On the other hand this compound is read as "emptiness and without characteristic marks" in Tibetan translations[7]. Both readings, *"śūnyatā-lakṣaṇa"* and *"śūnyatā-alakṣaṇa"*, are possible in Sanskrit. So it is necessary to discern which reading is appropriate in the history of Buddhist ideology. I cannot support the Chinese reading because Indian teachers who wrote the commentaries to this sūtra did not read this compound like Chinese translations but like Tibetan translations. In reading this compound, the most important consideration must be how those who spoke Sanskrit read it. One of the commentators, Vimalamitra, who translated this sūtra into Tibetan reads in his commentary:

> *All phenomena* are the sources and constituents. "Emptiness of their own entity" is affixed. Having set forth that [all phenomena] are to be seen to be empty of their own entity, [the sūtra] sets forth that they are to be seen to be empty of defining characteristic. Therefore, it says, *without defining characteristic.*[8]

He reads this compound as *"śūnyatā-alakṣaṇa"*, that is to say, "emptiness and without characteristic marks". Praśātrasena also reads in his commentary:

> *Without defining characteristic:* just as space is without defining characteristic, [phenomena] are without defining characteristic of affliction as well as without defining characteristic of purity.[9]

All Indian commentators read it as "emptiness and without characteristic marks", not "marked with emptiness".

Comparing the same context in the *Pañcaviṃśatisāhasrikā-prajñāpāramitāsūtra,* in the Chinese translation we can see that "all things are marked with emptiness, non arising and non-ceasing"[10]. But in the Sanskrit text we can see only that "all phenomena are non-arising and non-ceasing" and there is not the word "marked (*lakṣaṇa*)" there. Chinese Buddhist would intentionally accept the dogma of emptiness as characteristic. This emptiness was later put into one of the three truths as a positive idea of existence in T'ien-tai philosophy. This tendency to understand emptiness as existence seems to have been produced in the Chinese Buddhist tradition, but we can see it in the Indian Buddhist tradition as well. In early Buddhism emptiness was understood to be an omnipotential idea which could accept the existence of all beings.

II. *The Meaning of* "Śūnya"

It is necessary for us to reconsider the usage of the term, "*śūnya*" at first. Musashi Tachikawa criticizes the modern translations to the passage in the *Prajñāpāramitāhṛdayasūtra,* that is to say "*yad rūpaṃ sā śūnyatā, yā śūnyatā tad rūpam*".

> Should we read "*svabhāva-śūnya*" as "emptiness in its nature"? It is indeed possible to read it as "emptiness of self-existence (*svabhāva*)" and this seems to have been a orthodox reading. The term "*śūnyatā*" means originally emptiness of [something] or zero in number, in short, nothing or lacking. "X-śūnya" means generally "emptiness of X" (lacking of X). If we analyze this compound, it is śūnya with X in the instrumental case.[11]

He argues against readers, who read the compound "*svabhāvena śūnya*" as emptiness in its nature. Based on his opinion, it can be confirmed again that we must read the compound in the *Prajñāpāramitāhṛdayasūtra,* "*sarva-dharmāḥ* [*svabhāvena*] *śūnyatālakṣaṇa*", which I refer before, as "all things are emptiness or lacking of [their own entity (*svabhāva*)] and without defining characteristic".[12]

III. *Usage of "Śunya" in the Early Buddhist Texts*

The category of emptiness is not frequently taken up in the early texts of Buddhism. It is said in the *Saṃyuttanikāya:*

> Ānanda, eyes are emptiness of ātman or the vessel for ātman.[13]

This passage consists of a subject (*cakkhuṃ*) plus object in the instrumental (*attena* or *attaniyena*) with an adjective (*suññam*). The term of emptiness is used in order to express the idea of non-self (*anātman*). But it is not referring to the idea of dependence (*pratītyasamutpāda*) in this context.

And it is said in the *Cūḷasuññatasutta* collected in the *Majjhimanikāya*:

> It is perceived that when something does not exist there, the latter [the place] is empty with regard to the former. Further it is comprehended that something that remains there does exist as a real existent.[14]

This seems to be a wrong usage of emptiness. This passage is later frequently cited in the Yogācāra literature, that is say in the *Bodhisattvabhūmi* and the *Ratnagotravibhāga,* and so on. It seems to have been an authority which they cited in order to insist on the existence of emptiness. In the first part of this passage it is said to precept a emptiness of something, but the second half part it is said to precept an existence of what remains. These interpretations are relevant to the Yogācāra school which established the idea of suchness (*tathatā*) or *dharmadhātu* behind emptiness. But must the emptiness of something lead to the existence of what remains? This adjective, "empty," means only lacking of object in the instrumental case. The fixed form is, as above mentioned, "S+B (inst.)+śūnya" and this means that S is empty of B. Therefore it neve r means that somethings remains in S.

IV. *Usage of "Śūnya" in Mahāyānasūtra*

Next I will examine the usage in the *Aṣṭasāhasrikāprajñāpāramitāsūtra* as an example of the Mahāyāna. Though I had to refer to the *Laṅkāvatārasūtra* and so on, I will refer to it here because of the relation with the *Prajñāpāramitāhṛdayasūtra* which I refer to before. It is said in this sūtra:

> He courses in a sign when he courses in the idea of form.[15]

We must mind that "sign" is not *"lakṣaṇa"*, but "*nimitta*" in Sanskrit. It is interesting that emptiness has also a negative meaning in this context. There is a fear that to understand the form as emptiness becomes to cling a sign of emptiness. Therefore we must carefully reconsider again whether emptiness is a central idea in the *Prajñāpāramitāsūtra.*

V. *"Śūnya" in the Texts of Nāgārjuna*

Next I will consider the usage of emptiness in the texts of Nāgārjuna who established this idea philosophically. In his main text, the *Mūlamadhyamakakārikā,* he did not only related his own opinion, but also criticized the *sarvāstivādin* who insisted that everything is really existent. In the chapters 13, 24 and 25 we can see the term of emptiness in many places.

Firstly it is said in the third verse of chapter thirteen as follows:

> All things lack entity (hood), since change is perceived. There is nothing without entity because all things have emptiness.[16]

Most of its commentators interpreted this verse as that of an opponent and negative opinion which should be denied. Supplementing the last half of this verse with the commentary by Bhāviveka, the *Prajñāpradīpa,* it becomes as follows:

> Because all things are emptiness of self (*ātman*) or a vessel of self, they have emptiness, but they are not non-existence. Therefore all things exist.[17]

Emptiness is understood as a synonym of the idea of *anātman* relating the ultimate existence of all things. This position had to be criticized by Nāgārjuna, but it is interesting that it is understood as his position in the commentary of Sthiramati who is a master of the Yogācāra school and in that of Piṅgala which was translated into Chinese by Kumārajīva.

Next in the eighth verse of the same chapter it is said as follows:

> Emptiness has been declared by the Victors to be the issue from all views. But those who have a view of Emptiness they have said to be untreatable.[18]

He criticized those who have a wrong interpretation of the idea of emptiness. Based on this verse, Bhāviveka criticized the interpretation of the Yogācāra school which did not exist in the date of Nāgārjuna. He intended to criticize those who cling to the idea of emptiness positively. Or did *śūnyatāvādin* already exist then? In the last verse of the same chapter he criticized them, in establishing his own interpretation to emptiness. In his text the idea of emptiness appears in the negative context, and we can not judge that he insisted on the idea of emptiness. As for Nāgārjuna, emptiness is merely one of the means to express the idea of "without self nature (*niḥsvabhāva*)."

He applied the idea of emptiness as follows. In the eighteenth verse of the 24th chapter it is said:

> Whatever is dependently co-arisen, that is explained to be emptiness. That, being a dependent designation, is itself the middle way.[19]

The term of emptiness appears as a supplement to the term of originating of dependence (*pratītyasamutpāda*). Based on the commentary by Candrakīrti, emptiness is what does not arise from self-nature or is lacking of self-nature. This term, emptiness, is used in the context in which originating of dependence is related and it means only things which are lacking of self-nature. This relationship between originating of dependence and emptiness appears also in the twenty-second verse of the *Vigrahavyāvartanī* of Nāgārjuna. He answered the opponent who criticized the opinion of Mādhyamika as follows:

> The nature of the things which is dependent is called voidness, for that nature which is dependent is devoid of an intrinsic nature.[20]

Considering the subordinate relationship between them, it seems to be that originating of dependence is given a great deal of weight there and emptiness is only a supplementary term for it. In the 68th verse of the *Śūnyatāaptati* it is said:

> Since all things are void of an own being, the incomparable Tathāgata has taught the Dependent Origination of all things.[21]

The Tathāga uses the fixed phrase of emptiness and non-self-nature in order to express the idea of originating of dependence. Nāgārjuna used the term of emptiness in the context that all things have emptiness of self-nature and it appears with the idea of originating of dependence in his opinion.[22]

VI. *An Interpretation of Emptiness in the Yogācāra School*

Next I consider the usage of emptiness in the Yogācāra literature. At first we can see an example in the Tattvārtha chapter of the *Bodhisattvabhūmi,* based on the *Cūḷasuññatasutta.*[23] The author criticized the wrong interpretation of emptiness as follows:

> There are some śramaṇas, as well as brāhmaṇas, who do not agree concerning "owing to what there is a void"; nor do they agree concerning "that which is void."[24]

It is denied that the word "emptiness" means only lacking the nature of B in A and is not referred to as the existence of A. They define the right interpretation of emptiness as follows:

> Now, how is void rightly conceptualized? Wherever and in whatever place something is not, one rightly observes that [place] to be void of that [thing]. Moreover, whatever remains in that place one knows (*prajanati*) as it really is, that "here there is an existent." This is said to be engagement with voidness as it really is and without waywardness.[25]

They express in their opinion that something does not exist, but there is what remains. Following their interpretation, the sentence that A is empty of the nature of B means that there is what remains as C or D. They understand the word of emptiness positively as the existence of something and insist on the existence of emptiness. This is a basic guideline of the Yogācāra school and we can see the same statement in the thirteenth verse of the first chapter of the *Madhyāntavibhaṅgakārikā:*

> The non-being of duality, and the being of this non-being, is the characteristic of emptiness.[26]

The characteristic of emptiness is defined as non-existence of subjectivity and objectivity. Different from the definition by Nāgārjuna, who takes the critical point of view that emptiness is also lacking of self-nature, they admit that emptiness has its characteristic of non-existence and are thrown into an adherence to emptiness. This verse seems to make Xuangzang read the compound of '*śūnyatālakṣaṇa*' in the *Prajñāpāramitāsūtra* as "marked with emptiness," not 'emptiness and without defining characteristic'. In the next verse of the *Madhyāntavibhaṅgakārikā* synonyms for emptiness are related:

> Suchness, the reality-limit, the signless, the ultimate, the Ground of all events, are, in brief, synonyms for emptiness.[27]

By expression that emptiness is a synonym for suchness (*tathatā*), a basic concept of their idea, they declare certainly the existence of emptiness as substance. It is obvious for them that "all dharmas have the characteristic of emptiness". It is also related in the tenth chapter of the *Mahāyānasaṅgraha* as follows:

> [Dharma Body has] the characteristic of non-duality because, being characterized by the non-duality of existence and non-existence, all things are non-existent and the characteristic of emptiness is existent.[28]

They state that non-duality which has a characteristic of emptiness is existent.

VII. *An Interpretation of Emptiness in the Mādhyamika School*

Though emptiness had been positively understood as substance in the Yogācāra school, it was inevitably criticized whether this reading was the right interpretation as the orthodox idea of Buddhism. We can see these criticisms in Mādhyamika literature, among these the oldest in the works of Bhāviveka or Bhavya. He criticized their interpretations of emptiness in the thirteenth chapter of the *Prajñāpradīpa*. He spared one chapter in the *Madhyamakahṛdaya* in order to criticize them and defined his interpretation of emptiness in the 236th verse of its third chapter:

> What is emptiness is lacking of self-existence of emptiness.

> Therefore the wise man never sees emptiness as emptiness.[29]

He also understands that emptiness means lacking of self-nature as Nāgārjuna states in his *Mūlamadhyamakakārikā*. He never insists on the super logic of emptiness. His understanding is supported by his interpretation of two types of negation, that is to say presuppositional negation (*paryudāsa*) and non-presuppositional negation (*prasajyapratiṣedha*). It is related in the third chapter of the *Tarkajivāla,* the Commentary to his *Madhyamakahṛdaya:*

> Presuppositional negation is that which proves [another] nature of [that] thing which is [both] similar to it [and] different from it by negating the nature of [the first] thing. For example, by negation 'This [man] is not a Brahmin', it is proved that [he] is a non Brahmin who is different from what a Brahmin is like, viz., a low caste [man] inferior [to a Brahmin] as regards asceticism, learning, etc., who is [as a man] similar to a Brahmin but different from [a Brahmin].
>
> Non-presuppositional negation is that which merely negates the nature of a thing but does not prove [it to be] another thing which is similar to it but not identical with it. For example, [the negation] 'A Brahmin should not drink alcohol' merely negates that much, but does not imply either that [he should] drink a beverage which is different from that or that he [should] not drink [some other beverage].[30]

To understand emptiness in the way of the presuppositional negation seems to appear in the system of the Yogācāra. They negate the existence of self, but insist that there is what remains as emptiness. This interpretation is the same with the position of the presuppositional negation. Bhāviveka understood emptiness as lacking of self-existence in something and he negated only self-existence and never admitted what remained or something else. Of course he followed the standpoint of Nāgārjuna and this is the orthodox interpretation in the system of the Mādhyamika school. This distinction of the interpretations of emptiness between the two school is understood in the way of the distinction of two types of negation. In this context presuppositional negation is the right way of the negation in the Mādhyamika school and the interpretation by Yogācāra school is also to be neglected. It can be said that he apparently expressed the way to understand emptiness in the Mādhyamika system.

In the *Madhyamakāvatāra* Candrakīrti also criticizes the interpretation of emptiness that is based on the theory of the three self-existences (*trisvabhāva*) of the Yogācāra school. He relates in his *Prasannapadā* as follows:

> Your allegation derives from wrongly foisting the meaning of non-existence onto the idea of the absence of being. But we do not declare the meaning of non-existence and of absence of being to be the same; rather absence of being has the same meaning as dependent arising (*pratītyasamutpāda*); so this fault in the idea of devoidness does not make sense.[31]

He neglects them who misunderstand emptiness as no existence. And he expresses that emptiness means dependent arising.

Further Kamalaśīla, who was the one of great masters of the Mādhyamika school, criticized Dharmakīrti's theory of non-perception (*anupalabdhi*) in his *Madhyamakāloka* and said:

> It is not correct either to say: '[Once one] has perceptually apprehended a certain place as being free of another object, then something void of that which is other than it [i.e. place] will be understood by direct perception... and so forth'. This theory [of voidness] corresponds to the voidness of one thing by another (*itaretara-śūnyatā*), and not to the voidness concerning characters (*lakṣaṇa-śūnyatā*). Due to the voidness concerning characters, we accept that all things are ultimately without any nature. This is because ultimately their particular and universal characters as they are established are void.[32]

At first Dharmakīrti understood the interpretation of emptiness by Mādhyamika to be that they directly perceive the non-existence of A in B or the emptiness of A in B after perceiving B. Kamalaśīla interpreted this as the emptiness of one thing by another and rejected that it is established as a [conventionally] acknowledged nature, but not ultimately.[33] The Mādhyamika school understands that emptiness is the emptiness concerning characters and is ultimately established. And what is empty is self-existence and is not separated from a subject, for example, all things. He put the restriction of the term, 'ultimate (*paramārtha*)', on it.

VIII. *An Interpretation of Emptiness in the Tantric Text*

In the last of this paper I will show an example of the usage of emptiness from the tantric text. The idea of emptiness had been accepted in a widely different manner from that of the Mādhyamika school there. In the *Guhyasamājatantra* it is said as follows:

> Separated from the existence of all things, abandoning aggregates, the spiritual elements, bases, the objects apprehended and the subject apprehendor, and based on the non-substantiality of dharma and equality; one's own mind is non arising and has a nature of emptiness.[34]

This verse can be seen also in the *Mahāvairocanasūtra* and seems to be popular in the tantric school. The subject of the predicate, "has existence of emptiness", is the awakening mind (*bodhicitta*). In this context the awakening mind is not understood to be lacking of self-existence, but to have a special nature of emptiness. Using this interpretation positively, they state that the idea of emptiness is an essential idea of Buddhism. But this is what Nāgārjuna and his followers negated as the wrong interpretation of emptiness. Some modern scholars also insist on the idea of emptiness as substance. Does it translate as an essential idea of Buddhist philosophy?

IX. *Conclusion*

At first, we should read the compound in the *Prajñāpāramitāhṛdayasūtra, śūnyatālakṣaṇa,* that all things are empty [of self-existence] and without defining characteristic, not characteristic of emptiness. The reason why the Chinese translators read it as the characteristic of emptiness is that they were influenced by the idea of the Yogācāra tradition and their translations were also very popular in China. Of course we must reconsider that the influence of the idea of Lao-tsi in Taoism on them, making them understand emptiness as nothingless. At least they could not understand the original meaning of emptiness in the Indian Mādhyamika school.

Secondly, the concept of emptiness is to be validly used in the context that all things are empty of self-nature (*sarvadharmāḥ svabhāvena śūnyatā*). Because the subject is lacking of what is to be negated in the instrumental, this term is used in the negative meaning. This negation must be understood in the same way as non-presuppositional negation, therefore it never indicates the existence of what remains. If we judge from the basic idea of Buddhism, that is to say the idea of originating of dependence, the usage of emptiness in the Yogācāra school does not seem to be supported by Mādhyamika literature and it seems to deviate from the right interpretation of emptiness. On this ground we cannot accept the reading of the above mentioned compound as "marked with emptiness".

In the tradition of Tibetan Buddhism we can see a similar discussion between the emptiness of the heterogeneous (*g'zan stoṅ*) and the emptiness of own-nature (*raṅ stoṅ*). David Seyfort Ruegg calls the former "a positive or mystical current" and the latter "a negative or analytical one".[35] Though I cannot consider them in this paper, this standpoint based on the Mādhyamika literature was taken over by Tsonkhapa and he criticized the interpretation of emptiness based on the Yogācāra idea or that of Tathāgatagarbha.[36]

NOTES

1. Kamaleswar Bhattacharya, *The Dialectical Method of Nāgārjuna,* Motilal Banarsidass, Delhi, 1978, p. 83:
   trai-kālya-pratihetuś ca śūnyatāvādināṃ prāptaḥ //
2. Fernando Tola and Carmen Dragonetti, *Nāgārjuna's Refutation of Logic* (*Nyāya*), Motilal Banarsidass, Delhi, 1995, p. 21:
   stoṅ pa ñid du smra ba rnams kyis ni źen pa med pa'i phyir tshad ma la sogs pa'i don khas len par mi byed do źes zer ro /
   Saito, Akita: "Kūsho ronja kara eigi ronja he (From Śūnyatāvādin to Pratītyasamutpādavādin]", in *Kū to Jitsuzai* [*Śūnyatā and Existence*], Shunjūsha, Tokyo, 2000. According this paper, Buddhapālita called himself *pratītyasamutpādavādin.*
3. On the meaning of this term, see Lambert Schmithausen, "Śūnyatā," in Joachim Rittert and Karlfried Gründer (eds.), *Histotisches Wörterbuch der Philosophie,* Vol. 10, Basel, 1998, pp. 628-630.
4. Matsumoto Shiro, *Engi to Kū* [*Originating of dependence and Emptiness*],

Daizō Shupan, Tokyo, 1989. See also Noriaki Hakamaya, Kūshō rikai no mondaiten [Problems in Understanding Emptiness] in his *Hongaku shisō hihan* [*Critiques of the Doctrine of Original Enlightenment*], Daizō Shuppan, Tokyo, 1989, pp. 35-54.

5. Mochizuki Kaie, "Atīśa no *Prajñāhṛdayavyākhyā* ni tsuite [On the *Prajñāhṛdayavyākhyā* of Atīśa]," in *Indogaku Bukkyōgaku Kenkyū* 39(2), pp. 203-206.
6. Musashi Tachikawa, *Hannyashingyō no atarashii yomi kata* [*A New Way to Read the Prajñāpāramitāhṛdayasūtra*], Shunjūsha, Tokyo 2002, p.10.
7. Jonathan A. Silk, *The Heart Sūtra in Tibtan—A Critical Edition of the Two Recensions Contained in the Kanjur,* Arbeitskreis für tibetische und buddhistische Studien Universität Wien, Wien, 1994, pp. 122-123.
8. Donald S. Lopez, Jr., *Elaborations on Emptiness,* Princeton University Press, Princeton, 1996, p. 60. Gensui Shinba, *Saizōbun Hannyashingyō chushaku zenshū* [*The Collected Tibetan Translations of the Commentaries on the Prajñāpāramitāhṛdayasūtra*], Sagami Shobō, Tokyo, 1938; p.8:

   chos thams cad ni skye mched daṅ khams rnams te / raṅ gi ṅo bo stoṅ pa ñid de źes 'byung ba daṅ sbyar ro// raṅ gi ṅo bo stoṅ pa ñid la rnam par lta ba'i rnam pa bstan nas mtshan ñid med pa la rnam par lta ba'i rnam pa bstan pa'i phyir / mtshan ñid med pa źes bya ba gsuṅs so//
9. Lopez, *Elaboration on Emptiness,* p.145. Shinba, *Saizobun Hannyashingyo chushaku zenshu,* p.17:

   mtshan ñid med pa źes bya ba ni nam mkha' la mtshan ñid med pa ltar ñon moṅs pa'i mtshan ñid kyaṅ med rnam par byaṅ ba'i mtshan ñid kyan med pa'o//
10. *Pañcaviṃśatisāhasrikāprajñāpāramitāsūtra* (in *The Pañcaviṃśatisāhasrikā Prajñāpāramitā* ed. by Nalinaksha Dutt, Luzac and Co., London, 1934), p.46: *śūnyatā śāriputra notpadyate na nirudhyate.* Cf. Chin., Taishō ed., Vol. 5, No. 220, p.14a, Vol. 8, No. 223, p. 323a.
11. Tachikawa, Musashi: "Jishō ga kū de aru wo dō kaishaku suruka [How do we interpret *svabhāvaśūnya?*]," in *Bukkyo* 26, 1994, p.166.
12. David Seyfort Ruegg, *Three Studies in the History of Indian and Tibetan Madhuyamaka Philosophy, Part 1,* Arbeitskreis für tibetische und buddhistische Studien Universität Wien, Wien, 2000, pp. 38-39, n.71.
13. *Saṃyuttanikāya* (in *Saṃyutta-Nikāya* ed. by M. Leon Feer, Pali Text Society, London, 1894), p. 54:

   cakkhuṃ kho ānanda suññaṃ attena vā attaniyena vā/
14. Gājin M. Nagao, "What Remains in Śūnyatā," in his *Mādhyamika and Yogācāra,* State University of New York Press, Albany 1991, p.52. *Majjhimanikāya* (in *The Majjhima-Nikāya,* Vol. III ed. by Robert Chalmers, Pali Text Society, London, 1899), pp. 104-105:

   iti yaṃ hi kho tatha na hoti, tena taṃ suññaṃ samanupassati; yaṃ pana tatha avasiṭṭhaṃ hoti, taṃ santaṃ idam atthiti pajānāti.
15. Edward Conze, *The Perfection of Wisdom in Eight Thousand Lines & its Verse Summary,* Four Seasons Foundation, San Francisco, 1973, p.86. *Abhisamayālaṃkārālokā* (*in Abhisamayālaṃkār'ālokā Prajñāpāramitāvyākhyā,* ed. by Unrai Wogihara, Sankibo Busshorin, Tokyo 1973), p. 57:

   saced rūpaṃ śūnyam iti carati nimitte carati/

16. Jay L. Garfield, *The Fundamental Wisdom of the Middle Way*, Oxford University Press, Oxford, 1995, p. 208. *Mūlamadhyamakakārikā* (in *Nāgārjuna Mūlamadhyamakakārikāḥ* ed. by Jan Willem de Jong, The Adyar Library and Research Centre, Madras 1977), p. 17:

    bhāvānāṃ niḥsvabhāvatvām anyathābhāvadarśanāt /
    nāsvabhāvaś ca bhāvo 'sti bhāvānāṃ śūnyatā yataḥ //

17. *Prajñāpradīpa* (in Derge Edition), Tsha 149a 7-b1:

    gaṅ gi phyir dṅos po rnams bdag dang bdag gi ñid daṅ bral ba de'i phyir stoṅ pa ñid ces bya ba'i dṅos po med pa ni ma yin pas de'i phyir / dṅos po yod par źes par bya'o //

18. Seyfort Ruegg, *Three Studies in the History of Indian and Tibetan Madhyamaka Philosophy, Part 1*, p. 133, *Mūlamadhyamakakārikā*, p. 18:

    śūnyatā sarvadṛṣṭīnāṃ proktā niḥsaraṇaṃ jinaiḥ /
    yeṣāṃ tu śūnyatādṛṣṭiḥ tān asādhyān badhāṣire //

19. Garfield, *The Fundamental Wisdom of the Middle Way*, p. 304. *Mūlamadhyamakakārikā*, p. 35:

    yaḥ pratītyasamutpādaḥ śūnyatāṃ tāṃ pracakṣmahe /
    sā prajñaptir upādāya pratipat saiva madhyamā //

20. Bhattacharya, *The Dialectical Method of Nāgārjuna*, pp. 55 and 107:

    yaś ca pratītya-bhāvo bhāvānāṃ śūnyateri sā proktā /
    yaś ca pratītyā-bhāvo bhavati hi tasyāsvabhāvatvam //

21. Fernando Tola and Carmen Dragonetti, *On Voidness: A Study on Buddhist Nihilism*, Motilal Banarsidass, Delhi, 1995, p. 70 and 80:

    dṅos po thams cad raṅ bźin gyis //
    stoṅ pa yin pas dṅos rnams kyi //
    rten 'byuṅ de bźin gśes //
    mtshuṅs pa med par ñe bar bstan //

22. Fernando Tola and Carmen Dragoneti, Nāgārjuna's Concept of '*Voidness*' (*śūnyatā*), in *Journal of Indian Philosophy 9*, 1981.

23. Nagao, "What Remains in Śūnyatā," pp. 51-60. See also Dargyay, Lobsang, "What is non-existent and what is remanent in śūnyatā," in *Journal of Indian Philosophy* 18, pp. 81-91, 1990.

24. Janice Dean Willis, *On Knowing Reality*, repr., Motilal Banarsidass, Delhi, 1982, p. 162. *Bodhisattvabhūmi* (in *Bonbun Bosatsujikyō* ed, by Unrai Wogihara, repr., Sankibō Busshorin, Tokyo, 1971, p.47:

    kathaṃ punar dur-gṛhītā bhavati śūnyatā, yaḥ kaścic chramaṇo vā brāhmaṇo vā tac ca necchati yena śūnyaṃ, tad api necchati yat śūnyaṃ.

25. Willis, *On Knowing Reality*, p.163. *Bodhisattvabhūmi*, p. 47:

    kathaṃ ca punaḥ su-gṛhītā śūnyatā bhavati / yataś ca yad yatra na bhavati / tat tena śūnayam iti samanupaśyati / yat punar atrāvaśiṣṭaṃ bhavati / tat sad ihāstīti yathābhūtaṃ prajānāti / iyam ucyate śūnyatāvakrāntir yathābhūtā aviparītā /

26. Stefan Anacker, *Seven Works of Vasubandhu*, repr., Motilal Banarsidass, Delhi, 1984, p.217. *Madhyāntavibhāgabhāṣya* (in *Madhyāntavibhāgabhāṣya* ed. by Gajin M. Nagao, Suzuki Research Foundation, Tokyo, 1964, p.22.

    dvayābhāvo hy abhāvasya bhāvaḥ śūnyasya lakṣaṇaṃ /

27. Anacker, *Seven Works of Vasubandhu*, p. 218.

28 Paul J. Griffiths, Noriaki Hakamaya, John P, Keenan, and Pau L. Swanson, *The Realm of Awakening: Chapter Ten of Asanga's Mahāyānasaṅgraha*, Oxford University Press, Oxford, 1989, pp. 49 and 285:

gñis su med pa'i mtshan ñid ni yod pa daṅ med pa gñis su med pa'i mtshan ñid kyis chos thams cad dṅos po med pa daṅ / stoṅ pa ñid kyi mtshan ñid kyi dṅos po yin pa'i phyir ro //

Cf. also Etienne Lamotte, *La somme du grand vehicle d'Asaṅga* (*Mahāyānasaṃgraha*), tome I, Louvain, 1973, p.84 (tr. tome II, p. 271).

29. *Madhyamakahṛdaya* III, 263. Ejima. *Chūgan shisō no tenkai* [*Development of Mādhyamika Philosophy in India*], Shunjūsha, Tokyo, 1980, pp.334-335:

śūnyatādisvabhāvena yataḥ śūnyā hi śūnyatā /
na paśyati tato vidvāñ chūnyatety api śūnyatāṃ //

30. Kodo Yotsuya, *The Critique of Svatantra Reasoning by Candrakīrti and Tsong-kha-pa*, Franz Steiner Verlag, Stuttgart 1999, p.19. *Tarkajivāla*, Derge ed. Dza 59b4-6, Peking ed. Dza 63a6-bl:

ma yin par dgag pa ni dṅos po'i ṅo bo ñid dgag pas de daṅ 'dra ba de lag gźan pa'i dṅos po'i ṅo bo ñid sgrub par byed pa ste / dper na 'di bram ze ma yin no źes dgag pas bram ze 'dra ba de las gźam pa bram ze ma yin pa dka' thub daṅ thos daṅ thos pa la sogs pas dman pa'i dmaṅs rigs yin par sgrub pa lta bu'o // med par dgag pa ni dṅos po'i ṅo bo ñid tsam źig 'gog par zad kyi de daṅ 'dra ba de ma yin pa gźan gyi dṅos po sgrub par mi byed pa ste dper na bram zes chaṅ btuṅ bar mi bya'o / źes bya ba de tsam źig 'gog par zad kyi de las gźam pa'i btuṅ ba btuṅ ṅo źe'am mi btuṅ ṅo źes mi brjod pa lta bya'o//

31. Mervyn Sprung, *Lucid Exposition of the Middle Way*, Routledge & Kegan Paul, London, 1979, p. 235. Cf. also *Prasannapadā* (in *Mūlamadhyamakakārikās* (*Mādhyamikasūtras*) *de Nāgārjuna avec la Prasannapadā Commentaire de Candrakīrti* ed. by Louis de la Vallée Poussin, St. Petersburg, 1903-1913), p.499 (Tib. Jacque May, *Candrakīrti Prasannapadā Madhyamakavṛtti*, Adrien-Maisonneuve, Paris 1959, pp.437-438 (tr. p.234)):

abhāvārtham hi śūnyatārtham adhyāropya prasaṅga udbhāvito bhavatā / na ca ayam abhāvārthaṃ vyācakṣmahe / kiṃ tarhi pratītyasamutpādārtham ity ato na yuktam etac śūnyatā-darśana-dūṣaṇaṃ /

32. Kera Ryusei, "Kamalaśīla's Interpretation of *anupalabdhi* in the *Madhyamakāloka*," in Shoryu Katsura (eds.), *Dharmakīrti's Thought and Its Impact on Indian and Tibetan Philosophy*, Verlag der österreichischen Akademie der Wissenschaften, Wien. 1999, pp. 186-187:

gaṅ yaṅ don gźan gyis dben pa'i phyogs la sogs pa 'ga' źig mṅon sum gyis bzuṅ nas de las gźan pas stoṅ pa mṅon sum gyis rtogs par bya bar 'gyur źes bya ba la sogs pa smras pa de yaṅ rigs pa ma yin te / tshul 'di ni gcig gis gcig stoṅ pa ñid yin gyi / mtshan ñid stoṅ pa ñid ni ma yin no // mtshan ñid stoṅ pa ñid kyis ni don dam par chos thams cad ṅo bo ñid med par 'dod de / don dam par de dag gi raṅ daṅ spyi'i mtshan ñid ji ltar rnam par gźag pa stoṅ pa'i phyir ro //

See also Seitetsu Moriyama, "The Later Mādhyamika and Dharmakīrti," in Ernst Steinkellner (eds.). *Studies in the Buddhist Epistemological Tradition*, Verlag der österreichischen Akademie der Wissenschaften, Wien, 1991, pp. 207-209.

33. Candrakīrti had already criticized the idea of the emptiness of one thing by another in his *Madhyamakāvatārabhāṣya* (160, 17-20; 308, 17-309, 1). See Moriyama, "The Later Mādhyamika and Dharmakīrti." p. 209.
34. *Guhyasamājatantra* (in *The Gūhyasamāja Tantra* ed. by Yukei Matsunaga, Toho Shoten, Osaka, 1978) p. 10:
sarva-bhāva-vigataṃ skandha-dhātv-āyatana-grāhya-grāhaka-varjitam /
dharma-nairātmya-samatayā svacittam ādyanutpannaṃ śūnyatā-bhāvam /
35. David Seyfort Ruegg, *Buddha-nature, Mind and the Problem of Gradualism in a Comparative Perspective,* School of Oriental and African Studies, London, 1989, p. 10.
36. Cf. Helmut Tauscher, *Die Lehre von den zwei Wirklichkeiten in Tsoṅ kha pas Madhamaka-Werken,* Arbeitskreis für tibetische und buddhistische Studien Universität Wien, Wien, 1995, pp. 342-348.

Chapter 15

What are Mādhyamikas refuting? Śāntarakṣita, Kamalaśīla *et alii* on Superimpositions (*samāropa*)*

TOM TILLEMANS

Samāropa of X on Y, or superimposition of X on Y, is a widely attested concept in Indian thought, and consists in one attributing a property or nature, X, to Y, which Y does not have. It also, as I shall try to show, has an important role in Mādhyamika Buddhism, and in particular in the so-called "Svātantrika" system of Jñānagarbha, Śāntarakṣita and Kamalaśīla. In what follows, I'll have to presuppose a certain familiarity with basic Buddhist notions such as the two truth theory, i.e., customary truth (*saṃvṛtisatya*) and ultimate truth (*paramārthasatya*), as well as the basic Mādhyamika programme to show that nothing exists ultimately, or really, or by its intrinsic nature, and that things only exist for the world, i.e., they only have customary existence. I would maintain that there are, broadly speaking, two ways to take Mādhyamika Buddhist arguments, i.e., (1) as targeting things themselves and showing them to be inconsistent when analyzed, or (2) as targeting superimpositions and showing them to be inconsistent, but leaving the things untouched.

I

The first way to take Mādhyamika thought is to say that these philosophers show that the ordinary, or customary, things of our world, like tables, chairs, vases and atoms, are impossible because riddled with contradictions, and that these things are hence only thought to exist by people who are systematically unaware of all things' unreality. Who held this? Well, certainly a number of important writers in our secondary literature have thought that every Mādhyamika, or perhaps every true Mādhyamika, held it.[1] But, if we are looking for decisive unambiguous sources in Indian texts, it's not so easy to find sources that actually clearly prefer the first way over the second, although as we shall see there certainly are Indian and Tibetan sources which explicitly advocate the second and take the first as a total disaster. In any case, if we persist in our historical quest for advocates of the first scenario, this way of taking Mādhyamika is, I think, probably at its clearest in Tibetan Jo nang pa texts and Jo nang pa-inspired literature where it is asserted that customary things are "void of themselves" (*rang stong*) and that customary truth is only *blo 'khrul ba'i ngor yod pa* "existent from the perspective of mistaken understanding"—a table is void of tableness, or in other words, a table lacks the nature of being a table when we scrutinize it for its internal inconsistencies, and it only "exists" because people mistakenly think that it does.[2] The first way might even be thought to be a reading of certain passages in Śāntarakṣita and Kamalaśīla which speak of customary truth as "false appearances" (*brdzun pa'i snang ba*) that we have in common, similar to collective illusions; it also yields a reading of Candrakīrti's explanation of the etymology of *saṃvṛtsatya*, i.e., customary truth, as simply "truth for the benighted."[3] The textual exegesis on these passages would take me much too far afield, but suffice it to say that the first way is certainly not definitively ruled out, even though, as will be seen, it was perceived to have major philosophical difficulties.

In fact, the first way gives a rather clear (even if it is perhaps slightly shocking) account of what customary truth would be: it would be very much like a widespread shared error, having about the same the type of status as that which an ethical irrealist, or a so-called "error-theorist", like J.L. Mackie claimed for goodness and badness in his book *Ethics, Inventing Right and Wrong.*[4] In brief, according to an error theory, people understand and talk about goodness and badness and other ethical properties as if they existed, like gross physical entities or the entities of science that make up the "fabric of the world"; but actually goodness and badness don't exist in that way at all and we are just plain wrong; we invented them; they exist only in the eyes of those who are in error, or subscribers to a "metaphysical superstition" (to use J. Haldane's and C. Wright's phrase).[5] It looks pretty much the same for Buddhist customary truth when taken as a shared error and as existing only for the benighted: the first way of taking Mādhyamika yields an error theory, or irrealism. There is however a difference of scope: whereas Mackie limited his irrealism to ethics, the Mādhyamika approach, if it is understood along the lines of the first scenario, would generalize and apply irrealism to everything whatsoever. We are thus closer to a generalized irrealism like that of Nelson Goodman in his *Ways of Worldmaking,* than to the more restricted position of J.L. Mackie.

The obvious critique is to point out unpalatable relativistic consequences. Now, there are ways for a sophisticated modern irrealist, like J.L. Mackie or Nelson Goodman, to avoid the trap of having to say that anything goes so long as we simply think it goes, and yet still maintain that things, or at least some important things, are invented by us.[6] Perhaps a sophisticated first scenario Mādhyamika thinker could follow something like their approach in avoiding those unpalatable consequences, although I'm not sure that I know of one who did so. The minimalist historical claim I want to make now is simply that for many Mādhyamika Buddhists in India and Tibet, the irrealist theory, as formulated in terms of customary things themselves being inconsistent upon analysis and existing only because we generally think they do, was perceived to have (and is still perceived to have) an enormous danger of relativism. Śāntarakṣita's disciple, Kamalaśīla, repeatedly emphasizes the point that, even in the world, simply believing in something or accepting it (*dam bcas pa tsam*) is no guarantee for truth—in other words, the simple fact that something is generally acknowledged (*grags pa*) by the world need not have any bearing on its truth, even its customary truth.[7] We can acknowledge things and get them wrong, and thus customary truth being so simply because it is thought to be so is a woefully inadequate theory of how intelligent worldlings apply the concept of truth. Jñānagarbha, in his *Satyadvayavibhaṅgavṛtti* and Śāntarakṣita in his commentary upon this work, the *Satyadvayavibhaṅgapañjikā,* stress that if something is analysed and found to be impossible (*mi rung ba*) because contradictory, it is just plain impossible and that's the end of it (*mi rung du zad pa*)—thus we supposedly run the risk of refuting customary truth altogether (*gnod pa 'ba' zhig tu zad do*).[8] As for a Jo nang pa-style move of saying that customary truth does not exist, but just "exists for mistaken minds" (*blo 'khrul ba'i ngor yod pa*), this does not seem to have been explicitly argued against by Jñānagarbha, Śāntarakṣita and Kamalaśīla. In any case, the Jo nang pa's adversaries in Tibet, notably the dGe lugs pa, did point out problems with this latter move, criticizing it for its arbitrary and relativistic account of truth, or for dispensing with truth completely.

II

Let us now go to the second way of taking Mādhyamika Buddhist arguments. On this scenario the Mādhyamikas show that certain recurrent fictitious natures that people project, or superimpose, upon things are impossible and erroneous, but that things without these natures are not touched by these refutations at all.

It is quite clear that the second position is that of Śāntarakṣita, Kamalaśīla and Jñānagarbha, viz., some of the principal thinkers of the so-called Svātantrika Mādhyamika school. To bring this out consider the following two quotations. First of all, a passage from Jñānagarbha's *Satyadvayavibhaṅgavṛtti* (D. 12a-b):

> *gzugs la sogs pa'i lus rtog pa'i nyes pas ma sbags pa gzhan gyi dbang gi bdag nyid rnam par shes pa tsam snang ba dgag par mi nus pa 'ba' zhig tu ma zad kyi / byed na byed pa po la mngon sum la sogs pas phyir gnod pa kho na byed do //*
>
> "We cannot negate physical things, such as visible matter and the like, which are untainted by conceptualization's corruptions, are of a dependent nature, and which are appearances to simple [non-conceptual] cognition. Not only is this impossible, but if we did [negate such things] then the

> person who performed [this negation] would in fact be subsequently refuted by direct perception (*pratyakṣa*) and other [valid cognitions]."

Śāntarakṣita comments upon, and obviously accepts, these passages in his *Satyadvayavibhaṅgapañjikā*.

Next, compare what Śāntarakṣita's disciple, Kamalaśīla, has to say in the *Madhyamakāloka* (D. 180a):

> *des na dngos po rnams kyi ngo bo nyid kun rdzob pa la yang gnod pa ni mi byed kyi / 'on kyang de la bden pa'i rnam pa nyid du sgro btags pa sel ba'i phyir rab tu sgrub par byed pa kho na yin no //*
>
> "We do not invalidate the customary natures of entities, but instead just prove [the absence of real intrinsic nature] in order to exclude what is superimposed upon the [customary entities] as their aspect of being true (*bden pa'i rnam pa*)."

What we see in both these quotes is that it is an extremely important feature of these writers' philosophy that the Mādhyamika refutes only our superimpositions (*samāropa*), i.e., our inveterate tendencies to distort the world by systematically imposing upon it "intrinsic natures" (*svabhāva*). The Mādhyamika does not then refute ordinary things, so-called customary truth, because if he did, he would himself be simply refuted by empirical evidence, i.e., perception (*pratyakṣa*). *Svabhāva* is thus a false projection upon otherwise innocuous objects of our customary world that do not have such *svabhāva*, and the task of the Mādhyamika is to refute these projections, but not the customary world itself.

III

So much for the texts, at least for the moment. Let me however stay historically oriented and ask from a broader point of view what the issues between the rival ways of taking Mādhyamika might have come down to. I think we can profitably use some philosophy here to bring out the history of the ideas: the difference, at least to an important degree, came down to some rival Buddhist twists on anti-realist themes.

The first way, as I mentioned, was a type of generalized error-theory or irrealism, but it is much less obvious as to what sort of anti-realism the second way would yield. So let's backtrack a bit and look at possible varieties of anti-realism. The entry on "Realism and Antirealism" in the recently published *Routledge Encyclopedia of Philosophy,* after several disclaimers about how the terms are used differently by different philosophers, gives us a working idea as to what the issue is about:

> "A realist about Xs, for example, maintains that Xs (or facts or states of affairs involving them) exist independently of how anyone thinks or feels about them; whereas an anti-realist holds that they are so dependent."[9]

If we provisionally adopt John Haldane's and Crispin Wright's so-called "fair characterization of an intuitive realism",[10] the fundamental core of realism is a fusion of two ideas, deference to the independent and objective facts that make true beliefs true and the self-assurance that we can know these facts. The deference typically consists in an acceptance of an external world existing independently of us, of our concepts, attitudes, descriptions and beliefs; the self-assurance is the confidence that at least in some favorable circumstances we can come to know this independent world of facts as it is.

Now, straight off, we can say that no Mādhyamika, be he Svātantrika or Prāsaṅgika, will countenance there being a genuinely real external world completely independent of mind—in that sense, this philosophy clearly is *not* realist, when the term is used in the full sense following Haldane's and Wright's criteria. We can also understand how Mark Siderits would see the Mādhyamikas as all being *anti-realists* in their denial of a mind-independent reality to which beliefs, when true, must correspond.[11] The point of the doctrines of vacuity (*śūnyatā*), no substantial existence, things being unfindable under analysis and so forth is, at least in part, that there is actually no such fully independent world, but that the objects of the world are somehow created by minds. As the Tibetan dGe lugs pa scholastic would put it, everything for a Mādhyamika is *blo'i dbang gis bzhag pa,* "brought about by the mind." True, this phrase can supposedly be taken in different ways for Svātantrika and Prāsaṅgika, but there is a significant core element in common: it is an error to think that the world's objects, i.e., tables, chairs, atoms, buddhas, etc., could genuinely exist on their own and be determinate things without there being minds that grasp them as such.

There seem to be a variety of weaker and stronger anti-realist positions. Indeed Haldane and Wright distinguish three sorts of such anti-realism, including the semantic theories of Michael Dummett, the error-theory or irrealism of J.L. Mackie and a Wittgensteinian version turning on the difference in language-games. Although Haldane and Wright don't put things this way, amongst the weaker and certainly more exotic anti-realisms might possibly be a theory which would seem to have some holdovers from realism's deference to grounding facts and its self-assurance that these facts can be known, even if the theory didn't go so far as to subscribe to a *fully* real and *genuinely* mind-independent world. One way in which this type of anti-realism would be made possible is by the Buddhist tactic of an appeal to the two levels of truth, so that we would have the anti-realist views on one level and views more in keeping with realism on another. In the Buddhist case—where two levels of truth are indeed recognized—a Mādhyamika could thus be firm in saying there is no real, ultimately, or truly existing mind-independent world, but that on the level of customary truth some aspects of the realist picture are more or less the case. Notably, he would account for what is right in intelligent worldlings' views by saying that *customary* facts do have a certain objectivity, i.e., what they are is not *just* what we think, feel, say or imagine they are, that true beliefs are grounded upon or correspond to such facts, and that means of valid cognition give us access to those facts. This is of course a very, very delicate balancing act—as two-truth theories probably are—but *it is my contention that such is what is happening in Svātantrika Mādhyamika philosophies like those of Śāntarakṣita and Kamalaśīla.*[12] As I had mentioned in the beginning of this paper, these philosophers were strongly opposed to customary things being such and so *simply* because people might think they are, and thus they acutely felt the need for a kind of grounding for customary truth, some facts to which we defer and which make our ordinary beliefs about the world true, all be such facts only customary and not ultimate.

What is the connection between this Svātantrika Mādhyamika type of limited realism about customary truth and a second-scenario type of interpretation of what Mādhyamika argumentation is targeting? Here's how it looks to me: I would argue that for the Svātantrika their circumscribed realism was made possible largely by seeing Mādhyamika along the lines of the second way, i.e., refuting only superimpositions, because this way allows for customary facts to exist untouched and unrefuted by Mādhyamika arguments. The immunity of customary facts from Mādhyamika critique thus allowed the Svātantrika Mādhyamikas to make the short additional step in the direction of realism, because once these facts were left intact and unrefuted, the Mādhyamika could then also say that we can and should *defer* to these facts to *ground* or correct our ideas about them and that they are what make our beliefs on occasion true. In Indian terms, the second way of taking Mādhyamika, as developed by the Svātantrikas, makes it possible that there can be customary notions of accuracy or inaccuracy, or right and wrong (*tathyāsaṃvṛti* and *mithyāsaṃvṛti*), that are not *just* a matter of what the world *thinks*, but involve properties of objects themselves—the customary object does or does not behave in the expected ways, in short it has or does not have *arthakriyā* (causal efficacy). Objects having or not having *arthakriyā* are the facts to which we should defer, even if the Svātantrika saves his system from being a full-blown realism by placing these facts in the not-too-clear category of "customary truth" Once he grants that there are such facts, like objects causing such and such effects and generally behaving in such and such ways whether we think they do or not, the Svātantrika can also say that there are means of valid cognition (*pramāṇa*) which give access to them and whose truth is grounded by them. Both these themes are strongly present in Śāntarakṣita's philosophy, as they are in Jñānagarbha and Kamalaśīla's thought. I don't think we need to cite passage after passage—indeed, all this is largely the Svātantrikas common heritage from the seventh century thinker Dharmakīrti, whose philosophy they adopted and "Mādhyamika-ized" by making it bear upon only customary truth.[13]

IV

A final point. I have argued that the second way of taking Mādhyamika is clearly Svātantrika thought, and is at the heart of Jñānagarbha, Śāntarakṣita and Kamalaśīla's systems. But, it might be argued, is it only Svātantrika? Or does it more or less figure in so-called Prāsaṅgika Mādhyamika thought, such as that of Candrakīrti? Mightn't it even be hypothesized that the difference between Śāntarakṣita's school and that of Candrakīrti *is* just, or is essentially, that one is second-scenario Mādhyamika and the other is first-scenario? I think the response here would be "Nice try. But no." In fact, there are very strong indications that Candrakīrti *himself* saw the Mādhyamika arguments as targeting only superimpositions, and not targeting customary truth. Let me show what I take to be the strongest and most explicit quotation in favor of seeing Candrakīrti as also subscribing to the second scenario, i.e., refuting superimpositions. *Prasannapadā* 58.10-11:

> *tasmād anutpannā bhāvā ity evaṁ tāvad viparītasvarūpādhyāropapratipakṣeṇa prathamaprakaraṇārambhaḥ/ idānīṁ kvacid yaḥ kaścid viśeṣo 'dhyāropitas tadviśeṣāpākaraṇārthaṁ śeṣaprakaraṇārambhaḥ / gantṛgantavyagamanādiko 'pi niravaśeṣo viśeṣo nāsti pratītyasamutpādasyeti pratipādanārtham //*

> "Thus, when [Nāgārjuna] says 'entities do not arise' in this way first of all [it is pointed out that] the initial chapter [of the *Mūlamadhyamakakārikās*] was written as a counter to superimpositions of false intrinsic natures; and then that the remaining chapters were written in order to eliminate whatever distinctions are superimposed anywhere; the [passage] is designed to show that dependent arising has absolutely no distinctions at all like goers, places to be gone over and going, etc."

In a recent article, Teruyoshi Tanji says quite rightly about the passage cited from *Prasannapadā:*

> "... Candrakīrti asserts that, strictly speaking, the effect of *samāropa* is not a thing but the own-being [i.e., intrinsic nature] of a thing, as he observes that ... [*tasmād anutpannā bhāvā ity ... pratipādanārtham*]. This observation [i.e., the passage in *Prasannapadā* 58.10-11], being the summary of the subjects of the chapters in the MMK [i.e., *Mūlamadhyamakakārikās*], expresses aptly the core of Candrakīrti's philosophy of emptiness. It is so important and cardinal that the meaning of all the other statements in

> his commentary ought to be estimated by way of meeting the view of this observation."[14]

I agree fully. In brief: for Jñānagarbha, Śāntarakṣita, Kamalaśīla, and even Candrakīrti, at least, it looks like refuting superimpositions (i.e., reifications of things rather than customary things themselves) is what Mādhyamika is essentially about. Mādhyamika would thus refute superimposed versions of causes, parts, wholes, people, things, what have you, but not the causes, parts, wholes, etc., themselves upon which the superimpositions are made.

Nonetheless, although Candrakīrti was an advocate of the second scenario and targeted superimpositions, it looks like he did not make the same use of this scenario as did his Svātantrika coreligionists. I had said earlier that from the intactness of customary facts and their immunity to Mādhyamika refutation it is a short step to saying that we can and should defer to these facts to ground or correct our ideas about them, that they are what makes our beliefs on occasion true, etc., etc. Candrakīrti did not make that step. Indeed I think he refused it. In other words, as I have argued elsewhere,[15] he had a different version of *pramāṇas,* less place for objectivity, grounding and being right and wrong irrespective of what people think and, in short, did not subscribe to the holdovers of realism that we see in Svātantrika systems of thought like those of Śāntarakṣita and Kamalaśīla. He had his reasons, notably in his arguments with Bhāvaviveka and with the logicians, and I can't go into that here. I think the essential point for us here is that second scenario Mādhyamika does fit Candrakīrti too. Where his Prāsaṅgika philosophy comes in is, to quite a degree at least, that he thought he had to attack the holdovers of realism on the level of customary truth.

NOTES

* The present paper was first read at the panel on Śāntarakṣita at the meeting of the Central Division of the American Philosophical Association in Chicago, April 2002. The approach whereby Mādhyamika historical issues can be better discerned by seeing them above all philosophically is, I think, one which Musashi Tachikawa also appreciates. The article is a gesture of my esteem for his work.

1. It seems to have been the view of, e.g., Louis de la Vallée Poussin in his article "Madhyamaka" in *Mélanges Chinois et Bouddhiques* 1933, p. 18

where he speaks of "L'irréalité de l'expérience." Cf. J. May and K. Mimaki, *Chūdō, Hōbōgirin,* V, Paris-Tokyo, 1979, p. 461 : "L'irréalité de l'expérience, c'est la Vérité Mondaine annulée dans la Vérité du Sens-ultime", "... la Production-par-Conditions ... évacuée par les Huit Négations dans le sens d'une inconsistance généralisée..."

2. See, e.g., a modern Jo nang pa textbook, *the rGyu 'bras theg pa mchog gi gnas lugs zab mo'i don rnam par nges pa rje Jo nang pa chen po'i ring lugs 'jigs med gdong lnga' i nga ro* of Yon tan bzang po, published by Mi rigs dpe skrung khang, Beijing, 1990. In the section on the two truths (p. 116) we find statements like: *de ltar gyi kun rdzob bden pa / chos can/ khyod don dam bden pa ma yin te / khyod gshis kyi gnas lugs su ye shes dam pa'i spyod yul du mi bden pa'i phyir / der thal / khyod kyi rang bzhin na rnam shes 'khrul ngo tsam du zad pa gang zhig / 'phags pa mchog gi ye shes kyi gzigs ngor rnam yang ma grub pa'i phyir / kun brdzob bden pa yin na rnam shes 'khrul ngo tsam du zad pas khyab ste* ... "Take this type of customary truth as the topic: it is not ultimate truth, because it is not true as an object of the highest wisdom about the absolute. This follows because in its nature it is nothing more than a mere perspective of mistaken consciousness and is never established from the perspective of the noble, supreme wisdom. If something is a customary truth, this implies that it is nothing more than a mere perspective of mistaken consciousness."
3. See *Madhyamakāvatāra* VI.23-31 (ed. L. de la Vallée Poussin, Bibliotheca Buddhica IX, reprinted Osnabrück, 1970). thus, for example, Candrakīrti's own commentary, i.e., the *Madhyamakāvatārabhāṣya,* ad VI. 28: "That which appears as true because of the *saṃvṛti* (benighted) and appears as having a distinct intrinsic nature, but actually does not have an intrinsic nature, is true for the *saṃvṛti* (benighted) that make up the world which is in error."
4. J.L. Mackie, *Ethics, Inventing Right and Wrong,* Penguin Books (reprint), 1986.
5. J. Haldane and C. Wright, eds., *Reality, Representation and Projection.* Oxford University Press, 1993, p. 9.
6. Mackie himself (op cit. pp. 25-27) takes pains to argue that because good and bad, just, unjust, etc., are subjective in the sense of being mind-invented does not mean that the evaluations in terms of agreed upon standards become purely arbitrary so that "anything goes." There remains the possibility for argument and correction of opinions in the light of accepted standards, even though not in the light of any real ethical facts and properties. Something like this might conceivably be generalized by a first scenario Mādhyamika theorist, so that compliance with accepted standards would not be arbitrary, even if those standards themselves do not reflect anything real or "in the fabric of the world."
7. See, e.g., Kamalaśīla's *Sarvadharmaniḥsvabhāvasiddhi,* Peking 312a 8-312b 6: *de ni rigs pa ma yin te / tshad mas gtan la ma phab pa'i phyir dang/ grags pa yang log par srid pa'i phyir ro // de lta ma yin na rang la grags pa'i ngor byas te 'jug pa rnams su yang gang la yang bslu bar mi 'gyur ro //* "This is not reasonable, because there would be no ascertainment of things by *pramāṇas* ("means of valid cognition") and moreover it is possible that what is [generally] admitted is wrong. Otherwise [if analysis using

means of valid cognition were unnecessary], no-one who applied himself to what he had himself admitted would ever end up being unreliable about anything at all."

8. Indeed Jñānagarbha in the *Satyadvayavibhaṅgavṛtti* is preoccupied by what he sees as disastrous consequences in adopting the first way of taking Mādhyamika. D. 10b: *kho bo cag ni 'di la dpyod par mi byed kyi / dpyod par byed pa la ni 'gog par byed do // gal te dpyad par byas te ma rung na ma rung du zad do //* "We [Mādhyamikas] do not analyze this [customary truth]. Rather, we deny [the appropriateness of] analyzing. If something is impossible when analyzed, then it is nothing other than impossible." Śāntarakṣita accepts this view of Jñānagarbha.
9. p. 116, Vol. 8, *Routledge Encyclopedia of Philosophy,* ed. E. Craig, Routledge, London, 1998.
10. Haldane and Wright, *Reality, Representation and Projection,* pp. 3-5.
11. See M. Siderits, "Nāgārjuna as Anti-realist," *Journal of Indian Philosophy* 16, 1988, pp. 311-325 and "Thinking on Empty: Madhyamaka Anti-realism and Canons of Rationality," in Shlomo Biderman and Ben-Ami Scharfstein (eds.), *Rationality in Question.* On Eastern and Western Views of Rationality. Leiden, E.J. Brill, 1989, pp. 231-249. Note that Tibetan Mādhyamika writers themselves regularly use a term, i.e., *dngos por smra ba,* that we can quite justifiably translate by "realism"/"realist". The realism that they say the Mādhyamika is attacking is, as far as I can see, not significantly different from Siderits' characterization or that of Haldane and Wright, even though obviously the fine tuning of the comparison would take us too far afield.
12. The supporting textual passages from Indian and Tibetan sources, as well as the arguments for attribution of this two-tiered combination of anti-realism and realism to Śāntarakṣita and Kamalaśīla, have been elaborated upon in my article "Metaphysics for Mādhyamikas," in G. Dreyfus and S. McClintock (eds.), *The Svātantrika-Prāsaṅgika Distinction. What Difference does a Difference Make?* Studies in Indian and Tibetan Buddhism, Wisdom Publications, Boston, 2003, p. 93-123. Here it will have to suffice to give one passage from a fine Tibetan connoisseur of later Indian Buddhist philosophy, Sa skya Paṇḍita Kun dga' rgyal mtshan (1182-1251), who states the following in the first chapter of his *Tshad ma rigs gter rang 'grel* (Xizang xinhua shudian, Lhasa, 1992), p. 68: *dbu ma pa'ang don dam par spros pa dang bral zhing kun rdzob tu dngos por smra ba de dag gi rjes su 'jug kyang rung / 'jig rten grags sde dang bstun yang rung ste / de dag gang ltar yang kun tu tha snyad la don dang shes pa gnyis su kha tshon chod do //* "The Mādhyamika [hold] that ultimately things are free from [all] conceptual proliferation (*spros pa = prapañca*). And in terms of the customary, they may follow those realists (*dngos por smra ba de dag*) or may adhere [merely] to what the world recognizes, but in any case they will divide the customary into objects and consciousness." The realists (*dngos por smra ba*) being spoken of are the Sautrāntikas and Yogācāras; it is clear that the first type of Mādhyamika is thus the Svātantrika, including Yogācāra Svātantrikas like Śāntarakṣita and Kamalaśīla and Sautrāntika Svātantrikas like Bhāvaviveka, while the second type (who adhere to what the world recognizes) are Prāsaṅgikas, like Candrakīrti. Of course, dGe lugs writers too make a point of grouping Svātantrikas

along with realists (as opposed to Prāsaṅgikas), but as we see from the quote from Sa skya Paṇḍita, this is not *just* a later dGe lugs pa idea, but was also firmly endorsed by a Sa skya pa writer who was in direct contact with important Indian paṇḍits and prided himself on his "Indian authenticity."

13. See my "Metaphysics for Mādhyamikas."
14. p. 353 in T. Tanji, "On *samāropa*. Probing the Relationship of the Buddha's Silence and His Teaching," in J. Silk (ed.) *Wisdom, Compassion, and the Search for Understanding.* The Buddhist Studies Legacy of Gadjin M. Nagao, Honolulu; University of Hawai'i Press, 2000. See also our remarks on Tanji's article in our review in *Eastern Buddhist* 33, 1,2001, pp. 181-85.
15. "Metaphysics for Mādhyamikas," op. cit.

CHAPTER 16

Prāsaṅgika Interpretations of the Madhyamaka Theory of Freedom from Twin Extreme Positions

KODO YOTSUYA

I

"The Middle Way" means the way which is free from twin extreme positions. There are various interpretations of what this pair of concepts stands for. From a practical point of view, for instance, it comprises 'asceticism' and 'self-indulgence'; from a philosophical one, 'existence' and 'non-existence', the former of which is assumed to be 'eternalism', and the latter to be 'nihilism'. It is this philosophical interpretation that the Mādhyamikas mostly treat of. In this paper, we call the various ways in which they approach the problem the "Madhyamaka theory of freedom from twin extreme positions".

The Mādhyamikas have widely flourished throughout the history of Tibetan Buddhism. In the period of the later propagation (*pyi*[*r*] *dar*) the Prāsaṅgika-Mādhyamikas, a subschool opposed to the Svātantrika-Mādhyamikas, occupied the dominant position.

In this paper we focus on Tsong kha pa Blo bzang grags pa'i

dpal (1357-1419) and Go ram pa bSod nams seng ge (1429-1489), both highly influential exponents of the Prāsaṅgika-Mādhyamika school in the period of the later propagation, and examine their characteristic interpretations of the Madhyamaka theory of freedom from twin extreme positions, viz., existence and non-existence.[1]

II

We often come across the following verse from the *Jñānasāra-samuccaya* quoted in treatises which discuss the Madhyamaka theory of freedom from existence and non-existence:

> "[Things are] free from existence, non-existence, neither of them [and] both of them. Mādhyamikas who are released from these four extreme positions are true wise men."[2]

The negation of the two positions defined by such a directly contradictory pair as existence and non-existence aims at ultimately extinguishing all dichotomous thinking. If, however, existence and non-existence can be simultaneously negated without any condition, we may suspect that the principle of contradiction has been infringed.

Tsong kha pa's interpretation of this matter seems to presuppose this suspicion.[3]

He takes up the four extreme positions of the *Jñānasāra-samuccaya* and asserts that they should be conceived to be ultimate or hypostatized so that they all can be refuted without contradiction:

> "This [must be understood] as mentioned before. There are two kinds of existence (*dngos po*). [The first one is] existence established by own-being (*rang gi ngo bo*). Supposing that [it] is accepted on either level of the two truths, it can be negated. [The other one is] existence which has the capability of fulfilling its own purpose (*don byed nus pa*); it cannot be negated on the conventional level (*tha snyad du*). And it is also [the same] with respect to non-existence (*dngos po med pa*). If one claims that uncreated things (*'dus ma byas*) should be established by own-being, these too would be negated. Likewise, [if] what is at once existent and non-

> existent [could be] established by self-nature (*rang bzhin*), [it] would also be negated. Furthermore, [if] what is neither existent nor non-existent [could be] established by self-nature, [it] too would be negated. Consequently one should understand the way to negate the four alternatives (*mu bzhi*) in this way."[4]

We can understand more clearly from the following passage the reason why Tsong kha pa refuses to take the expression of the negation of the four extreme positions, existence, non-existence, etc. literally:

> "If [you] negate all of the four alternatives without appending such a qualification [as 'being established by self-nature',] that is, if [you] negate the existence of things and the non-existence of them, or if [you] negate both of them and then neither of them [without appending any qualification], you would directly contradict what you [yourself] have accepted. And if you say that even so there is no fault, we would not argue with such an insane person."[5]

Tsong kha pa here points out that it would infringe the principle of contradiction if the first two positions of the four alternatives, and the latter ones as well, were simply negated without any qualification. He therefore provides the qualification 'being ultimate' or 'being established by self-nature' to each position so that he can negate them all without any contradiction.

Thus, comprehending that self-nature or what is established by self-nature is non-existent, as the negation of them implies, is vitally important in Tsong kha pa's interpretation, under which every position of the four alternatives established by self-nature is negated. Such a comprehension cannot be abandoned without severe consequences. He explains this point as follows:

> "Moreover, discriminative wisdom (*prajñā, shes rab*) which understands that there is no self-nature (*rang bzhin*) or self (*bdag*) is generated when self-nature established by own-being (*rang gi ngo bos grub pa'i rang bzhin*) or the self of an aggregate is negated. However, if [an opponent claimed that] even the non-existence of self-nature which is the object of discriminative wisdom should be negated, [he would]

depreciate the correct view of the Madhyamaka (*dbu ma pa'i lta ba*). For [he] would depreciate the object of discriminative wisdom which comprehends that there is no self-nature in phenomena. [Such a] person that [simultaneously] depreciated both existence and non-existence should be challenged and replied to with the following question: Why should one depreciate the non-existence of self-nature which is the object of discriminative wisdom that judges (*nges pa*) that there is no self-nature in an aggregate?"[6]

We can find a clear-cut logical argument which reinforces his belief that one should not abandon discriminative wisdom (*prajñā, shes rab*) which comprehends that there is no self-nature, etc., in the following passage:

"Furthermore, when one of [two positions] which exclude [each other] (*dngos 'gal*), that is, which rule out a third alternative, cannot be established, there is no room to clinch a negation by inquiring whether [one alternative is] existent or non-existent, or single or many etc.; whereas when there is [such a possibility], the negation of one of [the two alternatives] which exclude [each other] is impossible without proving the other alternative."[7]

III

Go ram pa, who belonged to the Sa skya pa school, which was relatively faithful to the Indian Madhyamaka tradition, presents a critique of Tsong kha pa's unique interpretation of the problem:

"The mind which takes as real (*mngon par zhen va*) the non-existence of an hypostatized entity (*bden med*), having negated the hypostatized entity (*bden pa*) by analytical reasoning (*rigs pa*), comprehends the truth (*gnas lugs*) of the object, since [it] negates the hypostatized entity. However, [that mental operation] should [also] be negated by a following one (*blo phyi ma*) [employing analytical reasoning], since it is mistaken (*phyin ci log*) in its hypothesizing the non-existence of the hypostatized entity. This is because when one examines [the matter] by analytical reasoning, there is no non-existence of

> the hypostatized entity in the form of a conceptual object (*zhen yul*) arising from hypothesizing the hypostatized entity (*bden 'dzin*), even as there is no hypostatized entity in the form of a conceptual object which arises from taking the hypostatized entity as real."[8]

Go ram pa does not object to accepting tentatively the mental operation which negates an hypostatized entity (=self-nature or what is established by self-nature), but claims that it, too, should be finally abandoned by another mental operation employing analytical reasoning.

Again, according to him, if things are postulated by analytical reasoning, it follows that they are established in a substantialist sense. The non-existence of self-nature, for instance, which is the result of the negation of self-nature by analytical reasoning, might therefore be thought to be established in such a sense, having been postulated by analytical reasoning. Hence the non-existence of self-nature also needs to be negated by analytical reasoning.

Go ram pa, who believes that the non-existence of self-nature should also be negated as an instance of hypothesizing an hypostatized entity (*bden 'dzin*), illustrates his interpretation of the Madhyamaka theory of freedom from twin extreme positions in the following way:

> "When ordinary people examine the truth (*gnas lugs*), [they go through the following stages:] First of all, when the first position, i.e. the hypostatized entity, is negated by the logical reasons (*gtan tshigs*) of being neither one nor many (*gcig du bral*), etc., the mental operation that employs analytical reasoning serves the purpose of negating the hypostatized entity. Therefore [to this extent] it is not a fault to take as real the non-existence of the hypostatized entity, since the negation of the hypostatized entity by dialectic (*rtog pa*) is nothing but hypothesizing the non-existence of the hypostatized entity. [Moreover,] the conceptual object (*zhen yul*), viz. the non-existence of the hypostatized entity, is not found, because it is [regarded as] a fault [by] a following mental operation [employing analytical reasoning]. Hence it, too, needs to be negated in order to hypothesize the non-existence of the

hypostatized entity. And so it is not a fault to hypothesize that the non-existence of the hypostatized entity is not existent, since a mental operation [employing analytical reasoning] involves negating taking the non-existence of the hypostatized entity as real. This is similar to the previous [case where the hypostatized entity is negated]. It is also negated by a third [mental operation employing analytical reasoning,] one which grasps that the non-existence is not [existent], since this is also [regarded as] a fault [by] the third mental operation [employing analytical reasoning]. Furthermore it, too, is negated by a fourth [mental operation employing analytical reasoning], since that, [i.e. the negation of the non-existence,] is [again] regarded as a fault [by] a following mental operation [employing analytical reasoning]. In brief, the four extreme positions are [thus] negated in sequence. But there is not an infinite regress (*thug med*), since there cannot be any way of hypothesizing (*'dzin stangs*) beyond the fourth one."[9]

IV

Tsong kha pa refers to such a logical nexus whereby whatever is postulated by analytical reasoning must be established in a substantialist sense, that is, by self-nature,[10] and holds it to be untenable:

> "After examining first whether [or not] a sprout, etc., are truly existent (*bden par yod pa*), the non-existence of the hypostatized [sprout] is found by analytical reasoning. Therefore it is again examined whether the non-existence of the true [sprout] is truly existent or not. On this occasion, the non-existence of the hypostatized [sprout] is not found [to be truly existent by analytical reasoning]. But this does not mean that [the non-existence of the true sprout] has not been found [by analytical reasoning]."[11]

The self-nature of a sprout, etc., for instance, are investigated and negated by analytical reasoning. But even though the non-existence of the self-nature of the sprout, etc., which is postulated by the very process of negating their self-nature, is not established ultimately, this does not mean that the non-existence of *the* sprout, etc., is not existent at all. Tsong kha pa very probably thinks that it does not need to be established in a substantialist sense (ultimately), and can therefore be existent on the conventional level without having to be negated by analytical reasoning, since analytical reasoning involves exclusively hypostatized (ultimate) things, which it negates.[12]

This point that the non-existence of the self-nature of the sprout, etc., is ultimately not existent, but is not negated on the conventional level is closely related to another interpretation of his of the Madhyamaka theory of the freedom from twin extreme positions: the negation of existence means that things are not ultimately existent, whereas the negation of non- existence means that they are conventionally existent.[13]

V

Neither Tsong kha pa nor Go ram pa would probably deny the view that any mental construct must ultimately be extinguished. They differ, however, from each other in the interpretation of what is postulated by analytical reasoning. Tsong kha pa stresses that the non-existence of self-nature, once established in an act of negating self-nature by analytical reasoning need not be denied by another act of analytical reasoning, since indeed it cannot be existent ultimately, only conventionally. Go ram pa, on the contrary, believes that even the non-existence of self-nature, obtained by the same process, needs to be refuted by a separate act of analytical reasoning, since it must be postulated ultimately, that is, as an object taken as an hypostatized entity (*bden 'dzin*).

ABBREVIATIONS

BP: *rGyal ba thams cad kyi thugs kyi dgongs pa zab mo dbu ma'i de kgo na nyid spyi'i ngag gis stong pa nges don rab gsal,* Bibliotheca Tibetica 1-12 (ca), Tokyo, 1969.

CŚṭ: *Catuḥśataka-ṭīkā.* D. ed. dBu ma. vol. 8 (ya), 1978, Tokyo

D: sDe dGe ed. published by Sekai Seiten kyokai.

GR: *dBu ma la 'jug pa'i rgya cher bshad pa dGongs pa rab gsal,* bKra shis lhung po ed., *The Collected Works of rJe Tsong kha pa Blo bzang grags pa,* vol. 24 (ca), Delhi, 1979.

JSS: *Jñānasāra-samuccaya,* D. ed. dBu ma. vol. 2 (tsha), 1977, Tokyo.

LN: *Drang ba dang nges pa'i don rnam par phye ba'i bstan bcos Legs bshad snying po,* bKra shis lhung po ed., *The Collected Works of rJe Tsong kha pa Blo bzang grags pa,* vol. 21 (pha), Delhi, 1979.

LR: *Byang chub lam rim chen mo, bKra shis lhung po ed., The Collected Works of rJe Tsong kha pa Blo bzang grags pa,* vol. 20 (pa), Delhi, 1979.

RG: *dBu ma rtsa ba'i tshig le'ur byas pa shes rab ces bya ba'i rnam bshad rigs pa'i rgya pa mtsho,* bKra shis lhung po ed., *The Collected Works of rJe Tsong kha pa Blo bzang grags pa,* vol.23 (ba), Delhi, 1979.

TTh: *Zab mo stong pa nyid kyi de kho na nyid rab tu gsal bar byed pa'i bstan bcos. The Collected Works of the Loard mKhas grub dGe legs dpal bzang po,* (ka), Delhi, 1971.

NOTES

1. Shiro Matsumoto's significant contribution to this topic (*Chibetto Bukkyo Tetsugaku,* Daizo-shuppan, Tokyo, 1997, pp.205-228) deserves immediate mention.
2. yod min med min rod med mill //
gnyis ka'i bdag nyid kyang min pas //
mtha' bzhi las grol dbu ma pa //
mkhas pa rnams kyi de kho na'o // (JSS.D.tsha.27b3-4)
3. mKhas grub dge legs dpal bzang po (1305-1438), who is one of direct disciples of Tsong kha pa, elucidates this point in great detail in the *TTh* (TTh. ka.49b4-52b4).
4. di ni sngar bstan pa ltar dngos po la gnyis las rang gi ngo bas grub pa'i dngos po ni bden pa gnyis gang du rod par 'dod kyang 'gog la don byed nus pa'i dngos po ni tha snyad du 'gog pa ma yin no // dngos po med pa'ang 'dus ma byas rnams la rang gi ngo bas grub pa'i dngos med du 'dod na ni de 'dra ba'i dngos med kyang 'gog go // de bzhin du de 'dra ba'i dngos po yod med gnyis car yang 'gog la gnyis ka ma yin pa rang gi ngo bos grub pa'ang 'gog pas mu bzhi 'gog tshul thams cad ni de ltar du shes par bya'o // (LR.pa.382b5-383al)
5. de 'dra ba'i khyad par sbyar rgyu med par mu bzhi ga 'gog na dngos po yod pa dang dngos po med pa 'gog pa'i tshe de gnyis ka ma yin te zhes bkag na ni khas blangs dngos su 'gal ba yin la de ltar yin kyang skyon med do zhes bsnyon na ni kho ba cag smyon pa dang lhang cig tu mi rtsod do //(LR.pa.383a2-3)
6. gzhan yang phung po la rang gi ngo bos grub pa'i rang bzhin nam bdag bkag pa na rang bzhin nam bdag med do snyam pa'i shes rab skye la shes rab de'i yul rang bzhin med pa de yang' gog na ni dbu ma pa'i lta

ba sun 'byin pa yin te chos rnams rang bzhin med par rtog pa'i shes rab kyi yul sun 'byin pa'i phyir ro // rang bzhin yod med gnyis ka sun 'byin par 'dod pa de la 'di 'dri bar bya ste phung po la rang bzhin med do snyam du nges pa'i shes rab kyi yul rang bzhin med pa de ji ltar bras pas sun 'byin pa smros shig // (LR.pa.383a3-5)

7. gzhaṅ yang phung gsum sel ba'i dngos 'gal gcig ston rgyu med na ni yod med dam gcig dang du ma sogs gang 'dod do ces mtha' gnyis su kha tshon bcad pa'i brtag pa byas nas 'gog sa med la yod ma dngos 'gal gcig 'gog pa ni cig shos sgrub pa med na med pa yin te... (RG.ba.25b3-4) Tsong kha pa sets this out in more detail in the LN. (LN.pha.113b3-117b2). See also my study. (*The Critique of Svatantra reasoning by Candrakīrti and Tsong-kha-pa,* Tibetan and Indo-Tibetan Studies 8, Franz Steiner Verlag Stuttgart, Stuttgart, 1999, pp.15-25)
8. rigs pas bden pa bkag (?) nas bden med du mngon par zhen pa'i blo de bden pa bkag pa'i cha nas yul gyi gnas lugs rtogs pa yin kyang bden med du mngon par zhen pa'i cha nas phyin ci log yin pas blo phyi mas dgag dgos te/ rigs pas dpyad pa'i tshe bden 'dzin gyi zhen yul bden pa med pa ltar bden par du 'dzin pa'i zhen yul bden med de'ang med par mtshungs pa'i phyir ro// (BP.ca.87bl-3)
9. so so skye bos gnas lugs la dpyad pa'i tshe thog mar gcig du bral la sogs pa'i gtan tshigs kyis mtha' dang po bden pa bkag pa'i tshe rigs shes de'i byed pa ni bden pa bkag pa don yin pas bden med du mngon par zhen pa skyon ma yin te rtog pas bden pa bkag pa la bden med du mngon par zhen pa las ma 'das pa'i phyir blo phyi ma la ltos nas de nyid skyon yin pas zhen yul bden med nyid ma rnyed pa'i sgo nas bden med du zhen pa nyid kyang dgag dgos te / de'i tshe blo'i byed pa ni bden med du zhen pa bkag pa yin pas bden med ma yin no snyam du mngon par zhen pa skyon ma yin pa ni snga ma dang 'dra'o // de'ang blo gsum pa la ltos nas skyon du song bas gsum pas bden med ma yin par mngon par zhen pa'ang bkag la / de'ang blo zhi pa la ltos nas skyon du song bas bzhi pas de'ang bkag ste mdor na mtha' bzhi rim pa bzhin du 'gog pa'o // bzhi pa phan chad kyi 'dzin stangs mi srid pas thug med du mi 'gyur ro // (BP.ca.90b5-91a4)
10. ye shes des rnyed pa'am grub par bstan na des grub rgyu zhig byung na bden grub bo zhes 'dzin pa dgag pa'i phyir/. ...(GR.ma.107b5-6)
11. sngar myu gu la sogs pa bden par yod dam med btsal ba'i og tu bden med rigs shes kyis rnyed pas slar bden med bden par yod dam med btsal ba'i tshe bden med mi rnyed kyang de ma rnyed par mi 'gyur la/. ...(RG.ba.28b5-6)
12. On the point that analytical reasoning involves only the hypostatized thing, see CŚṭ.D.ya.201bl-4. On some functions of analytical reasoning in Tsong kha pa's philosophical system, see my study. (*op.cit.*, pp.8-15)
13. de yang sangs rgyas rnams kyis chos bstan pa // bden pa gnyis la yang dag brten / zhes skye 'jig sogs yod pa kun rdzob dang med pa don dam par yin pa'i bden gnyis dbye shes dgos par gsungs shing (RG.ba.18a2-3)

I am deeply obliged to Mr. Philip Pierce who checked the English of the final draft.

CHAPTER 17

Nāgārjuna, Shinran, and Whitehead

JOHN SHUNJI YOKOTA

Summary

The radical negativity of Buddhist emptiness is expressed throughout the tradition but is especially centered in the wisdom (*prajñā-pāramitā*) literature and Nāgārjuna. It is the basis of Buddhist ontology. The existence of reality is never negated in the tradition. Its fundamentally empty quality is made emphatic. This empty reality can and has been said to be free of all characterization. The Buddhist traditions have seen fit to characterize reality as embodying wisdom and compassion, however. Shinran's Pure Land Buddhist tradition especially emphasizes the primordial characterization of the Buddhist intuition into reality as that of a wise and compassionate saving power. The continuity of the emptiness tradition and Shinran's Pure Land tradition is discussed from certain perspectives of the process thought developed primarily by Alfred North Whitehead, Charles Hartshorne and their followers. John B. Cobb's *Beyond Dialogue* especially chapter six with its explicit Whiteheadian perspective has been a direct influence upon the ideas addressed in this paper. [John B. Cobb, Jr., *Beyond Dialogue: Toward a Mutual Transforma tion of Christianity and Buddhism* (Philadelphia: Fortress Press, 1982), pp.119-143.]

Introductory Remarks

The title of this essay covers much too much material for such a short endeavor. My academic concerns and its philosophy of religion perspective are, however, expressed by it. This is not an endeavor in traditional Buddhist Studies, rather it is an attempt at a critical, synthetic Buddhist theology. First, I will look at Nāgārjuna (second century C.E.) and try to understand the intent of his message. This will involve a critical overview of the development of the early tradition through Nāgārjuna, and beyond so as to see him within the context of what preceded and followed him. The interpretive work of Bhāvaviveka (sixth century C.E.) will be referred to in an attempt to see a 'positive' interpretation of Nāgārjuna and emptiness. Next, Shinran's emphasis on primordially characterizing reality as wise, compassionate activity is seen as the inevitable fulfilment of the tradition and expresses the primordial place of wisdom and compassion in the whole of the tradition. Put differently, the empty quality of reality inevitably leads to reality being wisely compassionate. Finally, certain emphases of process thought can help us positively develop this notion of a compassionate, empty reality.

I. *Nāgārjuna's Thought*

The question to be asked and answered is what Nāgārjuna is trying to say through a perplexingly redundant series of negative dialectical attacks on common sense assumptions as well as strictly Buddhist topics. On one level, the insistent negative dialectic points to the artificial nature of the linguistic process: having a word for an object or activity makes it seem to be substantially existent. This fallacy of concreteness projected by the linguistic process is, of course, one aspect of what Nāgārjuna is trying to make us aware of. Beyond this linguistic emptiness, however, Nāgārjuna is attempting to tell us that there is a phenomenal emptiness or non-substantiality of reality because of the impermanent flow of events that denies any substantial, unchanging substratum of reality. Obviously this does not mean that things do not exist, but that things that do exist are empty, ever-changing entities. As has been repeatedly stated by commentators, Nāgārjuna is not a nihilist denying the existence of things. He is developing an ontology of emptiness, an ontology of non-substantial existence.

A. *Understanding Nāgārjuna in the Development of the Tradition*

The exposition of the impermanence of existence and the subsequent corollary of non-substantiality are at the core of the tradition's teachings. The normative view of Nāgārjuna is that he revived the tradition by extending the negative logic of no-self to the entities of existence (*dharma*) themselves. He thereby rejected the insistence on the substantive view of the entities of existence that was formalized in the *Sarvāstivāda* position, his main doctrinal opponent. In denying the substantiality of these entities of existence, Nāgārjuna tried to show that the tradition should develop toward a fully realized emphasis of impermanence and non-substantiality. This is the standard understanding of the polemic of Nāgārjuna directed against a position alien to what he saw as the genuine spirit of the original teachings. However, if the insights of impermanence and its correlative of non-substantiality are so obvious and central to the original teachings, then, how could the tradition declare substantive being? Was the lure of substantiality as attractive as not to enable the full realization of the intuitions of early Buddhism? Put in a doctrinal context, if the impermanent, constitutive quality of the self was clearly recognized, how could the equally impermanent, constitutive quality of the entities of existence be ignored? This obvious lapse in thought and observation had long bothered me about the traditional understanding of the gradual doctrinal development from original Buddhism through Scholastic Buddhism to Mahāyāna Buddhism. In a paper related to this problem, I used Whitehead's basic intuition into reality—things change while enduring—to see the development of the tradition from a position outside of the traditional scholarship and understand the entities of existence advocated by the *Sarvāstivāda* position in a new light and thus question the traditional understanding of the intent of the message of Nāgārjuna. [John S. Ishihara, "Continuity and Novelty: A Contribution to the Dialogue between Buddhism and Process Thought", in *Charles Hartshorne's Concept of God: Philosophical and Theological Responses,* ed. Santiago Sia (Dordrecht: Kluwer Academic Publishers, 1990), pp. 163-184.]

The paper attempted to make three points. David Kalupahana [David Kalupahana, *Causality: The Central Philosophy of Buddhism* (Honolulu: University of Hawaii Press, 1975), pp. 49-86.] understood Nāgārjuna's polemic as misrepresenting the early tradition's understanding of the entities of existence. His argument is that there was no progression from emptying the self to emptying the constitutive entities of the self. In short, the logic and insight of seeing the emptiness of the self naturally and inevitably led to a similar insight into the emptiness of the constitutive entities of existence that make up the self. Nāgārjuna's insight into the emptiness of all elements of existence was present in the early tradition. For Kalupahana, it was the Sarvāstivāda tradition that made substantive these entities of existence. It was this school's misrepresentation of the earlier tradition's position that was the object of Nāgārjuna's polemic. Part of the first point I wanted to make, by relying on Kalupahana's insights into early Buddhism which coincided with my own dissatisfaction with the usual understanding of the progressive emptying of the objects of existence, was to emphasize the early tradition's claim to the emptiness of all entities of existence.

The second point was to look at *Sarvāstivāda's* claim of the substantive character of all constitutive entities of existence. This is admittedly a most problematic point, since it disregards the traditional, largely unquestioned understanding of the *Sarvāstivāda* view of the entities of existence. Here, Th. Stcherbatsky [Th. Stcherbatsky, *The Central Philosophy of Buddhism and the Meaning of the Word Dharma* (Calcutta: Sasil Gupta Ltd., 1961 (1923),) pp. 5, 22-24, 31-36, 66-70.] I. Funahashi [Issai Funahashi, *Gō no Kenkyu* (*A Study of Karma*) (Kyoto: Hozokan, 1954) pp. 376-380] and portions of the Chinese translation of the *Abhidharmakośa* (T xxix pp.152b and 304a) were referred to. I question the assumption that *Sarvāstivāda* in fact advocated the view that the entities of existence are substantive, unchanging monads of existence. Reading Stcherbatsky carefully, he puzzles over how to understand and express what a *dharma* really is: early on he notes that it is the 'real essence of the element' but finally must opt for 'subtle force'. This struggle attempts to convey that while things are forever arising and passing away, there is an enduring quality of these entities of existence as they arise and instantaneously disappear. He uses the image of a motion picture with each frame coming to light and disappearing yet leaving a continuity of being. The ultimate and meaningless fading away of all things is compensated by an insistence that there is a continuity of existence as well. Change is never denied nor the reality of enduring, continuing reality. Moreover, Funahashi is emphatic about denying substantive existence to the elements of existence. He clearly states that the notion of *dharma* that Nāgārjuna negates has no relation to the *dharma* advocated by *Sarvāstivāda.* Finally, the *Abhidharmakośa* selections note the continuity inherent in a self that is no-self. The intuition of both change and continuity were evident in Early as well as Scholastic Buddhism. Thus, Buddhism is true to our basic intuitions into life: things change and endure. Again, what, then, is the message of Nāgārjuna?

The third point and the point that has relationship to the present paper is what, indeed, was and is the point of Nāgārjuna's negative polemic against a substantive view of reality when the tradition more or less agreed with the insight into the impermanence and non-substantiality of the entities of existence. Looking at the development of the entire tradition, we can see Nāgārjuna's role as part of an ongoing dialectic in the tradition that began with an emphasis on impermanence, a swing toward continuity, back to impermanence again and to continuity a second time. I specifically have in mind the development from early Buddhism (change) to *Sarvāstivāda* (continuity) to *Mādhyamika* (change) and then on to *Yogācāra* (continuity). So we see Nāgārjuna as the one in the tradition that helped to re-emphasize the basic intuition into reality that things change in response to that other part of the tradition that emphasized that things endure. Buddhism as a whole, then, saw and articulated that basic human intuition into reality of change and continuity. It is in this context that Nāgārjuna's contribution to Buddhism can and should be seen.

In addition, to add a thought that was not articulated in the aforementioned paper, the discussion of impermanence and emptiness necessarily leads to the notion of non-attachment or non-grasping. Here, the spiritually therapeutic aspect of emptiness can be seen. That which is impermanent and inherently empty should not and, more importantly, cannot be grasped and be attached to. The freedom of non-attachment is being espoused which is the central *religious* meaning of Nāgārjuna's polemic of emptiness.

Finally, the paper makes the point that the Buddhist acknowledgement of both continuity and change, from a process philosophy perspective, does not fully confront the problem of perpetual perishing leading to mere insignificance. Here, process thought develops the idea of the preservation of all entities in the receptive nature of God (the consequent nature of God), so that they are preserved for eternity. Moreover, the process vision of reality sees a need for some input of novelty in the process of coming together so as to assure some development in the ever coming together of the past to form the present. They fault Buddhism with an inability to describe how things develop from the mere coming together of past events. They posit the notion of novelty introduced to the process by God (subjective aim). These two points will be discussed in the final section on process thought's contribution to the Buddhist articulation of reality.

The interpretation of Nāgārjuna that is brought to this paper, then, holds that it is imperative to see him in the flow of the development of the entire tradition. In his negative, dialectical attack on substantive existence, we see a pivotal accentuation of a central feature of the Buddhist tradition. However, it should be recognized that the tradition is not only this negative dialectic but also a tradition that sees continuity and endurance as equally important aspects of reality. Nāgārjuna, then, is a central figure in a major strand in the tradition but only one major strand. An alternating emphasis going back and forth from impermanence and non-substantiality to continuity and endurance is how the tradition should be viewed. We know that things change, but we also know and sense that there is an abidingness of these fleeting yet enduring entities of existence. Nāgārjuna's rhetoric of negation, then, makes us see the emptiness of our notions of reality, the emptiness of the actual entities of being and the appropriateness of non-attachment to these empty entities. Yet, it still tells us that there are things (empty things, yes, but nonetheless things) not just nothing. This point must always be acknowledged.

B. *Bhāvaviveka's Understanding of Nāgārjuna*

The central figure in the *Svātantrika* tradition of *Madhyamaka*.

Bhāvaviveka's work was, until recently, not as well documented as the more widely documented Candrakīrti (*ca.* 600 C.E.) and his *Prāsaṅgika* tradition of *Madhyamaka.* This was probably due to the fact that the former's work was essentially preserved in Tibetan and Chinese translations while the latter's central work was preserved in Sanskrit and happily had a critical edition of his main text available from early in the last century. The following is dependent on Malcolm David Eckel's *To See the Buddha* and specifically its translation of the third chapter ("The Ultimate Buddha") of Bhāvaviveka's *The Verses on the Essence of the Middle Way* (*Madhyamakahṛdayakārikā*) with its commentary, the *Flame of Reason* (*Tarkajvālā*) attributed to Bhāvaviveka. [Malcom David Eckel, *To See The Buddha: A Philosophers Quest for the Meaning of Emptiness* (Princeton: Princeton University Press, 1992.) pp. 158-194.] My interest centres on the relationship between emptiness and compassion, that is, the naturally compassionate activity of the buddhas and *bodhisattvas.*

There is a tendency to look at the ultimate reality that the buddha embodies as being beyond description and change, indeed, as being an absolute entity. The term absolute is used here in its Western philosophical sense: an entity independent and unto itself with only external relationships with other entities as a possibility. The traditional Western sense of real being is this changeless, affect-less entity complete unto itself. Buddhism rejects this view through the reality of dependent origination which is emptiness and the real quality of reality. The term ultimate would seem to be more appropriate and is the ideal translation for *paramārtha,* the utmost, that which has no higher. However, one can see an absolutistic description of reality in the following passages. "[The Buddha] is immeasurable because he understands the immeasurable. [The Buddha] is incalculable because he cannot be grasped. [The Buddha] is unthinkable because he cannot be an object of thought. [The Buddha] is incomparable because he cannot be compared." (V. 273) "Does not arise, does not have any form, and does not change. [The Buddha] is luminous, equal and not equal, unlimited, nonconceptual, and without characteristic." (V. 279) Although there is this definite tendency to absolutize the Buddha, there is an equally definite though paradoxical tendency to characterize the Buddha and, in a sense, make it relative. "[The Buddha] is called eternal for two reasons. He is eternally free from appearance and thus is completely free from concepts, and *he eternally accomplishes what is good.*" (emphasis mine) (V.275). The commentary for this verse states, "[The Buddha] is also called eternal because he eternally accomplishes what is good for sentient beings." The first half of verse 275 is a rather good description of the absolute freedom of an absolute being. The second half while surprising and seemingly out of place, is also the paradoxically logical rhetoric and practice of the Buddhist tradition in its primal orientation toward knowing and thus describing its ultimate as being a caring, compassionate activity that is far from being an absolute being. It is this natural activity of compassion that comes forth from the 'absolute' Buddha that makes it clear that an absolute being unto itself is not what a Buddha is but rather an existence that is in fundamental relationship with all other existence. Thus, naturally and non-problematically is the emptiness that is the Buddha, that is enlightenment, seen to be primordially a compassionate reality/activity.

While strictly speaking not a description of the Buddha or the enlightened one itself, the description of the *bodhisattva* offers explicit discussion of what the activity of enlightenment or more precisely activity toward enlightenment is. In a description of the progressive practice and attainments of the *bodhisattva,* the naturally flowing forth of compassion is explicitly enunciated. "[A *bodhisattva*] does not leave *saṃsāra,* (V. 294a), But [a *bodhisattva*] is free from the harm of *saṃsāra.* (V. 294b) [A *bodhisattva*] does not attain *nirvāṇa,* (V. 294c) But it is as if [a *bodhisattva*] were located in *nirvāṇa.* (V. 294d)... [The *bodhisattva*] has climbed the mountain peak of wisdom and is free from grief but looks with compassion on ordinary people who suffer and are burned by grief. (V. 296) Then, with an eye that is moist with compassion, [the *bodhisattva*] sees that the wisdom eyes of] ordinary people have been covered by an imaginary net created by the art of conceptual thought. (V. 297) An accomplished *bodhisattva,* who is tormented by compassion and dedicated to the welfare of these ordinary people, has a mind as hard as a diamond and is the greatest of beings. (V. 301) Finally, in the commentary of Verse 302, Bhāvaviveka quotes Nāgārjuna from the *Ratnāvali* IV.80abc and V.36-39, a discussion of the six perfections, which ends with the following conclusion, "... Compassion accomplishes everything."

On the one hand, the absolute independence from *sāṃsārika* existence, i.e., a transcendence of our environment, is declared for the enlightened one. On the other hand, an intimate relation of compassionate activity aimed at all other existents is assumed for these same enlightened ones. This is the paradox of enlightened or ideal existence. Enlightened existence is different from our ordinary existence, indeed, it is an importantly different form of existence. Nevertheless, it is intimately related to all forms of existence both socially and soteriologically and cannot simply be an absolute, isolated entity of existence. Thus, of a necessity and quite naturally, the compassion of interrelatedness flows from the enlightened one. Emptiness, then, is not simply an absolute form of existence but rather the freedom of engaging in existence. It is this dual reality that should be articulated when talking of the enlightenment of emptiness. The literature referred to above illustrates this dual aspect of reality in its insistence that reality has a transcendent quality as well as a compassionately active, soteriological quality.

II. *Shinran's Thought*

A. *Historical Actualization*

The fact that Shinran centered his thought on the saving, compassionate activity of Amida Buddha directed toward us—beings of karmic evil and blind passions—is an undeniable fact. The task of this section is to show that compassionate activity naturally flows from the reality of emptiness that Amida Buddha embodies. Admittedly, the relationship between the emptiness tradition and the tradition of Amida pietism is neither readily apparent nor abundantly documented. Many, if not most, Buddhist scholars and practitioners see the whole Pure Land tradition as an accommodation for the spiritually weak and slothful. That the practice and thought of the Pure Land tradition sometimes lends itself to that conclusion is the fault of its thinkers and practitioners. In careful expositions and expressions of the Pure Land tradition, however, the definite and abiding roots in the mainstream of the tradition with its basis in emptiness and non-attachment are clearly expressed.

Shinran was very concerned with having his thought seen as being continuous with the whole of the Buddhist tradition. Indeed, he had quite a deep sense of the importance of historical foundations for his statements. That this was a favorite way of many scholar priests, especially ones who wanted to authenticate their own teachings, goes without saying. He drew on the tradition to establish his doctrinal emphases. That he was sometimes mistaken in his textual assumptions because he adopted the textual-historical assumptions of his times also goes without saying. What is important to recognize is his conscious faithfulness to the tradition as was understood at that time. While this faithfulness toward the tradition can be seen only as a self-justifying exercise of form over substance, a look at the systematic development of his position reveals a sound and justified basis on emptiness as well as development of and from this basic position.

His sense of history is reflected in his understanding of the teachings of the Pure Land Buddhist masters as the core actualizations of the truth of Amida Buddha's reality of compassion. Shinran was concerned with the authentication of the reality of Amida's compassionate activity, and he did this by looking back through the tradition to see those past masters who talked of Amida's compassionate activity. He did not merely rely on the Amida story found in the Pure Land *Sūtras*. It is seen as the primal ground for the authentication of the compassionate activity of Amida. Yet beyond its important mythic authentication, I see Shinran seeking to go beyond this use of myth to an authenticity based upon historical manifestation. This is the rationale for his abundant quotation from the scriptures centering not only on the Pure Land *sūtras* but also on the writings of the masters of the Pure Land tradition to authenticate the story and reality of Amida Buddha. Granted, this method of scriptural verification had a power of persuasion that is no longer present, but it points to an important perspective. The exposition of the witness to the Dharmākara/Amida event is an attempt to actualize, in history, the acts of compassion that are the reality of Amida Buddha. In short, to talk of the compassionate activity of Amida Buddha is the most concrete and overt act of actualizing the compassion that is Amida Buddha. This does not negate the important if not central role of the existential and personal realization of Amida's saving activity and one's need for such compassion. Nevertheless, this less discussed aspect of Shinran's thought must also be declared and clarified.

Shinran saw the appearance of Śākyamuni Buddha as solely for the purpose of telling us the story of Amida Buddha and, thereby, authenticate the reality of Amida Buddha and Amida Buddha's compassionate activity. The Pure Land *Sūtras* authenticate the reality of Amida Buddha simply because they are the words of Śākyamuni Buddha. This scriptural authentication of the compassionate activity of Amida Buddha is a traditional method of Buddhism as well as all other religious traditions. This scriptural literalism or, if you will, orthodoxy need not be the only interpretive alternative, however. Shinran also saw two other Indian masters as vital to the articulation and actualization of the Amida reality. Nāgārjuna and Vasubandhu are the traditional Indian Pure Land masters. Then, there are the Chinese masters T'an-luan, Tao-ch'o, and Shan-tao and the Japanese masters Genshin and Honen. The Chinese and Japanese masters are definitely authors of their respective Pure Land Buddhist treatises. The problem is with the Buddha and the two Indian masters. There is no reasonable way to connect the former with the Pure Land *sūtras* or the two masters with the works purported to be by them. It is obvious that Shinran wished to verify the Amida story through reference to these works mistakenly believing them to have been 'authored' respectively by the three. The latter two are the principle architects of the northern Buddhist tradition. It is clear that someone used their names to give authenticity to their own claims. The works themselves are important in that key ideas or doctrines are introduced in them that will play important roles in the expansion of the doctrine. What I see as important about this authenticating process is the importance given to the fact of articulating the reality of the vow in the tradition, that is, in the historical narrative.

In all three cases, the fault does not lie with Shinran who only followed the then current, common understanding of authorship of the *sūtras* and discourses. Yet how are we, holders of at least a more correct idea of scriptural authorship, to understand this false attribution of authorship? As for Nāgārjuna and Vasubandhu, we are forced to say that followers or instigators of the Pure Land tradition followed an oft-practiced attribution of their ideas to famous masters. The same argument can be used for the supposed 'authorship' of the Pure Land Sūtras. Here, however, I see an important, though perhaps forced, relationship between the historical Buddha Gautama Siddhārtha and the Pure Land *sūtras.* The act of Siddhārtha Gautama to rise from the seat of enlightenment and go forth to talk of his understanding of reality in order to help others to gain enlightenment is the primordial act of compassion in our tradition and can, I believe, be seen as the actualization into history of the compassionate, saving activity of Amida Buddha. The religious intuition to secure the reality of one's religions commitments to historical actualization is but the abstraction of historical acts of going forth to teach and aid others. It is through these acts that the compassion of Amida Buddha is historically actualized.

B. *The Emptiness Tradition in Shinran's Thought*

The above reflects my conviction that a central character of Shinran's thought is its insistence on tradition or the historical actualization of the reality of Amida through the act of telling us about Amida's compassionate activity. The teaching of the vow, that is, Amida Buddha's intent, has the reality of actualizing the compassionate activity of Amida Buddha. This section will now attempt to make the connection between the emptiness and Pure Land traditions. Four texts will be looked at, T'an Luan's *Wang-Sheng Lun Chu* and specifically its notion of the two-fold *dharma* body, Shinran's development of T'an Luan's exposition on the two-fold *dharma* body is examined through passages from his *Yuishinsho Mon'i, Ichinen Tanen Mon'i* and the fifth letter of the *Mattosho* collection.

1. *T'an Luan and the Two-fold Dharma-body*

There is an obvious similarity between the *Yogācāra Vijñaptimātrā* doctrine of the *buddha*-body, The two doctrines were developed independently of each other, however. This doctrine represents a discussion of the compassionate, actualizing activity that is Amida Buddha which is unique to T'an Luan and the Pure Land tradition. In his major work, the *Wang-Sheng Lun Chu* (*Commentary on the Discourse on Birth in the Pure Land*), he discusses the two-fold *dharma*-body in the context of rhetorically asking himself why the one reality can actualize itself in manifold ways.

> For *buddhas* and *bodhisattvas*, there are two types of *dharma*-body. One is the *dharma*-body of *dharma* itself and the second is the *dharma*-body of *dharma*-for-us. Through the *dharma*-body of *dharma* itself, the *dharma*-body of *dharma*-for-us arises. Through the *dharma*-body of *dharma*-for-us, the *dharma*-body of *dharma* itself comes forth. The *dharma* bodies are different yet inseparable, one yet not the same. This is why the mutual interpenetration of the one and the manifold are united in the one word *dharma.* If *bodhisattvas* do not fathom the mutual interpenetration of the one and the many, then they cannot perform the practice of 'self-benefit and other-benefit' [SSZ I336-7 for the Chinese text; for another English translation, Roger Corless, *T'an Luan's Commentary on the Pure Land Discourse: An Annotated Translation and Soteriological Analysis of the Wang-Sheng-Lun* (T. 1819) (Ann Arbor: University Microfilms, Inc., 1973), p.297.]

T'an Luan clearly sees the answer to the question, how the manifold is actualized from the one, as centering on the two-fold quality of reality (the one). It is important to recognize that T'an Luan's doctrine is concerned with a discussion of *dharma*-body, the ultimate. To explain how the manifold comes to be actualized, T'an Luan introduces a dual notion of reality in which reality is that which is abiding in and of itself and also that which is actualizing itself outside of itself. The Chinese for the two aspects is *fa hsing fa shen* and *fang pien fa shen. Fa shen* indicates the *dharma* (*fa*) body (*shen*). *Fa hsing* is *dharma*-nature or *dharma*-ness and corresponds to the Sanskrit *dharmata. Fang pien* is the Chinese Buddhist technical term for *upaya,* compassionate means or as translated above the activity and quality of *dharma*-for-us. Thus, the first aspect of the *dharma*-body is that of *dharma* in and of itself and the second is that of compassionate coming forth from the *dharma, dharma*-for-us.

The rather complex non-duality of the two aspects is of central importance and occupies much of the discussion. Simply stated, the two aspects are mutually dependent. The first two bodies of the three-fold Buddha body doctrine are declared to be mutually dependent also. [Gadjin M. Nagao, *Mādhyamika and Yogācāra: A Study of Mahāyāna Philosophies.* Leslie S. Kawamura, tr. (Albany: State University of New York Press, 1991), pp. 107-11] Here, however, there is rather more amplification of what exactly this mutual dependence entails. Because of the aspect of *dharma*-itself, the *dharma*-for-us arises. Because of the aspect of *dharma*-for-us, the *dharma* itself comes forth. 'Arise' and 'come forth' clearly are synonyms. It is because of the one aspect that there is the other aspect. Putting it negatively, without the one, there cannot be the other. Indeed, the fullness of reality is not expressed unless both aspects are clearly declared. What is the implication of this mutual dependence? The *dharma* itself is the basis of the *dharma*-for-us. This is an understandable assertion in which the ultimate is seen as the ground from which this other aspect of reality arises. The *dharma*-for-us, on the other hand, is the basis of the ultimate. The ultimate can never be, unless it actualizes itself. The actualizing activity that is the *dharma*-for-us is the basis of the full reality of the ultimate. Put differently, there is no abstract ultimate unto itself. There is only the ultimate as it is related to the world. The two can never be identical, yet they can never be different. If identical, then why talk of the two aspects? If different, then what becomes of the unity of the ultimate? The focus of discussion is the one reality and its two-fold contrasting character. The *dharma* itself is the complete opposite of the *dharma*-for-us. It is only in the total negation of itself that the ultimate is actualized as the *dharma*-for-us. The *dharma* itself totally negated is the *dharma*-for-us. The ultimate is self-identical in its self-negation. It is because of this dynamic of identity in negation that the manifold appears. The *dharma* is not identical with the manifold. However, purged by the fire of negation, the *dharma* can be nothing but the manifold. This is the mutual interpenetration of the one and the manifold. T'an Luan seems to play with the word *dharma* and its dual meaning of reality (*dharmata*) and actualizations of reality (*dharmas*). The word *dharma* indicates both the ultimate and the manifold.

The final sentence of the T'an Luan passage connects the realization of this dynamic identity of opposites (the basis for the mutual interpenetration of the one and the manifold) with fulfilling the *bodhisattva* practice of self-benefit and other-benefit.

Self and other benefit refer to realization of enlightenment for oneself and the guiding of others to their own realization. In coming to see that there is no ultimate except in the actualization of the ultimate, the *bodhisattva* must realize that there can be no realization of enlightenment for oneself except in the realization of enlightenment for all existence. Using the image of light, a light is not a light until it illuminates the darkness. In the same manner, self-enlightenment is not enlightenment until all are enlightened. In other words, the ultimate is not the ultimate until it touches all with its ultimate quality through its actualizing activity. Thus, the inner dynamics of reality in its identity of opposites is expressed as the practice of self and other benefit, in short, as enlightenment and compassion.

While it is a cliché in Buddhist writings to state the inseparability of enlightenment and compassion, here, T'an Luan attempts to discuss the rationale for this inseparability. Thus, for T'an Luan, the discussion of how the manifold is actualized from 'the one' ends in an assertion that to see the true dynamics of the ultimate is to fulfil one's enlightenment in and through compassion.

2. *Shinran's Extension of T'an Luan's Thought*

(a) *Yuishinsho Mon'i*

Shinran bases much of his thought on Amida Buddha on T'an Luan's discussion. He moves beyond T'an Luan, however, in seeing the actualizing activity that is Amida Buddha's compassionate intent as being central to understanding what reality is. Amida Buddha, the coming worth of the ultimate, takes on central importance for Shinran and negates the notion of reality abiding unto itself. This aspect of compassion comes to the fore because of Shinran's vision of the radical impotency of the self to gain enlightenment. Realizing that one is soteriologically impotent, Shinran naturally centres attention on the soteriologically active Amida. While he cites T'an Luan in his major work, *Kyo Gyo Shin Sho,* it is little more than citation to validate the Pure Land position in the tradition. There is no real discussion of the content of T'an Luan's discussion. However, the two-fold *dharma* body is discussed in the *Yuishinsho Mon'i* wherein Shinran develops the concept of Amida beyond T'an Luan.

> ... This *tathāgata* pervades the countless worlds; in short, it fills the hearts and minds of the ocean of all beings. Thus, plants, trees, and land all attain Buddhahood.
>
> Since it is with this heart and mind of all sentient beings that they entrust themselves to the Vow of the *dharma*-body as compassionate means, this *shinjin* is none other than Buddha-nature. This Buddha-nature is *dharma*-nature. *Dharma*-nature is *dharma*-body. For this reason there are two kinds of *dharma*-body with regard to the Buddha. The first is called the *dharma*-body as suchness and the second, *dharma*- body as compassionate means. *Dharma*-body as suchness has neither color nor form; thus, the mind cannot grasp it nor words describe it. From this oneness, was manifested form, called *dharma*-body as compassionate means.
>
> Taking this form, the Buddha announced the name *Bhikṣu Dharmākara* and established the Forty-eight great Vows that surpass conceptual understanding. Among these vows are the Primal Vow of immeasurable light and the universal Vow of immeasurable life, and to the form manifesting these two Vows Bodhisattva Vasubandhu gave the title, "*Tathāgata* of unhindered light filling the ten quarters." This *Tathāgata* has fulfilled the Vows, which are the cause of that Buddhahood, and thus is called "*Tathāgata* of the fulfilled body." This is none other than Amida *Tathāgata*.
>
> "Fulfilled" means that the cause for enlightenment has been fulfilled. From the fulfilled body innumerable personified and accommodated bodies are manifested, radiating the unhindered light of wisdom throughout the countless worlds. Thus appearing in the form of light called "*Tathāgata* of unhindered light filling the ten quarters," it is without color and without form; that is, it is identical with the *dharma*-body as suchness, dispelling the darkness of ignorance and unobstructed by karmic evil. For this reason it is called "unhindered light". "Unhindered" means that it is not obstructed by the karmic evil and blind passions of beings. Know, therefore, that Amida Buddha is light and that light is the form taken by wisdom. (CWS I, 461-2)

This passage is taken from comments on the phrase, "The Land of bliss is the unconditioned, the realm of *nirvāṇa*." It is specifically explaining the realm of *nirvāṇa,* the realm where the illusions of ignorance are set aright and the highest wisdom is realized. A list of some synonyms of *nirvāṇa* follows. It ends with *buddhata* (*buddha*-nature) which is said to be nothing but *tathāgata* (going to or coming from thusness or the ultimate, a title of the Buddha). What is central to the passage is the emphasis on the activity of the ultimate in breaking through the darkness of ignorance and permeating the hearts and minds of all existence. It is a discussion of this saving activity that is the context of the discussion of the two-fold *dharma*-body. Unlike T'an Luan, in which the discussion of the two-fold *dharma*-body is in the context of understanding the relation of *dharma* (the one) and *dharmas* (the many instances of reality), here the context is entirely soteriological. It is with this soteriological emphasis in mind that I see Shinran giving priority to Amida Buddha as the *dharma*-body of *dharma*-for-us. T'an Luan begins with the ultimate in itself and thereby gives it priority even as he states their oneness in twoness. Shinran talks of the ultimate (*nirvāṇa* and its synonyms), yet what becomes quickly apparent is that the fundamental attribute of the ultimate is the coming out of itself to permeate all existence. For Shinran, there is no ultimate unless it is felt in one's heart and mind, until it comes out of itself and becomes that which is for us and with us. Thus, while Shinran can be said to begin also with the ultimate, this ultimate never really is except when it permeates all existence and is this *dharma*-for-us. It is because of this soteriologically active aspect of reality that Shinran introduces the topic of the two-fold *dharma*-body.

The richness of the passage precludes a fully exhaustive analysis, yet a closer look at it may be helpful. Shinran seems to be using the literal meaning of *tathāgata* (going to or coming from thusness) and interpreting it to mean the coming out of thusness to all existence, so that every single thing is enclosed by it. Through such contact, all things are enabled to gain enlightenment. It is interesting to note that Shinran, in accord with the Tendai thought he studied during his youth, enumerates inanimate things as examples of what can gain enlightenment. Universal enlightenment means that the whole world is enlightened. This coming forth to every single thing specifically envelops their hearts and minds. A pan-psychism is assumed here. Since the heart and mind is that in which true faith in the vow of Amida Buddha (the *dharma*-body of *dharma*-for-us) occurs, this faith can be nothing less than reality itself. This says, then, that the mind of faith, being awakened by this permeating activity, partakes of reality and is accordingly nothing less than reality. It is for this reason that there is the two-fold *dharma*-body. This activity that opens the hearts and minds of beings to the ultimate is the ultimate, and therefore there must be a dual quality about the ultimate. The point is that reality reaches out to embrace the whole world including all of us in such a way that it awakens the awareness of this coming forth to us in the hearts and minds of all beings. The mind of faith in the vow of Amida is the mind made aware of the compassionate intent of the ultimate. The *dharma*-body of *dharma* itself is formless and beyond the mind's grasp. Yet it is from this thusness that form is actualized.

What exactly is the nature of this form, however? It is called Dharmākara Bhikṣu by Śākyamuni in the *sūtra* account, and the essence of Dharmākara can be said to be the forty-eight vows he established. These vows themselves are of a wondrous nature beyond ordinary, conceptual understanding. They actualize the compassionate intent of the ultimate. Shinran uses the image of light to elaborate on this compassionate activity. Light and life are symbols for wisdom and compassion respectively, yet it is the light of wisdom dispelling ignorance and being unhindered by passion that enables all beings to see the reality of the vows and the intent they actualize. Thus, Shinran uses light as a metaphor for the compassionate enlightening of beings. This form of the *dharma*-body of, *dharma*-for-us is indeed no form (what is the form of light?). It is just like the *dharma*-body of *dharma*-itself in this respect. Its formless form is the activity of dispelling the darkness of ignorance. It is that wondrous activity that is not readily conceivable. The image of light, Dharmākara, and the vows while not within the ordinary mind's grasp are obviously not totally beyond conception and description. Here is the difference between the *dharma*-body of *dharma* itself and the *dharma*-body of *dharma*-for-us. What the two-fold *dharma*-body does is to present reality as a formless reality beyond all conception and description and a formless reality embodying the compassionate activity of reality. Note the parallel with the Bhāvaviveka material above. It is one reality grounded on the formless and the embodied (formless form).

As we have seen, the formlessness of both aspects is the ground upon which the discussion develops. There is mention of the specific bodies of actualization that appear from the *dharma*-body of *dharma*-for-us (fulfilled body). These are the historical actualizations of the ultimate, the forms that are actualized in history. By their actualization, the light of wisdom reaches throughout the world. The phrase, while mentioning these historical actualizations, places the emphasis on the formless activity of light enveloping all existence to rid beings of ignorance. The formlessness of Amida is emphasized to identify it with the ultimate. It is because Amida is founded on the formless that it is able to reach and touch all existence. Thus, the bodies of actualization while indicating historical bodies take on a rather ethereal quality and their physical actualization is really not important. Rather, the emphasis is on their function as the compassionate dispelling of ignorance.

(b) *Ichinen Tanen Mon'i*

A passage repeating the language and content of the above *Yuishinsho Mon'i* quotation is found in the *Ichinen Tanen Mon'i*. It also has an explanation of *dharma*-for-us that is not found in the above passage.

> From this treasure ocean of oneness form was manifested, taking the name of Bodhisattva Dharmākara, who, through establishing the unhindered Vow as the cause, became Amida Buddha. For this reason Amida is the "*Tathāgata* of fulfilled body". Amida has been called "Buddha of unhindered light filling the ten quarters". This *Tathāgata* is also known as *Namu-fukashikiko-butsu* (Namu-Buddha of inconceivable light) and is the "*dharma*-body as compassionate means". "Compassionate means" refers to manifesting form, revealing a name, and making itself known to sentient beings. It refers to Amida Buddha. This *Tathāgata* is light. Light is none other than wisdom; wisdom is the form of light. Wisdom is, in addition, formless; hence this *Tathāgata* is the Buddha of inconceivable light. This *Tathāgata* fills the countless worlds

> in the ten quarters, and so is called "Buddha of boundless light". Further, Bodhisattva Vasubandhu has given the name, "*Tathāgata* of unhindered light filling the ten quarters."(CWS I, 486-87)

Upāya, dharma-for-us or, as expressed in the above, compassionate means is explained as the actualization of the form (formless form of light) of the formless thusness. It is revealing the name of Buddha and making itself known to all beings. In short, it is the compassionate activity of coming forth that is the making known of this compassionate coming forth. *Dharma*-for-us is compassion that makes the compassionate intent known.

Again, my contention is that the formless form that is Amida, that is, the *dharma*-body of *dharma*-for-us becomes central to Shinran's interpretation of what reality is. The formless thusness from which the formless form is actualized is the basis of this coming forth, as the above passages indicate. On this basis, the central importance of the formless thusness can be argued. However, in these passages Shinran develops the notion that thusness in and of itself is nothing unless it is Amida compassionately coming out of itself to us. Put differently, Shinran is not interested in an abstract thusness but in Amida understood as *dharma*-itself compassionately coming to us, in short, the *dharma*-for-us. This is the full implication of thusness for Shinran. Therefore, the *dharma*-body of *dharma*-for-us is the basis of the *dharma*-body of *dharma* itself, because it makes the latter actual in the hearts and minds of all beings.

(c) *On Jinen Honi*

This centering on the compassionate activity that fulfills thusness is more clearly indicated in Shinran's short essay, *On Jinen Honi*. This is the fifth letter in the collection of Shinran's letters called *Mattosho*. *Jinen honi* is a phrase unique to Shinran referring to the ultimate, to the formless thusness. Shinran explicitly states this identification. "Supreme Buddha is formless. And because of being formless, it is called *jinen*". The function of Amida is to reveal the character of *jinen*, the formless. The above passage continues, "Buddha when appearing with form, is not called supreme *nirvāṇa*. In order to make it known that Supreme Buddha is formless, the name Amida Buddha is expressly used; so I have been taught. Amida Buddha fulfills the purpose of making us know the significance of *jinen.*" (CWS 1, 530)

[On *Jinen-Honi*]

Concerning *Jinen* [in the phrase *jinen honi*]:

Ji means "of itself"—not through the practicer's calculation. It signifies being made so.

Nen means "to be made so"—it is not through the practicer's calculation; it is through the working of the Tathāgata's Vow.

Concerning *honi*

Honi signifies being made so through the working of the Tathāgata's Vow. It is the working of the Tathāgata's Vow. It is the working of the Vow where there is no room for calculation on the part of the practicer. Know, therefore, that in Other Power, no working is true working.

Jinen signifies being made so from the very beginning. Amida's Vow is from the very beginning, designed to bring each of us to entrust ourselves to it—saying *"Namu-amida-butsu"*—and to receive us into the Pure Land; none of this is through our calculation. Thus, there is no room for the practicer to be concerned about being good or bad. This is the meaning of *jinen* as I have been taught.

As the essential purport of the Vow, [Amida] vowed to bring us all to become supreme Buddha. Supreme Buddha is formless, and because of being formless is called *jinen.* Buddha, when appearing with form, is not called supreme *nirvāṇa.* In order to make it known that supreme Buddha is formless, the name Amida Buddha is expressly used; so I have been taught. Amida Buddha fulfills the purpose of making us know the significance of *jinen.*

After we have realized this, we should not be forever talking about *jinen.* If we continuously discuss *jinen,* that no working is true working will again become a problem of working. It is a matter of inconceivable Buddha-wisdom. (CWS I, 530)

The explanation of *jinen* in the above points to a 'natural' activity, an activity beyond human intent. Of course, this is the working of Amida Buddha for the purpose of our salvation. This soteriological definition of the activity of Amida Buddha is the content of the first third of the letter and is reflected in the explanation of *honi* as well. It is in the latter half of the letter in which the subject of the supreme Buddha is discussed that the relationship of emptiness and Amida Buddha's compassionate activity comes to the fore. It is this passage that was cited before the whole letter was quoted and is the clearest statement of the formless taking the formless form of Amida Buddha.

At the very beginning, soteriological priority is emphasized, the whole point of Pure Land Buddhism is that Amida Buddha, through the vow, brings us all to become supreme Buddha. The supreme Buddha, the ultimate itself, is nothing but formless reality or emptiness itself. It is precisely this emptiness that is *jinen*. The reality of Amida Buddha is that Amida Buddha reveals the formless. Amida Buddha is expressly for making us know the significance of *jinen*, of the formless activity of *jinen honi*, the supreme Buddha. Without Amida Buddha, the reality of formless activity cannot be known, cannot be fully revealed. Thus, there is nothing known of the ultimate, formless, and supreme Buddha except as it is expressed in the reality of Amida Buddha, in the saving reality of wisdom and compassion. Amida Buddha primordially defines what the supreme Buddha is.

It is in this primordial defining of the reality of the formless Buddha by Amida Buddha that we see how Shinran makes central the reality of Amida Buddha. The primordial characterization of emptiness is nothing other than wisdom and compassion. For Shinran, there can be no other understanding and manifestation of emptiness but this compassionately wise/wisely compassionate reality that is Amida Buddha. Moreover, as the Bhāvaviveka text cited above in section IB makes clear, while there is the paradoxical assertion that an absolutely ultimate entity actualizes compassionate activity, the most simple and thereby most reasonable explanation would be to say that the ultimate entity is not absolute but is truly ultimate because it freely engages in the reality of the other so that compassionate activity is a natural and inevitable expression of ultimate, not absolute, reality.

III. Whitehead's Thought

Whitehead's thought has guided much if not all of the preceding discussion. The central point of the above discussion centres on the primordial characterization of emptiness as that of wisdom and compassion. Creativity is the corresponding reality to emptiness in the process thought of Whitehead. Creativity is the ultimate and characterizes reality. It is defined by Whitehead as "The many become one, and are increased by one". [Alfred North Whitehead, *Process and Reality: An Essay in Cosmology*, Corrected Edition, eds. David Ray Griffin and Donald W. Sherburne (New York: The Free Press, 1978 (1929.), p. 21.] It is not an abstract something but rather is always embodied with certain characteristics. There is no abstract reality called creativity. In the same way, emptiness is not a reality unto itself but always appears in form. The reality of the form is empty but there is no emptiness in and of itself. 'Emptiness is form and form is emptiness', this famous formula of the *Prajñāpāramitā* literature expresses the basic characterization of emptiness. There is no abstract reality called emptiness; things are empty. Again, the main thesis of this paper is that emptiness is not beyond expression but is always primordially characterized as wisdom and compassion. The embodiment of emptiness that is the *tathāgata* is nothing but wisdom and compassion actualized and engaging in wisely compassionate activity.

Two other points about the Buddhist conceptuality of reality, though partly addressed by the tradition, need to be discussed. The early discussion of the instantaneous arising, abiding and passing away of the entities of existence noted one point briefly. While the reinterpretation of the Sarvāstivāda notion of *dharma* developed above (IA) attempted to deal with the intuition into reality that saw things as not only impermanent but also as having a quality of continuity, there still is the ultimate problem of things eventually perishing or lingering on toward mere insignificance. It is with the process notion of objective immortality, the incorporation of all entities into God in every moment of the ever receding past, that we can observe a degree of permanence not fully actualized in only continuity. The second point is that although the coming together of the many to become the one is worked out in Buddhism, how the one from the many is determined or concretized is not worked out. In Whitehead's scheme, the notion of the subjective aim is introduced by God to guide this coming together to become this one, so that a novel, scant that it may be, entity arises to take its place in the ever passing parade of creation. In the process of creativity itself novelty is introduced so that the above definition ending with "increased by one" refers to the novel entity that is introduced into the world. Again, there is no mere repetition of the past, no mere repetition of preceding entities. God is not the ultimate in process thought, creativity is. God is the facilitating process of bringing coherence and novelty to the processes of coming to be and enduring. In short, it is through God that the chance of direction and endurance is possible. The Buddhist notion of emptiness/conditioned arising does not necessarily consider this aspect of existence. My suggestion is that perhaps it should.

Concluding Remarks

The thesis of this paper is that the Buddhist ultimate reality—emptiness/suchness—is primordially characterized as compassionate and wise regardless of the absolutist rhetoric that is sometimes found in the tradition. Shinran's primordial characterization of reality as compassionate means/*dharma*-for-us in his centering on Amida Buddha is therefore true to the tradition and need not be seen as a simplification of Buddhist teachings to cater to the spiritually weak and slothful.

ABBREVIATIONS

CWS I: *The Collected Works of Shinran, Volume I The Writings,* Kyoto: Jodo Shinshu Hongwanji-ha, 1997.

SSZ I: *Shinshu Shogyo Zensho* I, Kyoto: Oyagi Kobunsho, 1971.

T: *Taishō Shinshu Daizokyo,* Tokyo: Taishō Shinshu Daizo Kyo Kanko Kai, 1970.

IV

ICONOGRAPHY

CHAPTER 18

The Idea and Realization of the Colossal Buddhas: Maitreya and Vairocana*

AKIRA MIYAJI

I. *The Colossal Buddha Images Erected on the Trade Rout in the Ancient Time*

Buddhism is a comprehensive religion. In the process of the spreading of Buddhism and its culture from India to Central Asia and China, they have been adjusted to each region and people with transformation.

The Vairocana Buddha statue in the Tōdaiji temple known as *Daibutsu* (means—Great Buddha) is the most celebrated one for a colossal Buddha in Japan, so that every colossal image of Buddha is apt to be seen as Vairocana. However, a gigantic image of Buddha almost cannot be found inside India, even where was the origin of Buddhism. In fact, there is a pair of Buddhas carved at either end of the veranda of *caitya* hall (Cave 3) at Kānherī. These two images are more than 7 meters in height,[1] which are known as the largest images of Buddha in India. The *Da-tang Xiyuji* (*Records of the Western Regions of the Great T'ang Dynasty*) written by Xuanzang, provides descriptions about some colossal images of Buddha.[2] Even if its descriptions were accurate, we almost cannot assume that those images were over 10 meters high.

Emerged in the neighbouring area of India and Central Asia, colossal images of Buddha were popular in China, and those are mostly the images of Maitreya. It is not difficult to make the images in double or triple life-size for expressing the faith of devotee, but a huge image of Buddha over ten or twenty meters high, is suggestive of a special aim rather than just making a big statue: the idea of colossal Buddha. Based on the historical monuments and textual sources, the meaning of colossal Buddha images is about to be discussed.

1. *The Colossal Image of Maitreya in Darel as the Evidence by Fa-hsien and Xuanzang*

The earliest evidence about the colossal image of Buddha might be the wooden image of Maitreya Bodhisattva in Darel, where was the gateway to Indian subcontinent. It was witnessed by Fa-hsien who passed the western side of Karakorum Range from the Tarim Basin in the early fifth century[3] (the *Fa-hsien-Ch'uan*). The *Mei-sō-den-shō* by Sōshū in the Kamakura period, which quoted the *Ming-seng-Ch'uan* edited by Paoch'ang in the Liang, mentions that not only Pao-yun who travelled with Fa-hsien but Fasheng in the middle of fifth century observed the colossal image.[4] In addition to that, Xuanzang, who travelled in the early seventh century, stated about that image in his *Da-tang Xiyuji*.[5]

At present, the image in Darel no longer exists, which Fa-hsien reported that it was eight *jō* (80 feet) high. Xuanzang mentioned that it was around hundred feet, about thirty meters high. Both of them reported the legend regarding that image; that an *arhat* who dwelled there ascended to the Tuṣita Heaven accompanied by an artisan by his magical power and showed the holy figure of Maitreya. Then he asked the artisan to make that image in wood. After completing it, the *dharma* of Buddha was spread toward the east.

Darel, at the up-river of Indus in the north of Pakistan, is located in the intricate valleys of the Pamil-Karakorum. It is surprising that a colossal image of Buddha was erected in such mountainous area. Darel, however, was on the way of trade routes in the ancient time, from Gandhāra where was the centre of North Indian Buddhism, and passing over through the western part of Karakorum Range and the oasis area in the Taklimakan desert to China. Fa-hsien, Pao-yun and Fasheng used this way and witnessed the image of Buddha in Darel. Buddhist monks like Buddhabhadra, Chih-yen, Kumārajīva passed along this route between Gandhāra, the Tarim Basin and China in the early fifth century.

Compared with the area in the middle reaches of the Gaṅgā, where the Buddhism was sprouted, Darel is quite remote place. But it was once an important point on the route between India, Central Asia and China, where different parts of the world encountered. The colossal image in Darel indicates that Buddhists in such remote place tried to create a new idea of Buddhist world against the centre of Buddhism in India. The legend that the *dharma* of Buddha was spread toward the east after completing this image suggests that the colossal Maitreya might be the symbol of the New World.

2. *The Remaining Colossal Image of Maitreya in Mulbek*

The colossal image of Maitreya remains in Mulbek on the way from Kashmir to Leh of Ladakh, in the western Tibet. That image seems to have similar background to the image in Darel referred by Chinese monks. The big image in standing posture around ten meters in height is carved on the face of a solitary rock pinnacle. That image is shown the divine character as Bodhisattva Maitreya with four arms, a water flask in one left hand, *nāgakeśa* in the other left, *varada mudrā* in one right, and a rosary in the other right hand, and a *stūpa* crowned on the head. This relief might be assigned to be carved between the eighth and ninth century.[6]

In Kashmir, Buddhist art was developed in the eighth century, spread to Ladakh in the east where the Tibetan Buddhism was flourished since the tenth century. Mulbek is sited on the way of the trade route from Kashmir and Ladakh. The huge relief was created in Mulbek, a distant place from Kashmir, where can be called as the Gate to Ladakh geographically and historically for the spread of Buddhism.

3. *The Colossal Images of Buddha at Bāmiyān*

The most famous colossal image of Buddha around India is the Grand Buddhas of Bāmiyān in Afghanistan[7] (Unfortunately the two colossal Buddhas and the paintings have being destroyed by Taliban in 2001. In this paper, I will discuss the status before the destruction). Bāmiyān is located in the mountains of the Hindukush, dividing India and Central Asia. Since the ancient time, there are two routes connecting India, Central Asia and China: one goes up the Indus from Gandhāra, passing the west of Karakoram Range and Pamir, and entering to the Tarim Basin: the other goes west from Gandhāra, crossing the Hindukush, entering the Tarim Basin from Tokharestan (Northern Afghanistan). Analyzed the situations of these routes from the evidences by itinerant priests, the former route might be developed earlier, and the latter became active after the middle of sixth century.[8] While the colossal image of Buddha in Darel stood on the main route in the west of the Karakorum Range and Pamir, the Grand Buddhas in Bāmiyān were sited in the central point of the routes crossing the Hindukush.

Around 750 caves extend east and west about one and half kilometer along the cliff wall, with the two Grand Buddhas carved out and covered by plaster. While both colossal images lacked the face by probably vandalism, the east one is thirty-eight meters high and the west one is fifty-five meters high. In 629, Xuanzang visited at Fanyuan (Bāmiyān) and reported that Buddhism was flourishing remarkably there. He also referred to the two Grand Buddhas, and identified the East Grand Buddha as the standing Śākyamuni, the West one as the standing Buddha with descriptions that it was in gold and was bejewelled (without referring to its identity of the Buddha).

It is noteworthy that the two colossal images of Buddha have interesting mural paintings on the ceiling of their niches. On the ceiling of the niche above the East Grand Buddha, was represented the image of Sun God who rides the chariot with four winged horses in the sky, while the painting on the ceiling of the niche of the West Grand Buddha showed the geometric composition, arranging the figures of Bodhisattvas beneath of the niches, and heavenly being and maidens, celestial musicians, worshipping the seated Maitreya Bodhisattva in the centre, which figure was extinguished. Some celestial maidens are rendered even naked.

The *Kuan Mi-lo Pu-sa Shang-sheng Tou-shui-tien Ching* or the

"*Sūtra* of Meditation on Maitreya Bodhisattva's Rebirth on High in the Tuṣita Heaven" (Taishō vol. 14, No. 452) describes the sensual paradise of the heavenly world of the Tuṣita Heaven where Maitreya Bodhisattva dwells. The Tuṣita Heaven of Maitreya Bodhisattva and the Western Heaven of Amitābha are different: in the former heaven many celestial maidens decorate themselves by luxurious ornaments, jewels, and play the heavenly music: in the latter heaven, no maidens are there. The mural painting of the niche above the West Grand Buddha probably displays the Tuṣita Heaven of Maitreya Bodhisattva.[9] The West Grand Buddha might be Maitreya who would descend from the Tuṣita Heaven to this world, while the East Buddha is Śākyamuni.

As noted above, the colossal images of Buddha are located in such a remote region as Darel, Mulbek and Bāmiyān. In the ancient time, however, those places were at the crossroads of important land routes that linked India to the other areas.. Therefore, it is clear that the creation of those colossal Maitreyas lay in its strategical geographic location. Indeed, the lack of historical documentation makes it impossible to reveal the details of the creation of the Grand Buddhas. However, it can be easily presumed that they were erected with royal power which properties were gained by the advantage in the commercial trade between the East and the West. Not only the richness but also the powerful royalty must have promoted to erect those gigantic images. And now, the royal sovereignty has been absorbed into the cosmology of Buddhism. The question then arises about the relationship between the royal sovereignty and the Buddhist doctrine.

II. *Colossal Buddhas for the Spread of Buddhist Culture toward the East*

1. *The Adoration for the Emperor and the Erection of the Colossal Buddhas at Yungang*

The Yungang caves with famous images of Buddha; the earliest colossi in China, are located in the west of Pingcheng (Datong). There are around fifty caves and five images of Buddha in gigantic size on the cliff along the river of Wuzhou.[10] According to the *Weishu Shilaozhi Chronicles,* Tanyao who had been nominated to the *Shamentong,* or minister of the religion for the nation, petitioned to Emperor Wencheng for the excavation of the cave temples.[11] It states, "the five caves should be excavated in the cliff of the mountain ridge of Wuzhou, in the west of Pingcheng, with one central Buddhist statue carved in each cave. The tallest image was seventy feet and the second one sixty feet in height. The carving of their decoration is absolutely marvellous." It was the early Heping era (AD 460-65) that the construction of colossal images of Buddha started.

Those images of Buddha, showing the lively and robust representation with volume, are installed in the caves from Cave 16 to Cave 20, named as the Five Tanyao Caves. The largest one, in Cave 19, measures sixteen and half meters high and the shortest one, in Cave 20, is thirteen and half meters. The arrangement of five colossal images provokes us the assumption that each image was intended to honor the five emperors in the Northern Wei dynasty.

The Northern Wei, a dynasty founded by the tribe of a nomadic origin known as the Xianbei, established the idea that an emperor was a Buddha incarnate. The creation of colossal images might be strongly inspired by this conception. One historical episode justifies that idea: after the persecution of Buddhism by Emperor Taiwu, Emperor Wencheng ordered to make a statue of Buddha as large as the Emperor. After its completion, on the face and the foot of the statue, small black dots miraculously appeared in identical positions to moles on the face and the foot of the emperor. This happening was said to be a manifestation of the Buddha's gratitude for the emperor's devotion.

Each statue of Buddha in the Tanyao Five Caves has different appearance, which mingles the image of Buddha with emperor. Those statues present us an important feature regarding the motivation of creating the colossi Buddhas, that is the relationship between the adoration for emperor and the colossal Buddha. The attempt for identifying those images as historical emperors has been done and they are assumed to contain different characters as divinity, although it is not clearly identified yet.[12]

The standing Buddha (ht. 14 m.) in Cave 16 shows the *abhaya mudrā* in the right hand, the left hand is hung down with bending its thumb and middle finger. This Buddha wears the Chinese dress, differently from the other statues. Its oval face is also unique and it is generally assumed as Śākyamuni, however it could be identified with Amitābha who gives a welcome to the Pure Land, inspired by his *mudrā.*

The colossal image (ht. 16.3 m.) in Cave 17 is the leg-crossed Bodhisattva, wearing the jeweled crown and accessories. The leg-crossed Bodhisattva in the Northern Wei dynasty was commonly represented as Maitreya Bodhisattva in the Tuṣita Heaven. The fact above indicates that the image represents Maitreya.

The standing image of Buddha in Cave 18 (ht. 15.8 m.) lost its right hand, while the left hand holds a part of the garment. The characteristic expression here is that many small Buddha emanations carved on the drapery of Buddha. There is an interpretation that the colossal image is identified as Vairocana, inspired by the Buddhabhadra's translation of the *Ta Fang-kuang Fo Hua-yen Ching* (*Avataṃsaka Sūtra*) in which it is described that the cloud of Buddha emanations spouts out from the innumerable pores of Vairocana, when the Great Light is flashed out of Him. The identification, however, is not clear. Pointing out that the colossal image is attended by ten disciples and that other doctrinal sources mention Śākyamuni spreads the Buddha emanations on his body, A.F. Howard objected to the identification as Vairocana and concluded that this colossal is rendered Śākyamuni as the cosmological Buddha.[13]

The Buddha in Cave 19 (ht. 16.5 m.) shows the *abhaya mudrā* in the right hand and the other hand seizing the garment. That image is seated in cross-legged posture. The two other small caves were excavated on either side of Cave 19, and each has the images of Buddha seated in pendent legs, so that we can assume that this trinity depicts the Three Times Preach under the Nāgapuṣpa tree by Maitreya Buddha at His rebirth here below. This colossal, the largest statue in the Five Tanyao Caves, might be the earlier image of descending Maitreya which became popular in the T'ang dynasty in the representation of the seated trinity as the Three Times Preach.

The niche of Cave 20 was broken, thus the seated colossal Buddha (ht. 13.5 m.) is, present, exposed in the open air. With the *dhyāna mudrā,* it shows magnificent expression. The divine character in this image might be Amitābha (Amitāyus), however it is not clearly identified.

The colossal Buddhas in the Five Tanyao Caves could be presumed that they were produced as overlapping the features of historical emperors in the Northern Wei with the preferable character of Buddha and Bodhisattva for them. The Xianbei, newly coming nomadic people, tried to establish the Lord of the World as the core for their domination of the northern part of China. Applying the emperor adoration, which related to the worship for ancestor, to the universal idea of Buddhism, they endeavored to make the center of the world in a remote area. The strength filled with energy can be seen in the expression of those colossal Buddhas. Although the identities of Buddhas in Cave 16 and 20 are not clear, is possible to assume that the central one is Śākyamuni as the cosmological Buddha, accompanied with Maitreya Bodhisattva and Maitreya Buddha in the both sides, which show the outstanding representation.

Kucha in Xinjiang Uighur Region flourished as an important oasis kingdom on the Northern road in Central Asia. Many Buddhist sites are there, Kizil and Shimsim caves had ever contained colossal images of Buddha. Unfortunately, only niches have survived to the present time. But these niches suggest the existence of the images of Buddha in clay around ten meters high. They could be dated before the T'ang dynasty.

2. *Colossal Images of Buddha Remained on the Trade Routes in T'ang Dynasty*

The production of gigantic Buddha images became popular in the T'ang dynasty. Many images are found in the cave temples located along the He Xi Corridor, running from the western edge, Dunhuang to Xi'an and Luoyang. The core of statue was engraved out of the cliff, approximately modeled, and finished with thick clay and plaster. Most of images were represented Maitreya Buddha. Here, we list up the remaining colossal images from west.

(1) Colossal Images of Buddha in the Dunhuang Mogaoku

In Dunhuang, about five hundred caves have been excavated in the cliff face during the Northern Liang (in the second quarter of the fifth century) and the Yuan. In addition, there are two colossal Buddhas in the north and the south.[14] The northern figure (Cave 96), Buddha seated in pendent legs, measures thirty-three meters high. According to the *Mogaoku Ji* or the *Record of the Mogaoku* described in the antechamber of Cave 156, the northern image was constructed by Lingyin, a *dhyāna* master, with Yinzu, a lay Buddhist in the second year of the Yanzai era (AD 695) in the reign of Empress Wu. Although the identity of that Buddha is not mentioned, it might be represented Maitreya Buddha because the seated Buddhas in pendent legs in the Sui and the T'ang period were mostly rendered as Maitreya. The southern Buddha in Cave 130 (ht. 26 m.) is also seated image in pendent legs, assumed as Maitreya. The *Record of the Magaoku* states that it was erected by the dedication of Chuyan, a priest, and Ma Sizhong, a native, in the Kaiyuan era (AD 713-741).

(2) Colossal Image of Buddha in the Tientishan cave temple

The Tientishan temple in Wu-wei Ward is consisted of thirteen caves excavated during the northern Liang and T'ang dynasty.[15] The seated colossal image in pendent legs of Buddha in Cave 13 assigned to the late T'ang dynasty, measures twenty-six meters high. It was probably represented Maitreya Buddha accompanied by Bodhisattvas, *Arhats, Lokapālas* in the formation of Seven Deities.

(3) Colossal Image of Buddha in the Binglingsi cave

The Binglingsi in Yongjing Ward contains 184 caves excavated over a thousand years starting in the western Shin of the Sixteen Kingdoms.[16] The colossal seated image in Cave 171, twenty-seven meters high, is Maitreya. The multi-stories tower previously stood there. The *Qingtang Lu* edited by Li Yuan in the Song dynasty states, "Bao Chengtiao, an civil governor from Liangchou constructed the huge building of Lingyansi. Its length is seven *ri* along the mountain, the image was engraved from the rock of mountain. That measures around hundred feet high", describing the appearance of the colossal Buddha.

(4) Colossal Images of Buddha in the Maijishan Caves and other Caves

The Maijishan temple in Tianshui Ward was consisted of 194 caves excavated from the Northern Wei to the Ming period.[17] There are two colossal Buddhas in the eastern and the western sides of the cliff. The east image in Cave 13, fifteen meters high, is Maitreya Buddha seated in pendent legs accompanied with attendant Bodhisattvas, which are belonging to the Sui period. The west image in Cave 98 measures fourteen meters high in standing posture accompanied with attendant Bodhisattvas. Restored many times later, its construction is assigned to the Northern Wei dynasty.

The cave temples mentioned above are sited in Gansu Province and there are colossi of Buddha in other places: one in the Xumishan Yuanguangsi cave near Ku-yüan on the route from Lanzhou to Xi'an, in the Ningxia Hui Region.[18] That is Maitreya Buddha seated in pendent legs, created in the later T'ang. The other Buddha is a seated image in the Dafosi at Bin Ward of Shanxi Province. It measures twenty-five meters high and was erected in the T'ang period.

(5) *Colossal Image of Buddha in the Leshan Lingyunsi*

The largest image of Buddha in the world is installed in the Lingyunsi of Leshan at Sichuan Province.[19] It stands at the confluence of the Minjiang and Qingyijiang, engraved on the cliff of the Mount Lingyun in seventy-one meters high. It is the seated image in pendent legs of Maitreya with the inscription on its feet, the *Jiazhou Lingyunsi Dafoxiangji Bei*. It describes that it started to be created by the request of Haitong, a *dhyāna* master in the first year of Kaiyuan era (AD 713), in the reign of Xuanzong. With some interruptions, it was finally completed in the nineteenth year of the Zhengyuan era (AD 803) by the help of Wei Gao, a military governor. It took ninety years for its completion.

3. *The Descending Maitreya in Seated Posture with Pendent Legs*

As mentioned above, the erection of colossal Buddha was popular in the T'ang dynasty, and most of them were produced in the cave temples sited along the ancient trade route from Dunhuang to Xi'an. All these images are more than twenty meters high, except two Buddhas in the cave temples of Maijishan; erected in the Northern Wei and Sui period, are much smaller than other images.

The colossal images of Buddha must play an important role

as the symbol of the center in cave temples. And all images, i.e., the south and the north Buddhas in the Dunhuang Mogaoku, the colossal Buddhas in the temples Tiantishan, Binglingsi, Xumishan Yuanguangsi and Leshan Lingyunsi, were represented in seated with pendent legs, identified as Maitreya Buddha who would be reborn here below. In the scenes of the Maitreya's Pure Land on the wall of the T'ang period cave in Dunhuang, the figures of descending Maitreya are rendered in seated with pendent legs. Now, we have to search for the reason why the colossal images of Maitreya were created as the center of cave temples, and for the characteristic feature of Maitreya.

III. The Spread and the Transformation of Maitreya Cult

1. The Worship of Maitreya in Gandhāra, Central Asia and China

Maitreya is the Buddha-to-be who will appear next to Śākyamuni. In Gandhāra, the prominent characteristic of Maitreya is the image of Bodhisattva on the way towards Buddhahood to obtain the Enlightenment. Śākyamuni Bodhisattva and Avalokiteśvara Bodhisattva display the feature of royalty, wearing the turban-like crown. On the other hand, Maitreya Bodhisattva shows the feature of Brahman ascetic such as hair tied-up in topknot or bowknot and, a water flask in the hand. However, the feature and nature of Maitreya Bodhisattva has been dynamically transformed at the spread of Maitreya worship from Gandhāra to Central Asia and China.

In Central Asia, the character as savior was strongly projected on Maitreya. He will save many people who missed the preach by Śākyamuṇi. Some relieves in Gandhāra and Kāpiśī of Afghanistan invented the iconography of Maitreya Bodhisattva in the Tuṣita Heaven who was surrounded by heavenly beings and celestial maidens within a kind of trapezoidal architecture. This image was largely accepted in the cave temples of Kizil, Dunhuang in the Northern Wei, Yungang and Longmen.

The "*Sūtra* of Meditation on Maitreya Bodhisattva's Rebirth on High in the Tuṣita Heaven" or the *Guan Milepusa Shangsheng Doushuaitian Jing* (Taishō vol. 14, no. 452), which was translated by Juqu Jingsheng in Liu Song dynasty and completed in Central Asia, depicts the scene of the Tuṣita Heaven where Maitreya

Bodhisattva is surrounded by heavenly beings and celestial maidens in a palace. The worship of Maitreya at His rebirth on high is based on people's wish for reincarnating in the Tuṣita Heaven where Maitreya Bodhisattva dwells. That kind of worship widely developed the iconography of Maitreya in the Tuṣita Heaven.

Meanwhile the worship of Maitreya who will be reborn here below from the Tuṣita Heaven in far future was depicted in the *sūtras* of Maitreya, composed with the traditional legends of Maitreya. The legend of Maitreya is seen in the *Āgama-sūtras* and independent texts, so called, the *sūtras* on the Maitreya like the *Mi-lo Hsia Sheng Ch'eng Fo Ching* or the "*Sūtra* on Maitreya's Rebirth Here Below" (Taishō vol. 14, no. 454.), the *Mi-loTa Ch'eng Fo Ching* or the "Grand *Sūtra* on Maitreya's Becoming Buddha" (Taishō vol.14, no. 456.) translated by Kumārajīva in the later Chin, the *Maitreya-Vyākaraṇa* translated as the *"Sūtra* on Maitreya's Rebirth Here Below" by I-ching in the T'ang period. Although each *sūtra* differentiates, its main idea is same. In far future, there will be a bright and beautiful city called Ketumatī and one *Cakravartin* or Ruler of all the world, whose name is Śaṅkha will be born. The country will be peacefully ruled by *Cakravartin* Śaṅkha without using his four troops of army. He will hold the *sapta-ratna* or seven jewels that are symbols of *Cakravartin,* and thousand sons. At that time, Maitreya will be reborn in a Brahman family. After the renunciation, he will attain the Enlightenment under the *nāgapuṣpa* tree and become the Enlightened Buddha. King Śaṅkha will also renunciate under the guidance of Maitreya Buddha. Maitreya enters to the palace with King Śaṅkha and his followers, and turns the *dharma-cakra* (wheel of the Law). Maitreya will praise Śākyamuni Buddha and dedicate preaches three times (Three Times Preach under the *nāgapuṣpa* tree). And then he will lead countress people who missed the preach by Śākyamuni to salvation.

As above, the theme in the *sūtras* on Maitreya is that Maitreya will appear in far future and give salvation to the people who missed Śākyamuni's preach. And the appearance of Maitreya needs one basic condition that Śaṅkha, a *Cakravartin,* is born in the capital, Ketumatī. At the same time of his birth, Maitreya becomes Buddha. This idea reveals that the worship of Maitreya, a savior in future, is strongly connected the divine feature of *Cakravartin.* Maitreya is not only Buddha-to-be, but also relates with the ideal king as *Cakravartin.* He was worshipped in the symbolism of paradise where the ideal world could be realized both in sacred and secular. According to the traditional Buddhist context in India, the sacred world of Buddhism should be established in the monk's community *saṅgha,* while the worship of Maitreya was based on the concept of the ideal world linking with the royalty. That is the reason why Maitreya was represented in king-like feature, sitting in posture with pendent legs which may be followed the royal figure of nomadic people.

2. *The Background of Constructing the Colossal Buddha: The Worship of Maitreya*

The construction of colossal image of Maitreya was founded on the power and rich property of emperor. On the other hand, it included the significant feature in the history of Buddhist thought. That was related to the appearance of Maitreya in future.

In which kind of future will Maitreya appear? The *Chuan-lun Sheng-wang Hsiu-hsing Ching* in the chapter 6 of *the Dirghāgama* or the *Ch'ang-A-han Ching* (Taishō Vol.1, No.1) mentions that the world was flourished when the *Cakravartin* was born once. However, the world became worse and the human life span decreased from 40,000 to 100 years old. Gradually, the human age became shorter and shorter, finally to 10 years old when the world was in the worst stage. However, human life span will recover by degrees and the time when it reaches 80,000 years, Maitreya will be born. It suggests that the birth of Maitreya in future brings the best time of human life.[20]

We can find the traditional idea in India that the circuit of flourish and decadence in the world corresponds to the change of human life span. The visualization of this idea was introduced in the *Guanfo Sanmei Hai Jing* or the *Sūtra on the Ocean-Like Samādhi of the Visualization of* the *Buddha* (Taishō vol.15, no. 643; hereafter *Ocean Sūtra*) translated by Buddhabhadra. It mentions about the change of Buddha's bodily height instead of the change of human life span. This text is one of the meditation texts (*Guan Jing*), supposed it to be composed in the area around the north-western India and the Central Asia. Buddhabhadra, a high priest, who acquired the methods of Visualization in Gandhāra, shifted to China by the request of Chih-yen.[21]

The chapter 10 "Calling the seven Buddhas to mind" of the *Ocean Sūtra*,[22] gives an explanation of the method for visualizing Past Seven Buddhas with the details of the stature of each Buddha. The five Buddhas from Vipaśyin to Kanakamuni are measured in *yojana*, an imaginative unit, and Kāśyapa measures sixteen *jō* (=ten feet), finally the height of Maitreya is referred also as sixteen *jō*. The bodily height of Kāśyapa in sixteen *jō* in high, Śākyamuni in one *jō* and six feet, and Maitreya in sixteen *jō* corresponds to the change of the world: the glorious past, the decayed present and again the glorious future. The height of Śākyamuni Buddha, one *jō* and six feet, might be caused that four is believed as the complete number in India and sixteen, the multiple number of four, is important. The height of Kāśyapa in the past and Maitreya in the future may be calculated as ten times of Śākyamuni's height. The *Mi-lo Laishi Jing* (Taishō vol. 14, no. 457), an anonymous translation in the eastern Jin dynasty, also depicts that Maitreya is sixteen *jō* in high. That was the source to create a colossal image of Maitreya.

Buddhabhadra who translated the *Ocean Sūtra* encountered with Kumārajīva from Kucha in Chang'an. The "Grand *Sūtra* on Maitreya's Becoming Buddha" or the *Mi-lo Ta-ch'eng-fo Ching* (Taishō Vol. 14, No. 456) translated by Kumārajīva is the most completed version of the *Sūtras* of Maitreya together with his "*Sūtra* on Maitreya's Rebirth Here Below" or the *Mi-lo Hsia-sheng Ch'eng-fo Ching* (Taishō Vol. 14, No. 454). These two *sūtras* also mention that Maitreya will appear as colossal Buddha. The former text states that people will live to be 84,000 years old, and the bodily height be sixteen *jō* at the birth of Maitreya.[23] And it depicts that the color of His body is golden with thirty-two *lakṣaṇas*. Light miraculously radiates from the pores of His skin and shines without making any shadow. And His glorious body is referred as being larger than Śākyamuni and measured thirty-two *jō* as double of human height.

The "*Sūtra* on Maitreya's Rebirth Here Below", another translation of Kumārajīva, enlarged the height of Maitreya to thousand feet, thirty-two *jō* in width of the chest, twelve *jō* and four feet in length of the face.[24] Thousand, symbolizing a number in large quantity, is commonly used: thousand disciples of Maitreya, thousand sons of King *Cakravartin* and so on. This number might be adopted to the height of Maitreya, in fact, that is the most exaggerated height of Maitreya among every *sūtra.*

The erection of colossal image of Buddha means the establishment of ideal world in Buddhism. The monumental image of Maitreya was erected as the symbol of paradise. It is no wonder that the colossi of Maitreya were the Supreme in cave temples. Maitreya occupies the center of many caves, so-called, the Thousand Buddhas' Caves (Quianfodong). As *Cakravartin* has thousand sons, Maitreya is followed by thousand Buddhas. The last chapter of the *Miaofo Lianhua Jing* (*Saddharmapuṇḍarīka-sūtra,* Taishō vol. 9, no. 262) mentions that if one keeps the *sūtra* and understands its meanings, thousand Buddhas extend their hands to the believers.[25] He won't fall in bad reincarnation, and shall be reborn into Maitreya's Tuṣita Heaven. As discussed above, it can be said that the colossal image of Maitreya was constructed as the center of the whole caves having the Buddha images.

IV. Vairocana in the Longmen Cave Temple to the Great Buddha in the Tōdaiji Temple

1. *The Colossal Image of Vairocana Buddha in the Longmen Fengxiansidong*

Finally, we shall examine the colossal image of Buddha in the Longmen Fengxiansidong.[26] This image is not only the center of the cave temple but also serves as a manifestation of imperial grace. The identity of this Buddha is Vairocana, not Maitreya. The Longmen caves carved into the hills on the riverside of the Yi, are more than 1300 caves there. The peak of production at the site was the time when Luoyang was the imperial capital, namely the latter half of the Northern Wei and the T'ang dynasty. With magnificent scale as well as elegant and exquisite expression of the face, the colossal image of Buddha in the Fengxiansidong stands as the pinnacle achievement of the early T'ang period. The cave deeply and widely cut into the cliff face, there are nine images splendidly arrayed in the cave consisting of a central Vairocana image, symmetrically flanked with Bodhisattvas, *Arhats, Lokapālas* and guardians in pair.

This colossal Buddha, approximately 17 meters in high, contains the inscription carved on its pedestal and titled the "Record on the Great Vairocana", which informs the construction of the image. The Vairocana image was erected by an imperial order of Emperor Gaozong and it was completed on the 30th December in the second year of Shangyuan (AD 675). The inscription goes on to note that in the third year of Xianheng (AD 672), Empress Wu presented her funds for completion, the sum of 20,000 *guan,* to assist with the construction. The construction of Fengxiansidong Cave was supervised by two monks, Shandao of the Shijisi temple in Chang'an who was one of the patriarchs of Pure Land Teachings, and Huijian, a chief of the Fahaisi temple, the director was Wei Ji and the vice-director was Fan Xuanzeas. Those supreme people, nominated for the Fengxiansidong cave, reflects Emperor Gaozong's great enthusiasm for the national project. The monumental statue was completed with the elegant and magnificent expression. The inscription also records,

> With the help of Emperor, the representation of this statue was planned. The beauty of its face cannot be compared with anything. Its expression of mercy is like Sun and Moon. If we observed its figure, our impurity could be removed off. If we prayed for it, our wish could be accomplished. Around seven hundred years have passed since the real religion was spread toward the east. The propitiousness of this image is extreme.

The rounded face of the main statue is elegantly expressed with the elongated eyes which are drawn downward a little, the beautiful curved eyebrow like half-moon, the sharp nose, and the tense lips, which give the impression of grace and gentleness. Unfortunately the hands and laps are mostly corrupted, however, its robust body simply modeled and the thin garment with the expression of rhythmic drapery like waves render the unparalleled dignity.

The present image is seated on the octagonal pedestal with multi-piled lotus petals. It is worthy to notice that each petal has the relief of Śākyamuni Buddha on its surface.[27] That symbolizes the Lotus Repository World of Vairocana. The *Fan Wang Ching* (Taishō vol. 24, no. 1424) or the *Sūtra of the Perfect Net* depicts that Vairocana Buddha is seated on the gigantic lotus with thousand petals. On each petal there are worlds and Vairocana appears as Śākyamuni in each world. And each one world has ten billion worlds with Mount Sumeru, where Bodhisattva Śākyamuni appears. That image of Vairocana has the representation of Śākyamuni as Thousand Buddhas of Thousand Petals in the Lotus World on its pedestal. The meaning of Vairocana is 'One who widely shines', so to speak, Buddha of the Sun. This Buddha, residing in the center of the world, shines as the Sun in the world and governs it. With the image as the Master in the Lotus World, Vairocana spreads out His existence everywhere of the world, at the same time, He occupies its center.

The early T'ang period was the time when its power was extremely increased and the worldwide empire was established in the reign of Emperor Taizong and Gaozong. The colossal image of Vairocana, erected in the Fengxiansidong in the central plains of China (or at Chung-yüan) by the demand of Emperor Gaozong, was the monumental symbol of secular and sacred worlds, that is the domination of the actual world of the T'ang and the foundation of the center as an ideal world of Buddhism. It can be said that the importance of the colossal Buddha was fulfilled there.

2. *Maitreya Worship of Empress Zetian Wuhou*

After the expiration of Emperor Gaozong in 683, Zetian Wuhou dominated the political power. With the adhesion to the sect of Hsüeh Huai-i, a mysterious monk, she ordered to publish a fake Buddhist text titled the "*Sūtra* of Great Cloud" which describes that she was the reincarnation of Maitreya.[28] Based it on, she claimed to reign herself and then the Revolution of Wuhou was broken out (AD 690). She commanded to install the great sculpture of supposed Maitreya made in cloth and lacquer in a sacred hall of the palace at Luoyang. And she built the Dayunsi (Great Cloud Temple) in Chang'an, Luoyang and other provinces for dedicating the "*Sūtra* of Great Cloud". As a ruler, she used the worship of Maitreya and made it the ideology for her domination of the country. The Dayunsi was the first provincial temple in each places, and this system was followed to the Longxingsi at the reign of Emperor Zhongzong and the Kaiyuansi of Emperor Xuanzong.

In the later time of Zetian Wuhou, she tried to erect the colossal image of Buddha in bronze at the Baisimaban Hill.[29]

She planned to create the colossal Buddha and build the Dayunsi temples in provinces for her political ambition. The erection of the colossal Buddha in the Fengxiansidong by Emperor Gaozong, and her project to produce colossal images and the Dayunsi temples gave an impact to Japan, where the Great Vairocana Buddha was erected in the Tōdaiji temple and the system of provincial temples was executed.

The erection of colossal image of Buddha, based on the worship of Maitreya, is imbued with both to the worship of Emperor in the ancient time and to the Buddhist idealism. It reveals the ambiguous features in the actual world: peaceful and egoistic. Although the colossal image of Vairocana might be more dogmatic than Maitreya, it remains us the trace of the Maitreya Worship.

3. *The Erection of the Great Vairocana Buddha in the Tōdaiji Temple*

In Japan, the capital was transferred to Heijō in the third year of Wadō (AD 710), main temples in Asuka and Fujiwara were shifted to the new capital city. Ten years passing since the transfer of the capital, there were so magnificent forty-eight Buddhist sanctuaries dominated in rows the capital Heijō. At the reign of Emperor Shōmu (AD 724-749) who was a devout Buddhist, he decreed the edicts as follows[30]: to raise the seated image of Śākyamuni statues of *jōroku* size (about 2.4 m. high) at each province and to copy the complete set of *Daihannya-kyō* (*Mahāprajñāpāramitā-sūtra,* Taishō Vol. 5, No. 220) in the 9th year of Tenpyō (AD 737); to build the seven-storied pagoda in each province; to copy the *Hokekyō* (the *Lotus Sūtra: Saddharmapuṇḍarīka-sūtra*) in the 12th year of Tenpyō (AD 740); and to build the *kokubunji* (provincial temple) and the *kokubuniji* (provincial nunnery) in each province in the 13th year of Tenpyō (AD 741).

Under the unsteady political situation, Emperor Shōmu shifted the capital from Heijō to three other places one after another: the capital Kuni, Naniwa and Shigaraki. In the 15th year of Tenpyō (AD 743), he issued a proclamation to construct the colossal Vairocana in the Kōgaji temple at Shigaraki in the announcement as[31]:

> Even I am not virtuous, I am in the reign as emperor. My will is to provide the salvation to people widely, thus I endeavor to be affectionate to everyone. Although the affection and benefit of Buddha is spread in this country, His beneficence has not been supplied completely. I wish that the heaven and the earth would be peaceful for the sake of holy power under Three Jewels: *Buddha, dharma* and *saṅgha.* Promoting beneficial projects forever, I hope that every being could be prospered.
>
> Here, on the fifteenth of October in the fifteenth year of the Tenpyō era (AD 743), I make a vow of Bodhisattva and will produce the bronze statue of Vairocana with gilding. For that, it is necessary to expend every copper in the country, to cast the statue, and to build the hall by excavating the mountain. I spread the *dharma* of Buddha to the whole universe and devote myself for Buddhist. And finally, we will receive the benefit of Buddha and attain the Enlightenment for Buddhist life.

Although the flame work of the colossal Buddha was made in the Kōgaji temple at Shigaraki, the project to complete it was suspended. The project was then continued at the Konkōmyōji temple of Yamato, at the foot of Mount Mikasa in Heijō, which was finally selected to the seat of the central government. With the effort of Kuninakanomuraji Kimimaro, who was a superintendent of many engineers, and of Gyōki who was a sage widely supported by people, the project of colossal Buddha was accomplished with cruel labor and huge expenses.

It was so costly an enterprise that the resources of the Japanese nation were drained, as Emperor Shōmu proclaimed, "It was we who possess the wealth of the land; it was we who possess all power in the land. With this wealth and power at our command, we had resolved to create this venerable statue." And undoubtedly, same as the colossal image of Buddha in the Fengxiansidong was completed by Emperor Gaozong together with Empress Wu, Empress Kōmyō who was a pious Buddhist must have supported that project. The construction of the colossal Buddha could be considered as the establishment of the ideal State Buddhism which Emperor Shōmu had longed for.

This seated statue made in bronze and gold plated about

fourteen meters in height is Vairocana Buddha; the very shining One as Sun Buddha and the Cosmological Buddha located in the center of universe. That is because a lotus corresponds to one great world. In India, there is the tradition to take a lotus as the flower of light and as one universe. In Buddhism, the *Avataṃsaka-Sūtra* or the *Flower Garland Sūtra* and the *Fan Kang Ching* or the *Sūtra of the Perfect Net* put special emphasis on this idea.[32] According to "the Lotus Repository World" of the *Fan Kang Ching;* Vairocana exists in the Lotus World surrounded by a thousand petals. And a thousand Śākyamunis, as his manifestations, preside over these thousand petals. In each petal-universe, moreover, there are an infinite number of Sumeru World. And ten billion Bodhisattva-Śākyamunis as the manifestations of each Śākyamuni, preside over each Sumeru World.

The colossal image of Vairocana in the Fengxiansidong of Longmen visualizes the vision quoted above. But, in the other hand, the Great Buddha in the Tōdaiji temple portrays more sophisticated cosmological vision as the cosmology of Buddhism. The colossal statue is seated on the great pedestal consisting of the upward petals and the downwards petals, and twenty-eight of them, the upwards petals bear the incised drawings depicting Śākyamuni's World on the universe of Mount Sumeru.[33] According to the recent study,[34] it is said that the cosmological imagery is basically affiliated with the doctrine of the *Fan Kang Ching;* but the motifs on the petals such as the Mount Sumeru, the Heaven shown in its twenty-five registers and the world of Śākyamuni surrounded by twenty-two Bodhisattvas, might also be ascribed to the *Ta Chih-tu Lun* (*Mahāprajñāpāramitā-Śāstra*) which presents a well organized and most comprehensive summary of the Buddhist cosmos.

In any case, it is so magnificent vision that each petal corresponds to a world, Vairocana is seated on the Great Lotus pedestal and each petal contains Śākyamuni Buddha. The cosmological imagery on the petals is represented with smooth and vivid lines. That expression has the influence from the art at the peak of the T'ang dynasty and the unique idea of that cosmology astonishes us.

Namely, the construction of the colossal bronze statue of Vairocana in the Tōdaiji temple as the center of the local provincial *kokubunji* temples, to be located in the capital for governing the Śākyamuni statues enshrined in each *kokubunji* temples, was indisputably intended for the realization of the Lotus Repository World of Vairocana.

In the middle of the eighth century, when the system of centralized Autocracy having been just established in the model that used in the T'ang dynasty, it was already about to break down due to the struggle for power between the royal family and aristocracies. Under the political disorder, there can be little doubt that Emperor Shōmu erected the colossal Buddha as the symbol of his longing ideal Buddhist Nation.

In the fourth year of Tenpyō-Shōhō (AD 752), a brilliant ceremony of the inauguration of the Great Buddha was held under the leadership of an Indian monk, Bodhisena. That was the twice centennial anniversary of the official propagation of Buddhism to Japan (AD 552). It is fully convinced that Emperor Shōmu wished to declare the completion of the State Buddhism widely at that monumental occasion.

NOTES

* I express my deep gratitude to Ms. Yūko Fukuroi for her translation from my Japanese paper.

1. J. Fergusson and J. Burgess, *The Cave Temples of India,* 1880, rep. ed., Delhi, 1969, p. 352.
2. Taishō, vol. 51, p. 896a, 913b, 924b, 934b, 935b.
3. Taishō, vol. 51, p. 858a. cf. A. Stein, *Serindia,* vol. I, Oxford, 1921, pp. 5-6.
4. Taishō, vol. 59, p. 343c. Dainihon Zoku Zōkyō, vol. 7, part 1, p. 13.
5. Taishō, vol. 51, p. 884b.
6. D. Snellgrove and T. Skorupski, *The Cultural Heritage of Ladakh,* Warminster, 1977, pl. 4. S.L. Huntington, *The Art of Ancient India,* New York-Tokyo, 1985, pp. 376-77.
7. T. Higuchi (ed), *Bāmiyān: Art and Archaeological Researches on the Buddhist Cave Temples in Afghanistan 1970-1978,* 4 vols., Kyoto, 1983-84. D. Klimburg-Salter, *The Kingdom of Bāmiyān,* Naples-Rome, 1989. A Miyaji, *Bāmiyān harukanari,* Tokyo, 2002.
8. S. Kuwayama, "Bāmiyān Daibutsu ni kakawaru Futatsu no Michi (Two Routes relating to the Erection of the Grand Buddhas at Bāmiyān)", *Tōhōgakuhō,* Kyoto, vol. 57, 1985, pp. 109-209.
9. A. Miyaji, *Iconology of Parinirvāṇa and Maitreya—from India to Central Asia,* Tokyo, 1992, pp. 555-591.
10. S. Mizuno and T. Nagahiro, *Yungang Caves,* 16 vols., Kyoto University, 1951-56.

11. Z. Tsukamoto, *Sinabukkyo Shi : Hokugi-hen* (*History of Chinese Buddhism: a volume of Northern Wei period*), Tokyo, 1969, pp. 139-144.
12. R. Yoshimura, "Donyō Gokutsu Ron (A Study of Five Tanyao Caves)", *Bukkyō Geijutsu*, vol. 73, 1969, pp. 12-27. J.C. Huntington, "The Iconography and Iconology of the "Tan Yao Caves at Yungang", *Oriental Art,* 1986, Summer, pp. 142-160.
13. A.F. Howard, *The Imagery of the Cosmological Buddha,* Leiden, 1986, pp. 97-102.
14. K. Tō, "Tonkō Bakkōkutsu Saiso no Tenkai (Development of Painted Clay Sculptures of Dunhuang *Mogaoku*) ", *Chūgoku Sekkutsu Tonkō Bakkōkutsu,* vol. 3, Tokyo, 1981, pp. 224-227.
15. *Grotto Art of Gansu Sculpture,* Gansu Peeple's Fine Arts Publishing House, 1994, pl. 53.
16. *Chūgoku Sekkutsu, Heireiji Sekkutsu,* Tokyo, 1986.
17. *Chūgoku Sekkutsu, Bakusekizan Sekkutsu,* Tokyo, 1987.
18. *Comprehensive Record of Contents of Xumishan Grottoes,* Cultural Relics Publishing House, Beijing. 1997.
19. Y. Kegasawa, "Shisen Rakuzan Ryōunji Daibutsu no Rekishi to Genjo (History and Existing Condition of the Great Image of Buddha in the Lingyunsi of Leshan at Sichuan Province)", *Bukkyō Geijutsu,* 179, 1988, pp. 106-125.
20. Taishō, vol. 1, pp. 40-42.
21. Taishō, vol. 50, pp. 334-35, vol. 55, pp. 103-104.
22. Taishō, vol. 15, p. 613.
23. Taishō, vol. 14, pp. 429-430.
24. Taishō, vol. 14, pp. 423-424.
25. Taishō, vol. 9, p. 61c.
26. *Chūgoku Sekkutsu, Ryūmon Sekkutsu,* vol. 2, Tokyo, 1988, pls. 109-29, pp. 249-252.
27. S. Mizuno and T. Nagahiro, *Ryūmon Sekkutsu no Kenkyū,* Tokyo, 1941, pl. 56, p. 71.
28. S. Kamata, *Chūgoku Bukkyōshi* (History of Chinese Buddhism), vol. 5, 1994, Tokyo, pp. 76-86.
29. B. Matsumoto, *Bukkyōshi zakkō* (Studies on History of Buddhism), Osaka, 1944, pp. 351-388.
30. *Shoku Nihon gi,* vol. 2 (Shin Nihon Bungaku Taikei 13), Tokyo, 1990, pp. 312-313, 364-365, 390-391.
31. *Shoku Nihon gi,* op. cit., pp. 430-431.
32. A. Sadakata, *Buddhist Cosmology: Philosophy and Origins,* Tokyo, 1997, pp. 143-51.
33. *Nara Rokudaiji Taikan,* Tōdaiji, vol. 10 (Tōdaiji 2), Tokyo, 1998, revised ed. 2001, pls. 162-70, pp. 54-7.
34. N. Matsumoto, Tōdaiji Daibutsu Renben Senkokuga no Zuyō ni tsuite (Textual Sources of the Linear Engravings on the Lotus Petals of the Grand Buddha Statue at Tōdaiji Temple), *Nanto Bukkyō,* No. 55, 1986, pp. 52-70.

Chapter 19

Iconography of Sukhāvatī Lokeśvara

RURIKO SAKUMA

The cult of Avalokiteśvara originated in India, and has flourished in Asian countries such as India, Nepal, Tibet, China, Japan, etc. Various images of Avalokiteśvara represented in sculptures and paintings have appeared in these areas throughout centuries. For example, the carving of an eleven-headed figure in Kānheri cave in West India clearly shows the evolution of the Tantric form of Avalokiteśvara.

Sukhāvatī Lokeśvara is one of the Avalokiteśvaras in Tantric Buddhism. (Avalokiteśvara is also called Lokeśvara in India and Nepal.) This Lokeśvara was worshipped in India, Nepal and Tibet and is still now worshipped in Nepal[1]. As a contribution to Buddhist iconographical studies, this short essay aims at showing iconographical types of Sukhāvatī Lokeśvara based on textual sources including material unknown to preceding studies.

B. Bhattacharyya and D.C. Bhattacharyya refer to the iconography of the deity mentioned in the *Darmakoṣasaṃgraha* which was written by Vajrācārya Amṛtānanda.[2] Amṛtānanda wrote this work as the first Residency Pandit in Nepal at the request of Brian Hodgson in Newari era 946 (A.D. 1826).[3] The manuscript is preserved at the Library of the Asiatic Society, Calcutta (Ms. no. G.8055). D.C. Bhattacharyya points out that various materials, including earlier texts like the *Kriyāsamuccaya* are compiled into this work.[4] The image of the deity is as follows:

> "Sukhāvatī Lokeśvara is three-faced, white in color, and six-armed. One of his right hands is in the gesture of shooting an arrow, the remaining two have the rosary and the Varada pose. In two of his left hands he carries the bow and the lotus, and the third is placed on the thigh of Tārā who is on the god's lap. He sits in Lalitāsana[5] on the lotus, and is surrounded by the Goddesses Vajratārā, Ratnatārā, Padmatārā and Viśvatārā. There is a Caitya on the top".

For the translation above, I cite Bhattacharya, *Tantric Buddhist Iconographic Sources,* pp.22-23. A similar image of this form is found in a picture: one of the 108 forms of Lokeśvara in Seto Matsyendranāth temple, Kathmandu (Plate 1).[6] However, the goddesses of Vajratārā and so on are not depicted in it.

Plate 1
Three-faced and six-armed form
Sanskrit: Sukhāvatī Lokeśvara
Amoghavajra Vajrācārya, *Aṣṭottaraśatalokeśvaraparicaya,* p. 23 (no. 82).

In addition to this Nepalese description, we can find another six-armed form in Tibetan Buddhism. It is mentioned in the sādhana (visualization) of Sukhāvatī Lokeśvara which is included in the *Yi dam rgya mtsho'i sgrub thabs rin chen 'byun gnas kyi lhan thabs rin 'byuṅ don gsal (Rin lhan)*. This work was compiled by the Panchen Lama IV (1781-1852 or 1854).[7] The sādhana of Sukhāvatī Lokeśvara is one of the sādhanas handed down from an Indian Tantric Buddhist, Śākyarakṣita.[8] It is said that Śākyarakṣita learned the Hevajra, Cakrasaṃvara, Tārābhava and Mahākāla Tantras and belonged to Tārānatha's (born 1575) lineage of the Tārā Tantra.[9]

According to this sādhana, we can provide the iconographical characteristics of this deity. The Tibetan text and translation are as follows:

> ...'phags pa spyan ras gzigs jo bo su kha wa ti sku mdog dkar po źal gcig phyag drug pa / g'yas kyi daṅ po ba dan rtse gsum pa'i phyag rgya / gñis pa na bgraṅ 'phreṅ/ gsum pa na nor bu daṅ bcas pa'i mchog sbyin/ g'yon daṅ po padma dkar po'i sdoṅ bu nor bus mtshan pa/ gñis pa na dbyu gu rtse gsum/ tha ma na spyi blugs 'dzin pa / źabs rol pa'i stabs kyis bźugs śiṅ/ dar daṅ rin po ches brgyan pa / ral pa'i cod pan can/ g'yon phyogs su raṅ snaṅ gi yum u tpa la 'dzin pas 'khyud pa/ rgyal ba 'od dpag tu med pas dbu brgyan pa'o//(fol.99, 1-4)...
>
> ...the Lord Sukhāvatī Avalokiteśvara has a white body. [He is] one-faced and six-armed. The first right hand has a flag decorated with a trident. The second [right] hand holds a rosary. The third [right] hand has jewelry and displays the gesture of conferring boons. The first left hand holds a stalk of a white lotus decorated with jewelry. The second hand holds a trident. The last (third) hand has a golden goblet. He sits in the posture of relaxation. [He is] dressed in a cloth and adorned with jewelry. [He wears] a diadem consisted of twisted locks of hair. [He] holds a consort, his own mind, who has a blue lotus (utpala) in his left side. [His] head is adorned with the Buddha Amitābha...

Comparing the symbols and the gestures of hands of this form with that of the three-faced and six-armed form, we can find differences between the two. Whereas the three-faced and six-armed form has an arrow and a bow, the one-faced and six-armed form has a flag decorated with a trident, a trident and a golden goblet. Among these symbols, the trident is a well-known symbol of Śiva in Hinduism so we can clearly see an influence from the cult of Śiva in the one-faced and six-armed form.

This form is depicted in the wooden prints of the *Five Hundred Gods of Narthang* (Plate 2-1, 2-2).[10]

In addition to the six-armed form which is above mentioned, we can present the three-faced and ten-armed form based on two manuscripts of the *Sādhanamālā*. One manuscript is preserved at Kyoto University (K),[11] and the other is mentioned in

Plate 2-1
One-faced and six-armed form
Sanskrit: Sukhāvatī Avalokiteśvara
Tibetan: sPyan ras gzigs su kha va ti
Lokesh Chandra, *Buddhist Iconography,* p. 289 (no. 764)

A Microfilm Catalogue of the Buddhist Manuscripts in Nepal (BL)[12] The sādhana of Sukhāvatī Lokeśvara is written in folios 57b4-58a4 of the former manuscript and folio 37b[13] of the latter.

This three-faced and ten-armed form in the sādhana is not referred to by preceding studies of Foucher,[14] Mallmann,[15] Bhattacharyya[16] and Meisezahl.[17] The sādhana of Sukhāvatī Lokeśvara is not included in the Bhattacharya edition[18] of the *Sādhanamālā* and the sādhana collections in the Tanjur of the *Tibetan Tripiṭaka*.[19] The Sanskrit text and translation of the sādhana are provided below.

Plate 2-2
One-faced and six-armed form
Sanskrit: Sukhāvatī Avalokiteśvara
Tibetan: sPyan ras gzigs su kha va ti
Musashi Tachikawa and Masahide Mori and Shinobu Yamaguchi, *Five Hundred Buddhist Deities*, p. 298 (no. 255)

Sukhāvatīlokeśvaradhyānaṃ //

mūlamukhaṃ śaraccandragauraṃ[20] dakṣiṇamukhaṃ haritavarṇaṃ[21] vāmamukhaṃ raktavarṇaṃ[22] paṃcacīraśeṣaraṃ[23] jaṭāmitābhaśobhitaṃ[24] mayūrapicchābhavastrābharaṇam pītavarṇayā ekavadanayā dakṣiṇavaradakarayā[25] vāmābhayakarayā[26] vāmākasthayā[27] svaśaktyā virājitaṃ dakṣiṇaprathamakare jvālāmālāṃkitakhaḍgadharaṃ[28] vāmaprathamakare kamaladharaṃ dakṣiṇavāmayor dvitīye śaraśarāsanadharaṃ[29] tṛtīyayo dakṣiṇavāmayor[30] vajrāṃkitaparaśupāśadharaṃ[31] caturthayor dakṣiṇavāmayor[32] varadavāmāṃkasthaśaktyāliṃga-navātakarpaṭāṃkitatriśūladharaṃ[33] dakṣiṇavāmayor[34] paṃcamayor dharmacakramudrādharaṃ viśvapadmopari vidhumaṇḍale saṃsthaṃ saumyarūpaṃ sukhāvatīvyūhākhyaṃ lokeśvaraṃ sukhāvāptaye bhāvayet //[35]

Visualization of Sukhāvatī Lokeśvara

The front face [of Sukhāvatī Lokeśvara] is white as the moon in autumn, the right face is green and the left face is red. The top of his head is decorated with five pieces of cloth. He is adorned with matted hair and the Buddha Amitābha. He wears a cloth and ornaments having the colors of a tail of a peacock. He shines in company with his own consort (śakti) who sits on his left knee. She is yellow and has one face. She displays the gesture of conferring boons (varada) in her right hand and the gesture of protection (abhaya) in her left hand. His first right hand holds a sword featured with a ring of flame. The first left hand holds a lotus. The second right and left hands hold an arrow and a bow [respectively]. The third right hand holds an ax featured with a thunderbolt (vajra). The third left hand holds a lasso (pāśa). The fourth right hand displays the gesture of conferring boons (varada). The fourth left hand holding a trident, decorated with a rag blowing in the wind, embraces a consort (śakti) on his left side. The fifth right and left hands display the gesture of preaching the law (dharmacakramudrā). He sits on the disc of the moon in a double lotus (viśvapadma).[36] In order to obtain happiness, one should visualize the Lokeśvara having the tranquil image which is referred to in the *Sukhāvatīvyūha*.

Comparing the symbols and the gestures of hands of this form with that of the six-armed form, we can find some common and uncommon features between them. One similarity is that they are both accompanied by the consorts: Yum (Tib.), Tārā or Śakti.[37] The ten-armed form as well as the six-armed form includes the cult of the goddesses. Furthermore, we can also see that both have tridents (excluding the three-faced and six-armed form). The cult of Śiva is also reflected in the ten-armed form.

On the other hand, one of the differences is that the ten-armed form displays the gesture of preaching the law like the Lord Buddha, whereas the six-armed form does not.

As we have mentioned above, we can suggest that the ten-armed form has its originality in respect of having all three characteristics: the cult of the goddesses, the cult of Śiva and the appearence of a preacher like the Lord Buddha.

This ten-armed form can probably be traced back to Indian Tantric Buddhism as it is written in the *Sādhanamālā*. Furthermore, we can be fairly certain that this ten-armed form was also worshipped in Nepal because a very similar image of this form is found in a Nepalese picture which is included in Ekai Kawaguchi's collection of Tibetan and Nepalese Buddhist Art[38].

Finally, it is necessary to add an explanation of the relationship between Sukhāvatī Lokeśvara and the Pure Land of Amitābha (Amitāyus) in the *Sukhāvatī Vyūha*.

At the end of the sādhana of Sukhāvatī Lokeśvara, it is mentioned that one should visualize the deity which is referred to in the *Sukhāvatī Vyūha*. However, the name of Sukhāvatī Lokeśvara is not actually mentioned in the *Sukhāvatī Vyūha*. Furthermore, the similar forms (the six-armed and ten-armed forms) of Sukhāvatī Lokeśvara are also not mentioned in the *Sukhāvatī Vyūha*.[39] Indeed Sukhāvatī Lokeśvara has a relationship to the Pure Land of Amitābha, but the relationship seems to be thin and weak in respect of the iconography.

It should be concluded, from what has been said above, that we can provide three types of Sukhāvatī Lokeśvara based on the textual sources of India, Nepal and Tibet.

NOTES

* This is an expanded and revised version of the paper: "Iconographical Characteristics of Sukhāvatīlokeśvara" which first appeared in *Journal of Religious Studies,* vol. LXIX-4 (no.307), Japanese Association for Religious Studies, 1996, pp. 166-67 (in Japanese).

1. For example, Sukhāvatī Lokeśvara is worshipped at a ceremony on behalf of a dead person (śrāddha) in Nepal. This ceremony is performed six months or a year after the person's death. See Badri Ratna Bajracharya (translated by Kazumi Yoshizaki), *Buddhism of Nepal,* Kurokami Library, 1993 (1986), p. 59.
2. See Benoytosh Bhattacharyya, *The Indian Buddhist Iconography,* Firma K.L. Mukhopadhyay, Calcutta, 1968 (1924) (Reprint of Second Edition 1958, Revised and Enlarged with 357 Illustrations) p. 142 and Dipak Chandra Bhattacharyya, *Tantric Buddhist Iconographic Sources,* Munshiram Maṇoharlal Publishers Pvt. Ltd., New Delhi, 1974 (1973), pp. 22-23.
3. See Bhattacharyya, *Tantric Buddhist Iconographic Sources,* p. 9.
4. See Bhattacharyya, *Tantric Buddhist Iconographic Sources,* p. 9.
5. "Posture of relaxation". See Gösta Liebert, *Iconographic Dictionary of the Indian Religions,* Studies in South Asian Culture edited for the Institute of South Asian Archaeology University of Amsterdam by J.E. Van Lohuizen de Leeuw, vol.V, E.J. Brill, Leiden, 1976, p. 151.
6. See Amoghavajra Vajrācārya, *Aṣṭottārāśatalokeśvaraparicaya,* Lokeśvara saṃgha Nepal, 1980, p. 23 (no.82).
7. Lokesh Chandra, *Sadhana-mala of the Panchen Lama,* International Academy of Indian Culture, Part I, New Delhi, 1974, p. 7.
8. These sādhanas are included in the fifteenth section of the *Rin lhan.* Lokesh Chandra, *Sadhana-mala* of *the Panchen Lama,* Part II, New Delhi, 1974, pp. 66-143.
9. The reference to Śākyarakṣita can be found in *the sGrol ma'i rgyud kyi byuṅ khuṅs gsal bar byed pa'i lo rgyus gser gyi phreṅ ba źes bya ba (The Origin of Tārā Tantra,* trans. and ed. by David Templeman, Library of Tibetan Works and Archives, New Delhi, 1995 (1981), p. 26).
10. See Lokesh Chandra, *Buddhist Iconography,* (Śata-Piṭaka Series Indo-Asian Literatures vol. 342) 2 vols. Aditya Prakashan, New Delhi, 1987, p.289 (no. 764) and Musashi Tachikawa and Masahide Mori and Shinobu Yamaguchi, *Five Hundred Buddhist Deities.* Asian Iconography Series-I, Adroit Publishers, New Delhi, 2000, p. 298 (no. 255). The flag decorated with a trident mentioned in the text cannot be found in these wooden prints.
11. See Kiyotaka Goshima and Keiya Noguchi (compiled), *A Succinct Catalogue of the Sanskrit Manuscripts in the Possession of the Faculty of Letters, Kyoto University,* Kyoto, no. 119 (manuscript number). The date is Nepal Saṃvat 862? (A.D. 1742). See Zengyo Shimoizumi, "On the Kyoto University Manuscript of the *Sādhanamālā.*" (in Japanese) *Journal of Indian and Buddhist Studies* 30(1), pp. 136-137, no. 102 (manuscript number).
12. See Hidenobu Takaoka (ed.), *A Microfilm Catalogue of the Buddhist Manuscripts in Nepal.* Vol.1, Buddhist Library, Nagoya, 1981, KA30 (manuscript number).
13. The sādhana of Sukhāvatī Lokeśvara is written in the margin of the manuscript.

14. See A. Foucher, *Étude sur l'Iconographie Bouddhique* de *l'Inde*. Bibliothèque de l'École des Hautes Études Sciences Religieuses Treizième volume 2e partie, Ernst Leroux, Éditure, 1900, 1905, Paris.
15. See Marie-Thérèse de Mallmann, *Introduction a l'Étuede d'Avalokiteśvara,* Ministère de l'Éducation Nationale Annales du Musée Guimet Bobliothèque d'Étude-Tome Cinquante-Septième, Civilisations du Sud, 1948, Paris. *Introduction a l'Iconographie du Tantrisme Bouddhique,* Librairie d'Amérique et d'Orient, 1986, Paris.
16. See Bhattacharyya, *The Indian Buddhist Iconography.*
17. See R.O. Meisezahl, *Geist und Ikonographie des Vajrayāna-Buddhismus.* Beiträge Zentralasienforshung Band 2, VGH Wissenschaftsverlag, Sankt Augstin, 1980.
18. See Benoytosh Bhattacharyya, *The Sādhanamālā.* 2 vols. Gaekwad's Oriental Series nos. 26, 41, 1968 (1925, 1928) Oriental Institute, Baroda.
19. (1) *sGrub thabs brgya rtsa* translated by Pa tshab Tshul khrims rgyal mtshan (Peking no. 3964-4126, sDe dge no. 3143-3304); (2) *sGrub thabs brgya rtsa* translated by Ba ri ba (Peking no. 4127-4220, sDe dge no. 3306-3399); (3) *sGrub thabs rgya mtsho* translated by Grags pa rgyal mtshan (Peking no. 4221-4466, sDe dge no. 3400-3644).
20. BL saracandragauraṃ.
21. BL add. a central dot.
22. BL add. a central dot.
23. Confusion between the script of "kha" and "ṣa" is common in Nepalese manuscripts. See Kimiaki Tanaka and Kazumi Yoshizaki, *Neparu Bukkyo* (*Nepal Buddhism*). (in Japanese) Shunjusha , 1998, p. 245. The rendering is probably a misprint of "paṃcacīraśekharaṃ". BL paṃcacīrakaśeparaṃ?
24. BL add. a central dot.
25. BL -varadakayā.
26. The rendering follows the Sandhi rule. K vāma abhayakarayā; BL vāma abhayakareyā.
27. BL vāmāṃkasthyā.
28. BL dvālāmalāṃkitakhaḍgadharaṃ.
29. BL śaraśarāsanadhanaṃ.
30. BL dakṣavāmayor.
31. BL add. a central dot.
32. BL dakṣavāmayor.
33. BL illegible between varadavāmāṃkasthaśa and -liṃgana- vātakarpaṭāṃkitatriśūladharaṃ.
34. BL dakṣavāmayor.
35. BL bhāvayeha// //.
36. The lotus shows petals in both the upper and lower directions [Bhattacharyya 1968a: 437].
37. Whereas a consort of Hindu god is called "Śakti" or "Vidyā", a consort of a Buddhist diety is generally called "Vidyā". However, the name of "Śakti" is uncommonly used in the text.
38. The picture is classified as "Kawa 2-047" in the catalogue. See Kimiaki Tanaka, *A Catalogue of Ekai Kawaguchi's Collection of Tibetan and Nepalese Buddhist Art.* (in Japanese) Kosei Shuppansha, 1990, pp. 192-195. Tanaka suggests that Sukhāvatī Lokeśvara is depicted in it. Sukhāvatī Lokeśvara in the picture is three-faced (excluding the face of Buddha on top of

his head) and ten-armed. He sits in the vajraparyaṅka-āsana position (the two legs being firmly locked with both soles revealed. See Bhattacharyya, *Indian Buddhist Iconography,* p.435). While a sword and an ax decorated with a thunderbolt and the gesture of conferring boons are found in his right hands, a white lotus, a lasso, an arrow and a trident are found in his left hands. Two hands display the gesture of preaching the law. He embraces a consort who displays the gesture of conferring boons in her right hand and the gesture of protection in her left hand.'

39. For example, the larger *Sukhāvatī Vyūha* mentions that Bodhisattva Avalokiteśvara and Mahāsthāmaprāpta stand on both sides of Amitābha, and they illuminate the Pure Land. However, their iconographical details are not mentioned in it. See Unrai Wogiwara (translated), *Muryojukyo,* Jodoshutten Kankokai, Tokyo, 1931, pp. 118-119. Hajime Nakamura (translated), *Jodosanbukyo (Daimuryojukyo),* Iwanami Shoten, 1985 (1963), p. 74. The larger *Sukhāvatī Vyūha* regards "Lokeśvararāja" who is associated with Lokeśvara as an important teacher of Amitāyus (Nakamura, *Jodosanbukyo (Daimuryojukyo),* p. 223). However, iconographical details of Lokeśvararāja are not mentioned in it.

CHAPTER 20

The Origin and Evolution of the Caturvidyārāja (SHIDAI-MYÔOU)

MOTOHIRO YORITOMI

Introduction

It is a well-known fact that the past 50 years has seen much exciting progress in the study of Esoteric Buddhism, with respect to both philological study, based mainly on materials written in Sanskrit and Tibetan translation, as well as in doctrinal study having its basis in philosophical methodology and the history of Buddhist thought. Further, it is a most welcome phenomenon that many young researchers these days show much interest in Iconography, i.e. drawing use from visual media such as Buddhist sculpture, painting, and maṇḍalas for the examination of the history of Esoteric Buddhism, and in particular interest in Iconology, in order to go beyond mere study of reading description to a more deeper interpretation of Buddhist thought.

Following this spirit I, myself, have been focusing my research on the origin and evolution of the Buddhas/tathāgatas through my study of the Pañcatathāgata (Kongôkai-Gobutsu; Five Buddhas of Vajradhātu) which forms the basis of the *Sarvatathāgata-tattvasaṃgraha* (*Kongôchô-kyou*) and Vajradhātu-maṇḍala (Kongôkai-maṇḍala), in order to gain a more far-reaching perspective of the currents of Esoteric Buddhism as well as Buddhism as a whole.[1]

At present my research is concentrated on the study of the origin and evolution of the bodhisattvas, in order to provide a standing point from which to reexamine the evolution of Buddhist thought and culture.[2]

The intent of this paper is to propose a third approach to the historical study of Buddhist icons, by presenting the main currents of the tradition of the vidyārāja (Myôou), figures characteristic to Esoteric Buddhism, with particular emphasis on the origin of the grouped vidyārāja (Shūgou-Myôou) typified by Caturvidyārāja (Shidai-Myôou) and Pañcavidyārāja (Godai-Myôou).

Pertaining to the origin of the vidyārāja in India, I have in the past presented a rough outline at a workshop entitled "Iconography of vidyārājas" (Myôou no Zuzô) held in the Kyoto National Museum.[3]

Also, I have elsewhere substantiated the origin and popularity of the Caturvidyārāja and Pañcavidyārāja in China, focusing on the bells of "Vajraghaṇṭas relieved vidyārājas" (Myôou-rei) have treated in detail the difference between these two lineages.[4]

Further, at the 3rd workshop of the Buddhism in Heian Era (Heianbukkyô) which was held in Eizan-gakuin, 1998, I gave an explanation concerning the diversity of the various combinations of the Pañcavidyārāja accepted into Japan and affecting the two traditions of Japanese Esoteric Buddhism, "Tômitsu" and "Taimitsu".

My aim in this paper is to discuss, primarily utilizing philological materials together with some speculation, the process by which and text with which the fundamental group of vidyārāja—the Caturvidyārāja and Pañcavidyārāja came to be established.

1. *The Existence of "Vidyārāja"*

From our study of the Sanskrit text of the *Sarvatathāgatatattvasaṃgraha* which we will later see, there is no doubt that the origin of the word "Myôou" which we commonly use, is from the Sanskrit word "vidyārāja".

However, it is a pity that there are only very few Sanskrit texts which correspond to Chinese translations of the early and middle ages of Buddhist tantras, for these tantras may have had direct relations with the establishment of vidyārāja. As such, it is not easy to examine with strict thoroughness the circumstance of this age.

Also, there is an example of the icon Mahāmāyūri (Kujyaku-Myôou) which is classified under the category of vidyārāja even though the icon has quite a different circumstance of origin and evolution compared with other vidyārājas. This Mahāmāyūri may be the oldest vidyārāja (or vidyārājñī) in existence but it is a female figure and moreover, is basically not a wrathful figure.

As such, it would be good, here, to take some time to examine in some detail the context of the origin of the vidyārāja. Here, Chinese translations are the main materials of early Esoteric Buddhism, so we will use these texts mainly in our discussion.

It goes without saying that the word "Myôou" indicates a king (Ou) of vidyā (Myôjyu) and furthers that it is linked very strongly with mantra (shingon) and dhāraṇī. That is to say that there was first the power of mantra/dhāraṇī, and then later these were connected with particular icons, which also happened to correspond to the group of transformed Avalokiteśvara (Kannon) such as the Ekādaśamukha (Jyūichimen), Sahasrabhuja (Senju) or Amoghapāśa (Fukūkenzaku).

The factor, which made these icons into the group of vidyārāja when it was formed, was the existence of that which is called the "Vajra" (Kongô).

As already mentioned,[5] the first text of the icon group of Vajras to become distinguished was the *Dharanijikkyou* translated by central Indian monk Atikūṭa. This was in the 4th to 5th year of Yong huī i.e. 653-654. This text consists of twelve scrolls, the 7, 8 and 9th of which have been designated "Vajrakula" (Kongô-bu) i.e., the section of vajra. The contents of these three scrolls are as follows:

The 7th scroll:

Bussetsu Kongôzou-daiijinriki-sanmaihouin-bon, Ga-Kongôzoubosatsuzou-hou

Kongôzou-jyuhou-dan

Relatives of the Vajramāmākī (Kongômamakei) / Vajraśṛnkhala (Kongôsyoukara) etc.

The 8th scroll:

The mudrā, mantra and making maṇḍala of Vajrāmṛtkuṇḍalin (Kongô-AmiritaGundari-bosatsu)

The 9th scroll:

Ucchuṣma (Ususama), Daiseimenkongô

To explain in more detail, the group of "Kongô", the icons that are collected in the 7th scroll, are mainly bodhisattvas called Vajragarbha (Kongôzou) that appear in the *Avataṃsakasūtra* (*Kegon-kyou*) and their relatives. Further, the Vajrakula is found to be one of three parts, i.e., the Buddhakula (Butsu-bu), Padmakula (Renge-bu) and the Vajrakula (Kongô-bu), of both the *Susiddhikara-tantra* (*Soshicchi-kyou*) and the *Vairocanābhisaṃbodhi-tantra* (*Dainichi-kyou*) to be discuss more fully later. But it is not necessarily the case that these should be wrathful figures.

However, in the eighth and ninth scrolls we find three figures, the Amṛtakuṇḍalin (Kanro-Gundari), Ucchuṣma and Daiseimenkongô (i.e. Kôshin) standing in a wrathful pose, possessing several faces and hands.

On the *Dharanijikkyou* translated at the middle of 7th century AD at the time of Chinese emperor Tài zōng, there is no technical term of vidyārāja yet. However, there is no doubt that these powerful and fearful icons which appear in the 8th and 9th scrolls are the same as the vidyārāja we are familiar with-with the exception of the Daiseimenkongô, supposedly an icon from Taoism.

Concerning the history of Esoteric Buddhism in China, in the 3rd year of Jǐng lóng (709), the time of Chinese emperor Zhōng zōng, the thirty-scrolls of the *Amoghapāśakalparāja* (*Fukūkennjyakujinpensingon-kyou*) was translated by Bodhiruci and in it there are quite a number of references to the technical term vidyārāja.

It is thought that the texts in which the idea of the vidyārāja was truly established in China was with the series of tantric texts translated by Śubhakarasiṃha (637-735). Particularly at the beginning of the *Susiddhikara-tantra* there is an interesting description of two separate groups of icons as shown in the following.[6]

a. Vidyārāja (Myôou)

Buddhakula	Kinrinoubucchô
Padmakula	Hayagrīva (Batoukanjizai)
Vajrakula	Trailokyavijaya (Sanzesyou-Kongô)

b. Krodha (Fun'nu)

Buddhakula	Aparājita (Munousyou)
Padmakula	Renge-bu Fun'nu
Vajrakula	Kuṇḍalin (Gundali)

As is commonly known, the *Susiddhikara-tantra* analyses Buddhist doctrines having fixed numbers (Hossū) generally into the three sections: the Buddha-Padma-Vajra (Butsu-Ren-Kon).[7] As such, though some of the analyses are somewhat inappropriate, those, which grasp the essential point, are not few.

Firstly, in the part which enumerates the mantras of the vidyārājas, this tantra is assigned these icons in the following order: Kinrinoubucchô, Hayagrīva (Batoukanjizai) and Sanzesyou-Kongô, corresponding to the three above-mentioned sections. However, from an iconological point of view, this classification lacks unification, for each icon belongs to the category of Uṣṇīṣa (Bucchô), Avalokiteśvara and Vidyārāja, respectively.

Therefore, the meaning of "Myôou" here is in its most original, primal meaning, indicating something to the effect of "the sovereign of vidyā", i.e., "the keeper of powerful mantra".

As opposed to this, there exists no description of a concrete form of the Fun'nu. Only the names Aparājita, Renge-bu Fun'nu and Kuṇḍalin are given in this order. Within these, there is no certainty as to what is indicated by the Renge-bu Fun'nu, but judging by the mantra, it is probable that it refers to Hayagrīva.

In any case, both the vidyārāja and krodha are groups which appear alongside one another in the Gouzanze-bon of the *Sarvatathāgatatattvasaṃgraha,* to be discussed later. These groups therefore share common characteristics with one another.

Further, though the time is much later, the following is the way in which both Tsong-kha-pa and mKhas-grub-je sort the tantras of Kriyā-(Shosa) and Caryā-(Gyogi) in their summaries of Mantrayāna (Shingondou).[8]

1. The main icon (tathāgata) of the section (kula)

2. The master (bodhisattva) of the section
3. The mother (buddhamātṛ) of the section
4. The top of buddha's head (uṣṇīṣa) of the section
5. The wrathful king of vidyā of the section
6. The messenger of the section
7. The devas, nāgas and yakṣas of the section

In this categorization, it is possible to think of the 5th, the wrath king of vidyā and 6th, the messenger, as vidyārāja in a broad sense.

Therefore, to summarize, it is not a coincidence that *Susiddhikara-tantra* presents two groups of vidyārāja, but it rather suggests to us that the origin of the vidyārāja arises from several complex factors.

2. *The Origin of Caturvidyārāja*

The *Susiddhikara-tantra* is one of the main elements contributing to the images of "the grouped vidyārāja". In first chapter, we investigated the relation of Buddhakula, Padmakula and Vajrakula of *Susiddhikara-tantra* and the icon group of vidyārāja/krodha. Here, we must pay attention to the *Sarvatathāgatatattvasaṃgraha* a text, which has a slightly different genealogy.

Of especial interest are two groups of icons. One is the Gorui-Shoten, groups of five kinds of gods, classified iconicly as "Ten-bu", its existence linked deeply with the origin of vidyārāja. The other is the Caturvidyārāja which is found on each of the four comers of the maṇḍala of Eighty-one Buddhas (Hachijyūisson-maṇḍala), is considered one of the Vajradhātu-maṇḍala of the Tendai Sect's tradition in the field of art history of Japan.

It is considered that these two groups of icon are the roots for the vidyārāja group of the *Sarvatathāgatatattvasaṃgraha.*

On the Kongôkai-bon which is called the "*Syoekongôchô-kyou*", the first-chapter of the *Sarvatathāgatatattvasaṃgraha,* there are six different maṇḍalas which are mentioned. These are called the Vajradhātu-maṇḍala in a broad sense but none of them have images with a direct correlation with the vidyārāja.

The nine-block structured Vajradhātu-maṇḍala (Kue-maṇḍala) is called a Genzu-maṇḍala, the same type which Kôbôdaishi-Kūkai (Kūkai) brought back from China. In six blocks of the

Vajradhātu-maṇḍala are shown twenty guardian gods called the "Gekongôin-nijyutten", five on each of the four sides of the outer rim section (Gein). These can be seen on the six blocks called the Jyôsin-e, Samaya-e, Misai-e, Kuyou-e, Gouzanze-e and Gouzanzesamaya-e.

However, the icons of the nine block maṇḍala are not mentioned anywhere in the Kongôkai-bon, the first-chapter of the *Sarvatathāgatatattvasaṃgraha,* but appear for the first time in the Gouzanze-bon, the second-chapter of the *Sarvatathāgatatattvasaṃgraha.* The originator of the nine-block maṇḍala had arranged this group of icons along the outer rim section of the central block, the Jyôsin-e of the Vajradhātu-maṇḍala. This means that the originator had already mastered the Gouzanze-bon.

Further, upon examining the text of Gouzanze-bon, we find a difference between this and the corresponding place of the Genzu-maṇḍala. The difference is that there are five groups of icons grouped in the original text as follows, but it does not necessarily say that it is split into four sides.

I. Sarvatrailokyādhipati[9]

1. Maheśvara (Jizaiten)
2. Viṣṇu (Naraenten)[10]
3. Kumāra (Doujiten)
4. Brahman (Bonten)
5. Indra (Taisyakuten)

II. Antarīkṣacara

6. Vajrakuṇḍalin (Kongô-gundari) (Āditya: Nitten)
7. Candra (Gatten)
8. Daṇḍa (Daishôjyou) (Śani: Doseiten)
9. Piṅgala (Hyougaraten) (Maṅgala: Kaseiten)

III. Ākāśacara

10. Balabhadra (Madomataten)[11]
11. Mahākāla (Sakanroten)
12. Jaya (Saishô)[12]
13. Vijaya (Syougousaishô)

IV. Bhauma
   14. Shuzou
   15. Vāyu (Fūten)
   16. Agni (Katen)
   17. Kubera (Kubiraten/Bishamonten)

V. Pātāla
   18. Varāha (Chomenten)
   19. Yama (Enmaten)
   20. Pṛthivī (Jiten)
   21. Varuṇa (Suiten)

Thus, the number of gods in the "Gorui-Shoten" comes to 21 images in both the texts of Sanskrit and the Chinese-translations. Both texts refer to each images' partners, and the number of them also is 21.[13] Moreover, the text of the third chapter of the *Sarvatathāgatatattvasaṃgraha,* the *Vajraśekhara-tantra,* covers the same Hindu icons as the Gouzanze-bon and refers to the same number of pairs of icons. All the data therefore tells us that the number 21 is correct.

However, the icons of the existing Genzu-maṇḍala is divided into four sides as shown below, but because of this, omits the first image, the Maheśvara (Daijizaiten). If we remember the main story of the Gouzanze-bon in which Maheśvara and his wife, Umā are submitted to the wrathful Vajrapāṇi-mahābodhisattva, then it is logically consistent to omit the Maheśvara deliberately.

3. *The Origin of Vidyārāja*

These Hindu gods were imported into Esoteric Buddhism and were given abhiṣeka, received a mantra and esoteric name, and then in turn became protecting deities, exerting their power for the benefit of Esoteric Buddhism, the icon group vidyārāja.

In the past I have noted the following four points as criteria for the condition to be a vidyārāja.[14]

I. It must have certain mantra or dhāraṇī to be associated with it.

II. In principle, with the purpose of displaying its power, it must be a wrathful figure.

III. A certain Hindu god must have been submitted by it.

IV. It must be a transformation of certain deity of Buddhism.

To be sure, there is much variety in the group of vidyārāja, for example unique images like Mahāmāyūri. Yet in the case of the Gouzanze-bon, all of the Hindu gods had once been submitted and then were reborn into the vidyārāja group. This is indicated by the common noun, i.e. the name of the groups. Here, the names are quoted from the Chinese-translation.[15]

I. Sarvatrailokyādhipati—vidyārāja.

II. Antarīkṣacara—vajrakrodha.

III. Ākāśacara—gaṇapati.

IV. Bhauma—dūta.

V. Pātāla—ceṭaka

Of these Hindu gods, it is clearly understood that groups of the most powerful gods such as Viṣṇu or Indra are converted into Esoteric Buddhism to become vidyārāja.

Next, groups such as Vajrakuṇḍalin or Keiwakuten are converted into Esoteric Buddhism to become "vajrakrodha". I have already mentioned in the section of the *Susiddhikara-tantra,* the difference between vidyārāja and krodha, but both have characteristics of vidyārāja common, in the broad sense.

The groups of Madomata and Sakanro correspond to the Balabhadra and Mahākāla, if we follow the description of the commentary in the Tibetan-translation.[16] It is interesting that the former are of Viṣṇu's lineage and the latter are icons belonging to Śiva's lineage. In Japan these are referred to as the group Shôten, i.e., the Gaṇeśa or Vināyaka, the interfering gods. These are represented in the Gekongô-bu of Genzu-maṇḍala as the four Shôtens as follows: the Kangiten or ordinary Gaṇeśa, the Sangai-vināyaka Gaṇeśa holding sunshade, the Keman-vināyaka the Gaṇeśa holding a garland, and the Kyūsen-vināyaka the Gaṇeśa holding bow and arrow. Only this particular group may have some different characteristics from the vidyārāja in the strict sense.

If the fourth group of Jigoten, the group of Vāyu and Agni etc. and the fifth group of Suigoten, the group of Yama and

Pṛthivī etc. receive the abhiṣeka of Esoteric Buddhism, it is said that each of them shall receive the function of messenger (dūta or ceṭaka).

As in the example of the Acalanātha, the vidyārāja's function is to become messenger to important icons such as the tathāgata, and also it is a useful method for taking in heretical gods.

Thus, esoteric Buddhism either conquered or conciliated the Hindu gods, as typified in the Gorui-Shoten, into its own maṇḍala and in this way perhaps expanded its influence.

4. *The Icons on Four Corners*

Now, though we enter slightly the field of conjecture, I would like to examine the significance of the icons on the four corners of the Vajradhātu-maṇḍala, which are said to be connected to the origin of the Caturvidyārāja and Pañcavidyārāja.

In the case of Genzu-maṇḍala, there is an example of the Caturvidyārāja represented on the four corners of the outer most rim of the third part of Gouzanze-e. Though comparatively new, an example is found in Toji temple's "Genroku-bon". Here we find wrathful icons on the four corners of the maṇḍala, although they each have only one face and two arms.[17]

On the other hand, in another work found in Toji, regarded by many as unorthodox, is the Nishinoin-bon (Den-shingon'in-bon) of the Vajradhātu-maṇḍala, in which there are one faced and two armed female icons described on the four of corners of the Gouzanze-e's Gekongô-bu.

The reason for the existence of these two traditions shall now be considered. Here we see the case of the Sanskrit text and Chinese translation of the "Gouzanze-bon" of the *Sarvatathāgatatattvasaṃgraha:*

The Southeast corner: Śrī (Kichijyôten)

The Southwest corner: Sarasvatī (Benzaiten)

The Northwest corner: Gaurī (Byakueten or Umaten)

The Northeast corner: Bhairavī (Ifujyoten)

All of the above[18] icons are powerful Hindu female icons. As opposed to this there is a different tradition called the Hachijyūisson-kongôkai-maṇḍala which allocates the Caturvidyārāja at the four corners of the Vajradhātu-maṇḍala.

Prof. Osamu Takada[19] and Mr. Kei'ichi Kokubo[20] have been already studying the outline of Hachijyūisson-Kongôkai-maṇḍala, but in addition to this, I personally think there were at least two different traditions of it.

I. The tradition of Myôhouin-bon/Eizan-bon

The Southeast corner: Trailokyavijaya

The Southwest corner: Kuṇḍalin

The Northwest corner: Yamāntaka

The Northeast corner: Acalanātha

II. The tradition of Ishiyamadera-bon

The Southeast corner: Yamāntaka

The Southwest corner: Hayagrīva

The Northwest corner: Kuṇḍalin

The Northeast corner: Trailokyavijaya

Here is not the place for a detailed proof but I personally feel the tradition with the Caturvidyārāja possessing Acalanātha is newer than the other tradition possessing the Hayagrīva.

I speculate that even though both traditions are the Vajradhātu-maṇḍala, the Hachijyūisson-Kongôkai-maṇḍala concretely allocates the Caturvidyārāja at the four corners and that this had given its influence to the tradition of nine block structured Vajradhātu-maṇḍala (Kue-maṇḍala).

5. *The Origin of the Groups of Vidyārāja on Four Sides*

The allocation of the vidyārājas to the four sides of the maṇḍala, while being linked with the formation of the groups of vidyārāja on the four corners, evolved from the Gorui-Shoten.

In the text of the Gouzanze-bon of the *Sarvatathāgatatattvasaṃgraha,* there was no mention of any regulation pertaining to the correspondence between the five groups of the Gorui-Shoten and the directions. However, in the case of the Genzu-maṇḍala, the dividing of the group of the Gaṇeśa (Shotenshū) into four, and allotting them to each of the other groups and allocating them to the four sides of maṇḍala was already done. From this we can see that in the more clearly assembled maṇḍalas such as the *Vajraśekhara-tantra* and the Gouzanze-bon, the Gorui-Shoten had already been classified and allocated to the four corners.[21]

The East side:	Rudra, Viṣṇu, Kumāra, Brahman, Indra.
The South side:	Sun, Moon, Saturn, Mars.
The West side:	Madhumatta, Madhukara, Jaya, Vijaya, Vāyu, Agni, Kubera.
The North side:	Varāha, Yama, Gaṇeśa, Varuṇa.

The Hindu icons were thus allocated to each of the four directions in the above manner, and by this classification, the vidyārājas which conquered them were undoubtedly placed on each of the four sides. I suppose that such tendency brought the idea of the genealogy of the vidyārāja which evolved through the *Sarvatathāgatatattvasaṃgraha* (corresponding the first block), the *Vajraśekhara-tantra* (corresponding to the third block), etc. together with the idea to allocate them to the four sides of the directions in the *Durgatipariśodhana-tantra* which Dr. Shinten Sakai suggested was the fifth block of the Broad Kongôcho-kyo.[22]

Particularly, the maṇḍala of the Sarvavid-Vairocana (Chinese translation called the Issaichi-Dainichi or Fumyô-Dainichi) appears only on the earlier translation of the *Durgatipariśodhana-tantra,* however this tantra allocates the Caturvidyārāja to the four sides of the each directions in the following way:[23]

The East side:	Amṛtakuṇḍalin.
The South side:	Trailokyavijaya.
The West side:	Acalanātha.
The North side:	Hayagrīva.

Also, on the commentary of the *Durgatipariśodhana-tantra* by Vajravarman, the Caturvidyārāja appears as follows, with a slight difference in the allocation and the contents.[24]

The East side:	Trailokyavijaya.
The South side:	Amṛtakuṇḍalin.
The West side:	Yamāntaka.
The North side:	Hayagrīva.

As mentioned previously concerning the contents and the allocations, there is not always perfectly corresponding each other. But when we consider the correspondence between the icons of the Gorui-Shoten and the vidyārājas above, there is no doubt that the Trailokyavijaya's icon refers to the vidyārāja that conquers Maheśvara and Umā. Also, there is no doubt that the Amṛtakuṇḍalin corresponds directly to Amṛtakuṇḍalin, one of the icons of the Gorui-Shoten, and moreover, it is well-known that the image of the Yamāntaka conquered (antaka) the Hindu god of death Yama.[25]

Further, it is certain that the Acalakumāra (Fudou-douji) which is mentioned in the *Sarvatathāgatatattvasaṃgraha-tantra* is the same as the god Śiva's second son, Skanda. But if we take into consideration the fact that the image follows the pattern of a child figure and also the similarity of the name, there is still some possibility that it is linked with the Acalanātha, one of the main vidyārāja's of Esoteric Buddhism.

Anyway, I believe we can assume that the Caturvidyārāja formation having the Hayagrīva in the north side originated some time in India. Concerning the origin of Hayagrīva,[26] though there are still several points which need to be further examined, it is certain that its origination was much influenced by faith toward the god Viṣṇu. And also, that Hayagrīva was accepted into Buddhism as one of the relatives of Avalokiteśvara, whose origin was strongly linked with Viṣṇu. The process of Hayagrīva becoming a vidyārāja belonging to Padmakula can be easily seen when we study the *Susiddhikara-tantra* and the *Vairocanābhisaṃbodhi-tantra.*

Conclusion

In this paper, I introduced an outline of the origin of the Caturvidyārāja as part of a process of studying the grouped vidyārāja. As an interim report, we can conclude from the textual study that the Caturvidyārāja originated in India, and our research of relics leads us to China for the origin of the Pañcavidyārāja.

Furthermore there are the Hachidai-Myôou which evolved from the Hachidai-bosatsu and the Jyūdai-Myôou which evolved from the *Māyājāla-tantra* and the *Guhyasamāja-tantra,* but the examination of these groups of vidyārājas must be left to another paper.

NOTES

1. Yoritomi, Motohiro. *MIYYOBUTSU NO KENKYU,* Hozokan, 1990.
2. Regarding the origin and evolution of bodhisattvas, I consider the establishment of the Eight Bodhisattvas to be the significant turning point of Esoteric Buddhism.
3. Yoritomi, Motohiro. Icons of Myôô (vidyā-rāja)—around the establishment of collective images of Myôô—, *ICONOGRAPHY OF MYÔÔ,* Bukkyobijyutsukenkyu-uenokinenzaidan-zyoseikenkyuki, 1996.
4. Yoritomi, Motohiro. On Vajraghaṇṭās with reliefed Vidyārājas, *The Festschrift dedicated to Prof. Sato Ryuken in Commemoration of His Seventy Birthday,* 1998.
5. Yoritomi, Motohiro. Composition of the Buddhist Pantheon in the Dhāraṇī-saṃgraha, *Journal of Religious Studies* 276, 1988.
6. *Taishō* vol.18 p.604a.
7. Yoritomi, Motohiro. On the Development of the *Kulas* in Buddhist Tantras, *From Mahāyāna Buddhism to Tantric Buddhism: The Festschrift dedicated to Prof. Katsumata Shunkyo in Commemoration of His Seventy Birthday,* 1981.
8. Takada, Ninkaku. *A STUDY OF INDO-TIBETAN MANTRAYANA BUDDHISM;* Mikkyo Gakujutsu Sinkokai, 1978.
9. The Chinese notations are mainly based on Bussetsu-issainyoraishinjitsu-shôdaijyôgenshô-zanmaidaikyôu-kyo (*Taishō* vol.18 373a) translated by Shī hù.
10. The solutions of knotty Buddhist deities and the Sanskrit names are based by *Edited text of Tattvasaṃgraha-sūtra* (edited by Horiuchi, Kan'nin, Mikkyobunka-kenkyusho, 1983).
11. Balabhadra, equivalent to Madhumatta, is a son of Jagannātha who is one of Viṣṇu's varied forms, and popular with in the Orissa in East India.
12. Cf. Hatta, Yukio. On Esoteric Buddhist Maṇḍala composed of Five Hindu Deities in the Sarvatathāgatatattvasaṃgraha-sūtra, *Journal of Indian and Buddhist Studies* 15-2, 1967.
13. bSod nams rgya mtsho : *The Ngor Mandalas of Tibet,* The Center for East Asian Cultural Studies, 1991, pp. 34-38.
14. Yoritomi (1996) p. l.
15. *Taishō* vol. 18 p. 373 The Sanskrit names are based on *Horiuchi* (*1974*).
16. Horiuchi, op. cit., p. 359.
17. Supervised by Yoritomi. *Universe of Maṇḍalas,* Museum of Toji Temple, 1990 p. 54.
18. Horiuchi, op. cit., p. 506.
19. Takada, Osamu. The Pair of Maṇḍalas in Tendai Esoteric Buddhism, *The Festschrift dedicated to Tayama Honan in Commemoration of His Six Birthday,* Yoshikawa-kobunkan, 1965.
20. Kokubo, Keiichi. Maṇḍala of eighty-one Buddhas in Shingon Esoteric

Buddhism, *YAMTO BUNKA: Biannual Journal of Eastern Arts* 75.
21. bSod nams rgya mtsho, *TIBETAN MANDALAS*—The Ngor Collection—vol. 6, Kodansha, 1983.
22. Cf. Afterward on *SAKAI SHINTEN TYOSAKUSYU* vol. 3, Hozokan, 1985.
23. bSod nams rgya mtsho : op. cit., pp. 55-56.
24. T. Skorupski : *The Sarvadurgatipariśodhana Tantra,* Delhi, 1983, p. 54.
25. Miyasaka, Yusho. On the Yamāntaka, *Journal of Indian and Buddhist Studies* 19-2, 1971.
26. Koyama, Tenyū. Notes on Ḣayagrīva in Ancient India, *Journal of Esoteric Buddhist Studies.* 19, Yoritomi, Motohiro and Shimoizumi, Zengyo. *MIKKYÔ ZUZO ZUTEN,* Jinbunsho'in, 1994 pp. 164-65.

CHAPTER 21

The Chronology of Cave Temples at Elephanta

ATSUSHI ISHIGURO

No history of Elephanta is available except for very scanty material gathered from different sources. This situation is augmented further by the loss of important evidence. For example, (1) A stone panel with an inscription of large and well-written characters was removed to Europe in about 1540 by the Portuguese Viceroy Dom Joao de Casutro, and now there is no trace of it.[1] It is believed that the stone inscription if found and deciphered might prove to be of great help; (2) Similarly, two inscribed copper plates which were found in the north-east corner of the Island are believed to have been in England in the possession of one Mr. Harold Smith who carried them in 1865 A.D.[2] No information, however, is available either as to their contents or their whereabouts.

A large number of chronological studies of the cave temple at Elephanta by many scholars has failed to shed any further light because of the lack of unanimity of opinion. This situation has arisen, as can be expected, because of the different reference materials in question. Before going further, it would be helpful to look at the different views of scholars regarding the date of the cave temple at Elephanta.[3]

The earliest reference to the chronology of the cave temple

at Elephanta is found in the book *The Cave Temples of India* by J. Burgess. According to him the cave temple in question (at Elephanta) belongs to the latter part of the 8th century or the beginning of the 9th century. However, E.B. Harvell places it around the 7th century. In addition to these, many scholars such as V.A. Smith, A.K. Coomaraswamy, S. Kramrisch, B. Rowland, H. Zimmer, and P. Brown date it between the 7th and the 9th centuries. On the other hand C. Sivaramamurti places it under the Vākāṭakas, that is the 5th to the 6th century.[4] According to H. Goetz and W. Spink, it belongs to the Kalacuris who are well-known as Śaiva.[5] However, H. Goetz puts it in the latter part of the 6th century, whereas Spink refers it to the 6th century. From these it seems that the date of the cave temple at Elephanta lies between the 5th and 9th centuries.[6]

Now let us examine the historical background and religious condition of the Deccan Plateau including the Island of Elephanta from the 5th to 9th centuries. During this time numerous dynasties such as those of the Vākāṭakas, Kalacuris, the early Western Cālukyas and Rāṣṭrakūṭas flourished in different parts of the Deccan Plateau. But the main point to be noted here is existence of small kingdoms ruling different parts of the Deccan Plateau along with the main dynasty. For example, the Ajaṅtā Inscription no. 16 mentions Hariśena, who was the last great king of Vākāṭakas, conquering seven kingdoms: Kuṇtala, Avanti, Kaliṅga, Kosala, Turikūta, Lata and Andra.[7] Apart from these kingdoms, there were the Rāṣṭrakūṭas of Mānapura, who are to be distinguished from the Rāṣṭrakūṭas in the 9th century, and the Aśmaka who were ruling the neighboring area of the Vākāṭakas.[8] It is interesting to note that most scholars deal only with the main dynasties such as Vākāṭakas, Kalacuri, and the Early Western Cālukyas, etc., paying little or no attention to the small kingdoms that existed along with the main dynasties. However, I believe that these small kingdoms have also participated and played an important role in the history of fine arts on the Deccan Plateau. One of the purposes of this paper is to point out the role and importance of the small kingdoms in the history of fine arts on the Deccan Plateau.

After the fall of the Vākāṭakas in the beginning of the 6th century, the political situation is not at all clear. (A similar confusing situation is found in the history of north and central

India following the collapse of the Gupta dynasty).[9] However, some scholars attempted to place the Kalacuris as dominant rulers. This view is based on the copper coins found in many places on the Deccan Plateau. In the middle of the 6th century the Early Western Cālukyas, that is the Cālukyas of Bādāmi, became dominant, conquering the Kalacuris and some other small kingdoms. The Cālukyas, like Vākāṭakas ruled over many feudatories.[10] Over time the Rāṣṭrakūṭas, one of these feudatories, became powerful and in the middle of the 8th century conquered the Cālukyas. Thus, in the 9th century, the Rāṣṭrakūṭas were the dominant rulers on the Deccan Plateau.

Concerning religious beliefs, the main branch of the Vākāṭakas had faith in Brahmanism, especially in Śaivism. On the other hand, the Bāsim branch of the Vākāṭakas was devoted to Buddhism, but Buddhism on the Deccan Plateau was on the decline.[11] As I mentioned above the Kalacuris were devoted to the Pāśupatas. Further, under the Early Western Cālukyas, Brahmanism—both Śaivism and Vaiṣṇavism—prevailed along with flourishing artistic activities. Not only the many inscriptions belonging to the Early Western Cālukyas but also the sculptures depicted on many temples constructed under the Early Western Cālukyas show the worship of Kārttikeya, Saptamātṛkas, and Durgā.[12] The religious heritage of the Early Western Cālukyas was replaced by the Rāṣṭrakūṭas. It appears that Śaivism predominated over the Vaiṣṇavism among these four dynasties including the feudatories.

It may not possible to examine the different views of each of the scholars due to lack of time. So, I will discuss some of the main arguments regarding the patronage of the Elephanta excavation, especially about the Kalacuris dynasty as the patron of the cave temple at Elephanta.

According to Dr. Spink, the cave temple at Elephanta is attributed to the Kalacuris. This view is entirely based on the Kṛṣṇarājā's coins found there.[13] However the mere evidence of coins is insufficient to prove the Kalacuris patronage for the excavation of the cave temple at Elephanta. The possibility of the circulation of coins due to trade cannot be ruled out. This is supported by the fact that Kṛṣṇarājā's coins are found not only on the Island of Elephanta but also in various places extending in all directions, namely, Vidiśā in the north, Nāsik and Bombay in the west, Amrāvatī and Betole in the east, and Kalhāt in the south.[14] Further more, the sculpture of the so-called Lakulīśa, found inside the cave temple at Elephanta, cannot be considered as supporting the Kalacuris patronage. Along with the sculpture of Lakulīśa, other sculptures depicting different aspects of Lord Śiva's life are also found inside the cave temple at Elephanta. This fact can be used to argue for the patronage of other dynasties or small kingdoms, who also were devotees of Śiva, It seems far from logical that the Kalacuris excavated cave temples in a place far away from their own capital, Māhiṣmatī. It has been observed that many great monuments in India are found in or near the capital of the contemporary dynasty; for example, the Bādāmi of Early Western Cālukyas, and the Kāñchī of Pallvas. In addition, the geographical conditions were not favorable for the Kalacuris to excavate the cave temple at Elephanta. As it is known that the Māhiṣmatī was situated on the banks of the Narmadā river, the northern part of the Deccan Plateau.[15] It appears, therefore, to be a tedious task, and a difficult one too, to cross the Deccan Plateau and come down to an Island, namely, the Elephanta near Bombay harbor. Therefore, there seems to be neither reason nor profit for the Kalacuris to excavate the cave temples on the Island of Elephanta.

On the other hand, it is quite natural and logical to presume that the excavation of cave temple at Elephanta is the outcome of the patronage of the dynasty of kingdom which was closely related to the Konkan area, including the Island of Elephanta. It is an established historical fact that Western India formed a part of the vast Mauryan Empire during the reign of Aśoka. The Nausari (Baroda State) plates of the Gujarāt Cālukya Pulakeśinrājā dated in the Kalacuri year 490, i.e., 739 AD also show that the Konkaṇa Mauryas ruled in the west of India.[16] Elephanta is quite close to mainland and its very situation would suggest that whoever governed the coastal regions also governed it. The Aihole inscription of the Kīrtivarman's son show that the Mauryas were conquered by Kīrtivarman.[17] Another inscription, Aihole Praśasti, composed by the Jain poet Ravikīrtī, mentions that the Mauryas of Konkaṇa were again invaded by Pulakeśin II. The conquest of the Mauryas by the early Cālukyas is recorded in Kauthem grant of Vikramāditya V dated Śaka 931 (1009 AD). With the evidence of all these inscriptional records it stands to reason that the country lying around Bombay, that is Konkan including southern Gujarāt, was governed by the Mauryas even up to the 10th century after Christ, although it did not remain under the uninterrupted rule of the Mauryas. Though the Mauryas were subdued by Kīrtivarman, later the Mauryas became strong. Therefore, Pulakeśin II attacked them for a second time. Further, the Kanaswa stone inscription of Śivagaṇa dated in Malava year 796 expired, that is 738-9 A.D. glorifies the illustrious Maurya race and the king of that lineage named Dhavala, describing him as supreme ruler.

Furthermore, the Aihole Praśasti inscription describes the capital of the Mauryas called Śrīpurī as a prosperous sea-port town, 'the Lakṣmī of the western ocean'. Śrīpurī was evidently the capital of the Mauryas. The identity of Śrīpurī has not yet been determined but from what this Praśasti states, is not unreasonable to surmise that it stood on the sea. Presumably, it is located on the Island of Elephanta as this Island is rich in ancient remains.

This leads to the conclusion that the Mauryas were responsible for the excavation of the purpose behind it is also clear, that is to say, to adorn the capital city with beauty and demonstrate its prosperity.

NOTES

1. J. Fergusson and J. Burgess, *The Cave Temples of India,* London 1880 (Reprinted, Delhi, 1969) p. 467; B. Rowland, *The Art and Architecture of India,* Penguin Book, 1953, p. 189.
2. H. Shastri, *A Guide to Elephanta,* Delhi, 1934 (Reprinted, Delhi, 1978) p. 4.
3. V.A. Smith, *A History of Fine Art in India and Ceylon,* Oxford, 1911, p. 215; A.K. Coomaraswamy, *History of Indian and Indonesian Art,* New York, 1927 (Reprinted 1965), p. 100; S. Kramrisch, "Mahadeva of Elephanta Island with Dvarapala" *Ancient India,* No. 2, 1946; S. Kramrisch "App. The Greate Cave Temples of Śiva on the Island of Elephanta" *The Presence of Śiva,* Princeton, 1981, pp. 461-2 ; B. Rowland, op. cit., p. 189; H. Zimmer, *The Art of Indian Asia,* New York, 1955, Vol. 1, p. 9; P. Brown, *Indian Architecture* (Buddhist and Hindu Period), Bombay, Sixth Reprint, 1971, p. 73.
4. C. Sivaramamurti, *Nataraja in Art, Thought and Literature,* New Delhi, 1974, pp. 172-75; *The Art of India,* New York, 1977, pp. 473-4.
5. H. Goetz, "The Gupta School," *Encyclopedia of World Art,* Vol. VII, p. 261; W. Spink, *Ajanta to Ellora,* Bombay, 1967, pp. 8-10.

6. D.C. Sircar, "Deccan in the Gupta Age" "The Cālukyas" R.C. Majumdar (ed)., *The History and Culture of the Indian People,* vol. III, *The Classical Age,* 3rd ed., Bombay, 1970, pp. 177-201, pp. 227-49 ; K.A.N. Sastri, *A History of South India,* 3rd ed., Madras, 1966, pp. 146-73; G. Yazdani (ed)., *The Early History of the Deccan,* Reprint, Oxford University Press, 1960, pp. 149-314; R.G. Bhandarkar, *Early History of the Dekhan,* Calcutta, 1957, pp. 54-84; S. Chattopadhyaya, *Some Early Dynasties of South India,* Delhi, 1974, pp. 137-86; H.V.S. Murthy, *History of Karnataka.* New Delhi, 1974, pp. 47-101; V.A. Smith, *The Early History of India,* Oxford University Press, 4th ed., 1967, pp. 439-45.
7. V.V. Mirashi, *Corpus Inscriptionum Indicarum,* vol. V, *Inscriptions of the Vākāṭakas.* Ootagamund, 1963, p. XXX; J. Burgess, *Report on the Buddhist Cave Temples and their Inscriptions,* A.S.W.I., vol. IV, Varanasi, 1964, p. 127.
8. S.L. Weiner, *Ajaṅtā,* University of California Press, pp. 29-30.
9. J.C. Harle, *Gupta Sculpture,* Oxford, 1974, p. 6.
10. R.C. Majumdar, op. cit., pp. 199-201.
11. V.V. Mirashi, op. cit., pp. xl-xliii.
12. J. Burgess, op. cit., pp. 405-15 ; *Antiquities of the Belgaum and Kaladgi,* A. S. I. (New Imperial Series) vol. I, Varanasi, 1971, pp. 15-44; H. Cousens, *Cālukyan architecture of the Kanarese Districts,* A. S. I. (New Imperial Series) vol. 42, Calcutta, 1926; S. R. Balasubrahmaniyam, "The Date of the Lad Khan (*Sūrya-Nārāyan*) Temple at Aihole," Lalit Kalā. no. 10, 1961, pp. 41-4; R.S. Gupta, The A*rt and Architecture of Aihole,* Bombay, 1967; A. Lippe, "Some Sculptural Motifs on Early Cālukya Temples", *Artribus Asiae,* vol. XXIX, 1967, pp. 5-24; "Additions and Replacements in Early Cālukya Temples" *Archives of Asian Art,* 23, 1969-70, pp. 6-23; "Early Cālukya Ikons" *Artibus Asiae,* Vol. XXXIV, 4, 1972, pp. 273-330; J.C. Harle, "Some Remarks on Early Western Cālukya Sculpture," P. Pal (ed.), *Aspects of Indian Art,* Leiden, 1972, pp. 65-9; S.R. Rao, "A Note on the Chronology of Early Cālukyan Temples," *Lalit Kalā;* no. 15, 1972, pp. 9-18; G. Tarr, "Chronology and Development of the Cālukyan Cave Temples," *Ars Orientalis',* vol. VIII, 1970, pp. 155-84.
13. W. Spink, *Ajanta to Ellora,* Bombay, 1967, pp. 8-10.
14. V.V. Mirashi, op. cit., p. xxxii.
15. V. Mani, *Purāṇic Encyclopedia,* Delhi, Reprinted, 1979 pp. 467-8.
16. R. Sewell, A Sketch of the Dynastic of Southern India, Delhi 1975, p. 35 & 58; H.V.S. Murthy, op. cit., pp. 26-9.
17. R.C. Majumdar, op. cit., p. 232.
18. R.C. Majumdar, op. cit., p. 235.

V

JAINISM

CHAPTER 22

Reflections on Reflections: Shadow and Darkness in Jain Philosophical Texts

PHYLLIS GRANOFF

Sparkling jewels, reflections, and reflecting surfaces figure prominently in every aspect of Indian literature, in poetry and prose tales, in philosophical texts and in religious texts. In religious texts the body of the god may be likened to a jewel, or the god may appear in a jewelled pavilion, his reflection cast in all directions so that worshippers from every side can see him. Religious texts also engage in discussions of one particular type of reflection, *chāyā*, *pratimā*, or *pratibimba*, that is, images of the Jina, Buddha, or the Hindu deities.[1] There are many points of commonality in the discussions in the religious texts and speculation often crosses religious boundaries. Even more striking perhaps is the shared language of the poetic texts, in which jewels with their many-colored rays and their ability to serve as reflecting surfaces fascinate because they quite literally dazzle the mind. They confuse the human observer who mistakes a solid crystal surface for water; they may even befuddle a passing bird, which tries in vain to extract a blade of grass that reveals itself to be nothing more than the deep green rays of precious emeralds. Indeed, from the time of the *Mahābhārata*, when

Duryodhana is embarrassed by mistaking solid ground for water and water for solid ground in the marvellous jewelled palace that Maya has built for Yudhiṣṭhira, it would seem that using the special properties of jewels and objects made from them to confound a rival was one more means for a ruler to assert his power. If poets in the king's court could vie with each other in the fine crafting of verses with multiple meanings that only a select few could untangle, the king himself through the palace he built and the many objects he had made for his daily use could create an environment in which only the very clever indeed could discern the reality behind the brilliant appearances.

In this paper I begin with a brief exploration of jewels, reflections, and likenesses in the world of court literature, which I will argue presents one important way in which such things were understood by all of the different religious groups in medieval India, Hindus, Jains, and Buddhists.[2] I will argue that jewels and their rays and the reflections they occasion both befuddle and entrance; they are indications sometimes of unreality, and sometimes of greater reality. I will then look in some detail at Jain efforts to define the nature of reflections which undermine at least one aspect of this common understanding in which reflections are seen somehow to be deluding and false in essence. The Jain texts also offer us some insight into the early speculation in India on the nature of vision, transparencies, and mirror images, in other words, concerns shared by the science of optics, a field that remained otherwise underdeveloped. This discussion I will leave for a later date.

I. *Jewels, Reflections and Illusions*

The *Naiṣadhīyacarita* offers a convenient starting point for a discussion of reflections in court poetry and their deliberate use to confuse or provide an opportunity to convey multiple meanings.[3] In the *Naiṣadhīya* jewels and reflections belong to a larger group of things that can be used to create multiple perceptions, multiple meanings, allusions, and illusions. In sarga 16, Śrī Harṣa describes the grand feast that Damayantī's father has arranged for her on her marriage to Nala. Jewels, reflecting surfaces, and reflections abound among the many tools that Damayantī's father and brothers have at their command to delight, trick, and embarrass the groom and his guests. In verse 66, for example, we are told:

> *harinmaṇer bhojanabhājane 'rpite gatāḥ prakopaṃ kila vārayātrikāḥ/ bhṛtaṃ na śākāiḥ pravitīrṇam asti vas tviṣedam evam hariteti bodhitāḥ*//66
>
> "Members of the groom's party were absolutely furious when they were served their food in emerald bowls, for they thought that the bowls were filled with common spinach. But they were quickly made to see the truth as they were assured, 'The bowls are not filled with spinach; the green color is from the rays of the emeralds.' "

That the guests were meant to be deceived by the jewelled bowls seems clear from a subsequent verse in which we are told that the cooks deliberately prepared the food in such a way as to trick the guests into thinking that meat was vegetable and vegetable was meat:

> *yathāmiṣe jagmur anāmiṣabhramaṃ nirāmiṣe cāmiṣamoham ūhire/ tathā vidaghdaiḥ parikarmanirmitaṃ vicitram ete parihasya bhojitāḥ*//81
>
> "Skilled cooks prepared the food in such as way that the guests would mistake meat dishes for vegetarian dishes and vegetarian dishes for meat. Chided for their mistakes, the guests laughed good-humouredly as they ate delicately prepared dishes."

There are many such deliberate attempts to confound the guests. Nala's friends drop their betel leaves when they see scorpions on them, only to discover that the scorpion is part of the condiments, specially prepared for them by Damayantī's brother Dama.

> *mukhe nidhāya kramukaṃ nālānugair athājjhi parṇālir avekṣya vṛścikam/*
> *damārpitāntarmukhavāsanirmitam bhāyāvilaiḥ svabhramahāsitākhilaiḥ*//110
>
> "Everyone laughed at Nala's trembling friends as they quickly spat out the betel they had just put into their mouths, seeing the scorpions that Dama had made out of the fragrant condiments meant to sweeten their breath."

And this is not the only trick that the king of Vidarbha has for his guests.

> *Amīṣu tathyānṛtaratnajātayor varāṭarāṭ cārunitāntacāruṇoḥ/ svayaṃ gṛhāṇāikam ihety udīrya taddvayam dadāu śeṣajighṛkṣave hasan//*111
>
> "The king of Varāṭa held out to one of his guests two jewels, one false and one real, the false one even more beautiful than the true. 'Take one', he told them, and when he took the false jewel, the king laughed and gave him both."

The wedding feast is clearly also an arena for contest; guests are tricked with jewelled bowls into thinking they are being served common fare; they are duped by food made into likenesses of something else; they are asked to choose between a jewel and its fake counterpart. In each case the guests cannot tell the real object from the likeness; in the language of Sanskrit texts, the *bimba* from the *pratibimba*. It is also clear that fooling the guests is part of the host's way of maintaining his superiority over them; he maintains control over the party by deceiving them and then enlightening them with his greater knowledge of the true state of things.

Royal power is not the only kind of power that the confusion of likeness and prototype enhances; there is also a decidedly erotic tone to the party that the king of Vidarbha holds for his daughter's wedding and here too reflections allow the guests to communicate in a language of gesture and insinuation that would not be otherwise possible. In one verse a young man is offered a drink of water, but instead of drinking it he gently kisses the face of the serving girl that is reflected there:

> *papāu no ko 'pi kṣaṇam āsyamelitam jalasya gaṇḍūṣam uditasaṃmadaḥ/*
> *cucumba tatra pratibimbitaṃ mukhaṃ puraḥ sphuratyāḥ smarakārmukabhruvaḥ//*65
>
> "One young man, suddenly inflamed with passion, did not drink the water offered him. Instead he gently kissed the reflected face of the serving girl, who had eyebrows like the bow of the God of Love."

In another verse a reflection offers a young man the opportunity to express his passion and observe the visible signs that his desire is returned, in a complex image in which reflection and prototype can no longer be distinguished:

> *yuvā samāditsur amatragaṃ ghṛtaṃ vilokya tatraiṇadṛśo 'nubimbam/*
> *cakāra tannīviniveśinaṃ karaṃ babhūva tacca sphuṭa-kaṇṭakotkaram//*85
>
> "A young man, about to help himself to some ghee from a bowl, saw in it the reflection of some fawn-eyed beauty. Instead he let his finger slip into the reflection of her waist band and saw how instantly the reflection, with hair standing on end, bore one of the unmistakable signs of arousal."

In this verse, touching the reflection produces an effect on the prototype, the girl herself, which again is reflected in the shimmering ghee.

There are many verses like these, in which young men kiss the reflections of young woman or otherwise touch them in telling gestures of desire. As we might have expected from the verses cited above on the scorpions made of edible condiments, reflections are not the only substitutes offered young lovers. In one case a girl notices that her friend is too shy to serve a young man who clearly desires her. She makes a likeness of the girl (a *putrika*) out of sugar and places it in the young man's hands (verse 104), as the commentator tells us, signalling to the would-be lover that the girl's touch will be sweet and that she will deliver her over to him at the proper time.

The reflections of the young women are not confined to the limited surfaces of the serving bowls. Indeed the entire room seems to be filled with them. In a somewhat risqué verse, apparently not known to all the manuscripts of the poem, a young man feigns modesty, keeping his eyes down as a woman comes to serve him. He is in fact staring at the reflection of her private parts on the crystal floor!

> *dhruvaṃ vinītaḥ smitapūrvavāg yuvā kim apy apṛcchan na vilokayan mukham/*
> *sthitāṃ puraḥ sphāṭikakuṭṭime vadhūṃ tadaṅghriyugmāvani-madhyabaddhadṛk//*67
>
> "Smiling before he spoke, a well-mannered young man did

> not ask anything nor look up at the face of the woman standing in front of him. Instead he kept his eyes glued to the area of the crystal floor right between her legs."

The feast that Damayantī's father offers his guests is truly a dazzling affair. Reflections/likenesses are everywhere. Nothing is quite what it seems. The young man who appears to be modest is actually lustful; meat is actually vegetable and vegetable, meat; and a scorpion is actually a fragrant condiment. On one level, by manipulating the reflections/likenesses, the host delights his guests and maintains his superiority over them; on another, the young lovers assert their rights to the women who serve them. The reflections/deceptions at this party are tools in a political and erotic contest. At the same time, they are also clearly not what they purport to be. A man can touch the reflection of the face precisely because it is not the face that he would not dare to touch or kiss in public; the green rays are not spinach, or some common garden vegetable that it would be an insult to serve such noble guests.

The power of jewels and reflections to delude and the right of the king to use them for that purpose in his palace and the pleasure pavilions that he builds are clear from another medieval text, the *Śṛṅgāramañjarī kathā* of King Bhoja.[4] Reading this text one gets the impression that everything that is man-made in the king's city is part of a sparkling, dazzling, confusing dance of reflections and illusions. Thus the lac-painted feet of the women reflected on the crystal floors look like so many lotuses in ponds, for the crystal floor confuses the viewer to mistake solid stone for water (p. 3); ruby balconies reflected in ponds look like traces of saffron from the breasts of the women who had bathed there (p. 4), while the reflections of the women cast on crystal stones that border a pond make people think that snake maidens are emerging from the underworld to bathe there, and cakravāka birds, mistaking their own reflections for their mates, look longingly and expectantly at the ponds. The description of reflections and illusions reaches a climax as Bhoja describes his shower pavilion or *yantradhārāgṛha* (pp. 5-7), perhaps his ultimate achievement in exerting human control over the natural world[5]. The trees of the garden are reflected on its jewelled walls, so that the observer thinks they are inside the shower pavilion, having sought refuge there from the heat. Dark rays from emeralds seem to form a canopy of cloud, while sprouts from the forest trees reflected on the doors are taken for the bright burning feeling that people leave behind them when they enter the shower pavilion. Inside peacocks dance, thinking wrongly that the rainy season has come because the sky is darkened from the dark rays that come from the emeralds, and the beats of the drums struck by animated dolls sound to them like thunder; cakora birds try to drink the light that glitters from crystal pillars, thinking it to be moonbeams, which they are wont to sip; elsewhere the red flashing rays from the rubies delude the observer into thinking that lightning is flashing, while rays coming off various jewels are taken for sprays of water. Even the mechanical devices themselves are not free from perceptual illusions; the geese made of crystal try to eat the sprays of water, taking them for lotus fibers, while man-made cranes are tricked by tiny fish that elude their grasp. The pillars seem to combine their weight to support the structure as they are reflected one on the other; mechanical musicians delude even the clever into thinking a real band is playing, and so on. This crowning glory of the king's possessions is a veritable tangle of light rays, jewels, reflections, and illusions. In Bhoja's shower pavilion the man-made likenesses both create illusions and are subject to them; nothing can escape the deluding powers of the jewels and their rays, the reflecting surfaces and the reflections. With its dazzling jewels the shower pavilion recalls descriptions of the heavens of the gods; in his text on architecture and image making, the *Samarāṅganasūtradhāra*, when Bhoja describes the shower pavilion he makes this comparison explicit:[6]

ya etasmin gāḍhaglapitaghanagharmavyatikare
śucāu dhārādhāmni sphuṭasaliladhāre narapatiḥ/
sukhenāste paśyan vivdhajalaśilpāni sa bhavenna
martyaḥ kimtveṣa kṣitikṛtanivāsaḥ surapatiḥ//31.141

"The lord of men, who relaxes in this shining shower pavilion, water spurting all around him, freed from the wearying effects of the intense heat of the day, admiring all the ingenious and artful ways in which the water is made to flow, is surely not a mortal; no, he is the lord of gods, who has made earth his dwelling."

It would be possible to take any number of other medieval texts to show that jewels and reflections are essential in the descriptions of great cities, great rulers, and grand palaces. The *Kādambarī*, for example, in its description of the city of Ujjain makes it clear that Ujjain too is a city of jewelled palaces. It describes the reflections of the moon and sun on the jewelled floors; as the king longs for a son, he wonders when he will have the pleasure of seeing the child chasing after his own reflections on the jewelled floor or trying to grab ahold of the deer whose reflections he sees through the crystal walls (p. 132). When the king himself is described early in the text he is entirely studded with jewels and bathed in the reflections of the rays of the gems from his palace; red rays from the rubies make his thighs red so that he resembles Viṣṇu who has just killed the demons Madhu and Kaiṭabha; the sapphires on the floor cast their rays onto his nails, which look as if they have been darkened by the sighs of the enemy kings who bow at his feet. The king himself is reflected onto the jewelled floor, as if the earth were keeping him as her lover, pressed close to her heart (p. 12). Later the faces of women reflected on the crystal floor of the palace make the floor appear as if it were strewn with lotuses (181). The caṇḍāla girl who comes to the court is virtually transformed by the jewels she wears; the red from the jewels on her anklets makes it look as if she is bathed in fire in an effort to transform her caste. It is not just the court that is filled with reflections, gleaming rays from jewels, and crystal surfaces. Even a hermitage has its beguiling reflections. The stars reflected in the ponds appear as the seven sages themselves, come to see the hermitage (p. 80). A pond is described as bearing within it the reflection of all kinds of things, as Viṣṇu bears within his belly the entire universe (p. 231) When the prince Candrāpīḍa finds the maiden Mahāśvetā in a secluded Śiva temple, her many reflections on the crystal pillars make her seem as if she is surrounded by companions, although she is alone, while a lone reflection of her on the crystal liṅga makes it appear as if she has achieved liberation, having been absorbed into the liṅga (p. 249). The kingdom of the women to which the prince is taken is described in even more wondrous terms; there everything is made of jewels. A girl talks to her own reflection on the jewelled floor, while another girl tries to avoid stepping on what she thinks are flowers; they are really the reflections of her own face (p. 336). In the description of Kādambarī herself reflections are everywhere; with her reflections on the floor it looks as if she is being carried off by nāgas from the underworld; with her reflections on the sides of the room she appears to be in the process of being led away by the divine guadians of the quarters and with her reflections above her it seems as if the very gods are lifting her up. She is reflected on jewelled pillars and in jewelled mirrors. Her own jewels are reflected on the body of one of her servants, arousing her jealousy for she mistakes them for nail marks (p. 335-42). The examples could be multiplied. Kādambarī's world is the ultimate magical (heavenly) world of jewels and reflections. In this world the dazzling jewels and dizzying reflections are not merely the causes of illusions; they are also indicators of wealth and unearthly sensuous delights. At the same time as both Kādambarī's story and the saga of Nala and Damayantī are stories of illusions and deceptions, the jewels and their reflections function as indicators of higher and different realities that are concealed behind appearances.[7]

Kādambarī's world in addition recalls the magic kingdom of the lady Svayamprabhā, the daughter of the architect and demon Maya, in the *Kathāsaritsāgara.* Maya's world is entirely a world of illusion, nothing is what it seems. A visitor is deluded at every step; he thinks there are walls where there are none, and he perceives empty space as a solid barrier. Dry ground is mistaken for water and water for dry ground. But it is not just the delusiveness of these worlds of jewels that should arrest our attention; a verse from a later text written about King Bhoja, the *Bhojaprabandha,* reminds us that it is only god who can turn the world upside down in this way:[8]

ambhodhiḥ sthalatāṃ sthalam jaladhitām dhūlīlavaḥ śailatām
merur mṛtkaṇatāṃ tṛṇam kuliśatāṃ vajraṃ tṛṇaprāyatām/
vahniḥ śītalatāṃ himaṃ dahanatām āyāti yasyecchayā
līlādurlalitādbhutavyasanine devāya tasmai namaḥ //31

"Praise to that god, who just by the power of his own will can turn water into solid ground and solid ground into water; who can turn a grain of dust into a mountain and Mount Meru into a speck of dust; who can turn grass into a diamond

> weapon and make a diamond weapon not worth much more than a blade of grass; who can make fire cold and ice burn; praise to that god who, like a spoiled child, loves to work such wonders just because it amuses him."

There is something of the divine and the demonic, then, in the jewelled palaces of medieval poetry.

Reflections, jewelled structures and the delightful illusions they create are also part of the repertoire of the Jain poet. I cite here only one text, the *Kumāravihāraśataka*, a poem that celebrates the beauty of the Jain temple built by king Kumārapāla. The poet describes how the temple is reflected on its own outer walls, as if it wanted to observe its own beauty, that everyone was praising so highly, in a mirror (34).[9] In another verse the sun is reflected in the courtyard of the temple, as if it were throwing itself at the feet of the Jina, begging forgiveness for having been so bold as to touch with its rays the spires of the temple and for having committed the additional offense of frightening the worshippers inside by setting off a cascade of rays from the sunstones inside that made the worshippers fear the temple was on fire (35). In another verse, the moon, as it falls on the moonstone floors and the moonstone pots at the doorways, gives off rays that make the people think the floor is flooded with water, and the women modestly lift up their garments so as not to get them wet (56). Like Kādambarī's kingdom, the Jain temple is also a world of jewels, reflections, and glittering mirages.

Jewels, reflections, likenesses, then, are part of the standard repertoire of the medieval writer. While not all references to reflections or to jewels and their rays imply their power to delude, this is certainly one common theme. Signs of wealth and power, jewels dazzle the mind and suggest alternate realities. Given this concensus among poets, it is somewhat surprising, then, to realize that in the philosophical literature there was by no means a clear agreement on the nature of reflections or even on their inherent delusiveness. I would like now to examine briefly one way in which jewels/reflections entered into the discourse of medieval Indian philosophy, not simply as metaphor for ultimate reality or a simile to explain transmigratory existence, but as an object of debate. To my knowledge it is the Jains who argued most extensively about the nature and process of reflections. In doing so they took exception with other groups who argued either that a reflection was something false or that there was no such thing as a reflection at all; the perceiver in fact was simply grasping the prototype and mistakenly attaching it to the reflecting surface as its locus. The debate was not entirely trivial; the Jains used their discussion on the nature of reflections to refute a number of important tenets held by their rivals. They used it to defeat the Mīmāṃsaka doctrine of sound as one and eternal, although it appears in various places at various times. They also used it to refute the Buddhist concept that a valid inferential mark had to be either the product, *kārya*, or share the nature, *svabhāva*, of that which the debater wishes to infer. Finally, the Jains could also use their understanding of the nature of reflection to refute the Sāṃkhya/Vedānta theories of perception which involve the reflection of the soul in the inner-organ. If the discussion on the nature of reflections constitutes a footnote in the history of Jain philosophy, it is nonetheless one that could contribute to the discussion of more obviously fundamental issues as we shall now see.

II. *The Jain Debate on Reflections*

The *Nyāyakumudacandra* offers an extensive refutation of the non-Jain understandings of reflection.[10] The Jain position on reflection had been clearly stated in the *Tattvārthādhigamasūtra*, on which Akalaṅka had written an extensive commentary.[11] The *Tattvārthādhigamasūtra* and its commentary considered shade or shadow (chāyā) immediately after its discussion of darkness (*tamas*). In 5.15 *tamas* is defined as follows: *tamo dṛṣṭipratibandhahāraṇaṃ* Akalaṅka glosses this: *dṛṣṭeḥ pratibandhakaṃ vastu tama iti*, "*Tamas* is the substance that prevents vision". The Jain position is thus made clear: darkness is an independent and real substance and not merely the absence of light. 5.16 then defines shade: *chāyā prakāśāvaraṇanimittā* Akalaṅka glosses this as follows: *prakāśāvaraṇaṃ śarīrādi yasyā nimittaṃ bhavati sā chāyā*: "Shade is defined as that which has as its cause the obstruction of light, namely the body and other objects." This is further defined as of two sorts in 5.17:

sā dvedhā tadvarṇādivikāra-pratibimbamātragrahaṇavikalpāt Akalaṅka explains: *sā chāyā dvedhā vyavatiṣṭhate/kutaḥ tadvarṇādivikārāt pratibimbamātragrahaṇācca/ ādarśatalādiṣu prasannadravyeṣu mukhādicchāyā tadvarṇādipariṇatā upalabhyate. Itaratra pratibimbamātram eva* "Shade or shadow is two-fold, depending on whether there is grasped the mere reflection or whether there is also the transformation into the color, etc. of the prototype." Akalaṅka: "And shadow/shade is two-fold. Why? Because there can be transformation into the color, etc. of the prototype or the grasping of the mere prototype alone. In substances which are highly reflective, like the surfaces of mirrors, the reflection (shadow) of the face is perceived to have been transformed into the same color, etc. as the face itself. In other cases, only the bare reflection is perceived."

It is immediately clear that the Jain philosopher is talking not only of shadows cast by objects (one meaning of the word *chāyā*) but also about reflections (another meaning of the word *chāyā*) This dual meaning of *chāyā* is apparent in various contexts in Indian religious literature in which the term appears. There is even a third meaning of the word; in the *Divyāvadāna* when painters want to paint a likeness of the Buddha, they are unable to do so. They prepare a surface and the Buddha lets his shadow (*chāyā*) fall onto the prepared surface; the painters then color it in and the result is a likeness (*chāyā*) of the Buddha.[12] Akalaṅka in his interpretation of the text makes it clear that *chāyā* is both shadow and reflection, and we might want to keep in mind that *pratibimba*, reflection, is also the standard word for likeness or image. The discussion in Akalaṅka continues and it is worth citing here in full:

> *atrāha viparītagrahaṇaṃ kutaḥ prāṅmukhasya pratyaṅmukhā chāyā dṛśyate iti*
> *prasannadravyapariṇāmaviśeṣād bhavati. Atra codyate nādarśatalādicchāyāsadbhāvaḥ kiṃtarhi nayananirgatena raśminā ghanadravyāt pratihatanivṛttena svamukhasyaiva grahaṇam ity ayuktam viparyāsagrahaṇābhāvaprasaṅgāt, kuḍyādiṣu atiprasaṅgāt, grahaṇśaktyabhāvācca/ viparyāsagrahaṇābhāvaprasaṅgas tāvat yadi pratinivṛttena nayaraśminā svaśarīrasyaiva grahaṇam prāṅmukhasya prāṅmukham ityeva grahaṇam syāt viparyāsahetvabhāvāt Kuḍyādiṣu cātiprasaṅgaḥ syāt nayanaraśmeḥ pratighātasya tatrāpi sadbhāvāt/ nāpy asāu nayanaraśmiḥ śarīrān niṣkrāntaḥ manasānadhiṣthito grahītuṃ śaknoti*

"Now someone might interject, 'In that case then why is a mirror image always reversed, why is it that the reflection of a face which is actually looking in one direction always appears as if it is looking in the opposite direction?' The answer is that this is because of the peculiar nature of the transformation that takes place in the clear reflecting surface. Now someone might object, 'There is no real entity called a reflection on the surface of a mirror or other reflecting surface. What happens then? Well, the rays that go out from the eyes strike a hard object and are turned back to grasp the perceiver's own face.' This is illogical for three reasons: because it would then be impossible to explain why a mirror image always appears reversed; because the same would have to be true in the case of walls, and because the eye has no power to act in that way. First let me explain what I mean by saying that it would then be impossible to explain why a mirror image always appears reversed. If the rays of the eye were sent back and grasped the perceiver himself, then they should grasp a face looking in one direction as looking in that very direction; there would be no cause that could account for the reversal of the image. And it would result that the same should also happen in the case of a wall, because in that case too the rays would be striking a solid surface and be bent back to their origin. Nor does this so-called ray from the eyes that you speak of have the power to grasp anything outside the body, unassociated as it would then be with the mind."

The discussion here is instructive and can serve as a ready introduction into Jain views on the nature of reflection. A reflection is a transformation in the surface of the reflecting body; this alone, the Jain argues, can account for the fact that the image is reversed. It is the nature of the reflecting body to change in such a way that this occurs. This statement is reminiscent of a statement made by the Jain polyglot monk Hemacandra in his *Syādvādamañjarī,* where he discuses the nature of darkness.[13] There it is explained that atoms of light that have existed in the form of lamp light, when the oil is exhausted or when they are struck by a strong wind, leave off their form as light and become darkness. When an objector finds it odd that light should become darkness, given that one normally thinks of the two as opposites, Hemacandra replies that material things have the power to produce a wide range of products. After all fire, which is bright and glowing, is known to produce smoke, which is dark. In addition, the fact that a reflection implies a change in the reflecting surface will be used by the Jain to refute Sāṃkhya notions that the soul is not an enjoyer or an active agent. Thus in the *Ratnākarāvatārikā* of Vādi Devasūri, when the Sāṃkhya argues that the soul is not an agent; rather, pleasure and pain, which are reflected in the inner-organ, which is like a mirror, are then further reflected onto the soul so that the soul appears as if he enjoys pleasure and pain, the Jain retorts: *tasya tathāpariṇāmam antareṇa pratibimbodayasyāghaṭanāt,* "No, because it is impossible for a reflection to arise without having the reflecting surface be transformed into the reflected object."[14] This could equally serve as a refutation of the Vedānta theory of mutual superimposition.

Continuing with the passage from Akalaṅka, a second problem that the Jain poses is that reflections occur only with certain types of objects. If reflections were caused because the eye-rays hit a solid barrier and were cast back at the perceiver, they should also occur in the face of solid walls, but such is not the case.[15] Finally, the Jain argues that the eye rays imagined by the opponent to function in perception cannot in fact do so. The Jains argued vigorously against the notion that the sense-organs are *prāpyakāri,* that is, that the sense-organs must be in physical contact with their objects in order to grasp them. The Jain rejection of the theory that rays come out of the eye and are in contact with an object of course meant that they could not regard a reflection as somehow the result of rays that hit a solid object and were returned to grasp the perceiver himself.[16]

Let us turn now to the most extensive discussion of the nature of reflections and the process of reflections in a Jain philosophical text, Prabhācandra's *Nyāyakumudacandra.* I give here a summary of the argument. The discussion occurs in the larger context of a discussion of inference and valid inferential marks. The Jain states categorically that it is possible to infer the presence of the moon above from its reflection in a pond, and yet the moon in the pond is neither the product of the moon above nor does it share in its essence. The Jain wishes by these statements to refute the Buddhist insistence that valid marks are of only two types: where the mark is the product of what is to be inferred or where it shares the same nature as that which is to be inferred. An objector is allowed to argue that the debate is in fact pointless; there is no such thing as a reflection. A reflection cannot be something other than the moon, for in that case one would expect to see it in the absence of the moon. To this it is countered that the reflection is something that is produced in the presence of the moon and therefore we should not expect to see it in the absence of the moon. The objector continues by asking if this reflection is a quality or a substance. It cannot be a quality, because it is perceived to be a substance. It can also not be a substance. If it were a substance it would either have parts or have no parts. It is not true that it has no parts; the reflection appears to have the same parts as the prototype. If it were an independent substance with its own parts that arose in the reflecting surface, one would expect it to have its own qualities, but the reflected moon or face is cold to the touch, as is the water in which it is reflected. It does not have its own quality of touch. The next question that the objector raises is what would be the material causes of the new substance, the reflection. He raises two possibilities: the reflection is caused by the atoms of water (the atoms of the reflecting surface) or by something else. He dismisses the possibility that it is caused by something else, since two substances cannot occupy the same space at the same time. He also dismisses the idea that the reflection is made up of water atoms; he argues that we do not perceive the reflection to be made of water. In fact we perceive it to be different from the reflecting surface. In the case of a face reflected in a pond, the water is shimmering in color, while the face is flesh-colored. The objector also dismisses the idea that the color in the prototype is responsible for the color in the reflection; he argues that the prototype is simply the instrumental cause and that the color in an instrumental cause is never responsible for the color in the product. The brown color of the potter's stick is not transferred to the pot. Another argument he gives against regarding a reflection as something real that is produced in the reflecting surface is that the reflecting surface does not increase in weight or size. One would expect that if the reflection were something real, the reflecting object would be heavier with it than it was without it. The objector concludes that there is no such thing as a reflection; the rays from the eyes strike the reflecting surface and are cast back onto the prototype which they then grasp.

The text now proceeds to a discussion of the position advanced by Kumārila in the *Ślokavārttika* and to its refutation. The discussion in the *Ślokavārttika* occurs in the context of the discussion of sound. Kumārila uses what happens with reflections to show that sound though one can be perceived as many and in many different places. An objector is allowed to argue that if the eye-rays were simply deflected so that they perceived the face itself, one could not explain why mirror images are always seen as reversed. One could also not explain why the moon is perceived as down in the pond and not up in the sky. Kumārila's answer is that the rays of the eye proceed from the eye in several different directions. In the case of the moon, for example, rays go upward and downward. Because the body is bending downward, the soul does not grasp the image that was captured by the rays that went upward. These upward rays in fact transfer their image to the downward rays and so the moon is grasped as being down in the pool and not in the sky. In the case of the mirror image of the face, eye-rays go straight out in front of the face and in the other direction as well. The rays that are deflected from the surface of the mirror grasp the face and then transfer their image to the rays that were travelling in the opposite direction. The result is that the image appears to be reversed. The Mīmāṃsaka is also allowed to argue that if the reflection were something real, something other than the prototype, it would be impossible to explain why the reflection moves whenever the prototype moves, or why the reflection disappears when the prototype is gone. Even if one could argue that the reflection is destroyed when the prototype is taken away, one would still expect to see its parts; when a pot is destroyed the evidence of the potsherds remains.[17]

The Jain then begins his refutation. He first asks his opponent on what grounds he would deny the reality of the reflection: is it because there is no valid means of knowledge which makes it known or because there cannot be any cause that would bring the reflection into existence? He dismisses the first possibility easily; perception, after all, makes known the existence of the reflection. We see our faces in the mirror or the moon in the pond. He denies that the perception can be false, since it is shared by many perceivers and in exactly the same form. Everyone says, "I see the reflection of the moon in the water." There is also no subsequent cognition that denies the existence of the reflection as there is in the case of errors; when we wrongly perceive silver in the conch-shell, we later realize, "This is not silver. It is a conch." But we do not have such a cognition that later tells us, "This was not a reflection it was something else." He proceeds to argue that the reflection must be different from the prototype since they are perceived to be different. The mirror image is reversed. The Jain further argues that there are also causes to explain the existence of the reflection. The reflecting surface, water or the mirror, is the material cause, while the prototype is the instrumental cause. The product is a substance. The Jain also explains the fact that the face in the water is cold like the water on the basis of the fact that it is the water that has been transformed into the new substance, the reflection. In answer to the objection that the face in the water has a different color from the water (it has the color of the prototype) the Jain replies that matter has the ability to transmute in many different ways. In addition, because it is water that has changed into the reflection, the Jain argues that one would not expect the reflecting substance to be heavier with the reflection than without it; nor would he run into the problem that two substances cannot occupy the same space. This is one substance, water, in a new form. In answer to the question of why the mirror image is reversed, the Jain replies that this is simply the way in which it is produced from its own causes. Prabhācandra enlists distorted reflections to further his argument; if there were no such thing as a reflection, and the perceiver merely grasped his own face, then why would the face look elongated in a long reflecting object like a sword? Finally he argues that it is possible for something to follow its instrumental cause in behavior; there is nothing wrong with a theory in which the face is the instrumental cause of the reflection and yet when the face moves the reflection moves. He insists that this is what happens in certain cases (admittedly not in all; the pot does not move when the instrumental cause, the stick, is moved). Among those cases are shadows; when the umbrella moves, the shadow also moves. In such a case the product also disappears when the instrumental cause is removed. When the umbrella is taken away there is no more shadow; when the prototype disappears there is no more reflection. Prabhācandra thus concludes his argument, an argument that can be seen to be equally directed against the Buddhist for whom perceptions of reflections have no objective basis (*pratibimbadhiyaḥ sarvā yannirālambanāḥ sthitāḥ*, *Tattvasaṃgraha* 2576); against the Naiyāyikas for whom the rays of the eyes are deflected and return to grasp the prototype; against the Mīmāṃsakas, for whom rays go out from the eyes in various directions and the image from one set is transferred to another; and against the Sāṃkhyas and Vedāntas for whom reflections do not imply any transformation in the reflecting surface.

III. *Conclusions*

I began this paper with some examples of what I called a common discourse on jewels, reflections, and reflecting surfaces, the language of poets that is shared by Jains, Buddhists, and Hindus alike. For the poets reflections create an alternate reality in which things are never what they seem. The sun reflected on the temple courtyard is not just the sun, but a devotee, come to beg forgiveness of the Jina, while rays of light streaming from moonstones turn solid floor into the illusion of water. Reflected rays can seem to turn a dark caṇḍāla into a fair Brahmin lady, while the magical world of the heroine is a world of jewels and glitter, of reflections and illusions. At a court banquet, touching the body of a woman in a bowl before him, a lover sees her react as if had indeed touched not her reflection but her body itself, as the lines between reality and illusion, prototype and reflection are blurred. In a jewelled shower house trees reflected on a wall seem to have sought refuge inside the shower house from the heat outside, while the rays of gems are mistaken for grass, and light from pearls is mistaken for water. Pillars, reflected in each other, seem to pool their efforts to support a building, and so on. Jewels and their rays, reflecting surfaces and reflections, create a world in which the limits of ordinary reality are constantly being challenged. There is a wondrous quality to this world, an element of mystery that is not even exhausted when the deceived learns about the deception. He is left still to marvel at the skill of the artisan who could so deceive. In addition, the jewelled palaces and water pavilions of kings are recreations on earth of jewelled palaces in the worlds of the gods and demons. There is indeed a supernatural quality implied by the illusions and delusions of the jewels and reflections which seem to defy normal expectations of reality.

Religious and philosophical texts make various uses of many of these different aspects of reflection and jewelled surfaces. In this paper I confined myself to philosophers' explorations of what it is that actually takes place when something is reflected on another surface. In many religious texts authors are content to use reflecting surfaces or jewels as metaphors pointing to the nature of ultimate reality; the body of god is said to be crystal, the world is said to be within ultimate reality as mirror images in a mirror. In usages such as these little attention is paid to what a reflection actually is and how it comes about. It was this aspect that I wanted to investigate here. I focused on Jain discussions, which allowed us to review the diversity of views on reflections. For most philosophers as they analyze them reflections seem to evaporate; there is simply no such entity as a reflection, apart from the prototype. Only the Jains insist upon the substantial reality of the reflection and its ability to be perceived and appreciated as an independent entity. Perhaps in doing so they come a little closer to the texture of the mysterious reality that reflections create for the medieval poets and storytellers. Jewels that reflect or cast rays that then are reflected onto other objects, transfiguring them in the process, do seem to have unusual transformative properties. The Jain in his unique theory of the reflection as an independent substance, captures at least a hint of this mystery.

NOTES

1. I have discussed some of this material in my articles, "Portraits, Likenesses and Looking Glasses: Some Literary and Philosophical Reflections on Representation and Art in Medieval India", in Jan Assmann and Albert I. Baumgarten, *Representation in Religion: Studies in Honor of Moshe Barasch*, Brill, Leiden, 2001, pp. 63-107 and "Maitreya's Jewelled World: Some Remarks on Gems and Visions in Buddhist Texts", *Journal of Indian Philosophy*, 1998, pp. 347-371. On mirrors in particular see Jean Nadou, "Symbolisme du Miroir dans l'Inde", *Arts Asiatiques* XIII, 1966,

pp. 59-75, and the references in the articles cited here. It is not only palaces and man-made objects that are described as sparkling with jewels or made of jewels. This is also a common description of the marvellous mountains on which the gods dwell. See my article, "Medieval Jain Accounts of Mt. Girnar and Śatruñjaya: Visible and Invisible Sacred Realms" *Journal of the Oriental Institute. Baroda*, vol. 49. 1999 pp. 143-170.

2. I consider here jewels with their rays and their reflections as part and parcel of the same phenomenon; jewels in these passages from medieval literature are seen as both the passive agents of illusions in their capacity as reflecting surfaces and as the active agents of illusion in that through the rays which they project they engender illusion. Many texts indeed consider these two properties as related. I have discussed some of them in my articles cited above. The *Netratantra* chapter 9, verses 8-10 compares god to a wishing jewel or cintāmaṇi and a crystal with its reflective properties. A crystal, it says, strung on a thread of different colors takes on the appearance of those colors; furthermore it displays those colors so that others can see them and it is not altered in the least. Similarly god takes on the form in which the devotee imagines him and responds by granting the devotee's wishes. See the *Netratantra* of Kṣemarāja, ed. by Pandit Madhusudan Kaul Shastri, Bombay, Tattva Vivechaka Press, Kashmir Series of Texts and Studies no XLVI, 1926. Abhinavagupta in the *Paramārthasāra* similarly likens consciousness to a mirror and a crystal and emphasizes that supreme consciousness is also more than a mirror, which is passive and simply receives an image from outside; supreme consciousness also actively projects from within itself the objects that we perceive. In the language of poetry I would like to argue that both the projecting and the receiving of images are considered to have something of falsehood and the power to delude.

3. *Naiṣadhīyacarita* ed. by Nārāyaṇa Rāma Ācārya with the commentary of Nārāyaṇa, Nirṇayasāgara Press, Bombay, 1952. In my translations I have sometimes added a phrase to make the sense of the verse clearer; these are by no means literal translations.

4. *Śṛṅgāramañjarī kathā* of Bhoja ed. by Kumārī Dr. Kalpalatā Munśī, Singhi Jain Series no. 30, Bhāratīya Vidyā Pīṭha, 1959.

5. Indeed in the *Samarāṅganasūtradhāra* Bhoja defines a *yantra* as a device in which the elements, which would otherwise act in an untrammelled fashion, are made to operate in a totally controlled manner: *yadṛcchayā pravṛttāni bhūtāni svena vartmanā/ niyamyāsmin nayati yat tad yantram iti kīrtitam.* Bhoja also praises god as the invisible one within this whirling automaton that is the universe, who controls the motion of things. *Samarāṅganasūtradhāra* ed. by T. Gaṇapatiśāstrī, Baroda, Oriental Institute, 1966, p. 175, 31.3. On yantras see V. Raghavan, *Yantras or Mechanical Contrivances in Ancient India*, Bangalore, The Indian Institute of Culture, 1956. While there is no doubt an element of fantasy in Bhoja's descriptions of the shower pavilion, records of medieval courts in Europe indicate that rulers there too had a fascination with mechanical devices. The complex at Hesdin, for example included "ingenious devices, whereby guests were surprised by the sudden eruption of water-squirts, sprays, and deluges, floor soot and other unexpected happenings." See Malcolm

Vale, *The Princely Court: Medieval Courts and Culture in North-west Europe*, Oxford University Press, Oxford, 2001, p. 280. Vale suggests a Byzantine or Sicilian origin for the contraptions at Hesdin. On Byzantine automata see Gerard Brett, "The Automata in the Byzantine 'Throne of Solomon' ", *Speculum* XXIX(3), 1954, pp. 477-487. See also Derek J. de Solla Price, "Automata in History", *Technology and Culture* 5, 1964, pp. 9-42.

6. On the jewelled palaces of heaven see my article, "Heaven on Earth: Temples and Temple Cities of Medieval India", in Dick van der Meij (ed.), *India and Beyond: Aspects of Literature, Meaning, Ritual and Thought, Essays in Honour of Frits Staal*, International Institute for Asian Studies, Leiden and Amsterdam, 1997, pp. 170-194.
7. *Kādambarī*, ed. by Kāśīnāth Pāṇḍurang Parabh, Bombay, Nirṇayasāgara Press, 1896. From p. 231 references are to the second edition.
8. *Kathāsaritsāgara* ed. by Paṇḍit Jagadīśalāl Śāstrī, Motilal Banarsidass, Delhi, 1970, 6.3. *Bhoja Prabandha* ed. by Dr. Rāmeśvara Jhā, Prakāśana Kendra, Lucknow, n.d., p. 25.
9. *Kumāravihāraśataka* of Rāmcandragaṇi Śrī Ātmānanda Sabhā, Bhavnagar, 1911.
10. *Nyāyakumudacandra* of Prabhācandra, ed. By Pandit Mahendra Kumar Nyayacharya, Māṇikchandra Jaina Granthamālā 39, Bombay, Māṇik Chandra Digambara Jain Series, 1941, vol. II, pp. 451-59.
11. *Tattvārtharājavārtika*, ed. by Mahendrakumar Jain, Jñāna Pīṭha Mūrtidevī Jaina Granthamālā, Saṃskṛtagrantha 20, Bhāratīya Jñānapīṭha, Kāśī, 1957, p. 489.
12. I have discussed this story in "Divine Delicacies: Monks, Images and Miracles in the Contest between Jainism and Buddhism" in Richard Davis (ed.), *Images, Miracles and Authority in Asian Religious Traditions*, Westview Press, Boulder, 1998, pp. 121-141.
13. *Syādvādamañjarī*, ed. by Jagadīścandra Jain, Mahāvīra Press, Varanasi, 1970, pp. 17-18.
14. *Ratnaprabhasūri's Ratnākarāvātārikā* ed. by Pt. Dalsukh Malvania, L.D. Institute, Ahmedabad, 1969, vol. 3, p. 62.
15. The Naiyāyika at *Nyāyasūtra* III.1. 50 offered an answer not all that different from the Jains to justify why mirrors cause the rays of the eyes to come back and grasp the face and walls do not; they say that this is a peculiar feature of a reflecting surface that is not present in a wall. Both the Jain and the Naiyāyika, then, have resort to some unique property that belongs to the reflecting surface to explain features of the process of reflection. The Jain uses it to explain why the mirror image is reversed, while the Naiyāyika wants to explain why only some things give rise to the perception of reflections while others do not *Nyāyasūtra* commentaries ed. Taranath Nyayatarkatirtha, Delhi, Munshiram Manoharlal, 1985, p. 778.
16. Among the Jain arguments used to refute the Nyāya notion that the eye is in contact with its object is its inability to explain why we can see through transparent surfaces. The Naiyāyika argues that in such cases the rays are not stopped by the solid surface; they pierce the surface to grasp the object behind it or within it (*Nyāyasūtra. Nyāyavārttikatātparyaṭīkā* p. 775 on III. 1.47). The Jain argues that this is impossible; in such a case liquid should run out of a crystal vessel, but it does not For the Jain

refutation see *Nyāyaviniścayavivaraṇa of Vādirājasūri on Bhaṭṭākalaṅkadeva's Nyāyaviniścaya*, ed. Mahendra Kumar Jain, Jnānapīṭha Mūrtidevī Jaina Granthamālā, Saṃskṛta Grantha no 12; Bhārātiya Jñānapīṭha, Kāśi, 1954, vol. 2, p. 327 and *Prameyakamalamārtaṇḍa* of Prabhācandra, ed. Mahendra Kumar Jain, Nirṇayasāgara Press, Bombay, 1941, pp. 227-28. For the Buddhist argument against the notion that the sense-organs must be in contact with their objects see the discussion in Masaaki Hattori, *Dignāga on Perception*, Harvard University Press, Cambridge, 1968, p. 37ff.

17. The same section in the *Ślokavārttika* is also refuted by the Buddhist *Tattvasaṃgraha* verses 2209-2593. It is also worth noting that Prabhācandra in the *Prameyakamalamārtaṇḍa* refutation of the *Ślokavārttika* has a different reading for verse 178, reading *nānāika* instead of *nāneka*. Prabhācandra is also closer to the reading of the *Tattvasaṃgraha* 2209.

VI

LOGIC

CHAPTER 23

Prajñākaragupta's Proof of the Buddha's Authority

TAKASHI IWATA

In the Buddhist logical tradition a thesis is accepted only when it is proved to be true through reasoning that derives its consequence. This inevitably leads to the examination of those theses which are traditionally handed down and accepted as authoritative. Even descriptions of the Buddha himself are not an exception. In fact the thesis "The Buddha is a *pramāṇa*" which means that the Buddha is as trustworthy an authority as a means of cognition (*pramāṇa*), is an object of examination. Dharmakīrti (*ca.* 600-660 A.D.), following Dignāga's (*ca.* 480-540 A.D.) statement on four epithets of the Buddha, described a detailed proof of this thesis for the first time in the Buddhist logical tradition.[1] Among Dharmakīrti's followers, Prajñākaragupta (last half of the eighth century) expounded his own interpretation of Dharmakīrti's proof.[2] I shall deal with the analysis of Prajñākaragupta's argument on the proof of the Buddha's authority.

Examining the authority of the Buddha begins with Dignāga's allusion to the Buddha's four epithets.[3] The epithets are as follows: the Blessed One (*bhagavat*) seeks for the benefit of the world (*jagaddhitaiṣin*), is a teacher (*śāstṛ*), a *sugata*, and a protector (*tāyin*). He is a *pramāṇa* because he accomplished four actual stages which correspond to four epithets, namely, he accomplished intention (*āśaya*) to benefit all living beings, and then accomplished practice (*prayoga*) to become a true teacher; he accomplished his own objectives (*svārtha*) to be a *sugata*, and then accomplished the objectives of others (*parārtha*) to save the world. Dharmakīrti regards these four accomplishments as a causal sequence since each preceding stage causes succeeding stage.[4] As a result, Dharmakīrti argues, the Buddha has become a *pramāṇa*. This causal interpretation is already implied by his own explanation of the word "*pramāṇabhūta*",[5] which literally means that (he) is a *pramāṇa*. Intending to refute the objection that eternal entities like Īśvara, Viṣṇu etc. are *pramāṇas*, he explains that "the expression '*bhūta*' is [used] for the sake of excluding [the eternal entity, which] has not come into existence (*abhūta*)".[6] That is, the statement "The Buddha is a *pramāṇa*" means that he has become a *pramāṇa* after having accomplished the four stages mentioned above whereas in other schools an eternal entity like a god of Īśvara is assumed already to be a *pramāṇa*. The word "*bhūta*" in the compound *pramāṇabhūta* has the function of negating this view on the eternal authority assumed in other schools.

While explaining the proof of the Buddha's authority in accordance with Dharmakīrti's argument, Prajñākaragupta sporadically describes it in simplified forms. For the examination of Prajñākaragupta's view these descriptions are useful because some of them include his own interpretations. The simplified form of the proof which will be dealt with later in chapter II, consists of the following argument: The Buddha proclaims the truth (the Four Noble Truths) and hence is omniscient (*sarvajña*). In consequence, he is a *pramāṇa*. It is obvious that Prajñākaragupta's argument is different from that of Dharmakīrti in that the former includes the factor of "omniscience" which for Prajñākaragupta serves to divide his proof into two types, as will be seen in chapter I.1. In this paper I shall analyze Prajñākaragupta's description of the proof and point out several characteristic features of his argument.

I. Before going into the details of his proof, let us start with a basic description of the concept of *pramāṇa*.[7] According to Dharmakīrti's logical and epistemological system, there are two types of correct cognition: direct perception (*pratyakṣa*) and inference (*anumāna*). These are correct "because, when, having determined an object by means of these two (cognitions), one takes action [to the object], one is not belied (or thwarted— *na visaṃvādyate*) from attaining [one's] purpose (*arthakriyā*)".[8] The first thing that one notices is that the condition for correct cognition is that it be non-belying (*avisaṃvādana*), i.e., reliable. Only direct perception and inference are regarded as means of cognition (*pramāṇa*) in that they make a cognizer attain or cognize an aimed object and hence are non-belying, i.e., reliable. Dharmakīrti, using the concept "non-belying", defines *pramāṇa* as follows: "*Pramāṇa* is cognition which does not belie (*pramāṇam avisaṃvādi jñānam*)" (PV II 1ab'). "Being non-belying is [defined as] the establishment of attaining a purpose (*arthakriyāsthitiḥ/ avisaṃvādanam*)" (PV II 1b'c'). I shall consider the validity of this definition in detail in chapter 1.2. Dharmakīrti shows another definition of *pramāṇa:* "Or [*pramāṇa* is] illumination of a [previously] unapprehended object (*ajñātārthaprakāśo vā*)" (PV II 5c). Namely, it is neither cognition which conceptually constructs objects that are previously apprehended, nor is it recollection which recognizes the object that was known before.

I.1 Although the relationship between these two definitions is interpreted variously,[9] I shall not go into these interpretations in detail, but only allude to Prajñākaragupta's understanding, according to which these two are quite different. The second definition of the *pramāṇa* by "*ajñatarthaprakaśa*" is the definition of the *pramāṇa* related to supreme reality (*pāramārthika*), on the contrary, the first definition, by "*avisaṃvādana*" or "*arthakriyāsthiti*", is the definition of the *pramāṇa* related to verbal activities (*sāṃvyavahārika*),[10] namely, the conventional *pramāṇa*. This difference is applied to his proof of the Buddha's authority. It is a characteristic feature of his proof that he divided it into two types, conforming to the difference between two definitions of *pramāṇa*: the proof from the aspect of supreme reality and from that of convention.

Prajñākaragupta's argument in the first proof can be seen in his relatively simplified proof of the Buddha's authority discussed above. As will be analyzed in chapter II, it runs as follows: The Buddha is a *pramāṇa* because he proclaims the Four Noble Truths and is omniscient. Namely, he does not belie (i.e., is reliable), because he attains his purpose to save all living beings by means of both the proclamation of the truth and his omniscience. Generally speaking, the attainment of purpose of an object, however, occurs in the future (*bhāvinī*) but not at the time when one perceives the object,[11] just as the achievement of fire's purpose to burn firewood first occurs after the perception of fire itself. Therefore, the determination—that cognition which has a things to be arrived in the future as its object is non-belying — is possible on the level of verbal activities (*vyavahāra*). In other words, this determination is based on the assumption that, through the superimposition (*āropa*) of a thing to be arrived at in the future on a previously perceived thing, these two things, although actually different because of the doctrine of momentariness, are practically identical in the frame of everyday life, based on verbal activities.[12] This is what Dharmakīrti states on the matter: "[That cognition] is a *pramāṇa* is [recognized] by verbal activities" (PV II 5a: *prāmāṇyaṃ vyavahāreṇa*). That is, for Prajñākaragupta the recognition of "being non-belying" or "attainment of purpose" is of a conventional nature[13] in comparison with the direct perception of one's own form of cognition, i.e., self-cognition (*svasaṃvedana*) which is free from verbal activities and the one and only *pramāṇa* from the aspect of supreme reality.[14] This holds good, Prajñākaragupta admits, also for the Buddha's authority in the sense of being non-belying. He argues on the one hand that the Buddha is a *pramāṇa*, i.e., non-belying reliable authority, because he is omniscient, on the other hand, he argues that in order to distinguish supreme authority from conventional authority of being non-belying based on thorough knowledge, the thorough knowledge of all things (*sarvārthaparijñāna*) is possible in dependence on worldly verbal activities (*lokavyavahāra*) and is hence merely conventional (*sāṃvṛta*).[15] Thus, as far as the Buddha's authority is discussed in the frame of thorough knowledge based on verbal activities, it is conventional.

Since the thorough knowledge of all things and the concept of "non-belying" are conventional, it is easy to imagine that Prajñākaragupta does not apply them to the Buddha's authority from the aspect of supreme reality. In fact, in order to formulate his thesis that the Buddha is a *pramāṇa*, he makes use of the second definition of *pramāṇa*, i.e., illumination of an unapprehended object (*ajñātārthaprakāśa*), and glosses it as follows[16]:

the "object" (*artha*) in the term "unapprehended object" (*ajñātārtha*) means supreme reality (*paramārtha*); hence the "illumination of an unapprehended object" means the illumination of supreme reality (*paramārthaprakāśa*) which is not yet apprehended by conventional knowledge. The "supreme reality" in its turn means that cognition possesses a non-dual essence (*advaitarūpatā*), namely, an essence free from the duality of grasped and grasper (*grāhyagrāhaka*), unitariness and manifoldness, and so on. According to this interpretation, the Buddha is a *pramāṇa* from the aspect of supreme reality because he perceives the non-dual essence which is realized by himself alone, but not by others.

> Or, from the aspect of supreme reality (*paramārthataḥ*), the Blessed One also is a *pramāṇa* like that, [namely he is a *pramāṇa*] merely because [—just as correct cognition possesses the definition of *pramāṇa* — he possesses the definition "illumination of an unapprehended object", in other words] perceives the non-dual [essence] (*advaitāvabodha*), but not because he thoroughly knows all things. The thorough knowledge of all things, however, [is possible] by means of worldly verbal activities [and hence] is only conventional (*sāṃvṛta*) [knowledge] (PVBh 32, 14f.).[17]

This passage shows Prajñākaragupta's view on the difference between the two types of proof of the Buddha's authority: proof of his authority, i.e., non-belying reliability, from the conventional aspect on the grounds of his omniscience on the one hand, and on the other hand proof of his authority, i.e., his illumination of an unapprehended object, from the aspect of supreme reality on the grounds of his perception of non-dual essence.

I.2 Among the characteristic features of Prajñākaragupta's interpretation of *pramāṇa* it is interesting to note his examination of the validity of the definition of *pramāṇa*. Dharmakīrti, as we have seen, defines *pramāṇa* as cognition that possesses *avisaṃvādana*, and the latter as *arthakriyāsthiti*. There is, however, room for doubt about the latter definition, since in order to show the validity of this definition one must demonstrate that *avisaṃvādana* and *arthakriyāsthiti* are conceptually equal. Prajñākaragupta notices this problem and discusses it from the angle of the extension of these concepts. He paraphrases the concept *arthakriyā* of a thing as completion (*niṣpatti*) of function which is expected for a thing or for the sake of which a thing exists or is used, for example the *arthakriyā* of fire as the completion of burning or cooking. Then, he paraphrases the concept of *sthiti* as non-swaying (*avicalana*) or determination (*vyavasthiti*).[18] Finally, he studies the concept of *avisaṃvādana* as not deviating from the concept of *arthakriyāsthiti* and vice versa.

Let us look closely at his argument. The opponent (the Mīmāṃsaka) claims that *avisaṃvādana* cannot be defined by *arthakriyāsthiti*, because there is a case where in spite of the presence of *avisaṃvādana* (being non-belying) *arthakriyāsthiti* (establishment of the completion of function) is not present. For example, cognition of an object, perceiving it visibly, is non-belying but cannot establish completion of the object's function. This is because, as mentioned before, the completion of function occurs in the future. That is to say, at a point in time (t_{I}) in which cognition (j_{I}) perceives only fire but not fire's burning firewood; it is not yet certain whether the relevant fire can complete the function of burning firewood. This completion of burning can be ascertained only when later (t_{II}) the second cognition (j_{II}) recognizes that fire really burns firewood. Yet in order to ascertain this one must also ascertain the completion of the second cognition's function. The latter ascertainment is only possible when the third cognition (j_{II+1}) recognizes the completion of the second cognition's (j_{II}) function. In this way, one should seek for a third cognition (j_{II+1}) to ascertain the second cognition. However, this process would entail an infinite regression.[19] Thus, the first cognition, although being non-belying, does not establish the completion of function. Similarly the second cognition (j_{II}), though possessing the appearance of the completion of the object's function (e.g., fire's burning), does not possess the appearance of the completion of the cognition's (j_{II}) function. Therefore, this is also a case where cognition, although being non-belying with respect to its object, does not establish the completion of function with respect to the cognition itself. In consequence, the opponent claims that these are instances where the concept *arthakriyāsthiti* does not sufficiently pervade (**avyāpti, ma khyab pa*) the concept *avisaṃvādana*. To this objection Prajñākaragupta answers[20]:

"As far as the establishment of the completion of function with respect to the (cognition (j_I) of an object (a_I)) is attained by [cognition] other [than the cognition (j_I)], this (cognition (j_I)) is a correct cognition. When on the other hand the completion of function with respect to the (cognition (j_{II}) which recognizes the completion of the object's (a_I) function) is perceptively experienced (*anubhava*) by [the cognition (j_{II})] itself at the very time [of the cognition (j_{II})], this (cognition (j_{II})) is even more a correct cognition" (PVBh 4, 14f.).[21]

According to Yamāri's interpretation, "when the cognition (j_{II}) [which recognizes] the completion of [the object's (a_I)] function is determined as non-belying [and hence] possesses the capacity of proving even another (i.e., the previous object's (a_I) cognition (j_I)) to be a correct cognition, how cannot [the cognition (j_{II})] itself be a correct cognition?".[22]

As Yamāri points out, the argument to avoid the infinite regression is based on "the ground that the [subsequent] cognition (j_{II}), which possesses the appearance (**pratibhāsa*) of the completion of [the object's] function, is a correct cognition by itself".[23] To be sure, the subsequent cognition (j_{II}) would be an example where, as the opponent claims, *avisaṃvādana* (i.e., being non-belying with respect to an object) is present without *arthakriyāsthiti* (i.e., the establishment of the completion of the cognition's (j_{II}) function), if the cognition (j_{II}) could not complete its own function, i.e., the perception of the cognition (j_{II}) itself. In reality, however, this is not the case, because the cognition (j_{II}), while determining the completion of the object's (a_I) function, perceives simultaneously the cognition (j_{II}) itself, and hence completes its own function to perceive itself. Thus, since "[the definition of *avisaṃvādana* is] generally described [by saying] that *avisaṃvādana* is the establishment of the completion of function",[24] and the subsequent cognition (j_{II}) establishes not only the completion of the object's function but also the completion of its own function, i.e., self-cognition, it (j_{II}) is still more a *pramāṇa* (correct cognition).[25]

Here, the fundamental ground for Prajñākaragupta's argument for the affirmation of the view that in the later cognition (j_{II}) not only *avisaṃvādana* but also *arthakriyāsthiti* is present stems from his tenet of the cognition's self-cognition which makes it possible to determine the completion of its own function without dependence on any other factors.

As another example of the definition's fallacy that the concept *arthakriyāsthiti* does not sufficiently pervade the concept *avisaṃvādana*, the opponent adduces cognition of sound. Cognition of sound is non-belying but does not complete its function by the sound itself nor by another factor.[26] Let us look at the case of cognition of the sound "fire". Although one is not belied in regard to the perception of the sound "fire", neither the sound "fire" itself has the capacity to complete the function of burning firewood nor does the sound's cognition occurring after the pronunciation of the sound complete the function of arriving at the sound "fire", since as soon as it is spoken it falls away on account of its momentariness. According to Dharmakīrti, this objection is refuted: "Because in the case of (cognition) of sound also the intention (*abhiprāya*) [of the speaker] is indicated (*nivedana*) [by it and this indication of intention is an attainment of purpose, cognition of sound attains its purpose]".[27] According to Prajñākaragupta's explanation, "The indication of the essence of the completion of the intended function is really the 'being non-belying' in itself".[28] Here, the essence of the completion of function means direct perception of object.

> In this case [of cognition of an object], in reality, no kind of completion of function is recognized anywhere excepting the perception of the own form [of the object] (*svarūpasaṃvedana*) (PVBh 5, 22).[29]

Thus, since the perception of sound's own form is not only non-belying but also attains its purpose, i.e., completes the function intended by the speaker with regard to sound, the cognition of sound cannot be an example of the deviation in that without the completion of function a non-belying cognition is possible.

So far we have examined whether the concept *arthakriyāsthiti* does not extensionally sufficiently pervade the concept *avisaṃvādana* and have shown that Prajñākaragupta argues against the opponent's claim insisting on the possibility of a lack of sufficient pervasion. The next step in proving the identity of both concepts is to disprove the opponent's claim that the concept *arthakriyāsthiti* pervades exceedingly (*ativyāpti*), i.e., exceeds extensionally, the concept *avisaṃvādana*.[30] The opponent enumerates two examples of excessive pervasion, cognition in a dream and cognition of a yellow shell.[31] Cognition in a dream can sometimes exert an influence on reality and thereby complete its function, i.e., attain its purpose, yet the dream does not always come true and is not non-belying. Cognition of a yellow shell, although belying since the shell is not yellow but white, completes its function as long as one sees that an external form of the shell can hold water. Prajñākaragupta disproves these claims on the grounds that in each of these cases the opponents's assumption of the completion of function does not hold:

> Furthermore, this (i.e., mere appearance of the completion of function in the case of cognition in a dream) is not the establishment of the completion of function, because it is devoid of non-swaying. [In other words, the appearance of] the completion of function in a dream is attained by the force of mere repeated experience (i.e., a residual force infused by previous deeds). [Therefore] one is not satisfied with the (appearance of the completion of function) (PVBh 5, 8).[32]

In the case of cognition in a dream the completion of function is swaying and hence not established because it does not depend on real objects but only on a residual force. As concerns the cognition of a yellow shell, he argues, the completion of the function to recognize that the shell is yellow is not attained and hence not established, even though the mere recognition of the form of the shell could be a correct cognition, which is only an inference and not a direct perception.[33]

Thus, Prajñākaragupta demonstrates the validity of the definition "*pramāṇa* is cognition which possesses *avisaṃvādana* that is *arthakriyāsthiti*" by means of disproving the opponent's claims that *avisaṃvādana* is not extensionally the same as *arthakriyāsthiti*.[34] Due to this definition of *pramāṇa*, the statement that the Buddha is a *pramāṇa* means that he attains his own purpose, i.e., the liberation of all living beings from suffering, accordingly, he does not belie the expectation of realizing liberation and is therefore reliable.

II. Having considered Prajñākaragupta's arguments for the validity of the definition of *pramāṇa*, now we are able to look more carefully at his own proof of the Buddha's authority from a conventional aspect. A simplified structure of his proof can be derived from the following statement:

> Because the Blessed One proclaims the truth (*bhūtokti*) in order to exclude non-truth (*abhūtavinivṛttaye*), namely, to exclude error, he alone is omniscient (*sarvajña*), but not others (e.g., Īśvara, Viṣṇu etc.). Thus, [namely, because of his being omniscient, he is] a *pramāṇa* (PVBh 32, 8-11).[35]

While the word "*bhūtokti*" in the original context of Dharmakīrti's verse (PV II 7bc') means "the expression '*bhūta*' [in the compound *pramāṇabhūta]*", Prajñākaragupta interprets it differently as "proclamation (*ukti*) of the truth (*bhūta*)". He regards it as the ground for the Buddha's authority arguing that the Blessed One, i.e., the Buddha, is omniscient because he proclaims the truth, and therefore, he is a *pramāṇa*. Prajñākaragupta's thought pattern is abbreviated as follows.

> The Buddha: proclaiming the truth (*bhūtokti*) — omniscient (*sarvajña*) — *pramāṇa*

What comes before the colon indicates the subject of the proof.

Here, he makes use of two factors, i.e., proclamation of the truth and omniscience, for proof of the Buddha's authority. This pattern does not literally correspond to that of Dharmakīrti. The latter pattern consists of the following sequence of factors:

> The Buddha: seeking for the benefit of living beings — teacher — *sugata* — protector — *pramāṇa*.

In his commentary on Dharmakīrti's verse (PV II 34) Prajñākaragupta also mentions that compassion (*karuṇā*) is the fundamental ground (*sādhana*) for proof of the Buddha's authority[36] and this compassion corresponds to "seeking for the benefit of living beings". Furthermore, "proclaiming the truth" corresponds to the factor "protector" since the fact that he proclaims the Four Noble Truths which he discovered implies that by means of his sermon he protects living beings from suffering.[37] The remaining factor "omniscient" in Prajñākaragupta's thought pattern is the one which he himself inserts into the proof. Now the question arises as to what role this factor plays in his proof. Within the frame of the relationship between "omniscient" and "*pramāṇa*", the reason for his inserting the factor "omniscient" can be traced to the view that in order to be an authority in this world one must know all objects, otherwise one cannot attain one's own purpose.[38] Here, the relationship of the factor "omniscient" to the factor "*pramāṇa*" seems at least to be one of causality, since the statement that without being omniscient one cannot attain one's own purpose means that "being omniscient" is a cause for "being an authority" who is able to attain his own purpose.

It may be worth pointing out, in passing, that omniscience in the Buddhist logical tradition means not that he knows anything and everything as an omniscient being as is assumed in other schools, but that he knows everything with respect to the attainment of his intended purpose, namely, everything that is useful for the liberation of all living beings. According to Prajñākaragupta, omniscience is divided into two types: that of a person who knows the essential human purpose (*pradhānapuruṣārthajña*) and that of a person who knows all realities that are purified by a means of cognition (*pramāṇapariśuddhasakalatattvajña*).[39] Therefore, omniscience does not require the knowledge of things which are not indispensable to liberation, for example knowledge of the number of worms in this world. The essential human purpose is liberation from suffering; realities purified by a means of cognition are the momentariness (*kṣaṇikatva*) of all conditioned things, the non-existence of intrinsic nature (*nairātmya*) of things, and so on.[40]

In accordance with Dharmakīrti's causal relation among factors for proof of the Buddha's authority, one may also suppose that in Prajñākaragupta's thought pattern "proclaiming the truth—omniscient—*pramāṇa*", just as the factor "being omniscient" is a cause for the Buddha's authority, so the factor "proclaiming the truth" is a cause for the factor "being omniscient". However, contrary to our expectation, Prajñākaragupta thinks, according to Yamāri's commentary, that the relationship between the two is a logical one: The Buddha knows the Four Noble Truths and his knowledge of them, i.e., omniscience in the sense of the Buddhist logical tradition, motivates him to be actively engaged in proclaiming these Truths to protect all living beings. Namely, "[he] cannot protect all (living beings) unless [he] is omniscient".[41] In other words, from the cause "being omniscient" the effect "protection of all", i.e., "proclamation of the truth" arises. On the basis of the well-known relation that effect as reason implies cause as consequence, this causal relationship is formulated in the logical statement: whoever proclaims the truth is omniscient. Since the Buddha proclaims the Four Noble Truths, he is omniscient. Here, "proclamation of the truth" is an effect of "being omniscient". Therefore, the reason "proclaiming the truth", from which the consequence "being omniscient" of the Buddha is derived, is a reason as effect (*kāryahetu*).[42]

In short, it is Prajñākaragupta's unique argument that he inserts the factor "omniscient" as grounds for proof of the authority of the Buddha and regards the relationship between "proclaiming the truth" and "being omniscient" as logical. That is to say, he is of the view that from the reason as effect "proclaiming the truth" the consequence "omniscience" of the Buddha is derived, but he is not of the view that the former factor causes the latter.

From the examination mentioned above, it is clear that in Prajñākaragupta's thought pattern "the Buddha: proclaiming the truth—omniscient—*pramāṇa*" the first two factors, "proclaiming the truth" and "being omniscient", are related not causally or factually but logically. This would lead us to suppose the possibility that "proclaiming the truth" or "being omniscient" also can be logically related to "being a *pramāṇa*". Yet we confront a problem: According to Dharmakīrti's explanation, the fact that the Buddha has become an authority is an effect of his activities of proclaiming the truth, protecting all living beings and, so on. Since effect, however, is not always derived from cause, the problem arises as to how the derivation of the effect "Buddha's authority" can be derived logically from these causes.

In Prajñākaragupta's thought pattern "proclamation of the truth—omniscient—*pramāṇa*", the relationship between "proclamation of the truth" and "omniscience" is already known as a logical relation. Therefore, if the relationship between "omniscience" and "*pramāṇa*" can be understood logically, his thought pattern can be interpreted as a logical sequence. In the case of the relationship between "being omniscient" and "being a *pramāṇa*", the factor "omniscient" might facilitate us to understand this relationship without the nuance of causality, if we interpret it as follows. When a person is omniscient he knows all means to achieve his intention to protect living beings and hence is able to realize his intention; one who realizes one's own intention is a *pramāṇa*. In consequence, the Buddha, being omniscient, is a *pramāṇa*. That is, although the relationship between "being omniscient" and "being a *pramāṇa*" can be interpreted as causality, as mentioned above, we could also understand it without presupposing a causal relationship, provided that we neglect the difference between the knowledge or the ability to realize one's purpose and the realization itself.

If, however, one should take this difference into consideration, then the problem discussed above still remains. Namely, even if the Buddha knows the necessary means to protect all living beings, the knowledge itself as a cause does not always lead to the result of liberation of all living beings. A clue to answering this problem can be found in Dharmakīrti's theory of the inference of the possibility of effect from cause. According to his theory, the possibility or fitness (*yogyatā*) of the occurrence of effect can be derived logically from causes of effect under the condition that these are sufficient causes to produce their effect. That is, the proposition "Wherever there is a total complex (*sāmagrī*) of causes, there is the possibility of the occurrence of effect" is regarded as true[43]. The point to pay attention to is the description of the consequence, namely, that it consists not of mere "effect" but of the "possibility or fitness of the occurrence of effect". Therefore, in the case of proving the Buddha's authority, in order to infer his authority as an effect from the factors of omniscience etc., one needs, strictly speaking, to describe the consequence as "the possibility to be called a *pramāṇa*". This view is already suggested by Devendrabuddhi (last half of the seventh century) as pointed out in Inami/Tillemans 1986,[44] and is advocated by his disciple Śākyabuddhi.[45] When we take account of Dharmakīrti's theory of the inference of the possibility of effect from cause, we can formulate Prajñākaragupta's thought pattern from the conventional aspect in the following way:

> The Buddha: proclaiming the truth → omniscient → possibility to be called a *pramāṇa*

Here, the arrow indicates a logical implication.

Prajñākaragupta's tendency to interpret his own thought pattern as a logical sequence is implicitly reflected in his explanation of the factor "compassion". According to Dharmakīrti's causal thought pattern (the Buddha: seeking for the benefit of all living beings (i.e. possessing compassion)—teacher—*sugata*—protector—*pramāṇa*), the factor "compassion" is the cause for the succeeding factor "teacher" (i.e., practice to become a real teacher). In order to explain that compassion motivates the Buddha to practice the method to liberate living being from suffering, Dharmakīrti presupposes a spontaneously (increasing) function *svarasena pra √ vṛt*) of compassion.[46] Prajñākaragupta, following Dharmakīrti's causal thought pattern, discusses in detail the question of how this presumption of the spontaneous function of compassion is explained. He argues as follows. Compassion is a preeminent property of mind, i.e., an essential property (*svabhāva*) of mind, therefore, it possesses the continuance of mind as its stable basis (*sthirāśraya*) and does not depend upon any further effort (*punaryatna*), i.e., any factors other than its own seed (*bīja*) which is an immediate condition (*samanāntarapratyaya*) possessing a residual force of compassion. In consequence, he concludes, compassion increases infinitely when through repeated experience it is endowed with these two qualifications "possession of the continuance of mind as its stable basis" and "non-dependence upon any other factors".[47] This argument implies the necessity for the increase of compassion. Further, in regard to the relationship of the factor "compassion" to the factor "teacher" (i.e., practice of the method to liberate living beings from suffering in order to become a real teacher), he explains this relationship "on the grounds that [a compassionate person] who possesses the wish that other (living beings) are free from suffering necessarily (*avaśyam*) seeks for the means [for the liberation from suffering]".[48] Namely, when compassion, which wishes living beings' liberation from suffering, increases infinitely and attains the highest advance to excellence,[49] it necessarily causes the Buddha to seek for the method to realize liberation. Here, we can see Prajñākaragupta's view on the necessary occurrence of the effect, "the practice of the method to liberate living beings", i.e., "being a teacher" from the cause, "possession of compassion". The necessity of the occurrence of effect from cause could lead to the idea that this kind of cause is interpreted as a logical reason for the derivation of effect as consequence.[50]

Summary

In this paper I have analyzed Prajñākaragupta's proof of the Buddha's authority and pointed out three characteristic features. Firstly, he examines the validity of the definition of *pramāṇa.* According to Dharmakīrti's definition, *pramāṇa* is cognition which possesses *avisaṃvādana* (being non-belying) defined as *arthakriyāsthiti* (establishment of attaining purpose). Prajñākaragupta demonstrates that the concept *avisaṃvādana* does not deviate from the concept *arthakriyāsthiti* and vice versa. Secondly, he divides his proof into two types in conformity with the difference between two definitions of *pramāṇa:* A) proof of the Buddha's authority, i.e., non-belying reliability, from the conventional aspect on the grounds of his omniscience; and B) proof of his authority, i.e., his illumination of an unapprehended object, from the aspect of supreme reality on the grounds of his perception of non-dual essence. Thirdly, on the one hand he explains proof of the Buddha's authority in accordance with Dharmakīrti's thought pattern to interpret the Buddha's four epithets "seeking for the benefit of all living beings" (i.e., possession of compassion), "teacher", "*sugata*" and "protector" (i.e., proclamation of the truth) as a causal sequence, but on the other hand he sporadically describes Dharmakīrti's proof in simplified forms and implies the tendency to interpret these logically. As an example I have analyzed his thought pattern of proof of the Buddha's authority "proclamation of the truth—omniscient—*pramāṇa*" and showed his tendency to interpret it as a logical sequence. He suggests this tendency also in his interpretation of Dharmakīrti's causal relation between "possession of compassion" and "practice to become a real teacher".

NOTES

1. As for the synopsis of Dharmakīrti's proof of the Buddha's authority cf. Masahiro Inami and Tom J.F. Tillemans, "Another Look at the Framework of the *Pramāṇasiddhi* Chapter of *Pramāṇavārttika*," *Wiener Zeitschrift für die Kunde Südasiens* (hereafter **WZKS**) 30, 1986 (hereafter **Inami/Tillemans 1986**), pp. 128-141 and Yoichi Fukuda and Yumiko Ishihama, *A Comparative*

Table of Sa-bcad of the Pramāṇavārttika Found in Tibetan Commentaries on the Pramāṇavārttika, Studia Tibetica 12, The Toyo Bunko, 1986, pp. 21-36.

2. Cf. Takashi Iwata, "Seson ha ikanishite Kojyun (*pramāṇa*) to natta, no ka" (How has the Buddha become a *pramāṇa*), *Komazawa-tankidaigaku-Bukkyo-ronshu* 6, 2000 (hereafter **Iwata 2000**), pp. 9ff. and Takashi Iwata, "Seson no ryosei no shomei no ichikaishaku" (An Interpretation of proof of the Buddha's authority), *Indotetsugaku-Bukkyogaku*, 16, 2001 (hereafter **Iwata 2001**), pp. 46ff.
3. Cf. *Pramāṇasamuccayavṛtti*, tr. by Vasudhararakṣita and Seṅ (ge) rgyal (po), Peking edition (hereafter **P**) 5701, 13a7-b3 = *Pramāṇasamuccayavṛtti*, tr. by Kanakavarman and Dad pa(') śes rab, P 5702, 93b6-94a2 and Masaaki Hattori, *Dignāga, On Perception, being the Pratyakṣapariccheda of Dignāga's Pramāṇasamuccaya from the Sanskrit fragments and the Tibetan versions*, Harvard University Press, Cambridge, Massachusetts, 1968, p. 23 and pp. 73-75 (nn. I.1-3).
4. Cf. *Pramāṇavārttika* II (*pramāṇasiddhi*) (hereafter **PV II**) 280-282 (in Yusho Miyasaka, "*Pramāṇavārttika-kārikā* (Sanskrit and Tibetan)", *Acta Indologica* 2, 1971/72, pp. 1-206, as for the numbering of the verses of PV II, I follow Vetter's number), Tilmann Vetter, *Der Buddha und seine Lehre in Dharmakīrtis Pramāṇavārttika*, Arbeitskreis Für Tibetische und Buddhistische Studien Universität Wien (hereafter **ATBS**), Wien, 1984 (hereafter **Vetter 1984**), pp. 169ff. and Eli Franco, *Dharmakīrti on Compassion and Rebirth*, ATBS, Wien, 1997 (hereafter **Franco 1997**), pp. 19ff.
5. On studies treating the interpretation of the word *pramāṇabhūta* in the Buddhist logical tradition see Iwata 2001, p. 67, n.6.
6. PV II 7bc': *abhūtavinivṛttaye / bhūtoktiḥ* (translated in Toshihiko Kimura, *Dharmakīrti Shukyo-tetsugaku no Genten-kenkyu*, Tokyo, 1981, p. 38 and Masahiro Inami, "*Pramāṇavārttika Pramāṇasiddhi*-Sho no Kenkyu (3)," *Simane-kenritsu-Kokusai-tankidaigaku-Kiyo* 1, 1994 (hereafter **Inami 1994**), p. 17).
7. With regard to studies treating Dharmakīrti's definition of *pramāṇa* see Iwata 2001, p. 68, n. 13. For an English translation of the definition of *pramāṇa* cf. Franco 1997, p. 54, n. 21 & p. 56 and Vittorio A. van Bijlert, *Epistemology and Spiritual Authority* (hereafter **van Bijlert 1989**), ATBS, Wien, 1989, pp. 115ff.
8. Tilmann Vetter, *Dharmakīrti's Pramāṇaviniścayaḥ 1 Kapitel: Pratyakṣam*, Kommissionsverlag der Österreichischen Akademie der Wissenschaften, Wien, 1966, p. 30, 17f., see Iwata 2001, p. 67, n. 8.
9. See Helmut Krasser, "On Dharmakīrti's Understanding of *pramāṇabhūta* and his definitions of *pramāṇa*," WZKS 45, 2001, pp. 184ff.
10. See *Pramāṇavārttikabhāṣya* (in *Pramāṇavārtikabhāshyam or Vārtikālaṅkāraḥ of Prajñākaragupta*, ed. by R. Sāṅkṛtyāyana, Kashi Prasad Jayaswal Research Institute, Patna, 1953 (hereafter **PVBh**)) p. 30, 22 = Motoi Ono, *Prajñākaraguptas Erklärung der Definition gültiger Erkenntnis* (*Pramāṇavārttikālaṃkāra zu Pramāṇavārttika II 1-7*), *Teil I Sanskrit-Text und Materialien*, Verlag der Österreichischen Akademie der Wissenschaften (hereafter **VÖAW**), Wien, 2000 (hereafter **Ono (PVBh)**, p. 79, 18f.: *tatra pāramārthikapramāṇalakṣaṇam* etat (i.e., *ajñātārthaprakāśa*), *pūrvaṃ* (i.e. definition by *avisaṃvādana*) *tu sāṃvyavahārikasya*.

11. See PVBh, p. 4, 4f. = Ono (PVBh), p. 3, 11f.: *sā cārthakriyā bhāvinī, na tatkāle.*
12. Cf. PVBh, p. 5, 25; p. 26, 5ff (= Ono (PVBh), p. 8, 1f.; p. 67, 2ff), *Pramāṇavārttikavṛtti* (in *Pramāṇavārttika of Acharya Dharmakirtti with the Commentary 'Vritti' of Acharya Manorathanandin*, ed. by S. D. Shastri, Bauddha Bharati, Varanasi, 1968), p. 7, 14ff and Iwata 2000, p. 7.
13. See PVBh, p. 25, 19f.; p. 22, 10-17 = Ono (PVBh), p. 65, 4f.; pp. 55, 9-56,2.
14. See PVBh, p. 25, 24f.; p. 30, 20f. = Ono (PVBh), p. 65, 10-12; p. 79, 16-18.
15. Cf. PVBh, p. 32, 15 = Ono (PVBh), p. 84, 13f. (n. 17 infra) and Iwata 2001, p. 69, n. 20.
16. See PVBh, p. 30, 19f. = Ono (PVBh), p. 79, 15f.
17. See PVBh, p. 32, 14f. = Ono (PVBh), p. 84, 12-14: *atha vā paramārthatas* ***tadvad*** *advaitāvabodhād eva* ***pramāṇaṃ bhagavān*** *api, na sarvārthaparijñānataḥ. sarvārthaparijñānaṃ tu lokavyavahāreṇa sāṃvṛtam eva.* It is true that Prajñākaragupta distinguishes the knowledge of "omniscient" (*sarvajña*) from the knowledge of "a person who thoroughly knows everything" (see chapter II), but as far as the knowledge of omniscient is contextually related to the concept of "non-belying" which is conventional, the knowledge of omniscient is also conventional in comparison with the "illumination of supreme reality" which is his own interpretation of the second definition of *pramāṇa*, i.e., "*ajñātārthaprakāśa*" (illumination of an unapprehended object).
18. See PVBh, p. 4, 3f. = Ono (PVBh), p. 3, 10f.
19. Cf. PVBh, p. 4, 9-11 = Ono (PVBh), pp. 3,19-4, 2 and *Pramāṇavārttikālaṃkāraṭīkā Supariśuddhā*, P 5723 (hereafter **PVBhṬ(Ya)**), Phe 251b2f. = *Tattvasaṃgraha* (in *Tattvasaṅgraha of Ācārya Shāntarakṣita with the Commentary 'Pañjikā' of Shrī Kamalashīla*, ed. by S. D. Shatri, Bauddha Bharati, Varanasi, 1968), 2853 (Dr. Ono generously shared his private notes with me).
20. See PVBhṬ(Ya) 251b6 (ad PVBh, p. 4, 15f.): *des na ma khyab pa'i ñes pa* (*doṣa*) *med do źes bya ba'i don to//* and 252a3.
21. PVBh, p. 4, 14f. = Ono (PVBh), p. 4, 5-7: *yatrārthakriyāsthitir aparopakalpitā tad yāvat pramāṇam. yatra tu svatas tadaivārthakriyānubhavas tat sutarām eva pramāṇam.*
22. PVBhṬ(Ya) 251b4: *don byed pa ses pa de mi slu* (Derge edition (hereafter **D**) 209a2; *bslu* P) *ba ñid du ṅes pa na gźan yaṅ tshad mar bsgrub nus na ci ltar bdag ñid tshad ma ma yin/.*
23. See PVBhṬ(Ya) 251b3: (*grub mthar ni*) *don byed par snaṅ ba'i* (**pratibhāsa*) *śes pa* (*jñāna*) *ni / raṅ ñid kho nas tshad ma yin pa'i phyir /* (*thug* (D 209al; *'thug* P) *pa med pa* (D; *par* P) (*anavasthā*) *ma yin no źes bstan to //*).
24. PVBh, p. 4, 15f. = Ono (PVBh), p. 4, 7: (*tat sutarām eva pramāṇam,*) ***arthakriyāsthitir avisaṃvādanam*** *iti sāmānyenābhidhānāt.*
25. See *Pramāṇavārttikavṛtti* (of Ravigupta), P 5726 (hereafter **PVṬ(R)**) Tshe 139blf.: ... ... *gaṅ la tha dad pa'i don byed pa de la ji srid du tshad ma daṅ 'brel pa'i phyir daṅ / gaṅ du tha mi dad pa'i don byed pa yod pa de ñid ni śin tu yaṅ tshad ma yin no //* (... ... "When with respect to the (previous cognition (j_1) of an object (a_1)) [there is subsequently object (a_1)'s] *arthakriyā* (i.e., completion of the object (a_1)'s function) [which is]

different [from cognition (j_1)'s *arthakriyā*, i.e., completion of the cognition (j_1)'s function of perceiving the object (a_1)], so far the (previous cognition (j_1)) is connected with validity, therefore, when with respect to the (subsequent cognition (j_n) which recognizes the object (a_1)'s *arthakriyā*) there is [cognition (j_n)'s] *arthakriyā* (i.e., completion of the cognition (j_n)'s function of recognizing oneself) [which is] not different (i.e., not separated) [from the completion of the cognition (j_n)'s function of recognizing the object (a_1)'s *arthakriyā*], the (subsequent cognition (j_n)) itself is even more (*sutarām*) a *pramāṇa*". *yaṅ*). The idea of dividing *arthakriyā* into *arthakriyā* of object and that of cognition might relate to Devendrabuddhi's interpretation of dividing *avisaṃvādana* into *avisaṃvādana* of object and that of cognition. As for Devendrabuddhi's interpretation cf. *Pramāṇavārttikapañjikā*, P 5717(b) (hereafter **PVP),** Che 2a5-bl and van Bijlert 1989, pp. 121f.

26. See PVBh, p. 4, 17f. = Ono (PVBh), p. 4, 9f.
27. PV II 1c'd: *śābde 'py abhiprāyanivedanāt //*.
28. PVBh, p. 5, 20 = Ono (PVBh), p. 7, 6: *abhipretārthakriyāsvarūpanivedanam eva saṃvādanam.*
29. PVBh, p. 5, 22 = Ono (PVBh), p. 7, 9f.: *na khalu svarūpasaṃvedanād aparam atrārthakriyājātiḥ kvacid upalabhyate.*
30. See PVBhṬ(Ya) 252a3f. (*des na ma khyab pa'i skyon med do //*) *de ltar mi slu* (D 209a7; *bslu* P) *ba'i śes pa la brten nas ma khyab pa spaṅs pa na /* ***gal te*** (*nanu*) *źes bya ba la sogs pas ha caṅ khyab par dogs pa bsu bar byed do // yul gyi khyad par gyis yaṅ ma khyab pa smos pa ni /* ***sgra'i yul can gyi*** (*gyis* P D) (*śabdaviṣaye*) *źes bya ba'o //* ("Thus, [in PVBh, p. 4, 9-16] with respect to non-belying cognition [the fallacy that the concept *arthakriyāsthiti* does] not sufficiently pervade [the concept *avisaṃvādana*] is removed, then [the opponent] suspects [another fallacy that the concept *arthakriyāsthiti*] pervades exceedingly [the concept *avisaṃvādana*] by means of [the claim]: *nanu* ... (PVBh, p. 4, 17). On account of a peculiar object also [the opponent] claims [that the concept *arthakriyāsthiti* does] not sufficiently pervade [the concept *avisaṃvādana*]: *śabdaviṣaye*...(PVBh, p. 4, 17f.)").
31. Cf. PVBh, p. 4, 17 = Ono (PVBh), p. 4, 8f. and PVBhṬ(Ya) 252a3f. (see n. 30).
32. PVBh, p. 5, 8f. = Ono (PVBh), p. 6, 2-4: *na cāsāv arthakriyāsthitir avicalitatvābhāvāt. bhāvanāmātrabalāyātārthakriyā svapne. na tatra paritoṣaḥ.* This translation is based on PVBhṬ(Ya) 254b8-255a1.
33. Cf. PVBh, p. 5, 12ff. and PVṬ(R) 139b5-7.
34. The opponent (the Mīmāṃsaka) insists on his own definition of *pramāṇa* that "*pramāṇa* is cognition [which is] not annulled" (PVBh, p. 4, 18f. = Ono (PVBh), p. 4, 10f.: *abādhito bodhaḥ pramāṇam*).
35. PVBh, p. 32, 8-11 = Ono (PVBh), p. 84, 4-7: ***abhūtavinivṛttaye*** (PV II 7b)/ *bhrāntinivṛttyartham yatas tasya bhagavato* ***bhūtoktis tataḥ*** *sa eva sarvajño nāparaḥ. tathā ca pramāṇam.*
36. Cf. PVBh 53, 6-17 and Franco 1997, pp. 160f. As for the interpretation of the meaning of "ground" where compassion is the fundamental ground for proof of the Buddha's authority, see Iwata 2001, pp. 54-62.
37. Cf. PVBh, p. 118, 15f. & 24 and Iwata 2001, p. 69, nn. 23f.
38. See PVṬ(R) 164a4f. (ad PV II 34ab): *gaṅ źig tshad mar gyur par 'dod pa*

des śes bya thams cad mṅon sum du bya ba ste / gźan du na yoṅs su tshaṅ ba'i don mi srid pa'i phyir ro // ("Whoever wants to be a *pramāṇa* should directly perceive all (things) to be cognized, because otherwise no fulfilled purpose is possible").

39. See PVBh, p. 51, 22: *yo hi pradhānapuruṣārthajñaḥ pramāṇapariśuddhasakalatattvajñaś ca sa eva pramāṇam.*
40. See PVBhṬ(Ya) Be 51a6f. (ad PVBh, p. 51, 22).
41. PVBh 53, 16: (*tataḥ*) *sakalatrāṇam asarvajñatve na saṃbhavati.* Cf. Franco 1997, p. 161 and Iwata 2001, p. 57.
42. This interpretation is mentioned in Yamāri's commentary, cf. PVBhṬ(Ya) 2a1 (ad PVBh, p. 32, 11 = Ono (PVBh), p. 84, 8f.) and Iwata 2001, p. 71, n. 33. According to Dharmakīrti's interpretation the verbal root √*gam* in *sugata* has the meaning of "know" (see PV II 280c'). It is therefore possible for Prajñākaragupta that "omniscient" could correspond to "*sugata*". For example (PVBh, p. 164, 28); he glossed "*sugata*"-ness in the sense of "complete cognition" (*niḥśeṣajñāna*) as "cognition of all forms" (*sarvākārajñāna*) which implies a cognition of the omniscient, although in his interpretation of "*sugata*" (PVBh, p. 116, 10ff., ad PV II 139-144) he does not allude to omniscience. In this case Prajñākaragupta's view that "the Buddha's being omniscient" is the cause for "his proclamation of the truth (i.e., being a protector)" corresponds to Dharmakīrti's view that "the Buddha's being a *sugata*" is the cause for "his being a protector". Seen from the logical viewpoint, Prajñākaragupta's thought pattern—"the Buddha's proclamation of the truth" is a reason as effect for the consequence "his being omniscient"—is equal to Dharmakīrti's view that from "the Buddha's protection (i.e., proclamation of the truth)" "his being a *sugata*" is logically derived (for Dharmakīrti's view cf. PV II 280ab, Vetter 1984, p. 169 and Franco 1997, pp. 19-21).
43. On the inference of the possibility of the occurrence of effect from the total complex of causes, see Takashi Iwata, "On the Classification of Three Kinds of Reason in *Pramāṇaviniścaya* III", *Studies in the Buddhist Epistemological Tradition*, ed. by E. Steinkellner, VÖAW, Wien, 1991, pp. 86f.
44. See Inami/Tillemans 1986, pp. 126f., n. 10.
45. Cf. *Pramāṇavārttikaṭīkā* (of Śākyabuddhi), P 5718, 97b7-98a2 (ad PVP 8a1f. and PV II 7c'd), Inami 1994, p. 33f., n.7 and Iwata 2000, pp. 24ff., & p. 36, nn. 17-20.
46. Cf. PV II 124b'-d, Masahiro Inami, "Dharmakīrti no Jihi no Shujyu no Giron" (Dharmakīrti's discussion on the practice of compassion), *Indogaku-Bukkyogaku-Kenkyu* 35(1), 1986, p. 138 and Iwata 2001, p. 73, n. 49.
47. As for Prajñākaragupta's argument concerning the infinite increase of compassion cf. Iwata 2001, pp. 58ff. and Takashi Iwata, "Bukkyo-ronri-gakuha niyoru Seson no Ryusei no Shomei ni okeru Himin" (Compassion in proving the Buddha's authority within the Buddhist logical tradition), *Tohogaku* 104, pp. 131-133.
48. PVBh, p. 53, 12: *avaśyaṃ hi paraduḥkhaviyogecchāvatas tadupāyaparyeṣaṇam,* cf. Franco 1997, p. 160 and Iwata 2001, p. 61.
49. Cf. PVBh 53, 9: *sā karuṇā ... parāṃ prakarṣagatim āsādayati,* Franco 1997, p. 160 and Iwata 2001, pp. 58f.
50. This idea is not impossible for Prajñākaragupta because of his own theory

that an effect can be derived from the cause which necessarily produces the effect. According to Dharmakīrti's logical description of causality, logical consequence corresponds to "cause" in the sense that without cause no effect occurs, in other words, whenever there is an effect there is a cause, therefore, the consequence to be derived logically is "cause". In special cases of causality where an effect necessarily occurs in the future resulting from causes, Prajñākaragupta thinks, from the logical viewpoint, the effect is a consequence and its causes are a reason. In other words, he asserts that since consequence generally corresponds to "cause", an effect (which will) necessarily occur (in the future) [namely, a consequence] is precisely a "cause" (*avaśyaṃbhāvi kāryaṃ kāraṇam eva*), cf. PVBh, p. 27, 18ff., p. 28, 20ff. and Moti Ono, "Prajñākaragupta niyoru Dharmakīrti no *pramāṇa* no Teigi no Kaishaku" (Prajñākaragupta's Interpretation of Dharmakīrti's Definition of *pramāṇa*), *Indogaku-Bukkyogaku-Kenkyu* 42(2), 1994, pp. 201ff.

CHAPTER 24

Jñānaśrīmitra's Proof of the Momentary Destruction of Existence: A Philosophical Investigation from the Standpoint of Intuitionistic Logic

TADASHI TANI

1. *The Confrontation between Ratnākaraśānti and Jñānaśrīmitra in the Determination of Logical Pervasion*

In the final stage of Indian Buddhist logic, two sharply opposing interpretations arose concerning the determination of pervasion (*vyāpti:* logical necessity) in the proof of momentary existence, i.e., the thesis that whatever exists is momentary destruction. Ratnākaraśānti (*c.* 970-1020) maintained that pervasion could be determined on the basis of *antarvyāptivāda,* or the theory of internal (deductive) determination without any real and external exemplification, while Jñānaśrīmitra (*c.* 980-1030) sought to determine it by means of *bahirvyāptivāda,* or the theory of external (inductive) determination with exemplification by means of real and external existents such as rain clouds. It is commonly held that Ratnākaraśānti wrote his *Antarvyāptisamarthana* with the intention of criticizing the *bahirvyāptivāda* of Jñānaśrīmitra and

Ratnakīrti (*c.* 1000-1050). In a recent paper, however, I put forward a new hypothesis from the standpoint of philology that it was Jñānaśrīmitra who criticized Ratnākaraśānti, and not vice versa. In the same paper, I also suggested that Ratnakīrti was alienated from his teacher Jñānaśrīmitra and hoped to integrate Jñānaśrīmitra's and Ratnākaraśānti's proofs.[1] The purpose of this new paper is to substantiate my hypothesis from the standpoint of modern philosophical logic, since the logical significance of Jñānaśrīmitra's criticism of Ratnākaraśānti and Ratnakīrti's alienation cannot be revealed solely by means of philology.

2. *The Prior Determination of Negative Pervasion in Ratnākaraśānti's Proof by Internal Determination*

Ratnākaraśānti does not directly prove the positive pervasion (*anvaya:* A → B), i.e., "Whatever exists is momentary." But he dose independently prove negative pervasion (*vyatireka:* -B→ -A), i.e., "A non-momentary object cannot exist", which is the contraposition of positive pervasion. His proof has been translated by Kajiyama as follows:[2]

> (1) Here, 'existence' (*sattva*) 'making effective action' (*arthakriyā-kāritva*), because no other definition of existence is applicable. (2) And it is pervaded by 'succession and simultaneity' (*krama-yaugapadya*), because these two [alternatives] are characterized as being mutually excluded, and thus another case [as a way] of action is not possible. (3) [Effective actions in] succession and simultaneity do not exist in what is not momentary [permanent], for that which has a single, unchanging nature throughout the preceding and succeeding times cannot posses two contradictory properties, viz., being an agent of action and non-agent. Of these two, first, succession is impossible [in the permanent], since, each and every thing making action in succession will have [the difficulty] that it is the agent [of a particular action] and the non-agent [of it] in the preceding and succeeding [times] respectively. Thus, all successive [actions] being impossible [in the permanent], now it only remains possible that all actions would be [made] simultaneously [in the permanent]. In this case, [however,] the absolute contradiction would follow that [the permanent] is the agent [of all the

> actions] and the non-agent [of those actions] in the preceding and succeeding times respectively. As agency and non-agency are contradictory to each other, they are not possibly existent in one and the same locus (*dharmin*). (4) The permanent is known as what maintains one and the same nature during a given time, and it is proved to be impossible to possess succession and simultaneity. As said above, existence [i.e., ability of effective action], being negated in the permanent through non-cognition of its pervader (*vyāpakānupalabdhi*) [i.e., succession and simultaneity], abides only in the momentary. It means that existence is pervaded by momentariness (*kṣaṇikatva*). (5) Thus one can prove that a locus (*dharmin*), in which it [or, existence] is proved to be pervaded by momentariness, is momentary too.

The logical problems entailed in the above proof are as follows: (1) Here, existenceness (*sattva*) is defined quite simply as the operation of causal efficiency (*arthakriyā-kāritva*) only within the scope of a concept. The aim of Ratnākaraśānti's method of definition is to exclude realization by perception. (2) Ratnākaraśānti proves positive pervasion (A → B) through the prior determination of negative pervasion (-B → -A) as the contraposition of the former. This is because positive pervasion as a universal cannot be determined by inductive *bahirvyāptivāda* on the basis of finite exemplification. Furthermore, the succession and simultaneity (= non-succession) [of the operation] as the pervader of an efficient operation (*arthakriyā*) are divided by the law of excluded middle. (3) The negative cognition of the pervader is proved in the locus of non-existence, i.e., a non-momentary existent. This concerns the question of the "empty subject", which has become a hot topic of debate in modern philosophical logic. (4) Dharmakīrti initially restricted negative cognition (non-cognition: *anupalabdhi*) to perceivable objects (*dṛśyānupalabdhi*) because the non-existence of a non-perceivable object (i.e., transcendent object) cannot be determined by non-cognition of a non- perceivable object (*adṛśyānupalabdhi*). Thus, a property A should be negated only by the perception of the locus (property-possessor) as the perceivable counterpart (*pratiyogin:* -A) excluded by the relative negation (*paryudāsa*) of A. For example, the existence of a pot can be negated through the perception of the empty surface of table on which the pot ought to be perceived. But in the determination of the negative pervasion of proof of momentary existence, the non-momentary object as the locus where the efficient operation (and its pervader) is negated is a non-perceivable non-existent. Therefore, Dharmakīrti would later have to recognize the negative cognition of a non-perceivable object (*adṛśyānupalabdhi*) when proving momentary existence. But he must have noticed that this new negative cognition was incompatible with the hitherto negative cognition and the realization of a property in the real locus (*pakṣadharmatā*). Nevertheless, he added the new negative cognition to his logical system as an independent valid cognition (*pramāṇa*). Thus the negative cognition of the pervader as non-perceivable object (*adṛśyavyāpakānupalabdhi*) is termed by Dharmakīrti *sādhyaviparyaya/e bādhakapramāṇa* (hereafter: *svb-pramāṇa*), that is, the valid cognition (*pramāṇa*) of the negating (*bādhaka*) [of the hypothetical proving property (i.e., *hetu* or property to be pervaded [*vyāpya*]: the efficient operation)] if and only if [the hypothetical] property to be proved (*sādhya*) (i.e., the pervading property or pervader [*vyāpaka*]: momentary existence) is negated/reversed (*viparyaye*). *Antarvyāptivāda* is based on *svb-pramāṇa.* Here, an ambivalence occurs in Dharmakīrti's epistemological logic as to whether his logic represents *bahirvyāptivāda* dependent on perception or *antarvyāptivāda* independent of perception.[3] It was this ambivalence which caused a sharp confrontation between Dharmottara and Prajñākaragupta. This confrontation occurs in the interpretation of *prasaṅga* (indirect proof or *reductio ad bsurdum*). Dharmottara changes the *prasaṅga* as *vyāpakānupalabdhi* into a *svb-pramāṇa,* and he interprets *vyāpakānupalabdhi* by means of absolute negation (*prasajyapratiṣedha*). This absolute negation implies that non-existence of A can be determined without any locus. Thus the negative cognition of the pervader as non-perceivable object (*adṛśyavyāpakānupalabdhi*) can be regarded as a *svb-pramāṇa.* In contrast, Prajñākaragupta interprets *vyāpakānupalabdhi* by means of relative negation (*paryudāsa*). Relative negation implies that the non-existence of A is determined only by the perception of the counterpart of the perceivable A. Thus, *vyāpakānupalabdhi* is restricted to *dṛśyānupalabdhi.* Only in this case can the *prasaṅga* ($-B \rightarrow -A$) be transformed into its contraposition (*prasaṅgaviparyaya*) ($A \rightarrow B$). Otherwise, the *prasaṅga* cannot be transformed since the perceivable locus does not exist. According-ing to Prajñākaragupta, this latter case corresponds to Dharmottara's interpretation. Dharmottara's interpretation was accepted by Ratnākaraśānti, while Prajñākaragupta's was accepted by Jñānaśrīmitra.[4] (5) Ratnākaraśānti concludes (A → B) from the prior determination of (-B → -A). This transformation of the contraposition is valid in standard formal logic. Thus, Ratnākaraśānti's proof is based on the form "(-B → -A)→(A → B)".

3. *The Prior Determination of Positive Pervasion in Jñānaśrīmitra's Proof by External Determination*

By way of contrast, Jñānaśrīmitra first of all proves the positive pervasion (A → B) of the momentary destruction of existence, i.e., "Whatever exists is momentary, for example, a rain cloud." Negative pervasion (-B → -A) cannot be independently proved because (-B), "a non-momentary existent," cannot be perceived. As mentioned above, Jñānaśrīmitra restricts negative cognition to the sphere of perceivable objects. Therefore, he recognizes negative pervasion only as a contrapositive transformation of positive pervasion within the sphere of conceptualization. Jñānaśrīmitra's basic stance is that proof of positive pervasion must have as its locus perceivable examples such as a rain cloud. This positive pervasion can be proved by three pairs of *prasaṅga* and *prasaṅgaviparyaya.* The former is a hypothetical negative reasoning which proves a contradiction within the opponent's statement, while the latter is a direct reasoning which proves the momentary destruction of existent objects through the reversion of the *prasaṅga.* As noted earlier, this reversion is possible only when the *prasanga* has a perceivable locus such as a rain cloud. Jñānaśrīmitra's proof formulae are as follows:[5]

[1A] *Prasaṅga*

Whatever is capable of a certain action at a certain time makes the action at that time. For example, the totality of the cause and the conditions in its final moment is capable of producing its own effect.

[According to the opponent] one and the same [non-momentary] rain cloud [is capable of producing] its own effect while holding water in that very situation [i.e., before it rains], e.g., a farm labourer's eyes sparking with delight, or [it is capable of performing] such an operation when having sent forth the water [i.e., after it has rained]. And it is capable of producing both effects in both situations.

[Therefore, it produces both effects at any time, which is absurd]

[1B] *Prasaṅgaviparyaya*

Whatever does not perform a certain operation is not capable of performing that operation. For example, a grain seed not producing a rice sprout [is not capable of producing a rice sprout].

And the [rain cloud] neither performs from the second moment onwards an operation to be accomplished in the first moment, nor [does it perform] in the first moment [an operation] to be accomplished from the second moment onwards.

[Therefore, it produces at a certain moment only the effects belonging to that moment. Thus, it is momentary.]

Since two different essential properties (*svabhāva-bheda*) cannot occur in one and the same thing, one essential property should be restricted to one moment, and it cannot be extended to the next moment. The major premise of the above *prasaṅga* is proved by the simultaneity of semantic competency (*yogyatā*) between an action producing an effect and speaking (*vyavahāra*) about the power of that action. The denotation of "the power of action" is restricted to real action, which is in turn restricted to a certain time, place, and essential property.

[2A] *Prasaṅga*

[Premised on the same pervasion as lA]

[According to the opponent, this rain cloud] is capable [of performing an operation] even when all the operations have been completed.

[Therefore, it performs an operation even at a time of non-operation, which is absurd.]

[2B] *Prasaṅgaviparyaya*

[Premised on the same pervasion as 1B]

And at a time of non-operation [this rain cloud] does not perform an operation to be effected at the time of operation.

[Therefore, it is not capable of performing an operation at a time of non-operation, and hence it is unreal.]

[3A] *Prasaṅga*

Whatever is not capable of performing a certain operation does not perform that operation. For example, a grain seed [which is incapable of producing a rice sprout does not produce] a rice sprout.

[According to the opponent,] this rain cloud is not capable [of performing an operation] at other moments, either, just as [it is not capable of doing so] at a moment of non-operation.

[Therefore, it does not perform an operation at any time, which is absurd.]

[3B] *Prasaṅgaviparyaya*

Whatever performs a certain operation is not incapable of performing that operation, just like the final moment of the causal complex of a seed. And this cloud [performs] the action of holding water.

[Therefore, it is capable of holding water; and hence it is real.]

This conclusion can be generalized into a universally quantified pervasion (*sarvopasaṃhāravatī vyāpti*) by the simultaneity of semantic competency, since this semantic competency is not limited to a rain cloud. Therefore, the momentary destruction of existent entities can be universally proved.

Here, the logical indicator "existence" (*sattva*) is determined by the perception of the ability of efficient operation (*arthakriyāsāmarthya*) in the real object. This is not simply a definition of Ratnākaraśānti's, but the realization of "the power of an action" at a certain time and place. In this sense, Jñānaśrīmitra's statement "*yat sat tad kṣaṇikam*"[6] should not be translated as "All existence is momentary", but as "So far as/ whenever an object can be recognized as existent, that object is momentary." This is because the entire infinite sphere has not yet been perceived,[7] and also because the mere word (concept) "power of an action" cannot bring about an actual action. For Jñānaśrīmitra, a "rain cloud" as the locus of *a prasaṅga* and *prasaṅgaviparyaya* is not a stock example of a concept, but the vivid perception of the rumbling of thunder, the swirling spread of dynamic darkness, heavy rain, and flashes of lightning before one's eyes. Thus the premise of the pervasion of the *prasaṅga* is expressed as follows:

"Whatever is capable of a certain action at a certain time brings about the action at that time, as, for example, the totality of the cause and conditions in its final moment is capable of producing its own effect." Jñānaśrīmitra's premise is based on Dharmakīrti's following model:[8] "The causal complex of a seed grows through the accumulation of special power with the cooperation of earth, water and sunshine, etc., and as soon as the final moment of the causal complex of the seed is extinguished, the sprout is produced momentarily." The destruction of the cause and the production of the effect do not extend over two moments, but are simultaneous. Thus the relation of the cause cannot deviate from the effect. This necessity is called an "essential relation" (*svabhāvapratibandha*) which necessarily accomplishes its object as an effect. According to the proof of the spontaneous destruction of existence, Dharmakīrti and Jñānaśrīmitra regard nonexistence as an absolute negation (*prasajyapratiṣedha*). Absolute negation negates not only the property, but also the locus which possesses that property. Consequently any interval with an empty locus is excluded. Therefore, the final moment of destruction of the preceding existent as a causal complex is simultaneous with the moment of production of the new succeeding existent as its effect. Thus Jñānaśrīmitra recognizes the formula "(A→B)→(-B → -A)", but he does not recognize the formula "(-B→ -A)→(A →B)" as an independent form. This asymmetry of contraposition seems to be based on Dignāga's interpretation from the standpoint of inductive *bahirvyāptivāda*.

4. *Jñānaśrīmitra Criticized Ratnākaraśānti's Proof, and Not Vice Versa: The Reinstatement of the Theory of External Determination*

The main reasons that Jñānaśrīmitra criticized Ratnākaraśānti's proof, and not vice versa, are as follows: (1) Ratnākaraśānti refers neither to Jñānaśrīmitra's complex proofs based on *prasaṅga* and *prasaṅgaviparyaya* nor to Ratnakīrti's transformed versions of these proofs. If Ratnākaraśānti had meant to criticize Jñānaśrīmitra's or Ratnakīrti's proofs, he would naturally have referred to their main proofs. (2) Jñānaśrīmitra refers to opponent(s) "who is (/are) engrossed only in negative concomitance". The opponent(s), called *sādhyaviparyaye/a bādhakapramāṇavādin/-vādinaḥ*, maintain/s that pervasion must be deduced from *vyatireka*, which can be determined only independently by means of a *svb-pramāṇa*, and not by means of exemplification.[9] These opponent(s) could perhaps be identified with Ratnākaraśānti (and his followers). The important point to note is that the core of Ratnākaraśānti's proof of momentariness is, as we have seen, based on *vyatireka*, which is proved by a *svb-pramāṇa*, which is in turn independent of exemplification. Even though Dharmottara could be included among the targets of Jñānaśrīmitra's criticism, the latter would no doubt have been conscious of his elder contemporary, Ratnākaraśānti. We should not overlook the fact that pure deductive logic without external realization was criticized by Jñānaśrīmitra in the final stage of Indian Buddhist logic.

5. *Intuitionistic Logic and Jñānaśrīmitra's Proof of Momentary Existence*

We find a problem parallel to the proof of momentary existence in modern logical theory, that is, in Brouwer's "intuitionistic logic," which criticizes the symmetry of the contraposition. Like Jñānaśrīmitra, his logic does not recognize the formula "(-B→-A) → (A → B)".[10] Brouwer defines existence as the possibility of the real construction of the object. This constructivism is based on intuition of a perceivable object. This parallels Jñānaśrīmitra's determination of the ability of efficient operation on the basis of a perceivable object such as a real rain cloud. In "(-B → -A) → (A → B)", (-B → -A) implies that "if B cannot be constructed, A cannot be constructed," for the impossibility of the construction of A implies only the contradictoriness of A, and it cannot imply the possibility of the construction of A in (A → B). In order to deduce A from the impossibility of the construction of A, one must assume either the law of excluded middle (A ∨ -A) or its equivalent, double negation (–A → A). In intuitionistic logic, Ratnākaraśānti's proof form "(-B → -A) →(A →B)" based on *svb-pramāṇa* cannot be established. The law of excluded middle and double negation are not recognized in intuitionistic logic since all objects in the infinite scope have not yet been determined by the present perception. Brouwer does not regard infinity as a complete totality, the whole, or actual infinity, but regards it as potential infinity, an infinite process of repetition. Thus, standard logic with the law of excluded middle and double negation are seen by God's eyes, as it were, which can see a complete totality, the whole, and actual infinity all at once. Ratnākaraśānti applies these laws to actual infinity without any restrictions, whereas Brouwer and Jñānaśrīmitra restrict the infinite from the standpoint of finite human eyes. They recognize perceivable objects one-by-one in the endless process of human cognition. Although Jñānaśrīmitra's logical form of the transformation from *prasaṅga* to *prasaṅgaviparyaya* is "(-B → -A)→ (A→B)," he applies it to a real perceivable object, i.e., a rain cloud. The law of excluded middle and double negation are applicable within the finite perceivable sphere. As mentioned above, this theory is based on Prajñākaragupta's theory.[11] Ratnākaraśānti, on the other hand, applies them to a non-perceivable empty locus, i.e., a non-momentary existent. Here there arises the modern logical problem of the "empty subject". Furthermore, when considered from the standpoint of *bahirvyāptivāda*, the "paradox of Hempel's raven"[12] occurs in Ratnākaraśānti's theory of the priority of negative pervasion, since from the negative pervasion expressed as "all non-black swans are not ravens" its contraposition in the form of the positive pervasion "all ravens are black," cannot be deduced. Jñānaśrīmitra probably criticized Ratnākaraśānti's formalism from the standpoint of such intuitionism.

Intuition of Time

According to Brouwer, the construction of a number is base on the creative intuition of time: "The intuitionist mathematics is an essentially languageless activity of the mind having its origin in the perception of a *move of time*, i.e., of the falling apart of a life moment into two distinct things, one of which gives way to the other, but is retained by memory".[13] We must realize that Brouwer's intuition of the dual nature of time is not all that far removed from Jñānaśrīmitra's theory of the spontaneous destruction of existence. Both are based on the perception of momentary existence. Weyl, an intuitional logician, takes up the challenge of trying to describe momentary existence in the following manner: "This now is, but now no longer is. ... The view of a flow consisting of points and also dissolving points turns out to be false. Precisely what eludes us is the nature of the continuity, the flowing from point to point, in other words, the secret of how the continually enduring present can continually slip away into the receding past. Each one of us, at every moment, directly experiences the true character of this temporal continuity. But, because of the genuine primitiveness of phenomenal time, we cannot put our experiences into words. So we shall content ourselves with the following description. What I am conscious of is for me both a being-now and, in its essence, something which, with its temporal position, slips away."[14]

Proof of Momentary Destruction by Perception

The formation of formal logic within the sphere of conceptualization is separated from perception. Thus the inferred momentariness of existence cannot be identified with directly perceived momentary existence since perception itself excludes the conceptualizing on which inference is based. Nevertheless, Dharmakīrti states that inferred non-permanence (i.e., momentariness) is nothing other than perceived existence and that the non-permanence to be perceived has been proved by perception before non-permanence is inferred.[15] It is worth noting that Dharmakīrti states that it is "nothing other than perceived existence" (non-difference) rather than it is "identical with perceived existence" (identity). Therefore, Jñānaśrīmitra too never describes direct access to perceivable momentary existence, and instead describes the denial of the impossibility of access to it. The proof of momentary existence by means of perception (*pratyakṣasiddhaṃ kṣaṇikatvam*) is proved by the following *prasaṅga:* "Whatever manifests itself is complete as it is, like for instance the brilliant waters of the Gaṅgā. Otherwise, the [unique effective] operation corresponding to each real existent would be lost amidst commingled existents. Each construction of existence (*saṃskāra*) which manifests itself in each sense-organ continues for only one moment. Otherwise, an indistinct triple time-state (i.e., the confusion of past, present and future) would be perceived by the glimpse of one momentary present object"[16]. From this *prasaṅga* it is deduced that the perception is the *pramāṇa* for a momentary object, i.e., the momentary destruction of existence. The momentariness of the present operation of perception is determined within conceptualization by the perceptual judgement which immediately follows that perception. As noted above, this is proved not directly, but indirectly within the sphere of conceptualization. Thus Jñānaśrīmitra abandons any attempt to describe directly the momentariness of existence of the perceived object.

Kripke's Model of Intuitionistic Logic and Jñānaśrīmitra's Two-Dimensional Truth Theory

According to Kripke's idea of a counter-model of the law of excluded middle, "Intuitively, at the present situation G, we have not yet prove P; nor can we assert -P, since the possibility remains that we will get enough information later to advance to H and assert P, Thus, at the point G, we are not in a position to assert P ∨ -P".[17] In intuitionistic logic, proof depends on the level of cognition. Truth is not determined at a stroke from God's viewpoint, but in accordance with the human level of cognition. Jñānaśrīmitra, on the other hand, defines the ordinary level (i.e., that of conventional truth) as a state of cognition that is satisfied without investigation by means of *pramāṇa.* This means that the transformation from the ordinary level to the ultimate level is determined solely by investigation by means of *pramāṇa.* He thus transforms the static two-dimensional truth into a dynamic truth. From the standpoint of the new higher ultimate level, the preceding ultimate level is deemed to be ordinary.[18] This change of levels is based on the momentary destruction of existence. The proof of momentary existence implies that the destruction of the lower ordinary level reveals momentarily the new ultimate level. Astonishingly, Dharmakīrti had already reached the conviction that *pramāṇa* itself is not an eternal criterion, but a momentary existent, since the real object is momentary. Furthermore, his twofold definition of *pramāṇa* is based on the model of causal efficiency described above.[19] *Pramāṇa* is non-deviating cognition as an efficient operation, and it is the cognition of the revelation of a new momentary object as the effect. For Jñānaśrīmitra, enlightenment means interacting with momentary existence as an efficient act. This dynamic structure of truth would seem to be similar to Kripke's model.

6. *Ratnakīrti's Alienation from Jñānaśrīmitra: The Counterattack of Hilbert's Formalism*

Although Ratnakīrti's proof would seem to be merely a digest version of that of his teacher Jñānaśrīmitra, Ratnakīrti deliberately excludes the priority of positive pervasion found in Jñānaśrīmitra's proof. Ratnakīrti's proof consists of two symmetrical proofs of positive pervasion and negative pervasion. Thus, his *Kṣaṇabhaṅgasiddhi* has two symmetrical titles: "Proof on the basis of positive pervasion implying negative pervasion" and "Proof on the basis of negative pervasion implying positive pervasion." Ratnakīrti changes the scope of the application of *svb-pramāṇa* from conceptualization to a third meta-level which is neither pure concept nor pure perception. Its scope is indirectly determined (*adhyavaseya*) by the conception immediately following the perception. Therefore, the object of perception can be indirectly described by language on the meta-level of conceptualization. At the same time, he inserts the term *vyavahāra-yogyatā* (validity or semantic competency of the speech-act) into the two proof formulae.[20] Jñānaśrīmitra used the term *yogyatā* in the sense of the simultaneity of the connection of the real direct object of perception with a speech-act.[21] But by changing the direct object into an indirect object, Ratnakīrti changed the meaning of this term into the rules of word-usage on the meta-level. By doing so, he reinstated the principle of excluded middle and double negation on the meta-level, thereby obtaining symmetrical contrapositions. Ratnakīrti was alienated from Jñānaśrīmitra and attempted to synthesize Jñānaśrīmitra's proof with that of Ratnākaraśānti. Meanwhile, Hilbert attacked Brouwer, declaring, "Taking the principle of excluded middle from the mathematician would be the same, say, as proscribing the telescope to the astronomer or to the boxer the use of his fists".[22] Intuitionism rejects the principle of excluded middle, namely, that either A is proved or A is proved, because neither the affirmation nor negation of A can be proved. But it does not reject the principle that either A is proved or –A is not proved. This is because whether A is proved or not proved can be determined by our proof-act as a meta-level. Thus the law of excluded middle and its equivalent, double negation, are reinstated in Hilbert's metamathematics. According to Hilbert's plan, the coherence of an axiom should be able to be proved on the meta-level. With regard to the reinstatement of the law of excluded middle and double negation on the meta-level, Ratnakīrti's alienation and Hilbert's counterattack would seem to intersect with each other.

7. *The Impact of Gödel's Incompleteness Theory: A Return to Perception of Momentary Existence*

Hilbert's plan was undermined by Gödel's incompleteness theory. Gödel proved that a formal logical system cannot ultimately be placed on a firm basis.[23] If logic negates the external scope, i.e., perception, the circularity of self-reference then occurs. This includes the self-referent statement "I am a liar," or the paradox of a liar. Weyl expressed this in the following manner: "It confronts us with this alternative: either the reasoning by which consistency of the formalism is established must contain some argument that has no formal counterpart within the system, i.e., we have not succeeded in completely formalizing the procedure of mathematical induction; or the idea of strictly 'finistic' proof of consistency must be given up altogether."[24] Weyl also said, "Mathematizing may well be a creative activity of man, like music."[25] Thereafter, mathematics rejected foundationism and turned to constructivism. Gödel too, after having broken away from foundationism, advanced constructivism in the direction of the idea of mathematical reality. Ratnakīrti's formal consistency, on the other hand, seems to have been reduced once again to the perceivable scope of Jñānaśrīmitra, as is discussed below.

8. *Proof of Momentary Existence as the Creation of a Hypothesis (Abduction)*

Dharmakīrti cites the following *āgama:* "Whatever possesses the property of coming into existence (production) must possess the property of destroying itself."[26] He then decided to prove the Buddha's flash of insight by means of valid cognition (*pramāṇa*) on the basis of the essential relation (*svabhāvapratibandha*). He regards the *āgama* as a creative hypothesis, not as a dogma. Thus, through the definition of existence as an efficient operation, the above *āgama* is transformed into the following statement: "Whatever possesses the property of existence (efficient operation) must possess the property of momentarily destroying itself." Whereas Ratnākaraśānti proved the validity of this hypothesis by means of *svb-pramāṇa* from the standpoint of deductive *antarvyāptivāda,* Jñānaśrīmitra attempted to justify it by means *of prasaṅga* and *prasaṅgaviparyaya* from the standpoint of inductive *bahirvyāptivāda.* According to Matilal, "The general form of the arguments studied by the Indian logicians is : *A* is *B* because of *C*. The middle term or the 'reason' *hetu C* can be either adequate or inadequate (instead of being strictly valid or invalid)."[27]

Even though Ratnākaraśānti's proof may seem to be pure deduction, it would nonetheless be based on this general form. These proofs are similar to Peirce's 'abduction'. According to Peirce, "The abductive suggestion comes to us like a flash. It is an act of insight, although of extremely fallible insight."[28] The proof of momentary existence signifies the proof of creating a new hypothesis of momentary existence. In deduction a premise is necessarily connected to a conclusion, and in induction a premise is connected to a conclusion by a tendency to accept the conclusion. Neither deduction nor induction can create a new cognition other than that already included in their premises. In contrast, abduction creates a new cognition. The momentary destruction of existence should be regarded as a "creative hypothesis". The process of "abduction" is as follows: (1) When we cannot explain a fact by an existing theory, we creates a hypothesis (A → B); (2) we explain the hypothesis by deduction; and (3) the hypothesis and its explanation are verified by induction as a question of fact (by exemplification in a real perceivable object). In the process of justifying the validity of the hypothesis, deduction and induction are synthesized.

9. *The Realization of the Inferred Conceptual Momentariness of Existence by Means of a Yogin's Perception*

Up until now we have considered points in common between Jñānaśrīmitra's proof and intuitionistic logic. In bringing this enquiry to a close, the differences between the two should also be examined. The momentary object of perception cannot be identified with inferred momentariness. Jñānaśrīmitra eventually gave up trying to approach the former from the latter, and his epistemology now underwent a remarkable turnabout. Although inference is ultimately based on perception, ordinary perception can be deceived by a quick succession of similar objects. Therefore, the object of the deceived perception, i.e., non-momentary existence, must be rectified by means of inferred momentariness. This epistemological conversion is performed in the process of *yoga*-perception, in which the concept of momentariness can be perceived. Jñānaśrīmitra asserts that the object of a *yogin's* perception is an abstract property (*sāmānyalakṣaṇa*), i.e., momentariness, "*kṣaṇikatvam*".[29] The uninterrupted and continual concentration of a *yogin's* perception is performed on the general concept of the momentariness of existence. This momentariness is then gradually perceived as the perceived object, just as when the image of a loved one is vividly perceived. Next, the momentariness of the object of the *yogin*'s perception destroys the ordinary, everyday world, the non-momentary locus. In this manner, the perception gradually reveals the new ultimate momentary existent. Although the momentary destruction of existence (*kṣaṇabhaṅga*) to be proved is only a concept or word, this self-differentiating concept can destroy the self-identified object of the concept or word. This is the most noteworthy characteristic of the proof of momentary existence. The proof of the momentary destruction of existence destroys the concept and proceeds to reveal the ultimate emergence of momentary existence to be perceived. Intuitionistic constructivism, on the other hand, proceeds towards the ideal object of a concept by means of the construction of the concept based on perception. Although the two intersect at the point of the perception of momentary existence, they then diverge in opposite directions.

NOTES

1. Tani Tadashi, "Reinstatement of the Theory of External Determination of Pervasion (*bahirvyāptivāda*): Jñānaśrīmitra's Proof of Momentary Existence," in Katsura Shōryū (ed.), *Dharmakīrti's Thought and its Impact on the Indian and Tibetan Philosophy: Proceedings the Third International Dharmakīrti Conference. Hiroshima, November 4-6, 1997, Beiträge zur Kultur-und Geistesgeschichte Asiens,. Bd.* 32, *Denkschriften der philosophish-historischen Klasse, Bd. 281*, Wien, 1999, pp. 363-386.: Tani Tadashi, *Setsunametsu no Kenkyū* (A Study of the Momentary Destruction of Existence), Tōkyō: 2000, pp. 213-263: pp. 503-558.
2. Kajiyama Yūichi, *The Antarvyāptisamarthana of Ratnākaraśānti*. The International Research Institute for Advanced Buddhology Sōka University, Tōkyō. 1999. Text: pp. 58, 5-60, 8; Trans. : pp. 114, 2-115, 2.
3. Tani, *Setsunametsu no Kenkyū*, pp. 124-147.
4. Iwata Takashi, *Prasaṅga und Prasaṅgaviparyaya bei Dharmakīrti und seinen Kommentatoren*, Wien, 1993.; Tani, *Setsunametsu no Kenkyū*, pp. 178-195.; Tani, "Reinstatement of the Theory of External Determination of Pervasion (*bahirvyāptivāda*): Jñānaśrīmitra's Proof of Momentary Existence," pp. 361-364.

5. (A) *Jñānaśrīmitranibandhāvali,* (Buddhist Philosophical Works of Jñānaśrīmitra), ed. by Anantalal Thakur, Patna, [2nd ed.] 1987; [lst ed. 1959], p. 17,10-13; 17,23-18,2: Tani, *Setsunametsu no Kenkyū,* pp. 231-232; 234. (B) *Jñānaśrīmitranibandhāvali,* p. 17, 18-19; 18, 3-4: Tani, *Setsunametsu no Kenkyū,* p. 233; 234-235. (C) *Jñānaśrīmitranibandhāvali,* p.17, 20-22; 18, 4-6: Tani, *Setsunametsu no Kenkyū,* pp. 233-234; 235.
6. *Jñānaśrīmitranibandhāvali,* p. 1, 8.
7. Cf. Section 5 below.
8. Katsura Shōryū, "Dharmakīrti no Inga-ron," *Nanto-Bukkyō,* 50, pp. 96-114, 1983, pp. 100-104.; Ernst Steinkellner, *Dharmakīrti's Hetubinduḥ. Teil I. Tibetischer Text und rekonstruierter Sanskrit-Text.; Teil II. Übersetzung und Anmerkungen.* Wien, 1967, Teil 2, pp. 136-138; 127-129.
9. Tani, "Reinstatement of the Theory of External Determination of Pervasion (*bahirvyāptivāda*): Jñānaśrīmitra's Proof of Momentary Existence," pp. 363-369: Tani, *Setsunametsu no Kenkyū,* pp. 243-251.
10. A. Heyting, *Intuitionism, an introduction,* third revised ed. 1971, p. 104.
11. Cf. note 4.
12. Joerg Tuske, "Diṅnāga and the Raven Paradox," *Journal of Indian Philosophy,* 26, 1998, pp. 387-403.
13. Luitzen E.J. Brouwer, "Historical Background, Principles and Methods of Intuitionism," *South African Journal of Science,* 1952, pp. 140-141.; in A. Heyting (ed.), *L.E.J. Brouwer Collected Works I. Philosophy and Foundations of Mathematics,* 1975, pp. 509-510.
14. Hermann Weyl, *Das Kontinuum. Kritishe Untersuchungen über die Grundlagen der Analysis,* 1918, pp. 69-70: [Translated by Stephen Pollard and Thomas Bole, *The Continuum. A Critical Examination of the Foundation of Analysis,* 1987, pp. 91-92. (abstract)].
15. *Pramāṇvārttika,* Chapter III (pratyakṣa) in Tosaki Hiromasa, *Bukkyō-Ninshikiron no Kenkyū* (A study of Buddhist epistemology, 2 vols.). 1979/85. Vol. 1: pp. 153-183, [PV III. 80/101-107].
16. *Jñānaśrīmitranibandhāvali,* p. 155, 17-21; Tani, *Setsunametsu no Kenkyū,* p. 448.
17. Saul A. Kripke, "Semantical Analysis of Intuitionistic Logic I," in J.N. Crossley and M.A.E. Dummett (eds.), *Formal Systems and Recursive Functions,* pp. 92-130, 1965, p. 100.
18. Tani, *Setsunametsu no Kenkyū,* pp. 308-321.
19. Tani, *Setsunametsu no Kenkyū,* pp. 90-92.
20. *Ratnakīrtinibandhāvali* (Buddhist Nyāya Works of Ratnakīrti), Anantalal Thakur (ed.), Patna, [2nd ed.], 1975, [1st ed. 1957], pp. 68, 17-20.; Tani, *Setsunametsu no Kenkyū,* pp. 511-512.
21. *Jñānaśrīmitranibandhāvali,* p. 17, 13-17.; Tani, *Setsunametsu no Kenkyū,* pp. 232-233.
22. David Hilbert, *Grundlagen der Geometrie,* 1930, p. 307. [English Trans. "*The foundation of mathematics,*" in J.V. Heijenoort (ed.), *From Frege to Gödel, a source book in mathematical logic 1879-1931,* pp. 464-479, 1967, p. 476.]
23. Kurt Gödel, "Über formale unentscheidenbar Sätze der Principia Mathematica und verwandter Systeme I," 1931, in *Kürt Gödel Collected Works* I, 1986, pp. 145-195.

24. Hermann Weyl, *Philosophy of Mathematics and Natural Science,* 1949, p. 220.
25. Weyl, *Philosophy of Mathematics and Natural Science,* p. 219.
26. "yad kiñcid udayātmakam nirodha-dharmakaṃ sarvaṃ" *Pramāṇavārttika,* Chapter II (pramāṇasiddhi) 285b-c. in Yūshō Miyasaka (ed.) "Pramāṇavārttika-Kārikā (Sanskrit and Tibetan)," *Acta Indologica* 2, pp. 1-206, 1971/72, p. 40.
27. Bimal K. Matilal, "Reference and Existence in Nyāya and Buddhist Logic", in *Journal of Indian Philosophy,* 1, pp. 83-110, 1970, pp. 86-89.
28. Charls S. Peirce, "Lecture VII: Pragmatism and Abduction", in Charles Hartshone and Paul Weiss (eds.), *Collected Papers of Charls Sanders Peirce,* Vol. 5, 1974, p. 113.
29. Ernst Steinkellner, "Yogische Erkenntnis als Problem im Buddhismus," in G. Oberhammer (ed.), *Transzendenzerfahrung, Vollzugshorizont des Heils,* pp. 121-134, 1978, p. 130ff.

CHAPTER 25

The Propositional Logic of Uddyotakara

MICHIKO ISHITOBI

Uddyotakara, who is the author of the sub-commentary *Nyāyavārttika* on *Nyāyabhāṣya,* played a more important role in the development of the Nyāya theory of logic than is commonly recognized. He clearly incorporated epistemological thinking in Indian logic, and stood in opposition to Dignāga, a pioneer of Buddhist logic. In this paper I would like to clarify that Uddyotakara reformalized the five-membered syllogism (*pañca-avayava*) within an epistemological framework in the syllogistic theory of the Nyāya School. More concretely; it may be said that he established a kind of propositional logic, if such an expression being permitted, in Indian philosophy. It could be interpreted that Dignāga, on the other hand, constructed a kind of predicate logic, based not on propositions but on terms. The formalistic difference between the propositional logic of Uddyotakara and the predicate logic of Dignāga can be thought to be derived from the difference between the grounds of Realistic Epistemology on which the Nyāya School stands, and the grounds of Idealistic Ontology that the Dignāga School maintains. In this paper I will attempt to analyze Uddyotakara's interpretation of the syllogism on two topics: the inference of rainfall from clouds, and the inference of fire from smoke.

The Syllogism of Nyāya School in Indian Studies of the Past

Before turning to Uddyotakara's syllogism, I would like to take up an example of the syllogism of the Nyāya School which has been long considered to be implied in the *Nyāyasūtra* and *Nyāyabhāṣya* in studies of Indian logic in the past. According to Ganeri, it was Colebrooke that, for the first time, introduced the following example as the *Nyāyasūtra* analysis of an argument schema.[1]

> A regular argument or syllogism (*nyāya*) consists of five members (*avayava*) or component parts: 1st, the proposition (*pratijñā*); 2nd, the reason (*hetu* or *apadeśa*); 3rd, the instance (*udāharaṇa* or *nidarśana*); 4th, the application (*upanaya*); 5th, the conclusion (*nigamana*). Ex.:
>
> 1. This hill is fiery:
> 2. For it smokes.
> 3. What smokes is fiery: as a culinary hearth.
> 4. Accordingly; the hill is smoking:
> 5. Therefore it is fiery

This example of the five-membered syllogism was not an authentic quotation from the *Nyāyasūtra* or its *Bhāṣya.* While Vātsyāyana does give fire and smoke as an *instance* of inference (*anumāna*), as I mention below, fire and smoke are not made the *topic* of a syllogism. It might be said, indeed, that the history of misunderstandings about the earliest Nyāya reasoning began with Colebrooke's account. The following scholars of Indian logic have investigated the characteristics of the Nyāya syllogism using this example, considering it the argument schema of Nyāya reasoning which was consistently adopted since the *Nyāyasūtra.* Bochenski described this smoking-hill example as "the classic and constantly repeated example—as standard as the western 'all men are mortal, Socrates is a man, etc.'—",[2] and Matilal called it "the time-honored illustration" of "the Nyāya model".[3] While it may be oft-repeated, it is probably not as "time-honored" as Matilal would have us believe. Although Ingalls did not cite this example but the authentic one from the earliest Nyāya text, he was mistaken in saying that the classical Indian syllogism included a statement of invariable concomitance (*vyāpti*) in the third member of the syllogism, 'instance'.[4] For neither Gautama (the author of *Nyāyasūtra*) nor Vātsyāyana (the author of *Nyāyabhāṣya*) indicated the concept of *vyāpti*. It was not until later that Uddyotakara interpreted the inference of fire from smoke with the concept of inseparable relation (*avinābhāva*), not *vyāpti*. Colebrooke's example above, which, I think, was influenced by Dignāga's syllogistic theory, belongs to the later Nyāya-Vaiśeṣika texts, e.g. the *Tarkasaṅgraha*. In the period in which the *Nyāyasūtra* and *Nyāyabhāṣya* were composed, the Nyāya School had not yet formalized the inference of fire from smoke *with the syllogistic schema* (*nyāya*). Following Vātsyāyana, Uddyotakara eventually established a new interpretation of logic theory in order to formalize the three kinds of inference enumerated in *Nyāyasūtra* 1.1.5 with the syllogistic schema.

The law of causality, avinābhāva, and vyāpti

Gautama enumerated three kinds of inference (*anumāna*) in *Nyāyasūtra* 1.1.5:[5]

> Inference is preceded by perception and is of three kinds: *pūrvavat, śeṣavat,* and *sāmānyato dṛṣṭa.*

Vātsyāyana gave two alternative interpretations of the three kinds of inference. Of the three kinds, he interpreted two types of *pūrvavat* in *Nyāyabhāṣya* 1.1.5 as follows[6]:

(a) The *pūrvavat* inference is one in which the effect is inferred from the cause, e.g., when we see clouds rising, we infer that there will be rain.

(b) The *pūrvavat* inference is that in which, out of two things perceived on some former occasion, the one that is not perceived (at the time of inference) is inferred from the perception of the other, e.g., when fire is inferred from smoke.

In the Nyāya School, the inference is the second *pramāṇa,* or the means of true cognition, following the first *pramāṇa,* perception. A *pramāṇa* is, says Vātsyāyana, invariably connected with an object, because only when the object is known by means of a *pramāṇa,* it produces effective activity (*pramāṇataḥ arthapratipattau pravṛttisāmarthyāt arthavat pramāṇam*).[7] Therefore, these two examples must tell us two pieces of true knowledge.

In terms of modern Western logic, the inference of the effect from the cause is said to be an inductive inference, which leads us to conclusions which are not entailed by the premises. In that case, even though the premises are true, the conclusion can be false at times. In fact, we often experience that it does not rain when there are clouds. Because a line of inductive reasoning doesn't always lead us to a true conclusion, we must say it belongs to a science of probability. Therefore, from a modern logical perspective, this example might lead us to false conclusions.

In the Nyāya School, what kind of reasoning was *pūrvavat* inference of type (a)? I think, in India, it is basically considered deductive reasoning, which leads us to conclusions that are entailed by the premises. This is because the law of causality we find in this inference is recognized to be the absolute principle, on which the validity of this type of inference is firmly grounded. In *Nyāyasūtra* 2.2.3 and in its *Bhāṣya,* there is an objection argued about *arthāpatti* (postulation):[8]

> (Objection): Postulation cannot be treated as a *pramāṇa* because it leads to irregularity. (*Nyāyasūtra* 2.2.3) The proposition that 'there is rain when there are clouds', when it is made on the basis of another proposition that there is no rain when there are no clouds, is not valid. As a matter of fact, sometimes it so happens that even though clouds are present there is no rain. (*Nyāyabhāṣya,* 2.2.3)

In *Nyāyabhāṣya* 2.2.4, Vātsyāyana insists on the validity of postulation, but what is most notable here is how he uses the law of causality as an example to back up his assertion. Vātsyāyana's reply is as follows[9]:

> From the statement that 'when the cause is absent the effect is not present', we postulate that 'when the cause is present, the effect is present'. Existence is contrary to non-existence. Certainly, this postulation that the effect is produced when the cause is present is never found to fail in any single instance; that is to say, there is not a single instance where the effect is produced when the cause is not present.

According to Vātsyāyana, if it happens that even though clouds are present there is no rain, it doesn't come from the irregularity of causality, but it is just because there is an obstruction, namely, the contact of clouds with high winds, in the production of the effect. Thus the conclusion of the inference (a), 'it will rain' can be theoretically deduced on the basis of the principle of causality that 'when the cause is present, the effect is present' and that 'when the cause is absent, the effect is not present'. Therefore this deductive reasoning is valid, so it must be true knowledge.

The fact remains, however, that we sometimes fail to attain true conclusions by *pūrvavat* inferences. As a matter of fact, *pūrvavat* inferences, although lying on the sound basis of the law of causality, do not necessarily lead to true conclusions. On the other hand, the inference of type (b) cannot be reasoned from the law of causality, though smoke inevitably leads to the existence of fire. In order to remove these difficulties, it was the relation of *avinābhāva* that Uddyotakara adopted as the grounds of inferences.

According to Uddyotakara, an inseparable relation or *avinābhāva* is the basis for validating all three kinds of inferences enumerated in *Nyāyasūtra* 1.1.5. In other words, the word *avinābhāva* is a kind of logical term, like *vyāpti*, given in syllogistic interpretations. Uddyotakara used the concept of *avinābhāva* in his theory of syllogism, but nevertheless, he himself decisively refused to accept the validity of Dignāga's usage of *avinābhāva*, which says that, by reason of inseparable relation, the smoke does bring about the cognition of fire.[10] We do not know if this is truly Dignāga's position. It seems possible that Uddyotakara is putting words in to the mouth of his opponent in order to further his argument, or that he is merely anticipating Dignāga's response. For reasons which Uddyotakara did precisely mean by that refusal, I will address below by detailing his debate with Dignāga over the syllogism of smoke and fire. But first it seems necessary to clarify with what Uddyotakara identified Dignāga's inseparable relation.

He identified the following three possibilities for the relation between the smoke and fire and insisted that Dignāga's inseparable relation fall under at least one of them:[11]

1. The law of causality,
2. The relation of 'inherence' (*samavāya*), and
3. Mere relationship in general (= conjunction).

In Dignāga's inference, the inseparable relation must necessarily be understood as one of the three, but we may safely dispense with the third. Both the law of causality and inherence are close relationships between the two. The law of causality is almost universally explained in India as the fact that 'when the cause is present, the effect is present', and that 'when the cause is absent the effect is not present'.

I will make use of the formal notation of modern logic to define the logical features of such a relation, where 'p' stands for 'the cause is present', 'q' for 'the effect is present', and '$\sim p$' for the negation of 'p'. These propositions of the law of causality can be represented by:

(1) if p, then q

(2) if $\sim p$, then $\sim q$.

From (1) and (2), the following proposition can be deduced as follows:

(3) if and only if p, then q ($p \equiv q$) ('$\equiv$' is logical equivalence).

From a modern logical perspective, the relation between p and q is logical equivalence.

In case 2, it is interpreted to be 'established not to be separated' (*ayutasiddha*) by Praśastapāda.[12] For example, the cloth is inherent in the threads which are its parts. The *samavāya* holds between such entities as whole and part, attribute or action and substance, the universals and the individual, etc. Of these pairs, the first cannot exist without being related to the other. Therefore, in the case of inherence, the same interpretation can be also given; for example, if the part exists, then the whole exist, and, if the part doesn't exist, then the whole doesn't exist. We can see here conclusively that Uddyotakara understood *avinābhāva* to mean what we would call "logical equivalence".

On the other hand, as already described, the five-membered syllogism in Nyāya School has been thought to be built on the basis of the *vyāpti* relation. Back to Colebrooke's example, it is interpreted that 'what smokes is fiery' in the third member of syllogism, 'instance', expresses the *vyāpti* relation. As another expression of *vyāpti*, in a later Nyāya-Vaiśeṣika text, *Tarkasaṅgraha*, there is the proposition, 'whenever there is smoke, there is fire'.[13] *Vyāpti*, though usually translated as invariable concomitance, is a unilateral relation between smoke and fire. While fire is always found where smoke is present, smoke is not always observed along with fire, as in the case of a red-hot iron-ball.[14] I will formalize this relation of *vyāpti* using formal notation in order to differentiate it from *avinābhāva*, substituting 'p' for 'there is smoke', and 'q' for 'there is fire' as follows:

(4) if p, then q ($p \supset q$) ($\supset$: the symbol for implication).

From the logical point of view, there is a major difference between the conception of *avinābhāva* and that of *vyāpti*. It is significant to emphasize in further illustrating Uddyotakara's theory of logic that while *vyāpti* expresses the relation of implication, *avinābhāva* expresses that of logical equivalence.

In the *Tarkasaṅgraha*, *vyāpti* is defined as certainty of coexistence (*sāhacaryaniyama*),[15] but on the other hand, Uddyotakara maintains that *avinābhāva* is not treated as some kind of coexistence (*sāhacarya*) because it is observed that in some cases there is fire without smoke, and in other cases there is smoke without fire.[16] Furthermore, he asserts, the same reasoning holds against the inference that may be formulated as 'wherever there is smoke, there is fire'. It is certain that for Uddyotakara, *avinābhāva* is completely different from *vyāpti*. But even so, Uddyotaka's assertion, at least at first, seems puzzling. In the following I will try to ascertain the true intent of his assertion.

Epistemological Syllogism and Ontological Syllogism

In the earliest Nyāyaśāstra an argument or syllogism (*nyāya*) is explained in connection with an inference (*anumāna*), but not the converse, i.e. an inference with respect to a syllogism. In *Nyāyabhāṣya* 1.1.1, Vātsyāyana explains as follows:[17]

> An argument or syllogism (*nyāya*) is the examination of an object with the help of the means of true knowledge (*pramāṇa-s*). The inference (*anumāna*) which is not contradicted

> by perception and scripture is called *anvīkṣa* (investigation), because it consists in knowing over again (*anu-*) a thing already known (*īkṣita*) by perception and by scripture; this whole operation of investigation is called '*ānvīkṣikī*,' '*nyāyavidyā*,' and '*nyāyaśāstra*'.

Judging from these statements, an argument (*nyāya*) means the inference in which a thing already known by perception and scripture is known over again. This is why the theme of an argument is apt to relate to ontological subject matters because they are already known by perception and by scripture, and are still under discussion.

On the other hand, in *Nyāyabhāṣya* 1.1.5, Vātsyāyana explains Gautama's definition that an inference is preceded by perception as follows:[18]

> By the expression 'preceded by it' is meant '[preceded by] the perception of the relation between the sign (*liṅga*) and the significate (*liṅgin*) as well as the perception of the sign itself;' and the perception of the relation between the sign and the significate also implies the recollection of the sign. Thus it is by means of recollection and perception of the sign that the non-perceived object is inferred.

In the case of inference, we must emphasize that an inference is based on the perception of the relation between the sign and the significate, and on the perception of the sign, because it is a non-perceived object at the time of inference that we want to infer. In the early Nyāya School, the subjects of inference were always chosen from the regions of epistemology, never from that of ontology, because the inference was not yet connected with the argument form (*nyāya*). On *Nyāyabhāṣya* 1.1.5, mentioned above, Uddyotakara did not comment directly; but he did however completely accept Vātsyāyana's interpretation of the process of inference; and he further developed it epistemologically.

Let us now turn to his illustration in two examples of *pūrvavat* inference, viz. (a) the inference of rainfall from clouds, (b) the inference of fire from smoke, as mentioned above. First I will take up example (a) of the inference of effect from cause. Uddyotakara refers to two objections concerning Vātsyāyana's assertion that the effect is inferred from the cause. The objections state, in effect, that it means 'the presence of the effect is inferred from the perception of the cause' or that it means 'where the cause is, there the effect is'. Uddyotakara refutes these assertions, saying that they are not Nyāya views. It may be because they are based on the ontological interpretation. He says[19]:

> What the Sūtra actually means is that, what is inferred is the Effect as the qualifying property of the cause (*kāraṇa-viśeṣa*).

This requires further explanation. This statement tells us the inference of effect from cause is a problem of cognition, and is therefore naturally epistemological. As already described, in inferences Uddyotakara recognized an inseparable relation, by which he means logical equivalence. We shall see how this relation works in inference (a), which Uddyotakara illustrated in a kind syllogism, as follows[20]:

1 These clouds will bring rain,

2. Because they are rising, being, as they are, accompanied by deep rumbling, having many lines of cranes flying through them, flashing with lightning, and

3. Just like other rain-clouds perceived in the past.

Uddyotakara interprets the inference of rainfall from clouds in a syllogistic form, consisting of three members, instead of five members. He defines rainfall, or the effect, as the qualifying property of clouds, or the cause. That is to say; it is pointed out that there is the qualifier-qualificand relation between the cause and the effect. And this relation is that which is found on the stage of epistemology, and the qualifier (*viśeṣaṇa*) and the qualificand (*viśeṣya*) are inseparable. Only such clouds with many qualifiers like, accompanied by deep rumbling, having many lines of cranes flying through them, etc., bring rain. Why? Because rain is also a qualifier of such clouds, though not perceived at the time of inference. Rainfall is inevitably connected, as a qualifier, with such special clouds in the specific scene observed.

This epistemological inference was first formalized in syllogistic form by Uddyotakara. The third member of syllogism, called 'instance', consists of a very simple expression, that is, 'just like other rain-clouds perceived in the past', but I think it indicates the *avinābhāva* relation. Because a qualifier-qualificand relation is an inseparable one, and because we need only pick out some qualifiers from the whole situation we see, it is little easy to analyze the logical construction of such a situation. Furthermore, the third member of the syllogism, 'instance', is not a particular example of the kind that are used as proof in analogy or induction. It is the perceived knowledge, attained by a *pramāṇa*, or a means of true knowledge. Uddyotakara, I think, interpreted this syllogism as a form of deductive reasoning. His syllogism can be formalized again in the form of deductive reasoning, which says from p and $p \equiv q$, infer q, as follows:

– If and only if clouds are rising, being, as they are, accompanied by deep rumbling, having many lines of cranes flying through them, flashing with lightning, then they will bring rain.

– Clouds are rising, being, as they are, accompanied by deep rumbling, having many lines of cranes flying through them, flashing with lightning

– Therefore, these clouds will bring rain

Thus he introduced a kind of propositional logic in Indian theory of logic on epistemological grounds. His syllogism is fundamentally constructed by propositions and not by terms.

The same is the case with (b), the inference of fire from smoke. Uddyotakara says[21] :

> When we see certain peculiarities of smoke we infer the presence of smoke as qualified by fire. The fire becomes a qualification (*viśeṣaṇa*) of smoke, simply because the fire is subordinate (*guṇabhūta*) to the smoke.

Thus, the fire, not yet perceived, can be inferred by means of the smoke, with specific features, such as the continuity of its upward rising, volume, etc.

As I stated above, Uddyotakara rejects Dignāga's theory of syllogism regarding the inference of fire from smoke. Uddyotakara maintained that fire and smoke do not always coexist, i.e. he did not accept the assertion that wherever there is smoke, there is fire.[22] And as far as cognition is concerned, his assertion is not as awkward as it first may seem. It is possible to see smoke without fire, viz. a dying fire, or to see fire without smoke, viz. a hot coal. His point was to refute Dignāga's ontological interpretation.

I shall now illustrate the following example Vātsyāyana gave in his second interpretation of *pūrvavat* inference: 'Fire is inferred from smoke'. Uddyotakara asks what it is that is cognized by means of smoke is, and raises four possibilities, as follows[23]:

A) It is fire.

B) It is the particular place where the fire is.

C) It is the existence (*sattā*) of fire.

D) It is the particular place along with the fire.

Vācaspatimiśra, the commentator of *Nyāyavārttika*, comments that first three alternatives are rejected by Dignāga and that the last one is Dignāga's.[24] Uddyotakara, pointing out that the relation of *dharma* and *dharmin* cannot be established in this example, ultimately rejects all four alternatives.

As a good example of the ontological syllogism, we may recall the smoking-hill 'example of Colebrooke's syllogism. It is the relation of property (*dharma*) and property-possessor (*dharmin*) that covers such ontological syllogism, corresponding to the relation of qualifier and qualificand, covering the epistemological syllogism. Apart from the context of cognition, when we say, 'this hill is fiery', the hill is indicated as property-possessor or locus and fire is indicated as property.

In Vātsyāyana's example, however, the smoke simply leads us to the fire. In this example, what is the *dharma* and what is the *dharmin*? In the case of A), because there is not the relation of *dharma* and *dharmin* between smoke and fire, it is not possible that fire is cognized. In the cases of B) and C), they are already known. And in the case of D), the smoke is not a property of that place containing fire, and furthermore, the relation of fire to a place is not unknown.[25] The relation of *dharma* and *dharmin* cannot be decided so as to be the valid basis of the syllogism in any of the cases.

Moreover, Dignāga argues that the inference can be stated in the form: 'This place contains fire'. In this expression, he says, what is inferred is a particular place as containing fire. But Uddyotakara denies that the actual place is ever perceived. In his gloss of Uddyotakara's refutation,[26] adds that when one sees the smoke rising up in the sky, he may not see the actual place from where it issues.

Thus Uddyotakara indicates that the inference of fire from smoke cannot be logically interpreted by the ontological theory of syllogism.

Conclusion

Uddyotakara did not lose sight of the essential difference between the inference and the syllogism; the inference is epistemological, and the syllogism is ontological. The main point of Uddyotakara's argument is that the syllogism which is made on the basis of the inference, such as *pūrvavat,* etc, should be interpreted on epistemological grounds, and not ontological grounds. In other words, it should not be interpreted through relation of *dharma* and *dharmin,* but through the relation of *viśeṣaṇa* and *viśeṣya.* And therefore Colebrooke's ontological example of the smoking-hill inference should not have been held up in the interpretation of the syllogism of the early Nyāya School. For many investigators of Indian logic the syllogism of this example has been attractive as a convenient analogy to the Aristotelian syllogism. In fact, neither Vātsyāyana nor Uddyotakara ever described that example of inference in such an ontological syllogistic form. On the contrary, Uddyotakara constructed the syllogistic form in which a proposition is the basic constituent of logical theory, and epistemologically interpreted the example of inference using the concept of *avinābhāva,* viz. logical equivalence, though it seems that this fact has often been overlooked.

NOTES

1. H.T. Colebrooke, "The Philosophy of the Hindus: On the Nyāya and Vaiśeṣika Systems" (1824) (in *Indian Logic: A Reader,* ed. by Jonardon Ganeri, Curzon Press, Richmond, Surrey, 2001), pp. 47-8.
2. I.M. Bochenski, "The Indian Variety of Logic" (1956) (in *Indian Logic: A Reader,* ed. by Jonardon Ganeri, Curzon Press, Richimond, Surrey, 2001), p. 130.
3. Bimal Krishna Matilal, "Introducing Indian Logic" (1998) (in *Indian Logic: A Reader,* ed. by Jonardon Ganeri, Curzon Press, Richimond, Surrey, 2001), p. 186.
4. Daniel H.H. Ingalls, Logic in India (1955) (in *Indian Logic: A Reader,*

ed. by Jonardon Ganeri, Curzon Press, Richimond, Surrey, 2001), p. 111.

5. *Gutamīyanyāyadarśana with Bhāṣya of Vātsyāyana*, Nyayacaturgranthika Vol. I, ed. by Anantala Thakur, Indian Council of Philosophical Research, New Delhi, 1997, p. 12.
6. *Gutamīyanyāyadarśana with Bhāṣya of Vātsyāyana*, p. 12.
7. *Gutamīyanyāyadarśana with Bhāṣya of Vātsyāyana*, p. 1.
8. *Gutamīyanyāyadarśana with Bhāṣya of Vātsyāyana*, p. 100.
9. *Gutamīyanyāyadarśana with Bhāṣya of Vātsyāyana*, p. 101.
10. *Nyāyabhāṣyavārttika of Bharadvāja Uddyotakara*, Nyayacaturgranthika Vol. II, ed. by Anantala Thakur, Indian Council of Philosophical Research, New Delhi, 1997, p. 47.
11. *Nyāyabhāṣyavārttika of Bharadvāja Uddyotakara*, p. 47.
12. *Praśastapādabhāṣya (in Praśastapādabhāṣya with commentary Nyāyakandalī by Śrīdhara Bhaṭṭa, along with Hindi Translation*, ed. by Pt. Durgadhara Jha, Varanasi, 1977), p. 773.
13. *Tarkasaṅgraha of Annambhaṭṭa, with the Author's Own Dīpikā, and Govardhana's Nyāya-Bodhinī*. ed. by Yashwant Vasudev Athalye, Bombay Sanskrit Series, No. LV, Bhandarkar Oriental Research Institute, Poona, 1974, p. 34.
14. *Tarkasaṅgraha of Annambhaṭṭa*, p. 244.
15. *Tarkasaṅgraha of Annambhaṭṭa*, p. 34.
16. *Nyāyabhāṣyavārttika of Bharadvāja Uddyotakara*, p. 47
17. *Gutamīyanyāyadarśana with Bhāṣya of Vātsyāyana*, p. 3.
18. *Gutamīyanyāyadarśana with Bhāṣya of Vātsyāyana*, p. 12.
19. *Nyāyabhāṣyavārttika of Bharadvāja Uddyotakara*, p. 44.
20. *Nyāyabhāṣyavārttika of Bharadvāja Uddyotakara*, p. 44.
21. *Nyāyabhāṣyavārttika of Bharadvāja Uddyotakara*, p. 47.
22. *Nyāyabhāṣyavārttika of Bharadvāja Uddyotakara*, p. 47.
23. *Nyāyabhāṣyavārttika of Bharadvāja Uddyotakara*, p. 46.
24. *Nyāyabhāṣyavārttikatātparyaṭīkā of Vācaspatimiśra*, ed. by Anantalal Thakur, Vol. III, Indian Council of Philosophical Research, New Delhi, 1997, p. 148.
25. *Nyāyabhāṣyavārttika of Bharadvāja Uddyotakara*, pp. 46-7.
26. *Nyāyabhāṣyavārttikatātparyaṭīkā of Vācaspatimisra*, p. 148.

CHAPTER 26

Svasvāmisambandha in the Vaiśeṣika System

MASANOBU NOZAWA

1.1 The Vaiśeṣikas altered the theory of transmigration at the early stage of their history. At first they had the theory of movable *ātman* and believed in the transmigration of *ātman* from body to body, which was explained in the *Vaiśeṣikasūtra* (abbr. VS) 5.2.19.[1] But it came to be taken as explaining the transmigration of not *ātman* but *manas* at some time before the compilation of the *Nyāyasūtra* (abbr. NS) 3.2.68-70,[2] where the theory of transmigration of *manas* was criticized. The question in issue is what was it like the earliest Vaiśeṣika theory of transmigration and why the Vaiśeṣika abandoned the theory of *ātman* transmigrating from body to body.

1.2 A hypothetical answer would be like this:[3] The early Vaiśeṣikas regarded *ātman* as having some limited size. But the development of the atomic theory urged them to revise the theory of size of substances and to adopt a new notion of *ātman* with an unlimited size in line with the other immaterial substances such as *ākāśa,* etc.; accordingly they abandoned the theory of movable *ātman,* since they thought of it as impossible for omnipresent substances to have motion.

1.3 As has been pointed out by Adachi,[4] however, the textual evidence for the Vaiśeṣika *ātman* with a limited size is difficult to find. As far as we know there is only one dubious case of such evidence referring to seemingly Vaiśeṣika *ātman* finite in size. It is a passage of Piṅgala's commentary on the *Madhyamaka Śāstra* (*Zhōng lùn*)[5] in which appears a criticism against a view of *ātman* with a limited size following an assertion of existence *of ātman* that is similar to that of VS 3.2.4 or NS 1.1.10. Although the possibility exists that it reports a fairly unique opinion held by some factions within the Vaiśeṣika school, but the other possibility also remains that the commentator mixed up the Vaiśeṣika view with the Jaina one;[6] so that it is rather doubtful whether this text reflects the true picture of the Vaiśeṣika at the early period.

1.4 Miyamoto[7] and Bronkhorst[8] doubt the existence of the early Vaiśeṣika theory of *ātman* with a limited size and suggest that the *ātman* should be thought of as omnipresent by the Vaiśeṣikas from the very beginning as is explained by VS 7.1.28, 29. This suggestion seems persuasive so far as it is difficult to provide convincing evidence for alteration of the size of *ātman*.

2.1 On the supposition that there was no change in the theory of the size of *ātman* how should we understand the early Vaiśeṣikas' view of transmigration? Bronkhorst[9] proposes an interesting hypothesis by making use of a reference to the Vaiśeṣika *ātman* in the *Vākyapadīya*. It is as follows:

> There is no real evidence supporting the opinion that the soul of the primitive Vaiśeṣika was finite in size. The soul, although being omnipresent, can be active because it has a specific contact—described as 'contact of owner and owned' (*sva-svāmi-sambandha*)—with the own body and all that is contained in it. The action of *ātman* is not concerned to *ātman* itself but to a particular part of *ātman* constituted by the relation of owner and owned. But the implausibility of this way of speaking about the 'action' of an omnipresent soul is obvious, so that the idea was discarded with the interposition of *manas* between a soul and its body. Thus the mystery of the special relationship between the soul and its body disappears.

2.2 This explanation seems attractive, although the last part of it needs to be touched up, for the relation of *sva-svāmi-sambandha* referred to as Vaiśeṣika theory is found not only in the *Vākyapadīya* but also in later works, such as Dharmapāla's commentary on the *Catuḥśataka*[10] and the *Brahmasūtra-Śāṅkara-Bhāṣya*[11], which show that the relation of *sva-savāmi-sambandha* was not discarded even after the replacement of *ātman* by *manas* in the theory of transmigration. And there still remains a question what made them feel the old theory implausible and interpose *manas* between a soul and the body. But as a whole the concept of *sva-svāmi-sambandha* seems to work as a key to solve the apparent incompatibility of omnipresence and action of *ātman*.

First we will inquire what kind of relation *sva-svāmi-sambandha* is and next proceed to the question how it works in the early Vaiśeṣika theory of transmigration and then discuss what urged the Vaiśeṣikas to alter the theory.

3.1 *Svasvāmisambandha* is 'possessive relation' and translated as 'relation of owner and owned'. It is found not only in the context of the Vaiśeṣika theory but also in the literature of the other schools, such as the Yoga,[12] the Sāṃkhya,[13] and the Vedānta,[14] which shows that this relation is well-known and widely accepted among various schools.

3.2 It appears as a relation of *puruṣa* with knowable objects (*dṛśya*) in the *Yogasūtra.*

> *sva-svāmi-śaktyoḥ svarūpa-upalabdhi-hetuḥ saṃyogaḥ* //2.23//
> (Yogabhāṣya) *puruṣaḥ svāmi dṛśyena svena darśanārthaṃ saṃyuktaḥ*/ [15]
>
> YS 2.23. Conjunction is what causes cognition of the nature of the power of the owner and the owned.
>
> (Yogabhāṣya) *Puruṣa,* i.e. the owner, is conjoined with the knowable object, i.e. the owned, for the purpose of knowing.

3.3 Another reference to it is found in the *Yogabhāṣya.* Here the relation is formed between *puruṣa* and the mind (*citta*).[16]

> *cittam ayaskānta-maṇi-kalpaṃ saṃnidhi-mātropakāri dṛśyatvena svaṃ bhavati puruṣasya svāminaḥ tasmāc citta-vṛtti-bodhe puruṣasyānādih sambandho hetuḥ/*
>
> The mind, which, like a magnet or a jewel, performs function

(of attraction or cognition) with the help of proximity alone, is owned by the owner, i.e. *puruṣa,* by being seen. Therefore the eternal relation of *puruṣa* is the cause of knowing the operations of the mind.

3.4 It is also found in the *Śāṅkarabhāṣya* on BS 1.3.14, where the relation of an individual self and the body is compared to that of a king and his castle.[17]

athavā jīvo dahara iti prāptam, brahmapura-śabdāt / jīvasya hīdaṃ puraṃ sac charīraṃ brahmapuram ity ucyate / tasya svakarmaṇo-pārjitatvāt / bhaktyā ca tasya brahma-śabda-vācyatvam / na hi parasya brahmaṇaḥ śarīreṇa sva-svāmi-bhāvaḥ sambandho 'sti /

Or it should be understood that an individual self is meant by (the word) 'small', because the word 'castle of Brahman' (*brahma-pura*) is used. The body is the castle of an individual self and is called the 'castle of Brahman', because it is gained by means of its own action by an individual self. And the word '*brahma*' is used in a secondary sense, for there is no relation of owner and owned between the supreme Brahman and the body. And it is observed that the owner of a castle is seen to live in part of it just like a king.

3.5 The relation of owner and owned is a common relation widely accepted among various schools. The 'owner' is *ātman* or *puruṣa* or *jīva,* and the 'owned' is whatever are in connection to it or belong to it.[18] This relation is implicitly recognized so long as the possessive relation is referred to as in the case of calling *ātman* as 'the owner of the body' (*dehin*).

But it seems to have a special meaning for the Vaiśeṣikas, because it is a convenient means to explain away the difficult problems pertaining to their supposition of omnipresent *ātman.*

4.1 How was the *sva-svāmi-sambandha* conceived by the Vaiśeṣikas? Dharmapāla's commentary on the 14th verse in the chapter of 'refutation of *ātman'* of Āryadeva's **Catuḥśataka* (*Guǎg bǎi lùn shì lùn*)[19] gives a fairly clear answer to this question. It appears after a criticism against the Vaiśeṣika view of *ātman.* The criticism runs as this: The Vaiśeṣika *ātman* cannot be called conscious, since according to their view consciousness resides only in a very tiny part of *ātman* that is in contact with the mind which is atomic in size, and since the most part of *ātman* is lacking in consciousness.[20]

Translation: (200a22) Next, another tries to avoid the defect by not allowing the occurrence of function in part of a self and (a23) asserts that the depending qualities [consciousness etc.] pervade over the self on which they depend. But this is not right, either. If qualities pervaded over a self, (a24) the contact of sense organs would be of no use, because pleasure and so on should arise where there is no [contact with] sense organs. (a25) If some says that it is not the case, and that pleasure and so on arise through the contact of part of a self with sense organs etc. (a26) just like the light of a lamp is kindled by the disposition of the wick and brightness pervades over places.[21]

To such an assertion [Āryadeva] (a27) says in verse:

(200a28) If the self and its qualities are pervasive, why do not the others receive them?

(a29) Commentary: If the self and its qualities are both pervasive in size, one man's pleasure pervades over the other selves. (200bl) How can you say the other selves do not receive them? Even if you say that the self can perceive them, since the mind is in contact with the part of self (b2) where pain and pleasure arise, [then as far as the other selves are also in contact with them] how can it be flawless?

(b3) Again you may make an assertion as follows: My own property belongs only to myself and can be used by myself. Although one man's (b4) pleasure etc. pervade over all the selves, they belong to only one [self] and have no connection with the others, so that how could (b5) the others receive the pain and pleasure of one self! In the worldly life we observe that property is possessed only by the owner and (b6) not used by the others. If the places of possessions were different, this answer would do well. However they exist in the same place and (b7) nothing prevent them from being possessed by the others.

You may say that even if possessions exist in the same place, so long as they do not belong to me, they are discriminated and not (b8) used freely by me.

But [it is useless to say so, because] nothing can prevent

them from being enjoyed through the visual and tactile perception. Indeed, in the worldly life (b9) we are not prevented from seeing and touching what are not our possessions if they exist in the same place. Now that pain, pleasure, etc. are lacking in material form, (b10) we cannot discriminate them by the visual or tactile perception. This is why your assertion would not save your tenet.

4.2 Śaṅkara criticizes the Vaiśeṣika theory of *ātman* and refers to the *sva-svāmi-sambandha* which seems to occur in a quotation from a lost Vaiśeṣika work.[22]

Text: *kaṇādānām api yadaikenātmanā manaḥ saṃyujyate tadā ātmāntarair api nāntarīyakaḥ saṃyogaḥ syāt sannidhānādy-aviśeṣāt / tataś ca hetv-aviśeṣāt phalāviśaṣa ity ekasyātmanaḥ sukha-duḥkha-yoge sarvātmanām api samānaṃ sukha-duḥkhitvaṃ prasajyeta*// 50//

syād etat–adṛṣṭa-nimitto niyamo bhaviṣyatīti / nety āha— adṛṣṭāniyamāt //2.3.51//

bahuṣv ātmasv ākāśavat sarva-gateṣu prati-śarīraṃ bāhyābhyantarāviśeṣeṇa sannihiteṣu mano-vāk-kāyair dharmādharma-lakṣaṇam adṛṣṭam upārjyate / sāṃkhyānāṃ tāvat tad anātma-samavāyi pradhāna-varti, pradhāna-sādhāraṇyān na pratyātmaṃ sukha-duḥkhopabhogasya niyāmakam upapadyate / kāṇādānām api pūrvavat sādhāraṇenātma-manaḥ-saṃyogena nirvartitasyādṛṣṭasyāpy asyaivātmana idam adṛṣṭam iti niyame hetv-abhāvād eṣa eva doṣaḥ //51//

syād etad—aham idaṃ phalaṃ prāpnavānīdaṃ pariharāṇītthaṃ prayatā itthaṃ karavāṇīty evaṃ-vidhā abhisaṃdhy-ādayaḥ pratyātmaṃ pravartamānā adṛṣṭasyātmaṇāṃ ca sva-svāmi-bhāvaṃ niyaṃsyantīti /nety āha— abhisaṃdhyādiṣv api caivam//2.3.52//

abhisaṃdhy-ādīnām api sādhāraṇenaivātma-manaḥ-saṃyogena sarvātma-sannidhau kriyamāṇānāṃ niyama-hetutvānupapatter ukta-doṣānuṣaṅga eva //52//

Translation: In the case of the followers of Kaṇāda [there is a theoretical defect as follows]: When one mind (*manas*) is connected to one *ātman*, the direct connection with the other *ātmans* will be also formed, since there is no difference as regards proximity [of the mind to all *ātmans* that are omnipresent]. When there is no difference of cause, there is no difference of effect. Therefore it will lead an undesirable consequence that when one *ātman* is connected to pleasure and pain, the same pleasure and pain should arise in all *ātmans*.

If they say that regulation would be made by *adṛṣṭa,* it is not so.

Sūtra 2.3.51: Because *adṛṣṭa* makes no regulation.

The *ātmans* are numerous and omnipresent like ether and are equally close to every body without difference of inside and outside. *Adṛṣṭa* characterized as *dharmādharma* is obtained for them through mind and speech and body. For the Sāṃkhyas it does not inhere in *ātman* but subsists in the primal cause. Since the primal cause is common to [all the *ātmans*], it does not make any regulation for each *ātman* as regards who enjoys the pleasure and pain. The same defect applies to the followers of Kaṇāda, since even if *adṛṣṭa* is made by the connection of *ātman* and the mind, there is no cause of regulation that this *adṛṣṭa* belongs to this *ātman*.

A following opinion may be put forward: Every particular *ātman* executes wills such as 'I will obtain this result', 'I will avoid this', 'I will make such and such an effort', and 'I will make such and such a thing', and these [wills] regulate the relation of owner and owned between *ātman* and *adṛṣṭa*. —It is not so.

Sūtra 2.3.52: Wills etc. are also the case [as mentioned above].

Wills etc. are all formed by the connection of *ātman* with the mind, which is common [to all the *ātmans*]. As they are so close to all the *ātmans,* they cannot be the cause of regulation. Therefore the defect mentioned above will be a necessary consequence.

5.1 How does the relation of *sva-svāmi-sambandha* work in the theory of transmigration of the early Vaiśeṣika? We find a passage in the 1st chapter of the Śārīrasthāna of the *Carakasaṃhitā* (abbr. CS),[23] which seems to reflect the earliest Vaiśeṣika view of *ātman*. And the concept *sva-svāmi-sambandha* is, although not explicitly mentioned, serves as basis for the argument here.

1.75: *acetanaṃ kiriyāvac ca manaś cetayitā paraḥ/*
yutasya manasā tasya ṇirdiśyante vibhoḥ kriyāḥ //

76: *cetanāvān yataś cātmā tataḥ kartā nirucyate /*
acetanatvāc ca manaḥ kriyāvad api nocyate //

79: *dehī sarva-gato'py ātmā sve sve saṃsparśanendriye /*
sarvāḥ sarvāśraya-sthās tu nātmāto vetti vedanāḥ //

80: *vibhutvam ata evāsya yasmāt sarvagato mahān /*
manasaś ca samādhānāt paśyaty ātmā tiraskṛtam //

81: *nityānubandhaṃ manasā deha-karmānupātinā /*
sarva-yoni-gataṃ vidyād eka-yonāv api sthitam //

1.75. Without consciousness the mind has action. The owner of consciousness (*cetayitṛ*) is the superior one (*para*) [i.e. *ātman*]. The actions of the omnipresent one are describable when it is in contact with the mind.

76. The self is called 'doer' because of having consciousness, while the mind is not so in spite of having actions because it is devoid of consciousness.

79. The self, though omnipresent, is connected to his own particular sense organs as owner of the body; therefore the self does not have all sensation pertaining to all physical abodes.

80. It [*ātman*] is pervasive because it is omnipresent and huge. And the *ātman* perceives the hidden when the mind is fixed in contemplation.

81. It has an enduring bond with the mind that follows the actions of the body [to various forms of existence], so that, although stationed in one form of existence, it could know everything in all the forms of existence.

5.2 The passage of CS might be a textual evidence for the core of Bronkhorst's hypothesis mentioned above in § 2.1. It gives a picture of the early Vaiśeṣika theory of *ātman* as follows: *Ātman* is omnipresent (*vibhu,* VS 7.1.29) and numerous in number (VS 3.2.16). Each *ātman* has a specific relation with a particular body and mind as owner. Also each *ātman* is, as owner of knowledge or consciousness, the abode of each own experience of pleasure, pain and so on. This is why it does not concern anything outside of the body, and does not experience the others' sensations in spite of being omnipresent. And through the connection to its own particular body, it can be active as an agent (*kartṛ*), and has motion in this sense, and it is said that *ātman* transmigrates from body to body. It is entering of *manas* in the body that forms the relation of *ātman* with a particular body. What travels from one body to another is *manas*, while *ātman* also changes its relation to the body in accordance with the transition of *manas*, so that it could be said that *ātman* transmigrates from one body to another. This seems to be how the original intention of VS 5.2.19 was.

It might also open the possibility that the theory of body-sized *ātman* mentioned in the *Zhōng lún* quoted in § 1.2 was held by some faction of the Vaiśeṣika, since it might be the case that they concerned not the *ātman* in whole but only the part of *ātman* where the body is connected.[24]

6.1 A similar theory of transmigration of omnipresent soul is found in the *Bhagavadgītā* 2.22-24[25] and the *Nyāyabhāṣya* (abbr: NBh).[26] *Bhagavadgītā* 2.22-24 runs as follows:

> *vāsāṃsi jīrṇāni yathā vihāya navāṇi gṛhṇāti naro 'parāṇi /*
> *tathā śarīrāṇi vihāya jīrṇāny anyāni saṃyāti navāni dehī* // 22//
>
> *nainaṃ chindanti śastrāṇi nainaṃ dahati pāvakaḥ /*
> *na cainaṃ kledayanty āpo na śoṣayati mārutaḥ* // 23//
>
> *acchedo 'yam adāhyo 'yam akledyo 'śoṣya eva ca /*
> *nityaḥ sarvagataḥ sthāṇur acalo 'yam sanātanaḥ* // 24//

22. As leaving aside worn-out garments
A man takes other, new ones,
So leaving aside worn-out bodies
To other, new ones goes the embodied (soul).

23. Swords cut him not,
Fire burn him not,
Water wets him not,
Wind dries him not.

24. Not to be cut is he, not to be burnt is he,
Not to be wet nor yet dried;
Eternal, omnipresent, fixed,
Immovable, everlasting is he.

(F. Edgerton, *The Bhagavad Gītā*, Cambridge (MA), 1972, p.11.)

6.2 The notion of omnipresent *ātman* dates back as far as the age of the *Kaṭha* and the *Śvetāśvatara Upaniṣads.*[27] The conception of omnipresent *ātman* transmigrating from body to body was popular and confirmed by the authority of the scriptures; it caused no problem for the traditionalistic minds. They had no reason to change the theory and so it was sustained, but the circumstances were different with the Vaiśeṣikas. They elaborated the kinetic theory of substances, and so were faced with a difficult problem of motion of an omnipresent existence.

7.1 What urged the Vaiśeṣikas to discard the notion of active *ātman*? A clue seems to be in the interpretation of VS 5.2.23: *dik-kāla-ākāśaṃ ca kriyāvadbhyo vaidharmyān niṣkriyāṇi* (Direction, time and ether are inactive because of difference from what has action.) This *sūtra* does not include *ātman* among inactive substances, so that it must have been composed before the discarding of active *ātman.* Probably it is as old as VS 5.2.19 the original intention of which is to explain the transmigration of *ātman.*

Candrānanda annotates 'difference from what has action' as 'intangibility' (*amūrtatā*) but the understanding of the phrase at the earliest days seems to have been different from it, because it needs to exclude *ātman* from inactive substances. It is inferred that it contained some other element than *amūrtatā* or *vibhutva* which is in negative relation to activeness of *ātman,* such as unconsciousness (*ajñatva*), or not-agent-ness (*akartṛtva*) or something like that.

Note that the division of *karman* into five species (VS 1.1.6) is based on 'bodily action' such as throwing up etc. Although the term *karman* in VS is not restricted in the meaning of 'bodily action' but used in more genereal sense of 'motion', it is notable that VS shows a tendency of using the term in the former sense, for 13 among 18 sūtras of VS 5.1 deal with 'bodily action' rather than 'motion'. As far as they mainly took *karman* as 'action', the interpretation of the term 'difference' in VS 5.2.23 as *vibhutva* and *ajñatva* or *akartṛtva* caused no problem. But when *karman* became used in much more neutral sense as 'motion' in accordance with the systematization of the theory of categories, it came to be clear that intangibility or omnipresence should suffice to exclude active or movable substances, and that 'unconsciousness' or 'not-agent-ness' was regarded as redundant.

They noticed the incompatibility of action and omnipresence of *ātman* and questioned the mobility of *ātman*. As far as they kept the view of omnipresent *ātman*, it was difficult to sustain the notion of transmigrating soul; accordingly they gave up the notion of active *ātman* and appointed *manas* the role of traveling from body to body.

7.2 Once *ātman* was regarded as inactive because of being omnipresent, they stopped talking about the transmigration of *ātman*, and they changed the interpretations of the *sūtra* 5.2.19 and took it as explaining the transmigration of *manas*. The new interpretation was accepted without much friction, since it was not so much far apart from the old one as long as the transposition of *manas* caused the transmigration of *ātman*. The relation of *adṛṣṭa*, however, needed emendation. If it is *ātman* that transmigrates from body to body, then *adṛṣṭa* is related to *ātman*, but if it is *manas*, it belongs to *manas*. NS 3.2.69-70 and NBh on them record an interesting objection against the Vaiśeṣika view in which *adṛṣṭa* is regarded as belonging to *manas*.[28] This shows that the ascription of *adṛṣṭa* to *manas* survived for some time before the establishment of the classical theory according to which *adṛṣṭa* was identified with *dharmādharma* and designated as one of the specific qualities of *ātman*.

NOTES

1. *Vaiśeṣikasūtra of Kaṇāda with the Commentary of Candrānanda*, ed. by Jambūvijaya Muni, *GOS* 136, Baroda 1961.
2. *Nyāyasūtram*, ed. by Ganganath Jhā, *POS* 58, Poona 1939.
3. See Nozawa, Masanobu, "On Vaiśeṣika Theory of Metempsychosis," (in Japanese) *Journal of Nippon Buddhist Research Association*, vol.XLVI, 1981, pp. 459-472. Frauwallner conjectured that the *ātman* of the Vaiśeṣika was assigned some limited size at first. Frauwallner, Erich, *Geschichte der Indischen Philosophie*, Bd.2, Salzburg, 1956, p. 62.
4. Adachi, Toshihide, "On the Size and Mobility of the *ātman* in the Early Vaiśeṣika," *AS*, XLVIII.2, 1994, pp. 653-663.
5. Zhōng lùn (Kumārajīva's Chinese translation of the *Madhyamaka Śāstra* with Piṅgala's commentary), Taishō No. 1465, p. 13b22f. See Adachi, "On the Size and Mobility of the *ātman* in the Early Vaiśeṣika," p. 656, note. 17.

   Translation (Numerals in parentheses denote the page and line of text.): (13b22) Question: Some say breathing in, breathing out, blinking, (b23) life, cognition, pain, pleasure, aversion, affection and volition—these are the specific features of Soul (*ātman*). If it were not for (b24) Soul, how could these features, i.e., breathing in, breathing out and so on be possible? Therefore we should know that apart from the sense organs (such as) the eyes, the ears etc. (b25) there must be a certain fundamental existence (*vyavasthita*), and the qualities (such as) pain and pleasure etc.

Answer: If the Soul should exist, (b26) it must exist in the body just like a pillar existing in the wall, or it must exist outside of the body just like an armor worn by a person. (b27) First, if it existed in the body, the body would be imperishable, because it contains the Soul that is eternal. (b28) Therefore saying that the Soul exists in the body is nothing but a false and baseless assertion. (b29) Second, if the Soul existed outside of the body and shrouded the body just like an armor, the body would be invisible, (13cl) because the Soul shrouds it densely. And also it would become imperishable. But in fact we observe the body perishing. Therefore (c2) we should know that there is no other existence apart from pain and pleasure etc. If you should say that when the arm is cut off, (c3) the Soul shrinks into the body, then [killing by] cutting would be impossible, for if the Soul could shrink into the body when the head is cut off, (c4) there would be no death, but in fact death is real. Therefore we know saying that there is Soul apart from pain and pleasure etc., (c5) is nothing but a false and baseless assertion.

Someone may say that the Soul is as large as the body (c6) and when the body is big the Soul is big and when the body is small the Soul is small just as when a lamp is big the light is strong and when a lamp is small (c7) the light is weak. If it should be like this and the Soul should be in proportion to the body in size, then it could not be eternal. If the Soul were in proportion to the body in size, (c8) the Soul would disappear when the body disappears just as the light disappears when a lamp is put out. If the Soul is non-eternal, (c9) it would be the same with the eyes, the ears, pain, pleasure etc., therefore we know that there is no such existence as Soul apart from the eyes, the ears and so on.

6. The Jainas have a similar theory that the soul is in proportion to the body in size, and use the simile of *pradīpa*. See *Tattvārthādhigamasūtra* 5.16: *pradeśa-saṃhārāvisargābhyāṃ pradīpavat* / In proportion to contraction and expansion of space [the soul (*jīva*) occupies the space] as the light of a lamp. See Schubring, *The Doctrine of the Jainas*, Delhi 1962, p.131, and Frauwallner, *Geschichte der Indischen Philosophie*, Bd.2, p.258.
7. Miyamoto, Keiichi, *The Metaphysics and Epistemology of the Early Vaiśeṣika*, Pune, 1996, p.19f. The original paper in Japanese was published in 1991. Miyamoto, Keiichi, "Ātman no Okisa—Shoki Vaiśeṣika Gakuha no Kenkai wo megutte," *Journal of Kokugakuin University* 92-5, 1991, pp.1-15. See also Potter, K., *Encyclopedia of Indian Philosophies: Indian Metaphysics and Epistemology: The Tradition of Nyāya-Vaiśaṣika up to Gaṅgeśa*, Delhi, 1977, pp. 97-99.
8. Bronkhorst, Johannes, "Mysticisme et rationalité, en Inde: le cas du Vaiśeṣika," *AS*, XLVII.4, 1993, pp.565f. Bronkhorst, Johannes, *Karma and Teleology*, Studia Philologica Buddhica Monograph Series XV, Tokyo, 2000, p. 33f.
9. Bronkhorst, Johannes, "Studies on Bhartṛhari, 5: Bhartṛhari and Vaiśeṣika,"

AS, XLVII. 1, 1993, p.91, and Bronkhorst, "Mysticisme et rationalité, en Inde: le cas du Vaiśeṣika," p. 565.

10 *Guǎng bǎi lùn shì lùn,* (Xuán zàng's Chinese translation of Dharmapāla's commentary on Āryadeva's Catuḥśataka) Taisho No.1571, pp. 200a22-200b10.

11. *Brahmasūtra-Śāṅkarabhāṣyam,* ed. by J.L. Shastri, Delhi 1980, pp. 223-224 (1.3.14), p. 562 (2.3.51).

12. *Pātañjala Yogadarśanam,* ed. by Śrīnārayaṇamiśra, Varaṇasī 1971, YS 2.23, pp. 18, 221.

13. *Sāṃkhyapravacanabhāṣya,* ed. by Richard Garbe, HOS 2,1943, p. 163: *karma-nimittaḥ prakṛteḥ sva-svāmi-bhāvo 'py anādir, bījāṅkura-vat.* (The relation of owner and owned of *prakṛti,* which is caused by karma, has no beginning just like the relation of seed and sprout). Cf. *Yuktidīpikā,* ed. by Albrecht Wezler and Shujun Motegi, Stuttgart 1998, p. 161.4: *tathā ca bījād aṅkurādayo 'ṅkurādibhyo bījam ity anavasthā.* See also *Sāṃkhyapravacanabhāṣya* p. 12.26: "*citta-vṛtti-bodhe puruṣasyādiḥ sva-svāmibhāvaḥ sambandho hetur*" *iti Yogabhāṣyād ayaṃ siddhāntaḥ siddhaḥ.* On the *sva-svāmi-sambandha* of the Sāṃkhya see Garbe, *Richard, Die Sāṃkhya-philosophie,* Leibzig, 1894, p. 348.

14. See note 11.

15. *Yogabhāṣya* p. 221.

16. *Yogabhāṣya* on YS 1.4, p. 18.

17. *Brahmasūtra-Śāṅkarabhāṣyaṃ* pp. 223-224. The simile of a king and his castle reminds us of 'a beholder in a chamber with several windows' (*aneka-gavākṣāntargata-prekṣaka*) mentioned in *Padārthadharmasaṃgraha,* ed. by Vindhyeśvarīprasāda Dvivedin, *Viz.SS* 4, Benaras, 1895, (rpt. Delhi 1984), p. 70.4.

18. The Vaiśeṣikas adopt two kinds of relation, that is conjunction (*saṃyoga*) and inherence (*samavāya*). *Sva-svāmi-sambandha* does not matter whether it is *saṃyoga* or *samavāya.*

19. *Guǎng bǎi lùn shì lùn,* Taishō No.1571, pp. 200a22-200b10.

20. See Adachi, "On the Size and Mobility of the ātman in the Early Vaiśeṣika," p. 656, and Lang, Karen, *Āryadeva's Catuḥśataka,* Copenhagen, 1986, pp. 98, 99, and also Tillemans, Tom J.F., *Materials for the Study of Āryadeva, Darmapāda and Candrakīrti,* 2 vols., Wien, 1990.

21. See Note 6.

22. *Brahmasūtra-Śāṅkarabhāṣyam* on BS 2.3.50-52. p. 562, See Thibaut, *The Vedānta Sūtra,* New York 1890, vol. 2, p.69, V.M. Apte, *Brahma-Sūtra Shānkara-Bhāshya,* Bombay 1960, p. 495. Kanakura, *Shankara no Tetsugaku,* Tokyo 1984, vol. 2, p. 97. As to lost Vaiśeṣika works see Matilal, B.K., *A History of Indian Literature, Nyāya-Vaiśeṣika,* Wiesbaden, 1977, pp. 60f, and Bronkhorst, Johannes, "The Vaiśeṣika Vākya and Bhāṣya," *Annals* (B.O.R. Institute) *Amṛtamahotsava Volume,* 1993, pp. 145-169.

23. *Carakasaṃhitā,* ed. by Vaidya Jādavaji Trikamji Ācārya, Bombay, 1941, p. 294. *Carakasaṃhitā. Text with English Translation.* ed. by Sharma, P.V., Delhi, 1994, p. 404. Comba, A (1987): "Carakasaṃhitā. Śārīrasthāna I and Vaiśeṣika philosophy," *Studies on Indian Medical History,* Groningen, pp. 43-61. Nozawa, Masanobu, "Concept of *yoga* in the *Vaiśeṣikasūtra,*" *Indian Thoughts and Buddhist Culture, Essays in honor of Prof. J. Imanishi on his Sixtieth Birthday,* 1996, pp.(17)-(30).

24. The *sva-svāmi-sambandha* of *ātman* with the body might explain why the term '*ātman*' is used in the meaning of 'body' as in VS 5.1.6: *tathā cātma-karma hasta-saṃyogāc ca* (*ātma-karmeti śarīraikadeśaḥ*, Candrānanda p. 38.2) and VS 5.2.18: *kāyakarmaṇātmakarma vyākhyātam*. The usage of *ātman* in the sense of 'body' is not rare in the Upaniṣads as in *the Bṛhadāraṇyaka* 1.2.4, 7, 1.4.3, 14, etc. But the Vaiśeṣikas seem to have had some more reason of identifying *ātman* with the body, that is their early conception of body and mind formed by the help of *sva-svāmi-sambandha*.
25. J.A.B. van Buitenen, *The Bhagavadgītā in the Mahābhārata*, Chicago 1981, p. 74-76.
26. NBh defines *ātman* as omnipresent at the commentary on NS 3.2.20 (p. 206.1) and as transmigrating from body to body at NS 3.1.21, 3.2.66, 67 (pp. 170.18, 235.7, 236.8). See Nozawa (2000) p. 118.
27. *Kaṭha Upaniṣad* 2.22: *mahāntaṃ vibhum ātmānaṃ matvā. Śvetāśvatara Upaniṣad* 3.21: *sarvātmānaṃ sarvagataṃ vibhutvāt.*
28. See Ruben, Walter, *Die Nyāyasūtra's Text, Übersetzung, Erleuterung und Glossar*, Leipzig, 1928, p. 210, and Halbfass, Wilhelm, *Tradition and Reflection*, New York 1991, (Delhi, 1992), p. 313, and Bronkhorst, "Studies on Bhartṛhari, 5: Bhartṛhari and Vaiśeṣika," p. 90, and Halbfass, Wilhelm, *Karma und Wiedergeburt im indischen Denken*, Kreuzlingen, München, 2000, p. 136, and Nozawa, Masanobu, "Early Vaiśeṣika Theory of Transmigration Referred to by the Naiyāyikas," (in Japanese) *Hokkaido Journal of Indological and Buddhist Studies*, vol. 15, 2000, p. 116.

Chapter 27

The Two Types of Cognitive Process in the Vaiśeṣika Philosophy

KATSUNORI HIRANO

1. *Introduction*

Indian realism holds that the outer world is independent of cognition,[1] and that the existence of an outer object precedes the occurrence of its cognition. However, these principles do not appear to simultaneously hold true in all cognitions of the outer world in the Vaiśeṣika system whose standpoint is realism. When it is not the case that both principles simultaneously function in the cognitive process of the outer world, the Vaiśeṣikas discard the first one and devise a new process in explaining the process.

For an understanding of this process it is necessary to see how the Vaiśeṣikas analyze the object of cognition and how cognition takes place. In Vaiśeṣika the object of cognition is analyzed into three elements: a property (*dharma*), its property-possessor or substratum (*dharmin*), and the relation (*saṃbandha*) between the property and the property-possessor. To take an example, when there is a blue pot, the blue color (*nīlarūpa*) is called the property; the pot, the property-possessor; inherence (*samavāya*) between the blue color and the pot, the relation.

When we focus on the property in these three elements, we can assume the two types of the Vaiśeṣikā's cognitive process. The first type is a process through which cognition-independent property is grasped. For instance, in the cognition "this is a pot", potness (*ghaṭasāmānya* or *ghaṭatva*), which exists independently of the subject of the recognizer, is grasped. The second type is a process through which a property "produced" by the subject of the recognizer, a cognition-dependent property, is grasped. To give an example, in the cognition "there are two things", number two (*dvitva*), which is included in the category of quality (*guṇa*) and exists dependently upon the subject of the recognizer, is grasped. Thus, in the former case the property is grasped, while in the latter case the property is "produced" and grasped. In fact, such a distinction of those cognitive processes is not always clearly made in the Vaiśeṣika works.

This paper aims to point out that the number of cognition-dependent properties increases in the course of the early Vaiśeṣika period and trace the development of the Vaiśeṣika thought. For this task I have mainly utilized the *Padārthadharmasaṃgraha* (*PDhS*) or *Praśastapādabhāṣya* by Praśastapāda (ca. 550-600)[2], the *Vyomavatī* (*Vy*) by Vyomaśiva (ca. 900-960), the *Nyāyakandalī* by Śrīdhara (ca. 950-1000), and the *Kiraṇāvalī* by Udayana (ca. 1050-1100).

2. *Cognition-Dependent Properties*

The Vaiśeṣika school enumerates twenty-four kinds of quality,[3] which is the second of the six categories (*padārtha*) this school lists, and among them number (*saṃkhyā*), otherness (*pṛthaktva*), remoteness (*paratva*), and proximity (*aparatva*) are considered to be cognition-dependent qualities.[4] Praśastapāda gives the following brief description of them:

> Remoteness, proximity, number two, two-otherness, and so forth (*ādi*) are based on cognition (*buddhyapekṣa*).[5]

The term '*buddhyapekṣa*' (based on cognition)[6] indicates remoteness etc. are cognition-dependent qualities. Let us now look at the commentaries on the *PDhS*, which are the *Vy*, the *Nyāyakandalī*, and the *Kiraṇāvalī* for an understanding of the *PDhS's* passage quoted above. Vyomaśiva states the following in regards to the *PDhS*:

> Remoteness, proximity, number two, two-otherness, and so forth have need of cognition when they come into existence, and hence [Praśastapāda says:] "based on cognition" (*buddhyapekṣa*). The words "so forth" [in the *PDhS*] refers to other levels of number and otherness which both go from three to '100000 billion'. Then it is determined that they (remoteness and so forth) are always based on cognition; in this way, they are the very [qualities] based on cognition. Without cognition, [remoteness, etc.] do not come into existence.[7]

Śrīdhara interprets the *PDhS*'s passage the same as follows:

> The instrumental cause is cognition in the case where they (remoteness, etc.) come into existence. By the words "so forth" [in the *PDhS*], number three, three-otherness and so on is comprehended.[8]

Udayana likewise interprets it as follows:

> [The words in the *PDhS*] "based on cognition" mean that [remoteness, etc.] are produced by cognition as instrumental cause.[9] By the words "so forth" [in the *PDhS*], number three, three-otherness, and so on is understood, . . .[10]

From the interpretation of the above commentaries on the *PDhS* we can see that the added cognition-dependent qualities which Praśastapāda does not state definitely in the *PDhS*, in other words, the word '*ādi*' (so forth) in the *PDhS* refer to number and otherness, ranked from three on up. Furthermore, we notice that '*buddhi*' (cognition) in the term '*buddhyapekṣa*' is regarded as the instrumental cause (*nimittakāraṇa*) for the origination of cognition-dependent qualities. That is to say,[11] in the cognition "object *a* is farther than object *b* from me (the recognizer)", cognition as an instrumental cause is necessary for the origination of remoteness in object *a*.

It must, however, be noted that the cognition-dependent qualities do not exist in the mind but in the outer world, although the subject of the recognizer "produces" them. The reason for this is as follows: the philosophical standpoint of the Vaiśeṣika School is realism, so that any kind of property, which is grasped through either type of cognitive processes, exists in the outer world or has external realities.[12]

3. *The Two Types of Cognitive Process in the Vyomavatī*

The *Vy* is the oldest available commentary on the *PDhS.* When one recognizes that "a man is a cook", the two instrumental causes of this cognition are remarked in the *Vy*:

> The instrumental [cause] is the act of cooking or knowledge of that [act of cooking] with regards to the cognition "[a man is] a cook", since the cognition (or expression)[13] "[a man is] a cook" would occur [in the recognizer for the man] even in the case of the man, who cooks, ceasing the act of cooking.[14]

Of these two instrumental causes of the cognition "a man is a cook" in the above quotation, the first one is the act of cooking (*pacikriyā*), which belongs under the category of motion (*karman*), the third of the six categories in the Vaiśeṣika school. Now, suppose a man is cooking. The Vaiśeṣika authors interpret that the man possesses 'the act of cooking'. Then, depending upon the act of cooking which functions as an instrumental cause, the recognizer understands that the man is a cook. In this case, the property, which the recognizer grasps in the man (the property-possessor), is the act of cooking, and is a cognition-independent property in the sense that the subject of the recognizer does not "produce" it. Therefore, the cognition is of the same type as cognition "this is a pot", because, as I said earlier, potness (*ghaṭatva*), which is a cognition-independent property, is grasped in this cognitive process.

The second instrumental cause is knowledge (*abhijñatā*). Suppose that man, who is a cook, interrupts the action of cooking. In other words, the man does not have the act of cooking. Due to the instrumental cause, which is the knowledge "the man did cook once", the recognizer still has the cognition "the man is a cook". With regards to this cognition, the recognizer "produces" the property in the man who did cook, and grasps it. Therefore, it can be said that the cognition based on knowledge is of the same type as cognition "there are two things", because, as we have seen, number two (*dvitva*), which is a cognition-dependent property, is grasped in this cognitive process.

In the case of the second instrumental cause, Vyomaśiva does not state what kind of property is produced in the man, but we can say that the property is cookness (*pācakatva*), since the cognition "the man is a cook" occurs in the recognizer. In this case the "produced" property in the man cannot be the act of cooking. If it is so, the man must be actually cooking at the time the recognizer perceives him. Turning now to cookness, it is not a universal (*sāmānya, jāti*) but an imposed property (*upādhi*) in the later Vaiśeṣika thought.[15] There is no textual evidence to provide an answer whether Vyomaśiva makes a difference between universals and imposed properties. However, if the eternity (*nityatva*), which is one part of the definition of universal in the *Vy*,[16] is taken into consideration, we can say that Vyomaśiva does not regard cookness as universal, since cookness, according to the later Vaiśeṣika, is temporary. Thus, Vyomaśiva introduced the second type of cognitive process into the explanation of the cognition "the man is a cook" and added the new property, which seems to be cookness, to the list of the cognition-dependent properties that Praśastapāda had mentioned.

4. *The Views of Other Schools*

With regards to the cause of the cognition "a man is a cook", there are conflicts between Vaiśeṣika and Buddhism such as the Yogācāra and Mādhyamika schools. The conflicts seem to be caused by the different standpoints in how cognition and the outer world correlate to each other. Briefly speaking, the Vaiśeṣika standpoint is realism, which regards the outer world as existing independently of cognition. On the other hand, the Buddhist standpoint is nominalism, which regards it as a mere mental construction.[17] On such opposite standpoints, the Buddhists argue against the causes, which Vaiśeṣika asserts, of the cognition "a man is a cook". For example, in the *Pramāṇavārttika* by Dharmakīrti (ca. 640) and his commentary on it, the *Pramāṇavārttikasvavṛtti*, he introduces the opinion of the Vaiśeṣikas that "both (expression and cognition) occur from the instrumental cause [being an act] in the past or future"[18], and counters:

> The act which does not exist, is not the instrumental [cause] of cognition and expression, because [even if] having no cause, both [cognition and word] would occur.[19]

The *Tattvasaṃgraha* by Śāntarakṣita (ca. 750) provides another illustration of the same point.

> If [you the Vaiśeṣikas] said that the cognition and expression ["a man is a cook"] occur for them (the cooks) from the instrumental cause being the act in the past or future, [we reply] that (the act in the past or future) is not the cause, because it has not existed.[20]

The point of issue in the above objections can be summarized: the act of cooking in the past and future cannot be the instrumental cause of the present cognition and expression ("a man is a cook") on the ground that it has already disappeared in the man. Comparing these Buddhist views with Vyomaśiva's of the instrumental cause, we notice that his opinion describes *the knowledge* of the act in the past—not the act itself in the past—as the instrumental cause of the cognition. Let us then consider the gap in their opinions from a historical perspective.

The objections were addressed around the seventh and eighth centuries, and this period falls between Praśastapāda (the sixth cent.) and Vyomaśiva (the ninth or tenth cent.). This historical fact leads us to the assumption that the Vaiśeṣikas could not form the theory for replying to the above objections at that time, although the second type of cognitive process had already been acknowledged.[21] But in the ninth or tenth century, Vyomaśiva, in fact, put forward the new property to settle the objections, making the use of the second type of cognitive process. Here we can point out the contribution of Vyomaśiva toward the Vaiśeṣika thought: by applying the second type of cognitive process, Vyomaśiva defends the school principle, "every cognition must have a counterpart in the external world".[22]

5. *Conclusion*

In the Vaiśeṣika tradition there are two types of cognitive processes: the first type is a process through which cognition-independent property is grasped; the second is a process through which cognition-dependent property is grasped. With regards to the cognition-dependent property, Praśastapāda described the corresponding qualities (remoteness, etc.) with the term '*buddhyapekṣa*' (based on cognition) in the *PDhS.* Vyomaśiva made reference to the two types of cognitive processes in the *Vy* as to the cognition "a man is a cook". With respect to the second type of cognitive process, he introduced it for the reason why the cognition "a man is a cook" occurs for the man who cooked once but does not cook now. For this problem, which the Buddhists criticized, he furnished the knowledge "the man did cook once" as instrumental cause. This knowledge corresponds to '*buddhi*' in the term of '*buddhyapekṣa*'. By the '*buddhi*', the property, which seems to be *pācakatva*, is "produced" in the man. Having no definite reference in the *Vy* to what kind of the cognitive-dependent property Vy omaśiva bore in mind in this case, we conclude that Vyomaśiva accepted a new cognitive-dependent property, which Praśastapāda did not mention.

In the Vaiśeṣika school, an increase of the cognitive-dependent property or the wider applying the second type of cognitive process is the unavoidable result of holding realism against Buddhist nominalism. The Vaiśeṣikas had to point out the property in the outer world which property correlates with the cognition in order to maintain their realist standpoint. The significance of the Vyomaśiva's description can be understood as one progress in this stream of the Vaiśeṣika thought.

NOTES

1. On the concept of 'realism', see Stephen H. Phillips, *Classical Indian Metaphysics,* 1st Indian ed., Motilal Banarsidass, Delhi, 1997 (1996), p. 1; Toshihiro Wada, "The Action of the Subject towards the Outer World in Indian Realism", *Concepts of Knowledge: East and West,* Ramakrishna Mission Institute of Culture, Calcutta, 2000, pp. 310-311.
2. The dates of authors referred to in this paper are based on the book: K.H. Potter (ed.), *Encyclopedia of Indian Philosophies, Vol. I, Bibliography,* 3rd revised ed., Delhi, Motilal Banarsidass, 1995 (1970); K.H. Potter (ed.), *Encyclopedia of Indian Philosophy, Vol. II, Indian Metaphysics and Epistemology: The Tradition of Nyāya-Vaiśeṣika up to Gaṅgeśa,* Reprint, Motilal Banarsidass, Delhi, 1995 (1977), pp. 9-12.
3. The number of quality is different between Kaṇāda and Praśastapāda. According to Kaṇāda, who is the author of the *Vaiśeṣikasūtra,* it is seventeen. In contrast, Praśastapāda enumerates twenty-four qualities. The added seven qualities in the *PDhS* are heaviness (*gurutva*), fluidity (*dravatva*), viscidity (*sneha*), mental impression (*saṃskāra*), merit (*dharma*), demerit (*adharma*), and sound (*śabda*).
4. Shastri divides twenty-four qualities as either subjective and objective, and regards remoteness, proximity, number two etc. as subjective qualities depending on whether the quality has a subjective origin or not, and generated in thought or not. See Dharmendra Nath Shastri, *The Philosophy of Nyāya-Vaiśeṣika and its Conflict with The Buddhist Dignāga School: Critique of Indian Realism,* Reprint, Bharatiya Vidya Prakashan, New Delhi, 1976 (1964), pp. 287-295.

5. *Padārthadharmasaṃgraha* (in *Word Index to the Praśastapādabhāṣya edited with a Complete Word Index to the Printed Editions of Praśastapādabhāṣya* ed. by Johannes Bronkhorst & Yves Ramseier, Motilal Banarsidass, Delhi, 1994), p. 19, no.100: *paratvāparatvadvitvadvipṛthaktvādayo buddhyapekṣāh.*
6. Miyamoto interprets the compound '*buddhyapekṣa*', which is translated as 'based on cognition' in this paper, with reference to the usage of the term '*apekṣābuddhi*'. See Keiichi Miyamoto, *The Metaphysics and Epistemology of the Early Vaiśeṣikas,* Bhandarkar Oriental Research Institute, Pune, 1996, pp.78-84.
7. *Vyomavatī* (in *Vyomavatī of Vyomaśiva* ed. by Gaurinath Sastri, 2 vols., Sampurnanand Sanskrit University, Varanasi, 1983, 1984), vol. II, pp. 8, 25-9, 2: *paratvāparatvadvitvadvipṛthaktvādayaḥ buddhim apekṣante svotpattāv iti buddhyapekṣā iti. ādipadena tritvādikā parārdhāntā saṃkhyā tadavacchinnañ ca pṛthaktvaṃ gṛhyate. avaghāraṇan [avadhāraṇan] tu eta eva buddhyapekṣās tathaite buddhyapekṣā eva. buddhiṃ vinā na bhavantīti. avaghāraṇan* should be corrected to *avadhāraṇan* in accordance with *Vyomavatī* [*A*]. See *Vyomavatī* [*A*] (in *Praśastapādabhāṣyam of Praśasta with commentaries (up to Dravya) Sūktī by Jagadīśa Tarkālaṅkāra Setu by Padmanābha Miśra and Vyomavatī by Vyomaśiva (to the end)* ed. by Gopīnath Kavirāj and Panditraj Dhundhirāj Shāstri, 2nd ed., Chaukhamba Amarabharati Prakashan, Varanasi, 1983), p. 435,22.
8. *Nyāyakandalī* (in *The Praśastapāda Bhāshya with Commentary Nyāyakandalī of Śrīdhara* ed. by V.P. Dvivedin, Sri Satguru Publications, Delhi, 1984), p. 99,12-13: *eṣām utpattau nimittakāraṇaṃ buddhih. ādiśabdāt tritvatripṛthaktvādi–parigrahaḥ.*
9. On the meaning of the term '*apekṣābuddhi*' (cognition as instrument), see Miyamoto, *The Metaphysics and Epistemology of the Early Vaiśeṣikas,* pp. 78-84.
10. *Kiraṇāvalī* (in *Praśastapādabhāṣyam with the Commentary Kiraṇāvalī of Udayana* ed. by J.S. Jetly, 2nd ed., Oriental Institute, Vadodara, 1991), p. 108,23-24: *buddhyapekāḥ apekṣābuddhijanyā ity arthaḥ. ādigrahaṇāt tritvatripṛthaktvādayo grāhyāḥ, ...*
11. For more details of the origination of remoteness, see Miyamoto, *The Metaphysics and Epistemology of the Early Vaiśeṣikas,* pp. 79-82.
12. Of the characters of the Vaiśeṣika realism, as Murakami and Wada point out, there are some cases where nominalistic views are maintained. See Shinkan Murakami, *Indo no Jitsuzairon* (*Realistic Epistemology of Indian Philosophy*), Heirakuji Shoten, Kyoto, 1997, pp. 71-114; Wada, "The Action of the Subject towards the Outer World in Indian Realism", p. 315.
13. On the meaning of the term '*vyavahāra*', see Miyamoto, *The Metaphysics and Epistemology of the Early Vaiśeṣikas,* p. 59.
14. *Vyomavatī*, vol. II, p. 279, 5-7: *pācaka iti jñāne pacikriyā nimittam, tadabhijñatā vā, tatsadbhāve kriyoparame 'pi pācaka iti vyavahārāt.*
15. On the distinction between universals and imposed properties, see Raja Ram Dravid, *The Problem of Universals in Indian philosophy,* Motilal Banarsidass, Delhi/Patna/Varanasi, 1972, pp. 25-33; Shastri, *The Philosophy of Nyāya-Vaiśeṣika and its Conflict with The Buddhist Dignāga School: Critique of Indian Realism,* pp. 320-321; Musashi Tachikawa, *The Structure of the World in Udayana's Realism,* D. Reidel Publishing Company, Dordrecht, 1981, pp. 37-38.

16. On the definition of universals in the *Vy*, see Katsunori Hirano, "Vyomavatī niokeru Huhen no Teigi" (The definition of Universal in the *Vyomavatī*), *Tokai-Bukkyo* 43, pp. 75-88. Vyomaśiva defines universals as "universal is eternal, one, and inherent in many things". *Vyomavatī*, vol. II, p. 275, 3-4: ...*sāmānyasva* [*sāmānyasya*] *nityatvaikatve saty anekavṛttitvalakṣaṇātvāt.* The word '*sāmānyasva*' should be corrected to '*sāmānyasya*', since *Vyomavatī* [*A*] (p. 684,19) reads "*sāmānyasya*".
17. On the concepts of 'realism' and 'nominalism' (Phillips adopts the term 'idealism') in Indian philosophy, see Stephen H. Phillips, *Classical Indian Metaphysics*, p. 1; Wada, "The Action of the Subject towards the Outer World in Indian Realism", pp. 310-312.
18. *Pramāṇavārttika* (in *The Pramāṇavārttikam of Dharmakīrti with the first Chapter with the Autocommentary*, ed. by Raniero Gnoli, Instituto Italiano Per I/ Medio Ed Estremo Oriente, Roma, 1960), p. 80,16-17: *atītam anāgataṃ vā nimittikṛtya tayoḥ pravṛttir iti cet.*
19. *Pramāṇavārttika*, p. 80,18-20: *karmāpi nāsaj jñānābhidhānayoḥ / nimittam/ tayoḥ anaimittikatāpatteḥ* (k. 159 abc)
20. *Tattvasaṃgraha* (in *Tattvasaṅgraha of Śāntarakṣita with the commentary of Kamalaśīla* ed. by Embar Krishna, 2 vols., Reprint, Oriental Institute, Baroda, 1984, 1988), vol. I, p. 247, 5-6: *atītānāgataṃ karma nimittikṛtya teṣu cet / pācakādiṣu dhīśabdau, tanna hetur asattvataḥ* //(k. 754)
21. The term *apekṣābuddhi*, which is concerned with the second type of cognitive process to a great deal, is not used in the *Vaiśeṣikasūtra;* but the term is used in the *Daśapadārthī* and the *PDhS*. See Miyamoto, *The Metaphysics and Epistemology of the Early Vaiśeṣikas*, p. 78.
22. Shastri, *The Philosophy of Nyāya-Vaiśeṣika and its Conflict with The Buddhist Dignāga School: Critique of Indian Realism*, p. 293.

CHAPTER 28

Treatment of Natural Property and Contextual Property in *Navya-nyāya*

V. N. JHA

We all know that the *Navya Nyāya* Language was created out of a necessity to develop a medium of precise communication when it was realized through a long period of the close analytic and philosophical dialogue among various systems of Indian Philosophy that more natural the language of communication is, there arise more chances of ambiguity. The emergence of the definition of *pramāṇa* as *pramā–karaṇam pramāṇam* in the hands of Vācaspati Miśra in his *Nyāyabhāṣya-vārttika-tātparya ṭīkā* by substituting *upalabdhi* and *sādhana* in Vātsyāyana's statement *upalabdhi-sādhanam pramāṇam* (on *Gautamasūtra* 1.1.1) may be one of the ideal examples demonstrating such a necessity.

It does not matter whether one is an idealist or a realist or a materialist. All can sit around a table and take part in a discourse.

What is absolutely necessary to make the discourse meaningful is to use such a medium of dialogue as could be easily understood by all the participants in the discourse. It was soon realized that the use of ordinary Sanskrit language often resulted into ambiguity and thereby into misunderstanding. The tradition realized, therefore, a need to create a medium of precise communication. The *Nyāya-Vaiśeṣika* realists took the lead in this job and the result was the development of a language of precise philosophical communication and that language is the *Navya Nyāya* language.

The question that comes to our mind is how could the Nyāya-Vaiśeṣika Philosophers create such a language?

If we pay close attention to the texts written in *Navya Nyāya* Language we can observe that the authors of the texts are engaged in disambiguating the statements through a set of concepts through delimitations. Some such prominent concepts are *dharma* 'property', *dharmin* 'possessor of property', *sambandha* 'relation', *avacchedaka* 'delimitor' and *avacchinna* 'delimited'.

In this paper I would like to point out to a very fundamental and innovative contribution of the *Nyāya-Vaiśeṣika* System namely, the classification of *dharma* into *Svābhāvika* or natural and an *āgantuka* or contextual.[1]

It was observed that the world of our experience is what is presented by language (*padārtha*). Its acceptance or denial can be made only after it is presented in language. There is no other way to get access to the world of name and form. It is language that makes public the world of everyone's experience. Once the world is made public a speaker can speak about the world of his experience and the hearer can understand that and there can be rapport, or otherwise, between them.

Next question in order was; how could this world be named? The *Naiyāyikas* applied the principle of identifying the *pravṛttinimitta* (ground for application of a linguistic term) for naming the locus of that *pravṛttinimitta*. The entire world of form and name (*nāma-rūpa*) appeared before the Nyāya-Vaiśeṣikas with the following structure:

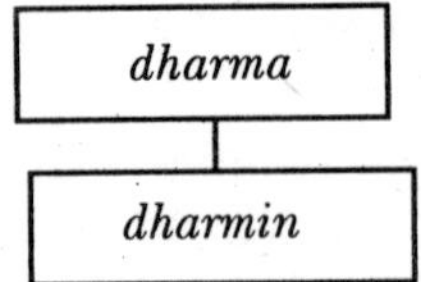

It was decided to name a *dharmin* through its *dharma*. Thus a pot was named as pot through its potness (*ghaṭatva*), *pṛthivī* was called so through its property namely, *pṛthivitva* (earthness), a *dravya* as *dravya* through *dravyatva* and so on. The whole world (*padārtha*) was named as such through *padārthatva*. The *dharmas* such as *ghaṭatva, pṛthivitva, dravyatva* and *padārthatva* are called *pravṛttinimittas* for the application of the terms *ghaṭa, pṛthivī dravya* and *padārtha* respectively. Thus, a *dharmin* was designated through its *dharma* and since the entire world of name and form reflected its structure of *dharma-dharmi-bhāva*, the whole world could be named through this method. To be precise, the *Nyāya-Vaiśeṣikas* discovered that human beings have designated this world through the process discussed above.

They further observed that the *dharmas* or *the pravṛtti-nimitta-s* through which their loci are designated are of two types — (i) *svābhāvika* or natural and (ii) *āgantuka* or contextual. For instance, *manuṣyatva* in *manuṣya* is a natural *dharma* or property whereas when that man will be designated as a teacher it will imply that a *dharma* namely, teacherness (*gurutva*) is produced in that man when he started teaching students and in this way *gurutva* can be called a contextual property. In the same manner, *ghaṭatva* is a natural property, but *pratiyogitā* in that *ghaṭa* will be born in the context of its absence and hence it will be a contextual or acquired or situational property. The same *ghaṭa* will acquire a property called *viṣayatā* when it will be an object or *ghaṭa-jñāna*. Similarly when one will start inferring *ghaṭa* it will acquire a property called *anumeyatā* in it. In the same way, when the potter is going to produce the *ghaṭa* as an effect it will have *kāryatā* in it. In this way, the *ghaṭa* can have different properties at different contexts or situations. But a *ghaṭa* will always have *ghaṭatva*. Thus, *ghaṭva* is a *svābhāvika-dharma* and *pratiyogitā, viṣayatā anumeyatā* and *kāryatā* are the contextual properties.

Another fact needs our attention. Since *pratiyogitā* is produced in *ghaṭa* in the context of *abhāva* it requires to be assumed that there is a relationship between *pratiyogitā* of *ghaṭa* and *abhāva* of *ghaṭa*. The *abhāva* of *ghaṭa* is the describer (*nirūpaka*) of the *pratiyogitā* of *ghaṭa*. Thus, it is necessary to assume that as *ghaṭa* has acquired a contextual property called *pratiyogitā* so also *abhāva* of *ghaṭa* has acquired a contextual property called *anuyogitā* in terms of its relation. Not only that; when we say that *abhāva* is the *nirūpaka* of the *pratiyogitā* in *ghaṭa*, it implies that *abhāva* has also acquired the property of *nirūpakata* in it and a contextual property called *nirūpitatā* is produced in *pratiyogitā* since we have said that this *pratiyogitā* is described (*nirūpita*) by the *abhāva*.

Thus, in the case of a contextual property we find pair terms such as :

(a) *kārya* – *kāraṇa*
(b) *sādhya* – *sādhana*
(c) *pratiyogin* – *anuyogin*
(d) *nirūpya* – *nirūpaka*
(e) *viṣaya* – *viṣayin*
(f) *prakāra* – *prakārin*
(g) *viśeṣya* – *viśeṣaṇa*
(h) *avacchedya* – *avacchedaka*

and so on and so forth.

Here in (a) the contextual properties are *Kāryatā* and *Kāraṇatā*:
in (b) they are *sādhyatā* and *sādhanatā*;
in (c) they are *pratiyogitā* and *anuyogitā*;
in (d) they are *nirūpyatā* and *nirūpakatā*;
in (e) they are *viṣayatā* and *viṣayitā*;
in (f) they are *prakāratā* and *prakāritā*;
in (g) they are *viśeṣyatā* and *viśeṣaṇatā*[2]; and
in (h) they are *avacchedyatā* and *avacchedakatā*[2].

Through these contextual properties their loci are designated. Thus, the locus of *kāryatā* is designated as *kārya* and the locus of *kāraṇatā* is designated as *kāraṇa*. In the same manner. in the remaining pairs also the terms are designated through the respective contextual properties produced in them.

It may be noted that these terms occur in pair because the contextual properties mutually describe each other.

After having described this fact, the *Nyāya-Vaiśeṣika* philosophers turned to identify another very important point. They observed that mostly an ambiguity occurs in the context of a contextual property. For instance, if it is a case that *agni* (fire) is produced from *tṛṇa* (grass), *araṇi* (wood) and *maṇi* (stone), there arises a case of ambiguity about the locus of the contextual property called *kāraṇatā* in this case. Whether the locus is *tṛṇa* or *araṇi* or *maṇi* needs to be specified to remove the ambiguity.[3] In this way in all cases of contextual properties it was felt necessary to specify the exact loci of these properties in order to make the statements in which they occur free from possible ambiguity. This was achieved by employing the concept of delimitation (*avacchedaka*) by *deśa* (space), *kāla* (time), *dharma* (property) and *sambandha* (relation).

Now the question was: which *dharma* should be employed as a delimitor? The attempt to answer this question must have guided the Indian logicians to classify *dharma* or properties into natural properties and contextual properties. Thus, if *agni* is produced from *tṛṇa*, the contextual property namely, *kāraṇatā* in *tṛṇa* is delimited by *tṛṇatva* of *tṛṇa* which is a natural property. In this way, the locus of *kāraṇatā* can be specified as *araṇi* or *maṇi* through the delimiting *dharma* such as *araṇitva* or *maṇitva* respectively.

Similarly, when one wants to specify the locus, *ādheyatā* in *ghaṭa* on the ground he can do so by delimiting it by the natural property namely, *ghaṭatva*. This is how we paraphrase the expression *ghaṭavad bhūtalaṃ* 'ground possessed of a pot' as *ghaṭatva-avacchinna-ādheyatā-nirūpita-ādhāratā-vat bhūtalaṃ* 'the ground possesses *ādhāratā* which is described by the *ādheyatā* in *ghaṭa* which is delimited by *ghaṭatva*'. This is how by paraphrasing the expression we specified the reality—referred to by that expression. This is how step-by-step the *Navya Nyāya* Language was created.

Let us take now the expression *bhūtale ghaṭo na* 'There is no pot on the ground' and try to expand the part *'ghaṭo na'* in the *Navya Nyāya* Language.

Bhūtale ghaṭo na

= *bhūtala-niṣṭha-ādhāratā-nirūpita-ādheyatāvān ghaṭābhāvaḥ*

Here, *ghaṭābhāvaḥ* is a paraphrase of *ghaṭo na*. Now, let us expand it to specify the reality referred to by the speaker through this expression.

ghaṭa-abhāva 'the absence of pot'

= *ghaṭa-pratiyogika-abhāva* 'the absence the counter-positive of which is pot'

= *ghaṭa-niṣṭha-pratiyogitā-nirūpaka-abhāva* 'the absence which describes the *pratiyogitā* existing in pot'

= *ghaṭatva-avacchinna-ghaṭa-niṣṭha-pratiyogitā-nirūpaka-abhāva* 'the absence which describes the *pratiyogitā* existing in pot which is delimited by '*ghaṭatva*'.'

This is how we have specified the locus of the contextual property such as *pratiyogitā* by delimiting it by the natural property such as *ghaṭatva.* Now we understand that the speaker is talking about the absence of pot only and not of anything else.

In the same way the remaining ambiguity can be removed by delimiting the *pratiyogitā* further by a specific relation like *saṃyoga* (contact) in which case it will become further clear that the speaker is talking about the absence of pot on the ground by denying its contact with ground. This is how *Navya-nyāya* Language was created to disambiguate a statement through paraphrasing, leading to the specification of the expressed reality. I shall not elaborate it further here.

The point that I wanted to make in this paper is only this that the *Navya Naiyāyikas* classified *dharmas* into two sets namely, *svābhāvika-dharmas* (natural properties) and *āgantuka-dharma-s* (acquired or contextual or situational properties) in order to create a language of precise communication which facilitated the precise philosophical discourse.

This classification does not come on the way of traditional classification. According to the traditional classification a *dharma* is either a *jāti* or an *upādhi.* In the classification presented above I have included *jāti* in 'natural property'. Not only that I have included properties like *akāśatva, kālatva* etc. under 'natural property'. Thus, we can re-classify the *dharmas* as follows:

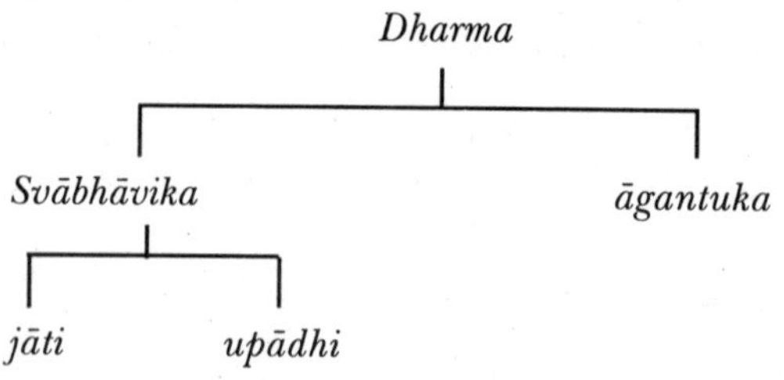

An *upādhi* can be distinguished from an *āgantuka-dharma* in the sense that an *upādhi* like ākāśatva is not derived out of a pair term whereas an *āgantuka dharma* is always derived out of a pair term like *ādhāra-ādheya, pratiyogin-anuyogin* and so on. The traditional classification can be understood as follows:

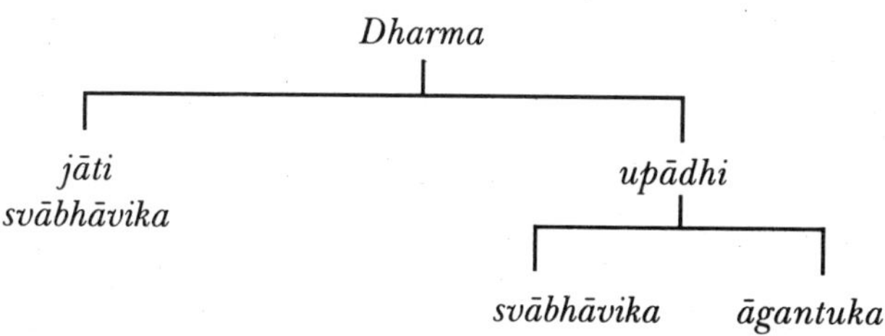

We have already seen that we need a *pravṛtti-nimitta* to name a *dharmin.* As *ghaṭatva* is a *pravṛttinimitta* for naming a *ghaṭa* and *akāśatva* is a *pravṛttinimitta* to name *ākāśa* so also *ādhāratā* or *ādheyatā* will function as a *pravṛttinimitta* for application of the term *ādhāra* or *ādheya.* Thus, any *dharma* or property can function as a ground for application of a linguistic term.

In a wider sense any entity can be a *dharma.* For instance, a *ghaṭa* can be called a *dharma* of *bhūtala* in the expression *ghaṭavat bhūtalaṃ.* Here too *ghaṭa* functions, in a way, like a *pravṛtti-nimitta* for the term *ghaṭatva,* although *ghaṭa* will be an *upādhi*[4], in this case.

Thus, the classification of *dharmas* presented in this paper does not disturb the traditional classification; rather it provides better understanding of the same.

NOTES

1. When this classification occurred to my mind I was using the term 'inherent' for 'natural' property. But since this term may create confusion in the case of properties like *ākāśatva, kālatva* etc. which do not exist by inherence, I am using the term 'natural' or *svābhāvika* for them. For earlier usage see *Viṣayatāvāda* of *Harirāma* Ed. and Tr. by V.N. Jha, CASS Publication, Class C, No. 16, University of Pune, 1987, pp. xvii–xxix.
2. For more details see *Viṣayatāvāda,* ibid. pp. xvii-xxvii.
3. The tradition accepted *phalavaijātya* by postulating $agni_1$, $agni_2$ and $agni_3$ and so on in order to avoid *kārya-kāraṇa-bhāva-vyabhicāra.*

4. The text *Navya-Nyāya-bhāṣāpradīpa* of *Mahesh Chandra Nyāyaratna* does use the term *dharma* in this wider sense and classified *dharma* as *Jāti* and *upādhi.* Whatever is inexhaustible in terms of its features is a *Jāti* and whatever could be expressed in terms of certain features is an *upādhi.* In this analysis even a *ghaṭa* can be an *upādhi* in certain situation since one can express *ghaṭa* as *ghaṭva-āśraya.* But listing of features of *ghaṭatva* is impossible and hence *ghaṭava* is a *jāti.*

CHAPTER 29

The Origin of Navya-nyāya and Its Place within the History of Indian Logic

TOSHIHIRO WADA

1. *Introduction*

'Navya-nyāya' is the name given to the new school of Nyāya, which preserved the traditions of both the Nyāya and Vaiśeṣika schools. Gaṅgeśa, who lived in the 14th century, is regarded as the representative philosopher of this school, though there are various views on who was the founder of this school. This question is inextricably linked to the question of what are the distinctive features of Navya-nyāya. Without taking these features into account, we cannot find the answer to the question of who was the founder. Therefore, I have devoted some amount of space in the present paper to a discussion of the features of Navya-nyāya's analytical method.

The term Nyāya, which means 'logic', also refers to a philosophical system which is concerned not only with the study of formal inference-patterns but also with the theory of how to get true cognition (*pramā*). In other words, Indian logic deals with both logical and epistemological issues.[1] The means of getting true cognition is called a *pramāṇa,* and the number of *pramāṇas* differs according to the various schools of Indian philosophy;

the Nyāya school recognizes all four *pramāṇas*. The term Nyāya can also refer specifically to the theory of inference, or *anumāna*, which is one of the four *pramāṇas*.

Keeping in mind the meaning of Nyāya as a system concerned with both logical and epistemological issues, we will first look at past research on the historical divisions of Indian logic and see how Navya-nyāya, or the New Logic, fits into these divisions. Then, we will look at past research on the question of who was the founder of Navya-nyāya. We will refer to the features of the Navya-nyāya method of analysis briefly, since I examined them somewhere else.[2] Finally I will conclude that Navya-nyāya originated with Udayana, who lived in the 11th century, and not with Gaṅgeśa.

2. *The Historical Divisions of Indian Logic*

It is commonly said that the final stage of Indian logic is Navya-nyāya, or the New Logic. Research on the historical divisions of Indian logic began with Satish Chandra Vidyabhusana's *History of Mediaeval School of Indian Logic* (1977 [1909], pp. xvii-xviii).[3] He presents three divisions: the Ancient School of Logic (600 B.C.-400 A.D.), the Mediaeval School of Logic (400 A.D.–1200 A.D.), and the Modern School of Logic (1200 A.D.–1850 A.D.). He says that the Mediaeval School originated with Dignāga, and the Modern School with Gaṅgeśa;[4] the foremost text of the first school is the *Nyāyasūtra* (3rd-4th centuries A.D.) by Akṣapāda, the representative work of the second is the *Pramāṇasamuccaya* by Dignāga (*ca.* 480-540), and the main text of the third is the *Tattvacintāmaṇi* (*TC*) by Gaṅgeśa (14th c.). Vidyabhusana does not discuss the first and second schools in detail, which follows from the title of his book. Vidyabhusana's *A History of Indian Logic* (1921, pp. xiii, 157-158, 401-404)[5] sets forth the same divisions as his *History of Mediaeval School of Indian Logic,* but modifies the beginning date of the Ancient School of Logic from 600 B.C. to 650 B.C., and the beginning date of the Modern School of Logic from 1200 A.D. to 900 A.D.

Ganganath Jha's *Sāḍholāl Lectures on Nyāya*(1994[1912-1916], p. 20)[6] presents three similar divisions: the Old Nyāya (logic) School[7] (*prācīna*) represented by Gautama and his commentators, the Medieval Nyāya School (*madhyama*) represented by the

Jaina and Buddhist authors, who confine their attention to the means of knowing (*pramāṇa*) but who do not investigate the verbal accuracy of its definition (*lakṣaṇa*), and the Modern Nyāya School (*navya*), which deals mainly with the means of knowing and its definition. Unlike Vidyabhusana, Jha does not provide a specific time frame for these divisions. He acknowledges that there is some overlapping between the Old and Medieval periods.

Janaki Vallabha Bhattacharyya's "Navya-Nyāya" (1975[1937?/1953], pp. 125-126)[8] refers not only to Vidyabhusana and Jha but also to Arthur B. Keith and Sarvepalli Radhakrishnan, J. Bhattacharyya, like Jha, acknowledges the general problem of overlapping of the periods, but he in the main follows Jha's divisions.[9] C. Goekoop's *The Logic of Invariable Concomitance in the Tattvacintāmaṇi* (1967, p. vii)[10] proposes three divisions: old Nyāya, Buddhist logic, and new Nyāya. Goekoop does not mention when and with whom New-Nyāya began but simply says that the principal text of the third period is the *TC* of Gaṅgeśa.[11]

The differences between Jha's and Vidyabhusana's classifications do not seem to be that great. Both Jha and Vidyabhusana designate the three historical divisions by the particular school of logic that existed during that period. This kind of designation obscures the fact that these schools overlap in time. The Old Nyāya School, used to designate the first period, in fact existed through the mediaeval period up to the advent of Navya-nyāya. Also, the Buddhist school of logic existed until about 1200 A.D., and Jaina logic continued much later than that.[12] But some scholars, such as Jha, move the beginning of the Navya-nyāya back to Udayana in the 10th century. Vidyabhusana by assigning specific dates to these divisions clarifies the divisions to some extent but does not really solve the problem of overlapping.

In the present paper, I have followed in general the classification given by Vidyabhusana and Jha, but without assigning a specific time frame. For the three divisions I have adopted Goekoop's terminology. Thus, Old Logic covers the period from the *Nyāyasūtra* to Dignāga, Buddhist Logic from Dignāga to Udayana, and New-Nyāya, or Navya-nyāya, begins with Udayana.[13] As noted before, I endorse the view that Udayana, and not Gaṅgeśa, is the originator of this school.

3. On the Question of Who is the founder of Navya-nyāya

Past research on this problem has mainly emphasized the following two differences: in Old Nyāya the basic text is the *Nyāyasūtra*, while in Navya-nyāya it is Gaṅgeśa's *TC*, and Navya-nyāya developed its own characteristic terminology. Based on these differences the prevalent view is that Gaṅgeśa is the founder of Navya-nyāya. Others maintain that Navya-nyāya originated with Udayana. In the present section we will investigate the three views on who is the founder of Navya-nyāya: (1) that it is someone unknown who lived between the time of Udayana and Gaṅgeśa, (2) Gaṅgeśa, or (3) Udayana.

The first view is held by Arthur B. Keith, Saileswar Sen, Dharmendra Nath Shastri, Dinesh Chandra Guha, Daniel H.H. Ingalls, Erich Frauwallner, Atsushi Uno, Keiichi Miyamoto, Michiko Ishitobi, John Vattanky, and so forth. Keith's *Indian Logic & Atomism* (1921 [1977], pp. 29-41)[14] states that the Nyāya and Vaiśeṣika schools were syncretized after Vācaspati Miśra (900-980), and he deliberately avoids using the term 'Navya-nyāya'. Keith says that Nyāya attains its final shape in Gaṅgeśa's *TC*,[15] but he does not describe what this shape is.[16] Saileswar Sen's *A Study on Mathurānātha's Tattva-cintāmaṇi-rahasya* (1924, pp. 5-6)[17] agrees with Keith's view on the historical relationship between Nyāya and Vaiśeṣika[18] but does not discuss who is the founder of Navya-nyāya. D.N. Shastri's *The Philosophy of Nyāya-Vaiśeṣika and its Conflict with the Buddhist Dignāga School: Critique of Indian Realism* (1976 [1964], p. 120)[19] does not deal with this question but says that in Udayana's works we find the method of subtle argumentation without much substance, which is the chief characteristic of Navya-nyāya. According to D.N. Shastri (1976 [1964], p. 121), Gaṅgeśa furnished the basis for a new methodology which made sharp and subtle distinctions in the connotations of logical terms, but Navya-nyāya made a contribution neither to the *prameya* part of the system (metaphysics) nor to the *pramāṇa-vāda* (epistemology). Shastri has on the whole a low estimate of Navya-nyāya.[20]

Guha's *Navya Nyāya System of Logic* (1968, pp. 1, 3)[21] states that the Navya-nyāya system of logic gradually flourished after Udayana and particularly at the time of Gaṅgeśa, and that it is very difficult to say when the logical treatises came to be known by the name of Navya-nyāya. Guha (1968, p. 5) points out that the outstanding features of Navya-nyāya are its extreme thoroughness of analysis and highest possible perfection. It is interestingly set forth by Guha (1968, p. 4) that the Prabhākara school of Mīmāṃsā paved the way for Gaṅgeśa's new method.[22] Ingalls' *Materials for the Study of Navya-Nyāya Logic* (1951)[23] takes the second view on the founder of Navya-nyāya, but he shifts to the present view without giving any reason in his two small writings.[24] We will see the view presented by Ingalls (1951) later. Frauwallner's *Die Lehre von der Zusätzlichen Bestimmung* (*upādhiḥ*) *in Gaṅgeśa's Tattvacintāmaṇiḥ* (1970, p. 5)[25] states that Udayana's school occupied the leading position in Nyāya for more than 200 years but was gradually superseded by the newly arising trend of Navya-nyāya. This implies that Frauwallner holds the view that Navya-nyāya originated after Udayana and before Gaṅgeśa. On who is the founder of Navya-nyāya, Frauwallner does not say anything more than this.

Uno's "Indo no ronriteki shiben" (Logical Speculation in India, 1973, pp. 119-120)[26] presents the popular view that Gaṅgeśa established Navya-nyāya but says that the trend of Navya-nyāya started before him. Uno also reports that among scholars the view prevails that Udayana founded Navya-nyāya while Gaṅgeśa organized it, which view corresponds to the third view on the founder of Navya-nyāya. Uno seems to include Dineshchandra Bhattacharya and Ingalls among those holding such a view.[27] Miyamoto and Ishitobi's "Indo ronrigaku no taikei (1)" (The System of Indian Logic, 1983, p. 211)[28] states that Navya-nyāya began during the time of Udayana and that Gaṅgeśa's *TC* exerted a great influence on later Nyāya literature. Miyamoto and Ishitobi regard Udayana as the final culmination of classical Nyāya but do not explicitly mention the relationship between Udayana and Navya-nyāya.

Vattanky's *Gaṅgeśa's Philosophy of God* (1984, pp. ix-x)[29] gives Udayana an intermediate position between classical Nyāya and Navya-nyāya, but does not say whether Navya-nyāya began with Udayana or Gaṅgeśa. However, Vattanky regards the *TC* as the basic text of Navya-nyāya and holds that this text reveals the features of the Navya-nyāya method of analysis. Vattanky does not specify what these features are but merely sums them up by saying that Navya-nyāya investigated "the nature, dimensions, and conditions of human knowledge with unparalleled rigor and exactitude."

The second view—that Gaṅgeśa is the founder of Navya-nyāya—is held by Maheśa Chandra Nyāyaratna, S.C. Vidyabhusana, Surendranath Dasgupta, Sarvepalli Radhakrishnan, Gopinath Kaviraj, Maysore Hiriyanna, J. V. Bhattacharyya, Daniel H.H. Ingalls, Jadunath Sinha, Karl H. Potter, S. Kuppuswami Sastri, Umesh Mishra, Sibajiban Bhattacharyya, Stephen H. Phillips, and so forth. Nyāyaratna's *Navyanyāya-Bhāṣāpradīpaḥ* (1973[1891?], pp. 1-3)[30] says that Navya-nyāya lays particular stress on the strict definition of technical terms and aims at ascertaining precisely the meanings of expressions in common use, and that Gaṅgeśa founded Navya-nyāya.

Vidyabhusana's *A History of Indian Logic* (1921, pp. 402-403) makes use of the term 'Tarka-śāstra' in the sense of Navya-nyāya and says that Gaṅgeśa originated Tarka-śāstra. Tarka-śāstra, according to Vidyabhusana, is characterized by the following five features: (1) discussion under the theme of the four means of valid knowledge (*pramāṇa*), i.e., perception (*pratyakṣa*), inference (*anumāna*), analogy (*upamāna*), and verbal testimony (*śabda*), (2) the adoption of the Vaiśeṣika categories, (3) hair-splitting discussion of the meaning of terms, (4) precise definition of terms, and (5) the use of technical terms[31] which makes features (3) and (4) possible. He enumerates several technical terms but does not explain why or how they represent the Tarka-śāstra method. It is interesting that he assigns the beginning of the Modern School, including Tarka-śāstra, at *ca.* 900, four centuries before Gaṅgeśa. Vidyabhusana (1921, pp. 356-357) says that between *ca.* 900 and the time of Gaṅgeśa, the manuals of logic called *prakaraṇa* were written, and their authors attempted to assimilate the six or seven Vaiśeṣika categories to the Nyāya categories of the means of valid knowledge; these authors inherited the Buddhist and Jaina tendency to discuss issues within the framework of the means of valid knowledge. Vidyabhusana (1921, p. 402) further states that such a tendency permeates Tarka-śāstra. In his opinion, Navya-nyāya, i.e., Tarka-śāstra, which represents the final stage of Indian logic, emerged during the period of Gaṅgeśa, but the Navya-nyāya tendency to give importance to the means of valid knowledge can be traced back to *ca.* 900.

Dasgupta's *A History of Indian Philosophy,* Vol. 1 (1975[1922], p. 308)[32] states that Navya-nyāya began with Gaṅgeśa, and that its main contribution lies in the development of a system of linguistic notations to specify accurately and precisely any concept or its relation with other concepts. Radhakrishnan's *Indian Philosophy,* Vol. 2 (1983[1923], pp. 41-42)[33] does not say with whom Navya-nyāya began, but says that its standard text is Gaṅgeśa's *TC.* According to him, "Navya-nyāya devotes much attention to the means of knowledge (*pramāṇa*) and the theory of definition, and indulges in scholastic subtleties, logical legerdemain, fine hair-splitting". Radhakrishnan thus describes the features of Navya-nyāya with negative connotation. Kaviraj's *Gleanings from the History and Bibliography of the Nyāya-Vaiśeṣika* (1961[1924], p. 33)[34] regards Gaṅgeśa as the starting point of Navya-nyāya. Hiriyanna's *Outline of Indian Philosophy* (1932[1983], p. 227)[35] also states that Navya-nyāya commenced with Gaṅgeśa, and that one of its chief characteristics is the cultivation of precision in thought as well as expression. Hiriyanna (1932[1983], pp. 227-228) categorizes Navya-nyāya after Gaṅgeśa as "confined more and more to matters of detail" and "for most part philosophically barren". In this respect he is as negative as Radhakrishnan. J. Bhattacharyya ("Navya-Nyāya", 1975[1937?/1953], pp. 126-127) takes the view that Gaṅgeśa laid the foundation of the revised metaphysics[36] of the Vaiśeṣika school by means of a new theory of knowledge, and that Navya-nyāya originated from Gaṅgeśa.

Ingalls (1951, p. 5) states that Gaṅgeśa refers to his teachings as the New Nyāya as distinguished from the Old Nyāya. It is one thing how Gaṅgeśa describes his own view, and it is another how we describe his view within the context of the history of Indian philosophy. On this matter Ingalls keeps silent, which seems to mean that he implicitly accepts Gaṅgeśa's description of his own view. Ingalls interestingly points out that many Indian scholars apply the term Navya-nyāya only to Raghunātha and his followers because of the originality of his work. Ingalls (1951, p. 1) states that Navya-nyāya, by means of abstract properties and the combination of negatives, expresses the same facts that we normally express by quantification. Later, Ingalls, as I mentioned before, changed his view on the founder of Navya-nyāya to the first view.

Sinha's *A History of Indian Philosophy,* Vol. 1 (1956, p. 699)[37] maintains that Gaṅgeśa founded Navya-nyāya, and that its features are the arrangement of argument under the four means of knowledge and the introduction of a new terminology for logical analysis. He adds that Gaṅgeśa developed Udayana's line of thought. Potter notes that the works of Navya-nyāya were produced between the 13th and 17th centuries, and that its greatest exponent was Gaṅgeśa.[38] This means that Potter regards him as the first author of Navya-nyāya, i.e., its founder, because following Ingalls Potter places Gaṅgeśa in the 13th century. This view of Potter remains unchanged in Potter's *Encyclopedia of Indian Philosophies,* Vol. 2 (1977) and Potter and S. Bhattacharyya's *Encyclopedia of Indian Philosophies,* Vol. 6 (1993).[39] S.K. Sastri states in his *A Primer of Indian Logic* (1961) that Gaṅgeśa shifted the emphasis from the categorical treatment of the topics of Nyāya to the epistemological treatment of the four means of valid cognition (*pramāṇa*) and established the terminology of Navya-nyāya, which enables elaborate analysis and discussion.[40] Sastri does not refer to the relationship between Udayana and Gaṅgeśa or between Udayana and Navya-nyāya.

Umesh Mishra's *History of Indian Philosophy,* Vol. 2 (1966, p. 238) takes the view that although the Navya-nyāya trend of thought can be found in Udayana,[41] it is proper to regard Gaṅgeśa as its founder. However, Mishra (1966, pp. 269-270) evaluates Udayana more highly than Gaṅgeśa in terms of substance and method of argumentation and adds in the final paragraph comparing both authors that we find much originality in Udayana and only subtle distinctions in Gaṅgeśa. According to Mishra (1966, pp. 237-238), Navya-nyāya is mainly concerned with the theory of knowledge, and its system is based on the four means of knowledge. We can infer the strong influence of the Prabhākara school of Mīmāṃsā on Gaṅgeśa from the statement in Mishra (1966, pp. 239, 249, 256-257).

Potter's *Encyclopedia of Indian Philosophies Vol. 2: Indian Metaphysics and Epistemology: The Tradition of Nyāya-Vaiśeṣika up to Gaṅgeśa* (1977, p. xi) states that with Gaṅgeśa a new start is made within the systems of Nyāya and Vaiśeṣika, the result coming to be known as Navya-nyāya. Moreover, Potter (1977, p. 8) says that Udayana looms so monumentally in the history of Nyāya and Vaiśeṣika that other writers in these traditions are overshadowed. Potter simply refers to the fact that there are some historians who hold the view that Udayana pioneered a new technique which Gaṅgeśa expertly wielded. Keeping the same basic position as in Potter (1977), Potter and S. Bhattacharyya's *Encyclopedia of Indian Philosophies Vol. 6: Indian Philosophical Analysis Nyāya-Vaiśeṣika from Gaṅgeśa to Raghunātha Śiromaṇi* (1993, p. 3)[42] deal with only the philosophy and authors of Navya-nyāya and clearly state that Gaṅgeśa is rightly viewed as its founder. Both authors point out that the term Navya-nyāya is employed to identify not only the Nyāya-Vaiśeṣika literature of Gaṅgeśa and later authors but also in particular those literary works, such as Gaṅgeśa's *TC*, which utilize a technical vocabulary to explicate the Nyāya-Vaiśeṣika concepts. Potter and Bhattacharyya (1993, pp. 15-18) say that Navya-nyāya is concerned mainly with the concepts of relation and awareness (*jñāna*) and analyze both concepts in Navya-nyāya before elucidating its metaphysics, epistemology, and logic in their book.

Phillips' *Classical Indian Metaphysics* (1997 [1996], p. 119)[43] regards Gaṅgeśa as the first Navya-nyāya philosopher and gives three main reasons. The first reason is that Udayana's work is not regarded by post-Gaṅgeśa Nyāya philosophers as part of Navya-nyāya. For the second reason, Phillips claims that it was Śrīharṣa, the 12th century Advaita-Vedānta philosopher's criticism of Nyāya and in particular Udayana that impelled Gaṅgeśa and others to make innovations in their analytical method.[44] The third reason is that Udayana's definitions suffer from an overall sterility. Explaining this point, Phillips further states that "Gaṅgeśa re-invigorates Nyāya by formulating new definitions that crystallize Nyāya insight and lead to a more profound appreciation of the system—in contrast with Udayana's excessive formalism, which seems blind to students' needs". However, on the same page Phillips says that "probably we should say then that Gaṅgeśa's monumental *TC* solidifies but does not, strictly speaking, originate Navya-nyāya".

Those who uphold the third view that Udayana is the founder of Navya-nyāya are: Ganganath Jha, Dineshchandra Bhattacharya, Musashi Tachikawa, Bimal Krishna Matilal, Akihiko Akamatsu, Toshihiro Wada, and so forth. We may include in this group Umesh Mishra, whose view was introduced before. Jha's *Sāḍholāl Lectures on Nyāya* (1994 [1912-1916], p. 18) appears to be the first to claim that Udayana was the founder of Navya-nyāya. Jha says that Udayana led the way for a rigid course of strict reasoning, which, beginning with his *Nyāyakusumāñjali* and *Ātmatattvaviveka,* reached its final stage in Gaṅgeśa's *TC.* According to Jha (1994[1912-1916], p. 20), classical Nyāya is concerned with the object of cognition (*prameya*), while Navya-nyāya is concerned with the definitions of the means of cognition (*pramāṇa*) and the definitions of things (or terms). D. Bhattacharya's *History of Navya-Nyāya in Mithilā* (1958, pp. 1-2, 39-40) takes the view that the real founder of Navya-nyāya is Udayana, but regrettably Bhattacharya does not clearly state the reasons for his view. We can infer them from his following statements: that Udayana's *Nyāyakusumāñjali* is a textbook of Navya-nyāya; that there is hardly any topic dealt with in the four major divisions of Gaṅgeśa's *Tattvacintāmaṇi* that has not already been discussed by Udayana in his main works and especially in the *Nyāyakusumāñjali;* and that Gaṅgeśa displayed his utmost veneration for Udayana by quoting his works in almost every section of his large work.

Tachikawa's "Udayana no Lakṣaṇāvalī ni tsuite (1)" (On Udayana's *Lakṣaṇāvalī,* 1973, p. 426),[45] claims that Udayana is the real starting point of Navya-nyāya while Gaṅgeśa is its consolidator. He says that Udayana was the first to employ the Navya-nyāya method of description: using long compounds with fewer of the so-called operating words such as *samaveta.* ('inhering'; an inhering entity) and *samavetavat* ('the possessor of an inhering entity'). Matilal's "Nyāya-Vaiśeṣika" (1977, p. 101), following D. Bhattacharya, maintains that Navya-nyāya began with Udayana but does not state his reason for this. Akamatsu (1988)[46] regards Udayana as the founder of Navya-nyāya, based upon G. Chemparathy's characterization of Udayana as an inspiring herald of Navya-nyāya. Chemparathy emphasizes in particular the influence of the *Nyāyakusumāñjali* on Navya-nyāya. Akamatsu employs the term Navya-nyāya in two senses: the syncretic school of Nyāya and Vaiśeṣika, and the authors who wrote the commentaries or subcommentaries on Gaṅgeśa's *TC.* Since he adds that Navya-nyāya generally carries the latter meaning, he takes a middle position between the second and third views on the founder of Navya-nyāya.[47] As far as the features of the Navya-nyāya analytical method are concerned, Akamatsu accepts the statement by Ingalls (1951, p. 1), which we have already seen. Wada's *Invariable Concomitance in Navya-Nyāya* (1990, p. 14)[48] supports D. Bhattacharya's statement that Udayana is the founder of Navya-nyāya and finds the origin of the Navya-nyāya method of analysis in Udayana's *Lakṣaṇāvalī*, as does Tachikawa. However, unlike Tachikawa, Wada (1990, p. 225) notes that the concept of relation plays an important role in Navya-nyāya analysis.

Taking together all the statements of the scholars discussed above, there appear to be three main points: that (1) the Indian tradition does not regard Udayana as a Navya-nyāya author; instead, the tradition considers the authors who wrote commentaries or subcommentaries on the *TC* as forming the stream of Navya-nyāya; (2) Udayana did not place the means of knowledge (*pramāṇa*) at the center of his philosophical system; (3) the Navya-nyāya terminology cannot be traced back to Udayana. The above three statements in and of themselves do not provide sufficient grounds for regarding Udayana as the founder of Navya-nyāya. If, on the other hand, one regards Gaṅgeśa as the founder, the above statements do not contradict this conclusion.

Among the scholars who hold that Gaṅgeśa is the founder, only Phillips' *Classical Indian Metaphysics* (1997[1996], p. 119) offers reasons that are substantially different from the above three. The first reason is that Śrīharṣa impelled Gaṅgeśa and others to make innovations in their analytical method. Phillips' contribution consists of employing the two concepts of idealism and realism to contrast Śrīharṣa's and Gaṅgeśa's standpoints respectively.[49] While he is aware that Udayana pioneered some techniques inherited by Navya-nyāya, he fails to investigate fully the similarity between Udayana's and Navya-nyāya's method of analysis.[50] On the whole Phillips relies too much on past research on Udayana's position and thus tends to overlook the continuity between Udayana and Gaṅgeśa.

The second reason given by Phillips is that "Gaṅgeśa reinvigorates Nyāya by formulating new definitions that crystallize Nyāya insight and lead to a more profound appreciation of the system in contrast with Udayana's excessive formalism". This reason is not persuasive either. We can, if anything, assume that Udayana's excessive formalism provided the model for Gaṅgeśa's or Navya-nyāya's method of analysis to a great extent, as Tachikawa points out.[51] Thus, we can conclude this section by stating that neither Phillips' reasons, nor those given by the other scholars, support the claim that Gaṅgeśa founded Navya-nyāya.

4. *The Features of Navya-nyāya*[52]

From the research discussed in the previous section we know the main features of Navya-nyāya to be the following: (1) its principal text is Gaṅgeśa's *TC*; (2) its arguments are organized under the framework of the means of valid cognition; (3) its elaborate arguments lead to precise definition of terms; (4) Navya-nyāya devised a terminology which makes (3) possible. At first glance, these four features might appear to bolster the claim that Gaṅgeśa is the founder of Navya-nyāya. But, leaving aside feature (1) for the moment, we can say that features (2), (3), and (4), each by itself, do not exclusively support this claim.

With regard to the second feature, it is Bhāsarvajña (860-920)[53] and not Gaṅgeśa who first argued under the framework of the means of valid cognition. His *Nyāyasāra* consists of three chapters entitled perception, inference, and verbal testimony respectively. It is unreasonable to contend that the third and fourth features are found only in Gaṅgeśa and later authors, because the Navya-nyāya term *avacchedaka* (delimitor) is employed in the works of pre-Gaṅgeśa authors, such as the *Nyāyasiddhāntadīpa* (*NSD*)[54] of Śaśadhara (1275-1325) and the *Nyāyaratna* (*NR*) of Maṇikaṇṭha Miśra (1275-1325).[55]

Thus, we can conclude that each of the three features does not exclusively support the view that Gaṅgeśa founded Navya-nyāya. The first feature—that the principal text is the *TC*—does not contradict the view that Navya-nyāya was founded by Udayana. That is because there is no rule that a text written by the founder must be the principal one of his school. If, however, we interpret feature (1) as an 'extrinsic' rather than 'intrinsic' feature, we might naturally conclude that Gaṅgeśa founded Navya-nyāya. This conclusion appears reasonable if we consider that it is Gaṅgeśa who simultaneously possesses the 'internal' features (2), (3), and (4).

Before proceeding further, we should stop to reflect on our method of solving the problem. We started out by investigating what are the features of Navya-nyāya, and enumerated four main ones. But in enumerating them we seem to have unconsciously taken into account only Gaṅgeśa and post-Gaṅgeśa authors. As a result we appear to have fallen into circular reasoning, and to avoid this we need to find a new starting point.

But in order to find a really new starting point, we must necessarily look again at the four main features of Navya-nyāya. None of the three views on who is the founder of Navya-nyāya casts any light on the connection among the 'internal' features (2), (3), and (4). These features, which at first glance appear unrelated to one another, do not give us a clear and coherent picture of the Navya-nyāya system. If we could arrive at one concept which would facilitate the connection among (2), (3), and (4) and give us a clear and coherent picture of the Navya-nyāya system, that concept will facilitate our understanding of the historical and philosophical significance of Navya-nyāya. Moreover, it might answer our question of who founded Navya-nyāya.

That single concept is 'relation' (*sambandha*). Navya-nyāya is interested in rationally explaining human experience of the world. Experience is based on cognition, which necessarily refers to relation. When one recognizes that there is a pot on the ground (*ghaṭavad bhūtalam*), classical Nyāya describes the object of this cognition within the framework of Vaiśeṣika ontology. The connection between potness (*ghaṭatva*) and the pot, and groundness (*bhūtalatva*) and the ground is inherence (*samavāya*); the connection between the pot and the ground is contact (*saṃyoga*). However, that framework cannot properly work in analyzing the structure of the object of a cognition such as the cognition that John is the father of Mary, because the relation of father or fatherness (*pitṛtva*) referred to by this cognition does not come under that framework. Navya-nyāya philosophers have to deal with such cognitions that are beyond the reach of that framework. Because they are *nirākāravādins,* who maintain that cognition has no content in itself, that which is called content is an object existing outside of the cognizer. They hold that the outer world originates the cognition of it, and that the existence of the outer world as object necessarily precedes the origination of its cognition. For Navya-nyāya, however, cognition is the only means to prove the existence of the outer world, which abounds in relations. Thus, the key term, or concept, 'relation', enables us to explain why feature (2) is characteristic of Navya-nyāya.

Furthermore, this key term can also explain why (3) and (4): elaborate argument about terms and their definitions, and a new terminology are the features of Navya-nyāya. Two terms characteristic of Navya-nyāya are *avacchedaka* (delimitor) and *nirūpaka* (describer), to which all modern scholars will agree. To my knowledge, these two terms are employed to specify, or 'identify', relation, and hence we can derive features (3) and (4) from the Navya-nyāya approach of interpreting the structure of the world in terms of relation. Since I analyzed the function of these two terms somewhere else,[56] I would like to avoid going into detailed analysis of them here.

If we stress this approach of Navya-nyāya, there is no necessity to regard Gaṅgeśa as the founder. If, on the other hand, we can demonstrate that Udayana takes such an approach and has exerted a strong influence on Gaṅgeśa, we will have sufficient reason to regard Udayana as the founder.[57]

5. *Definition in Terms of Relation*

To understand Udayana's method, we need to first see how he formulates definitions in terms of relation. For comparison, we will take Praśastapāda (550-600), who flourished long before him, and focus on their definitions of a substance (*dravya*). The question arises of whether it is meaningful to compare the definitions formulated by two persons belonging to different schools: Praśastapāda belongs to Vaiśeṣika, and Udayana to Navya-nyāya in my view. The latter school represents a synthesis of the Vaiśeṣika and Nyāya schools, and so it makes sense to compare Praśastapāda's and Udayana's definitions.

In his *Padārthadharmasaṃgraha* (*PDhS*), Praśastapāda enumerates five common features of a substance: (1) its being connected with substanceness (*dravyatva*), (2) its producing its own effect, (3) its possessing qualities (*guṇa*), (4) its not being destroyed by cause and effect, and (5) its possessing a particular (*viśeṣa*).[58] According to Vyomaśiva (900-960) and Śrīdhara (950-1000), feature (2) means that a substance is an inherent cause (*samavāyikāraṇa*) of a quality and an action (*karman*).[59]

Hence, feature (2) presupposes a quality and an action. As to feature (4), Śrīdhara is of the opinion that it is intended for discriminating a substance from sound,[60] and so feature (4) cannot be the substantial definition of a substance.[61] Features (1)-(3) and (5) are substantial and presuppose entities expressed by absolute general terms, i.e., 'substanceness', 'generic property' or 'universal' (*sāmānya, jāti*), 'quality', 'action', and 'particular'. Absolute general terms are those which apply to an individual thing such as a human being, a pot, and so on.[62] We have discussed the features common only to all substances, but they seem to be the definitions of a substance given by Praśastapāda. This is because in the Indian context, a definition is often given in terms of a feature peculiar only to the entity (or concept) to be defined.[63] Thus, Praśastapāda's definitions of a substance require absolute general terms.

Udayana, on the other hand, gives four definitions of a substance in his *Lakṣaṇāvalī,* and one of them contains only a relative general term. Relative general terms are those which, unlike absolute general terms, apply to things in a paired set, for instance, cause, father, and so on.[64] When we say that A is the cause, we presume its effect. The definition containing only a relative general term runs as follows: a substance is an entity which has inhering [in itself] a property which has inhering [in itself] another property: *samavetasamavetasamavetam.*[65] We need not concern ourselves here with what this definition means, for it is clearly analyzed and expounded by Tachikawa.[66] The relative general term contained in the definition is *samaveta,* which means 'inhering' or 'an inhering entity', and no other absolute general or relative general term is used in the definition. Udayana employs this term presuming the term *samavetavat,* which means 'the possessor of an inhering entity'. Since both terms apply to a set of two entities, one of which inheres in the other, they are relative general terms. Therefore, we can say that Udayana presents the definition only in terms of a relative general term. To apply a general term to an entity means that the entity is regarded as being related to another entity.

Let us look at the other three definitions formulated by Udayana. They run as follows: a substance is not the locus of a constant absence of a quality (*guṇātyantābhāvānadhikaraṇam*);[67] a substance is the possessor of a generic property which inheres in that which lacks corporeality and in that which lacks incorporeality and which (property) lacks the state of inhering in that which inheres in that which lacks corporeality (*mūrtatvarahitasamavetasamavetatvarahita-mūrtatvarahitāmūrtatvarahitasamavetajātimad*);[68] a substance is the possessor of a generic property which inheres in space and in a lotus but does not inhere in smell (*gandhāsamavetagaganāravindasamavetajātimad*).[69] These three definitions do not necessarily have relative general terms for their components, but in the second definition the term '*samaveta*' ('inhering') appears three times, and in the third twice. It is obvious that Udayana formulates these definitions by consciously and repeatedly employing this relative term.

All the definitions of a quality, an action, a generic property, a particular, and inherence in the *Lakṣaṇāvalī* also include the relative general term 'inhering' or 'sharing a locus with' (*samānādhikaraṇa*).[70] 'Sharing a locus with' denotes a symmetrical relation between x and y when x and y exist in one and the same locus z. We can say: x is that which shares a locus with y, and y is that which shares a locus with x. The term *samānādhikaraṇa'*, which means 'sharing a locus with', applies to x and y, and hence it is a relative general term. This term is not necessarily peculiar to Navya-nyāya, but its frequent use is characteristic of the Navya-nyāya method of description.

In the above discussion, we have seen how Udayana formulates his definition of a substance in terms of relation, i.e., by using relative general terms. We have focused here on his definition of a substance, but we note that he also formulates other definitions using relative general terms, i.e., his definitions of a quality, action, and so forth.

It should be pointed out that past research also supports the claim that relation plays an important role in the system. Guha calls Navya-nyāya relational logic, which shows that he recognizes the important function of relation in Navya-nyāya.[71] As mentioned in section 3, Potter and Bhattacharyya point out the central importance of both relation and awareness (*jñāna*) in Navya-nyāya and devote a chapter of their book to an analysis of these two concepts.[72] We note that many books on Navya-nyāya deal with the topic of relation, though they may not explicitly state its importance in the system.

6. *Conclusion*

Navya-nyāya describes the structure of the world in terms of relation. For this task it developed a specific terminology including the terms delimitor and describer. Udayana did not use either term, while Śaśadhara and Maṇikaṇṭha both used delimitor frequently in the technical sense. Gaṅgeśa in his *Tattvacintāmaṇi* made technical use of both delimitor and describer: the former term more frequently than the latter. The term describer appears more often in later Navya-nyāya texts, such as the *Nyāyabodhinī* of Govardhana in the 17th century. If we hold that Navya-nyāya is a system which describes the world in terms of relation, we can certainly trace this approach back to at least before Gaṅgeśa, and even further before Udayana if we can find a pre-Udayana author who noted the importance of relation in his system. But we cannot assert that Navya-nyāya was originated by any philosopher who first recognized its importance. To solve the problem of who adopted such an approach first, we should take into consideration other aspects of the relationship between such a philosopher and Gaṅgeśa. Past research on the relationship between Udayana and Gaṅgeśa has made it clear that Udayana's *Nyāyakusumāñjali* and *Ātmatattvaviveka* exerted great influence on Gaṅgeśa.[73] Taking this into account, we can claim at least that it is possible to find in Udayana the origin of analysis in terms of relation.

NOTES

1. On this point, see B.K. Matilal, *The Character of Indian Logic,* edited by J. Ganeri and H. Tiwari, State University of New York, New York, 1998, p. 14), which discusses the differences between Indian logic and Western logic.
2. For a detailed discussion of the features, see T. Wada, "The Analytical Method of Navya-Nyāya", *Journal of Indian Philosophy* 29, 2001, pp. 519-521.
3. S.C. Vidyabhusana, *History of Mediaeval School of Indian Logic,* Oriental Books Reprint Corporation, New Delhi, 1977(1909).
4. Vidyabhusana (*A History of Indian Logic,* p. 406) places Gaṅgeśa in the fourth quarter of the 12th century. But it has recently become the predominant view that he lived in the first half of the 14th century. For instance, Dinesh chandra Bhattacharya (*History of Navya-Nyāya in Mithilā,* Mithilā Institute of Post-Graduate Studies and Research in Sanskrit Learning, Darbhanga, 1958, p. 101) places him *ca.* 1325, and Potter and Bhattacharyya (*Encyclopedia of Indian Philosophies Vol. 6: Indian Philosophical*

Analysis Nyāya-Vaiśeṣika from Gaṅgeśa to Raghunātha Śiromaṇi, Motilal Banarsidass, Delhi, 1993, pp. 85-87) place him *ca.* 1320.

5. S.C. Vidyabhusana, *A History of Indian Logic,* The Calcutta University, Calcutta, 1921.
6. G. Jha, *Sāḍholāl Lectures on Nyāya,* Sri Satguru Publications, Delhi, 1994 (1912-1916).
7. Jha uses the term Nyāya in the sense of logic in his *Saḍholāl Lectures on Nyāya.*
8. J.V. Bhattacharyya, "Navya-Nyāya" in Haridas Bhattacharyya (ed.), *The Cultural Heritage of India,* Vol. 3, The Ramakrishna Mission Institute of Culture, Calcutta, 1975 (1937?/1953).
9. On the question of with whom Navya-nyāya began, G. Jha and J. Bhattacharyya hold different views, which will be referred to later. Jha marks its beginning with Udayana, and Bhattacharyya with Gaṅgeśa.
10. C. Goekoop, *The Logic of Invariable Concomitance in the Tattvacintāmaṇi,* D. Reidel Publishing Company, Dordrecht, 1967.
11. On the dates of the Nyāya and Vaiśeṣika authors, see K.H. Potter, *Encyclopedia of Indian Philosophies,* Vol. 2, Motilal Banarsidass, Delhi, 1977, pp. 9-12; Potter and Bhattacharyya, *Encyclopedia of Indian Philosophies,* Vol. 6, pp. 10-13.
12. Vidyabhusana (*A History of Indian Logic,* p. 157) assigns Jaina logic to the period 400 A.D.–1700 A.D.
13. It is an on-going problem whether it is proper or not to use historical designations like 'ancient', as Vidyabhusana does, for the divisions of the history of Indian logic. If we make use of such designations, we have to define them. Hence, I have avoided them here.
14. A.B. Keith, *Indian Logic & Atomism,* The Clarendon Press, Oxford, 1921 (rep. Oriental Books Reprint Corporation, New Delhi, 1977).
15. Keith (*Indian Logic & Atomism,* p. 33) says, "Probably within two centuries from Udayana and Śivāditya there flourished the famous Gaṅgeśa or Gaṅgeśvara, the author of the *Tattvacintāmaṇi,* in which the logic of Nyāya attains its final shape".
16. We cannot criticize him for not discussing its final shape, because he probably had limited access to research materials on Navya-nyāya.
17. S. Sen, *A Study on Mathurānātha's Tattvacintāmaṇi-rahasya,* Wageningen, 1924.
18. Sen calls the commentators on Gaṅgeśa syncretists, as does Keith, *Indian Logic and Atomism,* p. 33. Sen (*A Study on Mathurānātha's Tattvacintāmaṇi-rahasya,* p. 5 fn.3) refers to Keith.
19. D.N. Shastri, *The Philosophy of Nyāya-Vaiśeṣika and Its Conflict with the Buddhist Dignāga School,* Bharatiya Vidya Prakashan, Delhi/Varanasi, 1976(1964).
20. D.N. Shastri places less importance on Udayana and Navya-nyāya in the history of Indian philosophy. Chemparathy (*An Indian Rational Theology: Introduction to Udayana's Nyāyakusumāñjali,* Publications of the De Nobili Research Library 1, Gerold & Co., Vienna, 1972, p. 32), on the other hand, says that Shastri's statements regarding them are too harsh, and he holds Udayana in particularly high regard.
21. D.C. Guha, *Navya Nyāya System of Logic,* Bharatiya Vidya Prakashan, Varanasi, 1968 (rep., Motilal Banarsidass, Delhi, 1979).

22. Guha (*Navya Nyāya System of Logic,* p. 4, fn.2) provides the source of this view as: Paṇḍita Vāmācaraṇa Nyāyācārya, Introduction of Mahāmahopadhyāya Pañcānana Tarkaratna to *Vyāptipañcaka Māthurī* edited by Paṇḍita Vāmācaraṇa Nyāyācārya, p. 3. Umesh Mishra (*History of Indian Philosophy,* Vol. 2, Taribhukti Publications, Allahabad, 1966) also takes this view, which will be referred to in the discussion of the second view on who is the founder of Navya-nyāya.
23. D.H.H. Ingalls, *Materials for the Study of Navya-Nyāya Logic,* Harvard University Press, Cambridge, Mass., 1951.
24. D.H.H. Ingalls, "Preface", in Guha, *Navya Nyāya System of Logic,* pp. xvii-xviii; "Editor's Introduction", in B.K. Matilal, *The Navya-Nyāya Doctrine of Negation,* Harvard University Press, Cambridge, Mass., 1968, p. vii.
25. E. Frauwallner, *Die Lehre von der Zusätzlichen Bestimmung* (*upādhiḥ*) *in Gaṅgeśa's Tattvacintāmaṇi,* Kommisionsverlag der Österreichischen Akademie der Wissenschaften, Wien, 1970.
26. This article is included by A. Uno, *Indo ronrigaku* (Indian Logic), Hōzōkan, Kyoto, 1996, pp. 1-39 with revisions and partial deletions.
27. Uno must have read D. Bhattacharya, *History of Navya-Nyāya in Mithilā;* Ingalls, "Preface"; Ingalls, "Editor's Introduction", p. vii. These three were published before Uno, "Indo no ronriteki shiben" (Logical Speculation in India) in *Bunmei riron eno kokoromi* (An Approach to the Theory in Civilization), pp. 69-131. Later, Uno ("Shōri katsuron gakusetsu kenkyū" [A Study of the Nyāya and the Vaiśeṣika Philosophy (*sic*)], *The Hiroshima University Studies Faculty of Letters,* Special Issue 1, 1980) refers favourably to Matilal's opinion that Navya-nyāya was founded by Udayana, i.e., a few centuries before Gaṅgesa. This opinion is presented by B.K. Matilal, "Nyāya-Vaiśeṣika", *A History of Indian Literature,* Vol. 6, Fasc. 2, Otto Harrassowitz, Wiesbaden, 1977. Ingalls supports the second view in his *Materials for the Study of Navya-Nyāya Logic,* but he apparently favours the first in his "Preface" and "Editor's Introduction".
28. K. Miyamoto and M. Ishitobi, "Indo ronrigaku no taikei (1): *Maṇikaṇa* no wayaku to kaisetsu", *The Tōyō Gakujutsu Kenkyū* (The Journal of Oriental Studies), 22(1), 1983, pp. 210-231.
29. J. Vattanky, *Gaṅgeśa's Philosophy of God,* The Adyar Library and Research Centre, Madras, 1984.
30. M.C. Nyāyaratna, *Navya-nyāya-Bhāṣāpradīpah: Brief Notes on the Modern Nyāya System of Philosophy and Its Technical Terms,* Sanskrit College, Calcutta, 1973(1891?). This book is an introductory work on Navya-nyāya and includes, according to Uno ("Shinshōrigaku no jutsugo (1)" [Techincal terms in Navya-nyāya (*sic*)], *The Hiroshima University Studies Faculty of Letters* 37, 1977, pp. 85-105; *Indo ronrigaku,* p. 75), a paper read by Nyāyaratna on the occasion of the Ninth Orientalists Conference in 1891. (It is not known whether his paper was read in English, as it is reproduced in the book, or in Sanskrit.) The last colophon attached to the original Sanskrit in Uno, "Shinshōurigaku no jutsugo (1)", pp. 89-90, and written in English tells us that Nyāyaratna's book was published on 1 August 1891, by the publisher Jadu Nath Seal, and by the press Hare Press. Nyāyaratna's *Navyanyāya-Bhāṣāpradipaḥ* includes his paper in the section following his Sanskrit exposition on Navya-nyāya. This paper is assigned Arabic page numbers independent of the Sanskrit

numbers in the previous section. This paper and the Sanskrit exposition are translated into Japanese by Uno, "Shinshōrigaku no jutsugo (1) (2) (3)" (Techincal terms in Navya-nyāya [*sic*]), *The Hiroshima University Studies Faculty of Letters* 37, 1977, pp. 85-105; 38, 1978, pp. 89-109; 39, 1979, pp. 41-46+ pp. 23) and his translation is reprinted in Uno, *Indo ronrigaku*, pp. 71-119.

31. Vidyabhusana gives the following terms: *ativyāpti, anugatadharma, anugama, anuyogitā, anyathāsiddhi, avacchinna, avacchedaka, avyāpti, kurvadrūpatva, pratiyogi,* and *vyāpti.*
32. S. Dasgupta, *A History of Indian Philosophy,* Vol. 1, Motilal Banarsidass, Delhi, 1975(1922).
33. S. Radhakrishnan, *Indian Philosophy,* Vol. 2, Blackie & Son Publishers Pvt. Ltd., Bombay, 1983(1923).
34. G. Kaviraj, *Gleanings from the History and Bibliography of the Nyāya-Vaiśeṣika,* Calcutta, 1962(1924).
35. M. Hiriyanna, *Outline of Indian Philosophy,* Blackie & Son Publishers Pvt. Ltd., Bombay, 1983(1932).
36. Although Gaṅgeśa's *TC* is generally said to be a work on epistemology and logic, Bhattacharyya emphasizes Gaṅgeśa's metaphysical contribution. Bhattacharyya ("Navya-Nyāya", p. 127) deems that sound epistemology and logic should precede metaphysics and integrates the above common view into his view.
37. J. Sinha, *A History of Indian Philosophy,* Vol. 1, Sinha Publication House, Calcutta, 1956.
38. K.H. Potter, *Padārthatattvanirūpaṇaṃ of Raghunātha Śiromaṇi,* Harvard University Press, Cambridge, Mass., 1957, p. 3.
39. For the information of *Encyclopedia of Indian Philosophies,* Vols. 2 and 6, see notes 4 and 11.
40. S.K. Sastri, *A Primer of Indian Logic,* The Kuppuswami Sastri Research Institute, Madras, 1961, pp. xxxvi-xxxvii.
41. When Mishra (*History of Indian Philosophy,* Vol. 2, p. 150) discusses the date, native place, and so on of Udayana, he gives the heading 'Udayana and Gaṅgeśa, founders of the Neo-Nyāya School' and remarks that a careful study of the works of Udayana shows that the methodology of the Neo-Nyāya school had started at his time. Mishra further quotes the statement of Gopinath Kaviraj who *personally* held that the distinction between the Classical and New Nyāya dates from after Udayana and Śrīdhara. It seems difficult for Mishra to discard the view that Udayana is the founder of Navya-nyāya.
42. My review of this book appears in *Asiatische Studien* 50(4), 1996, pp. 1008-1015.
43. S.H. Phillips, *Classical Indian Metaphysics,* Motilal Banarsidass, Delhi, 1997 (rep., Open Court Publishing Company, Chicago, 1996).
44. Phillips's *Classical Indian Metaphysics* (p. 4) claims that the criticism by non-Vedāntic philosophers as well as Śrīharsa led the emergence of Navya-nyāya. Phillips (p. 118) also says that "since it is Udayana who receives the brunt of Śrīharṣa's criticism, the legend that Śrīharṣa provoked the writing of the *TC,* although strictly unwarranted, makes good folklore". Phyllis Granoff (*Philosophy and Argument in Late Vedānta: Śrī Harṣa's Khaṇḍanakhaṇḍakhadya,* D. Reidel Publishing Company, Dordrecht/Boston/

London, 1978), on the other hand, keeps silence on the relation between Śrīharṣa and Gaṅgeśa. Śrīharṣa's opponents referred to in the first chapter of his *Khaṇḍanakhaṇḍakhadya* are listed by Granoff (p. 3): the Naiyāyikas Udayana, Vācaspati Miśra, and Bhāsarvajña; the Mīmāṃsakas Kumārila and Prabhākara; the Buddhists Dharmakīrti, Dharmottara, and Prajñākaragupta, and the Jains Pujyapāda, Vidyānanda, Samantabhadra, and Akalaṅka.

45. M. Tachikawa, "Udayana no Lakṣaṇāvalī ni tsuite (1)(2)", *Journal of Indian Buddhist Studies* 22(1), 1973, pp. 426-431; 25(1), 1976, pp. 436-443.
46. A. Akamatsu, "(I) Niyāyagakuha no seiritsu, (2) Shoki no niyāyagakuha, (4) Shin niyāyagakuha no seiritsu to tenkai" ([1] Beginning of Nyāya, [2] Early Nyāya, [4] Establishment and Development of Navya-nyāya), in *Indo Shisō* (Indian Thought), Vol. 1, *Tōyō Shisō* (Oriental Thought), Vol. 5, Iwanamishoten, Tokyo, pp. 229-230.
47. On the origin of Navya-nyāya logic, Akamatsu ("[1] Niyāyagakuha no seiritsu, [2] Shoki no niyāyagakuha, [4] Shin niyāyagakuha no seiritsu to tenkai", p. 214) says "Uddyotakara takes the view that inference is possible only between two properties (*dharma*) when they simultaneously coexist in one and the same place, i.e., locus. The New Nyāya logic develops from the trends of formulating the structure of this inference, clarifying the relation between two properties as pervasion (*vyāpti*), and connecting pervasion with the reconsideration of the logical sign (*liṅgaparāmarśa*)". This statement explains to some extent the fact that Navya-nyāya literature includes a great deal of discussion on pervasion by post-Gaṅgeśa Navya-nyāya authors. We have to evaluate Akamatsu's attempt to answer the question of the origin of Navya-nyāya logic in a concrete context. However, it is an on going issue whether Navya-nyāya develops from the connection of pervasion with the reconsideration of the logical sign.
48. T. Wada, *Invariable Concomitance in Navya Nyāya,* Sri Satguru Publications, Delhi, 1990.
49. On Phillips' definitions of idealism and realism, see Phillips, *Classical Indian Metaphysics,* p. 1. His work is a valuable contribution to historical research on early Navya-nyāya, an area which on the whole has been neglected. This work also facilitates to a great extent our understanding of Indian philosophy from the viewpoint of the idealist and realist controversy.
50. Phillips (*Classical Indian Metaphysics,* pp. 118-119) states that "Udayana pioneered some of the techniques identified with New Logic". For instance, we know Udayana's method was inherited to Navya-nyāya in Phillips, *Classical Indian Metaphysics,* pp. 48, 56, 57-60, 63, 64-65, 66-69. Phillips (p. 97) is clearly aware of Udayana's method of formulating definition and says that "in early Nyāya, salient differentiating features are focused upon, while Udayana, in contrast, insists on mere differentiation". He does not mention this characteristic of Udayana as providing a link between Udayana and Navya-nyāya.
51. Tachikawa, "Udayana no Lakṣaṇāvalī ni tsuite (1)", p. 426.
52. This section mainly depends on Wada, "The Analytical Method of Navya-Nyāya".
53. On the dates of the Nyāya and Vaiśeṣika authors, see Potter, *Encyclopedia*

of Indian Philosophies, Vol. 2, pp. 9-12; Potter and Bhattacharyya, *Encyclopedia of Indian Philosophies*, Vol. 6, pp. 10-13.

54. Matilal ("Introduction" in B.K. Matilal, *Śaśadhara's Nyāyasiddhāntadīpa with Ṭippana by Guṇaratnasūri*, L.D. Institute of Indology, Ahmedabad, 1976, p. 17) presumes that the *NSD* was written no earlier than 1200 A.D.

55. The concept of *avacchedaka* is frequently used in the "Invariable Concomitance Chapter" (Vyāptivāda) of the *NSD* and in the "Reconsideration Chapter" (Parāmarśavāda) of the *NR*. In the former text the term *nirūpaka* appears twice, but at present we cannot determine whether it is used in the Navya-nyāya technical sense. For the Sanskrit texts of the *NSD* and the *NR*, see Matilal, *Śaśadhara's Nyāyasiddhāntadīpa with Ṭippaṇa by Guṇaratnasūri* and *Nyāyaratna by Maṇikaṇṭha Miśra with the Commentary Dyutimālikā of Nṛsiṃhayajvan* (edited by V. Subrahmanya Sastri and V. Krishnamacharya, Government Oriental Manuscripts Library, Madras, 1953) respectively.

56. For detailed analysis of the two terms, see Wada, *Invariable Concomitance in Navya-Nyāya*, pp. 66-98. For brief analysis of them, see Wada, "The Analytical Method of Navya-Nyāya", pp. 521-527.

57. We face another problem: why Udayana interprets the structure of the world in terms of relation. I propose as a solution to this problem the two working concepts: Indian realism and nominalism. The former presumes the reality of the external world, while the latter does not. Udayana defended the Nyāya-Vaiśeṣika realistic position against the Buddhist nominalistic position. On Indian realism and nominalism, see M. Tachikawa, *The Structure of the World in Udayana's Realism*, D. Reidel Publishing Company, Dordrecht/Boston/London, 1981, pp. 9-10. Gaṅgeśa wrote the *TC* in order to defend his realistic position against the nominalistic position of Śrīharṣa, an Advaita philosopher. To understand the opposition between Śrīharṣa and Gaṅgeśa, Phillips' *Classical Indian Metaphysics* is useful. Phillips employs the term idealist/idealism, while I use the term nominalist/nominalism with the similar meaning. Wada ("The Action of the Subject towards the Outer World", in *Concept of Knowledge: East and West* [Papers from a Seminar held from 4 January to 10 January 1995 at the Ramakrishna Mission Institute of Culture], the Ramakrishna Mission Institute of Culture, Calcutta, 2000, pp. 310-321) deals with the problem of the reality of the universal or generic property (*jāti, sāmānya*) in terms of the realism-nominalism dichotomy. It is also possible to analyze the problem of the property and property-possessor (*dharmadharmin*) relation under the framework of this dichotomy.

58. *PDhS* (in Johannes Bronkhorst and Yves Ramseier, *Word Index to the Praśastapādabhāṣya: a complete word index to the printed editions of the Praśastapādabhāṣya*, Motilal Banarsidass, Delhi, 1994), no. 16: *pṛthivyādīnāṃ navānām api dravyatvayogaḥ svātmany ārambhakatvam guṇavattvam kāryakāraṇavirodhitvam antyaviśeṣavattvam anāśritatvanityatve cānyatrāvayavidravyebhyaḥ.*

59. *Vyomavatī* (edited by Gaurinath Sastri, Sampurnananda Sanskrit University, Varanasi, 1983), p. 44,16-17: *evaṃ svaś cāsāv ātmā ceti svātmā, tasminn ārambhakatvam, svātmasamavetakāryajanakatvam samavāyikaraṇatvam iti yāvat. Nyāyakandalī* (in *The Praśastapāda Bhashya with Commentary*

Nyāyakandalī of Śrīdhara, edited by Vindhyesvari Prasad Dvivedin, Sri Satguru Publications, Delhi, 1984), p. 21, 2-3: *svātmany ārambhakatvam iti Svasamavetakāryajanakatvam ity arthaḥ. Kiraṇāvalī* (in *Praśastapādasyam with the Commentary Kiraṇāvalī of Udayanācārya,* edited by J.S. Jetly, Oriental Institute, Baroda, 1971), p. 23. 6-7: *svātmany ārambhakatvam - svasamavetakāryakāritvam samavāyikāraṇatvam it yarthaḥ.*

60. *Nyāyakandalī,* p. 21, 4-10: *kāryakāraṇāvirodhitvam. guṇo hi kvacit kāryeṇa vinaśyate yathādyaḥ śabdo dvitīyaśabdena kvacit kāraṇena vināśyate yathāntyaḥ śabda upāntyaśabdena karmāpi kāryeṇa vināśyate yathottarasaṃyogena dravyāṇi tu na vināśyante nāpi kāraṇeneti kāryakāraṇāvirodhīni nityānaṃ kāraṇavināśayor abhāvād eva kāraṇenavināśaḥ anityadravyāṇāṃ kāraṇavināśayoḥ sambhave 'pi kāraṇena na vināśaḥ kiṃ tv anyeneti vivekaḥ.*
61. Vyomaśiva clarifies feature (4) in two cases: when it consists of a single property (*Vyomavatī,* p. 44, 22-24) or two properties (*Vyomavatī,* pp. 44,25-45,15). In the former case, he does not make clear what this single property is. In the latter case, he concludes that neither property can be the definition of a substance.
62. On this term, see Matilal, *The Navya-Nyāya Doctrine of Negation,* p. 31. Matilal uses it by following W.V.O. Quine, *Word and Object,* The Technology Press of Massachusetts Institute of Technology and John Wiley & Sons, Inc., Cambridge, Mass., 1960, p. 105.
63. The word '*lakṣaṇa*', which corresponds to "definition", is sometimes rendered as "defining feature". The definition of *A* is generally given either in the form of "*A* is *B*" or by stating the defining character of *A*, i.e., "*B*-ness". On this point, see Wada, *Invariable Concomitance in Navya-Nyāya,* pp. 99-105. Over time Indian authors have preferred more and more the latter method to the fonner, especially when writing more difficult texts.
64. On this term, see Matilal, *The Navya-Nyāya Doctrine of Negation,* p. 31. Matilal uses it by following Quine, *Word and Object,* p. 105. A relative general term can naturally be used as an absolute general term.
65. *Lakṣaṇāvalī* (in M. Tachikawa, *The Structure of the World in Indian Realism,* D. Reidel Publishing Company, Dordrecht, 1981), p. 56, no. 12.
66. Tachikawa, "Udayana no Lakṣaṇavalī ni tsuite (1)", p. 426; *The Structure of the World in Udayana's Realism,* pp. 57, 91.
67. *Lakṣaṇāvalī,* p. 56, no. 9.
68. *Lakṣaṇāvalī,* p. 56, no. 10.
69. *Lakṣaṇāvalī,* p. 56, no. 11. These definitions are analyzed and explained by Tachikawa, "Udayana no Lakṣaṇāvalī ni tsuite (1)", pp. 427-429; *The Structure of the World in Indian Realism,* pp. 57, 89-91.
70. On the definitions of a quality, an action, a generic property, a particular, and inherence, see Tachikawa, "Udayana no Lakṣaṇāvalī ni tsuite (2)"; *The Structure of the World in Indian Realism,* pp. 73, 83, 85.
71. Guha, *Navya Nyāya System of Logic,* p. 56. He, however, does not make clear the connection between relation and Navya-nyāya terms such as delimitor (*avacchedaka*) and describer (*nirūpaka*).
72. Potter and Bhattacharyya, *Encyclopedia of Indian Philosophies,* Vol. 6, pp. 15-18.
73. Jha (*Sāḍholāl Lectures on Nyāya,* p. 18) and D. Bhattacharya (*History of*

Navya-Nyāya in Mithilā, pp. 1-2) discuss this influence. These two works are referred to in the second section of the present paper under the discussion of the third view that Udayana founded Navya-nyāya.

* The present paper is a revised English version of part of T. Wada, "Shin Niyāya Gakuha no Kigen to Bunseki Hōhō" (The Origin of Navya-nyāya and the Position of This School in the History of Indian Logic), *Indo-Shisōshi Kenkyū* (Studies in the History of Indian, Thought 11, 1999, pp. 15-41. T. Wada, "The Analytical Method of Navya-Nyāya", *Journal of Indian Philosophy* 29, 2001, pp. 519-521 is a revised English version of the other part of this Japanese paper. I wish to thank Charles Pain for his editorial assistance and his helpful comments.

CHAPTER 30

Logic and Culture

GREGOR PAUL

1. *The Problem: Its Aspects and Relevance*

Does logic depend on culture? To what extent is Aristotelian logic a function of ancient Greek culture? Does Aristotelian logic differ significantly from so-called non-Western logic, particularly so-called Indian, Chinese, Japanese and Buddhist logic? For decades, the question whether Aristotelian logic is a distinctively Western theory, or Western class of logical principles, has been a hotly debated issue. In intercultural discourse and comparative philosophy, this issue has remained an important topic. Sometimes, even politics is involved. The question of whether logic depends on culture, however, is a quite ambiguous one. The word "logic" can refer to (1) logical principles and rules such as the laws of non-contradiction and of transitivity, (2) particular theories of logic, especially theories of non-contradiction, inference and deduction, (3) applications of logical principles and rules and/or (4) logical thinking in general. Often, "logic" (also) refers to (5) forms of thinking which are determined by content. For example, sometimes people talk of the "logic of a soccer game", and even a term such as "quantum logics" designates structures, or theories of structures, that depend on a particular content, namely, on the relationship that exists between certain physical particles. In one of its most current versions the question whether Aristotelian logic is culturally determined and thus not universally valid, addresses the problem of whether logical form depends on the distinctive features of the language in which it is expressed. In other words, does logic, particularly logical structure, depend on linguistic properties particular to a specific human language, and if so, in what respect? Finally, the whole problem may also be phrased as the general question of whether there exists a class of logical principles and rules which, independently of time, place, and culture, have always been valid for all human beings. Thereby, "validity" is meant in a normative sense. Whether a logical rule is universally valid or not, is independent of whether or not it is violated. Though we often violate mathematical principles these principles remain valid.

All these questions are quite important. For suppose no class of universally valid logical principles but *only different classes of equally valid* logical principles would exist. Then people applying such incompatible—so to say, rival—principles, *to identical premises* could not but arrive at different conclusions. For example, one had to find out the shortest way from A to B, and had to pass either C or D. The distance between A and C be shorter than the distance between A and D, and that between C and B shorter than that between D and B. Then, according to the law of transitivity, going from A to B via C would be the best. However, people negating the law of transitivity and following different rules, would arrive at a different—though equally valid—conclusion. If such a thing were possible, international or intercultural discourse about ethical questions and moral norms would be doomed to failure. Even when starting from identical premises, members of different cultures could arrive at different though equally valid conclusions and justifications—they could even, in an equally valid way, justify sticking to fundamentally different norms and values. By pointing this out, I am not building up straw men. In an influential German newspaper one could read the following:

> Of course, the arguments [of non-European opponents] against the European view of human rights are based on reasons which can be explained very well by the different logics of these different cultures.
>
> Argumentation is a genuinly Occidental undertaking... which has always been tied to our method of formal logic.[1]

This is indeed to say that, in different cultures, the methods of argumentation, and in particular the principles of formal logical reasoning, differ to such an extent that it is virtually impossible to reach an understanding on ethical or moral norms, be it only the most fundamental norms.

I could easily quote a large number of statements that are in a similar relativistic vein, among them many remarks that favor racism, irrationalism, obscurantism, exotism and esotericism. Confronting Western logic and Eastern logic, or Western logic and Eastern intuition, they associate Western logic with coercion, lack of freedom, subjection of nature, logocentrism, scientism, rationality, lack of feeling, sobriety and so on, while connotating Eastern logic, or intuition, with notions such as freedom, avoidance of either-or-alternatives, harmony with nature, openness for non-scientific experience or knowledge, sensibility and sympathy. Thus, the question whether there exist universally valid logical principles or rules, is no mere academic problem but also one of practical and even political relevance.

Most of the culturalistic arguments questioning the existence of universally valid logical laws are easily dismissed. In the first place, if a word such as "logical" refers to structures of thinking and acting that are determined by content, the respective argument is quite irrelevant, for if there exist universally valid logical laws they must be laws of mere logical form, i.e., of a form independent of content. As indicated, so-called quantum logics are materially determined theories, and the same applies to, e.g., transcendental and dialectical logics. Since the principles (or theorems) generated by such theories cannot replace laws of formal logic, they cannot be used as counter-examples against such laws. Even if a scholar conceives of 'Eastern thought' as dialectical logic this does in no way imply that this 'Eastern thought' is less determined by principles of formal logic than is 'Western thought'.

Though confusion of material and formal logic is the main reason for the belief that there exists an Eastern logic significantly different from Western, Aristotelian, or two-valued logic, and for concluding that there exist no universally valid logical principles, there are also other important reasons for these convictions. Often, particular theoretical notions of logical laws, as for instance such formulated by Buddhist theories (namely, *hetu-vidyā, yinming, immyō*), are compared with general metatheoretical, or general methodological, notions. Even such different doctrines as Zen teachings and Aristotelian syllogistic are compared with each other. There are numerous examples for such categorical mistakes, some of them still very influential. Suzuki Daisetz has confronted Zen, i.e., doctrines he regarded as anti-logical, with Aristotelian logic, i.e., a set of theories that, in his view, promotes logocentrism. Instead, he should have compared (i) Zen and Western mystic, and (ii) *hetu-vidyā* (or *yinming* or *immyō*) and Aristotelian logic, especially Buddhist and Aristotelian notions of non-contradiction, inference and deduction. Beside his categorical mistakes, Suzuki committed another, equally grave mistake. For he virtually equated Eastern thought with Zen, and Western thought with Aristotelian logic, thus grossly overgeneralizing specific features. There is another problem. One ought not simply identify the question whether there exist universally valid logical laws with the question of whether Aristotelian logic is universally valid. Such identification invites misunderstanding and mistakes. Of course, if the latter is true then the former is also true. But if one wants to enter into an adequate and fruitful comparison of the ways logic was conceived of in different cultures, one needs to qualify terms such as "logic" and "Aristotelian".

(i) The meaning of the words "Aristotelian logic" must not be limited to the distinctive features of the respective theories. Put forward in Greek, and part of a particular historical context, Aristotle's logic is unique. Looking for exactly such a theory in, e.g., (early) Indian or Chinese cultures, would be absurd.

(ii) It would also be meaningless to compare distinctively Aristotelian concepts, e.g., of the principle of non-contradiction, with respective 'Indian' or 'Chinese' concepts, and then conclude that 'logic' varies according to culture and language. Even within the same culture, and at the same time, there can exist different theories of logic. One need only remember medieval scholasticism, or competing 20th century theories of intuitive, constructive, classic, and many-valued logic.

(iii) If the issue is universal validity, words like "Aristotelian" must be understood as designations of logical laws (axioms, rules, etc.) which in principle can be replaced by other, *equivalent* expressions, i.e., other expressions that refer to the same laws.

(iv) Hence, the question whether "*Aristotelian* logic" is universally valid, should be phrased as follows: Do certain Aristotelian sentences refer to logical laws and rules that are universally valid, namely principles that are normatively valid for all human beings of all times and places? If one denies this question it could still be possible that these sentences refer to specifications of universally valid laws or rules.

(v) Finally, one must discuss the question of whether there exist universally valid logical laws and rules on different levels. For, though some theories negate the universal validity of the *tertium non datur*, or—as for instance so-called para-consistent logics[2]—admit for isolated contradictions, this does not exclude the possibility that they could only be developed by applying, in one way or other, the *tertium non datur* and the law of non-contradiction. Certain laws of formal logic may be universally valid in the sense that—independent of the content of our reflections, and independent of the results we arrive at by reflecting—we cannot but acknowledge these laws (be it on the object-level or on a meta-level of speech), if we only want our reflections to refer to some identifiable thought (idea, object, etc.). To characterize this kind of universal validity, one can also speak of universally valid *methodological* principles. Instead of speaking of a universally valid law of non-contradiction, one could speak of a universally valid methodological principle, i.e., a principle indispensible for every kind of identifiable reflection. Thus one could easily discern a universally valid law of non-contradiction from those specific versions which are part (or result) of specific theories of logic.

In short, investigating the question of whether there exist universally valid logical laws requires distinguishing between at least two levels: (α) the level of indispensible methodological laws that are independent of the particular character of the various theories of logic, and (β) the empirical level of existent formulations and applications of logical laws. On the empirical level, one can for instance compare Aristotelian and Buddhist theories of logic, look for equivalent fonnulations of logical laws, and ask whether such equivalences indicate universal validity of the respective laws. To enable exact comparison, one had to interprete the formulations, rephrase all of them in one and the same language, and perhaps even formalize them—a difficult task which brings into play aspects belonging to the methodological level (α).

In the following, I try to show that there indeed exist universally valid logical principles and that, with regard to logical reflection, members of different cultures do not behave in significantly different ways. In my deliberations, I rely on, and further develop, arguments I have put forward in earlier publications.[3] First, I shall expound some basic and general arguments, i.e., anthropological, methodological, and empirico-inductive arguments. Then, secondly, I argue against the view that all logical principles depend on the linguistic particularities of the languages that express these principles. Thirdly, I want to refute the popular hypothesis that Eastern logic negates the *tertium non datur,* i.e., the principle, according to which every A is (a) B or non-B.

2. Basic arguments in favour of the existence of universally valid logical principles, and against the view that there exists a distinctively Eastern logic.

2.1 Judged from an anthropological point of view, man's capability for logical thinking is a function of his biological dispositions as *homo sapiens.* Without developing and employing this faculty he would simply not survive. Hence, if we use the word "logical" as referring to structures that accord with fundamental logical laws and rules, all cultures are equally 'logical.' By "fundamental logical laws and rules" I refer to such principles as the law of identity (A is A), the principle of non-contradiction (A is not non-A), the *tertium non datur* and the law of transitivity (or the *dictum de omni et nullo*). Thereby, I do not have in mind specific versions particular to certain theories of logic, but laws and rules of form that are, as I will try to show, methodologically indispensible.

2.2 For, if we want to understand a foreign culture, we must presuppose that its members are able to think logically, and that they usually try to do this. Actually, *this is an indispensible methodological and methodical principle for every kind of understanding.* When interpreting a text we must presuppose that it is—in one way or other, intentionally or unintentionally, consciously or unconsciously, on the level of object-language or meta-language—a function of the named logical principles. The same applies if we want to translate a text, for a translation is but a special kind of interpretation. By making such a presupposition, we do not read any logic into the respective text. We do not fall victim to a vicious circle, for our procedure permits for the conclusion that the respective text cannot be understood at all. This, then, could indeed imply that the text not only violates 'our' logical principles, but is a function, a result, or reflexion of 'something' completely different from them. As already pointed out, mere violations are irrelevant, for we also violate mathematical laws. In the second case, however, we would not be able to identify the 'something'. I do not know of any interpretation of a text which arrived at the conclusion that the text reflected, or was determined by, such a mysterious 'something', not to mention interpretations of a whole culture. Some Daoists and Zennists have attacked logical principles. However, certain Western philosophers did the same. One need only remember the so-called Greek sophists. But whoever thereby tried to convince his opponents, had himself to employ logical laws and rules.

2.3 There are also important empirico-inductive arguments indicating that the named logical principles are universally valid. These arguments must not be misunderstood. As pointed out, they do not prove that certain specific versions of these principles are identical, but can only show that some of the formulations are equivalent expressions of the principles, and thus indicate the principles' universal validity.

(i) Fundamental logical principles were articulated not only in ancient Greece but, independently from this, also in ancient China, and ancient India. In China, the later Mohists' logic of the 4th century B.C. includes formulations of the above named logical principles. The same applies to Buddhist logic (*hetu-vidyā*) developed in India from about the 1st through the 6th century A.D.[4]

(ii) Parts of Buddhist logic that are equivalent to Aristotelian logic in every logically relevant respect were taken over by Chinese and, only a little bit later, by Japanese Buddhist scholars. Copies of Chinese translations of Sanskrit *hetu-vidyā* treatises were brought to Japan already during the second half of the 7th century, and, under the name of *immyō.* soon became object of extensive and detailed studies.[5] In a similar way, from about the 9th century AD, Arabic (or Muslim) scholars embraced Aristotelian logic, and made it an object of investigation. The transmittance of 'Indian' and 'Greek' logic would have been impossible, if there were no universally valid logical principles that, in the sense indicated in 2.2, were not acknowledged as norms by the peoples of all times and places.

(iii) Many scholars who hold that Aristotelian theories of logic differ from traditional Chinese and Indian theories of logic even with regard to the acknowledgement of fundamental logical laws, try to justify their view by the following arguments: (α) "Logic" is a Western word, designating distinctively Western, especially Aristotelian notions and theories. Indian, Chinese, and Japanese scholars did not know of these notions before words such as "logic" were translated in their languages. (β) Further, traditional notions such as Chin. *mo bian,* Skt. *hetu-vidyā,* Chin. *yinming,* and Jap. *immyō* do not refer to such 'pure' theories as Aristotelian logic is, but to *comprehensive and pragmatic theories of discussion that include ontology, epistemology, and even ethics.* Also, these theories lack the Aristotelian formalizations. However, both arguments, (α) as well as (β), are easily refuted, or irrelevant. First of all, if the characteristics and the notion of a theory depend on its name, then Aristotle must not be credited with having developed, and comprehended, Aristotelian logic, for he never called his respective theory "logic". Actually, in European history, "logic" had various meanings, and it was probably not before the middle ages that the term "logic" became the standard designation for Aristotelian logics, particularly the doctrines developed in the *Organon,* and in interpretations of the *Organon.* Thus, if one ought not call, e.g., *hetu-vidyā,* logic, since traditionally it has not be called so, one ought not call Aristotelian logic "logic" either. Or one ought at least admit that there was no Aristotelian logic, before Cicero, Boethius, or some later medieval European scholars did not call it "logic". The whole idea that all characteristics of a notion, concept or theory must depend on a certain word, designation, or name for the notion, concept, or theory is ridiculous. Secondly, if, e.g., *mo bian* and *hetu-vidhyā,* are *comprehensive and pragmatic theories of discussion that include ontology, epistemology, and even ethics,* then this is also true of Aristotle's logic as developed in the *Organon,* and most, if not all, traditional Aristotelian logic until Leibniz and Kant. This becomes particularly clear from two characteristics *hetu-vidhyā* and Aristotelian logic have in common. Both (sets of) theories were developed to provide an efficient instrument for defending "the truth", or the doctrine one believed in, against opponents, for refuting opponents, and for successfully dealing with so-called sophists. It is for this reasons that both traditions, *hetu-vidyā* as well as Aristotelian logic, devoted much energy to answering the questions of how to avoid contradictions, to identify and disclose the contradictions of opponents, and to triumph over an opponent who argues inconsistently. Even Japanese *hetu-vidhyā* scholars (*immyō gakusha*) wrote treatises on what was called "the four kinds of contradiction (*shishu sōi*)" and "the 33 mistakes in argumentation (*sanjusan ka*)."[6] Generally speaking, they extensively and in detail discussed "fallacious means of proof" and "fallacious means of reputation."[7] On the other hand, an Aristotelian treatise as late as Raimundus Lullus' (1232-1316) *Nova Logica* still included large passages on para-syllogisms and fallicious inferences. And the same even applies to Antoine Arnaud's *La Logique ou L'Art de penser* of 1685, and Christian Wolff's so-called German Logic of 1713.[8] The second characteristic, many *hetu-vidhyā* and Aristotelian treatises on logic have in common, is their religious features. In some cases, it is only an eulogy devoted to Buddha, Dignāga, or the Christian god respectively. In other cases, the treatises possess an unmistakingly apologetic character. The most extreme example, however, I know of, is no Indian, or Sino-Asian, no *nyāya,* and no Buddhist treatise, but Lullus' Aristotelian *Nova Logica,* for Lullus maintains that "the true syllogism is a picture of the trinity." By saying this, Lullus wants to argue that a perfect syllogism must have three parts because the Christian god (though one) comprises three 'persons' within himself, namely, father, son, and holy spirit.[9] Finally, the argument that Aristotelian logic is formalized logic, and/or a theory of logical form, while Eastern logic is not, is wrong or irrelevant. One can very well adequately express a universal law of logical form without using variables or abstract symbols. Dignāga's concepts, or theories, of the wheel of reason (*hetu*), and the three marks of reason, may be regarded as an example. In sum, if one wants to distinguish traditional Western and Eastern logic by trying to point out differences in theoretical purity, one is doomed to failure.

(iv) Independent from each other, many ancient cultures developed impressive mathematical insights. Laws such as the *Theorem of Pythagoras* were detected and formulated in Egypt, Mesopotamia, Greece, and China. This indicates that the same logical laws were employed.

(v) One must not confuse the existence of expressly formulated theories of logic, and the interest in developing such theories, with logical competence and with actual acknowledgment or denial of logical laws. Most people argue logically without being interested in any theory of logic. Though Chinese and Japanese scholars did not write as many treatises on logic, as Western scholars did, this is irrelevant if it comes to the question of whether there exist universally valid logical principles.

(vi) Poetic or aesthetic expression must not be confused with inconsistency, or with a neglect of, or adversion to, logic. Even when reading verses such as the following from Goethe's *Faust*, it does not occur to us that they are illogical. We immediately recognize them as a methaphor:

> Alle theory, my friend, is grey.
> But green is life's glad golden tree.[10]

(vii) Logicalness must not be confused with systematism. Among, e.g., Chinese and Japanese philosophical texts, there are no systematic ensembles such as the writings of Aristotle or Kant's three *Critiques,* and there exists nothing similar to Spinoza's ethics *more geometrico.* But this does not indicate a lack of logical consistency. There may be inconsistencies in the Chinese and Japanese treatises. But this is of no significance, since most Western philosophical treatises of some length also contain logical mistakes, among them Spinoza's *Ethics.* So far nobody has shown that there exist significant differences in either number or degree. Besides, the human struggle for all-comprehensive consistency is perhaps characterized by effort rather than success.

Terms such as "logical" are inapt for indicating cultural

differences. However carefully they are defined or employed, usually they will be understood as also referring to fundamental logical laws, thus suggesting that the differences are much deeper and much more serious than it is actually possible for them to be. Obviously, this hampers cross-cultural understanding. Since usually words such as "logical" are also intended to refer to fundamental logical laws and logical consistency, their usage becomes even more difficult. Cases in which such a reference is explicitly excluded, are certainly rare, and hardly convincing. I myself do not know of any example. Indeed, whenever "logic" or "logical" is used with the intent to point out cultural differences, this inevitably calls forth an imagination of almost mysteriously different worlds. No wonder that this impression is invited by formulations and distinctions such as those I have quoted and referred to above.

What applies to terms such as "logical," similarily applies to terms intended to designate opposite notions, especially "aesthetical" and "emotional." Actually, they simply do not refer to opposite notions, i.e, contrary or contradictory concepts. Otherwise logical consistency and aesthetical expression could not be compatible with each other but even Japanese poems express philosophical ideas without violating logical rules. The *Genji monogatari,* "The Tale of [prince] Genji," a famous Japanese novel written about 1000 AD, includes a chapter which, in a rather argumentative and convincing manner, develops an aesthetical theory *innuce.*[11] Further, if a notion is faulty, its opposite notions are also faulty. If "black" designates yellow, than "not black" designates every colour not yellow, and hence also black.

3. *Some Arguments Against Linguistic Relativism*

3.0 Examination of the hypothesis that logical theory and practice depend on the particularities of the different human languages, confirms and strengthens my previous arguments.

3.1 Aristotle already made it clear that identifyable speech, including "reasoning with oneself," and, as a matter of consequence, communication and understanding are impossible without somehow acknowledging the laws of identity, non-contradiction, and/or excluded middle. Nobody, oneself included, would be able to identify a meaning, or reference, if A would also mean, or refer to, non-A, e.g., human also to non-human. The later Mohists put forward the same argument. This is to say, that these logical principles are of a more fundamental kind than every (natural) language and speech. Language and speech are a function of fundamental logical principles, and not *vice versa.* Since the arguments advanced by Aristotle and the later Mohists are of timeless relevance, I quote the most important parts:

> ... a principle which every one must have who understands anything that is, is not a hypothesis; and that which every one must know who knows anything, he must already have when he comes to a special study. Evidently then such a principle is the most certain of all; which principle this is, let us proceed to say. It is, that the same attribute cannot at the same time belong and not belong to the same subject and in the same respect; we must presuppose, to guard against dialectical objections, any further qualifications which might be added. This, then, is the most certain of all principles...
>
> For it is impossible for anyone to believe the same thing to be and not to be, as some think Heraclitus says. For what a man says, he does not necessarily believe ...
>
> We can ...demonstrate negatively even that this view [that it is possible for the same thing to be and not to be] is impossible, if our opponent will only say something...
>
> The starting-point for all such arguments is not the demand that our opponent shall say that something either is or is not (for this one might perhaps take to be a begging of the question), but that he shall say something which is significant both for himself and for another; for this is necessary, if he really is to say anything. For, if he means nothing, such a man will not be capable of reasoning, either with himself or with another. But if anyone grants this, demonstration will be possible; for we shall already have something definite. The person responsible for the proof, however, is not he who demonstrates but he who listens; for while disowning reason he listens to reason. And again he who admits this has admitted that something is true apart from demonstration (so that not everything will be 'so and not so').
>
> ...not to have one [definite, identifiable] meaning is to have no

> meaning, and if words have no meaning our reasoning with one another, and indeed with ourselves, has been annihilated; for it is impossible to think of anything if we do not think of one [definite] thing...
>
> ...if all contradictory statements are true of the same subject at the same time, evidently all things will be one [identical]...
>
> Again, is he in error who judges either that the thing is so or that it is not so, and is he right who judges both? ...if all are alike both wrong and right, one who is in this condition will not be able either to speak or to say anything intelligible; for he says at the same time both 'yes' and 'no.' And if he makes no judgement but 'thinks' and 'does not think', indifferently, what difference will there be between him and a vegetable?[12]

The later Mohists pointed out:

> To call this thing "crane" [*hao*] is admissible, but still it is no crane [*fei ...hao*]. To say that both that thing and this are this thing would not be admissible [*wei bi shi 'shi' ye buge*]; the sayer would have nothing which is specifically the thing it is called.[13]

As the contrast between "crane" and "no crane" indicates, *bi*, "that," is contradictory to *shi*, "this." Hence, to forbid calling both that and this "this," means to forbid calling both A and non-A "A." This is to say that one ought not violate the law of non-contradiction. Otherwise our speech would be empty. There would be nothing we would refer to. Besides this, the Mohist advance another reason because of which we ought abide by the law of non-contradiction. They emphasize that otherwise we could not use our speech as a basis for other expressions usually arrived at by substitution.[14]

Thus, like Aristotle, the Mohists justify the law of non-contradiction pragmatically. The Greek scholar and the Chinese scholars agree that we cannot reflect on an idea, and not pursue a line of thought, unless we do not identify an A as an A and distinguish it from non-A(s). If one holds that Aristotle, in his *Metaphysics,* also (though only more or less implicitly) refers to the law of identity, one must also hold that the later Mohists do the same.

3.2 Contrary to a widespread relativist view, Aristotle's logic is not, in any logically relevant sense, based on linguistic features particular to ancient Greek. In particular, it is not based on the grammatical distinction between subject and object. Aristotle's logic deals with the relations of identity and diversity that (can) exist between concepts, especially with the relations between general and specific concepts, *genera* and *species*. For example, the logical meaning of the proposition "Cranes are birds" is "The contents of the concept 'bird' is included in the contents of the concept 'crane,' " with "crane" being the *species,* and 'bird' the *genus.* In a similar way, Indian, Tibetan, Chinese, and Japanese Buddhist logicians distinguished between linguistic and logical categories. For instance, the Sanskrit *hetu-vidyā* terms *dharmin* and *dharma,* which mean "property-possessor" and "property," clearly refer to non-linguistic 'entities.' In particular, they do not refer to any syntactical categories. And the same holds true for the respective Chinese and Japanese translations and readings, *youfa* and *yǒu,* and *uhō* and *hō* respectively. The technical phrasing of one standard example of many *hetu-vidyā* treatises, "Sound is impermanent," was "There is impermanence in sound." Though in this sentence "sound" is no longer grammatical subject, it remaines *dharmin,* "property-possessor," which alone is logically relevant.[15]

3.3 There are indeed some specific logical rules that depend on linguistic particularities. But this does not limit the universal validity of such laws as the principle of non-contradiction. The Aristotelian rule of subaltemation is valid only if the words "*all* x" can also mean, or refer to, *some* x. The later Mohists, however, used a word "all (*jin*)" which excluded the meaning of "some (*huo*)." According to their definition and usage of "some," "some" meant "not all."[16] This notwithstanding, the logical structures constituted by the identity and diversity relations between concepts are not influenced by this particularities of language use. To put it differently, while Aristotle, in his usage of "some," developed a logical theory of particular statements (or propositions), the Mohists, in their usage of "some," developed a theory of so-called *strictly* particular statements.

3.4 The independent discovery and formulation of the same logical laws in various cultures the languages of which differed significantly from each other, would probably have been impossible if there existed no universally valid logical principles that do not depend on linguistic particularities. The same applies to the facts that Aristotelian texts on logic were translated into Syriac and Arabic, and that Sanskrit treatises on *hetu-vidyā* were translated into Chinese and Tibetan, and that these translations became the basis for further developments of logic in e.g. Muslim, Japanese and Tibetan cultures respectively.

3.5 Some relativists hold that languages such as Chinese and Japanese lead to, or at least further, a way of thinking that negates the *tertium non datur.* In earlier publications, I have quoted numerous passages from Chinese classics that refute this hypothesis.[17] In his "Language and Logic in Modern Japan,"[18] Carl Becker tries to justify his view of a distinctively Japanese logic by referring to Chad Hansen's characterization of Chinese nouns' as "mass nouns."[19] In Becker's opinion, this characterization applies also to Japanese nouns. "Mass nouns" are nouns that are not easily connected with numbers, or that refer to something that cannot easily be counted, such as "water" or "grass." Irrespectable of whether Hansen's characterization is true or not, the following must be said. First, a vocabulary and grammar of mass nouns simply cannot affect affirmation and negation of the *tertium non datur,* for there are numerous possibilities for sharply, and completely, distinguishing between parts, aspects, realms etc. of 'masses.' Further, that ancient Japanese, or so-called *Yamato kotoba,* possessed its particular features—as, by the way, every natural language does—does not call into question the notion of universally valid logical laws. Becker should have been aware of this, since, inspite of the linguistic particularities of old Germanic and old Finno-Ugric languages, he did not mind to speak of European, or Western, logic, instead restricting himself to speaking of Greek logic.

4. *The Tertium Non Datur as a Fundamental Principle of 'Eastern' Logic*

Most scholars who hold that there exists a distinctively Eastern logic, justify their view by stating that numerous relevant Eastern texts negate the *tertium non datur.* In particular, they refer to Buddhist treatises and scriptures, and especially to Nāgārjuna's works and Kumārajīva's (344-413) Chinese translation of an annotated version of Nāgārjuṇa's *Mūlamadhyamaka-kārikā,* the *Zhonglun.*[20] In Tibetan and Sino-Asian Buddhism, the *Mūlmadhyamaka-kārikā* and its translations were extremely influential. It is also because of this reason that many scholars believe that this treatise provides the most convincing example of a negation of the *tertium non datur.* The main reason for their view, however, is that the treatise makes abundant use of the *tetralemma* (Skt. *cātuskoṭi,* Jap. *shiku fumbetsu*) which they regard as the single most important, and as an (almost) formal and systematical, denial of the *tertium non datur.* Since I have already tried to refute this opinion,[21] in the following I confine myself to summing up my analyses of the *Zhonglun.*

One of the basic goals of the *Zhonglun* is to show that our common notions of existence are inadequate to characterize true reality, i.e., the text wants to prove that tnings do not exist in the way in which we usually express or describe their existence. In particular it tries to prove that nothing exists eternally and that nothing is "annihilated," i.e. perishes without traces. In most cases, the proof runs as follows:

Proposition:

A does not exist.

Proof:

(i) Suppose A exists.

(ii) Then A exists/must exist as B or non-B.[22]

(iii) This is impossible because of at least one of the following reasons: (α) There is no empirical evidence for the existence of B or non-B. (β) The proposition that B or non-B exists implies a contradiction, or a *regressus ad infinitum,* or an assumption which is as questionable and unproved as the proposition itself.[23]

Conclusion:

A does not exist.[24]

The following example contains an exemplary statement of the *tertium non datur:*

[Proposition:]

Goers do not exist. Why not?

[Proof:]

(i) If goers exist,

(ii) then there [can] exist [only] two kinds of goers, namely, those who go/start [by themselves?], and those who do not. Apart from these two kinds, there is no third one.[25]

According to the *Zhonglun,* (iii) neither of the two kinds exists, since otherwise reasoning would be inconsistent.

In some cases, (ii) is formulated as *tetralemma:*

(ii*) Then A exists/must exist as (1) B, or (2) non-B, or (3) B *and* non-B, or (4) neither B *nor* non-B.[26]

To give an example:

(ii*) The dharmas do not originate from (1) themselves,

nor from (2) others,

nor from (3) both, nor (4) without reasons.

(iii) Thus one knows that they do not originate at all.[27]

The examples should suffice to show that the *tetralemma* by no means negates the *tertium non* datur. For, in the first place, the *tetralemma* simply aims at combinatory perfection. It is used as a divice to cover every imaginable case, nonsensical cases included. Secondly, it actually contains an application of, and thus presupposes, the *tertium non datur.* Thirdly, the abstract formula of (ii*) which is so often used to prove the existence of a distinctively Eastern logic, presents the *tetralemma* in a generalized form rarely realized in the Buddhist texts. This applies in particular to the logical form suggested by the formula. In many cases, instances of "B *and* non-B" and "*neither* B *nor* non-B" are completely lacking. Furthermore, if a *phrase* like "B *and* non-B" actually occurs, it usually refers to a logical contrast such as "eternal" and "absolutely non-existent," or to different perspectives, but does not designate contradictories. If it does, however, then "B *and* non-B" often means a logical adjunction ("B *and/or* non-B"), i.e., a combination of B and non-B. The second example is a case in point: dharmas that do not originate from themselves, nor from others, may originate from both, that is, half from themselves and half from others. Cases, in which "B *and* non-B" occurs, and expresses a (self-)contradiction, are rare, and usually without much ado dismissed as untenable.

Furthermore, "*neither* B *nor* non-B" must not be confused with "neither B *exists nor* non-B *exists.*" The latter can be true. For example, neither blue dragons nor dragons which are not blue do exist. As far as the *Zhonglun* accepts "*neither* B *nor* non-B," the text refers to what it regards as untenable notions of existence. As already mentioned, one goal of the *Zhonglun* is to criticize such notions. None of all these cases implies the notion that "B *and* non-B" can be logically valid.

According to another interpretation of the *Zhonglun,* the treatise, following old Buddhist ontology, regards reality as a process of continuous change and hence as indeterminate. This could lead to the following two conclusions. (i) If one holds that the *Zhonglun* acknowledges only what is indeterminate, one could argue that it advocates a one-valued-logic (with "indeterminate" being the only value). (ii) If one concedes that the treatise also attributes a certain validity to the way in which we treat reality as determinate, one could argue that it advocates a many-valued logic, i.e., a logic that distinguishes between at least three values, for example the ontological "attributes" "eternal(ly existent)", "absolutely non-existent" and "indeterminate(ly existent)". In the light of the examples quoted above, the first conclusion can be savely dismissed, and as far as I know, has never been actually formulated.[28] Since the *Zhonglun* bases its ontology on an acknowledgement of the fundamental principles of logic, such an interpretation would be inconsistent. Nor does the second interpretation—though certainly a tenable one—permit for the view that the *Zhonglun* rejects the *tertium non datur.* For the hinted at many-valued logic would be but a conservative extension of a two-valued logic; it would presuppose and include a dichotomy between the values "determinate" and "indeterminate." One particular merit of the second interpretation is that it allows for reconstructing certain instances of the *tetralemma* as expressions of a many-valued logic, *thus* rendering the forth clause valid. As a matter of cosnequence, it also allows for a consistent explanation of an important argument often used by defenders of *Zhonglun*-philosophy, namely, that the negation of a proposition "A is B" need *not* be a contradicting proposition,[29] for, if B means (something) indeterminate, "non-B" would mean the same.

Whether the logic of Buddhist treatises is always sound, is a different problem irrelevant to the question of whether or not these treatises accept and/or employ the *tertium non datur*. To conclude, even the *Zhonglun* does not support the hypothesis that there exists a distinctively Eastern logic. It provides no evidence for any 'different logic.' In particular, according to this treatise the law of non-contradiction and the *tertium non datur* are indispensible instruments and criteria of valid argument, and especially ontological analysis. The much lauded result that logical principles are no ontological laws, and that we cannot grasp reality as it is—by the way, an insight that the Aristotelian logician Kant and many other Western philosophers also arrived at—is impressive evidence for a clear distinction between logical and ontological structures."

I cannot resist concluding my remarks on the *tertium non datur* by quoting from another Buddhist treatise which has also been very influential within the Sino-Asian Buddhist world, namely Xuan Zang's *Cheng wei shi lun,* "The Doctrine of Mere-Consciousness:"[30]

> ...that existent dharmas are neither identical nor different ...contradicts the common knowledge of the world that things are either identical with or different from other things ...[*you fei yi yi wei shi gong zhi you yi yi wu*][31]

5. *The Untenable Myth of a Culturally Distinctive Logic*

Most comparisons that confront Western and Eastern cultures by referring to differences in Western and Eastern logic, result from misunderstandings and terminological confusion. To preclude or at least reduce such faults, one ought distinguish between methodologically and meta-theoretically indispensible laws of logical form on the one hand, and ontological theories such as Buddhist notions of reality and so-called quantum logics on the other hand. One must not confuse the instrument logic with the theories that result from its employment, or with the objects that these theories try to explain. These theories may very well be theories of undeterminate or 'many-valued' structures. Further, one ought not use terms like "Eastern logic" in the vague sense of a materially (or intentionally) distinctive way of thinking, while employing the term 'Western logic' in the sense, e.g., of Aristotelian syllogistics. Buddhist ontologies, particularly Buddhist doctrines of true and provitional reality, ought not be called logics. Otherwise one would be obliged to call, e.g., European theories of a realization of a *unio mystica* logics too. Thirdly, one ought compare things of the *same kind,* for example Aristotelian logic to Buddhist *hetu-vidyā,* or, more precisely Aristotelian theories of logical consistence and inference to Buddhist doctrines of logical consistence and inference, and judge them *by applying the same standards.* If one describes and evaluates the historical circumstances which influenced *hetu-vidyā* and then maintains that these circumstances determined its character, one ought analyze and judge Aristotelian logic in the same way. Fourthly, one ought not overgeneralize, as for instance Suzuki Daisetz did in all his comparative studies. Finally, one ought carefully distinguish between grammatical, aesthetical, systematical, mathematical, and general laws, rules, and structures of rationality on the one hand, and logical laws, rules, and structures on the other.

Indeed, whenever terms like "logic" and "logical" are used to point out important cultural differences, they call forth the imagination of mysteriously different and unbridgeable worlds.

NOTES

1. Wolfgang Welsch and Detlef Horster in the *Frankfurter Rundschau* of the 3rd of September 1996, and the 11th of January 1997 respectively. My translation. A considerable number of German scholars hold similar views.
2. Scholars often misunderstand or overestimate the significance of such theories or instruments as "fuzzy logic" and "para-consistent logic." Though such systems seem to constitute radical alternatives to classical, or two valued, formal logic, this is not the case. As a kind of material logic, fuzzy logic belongs to a category radically different from formal logic. Also, as a set of particular theories of "logical" laws etc., it must not be confused with logical laws of universal methodological relevance. As to para-consistent logics, this is a set of theories which permit for contradictions but, by introducing respective rules, also preclude that these contradictions have relevant consequences, e.g., infect a whole theory and render it worthless. For example, applying the rule of *ex falso quod libet* is forbidden, since otherwise one could infer from the logical inconsistencies (the theories permit) that *every* proposition is true. Or any *reductio ad absurdum* is forbidden. In my opinion, however, such *ad hoc* devices are methodologically questionable. Apart from being designed to avoid unwelcome consequences, these devices also result from the development of so-called modern logic as for instance David Hilbert and Wilhelm Ackermann conceived of it in their famous *Grundzüge der Logik* (6. ed., Springer, Berlin, 1972).

Hilbert and Ackermann regard this development as a kind of progress. But this estimation must be qualified. The modern use of truth values and the introduction of a kind of existential import (i.e., of existential quantification) amount to limiting the scope of formal logic. If it comes to the question of how to conceive of *pure logical form,* perhaps the following solution is the best. Logical structures ought be understood as relations constituted by the identity and difference of concepts, independent of ontological, linguistic, psychological and mathematical particularities. This very approach precludes acceptance, and application, of the rule *ex falso quod libet.* And it also precludes acceptance of para-consistent logics, if such logics are thought to provide more than conventional and pragmatic systems or instruments, designed to fulfil particular goals and needs. Such systems can be no alternatives to a set of non-conventional laws of formal logic. Besides, certain theories of modern logic question the universal validity of the *reductio ad absurdum* because of *material* reasons, namely, because of problems of decision and application.

Probably, Bruno Baron von Freytag-Löringhoff has given the most comprehensive and convincing account of how and why 'pure formal logic' ought be conceived of as referring to the relations constituted by the identity and difference of concepts. Cf. his *Logik I,* 5th ed., Kohlhammer, Stuttgart, 1973, and *Neues System der Logik,* Meiner, Hamburg, 1985.

3. Paul, Gregor, *Mythos. Philosophie und Rationalität,* Lang, Frankfurt/M., 1988. *Aspects of Confucianism,* Lang, Frankfurt/M., New York, 1990. "Reflections on the Usage of the Terms 'Logic' and 'Logical'", *Journal of Chinese Philosophy* 1991 (18), pp. 73-87. *Philosophie in Japan,* iudicium, München, 1993 "Argumente für die Universalität der Logik, Mit einer Darstellung äquivalenter Axiome aristotelischer Syllogistik, spätmohistischer Logik und buddhistischer Begründungstheorie", *Hōrin* 1994 (1), pp. 57-86. "Reflections on the tertium non datur: Theories and Applications in Chinese and European Philosophies" in Michéle Schmiegelow (ed.), *Democracy in Asia,* St Martin's Press, New York, 1997, pp. 113-125. "The Myth of a Distinctively Chinese logic: Chinese Philosophy and the tertium non datur," *Studies in Central and East Asian Religions* 1997 (10), pp. 39-51. "Einheit der Logik und Einheit des Menschenbildes: Reflexionen über das Tertium non datur" in A. Baruzzi and A. Takeichi (eds.), *Ethos des Interkulturellen,* Ergon Verlag, Würzburg, 1998, pp. 15-29. "Probleme, Ziele und Relevanz einer Theorie universaler Logik, Unter besonderer Berücksichtigung sinologischer Interessen", *minima sinica* 1998 (1), pp. 40-69. "Neuere Literatur zur (buddhistischen) Begründungstheorie, Hōrin 1999 (6), pp. 249-259.
4. Cf. my "Argumente für die Universalität der Logik."
5. Cf. my *Philosophie in Japan.*
6. Cf. my *Philosophie in Japan,* pp. 164-192, and 349-365.
7. This is Tachikawa Musashi's translation of the respective Sanskrit terms. Cf. Tachikawa Musashi, "A Sixth-Century Manual of Indian Logic: A Translation of the Nyāyapraveśa," *Journal of Indian Philosophy* 1971 (1), no. 2, pp. 111-145.
8. Lullus, Raimundus, *Die neue Logik: Logica Nova,* (Lateinisch-Deutsch), ed. and trans. Victorio Hôsle, Wissenschaftliche Buchgesellschaft, Darmstadt, 2002, pp. 225-271. Arnould, Antoine, *La Logique ou L'Art de penser,* A

Amsterdam, Chez Abraham Wolfgang, 1685, chapters X, XIX, and XX. Wolff, Christian, *Vernünftige Gedanken von den Kräften des menschlichen Verstandes und ihrem richtigen Gebrauche in Erkenntnis der Wahrheit* [Reasonable Thoughts about the Power of the Human Mind and its Right Usage in Recognizing the Truth], ed. Hans Werner Arndt, Olms, Hildesheim, New York, 1978. Actually, the title of Wolff's treatise in Aristotelian logic is revealing.

9. Cf. Lullus, *Die neue Logik: Logica Nova,* pp. LI-LII.
10. Goethe, J.W., *Faust,* Part One, trans. P. Wayne. Penguin Books, Harmondsworth, 1979, p. 98.
11. Cf. my "Der Begriff des ästhetischen Scheins im *Genji monogatari.* Oder: Von der Vergeblichkeit der Suche nach einer 'spezifisch japanischen Ästhetik.'" *Hōrin* 1996 (3), pp. 57-74.
12. Aristotle, *Metaphysics,* ed. Jonathan Barnes, trans. W.D. Ross, Princeton University Press, 1984, 1005b, 1006a, 1006b, 1007b, 1008b.
13. Quoted from A.C. Graham, *Later Mohist Logic, Ethics and Science,* The Chinese University Press, Hong Kong, 1978, pp. 446-447.
14. Cf. Graham, *Later Mohist Logic, Ethics and Science,* pp. 40-44.
15. Cf. Tachikawa, "A Sixth-Century Manual of Indian Logic...," pp. 112-113.
16. Cf. Graham, *Later Mohist Logic, Ethics and Science,* pp. 294 and 470.
17. Cf. my "Reflections on the tertium non datur...," and "The Myth of a Distinctively Chinese logic..."
18. In Paul George Fendos, ed., *Cross-Cultural Communication: East and West,* Vol. III, Tainan, 1991, pp. 203-234.
19. Cf. Hansen, Chad, *Language and Logic in Ancient China,* The University of Michigan Press, Ann Arbor, 1983.
20. Cf. Bocking, Brian, *Nāgārjuna in China: A Translation of the Middle Treatise,* The Edwin Mellen Press, Lewiston, 1995. Also: Walleser, Max, trans., *Die Mittlere Lehre des Nāgārjuna, Nach der chinesischen Version übertragen,* Carl Winter's Universitätsbuchhandlung, Heidelberg, 1912.
21. Cf. my "Reflections on the tertium non datur...," "The Myth of a Distinctively Chinese logic..."
22. In most if not all cases, B refers to a concept and not to a sentence or statement. Hence "non-B" and not "not B." Further, "A is not B" can be reconstructed as "A is non-B." For example, "A is no chair," is equivalent to "A is a non-chair."
23. Cf. Walleser, *Die Mittlere Lehre des Nāgārjuna,* pp. 26 and 38. Cf. also my *Philosophy in Japan,* p. 131.
24. Max Walleser, *Die Mittlere Lehre des Nāgārjuna,* pp. 7-12, 14-18.
25. *Taishō Tripiṭaka,* vol. XXX, no. 1564, p. 4c; Walleser, *Die Mittlere Lehre des Nāgārjuna,* p. 14.
26. Walleser, *Die Mittlere Lehre des Nāgārjuna,* pp. 5, 47, 115 and 146.
27. *Zhonglun* I: 1; Walleser, *Die Mittlere Lehre des Nāgārjuna,* p. 5.
28. Besides this, a one-valued logic with "undeterminable" as the only value would make communication, and even individual reflection impossible. This should be clear from my above discussion of Aristotle's and the Mohists' pragmatic justification of fundamental logical, or methodological, laws.
29. Cf. for instance Kumārajīva's Chinese translation of Āryadeva's *Śata-*

sāstra, the *Bailun, Taishō Tripiṭaka,* vol. XXX, no. 1569, p. 181a; Tucci, Guiseppe (ed. and trans.), *Pre-Dinnāga Buddhist Texts on Logic from Chinese Sources,* Oriental Institute, Baroda, 1929, pp. 82-85, especially p. 85.

30. Wei Tat, *Cheng Wei-Shih Lun: The Doctrine of Mere-Consciousness. By Hsuan Tsang,* Hong Kong, 1973, pp. 44-45. Chinese text and English translation.

31. Cf. *Taishō Tripiṭaka,* vol. XXXI, no. 1585, pp. 3c-4a; Wei Tat, *Cheng Wei-Shih Lun: The Doctrine of Mere-Consciousness,* pp. 44-45; Chan Wing Tsit (ed. and trans.), *A Source Book in Chinese Philosophy,* Princeton University Press, 1969, pp. 379.

VII

POETICS

CHAPTER 31

Vāmana on Semantic Qualities: An Annotated Translation of the Kāvyālaṅkārasūtravṛtti (3.2.1-5.10-14)[1]

MARI HATTORI

The *guṇa*, or literary quality, is "mode of literary appreciation".[2] It was analyzed separately into verbal qualities (*śabda-guṇa*) and semantic qualities (*artha-guṇa*) for the first time by Vāmana, an 8th century's poetician and the author of the *Kāvyālaṅkārasūtra* (*KAS*) and his own commentary Kāvyālaṅkārasūtravṛtti (*KASV*).

After explaining ten verbal qualities (*śabda-guṇa*), Vāmana illustrates ten varieties of semantic qualities (*artha-guṇa*): floridity (*ojas*), lucidity (*prasāda*), coherence (*śleṣa*), equality (*samatā*), concentration (*samādhi*), delicacy (*mādhurya*), tenderness (*saukumārya*), nobleness (*udāratā*), clarity (*arthavyakti*), and splendor (*kānti*). The present article is an annotated translation of the *KAS* and *KASV* 3.2.1-5, 10-14,[3] the section of semantic qualities. In the notes I have referred to the *Kāmadhenu* of Gopendra Tripurahara Bhūpāla,[4] a commentary on the *KASV*.[5] I have explained also the *Abhinavabhāratī* of Abhinavagupta, where he quotes Vāmana while commenting on the *guṇa* of the *Nāṭyaśāstra*.[6]

As the basis of my translation I have used the edition of *Kāvyālaṅkārasūtrāṇi* edited by Nārāyaṇarāma, Motilal Banarsidass, Delhi, 1953.

Translation

As the consideration of the verbal qualities (*śabda-guṇa*) has been done, he says the following to distinguish the semantic qualities (*artha-guṇa*).

> Those same ones are semantic qualities (*artha-guṇa*).
> //*KAS* 3.2.1//

"Those same ones," that is, [those *guṇas* mentioned as verbal qualities] such as floridity (*ojas*), are also semantic qualities (*artha-guṇa*). The distinction between *śabda-guṇa* and *artha-guṇa* is shown by means of the signified and the signifier.[7]

> Floridity (*ojas*) is the boldness (*prauḍhi*) of meaning.
> // *KAS* 3.2.2//

"The boldness" (*prauḍhi*) "of meaning," that is, of that which is expressed (*abhidheya*), is the sublimity (*prauḍhatva*) and that is "floridity" (*ojas*).

Boldness (*prauḍhi*) of it (meaning) can be (1) expressing in a phrase (*vākyavacana*) the meaning of a word (*padārtha*), (2) mentioning in a word (*padābhidhā*) the meaning of a phrase (*vākyārtha*), (3) diffusion and contraction (*vyāsasamāsa*), or (4) having an intended implication (*sābhiprāyatva*).[8]

An example of the expressing in a phrase (*vākyavacana*) for the meaning of a word (*padārtha*) is as follows:

> Then, as the heaven, [bore] the light that arose from the eyes of Atri,[9]

Here, for the meaning that can be expressed by a word "moon," the phrase "the light that arose from the eyes of Atri" is used. And by "phrase" (*vākya*) is meant a collection of words.[10] Along these lines, other [passages] could also be shown.

For example:

> It was in the color of pale-white before. Afterwards, it was occupied by brownness. And then, due to the excess of ripeness, its body was mixed with a reddish property. /

> At the gradual onset of drying, its surface becomes uneven all over. In the forest, the jujube loses its fragrance and becomes tasteless. //[11]

There should not be an excessive attachment [for the floridity (*ojas*)]. Because the general definition of the quality (*guṇa*) has been fixed as to be the producer of the beauty of poetry.

An example of the mentioning in a word (*padābhidhāna*) for the meaning of a phrase (*vākyārtha*) is as follows:

For what could be said as "she is not a divine being but a human being", one says, "she blinks."[12]

There are both diffusion and contraction (*vyāsasamāsa*) for the meaning of a phrase (*vākyārtha*).[13] An example of the diffusion (*vyāsa*) is as follows:

> The mixture between pleasure and pain takes place in various ways. Either pleasure or pain is not there, and then, it is there. //
> However, afterwards there are some pleasure and pain together, and then still later, there is neither pain nor pleasure. //[14]

An example of the contraction (*samāsa*) is as follows:

> They said goodbye to Himalaya, went to see Śiva,/
> told him it was done, and, dismissed by him, went up in the sky.//[15]

An example of having an intended implication (*sābhiprayatva*)[16] is as follows:

> Now, this son of Candragupta, a young bright as the moon, has fortunately become a king who is a patron of the learned and has fulfilled his effort.

As there is a suggestion of [choosing] Vasubandhu[17] as a minister in "a patron of the learned," this is having an intended implication (*sābhiprāyatva*). In this manner,

> When the mass of hair of the lady with beautiful hair loosened due to love sport,

In this case, we can find also an intended implication in the expression "of the lady with beautiful hair."[18]

Lucidity (*prasāda*) is the clearness of meaning. // *KAS* 3.2.3//

The clearness of meaning consisting in using only what is effective (*prayojaka*) is "lucidity" (*prasāda*).[19] For example,

> A young girl of the same caste who is endowed with the onset of beauty and youthfulness.[20]

On the other hand, a counter-example of it is as follows:

> Let my hand approach this bright-jewel-belt-place.

As there is an indication of the loins by word "belt-place," the modifier ("bright-jewel") is not useful.[21]

Coherence (*śleṣa*) is the construction (*ghaṭanā*). //*KAS* 3.2.4//

A combination in which there is the logicalness due to a lack of disturbance in the sequence (of events) and the crookedness is "the construction (*ghaṭanā*)."[22] This is "coherence" (*śleṣa*). For example,

> Seeing his two lovers on the same bench, and coming up behind, he has closed the eyes of one lady. This man, mischievously playing a joke, /
> With his slightly-bent neck, thrilling, along with the heart jumping with love, kissed the broad cheek of the other lover who was shining with secret laughing. //[23]

More expansion of this [coherence (*śleṣa*)] can be seen in the compositions made by Śūdraka and so on.[24]

Equality (*samatā*) is evenness (*avaiṣamya*). //*KAS* 3.2.5//

"Evenness" (*avaiṣamya*) means the absence of difference in construction. Because in some places, the construction is broken. For example,

> The flowers of Kunda have fallen down. The trees are lazy in sending forth blossoms.
> These Malaya-winds glide gently disturbing the courage of separated lovers. /
> Then, the rays of sunlight cut the growth of the cold,
> But [they] do not hold the hardness that causes our fatigue.//

Here, in the second quarter of the stanza, which is meant to convey the juncture of two seasons,[25] there is a difference in construction, because the Malaya-winds are not (treated in) the same (way).[26] The second quarter of the stanza should be expressed as follows:

> *Kokilas*, composing songs in their minds, do not scatter [them] yet.

Or, the accessibility is the evenness (*avaiṣamya*). For example,

"There was [a mountain] of divine nature in the northern direction,"[27] etc.

The counter-examples are easy to find.

> Delicacy (*mādhurya*) is strikingness in expression (*uktivaicitrya*). // *KAS* 3.2.10//

What is striking in expression is "delicacy" (*mādhurya*).[28] For example,

> Nectars are sweet. There is no doubt. Honeys are not exceptional as well. A very juicy fruit of mango is also sweeter. / But, just once a man good at discrimination of taste must tell whether there is any sweeter thing than the teeth and lips of a lover. //[29]

> Tenderness (*saukumārya*) is a lack of harshness. // *KAS* 3.2.11//

A lack of harshness in a harsh meaning is "tenderness" (*saukumārya*).[30] For example, they say "having nothing left but glory" [instead of] "dead." Or, [instead of] "solitary," "Having God as a companion." And also instead of saying "go," [they say] "Carry on."

> Nobleness (*udāratā*) is not being vulgar (*agrāmayatva*). //*KAS* 3.2.12//

Not being vulgar when there is occasion to be vulgar is "nobleness" (*udāratā*).[31] For example,

> You are really beautiful and he is also famous for his brightness.
> Now, both of you possess the highest limit of arts. /
> Oh, thank heaven, how lucky this couple is! Then, when

what is left has been obtained,[32] it will be the victory of virtuousness.//[33]

The counter-example is as follows:

As long as this man sleeps, I will also sleep. What are you being deprived of? /
Declaring in this way, slowly she has prevented by her hand my hand that was moving towards the girdle. //

Clarity (*arthavyakti*) is the distinctiveness of the nature of objects. //*KAS* 3.2.13//

The distinctiveness of the nature of objects, that is, of things, is "clarity" (*arthavyakti*).[34] For example,

Having the luster of pieces in the form of conch-shell in the back, a water lily is fragrant in the water of a pond, with red streak marks of red resin on its cover, /
and with the tawny color of *gorocana* (bright yellow pigment prepared from the urine or bile of a cow) on the outside of its petals. //

Or, [an example of "clarity" (*arthavyakti*) is as follows.]

At first, its tip is scattered with the fatigue of broadened filaments, Next, it comes together slightly with loosened petals, /
Then, it contains pieces that are somehow just moving along with the outside petals. There was trouble in the action of closing for the aged lotuses. //[35]

Splendor (*kānti*) is having brilliant sentiment (*rasa*).
//*KAS* 3.2.14//

What has brilliant sentiments, that is the sentiment of love and so on, is "having brilliant sentiment" and to be that is "having brilliant sentiment" and this is "splendor" (*kānti*).[36] For example,

A lover, who was rejected by his beloved with an oath, and who has bowed down to her feet in the evening, and whose mind was disturbed, has gone out his house less than two to three steps, /
when [his beloved], holding her skirt together at the waist with

her hand, ran to the man and bowed to him. Ah, how striking the way of love is! //[37]

In this manner, other kinds of sentiments can be also illustrated.[38]

On this, there are verses:

It is called the maturity of poetry when the qualities (*guṇa*) are manifested entirely. /
And this is compared to the ripening of a mango (*cūta*).//[39]
If it is merely grammatically correct but is afflicted in its subjects and qualities /
that poem would be despised by the learned as the ripening of eggplant (*vṛntāka*). //[40]
What lacks ten varieties of the qualities (*guṇa*), is useless. /
Such a language is not worthy of consideration just like the "ten pomegranates." //[41]

Here ends the third chapter, called "on the constituent elements of the literature," of the *Kāvyālaṅkārasūtravṛtti*.

NOTES

1. I gratefully acknowledge helpful discussion with Prof. Gary Tubb on several points in this paper and his corrections of my English.
2. V. Raghavan, *Bhoja's Śṛṅgāraprakāśa*, Punarvasu, Madras, 1978, p. 244. Raghavan gives a comprehensive history of *guṇas* in the *Alaṅkāraśātras.* Cf. Raghavan, *Bhoja's Śṛṅgāraprakāśa*, pp. 244-343.
3. I have included the translation of the *KAS* and *KASV* 3.2.6-9, the section on "concentration" (*samādhi*) in my article, "Semantic Aspects of Vāmana's Poetics," *Cracow Indological Studies*, vol. 4 (in press).
4. *Kāmadhenu* (in *Kāvyālaṅkāra Sūtra of Ācārya Vāmana*, ed. with the *Kāvyālaṅkāra-Kāmadhenu* and Hindi Translation by Bechana Jha, the Kashi Sanskrit Series 209, Chowkhamba Sanskrit Series Office, Varanasi, 1971).
5. The translation of the *KAS* and *KASV* has already been done by Ganganatha Jha, *The Kāvyālaṅkārasūtras of Vāmana*, Sri Satguru Publications, Delhi (reprint edition), 1991. But Jha does not mention the *Kāmadhenu*.
6. *Abhinavabhāratī* (in the *Nāṭyaśāstra of Bharatamuni with the Commentary Abhinavabhāratī*, vol. II, ed. by Ramakrishna Kavi, Gaekwad's Oriental Series, vol. 68, Oriental Institute, Baroda 1956). Tubb has investigated Vāmana's *śabda-guṇas* along with the *Abhinavabhāratī*. Cf. "Gary A. Tubb, "Abhinavagupta on Phonetic Texture," *Journal of American Oriental Society* 105(3): 567-578. According to Tubb, "Abhinavagupta was surely in a better position to know the intentions of his fellow Kashimiri than the much later author of the printed commentary on Vāmana's work, the

Kāmadhenu of Gopendra Bhūpāla." Cf. Tubb, "Abhinavagupta on phonetic Texture" p. 567.

7. Jha translates "vācyavācakadvārrena" as "as due to the fact that the *word* is the *denoter* and the *idea* the *denoted.*" Cf. Jha, *The Kāvyālaṅkārasūtras of Vāmana,* p. 50. *Kāmadhenu* explains that "Though there is no difference by name between the verbal qualities and the semantic qualities, on account of the close connection between word and meaning there can be a difference [between verbal qualities and semantic qualities.] Cf. *Kāmadhenu,* p. 102, ll. 13-14.
8. Abhinavagupta refers to the examples of *KASV* in his commentary on the *Nāṭyaśāstra.* He gives Vāmana's example of "boldness" (*prauḍhi*) (i.e. *Raghuvaṃśa* 2.75) and his example of "diffusion" (*vyāsa*), but, according to Abhinavagupta, the former is called "expansion" (*vistara*) and the latter "brevity" (*saṃkṣepa*). Cf. *Abhinavabhāratī,* p. 341.
9. *Raghuvaṃśa* 2. 75a. See *Raghuvaṃśa* (ed. by M.R. Kale, Motilal Banarsidass, Delhi, 1991), p. 48.
10. *Kāmadhenu* explains that by '*vākya*', is meant simply a phrase rather than a sentence, as the word is defined in the *Amarakośa* 1.6.2 which *Kāmadhenu* quotes. Cf. *Kāmadhenu,* p. 105, ll. 3-4, *Amarakoṣa* (in *Nāmaliṅgānuśāsana of Amarakoṣa of Amarasiṃha with Rāmāśramī Commentary* ed. by Haragovinda Śāstrī, Kashi Sanskrit Series 198, Chaukambha Sanskrit Sansthan, Varanasi, 1997), p. 81.
11. *Kāmadhenu* explains that "Here, instead of what can be said as 'brownness' he has said as 'it was occupied by brownness.' Instead of what could be said as 'drying' he has said as 'at the gradual onset of drying.' As these statements are used, [this is an example of] 'the expressing in a phrase (*vākyavacana*) for the meaning of a word (*padārtha*)." Cf. *Kāmadhenu,* p. 105, ll. 7-9.
12. *Kāmadhenu* paraphrases "*iti vaktavye*" (for what is to be said) to "*iti naṣṭe*" (for what is in behind). Cf. *Kāmadhenu,* p. 105, l. 11. *Kāmadhenu* explains that "through this word which indicates the property of human being, she may not be a goddess." Cf. *Kāmadhenu,* p. 105, 1.13.
13. *Kāmadhenu* explains that "the meaning of word can take the status of the meaning of phrase and the meaning of phrase can take the status of the meaning of word." Cf. *Kāmadhenu,* p. 105, 1.16.
14. *Kāmadhenu* explains that "This experienced in the same way (by everyone)—intermixture takes place in various ways, or in variegated ways; this is the meaning of the phrase. There is an expansion of this, that is the diffusion made as 'There is either a pleasure or pain' and so on." Cf. *Kāmadhenu,* p. 105, ll.18-20.
15. *Kumārasaṃbhava* 6.94. Cf. *Kumārasaṃbhava* (in *Kālidāsa's Kumārasaṃbhava Cantos I-VIII,* edited with the Commentary of Mallinātha, a Literal English Translation, Notes and Introduction by M.R. Kale, Motilal Banarsidass, Delhi, 1995), p. 115.
16. *Kāmadhenu* explains that, "Without the use of another word, there is boldness conveying that meaning. This is 'having an intended implication' (*sābhiprāyatva*)." Cf. *Kāmadhenu,* p. 105, ll. 22-23.
17. Lahiri points out that there are two readings, that is 'Subandhu' and 'Vasubandhu.' Cf. Lahiri, P.C., *Concept of Rīti and Guṇa in Sanskrit Poetics,* V.K. Publishing House (first Indian edition), Delhi, 1987, p. 97.

18. *Kāmadhenu* explains that "In the passage of 'of a lady with beautiful hair', the excellence of hair is intended. It conveys the ability of her mass of hair to put to shame the trail of the peacock." Cf. *Kāmadhenu*, p. 105, ll. 24-26.
19. *Kāmadhenu* explains that "using only what is effective (*prayojaka*) means applying only the words that convey the intended meaning; from this, there is a clearness of meaning and this is lucidity (*prasāda*)." Cf. *Kāmadhenu*, p. 106, ll. 11-12.
20. Abhinavagupta refers to this passage in his commentary on the *Nāṭyaśāstra*. Cf. *Abhinavabhāratī* p. 335, ll. 22-24: *vivāhyatvaṃ prāpaṇīyatāhṛdyatvaṃ saṃbhogayogyatā, gṛhasthasahadharmacāriṇītvam ity upayogī sarvo 'yam arthaḥ*. (All the meaning is useful: marriageability, availability, charmingness, fitness for love, and capability to carry out the duties of a householder.)
21. *Kāmadhenu* explains that "'the modifier ("bright-jewel") is not useful' means the meaning is irrelevant." Cf. *Kāmadhenu*, p. 106, 1.17. Abhinavagupta refers to this verse in his commentary on the *Nāṭyaśāstra*. Cf. *Abhinavabhāratī*, p. 335, ll. 26-27: *atra vimalam anyathopayogāt pāṃsur iva jale 'trāprasannatāṃ karoti.* (Here, due to the unclear usage, there is an impurity just like dust in the water.)
22. *Kāmadhenu*, referring to the example of the *KASV*, explains that "As there is logicalness of fittingness in both the sequence or order [actions of] making eyes closed and so on, and the crookedness of the [actions] due to combined in a way lacking disturbance, so the combination or construction that is intended [here] is based on being free from questioning and being free from contradiction." *Kāmadhenu*, p. 107, ll. 10-12. Jha translates this passage of the *KASV* as "By 'commingling' is meant the mention of more than one action partaking of cunning not perceived (by the person concerned), and indicative of reasons (for the commingling of the acts and the non-perception of the cunning)." Cf. Jha, *The Kāvyālaṅkārasūtras of Vāmana*, p. 53. Lahiri points out that there are two interpretations for the word "*anulbaṇa*," that is, "lack of excessiveness" and "not perceived." Cf. Laḥiri, P.C., *Concepts of Rīti and Guṇa in Sanskrit Poetics*, p.101. Apte says on "anulvaṇa" that "free from disturbing circumstances." Cf. Vaman Shivaran Apte, *The Practical Sanskrit English Dictionary*, Rinsen Book Company, Kyoto, 1992 (third reprint), p. 106.
23. Amaruśataka 18, See Amaruśatakam (ed. by C.R. Devadhar, Motilal Banarsidass, Delhi, 1984) pp. 26-27. Abhinavagupta refers to this verse in his commentary on the *Nāṭyaśāstra*. Cf. *Abhinavabhāratī* p. 334, ll. 19-21: *atra manorathātīto 'py ekakālanāyikāyugalahṛdayagrahaṇalakṣaṇārthas tathopapādito yenāsaṃbhāvanāspadaṃ na bhavati tena kuṭilo 'py ayaṃ kramo na hṛdaye ulbaṇatvaṃ bhajate majjati* (Here, although, it is too much to wish for the meaning, characterized by pleasing the hearts of two heroines in a single moment, is in such a way that it is not unimaginable, so in spite of its crookedness, the sequence does not partake of or descend into a state of being disturbed in the heart [of a reader].)
24. Devadhar explains that "this *Arthaguṇa Śleṣa* is no other than a peculiarity of plot-construction; it is a definite pattern, and its repetition in Śūdraka's play is so frequent and so obvious as to justify Vāmana's remark that it is an outstanding characteristic of Śūdraka's play." Cf. C.R. Devadhar, "The Arthaguṇa Śleṣa," in S.M. Katre and P.K. Gode (eds.), *A Volume of Studies*

in Indology, Presented to Prof. P.V. Kane, M.A., LL.M, on his 61st Birthday 7th May 1941, Oriental Book Agency, Poona, 1941, p.154.

25. *Kāmadhenu* explains that "[This is] the juncture of the two seasons of early spring (*śiśira*) and spring (*vasanta*)." Cf. *Kāmadhenu*, p. 108, ll. 20. The six seasons are spring (*vasanta*) summer (*grīṣma*), rainy season (*varṣā*), autumn (*śarad*), winter (*hemanta*) and early spring (*śīśira*).
26. *Kāmadhenu* explains that "[the presence of Malaya-winds] is the property of spring only." (*Kāmadhenu*, p. 108, ll.20-21) Abhinavagupta refers to this verse in his commentary on the *Nāṭyaśāstra* and explains that the construction of the description of the juncture of two seasons is broken by 'Malaya-winds' but that they excite the [sentiment of love in] separation. Cf. *Abhinavabhāratī*, p.337, ll. 12-13.
27. *Kumārasaṃbhava* 1.1. Cf. *Kumārasaṃbhava*, p.1.
28. *Kāmadhenu* explains that "When excellence is to be achieved in something that is about to be described, strikingness is wording it in another way." Cf. *Kāmadhenu*, p. 113, ll. 19-20.
29. Abhinavagupta, referring to the expression of *Nāṭyaśāstra* as for delicacy (*mādhurya*) that is expressed repetedly and strikingly, interprets this verse as follow: Cf. *Abhinavabhāratī*, p. 340, ll. 8-9: *atra rasavad amṛtam iti ya evārthaḥ sa eva kaḥ sandeha ity uktayā vicitrayā pariniścayasthairyābhidhāyinyā niścayīkṛtaḥ*. (Here, in the expression of "Nectars are sweet" and so on, by the striking expression of "there is no doubt" that indicates ascertainment, for the meaning of "indeed" (*eva*), ascertainment is made.) On the other hand, *Kāmadhenu* explains that When what is to be expressed is that a kiss is superior to any other comparable things, because there is indication in another manner such as "Nectars are sweet," there is delicacy (*mādhurya*). Cf. *Kāmadhenu* p. 113, ll. 24-26. This verse occurs in Vidyākara's *Subhāṣitaratnakoṣa*. Cf. *The Subhāṣitaratnakoṣa* ed. by D.D. Kosambi and V.V. Gokhale, Cambridge (MA), Harvard University Press, 1957, p. 96. See also Daniel H.H. Ingalls, *An Anthology of Sanskrit Court Poetry Vidyākara's "Subhāṣitaratnakoṣa"* p. 48, 190.
30. *Kāmadhenu* explains that "What is lacking harshness when what is to be described is a harsh meaning that produces inauspiciousness and discomfort and so on, is tenderness (*saukumārya*). Cf. *Kāmadhenu*, p. 114, ll. 10-11.
31. *Kāmadhenu* explains that "When something is to be said that has a vulgar meaning, that is 'Oh, lady! You should love your beloved who loves (you)' presenting it with propriety is nobleness (*udāratā*)." Cf. *Kāmadhenu*, p. 115, ll. 4-5. Abhinavagupta, mentioning that "by others it (*udāratā*) is not being vulgar," and explains as follows. Cf. *Abhinavabhāratī*, p. 342, ll. 18-19: *grāmyaṃ hi yathāsthitam ayojitaracanāviśeṣaṃ prasiddhimātrapramāṇam ucyate, tato 'nyad agrāmyam.* (Being vulgar is when an object is mentioned just as it is, without special arrangement, and merely on well-known basis. What is the opposite of this is "not being vulgar.")
32. *Kāmadhenu* explains that "if the auspicious deed of marriage would be done." Cf. *Kāmadhenu*, p. 115, ll. 9-10.
33. *Kāmadhenu* explains that "Here, at first [they] are addressed individually as 'you and he,' then by the mixed way of 'both of you,' and immediately [they are addressed] as a 'couple.' Therefore, [the passage of] 'what is

left' is fruitful by means of suggestion having the intended meaning." Although *Kāmadhenu* explains that this verse is spoken by Kāmandākī to Mālatī, it is not found in the *Mālatīmādhava*. Cf. *Kāmadhenu*, p. 115, ll. 13-14. Cf. *Bhavabhūti's Mālatīmādhava with the Commentary of Jagaddhar*, ed. with Literal English Translation, Notes and Introduction by M.R. Kale, Delhi, Motilal Banarsidass, 1983.

34. *Kāmadhenu* explains that "In the description with complete adjectives, there is a situation similar to the appearance as if it were in front [of one.] Cf. *Kāmadhenu*, p. 116, ll. 12-13.

35. This verse occurs in Vidyākara's *Subhāṣitaratnakoṣa*. Cf. *The Subhāṣitaratnakoṣa*, p. 161. See also Ingalls, *An Anthology of Sanskrit Court Poetry Vidyākara's "Subhāṣitaratnakoṣa"*, p. 48, 267.

36. *Kāmadhenu* explains that " 'Brilliant' means what is revealed clearly with 'condition' (*vibhāva*), 'external indication of feeling' (*anubhāva*) and 'unsteady sensations' (*vyabhicāribhāva*)." Cf. *Kāmadhenu*, p. 118, ll. 1-2. Abhinavagupta refers to Vāmana in his commentary on the *Naṭyaśāstra* and explains that if it is the " 'condition' (*vibhāva*) and so on that are brilliant." Cf. *Abhinavabhāratī*, p. 343, l. 20.

37. *Kāmadhenu* explains that "There is 'love in union' (*saṃbhoga-śṛṅgāra*) preceded by 'love in separation' (*vipralambha-śṛṅgāra*)." Cf. *Kāmadhenu*, p. 118, l. 2. Abhinavagupta refers to this verse in his commentary on the *Nāṭyaśāstra*. Cf. *Abhinavabhāratī*, 344, ll. 13-14: *atra hīrṣyanubhāvasya ratyanubhāvasya, autsukyānubhāvasya ca diptatvam ity arthaguṇa*. (Here, the conditions of jealousy, affection, and anxiety are brilliant. Therefore, there is a semantic quality [of splendor (*kānti*)].)

38. *Kāmadhenu* shows, the examples of the other sentiments (*rasa*): heroism (*vīra*), grief (*karuṇa*), astonishment (*adbhuta*), humor (*hāsya*), terror (*bhayānaka*), wrath (*raudra*), disgust (*bībhatsa*) and quietism (*śānta*). Cf. *Kāmadhenu*. p. 118, l.ll-p. 119, l.8.

39. "Ripening of a mango" is one of nine varieties of poetic ripening in the *Kāvyamīmāṃsā*. Cf. *Kāvyamīmāṃsā*, (*Kāvyamīmāṃsā of Rājaśekhara, Original Text in Sanskrit and Translation with Explanatory Notes*, by Sadhana Prashar, D.K. Printworld (P) Ltd., New Delhi, 2000), p. 65, l. 5: *ādau madhyamam ante svādu sahakārapākam*. ([Poetry] that has a middle level [of taste] at first and becomes tasteful at the end can be [compared to] the ripening of a mango.) *Kāvyamīmāṃsā* also mentions that such poetry can be accepted [as good]. Cf. *Kāvyamīmāṃsā*, p. 65, l. 9.

40. "Ripening of an eggplant" is also one of nine varieties of poetic ripening in the *Kāvyamīmāṃsā*. Cf. *Kāvyamīmāṃsā*. p. 65, l.3: *ādau madhyam ante cāsvādu vārtākapākam*. ([Poetry] that has a middle level [of taste] at first and becomes tasteless at the end can be [compared to] the ripening of an eggplant.) *Kāvyamīmāṃsā* also mentions that such poetry should be rejected. Cf. *Kāvyamīmāṃsā* p. 65, l.9.

41. *Kāmadhenu* quotes a passage from the *Mahābhāṣya*: *daśa dāḍimāni ṣaḍapūpāḥ kuṇḍam ajājinaṃ palalapiṇḍa iti vākyaṃ vicārayogyaṃ na bhavati*. (Ten pomegranates, six cakes, a vessel, a cumin seed, and a lump of ground sesamum. This passage is not fit for consideration.) Cf. *Kāmadhenu*, p. 119, ll.17-18, *Mahābhāṣya* (in *Patañjali's Vyākaraṇa Mahābhāṣya with Kaiyaṭa's Pradīpa and Nāgojibhaṭṭa's Uddyota*, ed. by Bal Shastri, Delhi, Pratibha Prakashan, 2001), p. 58.

VIII

VEDIC THEMES

CHAPTER 32

Vedic Ritual: Kālidāsa and Bhavabhūti

GANESH THITE

One of the aspects of studies on classical Sanskrit poets is concerning the scholarship of a particular poet based on various references to a particular branch of knowledge in his works. Thus for example one may collect various references to music in the literature of Kālidāsa and conclude that he was well-versed in music. Another aspect of such studies is justification of a poet in connection with some discrepancies. One may refer Mallinātha's commentary on the word *dṛḍhabhakti* (Raghu. XII. 19). It will be seen there that this expression which is grammatically incorrect is justified in a very artificial manner. Having seen such cases one may remember a saying *tātasya kūpo'yamiti bruvāṇāḥ kṣāraṃ jalaṃ kāpuruṣaḥ pibanti.* In the present paper however this routine way of studying Sanskrit poetry is not followed. Having discussed some references to the Vedic ritual in the literature of Kālidāsa and Bhavabhūti discrepancies have been pointed out and it is concluded that these poets were not sufficiently abreast with the details of the Vedic rituals.

In the first act of Abhijñānaśākuntala, Kaṇva alias Kāśyapa is said to be unmarried (p. 440): *bhagavān kāśyapaḥ śaśvate brahmaṇi sthita iti prakāśaḥ.* In the fourth act however he is described as an Āhitāgni (one who has established fires)(p.486). He asks Śakuntalā to move around fires and then also blesses her in the verse in vedic meter. Earlier in the Miśra-viṣkambhaka it is said that he came to know about the love-marriage of Śakuntalā while he had entered in to the house containing fires (*agniśaraṇaṃ praviṣṭasya....* p.482). He even congratulated her with words—"Luckily even though the vision of the sacrificer was disturbed by smoke the libation fell in fire itself "(p.482). This metaphorical remark also indicates that he was an Āhitāgni. Here there is a serious discrepancy. According to the rules of Vedic ritual only a married man can be an Āhitāgni. Only he can perform various vedic rituals. Therefore we cannot accept Kāśyapa being an unmarried man performing Vedic ritual.

In Raghuvaṃśa 4.89 the sacrifice named Viśvajit is mentioned as a Sattra (sacrificial session). This description is not correct. The reason is that the sacrifice named Viśvajit is a one-day(Ekāha)—sacrifice. A Sattra, on the other hand, is a type of sacrifices the smallest of which can be of twelve days. It is thus obvious that Viśvajit can in no way be called a Sattra.

The case of Aśvamedha sacrifice is very complicated and deserves to be studied seriously. In Raghuvaṃśa Canto-III there is a reference to King Dilīpa trying to perform one hundred Aśvamedha sacrifices. He completed ninety-nine Aśvamedha sacrifices (III.38). At the time of the hundredth sacrifice Indra carried away the sacred horse. There was a fight between Indra and Raghu who was appointed as a guardian of the horse. Being pleased with the valor of Raghu, Indra became willing to compromise (III.63). Indra offered the merit of the hundredth sacrifice to Dilīpa without returning the horse, thus without allowing Dilīpa to perform the hundredth sacrifice. The reason why Indra did not allow Dilīpa to perform one hundred Aśvamedha sacrifices was that the performer of one hundred Aśvamedha sacrifices himself becomes Indra. Indra did not want any competitor for himself and thus he created hindrance in the last sacrifice of Dilīpa (III.49).

In the above mentioned story there is an obvious discrepancy. Indra had offered the merit of the hundredth sacrifice to Dilīpa. This means that the result of having performed one hundred sacrifices namely the position of being Indra was also indirectly granted. But it is not mentioned that Dilīpa became Indra. This is something contradictory.

There are however some extremely serious problems regarding the duration of Aśvamedha sacrifices performed by Dilīpa. Neither Kālidāsa nor Mallinātha nor the teachers nor the students have ever taken into consideration the question how much time the performance of one Aśvamedha sacrifice requires. According to the rules of the rituals the performance of one Aśvamedha sacrifice requires one year and almost one month. The horse wanders at its will for one year. After its return, for about three weeks the ritual of *Dīkṣā* and *Upasads* is performed. Then the Aśvamedha ritual proper is done for three days. After all this there will be some concluding rites like Avabhṛtha which will require approximately one day. Thus the 99 Aśvamedha sacrifices might have required one hundred and ten years. Dilīpa started the performance of Aśvamedha sacrifices only after his son Raghu had become young (*yuvarāja*). Before that Dilīpa had no progeny for a long time. Thus when Raghu was born, Dilīpa must have been at least about 30 years old. And when the actual performance of the first Aśvamedha started, Dilīpa must have been approximately 50 years old. At the time of the hundredth Aśvamedha sacrifice, Dilīpa must be 160 years old and Raghu must be 130 years old. Nowhere we read about the age of these two persons. Kālidāsa does not mention how long these two persons lived but it seems that each one lived approximately 170 years at least. This is something very difficult to believe. Even for the sake of argument, we accept that they lived extraordinarily long life or that in fiction persons may live a very long life, since Kālidāsa has not mentioned anything about their age the problem remains unsolved. The only possible conclusion in this connection is that Kālidāsa was not aware of the time required for the performance of one Aśvamedha sacrifice.

In Raghuvaṃśa III.66, Dilīpa is said to be '*sadogataḥ*'. It is said there that Dilīpa was in the '*sadas*' (a particular hall prepared at the time of the Soma sacrifice). It was expected that the incident which took place between Raghu and Indra should be known by Dilīpa situated in the '*sadas*' through a messenger of Indra. Now a question is how far the description '*sadogataḥ*' of Dilīpa is correct. The answer is "it is totally incorrect". From the day preceding the release of the horse for wandering up to its return after one year, the sacrificer (in this context, Dilīpa) has to sleep in the hall called '*prāgvaṃśa*', at the time of the night (Kātyāyana-Śrautasūtra XX. 1.17). 'Prāgvaṃśa' is the name of a hall, the central bamboo-beam of which points to the east. Here sacred fires are situated. Later on, after the Uttaravedī is built the 'Āhavanīya' fire is taken to the 'Uttaravedī'. 'Sadas' is situated on the 'Mahāvedī' (great altar) in a Soma sacrifice. In the 'Sadas' there are 'Dhiṣṇyas' (fire hearths). In the Sadas itself the priests of Sāmaveda, sit and sing. The sacrificer enters the Sadas not before the "Sutyā" (Soma pressing day). Even though the Sadas is prepared on the day earlier to the Sutyā day, the sacrificer is not allowed to stay there on the preceding night (see Āpastamba-Śrautasūtra XXI.21.8, Bhāradvāja-Śrautasūtra XII.20.11-13).

The Aśvamedha sacrifice is a three-day soma sacrifice. When the fight between Indra and Raghu took place, the soma sacrificial ritual proper had not yet commenced. Therefore, at the time of the battle, Dilīpa could not have been in the Sadas and therefore the description of Dilīpa as *sadogataḥ* is not correct.

Bhavabhūti is also a great Sanskrit poet, very famous in the history of Sanskrit poetry. He describes his family to be that of Āhitāgni-s. He claims himself to be a scholar of grammar, Mīmāṃsā and Nyāya. But as far as the Aśvamedha-sacrifice is considered, it seems that he did not know any details of it. In his Uttararāmacarita, it is said that Rāma used an idol of gold of Sītā because he had abandoned her. Rāma is very famous for his monogamy. His love for Sītā was so intense that he did not remarry and used a golden idol of Sītā at the time of Aśvamedha sacrifice. All this is very fine as poetry but creates problems from the point of view of ritual. In the first place, vedic ritual texts do not have the provision of using such an idol instead of the wife of the sacrificer. In the absence of Sītā if Rāma would have remarried, there might not have been any harm for the ritual. The second problem is more serious. In the Aśvamedha sacrifice, it is not simply one wife who has to carry out some duties in the ritual but rather four wives (see e.g. Śatapatha Brāhmaṇa XIII.4.1.12). Thus the performer king should have at least four wives. Neither the author of the epic Rāmāyaṇa nor the dramatist like Bhavabhūti seems to be aware of this technicality. No teacher or student of Sanskrit literature ever bothered for the details of Aśvamedha sacrifice. Therefore, nobody has pointed out this discrepancy.

Two conclusions seem to be following out of the details mentioned above. First, the great poets namely Kālidāsa and Bhavabhūti were not sufficiently acquainted with the details of the vedic ritual. Secondly, it is quite possible that the Aśvamedha sacrifice was never performed literally, strictly in accordance with the descriptions in the vedic texts. Always compromises must have been made in connection with the wandering of horse, as regards the space as well as time, the obscene details in the sacrifice etc. Since the Aśvamedha sacrifice was very prestigious, it is likely that many kings tried to get the credit of the performance of the sacrifice without performing it in all its details. The bards used to praise their patron kings by claiming that their patrons had done a lot of heroic or religious deeds. The performance of Aśvamedha might be one of such fictitious deeds.

(*The page references to the Kālidāsa's literature refer to Revaprasad Dwivedi's Kālidāsa Granthāvalī, Varanasi, 1976.*)

Chapter 33

The Role of the Brahman in the Sthālīpāka: with Special Reference to the Atharvaveda Ritual

SHRIKANT BAHULKAR

The *Sthālīpāka* is a domestic rite (*gṛhyakarman*) that forms the model (*tantra*) or norm (*prakṛti*) of all the *Pākayajñas*, where the main rite involves an oblation of a mess of rice or barley cooked in milk in an earthen dish or a cooking vessel (*sthālī*).[1] This sacrifice is a simplified, domestic form of the solemn sacrifice called *Iṣṭi*, to be performed on the full moon day (*pūrṇamāsa*) and the new moon day (*darśa*). This sacrifice, like the *Iṣṭi*, is also called *Darśapūrṇamāsa*.[2] This sacrifice is to be performed on one (domestic) fire (*ekāgnisādhya*)[3], established by the householder generally at the time of his wedding (ĀśvGS. 1.8.5, 9) or on the division of ancestral property (PārGS. 1.2.2) or the death of the head of the family, in which case the eldest son kindles a new fire[4]. The householder is the sacrificer (*yajamāna*) and is accompanied by his wife (*patnī*) who participates in the domestic rites, discharging certain duties assigned to her.[5]

In the *Iṣṭi*, the Adhvaryu performs most of the acts. Similarly, in the *Sthālīpāka*, there can be a priest—who is called the performer (*kartṛ*) or sometimes designated as Hotṛ (KhGS. 1.1.19;

GGS. 1.1.9; Dārila on KauśS. 3.10), besides the householder. However, it is not essential to employ a priest; the householder himself can perform the duties of the performer[6]. The deities of the *Sthālīpāka* are the same as those of the *Iṣṭi*, i.e., Agni and Agnīṣomau for the sacrifice on the full moon day and Agni and Indrāgni for that on the new moon day.

Since the *Sthālīpāka* is the domestic rite modelled after the *Iṣṭi*, the Gṛhyasūtras prescribe the choosing of the Brahman and assign certain duties to him. However, the role of the Brahman is optional. When the Brahman is not formally chosen, the householder himself performs the duties of the Brahman. Thus, virtually, the *Sthālīpāka* is performed by the Yajamāna accompanied by his wife. The ĀśvGS. (I.3.6) says that the Brahman may or may not be chosen (*kṛtākṛta*) in the *Pākayajñas*, except the sacrifice to Dhanvantari and the spit-ox sacrifice (*śūlagava*). KhGS. (I.1.26) prescribes that the Yajamāna, while discharging the duties of the Hotṛ and the Brahman by himself, should sit on the seat intended for the Brahman. It further says that, alternatively, an umbrella or a water-jar (*kamaṇḍalu*) may be placed on the seat of the Brahman. Bhavatrāta on KauṣīGS. (I.4.1) says that a water-jar may optionally be placed. He further says that the word *brahman* in the Sūtra does not denote a designation of the priest and that the sun itself is the Brahman. Harihara, on the PārGS. (I.1.2) says that in the absence of the Brahman a seat made of fifty *kuśa*-blades may be understood as the Brahman. Rāmacandra and Nārāyaṇa on the ŚāṅkhGS. (I.8.6) are of the same opinion. Some authorities prescribe that a grass-puppet (*kuśabaṭu*) should be made and placed on the seat of the Brahman (GobhGS.1.6.21). On the other hand, Karka and Gadādhara on ParGS. (1.1.2) say that it is essential to employ the Brahman. Gadādhara refers to Harihara who prescribes that the Brahman made of *kuśa*-grass be placed and says that this statement of Harihara has its origin in the Gṛhyasūtra of Sāmaveda (*chandogagṛhya*).

Thus we have seen that most of the authorities on the Gṛhyasūtras prescribe that the Brahman should be optional. Now let us see the position of the Brahman in the *Sthālīpāka* of Atharvavedins. This sacrifice is prescribed in the KauśS. (*kaṇḍikās* 1-6 and 137), the major ritual text in the Śaunakīya recension which is also the Gṛhyasūtra of the Atharvaveda.

In the case of the tradition of the Atharvaveda the relation between the Gṛhyasūtra and the Śrautasūtra is just the opposite of that between the Gṛhya and Śrauta Sūtras of the other Vedas. Other Gṛhyasūtras presuppose the Śrauta Sūtras of their recension. They are supposed to have been composed after the composition of the Śrauta Sūtras. As regards the Atharvaveda tradition, the Kauśika Sūtra is the first and the foremost Sūtra, rightly called the *Saṃhitāvidhi* "the ritual book dealing with the rites in which the hymns / verses of the Saṃhitā are to be employed". The Sūtra is based on the Śaunaka Saṃhitā of the AV. It also quotes in the *sakalapāṭha* verses from other texts, prominently the Paippalāda Saṃhitā of the AV. The Vaitāna Sūtra is the Śrauta Sūtra of the AV. It was composed after the composition of the KauśS. and presupposes the latter. At the outset, it says that the Brahman who is familiar with the Brahmaveda, i.e., the AV., (participating) in the ritual, sits to the south (of the Āhavanīya fire), with due procedure, restraining his speech." (VaitS. I.1.1). The VaitS. frequently refers to the KauśS. in which the relevant acts have already been prescribed. The duties of the Brahman in the *Iṣṭi* are thus to be understood on the basis of the KauśS. and the VaitS. as well. As regards the role of the Brahman in the *Sthālīpāka*, it is observed that the KauśS. lays down the relevant procedure to which certain details are added by the VaitS. The exegetical works on the KauśS. take into consideration those additions and explain the ritual accordingly.

According to Dārila, the Bhāṣyakāra, there are four persons taking part in the performance: the householder as the sacrificer (*yajamāna*), a priest as the performer (*kartṛ*), the wife of the sacrificer (*patnī*) and the Brahman[7]. The duties of the Brahman are prescribed by the KauśS. in the section on the *Darśapūrṇamāsa* (KauśS., *kaṇḍikās* 1-6). Some more details are also found in the section on *Ājyatantra* (*kaṇḍikā* 137), where a portion from the previous *kaṇḍikās*, is repeated *verbatim* or with certain modifications (KauśS. : 2.1 = 137.32; 2.18 = 137.33; 2.19 = 137.34; 2.41 = 137.30; 3.5 = 137.37; 3.6 = 137.38; 3.7 = 137.39; 3.8 = 137.40). The VaitS., at the outset, prescribes the qualifications and duties of the Brahman, in relation to the Śrauta sacrifices (VaitS. 1.1.1-2). It also prescribes the procedure of choosing the Brahman (VaitS. 1.1.17-18). This procedure is adopted by Dārila and Keśava, the authors of the *Bhāṣya* and of the

Paddhati respectively. The Prayoga texts dealing with the *Sthālīpāka* take into consideration all these details and explain the procedure, re-arranging the relevant portions in the *sūtras*. These texts also incorporate relevant material from other traditions.[8] The acts related to the role of the Brahman are as follows:

1. The householder or the priest strews *darbha*-grass for the seat of the Brahman to the south of the fire (KauśS. 2.18).
2. The householder stands to the north of the fire and with the formula—*bhūpate bhuvanapate*...formally chooses the Brahman (VaitS. 1.1.17).
3. The Brahman, thus chosen, mutters the formula—*ahaṁ bhūpatiḥ*... (VaitS. 1.1.18)[9].
4. The Brahman gives a call to the householder for strewing the sacrificial grass around the fire (KauśS. 2.20).
5. The householder strews the sacrificial grass around the fire, with the formula—*devasya tvā* (KauśS. 2.21).
6. With the formula—*ahe daidhiṣavya*..., the Brahman gazes at his seat (KauśS. 3.5).
7. He takes a *darbha*-blade from the *darbha*-grass strewn for his seat, and with the formula—*nirastaḥ parāgvasuḥ* ..., he throws it towards the south (KauśS. 3.6).
8. Having touched his seat, he mutters the formula—*idam aham*... (KauśS. 3.7).
9. With the verse—*vimṛgvarīm* ... (AV. 12.1.29), he takes his seat (KauśS. 3.8).

   According to Dārila, the priest (*kartṛ*) too takes his seat at this time.
10. With the verse—*pātaṁ mā dyāvāpṛthivī*..., he gazes at the heaven and the earth (KauśS. 137.41).
11. At the conclusion of the rite, the Brahman receives a vessel (*pūrṇapātra*) by way of his fees (and leaves the place) (KauśS. 6.21).

The commentators of the KauśS., namely, Dārila and Keśava, point out that the role of the Brahman in the *Sthālīpāka* is optional. Dārila says that when there is no Brahman, it is the householder who gives out a call to the performer for spreading the sacrificial grass[10]. Further he argues that the word *āsanīya*, an adjective of the word *brahmajapa,* in KauśS. 3.8, is used in order to denote that the act is to be done by the performer in the absence of the Brahman[11]. Keśava quotes from a text called Gobhilabrāhmaṇa, according to which, one should actually (*pratyakṣam*) place (the Brahman) on the seat intended for him, or, optionally, should place a seat made of *darbha*-grass or a water vessel[12].

While commenting on KauśS. 3.5, Dārila proposes a double meaning of the words *brahmāsanam anvīkṣate* : (i) the performer gazes at the seat of the Brahman and (ii) the Brahman gazes at (his own) seat[13]. All these explanations show that, according to the commentators, the role of the Brahman is optional.

If we carefully go through the KauśS., it appears that the Sūtrakāra does not really intend the actual participation of the Brahman. According to him, the acts that are supposed to be done by the Brahman are to be done by the householder who also performs the duties of the performer (*kartṛ*). The entire ritual of the *Sthālīpāka* is to be performed by the householder and his wife. The relevant *sūtras* are:

1. *dakṣiṇato'gner brahmāsanaṃ nidadhāti/* (KauśS. 2.18).
2. *pari stṛṇīhī'ti sampreṣyati/* (KauśS. 2.20).
3. *prapadya... brahmāsanam anvīkṣate/* (KauśS. 3.5).
4. *...dakṣiṇā tṛṇaṃ nirasyati/* (KauśS. 3.6).
5. *tad anvālabhya japati...* (KauśS. 3.7).
6. *vimṛgvarīm ity upaviśyā'sanīyaṃ brahmajapaṃ japati/* (KauśS. 3.8).

The act mentioned in *sūtra* 2.18 is to be done by the householder or the performer. All other acts mentioned by the other *sūtras* quoted above are supposed to be done by the Brahman, but virtually are done by the householder or the performer alone. These acts are modelled after the duties of the Brahman in the Śrauta *Darśapūrṇamāsa.* However, in the domestic ritual, the Brahman is not chosen. The commentators seem to have been influenced by other traditions where the role of the Brahman is normally optional in the *Pākayajñas.* Dārila's double interpretation of the words—*brahmāsanam anvīkṣate* in *sūtra* 3.5 is not convincing. It is more likely that it is the performer who gazes at the seat of the

Brahman and not the latter. Similarly, the sūtra—*āsanīyaṁ brahmajapaṁ japati* denotes that the performer mutters the formula that is originally to be muttered by the Brahman. On this sūtra, Dārila says that the word *āsanīya* is used in the *sūtra* in order that the act can be done by the performer, in the absence of the Brahman. He further points out that the word *brahmajapa* is used to denote the act specifically to be done by the Brahman or to indicate that this act is to be done by the Brahman in the *Indramaha* also. In the *Indramaha,* there is no mention of this *japa* (KauśS. 140.4)[14]. This explanation seems to be far-fetched, with a view to justifying the seemingly superfluous words, such as, *āsanīya* and *brahmajapa* used in that *sūtra.*

There are several instances in the KauśS. where the actual participation of the Brahman is essential:

1. The (concise) coronation of the king (KauśS. 17.6)
2. A *Śānti* rite for the consolation of a woman who has lost her child (34.7)
3. In the *Savayajñas* (68.7)
4. In the wedding ceremony (75. 9, 13, 18; 77.2, 6)
5. In the funeral rites (82.9, 12)
6. In the rites to ward off the effects of omens and portents (94.2; 126.2) and
7. In the *Indramaha* (140.4).

The *sūtras* prescribing the duties of the Brahman in all the rites, mentioned above, are unambiguous. On the other hand, the *sūtras* in the *Sthālīpāka* do not clearly indicate that the duties of the Brahman are to be performed by himself; nor does the Sūtrakāra, unlike those belonging to other recensions, prescribe any alternative for the Brahman. It is significant to note that the KauśS. does not prescribe the choosing of the Brahman. It is mentioned by the VaitS. It appears that according to the KauśS., the duties of the performer as well as of the Brahman in the *Sthālīpāka* are to be performed by the householder alone. The *Sthālīpāka* is a simple, domestic ritual, to be performed on every *parvan* day. It may not be practical to invite one or two priests to participate in the ritual as the performer and/or the Brahman on every *parvan* day. Their actual participation is not intended by the Sūtrakāra. The commentators, however, think that the Sūtrakāra prescribes the employment of the Brahman in the *Sthālīpāka* on formal basis. They therefore prescribe the option, probably under the influence of other traditions.

ABBREVIATIONS

AV	= Atharvaveda
ĀśvGS.	= Āśvalāyana Gṛhya Sūtra
GGS.	= Gobhila Gṛhya Sūtra
KauśS.	= Kauśika Sūtra
KauṣīGS.	= Kauṣītaki Gṛhya Sūtra
KhGS.	= Khādira Gṛhya Sūtra
PārGS.	= Pāraskara Gṛhya Sūtra
ŚāṅkhGS.	= Śāṅkhāyana Gṛhya Sūtra
VaitS.	= Vaitāna Sūtra

NOTES

1. According to the ĀśvGS. 1.1.2-3, there are three types of *Pākayajñas*: 1) *huta* 'the sacrifice where the main rite is the oblation into the fire,' e.g., *Sthālīpāka*; 2) *prahuta* 'the sacrifice where the oblation is not to be offered into the fire, but elsewhere', e.g., *Baliharaṇa* (ĀśvGS. 1.2.3) and 3) *brahmaṇihuta* 'the sacrifice involving mainly feeding of the Brahmins.'
2. In the Atharvaveda tradition, the *Pākayajñas* are divided in two categories, i.e., *Ājyatantra* in which the main oblation is that of the clarified butter and *Pākatantra* in which the main oblation is that of cooked food. See Keśava on KauśS. 1.9; 137.42-43; Sāyaṇa, introduction (*upodghāta*) to his commentary, *Atharvaveda Saṃhitā with Sāyaṇa's* commentary (ed. by Vishva Bandhu, Hoshiarpur, 1960), Vol. 1, p. 28. *The Atharvaṇīya Paddhati* describes the *Ājyatantra* under the name *Bṛhatkuśaṇḍikā*. See, KauśS., intro. (ed. by M. Bloomfield, *Journal of American Oriental Society*, 14, reprinted by Motilal Banarsidass, Delhi, 1972), p. xv. A correct word seems to be *kuśakaṇḍikā–*, see the title of works, *Kuśa(ka)ṇḍikā or Kuśaṇḍī, New Catalogus Catalogorum* (University of Madras, Madras, 1968), Vol. IV, p. 155.
3. KhGS. 1.1.16: *pākayajña ity ākhyā yaḥ kaścaikāgnau/* The commentary *Sūtrārthabodhinī* of Sri Paṭṭābhirāmārya explains: *ekāgnau gṛhyāgnau sādhyo yaḥ kaś ca yajñas tasya pākayajña iti saṁjñā/*
4. Nārāyaṇa on ĀśvGS. 1.8.3: *yadi vaivāhyo (agniḥ) na gṛhīto dāyavibhāgakāle gṛhyate/* For details, see A.B. Keith, *The Religion and Philosophy of the Veda and the Upaniṣads,* second half, Harvard Oriental Series no. 32, Oxford University Press, London, 1925, p. 358.
5. See, J. Gonda, *Vedic Ritual: The Non-solemn Rites,* E.J. Brill, Leiden-Köln, 1980, p. 200.

6. Bhavatrāta on KauśīGS. 1.4.1: *nanv iha eka eva hi pākayajñeṣu kartā/ pākayajñaḥ* (*°śabdaḥ?*) *alpavācī/tathā hy alpaṁ karma bhavati/ācāryo dvitīya iti cen na/ kartā ācāryavat draṣṭā saṃśayacchettā/ kvacit tu vacanād ācāryaḥ karoti/*
7. Dārila on KauśS. 1.26: *agniṃ prāpya nivartamānaḥ kartā brahmā yajamānaḥ patnī vā. pratīpamukha* (*°mukhaṃ?*) *nā'varteta śarīreṇa*) /
8. See, e.g., the *Sthālīpākaprayoga* (MS. no. 4242, Vaidika Saṃśodhana Maṇḍala, Pune).
9. In addition to the formula—*ahaṁ bhūpatiḥ*..., the VaitS. 1.1.18 prescribes the muttering of the *Apratiratha* hymn (AV. 19.13) that begins with *indrasya bāhū*... This is stated by Somāditya, the Bhāṣyakāra, see, *The Vaitāna-Śrauta-Sūtra with Somāditya's commentary Ākṣepānuvidhi*, ed. by Vishva Bandhu, Hoshiarpur, 1967, p. 7. The editors of the Śrautakośa (Vol. I, English Section, part 1, Vaidika Saṃśodhana Maṇḍala, Pune, 1958, p. 263) however think that it is the *apratiratha* verse (AV. 19.13.2).
10. Dārila on KauśS. 2.20: *brahmaṇa abhāve* (sic. *brahmaṇo'bhāve*) *yajamānaḥ sampreṣyati/*
11. Dārila on KauśS. 3.8: *āsanīyavacanaṃ brahmaṇo'bhāve'pi kartur yathā syāt/*
12. Keśava on KauśS. 2.18: *tathā ca gobhilabrāhmaṇam/ pratyakṣaṃ vā darbhamayaṃ vā'sanam udakakamaṇḍaluṁ vā brahmasthāne kuryāt/* There is no text called Gobhilabrāhmaṇa. The citation is not traced.
13. Dārila on KauśS. 3.5: *anena brahmaṇa āsanam anvīkṣate/ athavā brahmā 'tmīyam āsanam anvīkṣate/*
14. Dārila on KauśS. 3.8: *āsanīyavacanaṃ brahmaṇo'bhāve'pi kartur yathā syāt/ brahmajapavacanaṃ bhavati ca brahmaṇo'pi viśeṣārthatvāt/ athavā indramahe japaprāptyarthaṃ bhrhmajapagrahaṇam/*

CHAPTER 34

The Divine Origin of Kingship: It *is* Vedic

MADHAVI KOLHATKAR

In Vedic literature one comes across a variety of references to the origin and nature of kingship. In the Ṛgveda Saṃhitā: 4.42.8 and 9, the king Trasadasyu is eulogised as *ardhadeva* 'demigod'. In Atharvaveda King Parīkṣit is glorified as *yo devo martyān ati* 'who is a god surpassing the mortals.'

Further, in the Brāhmaṇa literature, there are various myths regarding kingship. The myth at AB. (Aitareyabrāhmaṇa) 1.14(3.3) tells us about the election or selection of the king. Thus it is, "The gods were losing the battles against the asuras. They realised that it was due to their not having a king. So, they elected Soma as their king and thereby won over the asuras."

TS. (Taittirīyasaṃhitā) 2.42 also narrates a story regarding the election of the king. There it is said, "The gods decided that they would follow the one who was the most strong among them. They said to Indra, 'You are the strongest among us. So, we will follow you.' "

The story in TB. (Taittirīyabrāhmaṇa) 2.2.7.2 actually tells about the creation of Indra by Prajāpati. "Prajāpati created the gods and the asuras, but he did not create Indra. Then the gods asked him to create Indra. Prajāpati saw Indra in him and created him. With him the gods defeated the asuras.

While discussing the origin of kingship various scholars have dealt mainly with these myths.[1] Ghoshal further has referred to some more myths. In TB. 2.2.10.1 it is stated that first the gods did not accept Indra as their king. He went to Prajāpati and complained about it. Prajāpati then gave his *hara* to Indra and then he was accepted as a king by the gods. According to the myth at the PB. (Pañcaviṃśabrāhmaṇa) 15.3.30 it was due to the *devasthānasāman* that the gods yielded to the supremacy of Varuṇa. Ghoshal next has referred to one more similar myth from the JB. (Jaiminīyabrāhmaṇa) 3.152. According to it the gods did not accept the supremacy of Varuṇa. So he observed celibacy for hundred years. Then Prajāpati bestowed upon him the *varuṇasāman* due to which the gods seated him on the royal seat and consecrated for sovereignty.

"This anticipates," according to Ghoshal, "in a remarkable fashion the doctrine of Divine creation of the human ruler which we find centuries later in the theories of Manu and of Bhīṣma in the Mahābhārata, a doctrine involving the idea of Divine creation of the ruler so as to invest him with divine attributes or even with divinity itself."[2]

As a matter of fact in some of the myths cited above, there is a clear reference to the creation of king by Prajāpati. All the scholars, however, have unanimously referred to the passages in Manusmṛti and Matsyapurāṇa as the first reference to divine origin of the king. In these passages, it is told, for the first time that the human ruler or king is formed with different elements taken from different gods.[3]

In Manusmṛti 7.1 ff., before stating the duties of the king, the author tells about the origin of the king. In the state of anarchy when all this world was running asunder due to fear, the God Almighty created the king for the protection of the world, taking certain measures from the gods, viz. Indra, the Wind, Yama, the Sun, the Fire, Varuṇa, the Moon and Kubera, the god of wealth. Since the king is thus created from the elements of the great gods, he overpowers all the beings with his brilliance. The passage in the Matsyapurāṇa 226.1 to 12 is similar to this.

In this connection, Ghoshal further has referred to a "remarkable extract (quoted anonymously by Viśvarūpa in his commentary on YājñaSm.1.350) relating to the origin of the human ruler, an extract which, to judge from its style and contents belongs to a lost Brāhmaṇa work..." He then narrates the passage, "The gods and the men (sages?)... failed to bring the people under their control... the gods disappeared. Prajāpati asked them who should protect the people after their disappearance, and he reminded them that the people not enjoying protection... would thenceforth cease to make the offerings on which depended their own livelihood; to this the gods replied by creating a king in human form after taking from the Moon, the Sun, Indra, Viṣṇu, Kubera, and Yama the qualities of beauty, lustre, prowess, victory, renunciation and restraint respectively..." Ghoshal next has remarked, "The above extract involves an advanced theory of Divine creation of the temporal ruler and his authority such as is not matched in the extant Yajus Saṃhitā and Brāhmaṇa texts."[4]

As will be seen further the last part of Ghoshal's statement is not true. Actually, among the scholars who have dealt with this topic, no scholar other than Ghoshal has referred to the JB. belonging to the Sāmaveda.[5] He is the only one who has discussed the story of consecration of Varuṇa as the king which occurs in connection with the *varuṇasāman* in JB.3.152. His book is published in 1959. Hence it is possible that while writing on this topic, he had before him only the selected passages of the JB. edited and translated by Caland and published in 1919.[6] The complete edited text published by Raghu Vira and Lokesh Chandra which is published in 1954 at Nagpur was perhaps not available to him.

The last portion of the third part of the JB. deals with cosmogony. In succession, it also cites a myth regarding the origin of kingship. Since these passages are very interesting and are not translated as yet, I am going to attempt the complete translation of it. The style of the text is very peculiar. It does not have any commentary on it and I know my limitations. All sorts of suggestions regarding the improvement of the translation and better options in the edition are most welcome.[7]

The Translation of the Passages JB.3.364 to 368 Describing the Origin of Kingship

These are deities, stomas, metres, seasons and oblations which are created.[8] These shining glories of them remained separate. They did not stand for the supremacy over each other. They said, "Let us not stand for the supremacy over each other. Come, let us ask for one who will rule over us." They came to Prajāpati, the creator and said, "We do not stand for the supremacy over each other. Hence, create someone for us who will rule over us." Prajāpati said, "That much only was the brilliance, power and valour in this person (i.e. in me) which has created you. Now you practise penance for one year. After practising penance for one year, come to me together and tell me what each one has secured." They practised penance for one year and came to him together. Whatever each one had secured they poured in the *manyu* 'wrath' which was his own abode. From that Indra was conceived.[9] Therefore, this is recited after it– *aśvād iyāyeti yad vadanty ojaso jātam uta manya enam/ manyor iyāya harmyeṣu tasthau yataḥ prajajña indro asya veda //*

It is said[10] that he has come forth from *manyu* 'wrath' since (it was) poured in *manyu* which is his own abode. It is said that he stayed in the palaces. The hearts indeed are the palaces. It indeed is the heart which gets angry. It is said "I regard that he is born of vigour." JB.I.364.

(They) asked Gaurvīta, "Have you indeed seen Indra being born?" Thus he said, "Since they say that he is born from a horse, I think him to be born of vigour. He came from *manyu* and stayed alone in palaces. Indra knows of what he is born."

He (i.e. Gaurvīta) said, "I think that he was born of vigour,"[11] so he (i.e. Gaurvīta) said, "Indra alone knows of what he is born."

He (Indra) took out his head and saw everywhere. He saw all this won over (i.e. pervaded or occupied) by these. He said, "Since all this is won over (that is occupied) by these give me the[12] world in which I should be born. These (JB. 3.365) two vernal months, give them to me." "These two I will give you," he (i.e. Prajāpati?) said. He rushed saying, "Food! food!" and got *rathantara,* the brilliance of the eastern direction.[13] That he placed here. One who knows this, gets the valour of the two even though he is alone. He entered (into it) again. He said to him, "Do please be born." He said, "Then[14] give me. Give me these two months of Grīṣma season (i.e. summer)." "I will give you these two," he said. He rushed, saying "Food! food!" and took *bṛhat,* the brilliance of the southern direction. That he placed here. One who knows this gets the valour of four though he is alone. He entered (into it) again. "Please do be born," he said. He said, "Then give me. Give me these two months of rainy season." He said, "These I will give you." He rushed saying "Food!food!" and took *vairūpa,* the brilliance of western direction. That he placed here. One who knows this acquires the valour of six though he is alone. He again entered (into it). To him he said,"Please do be born." He said,"Then give me. Give me these two months of autumn." "Thses two I will give you." He rushed saying "Food!food!" and took the brilliance *vairāj* of the northern direction. That he placed here. One who knows this acquires the valour of eight even if he is alone. He again entered (into it). To him he said, "Please do be born." "Then give me. Give me these two months of the season Hemanta." "I will give you these," he said. He rushed saying "Food!food!" and took the *śākvara* brilliance of the upper direction. That he placed here. One who knows this acquires the valour of the ten though he is alone. He entered (into it) again. To him he said, "Please do be born." He said, "Then give me. Give me these two months of the season *śiśira* (i.e. winter)." "I will give you these," he said. He rushed saying "Food!food!" and took the *raivata* brilliance of this direction (i.e downward direction). That he placed here. One who knows this acquires the valour of the twelve though he is alone. He pondered, "How should I bear all these seasons?" JB.3.366.

He saw those (*bhāḥ,* i.e. 'the brilliance from various directions') and the (way of) lying on the back (i.e. he thought of lying in that position and lay himself on the back). With his head[15] he held the two eastern ones (i.e. the two months of spring), with the two arms these (four, two from the southern and two from the northern direction) variously or separately, with his chest the two upper ones (i.e. the two from the upper direction), with the *praṣṭis* 'ankles' the two down ones (i.e. from the downward direction). Taking them in this way he pressed them below. Then he shines forth placed on these (six) seasons, the year and the glory. With all this he entered into it again. (He) said to him, "I was not able to take you out formerly even when you were alone. Surely I cannot take you out along with all this. Hence please do indeed be born". At that time he noticed around, the waters making noise. He said,"Then give me. Give me these waters. Then only I will take birth." He gave him six thousands of water. This is the verse regarding it—"Noone else crosses them. Nobody is capable of controlling them. The six thousand streams of water carry everywhere in this (world) honey, milk, ghee and curds." These *ambayā* 'the waters' indeed are these directions themselves. These alone trickle in thousands and thousands for him. These alone satisfy him. He was born. (He i.e. everybody) celebrated him who was born (i.e. his birth)—"The brilliance is born. The power is born. The valour is born. Brahma is born. Ksatra is born. The controller of the seven animals is born. The supporter of the seven directions is born. The born one is born. The father is born. The mother is born." He let himself be celebrated. He said,"Janitri (i.e. the mother)." One who knows this becomes the celebrity. They placed this royal seat for him who was born. On that they consecrated him with water. (JB.3.367)

The Vasus for kingdom, the Rudras for *vairājya* 'extended sovereignty', the Ādityas for *swārājya* 'independant rule', the Viśvedevas for sovereignty, the Maruts for *sārvavaśya* 'control over everybody', the Sādhyas and the Āptyas for *pārameṣṭhya* 'supremacy'.

Father Prajāpati attacked[16] him who became like this. He (i.e. Indra) said to the Vasus, "Give him unto me." They said, "we cannot harm father Prajāpati." he said (the same) to the Rudras. They did not wish (to comply with him). He said (so) to the Ādityas. They did not desire. He said (so)to the Viśvedevas. They did not desire. He said (so) to the Sādhyas and the Āptyas. They did not desire at all. Then he said (so) to the Maruts. (They asked him) "What will be there for us then?" "This my niṣkevalya śastra in the midday pressing will be common to me and you." "All right" (said the Maruts). They having attacked[17] (Prajāpati) gave him to him (i.e.to Indra). As he i.e. Prajāpati was saying, "*candram me! candam me*!" 'my brilliance! my brilliance!' he took that brilliance by which he burns this. As he said *candram me*, therefore (he is) *candramāḥ*. Since he again and again takes away (the brilliance) from him, he remains reduced accordingly.[18] Therefore this also has brilliance even today. As he illuminates this world by the day, so he shines on it at night. Him he understood to be non-perishable. He seized him. He said to him, "Do you not shine back on me." "No," he said, "I shall shine back on you." Hence they see him both the times in the day and at night. Hence they shine back on him.[19] These two, the sun and the moon indeed are the father and the son. Father is the moon, Āditya the son. Earlier is the moon, the later the son. They indeed attained the supremacy upon all the deities. As these two attained the supremacy over all gods, one who knows thus attains supremacy upon one's own kinsmen.

Concluding Remarks

1) This interesting passage has, at the end of the myth, suggested the origin of the two famous Indian aristocratic lineages, viz. *sūryavaṁśa* 'solar race' and *candravaṁśa* 'lunar race'. Prajāpati is the originator of the lunar race, whereas Indra is of the solar one.

The list of both these lineages comes in the Matsya Purāṇa and also in Bhāgavata Purāṇa, but the description in the lexicon Śabdakalpadruma is brief and precise. Regarding lunar lineage it states—Atri was the son of Brahman, his son was the moon, his son was Budha Ilā, the daughter of Vaivasvata Manu was the wife of Budha and gave birth to Pururavas, who became a sovereign king. His wife Urvaśī gave birth to six sons. Āyur was the eldest among them. His son was Nahuṣa, his Yayāti, his Puru and so on. The Kauravas, Pāṇḍavas, Yādavas are all from the descedents in this race. Regarding the solar race, it is stated—Parameśwara created Brahmā. He gave birth to Marīci, he to Kaśyapa, he to the Sun, the Sun to Vaivasvata Manu. Manu became the king in the Satyayuga. In Tretāyuga, his son Ikṣvāku became the king of Ayodhyā. At the rendezvous of the Tretā and Dvāparayuga, king Daśaratha, from the solar race gave birth to Rāma.

It will not be out of place here to note that in the Saṃhitā literature the word Ikṣvāku occurs only once and that also at ṚV.10.60.4 which is comparatively later. Besides this reference, in the whole of the Vedic literature it is only the JB.3.95; 168; 238 and the Lupta Śāṭyāyanaka 43.16; 66.1 and 43.15 where the word Ikṣvāku occurs.

The mention in the myth *paraś candramā, apara ādityaḥ* 'earlier is the moon, later, the Sun', is also significant in this regard and might perhaps shed some light on the history of these two races.

2) Here in these passages we find that the origin and the characteristics of the king, Indra and those of the sun are intermingled. The connection of Indra with the seasons, months, year etc. is in fact the characteristic of the Sun and is imposed on Indra. In Vedic lit. Viṣṇu is considered to be a form of the nature god, the Sun. Can we say that it is due to these mutual relations that in the later age the king was considered as an incarnation of Viṣṇu as is said in the floating verse—*nā viṣṇuḥ pṛthivīpatiḥ*.

3) One more point should be noted here. Much has been said regarding the relation of the Vedas and the Purāṇas[20]. There are some scholars who strongly believe in the sentence—*itihāsapurāṇābhyām vedaṁ samupabṛṃhayet.* 'The vedic texts should be elaborated with the help of history and the Purāṇas.'

The above Vedic passage in the JB. clearly highlights the dependence of the Purāṇas on the Veda. Further, the myth narrated in these passages and its connection with the Purāṇa and Smṛti passages indicates the later date of the JB., though exactly opposite conclusion is drawn sometimes on the basis of its language.

One thing, however, is very certain and that is—the close and careful study of this Brāhmaṇa is a desideratum.

NOTES

1. For the discussion regarding the origin and nature of kingship the important works are: K.P. Jayaswal, *Hindu Polity,* (2 volumes in 1), Calcutta, 1924, Part II, pp. 4ff.; U.N. Ghoshal, *A History of Indian Political Ideas,* Oxford University Press, Oxford, 1959, pp. 20 ff.; A.L. Basham, *The Wonder that was India,* Calcutta, 1991 (Reprint), pp. 82 ff.; R.N. Ḍandekar, *Sources of Indian Tradition,* (Editor Theodor de Bary, et al), Columbia University Press, New York, 1958, pp. 242 ff.; P.V. Kane, *History of Dharmashastra,* Vol. III, pp. 21 ff.
2. U.N. Ghoshal, *A History of Indian Political Ideas,* p. 28.
3. R.N. Dandekar, *Sources of Indian Tradition,* p. 475.
4. U.N. Ghoshal, *A History of Indian Political Ideas,* p. 29.
5. U.N. Ghoshal, *A History of Indian Political Ideas,* p. 28.
6. W. Caland, *Das Jaiminīya-Brāhmaṇa in Auswahl,* Johannes Müller, Amsterdam, 1919.
7. I am deeply indebted to my respected seniormost colleague Mr. D.B.

Polkam and also to my respected teacher Prof. Dr. G.B. Palsule who carefully went through each and every word of the text and the translation and made valuable suggestions.

8. As has been already pointed out this passage occurs in the context of cosmogony. The reference to the deities created is in JB. 3.363. The names of the deities mentioned are : the Vasus, the Ādityas, the Viśvedevas, the Maruts, the Sādhyas and the Āptyas. Trivṛt, Pañcadaśa, Saptadaśa, Ekaviṃśa, Triṇava and Trayastriṃśa are the Stomas. Gāyatrī, Triṣṭubh, Jagatī, Anuṣṭubh, Paṅkti and Aticchandas are the metres. Vasanta, Grīṣma, Varṣā, Śarad, Hemanta and the Śiśira are the seasons.
9. Better *samabhavat.*
10. The first part of the verse is not explained in the text. It can be translated, "as they say that he has come from the horse."
11. *ojaso'nvaham* is better than *ojaso'nvaham* or *ojaso'nvaha.*
12. *tam* is better than *sa* in the text.
13. *prācyai diśe* is better than *prācyai diśau* in the text, just as *dakṣiṇāyai diśo* etc. which follows. However, *prācyai diśaḥ* would have been preferable.
14. The meaning of *saḥ* here is 'therefore', 'then'; cf. the meaning No. 5 of *tad* pronoun in V.S. Apte's Sanskrit English Dictionary, ed. P.K. Gode, C.G. Karve (Revised ed. 1979).
15. Better *śīrṣṇaivemau.*
16. It seems that Prajāpati not only attacked Indra, but also took his brilliance away. Maruts took him to Indra and Indra took it back again and hence, at that time Prajāpati cried "*candram me*! *candram me*!"
17. *Abhiprapadya* or *abhipretya* instead of *abhipradya.*
18. Does it refer to the waning moon?
19. The meaning of the sentence is not clear to me.
20. For detailed discussion regarding the relation between the Vedas and the Purāṇas please see Ludo Rocher, *The Purāṇas,* Otto Harrassowitz, Wiesbaden, 1986, pp. 13 to 17; Frederick M. Smith, "Purāṇaveda", in *Authority, Anxiety and Canon,* ed. Lauri Patton, State University of New York Press, 1994, pp. 97 ff.

IX

SOCIAL PRACTICES

CHAPTER 35

Defying Blessings of the Goddess and the Community: Disputes over *Satī* (Widow Burning) in Contemporary India

MASAKAZU TANAKA

1. *Introduction*

This article aims to make clear the nature of ritual violence through the analysis of disputes over *satī* or sutte in contemporary India, pointing out the difficulties in defying it and investigating the possibilities of overcoming it. Originally, *sati* referred to chaste women and the goddess symbolising chastity and not to the custom of Hindu widows being burned or buried with the husband's corpse[1]. It was the British colonial rulers who understood the word *satī* as the act of burning widows. The idea is that the life on this earth literally comes to an end there and the husband and wife live together for ever in heaven. The British prohibited *satī* as a brutal custom in the beginning of the nineteenth century. Many researchers have already attempted analyses of *satī* in those days and of the disputes leading to the prohibition of *satī*[2]. Here I deal with the *satī* that took place in India in 1987 and its repercussions. I had visited the village concerned around six months after the incident, but the atmosphere was still such that no research could be conducted openly[3]. For this reason, newspaper and magazine articles on the incident will be used here as the objects of analysis. The number of articles on this topic comes to about two hundred ranging from those that just report the facts of the *satī* incident and the names of people arrested to special reports of several pages in length[4]. In addition to these there are many research articles by historians, religious studies specialists and anthropologists that have been published till recently. In this article, I first present a brief account of the incident in 1987 and then analyse the disputes over *satī* appearing in newspapers. What I want to focus on in particular are the beliefs behind *satī*, the pro-*satī* views of those who praise and defend *satī* and the anti-*satī* views of those who criticise it as an evil tradition of the past.

Ritual violence is a key concept here and it refers to two things: patterned or formalised violence and violent elements in ritual. In other words, this is community violence in the sense that it is socially sanctioned[5], and it is divine violence in the sense that it is linked to a supernatural being. As we will see later, *satī* is also ritualised violence which is worshipped by many people and blessed by the goddess. Widows who can receive the blessings of the goddess are limited. The widow must also show a miracle in the act of *satī*. Once this is accepted those who oppose the *satī* are cursed by the divine beings. Thus to reproach *satī* means the same as criticising the community and its system of belief. This is not just a matter of criticising violence as evil, since in order to criticise it, the community and the supernatural beings have to be reprimanded. Disputes over *satī* teach us the difficulties in this kind of criticism of violence.

2. *Deorala, a Site of satī*

On 4th September 1987 in Rajasthan, a state in north-east India, a young woman was cremated along with her husband who had died a few hours ago. To be more accurate, the word cremated applies only to the husband since the woman was still alive when she was burned. The first article in an English language newspaper reporting this incident was only a short one of about a hundred words (*Indian Express* 6th September 1987)[6]. In an article "A young woman commits *satī*, dated 5th September, it is said the police reported that an eighteen-year-old woman has committed *satī* and that four relatives have been arrested for aiding the suicide. There is no comment in particular.

Let me first present what were reported as facts. The village of Deorala is located eighty kilometres north of the state capital Jaipur and just twenty kilometres off the main road leading to Delhi, the capital city and it is by no means an isolated village in the middle of nowhere. The population is 13,000 and there are 300 households of Rajputs who are the dominant caste and own 70 per cent of the land in the entire village. The village is well off, it has five primary schools and the level of education is higher than in other regions[7].

Roop Kanwar's *satī* was the fourth one in this village as far as it is known and the last *satī* took place seventy years ago. Thirty-eight people have committed *satī* in Rajasthan since Independence and all have been in the Shekawati district which Deorala is a part of.

Roop Kanwar was eighteen years old, when she married the twenty-four-year-old Man Singh on 17th January 1987. The husband did not have a job. He had been trying to become a medical student, and had taken a university entrance examination before and after the marriage. He was taken into hospital on 3rd September with a stomach pain, but he died next morning[8]. This happened eight months after the marriage. Taking into account the period that she had spent in her fathers house after marriage, Roop Kanwar and Man Singh's time together seems to have been much shorter—some say just three weeks. She saw her husband's corpse and expressed her will to perform *satī*. She immediately put on her red wedding clothes and went with the funeral procession to the cremation ground. This was around one O'clock in the afternoon. As the villagers watched, she sat on the wood piled up to burn the corpse. The fifteen year-old younger brother of Singh lit the funeral pyre as the chief mourner[9]. There were said to have been four to five thousand spectators[10]. Roop Kanwar's parental house got to know about their daughter's *satī* in the newspapers next morning.

Roop Kanwar was born in a well-to-do family in Jaipur, the capital city of Rajasthan. Her father ran a transportation business there. She was born and brought up in Ranchi in the state of

Bihar, and there was a temple of *satī* nearby. Speculations that this might have influenced her were also reported. She was educated up to eighth class in Ranchi. She went on to high school in Jaipur, but she gave up her studies for marriage. Her father-in-law was an English teacher in Deorala village.

Roop Kanwar's *satī* attracted neighbouring villagers and several thousand worshippers visited every day even after the incident. The cremation place was called *satī stal* and was covered by a yellow canopy mixed with light pink. Four Rajput youths with open swords stood in front of the place and twenty-seven youths circled it without stop, guarding the cremation ashes twenty-four hours a day.[11]

The number of participants reached a climax on the morning of 16th September, when the ritual ending the mourning period called the *chunarī* festival took place. A *cunarī* (an expensive gold-embroidered silk shawl worn by a bride at her wedding) was taken along with other items from Roop Kanwar's natal house to her-in-law's house and then to the cremation ground. There the *cunarī* was burned in the sacred fire amidst the crowd shouting "Victory to goddess *Satī* !" and priests chanting the Gāyatrī mantra. The priests cooled down the ashes, gathered them in a pot and buried it. It was said that the ashes were saturated with sacred power (*śakti*). A trident was positioned where it was buried, worship was performed and more *cunarī* shawls were placed on top. Around 300,000 people participated and some had even walked barefoot from six hundred kilometres away.

Many souvenir shops were set up and many composite pictures were sold of Roop Kanwar and her husband showing the couple enveloped in flames. Even after the *cunarī* festival, two to three thousand people came to Deorala every day. In Roop Kanwar's house the wedding photograph was displayed on the veranda and in the room where she decided to commit *satī* the red and silver sari which she was wearing at the time was spread out on display. Elite members of the village decided to collect funds to build a temple for Roop Kanwar at the place of cremation. It is said 200,000–300,000 Rs. was collected just on the day of the *cunarī* festival.

Women activists reminded the Chief Minister of Rajasthan of

the anti-*satī* Act of 1827, demanding an explanation from him, but were turned away. On 14th September, around three hundred and fifty members of thirteen womens organisations took part in a silent demonstration in Jaipur criticising the government for not taking any action on 14th September. They took the matter to the Rajasthan High Court and on 15th September an order was passed banning the *cunarī* festival. However, this ban was not implemented, the government remained silent and there were even some members of the state assembly who participated in it. At this point, only Roop Kanwar's younger brother-in-law who had lit the funeral pyre was arrested. On 21st September a demonstration was organised in Delhi demanding that the Chief Minister should resign and that the central government should prevent the construction of the temple. On 26th over fifty widows joined a demonstration against *satī* and government relief measures for widows.

Rajiv Gandhi who was the Prime Minister at the time sent a minister on 22nd September for investigation into the incident and statement of the central government's position. The state government reacted under pressure, and on 19th September the father-in-law and three other relatives were arrested for aiding suicide. Twenty-eight people were arrested by 27th September. Policemen were posted in the village and all souvenir shops were banned by 2nd October. The state government issued a law prohibiting the practice and encouragement of *satī* on 1st October. On 20th October the police demolished a Roop Kanwar monument and on 31st October they arrested five people belonging to the Association for Protection of the Righteousness of Sati (Sati Dharma Raksha Samiti) for encouraging the glorification of *satī*.

Against these moves of the anti-*satī* lobby, the pro-*satī* groups responded by organising a demonstration of around five hundred Rajput men in Jaipur on 19th September as a protest against the arrests made on that day. They demanded that the government should not interfere in religious matters. On 27th September the first meeting of the Association for Protection of the Righteousness of Sati was held in Deorala, and the core members were the Rajputs living in Jaipur. On 8th October they hosted a pro-*satī* demonstration in Jaipur of about fifty thousand people, which was the largest demonstration organised after the incident. Kalyan Singh Kalvi who was a central figure in the Association for Protection of the Righteousness of Sati and the leader of the state's Janata Party also participated and gave a speech at the demonstration.

The influence of anti-*satī* movements went beyond Rajasthan and on 2nd October a women's organisation criticised the procession at a festival of a temple dedicated to *satī* in Bombay. Festivals were also banned in a *satī* temple in Calcutta. Thirty-six women's organisations demonstrated in Delhi on 4th November demanding the establishment of a law prohibiting *satī* for the whole of India. In response to this, a new prohibition law was passed in the Lower House and Upper House by 16th December. The Chief Minister of Rajasthan resigned on 18th January, and one of the reasons is said to be his inadequate response to Roop Kanwar's *satī* incident. However, those arrested were later released without bail and no trials have been carried out. Furthermore, in spite of the legal regulations, eight thousand people gathered in Deorala for the first anniversary of Roop Kanwar's death.

Let me make a brief summary of the points of dispute. First of all, the pro-*satī* viewpoint sees *satī* as an honoured tradition particular to the Rajputs or Hindus and is antagonistic to the state. By considering *satī* as religious, it criticises state intervention. The anti-*satī* viewpoint held most strongly by women's organisations, criticises *satī* as savage and emphasises the importance of education and the improvement in status of widows. For them, *satī* is a women's problem and a custom that symbolises the low status of women in India. There is no question of it being a miraculous divine deed and there is no such thing as voluntary *satī*. They argue that *satī* cannot be said to be religious and that it is a means of making money at the expense of women. Their attack is also directed against the government as they declare that the government is not sincerely trying to outlaw *satī* and that the legal prohibitions are merely a gesture. But what they actually did was to call for government action. They not only demanded the urgent arrest of the relatives involved in Roop Kanwar's *satī*, but also acted against temples commemorating *satī* in the past in Calcutta and Bombay, saying that they glorify *satī*.

3. *Satī as Miracle*

Here I would like to consider the beliefs behind *satī*. The anthropologist, Harlan gives the following explanation[12]. In Rajasthan, the value of a woman is determined by her chastity towards the husband (*pati*). By this the husband is protected from all kinds of danger. The practice of this value is called *pativrata*. The woman performs another practice when the husband dies. This is *satīvrata* and by this her body gets hot. That is why it is said that when she chooses her death on the funeral pyre, she does not feel the heat of the flames at all. When she dies, she is called *satī mātā* (*Satī* goddess). *Satī* is the manifestation of the moral goodness (*sat*) in women. In the newspapers, *sat* is expressed as something that takes hold of a widow, or it is explained that only a widow who has received a revelation from the goddess leaves everything behind and performs *satī* (*Telegraph* 10th October 1987).

Let us take a more detailed look at the process between the husband's death and the act of *satī*. When the widow tells her family of her intension to commit *satī*, she puts her finger near a candle flame and proves that it does not get burned. Next she takes a bath in a river and changes into her bridal clothes. If it is raining, it will stop and the suns rays will shine on the funeral pyre. The widow jumps on to the pile of wood. It is said that the husband comes to life for a moment to acknowledge his wife's *satī*. No one lights the pyre. Flames appear from the heat of the widows body itself, as she receives the goddess's blessing. For the widow, it feels like bathing in water and is literally called "bathing in flames" (*agni snāna*).

Roop Kanwar was filled with power and due to this power she was able to perform *satī*. Then, she became a goddess and gained the power to grant the wishes of other people. People came into contact with this sacred power at the cremation ground and sought for all kinds of worldly benefits.

From the point of view of other women, Roop Kanwar's *satī* signified her exceptional strength. The power of the widow who has decided to perform *satī* appears as a blessing and at the same time a curse to people. People cannot stop *satī* in fear of her curse. It is said that the lineage of the man who tried to prevent the *satī* in Deorala seventy years ago came to an end after that. It is also said that the policeman who arrested Roop Kanwar's father-in-law fell ill.

Whatever the status given to *satī* in the scriptures may be the explanations above seem to be enough to tell us about the beliefs that bring about *satī*. However, there is a contradiction here. For instance, a woman who commits *satī* is destined to be so, that means she is a chaste woman who has always been serving her husband. But, if that is the case, why the husband dies before her cannot be explained. Why didn't she die before her husband? This is surely a major contradiction if we take into consideration the fact that a widow is often said to be the cause of her husband's death.

Moreover, emphasis on the miracle may also lead to the denial of the *satī* that actually occurred. As some of the villagers point out, the fact that it was the younger brother-in-law who lit the funeral pyre and that there were some people arrested in Roop Kanwar's *satī* led to the denial of its authenticity (*Times of India* 11th December 1987). There is also a view that *sat* could not have manifested in Roop Kanwar since she was too young[13].

In this way, the logic of the people supporting *satī* seems comprehensive at first sight if we accept the concepts that are presupposed, such as the existence of *sat* and its power. But it is by no means so, and even if the beliefs themselves were not denied by facts, the authenticity of each of the incidents would be questioned. Roop Kanwar's *satī* was also not exempt from this inspection.

Furthermore, it is believed that the one who commits *satī* takes away not only the sins of her own, but also those of her husband, the ancestors and the descendents. This is a belief that deeply reflects the sacrificial nature of *satī*. I heard for instance that in the case of Roop Kanwar's *satī*, there was plenty of rain and abundant crops that year thanks to her. It would not be impossible here to identify the aspect of human sacrifice. There are various aspects to *satī* that cannot be understood simply as beliefs regarding chaste women.

4. *Satī as Resistance*

Roop Kanwar's father said that he was proud of what his daughter had done. She h as made both our family and the in-law's family immortal (*Indian Express* 11th September 1987). But this was not all. As we will see below, her death can be interpreted as not only making her family and relatives immortal, but also as being used politically to make the Rajputs and their land Rajasthan immortal.

As we have already seen, from the beginning of the *satī* incident, there was a conspicuous attempt to understand and defend this in relation to the Rajput caste. Demonstrations were organised many times with the Rajputs as the core. Why the Rajputs? If we take note of the fact that *satī* is a phenomenon particular to the Rajputs of Rajasthan, it is necessary to consider the conditions that the Rajputs are in when thinking about contemporary *satī*. Rajputs are a royal caste of northwestern India and were highly regarded as warriors even in the colonial period. They used to rule over Rajasthan, but their power has been weakened in recent years, externally due to the emergence of other castes and internally due to land reforms[14]. This is a crisis for the Rajputs. *Satī* originated from the act of women committing suicide after losing their husbands in battle to prevent being shamed by the enemy, thus, is a suitable symbol for demonstrating their past glory both internally and externally. *Satī* can be seen as a means of resistance to overcome the crisis of Rajput identity or tradition[15].

A member of a pro-*satī* organisation, Kalyan Singh Kalvi, did not stop defending *satī* as a part of his (Rajput) tradition, in spite of the criticisms of *satī* by the Congress party members in the centre (*Times of India* 16th September 1987). Kalvi later weakened his view a little and said that the Rajasthan state government should have deterred *satī* in accordance with the law, but it was not right that the government should intervene in the *chunarī* festival, and the construction of a memorial since these were only a part of family rituals (*Times of India* 29th September 1987). Here the relationship between politics and religion and that between the state and the family are put to question. Moreover, he even went on to state that the actions of the government and the police were wounding the religious sentiments of the Hindus, especially the Rajputs, and to hurt their pride would be very dangerous for the country since the Rajputs are emotional people and it is because of this that they have produced many martyrs as soldiers of the country (*Times of India* 30th September 1987).

Other pro-*satī* people emphasise similar points. According to them, enforced *satī* is a crime and should be reprimanded, but voluntary *satī* cannot be opposed or deterred. To do so, they say, would be government intervention in religious matters. They state that matters regarding religion should not be decided by the government or the courts, but by religious men such as the Shankaracharyas who head the four most important Hindu monasteries in India.

In this way, the defence of *satī* is reconsidered as the tradition of not only Rajputs but of Hindus in general, and its authority is sought in a sphere outside secular power. Here lies the reason why many articles point to the relationship between defenders of *satī* and contemporary Hindu nationalism, which calls to make Hinduism the state religion and India a Hindu state. It is thought that just as religion is only a tool for gaining political power in Hindu nationalism, *satī* is also only a tool in the power politics for politicians[16].

What I want to emphasise here is the point that it is not only because *satī* is a custom particular to India that it becomes a symbol. Not only this, but also more generally there is a historical relationship between Indian women and Hindu nationalism in the past. That is to say, in India as the anti-British movements became popular at the end of the nineteenth century, it came to be understood that women were the source and storehouse of Indian tradition. Unlike the men who worked outside, women who stayed at home were transformed into unpolluted beings, who were not influenced by the effects of modernisation and westernisation and were the basis of nationalism dreaming for a future independent state. Here the women who were idealised belonged to the upper castes observing social segregation (*purdah*). It was not only the British and Indian men who were put in opposition to this category. Westernised Hindu women and lower caste women who had no choice but to work outside along with men were also contrasted to these upper caste women. In this way, although it was paradoxical, a discourse was born according to which subjectivity was granted to the very women whose place was inside[17].

A similar rhetoric can be seen in the dispute regarding Roop Kanwar's *satī*. That is to say, *satī* contains the paradox that it recognises true subjectivity in women who are subjugated to their husbands. Moreover, *satī* differentiates Rajput women from other low caste women in the region ("Their *satī* is not real.")[18] and at the same time it functions to negate the urban and westernised women and the secularism that they represent. *Satī* becomes the ultimate tradition to be observed by Rajput women. This tradition is ultimate for women in the sense that they are its true heirs and thus to prove themselves as Rajput women they have to choose death. Their subjectivity can only be actualised by death.

5. *Resistance against satī*

Most of the English language newspapers reporting Roop Kanwar's *satī* all criticises it[19]. For instance, *Indian Express* dated 11th September published an editorial with a title saying that a "barbarian tradition" has come back to life. In the editorial titled "Savage and primitive" published on the fourteenth day after the incident when the *cunarī* ritual came to an end, it pointed out that, despite being an educated man, the father-in-law did not prevent the *satī* nor think that it was against the law. It also states that Roop Kanwar's death is related to violence against women, such as dowry murders and abortion of female foetus after testing for its sex. It deplores that this incident proves India to be still very far from the twenty-first century. In other newspapers, *satī* is seen as "savage act" (*Hindu* 17th September 1987) and expressions such as "shame" and "inhuman act" are used and the word superstition is repeatedly employed (*Hindustan Times* 18th September 1987). The many opinions published in the newspapers were much the same. What is common in these editorials is the significance of education and administrative leadership beyond political interests. They criticise that the state government did hardly anything after the *satī* occurred in fear of what might happen to the results of the next elections. They also approve of the establishment of the new legal measures, but question the efficacy of the law.

Satī was understood above all as the symbol of the pathetic condition of widows in India. The fact that demonstrations by widows were organised points to this. In Hindu society, particularly among upper castes, widows are considered to be most inauspicious[20]. This is because the cause of the husband's death is thought to be the wife who is still alive. Widow remarriage is accepted only among low castes. When a woman becomes a widow, various measures are taken to hide her sexuality which is potentially dangerous[21]. The widow must shave the long hair which is a symbol of womanhood, take off all her jewellery and wear white or plain light colour sari. She is prohibited from taking her meals with other family members and is not allowed to participate in her own son's wedding. She is considered very inauspicious and so is not fit for an auspicious occasion such as marriage. A married woman who dies before her husband is the complete opposite to the widow. If the couple has a son then she is perfect. A married woman whose husband is alive has important roles in rituals, such as marriage, as an auspicious being. So it was said that if there were no such discrimination against widows, no one would want to commit *satī*.

Moreover, *satī* is said to be a means of deterring the wife's inheritance right. Especially in the case of Roop Kanwar who had no children, the large amount of dowry in cash and kind given to the husband at the time of the wedding was supposed to be returned when she became a widow[22]. For this reason it was also interpreted and reported that the in-laws who did not want to do so forced the *satī* to take place.

There was also the criticism that contemporary *satī* is not a honourable tradition, but merely a religious show put up by the entire village aiming to gain the enormous amount of donations that would come from it. It was argued that this is not tradition but a contemporary phenomenon in a society penetrated by the market economy[23].

Furthermore, there were doubts regarding the incident itself. In a newspaper dated 25th September, a teacher who had taught Roop Kanwar in Ranchi was reported to have said that she was forced to sit on the funeral pyre and that she did not seem particularly religious when she was a student (*Times of India* 25th September 1987). But, the fact that she was forced has not been proved. A newspaper dated 29th September expresses doubts whether Roop Kanwar really committed *satī* of her own accord (*Hindu* 29th September 1987). According to one view, when

Man Singh's body was carried into the house, the members of the household blamed Roop Kanwar that she had brought misfortune to the house and said that even greater misfortunes will befall the house in the future. It was written that even if she had tried to escape, it would have been impossible due to the way in which the wood was piled up and her screaming would not have been heard due to the cheering of the crowds. Later, on 2nd October, a police report was published saying that Roop Kanwar had been trying to escape from the flames that were burning her body.

Reports based on actual statements began to appear only after mid-October. First, a report was published by three representatives of the Bombay Union of Journalists (*Indian Express* 23rd October 1987)[24]. There it was pointed out that Roop Kanwar was hiding in a shed. After this, the tendency to discuss Roop Kanwar's *satī* as murder grew stronger[25]. However, even in these reports the truth is obscure.

The above criticisms moved the government, but were nullified in the face of enthusiasm of those actually involved. Those who were against *satī* were to face some dilemmas themselves. These were the problems concerning the subjectivity of women and the fact that, however justified their argument was, it nonetheless could lead to supporting the control and punishment of minority groups, the Rajputs here, by state power.

To totally deny the existence of voluntary *satī* would be to accept the view of women as being powerless and as victims. In the case of *satī* the object of violence is a woman. But to criticise *satī* as the ultimate violence of patriarchal society and to talk of women as victims of evil customs could lead to denying the nature of women as agents from the start. As a result, one ends up supporting the typical view of women in patriarchal society, that they are dependent and cannot decide anything for themselves. It would then seem that the pro-*satī* discourse praising the heroism of women who commit *satī* was recognising the subjectivity of women, though it may not apply to women in general, as it denies the agency of those widows who have failed to commit *satī*.

On the other hand, if they accept voluntary *satī*, not only would they be unable to deny *satī* itself, but they would also be strengthening the image of women as being tied to tradition in this case as well. This is because the decision to commit *satī* is made by a woman who wants to be subjugated to her husband and sacrifice everything for him. This clearly shows that *satī* is literally the ultimate ideological apparatus which establishes a woman's subjected subjectivity[26]. There is a very fine line between seeing her as the victim of tradition and seeing her as the agent of positive choice, since the latter also aims at voluntary subjection. Thus highly educated urban women try to side with the woman and as a result end up constructing an image of women different from themselves[27].

Moreover, the anti-*satī* lobby emphasised the need for legal reforms prohibiting *satī* and the glorification of *satī*. This signifies the demand for state intervention and hence it differs little from the nineteenth century imperialist view. In the nineteenth century, legal system was prepared as a means to civilise India whose backwardness was symbolised by *satī* and thus colonial rule was legitimised[28]. At that time, episodes of British people rescuing widows just as they were about to throw themselves into the flames were often reported. It can be said that in 1987 this picture was replaced by that of urban intellectuals civilising savage rural Indians. In this way, the intellectuals, especially the activists in women's organisations in this case, came to be seen as the enemies of "nationalism". They were criticised as women poisoned by western thought who did not understand tradition, and also as agents of the state oppressing the local community. The Rajputs have come to positively accept the position as a minority opposing the modern state[29].

6. *From Blessing to Violence and to Pain*

Satī is violence in the name of blessing exercised by a goddess choosing one woman out of many widows. It is the family of her in-laws, the village, and the Rajputs who actually exercise the divine violence. *Satī* is carried out in the name of the goddess and the community. The chosen widow becomes a goddess, blesses the people in turn and chooses another widow.

In order to deny this belief and to accuse *satī* as being murder, one would have to deny the power of the goddess and of the community. This is rationalism and secularism which is anti-religious, and also individualism which is anti-community. This is indeed the anti-*satī* stance. It is said that only the spread of education based on these ideals will truly liberate women. However, in reality, those who are against *satī* have no choice but to appeal to the state to prohibit *satī*. From the point of view of the *satī* defenders, this is state interference in religion and against secularism (guarantee of religious freedom) and in so far as *satī* is seen as a family problem, it is state intervention in the private life. In other words, the pro-*satī* lobby also happens to respond using the same logic of secularism and individualism as the anti-*satī* lobby.

The dilemma against this violence called *satī* does not end here. For instance, if *satī* is seen as murder, the people who lit the fire or were directly involved in the *satī* would indeed be arrested and judged in the name of the law, but the collective nature of the violence would be ignored. Moreover, if the act of murder were emphasised, the violence at the symbolic level would be missed. The everyday discrimination or violence exercised against widows within the home would remain unseen. Furthermore, the power of discourse that distinguishes and differentiates between widows and married women whose husbands are alive would also be overlooked. These points can be said to illustrate the difficulties in criticising violence, especially ritual violence that is legitimised by religion (community) and which is usually only one element in a ritual.

The way to criticise ritual violence such as that represented by *satī* would be to deny the discourse that it is a divine blessing, that is to say, to make clear that it is not a blessing but violence, and that it does not involve happiness but pain for the one concerned and sorrow for the close relations[30].

For instance, *Asahi* newspaper dated 13th October 1987 reports Roop Kanwar's *satī* as follows. The headline was "A young wife in flames embracing her husband who died from illness". The story begins with the sentence 'Kanwar sat on the wood piled up for her husband's cremation and put his head on her lap. She smiled as her body burned in the raging fire and then fell collapsing'. The words "in flames" in the headline and "smiling" are indeed none else than expressions that mystify *satī*. In Japan, which is far away from India, *satī* was just a convenient incident to satisfy the curiosity about the mysterious country where anything goes. I will not question their irresponsible attitude here. The denial of mystification or of no pain typically found in the word "smiling", that is to say, the complete denial of the legitimacy of the violence by the divine beings is one of the few ways of going against the divine and communal violence. For this purpose, we have to ask questions regarding the body of Roop Kanwar which was enveloped in flames and not to take *satī* as an institution or representation of Hindu or Rajput nationalism. By doing so we can shift the point of discussion from the problem of rational subject who can make decisions to the problem of embodied subject who feels pain[31].

The dilemma faced by the anti-*satī* lobby, which emphasises the subjectivity of women, is similar to the dilemma that anthropologists feel when confronted with ritual violence of other cultures such as "female circumcision". This is because anthropologists cannot find a decisive solution as to how they can talk about the victims of violence, how they can resolve the violence itself, and whether in the first place, they as anthropologists should really say something. This difficulty lies in the fact that they have the beliefs and institutions legitimising violence as their framework of explanation. As long as cultural anthropology respects other cultures from the point of view of cultural relativism, it is not possible to criticise ritual violence. This is more so if it has to do with the identity making of individuals. It is probably necessary to somehow disengage the connection that the intention to understand violence leads to approving and defending it. To focus on pain here would be to point out that the individual is not necessarily totally bound to the systems of meanings or beliefs and social institutions, and does not necessarily become a completely subjected subject. The very fact of a body that responds to and resists pain shows us that there are aspects which cannot be subjectified. Desire and pain rooted in the body undermine the ideologically constructed subject. At that moment, the individual momentarily overcomes the subjected subject. We must not overlook this moment. The focus on pain, however, should not mean considering the individual as an isolated body. Rather, we should look for the "community of sorrow" which is made hidden by the mystification of pain[32]. This is not about accusing the relatives of acting out of self-interest and dividing up the pro-*satī* lobby which emphasises honour. It is rather about looking for people who accept the pain of *satī* as their own. It is by changing the analytic perspective from blessing to violence and then to pain, from the community of honour to the community of sorrow that the anthropology of violence can overcome many difficulties and open up new frontiers.

NOTES

1. For details of interpretation of sacred texts and historical sources regarding *satī*, see V.N. Datta, *Satī: Widow Burning in India,* Manohar, New Delhi, 1988, Sakuntala Narasimhan, *Satī: A Study of Widow Burning in India,* Viking, New Delhi, 1990, and Arvind Sharma, *Satī: Historical and Phenomenological Essays.* Motilal Banarsidass, New Delhi, 1988.
2. For instance, see Vasudha Dalmia-Luderitz, "'Sati' as a Religious Rite; Parliamentary Papers on Widow Immolation, 1821-30," *Economic and Political Weekly* 27(4), 1992, pp.58-64, Veena Das, "Gender Studies, Cross-Cultural Comparison and the Colonial Organization of Knowledge," *Berkshire Review* 21, 1986, pp. 58-76, Hanne Georgeson, "Representations of Hindu Women through Some of the Rewritings on Widow-burning," *TAJA* 3(3), 1992, pp. 150-174, Lata Mani, "Contentious Traditions: The Debate on SATI in Colonial India," *Cultural Critique* 7, 1887, pp. 119-156, "the Female Subject, the Colonial Gaze: Reading Eyewitness Accounts of Widow Burning," in Tejaswini Niranjana, P. Sudir and Vivek Dhareshwar (eds.), *Interrogating Modernity: Culture and Colonialism in India.* Seagull Books, Calcuttta, 1993, pp. 273-290, Gayatri Chakravorty Spavik, "Can the Subaltern Speak?" in Cary Nelson and Lawrence Grossberg (eds.), *Marxism and the Interpretation of Culture,* University of Illinois Press, Urbana, 1988, pp. 271-313, Dorothy K Stein, "Women to Burn: Suttee as a Normative Institution," *Signs* 4(2), 1978, pp. 253-273. Of course, although the nineteenth century disputes over *satī* centering in Bengal are not exactly the same as those I deal with in this article, they are not unrelated. In fact, in 1987 the nineteenth century disputes were often mentioned in the newspapers and there the British government was praised. In order to consider the post-colonial condition that India faces, it is necessary to keep the nineteenth century disputes on *satī* in view.
3. When I visited Deorala in March 1988, there was a police checkpoint on the road on the way to the village where I had to leave my camera.
4. Since I deal mainly with English language newspapers and magazines, the opinions are mostly against *satī*, but I have tried as much as possible to include the pro-*satī* views found in Hindi language newspapers through translation of them. I would also like to point out that I have not given the sources of the opinions which recur many times in different articles.
5. Already around a hundred years ago, Durkheim had declared *satī* to be a collective intentional suicide enforced by a group in his work *Suicide* [1897]. He says that this occurs in a society where individuals are almost buried in the society and individual personalities are not respected, and

when the society neglects life and takes it for granted that individuals give their lives for it without any important reason. See also for R.S. Gandhi, "Sati as Altruistic Suicide," *Contributions to Asian Studies* 10, 1977, pp.141-157. As it will become clear later on, those who criticise *satī* is faced with the dilemma of having to accept this kind of view of Indian society.

6. The first newspaper to report this incident was the local paper *Rajasthan Patrika* (5th September 1987), but it is said that it was treated in much the same way [Sharada Jain, Nirja Misra and Kavita Srivastava, "Deorala Episode: Women's Protest in Rajasthan," *Economic and Political Weekly* 22(45), 1987, pp. 1891-1894].
7. The literacy rate is 70 per cent and 40 per cent for women. This is very high considering that the average literacy rate in Rajasthan is only 2 per cent for women.
8. There are many speculations regarding the cause of death, such as intestinal inflammation and acute appendicitis. According to one speculation, he committed suicide due to the news he received, fifteen days before his death, of the failure in his repeated attempt at the entrance examination. The doctor who saw Man Singh's death went into hiding just afterwards and did not respond to police questions.
9. This is usually done by the eldest son, but the couple had no children. It is said that in the case of *satī,* a minor is usually chosen in fear of police arrest.
10. There are several views about the number of spectators. Some reports say that the number was four to five hundred since no one openly said that they saw it in fear of police arrest.
11. This was because it was feared that the ashes might be misused by magicians (*tantri*).
12. Here I have referred to Lindsey Harlan, "Perfection and Devotion: Sati Tradition in Rajasthan," in John S. Hawley (ed.), *Sati: The Blessing and the Curse: The Burning of Wives in India,* Oxford University Press, Oxford, 1994, pp.112-181 in particular. See also Kumkum Sangari and Sudesh Vaid, "Institutions, Beliefs, Ideologies: Widow Immolation in Contemporary Rajasthan," in Kumari Jayawardena and Malathi de Alwis (eds.), *Embodied Violence: Communalising Women's Sexuality in South Asia.* Zed Books, London, 1996, Sudesh Vaid, "Politics of Widow Immolation," *Seminar* 342, 1988, pp. 20-23.
13. Shobha, Kavita, Kanchan, Shobita and Sharada, "Rural Women Speak," *Seminar* 342, 1988, pp. 40-44. In this article many critical voices against *satī* by the general populace are recorded.
14. The Rajasthan Land Reform and Resumption of Jagirs Act was established in 1952. Two years later, the first *satī* after independence took place in Rajasthan.
15. See Vaid, "Politics of Widow Immolation" for this point.
16. For instance see the statement by a member of the communist party given in *Times of India* (27th September 1987). But at least Advani, the leader of the BJP (Bharatiya Janata Party) which is thought to represent Hindu nationalism, criticised *satī* and stood in opposition against the party members in Rajasthan. Moreover, the World Hindu Association (Viswa Hindu Parishad), which called for the demolition of the mosque

regarding the Ayodhya problem, also declared a position of opposing all *satī* since a distinction cannot be drawn between enforced and voluntary *satī* (*Indian Express* 17th October 1987). The same goes for the religious sphere, and all were silent except the Shankaracharya of Puri, or took the opposing position as the Arya Samaj did (*The Illustrated Weekly of India* 2nd May 1988). This exposes the fact that *satī* is not necessarily all mighty as the symbol of Hindus.

17. See Partha Chatterjee, "Colonialism, Nationalism, and Colonialized Women: the Contest in India." *American Ethnologist* 16(4), 1989, pp. 622-633, for this point.
18. *Satī* by low castes are criticised as just being a means for raising status by imitating Rajputs [Harlan, "Perfection and Devotion: Sati Tradition in Rajasthan," p. 82].
19. However, there are subtle differences in the same newspaper, for instance in the Rajasthan version there is a strong pro-*satī* view.
20. T.N. Kitchlu, *Widows in India.* Ashish, New Delhi, 1993, gives a detailed account of widows.
21. This is by no means an unrealistic anxiety. It was thought that young widows like Roop Kanwar would commit a "mistake" at some time or other, even if she were to remain in the in-law's house or go back to her parent's house and bring dishonour to both houses.
22. Since Roop Kanwar's parental house was well off, the dowry included around 460 grams of gold, a fixed bank deposit of 30,000 Rs., apart from radio, colour television, refrigerator and so on.
23. See Madhu Kishwar and Ruth Vanita, "the Burning of Roop Kanwar," *Race & Class* 30(1),1988, pp. 59-67, for this point.
24. I have not read the report Meena Menon, Geeta Sheshu and Sujata — Anandan *Trial on Fire: A Report on Roop Kanwar's Death,* Bombay: Bombay Union of Journalists, 1987, but its details can be estimated from Veena Talwar Oldenburg, "the Roop Kanwar Case: Feminist Responses," in John S. Hawley, (ed.), *Satī: The Blessing and the Curse.*
25. There were other reports that Roop Kanwar was drugged and she was hardly conscious (*Times of India* 3rd October 1987). It was also reported that her husband was impotent and she had a lover so there was no way she would have committed *satī* [Oldenburg, "the Roop Kanwar Case: Feminist Responses," p. 116].
26. It is indeed ultimate in the sense that the actual woman involved dies, but subjectification in the sense of Althusser and Foucault fails. Rather, we should say that *satī* as a spectacle functions as a pre-modern ideological apparatus that teaches other women how they should live or die.
27. Problems of women's subjectivity regarding *satī* have been pointed out by Das, Gender Studies, Dalmia-Luderitz, "Sati as a Religious Rite" Julie Leslie, "Suttee or Sati: Victim or Victor?" in J. Leslie (ed.), *Roles and Rituals for Hindu Women.* Pinter, London, 1991, Rajeswari Sunder Rajan, "The Subject of Sati: Pain and Death in the Contemporary Discourse on Sati," *Yale Journal of Criticism* 3(2), 1990, pp. 1-28.
28. See Krishna Iyer, V.R. "Maha Sati: Death to Innocents," *Main Stream* 26(4), 1987, pp. 22-26.
29. For this point, see Kishwar and Vanita, "The Burning of Roop Kanwar," pp. 61 65, In particular. Veena Das, *Critical Events: An Anthropological*

Perspective on Contemporary India. Oxford University Press, Delhi, 1995, considers similar problems regarding the glorification of *satī*.

30. On the one hand, we should not deny the heartfelt pain of the widow mourning her husband (not necessary due to the misery of the life as a widow) and the possibility of suicide as a reaction to this. The problem then no longer becomes the evaluation of *satī* but that of whether suicide is right or wrong. In cases such as female circumcision or female genital mutilation (FGM) where the pain is not denied or hidden and is positively valued as something to overcome, it seems that slightly different arguments to *satī* need to be made. For this point see C J. Walley, "Searching for "Voices": Feminism, Anthropology, and the Global Debate over Female Genital Operations," *Cultural Anthropology* 12(3),1997, pp. 405-438.
31. Rajan, "The Subject of Sati," focuses on pain from a similar point of view. Oldenburg, "the Roop Kanwar Case: Feminist Responses", p. 125, takes this up and points out that the widows body as a subject of desire is also hidden in the representation of *satī* and argues that the problem should focus on the widow as an embodied being. Of course, we should not forget the fact that the discourses about pain in social science, law and medicine transform pain as it is and disengage it from the people who experience it [Das, *Critical Events*. p. 175, also, "Language and Body: Transactions in the Construction of Pain," *Daedalus* 125(1), 1996, pp. 67-91, Arthur W. Frank, *The Wounded Storyteller: Body, Illness and Ethics*. The University of Chicago Press, Chicago, 1995, pp. 178-179, E. Scarry, *The Body in Pain: the Making and Unmaking of the World*, Oxford University Press, Oxford, 1985].
32. This corresponds to the concept of "a collective subjectivity of agents" by Ania Loomba, "Dead Women Tell no Tales: Issues of Female Subjectivity, Subaltern Agency and Tradition in Colonial and Post-Colonial Writings on Widow Immolation in India," *History Workshop* 36, 1993, pp. 209-227, which was triggered off by Rajan, "The Subject of Sati", Das *Critical Events*, pp. 194-196 proposes anthropology of pain and emphasises the significance of research on this kind of community.

CHAPTER 36

Historical Studies of Pharping, I: The Modern Celebration of Buddha Jayanti

WILL DOUGLAS

1. *Introduction*

Pharping is one of several small and ancient Newar cities which surround the Kathmandu Valley. On foot from Lalitpur, it is about three hours's walk: first south through the valley towards Khokna, then west across the Bagmati and up into the mountains. For Newars, Pharping is known as a lovely picnic spot blessed with three separate pilgrimages of great importance: Śeṣa Nārāyaṇa, Dakṣīṇ Kālī and Vajrayoginī. Śeṣa Nārāyaṇa is an ancient Vaiṣṇava shrine constructed around a series of fish-ponds just below Pharping proper. Dakṣīṇ Kālī, actually set in a deep valley beyond Pharping, is sacred to the ferocious form of the goddess and is an important centre for Śākta and Śaiva rituals. It is now a much larger site than either of the other two, with busloads of pilgrims coming for the bloody sacrifices. Vajrayoginī is a traditional Newar Buddhist monastery (bahāl) which holds one of the four manifestations of this wrathful deity that ring the Kathmandu Valley, the others being Vidyeśvarī, Vajravārāhī and the Saṅkhu Vajrayoginī. There is also at least one other Buddhist pilgrimage site in Pharping, the Asura Cave, which was the site of Padmasambhava's establishment of the Buddhist vajrakīla tantras in the 8th century; this is now entirely enclosed by a Tibetan monastic compound near Vajrayoginī.

There are probably fewer than five thousand people living in Pharping, but taken together with its surrounding settlements it is a thriving centre of transit and trade. The existing metalled road which now winds its way up from behind the Chobhar cement plant was built in the second quarter of the 20th century by the Ranas who wished to make the journey to Dakṣīṇ Kālī easier. In recent years there has been a tremendous influx of diaspora Tibetan lamas building retreat centres which has brought money into the market stalls and small businesses, but there is no industrial base, nor is there significant income from agriculture—though the taste of Pharping apples and oranges is justifiably famous.

In and around Pharping today there are three distinct resident ethnic groups with significant numbers of Buddhists: the Newars, the Tamangs and the recently arrived Tibetans. Only about half the Newars are Buddhists; there are many Śreṣṭhas, for example, running shops around the bus park. Of the traditionally Buddhist *jātis* Pharping has numerous Balāmī, sufficient to make up three *sī guthis* or funeral associations. Several Mānandhar households live along the main market road. There is one family of Vajrācāryas who live at Vajrayoginī, and one or two others who are absentee landowners in the town. Finally there is one family of Tulādhars living just above the market squạre. Few Tamang actually live in Pharping, but they are a constant presence in the social and economic life of the town, coming in from villages such as Huṇḍu and Lamagaũ scattered in the hills around Pharping. The Tibetans (and their foreign patrons and students), by contrast, now completely dominate the road which runs uphill from the bus park, although the oldest Tibetan monastery in or near Pharping is only about 40 years old.

In this paper I will look at the Buddha Jayanti celebrations of 2002. Buddha Jayanti is not a traditional Vajrayāna Buddhist holiday, but in the past decades it has become a noisy and playful festival which unites the otherwise rather dissociated Buddhist communities in the area. This year it was also the date chosen by the Tamangs of Huṇḍu to inaugurate a new *chos rten* and small shrine. Asking how and why Buddha Jayanti has become such a popular holiday, has lead me to this first of an anticipated series of papers on the history and present situation of Buddhism in Pharping.

2. *Early history*

The earliest mention of Pharping that I have so far found is in Pelliot Tibetan 44, a text from Dunhuang which describes the formulation of the Vajrakīla tantras by Padmasambhava and his collaborators. Opinions vary as to the antiquity of this document. Bischoff and Hartmann, in the original edition, speculate that it might have been written within two hundred years of the events described; Blondeau guesses that it might be a tenth-century document; while Richardson dates it to 'perhaps less than fifty years after the founding of the great monastery at bSam-yas' (=779CE).[1] Given the unanimity of all biographies of Padmasambhava in naming Pharping as the site of this innovation, we can be sure that there was already a settlement of some sort in Pharping around the end of the eighth century. In Pelliot 44, there are two distinct locations mentioned. The first, Yang le shod (*yang La shod* 1b), is where Padmasambhava was practicing, according to Boord,[2] with his Newar consort Śākaydevī when he decided to retrieve a text called the *phur bu'i bum sde* from his teacher Prabhāhasti at Nālandā. However, on setting out in the company of two Nepalese (Śākya Yur and Iso (?) (*shag kya yur dang i so* 5a), he found that a set of four malevolent female spirits (understood as a single being), the *bse'i lha mo bzhi* slew people in his party. He duly subdued them, took them in his hat to Nālandā, converted them into a (now single) guardian of the Vajrakīla practice and returned to Yang le shod with the desired texts. He then collected a team of scholar-yogis, with whom he retired to the Asura Cave (*a su ra'i brag pug* 6a-b)—our second site in Pharping—to perform sādhanas of this new protectress and in so doing codified the Vajrakīla materials for the first time.

The Asura cave is still well-known in Pharping today; there is even an Asura Cave Guest House. Although the name Yang le shod is also well-known, it is often mistakenly applied to the Asura cave. It appears rather to be located where the Śeṣa Nārāyaṇa temple is today. This identification is borne out in Tibetan pilgrimage guides such as the *bal yul gnas yig*[3], where *yang le shod* is identified as *seg nā rā yan sthan / phar ping gi lam na* (39) and the *a su ra yi brag phug* is within Pharping. While this identification has also been supported by informed Western and Tibetan scholars whom I have consulted, and Lévi encountered a party of 'Bhotiyas' who had come to install an inscribed stone at Śeṣa Nārāyaṇa, I have not so far found any pre-sixteenth-century sources which confirm the identification of Yang le shod with Śeṣa Nārāyaṇa.[4]

The list of Padmasambhava's collaborators varies as the history of the Vajrakīla material itself develops. In Pelliot 44, the list reads *a ca rgya sam ba bas bal po ser po dang in tra shu gu tu dang pra be se las bsogs pas* (6a), that is, 'Padmasambhava, the Newar Ser po, Intraśugutu, Prabese and others'. In an exhaustive study of the Vajrakīla origins, Boord takes Pelliot 44 together with several other sources and determines the list of collaborators as follows: Padmasambhava himself, Vimalamitra, and, the Newar Śīlamañju all working together with Prabhāhasti.[5]

Padmasambhava's residence in Pharping must have happened during the later eighth century. There are references to the activity of a second Tibetan yogi, sNubs sangs rgyas Ye shes, in Pharping in the ninth century. sNubs, who is an important figure in the Anuyoga lineages of Dzogchen, was among those Buddhists displaced from Tibet during the time of Ral pa can. Dudjom Rimpoche's history of the rNyings ma school gives his dates as 831 to 943.[6] A Tibetan, he was summoned to Yang le shod by a Nepalese king,[7] who was also his guru, and told to meditate on Yamāntaka in the cave there.

The next sources we have are the result of Petech's painstaking work reading colophons.[8] He identified a manuscript of the Kubjikāmata which was written in Kosabū Ṭol[9] in Pharping in the year 1092 CE. The colophon notes that Harṣadeva (?1085-1098 CE) was king,[10] but it tells us relatively little about the actual degree of control Harṣadeva may have exerted in Pharping. A second manuscript colophon noted by Petech dates from 1165 CE (Petech 1984 p. 63), and there is also an inscription, first published by Regmi[11] dating from 1260 CE.

The fourteenth-century chronicle of the Bhaktapur dynasty in Nepal called the *Gopālarājavaṃśāvalī* (GRV) has much to say about Pharping.[12] In that work, and in inscriptions from the period, Pharping is usually called *Phānapī* or *Phānapīga,* although sometimes it is also called Śikharapur. From the thirteenth century onwards it was an independent principality. The earliest entry for Pharping in the GRV (33b2) dates to NS 362 Pauṣa (1242 CE), when raiders from Bhaktapur attacked Pharping; across the course of several other entries, ending in 1384 CE (61b5), we can read the details of Pharping's place in the constant petty warfare among the many city-states of Nepal.

Pharping was also attacked, along with Nuwakoṭ, in 1328 by a force advancing under Ādityamalla (GRV 46a3). This king of the Khāśiyas appears to have been aligned with Sa sKya against Bri 'gung. There is some evidence that the Nepalese were more involved in Himalayan regional politics in the 14th century than has usually been thought;[13] but in any case, Ādityamalla failed to achieve his goal in the Kathmandu Valley. Although he did breach the western defensive line of the Nepalese, his attempts to capture fortified sites inside Lalitpur failed and he was forced to retreat.

Finally we may consider the 1793 report of Colonel Kirkpatrick, the leader of a British expeditionary force sent to assist the Nepalese court. In Kirkpatrick's time Pharping was a relatively small settlement and he says nothing about local authorities. Bearing in mind that the Kathmandu Valley, and especially the small fortress settlements to the west of the valley, had come under sustained attack throughout the mid-eighteenth century by the Gorkha troops who eventually subjugated all the Newar cities, this is not surprising. He remarks on the quality of the fruit and grain grown around Pharping, and notes carefully the trade route which passes through Pharping on its way from Lalitpur to Hetauda, the main staging point for trade with India. According to Kirkpatrick, the Pharping road was the main road in the late 18th century for the Indian trade. This is confirmed, without further discussion, by Sylvain Lévi who writes, 'Plus au Sud, dans le fond de la vallée, Phirping, au débouché de l'ancienne route de l'Inde.'[14] The Thankot road, which passes to the north of Pharping, became the usual way to Hetauda during the 19th century,[15] and no memory of the extensive mercantile traffic that must have passed through Pharping up to the 18th century remains today.

Summary: From this brief sketch of the sources certain conclusions emerge. Pharping has been an important commercial military and religious centre for over a millennium. Primarily a Newar settlement, it has drawn visitors or settlers from eastern and north western India, western and central Tibet. As a military outpost it has borne the brunt of invasions coming from the west; but equally, as a fortified medieval Nepalese town, it was attacked as part of internal Nepalese conflicts and in turn participated in attacks on other Nepalese city-states. After the consolidation of Gorkha rule in the 18th century its fortunes seem to have waned somewhat. The commercial traffic which passed through Pharping on its way to India was diverted, and along with all the other Newar city-states it lost its independence.

3. *The Modern Buddhist Communities of Pharping*

The Buddhists of Pharping in the year 2002 can be divided into five practice communities.

(1) The Tamangs who live in and around Pharping observe a form of Tibetan Buddhism. In this region they tend to patronize rNyings ma monks and lamas. The other indigenous group, the Newars, has two distinct forms of Buddhism, (2) a newer Theravāda form, distinguished in Pharping by the singing of the Jñāna Mālā devotional songs, and (3) the traditional Vajrayāna form. The actual practice of the Vajrayāna rituals is restricted to the incumbent Vajrācārya of Vajrayoginī Bahāl. He lives in the monastery with his family and performs the daily rituals for that monastery, and for the shrine of Vajrayoginī which is housed within. He is also called upon to perform life-cycle and occasional rituals for the Tulādhar and Mānandhar *jāti* members in Pharping. These *jātis* are traditionally Buddhist, and until the middle of the last century all of their religious ritual would have been performed by the resident Vajrācārya(s). However the development of popular devotional Theravāda Buddhism has led to the installation of images of Śākyamuni Buddha in public shrines in certain *ṭols* and the emergence of religious practices which do not require a Vajrācārya. Although in theory this form of Newar Buddhism is Theravādin, I have never yet actually seen a Theravāda monk or nun in Pharping, and it is the Vajrācārya who, for instance, performs their death rituals.

The (4) Tibetan lamas and their monasteries constitute the fourth group. The first monastery to be constructed in recent times was that of Chatral Rimpoche, an eminent teacher of Dzogchen, which was built at Yang le shod about 40 years ago. When the full flood of Tibetan refugees swept into Nepal, several other monasteries were built and the program of building has not stopped since. The most recent constructions were a retreat centre affiliated to Pal yul Monastery and the Ngagyur Nyingma Institute near Mysore in Karnataka, India, begun in 1997, and another new rNyings ma monastery, of the Ripa Ladrang foundation, which has only just been completed. The majority of these new centres are retreat centres. Finally there are usually (5) a number of foreign meditation students and long-term residents, both Western and East Asian, living in Pharping at any time. The number of such people has dropped dramatically since the declaration of the State of Emergency in Nepal at the end of 2001. On my last visit in June 2002 I saw only one other foreigner in Pharping. Almost all the foreigners in Pharping are affiliated to one or another of the new Tibetan monasteries, and indeed very few are aware of the presence of non-Tibetan Buddhists in Nepal at all.

3.1 Reasons for Conflict

These various communities do not necessarily cohere. A few examples will suffice to demonstrate the ways in which relations may be strained.

The Arrogance of Foreigners and Tibetans: While visiting Vajrayoginī one day, I found it full to bursting with a large group of Western students who had been brought from Boudha by senior lamas working for Lama Zopa, the founder of Kopan monastery. This is a monastery which is almost entirely devoted to the training of Western tourists. The Western students were apparently entirely unaware that this was not, in fact, a Tibetan site; and for their part, the lamas who were conducting the ritual made no effort to coordinate their activities with the Vajrācārya who is in charge of the shrine, nor did they leave the customary offering. When they had left, I helped to clean up the rubbish which had been left behind by the visitors.

The Problem with Vajrācāryas: Modernization has not been kind to the Vajrācāryas. They can no longer afford to work as ritual specialists and with the advent of an alternative Theravāda model of Buddhist righteousness, their social status is no longer guaranteed. The present Vajrācārya works in an office in Kathmandu and must make special arrangements if he is needed for a ritual during the working week. Moreover his family is new in the monastery; the previous lineage of Vajrācāryas, which died out about three decades ago, is still the subject of a number of spicey stories and they are certainly not remembered for their moral probity. Nonetheless, his clients still expect him to be able to perform a wide range of rituals with complete confidence. The difficulty of his situation is aggravated by his isolation; the single Pharping Vajrācārya is by birth and lineage a member of a monastery (Bu Bahāl) located about a dozen kilometres away, in Lalitpur.

The Unreliability of Mānandhars: When I spoke with the *thakāli* of the Mānandhars in Pharping, he assured me that all Mānandhars in Pharping were good Buddhists. Indeed, he and the Vajrācārya at Vajrayoginī are both concerned to preserve the strength of Buddhism in Pharping over against the constant threat of Hindu devotionalism. When I asked in the shops on the marketplace, I got a very different answer from the Mānandhar families who ran them; some people were devotees of Kṛṣṇa, some felt that the goddess of the nearby Dakṣīṇ-Kālī was their preferred deity and some identified themselves as Buddhist. When I asked the person who had named Kṛṣṇa why the *thakāli* had said Mānandhars were Buddhist, she replied 'We are! We celebrate Buddha Jayanti.'

The Inappropriate Behavior of Balāmīs: During the Buddha Jayanti procession a group of Balāmī men were happily inebriated and dancing with each other while their friends played percussion instruments. The group immediately in front of them was comprised of Tibetan monks, some of whom clearly disapproved of such a display in public.

The Invisibility of Newar Vajrayāna: In conversation with the Vajrācārya of Vajrayoginī Bahāl, I asked him if he had opportunities to work with visiting Tibetan teachers. This was, according to him, very rare, for very few of the high Tibetan lamas realized that the Newar Vajrayāna tradition was still alive and well. Once in the last year he had been invited to a major Tibetan teaching and pūjā and he rather hoped there would be more contact. I asked if he went out of his way to make contact; his working schedule made this difficult. Chatral Rimpoche, when he first came to Nepal, was regarded by the Newar Vajrācāryas with great warmth for his friendliness, but as he spent more and more time teaching in East and Southeast Asia, his contacts with, the Newar priestly community atrophied. From the other side, I have had conversations with senior Tibetan lamas, living in Pharping, who were completely unaware that Nepalese Vajrayāna still existed and that there was a community of skilled Vajrayāna priests who still used Sanskrit within a few hundred metres of their monasteries.

3.2 Other Factors Working Against an Integrated Buddhist Identity

Forgetting the Tibetans: The most obvious social divide in Pharping is between the Tibetan incomers and the Nepalis. The clear geographic seperation, which pushes the Tibetans uphill along the road to Huṇḍu, is matched by a cognitive failure to include the Tibetans in the Nepali mental map of Pharping. Most lists I elicited from Nepalis of the inhabitants of Pharping, their groups and numbers, simply omitted to mention the Tibetans at all. This is in opposition to their obvious presence in the market place, on the buses and indeed the pervasive sound of the Tibetan pūjās at various times of day.

The Decline of Newar Vajrayāna: The general decline of Newar Vajrayāna is keenly felt in Pharping. Although in present day Pharping there is only one Newar Buddhist monastery, that of Vajrayoginī, the *thakāli* of the Mānandhars who is something of a local historian was able to give me a list of nine other monasteries which were now lost. For at least two of these monasteries, place names in Pharping bear out the claim that there were once Bahāls; one of these places interestingly is Śeṣa Nārāyaṇa. However there are no local memories of Bahāls within the past hundred years and I have not so far been able to find inscriptional evidence for them. In any case, the isolation of the single remaining Vajrācārya is joined with a general sense that Newar Vajrayāna is on the defensive in Pharping.

Felt Oppression: This is paired with a strong sense among Newars and Tamangs, but not Tibetans, of the potential for oppression by non-Buddhists, and especially the officially Hindu state.[16] The explanation given for the loss of the monasteries was that they had been destroyed by Śaṅkarācārya. This is of course impossible. There was an eleventh-century ācārya from the maṭha at Benares who apparently gained great influence over the king in Nepal at that time, and the legends of oppression under Śaṅkara very likely can be traced to this historical figure. However it is also clear that Buddhist manuscripts were being copied well after the eleventh century in Pharping, and indeed the memory at least in toponyms of the Bahāls is such as to suggest that their demise is rather more recent. Unfortunately Kirkpatrick does not help us in this respect, and I do not know if any Pharping Bahāls survived the Gorkha conquest of Nepal. The general point, however, that the policies of the Gorkha state led to a dramatic reduction in patronage for the Vajrācāryas and Śākyas, appears to have had its effects in Pharping. Certainly the tendency among Mānandhars to find satisfying deities for devotion outside Buddhism, while grudgingly respecting the definition of their *thakāli* that they are, indeed, Buddhists, suggests that within two or three generations the Mānandhars of Pharping may well no longer be Buddhists even in name. Dakṣīṇ Kālī is a much more prestigious and popular pilgrimage site that any of the Buddhist shrines or monasteries in town.

The irony of a situation in which there is a tremendous influx of highly trained and charismatic Tibetan monks at the same time as respect for Buddhism is being eroded is not lost on the community leaders. Both the Vajrācārya and the *thakāli* of the Mānandhars remarked on their frustrating inability to draw on the Tibetan religious virtuosi to help them shore up Buddhism among the Newars of Pharping. This may change more young Tibetan monks and nuns grow up in the Newar community and build friendships. For the moment, though, the Tibetans are content to have commercial and social relations with the Nepalese of Pharping, while not attempting to engage them in religious discourse.

NAME	LOCATION	NOTES
Gaganakīrtivihāra	Vajrayoginī	Still exists.
Khāḥ Bahāl	Thalku ṭol	
Bosi Bahāl	above Gopāleśvara	Near the Asura cave.
So Bahāl	Kochu ṭol	
Taḥ Bahāl	Ṭipi ṭol	
Gola Bahāl	near the bus park	
Nanda Bahāl	Satīkhel	Just below Śeṣa Nārāyana.
(name lost)	Thalku ṭol	
Degu Bahāl	beyond Thalku ṭol	Signposted.

Figure 1: The Bahāls in Pharping

4. *How Unity was Displayed on Buddha Jayanti*

The festival of Buddha Jayanti is a new one in Nepal. It was first celebrated by the new Theravādins as part of their self-construction sometime around 1950, but it has rapidly become an important Buddhist holiday in many localities of Nepal. Śākyamuni Buddha, whose birth and enlightenment is celebrated on this day, is not thought ever to have come up to the Kathmandu Valley or Tibet, and the characters whose lives are realized in the surroundings of the Kathmandu Valley—for example, Nāgārjuna, Padmasambhava and Mañjuśrī—are all Mahāyāna or Vajrayāna figures. For Himalayan Buddhists Buddha Jayanti is a holiday with no history.

Buddha Jayanti this year (2002) fell on 12 June. From the early hours of the morning, images of the Buddha were displayed in at least two prominent locations, the main market square and a Ganesh shrine in the Balāmī quarter of town, which had a permanent Buddha image installed some years ago; and near each image a group of men sang devotional songs in the Jñāna Mālā style. Up beyond Pharping, in the Tamang community of Huṇḍu, a new stupa and shrine were being consecrated and at about 9:00 in the morning a procession wound its way down from Huṇḍu to Pharping, past all the Tibetan monasteries, into Pharping and right through the market square. This was the first of two processions, and it was comprised of Tamangs, both layfolk and their lama; monks from the nearest Tibetan monastery, which has substantial Tamang patronage; and Newars who live within Huṇḍu. In front of the procession walked a few small novices, carrying the Buddhist flags which one now sees all across the Kathmandu Valley as a mark of Buddhist solidarity. The image was a very simple metal Buddha image.

All day long the singing groups kept up their constant performance. Around 16:45, a number of different groups, all Newar, began to accumulate in the main market square in front of one of the Buddha images. The Vajrācārya from Vajrayoginī, who is an accomplished composer and singer, assembled with a group of Jñāna Mālā singers and musicians which he led. Other citizens of Pharping, including some Tamang, showed up. Schoolchildren lined up in long rows, all holding small Buddhist flags; a harmonium wheezed into life. Just before 17:00, with two Tibetan monks watching, a procession began, rather hesitantly, to move. The two monks were somewhat uncomfortable as they had expected a Tibetan element to be present, and within three minutes two senior lamas, one of who had also taken part in the morning's procession, appeared. The procession halted, having only made about 10 metres of progress, and several more Tibetan monks and lamas came down the road until a sizeable Tibetan contingent (mostly from Chatral Rimpoche's monastery) was present. They took up a place just ahead of the palanquin carrying the image of Śākyamuni. Then, with an astonishing noise of several different musical ensembles all starting to march at the same time, the newly re-ordered procession set off. The Tibetans had been awarded a place very much in the middle of the procession, and they marched with their long trumpets blaring away. By the time the procession had reached the end of the first street, it was, as with the morning's procession, comprised of all the major groups in Pharping: Newar, Tamang and Tibetan; and although I was the only foreigner present[17] I was duly given a badge indicating my participation. The *thakāli* of the Mānandhars, who was an important official in the Panchayat period and is now rather old, was remarkably spry as he moved around, smearing the face of every member of the procession and the audience with bright red powder.

The procession swooped its way around the lower half of town and set off up along the western side, traversing each *ṭol*, and reached a terminus at the Buddha image enshrined in the Balāmī quarter; there, all the participants took *darśana* of the image and then the procession regrouped and worked its way through the remaining *ṭols* of the upper and eastern half of town, finally returning to the market square. At moments, such as when the procession burst out of a long narrow street into the rather open area which contains the primary school, various spontaneous reorderings occurred; I saw a Tibetan cymbal playing monk leave his group and drift across to join Nepalese friends with their percussion troupe. Although the basic order of the main musician's groups, the palanquin and the high Tibetan lamas stayed the same throughout the walk, smaller clumps migrated back and forth along the length of the procession as it travelled along. The image which was carried during this procession was again, as is appropriate for Buddha Jayanti, a very simple image of Śākyamuni Buddha. The vocal songs were all of the Jñāna Mālā devotional style, in Newari. The Tibetan instruments heralded the arrival of the palanquin at each *ṭol.*

4.1 Negotiation

The performance of the Buddha Jayanti processions was a matter of deliberate beginnings and spontaneous enjoyment. Clearly, in the case of the second procession, there was a felt tension between the need to start the procession at the right ritual moment and the need to include the Tibetans.[18] Considerable relief was expressed by various leaders of the procession when the Tibetans showed up. The conspicuous display of the Buddhist flag in both processions was an overt marker of solidarity as Buddhists. The effect of daubing absolutely everyone's face with bright red powder was to erase the differences among the participants at the same time as it marked them out from all the other people in Pharping.

Perhaps the most striking negotiated feature of both processions, however, was the marked lack of any Vajrayāna iconography or ritual. Buddha Jayanti is a recent holiday in Nepal, and one which developed along with the institutionalization of Theravāda.[19] All the groups participating ordinarily have recourse to Vajrayāna iconography at some point during their life-cycle rituals (except, perhaps, the foreigners). Under the circumstances, however, they chose to assert their common religious identity through an image, that of Śākyamuni, which links them together not just with other Nepalese Buddhists but with Buddhists anywhere in the world. This also involves a suppression of the otherwise very strong understanding of Pharping as a Buddhist pilgrimage site, for all of the people and deities whose stories have created Pharping as a pilgrimage site are explicitly Vajrayāna figures. The virtue of Buddha Jayanti, then, is that it is a sort of lowest common denominator which makes no assertions beyond that of simply being Buddhist.

The other major Buddhist procession in Pharping, that of Vajrayoginī, is explicitly Vajrayānist. However, it attracts participation from non-Buddhist Newars living in Pharping who see Vajrayoginī as one of their local deities. It is not a moment in which Buddhist solidarity among many different groups of humans could be expressed; rather, it is a demonstration of the far-reaching compassion (and popularity) of a Buddhist deity.

4.2 Presentation

The question of presentation recurred when one of the organizers of the new Tamang *chos rten* in Huṇḍu explained why they had chosen Buddha Jayanti rather than some more traditional date, such as a Guru Rimpoche or Medicine Buddha festival, to inaugurate their new religious site. Because they were starting over, trying to restore a sense of religious performance and competence in a traditionally Buddhist society which had forgotten how to be Buddhist, they chose to found a new ritual, a procession, on a thoroughly Buddhist but otherwise unmarked day: Buddha Jayanti. If it stood for anything, it represented a sense of new beginnings, of returning to the origins of Buddhism in order to re-establish the Buddhist identity of the Tamang community. It was also extremely important to the organizers of this site that it be a resource for anyone, Tamang, Newar or even a Chetri who might be inclined to do pūjā at a Buddhist shrine.

If there were a genuinely powerful Theravāda community in Pharping, such that the celebration of Buddha Jayanti was in some sense a concession to that group, it would not be available as a shared holiday. In the absence of such a sociopolitical stress, the Vajrayāna understanding, that higher levels of Buddhist teaching include but transcend the lower levels, allows for Buddha Jayanti to be appropriated without any fear that it represents a genuine move towards Theravāda. Instead it is understood as a celebration of that which is held in common among Buddhists and that which is fundamental to Buddhism.

5. Modern, Antique and Eclectic Buddhism

5.1 Modernity and the State of Buddhism in Nepal

Such a demonstration of pan-Buddhist solidarity is only necessary in a place and time where the various Buddhist communities see themselves as threatened traditions. For each of the groups involved in the Buddha Jayanti celebration, the felt threat is slightly different; but in each case the threat has its roots in the political developments of modern Himalayan Asia. The Tibetans are in the process of diaspora as a result of the Chinese erasure of the Tibetan state. Both the Tamang and Newar Buddhist communities have suffered under two hundred years of the Gorkha state, the first modern nation-state to extend over the region which includes Pharping: the Tamangs through marginalization and exploitation, and the Vajrayāna Newars through diminishing patronage as a side-effect of the Gorkha state favoring Hinduism, as well as legal marginalization.

Newar Theravāda Buddhism emerged at least in part in response to oppression of the Newars, and specifically Newar Buddhism, under the early twentieth century Rana regime. Disaffected Newar Buddhists in India looking for ways to construct an identity drew on the Mahābodhi Society (a uniquely modern Buddhist institution) to do so, leading to an assertion of a Theravāda identity. Once a specifically Theravādin movement had taken root, it chose its opponents as much from the traditional forms of Newar Buddhism as from the Brahminical politico-religious authorities which had suppressed Newar Buddhism in the first place. Criticism of the costly and obligatory *jajmān* relations between agricultural or merchant caste clients and high-caste Vajrayāna priests became a strategy for expansion among possible Newar patrons. This competitive relationship between Theravāda and Vajrayāna Buddhism among the Newars is still a source of occasional antagonism in the press.

The response to a modern nation-state which has adopted an anti-Buddhist ideology has taken a few different forms. I mentioned the *janajāti* movement above, which argues for the distinctive authenticity of specific ethnic groups and frequently resorts to religion as a category, typically asserting that a specific group is either Buddhist or has an indigenous non-Buddhist, non-Brahminical tradition as part of that rhetoric. There is also an all-Nepal

Buddhist congress, which works to counteract government claims that the vast majority of Nepalese are Hindu. Newar Theravāda as I just described it can also be seen as response to the ideology (and indeed, coercive acts) of the Rana government exercising authority on behalf of the Nepalese state.

5.2 Before Modern Nepal

In a premodern Pharping, Newar, Tibetan and Tamang Buddhists would have interacted very differently. Political authority was both more local, vested in the princes or dukes of Pharping; and less pervasive, as there were a number of different polities in the region whose peoples visited and sponsored the religious institutions around Pharping. While there was competition with the Brahminical traditions for control of sacred sites around Pharping,[20] there would not have been the defensive attitude that one sees today. Tibetan lamas on pilgrimage to Pharping would have encountered a strong Newar tradition with several monasteries. From the evidence of Tibetan pilgrimage guides and Lévi's observation, while there appears to have been no permanent Tibetan presence in Pharping,[21] there was a steady stream of Tibetans coming to Pharping for pilgrimage. During the early Malla period, this relationship was not just local to the Kathmandu Valley; the Newar city-states and the developing Tibetan monastic states were closely engaged with each other.

The precise position of the Tamang in the premodern construction of Pharping's Buddhism is much less easy to discern. Charismatic Tamang lamas do figure in some Newar chronicles, and we may presume that some Tamang lamas became prestigious rNyings ma teachers. By and large, however, the history of Tamang religion, and their interaction with Newars or Tibetans around the Kathmandu Valley has as yet to be written. While the founding of the *chos rten* and shrine was couched in terms of a renewal of traditional Tamang Buddhism, premodern non-elite Tamang religion, as with contemporary forms, certainly consisted largely of shamanic rituals which occupy a specific relation to the high Tibetan tradition but are not simply derivable from that tradition.

5.3 Eclectic Buddhism in Late Modern Nepal

In 2002, the notion of a nation-state is everywhere disintegrating. In Nepal, where there is a serious civil war underway, as well as determined efforts by any number of ethnic communities to achieve recognition and power, the state, if we can even locate it, has become one among many possible authorities, with Maobadis, the new king (who acts together with the army in a way the elected government does not) or the threat of devastating and indiscriminate US military intervention all compete with the official parliamentary monarchy, for recognition. Moreover the Nepalese government is itself disintegrating, with the governing Congress party suffering a split which has resulted in the prime minister being expelled from his own party.

The Buddhists of Pharping have also recognized that their patrons and participants are no longer drawn from a Nepalese, Himalayan or even an Asian context. The Tamang committee formed to build the new *chos rten* raised money for the project from Tamang, Newar, Tibetan and European donors; the new Tibetan monasteries an retreat centres being built draw their funding from India, Taiwan, Singapore, Malaysia, Europe and North America. In this sense Pharping's celebration of Buddha Jayanti is immediately distinguishable from that of Lalitpur, the centre of Newar Buddhism, where the sense of links to the wider world, or even to non-Newar communities is much less strong. Turning again to the question of presentation, the stage on which the Tamangs of Huṇḍu are re-vitalizing their tradition is not just Pharping or Nepal; Pharping, by virtue of its ability to attract pilgrimage and patronage from across the world, is a site for the performance of global Buddhism.

This unexpectedly broad context is a feature of Eclectic Buddhism, the complex urban Buddhism which has developed in the last fifty years. It is characterized by the presence of multiple traditions of Buddhism occupying the same geographic and economic space without any predictable coherence, and indeed frequently with significant discontinuities. We saw above that Western tourists and dGe lugs Tibetan monks were able to deliberately ignore the Newar tradition which built and maintained the shrine in which they were performing their rituals, yet in the same town Tamangs, Newars and Tibetans express solidarity through an annual procession. While Eclectic Buddhism is easier to identify in Los Angeles or Singapore, we cannot explain Pharping's Buddha Jayanti celebrations without looking to this new form of Buddhism.

On the basis of the explicit rivalry between Theravāda and Vajrayāna Buddhism we might expect that the Vajrayānists, who are a numerical majority in Pharping, would reject Buddha Jayanti as a festival in which to express solidarity. In practice it is regarded as a holiday held in common by all Buddhist groups worldwide. Websites urge its celebration. The same holiday, referred to by its Pāli name 'Wesak', is also used as an expression of Buddhist solidarity in the US city of Chicago, where middle class Anglo convert Buddhists congregate together with the Japanese, Cambodian, Thai, Tibetan and Lao communities (to name a few) for an enormous cultural show. So also in many other cities worldwide, Buddha Jayanti has become the day on which the disjunct, yet earnest, urban communities of Eclectic Buddhism demonstrate and effect their solidarity. Dr. K. Sri Dhammananda Mahathera wrote the following for a group in Singapore:

> I am happy to say that perhaps we should follow the example of communities where Buddhists have been in the minority in a nation. Let us take Malaysia as an example. For the past fifty years or so, Malaysia Buddhists—Mahāyāna, Theravāda and Vajrayāna have been fostering close dialogue with each other—Perhaps most significantly they have all been celebrating Wesak together, thus presenting an image of great solidarity. On more intimate levels, I am happy to note, Buddhists have shown they can work together in unity. For example Theravāda ordination ceremonies were conducted in Mahayana temples in Singapore and Malaysia recently. Then, in August 1999, all Malaysian Buddhists freely joined in the Kalachakra event which was initiated by H.H. the Dalai Lama of Tibet. It is not an uncommon sight to see statues of Kuan Yin in Theravāda temples.[22]

Conversely we may expect that in countries where Mahāyāna or Vajrayāna Buddhism is the dominant religion, Buddha Jayanti would not be widely celebrated; and indeed this is so, for in Bhutan or Japan, it is barely acknowledged. Given the irreducible diversity of Pharping's Buddhist communities, a diversity which is as old as Pharping itself, in the present day the global community of Buddhists is the smallest shared context. The best festival for expressing solidarity among its communities has become precisely that one which is now a mark of Eclectic Buddhism.

NOTES

1. F.A. Bischoff, and Charles Hartman, "Padmasambhava's Invention of the Phur-Bu, Ms. Pelliot Tibétaine 44," in *Études Tibétaines Dédiées à la Mémoire de Marcelle Lalou,* Li-brairie d'Amérique et d'Orient, Paris 1971; Anne-Marie Blondeau, "Analysis of the Biographies of Padmasambava According to Tibetan Tradition," in *Tibetan Studies in Honour of Hugh Richardson,* Michael Aris and Aung San Suu Kyi (eds.), Aris and Westminster, Warminster 1980, pp. 45-52 (p. 47); Hugh E. Richardson, *High Peaks, Pure Earth: Collected writings* on *Tibetan history and culture* Michael Aris (ed.), Serindia, London, 1998, p. 140.
2. Martin Boord *The Cult of the Deity Vajrakīla* Buddhica Britannica Series Continua, 4, The Institute of Buddhist Studies, Tring, UK, 1993, p. 105.
3. Reproduced as appendix A in Turrell Wylie, ed. & trans., *A Tibetan Religious Geography of Nepal* ISMEO, Rome, 1970.
4. Sylvain Lévi, *Le Népal: Étude Historique d'un Royaume Hindou,* 3 vols., Annales de Mussée Guimet, 17-19, Ernest Leroux, Paris, 1905, vol. III p. 400. The *bal yul gnas yig* also takes notice of Vajrayoginī monastery and shrine, not mentioned in the Dunhuang sources.
5. Boord, *The Cult of the Deity Vajrakīla,* 109. The orthography in the early Tibetan sources is unstable; *in tra shu gu tu*(6a) becomes *shrī ri 'gugs ta* (8a). In any case, it would be difficult to arrive at Boord's list without resorting to later Tibetan hagiographic materials.
6. Dudjom Rimpoche, Michael Kapstein, and Gyurme Dorje, *History of the Nyingma School,* 2 vols. Wisdom, Cambridge, MA, 1991, p.109.
7. This was Vasudhara, the 'king of Nepal', about whom we know almost nothing. He may have been a member of the ruling family in Pharping.
8. Luciano Petech, *Mediaeval History of Nepal* (*c.* 750-1482), 2nd, thoroughly revised ed., Serie Orientale Roma, LIV, IsMEO, Rome, 1984.
9. The scribe describes himself as *śrī-phallpviṅga-viṣaye kosabūtollakādhivāsinā.* This ṭol, or locality, is otherwise unknown.
10. Petech, *Mediaeval History of Nepal,* p. 49.
11. D.R. Regmi, *Medieval Nepal,* 4 vols., K.L. Mukhopadhyaya, Calcutta, 1968, vol. III, pp. 12-13.
12. Dhanavajra Vajrācārya, and K.P. Malla, eds. & trans. *The Gopālarājavaṃśāvalī,* Nepal Research Centre Publications, 8. Franz Steiner Verlag, Weisbaden, 1985.
13. See the evidence contained in Petech, *Mediaeval History of Nepal* (c. 750-1482), Appendix A, for the Rāmavarddhana relations with Bri 'gung, and the discussion of changing Khāśiya-Newar relations in Will Douglas, "Washing Your Neighbour's God: Royal Ritual in 14th Century Nepal,"

in *Proceedings of the 1998 European Bulletin of Himalayan Research Conference, Meudon*, edited by Marie Lecomte-Tilouine and Pascal Dolfus, Oxford University Press India, New Delhi, 2002

14. Sylvain Lévi, *Le Népal: Étude Historique d'un Royaume Hindou*, vol. I. p. 67
15. William Kirkpatrick, *An account of the kingdom of Nepaul : being the substance of observations made during a mission to that country, in the year 1793*, printed for William Miller Albemarle-Street; by W. Bulmer and Co. Cleveland-Row St. James's, London, 1811, pp. 72 and 77.
16. For exile Tibetans, it is the Chinese state which oppresses them, and indeed periodically puts pressure on the Nepalese government to shift its attitude towards the Tibetans.
17. Because of the political tension very few foreigners were present in Nepal; I do not know if more foreigners would ordinarily have participated, although I was told they did not.
18. I was not able to watch the beginning of the morning procession.
19. The relationship between the Nepalese Buddha Jayanti and the Indian holiday, which was deeply influenced by the Mahābodhi Society, is something I cannot address here.
20. See Bikrama Jit Hasrat, ed. & trans., *History of Nepal, as told by its own and contemporary chroniclers*, VV Research Institute Press, Hoshiarpur, 1971, pp. 77-8, for the story of a brahmin named Narasiṃha Thākur̄ who recovered the *pīṭha* of Guhyeśvarī which the Bandyas (the usual term for Newar Vajrayāna priests) had obscured at the site of Dakṣīṇ Kālī. Such stories indicate the negotiated status of the *pīṭhas*, secret sites which are sacred to both the Śaiva/Śākta and Bauddha tantric traditions in Nepal.
21. In fact, it seems highly probable that there would have been a rNyings ma foundation of some sort around Pharping at some point, but I have so far not been able to find any material, textual or inscriptional evidence for this. Pharping is about a half-day's walk from Boudha. The pilgrimage guides and the account of sNubs Sangs rgyas Ye shes only mention the caves.
22. Ven Dr Dhammananda Mahathera. "Tolerance & Harmony in the Face of Religious Diversities", available from http://kbs.cdc.net.my/hongfa/english/update08/English0800.htm.

X
TIBETAN THEMES

CHAPTER 37

On the Characteristics of the Tibetan Buddhist Culture

SHUNZO ONODA

The many aspects of the Tibetan Culture that have been formed throughout the ages by its people stand out by its uniqueness at first glance. Compared to other cultures in Asia, as well as in the western world, it is undoubtedly evident that these differences felt from the first moment are not just a few. For example, there are the "Reincarnated Lamas", the "Polygamy", the "Shamans and Oracles", and the "Bird Funeral". One would wonder about the elements existing in the background that work to constitute the peculiarities of this culture. Yet, one would ask how was the formative process, taking into consideration their concept and view toward nature?

Now, I would like to study on the Tibetan culture considering all the features I have mentioned in order to allow ourselves to have a deeper insight. Our considerations mainly depend on those authoritic publications such as R.A. Stein's *Tibetan Civilization* and Zuiho Yamaguchi's *Tibet* [1].

1. *The Incarnations*

The singular feature in the Tibetan culture that we call now "Reincarnated Lamas", although the limitations that it take in terms of concept, it essentially means incarnation. Incarnation, here in this case, evokes the notion shared among the Tibetans that there is a supernatural and transcendental order that, whatever its objectives, it goes through a continuum in which human beings and animals are simply an actual appearance in a given time. Nevertheless, they make a clear-cut distinction between the notion of the transmigrated incarnation from the idea that a divine spirit can temporarily transposes from a body to another.

Though there is this notion that gods and Buddhas do appear in form of human beings, this idea does not validate the opposite, that the human beings are, at their best, viewed as divine or Buddha-like beings. Basically, the human beings are viewed as a receptacle for these divine Buddha-like beings, in which they continue to exist even though the flesh; the human body dies. The Dalai Lama, for example, is believed to be the incarnation of the Bodhisattva Avalokiteśvara, the deity of the great compassion, whose the cycle of transmigration enables him to stand for the salvation and relief of the people.[2]

In Tibet, the perception that a permanent and eternal divine being coexists with the human beings in such closeness is a given fact. Furthermore, one development of such notion led the Tibetan culture to hold its very originality. This is why a person who is believed to be or identified as the incarnation of a divine being or a Buddha-to-be spirit famed in a previous life is entitled to the "inheritance" in form of prestige and respect. This is recognized and institutionalized socially to the point of becoming a permanent cultural feature.[3]

I would like to point out a couple of indicators that show how and why the notion of the incarnation of it became institutionalized in such a way. The main indicator lies on how the inheritance or succession takes place. It happens from uncle to nephew, without necessarily consulting the clergy or the laity, and it is an indicator, which is very often noticed. One way to explain it, is by showing the particular form in which the marriage is structured.

In order to avoid the cattle, as the inheritance, to be scattered and dispersed, the polyandry, that is, having one wife for various husbands, was the form of polygamous marriage adopted. This custom is invariably surviving nowadays, where the male brothers, no matter how many, share the same wife, as it is instituted.[4] As one can imagine, it is difficult to define who is the actual father of the offspring. Therefore the child is conveniently treated as child of the eldest brother. In fact, even the actual father is referred to as uncle, and this is just part of the everyday life. One would observe that, in their lives, whatever they call father or uncle, son or nephew, often mean the same. That is how the labor force and the inherited cattle are kept together, avoiding the break-ups.

The Buddhist practitioner and monks are not immune to this notion, and they reproduce the same pattern of succession when the inheritance of a monastery is concerned. Those monks who do not get married will take a nephew to place as his disciple in the monastery in order to entitle him as a legitimate heir. This custom as a whole lead us to seriously consider that it has provided the psychological ground on which the institutionalized incarnation laid.

Once we have the incarnation responding institutionally, becoming a widely and a socially accepted custom, it provides the precedent to the notion of mind and body duality, that can be traced back to the ancient times, as far as the popular perception is concerned. I will return to this question later on.

2. *Shamanism*

In shamanism, one finds all the movements centered on the figure of the religious shaman, who, by acting in paranormal trance, has the supernatural ability to intermediate with the divine spirits, the souls, and the souls of the departed ones. Furthermore, the shaman also performs as oracle priest leading the ceremonies and celebrations a visionary priest by doing fortune telling and prophecies, as magician, and as a healer by treating his fellows medically.

Though the shaman performs such extra-natural tasks, it is interesting to notice that he is ultimately neither an incarnation nor a divine or Buddha-to-be figure. The shaman is commonly referred to as the "one who deals with the gods" due to his position of being in charge of mediating the supernatural forces with the worldly human beings. This situation, academically speaking, is called "trance". For a person to be seriously considered as a shaman, when he enters in trance, he should be in the state of ecstasy and possession. Nevertheless, these two featuring psychic states do vary depending on the region, the people, and the culture they take place. What is more important than that, however, is whether he delivers a service with positive results, so to speak. Even in a region that puts more emphasis on the ecstasy aspect, it does not mean they would not celebrate the possession side of the matter.

In Tibet, as well as in Mongolia and Central Asia, it is said that there are quite a number of shamans who perform as healer with the possession rituals. More interesting is the fact that the people in those regions think the cause for their illnesses lies upon the belief that their souls were lost or stolen. Illness, for them, happens because "something" may have entered the cursed body, or cure that, the only way is to call the wandering spirit back to the proper beholder, or by expelling the evil one. In this context, it is said that the shaman actually acts first as a transitory receptacle the wandering soul or of the evil one in order to transfers it into another animal.

Before Buddhist missionaries reached Tibet, there were some noticeable manifestatings of the shaman techniques and art due to the presence of the "Bon" religion and cults of "Shen". In Tun-huang, near Central Asia, documents related to Tibet were excavated, and they describe funeral rituals portraying the soul of the departed. Elements of Bon religion and Shen cult do appear randomly among the tantric Buddhist ceremonies, as it will be discussed later. The cause of the illnesses were believed to consist in someone having attached or incorporated to it, and the "spirit's mysterious voyages" were definitely ending their wandering trips in the figure of the religious shamans, but rather among the ordinary people.[5]

For a Tibetan shaman, his ultimate accomplishment is to be able to have someone recovered, and it surely is a reason for pride. As have mentioned before, the cause for many illness lies upon having someone possessed by a malign spirit, and it is up to the shaman to expel such spirit. That occurs as the shaman leaves aside his own spirit and calls or attracts the malign spirit to fulfil his own body. Then, he evokes a more powerful benign spirit to transfer that bad one into another animal and let it go. Finally, he calls back his own spirit, having accomplished his relief task.

3. *Bird Funeral*

Observing the Tibetan funeral procedures, one can notice there are four different ones. They are; the *"me sreg stong ba"*, or "fire funeral", which is equivalent to a cremation; the *"bya gtor"*, the "bird funeral"; the *"chu gtor"* or *"ña gtor"*, which mean "water funeral" or "fish funeral", respectively; and the *"sa sbas gtor"*, or the "earth funeral", that is the same as a burial

In general, the cremation "fire funeral" is allowed only for Lamas and the nobility. The "bird funeral" is performed to the common Tibetans, while the "water funeral" is done to the so-called miserable. Burial or the "earth funeral" is performed for those who died from diseases such as small pox and leprosy, or any other contagious disease. It is no coincidence that there is an expression that says: *(phuṅ po ri rtse'i rgod la ster, yaṅ na chu naṅ ña la sbyin)':* A dead body should either be given to the vultures from the top of the mountains, or be given to the fishes in the river".[6]

Among all these different funerals, the "bird funeral" became notorious due to its peculiar characteristics representative of the Tibetan region. Furthermore, not only "bird funeral", but the "fish funeral" as well were heatedly debated as far as their *raison d'etre* were concerned. In a situation where fuel is so scarce, a "fire funeral" is all owe, but justifiable unless a strong religious meaning is present there in order to make it widely accepted as a custom. Behind the custom of leaving the dead human body to be eaten by the starving animals, obstinacy towards the human body should not be the only factor, but more strongly the hope for revival or rebirth as a peaceful soul is much more evident.

Their attitude in relation to the eternal spirits that occupies the human body is full of offering procedures. Depending on the procedure, what they hope for is a gratifying reward in happiness. The good fortune waiting for in the next existence is the main hope and reason that works as a unquestionable reality, forming therefore as principle that has molded their own culture.

4. *The Origins of the Various Aspects of Tibetan Culture*

Considering the views towards life and spirits, in the Tibetan

Buddhist culture, there is a strong sense of the dualist perception soul and body lying at the bottom. For a Tibetan Buddhist practitioner whose objective is to free himself from all existence that includes the flesh. However, they acknowledge that in this existence, it would be possible to accomplish only a part of their practice towards freedom.

For the spirit that shelters himself in the body, the body itself is a limitation, therefore not essential. The Tibetan people have accepted this notion and they have carried it out to apply it in the social experiences. The death of the body is neither the absolute neither end nor a soul is completely an independent entity. Death is rather taken as a step necessary for the continuation of the eternal soul.

We might feel as a very different thing in terms of cultural development compared to the Tibetans is that the fundamental places for life and death are completely different, and separation of soul from the human body resulting in death is not a concept exclusive to the Tibetans, but something that expresses well their view on life and death is the practice of mummification of the Dalai Lama. In the Potala palace, there are stupa monuments with relics of the successional generations of Dalai Lama, and they serve as tomb with their mummies, they are famous for this reason. The culture of mummification, in general, can be seen as a manifestation of the importance placed on attaching spirit and body.

In a lifetime, when ruling authority, and influence were the surpassing forces that made people admire the shaman and that he is now dead. This fact per so is reason enough to mummify him in order to avoid the dread and the threat that such a mighty spirit takes a supernatural power against them. Rather than that, having these great spirits close enough as mummies, they would function securing and protecting themselves.

In the case of the living Buddhas, however, the spiritual force that Dalai Lama represents as a perpetuating force is generated upon the belief that they are here to relieve mankind. Therefore, at a first moment, it would be strange to observe such worship custom on dead one's mummy. In many other religions, it is believed that in the after life, the spirit departs from the body, but eventually it would return, constituting in rebirth. In the case of Tibetan mystique of living Buddhas, definitely there is no such thing.

The Dalai Lama, being associated to the deity figure of Avalokiteśvara, the Bodhisattva of great compassion, comes out of suffering transmigrational incarnation in order to save the worldly beings, as it is supposed as a devotee of the Buddha's law. Even as a divine creature who has transcended the mundane world, after his death in this world he would assure his existence in another body to keep continuing his mission and vow in accumulating virtuous deeds. Therefore he, the Dalai Lama, does not need to claim in attaining nirvāṇa by offering his dead body to another living being. In other words, as far as his transmigration goes, the Dalai Lama is not supposed to attain the nirvāṇa by being a Bodhisattva's incarnation. Yet, it is believed that his body is not impure, thus it is understandable that it is worshipped even as a mummified being.

Now, let us compare with, for example, Japanese Buddhist culture. In Japan, the notion of impermanence is often expressed as a state of having leaves falling from the trees. Such a view on impermanence and mutability is not recognized in Tibet. For the Tibetans the concept of impermanence in the cycle of transmigration has must more an animalesque precedent. For example, the calf born right in front of one's eyes or a scene of a yak's body weathering in open.

The Tibetan notion of karma-resulting transmigration is afar the Japanese view on life and death, where the perception on mutability and impermanence follows a nature-oriented tendency observing the seasonal cycle as it means for eternity. In fact, for the Tibetans, the transience of self is placed with humans and animal together as part of their usual custom. Such perception dictates that human beings are actually only one among others in the animal kingdom, and the body itself is taken instinctively that, eventually it will pass away. For those animals besides humans, they cannot neglect to be cautious against their threatening natural enemies. For them, they can dread the fiercest of their enemies and still run a but there is no motive to dread the death. It seems that there is an instinctive awareness that death is unavoidable, therefore there is no manifestation of dread and fear about it.

In Indian Buddhism as well as in Tibetan Buddhism, it is conceived that plants and vegetation do not hold suffering and they do not enter the "six path transmigration cycle" that all living-beings "with a soul" find themselves. Furthermore, the transience of self is not associated to the nature of transience at all. In Japan, in contrast, the cycle of one's life and death is put as analogous to the transformative cycle of the nature. The transience of self is extended by the transience of nature to the point of evading a more animal-like aspect of such mutability, avoiding the vivid views of blood and flesh.[7]

For the people in Tibet, living in a vastly wild nature, facing hardship to find food and water, moving from place to place, in a quasi-nomadic way is the only unavoidable lifestyle. Given such circumstances, questions of life and death were taken into account as a fact of life, with an attitude of "business as usual". For them, a body that cannot take control over that difficult environment should not be considered worthy. In the present world, however, there should be a meaning for having an existence in a human body, because, otherwise, there would be no chance to face the world of death in afterlife.

The idea of transient self in fine tune with the nature that Buddhist practitioners in Japan conceive does not make sense for Tibetans. For them, the animal-like view of transience is actually a need, which has to face a transmigration world where life and death are usually unpredictable.

The core of the transmigration issue has nothing to do with ancestor blood relation. Still, the ancestors themselves do not leave traces behind to hold on blood relations. In a polyandry world, where there is a wife for various husbands, therefore, making it difficult identify the actual father.

As we have noticed on the Tibetan "bird funeral", we cannot say that a soul is more important than the body generated by the parents, as a main core of transmigration cycle. In order to survive in a dry and scarce environment with such sparse vegetation, they have to rely on yak and lamb meat as main source of food. Even monks, after their ascetic training period, come to eat meat. They eat the yak and the lamb meat everyday. Killing is, for sure, a crime, and it is divided in many categories. Since a single yak can feed many people, the "crime" of killing it is outweighed. Thus, having an animal chopped into pieces and its meat sharing for the sake of other living being's survival, makes room for the opposite, where the human body is offered back to the animals, therefore to the nature, in form of funerals.

It would be really difficult to imagine a sensitive and intently transience in harmony with the nature in a way we Japanese are used to. The development of the Yoga practice was possible due to the duality of body and mind; yet, a radicalized concept of its absence would be unthinkable. The mysterious experience on death pursued by the "pho ba" practice, if fully mastered, is said to enable the soul to be detached from the living body.

The origins of various aspects in the Tibetan Buddhist culture such as the dualistic view of body and mind, as well as the animalesque sense of transience put in evidence that a self-possessed body is transience itself. At the same time, it gives a peculiar hope towards rebirth in the afterlife. In one's affairs in life, where a liberated spirit overcomes subjective instability, the main goal is to provide the situation of an eternal spirit, free from the body.

[This essay was originally written in Japanese, and once appeared as the title of "Chibettojin-no Shiseikan" in *Mandara and Samsāla* (Mandar-to Rinne) (M. Tachikawa ed.), Kosei-shuppansha, 1993. pp.60-74.]

NOTES

1. Stein, Rolf Alfred, *La Civilisation Tibetaine*, Paris, 1962 ; Yamaguchi Zuiho, *Tibet* (2 vols), Tokyo Univ., 1987.
2. See Yamaguchi Zuiho, "Katsubutsuni tsuite (On sPrul sku)," in *Hotokeno kennkyu* (Studies on Buddha), Shunjyu-sha), 1977, p. 285; "sprul" of "sprul-sku" (sometimes "phrul") originally means "transformation" or "change in quality". Probably which has some relations to the verb "brul (cast leaves)", or "khrul (distort)", and also this word might have the same origin as of the noun "sbrul (snake)" which make ecdysis. Yamaguchi says these might have come commonly from the verb "rul (rot)".
3. It is said that the very first sprul sku was Karma Rol pa'i rdo rje (1284-1339) who was believed as the incarnation of Karma Pakṣi (1204-82) the second Karma pa: Roerich G., *The Blue Annals*, The Asiatic Society, Calcutta, 1953, p. 494.
4. Cf. Nagano Sadako, "Chibetto go no Hahakatano oji wo shimesu Goi (Maternal Uncle in the Tibetan Kinship Terminology)" in *Studies on the Inner Asian Languages VIII*, the Society of Central Eurasian Studies (Kobe City University of Foreign Studies), 1993, p.114.

5. Cf. Nebesky-Wojkowitz, *Oracles and Demons of Tibet*, The Cult and Iconography of the Tibetan Protective Deities, Akademische Druck-u. Verlagsanstalt, Graz/Austria, 1975.
6. See Thupten Sangay, Tibetan Ceremonies of the Dead, Bod mi'i 'das mchod, LTWA, Dharamsala, 1974, pp.16-17.
7. Basically plants itself are not the subject of transformation (samsāla): cf. Lambert Schmithausen, *The Problem of the Sentience of Plants in Earliest Buddhism*, Studia Philologica Buddhica, Monograph series VI, The International Institute for Buddhist Studies, Tokyo, 1991.

CHAPTER 38

'The Story of How *bla-ma* Karma Chos-bzang Came to Yol-mo': A Family Document from Nepal

FRANZ-KARL EHRHARD

It was the *Thu'u bkvan grub mtha'*, the masterpiece of Blo-bzang Chos-kyi nyi-ma (1737-1802) from dGon-lung monastery in Amdo, which provided me with a first introduction into the philosophical doctrines of the bKa'-brgyud-pa school of Tibetan Buddhism. This happened during the classes of dGe-bshes dGe-'dun blo-gros (1924-1979) at Hamburg University and I still remember the charged atmosphere when "Rinpoche" laid out his intricate explanations before the small band of dedicated students. Shortly after the untimely death of this remarkable teacher, I met for the first time Musashi Tachikawa, a Humboldt Research Fellow at the institute and—like the rest of us—attracted to the subtleties of Madhyamaka philosophy and everything its manifold Tibetan traditions had to offer.

After I moved to Nepal in 1988 to work on the Nepal-German Manuscript Preservation Project (NGMPP) the contact was renewed, and Musashi Tachikawa joined more or less regularly the lunch table at the Nepal Research Center (NRC), always enthusiastic about his latest research activities. These included iconographical studies of Dharmadhātu and Vajradhātu maṇḍalas, the documentation of the Mother goddesses in the Kathmandu Valley, and the establishment of the Buddhist section at the National Museum of Nepal in Chauni. We also met at the National Archives of Nepal in Ramshah Path, where he was busy with a project to reprint important manuscripts from Asian countries. During one of these visits he brought along his Japanese translation of the chapter on the bKa'-brgyud-pa school in the *Thu'u bkvan grub mtha'*, and I was happy to see that my notes from the Hamburg classes had been of use for a fuller understanding of the text[1].

As a contribution to the felicitation volume of Musashi Tachikawa I would like to present a Tibetan-language document which throws some light on the spread of the bKa'-brgyud-pa school in an area of Nepal that once served the great yogin Mi-la-ras-pa as a place for his spiritual retreats. It is a token of gratitude for common interests shared, and accompanied by heart-felt wishes for many more years of fruitful work.

1. *The Document*

During an exploration tour of the NGMPP in the spring of 1989 to Yol-mo, *a bla-ma* from Kshaden offered his help and guided the team to his family monastery in the southern part of the region. There he produced the collection of his religious books, and also a document which he held in great esteem, relating as it did the story of how his family line had settled in Yolmo. The name of the *bla-ma* was Karma Ras-chung, and this name still kept alive the memory of the fact that the first of his line had arrived from the monastery of Ras-chung phug in Central Tibet to the Himalayan borderlands[2].

The document was filmed by the NGMPP under reel-no. E 2332/4 [=running-no. E 43183], its size being 44.5×59 cm; it is written in *dbu-can* and has 27 lines. Corrections to the text are either written over crossed-out passages or marked by boxes (in two cases). The composite structure of the document cannot be immediately recognized, but upon closer inspection, it is clearly seen to fall into two parts. The first part [=lines 1-17] relates the story of how *bla-ma* Karma Chos-bzang came to Yol-mo and provides a genealogy of his descendants, especially the branch of his son dKar-rgyud [bstan-pa'i rgyal-mtshan], who was himself the progenitor of seven sons, all of whom eventually moved to different areas in or around Yol-mo and settled there. The genealogy continues down to the fourth generation after dKar-rgyud [bstan-pa'i rgyal-mtshan] but refers to only those members of the family line of Karma Chos-bzang who stayed behind in the monastery of rGod-tshang gling. This was the monastery in Yol-mo where *bla-ma* Karma Chos-bzang had settled after his final journey from Ras-chung phug.

The second part [=lines 17-27] gives a short description of the renovation of rGod-tshang gling executed by *bla-ma* Karma Chos-bzang in a "bird year" (*bya-lo*) On the occasion of the consecration ceremony for this renovation the local donors supporting the *bla-ma* drew up a written contract which entitled Karma Chos-bzang to own the land around the monastery. The original version of this part of the document must have contained the thumb prints of the *bla-ma* and the different donors as a sign of their approval of the agreement. That we have a later copy before us can also be seen from the fact that the name of a copyist is given. As he can be identified as one of the sons of dKar-rgyud [bstan-pa'i rgyal-mtshan], the original copy of the written contract—set down by Karma Chos-bzang himself—was obviously still available during the time of the *bla-ma's* grandsons.

Those members of the family line who resided in the monastery of rGod-tshang gling eventually put together the two parts of the document, namely the arrival story-cum-genealogy and the land transfer, at the time of a descendant called dGra-'dul seng-ge. In the following I will first provide some historical details concerning rGod-tshang gling in order to arrive at the corresponding western date of the original land grant. On the basis of the transmission history of tne bKa'-brgyud-pa teachings associated with the monastery, I want then, secondly, to present a time frame within which the two parts of the document where joined by the descendants of *bla-ma* Karma Chos-bzang. It seems that the need to do so arose around the time when the Śāha dynasty was making its presence felt in the region of Yol-mo.

2. *The Monastery of rGod-tshang gling*

The importance of the monastery called "Island of the Vulture's

Nest" has already been noted by earlier research, a total of eighteen temples in Yol-mo having been traced back to rGod-tshang gling. It has also been noted that of the seven sons of dKar-rgyud [bstan-pa'i rgyal-mtshan] those who did not remain in the monastery were responsible for the founding of these temples; the family line of *bla-ma* Karma Chos-bzang thus became the major "lama lineage" of the region. The documentary source of these details is a Tibetan religious history of Yol-mo composed by one Karma 'Phrin-las dbang-po, who is none other than the eldest of the seven sons and the one who took over rGod-tshang gling from his father dKar-rgyud [bstan-pa'i rgyal-mtshan][3].

Once we leave the written sources of the local historiography and try to place the oldest bKa'-brgyud-pa monastery in Yol-mo in a wider context, it soon becomes clear that rGod-tshang gling derives its name from its founder, rGod-tshang ras-chen or rGod-tshang ras-pa sNa-tshogs rang-grol (1494-1559), one of the two more famous disciples of gTsang-smyon Heruka. The other disciple is lHa-btsun Rin-chen rnam-rgyal (1473-1557). Both left biographies of their master, and in composing such hagiographical literature thus followed in his footsteps. Although there exists a biographical tradition of the latter disciple, we are still not very well informed about the life of rGod-tshang ras-pa: the only commonly agreed point is that he kept up Ras-chung phug after the death of gTsang-smyon Heruka and propagated there the spiritual teachings associated with Ras-chung-pa rDo-rje grags-pa (he is known to have composed a biography of Ras-chung-pa as well and to have made available printed versions of the so-called *Ras chun snyan brgyud*).

But there has survived a biography of a disciple of both rGod-tshang ras-pa and lHa-btsun Rin-chen rnam-rgyal which gives us a view of rGod-tshang gling at a time when the founder of the site was still alive. The name of the disciple is Byams-pa phun-tshogs (1503-1581), a native of the sKyid-grong area in Mang-yul Gung-thang. During a journey from this area to the Nepal Valley he was present at the ceremony concluding the building of the first temple at the site founded by his teacher:

> Myself, at the age of fifty-four years, in the autumn of the dragon-year [=1556], when I went via Yol-mo for a

circumambulation of Nepal, [the land of] moisture, and came to [the valley of] Glang-'phrang, my host mTsho-skyes and others requested empowerments from me, and there was established a complete, pure union [between teacher and disciples], accompanied by marvellous services.

When I arrived then at rGod-tshang gling in Yol-mo, I thought: "This old *bla-ma* of mine—after he came here he acted extensively for the benefit of others!", and in that very moment of recalling the *bla-ma* many tears gushed forth. When there arose ever more memories of Chos-rje rGod-tshang-pa, in a state where my mind was overwhelmed by sorrow, [I saw] in a dream the master perform prodigiously, in a very majestic manner, adorned by the eight paraphernalia of [an ascetic living in] burial grounds. Afterwards he intoned spiritual songs in great number, and there came forth the following words:

"When the mind is without movement and artifice—this is the Prātimokṣa [vow].

When the mind of benefiting [others] is uninterrupted—[this] is the Bodhisattva [vow].

When the grasping of [individual] characteristics is purified—[this] is the Mantra[yāna] [vow].

Everything else is senseless behaviour: *Oṃ Āḥ, Hūṃ* !"

At that time I set up the guidance [for my spiritual practice] of the [*Phyag chen*] *yi ge bzhi pa* and the [*Na ro*] *chos drug* at rGod-tshang gling. For about one and a half months I made [the results] to come forth. On one occasion, in the *bla-brang* of rGod-tshang gling, I remembered again and again the course of the life of the lord [rGod-tshang ras-pa], and there was [even] stronger belief in [his] profound introduction [to the nature of the mind].

Once during that period *bla-ma* Kun-dga'-ba is said to have produced [a manuscript copy of] the extensive [version of the *Prajñāpāramitā*] in 100,000 verses and erected a temple, [but] he passed away without having completed these [things]. After his son and the donors tied up the ends of this [affair], I myself was called for the consecration, and they performed [acts of] congratulation and so forth. At

> that time *gaṇacakras,* offering substances and so forth, [all] marvellous [and] in accordance with the local customs, were forthcoming from the inhabitants of Yol-mo.[4]

At the time of the visit of Byams-pa phun-tshogs in the middle of the 16th century rGod-tshang gling had just been transformed from a simple "residence" (*bla brang*) of rGod-tshang ras-pa to a temple supervised by a caretaker and his family, and supported financially by local donors. When we look at the report of a later visitor to the site, we can see that the name of its founder was still embedded in people's memories, even though rGod-tshang gling itself was now referred to in more purely monastic terms. The following passage is from a travel account by the Sixth Zhva-dmar-pa Chos-kyi dbang-phyug (1584-1630), who felt an urge to see the different sacred sites of Yol-mo after returning from a journey to the Nepal Valley; this occurred in the final weeks of his life:

> The next day, when I went on continuously in a slow way, I arrived at what is called rGod-tshang gling, [the place where] rGod-tshang ras-chen had resided, the disciple of the noble gTsang-smyon [Heruka], a site where there had originally been established a *saṅgha* community with eight members. As I had been forgetful of the memorial services on the twenty-eighth day of the month before, being too busy with the way, I [now] performed the *maṇḍala* ritual of the five gods of *Śrī Cakrasaṃvara,* restoring the broken [commitment], and stayed for the night [there][5].

At this point I want to return to the "family document" from Yol-mo and its story of the two journeys of Karma Chos-bzang. The narrative starts with the *bla-ma's* initial arrival with a group of seven other monks, who were obviously under his supervision. The local headmen asked him to settle in Yol-mo, but he declined their request for the time being and returned to Ras-chung phug in Central Tibet; there he stayed for three years in the company of his teacher Zhabs-drung Grub-mchog dbang-po (1563-1618). Only after receiving the latter's permission to settle permanently in Yol-mo did he return for a second time and accept the offer of the local donors. When the narrative of *bla-ma* Karma Chos-bzang's activities in Yol-mo is taken up again in the second part of the document, it is mentioned that he had renovated the monastery of rGod-tshang gling when performing religious services for the three cities of the Nepal valley. These services for the Malla rulers seem to have been the main reason why the land around rGod-tshang gling was offered to *bla-ma* Karma Chos-bzang as "religious endowment" (*birtā*). This kind of land assignment in Nepal was by royal authority, and traditionally limited to Brahmins. As we have seen, the date of the renovation and the written title to the land was a "bird year".

If we take the "*saṅgha* community with eight members"—the original monastic community at rGod-tshang gling according to the Sixth Zhva-dmar-pa—to be the group of eight monks who had moved from Ras-chung phug to Yol-mo at the behest of Zhabs-drung Grub-mchog dbang-po, and take into account the return trip of *bla-ma* Karma Chos-bzang to Central Tibet, his three-year-stay in Ras-chung phug, and the final journey to rGod-tshang gling, then the renovation of the monastery and the "religious endowment" must have fallen in the period between the death of Zhabs-drung Grub-mchog dbang-po and the visit of Chos-kyi dbang-phyug to Yol-mo. As a corresponding western date for the "bird year" I would thus propose 1621 A.D.

3. *The Transmission of the Phyag chen yi ge bzhi pa and the Ras chung snyan brgyud*

When Byams-pa phun-tshogs visited the site of rGod-tshang gling his spiritual practice centered around a combination of a Mahāmudrā teaching called the "Four-lettered One" (*yi ge bzhi pa*) and the "Six Doctrines" (*chos drug*) according to the system of the Indian Mahāsiddha Nāḍapāda also known as Nāropa (956-1040). This combination shows that the disciple of rGod-tshang ras-chen and lHa-btsun Rin-chen rnam-rgyal practiced teachings of the Dvags-po bKa'-brgyud-pa, namely the instructions transmitted through sGam-po-pa bSod-nams rin-chen (1079-1153). If we consult the biographies of gTsang-smyon Heruka written by rGod-tshang ras-chen and lHa-btsun Rin-chen rnam-rgyal, we can see that this particular combination of teachings also formed the central spiritual practice of the "Madman from gTsang" who received them from his own guru, Sha-ra Rab-'byams-pa Sangs-rgyas seng-ge (1427-1470), at the mere age of seventeen years in the region of Dvags-po in south-eastern Tibet[6].

As there exists a biography of Sha-ra Rab-'byams-pa, we can trace back this transmission to his "main teacher" (*rtsa ba'i bla ma*), one Ngag-dbang grags-pa (1418-1496), who was the twelfth abbot of the sTag-lung monastery to the north of lHa-sa. Of the lineages of the *Phyag chen yi ge bzhi pa* which he conferred upon Sha-ra Rab-'byams-pa, two had passed through sGam-po-pa's disciple Phag-mo gru-pa rDo-rje rgyal-po (1110-1170) (here it should be noted that the twelfth abbot of sTag-lung was actually regarded by his contemporaries as the reincarnation of Phag-mo gru-pa rDo-rje rgyal-po). At their final meeting he particularly requested his disciple to spread the "oral lineage of the *Cakrasaṃvara* [Cycle]" (*bde mchog snyan brgyud*), the chief teaching of which is the so-called "oral lineage of Ras-chung[-pa]" (*ras chung snyan brgyud*), a specific tradition of the six doctrines of Nāropa fostered by Ras-chung-pa rDo-rje grags-pa. This task was later carried out mainly by gTsang-smyon Heruka, who compiled the twelve-volume *sNyan brgyud* collection and composed important textbooks for the further propagation of this specific tradition. The adherents of this tradition were known as the Ras-chung bKa'-brgyud-pa[7].

A good overview of the transmission of the *Phyag chen yi ge bzhi pa* and the *Ras chung snyan brgyud* is provided by a work of Kaḥ-tog Rig-'dzin Tshe-dbang nor-bu (1698-1755), who received these teachings in the region of Nub-ris, a Himalayan region to the south-west of Mang-yul Gung-thang, in the year 1729. According to this text the next person in the lineage after Byams-pa phun-tshogs (referred to by his alternative name gNas Rab-'byams-pa Blo-gros rab-yangs) was Grub-mchog dbang-po, the "incarnation from Ras-chung [phug]" (*ras chung sprul sku*). If one consults the biography of Byams-pa phun-tshogs, one finds indeed references to two visits of Grub-mchog dbang-po to sKyid-grong in order to receive the teachings of the *Phyag chen* [*yi ge bzhi pa*] and the [*Ras chung*] *snyan brgyud*. The young novice is identified as the reincarnation of rGod-tshang ras-chen, and his journeys from Ras-chung phug to the south-western border area were undertaken at the express wish of the Fifth Zhva-dmar-pa dKon-mchog yan-lag (1525-1583)[8].

The next two persons who passed on the teachings after Grub-mchog dbang-po were rNgog-ston Karma Blo-bzang (16th/17th cent.) and rGyal-dbang seng-ge (b. 1616). We are quite well informed about the life of the first figure, who had been a student at Ras-chung phug of both Grub-mchog dbang-po and the Sixth Zhva-dmar-pa Chos-kyi dbang-phyug. Upon the request of the latter teacher he became the resident priest of Brag-dkar rta-so, the famous Mi-la-ras-pa site in Mang-yul Gung-thang. This position had also been held by Byams-pa phun-tshogs for some time, and this might have contributed to Karma Blo-bzang's status of being the reincarnation of the lineage-holder from the sKyid-grong area. Karma Blo-bzang travelled extensively in the Himalayan valleys of Mustang, Dolpo and Manang, renovating old structures of the bKa'-brgyud-pa school and erecting new buildings. He paid two visits to the region of Yol-mo and the monastery of rGod-tshang gling; during the first visit he renovated the monastery, while regarding the second stay, the name of his main disciple in the region is given as Karma Gu-ru (the eldest son of *bla-ma* Karma Chos-bzang). These journeys can be placed in the middle of the 17th century, after the visit of the Sixth Zhav-dmar-pa and around the time when the family estate of rGod-tshang gling had been handed over by Karma Gu-ru to his brother dKar-rgyud [bstan-pa'i rgyal-mtshan][9].

Among the disciples of rNgog-ston Karma Blo-bzang, rGyal-dbang seng-ge is especially noted for having received the full transmission of the *Ras chung snyan brgyud*. Although a full-scale biography of him is not available, we know at least that he came from the region of Nub-ris; his place of origin there was called Zva-phug Brag-dmar chos-gling, which he had inherited from his father, Bya-btang 'Od-zer rgya-mtsho (1574-1661), a practitioner of bKa'-brgyud-pa teachings of local fame.[10] The disciple of rGyal-dbang seng-ge who kept the site of Zva-phug after the death of his teacher transmitted the *Phyag chen yi ge bzhi pa* and the *Ras chung snyan rgyud* teachings to Kaḥ-thog Rig-'dzin in 1729; it seems that the transmission had become already quite rare by that time.

As a final comment on the "family document" from Yol-mo it should now be pointed out that a reincarnation of rGyal-dbang seng-ge appeared and that he was born in rGod-tshang gling as the son of Karma 'Phrin-las dbang-po, the keeper of the family estate after dKar-rgyud [bstan-pa'i rgyal-mtshan]. While this person is referred to in the document as "grandfather" or "fore-father" Gar-dbang don-grub, in other literary sources he is called sPrul-sku Gar-dbang don-grub, the "reembodiment" (*sku'i skye ba*) of rGyal-dbang seng-ge from Zva-phug. I may also mention in this regard the autobiographies of three teachers from the re-gion of Kutang, to the south of Nub-ri̥s, who all travelled to Yol-mo to receive teachings from sPrul-sku Gar-dbang don-grub at the monastery of rGod-tshang gling. The names of these teachers are Padma don-grub (1668-1744), Padma dbang-'dus (b. 1697) and Padma lhun-grub (b. 1708). The first of these visits occurred in the 1730s, a period marked by the founding of further rNying-ma-pa religious institutions in Yol-mo. To the adherents of this school of Tibetan Buddhism the area is known as "Yol-mo, [which is] enclosed by glaciers" (*yol mo gangs r*[*v*]*a*).[11]

One cousin of *me-me* Gar-dbang don-grub was Karma rNam-mkhyen, and it was during the time of the latter's grandson that the written documents of the family monastery were put together in the form in which they are available to us now. The time frame for this final codification can safely be stated to be at the turn from the 18th to the 19th century. This was the period when old *birtā* land grants were being reexamined—and new ones given—by the rulers of the Śāha dynasty, and one such case involved a member of the "lama lineage" which traced back its history to the arrival of *bla-ma* Karma Chos-bzang in Yol-mo[12]. The investigation into the original land transfer (or the issue of a new title) must have triggered the need to authenticate the circumstances of the bestowal of the original "religious endowment" to the ancestor, and so to set down the genealogy of his succesors.

NOTES

1. See Musashi Tachikawa, *A Study of the Grub mtha' of Tibetan Buddhism. vol. 5: On the Chapter of the bKa' brgyud pa of Thu'u bkwan's Grub mtha'* (= *Studia Tibetica*, 13), The Toyo Bunko, Tokyo, 1987. In addition to the annotated translation of the chapter on the bKa'-brgyud-pa school, the publication includes a facsimile of the relevant section from the Zhol edition of the works of Blo-bzang Chos-kyi nyi-ma, different charts of transmission lineages of the Shangs-pa and Mar-pa traditions, and a hand list of the main bKa'-brgyud-pa works published in India. For the joint research between Tibetan and Japanese scholars conducted at The Toyo Bunko, which resulted in the publication of annotated Japanese translations of several chapters of the *Thu'u bkvan grub mtha'* see Yoichi Fukuda, "Japanese Research on Tibetan Buddhism, 1984-98," *Tibetan*

Studies in Japan (=*Asian Research Trends: A Humanities and Social Science Review* 9), 1999, p. 11.

2. The *bla-ma* from Kshaden also acted as an informant for a Tibetan-Newari lexicon which may have originated in the Yol-mo area; see Christoph Cüppers, "Some Remarks on a Tibetan-Newari Lexicon cum Phrase Book," in S. Ihara and Z. Yamaguchi (eds.), *Tibetan Studies*, vol. 2 (=*Monograph Series of the Naritasan Institute for Buddhist Studies. Occasional Papers*, 2), Naritasan Shinshoji,1992, p.416. The published version of this lexicon contains a photograph of Karma Ras-chung in front of his family monastery; see Christoph Cüppers, Kashinath Tamot, Philip Pierce, *A Tibetan-Newari Lexicon cum Phrase Book*, VGH Wissenschaftsverlag, Bonn, 1996, p. 238. For information on Ras-chung phug, located on a spur of the ridge separating the Yar-klungs and the 'Phyong-rgyas valleys, see Alfonsa Ferrari, *Mk'yen brtse's Guide to the Holy Places of Central Tibet* (= *Serie Orientale Roma*, 14), Istitutio Italiano Per Il Medio Ed Estremo Oriente, Rome, 1958, pp.51 & 127, note 265. This was the place where gTsang-smyon Heruka (1452-1507), the well-known promoter of the hagiographical traditions of Mi-la-ras-pa (1028-1111) and his teacher Mar-pa (1000-1081), passed away; gTsang-smyon Heruka was regarded as an incarnation of Mi-la-ras-pa's disciple Ras-chung-pa rDo-rje grags-pa (1083-1161). For a photograph of the monastery of Ras-chung phug (taken by H. Richardson) see Ferrari *Mk'yen brtse's Guide to the Holy Places of Central Tibet*, plate 26.

3. For the evidence that rGod-tshang gling is the "oldest Sermo Lama temple" in Yol-mo see Graham E. Clarke, "A Helambu History," *Journal of the Nepal Research Centre* 4, 1980, pp.19-21. The conditions in Yol-mo under which "*dgon-pa* (literally 'solitary place', also retreat/monastery/ religious centre) ... became *lha-khang* (temple)" has been described by Graham E. Clarke, "The Great and Little Traditions in the Study of Yolmo, Nepal," in E. Steinkellner and H. Tauscher (eds.), *Contributions on Tibetan Language, History and Culture*, vol. 1 (=*Wiener Studien zur Tibetologie und Buddhismuskunde*, 11), Arbeitskreis für Tibetische und Buddhistische Studien Universität Wien, Vienna 1983, p. 24. A facsimile of the documentary source for the history of rGod-tshang gling was published in Graham E. Clarke, "A Helambu History", pp. 26-27 [=Helambu Document 2]. Unfortunately Karma Chos-bzang's name was completely overlooked in the evaluation of this literary source, as was dKar-rgyud bstan-pa'i rgyal-mtshan's (his full name appears in this document). Karma Blo-bzang is recorded instead as the father of the seven sons. This misidentification resulted from a superficial reading of the document, which is structured around different "prophecies" (*lung bstan*) associated with the site; see Helambu Document 2, fol. 1a/3-5 (*pho brang chen po rgod tshang gling phyogs de ru/rgyal bas zhabs lcags* (=*bcags*) *lo rgyus zur tsam rjod* (=*brjod*) / *thub pas lung stan* (=*bstan*) *gu ru'i zhabs kyi* (=*kyis*) *lcags* (=*bcags*) / .../ *mar par* (=*ma pas*) *lung stan* (=*bstan*) *mi las* (=*mi la'i*) *zhabs kyi* (=*kyis*) *lcags* (=*bcags*) / .../ *tsang* (=*gtsang*) *smyon lung bstan rgod tshangs* (=*tshang*) *ra can* (=*ras chen*) *zhabs* [*kyis*] *lcags* (=*bcags*) / .../ *grub mchog lung bstan karma chos bzang zhabs kyi* (=*kyis*) *lcags* (=*bcags*) / .../ *mkhas grub chen po karma blo bzang gis* / *lung bstan* .../ *bka'* (=*dkar*) *rgyud stan pa'i* (=*bstan pa'i*) *rgyal mtshan zhabs kyi* (=*kyis*) *lcags* (=*bcags*). The last statement suggests that Karma Blo-bzang, the "great scholar and

siddha", was involved in installing dKar-rgyud bstan-pa'i rgyal-mtshan in rGod-tshang gling. For the person of [rNgog-ston] Karma Blo-bzang see note 9.

4. See *mKhas grub chen po byams pa phun tshogs kyi rnam thar,* NGMPP reel-no. L 783/3, fol. 83a/3-b/2 (*nged kyis kyang rang lo lnga bcud (=bcu) bzhi pa'i 'bryg lo'i ston ser bal yul skor ba la yol mo rgyud (=brgyud) te 'gro ba'i (= 'gro bas) glang 'brang du sleb tshe gnas po mtsho skyes sogs kyi (=kyis dbang zhus shing bsnyen bskur phun sum tshogs pa dang bcas rnams dkar gyi 'grel pa (= 'brel pa) bzhag nas / yol mo'i rgod tshang gling du sleb dus / nged kyi bla ma sgres po (=bgres po) des 'dir phebs nas gzhan don rgya cher mdzad yod bsam bla ma dran pa'i mod la mchin mang po shor // rig pa skyo chad de ba'i ngang la chos rje rgod tshang pa yang yang dran pa byung bas / rmi lam du rje nyid dur khrod kyis (=kyi) chas brgyad kyi (=kyis) brgyan pa'i rnam pa can shin tu gzi brjid che bar mdzad nas / mgur mang po cig gsung ba'i rjes la/ sems la g.yo sgyu med na so thar yin / phan ses rgyun chad med na byang sems yin / mtshan ma'i 'dzin pa dag na sngags sdom yin / gzhan mams bcal (=chal) le bcol (=chol) le oṃ āh hūṃ zhes gsung byung ngo / des dus rgod tshang gling du yi ge bzhi pa dang chos drug gi 'khrid btsugs / zla ba phyed gnyis tsam la thon pàr byas / de'i skabs cig rgod tshang gling gi bla brang du rje'i rnam thar yang yang dran zhing / zab mo'i ngo sprod la yid shar du ches so // de'i tshe skabs cig du (=tu) bla [83b] ma kun dga' bas / 'bum rgyas pa dang lha khang bzhengs 'dug pas de rnams ma tshar ba la khang (=khong) rang grongs/ de'i 'jug (=mjug) rnams sras po dang yon bdag rnams kyis bsdus nas rab gnas la nged bos nas bkra shis mnga'gsol sogs rgya cher byas / de'i tshe yol mo ba rnams kyis tshogs 'khor dang' 'bul cha sogs yul lugs dang mthun pa phun sum tshogs pa byung*). For the valley called "Bull's Passage" (*glang 'phrang*), the etymology of this toponym, and its status as a "hidden valley" (*sbas yul*), see Franz-*Karl Ehrhard,* "A 'Hidden Land' in the Nepal-Tibetan Borderlands," in A.W. Macdonald (ed.), *Maṇḍala and Landscape* (*=Emerging Perceptions in Buddhist Studies,* 6), D.K. Printworld, Delhi, 1997, pp. 345-346. This valley is located to the north of Yol-mo, and it is worth noting that in the 16th century Tibetan travellers passed through both areas on their way from Mang-yul Gung-thang to the Nepal Valley.

5. See *Bal yul bgrod pa'i lam yig nor bu'i spel ma'i 'phreng ba,* NGMPP reel-no. L 387/3, fol. 35a/5-b/2 (*de'i phyi nyin dal gyis song ba* [35b] *las / rgod tshang gling zhes bya ba / gtsang smyon pa'i slob ma / rgod tshang ras chen gyis bzhugs shing / dge 'dun gyi sde brgyad grva zhig thog mar 'dzugs par mdzad par gnas su slebs te / zla ba snga ma'i nyi shu brgyad kyi dus mchòd lam gyi brel bas g.yel te chad pa kha gso ba'i dpal 'khor lo sdom pa lha lnga'i dkyil chog rgyas pa shig bgyis shing zhag tu gnas so*). The monastery of rGod-tshang gling served as the base for the Sixth Zhva-dmar-pa's visits to the sacred sites of Yol-mo associated with Padmasambhava and Mi-la-ras-pa. The place of Padmasambhava is called Yang-dag mchog-gi sgrub-phug and the site where the great yogin stayed during his spiritual practice, sTag-phug Seng-ge rdzong; this latter toponym reminded pilgrims of the fact that the place had in earlier times been a "tiger den" (*stag gi tshang*). For an overview of the tour of Chos-kyi dbang-phyug in Yol-mo and the relevant passages of his travelogue see Franz-Karl Ehrhard, " 'The Lands Are like a Wiped Golden Basin': The Sixth Zhva-dmar-pa's Journey to Nepal and His Travelogue (1639/30)," in S.

Karmay and P. Sagant (eds.), *Les Habitants du toit du Monde: Etudes recueillies en hommage à Alexander W. Macdonald* (= *Recherches sur la Haute Asie,* 12), Société d'ethnologie, Nanterre, 1997, pp. 131-132.

6. The transmission of the teachings of the Dvags-po bKa'-brgyud-pa from Sha-ra Rab-'byams-pa to his young disciple in the year 1469 took place at Zur-mkhar, the residence of Zur-mkhar-ba mNyam-nyid rdo-rje (1439-1475). For the descriptions of the following period of spiritual practice see rGod-tshang ras-pa: *gTsang smyon he ru ka phyogs thams cad las rnam par rgyal ba'i rnam thar rdo rje theg pa'i gsal byed nyi ma'i snying po* (=Śata Piṭaka Series, 79), New Delhi, 1969, p. 22.2-4 (*phyag rgya chen po yi ge bzhi pa'i dmar khrid khyad chos kyi ngo sprod dang bcas pa gsan pas/ mnyam bzhag gi stogs* (=*rtogs pa*) *mngar* (=*sngar*) *zhal mjal dus su ngo 'phrod pas las na 'phar rgyu mi 'dug kyang Irjes thob la bogs dang brtsal* (=*rtsal*) *bsam gyis mi khyab pa thon / .../ de nas dpal na ro pa'i chos drug gi khrid yig rje mi las zin bris su mdzad pa'i steng nas dmar khrid du skyangs pas* (=*bskyangs pas*)*/ zhag bcvo lnga tsam song ba'i tshe...*); compare lHa-btsun Rill-chen rnam-rgyal: *Grub thob gtsang smyon pa'i rnam thar dad pa'i spu slong g.yo ba* in "Ras chung snyan brgyud", vol. 1 (=Smanrtsis Shesrig Spendzod, 11), Leh 1971, p. 11.7 (*da nas 'khrid kyi mgo btsugs nas / lta ba phyag rgya chen po yi ge bzhi pa / thabs lam na ro chos drug la zla ba gsum gyi bar du nyams khrid mdzad do*). A commentary on the Mahāmudrā teaching by lHa-btsun Rin-chen rnam-rgyal is available; see *rGyud kyi dgongs pa gtsor sngon pa phyag rgya chen po yi ge bzhi pa'i 'grel bshad gnyug ma'i gter mdzod,* 87 fols. (xylograph), NGMPP reel-no. L 956/8. For the definition of the Dvags-po bKa'-brgyud-pa as those adherents of the school who practice the *Phyag chen* and *Na ro chos drug* teachings passing through sGam-po-pa see E. Gene Smith, *Among Tibetan Texts: History and Literature of the Himalayan Plateau,* Wisdom Publications, Boston, 2001, p. 40.

7. The biography of the guru of gTsang-smyon Heruka bears the title *mKhas grub sha ra rab 'byams pa sangs rgyas seng ge'i rnam thar mthong ba don ldan ngo mtshar nor bu'i phreng ba thar 'dod yid 'phrog blo gsal mgul brgyan,* 26 fols. (xylograph); it was published in "Rare dKar-brgyud-pa Texts from Himachal Pradesh", New Delhi: Urgyan Dorje, 1976, pp. 451-501. According to the printing colophon, the block print was executed by Byams-pa phun-tshogs at his residence in Mang-yul Gung-thang in the year 1559; see ibid., pp. 500.6-501.4. In the same year, shortly after returning from his journey to Yol-mo and the Nepal Valley, he also printed the biography of Ras-chung-pa composed by his teacher rGod-tshang ras-chen; for the printing colophon see Jacques Bacot, "Titres et colophons d'ouvrages non canoniques tibetaines: textes et traduction," *Bulletin de l'École Francaise d'Extrême-Orient* 44, 1954, p. 292. The descriptions of the transmission of teachings from the sTag-lung abbot to Sha-ra Rab-'byams-pa can be found ibid., p. 461.2-4 (*khyad par phyag rgya chen po yi ge bzhi pa rgam po pa* (=*sgam po pa*) *nas dus gsum pa la brgyud pa dang / phag mo gru pa nas sgyer sgom zhig pa la brgyud pa dang / phag mo gru pa nas rnal 'byor gyi dbang phyug gling ras pa la brgyud pa'i lugs rnams nyams khrid du gsan ...*), and p. 479.4-5 (*bka' brgyud kyi chos bskor thams cad yongs su rdzogs par gnang / khyad par du bde mchog snyan brgyud 'di dar rgyas su spel tig gsung ngo*). For the circumstances surrounding the fact that Sha-ra Rab-'byams-pa and gTsang-smyon Heruka belonged to

the Ras-chung bKa'-brgyud-pa, a subsect of the bKa'-brgyud-pa school that has now completely disappeared as a separate entity, see E. Gene Smith, *Among Tibetan Texts: History and Literature of the Himalayan Plateau*, p.61.

8. The history of the transmission of the *Phyag chen yi ge bzhi pa* and the *Ras chung snyan brgyud* as it was received by Kaḥ-thog Rig-'dzin is contained in *lha rje mnyam med zla 'od gzhon nu'i bka' brygud phyag chen gdams pa ji tsam ṇod pa'i rtogs brjod legs bshad rin chen 'byung khungs in* "The Collected Works of Kaḥ-thog Rig-'dzin chen-po Tshe-dbang nor-bu", vol. 2, Dalhousie: Damchoe Sangpo, 1976, pp. 214.1-215.4 & 215.4-216.5. The descriptions of the two meetings between Grub-mchog dbang-po and Byams-pa phun-tshogs can be found in the latter's biography (as in note 4), fol 91b/3-4 (*de dus rje rin po che rgod tshang ras chen gyis* (=*gyi*) *sprul pa'i sku skyes grub mchog dbang po la / zhva dmar cod paṇ 'dzin pa lnga pa dkon mchog yan lag gis chos zhu dgos rnams zhu ba la skyid grong gnas su song gsung ba'i lung bstan nas / rgod tshang sprul sku 'dir phebs phyag chen snyan rgyud* (=*brgyud*) *dgongs 'dus sogs kyi chos yongs su rdzogs pa 'bul ba dang bcas thugs dgongs rdzogs par bsgrubs*), and fol. 92a/1-2 (*yang ras chung phug nas sprul sku rin po che dpon slob rnams kyi dogs gcod zhal gdams / ma song ma rnams kyis bka' lung yongs su rdzogs pa dang bsnyen bkur zhabs tog phul tu phyin bas dges bar mdzad nas / slar yang dbus gtsang du phebs song...*). Grub-mchog dbang-po set down in written form the teachings which he had received from Byams-pa phun-tshogs; see *Bla ma dam pa'i gsung rgyun gyi rim pa mthong dga'i nor bu'i phreng ba 'dod kun 'byung*, 89 fols. (manuscript), NGMPP reel no. L 957/2.

9. A sketch of the life of rNgog-ston Karma Blo-bzang, based on his autobiography, is given in Franz-Karl Ehrhard, "Religious Geography and Literay Traditions: The Foundation of the Monastery Brag-dkar bsam-gling," *Journal of the Nepal Research Centre* 12, 2001, pp. 101-106. Brag-dkar bsam-gling, the main monastery of the bKa'-brgyud-pa school in sNye-shang (present-day Manang), was established by Karma Blo-bzang in the year 1664. It is interesting to see that this *bla-ma* from Ras-chung phug was not only propagating the teachings of the *Ras chung snyan brgyud,* but also "treasure works" (*gter ma*) of the rNying-ma-pa master Rig-'dzin 'Ja'-tshon snying-po (1585-1656). His disciple Karma Gu-ru was equally eager to receive transmissions of rNying-ma-pa teachings and travelled for that purpose to Mang-yul Gung-thang; there he obtained from the rNying-ma-pa-master O-rgyan dpal-bzang (1617 -1677) treasure works of Rig-'dzin bDud-'dul rdo-rje (1615-1672). See *Rigs brgya dbang po 'dren mchog slob dpon dpal bzang po'i rnam par thar pa dad pa'i spu long g.yo b yed mthong bas yid 'phrog ngo mtshar 'phreng ba'i gtam rmad du byun ba*, NGMPP reel-no. L 83/1, fol 291a/2-4 (*de nas slar ran gi sgrub* [*gnas*] *u rgyan chos gling bzhugs dus su yol mo gangs ra nas bla ma karma gu ru dpon slob 'ga' 'byung ba la sprul sku snying thig dbang lung yongs su rdzogs su phul*). O-rgyan dpal-bzang had met rNgog-ston Karma Blo-bzang on several occasions and had founded the monastery of sKu-tshab gter-lnga in southern Mustang in the year 1668; see Franz-Karl Ehrhard, "Concepts of Religious Space in Southern Mustang: The Foundation of the Monastery sKu-tshab gter-lnga," *Giessener Geographische Schriften* 75 (in press).

10. A biography of Bya-btang 'Od-zer has survived, which gives the year 1637 as the date of his moving to the site Zva-phug Brag-dmar chos-gling; see *Bya btang 'od zer rgya mtsho'i rnam thar nges don rgya mtsho'i snying po,* NGMPP reel no. L 452/4, fols. 40b/4 ff. This text was composed by his son in the year 1665. His full name is given in the colophon as ['Chi-med] rGyal-dbang [phun-tshogs bstan-'dzin] seng-ge [bzang-po]; see ibid., fol. 59a/4. The autobiography of the rNying-ma-pa master O-rgyan dpal-bzang mentions an encounter with rGyal-dbang seng-ge; see the text (as in note 9), fol 314a/2-3 (*de mtshams su zva phug tu bla ma rgyal seng ge'i spyan 'dren zhus chos 'brel tsam phul bas gtang rag gis kyang mnyes par mdzad do*). For the transmissiion of the treasure-cycles of Rig-'dzin 'Ja'-tshon sning-po from rGyal-dbang seng-ge to O-rgyan bstan-'dzin (1657-1737), a disciple of O-rgyan dpal-bzang, see Franz-Karl Ehrhard, "Sa-'dul dgon-pa: A Temple at the Crossroads of Jumla, Dolpo and Mustang," *Ancient Nepal: Journal of the Department of Archaeology* 40, 1998, p. 4.
11. The three travel accounts are available in "Autobiographies of Three Spiritual Masters of Kutang", Thimphu: Kunsang Topgay and Mani Dorji, 1979. For the visit of Padma don-grub see ibid., p. 105.1-2 (*gnas yol mo gang (=gangs) ra la sprul sku gar dbang don grub la rta 'phags (=phag) yid bzhin nor bu'i lung thob*/ *'ja' mtshon (=tshon) snying po gter ma yin / dag po (=dvags po) mthar (=thar) rgya (=rgyan) gi lung thob*). The autobiography of Padma dbang-'dus devotes a whole chapter to the extended stay in Yol-mo and different meetings with sPrul-sku Gar-dbang don-grub. This master from Kutang used rGod-tshang gling as the starting and end point for a journey to the Nepal Valley; see ibid., pp. 313.1-345.2 (chapter title: *yol mo gangs ral (=ra) bal po'i dur khrod dang la phyi chu bar gsum gyis (=gyi) skor ro*). For the visit of Padma lhun-grub see ibid., pp. 729.5-730.1 (*sprul sku karma gar dbang don grub kyi drung du / bde mchog mkha' gro (='gro) snyan brgyud kyi lung / sngo ba' gyur gcig ma'i lung / bka' 'gyur ro mchog (=cog) kyi (=gi) lung /bsdom (=sdom) gsum kyi (=gyi) lung dang / dkon mchog spyi 'dus kyi tshe sgrub lcags kyi ri bo che'i dbang thog (=thob)*). A temple on the side of the mountain g.Yang-ri-ma and the monastery Padma'i chos-gling were founded in Yol-mo by the rNying-ma-pa teacher gTer-dbon Nyi-ma seng-ge (1687-1738); for these activities in the years 1723 and 1727 see Franz-Karl Ehrhard, "A Forgotten Incarnation Lineage: The Yol-mo-ba sPrul-skus (16th to 18th Centuries)", R.N. Prats (ed.), *The Paṇḍita and the Siddha: Tibetan Studies in Honour of E. Gene Smith,* Wisdom Publications, Boston (in press).
12. A land grant for Lhakhang Gyang, a village temple in one of the most beautiful parts of the whole region, was given by Gīrvāṇa Yuddha Vikrama Śāha (1789-1816) to one of the descendants of *bla-ma* Karma Chos-bzang. This land grant was later officialized by means of a copperplate in the year 1823. For the details of this copperplate see Graham E. Clarke, "A Helambu History," pp. 20-21 & 33 [=Helambu Document 8]; a description of this temple and its natural surroundings can be found in Corneille Jest, *Monuments of Northern Nepal,* UNESCO, Paris, 1981, pp. 81-83. Raṇa Bahādura Śāha (1777-1805), the father of Gīrvāṇa Yuddha Vikrama Śāha, had banished his first wife Rājārajeśvarī, also called Bijyālakṣmī, to Yol-mo in 1804. Her sad journey home after the murder of her husband became the topic of a Newari poem, one of the most popular

in the Nepal Valley; see Siegfried Lienhard, "*Songs of Nepal: An Anthology of Nevar Folksongs and Hymns*, Motilal Banarsidass, Delhi, 1992, pp. 98-99. It is possible that the land grant to Lhakang Gyang was connected with the exile of Gīrvāṇa Yuddha Vikrama Śāha's stepmother to Yol-mo. As early as 1787 Raṇa Bahādura Śāha had already begun to examine b*irtā* land grants in order to acertain who held land, how much was held, and who had granted it. For the troublesome period of the rule of Raṇa Bahādura Śāha, which also included the Nepal-Tibet war from 1788 to 1792, see, for example, Ludwig F. Stiller, S.J., *Nepal: Growth of a Nation,* Human Resources Development Research Center, Kathmandu,1993, pp. 33-45.

[I]

I prostrate before and take refuge in the Three Jewels [i.e. Buddha, Dharma, Saṅgha], the infallible objects of refuge!

Now, first, the story of how *bla-ma* Karma Chos-bzang came to [the region of] Yol-mo. The *bla-ma to* whom the donors of Yol-mo Gangs-rva adhered is from Ras-chung phug [in] upper [Tibet]. Although it is a place far away, yet, for the benefit of both the dead and the living, the *bla-ma* was invited to come [from there to Yol-mo]. And so eight masters and disciples, including *bla-ma* Karma Chos-bzang, the chant-leader Karma Thub-bstan and the head of discipline Karma dGe-legs, arrived in Yol-mo and stayed [there].

What would be of benefit for the donors having been addressed, the donors, headed by the elders of the land of Yol-mo, put a question in the following way: "Precious *bla-ma,* since the teacher to whom the donors of the sacred site Yol-mo adhere, has come [to live] in a far-away place, please consider to remaining [here] continuously! And take a wife as well!"

Then [Karma Chos-bzang] spoke: "I am a pure monk, but if you, my donors, say such a thing, I will ask my main teacher successively about all the causes of the happiness of the sponsors, and then I will only return if the *bla-ma* gives his consent."

And after installing the chant-leader Karma Thub-brtan in Yol-mo as the representative of the *bla-ma,* he went to Ras-chung phug [in] upper [Tibet]. When he had been there three years, Zhabs-drung Grub-mchog dbang-po said [to him]: "Karma Chos-bzang, as your family line and [your work of] benefitting beings is in Yol-mo, I allow you to take a wife!"

After [the *bla-ma*] gave this prophecy, [Karma Chos-bzang] returned to Yol-mo and married the nun *i-pi* Yi-dam and also [*i-pi*] Khrib-tse, the daughter of the elder brother of *i-pi* Yi-dam. The bone [i.e. paternal line] of the two "grandmothers" [was] Zhang-mo. To *i-pi* Yi-dam were born the sons *me-me* Karma Gu-ru and *me-me* dBang- chen; to *i-pi* Khrib-tse were born *me-me* dKar-rgyud and *me-me* Ngag-dbang. Then Karma Gu-ru spoke: "I am the eldest among us four! I am of a spiritual lineage where worldly deeds have been abandoned!" And [adding]: "Among you [younger] three kinsmen, you, brother dKar-rgyud, are the eldest", he bestowed upon him the family estate and the ownership of the monastery [rGod-tshang gling].

Then *me-me* dKar-rgyud took [as wives] the nun Zhing-skyong-ma and *i-pi* Chos-legs, and seven sons were born [to him]. The eldest son, *me-me* 'Phrin-las dbang-po, requested that a payment be given [to him in the form of] the ownership of the monastery of rGod-tshang gling. *Me-me* Don-grub rgyal-po stayed in sKyel-sdong, *Me me* Thar-pa rgyal-po stayed in Bod-thang. *Me-me* Kun-dga' rgyal-po stayed in Gu-ru-phug. *Me-me* mThong-ba rgyal-po stayed in Shab-ru. *Me-me* Chos rgyal-mtshan stayed in Shab-ru [as well]. [And] *me-me* Blo-gros dpal-bzang remained in rGod-tshang gling.

The son of *me-me* 'Phrin-las dbang-po was *me-me* Gar-dbang don-grub. The son of Blo-gros dpal-bzang [was] Karma rNam-mkhyen, [the latter's] son [was] 'Gyur-med rdo-rje, [and his] son [was] dGra-'dul seng-ge.

[II]

I prostrate before the *bla-ma*, the *yi-dam* and the beautiful *mkha' 'gro* [*ma*], who are accompanied by the entourage of an ocean of oath-bound guardians of the pronouncement [of the Buddha], [namely] the male and female Dharma protectors!

Please pay attention! I, *bla-ma* Karma Chos-bzang, I completed the renovation of the monastery of rGod-tshang gling, at the time when I was safeguarding from hail the three islands of Yam-bu [=Kathmandu], Ko-khom [=Bhaktapur] [and] Ye-rang [=Patan], on the fifteenth day of the tenth hor-month of the bird-year; afterwards, for the purpose of offering congratulations for the consecration [of the renovated structure], the households of the donors of the three districts of Yol-mo and the male and femal donors in their entirety [all] arrived for the consecration. At that time, after the elders held a discussion, [they said]: "The donors of Yol-mo Gangs-rva and the *bla-ma* [Karma Chos-bzang], [these] two, have to put down 100 *taṃ*[*ka*] [each], [together with] a binding document that the donors will not abandon the *bla-ma,* [and] a written contract that the *bla-ma* will not abandon the donors."

After the elders held a talk [once more], [they said]: "This rice field, a *bhir-ta* [=*birtā*] for a durable lineage, we will offer to *me-me* Karma Chos-bzang!"

And thus [followed] the hand signs [i.e. thumbprints] of *bla-ma* [Karma Chos-bzang], the elders [and] the chief estates of the east: at the beginning the thumbprint of *bla-ma* Karma Chos-bzang, below it the print of the elder Tshe-dbang grub-pa, below it the print of the elder Ri-skyabs, below it the print of the elder Bha-bu, below it the print of the elder Tsakka, below it the print of the elder dGos bsam-'phel, below it the print of the elder Nang-ga, below it the print of the elder lHa-sems, below it the print of the elder Nas-grub, below it the print of the elder Nang-ga thugs-rje, below it the print of the elder Nas-po, below it the print of the elder dGos-'joms, below it the print of [the elders oil the three chief estates of the three districts [of Yol-mo].

The copyist was *bla-ma* sNgags-ram-pa Don-grub rgyal-po [of sKyel-sdong]. The dharma field for a durable lineage, is a maṇḍalaic territory [the size] of a small cloth.

May it be virtuous!

[I]

// skyabs gnas bslu ba med pa dkon mchog gsum la phyag 'tshal zhing skyabs su mchi'o //

de yang dang po bla ma karma chos bzang yol mo la [2] phebs pa'i lo rgyus ni / gnas yol mo gangs rva'i sbyin bdag rnams kyi brten pa'i bla ma ni / stod ras chung phug yin / sa thag ring na yang gshin gson [3] gnyis kyi don la / bla ma drags phyin pa la / bla ma karma chos bzang / u (=dbu) mdzad karma thub bstan / chos khrims pa karma dge legs dang bca pa'i / [4] dpon slob brgyad yol mo la phebs nas bzhugs / sbyin bdag gi don gang yin pa mams zhu tshar ba dang/ yol mo yul gyi rgan po'i gtso mdzad pa'i sbyin bdag mams [5] kyis 'di ltar zhus / bla ma rin po che / gnas yol mos (=mo'i) sbyin bdag mams kyi brten pa'i bla ma / sa thag ring po 'dug pas / 'di ru brtan chag (=phyag) bzhugs [6] par thugs rjes gzigs pa dang / khyim thab gcig yang bzhes pa mdzod zhus pas / nga ni gtsang btsun zhig yin pas 'on kyang khyed sbyin bdag roams kyi (=kyis) 'di 'dra [7] gsungs na / nga yi rtsa ba'i bla ma la / sbyin bdag mams kyi skyid sdug gi rgyu mtshan thams cad rim par zhus nas / bla ma dgongs pa mi bkrol na mi yong gsungs [8] nas / yol mo la u (=dbu) mdzad karma thub bstan bla ma'i sku tshab la bzhugs nas / stod rag chung phug la phebs te lo gsum bzhugs nas zhabs drung grub [9] mchog dbang pos zhal nas / karma chos bzang khyod kyis (=kyi) mi brgyud dang 'gro don yolmo la yod pas / khyod rang khyim thab byed chog gsungs te lung bstan [10] gnang nas yol mo la phebs nas / i pi yi dam btsun mo dang i pi yi darp jo'i bu mo khrib tse yang tshun ma (=chung ma) bzhes / i pi gnyis kyi rug pa zhang mo / i pi yi dam [11] la / sras po me me karma gu ru dang me me dbang chen 'khrungs / i pi khrib tse la / me me dkar rgyud dang me me ngag dbang 'khrungs / de nas me me karma gu ru'i zhal nas / [12] 'o rang bzhi'i nang nas nga che ba yin te / nga ni bya btang rgyu (=rgyud) yin gsungs nas / nu'o khyed spun gsum gyi nang nas / nu'o dkar rgyud khyed che ba yin pas / [13] rgyal gzhi (=gzhis) dang dgon pa'i mnga' thang gnang nas / me me dkar rgyud kyi (=kyis) btsun mo zhing skyong ma / i pi chos legs bzhes nas sras po bdun 'khrungs / [14] sras che ba me me 'phrin lag dbang po rgod tshang gling dgon pa mnga' thang gnang phog zhu / me me don grub rgyal po skyel sdong la bzhugs / me me thar pa [15] rgyal po bod thang la bzhugs / me me kun dga' rgyal po gu ru phug la bzhugs / me me mthong ba rgyal po shah ru la bzhugs / [16] me me chos rgyal mtshan shah ru la bzhugs / me me blo gros dpal bzang rgod tshang gling la bzhugs/me me 'phrin las dbang pos (=po'i) sras po me me gar dbang don grub yin/ [17] blo gros dpal bzang gi sras / karma rnam mkhyen gyi sras 'gyur med rdo rje yi sras po / dgra 'dul seng ge yin no /

[II]

bla ma yi dam dpa' mkha' 'gro [18] chos skyong bsrung ma bka' bsrung dang dam can rgya mtsho 'khor dang bcas pa roams la phyag 'tshal lo //

dgongs su gsol / nga bla ma karma chos bzang gig yam bu [19] ko ba [=ko khom] ye rang gling gsum gyi ser bsrung mdzad dug rgod tshang gling gi dgon pa zhig gso la mdzad tshar nas bya lo'i hor zla bcu pa'i tshes bco lnga la rab gnas [20] bkra shis mnga' gsol mdzad pa'i don la yol mo'i yul sde gsum gyi sbyin bdag mi tshar (=tshang) dang sbyin bdag pho mo thams cad rab gnas la byon pa'i dug su [21] rgan parnams kyi (=kyis) bka' grog zhig mdzad nas yol mo gangs rva'i sbyin bdag dang bla ma gnyis ni sbyin bdag gig bla ma skyur sa med pa'i gaṃ (=gan) rgya / bla mas sbyin bdag [22] skyur sa med pa'i gaṃ (=gan) rgya taṃ brgya brgya bzhag pa yin / de nas rgan pa rnams kyi (=kyis) bka' grog gnang nas bla ma la mdung (=gdung) brtan pa'i bhir ta 'bras zhing de me me karma chos [23] bzang la 'phul ba yin pas / de nas bla ma dang rgan pa dang sha ra (=shar) dbu gzhi (=gzhis) rnams kyi phyag gi rtags / thog mar bla ma karma chos bzang gi phyag rtags [24] de 'og rgan pa tshe dbang grub pa'i rtags / de 'og rgan pa ri skyabs kyi rtags / de 'og rgan pa bha bu'i rtags / de 'og rgan pa tsakka'i rtags / de 'og [25] rgan pa dgongs bsam 'phel gyi rtags / de 'og rgan pa nang ga'i rtags/de 'og lha gems kyi rtags / de 'og rgan pa nas grub kyi rtags / de 'og [26] rgan pa nang thugs rje'i rtags / de 'og rgan pa nas po'i rtags / de 'og rgan pa dgos 'joms kyi rtags/ de 'og yul sde gsum gyi dbu gzhi (=gzhis) [27] gsum gyi rtags /

yi ge pa bla ma sngags ram pa don grub rgyal po yin lags / mdung (=gdung) brtan pa'i chos zhing yug chung gi maṇḍal sde yin no //

// dge'o //

CHAPTER 39

Brag-dkar-ba Chos-kyi dbang-phug's Reminder Notes for the Duties of a *dkon-gnyer*

CHRISTOPH CÜPPERS

Vol. Ca of the collected works of Brag-dkar rta-so sPrul-sku Chos-kyi dbang-phyug (1775-1837)[1] contains a short text of two fols. on the duties of the *dkon-gnyer* (caretaker of a temple). According to the title list of vol. Ca this text follows the short text no. 21, the *Maṇi skor chen sgril ba'i lag len.* This text proves to be quite interesting, particularly if one compares it with the duties of the *dkon-gnyer* written by sDe-srid Sangs-rgyas rgya-mtsho in his "Guidelines for Government Officials".[2] The regent gives seven short rules which are introduced by a quotation from the *Satipaṭṭhāna Sutta* in which the horrors of the hell are described in detail for those who fall into it as a karmic result of stealing things which are offered to the Buddha. The first four rules which follow deal with proper handling of offerings, taking care that no fire breaks out in the shrine room, and the handling of devotees who come to pray there. The next two rules prescribe that the *dkon-gnyer* has to avoid the consumption of smelling food like garlic and onions or tobacco. This rule is supported by a short quotation from the *Vinayasūtra.* Finally the chapter is ended with a general prescription to avoid behaviour which leads to bad karma and the advice to follow the example of Atiśa.

From the lines below it becomes obvious that the *rNying-ma-pa Bla-ma* is much more concerned with the spiritual practice of the *dkon-gnyer* than the regent in his guidelines. Chos-kyi dbang-phyug has organised a whole day into periods which the *dkon-gnyer* should fill with prayers and meditation. Self-discipline is emphasized more than the control of devotees who visit the shrines.

Text

[1r1] gtsug lag khang gi rten gsum rnams la mchod 'bul ba dkon gnyer rnams kyi bgyi 'os khrigs rim rjed thor bkod pa yod/

[1r2] {Zha}
Om svasti / bla ma dang dkon mchog gsum la gus pas phyag 'tshal lo // 'dir gtsug lag khang gi dkon mchog gsum gyi [1r3] rten gsum rnams la mchod 'bul ba dkon gnyer rnams kyi bgyi bar 'os pa'i rim pa khrigs su bkod par / dang por skya reng shar ma thag gam / de'i sngon du [1r4] gnyid las lang te tsog bur lus gnad bcas la thun la 'jug pa'i sngon 'gro nas bzung bla ma'i rnal 'byor rgyas bsdus gang rigs dang rgyun gyi bzlas [1r5] sgoms chag med byed dgos rnams byas la / de nas dngos gzhi skyabs sems tshad med bzhi dang bcas pa'i smar khrid kyi sngon 'gro rgyas pa'am / bsdu na mngon [1r6] rtogs yid bzhin nor bu'i bdag skyed blangs la yig drug stong phrag lnga tshun ci nus bzla ba'i ring maṇi gzung skor yod na bzlas pa dang gzung skor chab

[1v1] gcig tu byas pa'i thun mthar dge ba bsngo / de rjes ldang ba'i rnal 'byor gyis lang te phyag dar legs par bya zhing / spos kyi dud pas bdugs / rang nyid 'khrus [1v2] byas / chu gtsang ma blangs te yon chab 'bul / mar me / spos / me tog / lha bshos sogs mchod pa dngos 'byor gang bshams par chab kyis bsangs / ltung [1v3] bshags dang / phyag 'tshal gzhan shes na 'don zhing phyag 'tshal dang / dus bzang rnams su mchod 'bul rgyas par re / rgyun du bzang spyod yan lag bdun [1v4] pa dang spel ba'i mchod 'bul bsdus pa dang / sems bskyed / smon lam mdor bsdus ci ring brjod / de nas bza' btung bya ba'am / yang na nyi shar skabs [1v5] phyi rol du gtsang sar chu sbyin gtor ma gtang / bsangs bsur bsngo / smon lam gang rigs bya / thun

bzhir byed na mal du zhugs te lha'i (b)skyed rdzogs bzlas pa bya [1v6] zhing thun mthar dge ba sngo / nyin gung gi bza' btung zin nas bar der brel ba yod na bcad / de min gsol 'debs / le'u bdun ma / bshags

[2r1] pa smon lam gzung sngags sogs 'don bzhin du mchod rten dang / lha khang sogs la bskor ba byed / yang na dpe cha lta ba / bri [2r2] ba'am 'dzin pa / sgom shes na gnas lugs kyi rang ngo ma yengs par skyongs / dgongs thun snga thun bzhin la grol nas / mar me / yon chab / spos sogs [2r3] phul nas mchod 'bul snga gro bzhin byas la gtor bsngo dang / dmigs gsal gnas bdag gzhi bdag gi gtor bsngo gtang / tshes bcu sogs dus bzang rnams [2r4] su tshogs mchod re 'grub na legs / dgongs dang srod dus sgrol ma / sher snying / 'khor lo 'bar ba sogs bzlog rigs / gyo skol bza' btung zin nas mal du [2r5] zhugs te srod thun sngar bzhin dang gzung skor gang nus zhig skor nas phung po tshogs 'khor gyi mal gcod rgyas bsdus gang rigs mthar nyal ba'i rnal 'byor gyis [2r6] nyal / thun bzhi ma 'grub na snga dgongs gi thun gnyis cis kyang mi chag pa dang dus bzang rnams su dge sbyor lhag po gang 'grub bya / de ltar nyin zhag.

[2v1] 'phrugs gcig tu sgrigs su bcug pa dang / rgyun du sgo gsum spyod pa bag yod pa bag med chos min dang ma 'dres pa'i rang khrim(s) rang gi bsrung zhing sdig spongs [2v2] dge sgrubs chos mthun gyi bsam sbyor gong 'phel du bya ba gal che'o // ces pa'ang brag dkar ba chos kyi dbang phyug gis shar mar bris pa dge legs [2v3] 'phel // mangalam /

Translation

The duties for the *dkon-gnyer* who performs the offerings to the three supports of a temple, composed as well-arranged reminder notes :

Om svasti! To the *Bla-ma* and the Three Jewels I prostrate with respect. Here, with regard to the sequential arrangement of the duties of the *dkon-gnyer* who performs the offerings to the three supports[3] of a temple: at first he should rise from sleep at dawn or earlier and sit upright (on his bed) in meditation posture. After the preliminary practice which he enters in the morning he continues with the *Guruyoga,* either the extended or the abbreviated version, and performs what regular recitations and meditation he has to do without interruption. This is followed by the main practice, either the extended preliminaries of the essential instructions consisting of taking refuge, generating Bodhicitta, and the Four Immeasurable Ones[4], or if he takes the short version, realizing himself as *yid bzhin nor bu* (= Avalokiteśvara) and reciting the six syllables as much as he can up to five thousand times. During this, if he has a prayer wheel, he turns it simultaneously while reciting. At the final part he dedicates the merit.

After this the awakened yogī gets up (from his bed) and sweeps (the shrine room) well and scents it with the smoke of incense. Having washed himself he should take clean water and perform the water offering and sprinkle with water the well-arranged offerings that are there, such as butterlamps, incense flowers and food to the gods, etc. (Then) he confesses his transgressions and, if he knows another prostration prayer, recites it and prostrates himself.

On each of the special days[5] he performs the extended offerings. On ordinary days he performs the *bzang-spyod yan-lag bdun-pa* ([Pūja with] Seven parts)[6] and an additional short offering, generates Bodhicitta and recites the short *smon-lam*-prayer for as long as possible. After this he has his meal or, at sunrise he goes outside where he throws the *chu-sbyin gtor-ma* at a clean place and dedicates them to the *lha (bsangs)* and *'dre (bsur),* and says *smon-lam*-prayer of any variety.

If he does this at the fourth part of a day, he sits on his bed and recites the *lha'i bskyed(-rim)* and *rdzogs(- rim)* and at the final part he dedicates (the merit).

After his lunch, if he has some work to do in between, he should finish it; otherwise he circumambulates the stūpa and temple while praying or reciting prayers like the *Le'u-bdun-ma*[7] the confession, or *smon-lam,* or he studies books, writes or learns (texts) by heart. If he knows how to meditate, he should maintain, without an inattentive mind, (the meditation on) his own condition.

In the afternoon, after concluding it in the same way as in the morning, having offered butterlamps, water, incense, etc., he prays as in the morning and dedicates the *gtor-ma;* in particular he dedicates the *gtor-ma* to *gnas-bdag's* and *gzhi-bdag's.*

If he performs *tshogs* offerings on special days as the 10th day etc., this is good, as are the morning and evening recitations such as the *Tārā* prayer, *Prajñāpāramitāhṛdaya,* and the *'Khor-lo 'bar-ba*[8], etc.

After cooking and eating his meals and sitting on his bed he should perform the evening session in a similar way to the morning session by turning his prayer wheel as much as possible and practising a short or long version of (mentally) offering his body. At the end (of his practice) on his bed, he lies down finally in the sleep yoga position.

If he cannot practice four sessions, then he should practice the morning and evening sessions without interruption and on special days do additional virtuous acts as much as possible.

In this way the whole day is organised and it is of great importance that at all times he acts with his three gates (of body, speach and mind) with care and personally protects his self-discipline without mixing it carelessly with things other than *dharma,* that he abandons sins and practices virtue and develops thoughts and deeds which are in accordance with the *dharma.*

Chos kyi dbang phyug from Brag-dkar wrote this as it came to his mind. May perfectness increase! Mangalam!

NOTES

1. The collected works of Brag-dkar rta-so sPrul-sku Chos-kyi dbang-phyug have been microfilmed by the Nepal-German Manuscript Preservation Project under reel nos. L 376/1-L 381/8 [- vols. Ka-Ta] reel-no. AT 90/18-91/1 [= vol. Tha]; the size of the mss. is 45,5 X 7,5 cm.
2. See Christoph Cüppers, *Die Richtlinien für die tibetischen Beamten der dga'-ldan pho-brang-Regierung: sDe-srid Sangs-rgyas-rgya-mtsho's Blang dor gsal ba ston pa'i drang thig dvangs shel gyi me long nyer gcig pa* (forthcoming). The chapter on the dkon-gnyer's duties is chapter 15.
3. I.e. statues, books, and stūpas.
4. On the four *apramāṇas* see Mudagamuwe Maitrimurthi, *Wohlwollen, Mitleid, Freude und Gleichmut. Eine ideengeschichtliche Untersuchung der vier apramāṇas in der buddhistischen Ethik und Spiritualität von den Anfängen his zum frühen Yogācāra* (=Alt- und Neu-Indische Studie, 50), Stuttgart, 1999.
5. I.e. the 10th, the 15th, 25th and the 30th day of the lunar month.
6. The textual source for this seven-part-pūja which consists in 1. prostrating, 2. offering, 3. confessing, 4. rejoicing, 5. requesting, 6. praying and 7. dedicating is a vers from the *Ārya-bhadracārī-praṇidhāna-rājā.* Brag-dkar rta-so sPrul-sku treats these seven parts in a particular text, which he wrote on request by the *dkon-gnyer* of the 'Phags-pa lha-khang. See

Franz-Karl Ehrhard, *Die Statue und der Tempel des Ārya va-ti bzang-po: Ein Beitrag zur Geschichte und Geographie des Tibetischen Buddhismus* (in the press).

7. See Peter Schwieger, "Zur Rezeptionsgeschichte des gsol-'debs le'u bdun-ma und des gsol-'debs bsam-pa lhun-grub-ma," *Zentralasiatische Studien* 21 (1988/89), pp. 29-47. Also see Karl-Heinz Everding, *Das Königreich Mang yul Gung thang, Königtum und Herrschaftsgewalt im Tibet des 13.-17. Jahrhunderts,* Teil 2: Studien zur Geschichte des Reiches, Monumenta Tibetica Historica I, 6(2), Bonn, 2000. Appendix 5, pp. 618-627.
8. See PTT 3604, vol nyu fols 173b3-174a6. I am indebted to Burkhard Quessel for providing me with this reference. Sam van Schaik is thanked for reading a draft of this paper.

CHAPTER 40

The Life and Writings of Robert Brainerd Ekvall (1898-1983): Missionary, Soldier-Interpreter and Observer of Tibetan Nomadic Life

DAVID P. JACKSON

Since the mid-nineteenth century, dozens of Christian missionaries went from Europe and America to live for long periods in the Tibetan borderlands, where many studied Tibetan language and tried to proselytize. Besides the great Moravians H.A. Jäschke (1817-1883)[1] and H.A. Francke (1870-1930),[2] who excelled as scholars, few missionaries made noteworthy scholarly contributions or are remembered today outside their own circles. One exception is Robert Brainerd Ekvall (1898-1983), who lived a varied, colorful life and left behind a considerable legacy of publications.[3]

I met Robert Ekvall a few times during my student days in Seattle in the 1970s but did not pay much attention to him, discounting him in my youthful zeal as "an old ex-missionary." I did not begin to investigate his career more carefully until much later, when studying the life of Dezhung Rinpoche (1906-1987), a friend and valued informant of Ekvall in the 1960s and

1970s.[4] Since no detailed account of Ekvall's career has been published until now, I would like to sketch here what I could learn about his life and publications.[5]

1. *A Brief Biography*

Birth and Education

Robert Ekvall born on February 18, 1898, at Minhsien in Kansu province of China.[6] His parents were David P. Ekvall (d. May 18, 1912) and Helen (Galbraith) Ekvall (d. June 5, 1933), missionaries of the Christian and Missionary Alliance.[7] As a child he learned to speak Mandarin more fluently than English and also learned several other Chinese dialects. He was tutored at home by his parents, but he also learned a great deal simply growing up in the borderlands of western China during the first two decades of the twentieth century.

Following his father's death in 1912, he returned with his mother from China to the United States for secondary schooling at the Wilson Memorial Academy in Nyack, New York (1913-1916). After brief service in the Army near the end of World War I, he pursued four more years of studies at Wheaton College in Wheaton, Illinois, earning in 1920 a bachelor of arts degree. In 1921 he married his first wife, M. Elizabeth (Betty) Fischer, who was a fellow graduate of Wheaton. Together they attended the Nyack Missionary Institute in Nyack, New York, in 1921-1922.

Career as a Missionary

In 1922 Robert Ekvall departed with Betty (Tibetan name rDo-rje-mtsho) for China, where their son, David W. Ekvall (1925-1945, Tibetan name Zla-'od), was born. From January 1923 until 1926 Robert worked as mission teacher and school administrator. In 1926-1927 he mainly worked as "explorer" for the Christian and Missionary Alliance, investigating the possibilities for mission work in the Chinese-administrated borderlands of Northeastern Tibet (Amdo).[8] They were forced to evacuate from Amdo and China in 1927 because of fighting between Nationalist Chinese and the Muslim Hui warlords of Kansu.[9]

Back in the U.S.A., Ekvall sold to the Newark Museum in 1927 ethnographic objects (chiefly costumes) from the Amdo

Kokonor region that would later be their "Robert Ekvall collection." He was one of four missionaries to collect objects in eastern Tibet for that museum between 1910 and 1948. Collecting and selling art and artifacts was a means used by some missionaries to finance their mission work.[10]

After their American furlough in 1927-1928, Ekvall and family returned to the Tibetan borderlands in 1929. He learned the local Tibetan nomad dialect intensively, and from 1929 to 1935 he lived with his wife and son mainly in the isolated village of Lhamo (sTag-tshang-lha-mo), among the Samtsha nomads southeast of Labrang in southern Amdo (in present Luchu county on the border of Gansu and Sichuan).[11]

In 1936 they returned to the U.S.A. for a three-year furlough, during which time he wrote two histories for the mission society sponsoring him: *Gateway to Tibet: The Kansu-Tibetan Border* (Harrisburg: Christian Publications. 1938) and *After Fifty Years* (Harrisburg: Christian Publications, 1940). In 1937 he took a year off to attend the University of Chicago for graduate study of anthropology and to write his book *Cultural Relations on the Kansu-Tibetan Border* (University of Chicago Press. 1940). He also published his last articles in the *Alliance Weekly,* a Christian and Missionary Alliance periodical founded by A.B. Simpson (1844-1919) in 1882.

In 1939 Ekvall returned with his wife and son to Taktshang Lhamo among the Samtsha nomads between Labrang and Ngaba. The next year Betty, his beloved wife and companion of nineteen years, died after contracting in the nomadic borderlands a high fever that defied diagnosis (anthrax?).[12] Shaken by her death, he left western China in summer 1941 for French Indochina to visit his son, thus ending his missionary work.

Career as a Soldier-Interpreter

When Japan entered World War II in December, 1941, Robert Ekvall and his son were interred by the Japanese in Southeast Asia for about two years, but he managed to be repatriated on the ship Gripsholm through an exchange of internees, reaching New York in late 1943. To support the war effort he first joined the O.S.S. with a desk job as expert on Far-Eastern affairs. A few months later at the urging of Gen. Joseph W. "Vinegar Joe"

Stilwell and his chief of staff, Gen. Haydon Boatner (both of whom could speak Chinese), he was encouraged to join the U.S. Army with a commission as captain. They greatly needed Chinese-speaking Americans for military operations in northern Burma, where Chinese units were fighting in coordination with units from other allied countries.[13]

General Stillwell was then commanding general of the China theater and commanding general, U.S. Armed Forces in Burma. President Roosevelt had given support for a Burma theater with limited supplies, and by September, 1943, Stillwell was able to start his Galahad offensive with the help of the Kachin guerillas trained by the O.S.S., aimed at taking the airfield at Myitkyina, the largest city in Kachin province. By April, 1944, Ekvall joined this military action in Burma as a combat liaison officer, engaging for nine months in jungle warfare, commanding at one time a detachment of Merrill's Marauders. At the seige of Myitkyina (May-August 1944), he served on the staff of Gen. Boatner, his most important role being to check the English-Chinese interpretation at the daily staff conferences.[14]

In late 1944, after the end of the Burma campaign and the opening of the Burma Road, Ekvall moved to the wartime U.S. headquarters in China at Chungking, where he served as a staff officer in the U.S. China theatre headquarters. He was on the staff of Gen. Albert Coady Wedemeyer (1897-1989), who took over the China theatre in October, 1944.[15] He was assigned as liaison officer between G-2 (military intelligence) of the U.S. headquarters and Chinese military intelligence.[16]

On July 7, 1945, during the last months of the war, Ekvall took part in a special mission at the front in Luchow. He stumbled into a confused firefight in a village street and received a severe bullet wound in the arm. He returned to the U.S.A. for surgical treatment in Atlantic City.[17] While still recovering, he heard the news that his son, David, had been accidentally killed during military service in Korea by an ordnance explosion in December, 1945, several months after the end of World War II. The death of his only child, coming just a few years after the loss of his wife, troubled him spiritually. He never returned to being a missionary.[18]

Following nine months recuperation in the U.S.A., Ekvall

returned to China to serve in 1946-1947 in Peking on the staff of General George C. Marshall (1880-1959), who was then ambassador to China, attempting to reconcile the Nationalists and Communists. Afterward he was appointed assistant military attaché, one of three military attachés of the United States in China, in which capacity he served in 1947-1948, travelling through western China from Burma to central Asia.[19] From 1949 to 1951 he served as assistant G-2, Second Infantry Division, and then at Joint Army Forces PIO (Public Information Office?), Seattle.

In the late 1940s Ekvall married his second wife, Eva Kunfi, with whom he had two children, Erik (b. ca. 1950) and Karen (b. ca. 1956). He resigned from the U.S. Army in 1951, after the fall of the Kuomintang on the Chinese mainland in 1950, though remaining in the reserves.

In 1951-1952 Ekvall moved to West Virginia to work on a project of the Committee for Free Asia, an organization set up in San Francisco in 1951 to contain communism in East Asia.[20] (The committee changed its name to the Asia Foundation in 1954 and today, five decades later, still exists.)[21] Ekvall's job was to assist and translate for the committee's guest, the Dalai Lama's eldest brother, Thubten Jigme Norbu, Taktser Rinpoche (b. 1922), then about to arrive in the U.S.A.[22] In 1950 Norbu had fled from his homeland, Amdo, a Tibetan border province influenced by China for centuries, having received a foretaste of the communist nightmare that would befall central Tibet eight years later. He went first to Lhasa pretending to cooperate with a Chinese plan to overthrow the Dalai Lama. But instead of collaborating further with the communists, he revealed the plot at once to his brother and gave dire warnings to the central Tibetan government not to cooperate with the Chinese. Thereafter, on the pretext of receiving medical treatment, he secretly went to Kalimpong in June, 1951.[23] From there he travelled to Calcutta, trying to flee to the West–in an unofficial capacity but *de facto* as an emissary of his brother.[24] With the help of the Committee for Free Asia, which agreed to sponsor him for one year, Norbu managed to fly to New York City via London in early July, 1951.[25]

Ekvall was there to meet Norbu at Idlewild airport of New York, surprising the Amdo visitor by addressing him in a familiar nomad dialect. He helped Norbu as "mentor," assisting him adjust to life in the U.S.A. Norbu was taken to rural West Virginia where he received medical treatment for six months for a minor lung condition, staying in a farmhouse in Fairfax.[26] Six months later Norbu went to Berkeley, California, to learn English. Ekvall accompanied him, working on a study of the universals of Tibetan religious observances. Ekvall lived outside of Berkeley, California, and consulted Thubten Jigme Norbu as informant until Norbu left for Japan.[27]

Ekvall hoped to visit India and Tibet in the early 1950s, but this proved impossible. For a year (1952-53) he was officially a research associate of the anthropology department at the University of Chicago. His book *Tibetan Sky Lines* appeared in summer 1952 and was widely reviewed—mostly positively—in newspapers and journals.[28]

In spring, 1953, Ekvall was called back to military service as a Lt. Colonel to serve in the Korean War armistice talks. He was appointed principal language officer for the United Nations team at Panmunjom, Korea, where he worked at times in a tent placed athwart the 38th parallel of latitude.[29] In October, 1953, he began service as interpreter on loan to the State Department for ambassador Arthur H. Dean. In spring and summer of 1954, Ekvall served as interpreter at the Asian and Indochina conferences at Geneva.

The following year (1954-55) Ekvall served as staff officer in the intelligence division, Pentagon. In 1954 he also published his novel *Tents Against the Sky* (his second novel, *The Lama Knows,* would appear twenty-five years later in 1979).[30] From summer, 1955, until 1957 he served as interpreter on loan to the State Department for the Sino-American talks in Geneva. In 1957-58 he was posted to Paris as an assistant military attaché, presumably in an intelligence capacity.

Academic Career

In 1958 Ekvall was released from the army for being over-aged in grade as a sixty-year-old lieutenant colonel. The same year at the invitation of Prof. George E. Taylor he came to the University of Washington and joined the Inner Asia Research Project in the Far Eastern and Russian Institute, supported by a grant from the Carnegie Foundation. He came to the project as research fellow and also assumed its chairmanship.[31] He lived with wife and two small children in their house at 2015 E. Newton St. He was fond of taking his family camping and skiing in the Cascade mountains.[32]

In early 1960, Ekvall was slated to go to India accompanied by Turrell V. (Terry) Wylie (1927-1984), to select and invite a group of Tibetans to Seattle for Rockefeller Foundation-funded research.[33] But in about January 1960, his application for an Indian visa was refused, because the Indian consulate found out about his previous work as a U.S. Army interpreter and intelligence officer and suspected him of being a spy.[34] So the much younger Wylie, assistant professor of Tibetan language and history since 1959, became principal investigator for the grant and went to India and Nepal alone.[35]

Through Wylie's efforts, the University of Washington invited and hosted the largest group of Rockefeller-funded Tibetans, including the two lamas of the Phun-tshogs palace of Sakya. Ekvall quickly befriended the oldest of the Tibetans, the lama Dezhung Rinpoche (1906-1987), who was eight years younger than Ekvall. Dezhung Rinpoche had lived for long stretches among the nomads in two different parts of Kham—Dzachukha and Lithang—and had amazing powers of recall, making him a precious informant. Ekvall in his Christian writings published in the 1930s and 1940s had portrayed Buddhist monks and lamas as lazy, ignorant, hypocritic or worse.[36] But he did not doubt the integrity of Dezhung Rinpoche and until the end of his life continued to speak of him with highest respect and affection.[37] Ekvall dropped by almost every day to see the Sakya family residence where Dezhung Rinpoche stayed, and, notebook in hand, asked many questions.

During the three years of Rockefeller, support (1960-1963), Dezhung Rinpoche, together with the Sakya Jigdral Dagchen Rinpoche, his brother Thrinlay Rinpoche and Dagmo Kusho, participated in discussion groups led by Ekvall, in which they discussed the political and economic life in Sakya. Ekvall's work with the Tibetans in the Inner Asia Research Project during the years 1960-1962 eventually resulted in several books. The product of this work on Sakya with these informants and C.W. Cassinelli was published a few years later as C.W. Cassinelli and Robert B. Ekvall's *A Tibetan Principality: The Political System of Sa sKya* (Ithaca, NY: Cornell University Press, 1969). In the preface (p. v), the authors described the four main informants in the "continually functioning discussion group."

Another result of Robert Ekvall's work at the time was his *Religious Observances in Tibet: Patterns and Function* (Chicago and London: University of Chicago Press, 1964). In the preface (p. xii), Ekvall mentions his four main informants. A third book, a study of pilgrimage co-authored by James F. Downs (1923-1999), was published only twenty years later.[38]

On January 10, 1961, Ekvall's old friend and colleague Taktser Rinpoche, Thubten Jigme Norbu, arrived in Seattle.[39] Norbu came as research associate for the Tibetan project, after spending most of the previous year in India, trying to find solutions for the pressing refugee problem. He had visited Seattle about two years earlier.[40] During both visits he stayed with Ekvall. On this second visit, which lasted six months, Norbu worked primarily with Ekvall to translate the work: *The Younger Brother Don yod.... Being the Secret Biography, from the Words of the Glorious Lama, the Holy Reverend Blo bZang Ye Shes* (*dpal ldan bla ma dam pa rje btsun blo bzang ye shes kyi gsung las gsang ba'i rnam thar bzhugs so/*), which Norbu published eight years later from Bloomington (Indiana University Press, 1969).

Ekvall had a personality that one of his students later described as "gregarious, sometimes bombastic, and always adventurous," which stood him in good stead with the Amdo nomads in the 1930s and which the Tibetans in Seattle could also appreciate. Since he could speak with them, although in nomadic brogue, he was accepted by the visitors as an honorary Tibetan, who called him by his Tibetan name, "Sherab Tsondru" (*Shes-rab-brtson-'grus*). With his anthropological, military and diplomatic-interpreter experience, he was broader minded than most ex-missionaries, but there were gaps in his scholarly training, especially by the standards of the early 1960s.

Academic politics at the University of Washington were not always easy for the former missionary and retired officer/diplomatic interpreter.[41] The other Tibetologist in residence, Prof. T.V. Wylie, was not attracted by Ekvall's flamboyant or bombastic sides.[42] As time went by, Wylie—an unassuming Rocky Mountain native who never lost his rustic Colorado accent—developed an intense rivalry with Ekvall. Ekvall was Wylie's more urbane and socially self-assured senior by nearly thirty years, and his fluency in Amdo-nomad dialect of Tibetan (in addition to several Chinese dialects) gave him direct access to Tibetan informants. Wylie, by contrast, never spoke any dialect of Tibetan well.

Another factor working against Ekvall was his lack of an academic degree beyond his bachelor of arts from Wheaton. He had done some graduate work at Chicago and possessed an impressive personal background after so many years spent in the western Chinese borderlands and elsewhere in Asia. Even without a doctorate, Ekvall was clearly an old Asian hand, and by 1961 he had over twenty non-missionary articles and four non-missionary books to his credit, far more than the fledgling Wylie. For two years (1958-1960), he even served as chairman of the Inner Asia Research Project.[43] His knowledge of classical Tibetan and Buddhist high culture was, however, limited.

Wylie completed his Ph.D. at the University of Washington in 1958, and in 1959 he rose from the position of instructor to assistant professor of Tibetan language and history. He was interested almost exclusively in literary Tibetan and (mainly political) history, hardly concerning himself about the living culture or spoken language. By the early 1960s, he felt compelled to defend his academic turf. Though in other respects easygoing and amiable, Wylie emphasised academic formalities, and for him Ekvall lacked legitimate credentials.[44] One of Wylie's few claims to scholarly fame by then was his brief article in 1959 on romanization of Tibetan in which he had sketched a system already employed by the more established European scholars D.L. Snellgrove and R. de Nebesky-Wojkowitz. But Ekvall stubbornly insisted on devising his own unwieldy system, which not a single scholar later adopted. For these and other reasons, Wylie felt justified in criticizing Ekvall's scholarship.[45]

Wylie entrenched himself in August 1962 when Chang Kun resigned as co-chairman of the Inner Asia Project and Wylie was named "executive chairman."[46] The friction between Wylie and Ekvall came to a head in 1962 or 1963, when Ekvall and Cassinelli were to present a paper at a special enlarged meeting of the

Inner Asia Colloquium at which the director of the Far Eastern Institute, George Taylor, was to preside. Melvyn Goldstein, then an enthusiastic and ambitious anthropological graduate student of about twenty-five whose spoken Tibetan (in proper Lhasa dialect) was rapidly becoming good enough to check Ekvall's oral translations, read a copy of the paper that had been distributed in advance.[47] Goldstein was shocked by the paper, which argued, using dubious information, that Sakya had been an independent principality.[48] He therefore re-interviewed the informants Ekvall had used, mainly Jigdral Dagchen Rinpoche, and found that the latter's answers did not support everything Ekvall proposed (he believed Ekvall had asked leading questions). Goldstein had already developed doubts about some of Ekvall's methods and sources, learning that Jigdral Dagchen Rinpoche on more than one occasion had telephoned Tibetans from dBus Province to ask about customs and then passed on the information to Ekvall as Sakya tradition.[49] Goldstein's opinion that Ekvall's work was in some respects not up to current scholarly standards was, moreover, shared by more than one senior professor of anthropology at the university.[50]

Though Ekvall had left himself open to criticism in this case, his opponents seized this as a chance to put his whole scholarship on trial. To several graduate students, the proceedings smacked of a kangaroo court, and they boycotted the meeting.[51]

At the actual meeting, after Ekvall had read his paper Goldstein presented his misgivings in some detail. His main point was not that Ekvall's thesis was necessarily wrong or that he himself was correct: rather, he meant to demonstrate that this was a difficult and complex issue and that if Ekvall and his colleagues wanted to make a scientific contribution, they should go to India where there was no shortage of people from Sakya to interview, including the (very young) Sakya Trizin and entourage.[52]

Goldstein's critique of the much senior scholar's work (Ekvall was then sixty-four) caused a real stir and generated both friends and enemies for him.[53] In the Far Eastern Institute and Inner Asia Project, Ekvall was not seriously threatened, for he still had powerful friends such as George Taylor, another old China hand from the 1930s.[54] But Goldstein's criticisms may have resulted in one law professor deciding not to publish a book on Sakya law based on the same set of data.[55]

Ultimately Ekvall and Cassinelli decided not to go for further research to India. Ekvall had already been denied an Indian visa in 1960, as his critics knew full well, while Cassinelli said he was not responsible for the veracity of the data—that was Ekvall's job–but only for analyzing it. They went ahead and published their completed study as the book *A Tibetan Principality: The Political System of Sa sKya* in 1969.[56]

Through all the academic wrangling, the Sakyapa Tibetans maintained their close links with Ekvall. In 1964 after the Rockefeller Foundation funding ended, Ekvall, tried to revive his "Seminar on Tibetan Society and Culture."[57] He applied for a grant from the National Science Foundation, but by the time the grant was approved and work could be resumed, it was late fall of 1965 and most of his former Sakya informants had found other work. When they did resume some meetings, Jigdral Dagchen Rinpoche served as main informant. Ekvall, now honorary curator of Asian Ethnology at the Thomas Burke Memorial Museum in Seattle, did some additional interviews with Dezhung Rinpoche.[58]

In 1963 or 1964, tragedy struck again. Ekvall's charming Hungarian-Jewish wife, Eva, whom he deeply loved, died painfully of breast cancer. He wondered at the time whether by such extreme afflictions he was not being tested unfairly, like Job in the Bible.[59]

From 1965 to 1969 Ekvall continued to support his research through grants from the National Science Foundation. In ca. 1966 he spent about a year in Switzerland doing research among the Tibetans there.[60] He contributed editorials to the *Seattle Times* opinion page: "U.S. 'Open Door' to China Proposed" (November 24,1968) and "The 'Whys' of China's Willingness to Talk to Nixon" (December 12, 1971), the second based on a memorandum written for William Kintner at the Foreign Policy Research Institute.

From 1969-1974, even in his early seventies, Ekvall continued to keep nominal positions as research associate at either the Burke Museum or the Department of Anthropology at the University of Washington. Later in the 1960s he married a third time. That marriage, to a widow and accomplished yachtswoman, ended in divorce, according to Ekvall in part because his wife objected to his marching in protest of the Vietnam War.[61]

In these twilight years of his career, Ekvall still commanded respect as a senior China-watcher. Occasionally, he was sought out by idealistic young people, some of whom mistook him for an expert on Tibetan mysticism.[62]

Retirement and Death

Robert Ekvall officially retired in 1974 at age seventy-six. He lived in Carbondale, a hamlet in the Cascade Mountains, and continued to visit Seattle now and then, dropping by to visit his Tibetan friends such as Dezhung Rinpoche and giving them academic offprints inscribed with dedications written in his highly legible cursive Tibetan hand.[63]

Although his eyesight steadily worsened after his retirement (perhaps because of cataracts), he gave up driving only after he drove his car off the road and, in his words, "Pretty well destroyed it," forcing him to admit that driving was unsafe. Weakening eyesight made life difficult in his isolated mountain community, and he could only read with the help of a magnifying lens. After suffering a heart problem he moved to the small town of Enumclaw, in the foothills of Mt. Rainier, where he lived most of the last years of his life. On the advice of his physician he drank a single glass of French red wine with his lunch each day and took long walks, stepping with a peculiar bent-knee gait that he believed was easier on his knees.[64]

Near the end of his life he worked for several years on an account of his life as a missionary, dealing in part with his own struggles of faith. He expressed great respect for the strong Christian religious convictions of his daughter, Karen, with whom he occasionally attended church. But he gave some friends the impression that once he ceased to be a missionary, he made something of a break with that part of his life, and that from then on he viewed himself as an anthropologist and ethnographer, with perhaps a special insight into religious practices because of his own experiences. His Christian religious convictions appeared to be less doctrinaire and more tolerant than one would have expected from someone of his missionary background.[65]

Ekvall's last known article, addressing the subject of aging among the Tibetan nomads, appeared in 1980.[66] He passed away in a rest home on Capitol Hill in Seattle in May, 1983, at age eighty-five.

Methodologically, Ekvall's improvising style had been written off long before by certain academic colleagues. But he was fondly remembered by other colleagues, students and friends. As one recounted: "[Robert Ekvall was] a great character in all senses of the word, and someone I recall with great affection and appreciation. Quite human, quite nuanced, remarkably candid about himself, at least in the [last years of his life] when I knew him."[67] "Generous, prickly, challenging, patient and above all a great raconteur. There was about him, even when older, a resiliency and spirit that I hope to have at his age."[68]

Within the history of Tibetan studies in America, Robert Ekvall remains a colorful, rough-and-ready figure. His detailed observations of nomadic life have not lost their scholarly interest, nor have his missionary and ethnographic novels of eastern Tibet, the second of which appeared just four years before his death and featured a nomad protagonist who was "an improbable combination of saint and pretender."[69] Ekvall himself would probably not mind being remembered as one book reviewer described him in 1954: "an American missionary run wild, a good man and devout, but with a touch of piracy to offset the piety."[70]

2. *The Publications of Robert Ekvall*

By one account, R. Ekvall's writings included at least fourteen books, thirty-two articles and eight unpublished manuscripts.[71] Here I have tried to compile as complete a list as possible and have therefore included a number of titles I have not actually seen. For pre-1953 articles—mainly brief notes in the *Asia (and the Americas) Magazine*–I have relied on the bibliography of H.K. KulØy and Y. Imaeda (1986), p. 163f., while for many later scholarly articles and reviews I have relied upon one of Ekvall's own C.V.s. I found one or two additional publications in Dan Martin's unpublished bibliography of Tibetan studies, which here largely mirrors KulØy and Imaeda. I have also been able to locate several short pieces that Ekvall published in the Christian and Missionary Alliance periodical *Alliance Weekly* and the *New York Times* in the 1920s and 1930s.[72] Sources on Ekvall's life are listed below in the endnotes.

A. BOOKS OR MONOGRAPHS

Ekvall, Robert Brainerd (ca. 1928-1930). *Alliance Program of Advance in N.E Tibet.* 16pp. [In-house publication of the Christian and Missionary Alliance? Not seen.]

—(1936). *God's Miracle in the Heart of a Tibetan.* The Christian and Missionary Alliance. 29pp. [Not seen.]

—(1938). *Gateway to Tibet: The Kansu-Tibetan Border.* Harrisburg, Christian Publications. [Tibetan-border mission history.]

—(1938). *Monologues from the Chinese.* Harrisburg, Christian Publications. [Missionary verse.]

—(1939). *Cultural Relations on the Kansu-Tibetan Border.* Publications in Anthropology, occasional paper no. 1, University of Chicago. Chicago, University of Chicago Press.

—(1940). *After Forty Years.* Harrisburg, Christian Publications. [Tibetan-border mission history.]

—(1943). Two Japanese translations of Ekvall's book on cultural relations on the Kansu-Tibetan border appeared in Tokyo in 1943, see K&I nos. 2748 and 2749.

—(1946). *Tibetan Voices.* New York, Harper Brothers; reprint Wheaton, Tyndale House, 1968. [Missionary verse. Possibly first published in instalments in a missionary serial? Reviewed *New York Times* June 23, 1946, VII, p. 14, col. 4.]

—(1952). *Tibetan Skylines.* New York, Farrar, Straus and Young; reprint New York, Octagon Books, 1976. [Travel and ethnography. Reviewed *New York Times* June 20, 1952, p. 21, col. 6 and July 20, 1952, VII, p. 3, col. 1.]

—(1954). *Tents Against the Sky.* New York, Farrar, Straus and Young; reprint: Westchester, III., Good News Publishers, 1978. [Novel set among eastern-Tibetan nomads. Reviewed in the *New York Times* July 31, 1955, VII, p. 14, col. 2 "of indifferent quality as fiction, but most excellent ethnography."] French translation: *Tentes Contre le Ciel.* Paris, Stock, 1959. (See R. Ekvall 1968, p.99.)

[Set in Tibet with its "lamaseries," abbots, prayer wheels, and rosaries, this novel lets the reader taste the foods, feel the winds, and fear the sudden bandit attacks. It traces the pilgrimage of Dorje Rinchen, a seven-year-old boy-monk from a nomad region of eastern Tibet, as he thrusts into manhood, and, through wars, romance and suffering, comes to a confrontation with the One he called Complete Perfection–i.e., ending in his Christian conversion through contact with the missionary Sherab Dzondri (as Ekvall was called). It is dedicated to the memory of his son, David, who was with Ekvall in Saigon in 1942 when he wrote it.]

—(1960). *Faithful Echo.* New York, Twayne Publishers; reprint New Haven, Conn., College and University Press, 1975. Foreword by Arthur H. Dean. [Anecdotes about and principles of interpreting. Reviewed *New York Times,* January 8, 1961, VII, p. 38.]

—(1964). *Religious Observances in Tibet: Patterns and Function.* Chicago and London, University of Chicago Press.

—(1968). *Fields on the Hoof: Nexus of Tibetan Nomadic Pastoralism.* In the series G. and L. Spindler, eds., Case Studies in Cultural Anthropology, New York, Holt, Rinehart and Wilson.

Cassinelli, C.W., and Robert B. Ekvall (1969). *A Tibetan Principality: The Political System of Sa sKya.* Ithaca, N. Y., Cornell University Press.

Thubten Jigme Norbu and Robert B. Ekvall, translators (1969). *The Younger Brother Don yod.* ... Being the Secret Biography, from the Words of the Glorious Lama, the Holy Reverend Blo bZang Ye Shes (*dpal ldan bla ma dam pa rje btsun blo bzang ye shes kyi gsung las gsang ba'i rnam thar bzhugs so//.* Bloomington and London, Indiana University Press.

Ekvall, Robert Brainerd (1979). *The Lama Knows: A Tibetan Legend is Born.* New Delhi, Oxford and IBH. Second edition: Novato CA, Chandler and Sharp, 1981, with introduction by L.L. Langness. [The adventures of Aluk Shiang Cheung, "The Earless One," a lama from nomadic Amdo in ca. the 1930s whose spiritual attainments are matched by political ambitions–an improbable combination of saint and pretender. He was as much at home on a horse with a rifle–or his girl–across the saddle as when sitting, Buddha-like, in meditative trance. The story is told in Ekvall's individual style that evokes the Tibetan thoughts of the protagonist.]

Ekvall, Robert B., and James F. Downs (1987). *Tibetan Pilgrimage.* Tokyo, Institute for the Study of the Languages and Cultures of Asia and Africa.

B. ARTICLES

"Tikpah," *China Journal* (*of Science and Arts*) [Shanghai], vol. 3, 1925, pp. 422-424. [K&I no. 2736]

"The Opportunity in Northeast Tibet," *The Alliance Weekly*, August 27,1927, p. 570f. [Missionary report.]

"Westward Into Tibet," *The Alliance Weekly*, October 15, 1927, p. 681f. [Missionary report.]

"The Call of Far Interior Tibet," *The Alliance Weekly*, October 22, 1927, p. 698f. [Missionary report recording a visit to Ngapa and its king.]

"We Visit the King of Ngawa in Eastern Tibet," *Asia* (*and the Americas*) *Magazine* [New York], vol. 29, 1929, pp. 724-30 and 742-45. [K&.I no. 2737]

"Tibetan Ways," *The Alliance Weekly*, January 28, 1928, p. 58f. [Missionary report.]

"Tibetan Fires," *The Alliance Weekly*, February 18, 1928, p. 104 f. [Missionary report.]

"Tibetan Prayers," *The Alliance Weekly*, March 17, 1928, p. 170f. [Missionary report.]

"Tibetan Doors," *The Alliance Weekly*, April 14, 1928, p. 232f. [Missionary report.]

"Four Years After," *The Alliance Weekly*, July 11, 1931, p. 447f. [Missionary report.]

"The Ever Present Lord," *The Alliance Weekly*, May 6, 1933, pp. 276f. and 286. [Missionary report.]

"A Missionary Statesman," *Alliance Weekly*, in three parts: part 1, vol. 72, May 22, 1937; part 2, July 10, 1937; part 3, August 28, 1937. [Not seen. On A. B. Simpson and his vision of world evangelization?]

"Shadow of the Robber's God," *Asia* (*and the Americas*) *Magazine*, vol. 37, 1937, pp. 439-440. [K&I no. 2738]

"...Haunted House," *Asia* (*and the Americas*) *Magazine*, vol. 38, 1938, pp. 112-113. [K&I no. 2740]

"On the SkorBa Path," *Asia* (*and the Americas*) *Magazine*, vol. 38, 1938, pp. 491-493. [K&.I no. 2741]

"The Pugilism of Jamtzen," *Asia* (*and the Americas*) *Magazine*, vol. 38, 1938, pp. 440-442. [K&I no. 2742]

"Tam-dro Avenges His Father," *Asia (and the Americas) Magazine,* vol. 38, 1938, pp. 551-553. [K&I no. 2743]

"On the Road to Tibet: When the Traveler Jumps off into the Unknown Country Beyond China," *The New York Times,* Sunday, October 16, 1938, X p. 8, col. 4. [Description of traveling conditions among the eastern Tibetan nomads.]

"Tales from the Tibetan Border," *Asia (and the Americas) Magazine,* vol. 40, 1940, pp. 478-480. [K&I no. 2745]

"A Tibetan Hunt," *Asia (and the Americas) Magazine,* vol. 41, 1941, pp. 43-46. [K&I no. 2746]

"Tibet Pilgrim's Progress," *Asia (and the Americas) Magazine,* vol. 42, 1942, pp. 10-14 and 111-114. [K&I no. 2747]

"Culture Comes to Tibetans," *Asia (and the Americas) Magazine,* vol. 44, 1944, pp. 110-114. [K&I no. 2750]

"Five Universals of Tibetan Religious Observance," *Oriens,* vol. 6-2, 1953, pp. 334-343. [K&I no. 2753]

"Some Differences in Tibetan Land Tenure and Utilization," *Sinologica,* vol. 4-1, 1954/56, pp. 39-48. [K&I no. 2755]

"Mi sTong: The Tibetan Custom of Life Indemnity," *Sociologus,* vol. 4-2, 1954, pp. 136-145. [K&I no. 2754]

"Significance of Thirteen as a Symbolic Number in Tibetan and Mongolian Cultures," *Journal of the American Oriental Society,* vol. 79, 1959, pp. 188-192. [K&I no. 2757]

"The Double Role of the Panchen Lama," *Western World,* no. 12, 1959, pp. 41-44.

"Three Categories of Inmates within Tibetan Monasteries: Status and Function," *Central Asiatic Journal,* vol. 5-3, 1959/60, pp. 206-220. [K&I no. 2758]

"Tibetan Culture: in Raja Hutheesing ed., *Tibet Fights for Freedom,* Bombay, Orient Longmans. 1960, pp. i-iv. 1-10. Reprinted in F. Harper, ed., *This is China,* Hong Kong, Dragonfly Books, 1965, pp. 223-251.

"The Nomadic Pattern of Living among the Tibetans as Preparation for War," *American Anthropologist,* Dec., 1961, pp. 1250-1263.

"Historical Sites and Cultural Relics," *Current Scene,* no. 27, Mar. 20, 1962, pp. 1-11. Reprinted in F. Harper, ed., *This is China,* Hong Kong, Dragonfly Books. 1965, pp. 223-251.

"Role of the Interpreter," *The Texas Quarterly,* vol. 5-3, 1962, pp. 193-200.

"Role of the Dog in Tibetan Nomadic Society," *Central Asiatic Journal,* vol. 8-3, Sept. 1963, pp. 163-173. [K&I no. 2761]

"A Note on 'Live Blood' as Food Among the Tibetans," *Man,* no.175, Sept., 1963, pp. 45-46.

"Some Aspects of Divination in Tibetan Society," *Ethnology,* vol. 1-1, 1963, pp. 31-39.

Ekvall, Robert B., and James F. Downs (1963), "Note on Water Utilization and Rule in the Sakya Domain," *Journal of Asian Studies,* vol. 22-3, pp. 293-303. [K&I no. 2760]

"A Seminar on Tibetan Society and Culture," *Current Anthropology,* vol. 4-4, 1963, pp. 368-370.

"A Tibetan Performs the Circumambulation Rite," *Sociologus,* vol. 11-1, 1964, pp. 86-89.

"Law and the Individual among the Tibetan Nomads," *American Anthropologist* vol. 66-5, 1964, pp. 1110-1115. [K&I 2763]

"Peace and War among the Tibetan Nomads," *American Anthropologist,* vol. 66-5, Oct., 1964c, pp. 1119-1148.

James F. Downs and Ekvall, Robert B. (1965), "Animal and Social Types in the Exploitation of the Tibetan Plateau," in Anthony Leeds and Andrew P. Vayda, eds., *Man, Culture and Animals.* Symposium Series no. 78, American Association for the Advancement of Science, Washington, D.C., pp. 169-184.

"Tibetans in Switzerland," *The Tibet Society Newsletter,* vol. 1-2, 1967, pp. 113-117.

"P'iao-Drift," *The Texas Quarterly,* Vol. 12-2, 1969, pp. 22-25.

"Demographic Aspects of Tibetan Nomadic Pastoralism," in Brian Spooner, ed., *Population Growth: Anthropological Implications.* Cambridge, MIT Press, 1972, pp. 269-285.

"The Tibetan Nomad and His Horse," *Coyote's Journal,* no. 10, 1974, pp. 66-83.

"Tibetan Nomadic Pastoralists: Environments, Personality, and Ethos." *Proceedings of the American Philosophical Society,* vol. 118-6 (December), 1974, pp. 519-537.

"Correlation of contradictions: a Tibetan Semantic Device," in

W.C. McCormack and S.A. Wurm, eds., *Language and Thought: Anthropological Issues* (The Hague, 1977), pp. 325-6. Repr. in J.F. Fisher, ed., *Himalayan Anthropology* (The Hague,1978), pp. 251-26.

"The High-Pasturage Ones of Tibet also Grow Old," *Proceedings of the American Philosophical Society,* vol. 124-6, 1980, pp. 429-437.

C. REVIEWS

Review of Allen S. Whiting and Sheng Shih-ts'ai 1958, *Sinkiang: Pawn or Pivot? Journal of Asian Studies,* vol. 18-4, 1959.

Review of David Crockett Graham 1959, *The Customs and Religion of the Ch'iang. Journal of the American Oriental Society,* vol. 79, 1959, pp. 58-61.

Review of Peter Goullard 1959, *Land of the Lamas: Adventures in Secret Tibet. Journal of Asian Studies,* vol. 19, 1960, p. 115.

Review of Humphrey Clarke, tr. 1958, *The Message of Milarepa: New Light upon the Tibetan Way. Journal of Asian Studies,* vol. 19, 1960, pp. 60-61.

Review of Raja Hutheesing ed. 1960, *Tibet Fights For Freedom: A White Book.* review of Frank Moraes 1960, *The Revolt in Tibet; and* review of George N. Patterson 1960, *Tibet in Revolt. The China Quarterly,* no. 4, 1960, pp. 123-126.

Review of Chanakya Sen (pseud. of B. Sen Gupta) 1960, *Tibet Disappears: A Documentary History of Tibet's International Status the Great Rebellion and its Aftermath. Journal of Asian Studies,* vol. 20, 1961, p. 534.

Review of A.K. Gordon 1961, *The Hundred Thousand Songs : Selections from Milarepa, Poet-Saint of Tibet. Journal of Asian Studies,* vol. 20, Nov., 1961, pp. 88-89.

Review of Margaret W. Fisher, L. Rose and R.A. Huttenback 1963, *Himalayan Battleground: Sino-Indian Rivalry in Ladakh. Journal of Asian Studies,* vol. 23, 1964, pp. 313-314.

"Strangers in the Land; Chinese Colonialism in Tibet," review of Nai-min ling ed. 1964, *Tibetan Sourcebook. Current Scene,* vol. 3-11, Jan. 15, 1965, pp. 1-10.

Review of W.D. Shakabpa 1968, *Tibet: A Political History. The Asian Student,* March 30, 1968.

Review of G. Tucci 1967, *Tibet: Land of Snows. Journal of Asian Studies,* vol. 27-4, 1968.

Review of Thubten Jigme Norbu and Colin M. Turnbull 1968, *Tibet, its History, Religion and People. The Asian Student,* May 31, 1969.

Review of Fokke Sierksma 1966, *Tibet's Terrifying Deities: Sex and Agression in Religious Acculturation. Indo-Iranian Journal.* vol. 11-4, 1969, pp. 318-320.

Review of Union Research Institute 1968, *Tibet 1950-1967, The Asian Student,* September 27, 1969.

Review of Samten G. Karmay 1972, *The Treasury of Good Sayings: A Tibetan History of Bon. The Asian Student,* March 3, 1973, pp. 11-12.

Review of Stephen Beyer, *The Cult of Tara: Magic and Ritual in Tibet. The Asian Student,* January 4, 1975, p.12.

Review of Alex Wayman 1973, *The Buddhist Tantras: Light of Indo-Tibetan Esoterism. The Asian Student,* January 4, 1975, p. 12.

NOTES

1. Several accounts of Jäschke's life exist, one by Theodor Bechler (1930), *Heinrich August Jäschke, der geniale Sprachforscher, der Missionary der Brüdergemeine under den Tibetern im westlichen Himalaya, Erste Gabe zur 200. Jahrfeier der Brüdermission am 21. August 1930.* For other references, see J. Aschoff (1992), *Tibet, Nepal und der Kulturraum des Himalaya (mit Ladakh, Sikkim und Bhutan) : Kommentierte Bibliographie deutchsprachiger Bücher und Aufsätze 1627 bis 1990 (Aufsätze bis zum Jahre 1900)* (Dietikon, Garuda-Verlag), no. 955. Among the briefer more recent sketches see for instance John Bray (1983), "Heinrich August Jäschke: Pioneer Tibetan Scholar," *The Tibet Journal* vol, 8-?, pp. 50-55, and John Bray (1998), "The Contribution of the Moravian Mission to Tibetan Language and Literature," *Lungta* [Amnye Machen Institute, Dharamshala] 11, pp. 4-8.
2. For further details on H.A. Francke, see H. Walravens and M. Taube eds. (1992), *August Hermann Francke und die Westgunakata-Mission der Herrnhuter Brüdergemeinde Eine Bibliographie mit Standortnachweisen der tibetischen Druck,* Stuttgard, Steiner. For a bibliography of his works, see M. Hahn (1988), *August Hermann Francke (1870-1930) und sein Beitrag zu Tibetologie.*
3. Two other exceptional missionaries of the twentieth century who published numerous articles or books of scholarly value on the Khams and Amdo borderlands were the American Marion Herbert Duncan (1896-1977), who served for twelve years in Batang in Khams between 1921 and

1935, and the Australian John Huston Edgar (1872-1936) of the China Inland Mission, who was in Dar rtse mdo/Tachienlu or elsewhere on the Marches of Tibet from 1902 to 1936. Duncan's series of books in particular remains a much-underrated resource. See Hallvard Kare KulØy and Yoshiro Imaeda (1986), *Bibliography of Tibetan Studies* (Monograph Series of Naritasan Institute for Buddhist Studies, vol. 2, Narita, Narita Shinshoji), nos. 2539-2552 and 2631-2702. On Edgar's life and contributions, see David Templeman, "J.H. Edgar, an Australian Missionary in theTibetan Marches," *Lungta* 11, pp. 25-33, who based himself in part on Chris Elder, "The Man Who Found Shangri-La: James Edgar Huston [sic]," *New Zealand Journal of East Asian Studies,* vol. 1-2 (Dec. 1993).

4. See my biography of Dezhung Rinpoche, forthcoming from Wisdom Publications, from which this article has been expanded.
5. I am indebted to Arthur Leeper and Gene Smith for sharing their reminiscences of Ekvall.
6. Written sources on Ekvall's colorful life and career include the 'Appreciation' by James F. Downs and S. Iijima (pp. v–x) in the book by Robert B. Ekvall and James F. Downs (1987), *Tibetan Pilgrimage* (Tokyo, Institute for the Study of the Languages and Cultures of Asia and Africa). A biographical sketch by Mike Wyne, "A former missionary in Tibet, U.W. Researcher has 7 careers," appeared in the *Seattle Times,* 22 February 1959, Sunday supplement, p. 8, from which I have drawn a few details. Other details derive from Ekvall's curriculum vitae (C.V.) and other sources including newspaper clippings preserved in the archives of the Christian and Missionary Alliance, Colorado Springs, made available though the kind help of Mike Saunier. Further important data derived from two taped interviews (1979 and 1980) preserved in the archives of the Billy Graham Center, Wheaton, "Interviews with Robert Brainerd Ekvall–Collection 92." A sketch of Ekvall's life also appeared in William Carlsen (1985), *In Search of a Miracle* (Nyack, N.Y., Nyack College). Brief biographical citations are said in Ekvall's curriculum vitae to have appeared in *American Men of Science: The Social and Behavioral Sciences 1968; Who's Who in the West,* 12th edition, 1970-71; *The Writer's Dictionary 1974-1976; Men of Achievement* 1973-74; *The World Who's Who of Authors* 1975; and *The Dictionary of International Biography* 1975.
7. For references to David Ekvall and the Christian and Missionary Alliance, see William S. Martin (1998), "A Bibliographic Essay on American Missionaries to the Tibetans prior to 1950," in Jamyang Norbu ed., Christian Missionaries and Tibet, *Lungta* [Journal of the Amnye Machen Institute, McLeod Ganj, Dharamsala], no. 11 (Winter 1998), p. 14. See also R. Ekvall (1938), his history of this mission. Several of Ekvall's uncles, aunts and cousins were also missionaries.
8. Ekvall's life during this period is to some extent recorded in his travel memoirs *Tibetan Skylines* (London: 1952) and in his ethnographic novel *Tents Against the Sky* (New York: 1955).
9. P, Nietupski (1999), *Labrang: A Tibetan Buddhist Monastery at the Crossroads of Four Civilizations* (Ithaca, N.Y., Snow Lion Publications), p. 86-88, referring to sources including private correspondence from Ekvall, describes vividly the difficulties faced at this time by missionaries in Amdo, all of whom were forced to leave China in 1927.

10. Valrae Reynolds (1978), *Tibet a Lost World: The Newark Museum Collection of Tibetan Art and Ethnography* (New York, The American Federation of Arts), p. 13.
11. R. Ekvall's book *Tibetan Sky Lines* (1952) is a fascinating partly fictionalized account of his experiences during the years 1930-1935.
12. Living and traveling in the eastern Tibetan borderlands was dangerous in all periods, and no less so in the first half of the 20th century. Several missionaries were killed or threatened with death. Robert Ekvall's cousin Henry Ekvall was killed by bandits or renegade Chinese soldiers in 1932, as reported in the *New York Times* of that year.
13. Ekvall's joining and leaving the O.S.S. is recounted in R. Ekvall (1960), p. 29.
14. For some anecdotes about this period, see Ekvall (1960), pp. 29-34.
15. General Wedemeyer knew Brooke Dolan and Ilya Tolstoy, who traveled to Tibet in 1942 for the OSS. He published in 1958 his memoirs: *Wedemeyer Reports!*
16. R. Ekvall (1960), p. 37.
17. Ibid., p. 39.
18. Arthur Leeper, communication of June 25, 2002.
19. According to Arthur Leeper, communication of 25 June 2002, Ekvall had contact at this time in China with Rewi Alley, the New Zealander "foreign friend" who survived the transition to the PRC and became a noted author and pundit in Beijing.
20. George N. Patterson (1959), *Tragic Destiny,* pp. 85 and 90, mentions recommending "Colonel Robert Ekvall, a former missionary to Tibet," to help Norbu in the U.S.A. The Committee for Free Asia is described by Patterson, *ibid.*, as a "non-communist organization of businessmen."
21. This committee and its continuation after 1954, the Asia Foundation, are suspected to have received some funding from clandestine governmental organizations such as the CIA during the 1950s and 1960s, channeled through innocuous-sounding trusts. It produced a weekly publication called *The Asian Student* [San Francisco] during the academic year for sixteen years (1952-1978) as a service to Asian students in the U.S., edited by C.Y. Hsu. Ekvall contributed six brief book reviews to *The Asian Student* between 1968 and 1975.
22. Ekvall was assisted on this project by another American ex-missionary with great Tibetan expertise, Marion Duncan.
23. Thubten Jigme Norbu (1960), *Tibet is My Country, The Autobiography of Thubten Jigme Norbu, Brother of the Dalai Lama;* as told to Heinrich Harrer (London, Rupert Hart-Davis, 1960 and New York, 1961; reprint London, Wisdom, 1986, with postscript), tells the story of his escape from Amdo and Tibet. The help given Norbu by high levels of the U.S. State Department through their consulate in Calcutta is recorded in M. Goldstein (1989), *A History of Modern Tibet, 1913-1951* (Berkeley, University of California Press), p. 785. Thubten Jigme Norbu (1986), p. 259, records that already while still in Lhasa he had written his Mongolian friend from his early Kumbum years, Dilowa Hutuktu (1883-1965, who had left Peking for the U.S.A. in 1947), asking his advice on how best to come quickly to the U.S.A. Dilowa Hutuktu, who himself had been sponsored by an American businessman, replied by mail that he would try to help

arrange an invitation through American friends.

24. M. Goldstein (1989), p. 779, records the request given on 26 May by Shakabpa to American diplomats in India to facilitate Norbu's visit to the U.S.A., expressing this as the wish of the Dalai Lama himself.
25. The arrival of Taktser Rinpoche in the U.S.A. was reported in the *New York Times,* July 9, 1951, p. 8, col. 3: "Dalai Lama's Brother Taktser Rimpoche in U. S. to Study."
26. Thubten Jigme Norbu (1986), p. 253f. An interview from this period appeared in the *New York Times,* August 2, 1951, p. 4, col. 6: "Dalai Lama's brother interviewed at Virginia retreat, dislikes Chinese Communists, silent on brother's views." Six weeks later the visit of his younger brother is reported: "Dalai Lama's brother Gyalo Thondup to study in US," *New York Times,* Sept. 13, 1951, p. 10, col. 2.
27. Ekvall and Norbu's presence in Berkeley is mention in Ekvall (1960), p. 21. In Berkeley, Norbu met and befriended Prof. Lessing. By early July, 1952, Norbu left to attend the World Buddhist Conference in Tokyo, which opened in mid July, as reported in the *New York Times* of July 20, 1952, p. 65, col. 4. While in Japan his Indian travel documents lapsed. He was forced to remain in Japan until summer, 1955, when he received political asylum in America and sponsorship from the World Church Services (*New York Times,* Aug. 16, 1955, p. 3, col. 1; Oct. 5, 1955, p. 5, col. 1). He visited India again in autumn 1956 at the time of the Buddha Jayanti celebrating 2,500 years since the Buddha's birth, at which time the Dalai Lama also came. According to Tsering Shakya (2000), *The Dragon in the Land of Snows: A History of Modern Tibet Since 1947* (New York, Penguin Compass), p. 171, Thubten Jigme Norbu in India in autumn 1956–spring 1957 helped the CIA begin recruiting Tibetans who were to be trained in guerrilla warfare. A small number of fighters were later parachuted back into Tibet, though these CIA efforts resulted in nothing.
28. *Book Review Digest 1952* (New York, H.W. Wilson Co.), p. 281, lists 14 reviews of *Tibetan Sky Lines,* the longest by R.C. Andrews in the *New York Herald Tribune Book Review,* June 22, 1952, p. 3.
29. Ekvall relates the fascinating story of his experiences at this time in his book *The Faithful Echo* (New York: 1960). According to A. Leeper, communication of 7 July 2002, Ekvall later related how during his post Korean-War translation stint he met one Chinese Long-March veteran who spoke at length about his horrible experiences while struggling through Kham in Eastern Tibet, being hounded and picked off mercilessly by the local people a treatment that none of the survivors ever forgot. Ekvall remarked, "Who can say what effect that incident had on later Chinese treatment of Tibet and Tibetans?" Mike Wyne (1959) also recorded Ekvall's remarks on the Long–March incident.
30. The *Book Review Digest* 1955, p. 281, lists only two reviews of *Tents against the Sky,* including one by Peter Gervine in the *New York Herald Tribune Book Review,* July 10, 1955, p. 8,
31. In Robert B. Ekvall and James F. Downs (1987), p. 4, James Downs states that Ekvall was chairman of the Inner Asia Research Project from 1958 until being relieved of administrative responsibilities to devote himself fully to research [in ca. 1960]. In surviving correspondence

from this period, Ekvall signs himself as chairman of the project. See U. W. Archives, W.U. Inner Asia Colloquium, acc. no. 85-42, box 1, general correspondence, Ekvall. His occupying this position in 1958-1959 is also mentioned in the contemporaneous biographical sketch by Mike Wyne in the *Seattle Times,* February 22. 1959. Sunday supplement. p. 8.

32. Mike Wyne (1959), "A former missionary in Tibet, U. W. Researcher has 7 careers."
33. Both Ekvall and Wylie had attended the first conference on Tibetan studies in the U.S. held at the office of the Rockefeller Foundation. New York City, on September 22-23, 1959. It was proposed that both conduct a survey of the current situation in South Asia. The first Bellagio meeting was held October 24-25, 1959. An article in the *New York Times* (May 15, 1960, p. 119. col. 5) reported that the Rockefeller Foundation had made a grant of $250,000 to bring Tibetan refugee scholars to the U.S. and to foreign centers, to contribute to 'Western understanding of their unusual country and its culture.' Before the founding of the National Endowment for the Humanities in the mid-1960s, the Rockefeller and Ford foundations were the two main sources for funding such projects.
34. John Reynolds, interview, Fagernes. September 1992.
35. It is said that Franz Michael, then second only to George Taylor in the Far Eastern and Russian Institute and the author of political studies, had also wanted to do the job, but had not been able to go to India.
36. R. Ekvall (1938), p. 169f.; (1939), pp. 20-22; and (1946), pp. 10ff., 19ff., and 28ff.
37. Arthur Leeper, communication of 25 June 2002, Ekvall spoke admiringly of Dezhung Rinpoche as showing the strength of the Tibetan system of recognizing Tulkus, as someone who stood so far above the average in his character and ability that he had been retroactively "discovered." Ekvall's respect did not extend to Tibetans of another type: lamas by title or repute who lacked real substance.
38. R. Ekvall and James F. Downs (1987). p. 7.
39. Thubten Jigme Norbu's arrival was reported in the *Seattle Times* of January 11, 1961, p. 5.
40. Thubten Jigme Norbu was generally believed to have been the first Tibetan to set eyes on North America when he arrived in July, 1951, but he was not the first to establish permanent residence there. According to Thubten Samphel. "Tibetans in New York: Life between Two Cultures," *Tibetan Review,* vol. 14 no. 12 (Dec. 1989). p. 11: "The first Tibetan to immigrate to America is Tenki Tentuf Davis, who studied medicine at Columbia University. She came to the U.S. in 1951. She's now [1989] the director of a medical establishment in northern California. Tenki Tentuf is the granddaughter of S.W. Laden La, who organized the Tibetan police force in Lhasa in 1923." See also Ernest Dale, "Tibetan Immigration into the United States," *Tibet Society Bulletin* (*Bloomington*). no. 3 (1969), pp. 42-45. I am informed by A. Leeper that some Tibetans were brought to the U.S.A. for a visit four or five decades earlier by William Rockhill.
41. See also Downs and Iijima. "Appreciation," in Ekvall and Downs (1987), p. ix: "[Ekvall's] relations with the academic world were not always as smooth as he hoped they might be. In a field such as Asian Studies

based in no small part on the detached and meticulous reading of classical texts in little-known languages, his complete and flamboyantly demonstrated fluency in [spoken] Chinese and Tibetan was not always appreciated. There is no doubt that his development of a romanization system for Tibetan based on the spoken language did not meet with the approval [of] many scholars who spoke the language poorly, if at all. His interpretations of events in both China and Tibet based as they were on a life of observation and interaction did not always correspond to those of some of his more academically oriented colleagues."

42. For more details on Wylie's life and works, see the biographical sketch in the introduction to L. Epstein and R. Sherburne. eds., *Reflections on Tibetan Culture: Essays in Memory of Turrell V. Wylie* (Lewiston: Edwin Mellen Press, 1990), pp. ix-xiii. See also the similar obituary by R.A. Miller in the *Journal of the International Association of Buddhist Studies.* vol. 9-1 (1986). pp. 150-155, Brief biographical sketches of Wylie and most other U.W. professors in this period are found in the *Directory of American Scholars: A Biographical Directory* (4th edition, New York. R. R. Bowker, 1964).
43. Robert B. Ekvall and James F. Downs (1987), p. 4, state that Ekvall had acted as chairman of the Inner Asia Research Project from 1958 until he devoted himself more fully to research with the Tibetans.
44. Downs and Iijima in their "Appreciation," in Ekvall and Downs (1987), p. vi, refer to this without mentioning names: "[Ekvall's] efforts to produce [the book] *Cultural Relations* [*on the Kansu-Tibetan Border* (Chicago: 1939)] diverted him from his formal studies, and his goal of an advanced degree was not realized. In future years this would prove a handicap in dealing with some of the more hidebound academics who put greater faith in certification than they did in proven merit,"
45. See also T.V. Wylie's review article on Ekvall (1964). "A Propos of Tibetan Religious Observances." *Journal of the American Oriental Society* vol. 86-1 (1966). pp. 39-45, which concl uded with Wylie's regrets that Ekvall had not limited himself to an ethnographic description of the religious observances followed by the nomads he knew best. Wylie published another negative review in the *Journal of Religion*, vol. 45 (April 1965), p. 172. according to *Book Review Digest 1965,* Ekvall's book was also reviewed by E. Conze (*Further Buddhist Studies,* Oxford, 1975, p. 212), A. Bharati (*Central Asiatic Journal,* vol. 11, pp. 154-157), and Ingebord Woodcock (*Pacific Affairs,* vol. 38, Spring 1965, p. 73). The anthropologist Bharati (who had known Ekvall in Seattle in the late 1950s and early 1960s) faulted many of Ekvall's generalizations and interpretations, but considered the book very important and perhaps indispensable. Conze, the Buddhist scholar, was less positive overall.
46. Later, on May 23, 1969, Wylie was appointed chairman of the department of Asian Languages and Literature, to succeed George Taylor. This was reported in the *Seattle Times,* p. 6.
47. Melvyn Goldstein married Chunden Surkhang in Seattle on December 7. 1962, as reported in a *Seattle Times* front-page article by Julie Emery (December 10, 1962). The arrival of Chunden Surkhang (niece of the Surkhang cabinet minister) in Seattle in June 1961 from Cottey College, Nevada, Missouri, where she had been studying was reported in a *Seattle*

Times article dated June 7, 1961, p. 3. She was to assist in the research project in summer 1961.

48. Judging by the important criterion of taxation, Sakya was indeed independent of the Lhasa government, and I could not find its territories listed in the verification of tax registers *lCags stag zhib gzhung,* The anomalous "independent" status of Sakya was reported already by I. Desideri in the early 18th century and by G. Tucci in an article of 1940; see Cassinelli and Ekvall 1969. p. 44, n. 11. (In several other respects Sakya was also clearly a dependency of Lhasa, as Ekvall's Sakya informants acknowledged.) Presumably Goldstein rejected some other proofs of "independence" advanced by Ekvall.
49. Some of Ekvall's critics went further, maintaining that his "seminar" did not really exist in the way he had described it to other anthropologists. Most of his dealings and information gathering were done, they said, on an informal person-to-person basis. L. Epstein 1993 commented in retrospect: "There was too much money around in those days. A lot was wasted. The only ones who were really learning anything were Gene Smith and Mel Goldstein." A *Seattle Times* article of October 29, 1961, p. 20, reported that grants then totaled "some $150.000."
50. A mimeographed letter dated February 26, 1962, from Kenneth E. Read, one of the senior anthropologists at the university, to George Taylor (in U.W. Inner Asia Colloquium. acc. no. 85-42. general correspondence, miscellaneous) addressed the subject: "Anthropological research with members of the Tibetan group resident in Seattle, a collective opinion." Here Read stated that "culture at a distance" studies had largely fallen out of use after the war. He stressed the need for specialists who were conversant with the literary tradition and history. Ekvall could not, of course, claim to be a specialist in either field.
51. E. Gene Smith, communication of June 20, 2002.
52. M. Goldstein, letter of February 21, 1995. In Goldstein's opinion (ibid.): "There was no way to tease out [of their book] what is really Lhasa, what is hyperbole and what is correct."
53. M. Goldstein, letter of February 21, 1995.
54. George Taylor was born in Coventry, England, in 1905 but later became a U.S. citizen. He spent several years in China as a university professor in the 1930s and joined the University of Washington in 1939 as professor of Far Eastern history and political science and as executive officer of the Far Eastern department. During World War II he served for three years as deputy director for the Pacific area, U.S. Office of War Information. From 1946 onward he was chairman of the department of Far Eastern and Slavic languages and literature and director of the Far Eastern and Russian Institute.
55. M. Goldstein, letter of February 21, 1995. This professor was evidently Dan Fenno Henderson (b. Chelan, Wash., 1921: d. March 24, 2001), who from 1961 was professor of law and director of the Asian law program, School of Law, University of Washington. Henderson's main interest was in Japanese law, a field in which he later distinguished himself. He did go on to publish the article "Settlement of homicide disputes in Sakya (Tibet)," *American Anthropologist,* vol. 64 (Oct. 1964), pp. 1099-1105. Henderson had a military-intelligence background like Ekvall: he

served as a Lieutenant in the U.S. Army Intelligence Corps from 1943-1945, and from 1945-1947 was Japanese Language Officer censoring movies and broadcasts for General McArthur in Tokyo. From 1949-1955 he taught political science at Berkeley, before practicing law in California and Japan.

56. The reviews of this book included one by Owen Lattimore, *American Historical Review*, vol. 75, p. 570; and by Luciano Petech, *Pacific Affairs*, vol. 42 (winter 1969-70), p. 512.
57. The revival of Ekvall's "seminar" is mentioned in the introduction to Robert Ekvall and James F. Downs (1987).
58. Ibid., p. 11.
59. E. Gene Smith, conversation of June 20, 2002.
60. R. Ekvall (1968), pp. ix-x. See also R. Ekvall (1967), "Tibetans in Switzerland, "*The Tibet Society Newsletter*," vol. 1, no. 2, pp. 113-117.
61. Arthur Leeper, communication of June 25, 2002.
62. Darrell Houston, "Seattle's China Watcher," *The Seattle Times*, Magazine, May 7, 1972, p. 8f.
63. One such offprint was given to the author a few minutes later by Dezhung Rinpoche with the remark, "You can use this more than I can."
64. Arthur Leeper, communication of June 25, 2002.
65. Arthur Leeper, communication of June 25, 2002. Leeper perceived Ekvall's beliefs as seemingly not incompatible with Leeper's own liberal and humanist values. Ekvall's unpublished writings are probably the best sources on his beliefs at this stage of his life.
66. "The High-Pasturage Ones of Tibet also Grow Old," *Proceedings of the American Philosophical Society*, vol. 124-6 (1980), pp. 429-437.
67. Arthur Leeper, personal communication, June 18, 2002. A year before his death when he could no longer read, Ekvall gave his library to Leeper, instead of donating them to the local Enumclaw library. Some missionary-related material was donated by Leeper to the Newark Museum.
68. Arthur Leeper, communication of June 25, 2002.
69. See also the recent positive evaluation of R.B. Ekvall by John Bray (1997). "Das Tibetbild der Missionare im 19. und frühen 20. Jahrhundert," in Thierry Dodin and Heinz Räther eds. *Mythos Tibet: Wahrnehmungen, Projektionen, Phantasien* (Köln, Dumont), p. 45f.
70. Review of *Tibetan Sky Lines* in the *San Francisco Chronicle*, August 24, 1952, p. 22.
71. David Woodward (1991), "Examining a Significant Minority: Tibetan Christians," *Tibet Journal*, vol. 16-4, p. 64. One unpublished work was entitled "Tibetan religion as perceived by a missionary." It would be interesting to know the titles and length of the other unpublished manuscripts, and where they survive.
72. My thanks to Brian Wiggins at the Christian and Missionary Alliance national archives in Colorado Springs for locating and sending me these articles. Valrae Reynolds in Newark kindly shared a clipping of the 1938 article in the *New York Times*. The *New York Times* name index does not list Robert Ekvall in this period, though he may have published another article that same year: "[Tibetan] Nomad's life described," NYT, July 10, 1938, X, p. 11, col. 2.

XI

VEDĀNTA AND MĪMĀṂSĀ

CHAPTER 41

Bhāskara's Refutation of *Jīvanmukti*

LALITA DEODHAR

Indian philosophy has considered emancipation as the ultimate goal of human life and, therefore, it has emphasized various means to attain this goal. As such, among four aims of a person, viz. *dharma, artha, kāma* and *mokṣa,* the last one has acquired prime importance in *Vedānta* literature. In *Upaniṣads* also, the philosophers like Yājñavalkya, Naciketas, Jābāla have expressed earnest desire to attain immortality which is nothing else than realization of Brahman, the ultimate reality. Various systems of Indian philosophy have unanimously agreed with the nature of liberation; it is the final release of a person from this transmigratory existence after the bond of ignorance is removed by means of knowledge of the highest reality. Upaniṣadic literature has dealt with this topic very lucidly.

Indian tradition accepts that when a person realizes the true nature of the highest reality as all this is Brahman itself he becomes aware of the unity of the supreme soul and the embodied self. This self-realization can be possible in this very life, i.e. even before the death—this is *jīvanmukti* 'liberation in this life'. This concept became very much popular in *Vedānta* literature.

Bādarāyaṇa has composed the *Brahmasūtra* in order to establish the consequence among the statements of *Upaniṣads.* Eminent *ācāryas* of various systems of philosophy framed stand-points on the basis of the *Upaniṣads* and seeking the scriptural support wrote commentaries on the *Brahmasūtras* in accordance with their view-points. Śaṅkara advocated purely philosophical view apart from all theological considerations. According to Śaṅkara 'I'ness or ego of an embodied self is superimposition of worldly notions, such as body, attributes etc. on the soul. It signifies ignorance. Though, in reality, embodied self is not distinct from soul, ignorance causes the notion of diversity. Knowledge of the ultimate reality leads to the experience of unity setting aside the obstacle in the form of ignorance. Self-realization is, however, possible in this life itself. In this case the self achieves liberation even though the body exists. Therefore, it is called *jīvanmukti*. In ordinary life, the embodied self remains undetached from the world. He is bound with the notions of ego, agency, enjoyment; but in the state of *jīvanmukti*, though the enlightened self performs the same activities the motivation behind them changes, he becomes indifferent towards his surroundings. Advaita *Vedānta* advocates that self-realization causes destruction of the actions which are accumulated in number of births but the *prārabdha* actions, i.e. the actions which have started giving their results come to an end only after that process of enjoyment is complete. So the existing body continues till these actions give their effects.

The state of *jīvanmukti* is frequently described in *Upaniṣads*. Śaṅkara, while stating the characteristics of an enlightened person, has elaborately explained, in various places, the concept of *jīvanmukti*.

Bhāskara, who flourished in the 9th century A.D., i.e. shortly after Śaṅkara, has boldly attempted to oppose the recognized authority of Śaṅkara, on many issues. Bhāskara in his commentary on *Brahmasūtras*[1] has frequently mentioned the views of Śaṅkara and expressing difference of opinion he has contradicted Śaṅkara. Bhāskara is the follower of the theory of *Bhedābheda* (unity in diversity) and strongly advocates the combination of knowledge and action as the means of escaping from the transmigration. He states–*vedāntavākyaireva jñānasahakāritayā nityakarmopadeśāt tametaṃ vedānuvacaneneti/ tataścātmajñānādhikṛtasya karmabhirvināpavargānupapatteḥ jñānena karma samuccīyate* / (p. 16, *ll.* 21-22, on i.1.4)

While commenting on the *Brahmasūtra* (iii.4.26), *sarvāpekṣā ca yajñādiśruteraśvavat,* Bhāskara contradicts the views of Śaṅkara on the theory *jīvanmukti.* In the commentary on this sūtra Bhāskara quotes the Upaniṣadic statement[2]—*tametaṃ vedānuvacanena brāhmaṇā vividiṣanti yajñena dānena tapasānāśakena* and argues that this statement clearly enjoins the necessity of actions for realization of Brahman.

According to the monism advocated by Śaṅkara, knowledge is one and the only means of liberation. Therefore, the *jīvanmukta* who has attained self-realization need not continue to observe the path of activity; on the contrary he should renounce all the actions enjoined by the scriptures.

In the opinion of Bhāskara actions are absolutely necessary in every aspect of life. A person should necessarily perform actions enjoined by the Vedas. Also it is not possible to renounce all actions till the body exists. The body of the person is the result of his actions in previous births and even though he attains knowledge of the supreme soul his bodily state continues till the annihilation of his *prārabdha* actions. So embodiment is the characteristic feature of the self in this phenomenal world and embodied self cannot be totally released without leaving this limitation. Thus one is forced to conclude that liberation is not possible without giving up the body. When the enjoyment of the *prārabdha* actions comes to an end the necessity of body vanishes. Death releases the self from body and it is liberated.[3] This state is called as *videhamukti.*

Bhāskara is the first Indian philosopher who advocates *videhamukti* by refuting *jīvanmukti.* Bhāskara honours the opinion of Śaṅkara[4] that enlightened person is not tainted by any defilement caused by actions; but all the same opposes Śaṅkara's theory of renunciation of actions in the case of a knower. He considers that knowledge and action are not mutually contradicted,[5] therefore there is no question of renouncing actions after attaining self-realization. As a knower observes *śama, dama* etc. he should also perform the duties enjoined to him by the order of life. He clearly states—*na ca jñānasvarūpotpattau karma vyāpriyate śravaṇamananādi tadutpattikārakam/ tasmādyathaiva śamādayo yāvajjīvamanuvartante viduṣāmapavargaye tathāśramakarmāṇīti nāntarāle parityāgaḥ/* (p. 207, *ll.* 23-26, on iii.4.26). He further states—*api ca bhedadarśanāpagamāt karmatyāgācca muktimicchato muktireva na sidhyeta dhriyamāṇaśarīrasyobhayoravaśyaṃbhāvāt* (p. 209, *ll.* 5-7, on iii.4.26). Bhāskara objects the theory of renunciation of action mainly because Śaṅkara has not prescribed abandonment of all actions for *jīvanmukta*. Śaṅkara feels that mental activities such as *manana, nididhyāsana* are very much necessary. Also he has not asked to give up activities like going for alms etc. which are essential for the sustenance of a body. He seeks to renounce only those actions which are prescribed by the scriptures. Thus Bhāskara thinks that Śaṅkara follows *ardhajaratīnyāya* by asking renunciation of some actions and observance of some at the same time.[6] He has raised an objection that what is the harm in performing actions enjoined by the scriptures if a person is doing all the worldly activities. So he concludes—*sarvakarmatyāgasya ca mithyāsaṃkalpatvāt* (p. 206, *l.* 15, on iii.4.26).

In the discussion of such partial renunciation Bhāskara feels necessary to clarify some of his doubts.[7] Sarcastically he puts forth an argument that if in the state of *jīvanmukti*, an enlightened person becomes one with Brahman, what, indeed, is the necessity of going for alms to sustain the body; for Brahman is bodiless, is free from all attachments, nevertheless it is motivated by latent desires. The Upaniṣadic statement,[8] viz. *aśanāyāpipāse śokaṃ mohaṃ jarā mṛyumatyeti* expresses the same idea. Bhāskara argues that bodily impressions such as hunger, thrust should cease to exist in the case of *jīvanmukta* who is united with Brahman. If these impressions continue to exist, it is very much clear that he has not achieved unity in its true sense. Therefore, in the state of self-realization also an enlightened person cannot renounce mental as well as bodily activities. Bhāskara remarks—*parivrājakasya śaucācamanasnānabhikṣātanādikarma kāyikaṃ vācikaṃ mānasaṃ taccāparihāryaṃ dhriyamāṇaśarīrasyeti na kasyacinmuktiḥ syāt/ tasmāt sarveṣāṃ yathāyogaṃ brahmaniṣṭhatāparyaṃ tanniṣthatocyate na vyāpārāntaroparamam/* (*p.* 206, *ll.* 4-7, on iii.4.26).

Bhāskara is, thus, very firm about his views that knowledge alone cannot lead a person to liberation. The combination of knowledge and action is the only means for achievement of one's ultimate goal, as the actionless condition is not possible in this phenomenal world. Body is a *upādhi*. It distinguishes *jīva* from Brahman. It enforces modifications like birth, death etc. for *jīva*. When a self is delimited by body the natural awareness of non-descrimination is concealed—this is the very nature of ignorance. Knowledge destroys ignorance but it cannot remove the distinction which is the result of *upādhis*, important characteristics of phenomenal world. Modifications caused by *upādhis*, and their impressions cannot be terminated till the *upādhi* of body exists. Thus, though a person possesses self-realization he is not liberated as his body continues to exist; it is, according to Bhāskara, an obstruction for absolute unity. The notion of distinction automatically disappears as the body destroys and only then, complete oneness, devoid of any distraction and limitations is possible. Hence Bhāskara concludes—*ato jīvadavasthāyāṃ na mokṣo muktyupāyabhūtaṃ jñānakarma cānuṣṭheyaṃ* (*p*. 210, *ll*. 10-11, on iii.4.26).

Two widely distinct stand-points of Śaṅkara and Bhāskara are flashed explicitly in their discussion of *jīvanmukti* and *videhamukti* respectively. Both of them have no differences as regards the nature of emancipation. The contradiction, however, comes in respect of time as well as the status at the time of liberation. The phenomena of body proves to be the point of dispute. Śaṅkara approves the existence of body in the case of liberation whereas Bhāskara rejects it. Śaṅkara considers self-realization as an inward experience; it is cognition irrespective of bodily element. But Bhāskara's stand-point is more logical and theoretical. He accepts mental progression in the process of self-realization but he feels that in the bodily status a person cannot achieve absolute independence. Bhāskara treats liberation as being completely free from all sorts of limitations. When a person gets rid of body there remains no obstacle for liberation. So Bhāskara's notion of *videhamukti* is perfect liberation in its true sense.

The credit of elaborate treatment to the concept of *videhamukti* goes to the commentary of Bhāskara on *Brahmasūtras*. His later works, viz. commentary on *Bhagavadgītā* etc. reflect the same views. Following Bhāskara the later systems of Indian philosophy, like Viśiṣṭādvaita, Dvaita etc. also have adhered *videhamukti*. This very fact, no doubt, signifies the greatness of Bhāskara.

NOTES

1. *Brahmasūtrabhāṣyam* (*Brahmasūtra* with a Commentary by Bhāskarācārya). (ed.) Pandit Vidyesvarī Prasāda Dvivedin, Benares: Chowkhamba Sanskrit Series, nos. 70, 185 & 209, 1915.

2. *Bṛhadāraṇyakopaniṣad* 4.4.22.
3. *pretya viśeṣasaṃjñā nivartate muktaḥ paramātmā bhavati* (p. 84, *l.* 10, on i.4.22)
4. *jñānasyaitatsāmarthyaṃ yat jīve karma kurvati viduṣi na lepo bhavati* (p. 204, *l.* 1, on iv.1.14)
5. *na ca virodhātkarmatyāgaḥ* (p. 209, *ll.* 4-5, on iii.4.26)
6. *tasmādyāvadidaṃ me śarīramiti karmanibandhanāvṛttiranuvartate tāvadāśramakarmānuvṛttiraśakyā nivārayituṃ śāstraśaraṇena tiṣṭhatā* (p. 210, *ll.* 1-2, on iii.4.26)
7. p. 209, *ll.* 10-14, on iii.4.26)
8. *Bṛhadāraṇyakopaniṣad* 3.5.1.

CHAPTER 42

Rāmānuja's Theory of Three *Yogas*: The Way to *Mokṣa*

BUNKI KIMURA

I. "*From What*" and "*For What*"

In religious salvation, as Max Weber points out, one wishes to be saved from one state in the actual world, which is experienced as specifically "meaningless," for another state, which is regarded as "meaningful." This, however, depends on one's image of the world. He describes, furthermore, that the content of the striving for salvation will be different depending on "from what" and "for what" one wishes to escape.[1]

In Hinduism, especially in the ancient and medieval times, *saṃsāra* was regarded as the state from which one wished to be saved, and *mokṣa* as the state for which one wished to be saved. The meanings of "*saṃsāra*" and "*mokṣa,*" however, were not always fixed. They have changed as the times have changed and were interpreted differently by the leading masters of each school of Hinduism. In the 8th century, for example, Śaṅkara defines *saṃsāra* as the non-real state caused by the nescience, *avidyā,* and *mokṣa* as the only real state awakened by the knowledge, *vidyā.* We can say that Śaṅkara claims salvation from the realm of *avidyā* for the realm of *vidyā.*

Rāmānuja, in the 11th-12th centuries, agrees with Śaṅkara's

framework of salvation, but he insists on the reality not only of *mokṣa* but also of *saṃsāra,* both of which are created and ruled by the Supreme God, *Nārāyaṇa.* People in a state of *mokṣa,* according to Rāmānuja, blissfully enjoy eternity in Heaven by the infinite grace of God, while people in a state of *saṃsāra* experience a great deal of suffering in their mortal lives because of their ignorance of the greatness of God. He declares salvation from the earthly world filled with *avidyā* for a heavenly world attained with *vidyā.*

For the attainment of *mokṣa,* Hindu saints looked for and practiced several types of effective means based on the *Veda.* Since the 7th or 8th century, however, the *Bhagavadgītā* (abbr. Gītā) has been practically made as the principal source for the means for *mokṣa.* Gītā proposes three means: *Karma-yoga, Jñāna-yoga* and *Bhakti-yoga.* Masters have tried to explain the contents of these three types of *yoga* and the relation among them, which are not clearly explained in Gītā, and to formulate a system for the means for *mokṣa* on the basis of their images of both the world and the salvation "from what" and "for what."

Śaṅkara adopts only *Jñāna-yoga,* which is, according to him, the acquisition of knowledge, *vidyā,* as the direct means for *mokṣa,* and considers *Karma-yoga* to be subordinate to *Jñāna-yoga.* He ignores *Bhakti-yoga* because he does not acknowledge the reality of God to whom one devotes *bhakti.* Rāmānuja, on the other hand, explains the relationship among the three types of *yoga* by citing the following passage of Yāmuna: "[*Mokṣa* is] to be attained by the exclusive and excessive *Bhakti-yoga* of one whose inner faculty has been trained by both." He interprets the latter half of this passage as "of one whose internal organ has been purified by *Jñāna-yoga* and *Karma-yoga.*"[2] There is a suggestion here that Rāmānuja regards *Bhakti-yoga,* which he identifies with knowledge, *vidyā,* as the direct means, and considers *Karma-yoga* and *Jñāna-yoga* to be indispensable.

The purpose of this paper is to consider what function each *yoga* fulfills in the view of Rāmānuja. That is to say, "from what" and "for what" these three types of *yoga* respectively take one. This paper will also clarify which state Rāmānuja regards as meaningless and which state as meaningful. Our discussion will mainly rely on his three major works: the *Vedārthasaṃgraha,* the *Śrībhāṣya* and the *Bhagavadgītābhāṣya.*

II. *Karma-yoga*

A. *Renunciation of Earthly Concerns and Self-reliance*

Rāmānuja suggests one of the functions of *Karma-yoga* in the following passage:

> For the sake of producing that (knowledge), even the duties of *āśramas* (*āśramakarman*) have to undoubtedly be performed every day. Otherwise, the duties of *āśramas* being omitted, one, whose internal organ is soiled, will not have the origination of knowledge at all.[3]

We can say that the phrase "the duties of *āśramas*" means *Karma-yoga* because the passage of Yāmuna quoted above shows us that the internal organ is purified by *Karma-yoga*. It is, if true, likely that the activities performed as *Karma-yoga* are not special ones. This assumption is supported by the following passage of Rāmānuja.

> In any case, that is, both when they are meant for [the origination of] *vidyā* and when they are meant for [the observance of the duties of] *āśrama*, it is to be understood that the sacrifices and other activities are the same. There is no difference in the essential nature of the activities.[4]

It is not the contents of the activities themselves but the mental attitude of the person that distinguishes the activities of *Karma-yoga* from activities in general. To put it more clearly, these activities are changed into *Karma-yoga* by the mental renunciation of three things: the agency of the activity, the sense of possession of the activity and the fruits of the activity. Rāmānuja says:

> The [temporal] fruits of activities are obtained, after the performance of the activities, by those [who perform them] without the renunciation (*tyāga*) of the agency (*kartṛtva*), the sense of possession (*mamatā*) and the fruits (*phala*). ... But there are no fruits at all except *mokṣa* for those who have renounced the agency and others.[5]

He explains the grounds for the requirement of the renunciation in *Karma-yoga*:

> Now is taught the necessity for the performance of activities

> after attributing the agency, due to the *guṇas*, to God, who is the Supreme Person being the Soul of all, by showing that the essential nature of the *ātmans*, on account of their constituting the Body (*śarīra*) of the Supreme Person, is subservient to Him.[6]

It is clear from this passage that the renunciation of the agency, which is described as the attribution of it to God, is required because of the subservience of the *ātman* to Him. In other words, it is not the *ātman* but God as the Soul of all who really performs every activity, even though it apparently seems to be done by the *ātman.* "Therefore," says Rāmānuja, "there arises the renunciation of the sense of possession of both the fruits and the activities."[7]

What has to be noticed is that Rāmānuja never suggests renouncing the performance of activities. He asserts the necessity of the abandonment of desire and attachment to everything but God, and, as the basis of that, the necessity for the recognition of the relation between the *ātman* and God, which is compared to the relation between the body and soul (*śarīra-ātma-bhāva*) and the relation between the subordinate and principal (*śeṣa-śeṣi-bhāva*). To sum it up, practicing *Karma-yoga* brings one from a state filled with worldly concerns to a state without any concerns but God, and from a state of self-reliance to a state of reliance on God, thus, *bhakti* devoted to Him should be nourished by *Karma-yoga,* which is a point to be considered later.

In addition to this, *Karma-yoga,* as I mentioned earlier, also has the function to purify an internal organ. Earthly desire and delusion, according to Rāmānuja, are caused by *rajas* and *tamas* clinging to an internal organ, which prevent *sattva* from increasing to produce knowledge. By practicing *Karma-yoga,* which is the discipline to abandon worldly desire, one becomes "a person whose stains on his internal organ have been cleansed (*nirmalāntaḥkaraṇa*),"[8] because one's *rajas* and *tamas* have been removed.

We must, in this respect, draw attention to the fact that this purification is attained not by the performance of *Karma-yoga* itself, but by the grace of God who is pleased with it. Rāmānuja says:

> It is not in a visible way but through the grace (*prasāda*) of

> God that an activity becomes the cause of the purification of *manas.*[9]

For the purpose of analyzing this point, we will observe another aspect of *Karma-yoga* in the following.

B. General Concept of Bhakti and God's Grace

Rāmānuja frequently describes *Karma-yoga* as "that which has the nature of pleasing the Supreme Person (*paramapuruṣārādhana-rūpa*),"[10] and that pleasing (*ārādhana*) is "the behaviour of a complete subordinate (*paripūrṇaśeṣavṛtti*)."[11] He also states that the activities performed as *Karma-yoga* are ordained in "My commandment known as the *Veda* (*vedākhyaṃ madanuśāsanam*)."[12] From this viewpoint, we can say that God is pleased when His subordinate follows His orders.

Rāmānuja uses both words "*ārādhana*" and "*prīnaṇa*" interchangeably for the meaning of "pleasing." An important point to note is that Rāmānuja expresses the general concept of *bhakti*[13] not by the terms "*sneha*" nor "(*anu-*) *rāga*," which are preferred by the later masters,[14] but by the derivatives of "√ *prī*" including "*prīnaṇa*" after the diction of Gītā. According to Rāmānuja, we can recognize that pleasing God is one essence of *bhakti*, or love, and that *Karma-yoga*, which is called "the form of pleasing (*ārādhanaveṣa*),"[15] is a manifestation of *bhakti.*

To His follower who devotes *bhakti* to Him by performing the activities to please Him, God grants grace. Rāmānuja says:

> And that (the *Veda*) declares that good and evil activities have respectively the nature of pleasing the Supreme Person and the opposite, and that pleasure and pain, which are the results of those activities, depend on His grace (*anugraha*) and wrath (*nigraha*). ... Then, recognizing a person who performs activities of a good nature as one who follows His commandments, He blesses him with piety, riches, worldly pleasures and *mokṣa.* He, on the contrary, makes a person who does not follow His commandments experience the opposites of these.[16]

The contents of the grace God grants depend on what one wishes for, as can be seen in the following passage: "The Supreme Person, who is pleased with the activities of each person, grants the fruit that is wished for by each person."[17] To one who wishes to attain *mokṣa* without any other desire, God grants *mokṣa.* And to one who wishes for earthly fruits including the attainment of the heaven (*svarga*), He grants the fruits and the lives to enjoy them in *saṃsāra,* or to be more precise, *karman* that is the cause of *saṃsāra.* We can, therefore, say that even *karman* is bestowed by God.[18]

Here, we should consider Rāmānuja's view of *karman.* He often uses such expressions as the following: "*Karman* which has the nature of *avidyā* (*avidyārūpaṃ karman*)"[19] and also "*avidyā* which has the nature of *karman* (*karmarūpāvidyā*)."[20] It is clear from these examples that he identifies *karman* with the nescience, *avidyā.* He further explains that the function of *karman* or *avidyā,* is to envelope (√*veṣṭ*) the *ātman* and to conceal (*ā*-√*vṛ*) or contract (*saṃ*-√*kuc*) knowledge, *vidyā.*[21] In other words, one loses his complete knowledge because of his *karman.*

It follows from what has been said that, in order to attain *mokṣa,* it is required to please God, and to have Him remove his *karman* and recover his complete knowledge. When we look at this from the viewpoint of the purification of an internal organ, we can also say that one should have God fill his organ with *sattva,* which produces knowledge, through the removal of *rajas* and *tamas* as the causes of desire and delusion, which causes a man to do activities that produce *karman.*[22]

However, it is not possible for a person to directly attain *mokṣa* nor complete knowledge even if God is pleased with his practice of *Karma-yoga.* Rāmāṇuja describes:

> When the activities thus done for the purpose of sacrifices and others by one who is free from any attachment, the Supreme Person, who is pleased with the sacrifices and other activities, grants him the undisturbed intuition of the *ātman* (*ātmāvalokana*), after eradicating his subtle impressions of *karman* (*karmavāsanā*) which have continued from time immemorial.[23]

God stops the chain of his *karman* which contracts his knowledge, and grants first the intuition of the *ātman,* which is one definition of *Jñāna-yoga,* and, after that, the complete knowledge, which is called *Bhakti-yoga*, both of which will be discussed in the following chapters.

Before we go into that, there is a further point which needs to be clarified. In the writings of Rāmānuja, there seems to be some instances where the term "*pra-√pad*" meaning "to take refuge in" and the synonyms, that is, as van Buitenen stated,[24] "(*sam*) *ā-√śri*" and "*śaraṇam* (*upa-*) *√gam*," are used in the sense of *bhakti*. It shows that "taking refuge in God" is another essence of the concept of *bhakti*, or love.[25] Rāmānuja explains that "to take refuge in God" is "to follow God (*anu-√vṛt*)"[26] and also "to attribute the agency and others to God,"[27] which are, as mentioned earlier, always required in practicing *Karma-yoga*. We can, therefore, say that practicing *Karma-yoga* includes taking refuge in God.

This element is, moreover, presupposed by the practice of *Karma-yoga*, as can be seen in the following phrases: "In practicing *Karma-yoga* and others after taking refuge in Me (*matprapattipūrvakaṃ karmayogādiṣu*)"[28] and "Non-attachment and others based on taking refuge in God (*bhagavatprapattimūlam asaṅgādi*)."[29] It shows us that to take refuge in God is the beginning of the road to salvation.

Thus, it can be concluded that practicing *Karma-yoga*, which follows by taking refuge in God, makes Him pleased enough to grant grace. It takes one from a state of being filled with *karman* bestowed by God, to a state of being filled with knowledge granted by Him.

III. *Jñāna-yoga*

A. Ambiguous Description

Rāmānuja describes *Jñāna-yoga* as "that which has the nature of giving up the activities of all senses (*sarvendriyavyāpāroparatirūpa*)"[30] and "the [meditative] knowledge of the true nature of the *ātman* (*ātmayāthātmyajñānam*)."[31] However, his explanation of the role of *Jñāna-yoga* as the means for *mokṣa* seems to contradict itself, for it can be classified into three groups. First, he asserts that one should practice only *Karma-yoga* including *Jñāna-yoga*. Secondly, he advises against practicing *Jñāna-yoga*, though he acknowledges it as an alternative to *Karma-yoga*. Thirdly, he states that one will obtain qualification for *Jñāna-yoga* after accomplishing *Karma-yoga*. These statements throw us into confusion, and thus, opinions are divided among scholars on his intention.

P.N. Srinivasachari explains that "the Karma-yogin who does his duty in a disinterested way becomes a Jñāna-yogin, who prefers self-knowledge to activity." He also describes: "In the intuition of the *ātman* all activity is swallowed up. When the end is reached, there is no longer any need for endeavour."[32] We may, accordingly, say that he emphasizes the third statement mentioned above.

N.S. Anantharangachar abides by the second statement. He says that *Karma-yoga* "enables us to progress on the path of self-realization, either directly or through *Jñānayoga*," and says: "Viśiṣṭādvaita does not altogether dismiss the possibility of Jñānayoga, though it advises all aspirants to follow the path of Karmayoga itself."[33]

R.C. Lester regards the first statement as the intention of Rāmānuja, and asserts that *Jñāna-yoga* as an alternative to *Karma-yoga* is "at least a theoretical possibility." He says: "To summarize Rāmānuja's Means to Release as Karmayoga-Jñānayoga-Bhaktiyoga, as most writers on Rāmānuja do, is misleading, if not incorrect."[34]

J.A.B. van Buitenen tries to unite the first and the third statements and concludes as following: "Jñānayoga is now no longer a separate way—as such it is repeatedly condemned—but an advanced stage of karmayoga."[35]

It is worth examining the role of *Jñāna-yoga* more closely. The key to understanding it is the fact that Rāmānuja does not always use the same word in the same meaning

B. Three Meanings of "Jñāna-yoga"

We will begin by considering the first statement. Rāmānuja declares that one need not practice both *Karma-yoga* and *Jñāna-yoga* by showing that the goals of these *yogas* are the same, namely, the intuition of the *ātman* (*ātmāvalokana*). He says:

> As both (*Karma-yoga* and *Jñāna-yoga*) have only the intuition of the *ātman* as the fruit, one who practices only one [of them], on account of both having the same fruit, surely obtains that fruit.[36]

According to Rāmānuja, the reason for this is that *Jñāna-yoga* is included in *Karma-yoga.* He calls one who performs activities only to please God without any earthly desire as a "*yogin*" representing a person intent on *Karma-yoga,* and also as a "*saṃnyāsin*" representing a person intent on *Jñāna-yoga.*[37]

Rāmānuja finds the grounds of this argument in the diction of Gītā in which, he points out, the words "*tyāga*" and "*saṃnyāsa*" are used synonymously.[38] He explains that the word "*tyāga*" means the renunciation of the agency and others,[39] which is the core of *Karma-yoga,* and often regards the word "*saṃnyāsa*" as a synonym of "*Jñāna-yoga.*"[40] It is understood from this that *Jñāna-yoga* expressed by "*saṃnyāsa*" is the core of *Karma-yoga* expressed by "*tyāga.*"

It is also clear that this "*Jñāna-yoga*" implies the renunciation, in practicing *Karma-yoga,* of the agency misunderstood as the possession of the *ātman.* This renunciation shares the same meaning as the meditation of the *ātman* not being the agent. He says:

> Investigation of the true nature of the *ātman* is also included in *Karma-yoga* on account of [there being in it] the meditation on the *ātman* not being the agent.[41]

Moreover, he states: "*Karma-yoga* is preceded by the meditation on [the *atman*] not being the agent (*akartṛtvānusandhānapūrvakaṃ karma-yoga*)."[42] We can, therefore, say that the indispensability of *Jñāna-yoga* in practicing *Karma-yoga* is made explicit here.

Now let us proceed to the second statement in which Rāmānuja advises one against practicing *Jñāna-yoga.* He points out three major reasons for this. The first reason is that there is no need to practice *Jñāna-yoga* as an independent discipline because it is included in *Karma-yoga.* This is the same matter we have just discussed.

The second reason is that *Jñāna-yoga* as an alternative to *Karma-yoga* after renouncing all activities is too difficult to accomplish. The reason for it is that *Jñāna-yoga* is not one's own duty (*svadharma*) among the common people, while *Karma-yoga,* which consists of the activities of the sense organs made up of *prakṛti,* is one's own duty for any person who is associated with *prakṛti* as his body.[43] Thus, in practicing *Jñāna-yoga* without the purification of his *manas,* one does not devote oneself to it because his *manas* is addicted to the objects of his senses. Even if one purifies his *manas* and withdraws his other senses from the objects, he may still have desire and aversion. "These," says Rāmānuja, "bring one who strives for *Jñāna-yoga* ...under their control and violently direct him to their own activities. And then, he turns away from the experience of the nature of the *ātman*, and becomes completely lost."[44]

In order to escape from such a danger, one must eradicate desire and aversion. It is not possible to be achieved by any means except fixing his *manas* on God who grants him the purification of it.[45] This element, or fixing one's *manas* on God, is, however, not included in *Jñāna-yoga*, but essentially included in *Karma-yoga* which requires both pleasing God and taking refuge in Him.

The third reason is that one who is devoted to *Jñāna-yoga* after renouncing the sacrifices as *Karma-yoga*, cannot even sustain his body required for practicing *Jñāna-yoga*. Rāmānuja points out Gītā III.13 as the grounds for it:

> Good men who eat the remains of the sacrifices are released from all sins. But those wicked men, who cook for their own sakes, eat evil.

He explains this stanza and states that the people who support their bodies by eating the remains are "released from all sins which are inimical to the intuition of the true nature of the *ātman*."[46] He also says:

> One whose body and *manas* are not nourished by the remains of the sacrifices and whose *rajas* and *tamas* are consequently made predominant, turns away from the intuition of the *ātman* and becomes solely delighted in the enjoyments of the objects [of the senses].[47]

These passages show that one cannot remove his *rajas* and *tamas*, which cause desire and delusion, nor sustain his body filled with *sattva*, which produces knowledge, unless he eats the remains. Thus, one wishing to attain *mokṣa* must not give up performing the sacrifices even to obtain the remains of them as his foods.

It is clear from these examinations that Rāmānuja uses the

term "*Jñāna-yoga*" in the second statement to refer to the meditation of the *ātman* practiced after a renunciation of all activities. This *Jñāna-yoga* is advocated as the sole means for *mokṣa* by Śaṅkara. In other words, Rāmānuja here contradicts Śaṅkara's view on *Jñāna-yoga*.

We shall now discuss the third statement in which Rāmānuja admits that *Karma-yoga* is followed by *Jñāna-yoga*. He describes:

> *Karma-yoga*, which is preceded by knowledge of the *ātman* based on the sacred books,[48] leads to *Jñāna-niṣṭhā* known as *sthitaprajñatā* (the state of steady understanding). And, *sthitaprajñatā*, which has the nature of *Jñāna-niṣṭhā*, brings about the intuition of the *ātman* known as *yoga*.[49]

It is clear from this quotation that *sthitaprajñatā* is here called *Jñāna-niṣṭhā*, or *Jñāna-yoga*.[50] According to Rāmānuja, *sthitaprajñatā?* is "the climax of *Jñāna-yoga* (*Jñānaniṣṭhākāṣṭheyam*)," and it is the state where "one becomes pleased with his *manas* resting solely on the *ātman* and, in consequence of this pleasure, gives up entirely all other desires existing in his *manas*."[51] In other words, at this stage, one obtains the intuition of the *ātman* and the purification of his *manas*, both of which are also the fruits of *Karma-yoga*.

We may, therefore, say that this "*Jñāna yoga*" referred to as *sthitaprajñatā* represents not all stages of the discipline of meditation of the *ātman*, which is discussed in the first and the second statements, but represents the last stage of that. Furthermore, it is safe to say that Rāmānuja here follows Śaṅkara's view that *Karma-yoga* leads to *Jnana-yoga* through the purification of his *manas*[52] although Rāmānuja never admits the renunciation of activities even for the person who obtains *sthitaprajñatā*.

On the basis of these observations, we can conclude that Rāmānuja's view of *Jñāna-yoga* is not confusing but unified. He affirms that one who wishes to attain *mokṣa* should practice *Karma-yoga* including *Jñāna-yoga*, or the meditation of the *ātman* not being the agent, in order to obtain *Jñāna-yoga*, or *sthitaprajñatā*, in which the intuition of the *ātman* is acquired, though he always advises everyone not to be devoted to *Jñāna-yoga*, or the meditation after renouncing the practice of *Karma-yoga*.

There remains one last question concerning *Jñāna-yoga*. This is the question of what the intuition of the *ātman* is. By considering this matter, we will find what state *Jñāna-yoga* takes one to.[53] Rāmānuja declares that one obtaining the intuition of the *ātman* recognizes the true nature of the *ātman*, which is distinct from *prakṛti* constituting the body, and which has the sole form of uncontracted knowledge (*asaṅkucitajñānaikākāra*).[54] He is, in other words, released from the delusion to identify the *ātman* with *prakṛti*, or from the cause to unite the *ātman* with *prakṛti*. In consequence, he stops receiving new *karman* because he is now indifferent to any desire and activities caused by *prakṛti*.

Furthermore, in the intuition of the *ātman*, he recognizes the equality among all *ātmans*, and even the similarity between the *ātman* and God because of their uncontracted knowledge and their freedom from the bondage of *karman*. It makes him fix his *manas* firmly on God. He does not, however, recognize the *ātman* as the subordinate (*śeṣa*) to God, nor God as having the *ātman* as His subordinate, which is experienced in the stage of *Bhakti-yoga*.

IV. *Bhakti-yoga*

A. *Knowledge of God with the Nature of Bhakti*

Rāmānuja identifies *Bhakti-yoga*, which is in most cases called "*parabhakti* (higher *bhakti*)" or simply "*bhakti*" in his writings, with knowledge (*vidyā-jñāna*) of *Brahman*, or God, that has been traditionally accepted to be the direct means for *mokṣa* in the *Vedānta* school. According to Rāmānuja, this knowledge is "knowledge other than the mere knowledge of the sense of sentences (*vākyārthajñānād anyad*), and denoted by '*dhyāna*,' '*upāsana*' and similar terms."[55] These words imply meditation. We can, therefore, say that *Bhakti-yoga* is the meditation of God.

Bhakti-yoga is, moreover, defined as "the meditation which acquires the nature of *bhakti* (*bhaktirūpāpannaṃ dhyānam*)."[56] It is clear that *parabhakti* consists of two elements: knowledge and *bhakti*, or love. It is typically expressed as following:

> The word "*bhakti*" has the sense of a certain kind of love (*prītiviśeṣa*), and this love again that of a certain kind of knowledge (*jñānaviśeṣa*).[57]

The term "*bhakti*" here also implies both taking refuge in God and pleasing God. It is supported by the declaration that the person having knowledge (*jñānin*) takes refuge (*pra-√pad*) in God,[58] and by the following passage:

> The knowledge (*vidyā*) is ...of the nature of pleasing (*ārādhana*) the Supreme Person who is the object of the knowledge.[59]

Now arises the question of how *parabhakti*, or the meditation of God, is originated. God, according to Rāmānuja, possesses *māyā* with which He usually conceals His true nature and deludes the entire world. Rāmānuja advises the person, who firmly fixes his *manas* on God after acquiring the intuition of the *ātman*, to take refuge (*pra-√pad*) in God so as to be freed from His *māyā*.[60] He also says:

> Such meditation (*dhyāna*) is originated through the grace of the Supreme Person [pleased] with daily and occasional rituals, which are practiced day by day and which are of the nature of pleasing (*ārādhana*) the Supreme Person.[61]

We can conclude, from these examples, that *parabhakti* is granted by God to the person who takes refuge in God and pleases Him even after obtaining the intuition of the *ātman*.

Rāmānuja affirms that the person to whom God grants *parabhakti* is "the most beloved one (*priyatama*)" to Him, that is to say, "one to be chosen (*varaṇīya*)" by Him, by pointing out the following passage of the *Upaniṣad* as the grounds for it: "He is to be gained by only one whom He chooses (*yam evaiṣa vṛṇute tena labhyas*)."[62] The reason why God bestows it to one fixing his *manas* on Him is, in other words, that he cannot support himself without God, and that God, therefore, cannot maintain Himself without him, too.[63]

The next question we will discuss is what the object of the meditation known as *parabhakti* is. One who experiences the *ātman* of possessing the same character as God, and being freed from *māyā*, advances to the next level of the meditation of the *ātman* being the subordinate to God, in other words, to the meditation of God possessing the *ātman* as His subordinate. The realization of the relation between the *ātman* and God, compared to a subordinate and a principal (*śeṣa-śeṣi-bhāva*), is the basis of this meditation, and it is always involved in this meditation.[64] Because of that, the meditation of God is called "the service (*sevā*)"[65] performed by "one who is resolved on service to Me (God) (*maddāsyavyavasāyin*)."[66]

It is not only this relation but also God's attributes that should be meditated. However, the attributes to be meditated change as the meditation is improved. Rāmānuja says:

> [God] has been meditated in His essential nature (*svarūpa*) previously. For the purpose of the meditation of Him associated with [attributes like] "freedom from evil (*apahatapāpmatva*)" and others, repetition [of the meditation] should be made.[67]

When *parabhakti* is originated, God is to be meditated in "His essential nature," which consists of the five attributes determining the essential nature of the Entity (*arthasvarūpanirūpaṇadharma*): True Being (*satya*), Knowledge (*jñāna*), Bliss (*ānanda*), Stainlessness (*amalatva*) and Infinity (*anantatva*).[68] These attributes are to be experienced in all meditations of God from beginning to end together with the relation between the *ātman* and God because they are "equal to the Entity (*arthasāmānya*)" and "involved in the knowledge of the Entity (*arthapratītyanubandhin*)."[69]

On the other hand, His additional attributes (*upalakṣaṇa*) which are the innumerous auspicious attributes other than the five essential ones are to be meditated in a higher level of *parabhakti*. However, all of them are not required to be experienced. One should meditate only one aspect among the numerous forms of God, which is accompanied with some particular attributes, and taught in each branch (*śākhā*) of the *Veda*. Thus, the attributes to be meditated depend on the teaching of the branch one follows. For instance, the attribute of "freedom from evil (*apahatapāpmatva*)" is to be meditated only in the meditation called *Daharavidyā* taught in the *Vājasaneya* branch. Whichever teaching one follows, the object and the fruit of the meditation is the same, for the essential attributes of God are involved in every type of meditation.[70]

It is now clear that the meditation of God is not invariant forever nor identical for everyone. One should make continuous repetition of the meditation focusing on a definite aspect of God accompanied with some additional attributes, and thereby attempt to improve the meditation. For the purpose of improving that, Rāmānuja repeatedly advises one possessing *parabhakti* to practice *Karma-yoga*. He says:

> Because knowledge (*vidyā*), which becomes more perfect through practice up to death, is to be originated day by day, the duties of *āśramas* have to also be performed day by day for the sake of the origination of it (knowledge).[71]

The more perfect the meditation becomes, the more clearly the object is experienced. And, in consequence, the love, or *bhakti*, devoted to the object of the meditation also becomes stronger. Rāmānuja affirms that the improvement of both the meditation and the love is granted by God. He says:

> I (God) grant the improvement of the meditation which is required for the attainment of Me, the destruction of the obstacles to it, the condition of excessive love for Me and others.[72]

And finally, *parabhakti*, consisting of meditation and love, comes to perfection, by which the goal of *mokṣa* is obtained. He describes:

> The Supreme Person who is the Supreme *Brahman* ... is to be attained only by *bhakti*, which is of no other object [but God], uninterrupted and unsurpassed love (*ananyaprayojanānavaratanratiśayapriya*), and which possesses the nature of the meditation attaining the highest degree of immediate perception (*viśadatamapratyakṣatāpannānudhyāna-rūpa*).[73]

The last question to be addressed is why *parabhakti* is able to completely remove *karman* which is the cause of *saṃsāra*. We have seen before that even *karman* is bestowed by God. Furthermore, Rāmānuja says: "The power [of *karman*] is indeed displeasure (*aprīti*) of the Supreme Person."[74] It shows that God is not heartily pleased with one performing his duties with some earthly desire, and that He expresses His displeasure by giving *karman*. The only means to please God enough to stop His displeasure is to devote *parabhakti* to Him. Rāmānuja says:

> [Knowledge is] of the nature of pleasing the Supreme Person who is the object of knowledge. It destroys the displea-

> sure of the Supreme Person, which has been produced by an accumulation of *karman* (or activities) made before. And the same knowledge obstructs the origination of the displeasure of the Supreme Person caused by *karman* (or activities) which will be made after the origination of [knowledge] itself.[75]

Knowledge as *parabhakti*, however, cannot destroy all *karman*. Rāmānuja divides *karman*, whether good or bad, into two groups: the *karman* whose effects have not yet begun to operate (*anārabdhakārya*) and the *karman* whose effects have already begun to operate (*ārabdhakārya*). He affirms that only the former is destroyed by *parabhakti*, and that the latter must be completely exhausted through the enjoyment of its fruits in the bodies on the earth.[76] It means that *parabhakti* is not effective in destroying the latter *karman*. Thus, *parabhakti* does not come to perfection while the *karman* remains, and one cannot attain *mokṣa* while he lives with the body to enjoy the fruits of the *karman*. Rāmānuja denies the possibility of embodied liberation (*jīvanmukti*).

B. Additional Questions Concerning Bhakti-yoga

Concerning *Bhakti-yoga*, there remains two additional questions. The first is whether Rāmānuja allows an ascetic after renouncing the performance of sacrifices and others to attain *mokṣa*. The second is whether he recognizes a *śūdra* as one who is qualified for possessing knowledge and attaining *mokṣa*.

Let us start with the first question. As we have seen earlier, Rāmānuja emphasizes the necessity for practicing *Karma-yoga* and advises one against the renunciation of that. Nevertheless, it is said that Rāmānuja divorced his wife and became an ascetic at around the age of 30 years old. This apparent contradiction is to be solved. We find an idea for a solution in his explanation on the following passage of the *Upaniṣad*:

> Therefore, let a *brāhmaṇa*, after he has done with learning (*pāṇḍitya*), wish to stand by a childlike state (*bālya*). After having done with a childlike state and learning, then he becomes a sage (*muni*).[77]

Rāmānuja interprets the *brāhmaṇa* as one possessing knowledge (*vidyāvad*), and learning, the childlike state and the state of a sage (*mauna*) as auxiliaries to knowledge. The state of a sage, which is the highest among these three, is defined as "the reiterated representation before the mind of the object of the meditation (*upāsanālambanasya punaḥ punaḥ saṃśīlanaṃ*)." And Rāmānuja says: "One who acquires the state of a sage and them (the other two) in the proper manner will obtain the highest limit of knowledge (*vidyākāṣṭhā*), which is to be achieved only through them."[78]

Furthermore, he affirms that the state of a sage is "produced through the absorption in the duties of an ascetic (*pārivrājyadharmasthitihetukamauna*)" and that it is "preceded by wandering about begging for alms (*bhikṣācaraṇapūrvakamauna*)."[79] It shows that one cannot acquire both the state of a sage and the highest limit of knowledge unless he becomes an ascetic. It is clear from these examinations that Rāmānuja considers an ascetic as the ideal one for attaining *mokṣa*, although he usually advises to stay at the stage of a householder.

The reason Rāmānuja does not advise everyone to be an ascetic is probably because of the great difficulties in perfectly practicing the "austerities (*tapas*)," which are the essential duties prescribed to an ascetic[80] and which appear to mean the ceaseless renunciation of all desire.[81] Besides them, however, an ascetic has some other practices to be done, which are not exclusively connected with any *āśrama*, such as muttering prayer (*japa*), fasting (*upavāsa*), charity (*dāna*) and propitiation of deities (*devatārādhana*).[82] For an ascetic who does not do sacrifices and other things, the performance of these is the practice of *Karma yoga* which promotes knowledge.

Turning now to the second question on the qualification of a *śūdra*. Rāmānuja emphatically denies his qualification to acquire knowledge. The reason for this is that a *śūdra* is prohibited from studying the knowledge of the *Veda* and from performing the sacrifices, and he consequently does not know the manner to meditate God nor the nature of Him to be meditated.[83] Here, Rāmānuja faithfully follows the dicta of the *Brahmasūtras*, and his argument is quite similar to Śaṅkara's one.[84]

We should, however, notice that Rāmānuja is not only a master of the *Vedānta* school but also the third *ācārya* of the *Śrī*

Vaiṣṇava. In this community, twelve ancient devotees called *āḷvārs*, including *śūdras*, an untouchable and a female, are worshipped as saints who have attained to God. This fact leads us to doubt whether Rāmānuja completely excludes a *śūdra* from qualification to attain *mokṣa*. In this connection, we must not overlook the following passage:

> [*Śūdras* such as] *Vidura* and others possessed knowledge because they have not lost knowledge acquired by them in the previous births. Nevertheless, they were born in this class on account of their *karman* whose effects have already begun to operate (*prārabdhakarman*). Thus, they were devoted to *Brahman*.[85]

The *karman* whose effects have already begun to operate is, as stated above, not destroyed by *parabhakti*, and it forces one to be born in the next lives. There is, accordingly, a possibility that even one possessing knowledge could be a *śūdra*. In other words, Rāmānuja acknowledges that a *śūdra* possesses knowledge and attains *mokṣa* after all of his *karman* is exhausted, while he denies that a *śūdra* first acquires knowledge.

It follows from what has been said that both an ascetic and a *śūdra*, possessing knowledge, are compelled to continue their lives caused by their *karman*, and are devoted to meditate God constantly and to perform their own duties other than sacrifices, for the sake of the perfection of their knowledge. To put it another way, they long for the departure from the earthly world consuming the remains of their *karman*.

V. *For the Freedom from Karman*

It is traditionally accepted in the *Vedānta* school that the *ātman* having attained *mokṣa* manifests its own nature and realizes "oneness" between the *ātman* and *Brahman* represented by the dicta such as "That You Are (*tat tvam asi*)" and others. Śaṅkara strictly interprets this "oneness" and affirms that the *ātman* and *Brahman* are identical without difference. Rāmānuja rejects this view and asserts that the *ātman* does not give up its individual identity even in *mokṣa*. According to him, the "oneness" signifies that any *ātman* cannot exist independently of *Brahman* (*apṛthaksiddhi*), and, therefore, *Brahman* is "one without a second (*advitīya*)" because it is the only principal having all *ātmans* as subordinates.

Furthermore, Rāmānuja says that the *ātman* in *mokṣa* acquires the same qualities with God.[86] The *ātman* obtains True Being since it is no longer united with a mortal body by the force of *karman*. It obtains uncontracted Knowledge since it is not under the control of *karman* to contract it. It obtains Supreme Bliss since the *ātman* fully experiences the Bliss of God without any obstruction of *karman*. It obtains Stainlessness since it has no stain caused by *karman*. And it obtains Infinity since it possesses innumerable auspicious qualities, which have been lost in *saṃsāra* on account of *karman*. Thus we see that the *ātman*'s acquisition of all these qualities results from the complete freedom from *karman*, which is the essence of *mokṣa*.

In order to be freed from *karman*, Rāmānuja advises one wishing for *mokṣa* to practice the three types of *yoga*. He believes that *Karma-yoga* brings one from a state filled with worldly concerns to a state without any concerns but God, and from a state of self-reliance to a state of reliance on God. These functions nourish one's *bhakti*, for which both elements of pleasing God and taking refuge in Him are essential. *Karma-yoga* practiced with *bhakti* has God grant His followers the improvement of *sattva* producing knowledge through the removal of *rajas* and *tamas* as the cause of desire and delusion. Because of that, one practicing *Karma-yoga* advances from a state in which *karman* representing God's displeasure is successively bestowed by Him, to a state in which knowledge as *parabhakti* representing God's pleasure is granted by Him.

Jñāna-yoga, which is to be included in *Karma-yoga*, consists of two elements: one is the control of all senses and the other is the meditation of the *ātman*. It leads one to *sthitaprajñatā*, or the state of steady understanding, as the climax of both *Karma-yoga* and *Jñāna-yoga*, in which the intuition of the *ātman* is acquired. In this intuition, the *ātman* manifests its nature distinct from *prakṛti* to which *karman* originally belongs, and, therefore, its nature indifferent to *karman*. And one intuiting the *ātman* fixes his *manas* on God, which produces *parabhakti*.

Bhakti-yoga, or *parabhakti*, is the meditation of God associated with *bhakti*. This meditation is granted only to the person chosen by God, and it is further improved by His grace. *Parabhakti* has the functions to stop producing new *karman,* and to remove the *karman* which has been produced and whose effects have not yet begun to operate. One practicing *Bhakti-yoga* spends his time only for the sake of the exhaustion of the remains of his *karman* whose effects have already begun to operate. *Parabhakti* turns out to make all *karman* void and to bring one from a state where the *ātman* is united with a body to a state where it is separated from a body, or *mokṣa.*

Rāmānuja accepts Śaṅkara's theory that *mokṣa* is to be attained only through the destruction of *avidyā,* or the nescience, but he rejects Śaṅkara's declaration that *karman* is a false existence caused by *avidyā.* Rāmānuja identifies *karman* with *avidyā.* Madhva and Vallabha in the later times, on the other hand, consider that *mokṣa,* which is the blissful state in Heaven, can be achieved only through the grace of God. This is first theoretically supported by Rāmānuja, but he does not express the view given by them that the final grace to attain *mokṣa* solely relies on God's will independent of one's efforts, and that, therefore, *mokṣa* is not always attainable even for one acquiring the freedom from all *karman.* Rāmānuja regards the complete freedom from *karman* as the manifestation of the final grace of God granted to praise one's efforts. It is, thus, concluded that, according to Rāmānuja, the removal of all *karman* by the grace of God is the only way to escape from *saṃsāra* for *mokṣa.* Rāmānuja declares salvation from the earthly world filled with *karman* to the heavenly world free from *karman.*

NOTES

1. Max Weber, *Gesammelte Aufsätze zur Religionssoziologie,* vol. 1, J.C.B. Mohr, Tübingen, 1920, S.252; Max Weber, *Wirtschaft und Gesellschaft—Grundriss der Verstehenden Soziologie—,* vol. 1, J.C.B. Mohr, Tübingen, 1976, S. 319.
2. Rāmānuja's *Vedārthasaṃgraha* (abbr. VAS, in *Rāmānuja's Vedārthasaṃgraha,* ed. by J. A. B. van Buitenen, Deccan College Postgraduate and Research Institute, Poona, 1956) §.91, p. 126.
3. Rāmānuja's *Śrībhāṣya* ad *Brahmasūtras* (abbr. ŚBh, in *Brahmasūtra-Śrībhāṣya with Śrutaprakāśikā,* ed. by T. Viraraghavacarya, 2 vols., Ubhaya Vedanta Granthamala, Madras, 1967, rpt. Visishtadvaita Pracharini Sabha, Madras, 1989) IV. 1. 16, vol. 2, p. 588.
4. ŚBh III.4. 34, vol. 2, p. 556.
5. Rāmānuja's *Bhagavadgītābhāṣya* ad *Bhagavadgītā* (abbr. GBh, in *Bhagavad-Gītā with Eleven Commentaries,* ed. by Shastri Gajanana Shambhu Sadhale,

2nd ed., 3 vols., The Gujarati Printing Press, Bombay, 1938) XVIII.12, vol. 3, p. 308.

6. GBh III.30, vol. 1, p. 326.
7. GBh XVIII.13, vol. 3, p. 310.
8. GBh III.5, vol. 1, p. 279. Vedānta Deśika interprets this phrase as "the person whose plenty of *rajas* and *tamas* disappear, or the person without any desire, enmity and others caused by them" in his *Tātparyacandrikā* (in *The Bhagavad-Gītā with Eleven Commentaries*) ad Rāmānuja's GBh III.5, vol.l, p. 279.
9. GBh XVIII.8, vol. 3, p. 300.
10. ŚBh III.4.26, vol. 2, p. 551.
11. GBh XVIII.65, vol. 3, p. 398.
12. GBh XVI.23, vol. 3, p.231.
13. Rāmānuja acknowledges two kinds of *bhakti*: one is a general concept of devotion to God, and the other is a meditation of God, which is the direct means for *mokṣa* and called *parabhakti* or *Bhakti-yoga.*
14. Both Madhva in the 13th century and Vallabha in the 16th century define *bhakti* as "*sneha*" in the same passage as following:
    māhātmyajñānapūrvas tu sudṛḍhaḥ sarvato 'dhikaḥ/
    sneho bhaktir iti proktas tayā muktir na cānyathā//
    Madhva's *Mahābhāratatātparyanirṇaya* (in *Mahābhāratatātparyanirṇaya and Mahābhāratatātparyam*, ed. by B. Govindacharya, Akhila Bhārata Madhva Mahā Maṇḍala, Bangalore, 1971) I.85, p. 8; Vallabha's *Tattvārthadīpanibandha* (in *Tattvārthadīpanibandha with Prakāśā*, re-ed. by Goswami Shyam Manohar, 3 vols., Śrīvallabhavidyāpīṭh-Śrīviṭṭaleśaprabhucaraṇāśram Trust, Kolhapur, 1980) I.42, vol. 1, p. 80. Caitanya in the 16th century, on the other hand, regards the state filled with "*rāgātmikā-bhakti*" as the ideal one and "*rāgānugā-bhakti*" as the means for obtaining it.
15. VAS §.91, p. 126.
16. ŚBh II.2.3, vol. 2, pp. 282-283.
17. VAS §.124, p. 153.
18. On this point, Radhakrishnan says: "The law of karma expresses the will of God. The order of karma is set up by God, who is the ruler of karma. Since the law is dependent on God's nature, God himself may be regarded as rewarding the righteous and punishing the wicked." (S. Radhakrishnan, *Indian Philosophy*, Oxford University Press, Delhi, 1989, vol. 2, p.694.) It is also helpful to see Bharatan Kumarappa, *The Hindu Conception of the Deity*, Inter-India Publications, Delhi, 1979, pp. 298-300.
19. VAS §.43, p. 98.
20. VAS §.78, p. 116.
21. VAS §.78, p. 116, GBh V.15, vol. 1, p. 489.
22. In respect to the functions of the three types of *guṇa*, see GBh XIV.1ff.
23. GBh III.9, vol. 1, p. 286.
24. J.A.B. van Buitenen, *Rāmānuja on the Bhagavadgītā*, 2nd ed., Motilal Banarsidass, Delhi, 1968, p. 25n.
25. The term "*prapatti*" is a derivative of the verb "*pra-√pad.*" However, we should notice that Rāmānuja never advocates the doctrine of *prapatti*, "the complete self-surrender to God without any other efforts," which has grown so important in the later *Viśiṣṭādvaita* School, especially in the Southern School.

26. GBh XVIII.62, vol. 3, p. 393.
27. GBh XVIII.56, vol. 3, p. 385.
28. GBh XV.11, vol. 3, p. 176.
29. GBh XV.6, vol. 3, p. 166.
30. GBh III.41, vol. 1, p. 346.
31. GBh VI.2, vol. 1, p. 527.
32. P.N. Srinivasachari, *The Philosophy of Viśiṣṭādvaita*, The Adyar Library and Research Centre, Madras, 1943, p. 370 and p. 337.
33. N.S. Anantharangachar, *The Philosophy of Sādhana in Viśiṣṭādvaita*, University of Mysore, Mysore, 1967, p. 132 and p. 134.
34. Robert C. Lester, *Rāmānuja on the Yoga*, The Adyar Library and Research Centre, Madras, 1976, pp. 87-88.
35. J.A.B. van Buitenen, *Rāmānuja on the Bhagavadgītā*, p. 21.
36. GBh V.4, vol. 1, p. 468.
37. GBh VI.1, vol. 1, p. 524.
38. GBh XVIII.2, 7, 12, 49. In this paper, I will use the terms "*tyāga*" and "*saṃnyāsa*" to refer to the derivatives of the verbs √*tyaj* and *sam-ni-* √*as*.
39. GBh XVIII.1-4. Rāmānuja classifies "renunciation (*tyāga=saṃnyāsa*)" in three types according to *guṇas* in his GBh XVIII.7-9. The renunciation of the activities under the delusion that the activities bring one to bondage, is characterized by *tamas*. The renunciation of the sacrifices and others through the misunderstanding that *Jñāna-yoga* alone should be practiced for attaining the goal, is characterized by *rajas*. This corresponds to *Jñāna-yoga* advocated by Śaṅkara. The renunciation of the sense of possession and others of the activities in practicing *Karma-yoga*, is characterized by *sattva* and based on the knowledge of the purposes of the sacred books.
40. GBh V.1, 2, 6, VI.1, 2.
41. GBh III.8, vol. 1, p. 284.
42. GBh IV.1, vol. 1, p. 357.
43. See GBh III.8, 45, XVIII.47-48.
44. GBh III.34, vol. 1, p. 333. And see GBh III.33-42.
45. See GBh II.59-68.
46. GBh III.13, vol. 1, p. 293.
47. GBh III.16, vol. 1, p. 298.
48. This knowledge is not the direct (*aparokṣa*) or meditative one, but the indirect (*parokṣa*) one that is obtained by the study of the *Veda*.
49. GBh II.53, vol. 1, p. 208.
50. The term "*jñāna-niṣṭhā*" is, as van Buitenen points out, used synonymously with *Jñāna-yoga* by Rāmānuja. J.A.B. van Buitenen, *Rāmānuja on the Bhagavadgītā*, p. 66n.
51. GBh II.55, vol. 1, p. 214. Rāmānuja divides the state of *sthitaprajñatā* into four stages in his GBh II.55-58, among which the stage quoted here is the highest one.
52. Iwao Shima, "Śaṅkara's Interpretation of the Bhagavadgītā," *Journal of Indian and Buddhist Studies* 39(1), 1990, pp. 501-496.
53. My description of this part is mainly based on GBh VI.29-34.
54. GBh VI.32, vol. 1, p. 570.
55. ŚBh I.1.1, vol. 1, p. 52. Rāmānuja points out in his ŚBh I.1.1 and IV.1.1,

as the grounds, that √*vid*, √*dhyai* and *upa-* √*ās* are used synonymously in the *Upaniṣads*.

56. VAS §.91, p. 127.
57. VAS §.141, p. 170.
58. GBh VII. 19, vol. 2, p. 43.
59. ŚBh IV.1.13, vol. 2, p. 584.
60. GBh VII.14, vol. 2, pp. 29-30. Rāmānuja affirms that the word "māyā" does not mean the illusion (*mithyā*) or the nescience (*avidyā*) as explained in the *Advaita* school.
61. ŚBh III.4.26, vol. 2, p. 551.
62. VAS §.144, p. 173, GBh VIII.14, vol. 2, p. 97, ŚBh I.1.1, vol. 1, p. 60. This passage of the *Upaniṣad* is quoted from the *Muṇḍaka-Upaniṣad* III.2.3.
63. See GBh VII.17-18, VIII.14-15.
64. See GBh VII.16, 19.
65. VAS §.144, p. 173.
66. GBh IX.14, vol. 2, p. 159.
67. ŚBh III.3.42, vol. 2, p. 515.
68. ŚBh III.3.13, vol. 2, p. 474. Among these attributes, Knowledge is the fundamental one. Stainlessness implies "freedom from all imperfections (*nirastanikhiladoṣatva*)" which is the one of the two characteristics (*ubhayaliṅga*) of God, and Infinity includes the other, which is "possession of all auspicious qualities (*kalyāṇaguṇākaratva*)." On this point, it is helpful to see John Braisted Carman, *The Theology of Rāmānuja—An Essay in Interreligious Understanding*—, Yale University Press, New Haven, 1974, pp. 98-113.
69. ŚBh III.3.13, vol.2, p. 473.
70. My description of this part is besed on SBh III.3, particularly III.3.13 and 56-57.
71. ŚBh IV.1.16, vol. 2, p. 588.
72. GBh VIII.14, vol. 2, p. 97.
73. VAS §.91. p. 126.
74. ŚBh IV.1.13, vol. 2. p. 584.
75. ŚBh IV.1.13, vol. 2. p. 584. I translate the word "*agha*" in this quotation as "*karman*" according to the explanation in ŚBh IV.1.14 (vol.2, p. 587).
76. See ŚBh IV.1.15, 16, 19.
77. *Bṛhadāraṇyaka Upaniṣad* III.5.1, quoted in ŚBh III.4.46, vol. 2, p. 563.
78. ŚBh III.4.46, vol.2, pp. 563-564. The contents of learning, a childlike state and a state of a sage are not fully clear although explained in ŚBh III.4.46-49.
79. ŚBh III.4.48, vol. 2, p. 564.
80. ŚBh III.4.19, vol. 2, p. 545.
81. This inference is based on the description in ŚBh III.4.48 (vol.2, p. 564), which indicates that the renunciation of all desire is the only duty of an ascetic (*pārivrājya*).
82. ŚBh III.4.36, vol.2, p. 557.
83. See ŚBh I.3.3-39.
84. In his ŚBh I.3.39, Rāmānuja attacks the view of the *Advaita* school that a *śūdra* does not have qualification for knowledge. The purpose of it is, however, not to suggest that a *śūdra* has a chance to have qualification

for knowledge, but to manifest that the teachings of the *Advaita* school is inconsistent with the fundamentals of the *Vedānta* school and that only the view of Rāmānuja is the orthodox one consistent with that.

85. ŚBh I.3.33, vol.2, pp. 77-78.

86. The qualities of the *ātman* are, strictly speaking, not completely unlimited as the qualities of God, because the *ātman* has been or would be enveloped by *karman* to limit them. Moreover, the *ātman* never possesses the qualities like the power to create, to maintain and to destroy the entire world and the character of the principal of all, which are possessed only by God. See ŚBh IV.4.17-22. In respect to the condition of the *ātman* in a state of *mokṣa,* also see ŚBh IV.1.

CHAPTER 43

The *Jñāneśvarī* as a Commentary on the *Bhagavadgītā* (Chapters 1-6)

IWAO SHIMA

The thought of Jñānadeva has been discussed by scholars from the following three points of view.

1. Some scholars have pointed out the influence of Śaṅkara or Advaitavedānta on Jñānadeva's thought.[1]
2. Others have discussed *bhakti* elements in the thought of Jñānadeva in relation to the bhakti movement that developed through the Marāṭhī language in Mahārāṣṭra.[2]
3. Still others have found influences of the Nātha sect in Jñānadeva's thought.[3]

It is true that we find these three aspects in the *Jñāneśvarī* composed by Jñānadeva, but how are these three aspects interconnected and unified in one and the same work? It seems to me that a study on the *Jñāneśvarī* itself will be insufficient to clarify this point, because the *Jñāneśvarī* is a commentary on the *Bhagavadgītā* and its framework follows that of the *Bhagavadgītā*. Therefore, in this paper, I will discuss the interconnection and unification of the above-mentioned three aspects in the *Jñāneśvarī* (chapters 1-6) within the framework of the interpretation of the *Bhagavadgītā* in comparison with three previous commentaries on the *Bhagavadgītā*, i.e., the *Śaṅkarabhāṣya*, *Rāmānujabhāṣya* and *Madhvabhāṣya*.

Now let us first examine what kinds of religious traditions Jñānadeva succeeded in the *Jñāneśvarī*.

1. *Religious Traditions Succeeded by Jñānadeva in the Jñāneśvarī*

In the introduction of the *Jñāneśvarī* Jñānadeva pays homage to Gaṇapati and describes the different parts of Gaṇapati as corresponding to different religious traditions, as shown in table 1.

Table 1: Parts of Gaṇapati and their correspondence to religious traditions (Jñāneśvarī 1.3-14)

Parts of Gaṇapati	*Religious Traditions*
beautiful form	Śabdabrahma (Veda)
limbs	Smṛti
ornaments	eighteen Purāṇas
many-coloured garment	Sāhitya
jingling bells	Kāvyanāṭaka
waist-cloth and its tassled end	wisdom of Vyāsa etc.
six arms	six schools of Indian philosophy

Here Jñānadeva makes it clear that his work continues the orthodox Brahmanical religious traditions, such as the Veda, the Smṛti, the eighteen Purāṇas, the *Mahābhārata*[4] and the six schools of Indian philosophy.

The six schools of Indian philosophy are however not considered as opposing each other by Jñānadeva, although they are fighting each other in the orthodox Brahmanical religious traditions. Jñānadeva says:

> Impartial discussion [among these six schools of Indian philosophy] is the straight and white trunk [of Gaṇapati].[5]

Among the six schools of Indian philosophy, the Vedānta which continued the Upaniṣadic tradition, especially Dvaitavedānta and Advaitavedānta, seems to have special importance for Jñānadeva, as shown in table 2.

Table 2: Upper parts of Gaṇapati and their correspondance to religious traditions (Jñāneśvarī 1.16-18)

Parts of Gaṇapati	*Religious Traditions*
two ears	two Mīmāṃsas
temple	Dvaita and Advaita unified
fragrant flowers adorning the crown of the head	ten Upaniṣads

After having paid homage to the orthodox Brahmanical religious traditions, Jñānadeva ends his homage with paying homage to the Goddess Śāradā (1.21) and the Nātha yogin Nivṛtti (1.22-27). Then he talks about the excellence of the *Mahābhārata* and the *Bhagavadgītā* and makes references to *sants* (saints) and *bhaktas* (1.53-54) in Mahārāṣṭra.

From this introductory portion of the *Jñāneśvarī* we can infer the following three points. The *Jñāneśvarī* is,

1. based upon ten Upaniṣads on the scriptural level.
2. influenced by Dvaitavedānta and Advaitavedānta on the philosophical level.
3. influenced by the faith in the Goddess Śāradā, the Nātha sect and the *bhakti* of *sants* on the local religious tradition level.

Let us first examine the citations from the sacred texts.

1.1 Scriptural Level: Number of Citations from the Sacred Texts

As far as three Sanskrit commentaries on the *Bhagavadgītā* are concerned, we can trace the citations from the sacred texts and find out the degree of influence of each sacred text, as shown in table 3. This table shows the following:

1. All these commentaries are based upon the Upaniṣads as their religious authority.
2. The *Rāmānujabhāṣya* and the *Madhvabhāṣya* are also based upon Purāṇas as a religious authority.

Among Purāṇas, *Rāmānujabhāṣya* is influenced by the *Viṣṇupurāṇa*, while the *Madhvabhāṣya* is influenced by the *Bhāgavatapurāṇa*, as shown in table 4.

The *Jñāneśvarī*, however, does not cite any sacred texts. In this respect the *Jñāneśvarī* is quite different in its style of commentary from the previous three Sanskrit commentaries. Therefore, we cannot apply the same method to the *Jñāneśvarī* in order to know the influence of particular sacred texts on it.

Table 3: Number of Citations from the Sacred Texts (*Śaṅkara, Rāmānuja and Madhva*)

	Śaṅkara	*Rāmānuja*	*Madhva*
Saṃhitā	7	7	26
Brāhmaṇa	4	12	3
Āraṇyaka	3	5	3
Upaniṣad	72	101	106
Dharmaśāstra	10	6	7
Mahābhārata	19	6	60
Purāṇa	2	20	117
Brahmsūtra	1	8	12
Pañcarātra		1	
Gauḍapādakārikā			1
Gītārthasaṃgraha		2	
Pāṇinisūtra		1	
Etymology			30
Śruti, Śākhā, Khila			74
Other Works			42
Miscellaneous	5	7	105

Table 4: Number of Citations from the Purāṇas (*Śaṅkara, Rāmānuja and Madhva*)

	Śaṅkara	*Rāmānuja*	*Madhva*
Āditya			2
Bhāgavata		2	67
Brahma			8
Brahmavaivarta			6
Garuḍa		1	8
Kūrma			1
Liṅgottara		1	
Matsya			1
Nārasiṃha		1	
Padma			7
Skanda			9
Vāmana			1
Varāha			1
Viṣṇu	2	20	6

1.2 *Philosophical Level: Influence of Advaitavedānta?*

Among the six schools of Indian philosophy, it appears that we find influences of Advaitavedānta especially in the first six chapters of the *Jñāneśvarī*. For example,

> Within this adjunct all-pervading pure consciousness is hidden.[6]
>
> In the same way though the body may die, the Self does not. Therefore, O Beloved, do not superimpose this delusion [to the Self].[7]
>
> So you should realize that all that has form is made by illusion (*māyā*).[8]
>
> When he sees nothing but his own Self in the world, what action could there be for him?[9]
>
> And you should know that one whose internal organ has forgotten the memory of 'I' and 'mine' is the eternal renouncer, O Pārtha.[10]
>
> Therefore, [you should know that] he who sees equality always and everywhere has already become non-dual Brahman.[11]

Although we thus find many ideas of Advaitavedānta in the first six chapters of the *Jñāneśvarī*, it cannot be said for the present that these six chapters are influenced by Advaitavedānta. For even Rāmānuja, who opposed Śaṅkara, interprets these six chapters as preaching the realization (sākṣātkāra) of *ātman*, though his interpretation of the relationship, between action (*karma*) and knowledge (*jñāna*) is quite different from that of Śaṅkara. In order to understand this point we should first grasp the basic framework of the interpretation of the *Bhagavadgītā* by Jñānadeva in the historical development of the interpretations of the *Bhagavadgītā*. Let us first examine the basic framework of the interpretation of the *Bhagavadgītā* in the previous three Sanskrit commentaries.

2. *Basic Framework of the Interpretation of the Bhagavadgītā (Chapters 1-6) : From Śaṅkara to Madhva*

2.1 *Śaṅkara's Interpretation of the Bhagavadgītā*[12]

Śaṅkara interprets the *Bhagavadgītā* according to the following two *dharmas* : (1) the *dharma* characterized by non-action (i.e. *jñānayoga*) which directly leads to liberation, and (2) the *dharma* characterized by action (i.e. *karmayoga*) which indirectly leads to liberation through the purification of the mind, the attainment of knowledge and the renunciation (*saṃnyāsa*) of all actions, when it is practiced in a spirit of complete devotion to the Lord and without regard to its result. And these two types of *dharmas* are the two fundamental schemes of Śaṅkara's interpretation of the whole *Bhagavadgītā*.

Although the first of these two fundamental schemes is the most essentical one for Śaṅkara, when Śaṅkara follows the second fundamental scheme he argues in various places that *karmayoga* leads to *jñānayoga* through the purification of the mind and finally leads to liberation through *jñānayoga* [*Śaṅkarabhāṣya* III.3 etc.]. This process of liberation consists of the following four stages: (1) *karmayoga* dedicated to the Lord and practiced without regard to its result, (2) the purification of mind, (3) the attainment of the knowledge of *ātman*, (4) the renunciation of all actions, followed by liberation [*Śāṅkarabhāṣya* V.12; V.27].

Thus, in short, Śaṅkara interprets the whole *Bhagavadgītā* within the framework of *karma* and *jñāna*. In other words, he interprets the whole *Bhagavadgītā* within the double framework of the Vedic tradition of rituals and the Upaniṣadic tradition of knowledge.

2.2 *Rāmānuja's Interpretation of the Bhagavadgītā*[13]

In contrast to the dichotomic framework of Śaṅkara's interpretation, Rāmānuja uses a triadic framework of interpretation, namely, *karma, jñāna* and *bhakti*, following Yāmuna's interpretation. In the introduction to his *Gītābhāṣya*, Rāmānuja says: "Under the pretense of encouraging the son of Pāṇḍu to fight, the Lord Viṣṇu brought in this world the *bhaktiyoga*, which is fostered by *jñāna* and *karma*, has the Lord himself as its object, and is declared to be the means of attaining salvation (*mokṣa*) or the highest goal of human life in the Upaniṣad." Thus, according to Rāmānuja, the purport of the *Bhagavadgītā* is *bhaktiyoga* and this *bhaktiyoga* is fostered by *jñānayoga* and *karmayoga*. Based upon this relationship of the three means to salvation and following Yāmuna's idea [*Gītārthasaṃgraha* 2-4], Rāmānuja divides the chapters of the *Bhagavadgītā* into three groups according to their subject, as follows: *karmayoga* and *jñānayoga* (chapters 1-6), *bhaktiyoga* (chapters 7-12) and other miscellaneous topics (chapters 13-18). Let us first consider the first of these three groups.

After discussing the *sāṃkyabuddhi* (the consciousness of the difference between body and *ātman*) and the *yogabuddhi* (the application of the *sāṃkyabuddhi* to the daily performance of acts, presupposing the knowledge of *ātman*) in the second chapter, Rāmānuja briefly summarizes the stages to salvation in the introductory portion of the third chapter as follows: the knowledge of *ātman* combined with *karmayoga* (i.e. *yogabuddhi*) leads to *jñānayoga;* this *jñānayoga* (the constant consciousness of the knowledge of *ātman*) leads to the contemplation of *ātman* which culminates in the realization (*sākṣātkāra*) of *ātman;* this realization again leads to *bhaktiyoga;* and this *bhaktiyoga* alone leads to the attainment of God or *salvation. Rāmānuja* then discusses the relationship between *karmayoga* and *jñānayoga* in the remainder of chapter three, and *karmayoga* in the fourth and fifth chapters.[14]

In sum, Rāmānuja seems to distinguish the following stages to salvation: (1) the knowledge of *ātman* (discussed in chapter 2), (2) *karmayoga* or *jñānayoga* (discussed in chapters 3-5), (3) the contemplation of *ātman* culminating in the realization of *ātman*, (4) *bhaktiyoga*, and (5) the attainment of God or salvation. Accordingly, in the sixth chapter he explains the contemplation of *ātman* which presupposes *karmayoga* and/or *jñānayoga*, and in chapters 7-12 he proceeds to explain *bhaktiyoga* which presupposes the realization of *ātman*. Thus Rāmānuja interprets the *Bhagavadgītā* (chapters 1-12) according to the stages of salvation and places *bhakti* as the final stage after the realization of *atman*, which is the goal of Advaitavedānta.

2.3 *Madhva's Interpretation of the Bhagavadgītā*

Like Rāmānuja Madhva also follows a triadic framework of interpretation, namely, *karma, jñāna* and *bhakti*, and divides the chapters of the *Bhagavadgītā* into three groups, i.e., *karmayoga* and *jñānayoga* (chapters 1-6), *bhaktiyoga* (chapters 7-12) and other miscellaneous topics (chapters 13-18).

With regard to the topics of the second and the third chapter, Madhva says:

> [The knowledge of] *ātman* and the means of the knowledge

[of *ātman*] were discussed in the previous chapter (chapter 2).[15]

In the latter chapter (chapter 3), after criticizing non-action, action is ordered as the means of the knowledge.[16]

Thus the topic of the second chapter is the knowledge of *ātman* and the means of the knowledge of *ātman*, and the topic of the third chapter is the criticism of non-action and the performance of action (i.e. *karmayoga*) according to Madhva.

Next, about the fourth and the fifth chapter, Madhva says:

> The greatness of the highest intelligence, the difference of action (*karma*) [from the actions based upon desire (*kāmyakarma*)] and the greatness of the knowledge are discussed in this chapter (chapter 4).[17]
>
> [God] explains in this chapter (chapter 5) the *karmayoga* mentioned in the third chapter.[18]

Thus the topic of the fourth chapter is *jñāna* and *karma*, and that of the fifth chapter is *karmayoga*, which was discussed in relation to the renunciation of action (*karmasaṃnyāsa*) in the previous two chapters.[19]

Next, *Madhya* introduces the sixth chapter as follows:

> The contemplation (*samādhiyoga*), which is the inner part of the knowledge, will be discussed in this chapter (chapter 6).[20]

Thus the topic of the sixth chapter is the contemplation, and this contemplation finally culminates in the direct vision (*aparokṣajñāna*) of the Highest God, as shown at the beginning of the seventh chapter:[21]

> While the means [of *aparokṣajñāna*] were mainly discussed in the previous [six] chapters, the greatness of the Highest God will be mainly discussed in the following six chapters.[22]

Thus according to Madhva, *karmayoga* and *jñānayoga*, discussed in the first five chapters of the *Bhagavadgītā*, culminate in the contemplation which is discussed in the sixth chapter and leads to *aparokṣajñāna*. Next, *bhakti* to the Highest God, which presupposes this *aparokṣajñāna*, is discussed in the next six chapters (chapters 7-12).

3. *Jñānadeva's Interpretation of the Bhagavadgītā (Chapters 1-6)*

Like Rāmānuja and Madhva, Jñānadeva also follows a triadic framework of interpretation, namely, *karma, jñāna* and *bhakti,* and divides the chapters of the *Bhagavadgītā* into three groups, i.e., *karmayoga* and *jñānayoga* (chapters 1-6), *bhaktiyoga* (chapters 7-12) and other miscellaneous topics (chapters 13-18).

3.1 *Second Chapter: Buddhiyoga and Karmayoga*

In the second chapter Jñānadeva discusses *buddhiyoga* and *karmayoga* as follows:

> When we consider this yoga of pure intelligence, the part of action (*karmayoga*) appears in many ways to be inferior, O Partha.[23]
>
> But only when this action (*karmayoga*) is performed, this yoga (*buddhiyoga*) becomes attainable.[24]
>
> Therefore the yoga of pure intelligence is supported [by *karmayoga*]. O Arjuna, concentrate on it (*buddhiyoga*).[25]

Here Jñānadeva says that the yoga of pure intelligence (*buddhiyoga*= *jñānayoga*) presupposes *karmayoga,* and thus emphasizes the necessity of *karmayoga* which appears in many ways to be inferior to *buddhiyoga.*

3.2 *Third Chapter: Jñānayoga and Karmayoga*

In the third chapter Jñānadeva discusses *jñānayoga* and *karmayoga* as follows:

> These two paths appeared from Me in this world and have been established beginninglessly.[26]
>
> One is called *jñānayoga* and it is to be followed by philosophers, who immediately after realizing [the Self] become one with it.[27]
>
> The other is known as *karmayoga* in which practitioners become skillful and reach final release (*nirvāṇa*) in course of time.[28]
>
> Though these two paths are two, ultimately they become one.[29]
>
> Philosophers follow the path of knowledge and instantly attain final release.[30]

> The yogins, on the other hand, follow the path of action and, by performing their own prescribed duties, attain perfection in course of time.[31]

Here Jñānadeva shows two paths to final release, i.e., *jñānayoga* and *karmayoga*. Through *jñānayoga* philosophers instantly become one with the Self and attain final release (*mokṣa*), which appears to be the final goal of Advaitavedānta. Through *karmayoga*, on the other hand, practitioners or yogins attain final release (*nirvāṇa* or perfection) in course of time. But these two paths ultimately becomes one. Thus here also Jñānadeva emphasizes the necessity of *karmayoga*. This point is also clearly stated in the following verse:

> Therefore action should not be abandoned. Especially *sants* (sages) should continue to perform action.[32]

3.3 *Fourth Chapter: Jñānayoga*

At the beginning of the fourth chapter Jñānadeva describes the topic of this chapter as follows:

> First the topic [of this chapter] is the discrimination [of *ātman* and non-*ātman*].[33]

Here *jñānayoga* is considered to be the descrimination of *ātman* and non-*ātman*, which is the subject of Advaitavedānta.

3.4 *Fifth Chapter: Karmasaṃnyāsa and Karmayoga*

In the fifth chapter Jñānadeva discusses *karmasaṃnyāsa* and *karmayoga* as follows:

> If you consider renunciation and yoga, both are in fact means to attain final release.[34]
>
> Yet to all, the wise as well as the ignorant, this yoga of action (*karmayoga*) is indeed easy [to practice].[35]
>
> Whatever is gained by philosophers (= the renouncers of action), is likewise reached by *yogins*. Therefore these two are one by nature.[36]

Just as in the third chapter, Jñānadeva again emphasizes the oneness of *karmasaṃnyāsa* (i.e. *jñānayoga*) and *karmayoga*, and thus again points out the importance of *karmayoga* in the way to final release. What then is this *karmayoga*, which is easier to practice but takes more time to reach final release than *jñānayoga*? After a short explanation of *kuṇḍalinīyoga* by Lord Kṛṣṇa, Arjuna addresses Him as follows:

> Similarly, [the path of yoga] is easier than the path of knowledge for people as weak as we are. Though this [yoga] is attainable after a long time, we will be patient.[37]

Here the path of yoga (*karmayoga*), which is mentioned as being easier then the path of knowledge (*sāṃkhyayoga* = *jñānayoga*), is related to the *kuṇḍalinīyoga* of Nātha sect, which Jñānadeva's teacher Nivṛtti followed. In the sixth chapter this *kuṇḍalinīyoga* is explained in detail.

3.5 *Sixth Chapter: Karmayoga = Kuṇḍalinīyoga of the Nātha sect*[38]

At the beginning of the fourth chapter Jñānadeva describes the topic of this chapter as follows:

> This is the sixth discourse of the Gītā, of Sanjaya's narration. As nectar was born from the milky ocean,[39]
>
> so is laid before us here the essence of the meaning of the Gītā, the other shore of the ocean of discrimination, the treasure of the riches of yoga,[40]
>
> the resting place of primordial matter, which cannot be expressed by the Vedas, and from which springs the root of the creeper of the Gītā.[41]
>
> Such is this sixth discourse, which will be explained with literary beauty. Therefore listen to it attentively.[42]
>
> My language is Marāṭhī, but it easily surpasses nectar, with such beauty of words and the power of fragrance will be subdued by its charm.[43]

Here it is said that the topic of the sixth chapter is the essence of the meaning of the *Bhagavadgītā*, the other shore of the ocean of discrimination, the treasure of the riches of yoga, the resting place of primordial matter. And this topic cannot be expressed by Vedas, which means that it does not belong to the Vedic tradition. Jñānadeva talks about this topic in the local language Marāṭhī. This is indeed the *kuṇḍalinīyoga* of the Nātha sect, which will be discussed in detail in 6.152-330.[44]

In sum, according to Jñānadeva,

1. the topic of the first six chapters of the *Bhagavadgītā* are *jñānayoga* and *karmayoga.*
2. *Jñānayoga* is a quick but difficult way to final release and corresponds to the Advaitavedāntic way to final release.
3. *Karmayoga,* which is recommended to *sants,* is an easy but slow way to final release and is identical with the *kuṇḍalinīyoga* of the Nātha sect.

In this way Jñānadeva interprets the first six chapters of the *Bhagavadgītā* as culminating in the *kuṇḍalinīyoga* of the Nātha asect in the sixth chapter.

At the beginning of this paper I proposed the following three points. The *Jñāneśvarī* is,

1. based upon ten Upaniṣads on scriptural level.
2. influenced by Dvaitavedānta and Advaitavedānta on the philosophical level.
3. influenced by the faith in the Goddess Śāradā, the Nātha sect and the *bhakti* of *sants* on the local religious tradition level.

To conclude, we can say that among these three points,

1. Citations from ten Upaniṣads were not confirmed.
2. The influence of Advaitavedānta was confirmed.
3. The influence of the Nātha sect was confirmed.

Three topics remain to be discussed, namely, the influence of Dvaitavedānta on the philosophical level, and that of the faith in Goddess Śāradā and the *bhakti* of *sants* on the local religious tradition level. The influence of the *bhakti* of *sants* can be gathered from chapters 7-12, which deal with *bhakti.* I intend to discuss this issue in the near future.

Texts and Translations

The Bhagavadgītā with Eleven Commentaries, ed. by S.G.S. Sadhale. The Gujarati Printing Press, Bombay, 1933.

Śrī Jñāneśvarī, ed. by V.K. Rājavaḍe, Government Central Press, Mumbai, 1963.

Dandekar, S. V. (ed. & tr.), *Sārtha Jñāneśvarī,* Svānaṃd Prakāśan, Puṇe, 1986.

Maṃgarūṛkar, A. & Keḷkar, V.M. (ed. & tr.), *Jñāneśvarī* (3 vols), University of Bombay, Bombay, 1994.

Pradhan V.G. (tr.), *Jñāneśvarī: A Song-Sermon on the Bhagavadgītā* (2 vols), George Allen & Unwin Publication, Loṇdon, 1969.

Shima, I. (tr.), "A Japanese Translation of the Jñāneśvarī (Chapter 1)", *Mahārāṣṭra* 5, 1999, pp. 43-72.

Shima, I. (tr.), "A Japanese Translation of the Jñāneśvarī (Chapter 2)", *Mahārāṣṭra* 6, 2000, pp. 27-70.

Shima, I. (tr.), "A Japanese Translation of the Jñāneśvarī (Chapter 3)", *Mahārāṣṭra* 7, 2001, pp. 101-128.

Yārdī M. R. (tr.), *Surasa Jñāneśvarī*, Bharatīya Vidyabhavan, Puṇe, 1991.

NOTES

1. Cf. B.P. Bahirat, *The Philosophy of Jñānadeva*, Motilal Banarsidass, Delhi, 1984. R.D. Ranade, *Mysticism in Mahārāshtra*, Motilal Banarsidass, Delhi, 1982.
2. Cf. G.A. Deleury, *The Cult of Viṭhobā*, Deccan College, Poona, 1960. C. Kiehnle, *The Conservative Vaiṣṇava: Anonymous Songs of the Jñānadeva Gāthā*, Alt-und Neu-Indishe Studien herausgegeben vom Institute für Kulture und Geschichte Indiens und Tibets an der Universität Hamburg 48.2, Franz Steiner Verlag, Stuttgart, 1997. D.B. Mokashi, *Palkhi*, tr. by Philip Engblom, State University of New York Press, Albany, 1987. G.B. Sardar, *The Saint-Poets of Maharashtra*, tr. by K. A. Mehta, Orient Longmans, Bombay, 1969. C. Vaudeville, *L'Invocation, Le Haripāṭh de Dyāndev*, Publications de l'E'cole Francaise d'E'xtrême-Orient vol. LXXIII, Adrien-Maisonneuve, Paris, 1969. C. Vaudeville, *Myths, Saints and Legends in Medieval India*, Oxford University Press, Delhi, 1996. S.G. Tulpule, *Mysticism in Medieval India*, Otto Harrassowitz, Wiesbaden, 1984. E. Zelliot & M. Berntsen, *The Experience of Hinduism: Essays on Religion in Maharashtra*, State University of New York Press, New York, 1988.
3. Cf. C. Kiehnle, *Song on Yoga: Texts and Teachings of the Mahārāṣṭrian Nāthas*, Alt-und Neu-Indishe Studien herausgegeben vom Institute für Kulture und Geschichte Indiens unci Tibets an der Universität Hamburg 48.1, Franz Steiner Verlag, Stuttgart, 1997.
4. Wisdom of Vyāsa means the *Mahābhārata*.
5. *tari saṃvādu to ci daśanu / samatā śubhrāvarṇu /* (1.15ab)
6. *eyā upādhimājhi gupta / caitanya ase sarvagata /* (2.126ab)
7. *taiseṃ śarīrācāṃ lopīṃ / sarvathā nāśu nāhīṃ svarūpīṃ / hmaṇauni tuṃ heṃ nāropīṃ / bhrāṃti bāpā //* (2.143)
8. *taiseṃ sakaḷa heṃ mūrtta / jāṇa pāṃ māyākārita /* (2.168ab)
9. *jeyā āpaṇapeṃvāṃcūni nāhīṃ / karma teṃ kavaṇa kāi /* (4.111bc)
10. *āṇi mī mājheṃ he āṭhavaṇa/ visareleṃ jeyāceṃ aṃtaḥkaraṇa / to pārthā saṃnyāsī jāṇa / niraṃtara //* (5.20)

11. *hmaṇauni sarvatra sadā sama / teṃ āpaṇa ci advaya brahma* //(5.95ab)
12. Cf. I. Shima, "Śaṅkara's Interpretation of the *Bhagavadgītā*", *Journal of Indian and Buddhist Studies* 39-1, 1990, pp. 501-504.
13. Cf. I. Shima, "Historical Development of Salvation Theories Found in Commentaries on the *Bhagavadgītā* : From Śaṅkara to Rāmānuja", *Journal of the Japanese Association for South Asian Studies* 4, 1992, pp. 6-8.
14. In these three chapters, however, Rāmānuja explains the relationship between *karmayoga* and *jñānayoga* in a different way from that mentioned above. That is to say, he does not see them as successive stages (from *karmayoga* to *jñānayoga*), but as optional means to attain the next stage, i.e., the contemplation of *ātman*. Thus he attaches equal importance to *karmayoga* and to *jñānayoga* in the stages to salvation, and in that respect he is quite different from Śaṅkara.
15. *ātmarūpaṃ jñānasādhanaṃ coktaṃ pūrvatra* / (3.1)
16. *jñānasādhanatvenākarma vinindya karma vidhīyata uttarādhyāye* / (3.1)
17. *buddheḥ parasya māhātmyaṃ karmabhedo jñānamāhātmyaṃ cocyate asminn adhyāye* / (4.1-3)
18. *tṛtīyādhyāyoktam eva karmayogaṃ prapañcayaty anenādhyāyena* / (5.1)
19. Cf. "*yadṛcchālābhasantuṣṭaḥ*" (Gītā 4.22) *ityādi saṃnyāsaṃ "kuru karmaiva"* (Gītā 4.15) *ityādi karmayogṃ ca* / (5.1). Unlike for Śaṅkara, for Madhva *saṃnyāsa* does not mean the renunciation of all actions. It means only the renunciation of the actions based upon desire or the dedication of actions to God. Madhva says:

    saṃnyāsaḥ kāmyakarmaparityāgaḥ / (3.4)
    saṃnyāsas tu bhagavān karotīti / (3.20)

    Thus Madhva adheres to the importance of action in his understanding of the way to salvation.
20. *jñānāntaraṅgaṃ samādhiyogam āha anenādhyāyena* / (6.1)
21. With regard to *aparokṣajñāna* Madhva says:

    tasmāt sarvadā sarvarūpeṣv aparigaṇitān anataguṇagaṇaṃ nityanirastāśeṣadoṣaṃ ca nārāyaṇākhyaṃ paraṃ bra (2.72)
    ato'parokṣajñānād eva mokṣaḥ / (3.20)
    karma tu tatsādhanam eva // (3.20)
    ye tv evaṃ nivṛttakarmiṇas te'pi mucyante jñānadvārā, kimv aparokṣajñāninaḥ? (3.31-32)
    parameśvarasvarūpāṇāṃ sarvatra sāmyadarśanaṃ cāparokṣajñānasādhanam ity āśayavān āha// (5.18)
    tadā ca paramātmā samyagāhitaḥ hṛdi sannihito bhavati, aparokṣajñānī bhavatīty arthaḥ/ (6.7.8)

    Thus, *aparokṣajñāna*, which is the means of *mokṣa*, has as its object the Highest Brahman called Nārāyaṇa (3.20) or the Highest Ātman (6.7-8) and *aparokṣajñānins* are different from *nivṛttakarmins* (3.31-32). Judging from these passages, *aparokṣajñāna* means the direct vision of the God.
22. *sādhanaṃ prādhānyenoktam atītair adhyāyaiḥ, uttarais tu ṣaḍbhir bhagavanmāhātmyaṃ prādhānyena āha* (7.1)
23. *to buddhiyogu vivaritāṃ / bahuveṃ pāḍeṃ pārthā / dīse hā ārautā / karmabhāgu* // (2.274)
24. *pari teṃ ci karma ācarije / tarī ci hā yogu pāvije* / (2.275ab)
25. *hmaṇauni je buddhiyogeṃ yojale / te ci pāraṃgata jāle / ehīṃ ubhayabaṃdhīṃ sāṃḍileṃ / pāpapuṇyīṃ* // (2.277)

26. *iye lokīṃ iyā donhī niṣṭhā / maja ci pāsauni prakaṭā / anādisiddhā//* (3.35b-d)
27. *eka jñānayogu hmaṇije / to sāṃkhyiṃ anuṣṭhije / jetha voḷakhīsaveṃ pāvije / tadrūpatā //* (3.36)
28. *eru karmayogu jāṇa / jetha sādhakajana nipuṇa / houniyāṃ nirvāṇa / pavati veḷe //* (3.37)
29. *he mārga tari donhī / pari ekavaṭati nidānīṃ/* (3.38ab)
30. *adhiṣṭhūni jñānāteṃ / sāṃkhya sadya mokṣāteṃ/* (3.43bc)
31. *era yogiye karmādhāreṃ / vihiteṃ ci nijācāreṃ / pūrṇatā avasareṃ / pāvate hoṃti //* (3.44)
32. *hmaṇauni karma na saṃḍāveṃ / viśeṣeṃ ācarāveṃ / lāge saṃtīṃ //* (3.158b-d)
33. *ādī ci vivekācī goṭhī /* (4.2a)
34. *he saṃnyāsayoga vicāritāṃ / mokṣakara tattvatā / donhīṃ hoṃti //* (5.15b-d)
35. *tarhīṃ jāṇāṃ neṇāṃ sakaḷāṃ / hā karmayoga kira pāṃjaḷā /* (5.16)ab
36. *āṇi sāṃkhyīṃ jeṃ pāvije / teṃ ci yogiṃ gamije / hmaṇauni aikya dohoṃ sāhājeṃ / iyā hī pari //* (5.29)
37. *taisā sāṃkhyāhūni pāhā prāṃjaḷā / pari āhmāṃsārikheyāṃ jī abhoḷāṃ / etha āthi kāhiṃ prakāḷā / to sāhoṃ e vara* (5.165)
38. In the sixth chapter I followed Pradān's translation.
39. *to gītemāji ṣaṣṭicā / prasaṃgu ase āṇicā / jaisā kṣīrārṇaviṃ amṛtācā / nivāḍu jālā //* (6.10)
40. *taiseṃ gītārthāceṃ sāra / jeṃ vivekasiṃdhuceṃ pāra / nānā yogavibhavabhāṃḍāra / ughaḍaleṃ kāṃ //* (6.11)
41. *jeṃ ādiprakṛticeṃ visaṃvaṇeṃ / jeṃ śabdabrahmāsi na bolaṇeṃ / jethauni gītāvalliceṃ ṭhāṇeṃ / praroho pāve //* (6.12)
42. *to adhyāo hā sāhāvā / vari sāhityāciyā baravā / sāṃghijaila hmaṇauni pariyasāvā / citta deuni //* (6.13)
43. *mājhā marhāṭā ci bolu kavatikeṃ / pari amṛtāteṃ hīṃ paijeṃsīṃ jīṃkhe / asisīṃ akṣareṃ ci rasikeṃ / meḷavīna //* (6.14)
44. For more details on this portion on the *kuṇḍalinīyoga* of the Nātha sect, see I. Shima, "Jñāneśvara's Interpretation of the *Bhagavadgītā* V-VI", *Indian Thoughts and Buddhist Culture: Essays in Honour of Professor Junkichi Imanishi on His Sixtieth Birthday*, Shunjūsha, Tokyo, 1996. 12, pp. 29-42.

CHAPTER 44

Sadānanda's Criticism of Buddhism

SHINKAN MURAKAMI

I. The Advaitin Sadānanda Kāśmīraka's *Advaita-Brahma-Siddhi* (*ABS*) is a philosophical compendium of the Vedānta-schools, written at the beginning of the 18th century (see P.K. Gode 1949). It was completed on the second day of the latter half of the sixth month (=June 8) of the year [Vikrama]-saṃvat 1761 (=1704 C.E.), according to the colophon of the presumed original manuscript 'Ka' quoted by Vāmana Śāstrī Śarmā at page 9[8] of the Bhūmikā of the *ABS*. This is perhaps the last book that refers to and criticizes Buddhism in detail, written almost five centuries after the time when the Buddhist temples and monasteries were destroyed by the Moslem forces and Buddhism was lost in India Proper in the early 13th century. His sources seem to be the traditional understanding of Buddhism in the School of the Advaita-Vedānta. The very authentic text of the Vedānta-school, i.e. *Brahma-sūtra* (=*BS*) 2.2.18-32 refers critically to some fundamental Buddhist theories but so briefly that the exact meaning of the *BS* is to be understood only through its commentaries. The commentators and philosophers of the Vedānta-school elucidate diversely. Among them Śaṅkara's commentary: *Brahma-sūtra-Bhāṣya* (*BSBh*) is the oldest one written with full meaning (in the early 8th century). On Śaṅkara's *BSBh* Vācaspatimiśra (in the later 10th century) writes a voluminous sub-commentary *Bhāmatī* (*BM*), which explains, interprets and criticizes the Buddhist doctrines in detail. Of course, Sadānanda knows Śaṅkara's *BSBh*, Vācaspatimiśra's *Bhāmatī* Mādhava's *Sarva-darśana-saṃgraha* (*SDS:* A famous philosophical compendium, written in the 14th century) and *Pañcadaśī* as well as Appaya-Dīkṣita's *Śivārkamaṇi-Dīpikā* (17th century, on *Śrīkaṇṭha-Bhāṣya:* Śrīkaṇṭha's commentary on the *BS*), and others. Sadānanda condenses uniquely and criticizes the essential thoughts of four Buddhist schools (Vaibhāṣika = Sarvāsti-vādin, Sautrāntika, Vijñāna-vādin = Yogācāra, and Mādhyamika) which were already extinct in India Proper. According to the second chapter of his *ABS*, all of the four schools of Buddhism maintain that only the momentary consciousness or mind (*kṣaṇikaṃ vijñānam eva*) stands for the individual soul (*jīva-ātman, ABS.* p.54[1]), and Buddhism is the doctrine in which the momentary consciousness (cognition, mind) is the self (*kṣaṇika-vijñāna-ātma-vāda, ABS.*p.55[1]). His criticism is related to the Buddhist theories of aggregates (*skandha*), dependent origination (*pratītya-samutpāda*), universal momentariness (*kṣaṇikatva*), mere cognition or ideation (*vijñāna-mātrā*), voidness (*śūnyatā*, emptiness), etc. His criticism is chiefly against the universal momentariness and non-existence of the eternal soul (*cetana, ātman*). He is silent on the Buddhist theories of Buddha-body (*buddha-kāya: dharma-kāya, sambhoga-kāya, nirmāṇa-kāya,* etc.), some of which seem to be somewhat akin to or comparable with the concept of the absolute (*brahman,* or *ātman*) in the Vedānta-schools. Although Śaṅkara and his followers (Advaitins) have rarely criticized in full length the Mādhyamika's theory of voidness, Sadānanda comments on the Mādhyamika's theory. He says:

> "Is the so-called void something of truth or not? If in the first case [you say yes], then you come to take our side, because you have entered into our opinion of the Vedānta. And thus our debate is concerned with the name only" (*śūnyaṃ nāma kiñcit tattvaṃ asti na vā, ādye, āgato 'si mārge, vedānta-mata-praveśāt tathā ca nāma-mātre vivādaḥ ABS.* p. 85[18-19]).

Thus, he continues to criticize the Buddhist theory of voidness.

II. Chapter 2 of the *ABS* deals with the various theories of the principle of individual soul (*jīva-tattva*), and it begins with:

> "What is then called the individual soul (*jīva-ātman*)? Is it only the momentary consciousness (*kṣaṇikaṃ vijñāṇam*, cognition or mind) according to the reason that anything existing is momentary (transitory) just like a cloud? Because so is agreed by the Buddha-muni's disciples who are delivered from bondage, i.e., by [the proponents of the schools of] the Vaibhāṣika (Sarvāsti-vādin), the Sautrāntika, the Vijñāna-vādin (Yogācāra), and the Mādhyamika." (*hanta tarhi ko 'yaṃ jīvātmā vyavahrīyate? yat sat tat kṣaṇikaṃ yathā ghanaḥ iti nyāyena kṣaṇikaṃ vijñāṇam eva vā? Buddha-muni-śiṣyaiḥ mukta-kakṣair Vaibhāṣika-Sautrāntika-Yogācāra Mādhyamikaiḥ svīkārāt. ABS.* pp. 53[8]–54[2])

The expression 'anything existing is momentary just like a cloud' reminds us of Jñānaśrīmitra's logic of universal momentariness (10-11th century):

> "Anything existing is momentary just as a rain-cloud, and these things are existing, [so these are momentary]." (*yat sat tat kṣaṇikaṃ yathā-jala-dharaḥ. santaś ca bhāvā amī. Jñānaśrī* p.l)

This passage is quoted in Mādhava's *SDS* (Chap. II.*l.*117). Sadānanda seems to know this quotation of the *SDS*, however it must be his original opinion that Buddhism is the doctrine that momentary consciousness (cognition, mind) is the self (*kṣaṇika-vijñāna-ātma vāda, ABS.* p.55[1]). Jñānaśrīmitra's logic of universal momentariness has its origin in Dharmakīrti (6-7th century). As for one instance, Dharmakīrti's *Hetubindu* (according to E. Steinkellner's reconstruction) runs thus:

> "Anything existing is only momentary. If it is not momentary, it is contradictory to the efficient function (efficient operation), then the reality which is of the characteristics of that [efficient function] is to be lost" (*yat sat tat kṣaṇikam eva, akṣaṇikatve 'rtha-kriyā-virodhāt tal-lakṣaṇaṃ vastutvaṃ hīyate.* p.4*[6])
>
> "In case of no momentariness, there [would be] no existence." (*kṣaṇikatvābhāve sattvābhāvaḥ.* p.5*[20])

Dharmakīrti developed the doctrine of universal momentariness (or momentary destruction, *kṣaṇa-bhaṅga*) which Vasubandhu (4-5th century) had asserted in his *Abhidharmakośabhāṣya* (*AKBh*). Vasubandhu says in his *AKBh:*

> "[Any] conditioned [element] is momentary (*saṃskṛtaṃ kṣaṇikaṃ*)."
>
> "Destruction of existing [elements] is without cause. What is the reason why [destruction is without cause]? For effect has its cause, but destruction is non-existence. And what is to be done with whatever is non-existence? (i.e. non-existence has no cause)." (*ākasmiko hi bhāvānāṃ vināśaḥ. kiṃ kāraṇam, kāryasya hi kāraṇaṃ bhavati, vināśaś cābhāvaḥ yaś cābhāvas tasya kiṃ kartavyam AKBh* p.193$^{1, 7-8}$).
>
> "If there is no extinction of an existing element (*bhāva*, existence) which has just originated, without cause, there shall be no extinction, because an existing element is the same. If [an existing element] becomes different, it is not possible that the same thing is different. Because it is not possible that the same [existing element] is of a different characteristic from that [same thing]". (*so 'sāv ākasmiko vināśo, yadi bhāvasyotpanna-mātrasya syāt, paścād api na syād, bhāvasya tulyatvāt/ athānyathī-bhūtaḥ/na yuktaṃ tasyaivānyathātvaṃ/ na hi sa eva tasmād vilakṣaṇo yujyate, AKBh* p.193$^{8-10}$).

According to this doctrine an existing element (*bhāva*, existence) does not change or become different. If there is any change or difference there, there must be a series or a stream of existing elements, which are all momentary. He adduces such examples as fuel, a flame of fire, water, etc. in order to prove their momentariness. But it is said that fuel, fire, and water as well as an earthen pot are not a truly (substantially) existing thing (*paramārtha-sat, dravya-sat*) but only conventionally or provisionally existing (*saṃvṛti-sat*), but color (*rūpa*), etc. are truly existing. An earthen pot is only conventionally existing, because when it is divided into potsherds we have no consciousness of the pot any more. Water is only conventionally existing, because when elements (*dharma*) of color, etc. are removed by [our] consciousness we have no consciousness of water any more. But color (*rūpa*), etc. are not so, for they are truly existing (see *AKBh*. p.334$^{3-12}$). Vasubandhu denies the substantial existence of the unconditioned elements (*asaṃskṛta-dharma*). This implies that all that is existing is momentary. His theory of momentariness became developed into Dharmakīrti's demonstration that all that is existing is momentary as seen above. This doctrine also can be traced back to the teaching of impermanence of the early Buddhist Canon. i.e. 'everything (= any of five *skandhas*, twelve *āyatanas*, etc. i.e. our sense, body, consciousness, mental functions and elements) is impermanent (*anitya, anicca*)', 'anything that is impermanent is of pain or suffering (*duḥkha, dukkha*)', and 'anything that is of pain is not mine (*mama*). I (*ahaṃ*) am not this.' 'This is not my self or soul (*ātman, attan*).' So declares the Buddhist Canon repeatedly (See *Vin* I. pp.134 =*S.* III pp.66-8, *CPS* 15.2-18).

It is very difficult to understand the concept of *ātman* (*attan*, self, soul, ego) in Buddhism. Or in other words, the Buddhist doctrine of no-self (*nairātmya*) involves many difficulties. Since, however Buddhism denies the existence of 'self' (*ātman*), there must be some exceptions. That is to say, in ordinary life it is inevitable to use such words as I, myself, and you yourself, etc. According to the 'Chapter of self' (*atta-vagga*) of the *Dhammapāda* (*Dh.*) 'self (*attan*) is the lord of self' (*Dh.*160), 'each man should let himself be directed first to what is proper' (*Dh.*158). 'By oneself the evil is done, by oneself one suffers; by oneself evil is left undone, by oneself one is purified; purity and impurity belong to oneself, no one can purify another' (*Dh.165*). Buddhist Canon also knows the transmigration (*saṃsāra*) of living beings, however it does not use the word of 'soul' or 'life', which is generally expressed by *ātman, puruṣa or jīvātman* in the texts of literature and of the other philosophical schools. In telling many stories of previous lives or births of the Buddha, his disciples or other persons, Buddhist Canon uses personal pronouns (I, he, or she) or proper nouns (Devadatta, etc.) instead of the concept of soul or life. In the transmigrations of lives, these pronouns or proper nouns seem to stand for the concept of the subject of the transmigrations, which is very akin to the concept of *ātman* or *puruṣa* in the other schools. The concept of *ātman* or *puruṣa* is, in general, eternal and not transitory. On the other hand, in the Buddhist texts everything is transitory and nothing is eternal, so the subject of transmigration must be also transitory and non-eternal (*anitya, anicca*). What is, then, the subject of transmigrations in Buddhism? The answer is to be divided into two: (1) ever-changing and transitory mental and physical elements, or (2) ever-changing and transitory mind or consciousness (*citta*, or *vijñāna*) is continuous with intervals in every instant of transmigration just like a stream of a waterfall.

III. (1) The theory that ever-changing and transitory mental and physical elements (name-and-form, five aggregates) transmigrate is again divided into the following three types:

(a) Name-and-form (*nāma-rūpa*. our mental elements and functions, and color and form) transmigrates:

On this point the *Milinda-pañha* (*Mil*), a post Canonical text, runs as follows:

> "What is it that is reborn (reunites itself)? Name-and-form is reborn." (*ko paṭisandahatīti ...nāma-rūpaṃ ... paṭisandahatīti. Mil.* p.46[5-6])

Name (*nāma*) is "subtle elements of mind and mental functions" (*sukhumā citta-cetasikā dhammā*), and form (*rūpa*, color) is the "gross one" (*oḷārika*) (*Mil.* p.49[15-16]). Thus name means mental elements and functions, and form means gross physical elements, so name-and-form stands for a compound of our mind and body.

> "This same name-and-form is not reborn. But by this name-and-form good or evil work (*kamma*, deed) is done, and by this work another name-and-form is reborn." (*na ... imaṃ yeva nāma-rūpaṃ paṭisandahatī, iminā pana ... nāma-rūpena kammaṃ karoti sobhanaṃ vā pāpakaṃ vā, tena kammena aññaṃ nāma-rūpaṃ paṭisandahatīti. Mil.* p.46[7-11])

This relationship is explained with such illustrations as: (1) A planted small mango-tree and mango-fruits of the grown large mango-tree; (2) a small bonfire and its spreading up to a neighbor's farm; (3) a lamp and the great fire occasioned by that lamp; (4) a little girl and the later grown-up mature woman; (5) milk and its by-products of yoghurt, etc. In short:

> "The name-and-form that ends with death is different from the name-and-form that is reborn again in transmigration, but from the same former [name-and-form that ends with

death] the latter [name-and-form that is to be reborn] comes out." (*kiñcāpi aññaṃ maraṇantikaṃ nāma-rūpaṃ aññaṃ paṭisandhismiṃ nāma-rūpaṃ, api ca tato yeva taṃ nibbataṃ. Mil.* p.48[25-6])

(b) The stream of five aggregates of our physical and mental elements (*skandhas = rūpa, vedanā, saṃjñā, saṃskāra, vijñāna*) is transmigration: On this point the *AKBh* runs as follows:

"Because the aggregates of physical and mental elements (*skandha*) are momentary, so they have no faculty to transfer themselves. But the only cravings (*kleśa*) that are cherished by [former] cravings and works (*karman,* deed), in a stream that is called intermediate existence (*antarā-bhava*), enter a womb of mother. It is just like a light of a candle, though momentary, in a stream [of a light of a fire, continues to burn] up to another point (the bottom) [of the candle]. Then there is no logical error here. Therefore it is established that a stream of aggregates [of physical and mental elements] is prepared by the [former] cravings and works without soul (*ātman*)." (*kṣaṇikā hi skandhās teṣāṃ saṃcarituṃ nāsti śaktiḥ, kleśais tu paribhāvitaṃ karmabhiś ca kleśa-mātram antarā-bhava-saṃjñikayā saṃtatyā mātuḥ kukṣim āyati, tad yathā pradīpaḥ kṣaṇiko'pi saṃtatyā deśāntaram iti nāsti eṣa doṣaḥ, tasmāt siddham etad asaty apy ātmani kleśa-karmābhisaṃskṛtaḥ skandhānāṃ saṃtāno mātuḥ kukṣim āpadyata iti. AKBh* p.129[18-21])

"But just as it is said that a momentary fire transfers burning as in a stream [of fire], so is said that a combination of aggregates, which is called a sentient being, transmigrates also by dint of the [former] fervent desire (*tṛṣṇā*) and attachment (*upādāna*)." (*yathā tu kṣaṇiko 'gniḥ saṃtatyā saṃsaratīty ucyate tathā sattvākhyaḥ skandhākhya-samudāyas tṛṣṇopādānaḥ saṃsaratīty ucyate. AKBh.* p.472[2-3])

(c) The stream of our essential elements (*dharma, dhamma*) is transmigration: The *Mil* compares it to the flame of a candle-light which burns through all the night. Its first fire is not the same as the last fire at the end of the night but this last fire is nothing other than that first fire. It concludes as follows:

"Just like [the fire of a candle], so continues the stream of

> the essential elements (*dhamma-santati*) of living beings. As the one is born, and the other vanishes, like as without the former and without the latter, [the stream of these elements] continues. Therefore that [stream] is not the same but not the other, it comes to the grasp of the last consciousness." (*Evaṃ eva ...dhamma-santati sandahati, añño uppajjati añño nirujjhati, apubbaṃ acarimaṃ viya sandahati, tena na ca so na ca añño pacchima-viññāṇa-saṅgahaṃ gacchatīti. Mil.* p.40[28-31])

The mental and physical elements [of a dying person] come to the grasp of the last consciousness here, so the consciousness (mind) must be the centre for these elements. This understanding leads to the next case.

(2) Ever-changing and transitory mind or consciousness (*citta*, or *vijñāna*) is continuous with intervals in every instant of transmigration just like a stream of a waterfall.

(a) The stream of consciousness (*citta*, mind) is transmigration:

The consciousness (*viññāṇa*, cognition) as a member of the chain of dependent origination (*paṭicca-samuppāda, pratītya-samutpāda*) is explained as a life that enters the womb of mother (*Dīgha-nikāya=D.* II.p.63).

> "The consciousness (*citta*, mind) is called self (*ātman*, soul) metaphorically, because it is a substratum of self-attachment." (*ahaṃkāra-sanniśrayatvāc cittam ātmeti upacaryate. AKBh.* p.27[6])

The above passages imply that the consciousness (*citta, vijñāna*) transmigrates.

(b) The stream of store consciousness (*ālaya-vijñāna*, innermost consciousness) is transmigration:

> "Just as a flood flows carrying blades of grass, pieces of timber, cow-dung, etc., so continues the store-consciousness (*ālaya-vijñāna*) too, as a stream carrying the contact, attention, etc. [feeling, concept, will] together with the potential energies (persevering latent impressions) of meritorious, non-meritorious, or immovable works (*karman*, deed) up to the time when the transmigration stops." (*yathā hy oghas*

tṛṇa-kāṣṭha-gomayādīn ākarṣayan gacchati evam ālaya-vijñānam api puṇyāpuṇyāneñjya-karma-vāsanānugataṃ sparśa-manaskārādīn ākarṣayat srotasā saṃsāram avyuparataṃ pravartata iti. Sthiramati's *Triṃśikā-Vijñapti-Bhāṣya* p.22[3-5])

In this case, the consciousness (*vijñāna, ālaya-vijñāna*) must stand for the soul, but this consciousness is transitory and momentary, which is different from the concept of the eternal soul (*ātman, puruṣa, jīva*) that the other schools assert to exist. In Buddhism the consciousness (cognition) is accompanied with many other mental elements and functions (*caitta, caitasika*), all of which compose together a mental and psychical complex. Moreover, this mental complex is also accompanied with other essential elements [of our phenomenal word] (*dharma*). Then the difference between (1) and (2) becomes smaller, though the second theory gives more importance to the consciousness than the first.

The *ABS* deems that all the Buddhist schools admit the latter kind of concept of soul (*jīva-ātman*), although Buddhists seldom admit the existence of soul. As seen above, the author of *AKBh*, Vasubandhu admits that the consciousness (*citta*, mind) is called self (*ātman*, soul) metaphorically, because it is a substratum of self-attachment. He quotes, in this context, two half-verses, which show that *ātman* (self) is equivalent to *citta* (mind, consciousness) as in the following (*AKBh.* p.27[6-7]):

"The wise one attains surely to the heavenly world with [his] well-controlled self" (*ātmanā hi sudāntena svargaṃ prāpnoti paṇḍitaḥ. Udānavarga* = *Udv.*23.17cd)

"The control of [one's own] mind is good: the controlled mind brings forth the happiness." (*cittasya damanaṃ sādhu cittaṃ dāntaṃ sukhāvahaṃ. Udv.* 31.1 cd)

Prajñākaramati (10-11th century) of the Mādhyamika-school also conveys the same meaning and quotes the same verses (P.L. Vaidya ed., *Bodhicaryāvatāra* pp. 236-7). In this way the Buddhists admit that *citta* is equivalent to *ātman.*

IV. The *ABS* condenses each doctrine of the four Buddhist schools as follows:

"According to the reason that anything existing is momentary just like a cloud, it can be perceived directly and inferred too. So says the Vaibhāṣika[-school] (*yat sat tat kṣaṇikaṃ yathā jala-dhara-paṭalaṃ iti nyāyena pratyakṣaṃ anumeyañ ceti Vaibhāṣikaḥ*).

The object, though momentary, can be only inferred, because of the multifariousness of consciousness (*buddhi*). So says the Sautrāntika[-school]. Because a reflected image of a pot, etc. appears in the consciousness that has the image of the pot. That is to say: that reflected image is dependent on the real thing, because [the image of the pot in the consciousness] is the reflected image [of a real pot]. Just like a reflected image of a face, etc. (*buddhi-vaicitryāt kṣaṇiko 'py artho 'numeya eva iti sautrāntikaḥ. ghaṭākāre hi jñāne ghaṭādīnāṃ pratibimba-sambhavāt, tathā hi tat-pratibimbaṃ bimba-pūrvakam, pratibimbatvāt, mukhādi-pratibimbavat*).

All is only momentary consciousness (cognition). So says the Yogācāra[-school] (*sarvaṃ vijñāna-mātraṃ kṣaṇikaṃ iti Yogācāraḥ*).

Because the external [world] cannot be admitted, that [consciousness] is also only void (empty). So says the Mādhyamika[-school]"(*bāhyānaṅgikārāt tad api śūnyam eva iti Mādhyamikaḥ*)." (ABS.p.55[6-11])

At first the doctrines of the Vaibhāṣika[-school] and the Sautrāntika [-school] are introduced and criticized. Here the doctrine of combination (*samudāya*) [of physical and mental elements] comes first, which is introduced and criticized at the first time in the *BS.* 2.2.18 very briefly, and explained by Śaṅkara in his *BSBh.* The author of the *ABS* knows Śaṅkara's explanation, and Vācaspatimiśra's sub-commentary *Bhāmatī* (*BM*), etc., but his exposition is very unique and reasonable as can be seen from the following:

"The advocates of the existence of all the external [objects] (*bāhya-sarvāstitva-vādinaḥ*, i.e. *sarvāsti-vādinaḥ*) think of the two combinations—external and internal (*samudāya*). Among them, the former (external combination) comprises the [general] element (*bhūta*) and that which springs forth from the element (*bhautika*, elemental = special element). That is to say, the elements are earth, water, fire, wind, space, and seasons; those which spring forth from the elements (elementals, i.e. special elements) are the objects such as color, etc. and the organs of sense which grasp the objects, such as eyes, etc. The atoms or minutest particles (*paramāṇu*) of earth are of its own solid quality; the atoms of water are of its own wet quality; the atoms of fire are of its own hot quality; and the atoms of wind are of its own moving quality. By the union of these four kinds [of elements], the earth, etc., which are only heaps of atoms and which become the parts [of the whole], come into existence at the time of creation [of the world]. But there is no other whole than the parts, because there is no means of its cognition, and [if there is a whole other than parts] a perception of two qualities and heaviness, etc. shall be absurdly resulted." (*bāhya-sarvāstitva-vādino mayante dvau samudāyau. bāhya ābhyantaraś ceti tatra bhūtaṃ bhautikaṃ ca ādyaḥ. bhūtaṃ hi pṛthivy-ap-tejo-vāyv-ākāśa-ṛtavaḥ. bhautikaṃ ca rūpādi-viṣayās tad-grāhakāṇi cakṣur-ādīndriyāṇi ca. kaṭhina-svabhāvāḥ pṛthivī-paramāṇavaḥ. sneha-svabhāvā jala-paramāṇavaḥ. uṣṇa-svabhāvās tejasāḥ. calana-svabhāvā vāyavīyāḥ. eṣāṃ catur-vidhānāṃ sarga-kāle saṅghātena paramāṇu-puñjā evāvayava-bhūtaḥ pṛthivy-ādayo jāyate. na tv avayavātirikto avayavī. mānābhāvāt. dvi-guṇa-gurutvādy-upalabdhi-prasaṅgāc ca. ABS.*p.56[6-13])

The above theory of six elements (*bhūta*) seems to have come from the six elements (*dhātu*) of the *Śālistaṃba-sūtra* (*Śls.* R. 13), which Vācaspatimiśra quotes in his *BM* p.526[11]. Mādhava also refers to these six *dhātus* in his *SDS.*II.*l.* 298. The above theory of atoms seems to be traced in the *AKBh.*pp. 52-54. The *ABS* continues:

"The internal combination consists of mind (*citta*, consciousness) and mental functions (*caitta*), and its cause is the five-fold aggregate (*skandha*): aggregate of color or form (*rūpa-skandha*), aggregate of consciousness or cognition (*vijñāna-s.*), aggregate of feeling or sensation (*vedanā-s.*), aggregate of concept (*saṃjñā-s.*), and aggregate of latent forces (*saṃskāra-s.*)." (*ābhyantaraś ca samudāyaḥ citta-caittātmakaḥ. tasya ca kāraṇaṃ skandha-pañcakaṃ. rūpa-skandhaḥ. vijñāna-skandhaḥ. vedanā-skandhaḥ. saṃjñā-skandhaḥ. saṃskāra-skandhaś ceti. ABS.* p.56[14-15])

The internal combination stands for the mental complex, and

its cause is the five-fold aggregate, which seems to mean the complex of body and mind, that is to say, an individual person. The above order of the five aggregates, which is very usual in the Vedānta-schools, is different from the ordinary order of the Buddhist Canon (*rūpa, vedanā, saṃjñā, saṃskāra, vijñāna*). However, we find a similar order of the five aggregates in Harivarman's *Tattvasiddhi* (or *Satyasiddhi-śāstra*) translated into Chinese by Kumārajīva in 412 C.E. (*T.* 32, No.1646, vol. 3. 261a[7-8]: *rūpa, vijñāna, saṃjñā, vedanā and saṃskāra*). So, we must suppose an unknown source of their order in the Vedānta-schools. The next passage is an explanation of each aggregate.

> "Among them, that which is perceived (*rūpyate*) by these [organs of sense] is color (*rūpa*, color and form, physical element). By this etymological explanation, the aggregate of color is the sense organs together with their objects. Although earth, etc. which are perceived are external, as in case where they are perceived, they are in [our] body, or as they are associated with the organ of sense, they are internal." (*tatra rūpyate ebhir iti rūpaṃ iti vyutpattyā sa viṣayāṇi indriyāṇi rūpa-skandhaḥ yady api rūpyamāṇāḥ pṛthivy-ādayo bāhyāḥ tathāpi rūpyamāṇatā-daśāyāṃ kāya-sthatvād indriya-sambandhād vā bhavanty ādhyātmikāḥ. ABS.* p. 56[16-19] = *BM.* p. 524[3-5])

The Sanskrit word *rūpa* is in Buddhism traditionally explained by *rūpyate* (that which is destroyed), which seems, though, to be explained differently in the *ABS* as well as in the *BM* .

> "The aggregate of consciousness (cognition) is of two kinds: The first is called store-consciousness (*ālaya-vijñāna*), which has the image of conception of 'I (*ahaṃ*)'. This alone is self (*ātman*). The second is called activity-consciousness (*pravṛtti-vijñāna*), such as 'this', which is the concept of object, that is standing like a post, which comes from the organ of sense, etc. And that [activity-consciousness] is of six kinds according to the difference of sense-organs. Both consciousnesses are free from conceptional construction (*nirvikalpaka*), and momentary (*kṣaṇika*), because [both] are existing (*sattvāt*). In addition, momentariness (*kṣaṇikatva*) is correspondent to the vanishing of its existence in the second moment. Then by every former store-consciousness every later [store-con-

sciousness] comes into existence. In this way the stream [of consciousness] is without beginning and without end." (*vijñāna-skandho dvi-vidhaḥ aham-iti-pratyayākāra ālaya-vijñānākhyaḥ ādyaḥ ayam evātma. idam iti indriyādi-janyo viṣaya-pratyayo daṇḍāyamānaḥ pravṛtti-vijñānākhyaḥ dvitīyaḥ, sa cēndriya-bhedena ṣaḍ-vidhaḥ. etāv ubhayāv api nirvikalpakau kṣaṇikau ca. sattvāt. kṣaṇikatvaṃ ca dvitīya-kṣaṇa-vṛtti-dhvaṃsa-pratiyogitvam. tathā ca pūrva-pūrvālaya-vijñanenottarottaraṃ jāyata iti cānādy-anantaḥ pravāhaḥ. ABS.* pp. 56[19]-57[1])

This explanation of consciousness (= *SDS*, II.*ll*,.257-8) is different from that of Vasubandhu's *Triṃśikā*. where I-consciousness (*mano nāma vijñānam*) is added. The above explanation of consciousness seems to come from Dignāga's definition of direct perception (*pratyakṣaṃ kalpanāpoḍham*, direct perception is free from conceptional construction), which exerted a great influence not only on his followers (Dharmakīrti, etc.) but also on his opponents (Uddyotakara, etc.). And Dharmakīrti's theory of universal momentariness (as is seen above) seems to be referred to here. The universal momentariness is expounded in more detail.

"It should not be asserted that there is no possibility of activity for the momentary self in order to enjoy in other time. [Why?] Is the absence of activity to be caused before the knowledge of the truth, or after [that knowledge]? The first [alternative] is not [possible]. Because the activity is possiblc, as the beginningless persevering latent impression (*vāsanā*), whose object is eternity, is not annihilated, without coming to maturity of the meditation on momentariness (*kṣaṇikatva-bhāvanā*). The meditation on momentariness is of four kinds: (1) meditation on the peculiar characteristics [which is the object of direct perception], (2) meditation on momentariness, (3) meditation on suffering (*duḥkha*), and (4) meditation on the void (*śūnya*). Here the peculiar characteristic (*svalakṣaṇa*) is a pure real thing (*vastu*). By this [meditation on the peculiar chamcteristics] the relationship between quality and its subject is removed. By the meditation on momentariness, the [concept of] permanence is removed. The second [alternative] (absence of activity that is to be caused after the knowledge of the truth) is not [possible]. But when the four-fold meditation on momentariness is mature, as the continuity of the fluctuating store-consciousness stops, or by attaining to the deliverance which is, in appearance, included in the continuity of the non-fluctuating omniscient lord (god, *īśvara-santāna*), the absence of activity is to be hoped." (*na ca kṣaṇikasyātmanaḥ kālāntara-bhāvi-bhogārthaṃ pravṛtty-anupapattiḥ iti vācyam. pravṛtty-abhāvaḥ kiṃ tattva-jñānāt prāg āpadyate, ūrdhvaṃ vā? nādyam. kṣaṇikatva-bhāvanā-paripākaṃ vinā sthiratva-gocarānādi-dṛḍha-vāsanānucchedāt pravṛtty-upapatteḥ. kṣaṇikatva-bhāvanā ca catur-vidhā. svalakṣaṇa-bhāvanā kṣaṇikatva-bhāvanā duḥkha-bhāvanā śūnya-bhāvanā ceti. tatra śuddhaṃ vastu svalakṣaṇaṃ. anena dharma-dharmi-bhāva-nirāsaḥ. kṣaṇikatva-bhāvanāya sthāyitva-nirāsaḥ. na dvitīyaḥ catur-vidha-kṣaṇikatva-bhāvanā-paripāke tu sopaplavālaya-vijñāna-santānasyoparamād vā, nirūpaplava-sarvajñeśvara-santānāntarbhāva-rūpa-mokṣa-prāpyā vā pravṛtty-abhāvasyeṣṭatvāt, ABS.* p. 57[1-10])

The four-fold meditation is expounded by Mādhava (*SDS*.II.*ll*.47-174) in more detail, but the order of meditations is different and these meditations are ascribed to the Mādhyamika-school instead. The last description of deliverance seems to belong to the Vedāntic interpretation, because the omniscient god is mentioned here. The rest of the five aggregates are expounded as follows:

"The conception of happiness, pain, etc. which comes from the above-mentioned knowledge is the aggregate of feeling (sensation). The concept that is murmured by the words such as 'cow', 'horse', etc. is the aggregate of concept which is accompanied with conceptional construction (*savikalpaka*). Those which consist of the persevering latent impression of these (concepts), i.e. the cravings (*kleśa*) such as passion (*rāga*), etc. sub-cravings (*upakleśa*) such as arrogance (*mada*), pride (*māna*), etc., merit (*dharma*) and demerit (*adharma*) are the aggregate of latent forces (*saṃskāra*). Here the aggregate of consciousness (*vijñāna-skandha*) is the mind (*citta*), and the other [three aggregates] are mental functions (*caitta*). But to be a mental function (*caittatva*) is possible, only when the mind (consciousness) is colored with a special object, even if the aggregates of color (form), etc. are contained in a stream of mind (consciousness). But [the mental function] is not [possible], when [the mind] is not [colored with a special object], because it must be understood that the mental function is occasional. The combination of these is the five-fold aggregate, and only this is the cause of internal combination." (*pūrvōkta-jñāna-janyaḥ sukha-duḥkhādi-pratyayo vedanā-skandhaḥ. gaur aśva ity-ādi-śabda-jalpita-pratyayaḥ savikalpakaḥ saṃjñā-skandhaḥ. eteṣāṃ vāsanā-rūpā rāgādayaḥ kleśāḥ upakleśaś ca mada-mānādayo dharmādharma ceti saṃskāra skandhāḥ. atra vijñāna-skandhaś cittam. itare caittāḥ. caittatvaṃ tu rūpa-skandhādikaṃ citte pravāhāntargatam api cittasya viṣaya-viśeṣoparāge sati bhavati asati neti kādācitkatvād bodhyam. eṣāṃ samudāya-dvayaṃ pañca-skandho saivābhyantara-samudāya-hetuḥ. ABS.* p.57[10-17])

According to the system of the Sarvāsti-vādin-school, the aggregate of latent forces (*saṃskāra*) is divided into two: forces intimately combined with consciousness (*citta-samprayukta-saṃskāra*) and forces separated from consciousness (*citta-viprayukta-saṃskāra*). But the *ABS* does not refer to the latter (Here we remind of Vasubandhu's denial of its substantial existence). Merit and demerit are not included in the system of the *dharmas* (essential elements of our existence and phenomenal world) according to the Sarvāsti-vādin-school, and both correspond to the good work (deed) and evil work (deed) respectively. This explanation of the five aggregates is almost the same as in Mādhava's explanation of the Sautrāntika-school (*SDS.*II.*ll.*283-9).

The process of cognition in the Vaibhaṣika-system is expounded in the *ABS* as in the following:

"The two-fold combination is only momentary. So is established by perception and reasoning, because by perception that determines the present object, its own object is excluded from that which is not existing. For example, by the [perception] that determines [something blue], its own object is [excluded] from anything that is not blue." (*tac ca samudāya-dvayaṃ pratyakṣānumānābhyāṃ kṣaṇikatvam eva sidhyati, pratyakṣeṇa hi vartamānārtha-paricchedinā svaviṣayasyāvartamānād vyāvṛttiḥ kriyate, yathā nīla-paricchedinā svaviṣayasyānīlāt*).

And the reasoning is as follows (*anumānaṃ ca*):

(I) "Everything existing is momentary (*sarve bhavaḥ kṣaṇikāḥ*).

Because it has efficient function, and because it is existing (*artha-kriyā-kāritvāt, sattvāc ca*).

Those which are not momentary are not of efficient function and [not] existing, like the horn of a hare, etc. (*ye kṣaṇikā na bhavanti na te 'rtha-kriyā-kāriṇaḥ santaś ca yathā śaśa-viṣāṇādayaḥ*).

(2) Aṣ a jar is existing at the last moment, the existences that are restricted at every former moment are to vanish after the moment posterior to the moment of their own existence (*ghaṭasyāntya-kṣaṇa-sattvāt pūrva-pūrva-kṣaṇa-viśiṣṭa-sattvāni sva-sattā-kṣaṇād uttara-kṣaṇe vināśinī*).

Because a jar is existing (*ghaṭa-sattvāt*).

Like the existence restricted at the last moment (*antya-kṣaṇa-viśiṣṭa-sattvavat*).

In this way, there comes forth, in the momentary fluxes, the worldly affair which is caused by ignorance, etc. (*evaṃ kṣaṇikesv api pravāheṣu avidyādi-nimitto loka-vyavahāraḥ*)" (*ABS.* pp. 57[17]-58[3])

This passage is based on Dignāga's theory of language (*apoha*-theory, i.e. a theory that any word expresses its meaning by excluding other meanings than itself) and Dharmakīrti's theory of universal momentariness and efficient function. Ignorance (*avidyā*), which is, like as in the Advaita-school, the cause of worldly affairs, is expounded as follows:

> "Whereas ignorance iṣ the consciousness of pennanence (*sthāyitva-buddhi*) in the momentary, the consciousness of eternity (*nityatva-buddhi*) in one's body, the consciousness of happiness (pleasure) in the suffering (*duḥkha*), and the consciousness of a real thing in the void (*śūnya*). So in this way, inasmuch as every respective difference is possible by this two-fold combination, for what purpose the eternal spiritual soul (*ātman*) and lord (supreme god, *īśvara*) are admitted?" (*avidyā tu kṣaṇikeṣu sthāyitva-buddhiḥ, kārye nityatva-buddhiḥ, duḥkhe sukha-buddhiḥ, śūnye vastu-buddhiḥ iti, evaṃ ca sati samudāya-dvayena sarva-vyavasthōpapatteḥ, kim-arthaṃ nityaś cetana ātmā īśvaraś ceti svīkriyāte. ABS.* p. 58[3-6])

This denial of the eternal soul and supreme god is criticized in the following way :

> "You are erring, because [your opinion is] contradicted to reason and experience in every point. For without a spiritual eternal combining agent, the combination of the aggregates and atoms is not possible. It is not to be asserted that [their combination is possible] in consciousness. Because the momentary [consciousness] has no knowledge to achieve what is desired, any activity for creation is impossible, and because the combination of the atoms which have no parts is impossible. That [meaning] is declared as in the following (*bhrānto'si sarvathā yukty-anubhava-virodhāt, tathā hi saṃhantuś cetanasya sthirasyābhāvāt. skandhānāṃ aṇūnāṃ ca samudāyānupapatteḥ. na ca buddhāv astīti vācyam. kṣaṇikasya tasyeṣṭa-sādhanatva-jñānābhāvena sṛṣṭau pravṛtty-anupapatteḥ. niravayavānāṃ paramāṇūnāṃ samūhānupapatteś ca. tad uktaṃ*).
>
> 'Because of absence of eternal spiritual entity, and because of their being non-spiritual, the combination of the aggregates and atoms is not suitable (*sthira-cetana-rāhityāt svayaṃ cācetanatvataḥ. na skandhānām aṇūnāṃ ca samudāyo 'tra yujyate iti*)." (*ABS.* p.58[6-13])

The point of this criticism is that the combinations of the aggregates and atoms are not possible, without eternal spiritual agent (*ātman*) which combines the elements together. This point has often been repeated in the Advaita-school since Śaṅkara's *BSBh* (ad *BS.2.2.18*). On the other hand, the Buddhists argue that without spiritual agent these two combinations are possible by dint of dependent origination (*pratītya-samutpāda*). The theory of dependent origination here introduced (*ABS.* pp. 58[18]-61[19]) seems to come from the *Śls* (R.10~14, 21~25, 27; *MŚls.* pp. 108[19]-109[10], 110[1-23], 111[10-22]; cf. *T.* 16, 815b-816a, 817a-818a, 819b-820a, 822a-c, 824a-825a, *T.* 85, 550b-553b) originally, but perhaps actually from the *BM* (pp.526[4]-528[15]), which quotes the *Śls* in full length too. This dependent origination consists of external and internal ones, each of which is born from the causal relation (*hetu-upanibandha*) and the conditional relation (*pratyaya-upanibandha*). The causal relation is that each cause produces an effect, and the conditional relation is that the conditions, which are combinations of these causes, produce an effect. The external causal relation is, for example, a sprout is born from a seed, ... and a fruit is born from a flower. The external conditional relation is such as a sprout is born from a seed which is a cause in the combination of six elements (*dhātu*, = *bhūta*). The causal relation of the internal dependent origination is the twelve-fold chain of dependent origination, and the internal conditional relation is that a body is born from the combination of six elements, i.e. five elements (earth, etc.) and consciousness (*vijñāna*, instead of season). This interpretation of the internal dependent origination is an explanation of human existence in the transmigration, and nearly the same interpretation is found in the *BM*. This interpretation implies that there is no use of the soul (*ātman*) in explaining human existence.

The criticism of Buddhist dependent origination follows thus: each preceding member, such as ignorance (*avidyā*), etc., of the chain of dependent origination, becomes an efficient cause of the subsequent member of dependent origination, however, there is no possibility of any efficient cause of the origination of the combinations. This notion of criticism seems to come from Śaṅkara's *BSBh* (ad *BS*.2.2.19); i.e. in short,

> "Without a spiritual one (*ātman*), there is nothing else that makes the causes combine together." (*na ca cetanam antareṇa anyaḥ sannidhāpayitā asti kāraṇānām iti. ABS.* p.62[4-5])

Buddhists response: "By dint of the nearing relation (*upasarpaṇa-pratyaya*) these [elements, such as earth, etc.] combine themselves each other" (*teṣāṃ tūpasarpaṇa-pratyaya-vaśāt parasparaṃ samavadhānaṃ bhavati. ABS.* p.62[6-7]).

A criticism follows:

> "It is observed that the combining together of causes only presupposes an intelligent one who knows the differences of arrangements and their aim. Therefore it must be impossible that [the combinations of elements] originates from non-spiritual ones." (*tac cedaṃ samavadhānaṃ kāraṇānāṃ vinyāsa-bheda-tat-prayojanābhijña-prekṣāvat-pūrvakam eva dṛṣṭam iti nācetanād bhavitum arhati. ABS.* p.62[22-24])

That is to say: without a supreme god no combinations [of elements] are possible, and human existence is inexplicable.

The Buddhists give the following counter-argument:

> "Existences are not ever-lasting, but possible only by

combining together in the beginningless transmigrations. But not eternally existing ones are caused to be combined together by some one else. And ignorance, etc. are dependent on these [combinations]. Therefore, as there is no unifying spiritual one (*ātman*), only the dependent origination which has conditional relations is right." (*nanu asthirā api bhāvāḥ sadā saṃhatā eva anādi-saṃsāre udayante, na punar itas tato 'vasthitāḥ kenacit puñjī-kriyante. tad-āśrayāś cāvidyādayaḥ tataś ca saṃhantṛ-cetanābhāvāt pratyayopanibandhanaḥ pratītyasamutpāda eva yujyate. ABS.* p.63[16-19])

The essential point of Sadānanda's criticism is as follows. According to Buddhism, since no eternal spiritual agent (*ātman*) is admitted, and universal momentariness is presupposed, no relations of causes and effects are possible and the combinations of body and mind cannot come into existence, thus our human existence is inexplicable.

V. The above-quoted opinions of the schools of Vaibhāṣikas and Sautrāntikas, and their criticism are different from the Buddhist system as known in the *AKBh*, etc. They have maintained the store-consciousness (*ālaya-vijñāna*), universal momentariness and perception-theory, both of which seem to come back to Dharmakīrti and Dignāga respectively. We are confronted here to assume that these schools had been developing their philosophical views up till the very age of the extinction in India.

ABBREVIATIONS AND REFERENCED BOOKS AND ARTICLES

[See also the abbreviations of the Buddhist Texts in *A Critical Pāli Dictionary*]

ABS—*Advaita-Brahma-Siddhi of Sadānanda Yati* ed. by Vaman Shastri, An introduction in English by Dr. Haramohan Mishra, Delhi 1993 [page, line].

AKBh—*Abhidharma-kośa-bhāṣya*. P. Pradhan ed. *Abhidharm-Kośabhāṣya of Vasubandhu*, Patna 1967.

BM—*Bhāmatī*. see next.

BS—*The Brahmasūtra Śāṅkara Bhāṣya with the Commentries Bhāmatī*

Kalpataru and Parimala ed. by Anantkṛṣṇa Śāstrī. Nirṇaya Sāgar Press, Bombay 1938.

BSBh—Śaṅkara's Brahmasūtra-bhāṣya. see above.

CPS—Das Catuṣpariṣatsūtra ed. by Ernst Waldschmidt, Berlin 1952, -57, -62 [paragraph number].

P.K. Gode, The Date of the Advaitabrahmasiddhi of Sadānada Kāśmīraka—Between AD. 1600 and 1700, *Annals of the Bhandarkar Oriental Research Institute* (*ABORI*), XXX 1949, pp. 23-30 (= P.K. Gode, *Studies in Indian Literary History* Vol. II, *Singhi Jain Series* Number 38, Bombay 1954, pp. 203-210).

Hetubindu—Dharmakīrti's Hetubinduḥ Teil I Tibetischer Text und rekonstruirter Sanskrit-Text, ed. by Ernst Steinkellner, Wien 1967.

Jñānaśrī—Jñānaśrīmitra-nibandhāvalī ed. by Anantalal Thakur, 2nd ed. Patna 1987.

SDS—Sarvadarśana-saṃgraha ed. by Vasudev Shastri Abhyankar, Poona 1951 [chapter, line].

Śls (R)—*The Śālistamba Sūtra* (ed. and tr.) by N. Ross Reat, Delhi 1993 [paragraph number].

(BST) *Buddhist Sanskrit Text* No. 17 *Mahāyāna-Sūtrasaṃgraha* ed. by P.L. Vaidya, Part 1, Darbhanga 1961, pp. 100-106 (*Śālistaṃba-sūtram*, reconstructed from its Tibetan translation by N. Ayyaswami Sastri).

MŚls—Madhyamaka-Śālistamba-sūtram: Buddhist Sanskrit Text (*BST*) No. 17, Part 1, pp.107-116 (V.V. Gokhale ed.).

Sthiramati's *Triṃśikā-Vijñapti-bhāṣya*, see *Vijñaptimātratāsiddhi, Deux Traités de Vasubandhu: Viṃśatikā et Triṃśikā*, publiés par Sylvain Levi, Paris 1925.

T. Taishō Shinshū Daizokyō (Buddhist Tripiṭaka in Chinese, Taishō edition)

T. 16, No. 708, pp.815b-816c: *Leao-pen-cheng-sseu-king* (translated by Chih-ch'ien, 223-253).

T. 16, No. 709, pp. 816c-818c: *Tao-kan-king* (translated in Eastern Chin 317-420).

T. 16, No. 710, pp. 819a-821b: Ts'eu-che-p'ou-sa-so-chouo-ta-tch'eng-yuan-cheng-tao-kan-yu-king (translated by Amoghavajra, -774).

T. 16, No. 711, pp. 821b-823b: *Ta-tch'eng-chö-li-so-tan-mo-king* (translated by Dānapāla, 980-1000).

*T.*16, No. 712, pp. 823b-826a: *Ta-tch'eng-tao-kan-king* (Tunhuang version).

T. 85, No. 2782, pp. 543c-556b: *Ta-tch'eng-tao-kan-king souei-t'ing-chou* (translated and commented by Ḥgo Chos-grub, 8-9 century)

* My thanks are due to Mr. Toma Radev, a graduate student of Tohoku University, who was kind enough to correct my English.

** Concerning the *ABS* the author has written an article: Vedāntic Interpretation and Criticism of the Buddhist Dependent Origination (pratītya-samutpāda), *ZDMG.* 152, 2 (2002), pp. 269-294.

CHAPTER 45

The Simile of the Leech (*jalāyukā*) as Saṃsārin

NORIAKI HOSODA

Introduction

With respect to the thought of Ancient India, one extremely important task is to examine the relationship between the chronologically successive Early Upaniṣads and Early Buddhism. Buddhism constructed its own original (sometimes to the point of fastidiousness) system based on the doctrines of dependent origination, emptiness, and not-self. Yet while Buddhism critically dismantled conventional ideas, it is crucial to make clear that as Buddhist thought developed and carefully reconstructed its own system, it also absorbed some of those ideas.

Among these, the idea of transmigration was refined through a period spanning from the later Brāhmaṇas to the *Chāndogya* and *Bṛhadāraṇyaka* (*Bṛhad*) Upaniṣads in the form of the "five fires and two paths." Its cause was sought in good and bad *karman* and it is first recognized clearly and distinctly in the Early Upaniṣads. Transmigration itself was adopted as a natural idea in both Buddhism and Jainism. It is therefore worthwhile to make clear the position in Indian intellectual history of the Upaniṣadic thought that first distinctly expressed transmigration. In this paper I will take up as one example the simile of the leech from *Bṛhad* 4.4.3, which concerns "the thing that transmigrates," i.e.; what is referred to in later traditions, especially the Vedānta, as the *saṃsārin*. This simile describes the process of dying and then receiving the next life. With respect to transmigration, it appears in the following contexts in Abhidharma literature:

1. As a simile put forth in a proof, along with No. 957 of the Chinese *Saṃyuktāgama* (*SA*) as a "scriptural basis," by the Vibhajyavādin in discussions of "intermediate-existence" (*antarābhava*), or the interim state between death and the next life.
2. In discussions involving No. 287 of the Chinese *SA*, corresponding to *Nagara*, (*Saṃyutta-nikāya* 12.65), which deals with the ten-fold *pratītyasamutpāda* as it applies to transmigration. The simile is used to illustrate that the mind cannot observe beyond *vijñāna*. Needless to say, both issues are intimately connected to the problem of *vijñāna*. *Vijñāna* also has an important role in *Bṛhad*. One purpose of this paper is to clarify the context of this section of *Bṛhad* so that this may serve as one clue towards a better understanding of the meditation and world-view of Early Buddhism. Though I will take up the discussions mentioned above more fully elsewhere, in the following section I will address the first in order to illustrate the scope of the problem.

II. *Vātsyagotra-saṃyukta of the Chinese Saṃyuktāgama*

In the Chinese *SĀ*, the questions of the Vātsyagotra mendicant (P. *Vacchagottaparibbājaka*), who asked Gotama Buddha of the existence of *ātman*, are together collected into *Vātsyagotra-Saṃyukta* (Sūtra Nos. 957-964). In the Pāli canon these correspond to: the last four suttas *of Avyākata-saṃyutta* (*Saṃyutta-nikāya* 44, suttas 7-11), *Vacchagotta-saṃyutta* (*SN* 33), and the first three suttas of *Paribhājataka-vagga* (*MN* 71-73). In this Saṃyukta are concentrated examples of the "14 unanswered questions" (10 in Pāli) on four topics: the permanence and finiteness of the world, the unity of life and body, and the fate of a *tathāgata* after death. I have taken up this Saṃyukta elsewhere,[1] but because of space constraints I had to omit the original texts, which I will indicate below along with relevant portions of Abhidharmic treatises, the most significant of which is *Mahāvibhāṣā*.

Among the sūtras of the *Vātsyagotra-saṃyukta,* one sutra

answers neither yes nor no to the question of whether or not *ātman* exists. This sūtra is called "existence-of-*ātman sūtra*" in Chinese (No. 961) and is referred to *Vātsya-sūtra* in *Pudgalaviniścaya*, the ninth chapter of *Abhidharmakośabhāṣya*. In *SA* No. 957, following the simile of a fire and the idea of *sa-upādāna*, there is an exchange in which it is said that "beings, after their life is over, are carried by their body-made-of-mind, and are reborn elsewhere." For the Sarvāstivādin "made-of-mind" (*manomaya*) is synonymous with intermediate-existence (*antarābhava*). As I stated above, it is in a debate over this intermediate-existence that this sutta is used as a scriptural basis. The passages concerning this debate are as follows (It is impossible to print Chinese charactors, so that only Pāli passages are quoted and corresponding Chinese passages are indicated by Taishō Nos. and pages):

> *Saṃyutta-nikāya:*[2] *yasmiṃ kho Vaccha samaye imañ ca kāyam nikkhipati, satto ca aññataraṃ kāyam anupatto*[3] *hoti. tam ahaṃ taṇh'upādānaṃ vadāmi. taṇhā hi'ssa Vaccha tasmiṃ samaye upādānaṃ hotī'ti.*
>
> *SĀ* I, No. 99[4]; *SĀ* II, No. 100[5]; *Mahāvibhāṣā* (No. 1545, newer translation)[6]; *Mahāvibhāṣā* (No 1546, older translation)[7]; *Mahāvibhāṣā* (No. 1547, smaller translation)[8]; *Nyāyānusāra* (No. 1562)[9]; *Satyasiddhiśāstra* (No. 1646)[10]; *Saṃmatīya[nikāya]śāstra* (No. 1649)[11]

In the Pāli, which does not posit the idea of intermediate-existence, it is simply said, "when a being disposes of this body, and gains another body..." In *Mahāvibhāṣā* there is a debate on whether or not to interpret the body-made-of-mind as intermediate-existence, and in this debate the Vibhajyavādin side, whose members deny intermediate-existence, quote a scripture that includes a long passage not seen in *SĀ* in which it is stated that a :

> Vātsyagotra mendicant gains clairvoyance (*divyacakṣus*). His fellow mendicant died before him and is born into the formless-world (*ārūpya-dhātu*). With his clairvoyance he was unable to see his fellow in the form-world or the desire-world, and had the suspicion that he had disappeared into oblivion, so he asked the Exalted One.

The point of dispute between the Vibhajyavādin and the Yuktavādin is whether to see the body-made-of-mind as being born in the formless-world, or to see it as existing in the intermediate-state. Furthermore, as a basis for the assertion that there is no interval between death and the next existence, the Vibhajyavādin side puts forth the simile of the leech.

That which is translated in *Mahāvibhāṣā* (No. 1547, smaller translation) as "an inchworm" is, in the newer and older *Mahāvibhāṣā* (No. 1545 & 1546) translations rendered phonetically, which tells us that the original had *jalokā* or *jalūkā* i.e., a leech. The simile of the leech also occurs in connection with being reborn in the next life as part of Yājñavalkya's doctrine in *Bṛhad.*

III. *The Simile of the Leech in Bṛhadāraṇyakopaniṣad*

This simile, together with the succeeding simile of "embroidery," illustrates the transition of *ātman* (*puruṣa* in Mādhyandina, which I abbreviate throughout M and Kāṇva, K) from one life to the next. The two similes have the following structure:

> Just as a leech[12] on a blade of grass, having reached the tip of the blade, proceeds one more step to another [blade], and gathers itself in [on the next blade], in the same manner this *ātman* (*puruṣa* M), after casting off this body and leaving it void of knowledge, proceeds one more step to another [body], and gathers itself in [in the next body].
> *tad yathā tṛṇajalāyukā tṛṇasyā'ntaṃ gatvā, anyam ākramam ākramyā*[13] *"tmānam upasaṁharati, evam evā'yam ātmā* [*púruṣaḥ* M] *idaṁ śarīraṃ nihityā'vidyāṃ gamayitvā, anyam ākramam ākramyā*[17] *"tmānam upasaṁharati.* (*Bṛhad.* 4.4.3[4 M])[14]
>
> Just as a woman who embroiders[15] unravels a part of her embroidery and weaves another newer and better shape, in the same manner this *ātman* (*puruṣa* M), after casting off this body and leaving it void of knowledge, makes another newer and better form, that of an ancestor or gandharva or
>
> [K: of deities or Prajāpati or Brahman or that of any other living thing.]
>
> [M: of Brahman or Prajāpati or deities or man or that for any other living thing.]
>
> *tad yathā peśaskārī peśaso mātrām apādāya,*[16] *anyan navataraṃ*

> *kalyāṇataraṃ rūpaṃ tanute, evam evā'yam ātmā* [*púruṣaḥ* M] *idaṁ śarīraṃ nihityāvidyāṃ gamayitvā, anyan navataram* [*kalyāṇataraṃ* M omits] *rūpaṃ kurute, pitryaṃ vā gāndharvaṃ vā*
> [K: *daivaṃ vā prājāpatyaṃ vā brāhmaṃ vā 'nyeṣāṃ vā bhūtānām.*] (*Bṛhad.* 4.4.4.)
>
> [M: *brāhmáṃ vāprājāpatyáṃ vā daívaṃ vā mānuṣáṃ vā 'nyébhyo vā bhūtébhyaḥ*] (M 4.4.5)

While the two similes both describe the transition from the present life to the next, it is clear that the two differ in nuance, merely sharing the portion "this *ātman* (*puruṣa* M), after casting off this body and making it void of knowledge. ..."[17] In the simile of embroidery the imagery presented is that of "making another newer and better shape," and therefore it illustrates being reborn in a better world. In contrast, the leech simile presents the relationship between *ātman* (*puruṣa* M), "the essence of which is the *saṃsārin*",[18] and the physical body as follows:

blade of grass (*tṛṇa*)	leech on the blade of grass (*tṛṇajalāyukā*)
physical body (*śarīra*)	*ātman* [in the body] ([*śārīra*] *ātman*)

As is clear from its correspondence between the physical body and the blade of grass, *tṛṇajalāyukā* should not be translated as "caterpillar" or "inchworm" but as a locative-dependent *tatpuruṣa*, "leech on a blade of grass," and *ātman* here means *śarīrātman* or *jīvātman.*

Where this section of *Bṛhad.* (4.4.1) begins with "this *ātman* falls into powerlessness. . .," the Mādhyandina text gives *śārīra ātman.* Other examples of variants in Mādhyandina where the more commonly read Kāṇva has *ātman* or *puruṣa* are as follows:

	4.3.21[=M]	4.3.35[42 M]	4.3.36[41 M]	4.4.1[=M]
K:	*puruṣa*	*śārīra ātman*	*puruṣa*	*ātman*
M:	*śārīra ātman*	*śārīra ātman*	*śārīra ātman*	*śārīra ātman*

The reason why Kāṇva differs in its expression, whereas Mādhyandina is consistent with *śārīra ātman,* is that chapters three and four of *Bṛhad* (i.e. the Yājñavalkya section) are structured in a complicated manner against the backdrop of various intellectual developments of the previous age. For example in *Bṛhad.* 4.3.2[19] we can see, the influence of *Śatapatha Brāhmaṇa* in its conception of *puruṣa.* However *śārīra ātman* is here being contrasted with *prājña ātman,* and where the same contrast is made in 4.3.35,[20] both texts have *śārīra ātman.* In 4.3.36,[21] just as in the leech simile, the context is that of the process of dying, but the Kāṇva text posits *puruṣa.* Judging from the context *ātman* in *Bṛhad* 4.4.1 K,[22] also as in the leech simile, should be interpreted to mean *śārīra ātman.*[23] While generally in Upaniṣadic thought *ātman* is thought to have the representative role of the *saṃsārin,* the variant readings between the Kāṇva and Mādhyandina traditions are noteworthy.

One portion of the phrase "proceeds one more step to another [blade/body], and gathers itself in on the next [blade body] (*anyam ākramam ākramya*)," which is absent in Mādhyandina 4.4.4, illustrates the journey from this world to the next in the simile of sleep in *Bṛhad* :[24]

> Now this (dream state) is the path to the other world.
> As he advances along that path, he sees both the evil things and the joys.
>
> *atha yathākramo 'yaṃ paralokasthāne bhavati.*
> *tam ākramam ākramyo 'bhayān pāpmana ānandāṁś ca paśyati.*
>
> When he sleeps, taking a part of this world that holds all, destroying it himself, creating it himself, he sleeps with his own brilliance, with his own light.
> *sa yatra* [*ayam* M] *prasvapity asya lokasya sarvāvato mātrām apādāya svayaṃ vihitya svayaṃ nirmāya svena bhāsā svena jyotiṣā prasvapiti.*
> (*Bṛhad.* 4.3.9 [10 M])

This sleep state, called the third state, is the connecting point (*sandhya*) joining the states of world and the other world. *Puruṣa* presides over and traverses both worlds, and since *puruṣa* is separated from the inner self, it is warned that one must not wake suddenly the sleeping.[25] The latter part of the passage quoted above, "taking a part of this world that holds all" (*asya lokasya sarvāvato mātrām apādāya*) is in concert with "unravels a part of the embroidery" (*peśaso mātrām apādāya*) in the embroidery simile.

There are, however, fundamental differences in context between the leech/embroidery similes and that of sleep. Specifically, the former similes are a preamble to the idea of actions (*karman*). In awe of King Janaka, who asks for further instruction concerning emancipation, Yājñavalkya says, "the wise king has forced me out of every conclusion."[26] This indicates the same circumstances when Yājñavalkya, in chapter three, led Ārtabhāga away from the gathering and told him of principle of *karman*.

IV. *Transmigration, Actions and their Consequences*

The main function of these two similes is to explain *ātman* (or *puruṣa*) as the bearer of transmigration. Yet following these similes, it is thus further said of this *saṃsārin:*

> This *ātman* is truly *brahman*. He is made of awareness, made of mind, made of breath . . .[27] He who does good becomes good. He who does bad becomes bad. Through meritorious acts one becomes meritorious. Through bad acts one becomes bad.[28]
> *sa vā ayam ātmā brahma vijñānamayo manomayaḥ prāṇamayaś... sādhukārī sādhur bhavati, pāpakārī pāpo bhavati. puṇyaḥ puṇyena karmaṇā bhavati, pāpaḥ pāpena.* (*Bṛhad* 4.4.5 [6 M])

In the exchange with King Janaka the phrase beginning with "this *ātman* is truly" is used to summarize the preceding teachings,[29] and the descriptive "made of awareness" is at the focus.[30] Though I indicate the portion abbreviated here in the notes, the reason I list the three up to "made of breath" (*prāṇamaya*) is that they are of particular significance because they are thought to form the authority for the definition of the "subtle-body" in later Vedānta.[31] In addition, in the phrases used to summarize the teachings we see a change of subject from *puruṣa* to *ātman* with progressive sections of the text, i.e., as the teachings go to deeper levels, and at the foundation of these expressions is the phrase appearing in the dialogue with Maitreyī, *sa eṣa neti nety ātmā.*[32]

In the above we have a passage describing the idea that good moral acts bring about good consequences and bad acts produce bad consequences, which appeared in the dialogue with Ārtabhāga in chapter three as secret doctrine. Furthermore, *Bṛhad* 4.4.1-6, which begins this section, together with the idea of *karman* and its consequences, indicates the structure of transmigration and reincarnation. Accordingly, I would like to look at 4.4.1-2, which leads up to the leech simile.

> When this [bodily] *ātman* falls into powerlessness, and falls nearly into comatose state, then these vital functions gather around him. As he absorbs these elements of light, *he indeed descends into the heart.*
>
> *sa yatrā'yam* [*śārīrá* M] *ātmā'balayaṃ nyetya* (*nītya* M), *saṃmoham iva nyeti. athai'nam ete prāṇā abhisamāyanti. sa etās tejomātrāḥ samabhyādadāno* ***hṛdayam evā 'nvavakrāmati.*** (*Bṛhad* 4.4.1 [=M])
>
> As he departs, the breath follows and departs. As the breath follows and departs, all the vital functions follow and depart.
>
> *taṃ utkrāmantaṃ prāṇo 'nūtkrāmati. prāṇam anūtkrāmantaṃ sarve prāṇā anūtkrāmanti.*
>
> [K: He becomes one who has awareness. *He descends into that very thing which has awareness.*]
>
> [M: *Indeed he descends into that very* saṃjñāna. He is a sage. He becomes one who has awareness.]
>
> Knowledge, *karman*, and conciousness (memory) of the previous life accompany him.
>
> [K: *sa-vijñāno bhavati.* ***sa-vijñānam evā 'nvavakrāmati.***]
>
> [M: ***saṃjñānam evā'nvávakrāmati.*** *sá eṣá jñáḥ sávijñāno bhavati.*]
>
> *taṃ vidyā-karmaṇī samanvārabhete pūrvaprajñā ca.* (*Bṛhad* 4.4.2 [3 M])

The meaning up to the first half of 4.4.2 is perfectly clear. That is, [bodily] *ātman* is part of a relationship where breath is subordinate to *ātman*, and the vital functions subordinate to breath, and at the moment of death *ātman* descends (*anvavakrāmati*) into the heart. When this *ātman* departs, breath and the vital functions follow suit and depart respectively (*anūtkrāmanti*). The problem is how to interpret the latter half of 4.4.2. The passage "*sa-vijñāno bhavati, sa-vijñānam evā'nvavakrāmati*" is puzzling. As I have indicated by bold italic type above, the sentence structure here is the same that of "descends into the heart," and both the heart and *sa-vijñāna* phrases share the verb *anvavakrāmati.*[33] Yet as examples of various modern translations below show, scholars have interpreted these phrases in very different ways.

Kāṇva:

hṛdayam evā 'nvavakrāmati	*sa-vijñānam evā 'nvavakrāmati*
Müller: descends into the heart	being conscious he follows and departs
Hume: descends into the heart	What has intelligence departs with him
Radhakrishnan: descends into the heart	What has intelligence departs with him
Zaehner: descends right down into the heart	follows after the understanding
Senart: se concentre uniquement dans le coeur	sa migration est toute spirituelle
Deussen: ziehet sich zurück auf das Herz	was von Erkenntnisart ist, das ziehet ihm nach
Geldner: steigt in das Herzens hinab	während er bei klarem Bewußtsein ist, zieht ihm nach[34]
Ruben: steigt ins Herz selber hinab[35]	dem Erkenntnisvollen folgt es nach
Gelder: geht ein in das Herz	er geht in das Erkenntnisvolle ein
Hanefeld: steigt es [bzw.er] herab zum Herzen	er steigt entsprechend herab zu jemandem, der mit Erkennen versehen ist
Takakusu: shinzō ni kōka su	kare ha ninshiki ni nomi tsuizui su
Sahoda: shinzō nai ni taikyo suru toki ni ha	shiki wo guyū suru mono (jiga) ni gōitsu suru
Tsuji: shinzō ni kōka su	tada shiki wo gubi shite kare ha kōka su
Iwamoto: shinzō ni kōka suru	ninshiki wo motsu mono (*ātman*) no ato ni tsuzuite
Hattori: masashiku shinzō he to kōka shite ikimasu	masashiku ishiki wo motsu mono (tsugi no sei wo ukeru botai) he to kudatte ikimasu
Yuda: shinzō no naka ni oriru	ninshiki wo sonaeta mono ni shitagatte, sore (iki) ha saru

Mādhyandina:

hṛdayam evā 'nvavakrāmati	*saṃjñānam evā 'nvavakrāmati*
Müller: descends into the heart	Consciousness departs after him[36]
Edgerton: departs into the Heart	It is simply consciousness[37] that follow along with it[38]
Böhtlingk: zieht sich allmählich in's Herz	Darauf tritt das Bewuβtsein hinaus
Hillebrandt: begibt sich hinab in das Herz	folgt das Bewuβtsein
Gelder: geht ein das Herz	Er geht in das Verständnis ein
Matsunami: hoka naranu shinzō ni orite iku	hoka naranu ishiki aru mono he orite yuku

The heart houses *ātman*, has a central position among the various vital functions, and has a special significance in Yājñavalkya's teachings.[39] The various translations seem to agree in their understanding that *ātman* "descends into the heart" at the moment of death. While several Japanese translators render [*savijñānam/saṃjñānam*] *evā'nvavakrāmati* with words likewise denoting "descent," the majority of the translations listed above indicate "departing" and "following along."[40] However, as the passages I have listed also indicate, in *Bṛhad* (and also in the Upaniṣads in general) for words meaning "departure" *utkram-* (and *anūtkram-* in *Bṛhad*) is used, and in both cases Śaṅkara takes them to mean *anvāgacchati*. Compared to *anūtkram-*, *anvavakram-* expresses downward movement, and also implies entering a particular space, like the space of the heart.[41] Accordingly, *anvavakram-* may be translated in the same way in 4.4.1 and 4.4.2.

In this respect Hattori's translation, which renders *anvavakrāmati* both in 4.4.1 and 4.4.2 with words indicating descent, provides us with a clear interpretation in that "masashiku ishiki wo motsu mono (*savijñāna*)" is supplemented with the explanation "tsugi no sei wo ukeru botai," hence indicating that *savijñāna* is the womb of the next life.[42] In both texts, *ātman* departs from the physical body and takes the various vital functions with it, so it must necessarily go somewhere else. This interpretation is adopted by the latter Upaniṣads, which exhibit strong physiological overtones.[43] The Mādhyandina text has "descends into *saṃjñāna*," and "becomes one who has awareness," and if one adopts Hattori's interpretation here also (the place that has) *saṃjñāna* would mean the womb.

In most of the translations listed above *saṃjñāna* is rendered as "consciousness" or its equivalents, and is taken to be synonymous with *samjñā* in the phrase spoken to Maitreyī, "there is no consciousness after death" (*na pretya saṃjñā'sti*).[44] This dialogue is seen in chapters two and four, where "this great being/ *ātman*,[45] is called *vijñāna-ghana* in the former and *prajñāna-ghana* in the latter. It is not clear what degree of difference in meaning is imparted to *jñāna* by the change of prefixes, but *saṃjñāna* is known to have the meaning "agreement" in Vedic literature.[46]

The destination of the *saṃsārin* is *savijñāna* (K)/*samjñāna* (M), and though interpretation of this requires further examination, the *saṃsārin* becomes one who has awareness and attains the next life. Release for Yājñavalkya, on the other hand, is the dissolution of the perception of duality. This he calls the "mass of *vijñāna/prajñāna*" (*vijñāna-ghana/prajñāna-ghana*) and clearly states that for one who has attained release there is "no consciousness after death." This expression means that for one who perceives *ātman* about which one can only say "*neti neti*," consciousness becomes whole and one no longer perceives duality. In essence it is the same thing the assertion that the cause of transmigration/reincarnation is desire, and to leave behind desire is to "desire *ātman*" and to "have that desire fulfilled."

V. *The Dialogue with Ārtabhāga and Bṛhad 4.4.1-6*

It is against this backdrop of the structure of transmigration/ reincarnation that the object of transmigration, the *saṃsārin*, is likened to a leech. And in *Bṛhad* 4.4.5, I have quoted above, the idea seen in the dialogue with Ārtabhāga that good actions bear good consequences and bad actions bear bad consequences is repeated. The notion that action is based on desire is clear from the outlined process where desire leads to will, will to action, and action to result. Accordingly, release from the cycle of transmigration is achieved by the elimination of desire, or in other term, through the purification of that desire into desire for *ātman*.[47] The following is said of he who has no desire:

> [K: For one who has no desire, has left desire, has had desire fulfilled, and desires *ātman*, the vital functions do not depart.]
> [M: From one who has no desire, has left desire, desires *ātman*, and has had desire fulfilled, the vital functions do not depart. They gather around there.]
> Brahman he is and into Brahman he enters.
> [K: *yo 'kāmo niṣkāma āptakāma ātmakāmo na tasya prāṇāutkrāmanti.*]
> [M: *yo 'kāmó níṣkāma ātmákāma āptákāmo bhávati ná tasmắt prāṇắ útkrāmanti. átrai'vá samávanīyante.*]
> *brahmai'va san brahmāpyeti.* (*Bṛhad.* 4.4.6 [8M])

In contrast to the vital functions of a *saṃsārin*, which depart, the functions of one who has attained release do not. The Mādhyandina text also includes the phrase "they (the vital functions) gather around there" (*atrai'va samavanīyante*). This phrase is also seen in the dialogue with Ārtabhāga, where Ārtabhāga puts forth the question to Yājñavalkya, "when a man dies do his breaths depart from him?" To this Yājñavalkya answers in the negative.

> *yatrā'yaṃ puruṣo mriyate, ud asyāt prāṇāḥ krāmanty āho ne'ti. ne'ti ho'vāca Yājñavalkyaḥ. atrai'va samavanīyante.* (*Bṛhad.* 3.2.11 [12M])

The reason I have translated *prāṇāḥ* as "breaths" is that it is followed by the observation of a corpse "swelling and bloating," and therefore differs in context from 4.4.6. The debate among the Brahmins of chapter three was a competition to see who possessed the deepest knowledge, and the discussion and praising of *karman*, a problem of an entirely different nature, took place away from the public forum of debate.

VI. *Conclusions and Remaining Issues*

As I have shown above, the notion of *karman* seen in the well known dialogue with Ārtabhāga and *Bṛhad.* 4.4.1-6 are intimately related. And although this relationship requires further examination, I would like to make this paper an introductory or preliminary study with a view toward further investigation into the problems of *karman*, transmigration and the *saṃsārin*, particularly with respect to the problem of *vijñāna* in a Buddhist context.

As I briefly mentioned above (II), the leech simile appears in *Mahāvibhāṣā* where an attempt is made to answer the question put forth in SA No.287, "why can't the mind observe further than *vijñāna*?" The reason given is That there is no "support" (*ālambana*) on which the mind may rest past *vijñāna*, and just as the crawling leech returns after extending itself to where there is no next blade of grass on which to rest, so also the observing mind returns (to *vijñāna*).[48] Elsewhere in *Mahāvibhāṣā* the simile is invoked in a similar context, where the upper limit is said to be *nasaṃjñānāpyasaṃjñaka*.[49] This simile also has a role in *Mahāprajñāpāramitopadeśa* (No. 1509), where it is related to the problems of life in transmigration, and *vijñāna* in meditation.[50]

In connection with a closely related problem, the genesis of the questions of the Vātsyagotra is as I mention above actually a debate concerning the well known simile of the fire and its fuel. The question concerns the observation that while fire needs fuel to continue burning, the floating flame itself seems to require no fuel (*an-upādāna*). The answer given is that the flame also depends on fuel (*sa-upādāna*), and that fuel is the wind. This issue continued to remain relevant, as evidenced by its treatment in *Mahāprajñāpāramitopadeśa*.[51]

NOTES

1. N. Hosoda, "'Zōagon-kyō-Basashu-sōō' kō" ("*Vātsyagotra-saṃyukta of the Saṃyuktāgama*"), *Indogaku Bukkyōgaku Kenkyū* Vol. 43, No.1 (1994) pp. 200-204.
2. *SN* IV, p. 400.
3. Correcting *anuppanno*. See *SN* p. 400 n. 2.
4. T2, p. 244b.
5. T2, p. 443b.
6. T28, p. 357c.
7. T28, p. 264c.
8. T28, p. 516c.
9. T29, p. 475b-c.
10. T32, p. 256b.
11. T32, p. 470b.
12. *tṛṇajalāyukā*>*tṛṇajalaukā* "*au* aus *āyu*" *AG* I p.41. Volksetymologie: <*jala-āyuka* or *jala-okas*. Cf. *Suśrutasaṁhitā*, 1.13.6, 8; *AG* II, 1 p. 37.
13. M omits *anyam ākramam ākramya*. Cf. 4.3.9 [10M]: *atha yathākramo 'yaṃ paralokasthāne bhavati. tam ākramam ākramyo 'bhayān pāpmana ānandāṁś ca paśyati.*
14. Śaṅkara ad *Bṛhad* 4.4.3:

tat tatra dehāntara-saṁcāra idaṃ nidarśanam. yathā *yena prakāreṇa,* tṛṇajalāyukā *tṛṇajalūkā,* tṛṇasyāntam *avasānaṃ,* gatvā *prāpya,* anyaṃ *tṛṇāntaram* ākramam *ākramyata ity ākramas tam ākramam,* ākramya *āśritya,* ātmānam *ātmanaḥ pūrvāvayavam,* upasaṁharaty *antyāvayavasthāne.* evam evā'yam ātmā *yaḥ prakṛtaḥ saṁsārī,* idaṁ śarīraṃ *pūrvopāttaṃ,* nihitya *svapnaṃ pratiṣitsur iva pātayitvā,* avidyāṃ gamayitvā *acetanaṃ kṛtvā, svātmopasaṁhāreṇa,* anyam ākramaṃ *tṛṇāntaram iva tṛṇajalūkā śarīrāntaraṃ gṛhītvā, prasāritayā vāsanayā* ātmānam upasaṁharati.
tatrā "tmabhāvam ārabhate yathā svapne dehāntaram ārabhate svapnadehātarasya śarīrārambhadeśa ārabhayamāṇe dehe jaṅgame sthāvare vā.

15. Some translators follow Śāṅkara's gloss and take *peśaskārī* to mean goldsmith (Müllller, Hume, Radhakrishnan, Zaehner, Deussen, Ruben, Takakusu) or artist (Senart, Hillebrandt, Gelder), but as is clear from the accent indicated in M, it should be interpreted as embroiderer (Edgerton, Böhtlingk, Geldner, Thieme, Hanefeld, Sahoda, Tsuji, Iwamoto, Hattori, Yuda, Matsunami).
Śāṅkara: peśaskārī *peśaḥ suvarṇaṃ tat karotīti peśaskārī, suvarṇakāraḥ* peśasaḥ *suvarṇasya* mātrām apādāyā *'pacchidya gṛhitvā,* anyat *pūrvasmād racanāviśeṣān* navataraṃ *abhinavataraṃ kalyāṇāt* kalyāṇataraṃ rūpaṃ tanute *nirminoti.* . . . kurute pitryaṃ *vā pitṛbhyo hitaṃ pitṛlokopabhogayogyaṃ ity arthaḥ.*
16. There is also the variant *upādāya* which Senart follows.
17. Just as Śāṅkara glosses *avidyāṃ gamayitvā* with *acetanaṃ kṛtvā,* this refers to the state of the body after *ātman,* which has consciousness, has left it. The Various translations are as follows: "dispelled all ignorance" (Müller); "dispels its ignorance" (Hume); "dispelled ignorance"(Radhakrishnan); "cast off ignorance" (Edgerton); "dispelling ignorance" (Zaehner); "dépouillant le non-être" (Senart); "ihm um alles Wissen gebracht hat" (Böhtlingk); "nach vernichtung des Körpers" (Hillebrandt); "das Nichtwissen zeitweilig losgelassen hat" (Deussen); "die Unwissenheit hat fuhren lassen" (Geldner) [note 692: "Vom dem Moment des Todes bis zur neuen Geburt]; "läβt seine Unwissenheit gehen" (Ruben); "die Unwissenheit fortschickend" (Gelder); "ihn [den Körper] ins Nichtwissen hat eintreten lassen" (Thieme); "ins Nichtwissen hat eintreten lassen" (Hanefeld); "mumyō wo harai" (Takakusu); "muishiki ni nari, shikaru nochi ni" (Sahoda); "mumyō wo sari" (Tsuji); "shikichi suru nōryoku no nai jōtai wo hanarete" (Iwamoto); "muchi ni shita nochi" (Hattori) [note: "*ātman* ni fuzui shite, shokinō ya chishiki, kōi, kioku mo shintai wo dete iku no de, shintai ha muchi na mono to shite nokosareru"]; "muchi wo oiharatte kara" (Yuda); "[shintai wo] muchi no jōtai ni omomukase" (Matstunami). On the interpretations of this phrase, see Sengaku Maeda, "Mumyō, kono kokoro wo ōu mono : ko-Upaniṣad wo chūshin to shite," *Bukkyōgaku* Vol. 9/10 (1980), pp. 4-6.
18. *yaḥ prakṛtaḥ saṃsārī* Śāṅkara ad loc.
19. *tad yathā priyayā striyā saṃpariṣvakto na bāhyaṃ kiṃcana veda nā'ntaraṃ evam evā'yaṃ* puruṣaḥ [śārīra atmā·M] *prājñenā "tmanā saṃpariṣvakto na bāhyaṃ kiṃcana veda nā'ntaram.* On "knowing nothing inside or out" in a state of (deep) sleep, it is said in *ŚB* 10.5.2.11, *asaṃvida iva,* and likewise in 15, *na kasyacana veda.* See N. Hosoda, '*Bṛhadāraṇyakopaniṣad* kenkyū: dai-4-shō to *ŚB* X.5.2 no suimin-setsu, '*Indogaku Bukkyōgaku Kenkyū* Vol. 33, No.1 (1984) p. 382.

20. *tad yathā'naḥ susamāhitam utsarjad* [*°jam,* M] *yāyāt. evam evā'yaṁ śarīra ātma prājñnenā "tmanā'nvārūḍha utsarjan yāti.*
21. [*tad* K] *yathā'mraṃ vo'dumbaraṃ vā pippalaṃ vābandhanāt pramucyate* [*°cyeta* M] *evam evā'yaṃ* puruṣa [śārīra ātmā M] *ebhyo 'ṅgebhyaḥ saṃpramucya punaḥ pratinyāyaṃ pratiyony ādravati prāṇāyai'va.*
22. *sa yatrā'yam* ātmā [śārīra ātma M] *'balyaṃ nyetya* [nītya M] *saṃmoham iva nyeti.*
23. For another example of *śārīra: yaś cāyam asyāṃ* pṛthivyāṃ *tejomayo 'mṛtamayaḥ puruṣo yaś cā 'yam adhyātmaṃ* śarīras *tejomayo 'mṛtamayaḥ* puruṣo *'yam eva sa yo 'yam ātmā,* (*Bṛhad* 2.5.1). The correspondence of the words emphasized above is as follows (*Bṛhad.* 2.5.2-13): *ap=raitasa; agni=vāṅmaya;* [*ākāśa=hṛdy ākāśa* M]*; vāyu=prāṇa; āditya=cākṣuṣa;* [*candra =mānasa* M]*; diś=śrautaḥ prātiśrutka;* [*candra =mānasa* K]; *vidyut=taijasa; stanayitnu=śābdaḥ sauvará* [*ākāśa=hṛdy ākāśa* K]; *dharma=dhārma; satya=sātya; mānuṣa=mānuṣa.*
This list (*madhu-vidyā*) is thought by the author to be related to the list of "made of all" (*sarva-maya*) of 4.4.5, taken up in this paper (Cf. note 27), Furthermore, the correspondence between *pṛthivī* and *śārīra* is expressed in the following in Chapter three: *ya evā'yaṁ śārīraḥ puruṣaḥ sa eṣaḥ* (3.9.10 [11 M]) [*āyatana=pṛthivī; loka=agni* [*cakṣus* M]; *jyotis-manas; puruṣa=śārīra; devatā=amṛta* [*strī* M]). In the dialogue with Ārtabhāga it is said that *śārīra* goes into *pṛthivī.*
Furthermore, it is said in 4.2.3 [4 M] that '*puruṣa* eat more choice food than does this bodily *ātman*' (*asmāc chārīrād ātmanaḥ*), and in 4.3.11 [12 M], "through sleep he overcomes bodily things, and not sleeping himself, he observes that which sleeps (= the vital functions)" (*svapnena śārīram abhiprahatyā'suptaḥ suptān abhicākaśīti*).
24. The sleep and leech similes are connected in the later Upaniṣads.
bhūyas tenaiva svapnāya gacchati jalaukāvat. yathā jalaukā'gram agraṃ nayaty ātmānaṃ nayati. paraṃ saṃdhaya yat paraṃ, naparaṃ tyajati. (*Brahma-Up.* 1)
bhūyas tenaiva mārgeṇa svapnasthānaṃ niyacchati. jalaukā-bhāvavad yathākāmam ājāyate "svarā. (*Parabrahma-Up.* 1)
25. See Hosoda, op.cit. (See note 19), pp. 382-383.
26. *Bṛhad.* 4.3.33 [41 M].
27. The abbreviated portion is as follows: [*vāṅmaya* M], *cakṣurmaya, śrotramaya, pṛthivīmaya, āpomaya, vāyumaya, ākāśamaya, tejomaya,* [*atejomaya, kāmamaya, akāmamaya* K], *krodhamaya, akrodhamaya,* [*harṣamaya aharṣamaya* M] *dharmamaya, adharmamaya, sarvamaya, idaṃmaya, adomaya.*
From *pṛthivī* to *tejas,* M gives the following order: *ākāśamaya, vāyumaya, tejomaya, āpomaya, pṛthivīmaya.* With regard to this list, see note 23.
28. *puṇyaḥ puṇyena karmaṇā bhavati, pāpaḥ pāpena.* See also *Bṛhad* 3.2.13 [14M]. Cf. *ŚB* 13.5.3; *ŚŚ.*16.9.7. See P. Horsch, *Die vedische Gāthā- und Śloka-Literatur,* 1966, S. 140.
29. The following are set phrases in other places:
yo 'yaṃ vijñānamayaḥ prāneṣu hṛdy antarjyotiḥ puruṣaḥ (4.3. 7 [= M]). *puruṣaḥ* is however placed after *vijñānamaya.*
sa vā eṣa mahān aja ātmā yo yaṃ vijñānamayo prāṇeṣu (4.4.22K [*sa vā ayam atmā* 4.4.24 M]).
sa vā eṣa mahān aja ātmā'jaro 'maro 'mṛto 'bhayo brahma (*Bṛhad* 4.4.25 K

[30, 31 M]). Repeated twice in M, though 30 M as a whole corresponds to 23 in K. Also the order of *amṛta* and *abhaya* is reversed.

30. See previous note. Cf. *ya eṣa vijñānamayaḥ puruṣaḥ* (2.1.16, 17 [= M]).

31. In the *Vedāntasāra*, the suble-body (*sūkṣma śarīra* or *liṅga śarīra*) is divided into and applied to 17 parts as follows:
vijñānamaya: buddhi, pañca-jñānendriya.
manomaya: manas, pañca-karmendriya.
prāṇamaya: pañca-prāṇa (or *-vāyu*). (*Vedāntasāra*, 79-122)
In the Vedānta, in connection with *Brahmasūtra* 3.1.1, this, together with the "five fires and two paths" of the *Chāndogya-Up.*, is referenced as scriptiual basis, though a comparison of the different arguments of the various schools concerning the subtle-body is a separate problem. For further reference I will indicate here the Sāṅkhya, Buddhist, Vaiśeṣika and Jaina positions that Śaṅkara gives in his commentary on *Brahmasūtra*, Ānandagiri's sub-commentaty, plus the Jaina, Devatāvādin, Sāṅkhya, and Vaiśeṣika views that Śaṅkara lists in his *Bṛhad.* commentary 4.4.3.
evaṃ śrutyukte dehāntarapratipatti-prakāre sati yāḥ puruṣa-mati-prabhāvaḥ kalpanā:
i) [Sāṅkhya] *vyāpināṃ karaṇānāṃ ātmanaś ca dehāntarapratipattau karmavaśād vṛttilābhas tatra bhavati.*
(Ānandagiri) *karaṇānām āhaṃkārikatvāt tasya vyāpitvāt, teṣām ātmanāṃ ca vibhutve kim iti. śarīre vṛttilābho niyamyate tatrā"ha; karmeti.*
(Śaṅkara ad *Bṛhad*) *kiṃcātrasthasyai'va sarvagatānānāṃ karaṇāṃ vṛttilābho bhavati.*
ii) [Buddhist (Vijñānavādin)] *kevalasyai'vā"tmano vṛttilābhas tatra bhavati. indriyāṇi tu dehavad abhinavāny eva tatra tatra bhogasthāna utpadhyante.*
(Ānandagiri) *ātmā khalv ālayajñāna-saṃtānas tasya vṛttayaḥ śabdādi-jñānāni tal-lābhaḥ śarīrāntare bhavati. kevala-śabdas tu karaṇa-sāhityam ātmano vārayati. kathaṃ tarhi dehāntare karaṇānīty āśaṅkya pañcendriyāṇi cakṣurādīni golakamāratvān manasaś ca samanantara-pratyaya-mātratvād abhinavānām eva teṣāṃ śarīrāntare janmety āha; indriyānī'ti.*
iii) [Vaiśeṣika] *mana eva vā kevalaṃ bhogasthānam abhipratiṣṭheta.*
(Ānandagiri) *mana iti. kevalaṃ karaṇair ātmanā ca rahitam iti yāvat. karaṇāni nūtanāny eva tatrā"rabhyante ātmā tu vibhutvād akriyo 'pi tatra vṛtti-mātram āpnoti. bhogasthānaṃ bhogāyatanaṃ nūtana-śarīram ity arthaḥ.*
(Śaṅkara ad *Bṛhad*) *kiṃ ca manomātraṃ vaiśeṣikasamaya iva dehāntarārambhe deśaṃ prati gacchati.*
iv) [Jaina (Digambara)] *jīva evo 'tplutya dehād dehāntaraṃ pratipadyate śuka iva vṛkṣād vṛkṣāntaram.*
(Ānandagiri) *jīva iti. vedabāhyakalpanām upasaṃharati.*
(Śaṅkara ad *Bṛhad*) *evaṃ vidyādisaṃbhārasaṃbhṛto dehāntaraṃ pratipadyamāno muktvā pūrvaṃ dehaṃ pakṣī'va vṛksāntaraṃ pratipadyate.*
v) [Devatāvādin] (Śaṅkara ad *Bṛhad*) *atha vā' tivāhikena śarīrāntareṇa karmaphalajanmadeśaṃ nīyate.*
(Ānandagiri ad *Bṛhad*) *atha vā iti. devatā yena śarīreṇa viśiṣṭaṃ jīvaṃ paralokaṃ nayati, tad ātivāhikaṃ śarīrāntaraṃ tene'ti yāvat.*

32. Cf. *yo 'yaṃ vijñānamayaḥ puruṣaḥ prāṇeṣu, sa eṣa neti nety ātmā* (ŚĀ 13). The *neti neti* phrase is also seen in *Bṛhad* 2.3.6, where it is put forth as an *ādeśa* concerning *puruṣa*, and when viewed against *Bṛhad* as a whole it can be said to illustrate a transition from a *puruṣa*-centered view to an

ātman-centered view. Also on this phrase see N. Hosoda, "*Puruṣa* no kansō to Yājñavalkya," *Indo Tetsugaku Bukkyōgaku* Vol. 1, 1986, p. 52.

33. Śaṅkara's gloss on both as follows:
(Śaṅkara ad 4.4.1) hṛdayam eva *puṇḍarikākāśam* anvavakrāmaty *anvāgacchati, hṛdaye 'bhivyakta-vijñāno bhavatīty arthaḥ. buddhyādi-vikṣepopasaṃhāre sati. na hi tasya svataś calanaṃ vikṣepopasaṃhārādi-vikriyā vā. "dhyāyatī'va lelāyatī'va"* (4.3.7) *ity uktatvāt. buddhyādyupādhi-dvārai 'va hi sarva-vikriyā'dhyāropyate tasmin*
(Śaṅkara ad 4.4.2) *tadai'ṣa ātmā* savijñāno bhavati. *svapna iva viseṣa-vijñānavān bhavati. karmavaśān na svatantraḥ. svātantreyeṇa hi savjñānatve sarvaḥ kṛtakṛtyaḥ syāt. nai'va tu tal-labhyate. ata evā"ha Vyāsaḥ; "sadā tad-bhāva-bhāvitah."* (*BhG. 8.6*) *iti. karmaṇā tū'dbhāvyamānena antaḥkaraṇa-vṛtti-viśeṣāśrita–vāsanātmaka-viśesavijñānena sarvo loka etasmin kāle* savijñāno bhavati. savijñānam eva *ca gantavyam* anvavakrāmaty *anvāgacchati. viśeṣa-vijñānodbhāsitam eve 'ty arthaḥ. tasmāt tat-kāle svātantryārthaṃ yogadharmānusevanaṃ parisaṃkhyānabhyāsaś ca. viśiṣṭa-puṇyopacayaś ca śraddadhānaiḥ paralokārthibhir apramattaiḥ kartavya iti.*

34. [note 688 to the translation] "Zunächst hinab ins Herz. Oder: Er folgt seinem Bewuβtsein"
35. [note 51] "S.o. Indhas Weg nach oben: Adem."
36. Gives translation of M in notes. See p. 175, note 1.
37. [note 3] "*saṃjñāna*, which must mean or include the *prāṇa* and the several *prāṇas*" (in parenthesis) and "Cf. *Kauṣ Up.* 3.4 end, where it is definitely stated that *prāṇa* = *prajāñ* (which =*saṃjñāna* here)."
38. [note 1] "So Mādhyaṃdina text; perhaps better with Kāṇva text for this sentence: 'He becomes endowed with intelligence, and only what is (likewise) endowed with intelligence departs along with him."
39. See N. Hosoda, "Kodai Indo ni okeru kokoro no gainen –*hṛd- hṛdaya-* wo megutte," *Indo Tetsugaku Bukkyōgaku* Vol. 2, 1987, pp.148-154.
40. Edgerton's translation, which is based on M, supports K here (see note 38), while Gelder is the opposite. Zaehner read *sa vijñāna*. Senart intetprets *savijñānam* adverbially.
41. Cf. Edgerton, *Buddhist Hybrid Sanskrit Dictionary*, p. 70, s.v. *avakram-*.
42. Toshifumi Gotō's partial translation also adopts this interpretation. Katsuhiko Kamimura and Keiichi Miyamoto (eds.), *Indo no yume, Indo no ai*, Shunjū-sha, 1994, p. 79, note 3.
43. *Nirukta-Up.* 2.5 (= *Nirukta* 13.20/14.7 [*Pariśiṣṭa*]) Cf. *Garbha-Up.* 3 (~*Nirukta.* 13.19/14.6 [*Pariśiṣṭa*]). Furthermore, in commenting on the passage from *Brahmā-Up.* that I refer to in note 24, Nārāyana quotes a certain Śruti before quoting *Bṛhad:*
evaṃ maraṇe dehāntaram ālambyai'va pūrvadehaṃ tyajati. tad uktam. "yathā tṛṇajalaukai'vaṃ dehī karmānugo 'vaśah." iti.
tathā "yathā tṛṇajalaukā tṛṇasyā'ntaṃ gatvā" (*Bṛhad* 4.4.3)
A search in reference indices reveals this work to be *Bhavasaṃtānā-Up.* 2.24, and while I was unable to consult this Upaniṣad, the title suggests that its contents could be relevant to the topic of this paper.
44. "knowledge (name)" (Müller); "consciousness" (Hume, Zaehner, Edgerton); "(separate or particular) consciousness"(Radhakrishnan); "conscience" (Senart); "Bewuβtsein" (Böhtlingk, Hillebrandt, Deussen, Ruben, Gelder, Thieme, Frauwallner); "Selbstbewuβtsein" (Geldner); "Objektbewuβtsein"

(Hanefeld); "sō/ishiki" (Takakusu); "ishiki" (Sahoda, Tsuji, Iwamoto, Hattori, Yuda); "shikibetsu sayō" (Matsunami).

45. *idaṃ mahad bhūtam* (*Bṛhad* 2.4.12 [M]; 4.5.13 M) *ayam ātmā* (4.5.13 K).

46. *niṣkṛtyai peśaskārīṃ, saṃjñānâya smarakārîm* (*VSM* 30.9 = *VSK* 34.9;*TB* 3.4.4, 6). "for Representation, a woman who embroiders, for Agreement, a woman who deals in lovecharms" (Griffith). "To Restoration, a female embroiderer. To Agreement, a woman who deals in lovecharms" (Dumont).

47. See N. Hosoda, "Yājñavalkya ni okeru *hṛdaya* ni tsuite," *Indogaku Bukkyōgaku-Kenkyū* vol. 35 No. 2, 1987, p. 13.

48. T27, p. 124c; see also T28, p. 98a.

49. T27, p. 264c, p. 780a; T28, p. 336c.

50. T25, p. 192a, 532a.

51. T25, p. 696b-c.

Chapter 46

Liberation in Kashmir Śaiva Philosophy

SHOUN HINO

1. *History of Kashmir Śaiva Philosophy*

Kashmir Śaivism is an important school of Śaiva philosophy prevalent in India. It is named after the region to which it belongs—a peculiar feature not shared by any other school of Śaivism. It is a monistic Tantrism which developed from the 8th century A.D. onwards in the Kashmir valley. Before that Śaiva tantric ritual was preserved in the Āgamic literature. People were devoted to Śiva and performed tantric practices following the Āgamic tradition.

The text of *Śaṅkaradigvijaya* describes Śaṅkara's visit to Kashmir. It greatly influenced religious belief there, and was responsible for the monistic approach towards the Highest reality. It gave a new interpretation of the Āgamic teaching and the dualistic approach was converted to monistic idealism.

It is believed in Kashmir Śaivism that it was Śiva Himself who revealed the Śiva-sūtras to the sage Vasugupta. This event established monism in Kashmir and restricted the Buddhist and dualistic influence in the valley. The Śiva-sūtras presented the philosophical ideas of the Āgamas in a systematic form. So Vasugupta is considered to be the human founder of Kashmir Śaiva philosophy.

Vasugupta had two disciples, Kallaṭa and Somānanda. Kallaṭa wrote *Spanda Kārikā* and established the Spanda branch of the Kashmir Śaiva school. Somānanda's *Śiva Dṛṣṭi* and Utpaladeva's *Īśvara Pratyabhijñā* (or *Pratyabhijñā Sūtra*) led to the establishment of the Pratyabhijñā school. In this school, Abhinavagupta and Kṣemarāja flourished. Abhinavagupta, a versatile scholar, wrote on various fields and was regarded as an authority in every one. Abhinavagupta's *Īśvara Pratyabhijñā Vimarśinī,* a commentary on Utpal's *Īśvara Pratyabhijñā,* is the most important book in Kashmir Śaiva philosophy. It explains the original sūtras in detail and proved to be helpful for the understanding of the Pratyabhijñā school. He wrote *Paramārthasāra* a guide book, and *Tantrāloka,* a voluminous work which deals elaborately with the Āgamic and tāntric aspect of the Kashmir Śaiva school. Kṣemarāja was the direct disciple of Abhinavagupta. He devoted himself to the explanation of Abhinavagupta's teachings and wrote a concise introductory book, *Pratyabhijñā Hṛdaya.*

2. *Discussion on Liberation in Indian Religions*

Every religion expounds various types of performances—be they daily, incidental or for the fulfilment of desire—for its followers and the effect of these actions binds an individual to this world. Also, it sets up the aim of human life, i.e. liberation from this transmigratory existence. This is the excellent ultimate end of human life. Therefore, every individual desires it and subsequently tries to achieve it through the means prescribed by the respective religions.

Every religion expresses a relationship between 'the sacred', i.e. the divine, and 'the profane', i.e. human beings, which stand opposed and try to negate each other. This relationship between 'the sacred' and 'the profane' is divided into two types according to their stand-point and their prominence. In the first type the two are remote in distance, 'the sacred' transcends 'the profane' and both are essentially distinct. On the contrary, the other type is where both are in close proximity, sometimes overlapping, and the equal existence of the two is emphasised. An example of the former type is Calvinism in Christianity, and of the latter religions which have arisen in India.

In the former type, 'the sacred' and 'the profane' are the

creator and the created, the latter burdened by original sin. The two are considered to be wholly different. The 'sacred' God is beyond the 'profane' human beings and 'is regarded as 'the transcendental principle'. Therefore 'the profane' beings consider this world as a stage to materialize the God's glory as desired by the God itself, and have the feeling of being the 'instruments of God' and being supported by the God. They act for the God's will and also to attain liberation by the grace of the God *through* deeds based on a life-time attitude of austerity-in-the-world. Therefore, this type of religion is called the 'instrument type of religion' or the 'grace type of religion'.

In the latter case, 'the sacred' and 'the profane' are emphasised as being equal. The two overlap or 'the sacred' is described as 'the immanent principle'. In this type the 'profane' human being is *possessed of* liberation by nature, and therefore is not the 'instrument of God' but the 'vessel of God'. Accordingly, here 'the profane' who are possessed of 'the sacred' in themselves as the 'vessels of God' are to be *against* their own deeds in the world, to minimize their own acts and to endeavor to reveal 'the sacred' being hidden in the depths by negating themselves, i.e. to try to make themselves divine. This is called the 'vessel type' or 'self-reliance type' in contrast with 'instrument' or 'grace' respectively. Religions in India belonging to this type maintain essentially equal status of 'the sacred' and 'the profane' and try to secure the aim of life through knowledge only, and 'knowledge' (gnosis), the chief means to liberation. Among the eminent schools of Indian philosophy, i.e. Sāṃkhya and Vedānta, the former is a realistic dualism and the latter is an absolute monism, wherein the 'sacred' universal principle (Brahman) and the 'profane' individual principle (Ātman) are identical.

Śaṅkara, in the eighth century A.D., founded the Advaita Vedānta school, taking recourse to his Advaita theory (Absolute Monism). It is a religion of the vessel-type, which advocates negating 'the profane' by one's own individual religious practice and then revealing 'the sacred' within oneself. On realizing knowledge of the oneness of the universal spiritual principle Brahman and the individual Ātman and nullifying one's own 'profane' human existence (the individual self), one becomes the 'sacred' Brahman. It is a knowledge-oriented liberation theory in which 'knowing is but becoming'.

There is a process by which the gnosis-oriented liberation theory has been overlapped by the current of *bhakti*-oriented liberation theory. This is a process of transformation of the abstract to a personification of the 'sacred' ultimate Reality in which the 'vessel-type' religion is influenced by the 'instrument -type'. There is at the same time a process of change of the contents of *bhakti*.

For Śaṅkara, the 'sacred' Brahman is absolutely the abstract principle, but *bhakti* needs an object to which the act of devotion is directed and 'the sacred' necessarily becomes personified. For Rāmānuja (eleventh century A.D.) and Madhva (thirteenth century A.D.), 'the sacred' is thus the transcendental personified God Viṣṇu. While Śaṅkara tries to achieve mystical union with 'the sacred', negating 'the profane', Rāmānuja and Madhva consider the transcendent personified Viṣṇu as 'the sacred', and thereby appear to show an affinity with liberation based on a 'religion of faith'. Both of them consider 'the profane' equally as important as 'the sacred'.

But here *bhakti* retains a tinge of gnosis which is highly esteemed by Advaita. *Bhakti* has characteristics of religious practice on the part of 'the profane'. We find, in Rāmānuja, a tinge of the self-reliance-type of religion which plans to be liberated by means of the religious practice of *bhakti* on the part of 'the profane', while in Madhva the absoluteness of Viṣṇu is more emphasised, and therefore liberation owing to the God is more discussed and the significance of *bhakti* becomes less important; it becomes more like a grace-type of religion and closer to Calvinism.

This *bhakti,* having a tinge of gnosis, is characterized as the religion of the elite and practised only by a selected few. On the contrary, the *bhakti* which emphasises the aspect of love is supported by the masses and stresses the immense love of God and His grace. This leads to a way of negating effort on the part oneself as a human being and surrendering one's liberation to God's grace.

The *bhakti* so far referred to is what is directed to the God by human beings. In contrast, the Viraha *bhakti* is discussed in the *Bhāgavata Purāṇa.* The stronger the love or inclination to the God that the human beings have, the more they realise their incapability of being, one with the God, accept the ineffectiveness of effort on their own part and conclude that there is a rigid distinction between themselves and God. Therefore they do not look upon *bhakti* as a means but consider it as an object to achieve. In short, there is a giving up of effort, and thereby *bhakti* is not a means but an object. This is called Viraha *bhakti,* which later on develops into Prapatti, that gives up the notion of union with God by means of human effort and the complete surrender of one's liberation to the God. In the course of development of *bhakti,* this is something epoch-making in that the initiative of liberation is entrusted by individual beings to the God.

In contrast to this Viraha *bhakti,* we also find Tantric *bhakti,* which arose with Tantrism in the background. These two *bhakti*s are similar at the point of propagating their affirmation of 'this world'. This is the presupposition of the religion of the masses and the ultimate mode of religion in the sense that it signifies a state of liberation while a being is alive in this world. Moreover, they are two sides of one and the same coin. In other words, they show the culminations of the two types of religion mentioned so far, i.e. the 'grace type' and the 'self-reliance type'.

In Tantric *bhakti,* 'profane' individual existence is always emphasised as the subject of a loving God and through the proper rituals one is united with God. The 'profane' individual can become, as it were, the 'sacred' God. If we understand it is becoming God in the world by self-reliant endeavor on the part of 'the profane', it is a liberation theory of the self-reliance type of religious practice based on the 'vessel type' of religion. In the Advaita Vedānta 'the sacred' is the unlimited Brahman, and 'the profane', the vessel; it requires endeavor to negate oneself to reveal 'the sacred' in the depth of oneself. And here in Tantric *bhakti* 'profane' human beings are taken to be really existent apart from the God, since the real existence of the world is affirmed. Moreover 'the sacred' is not the unlimited Brahman but a personified God-idea like Śiva or Viṣṇu. It is quite distinct from Śaṅkara's Advaita. But as a result the vessel-type is maintained.

The discussion, thus, sets two opposites, Advaita (negation of the world, non-personified reality, vessel-type) and Calvinism (affirmation of the world, personified God, instrument-type). In the case of Viraha *bhakti,* the personified God Viṣṇu becomes the divinity of high absoluteness which is distinct from 'the profane' and shows a similarity to Calvinism. And Tantric *bhakti* maintains a personified God and the affirmation of the world, and at the same time is both instrument-type and 'vessel-type'. Further, accepting the personified God, it naturally talks about grace. Now, Kashmir Śaiva philosophy very peculiar in nature, for though under the influence of Tantric *bhakti,* it tries to justify the Advaita standpoints of the negation of the world and an un personified God.

3. *Cosmology and Liberation of Kashmir Śaiva Philosophy*

Kashmir Śaivism is also called Trika. Since *paśu* 'domestic animal', *pati* 'lord' and *pāśa* 'rope' are the three realities described in the Āgamas, the teaching of Āgama is therefore said to be dualistic or pluralistic. Kashmir Ṣaiva philosophy maintains dualism though it ultimately advocates monism.

According to Kashmir Śaiva philosophy, *pati* is Parama Śiva (the ultimate Reality), *paśu* is Jīva (the individual self) and this material world, and *pāśa* is the six veils (Māyā and five Kañcukas) which bring concealment of the powers of Paramaśiva The ultimate reality is the Brahman of Advaita Vedānta, whereas according to Kashmir Śaivism it is Paramaśiva; both these schools consider an abstract, unpersonified ultimate reality. Advaita regards Jīva and the world as false/unreal but the Kashmir Śaiva school regards the same, i.e. *paśu,* as true/real.

According to Advaita the Brahman is the only Reality and Jīva as embodied, distinct Ātman, and the world, which are the creations of Māyā, are unreal. But it the veil of Māyā is removed then the Brahman and the Ātman are cognised as one and the same. According to Kashmir Śaiva, Paramaśiva and the veiled Jīva are both real, for Jīva is the appearance of Paramaśiva. The moment Jīva realises himself as nothing else but Paramaśiva, in other words, when the veil is removed, Jīva realises that he is himself Paramaśiva and becomes one with it. In short, all is *ekarasa* with prevailing ultimate reality. The difference of understanding consists in whether the veil makes the world into something false, or is just a cover which makes reality unseen until the world manifests itself in its true perspective at a proper time.

Paramaśiva first manifests itself into Śiva and Śakti. Śiva and Śakti are inseparable and undistinguishable principles, and are two aspects of the manifestation of the abstract principle, Paramaśiva. Śiva is *prakāśa,* the omnicient aspect, while Śakti is the omnicient aspect of the Reality. Śiva is a pure Seer and just observes the manifold development of the world through Śakti's creative power. Śiva is the first principle of evolution and Śakti evolves 33 principles from Sadāśiva to Earth. As long as Śiva and Śakti are manifested, those 33 principles are in the process of either evolution or dissolution.

There are 36 principles from the top Paramaśiva down to Earth. This is considered to be a process of manifestation beginning with Śiva and continuing to the Earth. In relation to *pati/ paśu/pāśa, pati* is Paramaśiva and there are 5 principles, viz. (1) Śiva, (2) Śakti, (3) Sadāśiva, (4) Īśvara, and (5) Śuddhavidyā (Pure Knowledge)—this is called Śuddha Advan (pure path). (6)-(11), the 6 veils, viz. Māyā and the 5 Kañcukas, are equivalent to *pāśa,* (12)-(36) Puruṣa, Prakṛti and so on, are the same as in the Sāṃkhya theory of 25 principles, equivalent to *paśu.*

The world is thus the manifestation of Paramaśiva by his own free will. All is the outcome of five actions (*kriyā*) based on his voluntary will. The five are (1) *sṛṣṭi,* evolution, (2) *sthiti,* maintenance, (3) *laya,* dissolution, (4) *tirodhāna,* veiling, and (5) *anugraha,* grace. Due to the act of veiling among the five activities, the real nature of the soul and also of the world is concealed. In that case the primaeval material of evolution is Māyā. It veils the real nature of Śiva and consequently causes imperfection in his five powers, viz. *cid, ānanda, icchā, jñāna* and *kriyā.* The limitation of the nature of the Highest Reality , constitutes the three *malas,* 'impurities', or 'defilements', as the nature of the limited self. They are (1) Āṇavamala 'innate ignorance', (2) Māyīyāmala 'impurity created due to illusion' and (3) Kārmamala 'impurity caused by actions'. The first of these is the cause of the others.

Āṇavamala veils the nature of the self and thereby Jīva considers itself to be incomplete. Under these circumstances, Paramaśiva's voluntary (*svātantrya*) will and omniscience (*jñātṛtva*) are limited. This leads to a misapprehension of the nature of Paramaśiva and ultimately produces limited or imperfect knowledge, whereby Māyīyāmala is created. Consequently dualistic knowledge based on the subject-object relationship, i.e. *vyāvahārika* knowledge, is effective. It is Kārmamala that restricts the powers of the actions of Paramaśiva. Thus universal knowledge becomes individual knowledges and the objective world is made manifold. Due to primaeval ignorance we are in such a bondaged condition, but liberation is due to the voluntary will of Paramaśiva.

The bondage is being bereft of the knowledge of the identity of Paramaśiva and Jīva, and this knowledge itself is liberation. We regain perfection due to knowledge. Thus ignorance and its removal (knowledge) is thought to be the *līlā* of Paramaśiva. This, Paramaśiva's power of grace, reveals the true nature of the Self, possessing perfection, and leads to the obtaining of liberation, which is said to be "the realisation that an individual self is the same as the lord himself". (*Īśvarapratyabhijñāvimarśinī* 1.1.1) This knowledge is called *anugraha* and the individual illuminated by Paramaśiva's *anugraha* sees himself as the whole.

The *anugraha* the fifth action of Paramaśiva is caused by Paramaśiva's voluntary will. It is unconditional. Śaktipāta proved that this *anugraha* has actually taken place. And Śaktipāta itself leads an individual to the path of spiritual realisation. That is, *bhakti* to Śiva is Śaktipāta. When Śaktipāta takes place, *bhakti* arises in the mind of devotees. It is the sign of Śaktipāta that devotees feel like taking the Dīkṣā ritual. That is, *bhakti* arises in the mind of devotees who obtain Śaktipāta and then devotees want to have Dīkṣā, 'spiritual initiation'. In the Kashmir Śaiva school ignorance is considered as two-fold–spiritual and intellectual. The latter depends upon the body, and therefore exists while the body exists. But spiritual ignorance is the notion of self-limitation. Dīkṣā removes it, and only then can intellectual knowledge, together with spiritual knowledge, lead to liberation. From the viewpoint of *anugraha* in Kashmir Śaiva philosophy, the elevating process is thus: purification of Malas → Śaktipāta → *bhakti* → Dīkṣā.

In Kashmir Śaiva the Guru plays an important role in the process of liberation. A Guru is only an authoritative person and is identified with Parama Śiva, and therefore thought to be a guiding teacher who leads an individual devotee on the proper way to liberation. The Guru confers the knowledge of Paramaśiva after performing Dīkṣā. Jīva lessens the sucking power of impurities gradually while repeatingly being born and doing actions. And at the time when the power of Jīva's impurities is weakened, Śiva in the form of a Guru performs the Dīkṣā ritual and removes Jīva's impurities. Thereby Jīva is liberated from *pāśa* at the time of death, obtains union with Śiva and is liberated.

When ignorance is removed through Dīkṣā and the learning of Āgama, self-realization arises. It is a revelation of the powers of the self such as omnipotence, omniscience etc. When an individual knows that he is of the nature of Paramaśiva, he realises his own self and identifies himself with paramaśiva. This is the identification of Jīva with Paramaśiva. It is *sāmarasya*—this is liberation.

Kashmir Śaivism mentions four means of liberation. They are *anupāya, śāmbhavopāya/icchopāya, śāktopāya/jñānopāya* and *āṇavopāya/kriyopāya.* This school advocates the theory of *jñānakarmasamuccaya.* This means that a combination of knowledge and action is the proper means to attain liberation. Knowledge or action alone cannot lead to liberation. Kashmir Śaivites regard Śiva and Śakti as two inseparable aspects of one reality. According to them Śiva and Śakti represent knowledge and action respectively. So the realisation of the reality constitutes the combination of knowledge and action. So they emphasize the combination of these two as the only means for liberation.

When Jīva realises himself as completely independent and free, there remains no difference between Jīva and Paramaśiva. Jīva has 'forgotten' this true nature due to ignorance, and 'recognizes' or 'notices' the identity of Jīva and Paramaśiva. This is liberation. Thereby the Kashmir Śaiva school is called the Pratyabhijñā School 'school of recognizing'.

The standpoint of Kashmir Śaiva philosophy is the affirmation of the world which means it is not the obtaining of knowledge by the negation of the world (through nullifying actions), as Advaita Vedāntins think, but is attainment of knowledge by 'noticing' in its true nature what already exists.

Kashmir Śaiva philosophy is a school of Tantrism and has the Āgamas as authoritative texts, but it approaches Advaita Vedānta, which acknowledges the authority of the Vedas, by adopting a monistic interpretation. Though Śaivism is a religious philosophy, it acknowledges an unpersonified Paramaśiva which conceptually resembles the Brahman of the Advaita Vedānta. Both these systems are similar in their method of self-reliance as the nature of liberation. Thus, we may say that Kashmir Śaiva is a Tantric world of Śiva with an Advaitic interpretation and a similar type structure.

CHAPTER 47

Notes on Kumārila's Approach to the Ritual Scripture*

KIYOTAKA YOSHIMIZU

In the Vedic corpus the framework of a sacrifice is described by a series of injunctions (*vidhi*). Since the scholars of the Mīmāṃsā school, namely, the Mīmāṃsakas, developed their theory of the Vedic exegesis under the strong influence of the Yajurveda, they attached much importance to injunctions while assigning the other types of Vedic sentences as supplements subordinate to an injunction: A formula (*mantra*) is to be pronounced when the action provided in an injunction is performed; an explanatory passage (*arthavāda*) elucidates why one should perform an action as provided in the injunction. A hierarchical structure was assumed also among injunctions. For every sacrifice, the Veda was supposed to have a core-injunction called "direction" (*codanā*), which urges or enjoins (*codayati*) a person to undertake a session of the sacrifice; and the other injunctions describing the details of the sacrifice are subordinate to the direction. Introducing several innovations into the traditional exegesis, Kumārila (ca. 600 A.D.) opened up a new dimension in Indian theories about how to interpret various texts from various aspects. In this article I would like to point out a certain ambivalence in Kumārila's hermeneutic speculation about the relation between the human beings and the ritual scripture. Before we move on to this issue, two fundamental concepts in the Mīmāṃsā exegesis must be clarified.

I. *Bhāvanā and Apūrva*

The Mīmāṃsakas paid particular attention to the verb in an injunction. By the time of Śabarasvāmin, the meaning of "A causes B to occur" (*bhāv-ay-a-ti*), namely, the causative form of "B occurs" (*bhav-a-ti*), had been said to be implied in every verb used for referring to an act of a person. Human beings always carry out activities with the intention of pursuing their purpose. When we are engaged in an act, we work on an object to bring about a result. If the activity of an object a person works on to bring about a desired result can be called "*bhavati*" in general, the human activity intended to work on the object can be called "*bhāvayati*" in the causative. The noun "*bhāvanā*" is derived through adding the nominal suffix "*anā*" indicating an activity to the part of the verbal root √*bhū* in its causative form "*bhāv*". Because *bhāvanā* is thus what we might call "causing the object to perform its activity", we may render it simply as "exertion".[1] In the *Tantravārttika* Kumārila confined the part of a verb indicating a *bhāvanā* to its verbal ending as far as the *bhāvanā* is treated in the Vedic exegesis.[2]

When a person carries out an act, the general form of his activity called "exertion" (*bhāvanā*) requires the following three conditions to be fulfilled: First, *bhāvanā* requires a purpose, in other words, what is to be established (*sādhya*). Except for the cases of mental disturbance, people are aware of what they want to achieve when they take an action.[3] Secondly, *bhāvanā* requires a means (*sādhana*) one employs to acquire the aimed result. One must follow a particular pattern of human activity in order to accomplish a particular purpose. In a sacrifice one adopts an effective means for acquiring a desired result by offering a proper oblation to a particular deity. Thirdly, *bhāvanā* requires the manner of performance (*itikartavyatā*). In order to perform an act, one must carry out a proper procedure for procuring necessities beforehand and disposing of the remains afterwards. Mīmāṃsakas illustrate the manner of performance by a series of ritual acts preparing an oblation. It was the task assigned to Mīmāṃsakas to interpret ritual texts of the Veda as describing these three conditions by means of exegetic devices. Kumārila regards the activity of the Vedic direction to urge a person as a kind of *bhāvanā*, namely, "denotative exertion" (*abhidhābhāvanā*),[4] and adopted the scheme of the three conditions in order to describe the function of the Vedic injunction.[5]

On the other hand, the Mīmāṃsakas ascribed "non-redundancy" to the Veda. According to them, each injunction pertaining to a sacrifice has its own object, namely, it corresponds to a particular pattern of action not provided by any other injunctions. After having described an archetype (*prakṛti*) of a sacrifice in detail, the texts of the Yajurveda briefly describe its modification (*vikṛti*) to be performed for realizing a special desire. In this context, what the section of a modification provides without correspondence to its archetype was called "uniqueness" (*a-pūrva*).[6] The Mīmāṃsakas gave this term "*apūrva*" to the original pattern of each sacrifice including archetypes, considering what kind of oblation is to be offered to which deity at the sacrifice. And they believed that a direction (*codanā*), namely, a core-injunction containing the name of the sacrifice, corresponds one to one to an *apūrva*. By the time of Śabara, the *apūrva* of a sacrifice had been regarded as a kind of *causa finalis* urging a qualified person to have a session of the sacrifice. Śabara illustrated this aspect of *apūrva* by the simile of a garden and a gardener[7]: A gardener, employed by the owner of a garden, enters into his garden which has already been existing, and exerts himself to take care of it. In the same way, the *apūrva* has already been established in the Aryan society as a fixed pattern of a sacrifice. Individual persons are requested by the eternal Veda through its direction to keep the tradition of the sacrifice by following the procedure described in the ritual corpus. In this simile, however, it is affirmed that the gardener will receive his reward if he has accomplished his duties. By the time of Śabara, the *apūrva* had been assigned the role of intermediary leading to the result in the future.[8]

Kumārila, who was well acquainted with the various philosophical doctrines of his times, extensively introduced the notion of "disposition" (*saṃskāra*) into the theory of cognitive process as well as into the theory of ritual.[9] He changed the meaning of "*apūrva*" to a kind of disposition or "potency" (*śakti*) shared by the self (*ātman*) of individual persons; the *apūrva* came to be characterized as the intermediary for a result in the future rather than as the unique pattern of offering. As a result, the *apūrva*, which had been supposed to be inseparably related to a particular direction (*codanā*) of the eternal Veda, turned into a kind of disposition produced and accumulated in the self of an individual. Accordingly, Kumārila denied that the *apūrva* would exist prior to an individual as the ideal pattern of action to be followed.[10] We could say that Kumārila extended the notion of "exertion" (*bhāvanā*), namely, the form of an activity aiming at realizing a purpose, to apply it not only to human beings but also to the direction (*codanā*) of the eternal Veda, and at the same time he applied the idea of *apūrva* originally connected with the eternal Veda to an individual person.

II. *Anthropo-centric approach in Kumārila's exegesis*

Kumārila does not only generally consider the sacrifice as a human occupation in this world,[11] but he also pays much attention to the acts of individual persons in his discussion on each traditionally fixed topic of exegesis. We find an example in the *Tantravārttika* on the second volume (*adhyāya*) of the *Mīmāṃsāsūtra* where it is discussed how to discern a direction (*codanā*) from a pseudo-direction inserted into a complicated structure of ritual texts.[12] In its first section of the second chapter (*pāda*), it is discussed how to conceive the relation among the three injunctions "*somena yajeta*", "*dākṣiṇāni juhoti*" and "*hiraṇyam ātreyāya dadāti*" pertaining to one and the same Jyotiṣṭoma sacrifice.[13] When Śabarasvāmin calls the subject of the second *adhyāya* "discernment of an *apūrva*" in this section,[14] he views the discernment of a *codanā* from the side of *apūrva*, namely, from the side of the ideal pattern of a sacrifice inseparably connected with the eternal Veda. Kumārila, however, formulates the topic in this section in three ways as follows.

> [Is the topic of this section to be formulated as] "Do the three *bhāvanās* bring about a single *apūrva*, or three distinct ones?" Or "Do the referents of the three verbal roots qualify a single *bhāvanā*, or three distinct ones?" Or "Do the three verbal roots indicates a single referent, or three distinct ones?"[15]

The first formulation asks about the causality set in motion after an individual has performed a sacrifice at a sacrificial place.[16] Here Kumārila uses the term *apūrva* to refer to the intermediary produced through human activity. If, however, *apūrva* is considered to be the intermediary between the ephemeral session of a sacrifice and the result to be realized in the future, we cannot distinguish the *apūrvas* of various periodical sacrifices from each other through the description of their own form; for all the periodical sacrifices have no difference insofar as they carry the sacrificer to heaven after death. In fact, Kumārila rejects the first alternative and adopts the second, which asks about the structure of a human action as it is described in ritual texts.[17] By investigating the point at issue formulated in this way, Kumārila becomes engaged in the exegesis to discern a direction (*codanā*) from other types of sentences in ritual texts, sticking to his own view that *apūrva* is essentially an intermediary residing and accumulated in the individual self.

It must be noted that Śabarasvāmin had already introduced the notion of *bhāvanā* into the discussion of this section. First, the opponent of this section considers the three injunctions in question as forming a single large direction. He has recourse to a principle of exegesis called the economy of assumptions (*kalpanālāghava*) in later ages.[18] He insists, namely, that there must be a single large sentence comprising the three injunctions because assuming a single whole is, as far as such an assumption is possible, preferable to assuming many parts only.[19] Applying the notion of *bhāvanā,* he secondly advances another reason which would appear to be plausible even if the existence of the single whole is denied. Although the three finite verbs differ in their verbal roots, they equally enjoins the exertion of causing something to be realized (*bhāvayet*) through their verbal endings.[20]

We may therefore say that the *prima facie* view of the second formulation assumed in Kumārila's introduction was already stated by the opponent in Śabara's Bhāṣya. Nevertheless, Śabarasvāmin does not assert that the *bhāvanā* is differentiated in accordance with the verbal root; He accepts, on the contrary, the view of the opponent that the three verbs have a common ending which expresses a *bhāvanā;* and without going into whether this *bhāvanā* remains one and the same in each verb, Śabara derives a conclusion that each of the three injunctions forms a distinct direction enjoining its own *apūrva* respectively from the fact that the verb as a whole differs from each other in three injunctions.[21] This conclusion results from applying the first criterion for discerning a direction laid down in JS 2.2.1: "Where there is a different word (a verb), a different act [is enjoined]; because its attachment is established." (*śabdāntare karmabhedaḥ kṛtānubandhatvāt*). Śahara takes "*kṛtānubandha*" to refer to the fact that the meaning of a verb accomplishes its syntactical relation with the meanings of nouns (*kārakagrāma*) within each injunction.[22]

Kumārila, however, interprets this "*kṛtānubandha*" from a different angle in support of his own formulation of the point at issue. According to him, the *anubandha* in this context refers to the connection of a verbal ending to a verbal root. Because in a sentence a verbal ending is always attached to a verbal root and never used alone, it necessarily denotes its own meaning, namely, the exertion (*bhāvanā*), in a form connected to the referent of a verbal root. A verbal ending connected with a verbal root in a sentence does not need another verbal root forming a finite verb in other injunctions.[23] If there were any word used alone in a sentence for denoting a *bhāvanā* exclusively, it would be possible that one and the same *bhāvanā* is superficially coloured by each verb in the three injunctions. But because no word can denote a *bhāvanā* alone, we cannot but regard the *bhāvanās* denoted by each verb of the three injunctions as essentially different from each other.[24]

Kumārila compares the distinctiveness of *bhāvanās* to the distinctiveness of phonemes (*varṇa*). While "*g*", "*au*" and "*ḥ*" forming the word "*gauḥ*" (cow) equally fall into one and the same category of phoneme, we cannot deny that they are particular entities different from each other.[25] At the same time, he reminds us not to overlook the limit of this simile. Since the physical sound (*dhvani*) and the linguistic phoneme fall into different categories, the characteristic of the former such as rapidness (*druta*) should not be ascribed to the latter.[26] An act of individual persons such as sacrificing (*yāga*), on the other hand, is not totally different (*na . . .dūravyatirikta*) from the particular *bhāvanā* inhering in it.[27] While the *bhāvanā* of a sacrifice is described in ritual texts of the eternal Veda with regard to its three conditions, namely, its purpose, its means and its manner of performance, it is inherent, as a universal, in a number of distinct particular acts (*kriyā*) performed by individual persons in a particular place at a particular time in this world.

III. *Scripture-centered approach in Kumārila's exegesis*

Kumārila is not a person of one-sided thinking in favor of the anthropo-centrism. He does not forget the fundamental notion of the Mīmāṃsā school established by the time of Śabara that the Vedic corpus, consisting of a lot of sentences, prompts an individual to undertake a sacrifice after having integrated its whole parts centering around a direction (*codanā*).[28] The integration of a ritual text, according to Kumārila, results from the "transition" or "redirection" (*saṃkrānti/saṃcaraṇa*) of the injunctive force (*vidhāna*)[29] from the direction (*codanā*) to the whole of the injunctions describing the sacrifice.

It is from the ninth section of the second chapter to the tenth section of the third chapter of the second volume that the *Mīmāṃsāsūtra* deals with how to apply the fifth of the six kinds of criteria for discerning a direction, namely, the mention of a subsidiary (*guṇa*)[30] in ritual texts. In the eleventh section of the second chapter" it is argued whether the injunction "For someone who desires strength, one should make an offering with yoghurt" (*dadhnendriyakāmasya juhuyāt*) is a distinct direction different from that of the Agnihotra. This injunction is said to be included in ritual texts after the section of the Agnihotra sacrifice.[31]

The opponent in this section insists that the injunction in question is a distinct direction, based on the following principle of exegesis originally established in the first section of the first chapter of the second volume: In a direction enjoining a person desiring heaven to undertake a sacrifice, it is not any noun but only a verb that denotes the means of realizing heaven. Following this principle, the opponent interprets the injunction "*dadhnendriyakāmasya juhuyāt*" as revealing the means to acquire strength (*indriya*) through the verb "should make offering" (*juhuyāt*). The Siddhāntin (JS 2.2.26), however, rejects this interpretation on the grounds that this injunction does not belong to the type of the direction "*svargakāmaḥ ... yajeta*" although both equally refer to a result. On the contrary, he asserts, the injunction in question states that the yoghurt denoted by the noun "*dadhnā*" is the means to acquire strength. Kumārila summarizes the differences between these two types of injunction as follows in two verses:

> As far as the injunctive force is not removed from the referent of a verbal root [as in the case of "*svargakāmaḥ . . . yajeta*"], it is recognized that what is related to the result is the referent of the verbal root. When, however, [in such injunctions as "*dadhnendriyakāmasya juhuyāt*"] a result happens to be mentioned after the injunctive force has been redirected into a subsidiary (*guṇasaṃcarite*[32] *vidhau*), then, this (mention of the result) forms a syntactical unity with that (subsidiary) because it has a contact (*spṛṣṭa*) with the injunction related to that (subsidiary).[33]

Through a somewhat difficult expression, Kumārila emphasizes that these two injunctions direct the attention of the hearer to different objects: one to the act of offering, the other to a subsidiary. In the case of such a direction as "*svargakāmaḥ... yajeta*", the expectation for the means for achieving heaven is fulfilled by hearing the verbal root referring to an act of offering. In the case of "*dadhnendriyakāmasya juhuyāt*", however, it is fulfilled not by the verbal root, but by the noun "with yoghurt" (*dadhnā*). This difference, according to Kumārila, results from the fact that a phenomenon, "transition (redirection) of the injunctive force," takes place in the entirety of the latter injunction, in which the verb "should make offering" (*juhuyāt*) does not play such a role as it played in the former injunction.

In an earlier section, namely, the fifth, two types of injunctions pertaining to the Agnihotra were quoted: (A) "*agnihotraṃ juhoti*" and (B) "*dadhnā juhoti*", "*payasā juhoti*" etc.[34] Whereas the injunction (A) forms a direction (*codanā*) enjoining the Agnihotra offering as such, each injunction categorized in (B) prescribes one of the alternatives for the material of the oblation alone and is therefore called "injunction of a subsidiary" (*guṇavidhi*). It is, however, not right to suppose that the injunctions (B) have nothing to do with the exertion (*bhāvanā*) of a person. Raw materials would produce no effect in a sacrifice if nobody used them at all. A subsidiary plays the role of an instrument of action (*kāraka*) necessary for a person to make exertion in a sacrifice. The injunctions (B), accordingly, must have a contact (*saṃsparśa*) with the direction (A) enjoining the exertion directly. The verbs in the injunctions (B) do not enjoin any exertion by themselves, but reassert (*anuvāda*) the exertion enjoined by the verb of the direction (A).[35]

Also the injunction quoted in the eleventh section "*dadhnendriyakāmasya juhuyāt*" falls into the category of injunction of a subsidiary. While this injunction assigns the role of the means for acquiring strength to a kind of material (*dravya*), namely, yoghurt, through the instrumental noun "*dadhnā*", it has a verb "*juhuyāt*" referring to an exertion qualified from both the sides of the desired purpose and the means for it.[36] This verb has the verbal root "*hu*" appearing in the direction "*agnihotraṃ juhoti*", which is located close to the injunction in question.[37] Nevertheless, the verb in "*dadhnendriyakāmasya juhuyāt*" does not refer to the act of offering as the means for a special purpose because in this case the act of offering has another role, namely, a basis (*āśraya*) in which the yoghurt is integrated into the exertion of a sacrificer.[38]

Relating the injunction in question to the direction of the Agnihotra "*agnihotraṃ juhoti*", Kumārila begins to explain the above-mentioned two verses, applying the notion of the transition of the injunctive force as follows:

> The injunctive force (*vidhitva*), although residing in one and the same exertion, is redirected (*saṃkrāmati*) from one (ritual factor) to another in accordance with the fact that the latter subserves the former. Because [in the direction of "*agnihotraṃ juhoti*"] the exertion is understood as being able to bring out a result when it has been directed into the referent of the verbal root [i.e. the act of offering], it is only the referent of the verbal root that can be regarded as the means [of the exertion].[39]

The first step of the transition takes place within a direction. First, the injunctive force is issued from the verbal ending of the direction; the injunctive force, in a fundamental but abstract manner, requires the hearer to make his exertion (*bhāvanā*). As to the role of the name "*agnihotram*" in the direction, Kumārila remarks that owing to the name of the sacrifice it is revealed that the act of offering enjoined by the direction is of a particular type of sacrifice.[40] But in the case of the injunction quoted in the present section, the noun "*dadhnā*" cannot be treated as the name of a sacrifice because the noun "*dadhnā*" shares none of the characteristics of names of sacrifice.[41] Hence Kumārila continues:

> Since here [in the case of "*dadhnendriyakāmasya juhuyāt*"] the noun "yoghurt" shares none of the characteristics of names of sacrifice, it must necessarily be understood as indicating what is to be enjoined [by this injunction]; and hence it transfers (*uttārayati*) the injunctive force which has been directed to the referent of the verbal root.[42]

In the second stage, the injunctive force proceeds to subordinate injunctions of ritual details in order to integrate them into a corpus describing a whole program of a sacrifice. In each injunction of a subsidiary, the injunctive force is transferred from the act of offering to a subsidiary on account of the function of a word referring to the subsidiary. Continuing to urge one and the same exertion (*bhāvanā*) of pursuing a particular result, the injunctive force issued from the direction of a sacrifice pervades the whole of the injunctions providing various rites, oblations, utensils and other elements necessary for each scene of the sacrifice.

ABBREVIATIONS AND REFERENCES

ĀpŚS *Āpastambaśrautasūtra,* [Bibliotheca Indica 92], vol. 1, repr. New Delhi, 1983.

KŚS *Kātyāyanaśrautasūtra,* Chowkhamba Skt. Ser. 104, repr. Varanasi, 1972.

TKM *Trikāṇḍamaṇḍana* (in: Frederick M. Smith, *The Vedic Sacrifice in Transition,* Bhandarkar Oriental Series 22, Poona, 1987).

JS *Mīmāṃsāsūtra,* see TV.

TV *Tantravārttika* (in *Mīmāṃsādarśanam,* Ānandāśrama, Skt. Ser. 97, Poona, 1929-53).

TV' *Tantravārttika* (in *Mīmāṃsādarśanam,* 2nd ed., Ānandāśrama, Skt. Ser. 97, 7pts, Poona, 1971-81).

NBh *Nyāyabhāṣya* (in *Nyāyadarśanam,* Calcutta Sanskrit Series 18&29, Calcutta, 1936-44).

NRM *Nyāyaratnamālā,* Library Rare Text Publication Series 4, Varanasi, 1982.

NSu *Nyāyasudhā,* Chowkhamba Skt. Ser. 45 & 56, Benares, 1901-1902.

ŚBh *Śābarabhāṣya,* see TV.

ŚBh' *Śābarabhāṣya,* see TV'.

ŚBh(F) *Śābarabhāṣya* on JS 1.1.1-5 (in: Erich Frauwallner, *Materialien zur ältesten Erkenntnislehre der Karmamīmāṃsā,* Veröffentlichungen der Kommission für Sprachen und Kulturen Süd- und Ostasiens 6, Wien, 1968).

ŚV *Ślokavārttika,* Prāchyabhārati Series 10, Varanasi, 1978.

NOTES

* This article is based on my Japanese articles "genjitsuka no hataraki (*bhāvanā*) no gutaika to mikakunin taishō sōtei no gensoku" [Making *bhāvanā* Definite and the Principle of *adṛṣṭakalpanā*], *Hokkaido Journal of Indological and Buddhist Studies* 15, 2000, pp. (35)-(49) and "Kitei no hataraki no sen-i ni tsuite" [On the Transition of Injunction according to the Tantravārttika 2.2], *Hokkaido Journal of Indological and Buddhist Studies* 16, 2001, pp. (75)-(92). I express my gratitude to Mr. Christopher Nichols for improving English expressions.

1. "*bhāvanā*" could most literally be rendered as bringing into becoming.
2. In the TV, as investigated by Erich Frauwallner ("Bhāvanā und Vidhiḥ bei Maṇḍanamiśra", *Wiener Zeitschrift für Kunde Morgenlandes* 45, 1938, pp. 212-252: pp. 224-226) and Horoshi Kuroda ("Kumārila no *bhāvanā* setsu ni tsuite (2)" [Some problems Concerning the *bhāvanā* Theory of Kumārila (2)], *Journal of Indian and Buddhist Studies* 29-1, 1980, pp.(42)-(47): pp.(43)-(44)), Kumārila presents two theories about which part of a finite verb indicates *bhāvanā:* (1) a whole finite verb referring to an act directed to an object different from the agent of the act, and as a result, excluding intransitive verbs; (2) verbal endings of all verbs including intransitive verbs. Kumārila remarks that (2) is acknowledged in the exegesis of Vedic texts (*śāstra*). Cf. TV p.380, 23: TV' pt.2, p. 347, 3; TV p. 382, 23: TV' pt.2, p. 349, 12. Although Kumārila did not decide which theory is better in the ŚV Vākyādhikaraṇa k.250cd (cf. Kuroda, "Kumārila no *bhāvanā* setsu ni tsuite (2)," p.(43)); he definitively stands by (2) in the TV: After having remarked that the author of the JS and Śabara did not say that *bhāvanā* is the meaning of a verbal ending (TV p. 380, 21-23: TV' pt.2, p. 347, 1-3), Kumārila begins a long argument supporting (2), in which he also criticizes (1) in detail (TV p. 381, 6: p. 383, 18: TV' pt.2, p.347, 12-p. 350, 14).
3. Whereas all periodical sacrifices are believed to carry a sacrificer to heaven after his death, each optional sacrifice is expected to realize a particular secular wish; hence a sacrificer has to choose one of them in order to acquire what their private circumstances demand. Whichever sacrifice one may choose to perform, however, it is emphasized that one spontaneously wishes the result. A sacrificer is not forced to desire the result by the direction of the Veda. The direction instructs a person what to do if he wants to pursue an end inaccessible by secular means.

Cf. ŚBh(F) p. 20, 16-19; JS 4.1.2; Kiyotaka Yoshimizu, *Der 'Organismus' des urheberlosen Veda. Eine Studie der Niyoga-Lehre Prabhākaras mit ausgewählten Übersetzungen der Bṛhatī*, Publications of the De Nobili Research Library 25, Wien, 1997: pp. 133-134.

4. As pointed out by Kunio Harikai ("*abhidhābhāvanā* no kaishaku" [On the Interpretation of the Word "*abhidhābhāvanā*"], *Journal of Indian and Buddhist Studies* 18-2, 1970, pp. 164-165), Someśvara remarks that the "*abhidhā*" in "*abhidhābhāvanā*" means the agent or the instrument of denotation, namely, (*vidhi-*)*śabda* and regards the compound as a genitive *tatpuruṣa* (NSu p.559,24-26), whereas Pārthasārathi remarks that the "*abhidhā*" means the object of denotation, namely, *bhāvanā* itself, and regards the compound as a *karmadhāraya* (NRM p. 76, 17-p.77, 6).

5. Śabara had already defined the direction (*codanā*) as a declaration urging a person to take action*. Kumārila, accordingly, regarded the incitement of a person to performing an activity (*puruṣapravartana*) as the purpose to be established by the denotative exertion (TV p.114,18: TV pt.2, p.12,19-20). Mīmāṃsā scholars had investigated the characteristics of a verb making a sentence an injunction, and this investigation resulted in a verse quoted by Śabara**. As the means to be applied for the denotative exertion, Kumārila considered the grammatical knowledge acquired through the former experience about the relation (*pūrva-saṃbandhānubhavāpekṣa-vidhivijñāna*) between the verbal characteristics of injunction and the hearer's commencement of action (TV p.114,22-23: TV pt.2, p.12,24-25). Since the time of the compilation of the *Mīmāṃsāsūtra*, the explanatory passage (*arthavāda*) had been supposed to be contextually united (*ekavākyatva*) with an injunction because the former praises (*stuti*) the act provided by the latter***. Accordingly, Kumārila interpreted this contextual unity as a result of such an interrelation between an injunction and an explanatory passage that the former requires an assistance, which is afforded by the latter in recommending the hearer to follow it. Therefore, he regarded the function of an *arthavāda* supplying the knowledge of praiseworthiness (*praśastyajñāna*) of an enjoined act as the manner of performance for the denotative exertion (TV p.114,23-24: IV pt.2, p.12,25-p.13,2). Cf. Kunio Harikai, *Koten Indo Seiten Kaishakugaku Kenkyū* [*The Hermeneutics of Classical India — A Study of Arthavāda and Mantra of the Mīmāṃsā School*], Fukuoka, 1990: pp.119-122; pp. 329-332.

* ŚBh(F) p.16,9: *codanā iti kriyāyāḥ pravartakaṃ vacanam āhuḥ.*

** ŚBh p.1247,22-25: ŚBh' pt.5, p.62,17-20: *evaṃ hi padavākyārthanyāyavidaḥ ślokam āmananti, kuryāt kriyeta kartavyaṃ bhavet syād iti pañcamam / etat syāt sarvavedeṣu niyataṃ vidhilakṣaṇam // iti.*

*** JS 1.2.7: *vidhinā tv ekavākyatvāt stutyarthena vidhīnām syuḥ.*

6. Cf. ĀpŚS 24.4.15; Kiyotaka Yoshimizu, "Change of View on *Apūrva* from Śabarasvāmin to Kumārila," in S. Mayeda (ed.), *The Way to Liberation. Indological Studies in Japan, Japanese Studies on South Asia* No.3, New Delhi: Manohar, 2000, pp. 149-165: n.10.

7. ŚBh p.1641,3-5: ŚBh' pt.6, p.62,19-p.63,2; Kiyotaka Yoshimizu, "Mokuteki-in toshite no *Apūrva*" [*Apūrva* as a *causa finalis*], *Studies in the History of Indian Thought* 8, 1996, pp. 20-41: p.33; Yoshimizu, "Change of View on *Apūrva* from Śabarasvāmin to Kumārila": n.17.

8. Cf. Kiyotaka Yoshimizu, "Śabara ni yoru sūtra 2.1.5 chū no rikai ni mukete" [A New Approach to Śabarasvāmin's Commentary on JS 2.1.5], *Journal of Indian and Buddhist Studies* 47-2,1999, pp.(61)-(67): Yoshimizu, "Change of View on *Apūrva* from Śabarasvāmin to Kumārila": pp.153-154.
9. Since Kumārila introduces *apūrva* as a kind of *saṃskāra* in his TV although his notion of *apūrva* is very similar to that of *adṛṣṭa* in the Vaiśeṣika school, W. Halbfass proposes the chapter "examination of the fruit" (*phalaparīkṣā*) of the NBh as a possible source for Kumārila's use of *saṃskāra* in the discussion of *apūrva*. Cf. NBh p.955,10-11: "By means of activity, a disposition characterized as merit or demerit is produced. This (disposition), being produced and assisted by other instrumental causes, brings about a result in the future" (*pravṛttyā saṃskāro dharmādharmalakṣaṇo janyate, sa jāto nimittāntarānugṛhītaḥ kālāntare phalam niṣpādayatīti*); Wilhelm Halbfass, *Tradition and Reflection, Explorations in Indian Thought,* Albany, N.Y., 1991: p.308; n.71.
10. In ŚV Codanā kk. 197-200, Kumārila rejects the traditional theory of the transcendental *apūrva*. He also quotes the manifestation (*abhivyakti*) theory of *apūrva* held by "some scholars" (*eke*) in the Apūrvādhikaraṇa of the TV. Cf. Kiyotaka Yoshimizu, "Kumārila ni okeru saishiki kōzōron no tenkan" [Kumārila's Innovation in the Mīmāṃsā View on the Structure of a Sacrifice], *Journal of Japanese Association for South Asian Studies* 10, 1998, pp. 56-73: pp.60-62; Kiyotaka Yoshimizu, "Kumārila ga hihan suru *apūrva* setsu ni tsuite" [On the Theory *of apūrva* Criticized by Kumārila], *Hokkaido Journal of Indological and Buddhist Studies* 13, 1998: pp. (1)-(15): pp.(2)-(3); Yoshimizu, "Change of View on *Apūrva* from Śabarasvāmin to Kumārila": pp.154-157.
11. It is Francis X. Clooney (*Thinking Ritually Rediscovering the Pūrvamīmāṃsā of Jaimini,* Publications of the De Nobili Research Library 17, Vienna, 1990; p.239) that called Kumārila's thought "anthropocentric" which Clooney says he took over from Śabara. In Yoshimizu, "Change of View on *Apūrva* from Śabarasvāmin to Kumārila", I presented the difference in the way of interpretation of the term "*apūrva*" between Śabara and Kumārila, and I will point out another aspect of Kumārila's thought in the next section of the present article.
12. Some of the Siddhānta sūtras declare that the sentence at issue is a *codanā*. Cf. JS 2.2.6; 2.2.10; 2.2.16; 2.2.17.
13. In the Mīmāṃsā exegesis on the Jyotiṣṭoma ritual, "*somena yajeta*" is regarded as the injunction to offer *soma* juice into the sacrificial fire (cf. E. Edgerton, *The Mīmāṃsā Nyāya Prakāśa or Āpadevī : A Treatise on the Mīmāṃsā System by Āpadeva,* New Haven, 1929: p.43, n.11), "*dākṣiṇāni juhoti*" as the injunction of a *puroḍāśa* offering to be performed at presenting gifts to officiants (cf. W. Caland et V. Henry *L'agniṣṭoma,* Paris, 1906-07: p.289), and "*hiraṇyam ātreyāya dadāti*" as an example of the injunctions to present the gifts (cf. Caland et Henry, *L'agniṣṭoma,* p. 293).
14. ŚBh p. 464, 3-4: ŚBh' pt. 3, p. 5, 3: *evaṃ prāpte brūmaḥ. pratiśabdam apūrvabheda iti.*
15. TV p. 461, 19-21: TV' pt.3, p.1, 19-21: *tad yathā tisro bhāvanāḥ kim ekam apūrvaṃ kurvanty uta trīṇīti, tathā trayo dhātvarthāḥ kim ekāṃ bhāvanāṃ*

viśiṃṣanty uta tisraḥ, tathā trayo dhātavaḥ kim ekaṃ dhātvarthaṃ vadanty uta trīn iti.

16. In the first formulation *bhāvanā* is glossed with "what produces (*utpādana*) an *apūrva*", while in the second the referent of a verbal root (*dhātvartha*) is glossed with "what qualifies (*viśeṣaṇa*) a *bhāvanā*". Cf. TV p. 461, 22: TV' pt.3, p. 1, 22-23.
17. TV p. 461, 26-p. 462, 12: TV' pt.3, p. 2, 12-15: "In fact, however, there is only one real problem in this case: Is there only one *bhāvanā* coloured by the referents of the three verbal roots, or is there a distinct *bhāvanā* in accordance with the referent of each verbal root? It is only a *bhāvanā* coloured by the referent of a verbal root that is referred to with the word 'act' [in JS 2.1.1]. It is only that (*bhāvanā*) that is differentiated by means of [the six kinds of criteria] such as different words, whereas the *apūrva* [is differentiated] in accordance with the differentiation of acts, because an *apūrva* is not denoted [by any word]*. Hence the [first formulation] is not worthy of being investigated separately." (*atha vā pāramārthiko 'trāyam ekaḥ saṃśayaḥ kiṃ dhātvarthatrayānuraktaikā bhāvanā, atha vā pratidhātvarthaṃ bhāvanābheda iti, bhāvanaiva dhātvanuraktā karmaśabdenocyate. tasyā eva śabdāntarādi bhedakaṃ bhaviṣyati, apūrvasyānabhidheyatvāt karmabhedānuniṣpādy eva tad iti na pṛthag vicāram arhati*); TV p. 465, 2-3: TV' pt.3, p. 6, 8-9: "And whether the acts are different or the same does not depend on whether the *apūrvas* are different or the same; because the reverse is acknowledged" (*na cāpūrvabhedābhedapūrvakau karmabhedābhedau viparītābhyupagamāt*). Kumārila neglects the third formulation saying that it is just an incidental one (*prāsaṅgika*). Cf. TV p. 462, 12-13: TV' pt. 3, p. 2, 15-16.

 * As for the fact that Śabarasvāmin admits that an *apūrva* is denoted by the verbal ending in its optative mode in a direction, see Kiyotaka Yoshimizu, "The Means of Knowing *Apūrva* in Śabarasvāmin's Bhāṣya," *Journal of Indian and Buddhist Studies* 45-1, 1996, pp. (10)-(14): pp. (13)-(14). In his saying "*na tu kaścic chabdaḥ sākṣād apūrvasya vācako 'sti*" (ŚBh 376, 1-2: ŚBh' pt.2, 340, 9-341, 1), what Śabara denies seems to be the possibility that an *apūrva* would be distinguished by means of such a single verb as "*yajeta*" common to many directions of various sacrifices, since Śabara regards an *apūrva* as the unique pattern of a particular sacrifice. Cf. Yoshimizu, "Śabara ni yoru sūtra 2.1.5 chū no rikai ni mukete"; Yoshimizu, "Change of View on *Apūrva* from Śabarasvāmin to Kumārila": p. 154.

18. In ŚBh p. 462, 3-6: ŚBh' pt. 3, 2, 3-6, Śabara quotes two verses which explains two principles of exegesis: According to the first principle, an interpretation without assuming anything unobserved (*adṛṣṭa*) or not mentioned (*aśruta*) in the text is preferred to that with such an assumption; according to the second, an interpretation with fewer assumptions is preferred.
19. ŚBh p. 462, 7-10: ŚBh' p. 3, p. 2, 7-p. 3, 2. The opponent presents this interpretation applying the second of the two above-mentioned exegetic principles.
20. ŚBh p. 462, 10-11: ŚBh' pt. 3, p. 3, 2-3: *atha vā yajetety asya pūrvo bhāgo yajatyarthaṃ bravīti. uttaro bhāvayed iti.* According to Kumārila, the opponent proposes this alternative interpretation to escape the criticism (TV p.

463, 15-24: TV pt. 3, p. 4, 6-16) that the interpretation presented at first is not established on account of violating the first exegetic principle.

21. ŚBh p. 466, 6-8. ŚBh' pt. 3, p. 7, 5-7.
22. ŚBh p. 466, 13-14. ŚBh' pt. 3, p.8, 5-6.
23. TV p. 465, 8-11: TV' pt. 3, p. 6,14-18.
24. TV p. 464, 26-p. 465,1: TV' pt. 3, p. 6, 2-6; TV p. 465, 3-6: TV' pt. 3, p. 6, 9-12. Cf. Yoshimizu, "genjitsuka no hataraki (*bhāvanā*) no gutaika to mikakunin taishō sōtei no gensoku," n. (17) & (18).
25. TV p. 465, 20-22: TV' pt. 3, p. 7, 11-12.
26. ŚV Sphoṭa kk. 61cd-62.
27. TV p. 465, 22-23: TV pt. 3, p. 7, 12-13. The *avagraha* before the "*dūravyatiriktāḥ*" in the Ānandāśrama edition should be deleted. Commenting on the similarity between the act referred to by the root of a verb and the *bhāvanā* by its ending, Someśvara says that the incompleteness of successive change (*pūrvāparībhāvāniṣpannatva*), a character of an act, is not illusively projected on a *bhāvanā*, but exists in it (*vāstava*) (NSu p. 707, 8-10). As for Kumārila's statements about the "non-absolute-difference" (*atyantabhedābhāva*) between a universal and individuals, see Kunio Harikai, "Kumārila's Modification of Vaiśeṣika Categories," *Beyond Orientalism. The Work of Wilhelm Halbfass and its Impact on Indian and Cross-Cultural Studies,* Poznań Studies in the Philosophy of the Sciences and Humanities 59, Amsterdam-Atlanta, 1997, pp. 395-415: p. 404ff.
28. At the beginning of his explanation in the TV on JS 1.2.7 that the authority of an explanatory passage (*arthavāda*) depends on the injunction which enjoins the ritual act it praises, Kumārila emphasizes the important role of the injunction of the Vedic study (*adhyayanavidhi*), which prompts a person to study the whole Vedic corpus step by step so that the person can systematically perform the sacrifice. Cf. Harikai, *Koten Indo Seiten Kaishakugaku Kenkyū:* pp. 111-116; pp. 325-329. Kumārila makes some remarks about the integration of the Vedic corpus as follows: "Therefore, the Veda cannot be established as authoritative so far as it does not reveal that its whole corpus is valuable to a person" (TV p. 113,12-13: TV' pt. 2, p. 11, 6-7: *ato yāvad veda eva puruṣārthatayā sakalam ātmānam na pratipādayati tāvad apramāṇam*); "Thus it is established that all [parts of the Veda] are included in the [denotative] exertion [of the injunction of the Vedic study]" (TV p.114, 12-13: TV' pt. 2, p. 12, 13-14: *tena sarveṣāṃ bhāvanāntargatir upapannā*).
29. The "injunctive force" is also rendered in other word such as "the essence of injunction" (*vidhitva*) or "the ability of injunction" (*vidhisāmarthya*). Cf. footnote 33 & 39.
30. The identity of a sacrifice is established by the combination of the two main subsidiaries, namely, the oblation to be offered (*dravya*) and the deity (*devatā*) to be revered. Cf. the definition of the act of a sacrifice (*yāga*) in JS 4.2.27: *yajaticodanā dravyadevatākriyaṃ samudāye kṛtārthatvāt;* KŚS 1.2.2: *dravyaṃ devatā tyāgaḥ*. Concerning the two offerings in the spring session of the Cāturmāsya sacrifice, namely, the offering of whey (*vājina*) to the steeds (*vājin*) and the offering of curds to the Vaiśvadeva (JS 2.2.23), Kumārila summarizes the difference of subsidiaries as follows: "[The two sentences providing each offering are independent of each other;] for each of the two combinations of offering and deity enjoins

a distinct act because each allows no scope for the presence of the other, which would be incompatible with the former itself." (TV p. 533, 6-7: TV' pt. 3, p. 94, 9-10: *ubhau hi dravya-devatāsaṃyogāv ātmavirodhenā nyonyāvakāśam aprayacchantau pṛthakkarmaṇī vidhattaḥ*).

31. ŚBh p. 539, 11: ŚBh' pt. 3, p. 380, 23: *agnihotraṃ prakṛtya samāmananti.*

32. The reading "*guṇasaṃvarite*" in the Ānandāśrama edition should be corrected to "*guṇa-saṃcarite*".

33. TV p. 546, 20-23: TV' pt. 3, p. 111, 12-15: *yāvad dhi vidhisāmarthyaṃ dhātvarthād anapoddhṛtam / tāvad yaḥ phalasaṃbandhaḥ sa dhātvarthasya gamyate // bhavet phalaśrutir yā tu *guṇasaṃcarite vidhau / sā tadgatavidhispṛṣṭā tena yāty ekavākyatām //*

34. Śabara adduces the two ways of performing the Agnihotra with the oblation of yoghurt as an example for the exegetic theorem called "differentiation of connections" (*saṃyoga-pṛthaktvanyāya*). If one chooses yoghurt for the oblation in the normal periodical Agnihotra, the yoghurt is valuable to the ritual (*kratvartha*) on account of its connection with the act of offering. If, on the other hand, one offers yoghurt in the special Agnihotra desiring strength, the yoghurt turns to be valuable to the person (*puruṣārtha*) on account of its additional connection with the result. Cf. ŚBh on JS 4.3.5-7; Haruo Kurata, "Saṃyogapṛthaktvanyāya—as a basis of the theory of mokṣa—," *Journal of Indian and Buddhist Studies* 28-2, 1980, pp. (13)-(18): p. (13); Harikai, *Koten Indo Seiten Kaishakugaku Kenkyū:* pp.215-217. Kumārila states that there are ten alternatives of the oblation for the normal Agnihotra including yoghurt (TV p. 541, 23-24: TV' pt. 3, p. 105, 7-9). Commenting on this, Someśvara enumerates the following ten kinds, namely, *payas, dadhi, yavāgū, sarpis, odana, taṇḍulāḥ, soma, māṃsa, taila* and *āp* (NSu p. 837, 26-27). These are enumerated as the oblation without special desire (*akāma*[*taḥ*]) also in the commentary *Paddhati* on KŚS 4.14 (p. 415, 2-3) (*ghṛta* instead of *sarpis*). In the ritual literature, however, the oblation for the normal Agnihotra is restricted to the milk drawn and boiled each day. According to H. M. Bodewitz (*The Dairy Evening and Morning Offering* (*AGNIHOTRA*) *According to the Brāhmaṇas,* Orientalia Rheno-Traiectina 21, Leiden, 1976: p. 9; p. 52), yoghurt is included in the oblations enumerated in the *Taittirīya Brāhmaṇa* 2.1.5.5-6, where it is prescribed for the sacrificer desiring strength. Yoghurt is related only to *indriyakāma* also in the following Yajurveda Śrautasūtras: ĀpŚS 6.15.1; the *Hiraṇyakeśin* 3.7.114; the *Bhāradvāja* 6.14.14-15; the *Vaikhānasa* 2.9; the *Mānava* 1.6.1.23 (without mentioning *indriyakāma,* but milk is designated for the normal oblation); the *Vārāha* 1.5.3.1; KŚS 4.15.21-24 & 26; cf. P. E. Dumon, *L'agnihotra.* Baltimore, 1939. No mention of alternative oblations is found in the *Baudhāyana* 3.4-7 and the *Vādhūla* 1.15-18. According to Bhāskara Miśra, the author of the TKM (between the mid-11th century and the mid-12th century, cf. Smith, *The Vedic Sacrifice in Transition:* p. 54), one is allowed to use, in case that milk is occasionally unavailable for the daily Agnihotra, rice (*vrīhi*), barley, (*yava*), another domestic plant, wild plants, the fruits of a tree, or finally water in this order (TKM 2.35-37). Yoghurt does not count as a substitute for milk here. If most ritualists took for granted that offering yoghurt at the Agnihotra is inseparable from *indriyakāma,* then, we should say that in this case

the Mīmāṃsakas developed their speculation deviating from the real tradition of the Vedic ritual in order to establish their own exegetic theories.

35. TV p. 501, 7-9: TV' pt. 3, p. 54, 5-7; TV p. 504, 21-22: TV' pt. 3, p. 58, 16-18.
36. TV p. 548,18: TV' pt. 3, p. 113, 14.
37. TV p. 548, 20: TV' pt. 3, p. 113, 16-17.
38. TV p. 549, 11-13: TV' pt. 3, p. 114, 13-15.
39. TV p. 546, 24-25: TV' pt. 3, p.111, 16-17: *bhāvanāstham eva vidhitvaṃ tādarthyabhedena tatra tatra saṃkrāmati. tad yadā dhātvarthasaṃkrāntyavasthām phalavatīṃ bhāvanām āsādayati tadā dhātvartham eva karaṇīkaroti.*
40. TV p. 546, 25-27: TV' p. 3, p. 111, 18-19: "And everything else subserves that (act of offering). And this (interpretation) is not to be renounced in the case of such [a direction] as 'One who desires heaven should perform the Agnihotra-offering' because the name of a sacrifice cannot deprive of the injunctive force" (*anyac ca tadarthaṃ bhavati. tac ca "agnihotraṃ juhuyāt svargakāmaḥ" ityādiṣu nāmno vidhiśaktyapahārāsamarthatvād avihatam.*)
41. In the whole chapter of JS 1.4 it is investigated whether a noun used in a Vedic passage denotes its meaning in common usage or it is the name of a particular sacrifice.
42. TV p. 546, 27-p. 547, 10: TV' pt. 3, p. 111, 19-20: *iha tu dadhipadam aśeṣanāmadheya-lakṣaṇāsaṃsparśād avaśyaṃ vidhātavyaṃ sad uttārayati dhātvarthopanipatitaṃ vidhitvam.*

XII

SĀṂKHYA AND YOGA

CHAPTER 48

Bhūtātman Reconsidered[1]

SHUJUN MOTEGI

I. The origin or root of classical Sāṃkhya thoughts, transmitted in the Sāṃkhya-kārikā, a compendium of the Sāṃkhya school by Īśvarakṛṣṇa, is to be found in the old Upaniṣads.[2] But the Upaniṣads and the Sāṃkhya-Kārikā are separated by hundreds of years. Not only the early history of the Sāṃkhya school but also of other schools of philosophy which arose after the old Upaniṣads is rather difficult to trace, because of the lack of extant materials. It is, therefore, necessary to examine briefly the references to philosophical thoughts which occur in the literature of the earlier age. The Mokṣadharma of the Śānti-parvan of the Mahābhārata (abbr. MBh.[3]) is valuable in that it is replete with early philosophical concepts, one of the most important of which is self or soul (*ātman*). We occasionally encounter various terms meaning "self" or "soul" in a variety of occasionally confusing contexts, such as *adhyātma, puruṣa, jīva, bhūtātman, paramātman, kṣetrajña, antarātman, ātman* etc. These manifold expressions of self or soul imply that this was an important topic of the day, and this topic was discussed in many circles or groups of religio-philosophical thinkers, each of which must have expressed its own conception of "self" or "soul" with its own special terminology, influencing or being influenced by other groups. The systematization of philosophical thoughts must have been based upon the mutual influence of these groups of thinkers. Therefore, it is necessary to examine the meaning of these terms, in order to gain a clear notion of the nature of philosophical thought before the occurrence of systematization. On this occasion, I shall select the term *bhūtātman,* and examine it in detail. This term has chiefly been explained by modern scholars as element-self, which has to do with material affairs, but is occasionally identified with *jīva.*[4] It seems to me that this does not cover the multiple meanings of its various occurrences. While my examination of this term will be based upon its occurrences in the extant literature, it will, of necessity, focus largely upon the Mokṣadharma.

The main source of *bhūtātman* is no doubt the Mokṣadharma in which it appears with varied meanings in different contexts. Firstly, we must examine the usages of this term, and classify them into certain groups. This procedure might provide us with an explanation of how and why the differences in its usage occur.

Throughout the analysis, I shall refer to occurrences of this term in texts other than the Mokṣadharma, such as the Maitrāyaṇī Upaniṣad which offers the earliest reference to the term, giving two kinds of definition of it, the Manu Smṛti, which refers to the term as an agent in a person, and the Caraka Saṃhitā, which occasionally seems to regard it as being synonymous with *puruṣa, ātman* and *kṣetrajña* in its Śārīrasthāna, etc.

II. I shall now examine the occurrences of the term in the Mokṣadharma.

(1) MBh. XII.187.6

The first occurrence of *bhūtātman* in the Mokṣadharma is in the 6th verse of Chapter 187.[5] The subject of the beginning of this chapter is the constitution of a human being, that is, to enumerate all the elements that form a sentient being. Firstly, five material elements are identified with bodily components, and the relationship of the five material elements to the human body is explained by means of a simile that employs the sea and a wave. Then, the sense-organs and their director *ātman* or *jīva* are listed. Thus, all of the elements which form a human being are described. The term *bhūtātman* appears in the enumeration of the elements, which is as follows:

pṛthivī vāyur ākāśam āpo jyotiś ca pañcamam /
mahābhūtāni bhūtānāṃ sarveṣāṃ prabhavāpyayau //MBh.XII.187.4

tataḥ sṛṣṭāni tatraiva tāni yānti punaḥ punaḥ /
mahābhūtāni bhūteṣu sāgarasyormir yathā//MBh.XII.187.5

prasārya ca yathāṅgāni kūrmaḥ saṃharate punaḥ /
tadvad bhūtāni bhūtātmā sṛṣṭvā saṃharate punaḥ//MBh.XII.187.6

mahābhūtāni pañcaiva sarvabhūteṣu bhūtakṛt /
akarot teṣu vaiṣamyaṃ tat tu jīvo 'nu paśyati[6]//MBh.*XII*.187.7

Earth, wind, ether, water, and fire as the fifth are the five gross material elements, which are (the basis of) the appearance and disappearance of all existing beings. (187.4)

All beings which originate from them (material elements) repeatedly return to the same elements. The relationship of existing beings to the material elements is the same as that of the sea to its waves. (187.5)

The *bhūtātman,* creates and draws back existing beings like a tortoise extends and draws back its four limbs. (187.6)

The gross material elements are five in number. The creator of the (gross material) elements made them diversified. And *jīva,* sees the diversified forms (of the gross material elements) afterwards. (187.7)

Here, in this context, *bhūtātman,* appears in the process of creation with the analogy of a tortoise and its limbs. It creates five material elements, and also creates the diversity within them. Thus, the meaning of *bhūtātman,* includes the sense of creation. The role of *bhūtātman* is reminiscent of monism in which *ātman* is a creator of material elements.[7]

The term *jīva* here has the function of seeing. The relationship of *jīva* to *bhūtātman* is not immediately apparent, because there is no mention of *jīva* or of *bhūtātman* in the rest of the chapter. In other words, it is unclear whether *bhūtātman* is synonymous with *jīva* or not. Although the concept of *jīva* is ambiguous here, it is usually used to mean an empirical self which is responsible for ordinary actions in which "seeing" is included.[8] Taking this into account, it seems difficult to imagine that *jīva* has a faculty of creation like *bhūtātman*. Therefore, *bhūtātman* here differs from *jīva* in its relationship with the material elements.[9]

All that we can say about the features of the *bhūtātman* in this chapter is that they include the creation of existing beings. In so far as we are able to follow the implications of the simile, *bhūtātman* seems to be an originator of material elements and their differentiated forms.[10]

(2) *MBh. XII.196.6-7.*

A long discourse between Manu and Bṛhaspati begins in Chapter 194, and ends in Chapter 199. The main theme of the discourse is the essential nature of human beings. At the beginning of Chap. 194, Yudhiṣṭhira asks Bhīṣma what the result of *jñānayoga* and the vow of the Vedas is, and how *bhūtātman* is to be recognised (194.1). In order to answer these questions, Bhīṣma quotes the discourse of Manu and Bṛhaspati. Manu tries to prove the existence of a kind of knower in human beings. Human beings must have a knower in their bodies who is responsible for memory, even though such an entity is not clearly seen. Such a knower in human beings is variously called by the name of *svabhāva, śarīrin, kṣetrajña* and *bhūtātman*. Here, *bhūtātman,* is used synonymously with *svabhāva, śarīrin, kṣetrajña,* among which *śarīrin* is most frequently used. To prove the existence of *bhūtātman,* Manu employs a simile as follows:

> *yathā himavataḥ pārśvaṃ pṛṣṭhaṃ candramaso yathā /*
> *na dṛṣṭapūrvaṃ manujair na ca tan nāsti tāvatā //* MBh. XII.196.6
>
> *tadvat bhūteṣu bhūtātmā sūkṣmo jñānātmavān asau /*
> *adṛṣṭapūrvaśc cakṣusbhyāṃ na cāsau nāsti tāvatā //* MBh. XII.196.7
>
> The reverse side of the Himalaya or the other side of the moon has never been seen before by men, but it does not mean that it does not exist. (196.6)
> Likewise, *bhūtātman* whose essential function is recognition, exists in living beings without being recognized by eyes because of its subtlety. (196.7)

As *bhūtātman* here is used synonymously with *śarīrin,* meaning an empirical self, it must be a being of the same sort. It is an empirical self, that is, a positive individual principle. It is very subtle, and its essential function is recognition. It is not necessarily being treated as a lower existence, though it is involved in *jīva,* though the term *jīva* is not found among the terms used synonymously. The meaning of *bhūta* in the word *bhūtātman* in this context must not be material element, but rather living being or, more specifically speaking, a human being.

(*3*) *MBh. XII.200.11, 202.29, 31*

Chapters 200-202 of the Mokṣadharma describe the creation of the world by the supreme god Viṣṇu. In these chapters, the term *bhūtātman* appears to refer to an aspect of Viṣṇu or Saṃkarṣaṇa. Viṣṇu creates five *mahābhūtas* as the first step in the creation of the world. But why can Viṣṇu create them? The reason is described etymologically as follows:

> *mahābhūtāni bhūtātmā mahātmā puruṣottamaḥ /*
> *vāyur jyotis tathā cāpaḥ khaṃ gāṃ caivānvakalpayat //*
>
> MBh. XII.200.8
>
> The highest puruṣa (Viṣṇu) thought of the gross material elements, that is, wind, fire, water, ether, and earth, because he has elements (*bhūta*) as his essence and has greatness (*mahān*) as his essence.

In this way, the term *bhūtātman* is used to justify why Viṣṇu is able to create the world. According to the etymological explanation, Viṣṇu is able to think of *mahābhūtas* because he has them in his nature. In this explanation, the *bhūta* of *bhūtātman* must be material elements.

The God Viṣṇu then creates Saṃkarṣaṇa as the first existence by means of *saṃkalpa*. Saṃkarṣaṇa, a second self of Viṣṇu, is designated as *bhūtātman* because he is the last resort for all existing beings:

> *sarvatejomayas tasmin śayānaḥ śayane śubhe /*
> *so 'grajaṃ sarvabhūtānāṃ saṃkarśanam acintayat//*MBh.XII. 200.10
>
> *āśrayaṃ sarvabhūtānāṃ manaseti viśuśruma /*
> *sa dhārayati bhūtātmā ubhe bhūtabhaviṣyatī //* MBh. XII.200.11
>
> We heard that He (Viṣṇu) who had all the majesty, lying in the auspicious bed, thought of Saṃkarṣaṇa who was the first born of all the existent beings, the last resort for all the existent beings. (200.10-11ab)

> He (Saṃkarṣaṇa), who has the existent beings within himself (*bhūtātmā*), supports both the past and the future. (200.11cd)

Here, Saṃkarṣaṇa has the epithet *bhūtātman,* by which is meant that all existing beings are latent inside him. Therefore, the *bhūta* of *bhūtātman* here means existing beings. Furthermore, in Chapter 202, *bhūtātman* is used twice in rather formalized phrases of *mahāyogī bhūtātmā bhūtabhāvanaḥ* (vv.29, 31) to praise the greatness of Viṣṇu.[12] In these chapters, *bhūtātman* is used to describe the creative aspect of Viṣṇu and the character of Saṃkarṣaṇa. It could be said that, in this context, the term *bhūtātman* is used as an adjective and not as a noun, and that the *bhūta* signifies existent living beings.[13] It should be noted that *bhūtātman* occurs with *mahāyogin* here. In the 30th verse of this chapter, *yogin* appears with an adjective *sarvabhūteśvaro,* which could be seen as a specific feature of *bhūtātman.*

(*4*) *MBh. XII.231.11, 12, 21; 245.7, 11.*

Yoga practice is the main subject of Chapter 231. Śuka raises questions about *yoga* practice, and Vyāsa replies by showing him the condition of a human being who practices *yoga.* Vyāsa observes the physical and psychic formation of human beings and categorizes it into a certain number of elements, i.e., five material elements, five *guṇas,* five *indriyas, manas* and *bhūtātman.* Here *bhūtātman* appears in a simile about an obedient horse.

> *indriyāṇi mano yuṅkte vaśyān yanteva vājinaḥ /*
> *manaś cāpi sadā yuṅkte bhūtātmā hṛdayāśritaḥ* //MBh. XII. 231.11
>
> *indriyāṇāṃ tathaivaiṣāṃ sarveṣām īśvaraṃ manaḥ /*
> *niyame ca visarge ca bhūtātmā manasas tathā* //MBh. XII. 231.12
>
> *indriyānīndriyārthāś ca svabhāvaś cetanā manaḥ /*
> *prāṇāpānau ca jīvaś ca nityaṃ deheṣu dehinām* // MBh.XII.231.13
>
> *sarvabhūteṣu cātmānaṃ sarvabhūtāni cātmani /*
> *yadā paśyati bhūtātmā saṃpadyate tadā* // MBh. XII. 231.21
>
> The thought organ yokes the sense-organs, as a groom yokes obedient horses. And *bhūtātman,* who stays in the heart, yokes the thought organ. (231.11)
>
> As the thought organ is the lord of all the sense-organs, whenever they stop working or emit (toward objects), so *bhūtātman* is (the lord) of the thought organ[14]. (231.12)

> In the human body, there are always sense-organs, the objects of the sense-organs, one's own nature (*svabhāva*), consciousness, the thought organ, inspiration and aspiration, and the animating principle, whenever a soul is incorporated (*dehinām*). (231.13)
>
> When *bhūtātman* sees himself in all living beings and all living beings in himself, then he attains Brahman. (231.21)

Here, *bhūtātman* is the highest principle of a human being consisting of seventeen principles (v.15). Remaining in the heart, it regulates *manas* and reaches emancipation through *yoga* practice. This emancipation is the recognition that *bhūtātman* prevails throughout the entire universe and, with this knowledge, the *bhūtātman* of a *yogin* attains Brahman.[15] The *bhūtātman* in this chapter is an individual self called the seventeenth (v.15), which, without cosmic function, is involved in world affairs, and has the potential to be emancipated through the practice of yoga.[16]

We see the term *jīva* enumerated with the inner psychic organs, such as *indriya* and *manas* as a constituent of a body. *Bhūtātman* here is considered to be a higher principle of a human being which governs other psychic principles. As a self-concept, *bhūtātman* seems to be used synonymously with *dehin* (v.13) which occurs in a different context to *jīva* in the 13th verse. *Jīva* is used to mean a kind of animating principle within the body that keeps a person living: it does not have connotations of an individual self. As with the previous section, *bhūtātman* is used synonymously with *dehin*, an incorporated soul.

Nearly the same concept of *bhūtātman* is seen in Chapter 245. where it appears again in the context of *yoga* practice. The term *bhūtātman* appears in Chapter 245 in the following verses:

> *tesāṃ nityaṃ sadānityo bhūtāmā satataṃ guṇaiḥ /*
> *saptabhis tv anvitaḥ sūkṣmaiś cariṣṇur ajarāmaraḥ //*MBh.XII. 245.7
> *tam evam atitejo'ṃśaṃ bhūtātmanaṃ hṛdi sthitam /*
> *tamorajobhyām āviṣṭā nānupaśyanti mūrtiṣu //* MBh. XII. 245.11
>
> Their (*yogin*) eternal *bhūtātman* always goes around (the wombs) without old age and death, being associated with seven subtle *guṇas*. (245.7)
>
> Those who are covered by *tamas* and *rajas* do not see in

their bodies *bhūtātman* who stays in the heart as a part of great splendour. (245.11)

Here, it is said that the *bhūtātman* of a *yogin* is immortal and freed from aging, and accompanied by the seven subtle *guṇas* in the course of transmigration (245.7). The name Śāṇḍilya is quoted to define yoga (245.13). At the same time, it experiences pain and pleasure in both real life and dreams when it is conquered by *manas* and *buddhi* (245.8). *Bhūtātman* stays in the heart as a part of *atitejas* a super-human existence (245.11). When emancipated by *yoga* it attains Brahman (245.14).

The *bhūtātman* found in these chapters is the highest principle in a person which regulates *manas* and experiences pain and pleasure while staying in the heart. It has a part of the super human principle, perhaps Brahman. Sometimes, it is included within *manas* and *buddhi* but, at the same time, it has the potential of being emancipated through *yoga* practice.[17] When emancipated, it is said to attain Brahman. The *bhūtātman* in these chapters is an individual principle who is responsible for the ordinary activities of a human being, and is required to attain emancipation through the practice of *yoga*. Additionally, it also possesses a cosmic nature.[18] Thus, it can be assumed that *bhūtātman* has the nature of both *paramātman* and *jīva*. The emancipated condition is identified with Brahman, a cosmic principle that exists partially in *bhūtātman*. This concept is reminiscent of the Upaniṣadic doctrine of the identification of *ātman* and *brahman*: In addition, the concept of the *ātman's* staying in the heart is an ancient theory to be found in the old Upaniṣads.[19]

(5) *MBh.XII.286.18*

Connected with the question of the nature of welfare (*śreyas*) posed by Yudhiṣṭhira in the beginning of Chapter 279, Bhīṣma quotes a dialogue between King Janaka and Parāśara. Parāśara gives a long discourse whose topics include the prohibiton of killing, the inevitability of death, the condition of the soul after death, and so on. In the course of this discourse, he states that a human being consists of five material elements, *manas, indriya, buddhi* and *ātman*. *Ātman* is called *dehin* or *śarīrin* when it is connected with the physical body and is alive. However, when it is parted from the body, it must transmigrate until it is reborn.

The *ātman* of this condition, namely, after death, is referred to as *bhūtātman.* It is pictured as wandering around like a cloud as follows:

> *na jāyate tu nṛpati kañcitkālam ayaṃ punaḥ /*
> *paribhramati bhūtātmā dyām ivāṃbudharo mahān //*
>
> MBh.XII.286.18

> It (*śarīrin*) does not come to rebirth for a certain period. It wanders around as the *bhūtātman* as a big cloud wanders around in the sky. (286.18)

We may interpret these occurrences in the following manner: all human beings possess an eternal existence, that is, *ātman,* which is called *śarīrin* when it stays in a human body and gives life. On the other hand, it is called *bhūtātman* when it is separated from a human body. In this state, it wanders like a cloud in the sky until the next instance of rebirth. This usage occurs because of the thought that *bhūta* means an existence after death. This usage of *bhūtātman* may be related to *bhūta* as a spirit or goblin.

(*6*) *MBh.XII.291.34*

In Chapter 291, Yudhiṣṭhira asks Bhīṣma to define the *akṣara* that will not return to the *saṃsāra,* and the *kṣara* that will return to the *saṃsāra.* Bhīṣma answers by quoting a dialogue between Vaśiṣṭha and Karāra Janaka. Vaśiṣṭha gives the names of various living beings, and concludes that they all belong to *kṣara,* as they are named *vyakta* (things appeared). In his list of *kṣara,* the term *bhutatman* is used. The reason why it is identified with *kṣara* is that it perishes every day (291.34):

> *kṛtsnam etāvatas tāta kṣarate vyaktasaṃjñakam /*
> *ahany ahani bhūtātmā tataḥ kṣara iti smṛtaḥ//* MBh.XII.291.34

Vaśiṣṭha explains that human beings consist of two categories: *kṣára* and *akṣara, mūrti* and *amūrti,* and *vyakta* and *avyakta.* Here, *bhūtātman* is included in the category of *kṣara* (perishing), which is the mortal component of a human being, namely, the body. This usage is derived from the meaning of *bhūta* which is connected with materiality. Here, It is possible to say that *bhūtātman* is considered to be a negative aspect of human nature that could be an obstacle to those who pursue emancipation.

The same kind of usage of *bhūtātmam* often occurs in the Maitrāyaṇī Upaniṣad.[20] In the Maitrāyaṇī Upaniṣad 3.2, the term *bhūta* is given two definitions. First, it means the five *tanmātras* or the five material elements (*mahābhūtas*). Therefore, *bhūtātman* is nothing but a physical body which is made up of material elements. Second, it means "conquered" (*abhibhūta*). Therefore, *bhūtātman* is conquered by materials or an inner self (*antaḥ puruṣa*). In this way, *bhūtātman* is treated as a lower and impure self which is connected to or conquered by material things.[21]

Here, the usage of *bhūtātman* indicates that it should be considered as a lower, negative or perishing part of a human being, or as a lower self when contrasted with a higher self.[22]

III. As we have seen, the one term *bhūtātman* in the Mokṣadharma has several different usages, which may be summarized in the following way:

1. a creative function[23] (MBh.XII.187)
2. empirical self[24] to be emancipated by *yoga* practice (MBh.XII.196, 232, 245, Manu Smṛti, Caraka Saṃhitā)
3. a lower or perishing part of a human being (MBh.XII.291, Maitrāyaṇī Upaniṣad)
4. a separate being until rebirth (MBh.286)
5. an epithet of the highest being (MBh.XII.200)

How is this difference to be understood? Can we assume that each of these differences refers to aspects of the whole *bhūtātman*?

The various aspects of its character seem too contradictory to form a single entity. Moreover, it is rather difficult to imagine that there were originally different meanings for the same term. The meaning of the original concept, therefore, must have undergone a semantic change or development. I would like to propose one possible explanation for this shift.

In my view, one of the most important factors instrumental in causing this change in meaning was the multiple and often ambiguous meanings of *bhūta*. The many meanings of *bhūta* caused the development of different usages. In some usages, *bhūta* possesses a connotation of material things. However, in other usages, it means living or existing beings.

From a chronological perspective, the occurrences in MBh.XII. 187 and in the Mait. Up. are supposed to be comparatively old, but both seem to contradict each other: one is a kind of creator, while the other is an existence polluted by materials. It seems difficult to put these different usages into chronological order. But, through an examination of all instances of the term, it seems possible to postulate an older, underlying concept for the term, and to explain the presence of other usages in terms of derivations caused by the various meanings of *bhūta.*

Among the various expressions used to describe the functions of *bhūtātman,* I wish to focus upon a more primitive meaning that occurs twice, namely, "staying in the heart". This expression is reminiscent of the old Upaniṣadic concept of *ātman.* I would take this meaning of *bhūtātman* to be older. Thus, the characteristics of *bhūtātman* used with or related to the expression "staying in the heart" could indicate the older concept behind the term.

In Chapter 196, 231, 245, it is stated that *bhūtātman,* who stays in the heart, possesses knowledge and experiences both pain and pleasure, but is difficult to see because of its subtlety. It is possible to recognize it through *yoga* practice, and this process of recognition of *bhūtātman* leads to emancipation. The emancipated state of *ātman* is called *Brahman.* This was not unique at all but, rather, a frequently cited monistic method of conceptualizing ātman-brahman in the days of the old and middle Upaniṣads. I shall, therefore, assume that the original concept of *bhūtātman* was the subtle inner self that is responsible for knowledge and action, and was not divided into the two aspects of true self and empirical self until later. This being exists in all living beings, so it is called *bhūtātman,* or "the self in all the living beings". The purpose of a *yogin* is to recognize *bhūtātman* to be the essential being in himself, and, upon finding the same principle in all living beings, to become one with them (*sarvabhūtātmabhūta*). The original concept of *bhūtātman,* therefore, is not the same as that of *jīva,* which does not have a universal aspect to its essential nature.

At the same time, the creative function belongs to this *bhūtātman.* He is responsible for the creation of material beings in atheistic thought, which discounts the existence of such primordial materials as *prakṛti.*

The other usages of *bhūtātman* are presumed to have derived from the above assumed concept under the influence of developing philosophical thought and the various meanings of *bhūta*.

I shall conclude this paper by proposing some assumptions:

1. Under the effect of the two kinds of *ātman* prevalent in the middle Upaniṣads, *bhūtātman* is considered to be a lower self, because it is conditioned by the former member of the compound, that is, by those who have to distinguish true and unconditioned self from empirical self for the purpose of *mokṣa* theory. In this case, emphasis is placed upon the involvement of *bhūtātman* in the material world on the grounds that *bhūta* includes a sense of material element.[25] When *bhūtātman* is used to denote an empirical self, its meaning comes close to *jīva* which means life or animating principle in the body.
2. For the usage of an epithet of Viṣṇu, it is supposed to begin with the influence of theistic tendencies in the middle Upaniṣads. It is rather easy to apply a concept of omniscience to another omniscient principle. Therefore, we should assume that, in this case, *bhūtātman* is used adjectivally.
3. It is safe to assume that, before the days of the systematization of philosophical thought, there must have been many groups of thinkers who pursued the goal of emancipation, but expressed their ideas in different terms. In this situation, *bhūtātman* comes to be used synonymously with *dehin, śarīrin kṣetrajña* and *jīva.*[26]
4. When life and death is contrasted, it is easy to imagine that a living being is called *śarīrin,* and a dead being *bhūtātman.* In this case, the meaning of *bhūta* is "passed". This usage might be related to the hobgoblin (*bhūta*).
5. By the time of the development of the *ātman* and *mokṣa* theory, *bhūtātman* becomes obsolete, its role being replaced by other influential concepts or terms. This process seems to have been reflected in variants of MBh. More often than not, *bhūtātman* was replaced by other words.[27]
6. Texts such as the Manusmṛti and the Carakasaṃhitā retain the old term *bhūtātman* because they do not place primary importance on the pursuit of the real self and of emancipation.

NOTES

1. I presented a paper on the *bhūtātman* in the Mokṣadharma in 1995 at the 46th Conference of the Association of Japan Indology and Buddhist Studies, and published it in the *Journal of Indology and Buddhist Studies*, vol. 44-1.
2. Cf. E. Frauwallner, Die Geschichte der Indischen Philosophie, I.Band, Salzburg, 1953, p.283.
3. The Mahābhārata, for the first time critically edited by S.K. Belvalkar Poona, 1954. This text is referred to by P. when compared with B. (Śriman Mahābhāratam (7 vols.), with a commentary of Nīlakaṇṭha, reprint 1988 by Nag Publishers, Delhi) and K. (Śriman Mahābhāratam, first published 1901-1910 Kumbhakonam, reprint by Śri Satguru Publications, Delhi 1991.)
4. Cf. E.W. Hopkins, *The Great Epic of India, Its Character and Origin*, 1901, Reprint Calcutta 1978, p.39. F., Edgerton, *The Beginnings of Indian Philosophy*, London, 1965, p.256, fn.l. A. Malinar, Rājavidyā: das königliche Wissen um Herrshaft und Verzicht: Studien zur Bhagavadgītā, Wiesbaden, 1996, p.200. Johnston considers that the concept of *bhūtātman* was originally the same as *jīva* (E.H. Johnston, *Early Sāṃkhya*, London, 1937, pp.49-50).
5. Chapter 187 of the Mokṣadharma is often regarded by scholars as an important explication of early Sāṃkhya thought. (Cf. Hopkins, *Great Epic of India*, pp.120. 132, 160, 322; E. Frauwallner, *Untersuchungen zum Mokṣadharma. Die sāṃkhyistischen Taxte*, WZKM 32, 1925, pp.179-206. Edgerton, *The Beginnings of Indian Philosophy*, pp.256-260 J. A. B. van Buitenen, *Studies in Sāṃkhya (I)*, JAOS 76,1956, pp.153-157.)
6. P. *tat tu jīvo 'nu paśyati* B., K.: *tat tu jīvo na paśyati* The verse is quite similar to MBh.XII.239.6 which runs:
   mahābhūtani pancaiva sarvabhūteṣu bhūtakṛt/
   akarot tātavaiṣamyaṃ yasmin yad anupaśyati//
7. Concerning the occurrence of the term in MBh.XII.231, Frauwallner pointed out: Die individuelle Seele wird durch die Bezeichnug (*bhūtātman*) davon (*ātmā*, das oberste Princip) unterschieden. Aus dem ātmā sind die Elemente (*mahābhūtāni*) hervorgegangen. (E. Frauwallner, *Untersuchungen zum Mokṣadharma. Die nicht-sāṃkhyistischen Texte*, JAOS 45,1925, p. 55) But here material elements are born from *bhūtātman*.
8. But Johnston identifies the original *bhūtātman* with *jīva* (Johnston, *Early Sāṃkhya*, p. 45).
9. This is more easily understood from the variant readings of B., K.: *jīvo na paśyati*. This reading stresses that *jīva*. does not have the same function as that of *bhūtātman*.
10. Another occurrence of the same category, that is, creator, is seen in the variant readings of MBh.XII.224.45, which are as follows:
    sa vai sṛjati bhūtātmā sa eva puruṣaḥ paraḥ/ (P. *bhūtāni* B.K.: *bhūtātmā*)
11. A similar usage of the term is seen in MBh.III.203.34. In the 33rd verse, *jīva* is described as an agent and, in the following verse, *bhūtātman* is referred to as the higher principle as follows:
    evaṃ sarveṣu bhūtātmā na prakāśate/
    dṛśyate tv agryayā buddhyā sūkṣmayā jñānavedibhiḥ/

12. *eṣa devo mahāyogī bhūtātmā bhūtabhavanaḥ* /MBh.XII.202.29cd
padmanābho mahāyogī bhūtātmā bhūtabhavanaḥ./ MBh.XII.202.31cd
13. A similar usage of the term occurs in MBh.XIII.135.140 (=Śarabha Upaniṣad 24), as follows:
eko viṣṇur mahad bhūtaṃ pṛthag bhūtāny anekaśaḥ/
trīn lokān vyāpya bhūtātmā bhuṅkte viśvabhug avyayaḥ//
In the MBh.XII.Appendix I, No.28, 316(=Vāyupurāṇa (Ānandāśrama edition) 30.256, Brahmapurāṇa 40.71 (Brahmapurāṇa: Sanskrit Indices and Text of the Brahmapurāṇa, ed by P. Schreiner and R. Söhnen, Wiesbaden, 1987.)) *bhūtātman* is listed as one of the many epithets of Śiva. In the Gopālottaratapinī Upaniṣad, the term is used synonymously with *gopāla* (in the last ślokas No. 14). (cf. Hopkins, *Great Epic of India*, p.40.)
14. A sort of parallel passage is found in MBh.XIV:50.1 where *bhūtātman* is identified with *manas*, as follows:
bhūtānāṃ pañcānām īśvaraṃ manaḥ/
niyame ca visarge ca bhūtātmā mana eva ca//
Here, *manas* is supposed to be the controller of the material elements. *Bhūtātman* is used as an adjective that qualifies *manas*, in order to explain its specific nature. This is a later usage that is based upon the MBh. XII.231.12. (cf. Hopkins, Great Epic, p.40.)
In the following verse, namely, MBh.XIV.50.4, *bhūtātman* appears again as the charioteer of as chariot to which the material elements are yoked and whose rein is *buddhi*, which has almost the same appearance in MBh. XII.231.11.
mahābhūtasamāyuktaṃ buddhisaṃyamanaṃ ratham /
tam āruhya sa bhūtātmā samantāt paridhāvati //MBh.XIV:50.4
15. In the Śārīrasthāna of the Carakasaṃhitā, we find the same usage of this term in the arguement on emancipation:
ataḥ ataḥ paraṃ bramabhūto bhūtātmā nopalabhyate /
niḥsṛtaḥ sarvabhāvebhyaś cihnaṃ yasya na vidyate/
jñānaṃ brahmavidāṃ cātra nājñas taj jñātum arthati/
Caraka Saṃhitā, Śārīrasthāna I.155/
Here, *bhūtātman* comes to be identified with *brahman,* because of the removal of all the marks of existence. In the Śārīrasthāna, and only in the Śārīrasthāna, of the Carakasaṃhitā, *bhūtātman* appears as a doer (I.14,57), the supreme self (I.84), one of the conscious elements (4.8). As a whole, it is an inner self, responsible for both usual activity and emancipation, which implies that the concept is very close to that found in MBh.XII.231. In the Manu Smṛti 12.12 we also see *bhūtātman* as a performer of actions. Although the commentators vary in their interpretations, the term may perhaps have the sense of an inner self in the same text:
adbhir gātrāṇi śudhyanti manaḥ satyena śudhyati/
vidyātapobhyāṃ bhūtātmā buddhir jñānena śudhyati// Manu Smṛti 5.109
16. The context in which *bhūtātman* is used as an object of meditation is found in the MBh.XII. Appendix I, No.16, 27:
sarvabhūteṣu bhūtātmā tad tad buddhiṃ samāsthitaḥ/
tasmād buddhas tvam evainaṃ dhyāhi nityam atandritaḥ /
17. Although it is replaced by *bhūteṣu* in P. and K., the term *bhūtātman*

retained in MBh.(B.)XII.319.13 seems to have the same content, that is, being involved in transmigration:

evaṃbhūteṣu bhūteṣu (B. *bhūtātmā*) *nityabhūtādhruveṣu ca /*
kathaṃ hṛṣyeta jāteṣu mṛteṣu ca kathaṃ jvaret // MBh.XII.307.12

18. Although the meaning of *bhūta* is unclear, the cosmic attributes of the *bhūtātman* can be found in the Brahmabindhu Upaniṣad 12 (=Tripurātāpinyī Upaniṣad 5.12; Tattvasamāsasūtravṛtti (in Sāṃkhya-Saṅgraha, Chowkhamba Sanskrit Series, Nos. 246, 286 p.80):

eka eva hi bhūtātmā bhūte bhūte vyavasthitaḥ/
ekadhā bahudhā caiva dṛśyate jalacandravat /12/

One and the same *bhūtātman* exists in every living being(?), and is seen as one or many, like the moon in the water.

19. Cf. Bṛhadāraṇyaka Upaniṣad IV.4.22, Chāndogya Upaniṣad III.14 (Śāṇḍilya), et passim.

20. In the Maitrāyaṇī Upaniṣad, *bhūtātman* appears again in 4.1,2,3 and 6.10 with nearly the same semantic value. (Cf. Johnston, *Early Sāṃkhya,* p.48) In the Subāla Upaniṣad 5, *bhūtātman* appears with the adjective *annamayo.* Here, *bhūtātman* is considered to be involved in the material world, or is a material (food) itself.

21. Maitrāyaṇī Upaniṣad 3.2 states:

te hocur bhagavan yady evam asyātmano mahimān sūcyasīty anyo vā paraḥ ko 'yam ātmākhyo yo sitāsitaḥ karmaphalair abhibhūyamānaḥ sadasadyonim āpadyatā iti/ avāñcyordhvā vā gatir dvandvair abhibhūyamānaḥ paribhramati/ asti khalv anyo 'paro bhūtātmākhyo yo 'yaṃ sitāsitaḥ karmaphalair abhibhūyamānaḥ sadasadyonim āpadyatā iti/ avāñcyordhvā vā gatir abhibhūyamānaḥ paribhramatī/

Up to 3.5, *bhūtātman* continues to have strongly negative connotations, in that the material meaning of *bhūta* is variously stressed.

22. Cf. Frauwallner, Die Geschichte der Indischen Philosophie, p.106. The usage of *bhūtātman* which appears with *paramātman* is found in the MBh.XIII. Appendix I, No. 26.54:

eṣām(=ten *indriyas*) *uddhartakaḥ kālo nānābhedavad āsthitaḥ /*
paramātmā ca bhūtātmā guṇabhedena saṃsthitaḥ /

In the MBh.(B.)XII.204.5, Manu refers to *bhūtātman* as being satisfied in ignorance and involved in material things. With this reading, the empirical aspect of *bhūtātman* is treated rather negatively. This usage may be close to that of the Maitrāyaṇī Upaniṣad (cf. Hopkins, *Great Epic of India,* p.41, fn.1). The reading of P. and K. is *pūtātma* instead of *bhūtātmā.* The verse in question is as follows:

ajñānatṛpto viṣayeṣv avagāḍho na dṛśyate/
adṛṣtvaiva tu bhūtātmā viṣayebhyo nivartate // (=P.XII.197.5, K.XII.202.5)

23. In MBh.(B.) XII.313.12 *bhūtātman* is identified with *ahaṃkāra* and *prajāpati.* This reading is not retained in P. and K., both of which read *sarvātmā* instead of *bhūtātmā.*

mano grasati sarvātmā (B. *bhūtātmā*) *so 'haṃkāraḥ prajāpatiḥ /*
ahaṃkāraṃ mahān ātmā bhūtabhavyabhaviṣyavit // MBh.XII.300.12

In this verse which explains the process of reabsorption, *manas* is swallowed by *bhūtātman,* which is *ahaṃkāra,* that is, *prajāpati.* It is, therefore, identified with a being of a creative function. Buitenen pointed out the usage of *ahaṃkāra* in the context of creation (J.A.B. van Buitenen, *Studies in Sāṃkhya (II),* JAOS 77, 1957 pp.15-25)

24. Śaṅkara seems to refer to this usage of *bhūtātman* in his Brahmasūtra Bhāṣya when he explains that *ātman* is used to denote a being of consciousness. The passages in question are as follows:
athavaika evātmaśabdaś cetanācetanaviṣayo bhaviṣyati; bhūtātmendriyātmeti ca prayogadarśanāt / Brahmasūtra Śāṅkara Bhāṣya (Parimala Sanskrit Series No.1, ed. by E.A. Solomon) I.1.6 (p. 173)
tamāc cetanaviṣaya eva mukhya ātmaśabdaś cetanatvopacārād bhūtādiṣu prayujyate bhūtāmendriyātmeti ca/ op. cit., I.1.7 (pp. 173-174)
25. Interpreting the term of MBh.XII.187.6, Edgerton proposes that it should be read in the following way: *bhūtātman*, 'self of (or appearing in) the (material) elements; it seems to mean an empirically observed living being, without distinction of body and soul. (Edgerton, *The Beginnings of Indian Philosophy*, p. 256, fn.l)
26. In MBh.XII.121.40, *bhūtātman* is listed together with *jīva* as one of the eight synonyms of *akṣara*.
īśvaraḥ puruṣaḥ prāṇaḥ sattvaṃ vittaṃ prajāpatiḥ/
bhūtātmā jīva ity eva nāmabhiḥ procyate 'ṣṭabhiḥ// MBh.XII.121.40
27. Cf. MBh.XII.197.5 (K.202.5) (B. reads *bhūtātmā* instead of *pūtātmā*), XII.224.45 (The Manuscripts K7, D4, 9 in the critical apparatus of P. read *bhūtātmā* instead of *bhūtāni* of P., B., K. XII.300.12 (K.317.12) (B. *bhūtātma*, replaced by *sarvātmā*), XII.307.12 (K.324.13) (B. *bhūtātmā*, replaced by *bhūteṣu*) XIII.34.14 (B. *bhūtātmāno*, replaced by *kṛtātmāno*)

CHAPTER 49

A Study on the Relation between Ātmadarśana and Yogic Practice

GENSEI ASANO

I. *Introduction*

It is said that Gotama Buddha learned ākiṃcanyāyatana-dhyāna as soon as he became a monk and that he acquired nasaṃjñānapyasaṃjñaka-dhyāna next. But he soon rejected tapas because he was not satisfied with results of either of these dhyānas. He finally awoke to the realities of universe through his the last dhyāna under the bodhi tree. The starting point of this research is thus the question: what are the differences between these two types of dhyāna, one of which Gotama renounced and the other through which he acquired enlightenment?

In the course of my research into the history of yogic practices and its changing value in Indian society, I have come to some conclusions about why yogic practice came to be introduced into Indian thought. Already from the age of Veda, Āryan culture had begun to show philosophical interest in ultimate and invisible subjects.[1] When the logical methods of contemplation and the sciences are not sufficiently developed in a society, however, we tend to imagine ideal worlds through speculative or theological thinking. To a certain extent, Hinduism also shows this development. In India, however, attempts to clarify abstract subjects through logical methods occurred earlier than attempts to explain things by theological or metaphysical means. Even theistic explanations of the universe were excluded in the earliest times. A creator as a primary cause is not recognized in the creation myths passed down from the Vedas to the Upaniṣads. For example, Prajāpati and Parameṣṭhin are only mere saṃskṛta, in the sense of something that is itself a product of other causes.

Because these occurred in an earlier, still immature age, however, such logical attempts did not fully satisfy either the persons who were studying it or the person imagining it himself. Yogic practice and tapas, which may well predate the Āryan invasion, could be thought to have shouldered the burden of filling this gap.

Even when the methods of logical thought were more developed, Yogic practice did not lose this important role. On the contrary, its value increased more and more. Yogic practitioners did not only investigate and analyze external phenomena. Rather, the main purpose of their investigations was to find out how the self, which embodies a worldly awakening, can be connected with the invisible, ineffable and cosmic sacred-space. In other words, they sought enlightenment as an ultimate awakening in which the conversion from worldly existence to sacred existence is realized.

We should call those people who seek to accomplish by yogic practices the enlightenment that is otherwise accomplished by logical or metaphysical methods, śramaṇas. For example, most thinking in the older Upaniṣads and classical Darśanas can be regarded as śramaṇic regardless of its modality. We thus propose to extend the meaning of the term śramaṇa. We shall call all those primarily concerned with the practices aimed toward mokṣa śramaṇa, because they did not arrive at the same conclusions later Hinduism did, that is, of monotheism and the worship of Īśvara. This reflects the actual situation of the śramaṇas who appeared in Indian history from the 6th century BC on.

Yogic practices were taken more seriously in śramaṇic thinking. But when brāhmaṇism was revived in later Hinduism and the Darśanas became its reigning ideology, the role of Yoga also changed, dividing the current of śramaṇic ideas into various tributaries.

2. *Śramaṇic Thought and the Purpose of Yoga*

2.1. Two Streams of Sāṃkhya and Yoga

One of the unique characteristics of Indian thought was that it transformed the concept of ātman, which has no stable or definite form, into something homogeneous. Ātman is often recognized as the whole universe, which transcends the repetitive cycle of utpāda-sthiti-bhaṅga. It is an invisible and indefinite substance, both spatially and temporally. No other transcendent and absolute existence free from the repetition of utpāda-sthiti-bhaṅga was conceived of and, in this way, a spiritual absolute as a sacred entity came to be discovered within the experiential world. After the theory of Īśvara developed during the succeeding growth of Hinduism, however, the purposes of yogic practice were transformed. These purposes can be roughly divided into two types. One was the attempt to make the Self return to the universal entity and the other is the attempt to realize the sacred universe within oneself. The former recognizes the absolute of a universal entity, while the latter does not.[2]

We can analyze this matter from a historical point of view. Although Indian thought had the above-mentioned characteristics, Āryan thought also included the factor from which the theory of Īśvara eventually developed. That is, the disorder in the history of Indian thought from B.C. sixth to fifth century—the age in which the most typical ideas in Indian thought appeared—was caused by two factors: the dissolution, of Vedic sacrifice and the immaturity of the Īśvara-like idea already implicit within Āryan thought. Philosophers, for example, admitted no transcendent and absolute entity like Īśvara separate from oneself and so they attempted to either make themselves return to the universal entity or to find the sacred universe within. These possible positions concerning these questions gave rise to a variety of disputes, all of which we can call śramaṇic because these were the circumstances in which śramaṇic thought first came to the forefront.

Vijñānabhikṣu commented on these various viewpoints, these Darśanas, as follows in his *Sāṃkhyapravacanabhāṣya,* his commentary on the *Sāṃkhyasūtra.*[3]

(1) An objector may say 'Nyāya and Vaiśeṣika also have their

> own way of thinking about these objects. And the Sāṃkhya position has been rendered meaningless by these two schools. Sāṃkhya and Nyāya-Vaiśeṣika prove the Self under the contradictory forms of saguṇa and niguṇa. Since there is opposition between the arguments of the Nyāya-Vaiśeṣika systems and the arguments of Sāṃkhya, no common understanding is possible.' If someone were to speak like this, it would not be so.
>
> Response: They are not meaningless and contradictory because their subject-matter is different: the Nyāya-Vaiśeṣikas are speaking about the vyāvahārika [level] and the Sāṃkhyas about the pāramārthika. According to both Nyāya and Vaiśeṣika, distinguishing the Self from simple physical existence is considered to be only an initial stage, because [ātman] is the repeatedly [defined in terms] of happiness (sukhin) and suffering (dukhin).[4]
>
> (2) But there certainly is contradiction between Sāṃkhya and both Brahma-mīmāṃsā, i.e., Vedānta, and Yoga. For, although both Vedānta and Yoga prove an eternal Īśvara, it should be denied by Sāṃkhya... .
>
> To this counterargument we should reply as follows. This too is limited by the differences in [their levels], i.e. the vyāvahārika of Sāṃkhya and the pāramārthika of Vedānta and Yoga... . In Sāṃkhya, one trains over and over again in the negation of worldly gods for the sake of freedom from all worldly desires toward those deities. If eternal Īśvara is not also disregarded, in accordance with the position of the Lokāyatas, then one would be blocked from obtaining discriminating wisdom (viveka) from devoting one's mind to [Īśvara] by acknowledging a supreme sacred reality which is perfect, eternal and inerrant. Sāṃkhya's scholars explained it in this way and never criticized theism itself.[5]

Vijñānabhikṣu's opinions presented here are very interesting. Nyāya-Vaiśeṣika and Sāṃkhya are compared in part 1. The only difference between them is the viewpoints of vyāvahārika and of pāramārthika they are based on. Vijñānabhikṣu explains that there is no other essential difference between them. In this case, Nyāya-Vaiśeṣika is based on vyāvahārika and Sāṃkhya on pāramārthika.

In part 2, the Sāṃkhya is compared with Vedānta and Yoga according to the distinction between theism and atheism. Here also, he explains that there is no essential difference between them, only the insignificant differences relating to their respective viewpoints of vyāvahārika or pāramārthika. In this case, too, Vedānta and Yoga are based on vyāvahārika and Sāṃkhya on pāramārthika.

Vijñānabhikṣu aims to return to Upaniṣadic thought and to unify the various Darśanas based on its viewpoints. Although his works were written with these ultimate purposes in mind, his understanding does not contradict the historical specifics of Indian thought. He was, rather, attempting to clarify the latent and indistinct currents lying within traditional Indian thinking.

For example, we shall now discuss the history of Vindhyavāsin and Pañcaśikha, who are early thinkers of the Sāṃkhya tradition. We can find fragments of their work in the *Yogasūtrabhāṣya,* the *Sāṃkhyasūtra* and the latter commentary of the *Sāṃkhyakārikā.*[6] More specifically, their thinking lay behind the explanations of Sāṃkhya-Yoga found in the *Yogabindu*[7] by the later Jain scholar, Haribhadrasūri. We will focus more directly on this text below, so we need not address this problem in detail here, but only indicate our general conclusions. There are at least two currents in the history of Sāṃkhya-Yoga. One flows from the stream of former scholars, and from it to the *Yogasūtrabhāṣya,* then to the latter commentaries of the *Sāṃkhyakārikā,* and on to the *Tattvavaiśaradī* by Vijñānabhikṣu. The other is the thought of the *Sāṃkhyakārikā* and its early commentators. The former can be said to be practical and realist, and the latter could be said to be theoretical and logical.

Yoga played an important and complex role in the interaction between theoretical study and disciplined practice. Yogic practice serves as a practical method of experientially discovering the spiritual absolute within, as opposed to a theological theory concerning an absolute entity cut off from empirical reality. Nevertheless, it also shows a tendency to lean toward either pāramārthika or vyavahārika, which is one of the reasons that various currents of thought arose. The Upaniṣads were also born in the interaction between theoretical study and disciplined practice, which is why they are also śramaṇic-like. But the Upaniṣads developed in a direction which reinforced the shift from the discovery of the subject in oneself to a consideration of objective factors. Yājñavalkya's theories typifies this. He characterized the ātman as immortal and fearless, and considered it is as of the same nature as brahman, a universal absolute. We can see that the sages of the Upaniṣads gradually shifted their interest to an external ideal entity and away from their investigation of an internal spiritual absolute.[8]

Dedicated śramaṇic movements, on the other hand, moved in the opposite direction. Buddhism, for example, established its identity by insisting on the centrality of the internal quest. A Buddhist often extraordinarily clings to this way of thinking and categorically denies all kinds of external entities. In this respect, Buddhism cannot be said to have a particular way of thinking, but rather played the historical role strengthening and clarifying the śramaṇic tendency. Both of these directions in śramaṇic thought, however, influenced the purposes and practices of Yoga, for they were deeply connected with the śramaṇa's very reason for being a śramaṇa.

2.2. Śramaṇic Thought in Opposition to Traditional Theism

Śramaṇic thought should not be characterized by the strange appearances or peculiar practices of the śramaṇas. Rather, we should think of it as having established its own identity by its concentrated focus upon the internal quest, as opposed to the extremism of either the theory of Īśvara as an external factor and of the idealism of those who would grasp every internal principle abstractly. It is in accordance with this middle ground that yogic mentalism developed, as we have explained above.

Unfortunately, few texts remain which can confirm this character of the śramaṇic movements. Even the *Yogasūtra,* though a main text for Yoga, did not inherit a purely śramāṇic character, because it was strongly influenced from the theistic directions Āryan thought took in the process of developing the Darśana systems.

Now we take up a work by Haribhadrasūri, who rejuvenated the theory of practice in Jainism. Jainism is characterized by typical śramaṇic thinking, and there is even a Jain sect which preserves this śramaṇic color to this day.[9] Haribhadrasūri's works are not antiquated, however, but remain important materials for our understanding of classical śramaṇic thinking. He presented his criticisms on the logic of Īśvara in the *Yogabindu* as follows, a logic that has to be denied by the śramaṇic practice.

> A soul is saṃsārin while it is being connected with something other than itself. When it breaks free from this connection, it will experience mokṣa. And saṃsāra and mokṣa are caused because connection and dis-connection is the very nature of each.[10]

This refers to the realistic relationship between niyoga and saṃyoga mediated by jīva. With these ideas in the background, Haribhadrasūri criticizes those who hold to Maheśvara or Śiva, as well as the Vedāntin school.

> (criticism of Maheśavādin)
> Because a soul connects with its very nature or svabhāva to receive this boon, it receives the boon from somebody else, i.e. Maheśvara. If that weren't so, then all this would not be worth telling.[11]
>
> (criticism of Vedāntin)
>
> By the logic of an ātman unconnected with anything else, it is always necessary that this soul be in a state of nondiscrimination. These two, saṃsāra and mokṣa, however, are only formed through discrimination.[12]
>
> Even though the nature of gold is in the state of nondiscrimination, the purity and impurity of genuine gold cannot be established without words or śabda. There is no doubt about this.[13]

In this opening part of the *Yogabindu,* Haribhadrasūri surveys Indian thought in general, and, while critical of it, mentions the importance and value of yogic practice in particular. Especially in a series of verses from kārikā 6 to 15, he attempts to defeat his opponents like Maheśavādins or Vedāntins. The auto-commentary on these kārikās suggests the viewpoint from which he recognizes the superiority of yogic practice over that of Maheśavāda. His reasons are based upon a realist theory concerning the relationship between saṃyoga and niyoga and between saṃsāra and mokṣa. Both Maheśavāda and Vedāntin are treated in parallel, here. For the ātman that is defended by them both is not reflected in any of the realities of individual existence; this ātman only exists at the level of absolute ideation. On this point, both of these sects share a common denominator.

We have already introduced the example by Vijñānabhikṣu mentioned in his *Pravacanabhāṣya*. There he applied the distinction between vyāvahārika and pāramārthika. Now, Haribhadrasūri also distinguishes the vyāvahārika reality established by śabda and the very nature of gold as pāramārthika proved by abstraction. He refutes the latter as idealism and treats Maheśavāda and Vedāntin as targets of the same kind of attack.

Haribhadrasūri seems to conduct his critique on the assumption that both vyāvahārika phenomenal reality and pāramārthika ultimate reality traffic with each other in accordance with the relationship of saṃyoga and niyoga. He does not accept paramārtha as a changeless kevalin in its own nature. And he refutes an unchanging vyavahāra in the same way. Saṃyoga means impurity of jīva and causes saṃsāra. On the other hand, efforts at practice in the worldly state of saṃsāra lead to purification, which is established by niyoga, and opens the way to reach paramārtha. The role of agent is performed here by jīva.[14] In this situation, we need to discover the existential reason why śramaṇic thought accompanies yogic practice in this way. Most of Indian thought, however, developed in the direction of a transcendentalism which placed Īśvara at its center.

2.3. Yogic Practice as Self-validating One's Internal True Nature

Yogic practice was a typical śramaṇic method and served an important function as the background supporting one current of Indian thought. It aimed to discover the Self as one's internal true nature. However, when someone attempts to verify his own ātman, two problems arise. One is the contradiction that ātman as the object to be verified is also the subject that verifies itself. The other is how such a practice can be distinguished from one that causes saṅga or attachments. It was due to the problems solving these contradictions that Īśvaravāda came to be accepted all the more and similar ways of thinking arose even within śramaṇic thought. This makes it much more difficult to research the history of yoga. To investigate these questions, we will again take up the work by Haribhadrasūri, the *Yogabindu*. We consider it adequate for reconstructing traditional methods of śramaṇic practice; plus, it is written very logically. Haribhadrasūri enumerates the main theses of various traditions concerning worldly bondage and mokṣa as follows:

> Something referring to ātman was named by the different schools of thought, as, for instance, puruṣa, kṣetravit and jñāna. On the other hand, something referring to an external entity was named, such as avidyā, prakṛti and karman.[15]

According to Haribhadrasūri's own commentary on this kārikā, the term puruṣa is used by Jainism and Vedānta. Sāṃkhya calls it kṣetravit or kṣetrajña and Buddhism uses jñāna. While the external entity which is separate from ātman is called avidyā by Buddhism and Vedānta, prakṛti by Sāṃkhya and karman by Jainism.[16]

This classification suggests a variety of things. It is interesting to see the Jain perspective on ātmavāda based on puruṣa theory, while kṣetravit is given for ātmavāda of Sāṃkhya, which is usually recognized as the prototype of puruṣa theory. Although jñāna for Buddhism may be acceptable if we take an historical point of view and regard the Buddhism in question as Vijñaptimātratā. But how can, we understand the difference between puruṣa as an internal spiritual reality and kṣetravit? In this case, puruṣa does not mean only abstract spirituality but also an embodied absolute in life. In other words, Haribhadrasūri intended to enlarge the simple meaning of puruṣa as a spiritual subject to encompass one's entire spiritual and material life. In the case of Sāṃkhya, however, although puruṣa is *bhoktṛ* or enjoyer, it never becomes kartṛ or doer. Sāṃkhya differs greatly from Vedānta on this point related to ātman. Haribhadrasūri seems to have expressly chosen a topic, ātman, with which Jainism conforms with Vedānta but is distinguished from Sāṃkhya.

However, he does differentiate his standpoint from Vedānta on the question of an external entity which is separate from ātman here. He equates Buddhism with Vedānta, and allocates the term 'avidyā' to both of them. Jaina receives karman and, needless to say, Sāṃkhya is given prakṛti.

We will now discuss how the various schools view Saṃyoga as the association between ātman and this external entity.

> Similarly, concerning the connection between ātman and some external entity, names like bhrānti, pravṛtti and bandha are mentioned. While the agent who grants boons is called names like śāstṛ, vandya and avikārin.[17]

Buddhism and Vedānta are combined again, here by the term 'bhavānti'. Sāṃkhya used *pravṛtti* and Jainism bandha.[18] Bhavānti is simply allocated to Buddhism and bandha induced by bhavānti is given only to Jainism, indicating that Haribhadrasūri is ignoring the theory of anātman in early Buddhism on the apparent assumption that only the Vijñaptimātratā form of Buddhism need be considered. Here we are hampered by the fact that the *Yogabindu* is not such an old text. Moreover, what is mentioned in the work does not reflect only the pure classical state of śramaṇic thinking, but is also influenced by contemporary developments and disputes. In this sense, we can imagine that it was due to his repulsion for the Buddhism which had by then been transformed into Vijñaptimātratā that he purposely avoided the characteristics that were shared by Buddhism and Jainism and did not mention that terms like karman or bandha were also Buddhist ideas. Or we might suppose that Jainism and Buddhism must have had a fundamental estrangement from each other from early times.

Although the *Yogabindu* is not clear enough for any solid conclusion, we can say at least the following. It conforms to an ancient Jain tradition which admitted an entity called *jīva*, to which the *Yogabindu* gave the name 'puruṣa' as an internal spiritual subject, acknowledging some commonality between Jainism and Advaita. The term 'jñāna', which was given to Buddhism in this section, might have been altered to nairātmya if the *Yogabindu* had considered early Buddhism instead. We should know in any case that Jainism and Buddhism, though they were equally śramaṇic movements, had I differing standpoints from early times.

Concerning the issue of material entities external to ātman, Buddhism is, along with Vedānta, allotted avidyā, while only Jainism is given karman. In short, Buddhism is not treated as a śramaṇaic movement here like Jainism, but is categorized as a kind of philosophical epistemology. This treatment is extended to the issue of saṃyoga, the connection between *ātman* and some external entity. As we have seen, bhavānti is allocated to

Buddhism and Vedānta, while only Jainism is accorded bandha induced by bhavānti. According to this analysis, Buddhism only analyzes the bitter existence of saṃsāra, using a term like bhavānti, while it is Jainism that maintains an interest in the object to be released from, i.e. bandha, and therefore the purpose of mokṣa. It is very interesting that Buddhists, who insist on a theory of anātman, are identified with Vedāntins, who maintain a form of monotheistic ātmavāda.

3. *The Role of Theories of Practice in Establishing Spiritual Hypostasi*

3.1. Co-existence of Embodied Soul and Mokṣa

We cannot overlook Haribhadrasūri's intentional distortion or dislike for a Buddhism that had been transformed into Vijñaptimātratā. But we may also be able to see the dilemma existing inside the śramaṇic theory of practice that transformed Buddhism into Vijñaptimātratā. So we need to reevaluate the various śramaṇic positions regarding internal entities or spiritual hypostasis.

According to Haribhadrasūri's thought, Jainism and Vedānta use the term 'puruṣa' for internal spirituality, while Buddhism applies 'jñāna' to it. Jainism, which uncritically admits a trans-historical spirituality entity like *jīva,* is commonplace in this regard. There is no basis for the transhistorical existence of *jīva,* however, it only exists in traditional legends which refer to it. But behind Haribhadrasūri's insistent acceptance of the reality of *jīva,* we can detect an intent to preserve a subject which must be purged and ultimately released by disciplined practice. On the other hand, Buddhism lost the opportunity to explicate the subject of *mokṣa* through disciplined practice because it denied the personal spiritual subject in favor of a rational and impersonal notion like jñāna. This was not an exceptional problem, but one of the most important problems in the history of Indian thought.

We can now examine the *Bhagavadgītā* on this question. The *Bhagavadgītā* began to be composed during the śramaṇic era, and soon provided the foundation of Hinduism on the basis of Īśvaravāda. We find theistic ātmavāda highlighted in the *Bhagavadgīta.* The actions of embodied souls are recognized as a cause of saṃsāra by the *Bhagavadgītā*. At the same time, however, the religious practices of embodied souls are also causes of mokṣa. The *Bhagavadgītā* intended to solve this problem as follows.

> After renouncing all action by manas, the embodied soul lives happily in the city of nine gates, neither working nor making work.[19]

The *Bhagavadgītā* explains here that embodied souls are not concerned with any actions, because the actions which either cause an attachment for fruits, i.e. the cause of saṃsāra, or the actions which renounce the attachment for fruits, i.e. the cause of mokṣa, all arise associated with a form of mind called 'manas'. In other words, the contradiction between kartṛtva and bhoktṛtva of ātman is handily avoided and the responsibility for both falls only upon the manas.

> The Self does not act and does not create worldly actions. Nor does He connect actions with their fruits. However his own nature is working there.[20]

Since the Sovereign Self does not act, it can evade responsibility for any connection between acts and their fruits. Although it maintains its purity this way, it also loses its role as the basis for embodied existence. Thus, the *Bhagavadgītā* admits acts only by its own nature, i.e. "*svabhāvas tu pravartate*". In short, insofar as the *Bhagavadgītā* regards the own nature (*svabhāva*) of the ātman as merely one of its attributes, the *Bhagavadgītā* is able to hold this apart from ātman itself. It is very clear that the text intends to avoid the Sovereign Self's becoming stained by acting or enjoying the fruits of actions.[21]

> The Self as universal entity doesn't accept any sins or beneficences. Wisdom is enveloped by ignorance. All creatures are wandering thereby.[22]

Following the *Bhagavadgītā* V-14, which insists that the Self does not become a doer, verse 15 declares that the Self does not enjoy any fruits of actions either. Thereby the Self is not responsible for either sins or virtues. This avoids regarding the Self as an agent, which can give rise to illusions. However, the Self may paradoxically lose even the ability for mokṣa. Buddhism adopted anātmavāda to overcome this contradictory problem. This anātmavāda theory negates every theory of an embodied soul from the beginning. And they constructed a structure with which to explain the connection or saṃyoga between cause and effect, i.e. by concepts like jñāna and ajñāna.[23] The *Bhagavadgītā* introduces this Buddhist-like method here, which the next verse, V-16, shows more distinctly.

> When someone's ignorance is destroyed by wisdom, the wisdom of such a person makes the Supreme Self like the sun.[24]

This concept above is Buddhist-like and, similar to the early Upaniṣads as well. We could even say that this way of thinking was already the basis of śramaṇic thought. Those who accept this thinking have no need for the idea of ātman as embodied soul. The concept of jñāna originated in the Upaniṣads and when Buddhist developed it, they arrived at anātmavāda. This kārikā follows this way of thinking. The main challenge in this way of thinking is the embodied soul must purify itself by disciplined practice. On the other hand, it has the advantage that it avoids the difficulties entailed by the idea that ātman as embodied soul both generates saṃsāric existence by its kartṛtva and is stained by his own bhoktṛtva. Jñāna is a process which was established to correspond to atman, but it is just a function and does not possess any absolute spiritual reality like āṭman. That jñāna is the only function necessary to cause mokṣa was a great discovery. However, as jñāna is emphasized more and more, the existential meaning of ātman becomes less and less necessary. The *Bhagavadgītā* is contradictory on this point. For relative concepts like jñāna and ajñāna do not fit well with ātmavāda, which insists on personalized identity of ātman. We have to realize that this usage of jñāna and ajñāna is different from that of the Buddhists.

3.2. The Solution by the Yogabindu

The following kārikās of the *Yogabindu* investigate this paradoxical problem and attempt to solve it by some means.

> A complete accomplishment of yoga according to all the factors just mentioned, for example paripāka, etc., should be understood by not hindering the proper potential of each.[25]

> When the Self is assumed to have an absolute existence, as in Vedānta, as well as when it isn't, as in Cārvāka, all spiritual practice is fruitless. However, if the Self is established owing to yogyatā, appropriate to its circumstances, spiritual practice will come to accomplish its purpose.[26]

Vedānta admits the value of ātman as absolute existence, while Cārvāka denies such an ātman. Neither extreme view about ātman, however, is able to establish the effectiveness of spiritual practice. By philosophical perspective, then, can spiritual practice contribute to the ultimate purpose of mokṣa? Haribhadrasūri insists that this will be accomplished in accordance with yogyatā theory.

He understands well that a simplistic ātmavāda theory in which ātman comes to possess both kartṛtva and bhoktṛtva results in the inconsistency that actions can be transcended by other actions. On the other hand, he is concerned that the true existence of the subject who must be liberated cannot be adequately specified in an idealist theory such as expressed in the Buddhist concepts of jñāna and ajñāna. Haribhadrasūri wanted to find out an appropriate way to solve both sides of this problem, which, he thought, is the only effective way to establish the ultimate purpose of yogic practice, i.e. mokṣa. This is why he developed the theory of yogyatā. This theory was used as a magic pill to bring about a compromise between the two opposing tendencies, i.e. the idealism of Buddhism or the early Upaniṣads and the Īśvaravāda of later Vedānta or Hinduism.[27] Haribhadrasūri thus explains how yogyatā can establish the validity of yogic practice:

> *tarhi katham na vṛthāiṣa syād ity āha—tasyātmanaḥ tathāyogyatāyāṃ tu—svarūpa-pararūpāpekṣayā sattvāsattva-yogyatāyāṃ satyāṃ punaḥ kim ity āha tadbhāvena-ātmanaḥ phala-rūpatayā pariṇāma-lakṣaṇena, eṣa—yogaḥ, sārthakaḥ—svasādhya-niṣpādaka iti/ yadā hi svarūpeṇa san pararūpeṇa cāsan nātmā pariṇāmī cêṣyate, tadāyam avṛthā yogaḥ syāt, na punar anyathêti//*[28]

Haribhadrasūri declares here that yogic practice does not concern ātman directly but rather effects that situation which exists as a result of previous transformations and the yogyatā, the potentialities or capacities, that are implicit within it. He thus urges one to look more closely at the meaning and value of transformative practice in terms of pararūpa rather than in terms of a purely idealistic entity such as svarūpa.

4. *The Troublesome Problem between Spirituality and the Theory of Practice*

We have researched theories of practice using Jain texts in order to understand its historical meaning and value in the most accurate way. We must note that as the purpose of spiritual practice became higher and higher, it became less and less concrete. In other words, it come to be treated as fanciful theory. It is very difficult to keep spiritual themes purely spiritual. If it is taken as a concrete object, it loses its spiritual sense. The following passage from *Bhagavadgītā* is an example of this problem:

> However, Oh Mighty-armed Arjuna, it is difficult to attain renunciation without yoga. The sage who accomplishes meditation by yogic practice will attain to Brahman quickly.[29]

This verse addressed the contradiction between saṃnyāsa or renunciation and yukta or meditation on the supreme being. The former means renouncing all actions, the latter is action itself. Because the *Bhagavadgītā* already mentioned that both methods were ways to mokṣa, it must explain what the relations between them are and which is the more beneficial for achieving mokṣa.

Saṃnyāsa and yukta influence each other closely, so it is impossible to separate one from the other. Though the *Bhagavadgītā* must understand this, in the latter half of this verse renunciation is replaced by the attainment of Brahman. We may say that this deviates from theory of practice in that it forgets the essential meaning of renunciation—abandoning everything and seeking to obtain nothing—and aims instead to attain to permanent supreme power out of its respect for Īśvaravāda. Of course, the *Bhagavadgītā,* which was influenced by the śramaṇic thought, also explains the way of śramaṇas to accomplish meditation and the purposes of this practice,[30] a matter we have investigated already. That is, it shifted the responsibility for both the attachment to results and the renunciation of that attachment to manas alone. In this way, it attempted to separate the role of agent of action (karman), which causes attachments, from the concept of ātman itself. The karman for renunciation was also separated from ātman because it wanted to keep it ātman absolutely independent.

We may recognize this theory as an expedient to avoid problems entailed by the concept of ātman. But, as we have seen, it also functions to indicate the existential sense of ātman as svabhāva. We know this from the *Bhagavadgītā* V-14. But when we admit the ātman as subject, along with the existential sense of svabhāva as that which makes the self become the self, the practice will lose its meaning as purely spiritual discipline. If a spirit exists and works according to its own nature, and therefore does not itself have kartṛtva and it does not create kartṛtva for others, then that spirit is already released and any reality that accompanied by an attachment to results can only be a product of playful imagination. In this way, the svabhāva theory in the *Bhagavadgītā* functions as a basis of Īśvaravāda. Though opposed to this in theory, the Buddhists, insofar as they emphasized anātmavāda, also ended up introducing idealism by a similar method.

Syādvāda of Jainism is a theory of relative affirmation, while Buddhism tends toward a theory of absolute negation. But they are similar in that they definition existence as changeable in dependence upon changing conditions. In short, syādvāda or anekānta as an affirmative theory of Jainism and anātmavāda as a negating theory of Buddhism are structurally similar though different in details. So we can say that two streams of śramaṇic thought have appeared. These are a standpoint of absolute negation and a standpoint of relative affirmation. Their ideas about the attainment of cessation (nirodha) by samādhi are also influenced by these considerations, and hence their methods are distinguished by emphasis the discovery of relative affirmation, or, conversely, upon arriving at absolute negation.[31]

In case of Buddhism, because it has transformed into Mahāyāna, its original character as a śramaṇic movement has been lost. While Jainism, on the other hand, has maintained a classical śramaṇic tradition to this day. The yogyatā theory by Haribhadrasūri has also served the important role of articulating purposes and methods of practice.

NOTES

1. We can get the good sources to indicate immature thinkings about phenomena of creation and existence at *Ṛg-veda* x.129. At *Atharva-veda* x, 7, the abstract concept like skambha came to be used and internal investigation developed in this age.
2. Musashi Tachikawa, *Hajimete no indo tetsugaku* (in Japanese), Kodansha, 1992.
3. Sūtra itself isn't so old and *Pravacanabhāṣya* was written after 1550 A.D. But this bhāṣya is very important to investigate the true purpose of various Indian philosophies.
4. *Sāṃkhya-pravacana-bhāṣya* (in *The Sāṃkhya-pravacana-bhāṣya* or commentary on the exposition of the Sāṃkhya philosophy by Vijñānabhikṣu ed. by Richard Garbe, Harvard University, Cambridge, Mass., U.S.A., 1895) p.1, ll.27-33.
5. *Sāṃkhya-pravacana-bhāṣya* 1895, p.2, ll.24-39.
6. Cf. The *Sāṃkhyasūtra* I-59, VI-59; The *Yogasūtrabhāṣya* ad the *Yogasūtra* 1-25, the *Sāṃkhyatattvakaumudī* on the *Sāṃkhyakārikā* 2.
7. cf. *Yogabindu* 449-450 (in *Haribhadra sūri's Yogabindu with commentary,* ed. by Luigi Suali, Ph.D., The Jain Dharma Prasaraka Sabha, Bhavnagar, 1911)
8. cf. *Chāndogya-Upaniṣad* IV, 15, 1-5 (in *The Principal Upaniṣads,* ed. with introduction, text, translation and notes by S. Radhakrishnan, George Allen & Unvin Ltd., London, Humanities Press Inc., New York, 1978)
9. Because Jainism hadn't became a main stream of Indian thoughts, they were able to inherit particular śramaṇic characters. For example, a sect of Jainism 'Therapanti' in Ladnun keeps classical practice like caryā or wandering until today.
10. *Yogabindu* 6.
11. *Yogabindu* 7.
12. *Yogabindu* 8. Haribhadrasūri supposes the Vedāntin's assertion in this verse.
13. *Yogabindu* 9. Haribhadra replies to supposed Vedāntin's assertion in former verse by this verse
14. We can find this kind of controversy between the commentary by Śaṅkara and one by Ramanuja on the *Bhagavadgītā.* Rāmānuja accomplished Īśvaravāda by a clever theory. This theory may be said to have surpassed the viewpoint of ātman as independent absoluteness. This theory of Īśvara came to the mainstream in the later Hinduism.

    cf. Bunki Kimura, "Jñāna-yoga of Rāmānuja (1)", *Journal of Tokai Association of Indian and Buddhist Studies* no.38, pp.25-41; "Jñāna-yoga of Rāmānuja (2)" *Journal of Tokai Association of Indian and Buddhist Studies* no.39, pp. 34-48.
15. *Yogabindu* 17.
16. See Haribhadrasūri's auto-commentary on the *Yogabindu* 17.
17. *Yogabindu* 18.
18. Cf. Haribhadrasūri's auto-commentary on the *Yogabindu* 18.
19. *Bhagavadgītā* V-13 (in The *Bhagavadgītā* with an Introductory Essay, Sanskrit Text, English Translation and Notes by S. Radhakrishnan, INDUS An imprint of Harper Collins Publishers India, New Delhi, 1996.)

20. *Bhagavadgītā* V-14 .
21. Haribhadrasūri often uses the term yogyatā which indicates an ability to make existence manifest. The theory of yogyatā has some analogy with this. Refer to my essay.
cf. Gensei Asano, "The Meaning of Vṛttisaṃkṣaya by Haribhadra's Yoga Thought", *Journal of Jaina Studies* no.5, pp.1-27.
22. *Bhagavadgītā* V-15.
23. But this way by Buddhists also arrived at the paradoxical conclusion. According to practical standpoints, the Self is refused by the Self itself which has denied already. This problem induced amendatory means like Mahāyāna. So Mahāyāna has inclinations to practical methods.
24. *Bhagavadgītā* V-16.
25. *Yogabindu* 19.
26. *Yogabindu* 20.
27. I had suggested by Dr. Shailaja Bapat in Poona University that a transition as anuśaya or relationship with fruits should be divided vipāka and paripāka oppositively. Paripāka is discussed here like *Yogabindu* 19. Still more, we should notice that this theory showed here is similar to Sāṃkhya if we can replace the relation of karman and jīva with the relation of puruṣa and prakṛti.
28. Haribhadrasūri's auto-commentary on the *Yogabindu* 20. p.12, ll.15-21.
29. *Bhagavadgītā* V-6.
30. cf. *Bhagavadgītā* V-11–13.
31. It is very interesting to replace this matter with a dispute between karmayoga and jñānayoga in the *Bhagavadgītā*. Śaṅkara's commentary explained karmayoga at first and after its understanding jñānayoga was considered in due order. While Rāmānuja intended to involve an accomplishment of jñānayoga in karmayoga or recognized that a an accomplishment of jñānayoga wouldn't complete without karmayoga. (ibid. Bunki Kimura).

CHAPTER 50

The Eight-limbed Yoga in Vācaspatimiśra's Understanding of the Advaitavedānta*

KO ENDO

Introduction

In the Advaitavedānta school's theory on the path to liberation, the passage of the *Bṛhadāraṇyaka-upaniṣad* (*BĀU*) 2.4.5[1], *ātmā vā are draṣṭavyaḥ śrotavyo mantavyo nididhyāsitavyo*, plays an important role as a scriptural sentence that teaches hearing (*śravaṇa*), thinking (*manana*), meditation (*nididhyāsana*) and seeing (*darśana*) of the Self (*ātman*). On this significant passage of *BĀU* 2.4.5, Vācaspatimiśra presents his interpretation by linking the passage with the eight-limbed yoga (*aṣṭāṅga-yoga*) of the *Yogasūtra* (*YS*)[2], in his commentary *Bhāmatī* on Śaṅkara's *Brahmasūtrabhāṣya* (*BSBh*) 2.3.39[3]. This paper aims at to examine Vācaspatimiśra's interpretation of *BĀU* 2.4.5 in the *Bhāmatī* 2.3.39 and consider his underlying intention there.

Scholars such as Hino[4] and others have made several attempts to clarify Advaitins' interpretations of the practices of the hearing, the thinking and the meditation presented by the above-quoted *BĀU* 2.4.5. Light has been thrown on Vācaspatimiśra's idea about the path to liberation in the Advaitavedānta particularly by Shima[5]. Before moving on to the main task, it is helpful to describe briefly the point at issue regarding these practices in the history of the Advaitavedānta[6]. Although the Advaita school insists that the direct knowledge of Brahman is the cause of final release (*mokṣa*), there are roughly speaking two different positions in this school regarding what brings about the direct knowledge, that is to say, what is the principal cause, or the immediate means (*karaṇa*) for the direct knowledge of Brahman[7]. One is the position which claims the direct knowledge of Brahman arises only from the scriptures, following Śaṅkara who does not admit action (*kriyā*) as the means for final release. This position is represented by Sureśvara, Padmapāda and their adherents. Another position maintains that the knowledge which arises from the scriptures such as the Upaniṣads is merely indirect (*parokṣa*) and therefore the scriptures cannot be the cause for the direct knowledge of Brahman. Maṇḍanamiśra as well as Vācaspatimiśra and his followers represent this position. Later, the former position is called *śabdāparokṣa-prasthāna* (the sect that holds scriptural knowledge is direct), the later *śabdaparokṣaprasthāna* (the sect that holds scriptural knowledge is indirect)[8]. Against Maṇḍanamiśra's opinion that the direct knowledge of Brahman originates from meditation (*upāsanā*)[9], Sureśvara does not admit the action of meditation as means to final release. As Hino pointed out, this view of Sureśvara is well demonstrated in his interpretation of the above quoted passage of *BĀU* 2.4.5, in which he asserts that *nididhyāsana* is not an action of meditation, but a culmination of the hearing (*śravaṇa*) and the thinking (*manana*)[10]. Vācaspatimiśra, who takes the position of *śabdaparokṣaprasthāna* like Maṇḍanamiśra, presents a unique theory. He asserts that the immediate cause (*karaṇa*) of the direct knowledge of Brahman is the internal organ (*antaḥkaraṇa*), or mind (*manas*)[11]. According to the *Bhāmatī*, the means of valid knowledge (*pramāṇa*) that produces the direct perception (*sākṣātkāra*) of Brahman is perception (*pratyakṣa*), and since perception as the means of valid knowledge is a particular transformation of the internal organ (*antaḥkaraṇavṛttibheda*), it is the internal organ that is the immediate cause (*karaṇa*) for the knowledge. Vācaspati says that this particular transformation of the internal organ arises with the assistance of the completion of meditation on the meaning of *mahāvākya* (major [complex] sentence)[12], or it arises with the assistance of the latent impression (*saṃskāra*) accumulated through meditation (*dhyānābhyāsa*) following the hearing (*śravaṇa*) and the thinking (*manana*)[13].

As noted above, in Vācaspatimiśra's Advaita theory on the path to liberation, meditation plays a very important role to accomplish the direct knowledge of Brahman. For this very reason, Vācaspati's interpretation *BĀU* 2.4.5 in the *Bhāmatī* 2.3.39, i.e., the interpretation which adduces the eight-limbed yoga (*aṣṭāṅga-yoga*) of *YS*, offers the key to a better understanding of his Advaitavedānta theory. Let us examine this interpretation next.

1. *Bhāmatī 2.3.39*

The *Brahmasūtra* 2.3.33-40 are the sūtras aiming at establishing the individual self (*jīva*) as the agent of action (*kartṛ*)[14]. Among them, the sūtra 2.3.39, *samādhyabhāvāc ca*, is the one that establishes it through the necessity of the agent of *samādhi*. In *BSBh* 2.3.39, Śaṅkara interprets this word *samādhi* as that which is taught in the Upaniṣads such as *ātmā vā are draṣṭavyaḥ śrotavyo mantavyo nididhyāsitavyo* (*BĀU* 2.4.5), *so 'nveṣṭavyaḥ sa vijijñāsitavyaḥ* (*Chāndogya-upaniṣad* 8.7.1), or *om ity evam dhyāyatha ātmānaṃ* (*Muṇḍaka-upaniṣad* 2.2.6) to let learners understand the Self (*ātman*) which is the subject matter of the Upaniṣads. One may say that here Śaṅkara understands *samādhi* as meditation on the Self. However, as compared with Śaṅkara, Vācaspatimiśra applies a far more specific meaning to this word *samādhi* in 2.3.39 of his *Bhāmatī*, a commentary on *BSBh*. He says that this *samādhi* means the "constraint (*saṃyama*)" i.e., the last three of the eight constituent parts of the yoga expounded in *YS*. It is well-known that the yoga expounded by *YS* consists of the eight constituent parts, namely, abstentions (*yama*), observances (*niyama*), postures (*āsana*), regulations-of-the-breath (*prāṇāyāma*), withdrawal-of-the-senses (*pratyāhāra*), fixed-attention (*dhāraṇā*), contemplation (*dhyāna*) and concentration (*samādhi*)[15]. This yoga is called the eight-limbed yoga (*aṣṭāṅga-yoga*). Let us see *Bhāmatī* 2.3.39 in tentative English translation.

[The word] "*samādhi*" [in *BSBh*[16]] implies (*upalakṣayati*) the constraint (*saṃyama*). This is because fixed-attention (*dhāraṇā*), contemplation (*dhyāna*) and concentration (*samādhi*) are denoted by the word constraint (*saṃyama*). As has been said [by the author of *YS*]: "The three [exercised] in one [object] are constraint (*YS* 3.4)." In this [*BĀU* 2.4.5 quoted in *BSBh]* (*atra*), the sentence "to be heard, to be thought (*śrotavyo mantavyaḥ*)" is the teaching of fixed-attention (*dhāraṇā*), "to be meditated on (*nididhyāsitavyaḥ*)" is the teaching of contemplation (*dhyāna*), and "to be seen (*draṣṭavyaḥ*)" is the teaching of concentration (*samādhi*). As has been said [by the author of *YS*]: "That same contemplation[17] [becomes] having only the manifestation of the object [in itself], as if it did not have its own form. It is concentration (*samādhi*) (*YS* 3.3)." Therefore, here (*iha*) this agent of action (*kartṛ*) is being taught in point of *samādhi* [i.e., the constraint (*saṃyama*),] and [hence] one understands (*avaiti*) the nature of the agent of action (*kartṛtva*) in the Self (*ātman*) [i.e., the individual self]. This is the meaning of the sūtra[18].

In the eight-limbed yoga of *YS*, the last three members, namely, fixed-attention (*dhāraṇā*), contemplation (*dhyāna*) and concentration (*samādhi*), are called constraint (*saṃyama*) when they are applied to the same object[19]. These three applied to the same object can be regarded as the three deepening steps of meditation. Therefore, we can represent the contents of the *Bhāmatī* 2.3.39 in a simple figure as follows:

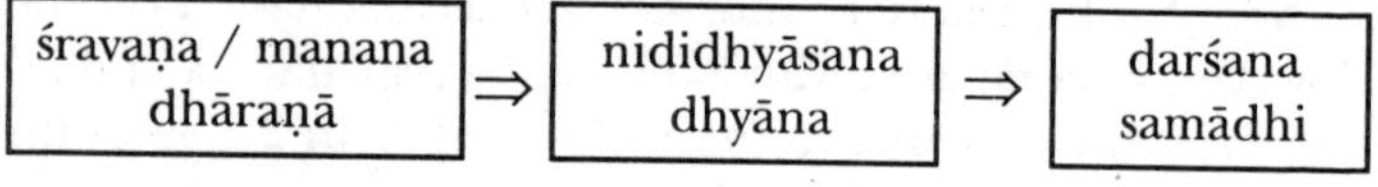

Figure 1

The *Kalpataru*, a commentary on the *Bhāmatī*, characterizes this *Bhāmatī* 2.3.39 as a note that clarifies why Śaṅkara refers to the hearing (*śravaṇa*) and others in relation to *samādhi*. However, as we noted above, it appears that Śaṅkara understands *samādhi* as close in meaning to 'meditation,' and therefore he quotes the scriptural passage of *BĀU* 2.4.5 that refers to meditation (*nididhyāsana*).

To understand the two words, *samādhi* and *nididhyāsana*, as meaning 'meditation' is not at all rare. In fact, other commentaries on *BSBh* such as *Nyāyanirṇaya* or *Ratnaprabhā* do not make any particular reference to the relation of the two words. On the other hand, *Bhāmatī*'s interpretation that explains hearing etc., with the theory of the eight-limbed yoga should be recognized as unusual. Moreover, although *BSBh* quotes not only*BĀU* 2.4.5 but also *Chāndogya-upaniṣad* 8.7.1 and *Muṇḍaka-upaniṣad* 2.2.6, the *Bhāmati* says nothing about these two scriptural sentences. How is the constraint (*saṃyama*) related to the two scriptural sentences? The answer is not found. Judging from the above, it is likely that the *Bhāmatī* relates *BĀU* 2.4.5 to the eight-limbed yoga theory of the Yoga school with a specific purpose in view.

To elucidate this interpretation of Vācaspatimiśra further, let us attempt in the next section to extend the discussion to his *Tattvavaiśāradī* (*TV*) commentary on the *Yogabhāṣya* (*YBh*) and his idea on hearing (*śravaṇa*), thinking (*manana*) and meditation (*nididhyāsana*) in it.

2. *The Yoga school's interpretation of the Bṛhadāraṇyaka-Upaniṣad 2.4.5.*

So far as *YS* and *YBh* are concerned, the hearing (*śravaṇa*), thinking (*manana*), meditation (*nididhyāsana*) and seeing (*darśana*) taught in *BĀU* 2.4.5 do not seem to appear as a subject for discussion. Yet in *TV* 1.48 Vācaspatimiśra thinks that the first three are mentioned in *YBh* 1.48.

At first, we have to inquire, to some extent, into the contents of the relevant portion of *YS* and *YBh*. *YS* 1.41-51 are the sūtras embodying the teaching about knowledge and the objects of knowledge in "conscious concentration (*saṃprajñāta-samādhi*)" through the concept of the four "balanced states (*samāpatti*)," namely, "deliberative (*savitarka*)," "super-deliberative (*nirvitarka*)," "reflective (*savicāra*)" and "super-reflective (*nirvicāra*)"[20]. Among these sūtras, *YS* 1.47 says that "clarity in respect of *ātman* (*adhyātmaprasāda*)" arises in clarity (*vaiśāradya*) of the super-reflective balanced state (*nirvicāra-samāpatti*), and *YS* 1.48 teaches that an insight (*prajñā*) called "bearing truth (*ṛtambharā*)" arises in that state. Commenting on this sūtra 1.48, *YBh* quotes the following verse to explain the sūtra and presumably to introduce the contrast between scriptural or inferential knowledge and perceptual knowledge arising from meditation stated in the next sūtra 1.49:

> *"āgamenānumānena dhyānābhyāsarasena ca /*
> *tridhā prakalpayan prajñāṃ labhate yogam uttamam //"*
>
> By scripture, by inference, and by having a high regard for practicing meditation, determining wisdom in [these] three ways, [a yogin] obtains the best yoga.

It is not easily intelligible in what sense this verse explains the contents of *YS* 1.48. Yet it seems reasonable to suppose that the portion in the verse that reads "by having a high regard for practicing meditation, determining wisdom..." fits the contents of the sūtra best, since the truth-bearing insight (*ṛtambhara-prajñā*) arising in the super-reflective balanced state (*nirvicāra-samāpatti*), which is a state of meditation concerning subtle objects, is the subject of the sūtra. Thus the wisdom mentioned in the verse is understood to correspond to the truth-bearing insight. What has to be noticed is that the ensuing *YS* and *YBh* 1.49 distinguish the knowledge arising from concentration (*samādhi*), which has the particular (*viśeṣa*) as its object, from scriptural and inferential knowledge having the universal (*sāmānya*) as their object. The Yoga school regards the knowledge arising from *samādhi* as direct perception (*pratyakṣa*). It is rigorously distinguished from scriptural knowledge, which is verbal cognition, or from inferential knowledge. Therefore, we can be fairly certain that *YBh* 1.48 identifies the truth-bearing insight (*ṛtambhara-prajñā*) as not arising directly from scripture or from inference, but arising primarily from meditation, or from having a high regard for practicing meditation. If the object of the meditation is something verbally cognized from scriptures or something inferred, scriptures and inference can be regarded as indirect causes for the knowledge arising from the meditation.

The wisdom (*prajñā*) mentioned in the above quoted verse is the *ṛtambhara-prajñā*. As we have seen, it arises in the clarity in respect of *ātman* (*adhyātmaprasāda*), which in turn occurs in the clarity (*vaiśāradya*) of the super-reflective balanced state (*nirvicāra-samāpatti*). This super-reflective balanced state (*nirvicāra-samāpatti*) is a form of conscious concentration (*saṃprajñāta-samādhi*). Accordingly, it seems reasonable to suppose that the *ṛtambhara-prajñā* is a state of deep conscious concentration. Then, what is "the best yoga (*uttama-yoga*)" which is taught by the verse to be obtained after the wisdom? *YS* 1.50-51 state that the latent impressions (*saṃskāra*) produced by the knowledge arising from *samādhi*, i.e., produced by the *ṛtambhara-prajñā*, obstruct the latent impressions produced by other mental activities, further that "seedless concentration (*nirbīja-samādhi*)" arises when the latent impressions produced from the insight become restrained. This seedless concentration (*nirbīja-samādhi*) is, according to *YBh* 1.18, "non-conscious concentration (*asaṃprajñāta-samādhi*)." Consequently, we may say that the best yoga in the above quoted verse is the *asaṃprajñāta-samādhi*. We can represent this idea of *YBh* in a figure as follows, in which the point that scripture and inference are merely indirect causes for the *ṛtambhara-prajñā* is represented by a simple arrow "→":

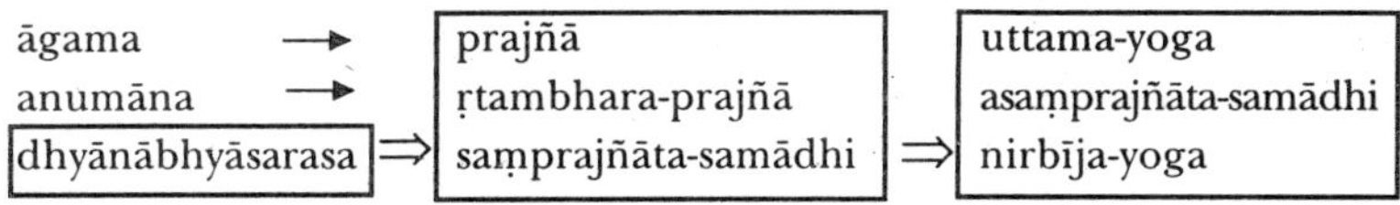

Figure 2

We are now able to examine Vācaspatimiśra's interpretation. Vācaspatimiśra thinks, as has been mentioned, that *YBh* 1.48 refers to the hearing (*śravaṇa*), thinking (*manana*) and meditation (*nididhyāsana*) taught in *BĀU* 2.4.5. In his *TV* 1.48, he interprets the three words mentioned in the above quoted verse, namely, scripture (*āgama*), inference (*anumāna*) and having a high regard for practicing meditation (*dhyānābhyāsarasa*), as hearing (*śravaṇa*), thinking (*manana*) and meditation (*nididhyāsana*) respectively. If we add this interpretation of Vācaspatimiśra to the above figure 2, we can obtain the following:

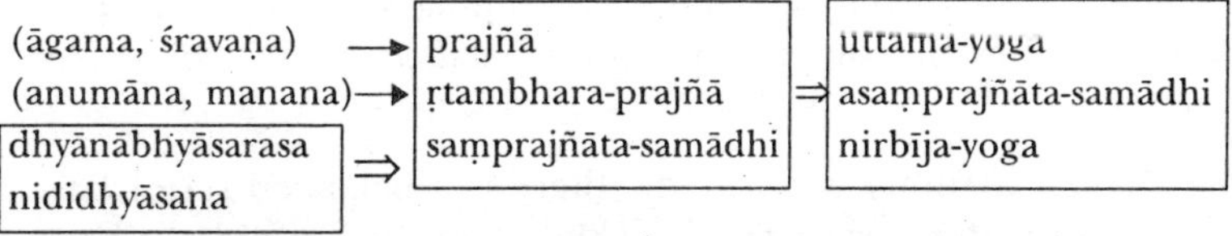

Figure 3

According to Vācaspatimiśra, thus, in the system of the Pātañjala-yoga, hearing, thinking and meditation are given the positions of preliminary stages for acquiring knowledge in the deep conscious concentration (*saṃprajñāta-samādhi*).

3. *The Stage after the Realization of Ātman: Asaṃprajñāta-samādhi*

In the previous section, we have seen how Vācaspatimiśra interprets the hearing, thinking and meditation of *BĀU* 2.4.5 in *TV* which presents his understanding of Pātañjala-yoga. In *TV*, hearing, thinking and meditation do not seem to constitute a step-by-step causal relation in which the hearing is a cause for the thinking and the thinking is that for the meditation as we found in the *Bhāmatī* 2.3.39. Nevertheless, they are regarded as causes for the appearance of insight in conscious concentration (*saṃprajñāta-samādhi*). If we assume this insight corresponds to "seeing (*darśana*)" stated in *BĀU* 2.4.5, we will be able to see the similarity between *TV* 1.48 and *Bhāmatī* 2.3.39 clearly. We shall now look into this point.

Bhāmatī 2.3.39, as we have seen, interprets hearing (*śravaṇa*) and thinking (*manana*) as the fixed-attention (*dhāraṇā*) of the eight-limbed yoga, meditation (*nididhyāsana*) as the contemplation (*dhyāna*), and seeing (*darśana*) as the concentration (*samādhi*). To this *samādhi* of the eight-limbed yoga, *YS* 3.3 gives the following definition, which is quoted in the *Bhāmatī* 2.3.39 also:

> "That same [contemplation (*dhyāna*)] comes to have only the manifestation of the object [in itself], as if it did not have its own form. It is concentration. (*tad evārthamātranirbhāsaṃ svarūpaśūnyam iva samādhiḥ*)."

Further, among the sūtras denoting the knowledge and objects of knowledge in the conscious concentration (*saṃprajñāta-samādhi*), namely, sūtras 1.41-51, we find a very similar sentence in *YS* 1.43 which defines the super-deliberative balanced state (*nirvitarka-samāpatti*):

> "When memory is purified, [there is a balanced state] having only the manifestation of the object as if it did not have its own fonn. It is the super-deliberative [balanced state] (*svarūpaśūnyevārthamātranirbhāsā nirvitarkā*)."

Moreover, *YBh* 1.44, while explaining the super-reflective balanced state (*nirvicāra-samāpatti*), says as follows:

> "And when the wisdom [arising in concentration] comes to have only [the manifestation of] the object, as if it did not

> have its own form, it is called the super-reflective [balanced state] (*prajñā ca svarūpaśūnyevārthamātrā yadā bhavati tadā nirvicārety ucyate*)."

According to *YBh* 1.44, the difference between *vitarka* and *vicāra* lies in the nature of their objects. *Vicāra* concerns more subtle objects than *vitarka*. Therefore, the super-deliberative balanced state and the super-reflective balanced state are not distinguished in their essential nature of meditative concentration. From the above quoted *YS* 1.43 and *YBh* 1.44, we can say without difficulty that the super-deliberative balanced state and the super-reflective balanced state are the mental state that is defined as concentration (*samādhi*) in the eight-limbed yoga by *YS* 3.3. This means, in other words, that the eighth element of the eight-limbed yoga, namely, *samādhi*, is a state described as the super-deliberative or the super-reflective balanced state, both of which are forms of the conscious concentration (*saṃprajñāta-samādhi*), or the knowledge arising in such mental concentration. Thus, it follows that if the *darśana* (seeing, knowing) set forth by *BĀU* 2.4.5 is understood, like Vācaspati' s interpretation in the *Bhāmatī* 2.3.39, to be the *samādhi* in the eight limbs, then this *darśana* is a knowing process arising in *saṃprajñāta-samādhi*. As we have seen already, the Yoga school regards the non-conscious concentration (*asaṃprajñāta-samādhi*) as a deeper state of meditation compared to the conscious concentration (*saṃprajñāta-samādhi*). If we add these points to the previously shown figure 1 to reconstruct Vācaspati's idea in the *Bhāmatī* 2.3.39, we get the following figure:

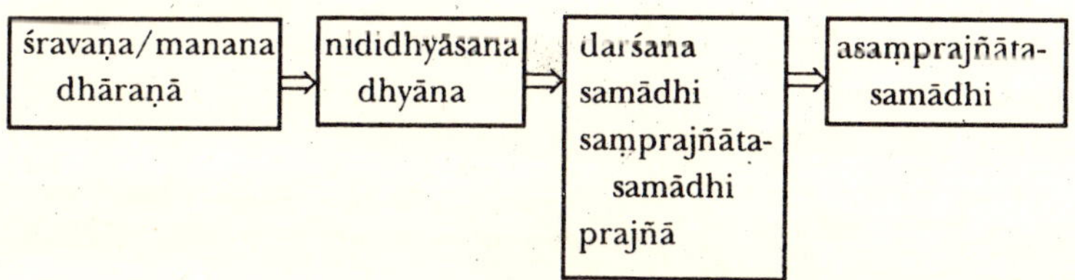

Figure 4

We can say that the idea represented by this figure 4 resembles very closely the interpretation found in *TV* 1.48 represented by figure 3, except for the internal relation among hearing, thinking and meditation. In the figure above, the *darśana* stated in

BĀU 2.4.5 corresponds to the truth-bearing insight (*ṛtambhara-prajñā*) of the figure 3, and appears instead of it.

However, we must not forget that Vācaspati's idea represented by the above figure 4 is merely a hypothetical reconstruction prepared for this article. In his *Bhāmatī*, does he really identify *darśana* with *saṃprajñāta-samādhi* and acknowledge the deeper meditative stage thereafter, i.e., the *asaṃprajñāta-samādhi*, as shown by this figure? To give a sure answer to this question may be possible after a thorough investigation of the entire *Bhāmatī*, and we are unable to do it at the moment. Nevertheless, it seems reasonable to suppose that Vācaspatimiśra admitted some stage similar to the *asaṃprajñāta-samādhi* after the *darśana* on for the following reasons. Vācaspati wrote *TV* before the *Bhāmatī*.[21] Therefore, we can infer that when he in his *Bhāmatī* 2.3.39 interpreted "the knowledge (*darśana*) on the identity of Brahman and the Self (*ātman*)" stated in *BĀU* 2.4.5 as the *samādhi* of the eight-limbed yoga, he clearly understood the knowledge (*darśana*) to correspond to the knowledge produced by conscious concentration (*saṃprajñāta-samādhi*). Of course he had known that Pātañjala-yoga admits a higher or deeper state of meditative concentration than *saṃprajñāta-samādhi*. That state is non-conscious concentration (*asaṃprajñāta-samādhi*). From these points, we may say that when Vācaspatimiśra wrote *Bhāmatī* 2.3.39, he already had an understanding that a deeper state of meditative concentration than the *darśana* of *BĀU* 2.4.5 exists, though he did not mention it explicitly. Moreover, it appears to me that the intention he had when he interpreted *BĀU* 2.4.5 in *Bhāmatī* 2.3.39 was to characterize hearing (*śravaṇa*), thinking (*manana*), meditation (*nididhyāsana*) and seeing (*darśana*) and to place them in an order based upon an understanding of meditative practice that admits a stage after the *darśana*.

As we noted earlier, in the theory of the Yoga school expounded in *YS* 1.50-51, *asaṃprajñāta-samādhi* is accomplished when the latent impressions (*saṃskāra*) produced by *ṛtambhara-prajñā* in the *saṃprajñāta-samādhi* stage become restrained. Shima points out that when we consider Vācaspatimiśra's Advaita theory on the path to liberation as a ladder of practical stages, two further stages, namely, destruction of the latent impressions produced by nescience (*avidyā*) and manifestation of the essential nature of Brahman, seem to follow from the knowledge (*darśana*) of the identity of Brahman and the Self (*ātman*)[22]. This may be related to the interpretation, which Vācaspati perhaps intended in *Bhāmatī* 2.3.39, that non-conscious concentration (*asaṃprajñāta-samādhi*) exists as a deeper meditative stage than the knowledge of the Self. To discuss the issue is beyond the scope of this brief paper. However, at the moment, it appears to me possible to understand that the destruction of nescience (*avidyā*) pointed out by Shima as a stage after the *darśana* is in fact conceived by Vācaspatimiśra in dependence not only on the opinion of Maṇḍanamiśra but also on the theory of the Yoga school, although Shima points out only Maṇḍanamiśra's influence on this point.

NOTES

* This paper was originally written in Japanese and published as "Chōmon, shi-i, meisō, ninshiki to hasshi yōga: *Bhāmatī* 2.3.39 ni tsuite" in *Aichi Bunkyō Daigaku Ronsō* (*Aichi Bunkyo University Review*), 2, 1999. I express my gratitude to Prof. Ian Mabbett, Aichi Bunkyo University, who kindly took trouble to revise and correct my English.

1. *Bṛhadāraṇyaka-upaniṣad* (in *Eighteen Principal Upaniṣads*, vol.1, ed. by V.P. Limaye and R.D. Vadekar, Vaidika Saṃśodhana Maṇḍala, Poona, 1958), p.206. The same sentence is found in *BĀU* 4.5.6 also.
2. In this paper, *Vācaspatimiśraviracitaṭīkāsaṃvalitavyāsabhāṣyasametāni Pātañjalayogasūtrāṇi, tathā Bhojadevaviracitarājamārtaṇḍābhidhavṛttisametāni Pātañjalayogasūtrāṇi*, Ānandāśrama Sanskrit series 47, ed. by Kāśīnātha Śāstrī Āgāśe, Ānandāśrama, Puṇyākhyapattana, 1919 (2nd), is used for the texts of the *Yogasūtra*, the *Yogabhāṣya* and the *Tattvavaiśāradī*.
3. *The Brahmasūtra Śāṅkara Bhāṣya with the commentaries Bhāmatī, Kalpataru and Parimala*, Parimal Sanskrit series 1, ed. by K.L. Joshi, Parimal Publications, Delhi, 1996, 3rd [reprint.?], is used in this paper for the texts of the *Brahmasūtra*, the *Brahmasūtraśāṅkarabhāṣya*, the *Bhāmatī* and the *Kalpataru*.
4. Shoun Hino, *Sureśvara's Vārttika of Yājñavalkya Maitreyī Dialogue*, Motilal Banarsidass, Delhi, 1982, pp.24-25.
5. Iwao Shima, "Huniichigenron gakuha ni okeru gedatsu e no michi (The Path toward Release in the Advaita Vedānta School)," *Shūkyō Kenkyū* (*Journal of Religious Studies*), 60(2), no. 269, 1986.
6. For a discussion of the influence of this issue to the Yoga school, see Ko Endo, "Ātman ninshiki shudan to shire no yōga: Nārāyaṇa Tīrtha no *Yogasūtra* kaishaku (2) (Pātañjala-yoga Functioning as the Means of Realizing Ātman: Nārāyaṇatīrtha's Interpretation of the *Yogasūtra* (2))" in *Abhidharma Bukkyō to Indo Tetsugaku: Katō Junshō Hahase Kanreki Kinen Ronbunshū* (*Abhidharma and Indian Thought: Essays in Honor of Professor Doctor Junsho Kato on His Sixtieth Birthday*), Shunju-sha, Tokyo, 2000.

7. K. Satchidananda Murti, *Revelation and Reason in Advaita Vedānta*, Motilal Banarsidass, Delhi, rpt. 1974, pp.103-109.
8. Tilmann Vetter, *Maṇḍanamiśra's Brahmasiddhiḥ: Brahmakāṇḍaḥ*, Hermann Böhlaus Nachf., Wien, 1969, p.18. Shima, "Huniichigenron gakuha ni okeru gedatsu e no michi," p.111. Both the positions are described briefly in the *Vedāntaparibhāṣā* (in *Vedāntaparibhāṣā by Dharmarāja Adhvarin* ed. with Eng. tr. by S.S. Suryanaryana Sastri, Adyar Library and Research Centre, Madras, rpt. 1984), pp.156-159.
9. On Maṇḍanamiśra's view that knowledge must be combined with actions to attain final release (*jñānakarmasamuccayavāda*), see S. Kuppuswami Sastri, *Brahmasiddhi by Acharya Maṇḍanamiśra: with Commentary by Saṅkhapāṇi*, Sri Satguru Publications, Delhi, 2nd ed. 1984, pp.xxviii-xxxi, xxxiii-xxxvi, Shōun Hino, "Sureśvara ni okeru nididhyāsana ni tsuite (Sureśvara on *nididhyāsana*)," *Indogaku Bukkyōgaku Kenkyū* (*Journal of Indian and Buddhist Studies*, 29 (2), 1981, pp.646-647, and Shima, "Huniichigenron gakuha ni okeru gedatsu e no michi," p.98.
10. See Hino, "Sureśvara ni okeru nididhyāsana ni tsuite (Sureśvara on *nididhyāsana*)," p.165 and Hino, *Sureśvara's Vārttika of Yājñavalkya Maitreyī Dialogue*, pp.24-25.
11. Shima remarks that this is the only original contribution of Vācaspati to the Advaita theory of the path to final release. See Shima, "Huniichigenron gakuha ni okeru gedatsu e no michi," p. 112 and the English abstract, p.v.
12. On the meaning of the term *"mahāvākya,"* see Atsushi Kanazawa, "Vedānta gakuha to daibunshō," in *Indogaku Bukkyōgaku Ronshū: Takasaki Jikidō Hakase Kanreki Kinen Ronshū*, Shunju-sha, Tokyo, 1987. In this article written in Japanese, Kanazawa clarified that Advaitins employed this term *"mahāvākya,"* following the terminology of Mīmāṃsakas, in the sense of a "major [complex] sentence" comprising a "lengthy, or compound sentence" together with "minor [subordinate] texts (*avāntavākya*)," but not in the sense of "great sentence." Since Kanazawa's article is written in Japanese, for English equivalents to the words *mahāvākya* and *avāntaravākya* I follow *S.S.* Suryanarayana Sastri's translation found in *Vedāntaparibhāṣā by Dharmarāja Adhvarin* (Adyar Library series 34), Adyar Library and Research Centre, Madras, rpt. 1984, pp.79-81.
13. *Bhāmatī* 1.1.1, p.55, 1.4-p.57, 1.3; 1.1.4, p.114, ll.5-6, p.115, ll.5-7, p.150, ll.16-18; 2.2.10, p.502, ll.16-18.
14. According to V.S. Ghate, among the commentators on the *Brahmasūtra*, Rāmānuja, Nimbārka, Madhva and Vallabha agree in regarding sūtras 2.3.33-40 as forming one *adhikaraṇa* that establishes agent-ness (*kartṛtva*) as a natural attribute of the individual soul. However, Śaṅkara thinks sūtra 2.3.40 forms one different *adhikaraṇa* with the subject of "superimposition (*adhyāsa*)" being the cause for *kartṛtva* of the individual self. See Ghate, *The Vedānta: a Study of the Brahma-Sūtras with the Bhāṣya of Śaṁkara, Rāmānuja, Nimbārka, Madhva, and Vallabha*, B.O.R.I., Poona, 3rd ed. 1981, pp.98-101.
15. For the English equivalents for the eight constituent parts of the yoga, I follow J.W. Woods, *The Yoga-system of Patañjali* (Harvard Oriental series 17), Motilal Banarsidass, Delhi, rpt. 1977.
16. I understand this "*samādhi*" to refer to the word in *BSBh*, on the grounds

that the *Bhāmatī* is a commentary to *BSBh,* and that the word "*atra*" appearing in a later sentence clearly refers to *BĀU* 2.4.5 quoted in *BSBh,* and also on the bases of the contents of the sub-commentary *Kalpataru* 2.3.39 that will be mentioned below. However, this word may refer to the word in the sūtra.

17. Although the *Bhāmatī* quotes *YS* 3.3 as "*tad eva dhyānam arthamātranirbhāsaṃ...,*" *YS* 3.3 generally does not read the word "*dhyāna.*"
18. Unfortunately, I cannot understand well the meaning of the last sentence "*so 'yam iha kartā samādhāv upadiśyamāna ātmanaḥ kartṛtvam avaitīti sūtrārthaḥ,*" especially the subject of the verb "*avaiti.*" Therefore, the translation presented here is merely tentative and subject to correction.
19. *YS* 3.4: *trayam ekatra saṃyamah..*
20. I follow J.W. Woods, *The Yoga-system of Patañjali,* for the English equivalents of *samāpatti, savitarka, nirvitarka, savicāra* and *nirvicāra.*
21. About the order of Vācaspatimiśra's writings, see Ensho Kanakura, "Tetsujin Vācaspatimiśra," in *Indotetsugaku Bukkyōgaku Kenkyū III Indotetsugaku hen 2,* Shunju-sha, Tokyo, 1976, p. 280, and Atsushi Kanazawa, "Vācaspatimiśra no nendai ron (A Note on Discussions of Vācaspatimiśra's Date)," *The Toyo Gakuho* 68 (3, 4), 1987, pp. 01-02.
22. Shima, "Huniichigenron gakuha ni okeru gedatsu e no michi," pp. 108-113.

XIII

TANTRISM

Chapter 51

Sanctification of the Sacrificial Ground

HIROMICHI HIKITA

In the ritual worship (*pūjā*), a tantric worshipper is obliged to perform the purification (*śuddhi*) of all the necessities for the worship. This is the preliminary act preceding the main program of the worship. This purification act is concerned with five objects: (1) the worshipper himself; (2) the place (*sthāna*) of worship; (3) the mantra used; (4) all utensils and objects (*dravya*) used for the offering; and (5) the deity to be worshipped. This is the opinion stated in the Kulārṇavatantra 6.16, a text belonging to the Śākta sect.[1]

This article deals mainly with the second object, i.e. the purification of the place of worship. Gupta shows us several acts of purification, which can be divided into two groups. Acts of the first group are based on propitiating the spirits, the semi-gods, etc. Food is offered to the spirits (*bhūtabali*) to ensure correct and safe performance of the ritual worship. The guardians of the quarters (*dikpālas*) or the lord of the place (*kṣetrapāla*) are invoked and asked to safeguard the worship.[2] The acts of the second group are based on fencing the ground in order to ward off evil spirits. They are considered to pollute the site or other ingredients of the worship. These acts are represented by *digbandhana,* the rite of enclosing the site of worship within a fixed boundary by meditating on magic arrows (*nārāca*) shot by the goddess. There are also similar acts such as casting divine glances all around, stamping the floor to drive away spirits, and snapping the fingers.[3] Gupta introduces this *digbandhana* rite as belonging to the Tantric one, but I want to consider it not only belonging to the Śākta sect but also to other sects like the Pāñcarātra, the Śaivasiddhānta, etc. As Gonda says,[4] it is rather the pan-Hindu rite. So the main purpose of this article is to explain the rite of *digbandhana* based mainly on the Pāñcarātra texts and also to reconfirm Gonda's opinion by referring to some Paurāṇic texts.

1

The rite of *digbandhana* is performed with the recitation of any mantra. In the Sātvatasaṃhitā, one of the oldest texts of the Pāñcarātra, we can find the Sanskrit term *digbandha* in the ritual to be performed for the attainment of worldly prosperity (*pauṣṭikavidhi*). The SātvataS 17.191 says as follows.

nidhāya pūrvavat kuryād digbandhaṃ hṛdayādikaiḥ/
astreṇa tu vidigbandhaṃ netreṇordhvam adhas tathā//

Here, the *sādhaka* type of priest performs the fencing of the four quarters (*digbandha*) with the *hṛdaya-*, *śiraḥ-*, *śikhā-*, and *kavaca-mantra,* the four intermediate points of compass (*vidigbandha*) with the *astramantra,* and upwards and downwards (*ūrdhva, adhas*) with the *netramantra.* In this way, he fences the ten directions with the six limb-mantras (*aṅgamantras*). Thereafter he invokes (*āvāhya*) the mantra-formed god and worships (*yajet*) him. The purpose of this act is to mentally ward off all evils at the site of worship.[5]

Then in the Jayākhyasaṃhitā, a text traditionally regarded as one of the "three gems" along with the SātvataS and the Pauṣkarasaṃhitā in the Pāñcarātra sect, we can see the act of the *digbandha* in the ritual of acquisition of dominion over *śaktimantra* (*śaktimantrasādhana*).

vīrasthānaṃ samāsādya niśśaṅko janavarjitam //
(the JayākhyaS 27.112cd)
varmaṇā 'streṇa digbandhaṃ kṛtvā duṣṭanirvahaṇaṃ/(113ab)[6]

> Free from fear he (= *sādhaka*) should come to a place of a hero without any people and perform the closing of the direction by means of the *varma-* (i.e., *kavaca-mantra*) and the *astramantra*, which destroys evil (beings).[7]

The above-mentioned procedure of this ritual is to perform it by uttering the six limb-mantras, especially the *astra-* and *kavaca-mantra.*[8] The Padmapurāṇa 7.11.79cd-80ab mentions that *svastivācana* is recited with Vedic mantras and the *digbandhana* with Paurāṇic mantras.[9] The mantra is; *"kṛṣṇo rakṣatu pūrvasyām āgneyyāṃ devakīsutaḥ* // (7.11.80cd) *yāmyāṃ rakṣatu daityārir nairṛtyāṃ madhusūdhanaḥ/ vidikṣu rakṣatu śrīmān ūrdhvaṃ ca śrīdharaḥ prabhuḥ//* (81) *adho rakṣatu viśvātmā kūrmamūrtiḥ kṛpāmayaḥ/ ye vighnakārakāḥ sarve pūjākāle bhavanti ha//* (82) *dūraṃ gacchantu te sarve harināmāstratāḍitāḥ/."* Having performed the *digbandhana* in this way, the worshipper makes the due announcement to accomplish (*saṃkalpa*) the worship of Hari.

This rite is sometimes performed immediately after the rite of infusing a root-mantra and its six limb-mantras into the body of a worshipper (*nyāsa*). In this time, he raises his right hand above the head while making a sound with the snapping of the thumb against the middle finger.[10] The GaruḍaP 1.11.13-14 also states that the *nyāsa* is followed by the *digbandha.*[11] In the Hiraṇyakeśigṛhyaśeṣasūtra 1.2.11, the rite of *digbandha* is connected with the *nyāsa* act.[12] The mantra used there is the *vyāhṛti* (= *bhūr bhuvaḥ suvar*) and *oṃ.*[13]

The recitation of mantras is sometimes accompanied by casting of seeds, clay, etc. Or as I will describe later, the seeds having been empowered by the *astramantra* beforehand can be scattered around without recitation of mantras.[14] Firstly the seeds are scattered around in this ritual. For example the term *digbandha* is connected with white mustard and unhusked rice: *saṃpraviśya ca digbandhaṃ kuryāt siddhārthakākṣataiḥ* // (the JayākhyaS 20.144cd). This ritual appears at the beginning of the *pratiṣṭhā* ceremony,[15] where it is followed by bathing to remove the crime of artisans (*śilpidoṣavināśārthasnapanavidhāna*). Secondly it is performed with ash empowered by the *astramantra*: *bhasmanā cāstrajaptena digbandhaṃ cātra kārayet* // (the JayākhyaS 26.15cd). Thirdly clay is scattered around in this ritual. In the chapter describing the manner of worship of the highest God (*bhagavadārādhanavidhinirūpaṇa*) of the Ahirbudhnyasaṃhitā (= AhiS), a worshipper first goes to a pure place, takes a handful of clay and divides it into two. He cleanses himself with half of the clay and bathes himself. Dividing another half into three, he places one third on his left hand and performs the *digbandha.*[16]

2

Although terms like *digbandha* do not appear, we can find similar acts to it. We show some examples here. First, a worshipper scatters seeds, etc. around the sacrificial ground. For example, in the initiation ceremony (*dīkṣā*) as seen in the SātvataS, the preceptor scatters all kinds of seeds empowered by the *astramantra* in ten directions. These seeds, representing the *astramantra* itself, are deemed to remove obstacles on the site for the initiation.[17] Second, in the initiation ceremony as seen in the AgniP, mustard seeds destructive of evil spirits, are scattered around with the recitation of the mantra ending with *phaṭ* (= *astramantra*).[18] Thereafter Viṣṇu along with His limbs are worshipped in the main water jar and the *vardhanī* jar. A worshipper recites the *astramantra* to the *vardhanī* jar a hundred times. Then he sprinkles a continuous downpour of water from its jar around the site. This is considered a kind of fencing of the site with the water empowered by the *astramantra.*[19] Third, in the rite for the attainment of protection (*rakṣāvidhi*) as seen in the SātvataS, a *sādhaka* worshipper places eight red arrows decorated with various items like peacock feather, etc. on their neck parts and then performs the *digbandha* act.[20] Fourth, the right heel is stamped thrice to remove evil spirits on the ground.[21] Fifth, the GaruḍaP 2.2.11-14; 2.32.97 states that a dying man or a dead body should be placed within a circle (*maṇḍala*) drawn on the ground in order that the spirits cannot go into it in. The reason is that Brahmā, Viṣṇu, Rudra, Śrī and the sacrificial fire preside over the circle.[22]

3

The LakṣmīT 49.72 shows an interesting term *diksthāpana.* It states that one covers an image with a cloth while reciting the Vedic hymns and he performs *diksthāpana* when the pure sun has risen. This is performed at the beginning of the *pratiṣṭhā* ceremony.[23] Gupta assumes that this may indicate the *digbandhana* rite.[24] But it seems that the *diksthāpana* is far more similar to *digupasthāna*, the rite of worshipping the quarters than the *digbandhana*. The *diksthāpana* may be the rite of worshipping and propitiating the gods presiding over each quarter. According to the Śrauta texts, the *digupasthāna* is performed at the first rite called *prāyanīyā* (opening) *iṣṭi* after the day of the Vedic *dīkṣā*. In this *iṣṭi caru* (rice) cooked in milk is offered to Aditi and four offerings of *ājya* to four more directions, viz. Pathyā Svasti, Agni, Soma and Savitṛ in the four directions, viz. east, south, west and north respectively.[25]

As Gonda states, orientation is one of the most striking features of Vedic and post-Vedic ritual.[26] The direction (*diś* / *pratidiś*) has been deified since the latter half of the Ṛgveda and the Atharvaveda. Particularly, in the Atharvaveda, the deified direction appears as the subject who approved the authority of a king who ascended to the throne.[27] For instance, in the *rājasūya* ceremony, a new king mounts the quarters of space (*digvyāsthāpana*) before inauguration. This is considered the ritual in which a king seeks support from the divinities, metres, etc., arranged in the directions.[28] Many expressions of worshipping the directions can be found. For instance the expression *"diśaḥ pratiyajati"* is found in the Śrauta texts,[29] and "One worships each direction" (*pratidiśam upatiṣṭhate*) in the Kauśikasūtra of Atharvaveda 8.4; 51.4; 61.3,[30] in which one offers *bali*-food to the directions (8.3: *ijyānāṃ diśyān balīn harati* 51.3: *diśyān balīn harati*). The Śaṅkhāyanagṛhyasūtra 2.14.6-7 also states the offering of *bali*-food to the deities presiding over the direction.[31] The Āśvalāyanagṛhyasūtra 4.9.20 also states the same kind of *bali*-offering. There is an instance in which one throws clods of earth to the ground to the different quarters of the horizon, from the left to the right, with the hymn, 'A ruler indeed' (RV 10.152) verse by verse (the ŚāṅkhāyanaGS 4.6.5).[32]

The act of offering *bali*-food to the directions or the deities presiding over the directions can be found in the Paurāṇic and tantric texts.[33] The GaruḍaP 1.48.79d, 99b gives such an expression as "one should offer *bali*-food to the guardians of directions" (*dikpālānāṃ baliṃ haret*). The NarasiṃhaP 56.30cd-33 also states the *bali*-offering to the guardians of directions in the *pratiṣṭhā* ceremony. It is often called *digbali*. The AgniP 103.8-10 states that after performing the *digbali* outside, the preceptor rinses his mouth, feeds brahmins and prays to Śiva for substituting an old phallic emblem (*duṣṭaliṅga*) for the new one.[34] This kind of *bali* is connected with *bhūmiparigraha* (taking hold of the ground), a ritual performed at the beginning of an initiation ceremony (*dīkṣā*) or an installation ceremony of an image (*pratiṣṭhā*).[35] It is done for the purification of the ground for the ceremony. The Nāradasaṃhitā of the Pāñcarātra sect 14.58cd-59 states in the chapter describing the characteristics of a temple that one propitiates deities on the ground with the *bali*-food and then performs the fire-offering.[36] The SomaśP states the term *digbali* several times in the *pratiṣṭhā part* (Vol. 4).[37] Brunner states that the *digbali* is equal with "*bali* for entrance" (*praveśabali*) and that the three rites like *praveśabali*, *bhūparīkṣā* (examination of the earth) and *bhūparigraha* are not performed separately in the installation ceremony of the god if they install him at the same time as they found a village.[38] The PauṣkaraS 2.30-34 states that when performing the *bhūmiparigraha*, one offers *bali*-food towards the directions and expels the spirits while regarding one's own body as the *astramantra*.[39] In the SātvataS 18.4-13, one takes hold of the ground (*kṣmāparigraha*) at the beginning of the initiation ceremony. Then one levels the ground and erects an open hall (*maṇḍapa*). On this occasion one offers *bali*-food to the spirits (*bhūta*).[40]

On the other hand, the similar rite to the *digbandha* can be found in the Vedic works. The Ṛgveda 7.104.23 prohibits the demons or the evil spirits from coming near those who practice witchcraft.[41] This is the hymn for chasing away the evils. The Atharvaveda 8.3.1-2 states that Agni is a protector from dangers originating in various directions.[42] The Atharvaveda 7.51.1 states that Bṛhaspati must protect us from above, from below, against the malignant one; Indra must make wide space for us from the front and from the centre, etc.[43] The ŚāṅkhāyanaGS 6.5.6 states that they just look to the four directions and the sky without offering anything, while reciting their relevant Vedic hymns, namely the Ṛgveda 10.152, which is a prayer for protection against threats and the occurrence of something undesired.[44] In this way, such rites as *digbandha* and *digbali* can be traced back to the time of the Vedic works.

NOTES

1. S. Gupta et al., *Hindu Tantrism*, Handbuch der Orientalistik, Zweite Abteilung, 4. Band, 2. Abschnitt, Leiden / Köln: E.J. Brill, 1979, p. 134.
2. Prof S. Einoo describes the development of the *dikpālas* from the time of the Atharvaveda. See S. Einoo, "Guardians of the Directions", *Pratiṣṭhā*, edited by S. Einoo (in press).
3. See Gupta et al., *Hindu Tantrism*, p. 137.
4. This *digbandhana* is said not to be restricted to the Tantric one but to the pan-Hindu one. It is parallel to the Vedic rite of looking towards the four points of the compass. See J. Gonda, *Vedic Ritual. The Non-solemn Rites*, Handbuch der Orientalistik, Zweite Abteilung, 4. Band, 1. Abschnitt, Leiden / Köln: E. J. Brill, 1980, p. 76. Even in the Buddhist texts, the term *digbandha* is found. For example, see the Avadānakalpalatā 64 (Sudhanakinnaryavadāna). 42-43.
5. See the SātvataS 17.250: *atha baddhaśikho maunī prāgvad digbandham ācaret / abhisandhāya manasā sarvadoṣapalāyanam //* in the rite for the attainment of protection (*rakṣāvidhi*) by the *sādhaka*.
6. Cf. the Lakṣmītantra 47.11cd-12ab.
7. I refer to M. Rastelli, "The Religious Practice of the *Sādhaka*, according to the Jayākhyasaṃhitā", *IIJ*, vol. 43 (2000), p. 332; p. 379, n. 129.
8. Brunner distinguishes the function of the *astramantra* and *the kavacamantra*. Though both mantras are used as purification rites, strictly speaking, the former is recited in the rite of *digbandhana* (= *rakṣaṇa*), whereas the latter in the rite of *avakuṇṭhana* (protective encirclement) while making a design of circle over each object with the fingers. See the Somaśambhupaddhati (= the SomaśP), translation and notes by Hélène Brunner-Lachaux, Pondichéry: Institut Français d'Indologie, vol. 1, 1963, p. 74, fn. 2.
9. *tatas tu vaidikair mantraiḥ kartavyaṃ svastivācanam //* (7. 11.79cd) ***digbandhanaṃ*** *ca kartavyaṃ mantraiḥ pauraṇikair budhaiḥ* /(80ab). The GaruḍaP 1.38.7 states the expression "Fence the quarters, etc." in the repeating prayers of the mantra of Durgā (*durgājapa*): *oṃ namo bhagavati cāmuṇḍe ... bandha bandha duṣṭagrahān sarvān* ***bandha bandha diśāṃ bandha bandha vidiśāṃ bandha bandha ūrdhvaṃ bandha bandha adhastād*** *bandha bandha bhasmanā pānīyena mṛttikayā ...* (1.38.7).
10. See G. Bühnemann, *Pūjā. A Study in Smarta Ritual*, Publications of the De Nobili Research Library, vol. 15, Vienna, 1988, p. 123. She uses the Ṛgvedīyabrahmakarmasamuccaya, a comprehensive practical handbook of rituals for the use of Mahārāṣṭrian Brahmins belonging to the śakala school of the Ṛgveda.
11. The eleventh chapter of this Purāṇa deals with worship of the nine Vyūha of Viṣṇu (*navavyūhārcana*). First the worshipper performs *bhūtaśuddhi*, then *nyāsa* and meditates on *yogapīṭha* of the supreme Lord. The GaruḍaP states; *śikhāyāṃ tu śikhāṃ nyasya kavacaṃ sarvatas tanau / netraṃ netre vidhātavyam astrañ ca karayor dvayoḥ //* (1.11.13) *tenaiva ca* ***diśo baddhvā*** *pūjāvidhim athācaret / hṛdaye cintayet pūrvaṃ yogapīṭhaṃ samāhitaḥ //* (14). In the Appendix I (*sakalīkaraṇavidhi*) of the SomaśP (pp. 322-25), a worshipper performs *karanyāsa* and *aṅganyāsa*. Then having clapped

his hands thrice, he performs the *digbandhana* with the *astramantra*, encloses himself (*avakuṇṭhya*) with the *kavacamantra* and shows the *mahāmudrā* while reciting the *mūlamantra* accompanied by *vauṣaṭ*.

12. [15, 2-4] *adhyavocad iti kavacam / namo bilmina ity upakavacam / namo astu nīlagrīvāyeti tṛtīyanetram / pramuñca dhanvana ity astram / ya etāvantaś ceti* **digbandha** *iti / oṃ namo bhagavate rudrāyeti namaskāraṃ nyaset / evaṃ nyāsavidhiṃ kṛtvā.*
13. [15, 21-26] *śivasaṃkalpaṃ hṛdayam / puruṣasūktaṃ śiraḥ / uttaranārāyaṇaṃ śikhā / apratirathaṃ kavacam / pratipuruṣam iti netram / śatarudrīyam ity astram / bhūr bhuvaḥ suvar om iti* **digbandha** *iti /.*
14. See also the SomaśP vol. 1, p. 22, fn. 4.
15. See H. Hikita "Consecration of an Divine Image", *Pratiṣṭhā* edited by S. Einoo (in press).
16. The AhirbudhnyaS states: *tīrthaṃ gatvā śucau deśe mṛdam ādāya mantrataḥ / dvidhā kṛtvaikabhāgena kuryād dehasya śodhanam //* (28.3) *snātvācamya gṛhītvānyaṃ mṛdbhāgaṃ vinyaset tridhā / vāme pāṇau diśābandhaṃ vidadhyād ekabhāgataḥ //* (4) *gātrālepaṃ tataḥ kuryād anyenāṃśena nārada / saṃkalpayet tṛtīyāṃśāṃ tīrthapīṭham ataḥ param //* (5). The similar expression can be found in the AgniP 22 describing bathing ritual (*snānavidhi*)*: vakṣye snānaṃ kriyādyarthaṃ nṛsiṃhena tu mṛttikām / gṛhītvā tāṃ dvidhā kṛtvā malasnānam athaikayā //* (22.1) *nimājyācamya vinyasya siṃhena kṛtarakṣakaḥ / vidhisnānaṃ tataḥ kuryāt prāṇāyāmapuraḥsaram //* (2) *hṛdi dhyāyan hariṃ devaṃ mantreṇāṣṭākṣareṇa hi / tridhā pāṇitale mṛtsnāṃ* ***digbandhaṃ*** *asiṃhajaptatāḥ //* (3) *vāsudevaprajaptena tīrthaṃ saṅkalpya cālabhet /* (4ab). The Nāradasaṃhitā 2.13cd states that he scatters clay empowered by the *astramantra* around: *mṛdāstrayuktayā kuryāt dikṣu digbandhaṃ ātmanaḥ //*. A similar expression is found in the bathing ritual in the Pādmasaṃhitā, chapter 13 describing the five daily duties (*pañcakāla*) (13.34-38, p. 169).
17. The SātvataS states: *sarvabījāni dhānyāni siddhārthakayutāny atha / kṛtvāstraparijaptāni dhyātvā cāstrasamāni ca //* (18.81) *vighnopaśāntaye vegād daśadikṣu vinikṣipet / saṃhṛtya barhikūrcena prācyāṃ dikṣi nidhāya vai //* (82). The worshipper also scatters sesame empowered by the *hṛnmantra* all around. See the SātvataS 18.227d-228ab.
18. The AgniP 27.2cd states: *sarṣapāṃs tu phaḍantena rakṣoghnān sarvatāḥ kṣipet //*.
19. The AgniP states: *varhanyā sahite kumbhe sāṅgaṃ viṣṇuṃ prapūjayet //* (27.6cd) *śatavāraṃ mantrayitvā tv astreṇaiva ca vardhanīm / acchinnadhārayā siñcann īśānāntaṃ nayec ca tam //* (7). See also the AgniP 34.14-15. For the similar act in the initiation ceremony, see the SātvataS 18.89-93; the JayākhyaS 16.100cd-102; the PauṣkaraS 12.232; the PādmaS 2.10-12 (the term *vardhanī* is replaced by *karaka* here).
20. The SātvataS states: *susamaṃ tad bahir dadhyād dikṣu lohaśarāṣṭakam / kaṇṭhadeśeṣu badhnīyāc charāṇāṃ dṛḍhatantunā //* (17.245) *barhipakṣasamāyuktāṃ sarṣakañcukabhūṣitām / sauṣadhīṃ bhūtajaṭāṃ śamīśākhāsamanvitāṃ //* (246) *pañcarāgeṇa sūtreṇa udagāśāditaḥ kramāt / prādakṣiṇyena tu tredhā veṣṭayet taccharāṣṭakam //* (247). See also the SomaśP 3.2-3 (vol. 1, p. 96), in which in order to removes obstacles (*vighnoccāṭana*), a worshipper casts down divine glances (*divyadṛṣṭinipāta*) with "*oṃ hāṃ hauṃ śivāya namaḥ*" and the *astramantra*, and stamps the

right heel thrice. See the KālikāP 59.18, 22, 28, 59, 80, 109, 143, 150, 182 quoted in J. Gonda, *Eye and Gaze in the Veda*, Amsterdam-London: North-Holland Publishing Company, 1969, p. 46.

21. The AgniP states: *utsārya divyān vighnāṃś ca puṣpakṣepāntarikṣagān //* (74.3cd) *dakṣapārṣṇitribhir ghātair bhūmiṣṭhān yāgamandiram /* (4ab).
22. The GaruḍaP states: *āturo mucyate naiva maṇḍalena vinā bhuvi / brahmā rudraś ca viṣṇuś ca śrīr hutāśana eva ca / maṇḍale copatiṣṭhantas tasmāt kurvīta maṇḍalam //* (2.29.12). The GaruḍaP 2.27.58 states that Brahmā and Viṣṇu should be worshipped in the middle of a special jar named *pretaghaṭa*, Śiva in the east, and the guardians of the directions in the neck in their serial order. This jar is donated to a Brahmin for the deceased. See also the GaruḍaP 2.28.2.
23. *udgate vimale sūrye kuryād* ***diksthāpanaṃ*** *tataḥ //* (49. 72cd).
24. S. Gupta, *Lakṣmī Tantra. A Pāñcarātra Text*, Delhi: Motilal Banarsidass, 1st Indian Edition (1972) 2000, p. 326, fn. 11.
25. P.V. Kane, *History of Dharmaśāstra*, vol. 2, Poona: Bhandarkar Oriental Research Institute p. 1140.
26. J. Gonda, *Vedic Ritual*, p. 52. See J. Gonda, *The Mantras of the Agnyupasthāna and the Sautrāmaṇī*, Amsterdam, Oxford, New York: North-Holland Publishing Company, 1980, pp 48-9 and S. Einoo, "Guardians of Directions", n. 1 (in press).
27. Yasuhiro Tuchiyama, "kodai indo ni okeru kanjyou no igi" (the meaning of inauguration in the ancient India, in Japanese) *Indotetsugaku Bukkyougaku*, vol. 16, p. 4.
28. J.C. Heesterman, *The Ancient Indian Royal Consecration, the Rājasūya described according to the Yajus texts and annoted*, 's-Gravenhage: Mouton and Co., 1957, pp. 103-5.
29. Naoshiro Tsuji, *Burāhumana to Shurautasūtra no Kankei* (The relation between the Brāhmaṇa and the Śrautasūtra, in Japanese), p. 105, § 31, *diśāṃ pratījyā*.
30. See also the Āśvalāyanagṛhyasūtra 1.9.21-22: *caturbhiḥ sūktaiś* ***catasro diśa upatiṣṭheta*** *kad rudrāyemā rudrāyāte pitar imā rudrāya sthiradhanvana iti /21/ sarvarudrayajñeṣu* ***diśām*** *upasthānam /22/* (in the *śūlagava*). The Hiraṇyakeśigṛhyasūtra states: *saṃsravantu diśo mayi samāgacchantu sūnṛtāḥ/ sarve kāmā abhiyantu naḥ priyā abhisravantu naḥ priyā iti* ***diśa upatiṣṭhate*** *//* (1.4.5, *madhuparka*); *udite nakṣatre prācīm udīcīṃ vā diśam upaniṣkramya devīḥ ṣaḍ urvīr iti diśa upatiṣṭhate //* (1.7.10, *vivāha*); *athopatiṣthate samīcī nāmāsi prācī dig ity etair mantraiḥ pratidiśaṃ //* (2.6.7, *śravaṇākarma*). The Pāraskaragṛhyasūtra states: *niṣkramya diśa upatiṣṭhate /* (3.4.14).
31. *atha diśāṃ pradakṣiṇaṃ yathārūpaṃ baliṃ harati /6/ nama indrāyaindrebhyaś ca, namo yamāya yāmebhyaś ca, namo varuṇāya vāruṇebhyaś ca, namaḥ somāya saumyebhyaś ca, namo bṛhaspate bārhaspatyebhyaś ca /7/* (in the *viśvedeva*).
32. I follow the translation of H. Oldenberg (SBE, vol. 29, pt. 1, p. 115).
33. Offering *bali*-food to the presiding deities over the directions are already found in the Āśvalāyanagṛhyasūtra. See Kane, *History of Dharmaśāstra*, vol. 2, p. 745, fn. 1777. See the Manusmṛti 3.87-93.
34. See also the AgniP 97.17a: *dikpālebhyo baliṃ dattvā samācānto 'tha deśikaḥ /*
35. The AgniP 57.1 states that one performs the *bhūmiparigraha* by scattering rice and mustard seeds which keep off the demons (*rakṣoghna*) with

narasiṃhamantra. This seems fencing the directions with seeds but not propitiating the demons with *bali*-food.

36. *etāṃs tu devān saṃpūjya vāstudehagatān dvija* // (14.58cd) *digbaliṃ ca tato dattvā iṣṭakāhomam ācaret / madhye tu maṇḍalaṃ kṛtvā dvādaśākṣara-vidyayā* // (59).
37. See 1.15ab; 2.245cd; 3.9cd; 9.31; 10.13; 11.10ab (vol. 4).
38. See the SomaśP, vol. 4, p. 14, fn. 44.
39. *śubhe 'nukūle 'tha dine kuryād* ***bhūmiparigraham*** */ ahiṃsitena māṃsena saktunā sodakena* tu // (2.30) *phalapuṣpasametena tailakṣārānvitena ca / svinne saṃsparśasaṅghena dadhikṣīraguḍena ca* // (31) *rajanīcūrṇayuktena śāḍvalena tilena ca / digvidikṣu tathā madhye tv idam uktvā* ***baliṃ kṣipet*** // (32) *yeṣāṃ vai krūrasattvānām ayaṃ bhūbhāga āśrayaḥ / te prayacchantu me tuṣṭiṃ prayāntu paramālayam* // (33) *dhyātvā 'sya sadṛśaṃ deham astramantreṇa cojjvalam / bhūtāny ājñāpayet paścāt toyāntāṃ nikhanen mahīm*// (34).
40. See the SātvataS 18.23 concerning the materials for propitiation of the spirits (*bhūtatarpaṇa*).
41. See J. Gonda, *Prayer and Blessing*, 1989, pp. 82-4.
42. See J. Gonda, "Purohita", *Selected Studies*, vol. 2, Leiden: E.J. Brill, 1975, p. 323.
43. The KauśS 47.16 mentions: *sa na indra purohita viśvataḥ pāhi rakṣasaḥ / abhi gāvo anūṣatābhi dyumnaṃ bṛhaspate* // (in the so-called *dīkṣā* for the *abhicāra*). See also the Ṛgveda 10.42.11; the KauśS 46.54.
44. See J. Gonda, *Eye and Gaze in the Veda*, p. 11.

Chapter 52

Another Version of Prajñārakṣita's *Balividhi*

MUNENOBU SAKURAI

I *Introductory Note*

Prajñārakṣita alias Śāśvatavajra[1] is a famous tantric buddhist scholar acting around the middle of the 11th century, and is said to be one of the four great disciples of Nāḍapāda (Nā ro paṇ chen) together with Maṇikaśrī, Bodhibhadra and Abhayakīrti.[2] He followed the doctrines of the Lūyīpāda School belonging to the Cakrasaṃvara cycle from Nāḍapāda and became an authority on that School.

As has been already known, Bu ston Rin chen grub listed up his four masterpieces under the name "The Four Religious Works of Prajñārakṣita (Pra dsñā ra kṣitaḥi chos bshi) / Śāśvatavajra (rTag paḥi rdo rje)".[3] These works have been regarded as the canonical texts among the Indo-Tibetan tantric buddhists for practising meditations and offerings according to the tradition of the School. Below is the list of "The Four Religious Works" :

> bDe mchog gi sgrub thabs Lū i pas mdsad paḥi ḥgrel pa Pra dsñā ra kṣitas mdsad pa (*Pañjikā*)
>
> ḥKhor lo sdom paḥi phyi rol mchod paḥi cho ga (*Bāhyapūjāvidhi*)

gTor maḥi cho ga (*Balividhi*)
Lag mchod kyi cho ga (*Hastapūjāvidhi*).[4]

In 1934 L. Finot published some Indian Buddhist Tantric Ritual Works, in which a Critical Skt. text of the *Balividhi* (F) was included, based on the P'ou-ngan sseu Manuscript.[5] Finot called the work "CAKRASAMVARABALIVIDHI" following the description of its colophon: "*saṃkṣipta-Śrī-Cakrasamvarabalividhiḥ samāptaḥ. kṛtiḥ Śāśvatavajrapādānām iti*". This text has, so to speak, the right form as an independent buddhist work; i.e. having both *namaskāra*-verse and *pariṇāmanā*-verse, as well as making clear its proper title and author's name in the colophon. The same matters are seen in the text included in a Skt. MS. belonging to The Asiatic Society of Bengal (C)[6] and a Tibetan translation (Tib.1).

In addition to these three materilas, three more Skt.MSS. (N_1, N_2, N_3) and one Tibetan translation (Tib.2) are proved to be preserved. Among these four materials N_2 and N_3 are identical with above-mentioned three ones for having "the right form". But N_1 and Tib.2 have neither *namaskāra*-verse, *pariṇāmanā*-verse, nor the colophon, thus seeming to be a component of a larger work. And insofar as Tib.2 shows, there was a tradition regarding the larger work as a Commentary of *Cakrasaṃvarābhisamaya*, written by "Lwa baḥi na bzaḥ can".[7] This, however, should be incorrect since the traditon of taking the name "Lwa baḥi na bzaḥ can" as the author of the whole works is supposed to be a misunderstanding. Reasoning from the contents of Skt.MS.C, a short supplemental memorundum by "Kaṃbalīpāda" on the abhiṣeka practising in meditation had been coming down accompanied with the four works.[8] And there is a strong possibility that the memorundum once operated as the cause to give rise to misunderstanding that all the four works, not only the memorundum, were written by Kaṃbalīpāda himself.[9]

From the structural distinctions among these seven materials we can divide the materials into these two groups: (a) C, F, N_2, N_3, Tib.1 (b) N_1, Tib.2. But when regarding the variant readings which the five Skt. materials and the two Tibetan translations show each other in the commonly included part, another grouping can be possible like this: (α) C, F, N_3 (β) N_1, N_2, Tib.1,

Tib.2. And we can see a general tendency between (α) and (β) that the former details the ritual procedures more than the latter. But also we should notice that all the readings shown in each group are not thoroughly identical. For example some readings in F are identical with the ones preserved in N_1 and Tibetan translations; some variants in N_2 are identical with those of C or C and N_3 ; there is a variant shown in C, N_1 and Tib.2 identically; some readings in Tib.2 are identical with the ones preserved in (α), all of which will be confirmed by the notes for II (p.822f.).

Judging from the facts mentioned above, the text of the *Balividhi* seems to have prevailed under more than one tradition. And this is the same case with the *Bāhyapūjāvidhi*[10] which is one of "The Four Religious Works".

In this paper I am presenting a critical Skt. text of the *Balividhi*—a Buddhist tantric ritual manual for doing *bali*-offering according to the Cakrasaṃvara cycle—together with its English translation mainly based on MS. N_1 to show concretely the existence of another traditon on the *Balividhi* regarding the differences from the other traditon represented by F.

II *A Critical Sanskrit Text of Prajñārakṣita's Balividhi*

The Sources of the Present Text

- Skt. MSS and Published Ed.

C	Included in a palm-leaf MS. belonging to The Asiatic Society of Bengal.	Shastri 100(4751)19b[3]-22a[6]
F	A critical ed. by L. Finot, *Journal Asiatique* 22, pp.56-58.	
N_1	Included in a palm-leaf MS. belonging to the National Archives Nepal.	Moriguchi 210. 7b[3-7].
N_2	Ibid.	Moriguchi 351. 19a[2]-20a[2].
N_3	Ibid.	Moriguchi 139. 19a[2]-20a[2].

- Tibetan translations

Tib.1 *Śrī-Cakrasaṃvarabalividhi.* [Tohoku 1467; Otani 2184].

Tib.2 A part of the *Cakrasaṃvarābhisamavaṭikā*. [Otani 4661] 288b[3]-290a[8].

[0] balir [1] ucyate //

[1] śrī-Saṃvarayogavān mantrī [2] bhaktādikam purataḥ saṃsthāpya viśodhayet //

[3] tat purato [4] Yaṁ-kāreṇa vāyumaṇḍalam / tadupari Raṁ-[5]kārajāgnimaṇḍalam / [6] tatra [7 →] śukla-Āḥ-kārajaṃ padmabhājanaṃ muṇḍatritaya[← 7]kṛtacullikāvyavasthitam / [8] tatra bhaktādikaṃ Oṁ-Trāṁ-[9]Āṁ-Khaṁ-Hūṁ-Lāṁ-Māṁ-Yāṁ-[10]Tāṁ-kārajatadadhiṣṭhitapa-[11]ñcāmṛta[12]pañcapradīparūpeṇa niṣpādya [13] vāyupreritāgnitāpavilīna-bījākṣarādikam abhinavabhānuvarṇadravarūpaṃ dṛṣṭvā / [14] tataḥ [15] pārada[16]varṇa-Hūṁ-[17]bhavādhomukhāmṛtamaya[18]śuklakhaṭvāṅgavilīne taṃ [19] dravaṃ pāradavarṇaṃ śītalaṃ [20] dṛṣṭvā / tadupari ālikāli-[21]pariṇatebhya Oṁ-Āḥ-[22]Hūṁ-[23]kārebhyo 'nukrameṇ[24]oparyupari[25]sthitebhyas [26 →] tricakradevatāḥ spharitvā [← 26] jagadarthaṃ kṛtvā [27] samāpattipūrvakaṃ [28] dravībhūya / [29] yathāyathaṃ [30] teṣu [31] praviṣṭāḥ // [32] tatra [33] Oṁ-kārādikam [34] api [35] kramaśo vilīnam avalokya [36] tryakṣareṇādhiṣṭhāya/[37]tato [38] jvālāmudrātanmantrābhyām [39] ānītaṃ sarvākāra[40]niṣpannaṃ maṇḍalaṃ purato 'vasthāpy[41]ārghādipuraḥ[42]saraṃ sampūjya / [43 →] ālikā-lipariṇatacandrasūryasvabhāvakaradvay[44]āntargataṃ Hūṁ-kāraṃ [← 43] dṛṣṭvā / <Oṁ anyonyānugatāḥ sarvadharmāḥ atyantānupraviṣṭāḥ sarvadharmāḥ Hūṁ> ity [45] uccāraṇa[46]pūrvaka[47 →]candrasūryārūḍha-[48]Hūṁ-[49]kārapariṇāmena [← 47] vajrāñjalikṛtakaratale tadamṛtabhāṇḍam avasthāpya

dhyātvā[50] vā / [51→]tato balisvīkārārthaṃ idaṃ[←51] paṭhet //

> devyaḥ pramāṇaṃ samayaḥ pramāṇaṃ taduktavācaś ca param pramānam /
>
> etena satyena bhaveyur etā devyo mamānugrahahetubhūtāḥ// 1 //

[2] tataḥ [52→]pūjyapūjakapujānām abhedam[53] [←52]paśyan tadamṛta[54]bhāṇḍaṃ dikṣu vāmāvartena [55→]pūrvādidiśam ārabhya[←55] / vidikṣv agnikoṇam ārabhya [#]diṣiṇāvartena bhrāmayan[56] / Hūṁ-bhavaśuklavajrajihvānāṃ[57] [58]tricakradevatānām <Oṁ kara 2 / kuru 2 / bandha 2 / trāsaya 2 bhaya 2 / Hrauṁ 2[59] / Hraḥ 2 /[60] Pheṁ 2 / Phaṭ 2 / daha 2 / paca 2 / bhakṣa 2 / vaśarudhira[61]ntramālāvalambine[62] / gṛhṇa 2 saptapātāla[63]gatabhujaṃgaṃ[64] sarpaṃ vā / tarjaya 2 / ākaṭya 2[65] / [66→]Hrīṁ[67] 2 / Jñauṁ 2 / Kṣauṁ[68] 2 / [←66]Hāṁ 2 / Hīṁ 2[69] / Hūṁ Hūṁ[70] / .kili 2 sili[71] 2 hili 2 dhili 2 Hūṁ Hūṁ Phaṭ[72]> ity anenaikavāroccāri-teṇa[73] / bhagavataḥ[74] saprajñasya Ḍākinyādīnāṃ Kākāsyādīnāñ ca yathāyogaṃ bhrāmayan[75] <Oṁ[76] vajrārali Hoḥ JaH Hūṁ Vaṁ Hoḥ Vajraḍākinyaḥ samayas tvaṃ dṛśya Hoḥ> ity anenaikadvitricatuḥpañcavāroccāriteṇa ḍhaukayitvā/tata ācamana[77]hasta-prokṣaṇa[78]tāmbūlādikaṃ dattvā Vīṇādibhiḥ saṃpūjya [79→]stutvābhimatasiddhiṃ prārthayet[←79] //

> bhavaśamasamasaṅgā bhagnasaṃkalpabhaṅgāḥ[80] kham iva sakalabhāvaṃ bhāvato vīkṣamāṇāḥ[81] /
>
> gurutarakaruṇā[82]mbhaḥsphīta[83]cittāmbunāthāḥ[84] kuruta kuruta devyo mayā[85]tīvānukampām // 2 //

tato 'ṣṭaśmaśāna[86]sthitadikpālānāṃ[87] pūrvavad bhrāmayan <Oṁ kha 2 khāhi 2 sarvayakṣa rākṣasabhūtapretapiśāconmādāpa-smāra[88]ḍākinyādaya imam balim gṛhṇantu[89] / samayaṃ rakṣantu / mama sarvasiddhiṃ[90] prayacchantu / yathaivaṃ yatheṣṭaṃ bhuñjatha[91] pibatha jighratha[92] mātikramatha mama sarvākāratayā[93] satsukhaviśuddhaye sahāyakā bhavantu [94→]Hūṁ Hūṁ Phaṭ Phaṭ[←94] Svāhā> ity anena vāradvayoccāritena ḍhaukayet // tadamṛtabhakṣaṇād[95] dikpālādayo[96] yathāvat[97] mahāsukhasamarpitavigrahā[98] bhāvyāḥ //

[3] tadanu samudāyena tāṃbūlādikaṃ dattvā hṛdbījanirgata[99]-Vīṇādibhiḥ[100] saṃpūjyā[101→]ṣṭapadamantreṇa[102] [←101]saṃstutyābhimataṃ prārthya[103] [←&→] & cchomakahastena saṃcchomya nyūnādhikavidhipūraṇārtham <Oṁ Vajraheruka samayam anupālaya Herukatvenopati[104]-ṣṭha/ dṛḍho[105→] me bhava / [106→]sutoṣyo me bhava[←105] / supoṣyo me bhava / anurakto me bhava[←106] / sarvasiddhim me prayaccha / sarvakarmasu ca me cittaṃ śreyaḥ[107] kuru Hūṁ Ha Ha Ha Ha Hoḥ[108] bhagavan Vajraheruka mā me muñca[109] Heruko bhava mahāsamayasattva Āḥ Hūṁ Phaṭ> iti śatākṣaramantraṃ ghaṇṭāvādanapūrvakam paṭhet //

tata[110] <Oṁ yogaśuddhāḥ sarvadharmā yogaśuddho 'ham> iti paṭhan kamalāvartena[111] paritoṣya mudropasaṃhāra[112] āliṅganābhinayapūrvakā[113]nāmikāṅguṣṭacchoṭikādānapūrvakam <Oṁ vajra muḥ> iti paṭhan visarjya taccakram ātmani sarvātmanā[114] praveśayet[115] // //

III *English Translation*

[0] [Now the ritual of] *bali* is explained [as follows].

[1] A tantric yogin uniting with Śrī-Saṃvara, putting the boiled rice etc. in front of him, should purify them.

In that case [he at first should meditate] the Wind-circle from the syllable Yaṁ, upon it the Fire-circle from the syllable Raṁ. And there from the syllable Āḥ is prepared a skull-bowl seated on the tripod fire-place the three legs of which are human heads. Within the [bowl he] meditates the boiled rice etc., which have been arised from the syllables Oṁ Trāṁ Āṁ Khaṁ Hūṁ Lāṁ Māṁ Yāṁ Tāṁ and have been put [with these syllables], to be The Five Ambrosias & The Five Lamps, and then [he continues meditating that] the syllables etc. melting by the heat of the inflaming Fire-circle fanned by the Wind-circle transform into the liquid with the colour of the sun just risen. And he sees [in the meditation that] the mercury-colored liquid, into which a white ambrosia-natured Skull-topped-staff arisen from the syllable Hūṁ and being upside down has melted, has got cold; and the deities who are the members of the Three Wheels [in the Cakrasaṃvaramaṇḍala] emanate from the syllables Oṁ Āḥ Hūṁ which arose from *Āli-Kāli* and are piled up in this order on the [surface of the] liquid, work for the benefit of the creatures, enter in *samāpatti* (meaning 'sexual yogic practice' in this context), melt out, and enter back to that [three syllables]. After that, meditating the syllables Oṁ etc. melting again [into the liquid], he blesses [the liquid] with the three syllables. Then inviting the [Cakrasaṃvaramaṇḍala] with the Flame hand-sign and its mantra, he sets it in front of him [in imagining], offers *argha* etc. [And he] settles or imagines the skull-bowl on the *vajrāñjali* after uttering <Oṁ all the substances are possessing each other, and [also] all the substances are entering into each other Hūṁ> and contemplating his *vajrāñjali* changing from the syllable Hūṁ on the sun- and the moon-disk. Then he should recite [this verse] to make the *bali*-offerings be acceptable [for the deities] :

> The Goddesses are authority, the pledge is authority, and also their words are supreme authority.

By this truth may the Goddesses be the one showing me a favor! //1//

[2] Afterwards thinking the equality between offering items, offerers, and offerings, he offers [the liquid] to the Three Wheel deities [one by one], who have the white diamond tongue changed from the syllable Hūṁ, with turning the [above-mentioned] skull-bowl at the four corners [of the maṇḍala] beginning with the east counterclockwise and at the four intermediate points of the compass beginning with the south-east clockwise, also uttering this mantra one time: < Oṁ kara 2 , do do, bind bind, wave wave, shake shake, Hrauṁ 2, Hraḥ 2, Pheṁ 2, Phaṭ 2, burn burn, bake bake, eat eat, [homage to] the one hanging down guts-made-garland filled with fat and blood! catch catch, serpents living in the seven regions under the earth or snakes, threaten threaten, surround surround, Hrīṁ 2, Jñāuṁ 2, Kṣauṁ 2, Hūṁ 2, Hūṁ 2 , Hūṁ Hūṁ, kili 2 , sili 2, hili 2, dhili 2, Hūṁ Hūṁ Phaṭ> . And offering [the liquid] to the Bhagavat together with his Prajñā-consort, Ḍākinī etc., and Kākāsyā etc. with [the skull-bowl] turning accordingly and uttering following [mantra] one, two, three, four or five times: <Oṁ Vajrārali, Hoḥ Jaḥ Hūṁ Vaṁ Hoḥ, Vajraḍākinī-s ! you are the [embodiment of the] pledge. See! Hoḥ>, then offering mouth-rinsing-water, hand-washing-water, sprinkling-water, betel etc., praising [them] with [the performance by the Goddeses] Vīnā etc., [he] should ask his wishing supernatural acquisition [to utter this verse] :

May the Goddesses who make the worldly lives be calm, treat them equally, break [their] impaired thought, and are considering all the existences like the sky as they really are, with the ocean of the mind filled with the water of the supreme guru's mercy, take much compassion on me ! //2//

Then turning [the Skull-bowl] in the above-mentioned way he should offer [the liquid] to the Guardians of quarter living in the eight cemeteries uttering this [mantra] one time: < Oṁ kha 2, khāhi 2, all the *yakṣa*-s, *rākṣasa*-s, *bhūta*-s, *preta*-s, *piśāca*-s, *unmāda*-s, *apasmāra*-s, and *ḍākinī*-s ! Take this bali-offering! Keep [your] pledges! Give me all supernatural acquisitions! Eat, drink, and smell [the offerings] as long as we have at will! Don't overstep!

May you be my freinds to purify the real joy completely! Hūṁ Hūṁ Phaṭ Svāhā>. By eating the ambrosia, the Guardians etc. will surely be [the ones whose] bodies are filled with the Great Joy.

[3] Afterwards offering the betel etc. all together, praising [them] with [the performance by the Goddesses] Vīnā etc. emancipated from [the yogin's] *bīja* placing on [his] breast, asking own wishing, and performing the secret gesture by hands, he should utter the [following] One-Hundred-Syllable-mantra after ringing bell to compensate for the excess and lack of the rituals: <Oṁ Vajraheruka! Keep the pledges! Be beside [me] as the Heruka ! Be firm for me! Make me satisfied! Lead me prosperity! Make me delighted! Give me all the supernatural acquisitions! And make my mind more blessed on [doing] all actions! Hūṁ Ha Ha Ha Ha Hoḥ Bhagavat Vajraheruka ! Don't emancipate me! Make [me] the Heruka ! The Great-Pledge-person! Āḥ Hūṁ Phaṭ>

Then [he should] satisfy [them] with the Lotus-turning hand-sign uttering [this mantra]: < Oṁ all the existences are joining with pureness, and I am [also] joining with pureness>. And on the occasion of untying the hand-sign, performing the gesture of embrace and snapping with thumb and the ring finger, [he should] send away [the deities] uttering the mantra :<Oṁ [The One whose nature is equal to] the Diamond! Untei !>, and he should enter [the deities placing on the] circle [of the Cakrasaṃvaramaṇḍala] into himself.

NOTES

< For I >

1. Śāśvatavajra may be Prajñārakṣita's *guhya*-name given on the *abhiṣeka* rites.
2. Cf. Bu ston's *bDe mchog sphyi rnam* [Tohoku 5042] 51a[3]. Here Bu ston says that Prajñārakṣita was one of "the four disciples who had adhered and adored to Nāḍapāda during a long time in particular (*Nā ro paḥi slob ma khyad par du yun riṅ du bsten ciṅ mñes par byas oa bshi*)".
3. Cf. Bu ston's *bsTan hgyur dkar chag* [Tohoku 5205]:17a[7]-b[1] and *gSan yid* [*Tohoku* 5199]:43b[4].
4. R.O. Meisezahl has already listed up these four works under the title "vier religiösen Lehrschriften". See *Hastapūjāvidhi-texte Der Handritus*

im anuttarayogischen Kult des Götterpaares Cakrasambara und Vajravārāhī, VGH Wissenschafsverlag, Sankt Augustin, 1985, p. 7.

5. L. Finot, "Manuscripts Sanskrits de Sādhana's retrouves en Chine", *Journal Asiatique* 22, 1934, pp.56-58. Its French translation by Finot himself also appears on pp. 71-74.
6. About all the abbreviations for Skt. MSS. & Tib. Tr. using in I, see "The Sources of the Present Text" in II.
7. The structure of Tib.2 is as follows:
   [a] The part corresponding to the *Pañjikā*
   [b] The part corresponding to the *Bāhyapūjāvidhi*
   [c] The part corresponding to the *Balividhi*
   [d] The part corresponding to the *Hastapūjāvidhi*
   [e] A memorundum
   [f] Colophon
   According to the colophon all part of this work was written by "Lwa baḥi na bzaḥ can". And there is no reference to the name 'Prajñārakṣita' anywhere in it.
8. MS.C:25b³-26a¹. The content of this part is completely identical with that of "A memorundum" in Tib.2 (→ n.7 [e]).
9. The relationship between Kaṃbalīpāda (/Lwa baḥi na bzaḥ can) and "The Four Religious Works" by Prajñārakṣita here-mentioned has already been treated in my preceding paper. Sakurai Munenobu, "On the Cakrasaṃvarābhisamaya(1)-Bibliographical Survey-"(in Japanese), *The Journal of Esoteric Buddhist Study No.29*, March, 1977, pp.40-42.
10. Cf. Sakurai Munenobu(Soshin), "A Study on the Bāhyapūjāvidhi", *Journal of Chisan Studies No.65*, March 2002, pp.(37)-(38).

< For II >

1. C, F, N_2, N_3 add here the *namaskāra*-verse and a definition on the timing of doing *bali*-offering as follows:
   praṇammya saṃvaraṃ vīraṃ sarvvabhāvaikasamvaraṃ /
   saṃlikhyate yathāmnāyam balitatvaṃ samāsataḥ //
   prathamato mahāyogālambanotthitaḥ* (N_2, *-otthitaś ca*) /
   "Bowing down to the Saṃvara, a hero of concentrating all the existences into one, the truth about the *bāli*-offering is briefly written down in accordance with the traditional instruction [handed down to the author of this work]. At first getting up from the exercise of *mahāyoga* ..."
   Tib.1 also has the passage corresponding with this text, and in addition a word *ācāryaḥ* must be put the place * : cf. *slob dpon rnal ḥbyor chen pos.*
2. F *bhakṣabhojyā-* ; N_3, *bhakṣyābhoktā-*.
3. N_2, N_3 *tatra.*
4. F *yāṃ.*
5. C *-kāreṇā-.*
6. C tat. Tib.l : *deḥi steṅ du = tadupari.*

7. C, F, N_3 *śukla-Āḥ-kārajaṃ* (F, N_3 *-kāraja*) *muṇḍatritayakṛtacullikārūḍhaṃ śuklapadmabhājanaṃ*; N_2 *-Āḥ-kāraja-*. Tib.l, Tib.2 *yi ge gsum las skyes pa* (*Tib.2 byuṅ ba*) = *tryakṣarajamuṇḍa-*. In addition about the figure of the skull-bowl Tib.l adds this passage: *naṅ dmar ba phyi dkar po.*
8. Tib.l *deḥi naṅ du* = *tadantare.*
9. N_1 *-Āṁ-Trāṁ-.*
10. N_3 adds here *Nāṁ.*
11. N_2 *-āmṛtaḥ.*
12. N_3 omits *pañca.*
13. C, F, N_2, N_3 *-preritaprajvalitāgni-.*
14. C *tatra*; F, N_3 omit this word.
15. N_2 *pādara-.*
16. C *-varṇṇaṃ.*
17. F *huṃbhāvā-.*
18. N_3 omits *maya.*
19. N_3 *ḍrava.*
20. C, N_2 add here *tataṣ*
21. C, F, N_3 *-ṇatān* ; N_2 *-ṇatebhyodi.*
22. F *-huṃ-.*
23. C, F, N_3 *- kārān.*
24. N_3 omits *anukrameṇa.*
25. C, F, N_3 *-sthitān tebhyaḥ.*
26. The passage equivalent here in C, F, N_3 is as follows: *spharitaraśminā daśadigvarttivīravīreśvarīṇāṃ jñānāmṛtaṃ,* (C, F *-āmṛta*) *pradīpa* (F-*dīpaṁ*) *saṃkramaṇanyāyena* (C *-kramaṇaṃ* / *tyāgena*) *tricakram* (F, N_3 *-cakrākāram*) *ākṛṣya* / "with [the yogin's] emanating rays, entering the gnostic essence of the Heroes and Heroines residing in the ten directions into The Theree Wheels [of the Cakrasaṃvaramaṇḍala] in the way of passing through a lamp". This is supposed to be the result of augmenting the textual contents for the purpose of giving more particular explanation about the meditation practising on this step. Tib.1 is in accordance with N_1 & N_2, while Tib.2 with C etc.
27. C, F, N_3 *kārayitvā.*
28. N_2 *dravīkṛtyabhūya.*
29. N_2 *yathāsamarthaṃ.* Tib.1: *yi ge gsum po ji lta ba bshin* = *tryakṣareṣu yathā.*
30. N_2, Tib.1 omit this word. C, Tib.2 add *bījeṣu.*
31. C, F, N_3 *-viṣṭaṃ* ; N_2 *-visyās.*
32. C, F, N_3 add *sakalasāgaādisthaṅ ca.*
33. F, N_3, Tib.2 *tata*
34. N_3 omits this word.
35. F ; N_3 *krama* ; N_3 *Krameṇo.*
36. All the MSS. except N_1 & F add *yāvadiccham* (= Tib.1 *ji srid ḥdod par*).
37. F, N_3, Tib.1, Tib.2 *adhitiṣṭhet* (= Tib.1 *byin gyis brlab bo* and Tib.2 *byin gyis*

brlab par byaḥo); C *adhiṣṭhet* should derive from miswriting the same word.

38. F, Tib.2 *jālā-*.
39. C *ānīta*.
40. C, N_2, N_3 *-panna*.
41. C, F, N_3 *-arghapādyā*. Tib.1 *yon chab daṅ shal bsil la sogs pa = -arghācamanādi*.
42. F, N_3 *pūrvvkaṃ* instead of *puraḥsaraṃ*.
43. This passage, while omitted in N_1, is supplemented from the context.
44. F, N_2 - *gata*.
45. C *-cāraṇāṃ*.
46. C, F *-pūrvvakaṃ*.
47. N_3 omits this passage.
48. C, N_2, N_3 *-rūḍhaṃ*.
49. C, N_3 *-kāraṃ*.
50. F *ca*
51. N_1 omits this passage; N_3 omits *tato*, and reads *baliṃ svī* ; N_3 *tato baliṃ svī-*. Tib.1 doesn't translate *bali*.
52. F, N_3, while omitting this passage, insert *pūjyapūjāpūjakānām abhedādhimokṣapūrvvakaṃ* which virtually corresponds to the omitted one in the place #.
53. N_2 *paśyet*
54. N_2 *-bhāṇḍa*.
55. N_2 omits this word.
56. F *bhāvayan*.
57. F *-vajrarasānāṃ* ; N_3 *-vajrarasaṃ*.
58. N_2 *nānātri-*.
59. C *Hroṁ*; N_2 *Hrau*.
60. C *Hra Hraḥ*; N_2 *Hra 2*.
61. F. *vama-*.
62. F *-lambino*.
63. N_2 - *gatān*.
64. N_2, N_3 *-bhujaṃgān*.
65. F *ākaṭṭha* ; N_2 *ākaṭaya*.
66. N_2 not readable on this part because of the damage.
67. C *Hrī Hraṁ*.
68. C *Kṣoṁ* ; F *kṣyām*.
69. F *haṃ* 2.
70. N_2 omits this word.
71. F *mili* 2.
72. F *ṅgam* 2(?).
73. All the MSS. except N_1 & F add here *nivedayet* (=Tib.1 *dbul lo* and Tib.2 *bstab par byaḥo*).
74. C, F, N_3 add *tu*.
75. N_1 *brāmayanaṃ* ; N_2 *bhāvayan*.
76. N_3, adds *Āḥ*.

77. N_2 *tatra;* N_3 omits this word.
78. F *-proñcana* instead of *prokṣana.*
79. C adds *vā* before *abimata* ; F *saṃstutya iti.* N_2 *saṃstutveti* and both omitting *abhimatasiddhim.*
80. N_1 *saṅgāḥ* instead of *bhaṅgāḥ.*
81. N_2 *vīkṣamānā.*
82. C, N_2 *-āmbha.*
83. F *-sphuṭā-.*
84. N_2 *-nāthā.*
85. C *-kampāt* ; N_1 *-kapāṃ* ; N_2 *-kampā.*
86. F *-sthānāṃ* ; N_3 *-sthānād.*
87. F, N_3 *-pālādīnāṃ.*
88. F, N_2, N_3, Tib.1 *-ḍākaḍākiny-.*
89. N_2 adds here *bhuñjantu.*
90. F, N_1 omit *sarva.*
91. F *bhuñjītha.*
92. C, F omit this.
93. F *sarvvākārasatsukha-* ; C should originally have adopted the same reading as F since *tayā* is supplemented on the upper margin by another scribe.
94. F *ṅgaṃ* 2 *phaṭ* ; N_2 writes *Phaṭ* one time.
95. N_2 *-bhakṣaṇā* ; N_3 *-bhakṣaṇāta.*
96. C *-pālānādayo.*
97. C, F insert here *dharmmadhātupūrvvakaṃ* (= Tib.1 *chos kyi dbyiṅs sṅon du ḥgro ba can*).
98. N_2 *-samarppitā* lacking *vigraha.*
99. C, F-*bījān* ; N_2- *bījan.*
100. F *-ādiḥ.*
101. In spite of N_1's lacking *aṣṭapadamantreṇa saṃstutya,* this passage is supplemented based on the other materials since there is high probablity that the praise with the *Aṣṭapadamantra* is practiced here judging from the ritual context. On the other hand C and N_3, putting the passage "& → ←&" just after this word *saṃstutya,* show the different word order from the text here presented, while Tib.1 being identical with C&N_3 and Tib.2 with my text.
102. *F -pādādimantraiḥ* ; N_3 *-mantraiḥ.*
103. All the MSS. except N_1 & F *abhimatasiddhim* (= Tib.1 *mṅon par ḥdod paḥi dṅos grub*).
104. C *Herukatveno pratiṣṭha.*
105. N_2 not readable here for the damage of the right corner in 7b.
106. F omits this passage; N_3 *anurakto me bhava / suposyo me bhava* (showing different word order).
107. F *hṛṃ.*
108. N_2 reduplicates *Ha* twice.
109. N_1 *muca*

110. N_3 omits this.

111. C, F, N_2 *-varttamudrayā* (= Tib.1. *pad skor gyi phyag rgyas* & Tib.2 *pad skor gyi phyag gis*).

112. N_1 *-hāreṇa.*

113. F, N_3 *-pūrvvakaṃ.*

114. Tib.1&Tib.2 don't translate *sarva.*

115. All the MSS. except N_2, &F, after "*praveśayed iti*", put a *pariṇāmanā*-verse as follows:

puṇyam ajāyata yan me balividhilikhanāj; (C *-likhaj* ; N_2, *-likhāj*) *jagattravaṃ tvaritam /*

paridhūya kalpanājālaṃ tricakrarūpaṃ tato bhavatāt (*C bhagavatāt*; N_2, *bhavatāt*) *//*

"By the merit which was produced from my writing [this] *Balividhi,* may inhabitants living in the Three Worlds speedily remove the net of wrong imagination and become the ones whose nature is [equal with] the Three Wheel [of Cakrasaṃvaramaṇḍala] !"

CHAPTER 53

A Nepalese Buddhist Fire Ritual: Sahasrāhutihoma

SHINOBU YAMAGUCHI

1. *Fire Rituals in Kathmandu Valley*

In Kathmandu Valley, Newar Buddhism, which inherits the tradition of Indian Tantric Buddhism, survives among the Newar people. In Newar Buddhism, pūjā (offering worship) and homa (fire offering ritual) are popular. Newar Buddhists perform several kinds of homas such as Śirāhutihoma and Māṃsāhutihoma.

In August 1994, I had the opportunity to observe one of the most popular homa rituals in Newar Buddhism called Sahasrāhutihoma (one thousand offering homa ritual). Newar Buddhist priests perform Sahasrāhutihoma in various occasions such as the time of the construction of stūpas and the celebration of one's seventy-seventh birthday.

This paper contains the description of the Sahasrāhutihoma performed by a Newar Buddhist priest, Rev. Ratnakajī Vajrācārya, on the second of August 1994. In that year, his first and second sons were married. The homa was performed in order to ask for the happiness of the new couples.

2. *The Sahasrāhutihoma*

The Sahasrāhutihoma was performed at the house of Rev. Ratnakajī

Vajrācārya, which is situated in the Demelohn area near Svayambhūnāth Temple. The house was three-storied, and the homa was performed in the second son's room on the third floor. On that day, I visited the house at seven o'clock in the morning. At that time, the fireplace was already placed in the center of the room.

Rev. Ratnakajī was drawing a vajra, a flag, a sword and the like in the eight directions on the fireplace. It is believed that eight guardian deities (Skt. dikpāla or lokapāla) protect the eight directions of the fireplace. The vajra, the flag, etc. are symbols of the guardian deities. After completing these drawings, Rev. Ratnakajī placed thirty-two small clay vessels (Nw. sali), in which thirty-two kinds of grains and beans were placed for offerings. By eight o'clock, the fireplace, offerings and utensils were set for the ceremony (Fig. 1).[1]

The Sahasrāhutihoma was performed on that day according to the following procedure. The guru, or priest, who mainly performed the ritual was Rev. Ratnakajī Vajrācārya. The yajamāna, or

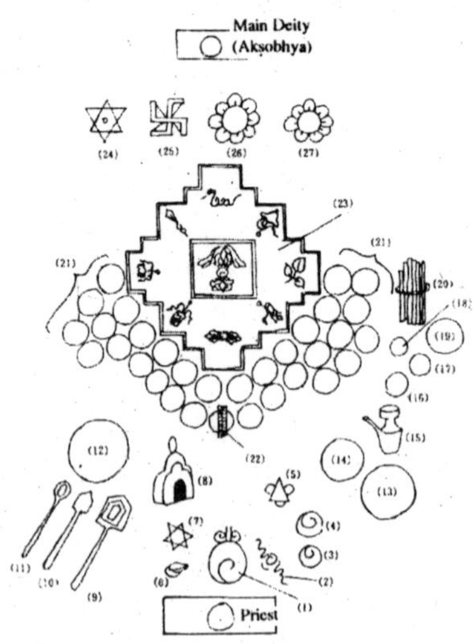

(1) Gurumaṇḍala (2) Spāṃya goja (3) Vessel of pañcāmṛta (pātra) (4) Five kinds of cow products (pañcagavya) (5) Lamp (mata) (6) Conch shell (śaṅkha) (7) samādhibali (8) Crown (mukuṭa) (9) Sulpā ladle (10) Catvā ladle (11) Dhagaḥ ladle (12) Container of incense (13) Container of offerings (14) Plate of fruits (15) Water jar (nīlaḥ thal) (16) Container of clarified butter (17) Container of red powder (18) Container of lamps (19) Goja (a kind of offering made of rice powder in the shape of Mt. Meru) (20) Fuel sticks (sintā) (21) Thirty-two grains and beans (22) Hoṃvī (cigar figured sticks for offering) (23) Fireplace (kuṇḍa) (24) Bali offering (25) Container of yogurt (daupati) (26) Jar (kalaśa) (27) Nāgapan

Fig. 1. Fireplace, utensils, and offerings used in the Sahasrāhutihoma ritual

patron, was his second son Rev. Gautam Ratna Vajrācārya. The priest performed the ritual according to the Sanskrit text named *Kalaśārcanahomavidhi*.[2]

(1) Preliminary Rite: Kalaśārcanapūjā

(1.1) Gurumaṇḍalapūjā

(1.2) Trisamādhi

(1.3) Kalaśapūjā

(2) Main Rite: Homa

(2.1) Purification and Lighting of the Fireplace (Agnisthāpana).

(2.2) Fire Offering (āhuti) to the Fire God Agni (Agnyāhuti).

(2.3) Fire Offering to the Main Deity.

(2.4) Bali Offering (Balipūjā), Worship of Holy Places (Pīṭhādipūjā) and Sacred Places located in the Eight Directions (Cākrapūjā).

(2.5) Purification of Disciples (Śiṣyādhivāsana).

(2.6) Filling the Fireplace with Offerings (Pūrṇāhuti).

(2.7) Offering the Remainders of Oblations (Śeṣāhuti).

(2.8) Sending forth the Gods (Visarjana).

(1) Preliminary Rite: Kalaśārcanapūjā (8:09 a.m. ~ 9:01 a.m.)

The preliminary rite of the Sahasrāhutihoma, Kalaśārcanapūjā, consists of three rituals: (1.1) Gurumaṇḍalapūjā, (1.2) Trisamādhi, and (1.3) Kalaśapūjā. Gurumaṇḍalapuja is the most fundamental ritual in Newar Buddhism. Newar Buddhist priests perform the Gurumaṇḍalapūjā before all other rituals.

In the Gurumaṇḍalapūjā, the priest first draws a small circle, which is the symbol of the Gurumaṇḍala. In Newar Buddhism, the deity Vajrasattva is considered as a master (guru) of Newar Buddhist priests. In this ritual, the priest invites Vajrasattva into the Gurumaṇḍala and offers flowers, incense and the like to the deity.

During my observation, after sipping water for the purification of his body, the priest, Rev. Ratnakajī declared the date and the purpose of the Sahasrāhutihoma. At that time, the family members of the yajamāna silently touched the vessel in which offerings such as flowers, incense and so on were (Fig. 2).

Then the priest dropped flowers into the Gurumaṇḍala reciting, "Oṃ, I salute the central Mount Meru (Oṃ madhyamerave namaḥ)", "Oṃ, I salute the fine Mount Meru (oṃ sūkṣmamerave

Fig. 2. Declaration in the Gurumaṇḍalapūjā

namaḥ)", etc. This action was done in order to establish the world on the Gurumaṇḍala where Mt. Meru is the center. Then he offered the Gurumaṇḍala to Vajrasattva. At the end of the Gurumaṇḍalapūjā, he offered rice and flowers to the guardian deities.

After the Gurumaṇḍalapūjā, the second ritual Trisamādhi began. Trisamādhi consists of the three processes of meditation of the maṇḍala. The three processes are (1) Ādiyogasamādhi (Meditation of the First Yoga), (2) Maṇḍalarājāgrīsamādhi (Meditation of Highest King of the Maṇḍala), and (3) Karmarājāgrīsamādhi (Meditation of Highest King of the Ritual) or Sūkṣmayogasamādhi (Meditation of the Fine Yoga). On the day, in the Trisamādhi of the Sahasrāhutihoma, the meditations and the offering worship of the Cakrasaṃvaramaṇḍala were performed.

After Trisamādhi, the third ritual Kalaśapūjā began. In Kalaśapūjā, the priest invites the main deity, who becomes the main god in the main rite Homa, into the jar (kalaśa) put on the figure of the lotus. Kalaśapūjā is performed in order to invite the deity to the ritual place and make him stay there during the performance of Sahasrāhutihoma.

In Kalaśapūjā, the priest first meditated on a jar, which was transformed from the letter (bīja) ā and made of various kinds of jewels. He then offered sindūra, milk, fruits, etc. to the goddess Kaṇḍarohā and asked her to take away all the obstacles for the yajamāna. After that, he handed a five-colored string to the yajamāna, while holding one end. The yajamāna put the string's other end on the jar, in which the main deity was invited (Fig. 3). This act mean that the priest tries to identify himself with the main god, or that the main god comes to the priest through the five-colored string. Kalaśārcanapūjā ended with this act.

Fig. 3. Identifying the priest with the main god

(2) *Main Rite: Homa* (*9:02 a.m. ~ 11:00 a.m.*)

The main rite, Homa, contains two kinds of fire offerings: one to the fire god Agni, and the other to the main deity. The Homa, however, is not only a fire offering, but it also contains some offering worship (pūjā). Therefore, homa rituals in Newar Buddhism are often called homapūjā.

2.1 *Purification and Lighting of the Fireplace* (*Agnisthāpana*)

First, the priest touched the center of the fireplace, reciting "oṃ Vajrasattva āḥ" three times. Next, the yajamāna placed a substitution for kuśa grass in the form of a swastika inside the fireplace for purification. At that time, the priest asked the kuśa grass, which is identified with the god Brahmā here, to take away all the obstacles for the yajamāna.

After the purification of the fireplace, the priest handed the fuel sticks (Nw. soṃsi) to the yajamāna. The yajamāna arranged them in parallel crosses. Then the priest put another kind of fuel stick (Nw. sintā) on the small clay vessel and lit the sticks. After receiving the small vessel, the yajamāna lit the fuel sticks placed in the center of the fireplace. At that time, the priest meditated upon Samayāgni (the fire god of promise) after reciting a prayer asking for accomplishment of the yajamāna's desires.

2.2 *Fire Offering to the Fire God Agni* (*Agnyāhuti*)

After lighting the fireplace, Agnyāhuti, which is the fire offering to the fire god Agni started. In the Śrauta homa, from which Buddhist Tantric homa was originated, the clarified butter (ghī) is offered into the fire several times. The offering to Agni here is similar to the one of Śrauta homa.

First, the priest worshipped eight guardian gods, who are considered to reside at the eight corners of the fireplace, with rice, water in a conch shell, red powder (sindūra), popped rice and a lamp. Next, the priest put the clarified butter in a ladle called dhagaḥ and handed the dhagaḥ ladle to the yajamāna. The yajamāna melted the butter with the fire of the fireplace. Then the priest took another ladle called catvā in his right hand. With it, he stirred the clarified butter in the dhagaḥ ladle, which is in the yajamāna's hand, reciting "oṃ śrīḥ svāhā" one hundred eight times.

After the butter in the dhagaḥ ladle was melted completely, the yajamāna looked into the butter, which had become transparent, in order to reflect his face in the butter. At that time, the priest recited a prayer to burn all the sins of the yajamāna. Here the yajamāna imagined that his sins should melt into the butter, which reflects like a mirror.

Then, the priest received the dhagaḥ ladle from the yajamāna. Next, he put butter from the dhagaḥ ladle into the catvā ladle, poured the butter from the catvā ladle into the fire three times, and recited "Oṃ, for the god Agni, svāhā" (Fig. 4). Then he offered hoṃvī, in which eighteen kinds of fuel sticks are rolled in the figure of a cigar, to the god Agni.

After offering hoṃvī, the priest took grains and beans with the sulpā ladle and offered them into the fire. Then the priest put butter in the sulpā ladle. After reciting "This offering is for the god Agni, who carries offerings to the gods and ancestors.

Fig. 4. Offering the butter to the god Agni

Accept the offering for Agni", he poured butter into the fire. Then he offered two balls made of rice powder named hoja boja (Skt. proḍāśa) into the fire.

After that, the priest meditated on Jñānāgni (the fire god of knowledge). Later on, he meditated that Jñānāgni should be united with Samayāgni, which was meditated upon in the previous process, namely, Agnisthāpana. After the meditation, the priest offered grains and beans. At the same time, the yajamāna put the fuel sticks (sintā) into the fire.

2.3 *Fire Offering to the Main Deity*

After the offering to the god Agni, the offering to the main god, Akṣobhya started. The offering here consists of three parts: (2.3.1) Worship of the Main Deity (Devapūjā), (2.3.2) Fire Offering to the Main Deity (Devatāhuti), and (2.3.3) One Thousand Offerings to the Main Deity (Sahasrāhuti).

In the first process, namely, Devapūjā, the yajamāna put incense in front of the image of Akṣobhya Buddha. Next, he put the small plate, consisting of flowers, milk and butter, before the image. After that, he dropped pañcāmṛta (here he used beaten rice sprinkled with sugar) into the small plate. During this, the priest recited the mantra for the consecration (abhiṣeka). Next, the yajamāna sprinkled purification water on his family members.

After the worship of the main deity, the second process, namely, Devatāhuti started. First, the yajamāna threw grains and beans into the fireplace. The priest melted the clarified butter in the dhagaḥ ladle. Next, he declared the purpose of the Devatāhuti, holding both sulpā ladle and dhagaḥ ladle in his right hand. After declaring this, the priest then poured butter into the fire. At the same time, the yajamāna offered flowers and popped rice to the main god. After that, the priest recited the mantra of one hundred syllables.

After the fire offering to the main deity, the one thousand offerings (sahasrāhuti), which is core of the Sahasrāhutihoma, started. The priest filled a brass plate with beaten rice and puts a kind of barley (Nw. tacho) on it. Then he placed a red cloth and a bill as an offering on it. The red cloth is called Kasāy-gā in Newari (Skt. kaṣāyavastra). He then handed the brass plate to the yajamāna. Next, he declared the date and the purposes of the Kasāy-gā-āhuti (fire offering to the red cloth) and the Sahasrāhuti. After this declaration, he poured butter into the fire, while the yajamāna threw the grains and beans into the fire.

Then, the priest put on the red cloth. According to Rev. Gautam Ratna Vajrācārya, the priest gets divine power by wearing the red cloth. Next, the priest mixed beaten rice, black sesame, barley, clarified butter and milk on a plate for offering into the fire. Reciting the mantra, the priest offered the mixture into the fire many times (Fig. 5). This is the main act in the Sahasrāhutihoma. After the offering of the mixture of beaten rice and the like, the priest put the clarified butter into the sulpā ladle. While holding the ladle in his right hand, he recited the mantra of one hundred syllables. At that time, the yajamāna silently joined his palms together.

2.4 *Bali Offering* (*Balipūjā*), *Worship of Holy Places* (*Pīṭhādipūjā*) *and Sacred Places Located in the Eight Directions* (*Cākrapūjā*)

After the Sahasrāhuti ended, the Bali offering (Balipūjā) started. Here the Bali offering, which consists of cooked rice, beans, etc.

Fig. 5. Sahasrāhuti

was offered to lokapālas, goddesses yoginīs and ḍākinīs. They are believed to come to the ritual place accompanying the main deity. In the Balipūjā, the priest first meditated upon the Bali as a deity. By meditating on it, divine power is added to the Bali. Next, the priest recited the hymn to the goddesses, while the yajamāna poured the beer into the Bali.

Next, the worship of holy places started. First, the yajamāna and his younger brother went up to the rooftop, holding gojas (a kind of offering made with rice powder), incense, flowers and the like in their hands. On the rooftop, they put the gojas in the four corners of the terrace and stuck the incense into each goja. It is believed that there are eight sacred places at the eight directions of Kathmandu. For example, there is Svayambhūnāth Temple in the west and Bījeśvari Temple in the east. Here the yajamāna and his brother worshipped those eight sacred places.

2.5 *Purification of Disciples* (*Śiṣyādhivāsana*)

After the worship of the sacred places, the purification of the disciples was performed. Here the family members of the yajamāna were recognized as disciples of the priest. First, yajamāna's younger brother placed a lamp on the bell, which was turned upside-down. Then he took it to each member of the yajamāna's family. After this the priest recited the hymn of Aṣṭamātṛkās, such as Brahmāyanī and Indrāyanī, who are considered to protect the eight directions of Kathmandu Valley. At the same time, family members threw rice into the fireplace. After that, the yajamāna's younger brother put flowers into the bell. Then he touched the members with the bell (Fig. 6).

2.6 *Filling the Fireplace with Offerings* (*Pūrṇāhuti*)

After the purification of the disciples, the fire offering for filling the fireplace with offerings (pūrṇāhuti) began. In Newar Buddhism, most of the rituals end with Bali offerings. In the Sahasrāhutihoma, however, some additional fire offerings follow the Bali offering. Here thirty-two kinds of medicinal plants and seeds are offered into the fire, in addition to the grains, beans and hoṃvīs.

While reciting the mantra, the priest put the medicinal plants

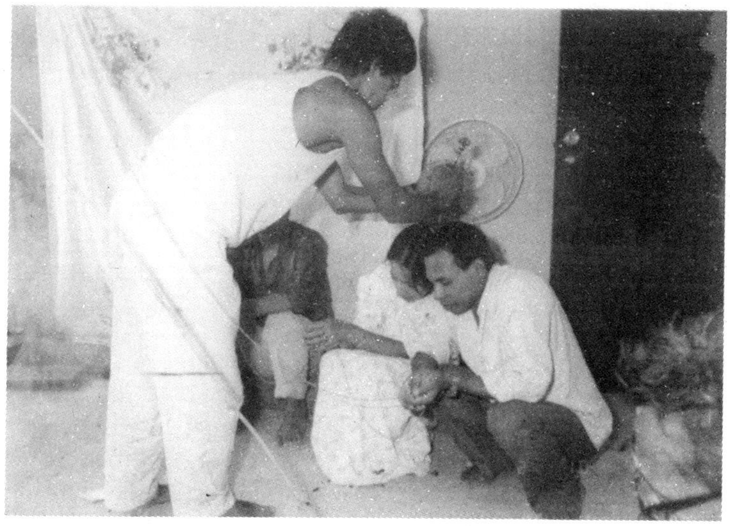

Fig. 6. A Scene of Śiṣyādhivāsana

and seeds, which were put in a basket called dhaki, into the fireplace (Fig. 7). The priest then threw grains and beans with the catvā ladle. After putting a red-colored pūrī (a kind of bread), hoṃvī, clarified butter and a ring on the sulpā ladle, the priest recited the mantra. Then family members of the yajamāna gave money as an offering to the priest. In return, the priest put the tikas on the foreheads of the members.

2.7 *Offering the Remainders of Oblations* (*Śeṣāhuti*)

2.8 *Sending forth the Gods* (*Visarjana*)

After the Pūrṇāhuti, the remnants of the offerings such as grains and beans were offered to the fire to clean the place of the ritual. In the Agnyāhuti, the priest meditated that Samayāgni and Jñānāgni should be united. Here the priest meditated that he should draw the maṇḍala of Agni, who was united in the previous process, into his own body. Next, the priest put the clarified butter into the sulpā ladle and put flowers into it. Then, holding the ladle in his hand, the priest recited a prayer asking that all creatures should be happy. After reciting the prayer, he poured butter into the fire.

At the same time, the yajamāna offered all remaining grains and beans to the fire. After the priest offered five kinds of offerings to the fireplace, he performed the hand gestures of

Fig. 7. A Scene of Pūrṇāhuti

the sixteen worshipping goddesses (ṣoḍaśalāsyāmudrā), and recited the hymns. In the end, the priest recited the words for sending off all the Buddhas, gods, goddesses who were invited into the ritual place, together with their families.

3. Conclusion

The Sahasrāhutihoma is one of the most popular rituals in Newar Buddhism. The Sahasrāhutihoma consists of two parts: the Kalaśārcanapūjā and the Homa. The latter contains not only the fire offerings, but also some offering worships (pūjās), in which five kinds of offerings and the like are offered to the main deity and guardian deities. In the Śrauta Homa rituals, from which the Buddhist Tantric homa is originated, the clarified butter is offered into the fire, In the Sahasrāhutihoma here, various kinds of raw materials such as grains, beans, and medicinal plants are offered in addition to the clarified butter.

In the Agnisthāpana of the Homa, the priest meditates upon Samayāgni. Then, in the Agnyāhuti he meditates upon Jñānāgni. After this, he unites Samayāgni and Jñānāgni. Finally, the priest draws the unity of Samayāgni and Jñānāgni into his body in the Śeṣāhuti. The concepts of Samayāgni and Jñānāgni are based upon two famous concepts of Buddhist Tantric realization (sādhana): Samayasattva and Jñānasattva. The realizations and the uniting of Samayāgni and Jñānāgni are found in the Indian Buddhist Tantric text such as the *Saṃvarodayatantra*.[3] However, the meditation of drawing the unity of Samayāgni and Jñānāgni into one's body is not mentioned in the *Saṃvarodayatantra*. The system of the realization of Samayāgni and Jñānāgni in Newar Buddhism needs to be further studied in detail.

NOTES

1. Fig. 1 was drawn based on Ratnakajī Vajrācārya, *Yeṃ Deya Bauddha Pūjā Kriyā yā Halaṃjvalaṃ*. Nepal Bauddha Prakashan, Kathmandu, 1980, p.10. Fig. 2, 3, 4, 5, 6, 7 are the photographs taken in cooperation with Prof. Musashi Tachikawa and Mr. Kenji Yokota.
2. Amoghavajra Vajrācārya (ed.), *Kalaśārcanahomavidhi*, Vajrācārya Saṃgha, Kathmandu, 1980.
3. Shinichi Tsuda, *The Saṃvarodayatantra*, The Hokuseido Press, Tokyo, 1974, p.139.

CHAPTER 54

The Vāstunāga Ritual Described in Tsong-kha-pa's *sNgags-rim chen-po*

MASAHIDE MORI

This article presents the Tibetan text and its translation of the part concerning *vāstunāga* (serpent of building site) ritual in Tsong-kha-pa's *sNgags-rim chen-po*.

Abbreviations

G: Tsong-kha-pa Blo-bzang grags-pa, *rGyal-ba khyab-bdag rdo rje 'chang chen-po'i lam-gyi rim-pa, gSang-ba kun-gyi gnad mam-par phye-ba (sNgags-rim chen-po),* The Collected Works (gSuṅ 'bum) of rJe Tsoṅ-kha-pa Blo-bzaṅ-grags-pa, Vols. 4, 5, Gedan Sungrab Minyam Gyunphel Series, Vols. 82-83. New Delhi, Ngawan Gelek Demo, 1975.

P: —,—, TibetanTripiṭaka, the Peking Edition, No. 6210, Vol. 161, 53.1.1-226.2.7.

TTP: Tibetan Tripiṭaka, the Peking Edition, Tokyo, Suzuki Foundation.

Remarks on Text and Translation

1. The Tibetan text is based on two blockprints: P and G. The

corresponding part appears in 103.3.7-104.5.2 (P) and 281.2-288.6 (G).

(2. The numbering system (e. g. <1.3.1.2>) follows M. Mori, "The Synopsis of the Consecration Ceremony in the *sNgags-rim chen-po* (Chapters V-X)". *Mikkyo Bunka (Journal of Esoteric Buddhism)* 199/200, 1998, pp.1-19.

(3) In the Tibetan text, the bold words indicate personal names and the bold italic words indicates text titles.

(4) The numbers in ( ) indicates the pagination of P.

(5) The passages and sentences in < > indicate the quotations from other works.

(6) I provide supplementary word(s) in [ ] in the translation.

Tibetan Text

< 1.3.1.2> gnyis pa la gsum / lto 'phye gang la brtag cing gnas pa dang rgyu ba'i tshul dang / de shes nas ji ltar brko ba'i tshul dang / brkos legs nyes kyi skyon yon bstan pa'o //

<1.3.1.2.1> dang po ni / lto 'phye brtag par ***rDo rje mkha' 'gro*** las gsungs shing / **Mi thub zla ba** dang **A bhya** dang **Pradznyā rakṣi ta** dang **Ratna rakṣi ta** dang **Nyin mo 'byung gnas** dang **De bzhin gshegs pa'i rdo rje** sogs kyi ***dkyil chog*** las kyang brtag par bshad do //

lto 'phye brtag pa gang la dgos pa ni / ***rDo rje mkha' 'gro*** las/

<gtsug lag khang dang khang bzang dang // mchod rten dkyil 'khor grong khyer dang //

khyim dang ldum ra la sogs la // lto 'phye'i lto bar brko ba dang //>

zhes gsungs shing ***Phreng bar*** dgon gnas byed pa la yang brtag par bshad do // **Bi bhū tī'i** ***dkyil chog*** las kyang/ <lha khang mchod rten khang bzang khang brtsegs dang / rab gnas dkyil chog la sogs byed 'dod pas // 'dir ni sa yi lto 'phye brtag bya ste//> zhes gsungs pas / 'di brtag pa ni mang po zhig la mkho bar snang ngo // de la dkyil 'khor gyi khang pa byed pa la ni nges par dgos la / sngar bshad pa ltar brkos nas sbyangs te dkyil 'khor gyi stegs bu byed pa la yang dgos so // sa brko ba'i sngon du sngar bshad pa ltar< sa gzhi bgegs dang bral bar byas nas gtor ma byin te sa bdag klu brtag par > gsungs pa ltar bya'o // 'dir ***Phreng ba*** las < rdo rje khu tshur gyis thig skud bzung ste/

sgrub grogs dang bcas pas g'yas skor gyi 'gros kyis slob dpon me dang rlung du gnas la shar dang nub dang byang dang lho phyogs kyi thig btab nas /> < gtsug lag khang la sogs pa gang du byed pa'i gzhi de gru bzhir byas te /> < ston zla gsum la sogs pa zla ba gsum gsum du rim pa bzhin shar lho nub byang rnams su mgo bstan cing lho la sogs par kha phyogs nas nyal ba brtags te /> < nyi ma shar ba nas brtsams nas klu'i mchan[1] las khru gang dor ba'i mchan[2] gyi char g'yas skor du rtsig rmang brko bar bya > zhes rags pa tsam zhig las ma gsungs kyang / **Bi bhū tīs** shib par gsungs pa (P 103.5) ltar bshad na / gzhi gang yin gru bzhir byas la de'i phyogs bzhi po re rer yang zla ba gsum gyi zhag grangs dang mthun par re'u[3] mig dgu bcu re bya'o //

de la lto 'phye gnas pa dang rgyu ba'i tshul ni / ston zla ra ba'i tshes gcig la mgo byang shar gyi mtshams kyi re'u mig tu bzhag nas mjug rtse lho nub kyi re'u mig tu bzhag ste kha lhor bltas nas gnas so // de nas zhag re song ba na mgos lho ngos su re'u mig re dang mjug rtse byang ngos su re'u mig re bgrod nas g'yas skor gyis 'pho'o // zla ba gsum la phyogs re'u re'u mig dgu bcu re bgrod pas lo gcig la phyogs bzhi'i re'u mig dgu bcu pa phrag bzhi kha[4] 'khor ro //

de yang gzhogs g'yon 'og tu bcug nas nyal ba'i gdengs ka nas mjug rtse'i bar la mtho bcu yod la mtho re re'u[5] mig dgu re non pas phyogs dang mtshams gang du gnas pa'i tshe yang re'u mig dgu bcu re non no // lus kyi zheng gis ni sa'i re'u mig gi cha dgu khyab par nyal zhing gsang gnas ni phyogs mtshams gang la gnas pa'i tshe na'ang de'i dbus su bzhag nas gnas te / **Bi bhū tī'i** ***dkyil chog*** las

<sa gzhi gang yin de ni gru bzhir bya // zla ba gsum gyi nyin mo'i grangs kyis 'dir //

phyogs ni so sor sa de rnam par dbye // dbang ldan nas ni me yi mtshams kyi bar //

shar gyi sa de dgu bcur rnam par dbyed // me nas bden bral mtshams kyi bar dang ni //

bden bral nas ni rlung gi mtshams bar dang // rlung nas 'byung po'i bdag po'i mtshams kyi bar //

de bzhin kho nar dgu bcur rnam dbye bya //

ston zla ra ba 'bring dang tha ma'i bar // dbang ldan mtshams la sogs par mgo bo gnas //

bden bral mtshams la sogs par mjug ma'i cha // gsang ba'i gnas ni sa yi dbus su gzhag[6] //

lte ba'i 'og (104.1) gi cha ni lto 'phye'i lus // steng cha gdengs ka dang ldan mi yi gzugs //

lhor lta lag pa g'yon pa rna bar bzhag // g'yas pa rin chen[7] thogs pas dkur bkab nas //

sa yi cha dgu khyab[8] par nyal nas gnas // klu yi rgyal po[9] lus tshad mtho bcu pa'o //

shar dang nub kyi mtha' mar gnas na yang // sa yi dum[10] bu de ni 'jal ba ltar //

nyi ma'i bgrod pas tshes gcig la sogs par // nyin zhag re re zhing ni cha re rer //

ji ltar rigs pas shar gyi cha ru rgyu // lho dang nub dang byang du'ang de bzhin no //

dgun zla ra ba 'bring dang tha ma yi // dkar phyogs la sogs nub tu kha mig lta //

me yi mtshams su yan lag mchog bstan te // rlung gi mtshams la sogs par mjug ma gnas //

dpyid zla ra ba 'bring dang tha ma de'i // gnod sbyin bdag phyogs[11] kha dang mig gis lta /

bden bral mtshams la sogs par mgo bo gnas // dbang ldan mtshams la sogs par mjug ma'i cha //

dbyar zla ra ba 'bring dang tha ma ru // shar phyogs su ni kha dang mig gis lta //

rlung gi mtshams la sogs par mgo bo gnas // me yi mtshams la sogs par mjug ma'i cha //

lo gcig la ni sa gzhi mtha' dag tu // 'khor gcig gis ni 'bad pas kun tu khyab //>

ces so //

gzhan yang klu chen po brgyad kyang de'i mjug rtse sogs gnas brgyad na gnas te / ***de nyid*** las /

<lto 'phye'i rgyal po'i rgyu ba'i dbye ba ni // zla ba re re'i bye brag shes nas su //

mtha' yas bdag nyid dkar po mdzes pa'i sku // mjug ma la sogs rim gyis bsams nas su //

de yi lus la klu yi bdag po brgyad // 'o ma la sogs nye bar spyod pas mchod //

mjug ma'i rtse mor rigs ldan shin tu sngo // gsang gnas dur ba ltar ljang stobs[12] kyi rgyu //

lte bar dung (104.2) skyong padma'i rtsa ba bzhin // dpung bar padma chen po gser dang mtshungs //

nor rgyas snying gar gnas pa ljang khu ste // 'jog po zhes bya dmar po mgrin par gnas //

rna bar padma dkar po'i 'od zer can // spyi bo ru ni mtha' yas sngon po gnas // >

zhes so // lto 'phye yang mtha' yas yin te mdog dkar la mdzes pa'o //

'o na sa gzhi che chung gang yin yang des de ltar khyab nas nyal ba ji ltar yin snyam na / bod kyi bla ma dag zla ba shar ba'i gzugs brnyan snod che chung gi chu nang du snang ba dang 'dra bas mi 'gal bar 'chad mod kyang mi 'thad de / lto 'phye gcig nyid kyis sa'i cha kun tu de ltar khyab pa ni 'gal la rang gi ngo bo gcig yin yang sa so so la gzugs brnyan so sor shar ba yang ma bshad pa'i phyir ro // des na gang du brkos pas sa bdag la mi 'phrod pa 'ong ba dang mi 'ong ba'i gnas shes pa'i phyir du sa che chung gang yin pa'i gzhi der rtog lugs de 'dra zhig gsungs kyi gar rtog pa'i sa thams cad du de ltar gnas mi dgos so //

< 1.3.1.2.2 >gnyis pa ni / 'o na thog mar brko ba'i gnas de gang yin snyam na / ***de nyid*** las /

< shar nas cha ni nyi shu rtsa bdun dor // byang nas phyed dang bcu bzhi'i cha dor bar //

shar nub cha dgu lho byang phyed dang lnga // 'di ni mchan[13] gyi mdun du thog mar brko //>

zhes gsungs so //

de'i don ni mgo shar du bstan pa'i dbang du byas na mgos re'u mig gang non pa'i phyogs de nas nub tu re'u mig dgu gsum nyer bdun dor pa'i bar la brkor mi rung bas / mtshams de nas nub tu re'u mig dgu dang rgyab kyi lus kyis non pa'i sa nas mdun du re'u mig phyed dang bcu bzhi'i bar la brkor mi rung bas mtshams de nas lhor re'u mig phyed dang lnga ni dang por brko ba'i dmigs so // de ni mchan[14] gyi mdun du bshed pas mchan[15] gyi (104.3) thad du re'u mig dgu spangs par brko ba'i lugs so //

Phreng ba las khru gang spangs pa'i[16] mchan gyi thad du brko ba’i rang lugs dang mthong ba’i thad kar brko ba’i gzhan lugs gnyis bshad do // ***sDom ’byung ’grel pa*** las /

<mgo’i phyogs la re’u mig nyi shu’am nyi shu rtsa gcig dang lto bar yang re’u mig gnyis sam gsum yongs su spangs te rgyab dang mjug ma yang nges par byas nas lto bar brko bar bya ste/> zhes gsungs te / lus kyi mgo mjug gis re’u mig dgu bcu non[17] pa dang ’gal mi ’gal brtag go //

<gdengs ka la ni zhal gang ste // zhal la cha phran dgu ru shes //

de ltar mgrin dang thugs ka nyid // lte ba la ni de yi tshad //

de nas mtshan ma’ang de tsam yin // lhag ma lto ’phye’i rnam pa’o //>

zhes zer ba bzhin du lus tshad nges par bya zhes gsung ba ni gsang gnas sa’i dbus su ’ong ba’i lugs dang ’gal lam[18] snyam mo // de ’dra ba’i lto ’phye bsams la ’o ma la sogs pa’i mchod pas mchod/ rko mkhan bgegs mthar byed du bskyed / tog tse rdo rjes mtshan par bsam lag pa g’yas steng dang g’yon ’og tu byas la bzung ste[19] kha shar dang byang du blta / ’jor kham bzhi brgyab pa’i sa blangs nas zhi ba’i sems kyis gtor ma’i nang du blug pa’am me mtshams la sogs pa’i phyi rol tu dor bar bya’o// kham lnga brgyab pa’i sa ni / sa de’i dbus su dgram de’i rjes nas phyogs mtshams kun tu las mi thams cad kyis brkos pas chog ste / **Bi bhū tīs** /

< mi ni bgegs mthar byed kyi rnam par bsgom // dpa’ po’i lag pa tog tse rdo rjes mtshan //

lag pa g’yon pa ’og tu byas nas gzung // de yis bdud kyi tshogs ni skrag cing zlog[20] //

shar dang byang gi phyogs su kha bltas pas // tog tse kham bzhi brgyab pas blangs pa’i sa //

zhi ba’i sems kyis gtor ma’i nang du ni // gzhag pa’am me mtshams la sogs phyi rol dor // (104.4)

’bad pas de yi kham lnga pa yi sa // sa gzhi’i dbus su legs pa’i yid kyis dgram //

kham lnga pa der las mi du ma yis // phyogs dang mtshams su kun nas brko bar bya //>

zhes so //

< 1.3.1.2.3 > gsum pa ni / sngar bshad pa ltar gyi gnas su brkos

na ni / chos dang nor dang 'dod don thams cad 'grub cing 'phel bar 'gyur la de las gzhan pa'i gnas su brkos na ni / nyes dmigs mang po 'byung ste ***de nyid*** las /

< de yis chos nor 'dod dong 'phel zhing 'grub // gal te lto 'phye'i rgyal po gnas pa yi //

cha dgu'i sa yi cha la brkos na ni // pha ma bu dang bu mo spun[21] chung ma //

mna' ma rang gi skye bo mdza' bshes 'chi // gal te rgyab tu brkos na rang 'chi zhing //

yang na rang gnas nas 'pho nor brlag 'gyur // mjug mar glang chen rta dang ma he ra //

ba lang 'chi zhing slobs kyang nyams par 'gyur // gal te kham lnga'i nang du shing dang skra //

grog mkhar skra sen thal bas good pa 'byung // rdo bas rlung gi 'jigs pa phub ma dang //

mgal dum gyis rims[22] rus pas zug gzer ro //>

zhes so //

kham lnga'i sa'i nang du shing la sogs pa byung na skyon skyed par gsungs pa ni / ma bsal ba'i nyes pa yin gyi yod pa tsam gyi min te / ***Phreng ba*** nas sngar ltar gsungs pa yang lto 'phye brtags nas brkos pa'i sa la gsungs pa dang / **Bi bhū tīs** kyang / <de nas rdo ba la sogs pa bsal te sa de nyid kyis sam des mi ldang na gzhan gyi sa la yang dri bzang gi chus btab ste dong dgang bar bya'o //> zhes sa'i zug rngu de dag bsal nas bya bar gsungs kyi / de las gzhan du spo ba'am mtshan ma ngan pa bzlog pa'i thabs ma bshad pa'i phyir ro // **Nyin mo 'byung gnas** kyis kyang /

< gal te zug mgu de[23] ma bsal // nyes pa dag ni skyed par 'gyur //>

zhes dang /

< zug rngu legs gsal des ni nyon mongs (104.5) ma lus sel //>

zhes lto 'phye brtags nas brkos pa'i sa la gsungs pa'i phyir ro// **Pradznārakṣitas** dngos grub kyi don du brko ba dang sa bdag brtags nas brko ba gnyis so sor bshad la / ***Phreng ba*** dang **Ratnarakṣitas** de gnyis 'jug pa gcig tu byas pa ni / dkyil 'khor gyi skabs la dgongs pas de las gzhan pa'i sa bdag brtags nas brko ba'i skabs su dngos grub gsum gyi don du brko ba'i tshul rnams mi dngos so //

Variant readings

1. P mtshan. 2. P mtshan. 3. P ri'u. P *reads* ri'u *for* re'u *in the following paragraphs.* 4. P ga. 5. P mtho res ri'u. 6. P bzhag. 7. P cen. 8. P khyad. 9. P bdag po. 10. G dus. 11. P phyegs. 12. P stebs. 13. P mtshan. 14. P mtshan. 15. P mtshan. 16. P spang ba'i. 17. G nan. 18. P la ma.19. G bzungs te. 20. P bzlog. 21. G span. 22. P rim. 23. G re.

Translation

<1.3.1.2.> As for the second, there are three [topics]: (1) where the serpent(= *vāstunāga)* is to be examined, its location and the manner of shifting, (2) after understanding it, the manner of how to dig up [the ground], and (3) showing the merit and demerit of auspicious or inauspicious [features in] the place dug out.

<1.3.1.2.1.> The first: the *Vajraḍākā-tantra* states that the serpent is to be examined[1], and the ritual texts by Durjayacandra, Abhaya[ākaragupta], Prajñārakṣita, Ratnarakṣita, Divākaracandra and Tathāgatavajra also state that [it is to be] examined[2].

Where the examination of the serpent is necessary, the *Vajraḍāka-tantra* says: "In a monastery, religious hall (*gandhakūṭī*), *stūpa, maṇḍala,* town, house, garden and others, dig at the belly of the serpent and..."[3]; the *Vajrāvalī* insists on examining the serpent where a monastery is constructed. Vibhūti[candra]'s *Maṇḍalavidhi* also states, "one who wishes to [construct] a shrine, *stūpa,* religious hall, or mansion, and perform the installation ceremony (*pratiṣṭhā*) or the *maṇḍala* ritual, should examine the serpent of the ground there"[4], therefore it is obvious that its examination is necessary in many cases. [The examination] is certainly necessary where the house of *maṇḍala* (*maṇḍalagṛha*) is to be constructed, it is also necessary when the *maṇḍala* altar is to be made after having dug out [the ground] and purified it, as mentioned above.

Before digging out the ground, as stated above, one should perform [the following] as [the *Vajrāvalī*] says in order to expel the impediments from the site, perform the oblation and examine the serpent[5]. As to this the *Vajrāvalī* provides an outline summary as follows: "After having held the thread with the *vajra*-fist, the *ācārya,* standing in the southeast then northwest corners, draws lines in the east, west, north and south directions respectively, shifting clockwise with an assistant[6]. After having the place where the monastery or other is to be constructed measured out in a square[7], one should examine the *vāstunāga* which lies [on the site] directing its head to the east, south, west and north in turn, respectively facing south etc., every three months starting with Bhādra month.[8] Starting [the process] at sunrise, he is to dig up a place onecubit (*hasta*) apart from the side of *nāga*'s breast in a clockwise direction for the foundation [of the building]"[9].

However, as Vibhūti[candra] explains in detail, we shall show that after measuring any place square, each side is to be divided into ninety parts in accordance with the number of days in the corresponding three months.

In that case, *vāstunāga*'s location and the manner of shifting are [as follows]. On the first day of Bhādra month, it faces the south with its head located in the north-eastern corner unit and its tail in the south-western corner unit. It then shifts the direction of its head southwards daily one unit at a time, and its tail one unit northwards in a clockwise direction. In three months, it shifts over the ninety units on each side, and in one year it shift over all ninety units on the four sides. This [serpent] lies with the left side of its body down, and it is ten spans (*vitasi*) in length from hood to tail, each span occupying nine units, therefore it occupies ninety units in any direction or corner it faces. The width of its recumbent body occupies ten units, and its secret spot occupies the centre of the site in any direction or corner where [the serpent] lies.

According to Vibhūti[candra]'s *maṇḍalavidhi*,

> "Measure any site square. Divide the site on each side by the number of the days of three months. From the northeast to the southeast, the eastern side of this site should be divided into ninety parts. From the southeast to the southwest, from the southwest to the northwest, from the northwest to the northeast, [each side of the site] should be divided into ninety parts in the same way. In the first, middle and last months of autumn, [the serpent] positions its head from the northeast corner and so on, its tail from the southwest corner and so on, with its secret spot in the centre of the site. The part below the navel takes the form of a serpent; the upper part takes the form of human

> being with a serpent hood. [The serpent] faces south and puts its left hand on its ear and its right hand at the waist holding a jewel pot. The king of serpent lies occupying nine parts of the site, and the length of its body is ten spans. It spreads [its body] between the east side and the west side, as if to measure the parts of the site. In accordance with the movement of the sun, as each day [passes], [the serpent] shifts unit by unit each day. Accordingly, it shifts on the east side, then south, west and north in the same way. In the first, middle and last months of winter, starting from the white half part [of the month], [the serpent] faces west and shows its best part (=head) in the southeast corner, placing its tail in the northwest corner and so on. In the first, middle and last months of spring, [the serpent] looks at the direction of *yakṣa*'s leader (=north) with its face and eyes, placing its head in the southwest corner and so on, and its tail in the northeast corner. In the first, middle and last months of summer, [the serpent] looks east with its face and eyes, placing its head in the northwest corner and so on, and its tail in the southeast corner. In one year [the serpent] makes a circuit of all the corners of the site."[10]

Alternatively, the eight *nāgas* occupy eight places such as the tail point etc. of the serpent. According to the same text (=Vibhūticandra's work),

> "As for the particularities of the shifting of the serpent king, one should know the differences according to each month. One should envisage [the serpent] whose nature is Ananta adorned in white, step by step beginning with the tail. By the offerings of milk etc., worship [the serpent], whose body is occupied by eight *nāgas*. Blue Kulika occupies the tail point, green Karkoṭaka like *dūrvā*-grass occupies the secret spot, Śaṅkapāla like [the white colour] of lotus root occupies the navel, Mahāpadma equal to gold occupies the arms, Māṇibhadra occupying the heart is green, red so-called Takṣaka occupies the neck, Padma with white splendour occupies the ears, blue Ananta occupies the top of the head."[11]

The serpent is also Ananta and is adorned in white.

Then, if one wonder how the serpent occupies and spreads over a site of any size, Tibetan teachers explain that there is no contradiction because it is similar to the situation of the risen moon reflected on the surface of water in vessels of any size. However, this is incorrect, because it is impossible that a single serpent thus occupies all sites, and because [the texts] do not insist that the serpent shows its body separately in each site even though [the serpent] has single nature. Therefore, one does not encounter the serpent when one digs at any site. In order to know an adequate or inadequate site [the Buddha] explains such a method of examining a site of any size. It is not necessary that the serpent occupy all the sites that are to be examined.

<1.3.1.2.2> The second (=the manner of how to dig up [the ground]): then if you consider the place to dig up first, this text (=Vibhūticandra's work) says,

> "Apart from the east side by twenty-seven parts, and from the north side by thirteen and a half parts, [the hole has] nine parts between east and west, and four and half parts between south and north. This is [the hole] in front of the armpit which you should dig up first."[12]

The meaning is thus: for example, when [the serpent] places its head in the east, it is inadequate that one digs up for nine [multiplied] by three, i.e. twenty-seven units from the side, one unit of which the head occupies, to the west, but one [digs up] for nine units from the edge [of the twenty-seven units]. It is inadequate that one digs up for thirteen and a half units in front of the place occupied by the back of the body, but one [digs up] for four and a half units from the edge to the south to begin. This is the [authentic] idea. As was explained regarding [to dig up] in front of the armpit, this is the manner of digging up the place apart from the armpit by nine units.

The *Vajrāvalī* refers to two methods: its own manner of digging up the place apart from the armpit by one cubit, and another manner of [digging up] the place in front of the eyes. The commentary of *Saṃvarodaya-*[*tantra*] says,

"Twenty or twenty-one units away in the direction of the head, two or three units away from the belly, fixing the positions of back and tail, one should dig at the belly."[13]

It should be considered whether this contradicts the fact that the body between head and tail occupies ninety units.

"The face fills the hood, and you should know that the face has nine units. Thus, the throat, breast and navel have the same size. The attribute also has the same size. The remaining parts have the shape of a serpent."[14]

As explained thus, the statement "define the size of the body" seems to contradict the manner of locating the secret spot in the centre of the site.

When such a serpent is envisaged, it is to be worshipped with the offering of milk etc., and then one should conceive of the digging person as Vighnāntaka, who holds a *vajra*-hoe with the right hand upward and the left hand downward. He faces the eastern and northern directions. He takes the soil dug out four times with the blade of the hoe, then he puts it in the oblation with a calm mind, or else he scatters it outside in the southeast corner and so on. The soil dug out the fifth time is to be spread over the centre of the site, and then all the workers may dig from any direction. Vibhūti[candra] says,

> "One should envisage the man as Vighnāntaka. The hero's hands hold a *vajra*-hoe. He holds the left hand downward to dig, by which he terrifies and disperses the group of demons. Facing the eastern and northern directions, he should put the soil dug out by the hoe four times in the oblation with a calm mind, or else he should scatter it outside in the southeast corner and so on. He should spread the soil dug out the fifth time in the centre of the site with a proper mind. From all directions many workers should dig up the place where the soil dug out five times [is scattered]."[15]

<1.3.1.2.3> The third (=showing the merit and demerit of the auspicious or inauspicious [features in] the dug out place): when one digs up the site above mentioned, the teaching, wealth and all purposes will be accomplished and increased, but when one digs out a different place, many disasters will occur. This text (= Vibhūticandra's work) says,

> "The teaching, wealth and all purposes will be accomplished by it. If one digs up the nine parts of the serpent king, father, mother, sons, daughters, brothers, sisters, daughters-

in-law, blood relatives or friends will die. If one digs up its back, he himself will die, or he will be expelled from his own position and his wealth will be confisçated. [If one digs up] the tail, elephants, horses, buffaloes and oxen will die and power will be lost. If there are wood pieces, hairs, anthills, fingernails, ashes in [the soil dug out] five times, harm occurs. A stone causes the danger of wind. A short straw or billet of wood causes epidemic. A bone causes pain."[16]

The statement that if a wood piece or the others are found in the soil [dug out] five times harm will occur does not mean the fault caused by its appearance alone, but the fault caused by neglecting its removal. The reasons are as follows. What the *Vajrāvalī* says above concerns the soil dug out after the examination of the serpent. Vibhūti[candra] also says, "Then after one has removed stones etc., he pours into the hole the [dug out] soil, or if it is insufficient, different soil, on which fragrant water has been scattered."[17] Thus he recommends removing these faults from the soil, but he does not mention moving to another place, or the method of expelling the inauspicious feature. Again, because Divākaracandra also says, "if the faults cannot be removed, evil will occur,"[18] and "by removal of the faults, all the sins will disappear"[19], thus [Divākaracandra] mentions the soil dug out after the examination of the serpent.

Although Prajñārakṣita twice refers to the processes of digging: one for accomplishment (*siddhi*) and the other after the examination of the earth ruler (=*vāstunāga*)[20], the *Vajrāvalī* and Ratnarakṣita combine both together[21], because their intention is the occasion of *maṇḍala*; therefore, when one examines an earth ruler different from it and digs up the site, the process of digging for the purpose of three kinds of accomplishment is not needed.

NOTES

1. See note no. 3.
2. Mi thub zla ba (Dujrayacandra), TTP, No. 2369, Vol. 56, 142.4.2-3; Pradznyārakṣita (Prajñārakṣita), No. 2186, Vol. 51, 263.1.6-7; Ratna rakṣita (Ratnarakṣita), No. 2137, Vol. 51, 95.5.4-8; Nyin mo 'byung gnas (Divākaracandra), No. 2390, Vol. 56, 223.4.2ff. "Abhya" means Abhayākragupta and his work *Vajrāvalī-nāma-maṇḍalopāyikā* (TTP, No.

3961). I cannot identify the work by De bzhin gshegs pa'i rdo rje (Tathāgatavajra).

3. TTP, No. 18. This passage is included in fol. 328b in the Peking edition, but the TTP wrongly repeats fol. 328a instead of fol. 328b. In the Derge edition, this passage can be found in vol. kha, fol. No. 97a, *ll.* 3-4.
4. TTP, No. 2226, Vol. 52, 74.5.4-5. Tsong-kha-pa attributes this passage to "*Bi bhū ti'i dkyil chog*" (Vibhūti[candra]'s *maṇḍalavidhi*), but the quated passages are included in Tathāgatavajra's *maṇḍalavidhi* (TTP, No. 2226), which is translated into Tibetan by Vibhūticandra.
5. I present a temporary Sanskrit text of the *Vajrāvalī* based on several manuscripts. *tato nirdalitavighnāśayo vāstunāgaṃ parīkṣet.* Performing the oblatin is not mentioned in the *Vajrāvalī.*
6. *vajramuṣṭyā sūtram ādāyottarasādhakena sārdhaṃ pradakṣiṇagatir analānilāvasthitaḥ prākpratīcyuttarāvāgdiśaḥ sūtrayitvā.*
7. *bhūmau vihārādikaṃ kartavyaṃ tāṃ sopacārāṃ caturasreṇa māpayitvā.*
8. *bhādrādīṃs trīṃs trīn māsān yathākramaṃ pūrvadakṣiṇapaścimottaradikśirasā dakṣiṇādimukhas tanmadhyabhūmau vāstunāgaḥ kila svapiti.*
9. *sūryodayam ārabhya pradakṣiṇato gartāpūraṃ khānayet / nāgasya kroḍabhāge kroḍaṃ hastaikena parityajya.*
10. TTP, No. 2226, Vol. 52,74.5.5-75.1.5.
11. TTP, No. 2226, Vol. 52, 75.1.5-7.
12. TTP, No. 2226, Vol. 52, 75.2.2-3.
13. Ratnarakṣita, TTP, No. 2137. Vol. 51, 95.5.6-7.
14. The infromation source of this passage is not clear.
15. TTP, No. 2226, Vol. 52, 75.1.8-2.2.
16. TTP, No. 2226, Vol. 52, 75.2.3-6.
17. TTP, No. 2226, Vol. 52, 75.2.4.2-3. The Tibetan version of this text reads as follows.
    de nas rdo ba la sogs pa bsal te sa de nyid kyis sam des mi ldang na gzhan gyi sa la yang dri bzangs kyi chus btab ste / dong dgang bar bya'o //
18. TTP, No. 2390, Vol. 56, 223.5.2.
19. TTP, No. 2390, Vol. 56, 223.5.4.
20. TTP, No. 2137, Vol. 51, 95.5.6-8.
21. TTP, No. 2186, Vol. 51, 23.1.4-5, 6-7.

Chapter 55

Nāgabodhi's *Śrī-guhyasamāja-maṇḍalopāyikā-viṃśati-vidhi*: The Tibetan Translation and Sanskrit Text of Chapters 5 and 6

KIMIAKI TANAKA

1. *Preamble*

The *Śrī-guhyasamājamaṇḍalopāyikā-viṃśati-vidhi* (hereafter: *Viṃśatividhi* attributed to Nāgabodhi/Nāgabuddhi,[1] who belonged to the Ārya school of interpretation of the *Guhyasamāja-tantra,* is a ritual manual for the 32-deity maṇḍala of the *Guhyasamāja-tantra* centred on Akṣobhyavajra, and it is one of the basic texts for maṇḍala rites in late Tantric Buddhism. Some time ago I discovered that the *Vajrācāryanayottama,* a Sanskrit manuscript in a private collection photographed by the Nepal-German Manuscript Preservation Project,[2] includes a work combining the text of the *Viṃśatividhi* with explanatory comments, and I have already published several chapters of the *Viṃśatividhi* recovered from this manuscript.[3] In the present article I propose to present the romanized text of Chapter 5 "Pṛthivīdevatākalaśādhivāsanavidhi" and Chapter 6 "Vijñānavidhi."

I have already described the said text in my earlier articles, but because this is my first treatment of this text in English, I will briefly summarize its content once again. The *Vajrācāryanayottama* is a palm-leaf manuscript consisting of 46 folios, and on the basis of the handwriting the folios can be divided into three groups: A (4 folios), B (22 folios), and C (20 folios). The text of the *Viṃśatividhi* belongs to Group B, and the *Vajrācāryanayottama* also contains several valuable fragments of other texts of the Ārya school.[4] As is suggested by its title, the *Viṃśatividhi* is composed of instructions for twenty rites (*vidhi*), but there are differences in their names and order as given in the manuscript of the *Vajrācāryanayottama,* as listed by Alex Wayman,[5] and as found in the *Viṃśatividhi* included in the bsTan-'gyur edited by the National Center for Tibetan Studies in China.[6]

2. *Chapters 5 and 6 of the Viṃśatividhi*

Let us now consider Chapters 5 and 6 of the *Viṃśatividhi.* If one disregards the chapter titles and interpolated passages, the Sanskrit text of Chapter 5 as recovered from the *Vajrācāryanayottama* consists of 13 verses and Chapter 6 of 15½ verses. In the Tibetan translation, the fourth *pāda* of verse 10 in Chapter 6 is missing.

The chapters which I have already published in romanized form have included a number of verses in metres other than the *śloka,* but in Chapters 5 and 6 all verses are *ślokas*. In some cases the number of syllables or the length of vowels does not conform with metrical requirements, and in such cases I have emended the text as best as possible with reference to identical or similar verses in other texts and the Tibetan translation.

Explanatory comments not found in the Tibetan translation have been inserted in the manuscript between verses 1 and 2, 5 and 6, 11 and 12, and 12 and 13 of Chapter 5. In the case of Chapter 6, on the other hand, the Sanskrit text and Tibetan translation tally fairly closely. The interpolated comments in Chapter 5 include instructions that have parallels in maṇḍala manuals of the Guhyasamāja cycle[7] and Kriyā texts.

Chapters 5 and 6 contain no direct quotations from the *Guhyasamāja-tantra,* but the *Vajrāvalī* (*VA*), *Ācāryakriyāsamuccaya* (*AKṢ*), *Kriyāsaṅgrahapañjikā* (*KSP*),[8] and *Sarvavajrodaya* (*SVD*) include quotations from our text and identical or similar verses. In the accompanying table a double circle (◎) indicates the presence of an identical or similar verse in another text, while a single circle (○) indicates a partial correspondence.

3. *The Content of Chapter 5*

Verse 1 of Chapter 5 is preceded in the manuscript by explanatory comments relating to the measurements of the maṇḍala, and these I intend dealing with when I publish the text of Chapter 4.

First, in verse 1, following on from the laying out of the maṇḍala in Chapter 4, stakes are driven into the ground to ward off obstacles (*vighna*).

Next, verses 2 and 3 correspond to the verses whereby the officiant seeks permission from the earth goddess to construct the maṇḍala, and in the Japanese Shingon sect they are known as the "Verses for Arousing the Earth Deity." They appear in the *Vairocanābhisaṃbodhi-sūtra,* and in the Chinese commentary by Śubhākarasiṃha and Yixing *(Darijing su)* the original Sanskrit has been transcribed in Chinese characters. In the Sanskrit manuscript, on the other hand, verse 2 is preceded by instructions for visualizing the earth goddess.

In later Kriyā texts the rite for invoking the earth goddess came to be separated from the *kulaśādhivāsanavidhi,* and in the *VA* and *AKS* it is called the *vasudhārādhivāsanavidhi,* dedicated to Vasudhārā, who was widely worshipped during the Pāla dynasty. The present text, on the other hand, retains an awareness of Sthāvarā, the earth goddess who acts as witness to the Buddha's defeat of Māra in the *Lalitavistara,* and it would appear to preserve an old tradition going back to the *Vairocanābhisaṃbodhi-sūtra.*

In verse 4 unguent is smeared on the ground and flowers are scattered over the ritual site, and then in verse 5 the preparing of the flask, the main topic of this chapter, begins. Verses 5-12 are quoted in an almost identical form and in the same order in the "Kalaśādhivāsanavidhi" of the *AKS.*[9]

In verse 5 the material for the flask is first prescribed. The manuscript then inserts three verses relating to the *vijayakalaśa,* an especially important type of flask used in maṇḍala rites, and

I have been able to determine that these verses have parallels in the *Yuganaddhaprakāśa* (Peking No. 2682), an initiation manual also deriving from the Ārya school.[10] Accordingly, I have added the corresponding section of the Tibetan translation of the *Yuganaddhaprakāśa* in square brackets to provide a comparison with the Sanskrit manuscript.

Next, verses 6-8 describe the five precious substances, five grains, and five drugs to be placed inside the flask. Sakurai Munenobu has published a study of the flasks used in initiation rites,[11] and the prescriptions of our text more or less tally with the results of Sakurai's research. Verses 9 and 10 describe the adornments attached to the mouth of the flask and the string tied around its neck. Verse 11 gives instructions for drawing the seed-syllables (*bīja*) or symbols (*cihna*) of the maṇḍala deities around the flask, while verse 12 states that the number of flasks should correspond to the number of deities. In later Kriyā texts the number of flasks came to be prescribed in great detail according to the type of maṇḍala.

The passage inserted between verses 12 and 13 merits special attention in that it describes the process for generating the maṇḍala deities by unifying the knowledge-circle *(jñānacakra)* visualized in the sky with the *samayacakra* inside the flask.

4. *The Content of Chapter 6*

In Chapter 6, verse 1 first prescribes the *ācārya*'s vestments, and then in verse 2 he proclaims his intention of constructing the maṇḍala to the maṇḍala deities visualized in the sky. In content, his pronouncements can be divided into four sections, namely, verses 3-5, 7-8, 10-11, and 13-finis.

Verses similar to those of the first pronouncement can also be found in other texts, but the only text in which the same verses appear in the same order is Ānandagarbha's *SVU*, a manual for the Vajradhātu-maṇḍala.[12] The second pronouncement (as far as the first half of verse 8) and third pronouncement also tally with the *SVU*.[13] When one considers that the text which is the next closest in content is the *KSP* (6th *prakaraṇa)*, also concerned with the Vajradhātu-maṇḍala, it is to be surmised that these pronouncements evolved within the Yoga Tantras, antecedent to the *Guhyasamāja-tantra,* and were incorporated into the *Viṃśatividhi.*

By way of contrast, the fourth pronouncement has no parallel in the *SVU*, but identical or similar verses appear in the *VA*, *AKS* and *KSP*.[14] A comparison of these texts reveals that whereas the *VA*, *AKS* and *KSP* generally tally in their wording, the *Viṃśatividhi* shows many differences, and a further two verses have been inserted between the second and third *pādas* of verse 14.

Thus, when compared with the *VA*, dating from the late eleventh to early twelfth centuries, and Kriyā texts that developed under its influence from the twelfth century onwards, the *Viṃśatividhi*, which was produced some time in the second half of the eighth century and first half of the ninth century, retains evidence of the influence of the middle period of Tantric Buddhism typified by the *Vairocanābhisaṃbodhi-sūtra* and *Sarvatathāgatatattvasaṃgraha*. Furthermore, as is shown by the fact that it is quoted several times in the *VA*, with the quotations attributed to Nāgabuddhipāda,[15] it exerted considerable influence in later times, and it may be regarded as an important text for understanding the historical development of maṇḍala rites.

5. *The Sanskrit Text Recovered from the Vajrācāryanayottama*

Below I have presented the romanized Sanskrit text of Chapters 5 and 6 of the *Viṃśatividhi* as recovered from the *Vajrācāryanayottama* along with the Tibetan translation (left side of page) as given in the bsTan-'gyur edited by the National Center for Tibetan Studies. It should be pointed out that some parts of the romanization remain tentative. Rāhula Sāṅkṛtyāyana writes that he discovered a Sanskrit manuscript of the *Viṃśatividhi* in Tibet,[16] but it went missing during the Cultural Revolution. Consequently, the romanization given below is based on the single extant manuscript of the *Vajrācāryanayottama* and has been emended with reference to the accompanying Tibetan translation and identical or similar verses found in other works.

As is common in Nepalese manuscripts, the manuscript does not distinguish between *ba* and *va*, and there is also frequent confusion of *sa*, *śa* and *ṣa*. The *virāmā* is missing in most cases, but has been supplied when deemed necessary. In addition, *sattva* and *dattvā* are regularly written *satva* and *datvā*, while a consonant after *r* is doubled, but these and other discrepancies with standard orthographical practice have been transcribed as they are, and the comment (sic) has been added only when they might be mistaken for a typographical error.

Graphs illegible on account of soiling of the palm leaves have been indicated by an ellipsis (...), while missing graphs supplied on the basis of similar verses in other texts or for metrical reasons have been enclosed in square brackets ([ ]), and only in cases where the manuscript's reading has been altered have these changes been signalled in the notes. Redundant graphs and symbols in the manuscript have been enclosed in braces ({ }), while redundant graphs that have been deleted in the manuscript with the deletion sign *(parimārjitasaṅketa)* have been enclosed in braces and underlined ({ — }).

Nāgabodhi's *Śrī-guhyasamājamaṇḍalopāyikā-viṃśati-vidhi, 5, 6*

bgegs rnams phur pas btab byas te/	kīlayitvā tato vighnān
de nas ra ba dra ba sogs/	prākāra{ka}ṃ pañjarādikaṃ/
bsams nas rdo rje'i raṅ bźin sa/	dhyātvā vajramayīṃ bhūmiṃ
thig btab lhag par gnas par bya//1//	sūtri{ka}tām adhivāsayet//

tatra vaṃkāraniṣpannāṃ pṛthivīdevatā[ṃ] ni[ḥ] (12a6) sṛtām arddhakāyikāṃ pītām ekamukhāṃ dhānyabindudharāṃ savye/ vāme ka [ ] dhāriṇotsavaṃbhūtāṃ vīkṣyārghapādyādikaṃ datvā saṃpūjya ca evaṃ vadet/

skyob pa saṅs rgyas thams cad kyis/	tvaṃ devi sākṣibhūtāsi
spyod pa'i tshul gyi khyad par daṅ/	sarvabuddhāna[17] tāyināṃ/
sa daṅ pha rol phyin rnams la/	caryānayaviśeṣeṣu
lha mo khyod ni dpaṅ du 'gyur//2//	bhūmipāramitā(12a7)ṣu(sic) ca/
skyob pa śākya seṅ ge yis/	yathā māra{ma}bala[ṃ] bhagnaṃ
ji ltar bdud kyi dpuṅ bcom ltar/	śākyasiṃhena tāyinā/
de bźin bdag gis bdud kyi dpuṅ/	tathā mārabalaṃ jitvā
pham par byas te dkyil 'khor bri//3//	maṇḍalaṃ lelikhāmy[18] ahaṃ//
dri źim sogs kyis sa byugs te/	kṣmām vilipya sugandhādyaiś
me tog sna tshogs kyis bkram nas/	citraiḥ puṣpaiḥ prakīrya ca/
tsa ndan sogs kyis lha gnas su/	candanaiś cakriṇyāṃ sthāne
mkhas pas mandal rab tu bya//4//	[pra]kuryān[19] maṇḍalam budhaḥ//
gser gyi'am yaṅ na dṅul gyi'am/	sauvarṇṇaṃ rājataṃ cāpi
zaṅs sam sa yi raṇ bźin ñid/	tāmraṃ mṛnma(12a8)yam eva vā/

ji ltar rñed pa bzuṅ nas ni/	yathālabdhañ ca saṃgṛhya
brtul źugs can gyis bum pa gźag//5//	sthāpayet kalasān(sic) vratī//
[bum pa de dag naṅ nas ni/]	kalaśānān tu madhye vai
[rnam rgyal mtshan ñid ldan par bya/]	vijayo lakṣaṇair yutaḥ/
[sor mo brgyad kyi tshad kyis ni/]	saptāṅgula[20] pramāṇena
[mgrin pa mtho źiṅ rnam par mdzes//]	u[c]cagrīvo virājate//
[sor mo gñis kyis mchu 'phyaṅ ba/]	lamboṣṭho dvyaṅgulaś caiva
[lto ba'i rgyar ni sor lṅa'o/]	garbbho vitastipañcakaḥ/
[gal te de las tshad źan[21] na/]	yady asau mānahīnaḥ syān
[yon bdag dge bar 'gyur ma yin//]	na tu dānapateḥ śi(19b1)vaṃ//
[baṃ gyi yi ge las byuṅ ba/]	vaṃkārākṣarasaṃbhūto
[rin chen rnam pa cher 'bar ba'o/]	ratna(sic)kāro maho[j]jvalaḥ/
[gźan pa rnams la ṅes med de/]	anyeṣāniyamo nāsti
[ji ltar mdzes pa rab tu brtag/]	yathāśobhaṃ prakalpayet//
byi ru dṅul daṅ gser daṅ ni/	pravāḍaṃ[22] rajataṃ hema
padma rā ga mu tig ste/	padmarāgaṃ ca śuktijaṃ/
rin chen śis pa lṅa po rnams/	śastāni pañcaratnāni
bum pa'i chu yi naṅ du gźug//6//	prakṣipet kalaśodare[23]//
nas daṅ gro daṅ mo sran gre'u/	pavagodhūmamāṣāś ca
til daṅ de bźin mon sran sde'u/	tila(19b2)mu[dras ta]thaiva ca/
'bru ni śis pa lṅa po rnams/	pañcadhānyāni śastāni
bum pa'i naṅ du gźug par bya//7//	sthāpayet kalaśodare//
chen po tsher ma'i dgra dan ni/	bṛhatı kaṇṭakārı ca
lhar bcas gźan gyis mi thub daṅ/	sahadevāparājitā/
daṇḍo {ta} utpal rtsa ba ste/	daṇḍotpalānāṃ mūlāni
sman lṅa po ni gźug par bya//8//	prakṣipet pañcauṣadhīḥ//
a mra u dumvā ra daṅ/	āmram udumvarāśokam
mya ṅan 'tshaṅ daṅ a śva ka/	aśvatthaṃ nāgajan tat[h]ā/
de bźin klu śiṅ skyes yal ga/	pañcapallavaṃ ādadyāt
bum pa'i kha mdzes lṅa gzugs so//9//	kala(19b3)śānāṃ
	mukhaśobhanaṃ//
gos ni dkar po chen po yis/	veṣṭayet kalaśagrīvāṃ
bum pa'i ṃgrin pa bciṅ bar bya/	mahatā śvetavāsasā/
gos kyi steṅ du srad bu dag/	[vastro]pari nyaset sūtrān
dkar po cho ga mkhas pas dgod//10//	suśuklān vidhikovidaḥ//

mkhas pas gur kum la sogs pa/
mṅon 'dus byas pas dkyil 'khor pa/
kun gyi sa bon nam mtshan ma/
bum pa'i ṅos la ṅes par bri//11//

sarvveṣāṃ māṇḍaleyānāṃ
bījaṃ cihnam athāpi ca/
ghaṭapā[r]śve likhed dhīmān
kuṃkumādy abhisaṃskṛtaṃ
(19b4)//

utsa[r]ggamaṇḍale viśvapadmopari sūryādyāsananiyama uktaḥ/ tadupari likhitavyaṃ ghaṭānāṃ pārśve vajrādicihnādikaṃ/ viśvapadmasya lakṣaṇam ucyate[24] //pūrvvādi digvāsidalāruṇābhaṃ vātānalāsā(sic)dalapītabhāvaṃ (19b5) pretādhipeśānadiśoś ca dūrvvāśyāmābdakṛṣṇaṃ khalu viśvapadmaṃ//

rin po che la sags ldan źiṅ//
raṅ gi sṅags kyis mṅon bsṅags pa/
chu bcas 'di rnams blo ldan gyis/
lha yi graṅs kyis gźag par bya//12//

ratnādisaṃyutān etān
svamantreṇābhimantritān[/]
sodakān{/} sthāpayed dhīmān
devatāparisaṃkhyayā//

maṇḍalasyeśānakoṇe cakro vedīṃ kṛ(19b6)tvā tatra saṃsthāpya vijayādi kalaśān adhivāsayet/ tatrādau baliṃ da{/}tvā gaganatale jñānacakraṃ saṃsthāpyārghādidāna puraḥsaraṃ vijayādi kala{sa}śasthasamaya cakreṇādvayībhūya devatāsvarūpṇa jñānacakram eva sthitaṃ/ tad ana(19b7)ntaraṃ mūrddhni vijayādīnāṃ śarāvopari sthāpya vajraṃ nānāpuṣpāviracitamālānibaddhaṃ/ tāñ ca mā{??}lāṃ vāma[25] muṣṭyā saṃgṛhya ghaṇṭāyā saha svadevatotsa[r]ggamantreṇa vajradhṛg ityādinā hṛnmantreṇa vā Hūṃkārādinā uṣṇīṣavijayā(19b8)[athavā pra]tyaṅgireṇa vābhimantrayed aṣṭottaraśataṃ/ kalaśasthajñānacakraṃ saṃpūjya puṣpādinā nīrājayitvā tu vijayādiṣu jñānāmṛtadravarūpeṇa saṃsthāpayet/

dkyil 'khor gyi ni grva bźi daṅ/
'khor yug gi ni naṅ dag tu/
blo daṅ ldan pas bum pa gźag/
gcig ni sgo la gźag par bya //13//

tato
maṇḍalasya catuḥkoṇā
{va}sthitacakravāḍāntare
kalaśān s[thā]paye(20a1)[d]
[e]kaṃ sthāpayet punaḥ//

sa'i lha mo daṅ
bum pa lhag par gnas pa'i cho ga'o//

pṛthivīdevatā-
kalaśādhivācanā(sic)vidhi//

phyi nas gos dmar 'dzin ciṅ rgyan/
thams cad kyis ni brgyan gyur ciṅ/
dril bu daṅ bcas bla ma yis/
bsñems bcas rdo rje gsor byas te//1//

(20a1)raktāmbaradharaḥ paścāt
sarvvālaṅkārabhūṣitaḥ/
sagarvvaṃ vajram ullā{la}yan
ghaṇṭayā sahito guru[ḥ//]

bar snaṅ la gnas saṅs rgyas daṅ/
dkyil 'khor pa rnams go rims bźin/
bltas nas mig rgyas 'gyur ba yis/
tshig 'di dag ni gsal bar brjod//2//

antarīkṣe sthitān buddhān
māṇḍaleyān yathākramaṃ
dṛṣṭvā protphullanayane
...giraṃ /

deṅ du bdag tshe 'bras bur bcas/
bdag gi gson pa 'bras bur bcas/
bdag ni dam tshig lha rnams daṅ/
mñam par gyur pa the tshom med//3//

(20a2)adya me saphala[ṃ] janma
saphalaṃ jīvitañ ca me/
samaḥ samayabuddhānāṃ
bhavitāhaṃ na saṃśayaḥ//

byaṅ chub sems dpa' sems gcig pa/
bdag ni phyir mi ldog par 'gyur/
bdag deṅ de bźin gśegs pa yi/
ris su skye bar gdon mi za//4//

avaivartto[26] bhaviṣyāmi
bodhisatvaikacetanaḥ//
tathāgatakulotpattir
mamādyaiva na saṃsa(sic)yaḥ//

saṅs rgyas thams cad spyan draṅs pas/
deṅ du bdag gi ñi ma mchog/
deṅ bdag mchod sbyin bla na med/
deṅ du bdag gi 'dus pa mchog//5//

agro me divaso hy adya
yajño me[']dya niruttaraḥ/
sannipāto[']dya me [hy agra]ḥ
sarvvabuddha(20a3) nimantraṇāt
iti/

de nas saṅs rgyas de dag la/
btud de mchod yon phul nas ni/
blo daṅ ldaṅ pas phyi naṅ gi/
mchod pas mchod de 'di skad brjod//6//

tataḥ praṇatān buddhānn
arghaṃ datvā viśuddhadhīḥ/
bāhyābhyantarapūjābhiḥ
pūjayitvā vaded idaṃ//

ma lus phyogs na bźugs pa yi/
saṅs rgyas rnams ni bdag la dgoṅs/
rdo rje can bdag che ge mo/
źes ni bgyi ba'i dkyil 'khor 'dri//7//

samanvāharantu māṃ buddhā
aśeṣādikṣu saṃsthitāḥ/
amukanāmāhaṃ vajrī
maṇḍalaṃ lelikhāmy[27] ahaṃ//

saṅs rgyas kun deṅ gśegs su gsol/
dṅos grub 'di ni stsal du gsol/
dkyil 'khor chen po'i las la ni/
ci nus bźin du rab tu bgyi//8//

āyāntu sarvvabuddhādyāḥ
siddhim enāṃ pradāsyatha/
yathā śaktyā(20a4) [pra]kurvvīta
mahāmaṇḍalakarmmaṇi//

de nas bsñems bcas laṅs nas ni/
rdzogs rim rnal 'byor daṅ ldan pa'i/
brtul źugs can gyis 'gro byed ciṅ/
dril bu dkrol bźin 'di skad brjod//9//

[tataḥ] sagarvvaṃ utthāya
niṣpannakramayogavān/
parikraman vaded evaṃ
ghaṇṭāñ ca[28] vādayan vratī//

bdag ni raṅ ñid rdo rje can/
rdo rje sems dpa' bdag raṅ ñid/

ahaṃ eva svayaṃ vajrī
vajrasatvo['smy a]haṃ svayaṃ

bdag ni saṅs rgyas rgyal po che/	ahaṃ buddho mahārājā
//10//	ahaṃ vajrī mahābalaḥ//
bdag ni rnal 'byor dbaṅ phyug rgyal/	ahaṃ yogīśvaro rājā
bdag ni phyag na rdo rje brtan/	vajrapāṇir ahaṃ dṛḍhaṃ/
bdag ni bdag po rdo rje che/	(20a5)ahaṃ svāmī mahāvajrī
deṅ bdag rdo rje sems dpar grub//11//	vajrasatvādya siddhya māṃ/
de nas saṅs rgyas saṅs rgyas lṅa'i/	vijñāpaye[t] tato buddhān
rigs 'byuṅ rnams la gsol ba gdab/	pañcabuddhakulodbhavān/
de dag bar snaṅ gnas bsams nas/	antarīkṣagatān dhyātvā
'di skad brjod ciṅ bskul bar bya//12//	codayet tān idaṃ bruvan/
thugs rje yi ni bdag can bdag/	svo(sic)[']ha[ṃ]likhitum icchāmi
slob ma rnams la rjes brtse daṅ/	maṇḍalaṃ karuṇātmakaḥ/
khyed cag la yaṅ mchod slad du/	śiṣyāṇām anukampāya
saṅ ni dkyil 'khor bri bar 'tshal//13//	yuṣmākaṃ pūjanāya ca/
bcom ldan gus pas bdag la ni/	(20a6)tan me bhaktasya bhagavan
de'i phyir bka' drin mdzad pa'i 'os/	prasādaṃ kartum arhasi/
rdo rje can bdag che ge mo/	amukanāmāhaṃ vajrī
źes bgyi'i dkyil 'khor mdzes pa ni//14//	amukaṃ maṇḍalaṃ śubhaṃ//
che ge ci nus yo byad kyis/	śvobhūte tu likhiṣyāmi
saṅ ni yaṅ dag 'dri bar 'gyur/	yathāśaktyupacārataḥ/
de phyir slob mar bcas bdag la/	anukampām upādāya
rjes su brtse bas ñer bzuṅ nas//15//	saśiṣyasya tu tan mama//
'khor bcas kun gyis dkyil 'khor la/	maṇḍalaṃ sahitā sarvve[29]
byiṅ gyis brlab par mdzad par 'os//	sānnidhyaṃ karttum arhatha iti//
[gsol ba gdab pa'i cho ga'o]	vijña(20a7)navidhiḥ//

NOTES

1. Nāgabodhi has the same name as one of the eight patriarchs of the Japanese Shingon sect, but it is not clear whether they are one and the same person. In some manuscripts his name is given as Nāgabuddhi. In Tibet, Tsoṅ-kha-pa is said to have wanted to visit India in order to study

the difficult points of the Ārya school under Klu-byaṅ (i.e., Nāgabodhi), but was dissuaded from doing so by lHo-brag Grub-chen, and it is evident that the legend of Nāgabodhi's longevity had been widely disseminated.

2. N.G.M.P.P., Running No. E-18322, Reel No. E 920/12.
3. See the following articles (all in Japanese): "Nāgabodhi's *Śrī-guhyasamājamaṇḍalopāyikā-viṃśati-vidhi* (10/11) āvāhavidhi: A Romanized Text of a Newly Identified Sanskrit Manuscript," *Mikkyō Bunka* 203 (1999); "Nāgabodhi's *Śrī-guhyasamājamaṇḍalopāyikā-viṃśati-vidhi,* śiṣyapraveśavidhi," *Mikkyō Bunka* 205 (2000); "Nāgabodhi's *Śrī-guhyasamājamaṇḍalopāyikā-viṃśati-vidhi,* 9 raṅgajāpavidhi and 10 raṅgapātanavidhi," *Indogaku Bukkyōgaku Kenkyū* 49-1 (2000); "Nāgabodhi's *Śrī-guhyasamājamaṇḍalopāyikā-viṃśati-vidhi,* 8 ākāśasūtrapātanavidhi," *Indogaku Bukkyōgaku Kenkyū* 50-1 (2001).
4. On texts in Group C related to the *niṣpannakrama,* see my following article (in Japanese): "Self-Styled Mādhyamika Tantrists: The Thought and Practices of the Ārya School of the Guhyasamāja Cycle," in *Śūnyatā and Reality: Volume in Memory of Prof. Ejima Yasunori,* Shunjūsha, Tokyo, 2000 (CD-ROM). Another text of the Guhyasamāja cycle included in Group C (referred to as "Ms. C" in the accompanying table) also includes several verses identical or similar to verses in the *Viṃśatividhi.*
5. Alex Wayman, *Yoga of the Guhyasamājatantra,* Motilal Banarsidass, Delhi, 1977, pp. 161-162.
6. Zhongguo Zangxue Zhongxin, ed., *Daṅzhur* (Collated Version), Vol. 18, Zhongguo Zangxue Chubanshe, Beijing, 1997, pp. 364-408.
7. A passage similar to the comments inserted between verses 11 and 12 is to be found in the Tokyo University Library manuscript of Padmaśrīmitra's *Maṇḍalopāyikā* (No. 280; "*SMU*" in the accompanying table).
8. Because the *KSP* is a voluminous work, I have been unable to examine the entire text and confined myself to the sixth *prakaraṇa,* which has close connections with the *Viṃśatividhi.*
9. *Kriyāsamuccaya* (Śata-piṭaka, Vol. 237), p. 81,ll.2-7.
10. *Yuganaddhaprakāśa* (Zhongguo Zangxue Zhongxin, ed., *Danzhur,* Vol. 18), p. 641, *ll.* 115-12.
11. Sakurai Munenobu, "Kanjō shidai de mochiiru byō-Sekaprakriyā byō junbi giki yakuchū", in *id., Indo Mikkyō girei kenkyū–kōki Indo Mikkyō no kanjō,* Hōzōkan, Kyoto, 1996.
12. Mikkyō Seiten Kenkyūkai, "Vajradhātumahamaṇḍalopāyikā-Sarvavajrodaya-Bonbun tekisuto to wayaku (II) kan", *Taishō Daiaku Sōgō Bukkyō Kenkyūjo Nenpō* (1987), p. 289.
13. *Ibid.,* pp. 289-287.
14. *Vajrāvalī* (Śata-piṭaka, Vol. 239), p. 49, *l.* 5 -p. 50, *l.* 1; *Kriyāsamuccaya* (Śata-piṭaka, Vol. 237), p. 87, *ll.* 1-5; *Kriyāsaṅgraha* (Śata-piṭaka, Vol. 236), p. 144, *l.* 6 -p. 145, *l.*4.
15. Six such quotations are pointed out in the *Lupta Buddha Vacana Samgraha,* Part 1 (Sarnath, 1990, pp. 29-30), and three of these correspond to verses 5, 10 (second half) and 11 (first three *pādas*) in Chapter 5 of the *Viṃśatividhi.* The *VA* also includes verses identical or similar to verses in Chapter 6 of the *Viṃśatividhi,* but they are not explicitly attributed to Nāgabuddhipāda.
16. Rāhula Sāṅkṛtyāyana, "Second Search of Sanskrit Palm-leaf Mss. in Tibet," *J.B.O.R.S.* 23-1 (1937), p. 45, Manuscript No. 302.

17. I have interpreted this as BHS gen. pl. *metri causa* and have accordingly not emended it.
18. The form *lelikhāmi* is grammatically problematical, but it also appears in verse 7 of Chapter 6 and in the Tokyo University Library manuscript of Padma-śrīmitra's *Maṇḍalopāyikā* (No. 280), and the transliteration 隸履佉頡痕 in the *Darijing su* (Taishō Vol. 39, p. 619b25) also supports this.
19. Ms.: [*pra*]*kuryan.*
20. The Tibetan translation would suggest *aṣṭāṅgula.*
21. *gźan* has been emended to the variant *źan* on the basis of the Sanskrit *mānahīna.*
22. Ms.: *pravālaṃ.*
23. The Tibetan translation would suggest *kalaśodake.*
24. Ms.: *ucyatu.*
25. Ms.: *vama.*
26. Ms.: *avaivarttā.*
27. See n. 18.
28. Ms.: *ghaṇṭām vādayan.*
29. Ms.: *servva.*

Synopsis of Nāgabodhi's *Śrī-guhyasamājamaṇḍalopāyikā-viṃśati-vidhi*, Chapter 5 & 6

Verse Number	Ms. Folio	Content	VA	KSP	AKS	SVU	SMU	Ms.C	Other Texts
1.	12a5	Stakes							
	12a5	Visualization of earth goddess							
2.	12a6	Verses for arousing		◎			◎	◎	*Darijing su*
3.	12a7	earth goddess		◎			◎	○	*Darijing su*
4.	12a7	Unguent and flowers							
5.	12a7	Flask material	◎		◎				
	12a8	Characteristics of *vijayakalaśa*							*Yuganaddhaprakāśa*
6.	19b1	Placing of five precious substances in flask			◎				
7.	19b1	Placing of five grains in flask			◎				
8.	19b2	Placing of five drugs in flask			◎				
9.	19b2	Decoration of mouth of flask			◎				
10.	19b3	Cloth and string for neck of flask	○		◎				
11.	19b3	Arrangement of deities' seed-syllables	◎		◎				
	19b4	Characteristics of multicoloured lotus							
12.	19b5	Number of flasks			◎				
	19b5	Generation of deity in flask							
13.	19b8	Arrangement of flasks							

Verse Number	Ms. Folio	Content	VA	KSP	AKS	SVU	SMU	Ms.C	Other Texts
1.	20a1	*Ācārya*'s vestments							
2.	20a1	Visualization of deities							
3.	20a2	First pronouncement	○	◎		◎			
4.	20a2			◎		◎			
5.	20a2			◎		◎			
6.	20a3	Offering of *argha* and worship							
7.	20a3	Second pronouncement		◎		◎			
8.	20a3			○		○			
9.	20a4	Perambulation and ringing of bell							
10.	20a4	Third pronouncement		◎		◎			
11.	20a4			○		◎			
12.	20a5	Visualization of deities in sky							
13.	20a5	Fourth pronouncement	○	○	○		○	○	
14.	20a6		◎	◎	◎		○	○	
15.	20a6		◎	◎	◎		○	○	
half verse	20a6		◎	◎	◎		◎	○	

CHAPTER 56

The Signs of Death and Their Contexts

SHINGO EINOO

The Ḥauḍ al-Ḥayāt is an Arabic or Persian translation of a Sanskrit text called Amṛtakuṇḍa the original of which has not yet been found.[1] The eighth chapter of the Ḥauḍ al-Ḥayāt is titled the knowledge of death and the method to conquer it. Here three signs of death are described and the practice of the yogic meditation laid down in the seventh chapter is recommended to avert the approaching death.

The Ḥauḍ al-Ḥayāt, a text studied among the circles of Sufism, is a very interesting text which involves a number of tantric elements. The treatment of the signs of death in this text can be counted among these tantric elements. But the description of the signs of death is not only confined to the tantric tradition but they can be found in a wider range of ancient Indian literature at least in three different contexts. In this paper I will, at first, collect the passages where the signs of death are described, and then examine the contexts in which they appear and lastly I will try to clarify the position of the Ḥauḍ al-Ḥayāt in the cultural tradition of India.

A.S. Gopani seems to be the only scholar who studied the signs of death in great detail and collected many texts which deal with them.[2] Besides A.S. Gopani there are a number of scholars who touched upon this subject more or less briefly.

They are, for example, Th. Aufrecht[3], P. V. Kane[4], S. Beyer[5], Lallanji Gopal[6], T. Goudriaan[7], G. Jan Meulenbeld[8] and others. According to their statements and informations given by my friends we have now the following list of the text passages which deal with the signs of death:

> Aitareya Āraṇyaka 3.2. 4 [136, 137, 4][9], Śāṅkhāyana Āraṇyaka 8.7 and 11.3-4[10], Caraka Saṃhitā, Indriyasthāna[11], Mahābhārata 12.305.8-17[12], Liṅga Purāṇa 1.91.1-35[13], Mārkaṇḍeya Purāṇa 40.1-36[14], Skanda Purāṇa 4.1. 42[15], Vāyu Purāṇa 19.1-32[16], Viṣṇudharmottara Purāṇa 3.238.1-33[17], Śiva Purāṇa 5. 25. 9-28[18], Vṛddhayavana jātaka 64.1-45[19], Bṛhajjātaka 6.1-12 and Laghu jātaka 7.1-11[20], Kṛtyakalpataru, 14. Mokṣakāṇḍa 25[21], Adbhutasāgara, Kāyariṣṭādbhutāvarta[22], Dharmasindhu 3.1[23], Śārṅgadharapaddhati 162[24], Śivatattvaratnākara 5. 1. 62-84[25], Kubjikāmata Tantra 23. 16-43[26], Saṃvarodaya Tantra 19. 1-25[27], Vimalaprabhā 2.4. 79-81[28], Commentaries on Yogasūtra 3.22[29], Yogaratnākara[30], Riṣṭasamuccaya[31], Ḥauḍ al-Ḥayāt, chapt. 8[32]

A detailed analysis of the signs of death described in the texts, listed above, would show their variety, and some relationship between the texts which reveal line of development of this subject. But, in this paper, I will not go into their detailed analysis. I propose to examine here only the three signs of death which are discussed in the Ḥauḍ al-Ḥayāt. They are as follows:[33]

> The first study: One gets up in the morning and goes out when the sun has come out. When it rises high, he turns his face towards west, so that his shadow will be equal to his height. He should sit down straight and without moving on the ground with his two arms stretched downward and seeing no directions than his own shadow. When he turns his eyes from his shadow and sees in the air, he will see his own shadow like a white big man. If the shadow will be complete and with no defect, he will live for long years. If he sees his shadow without a head, his life will be left three days. If one ear is lacking, six months will remain. If two ears are lacking, fifteen days will remain. If he sees it without a neck, seven days will remain. If he sees it without arms, six months

> remain. If he sees it without legs, one year will remain. If one leg is lacking, two years will remain. And the same applies to the fingers, too.
>
> The second study: He looks into the mirror and fixes his eyes on his reflection. If he sees nothing, his death has come close to him. The judgement is to be done according to the first study. For two eyes the judgement of the two ears is applied. For two ears the judgement of the two arms is applied. For two eyebrows the judgement of the two legs is applied. For the leg the judgement of the fingers is applied. The judgement of the forehead will be the judgement of all. This judgement concerns diseases.
>
> The third study: If urine and feces come out without consciousness, the death has come close to him.

The first examination of the remaining time of one's life is done by seeing the afterimage of one's shadow in the air, and the second examination is based on the conditions of one's reflection in the mirror. We have similar examples of the examination of the approaching death by using the afterimage of one's shadow in the air in several texts listed above. They are Śiva Purāṇa 5.28.3-13, Adbhutasāgara 552, 7-13 quoting from the Kālāvalī, Riṣṭasamuccaya 95cd-105, and Yogaśāstra 5.168-172 quoted by Gopani in the Riṣṭasamuccaya of Durgadeva on p. 106.[34] Apart from these texts there are other texts which foretell the moment of death by observing the person's shadow itself. They are Adbhutasāgara 552, 15-18 quoting the Ādi Purāṇa, the same 552, 20-24 quoting the Kalāvalī, Kṛtyakalpataru, XIV Mokṣakāṇḍa, 25 (252, 10-17) quoting the Brahma Purāṇa, Yogaśāstra 5.211-223 quoted in Gopani, The Riṣṭasamuccaya of Durgadeva, p. 107, Riṣṭasamuccaya 70-84, Saṃvarodaya Tantra 19.18-19 and Mṛtyuvañcanopadeśa 1 (NGMPP, B 90/12, folio 5a, 2-4). The parts of the body or the points to be checked to determine the remaining lifetime vary very largely according to the different texts so that it is almost impossible to establish the common feature of the prognostication of approaching death shared by these texts.

Śiva Purāṇa 5.28.8-11ab, for example, says as follows: If one sees the shadow without a head, the death takes place in six months. Then the Śiva Purāṇa discusses the colours of the shadow. If the shadow is white, it indicates religious merit (*dharma*). But the black color suggests the evil (*pāpa*), while the red foretells the imprisonment (*bandha*) and the yellow points to the existence of a foe (*vidviṣa*). Then this text comes back to the analysis of the lacking parts of the body in the shadow. The lack of the arms indicates the loss of kinsmen *(bandhunāśa)*, the shadow without a mouth (*vituṇḍa*) causes fear from hunger. If there is not the hip in the shadow, the wife will die. If one does not see the leg from the ankle to the knee, wealth will perish and the footless shadow results in the flight in the foreign country (*videśa*). The Ḥauḍ al-Ḥayāt foretells only the remaining lifespan, but the Śiva Purāṇa prognosticates very different results.

In the description of the signs of death the Riṣṭasamuccaya 100-104 and the Yogaśāstra 5.211-223 are most similar to the Ḥauḍ al-Ḥayāt in that these texts mention only the remaining lifespan of the person concerned. To itemize the lacking parts of the body and the remaining lifetime, the statement of the Riṣṭasamuccaya 100-104 is summarized as follows: head, six months; feet, three years; eyes, two years; knee, one year; shanks, twenty-eight months; hip, fifteen months; heart, eight months; pubes, six days; hands, four days; arms, two days; shoulders, one day. Yogaśāstra 5.211-223 says as follows: ears, fifteen years; hands, ten years; fingers, eight years; shoulders, seven years; hair, five years; the side and nose, one year; head, six months; neck, one month; eyes, ten days; holed heart, seven days; two shadows, sudden death. But the comparison of the description of these three texts shows only diversity differing in the choice of the parts of the body and the statement of the remainder of one's life.[35]

Apart from these descriptions which refer to various parts of the body in order to foretell the approach of one's death, there are many passages where single aspect of the shadow is pointed out. We have the following cases. One does not see one's own shadow.[36] Or one sees the deformed shadow.[37] The shadow is holed.[38] The shadow is headless.[39] One sees one's shadow in the southern direction.[40]

The second study in the Ḥauḍ al-Ḥayāt concerns the reflection in a mirror. Here the Ḥauḍ al-Ḥayāt gives various symptoms of approaching death on the analogy of the cases of the afterimage of one's shadow in the sky. But in other texts listed above we cannot find such a systematic prognostication of comming death. Naturally we have many texts which describe the reflection of one's form in a mirror or in the water. For example, from Aitareya Āraṇyaka 3.2.4 [136, 8-9] we read:

> *athāpy ādarśe vodake vā jihmaśirasaṃ vāśirasaṃ vātmānaṃ paśyet*
> "And again when he sees himself in a mirror or in the water with a crooked head or without a head."

Śāṅkhāyana Āraṇyaka. 7 [314, 1] adds to these two cases another case: *vā na paśyet* "Or if he does not see himself." As regards the reflection we have several variations.The first case is that one does not see oneself.[41] Secondly, one does not see one's own face.[42] Thirdly, there are cases where it is said that one does not see oneself or one sees oneself without a head.[43] In the fourth case, instead of the reflection without a head the deformed reflection is mentioned.[44] In the fifth case it is said that one does not see oneself in the pupil reflected in a mirror.[45] Finally, we have a case that one does not see oneself in the eye of another person.[46]

In the third study of the Ḥauḍ al-Ḥayāt the sign of death is that urine and feces come out without consciousness. In other texts we have several varieties of the signs of death concerning the excrement. But they are different from that given in the Ḥauḍ al-Ḥayāt. In one case it is said that urine and feces are like gold or silver.[47] Second is the case when urine, feces and other excrement come out simultaneously.[48] And several kinds of changes of excrement are enumerated.[49]

Thus, regarding the second and third studies of the sings of death laid down in the Ḥauḍ al-Ḥayāt we have no corresponding descriptions in other texts.

After describing these signs of death the Ḥauḍ al-Ḥayāt goes on to say:

> If someone finds these signs within himself and desires that he wards them off, he should turn his face toward the east and sit cross-legged as I have described in the chapter on the mortification regarding the first method of sitting. In the thought the shapes and their positions are provided with their colors and outer appearances.[50] Likewise he should

> think over the position one by one as mentioned in the seventh chapter with its shape and the word (namely mantra) so that he could see the seventh position that is the moon. And he sees the light with the inner eye in the middle of the head. With a correct imagination he should pull up the *suṣumnā*[51] from the navel and carry up and bring it to the moon so that the *suṣumnā* and the moon may unite. Then he should imagine that from them the water of life drips in the same way as at the time of coition the sperm comes out among the wife and husband. He should imagine that both the moon and the *suṣumnā* unite on the journey and from them the water falls out and pours on the body. By being engaged in this imagination night and day, he extinguishes the signs which appeared and obtains the knowledge of death.

Here the Ḥauḍ al-Ḥayāt describes, to use the Indian expression, a yogic practice to extinguish the signs of death and consequently to overcome death. It is, therefore, important to see in which contexts the signs of death are described in other texts.[52] Carakasaṃhitā, Indriyasthāna, 12.90cd clearly expresses the utility of the knowledge of the signs of death as follows:

> *tathā hi siddhiṃ ca yaśaś ca śāśvataṃ sa siddhakarma labhate dhanāni ca //*
>
> "Because he, as a physician who is successful in his treatments, obtains success, everlasting fame, and so wealth as well."

So it is recommended in the text with various expressions that a wise physician should avoid a patient who shows fatal signs[53], or he should not give medicine to such a patient[54], or he should not treat such a patient medically[55], or he should not even go to such a patient.[56] Here we can see a realistic and sober standpoint of the ancient Indian medical texts.

Other texts, on the other hand, show more religious or rather magicoritualistic attitudes.We can here distinguish two categories. One is the final preparation for the departure of the soul so that the soul can attain liberation from the bondage of being, which is called *utkramaṇa* or *utkrānti.* And the other is a ritual device or means to prolong life of one who is assailed by the imminent death. This is called either cheating death (*kālavañcana*) or conquering death (*mṛtyuñjaya*). The case of the Ḥauḍ al-Ḥayāt can be classified into the second category. But the dividing line between the two is sometimes difficult to draw.

Into the first category can be classified at first Mahābhārata 12.305.1-7 and 17-21 that are given before and after the descriptions of the signs of death and the whole chapter 12.305 is preceded by the chapter 12.304 which describes the teachings of *yoga* practice.[57] Mahābhārata 12.305.1 reads as follows: *tathaivotkramamāṇaṃ tu śṛṇuṣvāhito nṛpa / padbhyām utkramamāṇasya vaiṣṇavaṃ sthānaṃ ucyate//* "Listen to carefully, O king, saying about one who is departing as follows. The world of Viṣṇu is assigned to one who departs through the feet." In the following six verses the parts of the body through which the soul of a dying person passes out and the worlds of deities to which the departed go are enumerated. They can be listed as follows: shanks, Vasus; knees, Sādhyas; anus, Mitra; hip, Pṛthivī; thighs, Prajāpati; sides of the body, Maruts; nostrils, the Moon; arms, Indra; breast, Rudra; neck, Nara; mouth, Viśve devās; ear, the Directions; nose, Gandhavahana; eyes, the Sun; eyebrows, Aśvins; the forehead, the Pitṛs; the head, Brahmā.[58]

We have descriptions more or less similar to Mahābhārata 12.305.17-21 in the following texts: Liṅga Purāṇa 1.91. 36-45ab (almost same with Vāyu Purāna 19.33-40), Mārkaṇḍeya Purāṇa 40.40-46, Kubjikāmata Tantra 23. 98cd-125; Kṛtyakalpataru, XIV Mokṣakāṇḍa, 255, 4-18; Śārṅgadharapaddhati 163.1-7; Saṃvarodaya Tantra 19. 27cd-39. They show some common features. In order to accomplish the *utkranti* certain yogic practice is to be performed.[59] The person who saw the signs of death should not have fear caused by comming death.[60] By practising the *utkrānti* he attains the final liberation which is expressed variously.[61]

Now we turn to the second category of ritual device or means to prolong life which is called either cheating death (*kālavañcana*) or conquering death (*mṛtyuñjaya*). We find it in the following texts: Skanda Purāṇa 4. 1. 42.40-41; Śiva Purāṇa 5.26. 24-54, 27.2-15ab, 27.15cd-26, 27.27-33, and 27.34-37;[62] Śārṅgadharapaddhati 163.8-21; Śivatattvaratnākara 5.1.85-90; Kubjikāmata Tantra 23.80cd-98, 161-172ab; Saṃvarodaya Tantra 29.26-27ab; Mṛtyuvañcanopadeśa, *pariccheda* 3 and 4.[63]

The distinction between the first and the second category is, however, floating. In Mahābhārata 12.305.19c and 20c, where the *utkrānti* is described, we come across the expression of conquering death.[64] Skanda Purāṇa 4. 1.42.40-41 recommends as a means of cheating death *(kālavañcanopāya)* the pilgrimage to Kāśīnātha who conquers death (*mṛtyuñjaya*), who has another epithet *garbhāvarodhaka* or one who obstructs further birth. Śiva Purāṇa 5.26. 29ab says as a result of conquering death the *yogin* is liberated from the bondage of transmigration.[65] But in other texts we find expressions which do not seem to suggest the final emancipation. The *yogin* obtains immortality.[66] The *yogin* is not submitted to death and lives one hundred years.[67] Or the death turns the face away from him.[68] In Śiva Purāṇa 5.27.20cd-22 and 32-32 we read of the attainment of the supernatural powers (*siddhis*) by the *yogin*.

The Ḥauḍ al-Ḥayāt says that after performing a yogic practice the water of life comes out of the moon united with the *suṣumnā*. Three text passages suggest the pouring out of the water of life. They are Śiva Purāṇa 5.27. 29cd-30ab; 35-36ab; Śārṅgadharapaddhati 163. 13-17ab.[69] This pouring out of the water of life seems to be a well-known theme in the tantric yoga, not only in the Haṭhayoga tradition but also in other Hindu and Buddhist tantras.[70] It is interesting to note that the yogic practice described in Śiva Purāṇa 5.27.35-36 seems to be identical with the haṭhayogic practice called *khecarīmudrā* which is performed by turning the tongue upward to the palate and further to the uvula and which is said to be the best method to produce the water of life.[71] But, besides Śiva Purāṇa 5.27.35-36 where the *khecarīmudrā* is alluded, there are several texts belonging to both Hindu and Buddhist tantras which explicitly or implicitly mention this yogic practice.[72] Here we have again examples of common sharing of religious elements by both Hindu and Buddhist tantric texts.

After describing the signs of death Aitareya Āraṇyaka 3.2.4 [137, 5-6] prescribes a burnt-offering of milk gruel (*pāyasa*) to the accompaniment of the *rātrīsūkta* (Ṛgveda 10. 127) according to the basic pattern of the Gṛhya ritual. Śāṅkhāyana Āraṇyaka 11.4-5 [319, 21-34] prescribes a similar offering without using the *rātrīsūkta* but with another set of mantras given in 11.5 [319, 28-34]. Śāṅkhāyana Āraṇyaka 11.5-6 [319, 34-320, 22] prescribes still another kind of offering and its purport can be understood from a repeated phrase in the accompanying mantra: *māham akāmo mariṣyāmi* "I will not die an undesired death." In these texts there are no expressions such as cheating death and conquering death, but we can certainly see here a certain ritual device to avert an untimely death. Apart from the yogic practice there is another means to overcome death. Kubjikāmata Tantra 23.80cd says *ariṣṭadarśanaṃ nāthe japahomopāśāmyati* "Recitation of a mantra and an offering pacifies the sight of the signs of death, O mistress," and then gives a short mantra called *mṛtyuñjaya*, conqueror of death.[73] Śivatattvaratnākara 5.1.88 lays down also an offering and a recitation of a mantra to defeat death.[74]

The name of the mantra *mṛtyuñjaya* reminds us of a Ṛgvedic mantra (Ṛgveda 7.59.12) which is also named *mṛtyuñjaya*. Some Vedic texts know a ritual which is called *mṛtyuñjaya*.[75] We must here take into consideration the Atharvavedic hymns classified as *āyuṣyāni* or prayers for long life and health.[76] The two cases of the Aitareya Āraṇyaka and Śāṅkhāyana Āraṇyaka belong to this tradition.

Thus from the time of Vedic period the people of ancient India developed some ritual devices for prolonging life at least up to one hundred years as their ideal lifespan. Broadly speaking, religious and magico-ritualistic methods to overcome death which are laid down after the descriptions of the signs of death in the texts investigated in this paper belong to the old tradition observable already in the Vedic period. But, on the other hand, they show their own developments which are based on the long history of the yogic practice and tantric ritualism. The very tradition of the yogic practice and tantric ritualism has, however, developed into very much diverse directions like Hindu tantras and Buddhist tantras, involving also certainly Jainism[77] and, as the Ḥauḍ al-Ḥayāt shows, Indian Sufism. And these new developments share many common features, although they naturally have their own peculiarities.

One of the purposes of this article is to locate the Ḥauḍ al-Ḥayāt in the yogic and tantric tradition or to find out any close affinity of it with a peculiar religious trend. But the analysis of both the signs of death and the yogic practice to overcome the approaching death described by it dispersed into wider contexts of religious development in medieval India. A further investigation of the development of tantric religions in India and the contents of the Ḥauḍ al-Ḥayāt will any time in future result in gaining a more clear idea about the origin and affiliation of this interesting text, the Ḥauḍ al-Ḥayāt.

NOTES

1. See Kazuyo Sakaki, "The Amṛtakuṇḍa (The Vessel Containing the Nectar) and Sufic Practices," *The Memoirs of the Institute of Oriental Culture* 139, pp. (173)-(206). Here she discusses the genesis of the Ḥauḍ al-Ḥayāt in various versions, analyses its contents and points out the close relation to the tantric yoga, especially the Nath cult.
2. A. S. Gopani, *The Riṣṭasamuccaya of Durgadeva, Critically edited with Exhaustive Introduction, English Translation, Sanskrit Chāyā, Notes, Appendix, Indices, etc.*, Bharatiya Vidya Bhavan, Bombay, 1945.
3. Th. Aufrecht, "Ueber eine Stelle des Aitareyāraṇyaka," *Zeitschrift der Deutschen Morgenländischen Gesellschaft* 32, p. 573.
4. P.V. Kane, *History of Dharmaśāstra* (*Ancient and Mediaeval Religious and Civil Law*), Vol. IV, Second Edition, Bhandarkar Oriental Research Institute, Poona, 1973, p. 181.
5. Stephan Beyer, 1973, *Magic and Ritual in Tibet: The Cult of Tārā*, University of California Press, Berkeley pp. 367-375.
6. Lallanji Gopal, "Viṣṇudharmottara Purāṇa on Ariṣṭas," *Purāṇa* 24(1), pp. 63-78 and "The Vāyupurāṇa and the Mārkaṇḍeyapurāṇa: A Comparative Study," *Purāṇa* 24(2), pp. 338-352.
7. T. Goudriaan, "Some Beliefs and Rituals Concerning Time and Death in the Kubjikāmata," in Ria Kloppenborg, ed., *Selected Studies on Ritual in the Indian Religions, Essays to D.J. Hoens*, Leiden, 1983, pp. 95-117.
8. G. Jan Meulenbeld, *A History of Indian Medical Literature*, Vol. IB Annotation, Egbert Forsten, Groningen, 1999, p. 94, n. 1 and 2.
9. A.B. Keith, *The Aitareya Āraṇyaka*, Oxford, The Clarendon Press, (1909), 1969, pp. 136-137.
10. Keith, *The Aitareya Āraṇyaka*, pp. 313-314 and p. 319. Cf. LāṭyŚS 3.3.6-8: (6) One should let those who will undertake the *dīkṣā* see a mirror, Arundhatī, the polar star, a water vessel, and the man who is seen in the eye. (7) One whose life is over does not see them. (8) One should not allow them to undertake the *dīkṣā*, and ĀpŚS 9.20.10: When the oblation is offered in the fire and black smoke spreads toward the southern direction or wind surrounds the smoke anti-clockwise, the sacrificer will die. See A. Hillebrandt, 1897, *Ritual-Litteratur, Vedische Opfer und Zauber*, Karl J. Trübner, Strassburg, p. 184. See further VaikhGS 5.1 [68,2-3] *yathoktair vārṣikair ariṣṭair āyur ātmīyaṃ parīkṣya*. Among the Vedic texts this seems to be the place where the word *ariṣṭa* denoting the signs of death occurs for the first time. W. Caland in his *Vaikhānasasmārtasūtram. The Domestic Rules and Sacred Laws of the Vaikhānasa School Belonging to the Black Yajurveda*, The Asiatic Society of Bengal, Calcutta, 1929, p. 121 translates it as follows: "When he has carefully ascertained the duration of his own life by (consulting) the symptoms of death coming within three years, as they are treated (in the *jyotiḥśāstras*)."

In his note 3 on the *jyotiḥśāstras* he remarks "So according to the Bhāṣya. Perhaps some medical texts are to be understood." But see, for example, the Vṛddhayavanajātaka, the Bṛhajjātaka, and the Laghujātaka in this list.

11. For other ancient Indian medical texts see Meulenbeld, *A History of Indian Medical Literature*, Vol. IB Annotation, p. 94.
12. *The Śāntiparvan [Part III: Mokṣadharma, A] Being the Twelfth Book of the Mahābhārata for the First Time* Critically Edited by Shripad Krishna Belvalkar, Bhandarkar Oriental Research Institute, Poona, 1954, pp. 1682-1683.
13. *Liṅga Purāṇa with Sanskrit Commentary Śivatoṣinī of Gaṇeśa Nātu* ed. by J.L. Shastri, Motilal Banarsidass, Delhi, 1980, p. 114.
14. *The Mārkaṇḍeyamahāpurāṇam*, Nag Publishers, Delhi, n.d., pp. 143b-145a.
15. *The Skandamahāpurāṇam*, Nag Publishers, Delhi, 1987, pp. 200b-201b.
16. *The Vāyumahāpurāṇam*, Nag Publishers, Delhi, 1983, pp. 24a-b.
17. *The Viṣṇudharmottarapurāṇam*, Nag Publishers, Delhi, 1985, pp. 412b-413a.
18. *The Śivamahāpurāṇam*, Part II, Nag Publishers, Delhi, 1986, pp. 434b-435a. A difficult discussion given in Śiva Purāṇa 5.25.37-75 seems to have a similarity to an also difficult discussion given in Vimalāprabhā 2.4, pp. 190ff. For the Vimalāprabhā see note 28.
19. *Vṛddhayavanajātaka of Mīnarāja*, Vol. II, ed. by D. Pingree, Oriental Institute, Baroda, 1979, pp. 359-364.
20. *Bṛhajjātaka, Avantikācārya Varāhamihirakṛta, Paṇḍitamahīdharakṛtabhāṣāsahita*, ed. by Khemarāja Śrī Kṛṣṇadāsa, Venkateshvara Press, Bombay, 1892, pp. 58-63 and *Laghujātaka of Varāhamihirācārya*, ed. by Pt. Lasanalal Jha, Krishnadas Academy, Varanasi, 1983, pp. 43-50.
21. *Kṛtyakalpataru of Bhaṭṭa Lakṣmīdhara, Vol. XIV. Mokṣakāṇḍa*, ed. by K.V. Rangaswami Aiyangar, Oriental Institute, Baroda, 1945, pp. 248-254. Devala, Vāyu Purāṇa, Mārkaṇḍeya Purāṇa, and Brahma Purāṇa are quoted.
22. *The Adbhutasāgara by Vallāla Sena Deva* ed. by Murali Dhara Jha, The Prabhakari & Co., Benares, 1905, pp. 515-557. Many Sanskrit Texts are drawn upon as sources. They are Ādipurāṇa, Bārhaspatya, Bhāgavata Purāṇa, Brahmāṇḍa Purāṇa, Bṛhadyātrā, Caraka Saṃhitā, Devala, Hārīta Riṣṭaprakaraṇa, Kālāvalī, Liṅga Purāṇa, Mahābhārata, Mārkaṇḍeya Purāṇa, Mayūracitra, Nārada, Parāśara, Suśruta Samhitā, and Viṣṇudharmottara Purāṇa.
23. *Dharmasindhu* ed. by Vasudeva Sarma, Nirnaya Sagar Press, Bombay, 1936, p. 313.
24. *Śārṅgadhara Paddhati being an Anthology of Sanskrit Verses compiled by Śārṅgadhara* ed. by Peter Peterson, Nirnaya Sagar Press, Bombay, 1915 (Chaukhamba Sanskrit Pratishthan, Delhi, 1987), pp. 686-689. As is clear from the comment given after stanza 27: *ete mārkaṇḍeyapurāṇāt* 'These are from the Mārkaṇḍeya Purāṇa.' this is a quotation from the Mārkaṇḍeya Purāṇa. See Aufrecht, "Ueber eine Stelle des Aitareyāraṇyaka," p. 573.
25. *Śivatattva Ratnākara of Basavarāja of Keḷadi*, Vol. I, ed. by S. Narayanaswamy Sastry, Oriental Research Institute, University of Mysore, Mysore, 1964, pp. 304-306.
26. *The Ḳubjikāmatatantra, Kulālikāmnāya Version, Critical Edition* by T. Goudriaan and J.A. Schoterman, E.J. Brill, Leiden, New York, Kobenhavn, Köln,

1988, pp. 421-424. According to T. Goudriaan, *Hindu Tantric and Śākta Literature,* Otto Harrassowitz, 1981, p. 51 the Kaulajñānanirṇaya seems to have some chapters dealing with "the symptoms of old age, disease and death" and "the exercise of supernatural powers, especially the conquering of death".

27. *The Saṃvarodaya-Tantra, Selected Chapters* ed. by Shiníchi Tsuda, The Hokuseido Press, Tokyo, 1974, pp. 129-132.

28. *Vimalāprabhā,* Part I ed. by Jagannath Upadhyaya, Central Institute of Higher Tibetan Studies, Sarnath, 1986, pp. 213-214. According to Kimiaki Tanaka, *Sexology and Thanatology of Buddhism,* Shunjusha, Tokyo, 1997, pp. 202-203 Catuṣpīṭha Tantra 1.2.2-9 describes the signs of death. Here Mr. Tanaka gives the Japanese translation of the text. And according to Munenobu Sakurai, "Mṛtyuvañcana-Tārā and its Sādhana," *Mikkyogaku Kenkyu* 32, p. 3 the Mṛtyuvañcanopadeśa, *pariccheda* 1 lays down the external signs of death and *pariccheda* 2 the internal signs of death. Dr. Sakurai was kind enough to allowe me to read one manuscript of the Mṛtyuvañcanopadeśa, namely NGMPP B 90/12. In the following discussion I sometimes refer to this manuscript.

29. Yogasūtra 3.22 reads *sopakramaṃ nirūpakramaṃ ca karma tatsamayād aparānta jñānam ariṣṭebhyo vā //* The Yogasūtra itself alludes to the *ariṣṭas* but does not mention concrete examples. Gopani, *The Riṣṭasamuccaya of Durgadeva,* pp. 99-100, refers to three commentaries: Vyāsabhāṣya, Vācaspatya, and Bhojadevīya and they enumerate a limited numbers of the signs of approaching death.

30. *Yogaratnākara,* Ananda Ashrama Sanskrit Series, 4, 1900, pp. 8-9 (this passage is quoted by A. S. Gopani in his *The Riṣṭasamuccaya of Durgadeva,* p. 108) and pp. 26-27 under the title of *svalpāyuṣo lakṣaṇāni* or characteristics of very short life.

31. Gopani, *The Riṣṭasamuccaya of Durgadeva,* pp. 1-46. Analysis of the contents of the Riṣṭasamuccaya reveals that this text consists of at least two parts and the dividing line is verse 148. The first part describes the signs of death which can be observed in many other texts listed till now and the second part contains many examples of astrological prognostications usually called *praśna* regarding the coming death. See Gopani, *The Riṣṭasamuccaya of Durgadeva,* pp. 12-13. Among sixteen texts which A.S. Gopani quoted in Appendix the Yogaśāstra of Hemacandra, 5.129-224 (quoted in *The Riṣṭasamuccaya of Durgadeva,* pp. 104-108) was not available to me.

32. Yusuf Husain, "Ḥauḍ al-Ḥayāt: La version arabe de l'amratkund," *Journal Asiatique* 208, pp. 335-337. Muhammad Enamul Haq, *A History of Sufism in Bengal,* Asiatic Society of Bangladesh, Dacca, 1975, pp. 394-396 gives a English translation of chapter 18 of the Yogakalandar of Sayyad Murtaza which was originally written in old Bengali where we can find the descriptions of many signs of death.

33. This paraphrase of the eighth chapter of the Ḥauḍ al-Ḥayāt is based on the Persian version of it prepared by Dr. Sakaki using mainly the manuscript of Majmū'a-yi Rasā'il 2, Salar Jung Museum, cat. XI 4435 with her Japanese translation and the English paraphrase made by Prof. Nazir Ahmad which Dr. Sakaki allowed me to use.

34. In these texts the afterimage is indicated explicitly: Śiva Purāṇa 5.28.

6a *dṛṣṭvā taṃ punar ākāśe* "after seeing it again in the air"; Adbhutasāgara 552, 9 *śanair uttolite netre svacchāya dṛśyate 'mbare* "The eyes are slowly raised. His own shadow is seen in the sky."; Riṣṭasamuccaya 99ab *ni jachāyāṃ gaganatale paśyati pratibimbitāṃ sphuṭam* "He sees his own shadow clearly reflected in the surface of the sky."; Yogaśāstra 5.169ab *śanair utkṣipya netre svacchāyāṃ paśyet tato 'mbare* "After having slowly raised his eyes he should then see his own shadow in the sky." Stephan Beyer reports also the same method in his *The Cult of Tārā* on pages 371-373. The following sentence clearly suggests the afterimage: "then he looks into the center of the cloudless sky, whereupon he sees an optical afterimage of his own form." (Beyer, *The Cult of Tārā,* p. 372.)

35. A similarity of the descriptions of the Saṃvarodaya Tantra 19.18-19 and Mṛtyuvañcanopadeśa 1 (NGMPP, B 90/12, folio 5a, 2-4), both being Buddhist tantra texts, is easily understandable. They mention three cases: if one does not see the head, one dies within a year, whereas the lack of the left arm and right arm indicates the death of the son and the wife on the one hand and the death of the father and the brother on the other. Almost the same prognostication is found in Yogaśāstra 5.169cd-170, a Jain text, and Adbhutasāgara 552,10-13, a Hindu text, referring to the Kālāvalī. In the latter two texts the mention of the father is absent. It is, thus, interesting to note that the textual correspondence is observable not only within the Buddhist tradition, but it extends also into the Jain and Hindu traditions.
36. See, for example, Śiva Purāṇa 5. 25. 19cd; Adbhutasāgara 553, 3; 553, 8; 554, 14.
37. See, for example, Vṛddhayavanajātaka 64. 13ac; Liṅga Purāṇa 91.9cd; Vāyu Purāṇa 19.7cd; Viṣṇudharmottara Purāṇa 3.238. 12cd; Kubjikāmata Tantra 23.40cd; Adbhutasāgara 553,10 and 556,3.
38. Aitareya Āraṇyaka 3.2.4 [136, 7-8]; Śāṅkhāyana Āraṇyaka 8.7 [314,1-2] and 11.3 [319,9] .
39. Kubjikāmata Tantra 23.30cd; 43cd; Śivatattvaratnākara 5. 1.75cd.
40. Kubjikāmata Tantra 23. 38cd-39ab; Skanda Purāṇa 4. 1. 42. 29; Adbhutasāgara 555, 11; I 13-14; Mṛtyuvañcanopadeśa 1 (NGMPP, B 90/12, folio 3b, 6 and folio 6a, 5); Riṣṭasamuccaya 142cd.
41. Saṃvarodaya Tantra 19.10cd = Mṛtyuvañcanopadeśa 1, folio 3b, 5.
42. Riṣṭasamuccaya 143; 147; Adbhutasāgara 554, 3-4; 555, 2.
43. Mārkaṇḍeya Purāṇa 40. 11; Liṅga Purāṇa 91 11; Vāyu Purāṇa 19. 9; Kubjikāmata Tantra 23.30;
44. Śiva Purāṇa 5. 25. 17; Adbhutasāgara 554, 9-10; Yogaratnākara 27, 7-8. Dharmasindhu 313, 19 only refers to the reflection without a head.
45. Adbhutasāgara 553,16; Saṃvarodaya Tantra 19. 6 = Mṛtyuvañcanopadeśa 1, folio 3a, 2.
46. Mahābhārata 12.305.10; Mṛtyuvañcanopadeśa 1, folio 5b,6.
47. Liṅga Purāṇa 91.4; Mārkaṇḍeya Purāṇa 40.4; Viṣṇudharmottara Purāṇa 3.238.7; Mṛtyuvañcanopadeśa 1, folio 4a,1.
48. Skanda Purāṇa 4.1.42.10; Adbhutasāgara 556, 16-17; Saṃvarodaya Tantra 19.17; Mṛtyuvañcanopadeśa 1, folio 4a,7.
49. According to Vṛddhayavanajātaka 64.19ab one excretes excessively. Mṛtyuvañcanopadeśa 1, folio 6a, 1-3 describes changes of urine in taste and color and says further that urine flows in five streams, turning to

left, giving out a bad smell. Saṃvarodaya Tantra 19.20 similarly says that urine flows in five streams, turning to left, giving out a bad smell and it shows the change in taste.

50. *wa fikr rā wa shakl waz'-i o bā rang wa sūrat-i o bayand.* This sentence is not clear. In the seventh chapter seven mantras beginning with *hom* are discussed. Each mantra has its own shape and position in the body and its own colour. The mantra *hom,* for example, is of a definite shape and assigned to the anus and its colour is black with yellow inside it.
51. In the text *suṣumna* is written as *sukhmunā.*
52. It seems that the Viṣṇudharmottara Purāṇa, Vṛddhayavanajātaka, Bṛhajjātaka, Laghujātaka, Adbhutasāgara and Dharmasindhu collect these signs of death without any purpose. We do not know the purpose for which the knowledge of these signs is used in these texts.
53. Carakasaṃhitā, Indriyasthāna, 6.6d *taṃ bhiṣak parivarjayet.* See also 6. 13d; 6. 15d; 7. 18d; 7.21d; 8.9d; 8. 15d; 9.9d; 9. 13d; 9. 14d.
54. Carakasaṃhitā, Indriyasthāna, 6.7c *na tasmai bheṣajaṃ dadyāt.* See also 8.4cd; 11.22d; 12.6.
55. Carakasaṃhitā, Indriyasthāna, 7. 3d *nainam icched cikitsitum.* See also 8.3d; 12. 64b; 6. 17d; 12.7d.
56. Carakasaṃhitā, Indriyasthāna, 12.17d *na vaidyo gantum arhati.* See also 12.21d; 12.31.
57. A text very similar to Mahābhārata 12.305. 17-21 is quoted in Kṛtyakalpataru, XIV Mokṣakāṇḍa, 253, 16- 254, 3 as originated from the Brahma Purāṇa.
58. This assignment of the deities to various parts of the body is peculiar. Compare, for example, Hiraṇyakeśi Gṛhyaśeṣasūtra 1.2.12. Saṃvarodaya Tantra 19. 34-38a gives a Buddhist version of the enumeration of the parts of the body through which the consciousness (*cetas*) passes out and of the worlds obtained by it. They can be listed as follows: navel, realm of desire; the spot between the eyebrows, birth as a corporeal being *(rūpadehin);* the upper part (*ūrdhva*), formless realm; nostrils, abode of *yakṣas*; ears, abode of *kinnaras*; eyes, birth as a king of men; mouth, the existence of *pretas;* penis, birth as an animal; anus, birth in a hell. For the Buddhist version see Alex Wayman, *The Buddhist Tantras: Light on Indo-Tibetan Esotericism,* Samuel Weiser, New York, 1913, pp. 140-141.
59. Mahābhārata 12.305. 17cd *ātmānam yojayet paramātmani.* Liṅga Purāṇa 1.91. 40b *yuñjīta.* Mārkaṇḍeya Purāṇa 40.40c *yuñjīta yogī.* Kṛtyakalpataru, Mokṣakāṇḍa 255, 8 *dhāraṇāṃ mūrdhni dhārayet.* Śārṅgadharapaddhati 163.2b *yogaṃ yuñjīta yogavit.* Saṃvarodaya Tantra 19.29b *utkrāntiyogam uttamam* and in the following 29cd-30 is explained the *prāṇāyāma* consisting of *pūraka, kumbhaka* and *recaka.* For the Kubjikāmata Tantra see Goudriaan, "Some Beliefs and Rituals Concerning Time and Death in the Kubjikāmata," p. 100: "The way in which the *utkrānti* method is described in this fragment suggests that we are confronted here with a variety of raising *kuṇḍalinī.*"
60. Liṅga Purāṇa 1.91.36c *tyaktvā khedaṃ viṣadaṃ ca.* Mārkaṇḍeya Purāṇa 40.41b = Śārṅgadharapaddhati 163.2d *tyaktvā maraṇajaṃ bhayaṃ.* Kṛtyakalpataru, Mokṣakāṇḍa, 255, 4 *tyaktvā bhayaṃ viṣadam.* Cf. Kubjikāmata Tantra 23. 102cd *na duḥkhito na kopena kuryād utkrāntikaraṇam.*
61. Mahābhārata 12. 305. 21ac *gacchet prāpyākṣayaṃ kṛtsnam ajanma śivam*

avyayam / śāśvataṃ sthānam acalam. Liṅga Purāṇa 1.91. 45ab *tathoṃkāramayo yogī akṣare tv akṣarī bhavet.* Mārkaṇḍeya Purāṇa 40.46 *tataḥ paramanirvāṇaṃ ...aśnute.* Kṛtyakalpataru, Mokṣakāṇḍa, 255, 12 *evaṃ nirvāṇaṃ āpnoti.* Śārṅgadharapaddhati 163.6d *paramātmani līyate.* Saṃvarodaya Tantra 19. 38b says *mokṣāṇāṃ gatir anyathā* "Different is the way to the liberations" after describing the various ways reached by the consciousness by passing out through different parts of the body as mentioned in note 58.

62. Concrete practices described in these passages are summed up as cheating death (*kālavañcana*) in Śiva Purāṇa 5.28.1ab *devadeva mahādeva kathitaṃ kālavañcanaṃ* "O god of gods, the cheating of death is told."

63. Mṛtyuvañcanopadeśa, *pariccheda* 3 and 4 describes thirteen ways of cheating death. For the detailed analysis of them see Michael Walter, "Cheating Death," in David Gordon White (ed.), *Tantra in Practice*, Princeton University Press, Princeton and London, 2000, pp. 605-624. In note 52 I included the Adbhutasāgara in the texts which collect the signs of death without showing definite purposes. But in the Adbhutasāgara we find several quotations which prescribe some ritual rites to pacify the approach of death. They are as follows (in round brackets the title of the texts quoted is given): 520, 16-20 (Mayūracitra); 521,21-26 (Mayūracitra); 522, 4-6 (Nārada); 524, 20-21 (Mayūracitra); 525, 2 (Mayūracitra); 534, 17 (Vasantarāja); 554, 13 (Mayūracitra); 554, 15 (Mayūracitra); 554, 19-20 (Nārada); 557,12 (Mayūracitra). Most of the passages are quoted from the Mayūracitra. According to D. Pingree, *Jyotiḥśāstra*, Otto Harrassowitz, Wiesbaden, 1981, p. 72, Varāhamihira cites Nārada's Mayūracitraka as an earlier authority. Nārada which occurs two times and the Mayūracitra may be the same work. For Vasantarāja see Pingree, *Jyotiḥśāstra*, p. 76. Jaghujātaka, chapter 8, where malignant combinations of stars which predict the approaching death is dealt with, is followed by chapter 9 which describes the celestial combinations that pacify the predicted death

64. Mahābhārata 12.305.19c *tathā hi mṛtyuṃ jayati*; 20c *jayec ca mṛtyuṃ yogena.*

65. Śiva Purāṇa 5. 26. 29ab *mucyate yogī sadyaḥ saṃsārabandhanāt.* According to Śiva Purāṇa 5.27.12d one who practises the breath control (*prāṇāyāma*) goes to the world of Brahman (*āśu brahmalokaṃ sa gacchati*). Śārṅgadharapaddhati 163. 17b says that the yogin goes to the unity with Śiva (*yogī áivenaikātmatāṃ vrajet*).

66. Śiva Purāṇa 5. 27. 26d *yogī cāmṛtatvaṃ prapadyate.* Śiva Purāṇa 5.27. 36cd *yogī so 'mṛtatvaṃ hi gacchati.*

67. Śiva Purāṇa 5. 27. 31ab and 33a *yogī na mṛtyuvaśago bhavet ...jīven naro varṣaśatam.* For the idea that life of one hundred years is the immortality for the human beings see, for example, J.Fr. Sprockhoff, "Die Alten im alten Indien: Ein Versuch nach brahmanischen Quellen," *Saeculum* 30(4), p. 378, and n. 7.

68. Śivatattvaratnākara 5.1.87c *kālo vimukhato yāti.*

69. Śiva Purāṇa 5.27. 29cd-30ab *cañcvākāreṇa vaktreṇa piban vāyuṃ śanaiḥ śanaiḥ /29/ prasravanti kṣaṇād āpas tālusthā jīvadāyikāḥ.* Śiva Purāṇa 5.27. 35-36ab *samākuñcyābhyased yogī rasanāṃ tālukaṃ prati / kiñcit kālāntareṇaiva kramāt prāpnoti lambikām /35/ tataḥ prasravate sā tu saṃspṛṣṭā śītalāṃ sudhām. Śārṅgadharapaddhati* 163-13-16 *bandhayet khecarīm mudrāṃ /13/... pītvā sudhākarodbhūtaṃ amṛtaṃ tena mūlataḥ / siñcantīṃ*

sakalaṃ dehaṃ plāvayantīm vicintayet /16/ In the Mṛtyuvañcanopadeśa we find similar passages. They are Mṛtyuvañcanopadeśa 4, NGMPP, B90/12, folio 15b, 5-6; folio 16a, 1-3 and folio 16a, 3-6.

70. See, for example, Shashibhusana Das Gupta, *Obscure Religious Cults*, Firma KLM, Calcutta, 1976, pp. 239-243; K.R. van Kooij, *Worship of the Goddess According to the Kālikāpurāṇa, pt. I, A Translation with an Introduction and Notes of Chapters 54-69*, Leiden: Brill, 1972, p. 16; Helene Brunner, "Un Tantra du Nord: Le Netra Tantra," *Bulletin de l'École Française d'Extrême-Orient*, LXI, p. 143; Wayman, *The Buddhist Tantras*, p. 181.

71. See Das Gupta, *Obscure Religious Cults*, p. 242. According to the information given by Dr. K. Sakaki, the *khecarīmudrā* is defined, among the Haṭhayoga texts, for example by Haṭhayogapradīpikā 3.32, Gheraṇḍasaṃhitā 3.27 and Gorakṣaśataka 64.

72. As noted above in note 69 Śārṅgadharapaddhati 163.13a explicitly mentions the *khecarīmudrā*. Mṛtyuvañcanopadeśa 4, NGMPP, B90/12, folio 16a, I mentioned above in note 69 also alludes to it as follows: *jihvāṃ tālugatāṃ kṛtvā dantair dantān na saṃspṛśet.* Devībhāgavata Purāṇa 11.1. 35cd-36ab *dantair dantān na saṃspṛśet //35// tālusthācalajihvaś ca saṃvṛtāsyaḥ suniścalaḥ* Cf. Kubjikāmata Tantra 6.62cd *dvādaśāarordhvanālena lambikānte niveśayet* and 23. 161 *rasanāṃ śūnyamadhyasthāṃ kṛtvā caiva nirāśrayaṃ / na dantair daśanān spṛṣṭvā oṣṭhau naiva parasparaṃ //*

73. Kubjikāmata Tantra 23. 81cd *juṃ saḥ sampuṭanāmādyaṃ saḥ juṃ ante niyojayet.* I can not "pull out" the proper mantra. For a similar mantra *oṃ juṃ saḥ* and the *saṃpuṭa* method of pulling out a mantra from the encoded text see H. Brunner, 1974, "Un Tantra du Nord: Le Netra Tantra," *BEFEO*, LXI, p. 139 and p. 140.

74. The mantra given in Śivatattvaratnākara 5. 1. 88ab+ reads as follows: *hrīṃ sraṃ kṣrām drauṃ drāṃ kroṃ saṃmohinī caṇḍe kālasaṃkarṣaṇi namaḥ//* Mṛtyuvañcanopadeśa, *pariccheda* 3 and 4, give many examples of mantras to be used to cheat death. Among them is one mantra given in folio 15a, 5: *om tāre tuttāre ture svāhā.* According to G. Bühnemann, "Buddhist Deities and Mantras," *Indo-Iranian Journal* 43, p. 31-32 mantras corresponding to it are given in various Hindu and Buddhist tantras such as Śrīvidyārṇava Tantra 2, p. 277, 10-11; Tantrasāra, p. 280, 21-22; Tārabhaktisudhārṇava, chapter 11 (p. 422, 25-26); Siddhaikavīramahātantra, p. 150, 5; Tantrarāja 22. 25-27ab; Guhyasamāja Tantra 14.6+; Sādhanamālā, no. 97, p. 197, 7. Śiva Purāṇa 2. 2. 38. 22-29 records a *mahāmṛtyuṃjaya mantra*. (See Ludo Rocher, "Mantras in the Śivapurāṇa," in Harvey, P. Alper (ed.), *Understanding Mantras*, Motilal Banarsidass, Delhi, 1991, p. 189.) Narasiṃha Purāṇa 7.44 prescribes the use of mantra: *oṃ namo bhagavate vāsudevāya*, a famous twelve-syllabled mantra of Viṣṇu, to expel death.

75. See Jan Gonda, *Vedic Ritual: The Non-solemn Ritual*, E.J. Brill, Leiden-Köln, 1980, p. 474. See further, for example, Bhāradvāja Paitrimedhikasūtra 1.8-13; Gobhila Gṛhyasūtra 4. 6. 1.

76. See M. Bloomfield, *The Atharvaveda and the Gopatha Brāhmaṇa*, Karl J. Trübner, Strassburg, 1899, pp. 63-65.

77. For Jain tantrism see, for example, Olle Qvarnstrom, "Jain Tantra: Divinatory and Meditative Practices in the Twelfth-Century Yogaśāstra of Hemacandra," in White (ed.), *Tantra in Practice*, pp. 595-604.

Curriculum Vitae of Prof. M. Tachikawa

NAME: TACHIKAWA Musashi
DATE OF BIRTH: February 6, 1942

EDUCATION

1967-70	Ph.D. Course at Graduate School of Arts and Sciences, Harvard University (Ph.D. in Sanskrit and Indian Studies)
1966-67	Ph.D. Course at Faculty of Letters, Nagoya University (Doctor of Literature, 1985)
1964-66	M.A. Course, Nagoya University (M.A. in Literature, 1966)
1960-64	B.A. Course, Nagoya University (B.A. in Literature, 1964)

OCCUPATION

2004-present	Professor, Faculty of Letters, Aichi Gakuin University
1992-2004	Professor, National Museum of Ethnology
1989-1992	Professor, Faculty of Letters, Nagoya University
1973-1989	Associate Professor, Faculty of Letters, Nagoya University
1970-1973	Lecturer, Faculty of Letters, Nagoya University

OTHER AFFLIATIONS AND PROFESSIONAL EXPERIENCE

Member, Japanese Association for South Asian Studies
Member, Japanese Association of Indian and Buddhist Studies
Member, Japanese Association for Tibetan Studies
Member, International Association for Buddhist Studies

AWARDS

2001 The 11th Nakamura Hajime Eastern Study Prize from the Eastern Institute, Inc.

1997 The 50th Chunichi Culture Prize from Chunichi Newspapers

1991 The 3rd Asia-Pacific Special Prize from Mainichi Newspapers

MAIN RESEARCH AND TEACHING CONDUCTED ABROAD

2002 (Sep.)	Research of Hinduism in Bali.
2001 (May-Jun.)	Siebold Professor at Bonn University
2001 (Feb.-Mar.)	Numata Professor at Leiden University
1995 (July-Aug.)	Research of Hinduism in Maharashtra.
1992 (Feb.-May)	Numata Professor at University of Chicago.
1987 (Jan.-May)	Numata Professor at University of California, Berkeley.
1984 (July-Sept.)	Research of Newar Buddhism in Kathmandu.
1982 (July-Sept.)	Research of Tibetan Buddhism in Kathmandu.
1979 (July)-1980(Sept.)	Research of Indian Buddhism at Hamburg University as a Humboldt Researcher.
1977 (July-Sept.)	Research of Indian Philosophy at Pune.
1975 (July-Aug.)	Research of Indian Philosophy at Pune.

Publications of Prof. M. Tachikawa

A-1. Books

(1) *Chibetto Bukkyou Shuugi Kenkyuu* (*A study of the Grub mtha' of Tibetan Buddhism*, Vol.1, The Sa skya pa Chapter of Thu'u bkwan's *Shel gyi me long*), Oriental Library, Tokyo, 1974.

(2) *The Structure of the World in Udayana's Realism*, Reidel, Holland, 1981 (Harvard Ph. D. Thesis).

(3) *Kuu no Kouzou: Chuuron no Ronri* (*The Structure of Emptiness: The Logic of the Madhyamakakārikā*), Daisan Bunmeisha, 1986.

(4) *Mandara no Kamigami* (*Maṇḍala Deities*), Arina Shobou, 1987.

(5) *Chibetto Bukkyou Shuugi Kenkyuu* (*A study of the Grub mtha' of Tibetan Buddhism*, Vol. 5, The bKa' brgyud pa Chapter of Thu'u bkwan's Shel gyi me long), Oriental Library, Tokyo, 1987.

(6) *Yooga no Tetsugaku* (*Philosophy of Yoga*), Koudansha, Gendaishinsho No.924, 1998.

(7) *Megamitachi no Indo* (*India of Goddesses*), Serika Shobou, 1990.

(8) *Hajimete no Indo Tetsugaku* (*An Introduction to Indian Philosophy*), Koudansha, Gendaishinsho No.1123, 1992.

(9) *Chuuron no Shisou* (*The Thought of the Madhyamakakārikā*), Houzoukan, 1994 (Nagoya University Dr. Thesis).

(10) *Nihon Bukkyou no Shisou* (*A History of Japanese Buddhism*), Koudansha, Gendaishinsho No.1254, 1994.

(11) *Seinarumono eno Tabi* (*A Journey to the Sacred*), Jinbun Shoin, 1994.

(12) *Mandara* (*Maṇḍala*), Gakushuu Kenkyuusha, 1996.

(13) *An Introduction to the Philosophy of Nāgārjuna*, tr. by R. Giebel, Motilal Banarsidass, Delhi, 1997.
(14) *Mandara Meisouhou* (*Meditation on Maṇḍala*), Kadokawa Shoten, 1997.
(15) *Budda no Tetsugaku* (*Philosophy of Buddha*), Houzoukan, 1998.
(16) *Mandara towa Nanika* (*What is the Maṇḍala*), Kouyasan University, 1998.
(17) *Mikkyou no Shisou* (*Thought of Tantrism*), Yoshikawa Koubunkan, 1998.
(18) *Saichou to Kuukai* (*Saicho and Kukai*), Koudansha, 1998.
(19) *Hannyashingyou no Atarashii Yomikata* (*A New Light on the Heart Sūtra*), Shunjuusha, 2001.
(20) *Kuu no Shisoushi* (*A History of the Thought of Emptiness*), Koudansha, 2003.

A-2. Books with Co-author(s)

(1) *Bukkyou to Gendaishisou* (*Buddhism and the Modern Thought*), (Co-authors: K. Ikuta, K. Kanbe and M. Usami) Shindoukaikan, Nagoya, 1975.
(2) *Nyi 'ong chos 'byung chogs bsdus* (*A Short History of Japanese Buddhism*) (in Tibetan), (Co-author: Tsultrim Kelsang) International Buddhist Association, Hamamatsu, 1977.
(3) *Hinzuu no Kamigami* (*Hindu Deities*), (Co-authors: A. Ishiguro, K. Hishida and I. Shima) Serika Shobou, 1980.
(4) *Niṣpannayogāvālī*, (Co-author: G. Buehnemann) The Center for East Asian Cultural Studies, 1991.
(5) *Chibetto Mikkyou no Shinpi* (*Mysteries of Tibetan Buddhism*), (Co-author: A. Masaki) Gakushuu Kenkyuusha, 1997.
(6) *Pūjā and Saṃskāra*, (Co-authors: S. Hino and L. Deodhar) Motilal Banarsidass, Delhi, 2001.
(7) *Ancient Indian Fire Ritual*, (Co-authors: S. Bahulkar and M. Kolhatkar) Motilal Banarsidass, Delhi, 2001.
(8) *Chibetto Bukkyou Shuugi Kenkyuu* (*A study of the Grub mtha' of Tibetan Buddhism*, Vol.7, The dGe lugs pa Chapter of Thu'u bkwan's Shel gyi me long), (Co-authors: Y. Fukuda and Y. Ishihama) Oriental Library, Tokyo (in print).
(9) *Ajanta to Eroora* (*Ajanata and Ellora*), (Photo: T. Omura) Shuueisha, 2000.

(10). *Shiva to Nyoshintachi* (*Śiva and Goddesses*), (Photo: T. Omura) Yamakawa Shuppan, 2002.

A-3. Compiled Books

(1) *Bukkyou no Juyou to Henyou* (*The Acceptance and Change of Buddhism*), Vol. 3, Kousei Shuppansha, 1991.

(2) *Mandara Uchuuron* (*The Cosmology of Maṇḍala*), Houzoukan, 1996.

(3) *Iyashi to Sukui* (*Healing and Salvation*), Tamagawa University Press, 2000.

B-1. Edited Books

(1) *Catalogue of Tibetan Works kept in Joraku-ji Temple Library*, Studia Asiatica No.4, The Department of Indian Philosophy, Nagoya University, 1979.

(2) *A Catalogue of the Gedan Sungrab Minyam Gyunphel Series*, Part 1, Studia Asiatica No.7, The Department of Indian Philosophy, Nagoya University, 1985.

(3) *Mandara: Chibetto to Nepaaru no Hotoketachi* (*Maṇḍala: Deities of Tibetan and Nepalese Buddhism*), National Museum of Ethnology and Senri Bunka Zaidan, 2003.

(4) *A KWIC Index to the Mūlamadhyamakakārikā*, Houzoukan (in print).

With Co-editor(s)

(1) *A Comparative Text of the Samantamukha Chapter of the Lotus Sūtra*, Report of the Fund of the Ministry of Education, The Oriental Library, H. Kitamura and others (co-ed.), 1891, 3 vols.

(2) *A Catalogue of the United States Library of Congress Collection of Tibetan Literature in Microfiche*, Part 1, The International Institute for Buddhist Studies, Tokyo, Tsultrim Kelsang and T. Onoda (co-ed.), 1983.

(3) *A Catalogue of the United States Library of Congress Collection of Tibetan Literature in Microfiche*, Part 2, The International Institute for Buddhist Studies, Tokyo, Y. Nagano, F. Taniguchi and S. Onoda (co-ed.), 1988.

(4) *Chibetto no Gengo to Bunka* (*Language and Culture of Tibet*), Felicitation Volume of Prof. H. Kitamura, Y. Nagano (co-ed.), Toujusha, 1987.
(5) *The Deities of the Dharmadhātu Maṇḍala,* Bulletin of the National Museum of Ethnology, Special Issue 7, Y. Nagano (co-ed.), 1989.
(6) *Three Works of Vasubandhu in Sanskrit Manuscript,* K. Mimaki and A. Yuyama (co-ed.), The Center for East Asian Cultural Studies, 1989.
(7) *The Ngor Maṇḍalas of Tibet, Listings of the Names of Deities,* S. Onoda, K. Noguchi and K. Tanaka (co-ed.), The Center for East Asian Cultural Studies, 1991.
(8) *Iconographic Studies of the Stūpa of Gyantse,* Bulletin of the National Museum of Ethnology, Special Issue No.18, A. Masaki (co-ed.) National Museum of Ethnology, 1997.
(9) *Series Mikkyou 1: Indo Mikkyou* (*Studies in Tantrism: India*), M. Yoritomi (co-ed.), Shunjuusha, 1999.
(10) *Series Mikkyou 2: Chibetto Mikkyou* (*Studies in Tantrism: Tibet*), M. Yoritomi (co-ed.), Shunjuusha, 1999.
(11) *Series Mikkyou 3: Chuugoku Mikkyou* (*Studies in Tantrism: China*), M. Yoritomi (co-ed.), Shunjuusha, 1999.
(12) *Series-Mikkyou 4: Nihon Mikkyou* (*Studies in Tantrism: Japan*), M. Yoritomi (co-ed.), Shunjuusha, 2000.
(13) *Five Hundred Buddhist Deities,* M. Mori and S. Yamaguchi (co-ed.), Asian Iconography Series I, Adroit Publishers, Delhi, 2000.
(14) *Maṇḍalas of the Bon Religion,* Tenzin Namdak and Y. Nagano (co-ed.), Senri Ethnological Reports 12, National Museum of Ethnology, 2000.
(15) *Three Hundred and Sixty Buddhist Deities,* M. Mori and S. Yamaguchi (co-ed.), Asian Iconography Series II, Adroit Publishers, Delhi, 2001.

C. Papers

(1) Chuuron ni okeru Soue ni tsuite (Mutual Dependence in the Madhyamakakārikā), *Toukai Bukkyou* No. 12, 1967, pp.13-20.
(2) A Sixth-Century Manual of Indian Logic, *Journal of Indian Philosophy* Vol.1, part 2, Dordrecht-Holland, 1971, pp. 111-145.

(3) Chibetto Shiryou ni Mirareru Chuugan Puraasangikaha no Keihu (The Prāsaṅgika Tradition in Tibetan Buddhism), *Ajia Bunka* No.10, Part 1, 1973, pp.66-74.
(4) Bukkyou no Ronrigaku (Buddhist Logic), *Touyou Gakujutsu Kenkyuu* Vol.12, No.1, 1973, pp.21-38.
(5) Udayana no Lakṣaṇāvalī ni tsuite (On Udayana's Lakṣaṇāvalī) 1, *Journal of Indian and Buddhist Studies* Vol.22, No.1, 1974, pp.431-426.
(6) Yooga no Dentou (Tradition of Yoga), *Chuuou Kouron*, Chuuou Kouronsha, May 1974, pp.352-359.
(7) A Study of Buddhapālita's Mūlamadhyamakakārikāvṛtti, *The Journal of the Faculty of Literature Nagoya University*, No.63, 1974, pp.1-19.
(8) A Note on Sa skya pa's Lam 'bras Doctrine, *Report of the Japanese Association for Tibetan Studies*, No. 20, 1974, pp.7-8.
(9) The Tantric Doctrine of the Sa skya pa according to the Shel gyi me long, *Acta Asiatica* Vol.29, 1975, pp.95-106.
(10) Udayana no Lakṣaṇāvalī ni tsuite (On Udayana's Lakṣaṇāvalī) 2, *Journal of Indian and Buddhist Studies* Vol. 25, No. 1, 1976, pp. 443-437.
(11) Shuukyouteki Ketsudan ni okeru Ishi to Jikan (Will and Time at Religious Decision), *The Journal of the Nippon Buddhist Research Association* No. 42, 1976, pp. 375-388.
(12) Shiva to Heeruka (Siva and Heruka), *Mikkyou no Bunka* (*Culture of Tantrism*), Shunjuusha, 1977, pp. 260-281.
(13) Chuuron ni okeru Sezoku to Shougi (Ultimate Truth and Convensional Truth in the Madhyamakakārikā), *Touyou Gakujutsu Kenkyuu* No.16, Part 5, 1977, pp. 1-22.
(14) Chuuron Happuge ni tsuite (On the Dedication Verse of the Madhyamakakārikā), *Journal of Religion Studies* No.234, 1977, pp.324-325.
(15) Mikkyou to Jujutsu (Tantrism and Magic), *Mikkyou no Riron to Jissen, Shunjuusha,* 1978, pp.196-222.
(16) Chuuron ni okeru Engi (Dependent Co-arising in the Madhyamakakārikā), *The Journal of the Faculty of Literature Nagoya University*, Thirtieth Anniversary Volume, 1979, pp. 550-535.
(17) Gengokatsudou no Shimetsu to Kuushou (Cessation of Verbal Activities and Emptiness), *Bukkyougaku* Nos. 9-10, 1980, pp. 145-163.

(18) A Logical Analysis of the Mūlamadhyamakakārikā, *Sanskrit and Indian Studies: essays in honor of Daniel H. H. Ingalls*, Reidel, 1980, pp. 159-181.

(19) Pratītyasamutpāda in the Dedication of the *Mūlamadhyamakakārikā, The Adyar Library Bulletin, Dr. K. Kunjunni Rāja Felicitation Volume* Vols. 44-45, 1980-1981, pp. 639-653.

(20) Kuushisou Kenkyuu no tameno Shosuihei (Horizons for Studies of Emptiness Thought) 1, *Touyou Gakujutsu Kenkyuu* No. 20, Part 1, 1981, pp. 86-100.

(21) Ibid. 2, No. 20, Part 2, 1981, pp. 120-136.

(22) Genshou Sekai no Seika (Sanctification of the Phenomenal World), *Buddhist Seminar* No. 35, 1982, pp. 73-88.

(23) Kamigami to Hinzuu Kyouto (Deities and Hindus), *Kami to Hotoke no Daichi Indo*, Kousei Shuppan, 1982, pp. 54-87.

(24) Shuukyou Jissen ni okeru Jiko Kuukan no Henyou (Changes of the Self-space in Religious Practices), *The Journal of the Nippon Buddhist Research Association*, 1982, pp. 345-360.

(25) Shouben cho, Chie no Tomoshibi, Chap.2 Wayaku Kaisetsu (A Japanese Translation of the Second Chapter of Bhāvaviveka's Prajñāpradīpa) 1, *The Journal of the Faculty of Literature Nagoya University*, No. 84, 1982, pp. 1-26.

(26) Kibyuuronshouha: Butsugo to Gesshou (Prāsaṅgikas: Buddhapālita and Candrakīrti), *Kouza Daijou Bukkyou* 7, Shunjuusha, 1982, pp. 117-145.

(27) Kagyuuha no Tenseki to Kyougi (The Literature and Doctrine of the Kagyud School), *Touyou Gakujutsu Kenkyuu* No. 21, Part 2, 1982, pp. 99-111.

(28) A Hindu Worship Service in Sixteen Steps, *Bulletin of the National Museum of Ethnology* Special Issue Vol. 8, No. 1, 1983, pp. 104-186.

(29) Engi wo Kataru Meidai ni okeru Hitei to Koutei (Negation and Affirmation in the Sentences Describing Pratītyasamutpāda), *Nanto Bukkyou* No. 51, 1983, pp. 43-61.

(30) Shouben cho, Chie no Tomoshibi, Chap.2 Wayaku Kaisetsu (A Japanese Translation of the Second Chapter of Bhāvaviveka's Prajñāpradīpa) 2, *The Journal of the Faculty of Literature Nagoya University* No. 87, 1983, pp. 31-58.

(31) Shouben cho, Chie no Tomoshibi, Chap.2 Wayaku Kaisetsu (A Japanese Translation of the Second Chapter of Bhāvaviveka's

Prajñāpradīpa) 3, *Sambhāṣā* No.5, Association of Indian and Buddhist Studies at Nagoya University, 1983, pp. 111-128.

(32) Two Kinds of Negations in the Mūlamadhyamakakārikā, Proceedings of the Thirty-First International Congress of Human Sciences in Asia and North Africa, Toho Gakkai, 1984, pp. 204-205.

(33) Shouben cho, Chie no Tomoshibi, Chap.2 Wayaku Kaisetsu (A Japanese Translation of the Second Chapter of Bhāvaviveka's Prajñāpradīpa) 4-1, *The Journal of the Faculty of Literature Nagoya University* No. 90, 1984, pp. 1-22.

(34) Engi wo Kousei suru Futatsu no Kou ni tsuite (Two Factors Comprising Pratītyasamutpāda), *Shinpi Shisou Ronshuu*, Naritasan Bukkyou Kenkyuujo, 1984, pp. 281-295.

(35) Shoki Chuugan ni okeru Kuu (Emptiness in the Early Madhyamikas), *Risou* No. 610, 1984, pp. 3-96.

(36) Chibetto Bukkyou ni okeru Kokoro no Honshitsu (The Essence of the Mind in Tibetan Buddhism) *Bukkyou Shisou: Kokoro* (*Buddhist Thought: Mind*), Heirakuji Shoten, 1984, pp.277-320.

(37) Shouben cho, Chie no Tomoshibi, Chap.2 Wayaku Kaisetsu (A Japanese Translation of the Second Chapter of Bhāvaviveka's Prajñāpradīpa) 4-2 *Sambhāṣā* No. 6, Association of Indian and Buddhist Studies at Nagoya University, 1985, pp. 44-55.

(38) Chuuron ni okeru Nishu no Hitei (Two Kinds of Negations in the Madhyamakakārikā), *Felicitation Volume of Rev. S. Nasu*, Naritasan Shinshouji, 1985, pp. 632-656.

(39) Chuuron ni okeru Jishou ni tsuite (On Svabhāva in the Madhyamakakārikā), History and Thought of Buddhism, *Felicitation Volume of Prof. T. Mibu*, Daizou Shuppan 1985, pp. 123-140.

(40) Shouben cho, Chie no Tomoshibi, Chap.2 Wayaku Kaisetsu (A Japanese Translation of the Second Chapter of Bhāvaviveka's Prajñāpradīpa) 5, *The Journal of the Faculty of Literature Nagoya University* No. 93, 1985, pp. 21-41.

(41) Kegon Gokyoushou ni okeru Shiku Hunbetsu (Catuskotis in the Hua yen wu chicao chang), *Felicitation Volume of Prof. S. Kumoi*, Heirakuji Shoten, 1985, pp. 249-265.

(42) Kongou Taaraa no Kansouhou (Visualization of Vajratārā),

Felicitation Volume of Prof. K. Machida, Yoshikawa Koubunkan, 1986, pp. 65-97.

(43) Katomanzu ni okeru Hachi Boshin to Hachi Bairaba (The Eight Matrkas and the Eight Bhairavas in Kathmandu), *Mikkyou Zuzou* (*The Journal of Buddhist Iconography*) No. 4, 1986, pp. 29-45.

(44) Bukkyou Zuzou (Buddhist Iconography), *Chibetto no Gengo to Bunka* (*Language and Culture of Tibet*), Toujusha, 1987, pp.336-363.

(45) Daijiboshin no Sugata (Forms of Great Mother-Goddesses), *Shizen to Bunka* (*Nature and Culture*), Spring Issue, Nihon National Trust, 1987, pp. 46-51.

(46) Akirakana Kotoba, Chap.2 Wayaku Kaisetsu (A Japanese Translation of the Second Chapter of the Prasannapadā) 1, *Journal of Naritasan Institute for Buddhist Studies* No. 11, Naritasan Shinshouji, 1988, pp. 195-218.

(47) Akirakana Kotoba, Chap.2 Wayaku Kaisetsu (A Japanese Translation of the Second Chapter of Prasannapada) 2, *Felicitation Volume of Prof. K. Hujita*, Shunjuusha 1989, pp. 433-455.

(48) Sakyaha (On the Sakya School), *Iwanami Kouza Touyoushisou* Vol. 11, Iwanami Shoten, 1989, pp. 153-170.

(49) Kagyuha (On the Kagyud School), *Iwanami Kouza Touyoushisou* Vol. 11, Iwanami Shoten, 1989, pp. 172-189.

(50) Katomanzu ni okeru Hokkai Mandara (The Dharmadhātu Maṇḍala in Kathmandu), *Bulletin of the National Museum of Ethnology* Special Issue No. 7, National Museum of Ethnology, 1989, pp. 5-44.

(51) Chibetto no Maniishi (Mani-stone of Tibet with Special Reference to the Maṇi-stone Presented to Mr. T. Furukawa in Celebration of his 99th Birthday), *Nagoya University Furukawa Museum* No. 5, 1989, pp. 85-95.(Co-author: F. Taniguchi)

(52) Mandara: Kouzou to Kinou (The Structure and Function of Maṇḍala), *Iwanami Kouza Touyoushisou* Vol. 10, Iwanami Shoten, 1989, pp. 289-314.

(53) Sei to Shi wo Housetsu suru Boshin (Mother-Goddesses Embracing Life and Death), *Sei to Shi no Bunkashi* (*Cultural History of Life and Death*), Nagoya University Press, 1989, pp. 31-60.

(54) The logical Structure of the Tetralemma in the *Mūlamadhyamakakārikā, Studies on the Cultural and Structure of the Countries Surrounding the Pacific Ocean*, Nagoya University, 1990, pp. 1-17.

(55) The Maṇḍala: Its Structure and Function, *The Ngor Maṇḍalas of Tibet*, The Center for East Asian Cultural Studies, Tokyo, 1990, pp. xxxi-xxxv.

(56) Seimeitai to shiteno Uchuu (The Cosmos as an Organic Body), *The Journal of the Nippon Buddhist Research Association* No. 56, 1991, pp. 213-227.

(57) Kongouhannyakyou ni Mirareru Sokuhi no Ronri Hihan (Logical Analysis of the Vajracchedikā), *Journal of Indian and Buddhist Studies* Vol. 41, No. 2, 1993, pp. 984-987.

(58) Ryuuju no Kuushisou (The Emptiness Thought of Nāgārjuna), *Gakushikai Kaihou* No. 799, 1993, pp. 97-100.

(59) The Tetralemma in the Mūlamadhyamakakārikā, *Felicitation Volume of Prof. Y. Miyasaka*, Houzoukan, 1993, pp. 401-421.

(60) Mahāyāna Philosophies I. Mādhyamika Tradition, *Encyclopedia of Spirituality*, Nanzan Institute for Religion and Culture, 1993, pp.188-202.

(61) Homa in Vedic Ritual: The Structure of the Darśapūrṇamāsa, *Senri Ethnological Studies* No. 36, 1993, pp. 239-267.

(62) Veeda Saishiki ni okeru Hooma (Homa in Vedic Rituals), *Indo Fukugou Bunka no Kouzou* (*The Structure of Complex Culture of India*), Houzoukan, 1993, p. 319-356.

(63) Kuushisou ni okeru Shi to Saisei (The Death and Rebirth in Emptiness Thought), *Yuriika* Vol. 26, No. 13, Seidosha, 1994, pp. 294-301.

(64) Jishou ga Kuu de aru wo dou Kaishaku suruka (How to interpret the Expression of Svabhāva-śūnya), *Bukkyou* No. 26, Houzoukan, 1994, pp. 164-177.

(65) Interpretation of Emptiness, *Horin* No. 2, das Haus der Japanischen Kultur, Duesseldorf, 1995, pp. 81-92.

(66) The Concept of Universal in Bhāvaviveka's Writings, *Asiatische Studien* XLVb-2, Berlin, 1994, pp. 891-902.

(67) Svabhāva and Śūnyatā, *Journal of Indian and Buddhist Studies* Vol.43, No. 2, 1995, pp. 1027-1021.

(68) Nihon Bukkyou ni okeru Shizen (The Concept of Nature in Japanese Buddhism), *Bunmei to Kankyou* (*Civilization and Environment*) Vol. 13, Asakura Shoten, 1996, pp. 109-121.

(69) Kansei seru Yooga no Wa, 19shou Wayaku (A Japanese Translation of the 19th Chapter of the *Niṣpannayogāvalī*), *Mikkyou Zuzou* (*The Journal of Buddhist Iconography*) No. 14, 1995, pp. 1-33.
(70) Yuishiki Sanjuuju ni okeru Kesetsu to Shiki ni tsuite (Vijñapti and Vijñāna in the Triṃśikā), *Felicitation Volume of Prof. J. Imanishi*, Shunjuusha, 1996, pp. 345-356.
(71) Sekai to Kami no Kankei (The Relation between the World and God), *The Journal of the Nippon Buddhist Research Association* No. 62, 1997, pp. 133-146.
(72) Kongoukai Mandara no Kansouhou (Meditation of Vajradhātu Maṇḍala), *Bulletin of the National Museum of Ethnology* Special Issue No. 18, 1997, pp. 319-336.
(73) Time in Buddhism, *Senri Ethnological Studies* No. 45, National Museum of Ethnology, 1998, pp. 123-142.
(74) On the Introduction of Buddhism of Buddhist Thought to Japan, *Japan in a Comparative Perspective, International Symposium* No. 12, International Research Center for Japanese Studies, 1998, pp. 63-75.
(75) Indo no Nyoshintachi no Henyou (Development of the Goddess Cult in India), *Yuriika* Vol. 30-15, Seidosha, 1998, pp. 102-108.
(76) Sekai no Seika wa Ikanishite Kanouka (How is World Sanctification Possible?), *Ajia no Kankyou-Bunmei-Ningen* (*Environment, Civilization, and Human Beings in Asia*), Houzoukan, 1998, pp. 275-288.
(77) How is World Sanctification Possible, *Views of the Environment in Asian Countries, Asian Pacific Center*, The United Nations University, 1999, pp. 153-160.
(78) Hindu Thinking on Śakti, *Senri Ethnological Studies* 50, National Museum of Ethnology, 1999, pp. 21-32.
(79) Sanjuuju Annechuu ni okeru Shiki no Tenpen (Vijñāna-pariṇāma in Sthiramati's Commentary on the *Triṃśikā*), *Journal of Indian and Buddhist Studies* Vol. 48, Part 1, 1999, pp. 249-257.
(80) Mikkyou towa Nanika (What is Tantrism?), *Series Mikkyou 1: Indo Mikkyou* (*Studies in Tantrism: India*), Shunjuusha, 1999, pp.3-13.
(81) Indo Mikkyou no Rekishiteki Haikei (Histrorical Background

of Indian Tantrism), *Series Mikkyou 1: Indo Mikkyo* (*Studies in Tantrism: India*), Shunjuusha, 1999, pp. 19-31.

(82) Hinzuu Tantorizumu (Hindu Tantrism), *Series Mikkyou 1 : Indo Mikkyou* (*Studies in Tantrism: India*), Shunjuusha, 1999, pp. 225-236.

(83) Chibetto Mikkyou towa Nanika (What is Tibetan Tantrism), *Series Mikkyou 2: Chibetto Mikkyou* (*Studies in Tantrism:Tibet*), Shunjuusha, 1999, pp. 3-23.

(84) Tsonkapa no Shougai to Mikkyou Shisou (The Life and Thought of Tsong kha pa), *Series Mikkyou 2: Chibetto Mikkyou* (*Studies in Tantrism: Tibet*), Shunjuusha, 1999, pp. 51-63.

(85) Katomanzu Bonchi no Nepaaru Mikkyou (Nepalese Tantrism in Kathmandu), *Series Mikkyou 2 : Chibetto Mikkyou* (*Studies in Tantrism: Tibet*), Shunjuusha, 1999, pp. 239-252.

(86) Bukkyou ni okeru Jikan (Time in Buddhism), *Jikan-Kotoba-Ninshiki* (*Time, Language, and Cognition*), Hitsuji Shobou, 1999, pp. 121-142.

(87) Inoue Enryou no Bukkyou Shisou (Buddhist Thought of E. Inoue) *Journal of Indian and Buddhist Studies* Vol. 49, Part 1, 2000, pp. 12-20.

(88) Maṇḍala Contemplation and Pure Land Practice, *Toward a Contemporary Understanding of Pure Land Buddhism,* State University of New York Press, 2000, pp. 101-124.

(89) The World of Amida Buddha, *Toward a Contemporary Understanding of Pure Land Buddhism,* State University of New York Press, 2000, pp. 223-240.

(90) Maṇḍala Visualization and Possession, *New Horizon in Bon Studies,* National Museum of Ethnology, 2000, pp. 227-247.

(91) The Sixteen Bodhisattvas in the Dharmadhātu Maṇḍalas, *Bulletin of the National Museum of Ethnology* Vol. 25, No. 4, 2001, pp. 537-623.

(92) The Introduction Part of the Kiraṇāvalī, *Journal of Indian Philosophy* No.29, Kluwer Academic Publishers, pp.275-291, 2001.

(93) Seinarumono to Shi (The Sacred and Death), *Journal of Religious Studies* No. 333, 2002, pp. 259-286.

(94) Nature and Dependent Origination, *Buddhist and Indian Studies in Honour of Professor S. Mori,* International Buddhist Association, 2002, pp. 413-424.

D. Reports of Field Works

(1) Katomanzu no Kamigami (Deities in Kathmandu), *Kikan Minzokugaku* No.26, National Museum of Ethnology, 1983, pp.115-125.

(2) Materials for Iconographic Studies of Eight Mother-Goddesses in the Kathmandu Valley Part I-1, *Monumenta Serindica* No. 14-2, Institute for the Study of Languages and Cultures of Asia and Africa, 1984, pp. 1-122.

(3) *An Ancient Indian Homa Ritual*, The Department of Indian Philosophy Nagoya University, 1985, pp.1-91.

(4) Materials for Iconographic Studies of Mother-Goddesses in Kathmandu Valley, Part I-2, *Monumenta Serindica* No. 15, Institute for the Study of Languages and Cultures of Asia and Africa, 1985, pp. 41-116.

(5) Fudougoma no Kiroku (A Record of Japanese Homa), *Sambhāṣā* No. 8, Association of Indian and Buddhist Studies at Nagoya University, 1986, pp. 1-48.

(6) Matyendora-naato-ji no Hyakuhachi-Kanjizai ni tsuite (The 108 Lokeśvaras at Matsyendranāth Temple), *Mikkyou Zuzou* (*The Journal of Buddhist Iconography*) No.8, 1990, pp. 6-79 (together with S. Yamaguchi)

(7) A Study of the Vajradhātu-Maṇḍala of the Niṣpannayogāvalī, *Bulletin of the National Museum of Ethnology* Vol. 14, No. 2, 1991, pp. 1073-1120.

(8) Newaaru Hokkai mandara Zuzoushiryou, (Materials for Iconographic Studies of Newar Dharmadhātu Maṇḍalas), *Bulletin of the National Museum of Ethnology* Vol. 23, No. 4, 1999, pp. 699-808.

E. Translation

(1) A Japanese Translation of the Amaruśataka 1, *Toukai Bukkyou* Nos. 14-15, 1970, pp. 3-14.

(2) A Japanese Translation of the Amaruśataka 2, *Toukai Bukkyou* No. 16, 1971, pp. 22-31.

(3) M.Eliade's Yoga, 2 vols., Serika Shobou, 1975.

(4) bSod nams rgya mtsho, *Maṇḍala, Asia no Kosumosu Mandara*, (*The Cosmos in Asia: Maṇḍala*), Koudansha, 1982.

(5) Buddhacarita Chap.1-7, *Genshi Butten* (*Early Buddhist Scriptures*) Vol. 10, Koudansha, 1978, pp. 3-78.

(6) The Chapter on the dGe lugs pa of Thu'u bkwan's Grub mthah (1), *Felicitation Volume of Prof. Z. Yamaguchi*, Shunjuusha, 1986, pp. 431-451.

(7) R. Otto, *Indo no Kami to Hito* (A Translation of *Die Gnadenreligion des Indiens und das Christentum*), Jinbun Shoin, 1988 (together with K. Tachikawa).

(8) A Japanese Translation of Chap.2 of the *Kumārasambhava*, *Felicitation Volume of Prof. J. Kato*, Shunjuusha, 2000, pp. 499-519.

F. Others

(1) Hanmon (Inquiry), *Toukai Bukkyou* No. 19, 1974, pp.95-114.

(2) Jumoku to Seinarumono (Trees and the Sacred), *Is* Vol. 15, 1974, pp. 24-25.

(3) Chibetto Minzoku Shiryou Mokuroku (A Catalogue of the B. Aoki's Tibet Collection at the National Museum of Ethnology), *Bulletin of the National Museum of Ethnology* Special Issue No. 1, Nos. 4, 5, 6, 13, 14, 15, etc., 1983.

(4) Nepaaru no Bukkyou (Buddhism in Nepal), Bukkyou no Ruden to Henyou (Spread and Change of Buddhism), Osaka Shoseki, 1986, pp. 107-131.

(5) Chibetto no Bukkyou (Buddhism in Tibet), *Bukkyou no Ruden to Henyou* (*Spread and Change of Buddhism*), Osaka Shoseki, 1986, pp. 167-186.

(6) Mandara to Shiteno Katomanzu Bonchi (The Kathmandu Valley as a Maṇḍala), *Himaraya Bukkyou Oukoku 2*, Sanseidou, 1986, pp. 212-223.

(7) Boshintachi no Kosumosu (A Cosmos of Goddesses), *Subaru*, Aug. 1987, pp. 169-178.

(8) Ajia no Shuukyou ni okeru Sei to Zoku (The Sacred and the Profane in Asian Religions), *University and Science* No. 2, Open Symposium Organization Committee, Asahi Shuppansha, 1988, pp. 14-24.

(9) Jiko Kuukan to Koui no Kijun (Self-space and Criteria of Actions), Bukkyou No. 9, Houzoukan, 1989, pp. 167-176.

(10) Koui no Jikankouzou to Engi (The Time-Structure of Actions and Dependent Co-arising) 1, *Bukkyou* No. 11, Houzoukan, 1991, pp. 171-181.

(11) Koui no Jikankouzou to Engi (The Time-Structure of Actions and Dependent Co-arising) 2, *Bukkyou* No. 17, Houzoukan, 1991, pp. 176-187.
(12) Tantora ni okeru Shintai Uchuuron (Cosmic Body in Tantrism), *Mandara Runnesansu,* Asahi Shinbunsha, 1991, pp. 66-67.
(13) Chibetto ni okeru Bukkyou no Juyou to Henyou (The Acceptance and Change of Buddhism in Tibet), *Kouza Bukkyou* Vol. 3, Kousei Shuppansha, 1991 pp. 12-44.
(14) Nepaaru ni okeru Bukkyou no Juyou to Henyou (The Acceptance and Change of Buddhism in Nepal), *Kouza Bukkyou* Vol.3, Kousei Shuppansha, 1991 pp. 186-204.
(15) Indo Tantora (Indian Tantrism), *Bukkyou* No. 19, Houzoukan, 1992, pp.44-56.
(16) Mandara no Uchuukan (The Concept of Cosmos in Maṇḍala), *Souzou no Sekai* No.84, Shougakkan, 1992, pp. 6-25.
(17) Bijutsu (Survey of Indian Art), *Indo,* Shinchousha, 1992, pp. 92-108.
(18) Mandara no Kouzougaku, *Books Esoterica* Vol. 11, Gakushuu Kenkyuusha, 1994 (together with S. Yamaguchi).
(19) Buutan no Zuzou (Bhutanese Iconography), *Asia Forum* No. 73, Ajia Kurabu, 1994.
(20) Hinzuu no Joujuhou (Visualization in Hinduism), *Books Esoterica* Vol.12, Gakushuu Kenkyuusha, 1994, pp. 124-132.
(21) Kinnen no Kaigai ni okeru Kuushisou Kenkyuu (Contemporary Studies of Emptiness Thought), *Bukkyougaku* No. 36, 1994, pp. 1-17.
(22) Shiki soku ze Kuu ni tsuite (On the Expression "Form is Emptiness"), *Hikari* No. 3, Chikushi Women College, 1995, pp. 16-47.
(23) Mandara to Jiko (Maṇḍala and Self), *Minpaku Tsuushin* No.70, National Museum of Ethnology, 1995, pp. 44-65.
(24) Oubei no Touyougaku: G. Tucci (Oriental Studies in the West: G. Tucci), *Shinika,* Taishuukan Shoten, Nov. 1995, pp. 102-107.
(25) Seimeitai to shiteno Kosumosu (Organic Body: Maṇḍala), *Mandara Uchuuron* (*The Cosmology of Maṇḍala*), Houzoukan, 1996, pp. 397-426.
(26) Inoue Enryou no Bukkyoukan to sono Igi (E. Inoue's Understanding of Buddhism and its Significance), *Satia*

No. 24, Touyou University Inoue Enryou Commemoration Center, 1996, pp.34-36.

(27) Mikkyou to Kegare (Tantrism and Impurity), *Hongou* No. 20, Yoshikawa Koubunkan, 1999, pp.19-21.

(28) Shiki soku ze Kuu no Kaishaku (Interpretations of the Expression "Form is Emptiness"), *Collected Works of Daisetsu Suzuki Vol. 8 Monthly Report 1*, Iwanami Shoten, 1999, pp. 5-8.

(29) Hannyashingyou to Kuu (The Heart Sūtra and Emptiness), *Bukkyou Bunka* No.39, Tokyo University Young Buddhist Association, 1999, pp. 5-8.

(30) Saichou, *AERA Mook: Bukkyou ga Wakaru*, Asahi Shinbunsha, 2000, pp. 16-20.

(31) Mandara : Uchuu to Koga no Gouitsu (Maṇḍala: The Unity of the Self with the Cosmos), *Gekkan Minpaku*, 4, Senri Bunka Zaidan, April 2000, pp. 16-18.

(32) Hyoui ni tsuite (On Possession), *Higashi Ajia no Shintai Gihou* (*Somatic Technique in East Asia*), Bensei Shuppan, 2000, pp. 8-17.

(33) Indo Tetsugaku to IT (Indian philosophy and IT), *Kouryuu* No. 57, Chuubu Denryoku, 2001, pp. 9-12.

(34) Joudo ni tsuite (On Pure Land), *Indo Tetsugaku Bukkyougaku* No. 16, Hokkaidou Association of Indian and Buddhist Studies, 2001, pp. 354-373.

(35) Nijuuisseiki no Budda (Buddha in the 21st Century), *Bukkyou* No. 52, Houzoukan, 2001, pp. 28-37.